Poetry Criticism

Guide to Gale Literary Criticism Series

For criticism on	Consult these Gale series
Authors now living or who died after December 31, 1999	*CONTEMPORARY LITERARY CRITICISM (CLC)*
Authors who died between 1900 and 1999	*TWENTIETH-CENTURY LITERARY CRITICISM (TCLC)*
Authors who died between 1800 and 1899	*NINETEENTH-CENTURY LITERATURE CRITICISM (NCLC)*
Authors who died between 1400 and 1799	*LITERATURE CRITICISM FROM 1400 TO 1800 (LC)* *SHAKESPEAREAN CRITICISM (SC)*
Authors who died before 1400	*CLASSICAL AND MEDIEVAL LITERATURE CRITICISM (CMLC)*
Authors of books for children and young adults	*CHILDREN'S LITERATURE REVIEW (CLR)*
Dramatists	*DRAMA CRITICISM (DC)*
Poets	*POETRY CRITICISM (PC)*
Short story writers	*SHORT STORY CRITICISM (SSC)*
Literary topics and movements	*HARLEM RENAISSANCE: A GALE CRITICAL COMPANION (HR)* *THE BEAT GENERATION: A GALE CRITICAL COMPANION (BG)*
Asian American writers of the last two hundred years	*ASIAN AMERICAN LITERATURE (AAL)*
Black writers of the past two hundred years	*BLACK LITERATURE CRITICISM (BLC)* *BLACK LITERATURE CRITICISM SUPPLEMENT (BLCS)*
Hispanic writers of the late nineteenth and twentieth centuries	*HISPANIC LITERATURE CRITICISM (HLC)* *HISPANIC LITERATURE CRITICISM SUPPLEMENT (HLCS)*
Native North American writers and orators of the eighteenth, nineteenth, and twentieth centuries	*NATIVE NORTH AMERICAN LITERATURE (NNAL)*
Major authors from the Renaissance to the present	*WORLD LITERATURE CRITICISM, 1500 TO THE PRESENT (WLC)* *WORLD LITERATURE CRITICISM SUPPLEMENT (WLCS)*

ISSN 1052-4851

Poetry Criticism

Excerpts from Criticism of the Works of the Most Significant and Widely Studied Poets of World Literature

Volume 66

Michelle Lee
Project Editor

THOMSON

GALE

Detroit • New York • San Francisco • San Diego • New Haven, Conn. • Waterville, Maine • London • Munich

Poetry Criticism, Vol. 66

Project Editor
Michelle Lee

Editorial
Jessica Bomarito, Kathy D. Darrow, Jeffrey Hunter, Jelena O. Krstović, Thomas J. Schoenberg, Lawrence J. Trudeau, Russel Whitaker

Data Capture
Francis Monroe, Gwen Tucker

Indexing Services
Synapse, the Knowledge Link Corporation

Rights and Acquisitions
Ron Montgomery, Sue Rudolph, Shalice Shah-Caldwell

Imaging and Multimedia
Dean Dauphinais, Leitha Etheridge-Sims, Lezlie Light, Mike Logusz, Dan Newell, Christine O'Bryan, Kelly A. Quin, Denay Wilding, Robyn Young

Composition and Electronic Capture
Kathy Sauer

Manufacturing
Rhonda Dover

Associate Product Manager
Marc Cormier

LIBRARY OF CONGRESS CATALOG CARD NUMBER 91-118494

ISBN 0-7876-8700-6
ISSN 1052-4851

Printed in the United States of America
10 9 8 7 6 5 4 3 2 1

Contents

Preface vii

Acknowledgments ix

Literary Criticism Series Advisory Board xi

Preface

*P*oetry Criticism (*PC*) presents significant criticism of the world's greatest poets and provides supplementary biographical and bibliographical material to guide the interested reader to a greater understanding of the genre and its creators. Although major poets and literary movements are covered in such Gale Literary Criticism series as *Contemporary Literary Criticism* (*CLC*), *Twentieth-Century Literary Criticism* (*TCLC*), *Nineteenth-Century Literature Criticism* (*NCLC*), *Literature Criticism from 1400 to 1800* (*LC*), and *Classical and Medieval Literature Criticism* (*CMLC*), *PC* offers more focused attention on poetry than is possible in the broader, survey-oriented entries on writers in these Thomson Gale series. Students, teachers, librarians, and researchers will find that the generous excerpts and supplementary material provided by *PC* supply them with the vital information needed to write a term paper on poetic technique, to examine a poet's most prominent themes, or to lead a poetry discussion group.

Scope of the Series

PC is designed to serve as an introduction to major poets of all eras and nationalities. Since these authors have inspired a great deal of relevant critical material, *PC* is necessarily selective, and the editors have chosen the most important published criticism to aid readers and students in their research. Each author entry presents a historical survey of the critical response to that author's work. The length of an entry is intended to reflect the amount of critical attention the author has received from critics writing in English and from foreign critics in translation. Every attempt has been made to identify and include the most significant essays on each author's work. In order to provide these important critical pieces, the editors sometimes reprint essays that have appeared elsewhere in Thomson Gale's Literary Criticism Series. Such duplication, however, never exceeds twenty percent of a *PC* volume.

Organization of the Book

Each *PC* entry consists of the following elements:

- The **Author Heading** cites the name under which the author most commonly wrote, followed by birth and death dates. Also located here are any name variations under which an author wrote, including transliterated forms for authors whose native languages use nonroman alphabets. If the author wrote consistently under a pseudonym, the pseudonym will be listed in the author heading and the author's actual name given in parenthesis on the first line of the biographical and critical introduction. Uncertain birth or death dates are indicated by question marks. Single-work entries are preceded by the title of the work and its date of publication.

- The **Introduction** contains background information that introduces the reader to the author and the critical debates surrounding his or her work.

- A **Portrait of the Author** is included when available.

- The list of **Principal Works** is ordered chronologically by date of first publication and lists the most important works by the author. The first section comprises poetry collections and book-length poems. The second section gives information on other major works by the author. For foreign authors, the editors have provided original foreign-language publication information and have selected what are considered the best and most complete English-language editions of their works.

- Reprinted **Criticism** is arranged chronologically in each entry to provide a useful perspective on changes in critical evaluation over time. All individual titles of poems and poetry collections by the author featured in the entry are printed in boldface type. The critic's name and the date of composition or publication of the critical work are given at the beginning of each piece of criticism. Unsigned criticism is preceded by the title of the source in which it appeared. Footnotes are reprinted at the end of each essay or excerpt. In the case of excerpted criticism, only those footnotes that pertain to the excerpted texts are included.

- Critical essays are prefaced by brief **Annotations** explicating each piece.

- A complete **Bibliographical Citation** of the original essay or book precedes each piece of criticism.

- An annotated bibliography of **Further Reading** appears at the end of each entry and suggests resources for additional study. In some cases, significant essays for which the editors could not obtain reprint rights are included here. Boxed material following the further reading list provides references to other biographical and critical sources on the author in series published by Thomson Gale.

Cumulative Indexes

A **Cumulative Author Index** lists all of the authors that appear in a wide variety of reference sources published by Thomson Gale, including *PC*. A complete list of these sources is found facing the first page of the Author Index. The index also includes birth and death dates and cross references between pseudonyms and actual names.

A **Cumulative Nationality Index** lists all authors featured in *PC* by nationality, followed by the number of the *PC* volume in which their entry appears.

A **Cumulative Title Index** lists in alphabetical order all individual poems, book-length poems, and collection titles contained in the *PC* series. Titles of poetry collections and separately published poems are printed in italics, while titles of individual poems are printed in roman type with quotation marks. Each title is followed by the author's last name and corresponding volume and page numbers where commentary on the work is located. English-language translations of original foreign-language titles are cross-referenced to the foreign titles so that all references to discussion of a work are combined in one listing.

Citing *Poetry Criticism*

When writing papers, students who quote directly from any volume in the Literary Criticism Series may use the following general format to footnote reprinted criticism. The first example pertains to material drawn from periodicals, the second to material reprinted from books.

Sylvia Kasey Marks, "A Brief Glance at George Eliot's *The Spanish Gypsy*," *Victorian Poetry* 20, no. 2 (Summer 1983), 184-90; reprinted in *Poetry Criticism*, vol. 20, ed. Ellen McGeagh (Detroit: The Gale Group), 128-31.

Linden Peach, "Man, Nature and Wordsworth: American Versions," *British Influence on the Birth of American Literature*, (Macmillan Press Ltd., 1982), 29-57; reprinted in *Poetry Criticism*, vol. 20, ed. Ellen McGeagh (Detroit: The Gale Group), 37-40.

Suggestions are Welcome

Readers who wish to suggest new features, topics, or authors to appear in future volumes, or who have other suggestions or comments are cordially invited to call, write, or fax the Associate Product Manager:

Associate Product Manager, Literary Criticism Series
Thomson Gale
27500 Drake Road
Farmington Hills, MI 48331-3535
1-800-347-4253 (GALE)
Fax: 248-699-8054

Acknowledgments

The editors wish to thank the copyright holders of the criticism included in this volume and the permissions managers of many book and magazine publishing companies for assisting us in securing reproduction rights. We are also grateful to the staffs of the Detroit Public Library, the Library of Congress, the University of Detroit Mercy Library, Wayne State University Purdy/Kresge Library Complex, and the University of Michigan Libraries for making their resources available to us. Following is a list of the copyright holders who have granted us permission to reproduce material in this volume of *PC*. Every effort has been made to trace copyright, but if omissions have been made, please let us know.

COPYRIGHTED MATERIAL IN *PC*, VOLUME 66, WAS REPRODUCED FROM THE FOLLOWING PERIODICALS:

American Imago, v. 41, summer, 1984. Copyright © 1984 by the Johns Hopkins University Press. Reproduced by permission.—*Books Abroad,* v. 42, spring, 1968. Copyright © 1968 by the University of Oklahoma Press. Reproduced by permission.—*Books at Iowa,* April, 1980. Reproduced by permission.—*Charioteer,* spring, 1964. Copyright © 1964 by Parnassos. All rights reserved. Reproduced by permission from Pella Publishing Co., New York, NY.—*CLA Journal,* v. 32, September, 1988. Copyright © 1988 by the College Language Association. Used by permission of the College Language Association.—*Contemporary Review,* v. 225, October, 1974. Copyright © 1974 Contemporary Review Co., Ltd. Reproduced by the permission of Contemporary Review Ltd.—*Durham University Journal,* January, 1994. Reproduced by permission.—*ELH,* v. 69, summer, 2002; v. 69, fall, 2002. Copyright © 2002 by the Johns Hopkins University Press. Both reproduced by permission.—*English,* v. XVII, spring, 1968. Copyright © by the English Association 1968. Reproduced by permission.—*English Studies,* v. 69, October, 1988. Copyright © 1988 Swets & Zeitlinger. Reproduced by permission.—*English Studies in Canada,* v. 4, summer, 1978. Copyright © 1978 by the Association of Canadian University Teachers of English. Reproduced by permission of the publisher.—*Essays in Literature,* v. 6, spring, 1979; v. 9, fall, 1982. Copyright © 1979, 1982 by Western Illinois University. Both reproduced by permission.—*Explicator,* v. 53, summer, 1995; v. 57, winter, 1999. Copyright © 1995, 1999 by Helen Dwight Reid Educational Foundation. Both reproduced with permission of the Helen Dwight Reid Educational Foundation, published by Heldref Publications, 1319 18th Street, NW, Washington, DC 20036-1802.—*Grand Street,* v. 5, winter, 1986. Copyright © 1986 by Grand Street Publications, Inc. Reproduced by permission.—*Journal of English and Germanic Philology,* v. 73, July, 1974. Copyright © 1974 by the Board of Trustees of the University of Illinois. Reproduced by permission of the University of Illinois Press.—*Journal of European Studies,* v. 19, 1989. Copyright © Sage Publications, 1989. Reproduced by permission of Sage Publications. www.sagepub.co.uk—*Journal of the Hellenic Diaspora,* v. 26, 2000. Copyright © 2000 by Pella Publishing Company, Inc. Reproduced by permission from Pella Publishing Co., New York, NY.—*Journal of Modern Greek Studies,* v. 5, May, 1987; v. 5, October, 1987; v. 20, October, 2002. Copyright © 1987, 2002 by the Johns Hopkins University Press. All reproduced by permission.—*P.N. Review,* v. 25, January-February, 1999 for "Shelf Lives: Edmund Blunden" by Peter Scupham. Reproduced by permission of the author.—*Papers on Language & Literature,* v. 12, summer, 1976. Copyright © 1976 by the Board of Trustees, Southern Illinois University. Reproduced by permission.—*Parnassus: Poetry in Review,* v. 3, spring/summer, 1975 for "Greek Light" by Stavros Deligiorgis. Copyright © 1975 by the Poetry in Review Foundation, NY. Reproduced by permission of the author.—*Restoration,* v. 5, spring, 1981. Reproduced by permission.—*South Atlantic Review,* v. 47, January, 1982. Copyright © 1982 by the South Atlantic Modern Language Association. Reproduced by permission.—*Studies in English Literature 1500-1900,* v. 15, summer, 1975; v. 24, summer, 1984. Copyright © 1975, 1984 by William Marsh Rice University. Both reproduced by permission.—*Texas Quarterly,* v. VII, spring, 1964; v. XI, winter, 1968. © 1964, 1968 by the University of Texas at Austin. Both reproduced by permission.—*Texas Studies in Literature and Language,* v. 23, winter, 1981 for "Mind Against Itself: Theme and Structure in Rochester's *Satyr Against Reason and Mankind*" by James E. Gill. Copyright © 1981 by the University of Texas Press. All rights reserved. Reproduced by permission of the publisher and the author.—*War, Literature, and the Arts,* fall/winter, 1993 for "An I for an Eye: Edmund Blunden's War" by Thomas G. Bowie, Jr. Reproduced by permission of the author.

COPYRIGHTED MATERIAL IN *PC*, VOLUME 66, WAS REPRODUCED FROM THE FOLLOWING BOOKS:

Beaton, Roderick. From *George Seferis.* Bristol Classical Press, 1991. Copyright © Roderick Beaton. Reproduced by permission of the author.—Capri-Karka, C. From *Love and the Symbolic Journey in the Poetry of Cavafy, Eliot, and Sef-

Thomson Gale Literature Product Advisory Board

The members of the Thomson Gale Literature Product Advisory Board—reference librarians from public and academic library systems—represent a cross-section of our customer base and offer a variety of informed perspectives on both the presentation and content of our literature products. Advisory board members assess and define such quality issues as the relevance, currency, and usefulness of the author coverage, critical content, and literary topics included in our series; evaluate the layout, presentation, and general quality of our printed volumes; provide feedback on the criteria used for selecting authors and topics covered in our series; provide suggestions for potential enhancements to our series; identify any gaps in our coverage of authors or literary topics, recommending authors or topics for inclusion; analyze the appropriateness of our content and presentation for various user audiences, such as high school students, undergraduates, graduate students, librarians, and educators; and offer feedback on any proposed changes/enhancements to our series. We wish to thank the following advisors for their advice throughout the year.

Edmund Blunden
1896-1974

English poet, critic, biographer, essayist, novelist, and travel writer.

INTRODUCTION

Blunden is primarily known for his use of the pastoral form to express in verse his deep appreciation of the English countryside—which he knew intimately—and for his war poetry, inspired by his experiences serving in the British army in France and Belgium from 1914 to 1918.

BIOGRAPHICAL INFORMATION

Blunden was born November 1, 1896, in London, but was raised in a small village in Kent where his parents, Charles and Georgina Tyler Blunden, were teachers. In 1913 the family moved to Sussex, where his parents took positions at the Framfield School. He attended Christ's Hospital, recently relocated from London to Sussex, and developed a fierce loyalty to his fellow Blues, as the students were called, from his own time as well as from years past—a group that included Charles Lamb, Samuel Taylor Coleridge, and Leigh Hunt. Blunden received a scholarship to Oxford and enrolled in Queen's College in 1914, but he left soon afterwards to serve as a lieutenant in the Royal Sussex Regiment. He saw action in France and Belgium and survived the third battle of Ypres, a failed offensive that claimed more than 300,000 lives. Repeated exposure to poisonous gas left him unfit for further military duty and he returned to England in 1918, married Mary Davies, and resumed his studies at Oxford. However, memories of his combat experiences made him unable to adjust to life as a student and he left the university in 1919.

In 1920 Blunden moved to London and resumed the writing career he had started prior to the war. He contributed several essays and literary reviews to the *Athenaeum* and began publishing collections of his poetry. He traveled to South America in an effort to regain his health and then accepted a teaching position in Tokyo. His wife refused to accompany him to Japan, and when Blunden returned to England in 1927 he discovered that she had been unfaithful during his absence; he had himself engaged in an extended affair

with a Japanese school teacher, Aki Hayashi, who returned to England with him and worked as his secretary and research assistant. He and his wife separated in 1928 and divorced in 1931, but his intimate relationship with Hayashi did not continue once Blunden was free. In 1933 he married Sylva Norman, with whom he collaborated on his only novel; that marriage also ended in divorce. In 1945 Blunden married Claire Margaret Poynting.

After his return from Japan, Blunden resumed work at the *Nation and Athenaeum,* as the periodical was then called, and began publishing some of the poetry he composed in Japan. In 1931 he joined Merton College, Oxford, as a fellow and tutor, and continued writing—concentrating more on essays, literary criticism, and biography than on the poetry that dominated his early career. In 1943 Blunden left Oxford for London, where he began a long association with the *Times Literary Supplement.* From 1947 to 1950 he served as cultural liaison officer to the British Mission in Japan, and in

1953 he joined the faculty of the University of Hong Kong as a professor of English literature, a post he held until 1964. In 1966 he became professor of poetry at Oxford, but resigned after two years because of failing health. Blunden died on January 20, 1974.

MAJOR WORKS

Prior to World War I, Blunden produced some of his verse in chapbook form, but his first significant publication was *The Waggoner and Other Poems* (1920), followed by *The Shepherd and Other Poems of Peace and War* (1922). Although few of the poems in the two volumes are directly connected to Blunden's war experiences, the collections nonetheless reflect the violence and disillusionment he associated with combat. While teaching in Japan, Blunden was apparently able to establish enough distance from his war experiences to write about them more overtly in *Undertones of War* (1928), which many critics consider his masterpiece. The work consists of a prose narrative of episodes in his life as a soldier, accompanied by several new poems. Some critics have categorized the entire work as a narrative prose poem. Although the book was published in 1928, Blunden continued to revise it for two years after its publication.

The collections *Japanese Garland* and *Near and Far* reflect Blunden's complicated relationship with Japan. Many of the poems in the two collections were written during his stay in Japan although they were published in 1928 and 1929, respectively—long after his return to England. *Near and Far* contains the sonnet "Values," originally published in *The Observer* a year earlier; it is considered one of Blunden's most important individual poems. Also highly esteemed is a series of six elegiac poems on the death of his infant daughter Joy composed over a period of forty years. Known collectively as the "Joy Poems," they convey various intensities and aspects of grief and include "The Child's Grave," "Achronos," "To Joy," "A First Impression," "In a Country Churchyard," and "But at Last." The first appeared shortly after the child's death in 1922 and the last was published in 1962.

CRITICAL RECEPTION

Most critical commentary on Blunden's poetry has concentrated on the three main elements of his life that most informed his work: his childhood in rural England, his war experiences, and his extended residence in Japan. His early work, with its emphasis on nature, has often been compared to the poetry of John Clare, and his ability to depict rural life with detachment has been likened to that of Thomas Hardy. J. C. Squire notes that

Blunden, unlike many of his contemporaries, truly deserves the designation of "landscape poet" because of his intimate knowledge of the countryside. John Studley has also studied Blunden's nature poems and maintains that they are not merely representations of "country life"; rather, they are "meditations on the cultural and moral conditions of man." Michael Thorpe, however, finds Blunden's landscape poetry less laudable, contending that the poet "has versified copiously, multiplied and variegated his trees so generously that any but the most patient and diligent reader may be forgiven for questioning the existence of any definable wood."

Squire, like many other critics, has also commented on the conflation of nature and war themes in much of Blunden's poetry. According to Squire, Blunden saw war "as a cruel disturbance of rural peace." Bernard Schweizer has examined Blunden's juxtaposition of war imagery and pastoral elements in two of his war poems, "Two Voices" and "Preparations for Victory," and concludes that in the former, "the pastoral is an elusive phantom," and in the latter, "the sights of rural beauty become ironically undermined the minute they are invoked." Thomas G. Bowie, Jr., who has studied *Undertones of War,* asserts that Blunden is World War I's foremost spokesman, in both poetry and prose. Several of the poems in the collection, as well as sections of the prose narrative of *Undertones,* seem to confuse narrator and reader; according to Bowie: "The world of the war becomes Blunden's world, a world he leaves only infrequently and reluctantly, thus a world he places readers resolutely within." A. D. Burnett claims that "for Blunden, as for others, the war which had begun in 1914 did not end in 1918." Peter Scupham finds Blunden's obvious and genuine affection for his fellow soldiers, apparent throughout his war poetry, oddly comforting. He reports that "a self-effacing, undramatic love for them shines through his diction and in a curious way calms and balances the cataclysmic events of 1914-1918 in a way no other poet quite does for me."

The years Blunden spent teaching in Japan had a profound influence on his work, according to Miriam J. Benkovitz, who contends that the verse he wrote in the Far East, particularly the poetry in the collection *Japanese Garland,* "puts Blunden in the mainstream of English poets classified as romantic: Clare, Shelley, Keats." Benkovitz reports that, despite Blunden's initial belief that he could find nothing in Japan to inspire him to produce poetry, he eventually managed to write on the same topics that he wrote about in England: the death of his child, loneliness, and his own emotional responses to those events and conditions. Sumie Okada has studied the love poetry that Blunden wrote in Japan, influenced in part by his relationship with Hayashi. Okada cites in particular "Lonely Love" and "Ainu Child," as well as the poems published in *Near and Far,* which "record his first impressions of Japan, the shock he experienced in assimilating the different culture and sensibility, and above all, his clandestine love for Aki Hayashi." Burnett suggests that the poem "Values" may be addressed to Hayashi to hint that their relationship was ending and that "he would prefer her to be—as he sees her—an 'angel' who can accept this alteration without anger and become his assistant and not his mistress." Burnett further points out the conflict inherent in the reception of the poem by his Japanese students and readers given Blunden's "insistence upon an individual and authentic response to experience and upon a refusal of conventional certainties" in a culture that values deference to authority and conformity to social conventions.

PRINCIPAL WORKS

Poetry

Poems 1913 and 1914 1914
Pastorals: A Book of Verses 1916
The Waggoner and Other Poems 1920
Old Homes: A Poem 1922
The Shepherd and Other Poems of Peace and War 1922
To Nature 1923
Masks of Time 1925
English Poems 1926
Japanese Garland 1928
Retreat 1928
Undertones of War (poetry and prose) 1928
Near and Far: New Poems 1929
The Poems of Edmund Blunden, 1914-1930 1930
Halfway House: A Miscellany of New Poems 1932
Choice or Chance: New Poems 1934
Verses to H. R. H. the Duke of Windsor 1936
An Elegy and Other Poems 1937
Poems 1930-1940 1940
Shells by a Stream: New Poems 1944
After the Bombing and Other Short Poems 1949
Eastward: A Selection of Verses Original and Translated 1950
Edmund Blunden: A Selection of His Poetry and Prose (poetry and prose) 1950
Records of Friendship: Occasional and Epistolary Poems Written during Visits to Kyushu 1950
Poems of Many Years 1957
A Hong Kong House: Poems 1951-1961 1962
Eleven Poems 1965
A Selection of the Shorter Poems 1966
Poems on Japan, Hitherto Uncollected and Mostly Unprinted: Compiled and Edited in Honour of His Seventieth Birthday [edited by Takeshi Saito] 1967
The Midnight Skaters: Poems for Young Children [edited by C. Day Lewis] 1968
A Selection from the Poems [edited by Jim White] 1969

Other Major Works

The Appreciation of Literary Prose: Being One of the Special Courses of the Art of Life (essay) 1921
The Bonadventure: A Random Journal of an Atlantic Holiday (travel journal) 1922
Christ's Hospital: A Retrospect (essay) 1923
Leigh Hunt: A Biography (biography) 1930
We'll Shift Our Ground; or, Two on a Tour [with Sylva Norman] (novel) 1933
Thomas Hardy (biography) 1941
Cricket Country (essay) 1944
Shelley: A Life Story (biography) 1946
John Keats (biography) 1950
Charles Lamb (biography) 1954
Three Young Poets: Critical Sketches of Byron, Shelley, and Keats (criticism) 1959
John Clare: Beginner's Luck (criticism) 1971

CRITICISM

J. C. Squire (essay date 1923)

SOURCE: Squire, J. C. "Mr. Edmund Blunden." *Essays on Poetry*, pp. 171-81. New York: George H. Doran Company, 1923.

[*In the following essay, Squire distinguishes between landscape poets and true country poets, maintaining that, based on his intimate knowledge of the countryside, Blunden is the latter.*]

Mr. Blunden was, is, and probably always will be, a poet mainly of the countryside. "Landscape poet" is a misnomer. Landscape poets are very often townsmen, with an eye for colour and shape and a feeling for nature in general, but not necessarily a knowledge of the characters or even the names of any but the commonest and most conspicuous country things, who have never shared in the occupations of a farm or the sports of a village. Lark and nightingale are well enough; Jones's Warbler is another matter; there is no reason to expect that poets should be expert ornithologists; nor do they necessarily suffer by the defect. We have a very great wealth of "landscape poetry" in English, but not much has been done from the habitual countryman's angle. Mr. Blunden's work is so done. It has affinities with certain parts of Wordsworth; but the poets nearest him are Edward Thomas, and still more John Clare, whom he has enthusiastically edited, and he often reminds us of Richard Jefferies, the essayist. The life of the country is his own life, and he finds the beautiful where a transient passenger would fail to find the picturesque. He does not, as a rule, wait for the remarkable natural conformation, or the remarkable natural effect; and he does not usually wait for a great emotional moment in himself. But he has a steady love of the South English rural scene in all its changes and in all its details: barns with sagging roofs, cornfields, oast-houses, clay pastures, mills, small rivers, fish pools, grass, nettles and the wild flowers of the downs. Anything in that world may give him a poem. Characteristic instances are to be found in these two extracts:

> And nigh this toppling reed, still as the dead
>   The great pike lies, the murderous patriarch
>   Watching the waterpit sheer-shelving dark,
> Where through the plash his lithe bright vassals thread.
> The rose-fumed roach and bluish bream
> And staring ruff steal up the stream
> Hard by their glutted tyrant, now
> Still as a sunken bough.
>
> Up the slow stream the immemorial bream
> (For when had Death dominion over them?)
> Through green pavilions of ghost leaf and stem,
> A conclave of blue shadows in a dream,
> Glide on; idola that forgotten plan,
> Incomparably wise, the doom of man.

These are typical lines from the many poems in which the poet muses over small slow streams full of fish—full, if one may say so, in one instance, of too many sorts of fish. This again is from **"The Barn"**:

> The smell of apples stored in hay
> And homely cattle-cake is there.
> Use and disuse have come to terms,
> The walls are hollowed out by worms,
> But men's feet keep the mid-floor bare
>   And free from worse decay.
>
> All merry noise of hens astir,
> Of sparrows squabbling on the roof
> Comes to the barn's broad open door;
> You hear upon the stable floor
> Old hungry Dapple strike his hoof,
>   And the blue fan-tail's whir.

In **"Leisure"** he watches dawn come over the earth and, with delicious whimsicality, pictures "the delighted Spirit in the dells" who

> Woos the sun's opening eye
> With his droll night-whims, puffballs' pepper-gourds,
> Startling white mushrooms and bronze chantarelles.

In **"The Giant Puffball"** one of these "drolls" is taken singly. **"Perch-fishing"** has an amazingly vivid and watery description of a catch; **"Storm at Hoptime"** describes all the movement of hopping. A complete example is **"The Poor Man's Pig"**:

> Already fallen plum-bloom stars the green
>   And apple-boughs as knarred as old toads' backs,
> Wear their small roses ere a rose is seen;
>   The building thrush watches old Job who stacks
> The bright-peeled osiers on the sunny fence,
>   The pent sow grunts to hear him stumping by,
> And tries to push the bolt and scamper thence,
>   But her ringed snout still keeps her to the sty.
>
> Then out he lets her run; away she snorts
>   In bundling gallop for the cottage door,
> With hungry hubbub begging crusts and orts;
> Then like the whirlwind bumping round once more;
> Nuzzling the dog, making the pullets run,
>   And sulky as a child when her play's done.

This is not landscape, though there are fragments of landscape in it; it is a reproduction of a part of rusticity, of rural life. Just above it is a sketch of the village green. The yokels are playing football:

> Who on the wet green whirl the ball about
> With monstrous shambling kicks; and in and out
> Among them plays the mongrel black and young,
> As pleased as any there, and lolls his tongue,
> But near the postman, watching "how she flies,"
> The older dog looks on with pitying eyes,
> And thinks it only folly play, and droops
> His weary head away when laughter whoops
> To see tripped Longshanks floundering on his back,
> With trousers daubed in mire and face all black.

Writing like this springs from daily familiarity. But it also springs from daily delight. It is not "mere description," as some modern writing is. Feeling is implicit everywhere; it is explicit in such phrases as "sulky as a child," and "as pleased as any there"; a pervading sentiment and awareness of the goodness of it all, a relish of the quality in everything seen, all these perennial trifles, all these day-to-day occurrences. These quotations are extreme examples of reticence; there are many poems in which the poet makes himself much more clearly evident, and some in which the life he reflects is a background for emotions externally derived by himself or other persons. But it is almost always there. When you have read his books there have been recalled to you innumerable sounds, sights, and scents which you have experienced in the English countryside, and many which you never consciously recorded or recalled: the smells of the farmyard, the ways of poultry and cattle, the dim and stealthy movements of fish, black weeds hanging on sun-dried sluices, the texture of stone drinking-troughs, the colour of alehouse benches and the pictures on the walls, the scurryings and crawlings of insects under stones, the tone of bells, the casual encounters with way-farers on woodland paths, the dippings of dragonflies in ponds, the aspect of a village street at noon, the writhings of worms in new-turned mole-heaps, the taste of ale under a hedge, the feel of an old dog's tongue. I huddle them together without order; so, sometimes, does Mr. Blunden; but he delights in them all, and he makes the reader delight too. He might say of ten thousand things what he says of the not conventionally musical practice of the woodpecker:

> From all these happy folk I find
> Life's radiance kindle in my mind,
> And even when homeward last I turn,
> How bright the hawthorn berries burn,
> How steady in the old elm still
> The great woodpecker strikes his bill;
> Whose labour oft in vain is given,
> Yet never he upbraids high heaven:
> Such trust is his. O I have heard
> No sweeter from a singing bird
> Than his tap-tapping there this day,
> That said what words will never say.

The last line echoes the accents of a hundred poets; but Mr. Blunden differs from most of them in that he never attempts to say this inexpressible thing. He speculates and reasons hardly at all; his philosophy or his search for a philosophy is to be guessed; he does not even incite to the guessing. He is content to recount his loves and leave the argument to someone else.

For Poetry is an expression of gratitude for things enjoyed. The elements of Life in which the spirit takes most intense delight and on which the memory broods most fondly, vary from poet to poet. A man's dominant preoccupation may be his own capacity for action, the spectacle of other men, or of the race, in action, the pursuit of knowledge, personal grief and regret, the perception of the eternal behind appearances; there are many more. Mr. Blunden's is rural Nature; not Nature the personification, or Nature the instrument of the Almighty; the manifestations, not the power behind, though it may be the instinctive perception of that power that gives wonder and beauty to those manifestations. Mr. Blunden is not entirely concentrated on this one aspect of Life. He has written some powerful war-poems, some exquisite love poems, a touching elegy on a child. Yet war he sees most clearly as a cruel disturbance of rural peace, and he is continually driven to exhibit its vileness by contrasting it with pictures of the natural beauty which it destroys and from which it drags its victims. The loves he felt (his poems are all dated) in 1914 had become intensified when he returned after his years in France, to watch the lightest gossamer and the hungriest pike with a renewed and deepened affection. A country parish will serve as a symbol for all he deals with; and he writes of war as something inimical to the country parish. And his recollections of human relations are always thickly intertwined with wild-wood flowers and mingled with the racing of mill streams and the noises of birds and beasts. There is merit in the rather Wordsworthian story of **"The Silver Bird of Herndyke Mill."** There are some admirably

sympathetic portraits of rural characters: in **"The Shepherd"** for example, and in the Arcadian **"Almswomen,"** a poem about two old women in a cottage with a flower-garden. They and their small possessions are described quietly and affectionately:

> Many a time they kiss and cry, and pray
> That both be summoned on the selfsame day,
> And wiseman linnet tinkling in his cage
> End too with them the friendship of old age,
> And all together leave their treasured room
> Some bell-like evening when the may's in bloom.

Yet if there be no strong force diverting him he will always return to the contemplation of country life. Not landscape in the ordinary sense. He does occasionally make a generalised picture, a few large lines and a few selected details. But, as a rule, he does not "compose" in that way. He sees every detail with acute clearness, but they are all of equal importance to him. They are important in themselves, not merely as contributions to a picture. He loves every sound and scent, every form of animal and plant and insect; each thing that lives has character to him, and he discriminates very little between people and beasts and flowers. They all live, ploughman and whistling boy, heifer and fish; they all have pleasure in their lives, and suffer; they all are beautiful and die. Even timbers and stones, bells, carts, and tools seem animated to him; so intense is the quality of each, so characteristic its function, so like its progress from newness to decay to that of all things that live.

Varied as his second book is, he showed a sound instinct when he placed at the end of it **"The Last of Autumn,"** a poem in which his most prevalent mood and most habitual joy are expressed as it were in a summary. The sun is gilding autumnal oaks. The fields are shorn of the harvest, sheep "dapple the broad pale green, nabbing or resting," haystacks and hurdles gleam, and the heart, conscious of transience,

> Cannot let a bird
> Chance by but counts him into memory's tribe.

He exhorts himself to note everything, however slowly the shadows may seem to move:

> Ivy with wasp and hornet buzzes still,
> Blue glittering flies are sunning on the stones,
> And the hives among the nettles' chalky flowers
> Are toiling: welcome, wayside thistles' crown,
> And rare-grown daisy in the meadow, shine,
> Though your pale cheeks have lost their lovely red.
>
> But the wind that frets the old and clinging leaves
> Arises deep, the very dirge and knell
> Of this doomed dream:
> And sets the weasel, where she hangs and dries
> To skin and bone, still with her whiskered snarl,
> A-swaying on the barren sloe-tree's thorn. . . .

> But who may tell
> When spring shall come again? And if these eyes
> Should then be shut to the brightness of her coming?
> So for her phantom violets I'll not lose
> These rich, these poor, these fading, glowing hills
> Nor drown my joy in boding. Better it were
> To be dull Thrift, than squander thus this day:
> Dull Thrift, who now has sown his mite of land,
> Has thrashed his corn and beans, and where the dew's
> Quicksilver bubbles lodge and shine all day
> In the cabbage leaves, and the last ladybird
> Beats her bright rosy way, leans reckoning coombs
> And pence upon his garden palisades.

Mr. Blunden does not "drown his joy with boding." He is one of the least sorrowful of poets; when he is sad there is a specific reason for it. He communicates a steady joy, "the harvest of a quiet eye." His work had the marks of permanence from the start; apart from the general merits of his early poems, they showed an unmistakable and rare gift for the timeless phrase. "All things they have in common, being so poor," he wrote, with classic inevitability, of his two old Almswomen; and, lying at leisure in an autumn landscape, he idly watched

> The feather's fall, the doomed red leaf delaying,
> And all the tiny circumstance of peace.

Those last lines, with their touch of Keats, anticipate, by the way, one of the loveliest passages in the later book, a stanza beginning:

> Here joy shall muse what melancholy tells,
>   And melancholy smile because of joy,
> Whether the poppy breathe Arabian spells,
>   To make them friends, or whistling gipsy-boy
>   Sound them a truce that nothing comes to cloy.

But the second book is very much more impressive than the first, and the third will probably be better still. A tendency to overdo dialect words and neologisms—for coining which Mr. Blunden has an extraordinary talent—has disappeared (though "slats the weazen bine" may defeat some readers); but he has still to make some sacrifices to euphony. Some of his lines are so crowded with consonants as to be almost unpronounceable (he lacks that strange power of Mr. Hardy's which fuses the most intractable material into music), and he still inclines to crowd his epithets and his images so that one cannot see the wood for the trees. The crowding comes from his very eagerness, the variety of his affections: everything reminds him of something else, and everything he thinks of is a thing he has seen and noted and savoured, distinguishing its character. Nevertheless the music of the verse is growing more certain and more varied; and the shape of the poems is better. There is still room for development, I think, in this last regard. The defects of Mr. Blunden's qualities are obvious and not easy to fight. A man whose eyes are on the near thing and not on the far horizon, will naturally be tempted to crowd his admirable details too much together; a man so acutely sensitive to those details will sometimes dispense with a theme, and will sometimes be drawn from one to another regardless of beginning, middle, and end. One may still say of some of his poems that each line taken separately is perfect, but that the poems are not perfect. But there is no writer against whom something—usually much—cannot be said.

Work Cited

"The Shepherd and Other Poems of Peace and War," by Edmund Blunden. 1922. "The Waggoner," 1921.

Michael Thorpe (essay date spring 1968)

SOURCE: Thorpe, Michael. "Edmund Blunden's 'Joy' Poems." *English* 17, no. 97 (spring 1968): 9-14.

[*In the following essay, Thorpe examines Blunden's six elegiac poems, written over a period of forty years for his daughter, Joy, who died in infancy.*]

Reviewing Edmund Blunden's **Eleven Poems** in *The Times Literary Supplement* (31 March 1966), an anonymous writer noted his relative neglect by 'the writers of learned articles or academic monographs' and went on to suggest that 'Mr. Blunden may, like Mr. Graves or Robert Frost, in the end prove just as attractive to close critics as such poets as Ezra Pound, say, or T. S. Eliot'. This may seem doubtful: Blunden has versified copiously, multiplied and variegated his trees so generously that any but the most patient and diligent reader may be forgiven for questioning the existence of any definable wood. Unlike Eliot, Pound, and Graves, he has not chosen to segregate his 'poetry' severely from his 'verse'; in fact, he often refers to his whole output as 'verse' as though unaware of its usual pejorative connotation. His level of writing is less consistently high than Frost's: though both had time for 'verse', more of his poems than Frost's would fit readily into a category labelled 'simple, unpretentious observation and reflection'; like Frost, he has always written from a convinced religious standpoint. This is uncommon amongst notable poets nowadays, when the religious poetry that in any case tends to appeal most strongly is that which issues from an intense inward struggle towards a belief radically qualified by anxiety, scepticism, and self-doubt, as in Muir and T. S. Eliot. Frost's religious poetry is more akin to these poets' than to Blunden's, much of which is of the 'devotional' kind and, though it often has a serene beauty, it will never satisfy the 'close critics' whomever else it pleases. Yet, even touching this area of his writing, a rewarding complexity may be found: a complexity that results from a conflict between Blunden's conscious beliefs and wishes and his deeply felt emotion, so giving rise to the 'true voice of feeling'.

To explore this, I have chosen here to discuss the six elegiac poems for his infant daughter Joy, of which the earliest appeared in 1922, the latest in 1962. I could equally well have selected a number of his nature poems, war poems, or some pieces which show a more explicitly religious concern: but the 'Joy' elegies can more readily be treated as a self-contained group and provide at the same time a testing example of one of the most exacting personal themes imaginable, the death of a loved child (Joy died in the summer of 1919, aged forty days). Laments for those who have lived out a life can be more individualized and more substantial: their achievements, their name, may make the loss more supportable—so Dryden could laud Oldham as a lamented peer and Johnson's elegy on Levet, the slum doctor, became a grave monument to a good long life—while such poems as 'Lycidas' and 'Adonais' can mingle, without incongruity, the poet's fate with his subject's. Elegizing the young unformed child, the poet is prone to fall back upon the lax conventional consolations: thus, the classical buttressing and crass sententiousness of the young Milton's poem, despite the beautiful promise of its opening—'O fairest flower no sooner blown but blasted / Soft silken primrose fading timelesslie'. Whatever convention may offer, the bereaved parent has never found the matter easy. Ben Jonson elegized two children: in the first case convention served, 'At six months' end she parted hence / With safety of her innocence' ('On My First Daughter'), but in the second, grief for a more deeply known seven-year-old son almost overpowers him and only by stern self-castigation can he choke back the emotion ('On My First Son'). This moves by its very restraint, but a single flaw can undo all dignity and control, as in Bridges's mawkish line, 'Go lie thou there in thy coffin, thy last little bed!' ('On a Dead Child'). In Blunden's 'Joy' poems we find, as in 'In Memoriam', responses of greatly varying intensity and moving power to a single cause of suffering, two of which at least must live as memorable poems of their kind.

The poems are: **'The Child's Grave'** (*The Shepherd*, 1922); **'Achronos', 'To Joy', 'A First Impression (Tokyo)'**, and **'In a Country Churchyard'** (*English Poems*, 1925), and **'But at Last'** (*A Hong Kong House*, 1962). I shall discuss the poems in the order of their placing in *Poems of Many Years*,[1] taking this as the order in which they were composed; I must assume that the reader has access to all the texts, except **'But at Last'**, which I quote in full for the sake of detailed comment.

Of all these poems the first, though nearest to the child's death, seems the most controlled—though this should not surprise us. The poet describes an April morning walk to visit the grave, his reflections there and on his way home. It is neatly balanced and falls into three clear movements. Stanzas 1-5 describe the peace and beauty of the walk which fill him with so overpowering a sense of life that 'I sang for delight in the ripening of spring'. As often in Blunden's poetry this is richly evoked by precise and colourful detail—'pairing goldfinches gleaming abroad' and 'yellow-hammers sunning on paling and sty'—but this shades into

> The lazy white owls in the glade cool and lone
>   Paid calls on their cousins in the elm's chambered
>   core.

So he comes

>   to the gate of that overgrown ground
>   Where scarce once a year sees the priest come to bury

—here 'overgrown' and the indication that deaths here are infrequent allow, but do not enforce, the mind's adjustment to a darker note. The description of the grave in the next stanza, where the first line arrests the hitherto flowing anapaestic metre, succeeds through the unsentimental presentation of disturbing detail:

> Over the mounds stood the nettles in pride,
>   And, where no fine flowers, there kind weeds dared
>   to wave;
> It seemed but as yesterday she lay by my side,
>   And now my dog ate of the grass on her grave.

He stands by the grave, the dog impatiently licking his hand, and inwardly questions her spirit to know what had become of it since the burial day, 'But the grave held no answer . . .'. The enigma cannot be solved there, in the dull earth itself—'strange that this clay should mingle with hers!'—but, as he returns home, she seems to live again in the beauty that springs from that same earth:

> Joy's spirit shone then in each flower I went by,
>   And clear as the noon, in coppice and ley,
>   Her sweet dawning smile and her violet eye.

At first glance one says, 'Yes, the inevitable pantheistic consolation of the nature worshipper': but this could equally well express a Christian sense of life everlasting granted to the pure in spirit—and here, naturally, felt in the outward symbols of a regenerated universe. The situation and the reflections it prompts strongly remind one of Shelley's 'To William Shelley',

> Let me think thy spirit feeds,
> With its life intense and mild,
>   The love of living leaves and weeds

—but Shelley's poem ends brokenly, tentatively, as his sceptical mind dictates. **'The Child's Grave'**, on the other hand, is doubtless to the steady eye of faith a beautiful and satisfying poem, but our sufferings do not always bow to the rule of our beliefs, nor do they find more than temporary relief, if we feel strongly, in the consolations they supply.

The four poems included in **English Poems** were probably written under less soothing conditions, and two of them fall into the morbid strain which is an ever-present hazard at the ground level of all Romantic poetry. 'Achronos' is the least impressive. At first sight a sonnet (but it has fifteen lines), it is in fact a loosely strung series of visual images representing transience, hastening time, pointing the nothingness of the past. The 'properties', as it were, are trees that 'felled last year, already show / Rust-red their rounds', a 'plough I saw my friend so often guide' lying broken, bramble-covered, and at the poem's turning-point an image suspended in time: 'The spider dates it not but spins in the heat.' It concludes:

> For what's time past? But present time is sweet.
> Think, in that churchyard lies fruit of our loins—
> The child who bright as pearl shone into breath
> With the Egyptian's first-born shares coeval death.

One wonders whether the poem might not have taken a different turn or whether, with this closing reflection, a break came in the feeling. The first of these lines ill prepares one for the last three, where the child is introduced as the final example of the flat opposition between green youth, beauty, use and death or destruction, a passing beyond time's values. The feeling controlled is strong, as the images suggest, but thought is functioning at relatively low pressure.

'To Joy' utterly contrasts with the poems so far discussed: setting the habitual rhyme aside, it lacks all suggestion of contrivance; it is emotional but not strained, bare yet imaginative, as moving as any brief elegy in English. It can be quoted entire:

> Is not this enough for moan
> To see this babe all motherless—
> A babe beloved—thrust out alone
>   Upon death's wilderness?
> Our tears fall, fall, fall—I would weep
> My blood away to make her warm,
> Who never went on earth one step,
>   Nor heard the breath of the storm.
> How shall you go, my little child,
> Alone on that most wintry wild?

The wilderness, the storm, the solitude of the unprotected child: readers may recall 'Alice Fell' and 'Lucy Gray', where the ballad-like rhythms and the bare, essential imagery also seize upon our feelings as soon as uttered. There are some verbal correspondences: the 'lonesome wild' of 'Lucy Gray', and in 'Alice Fell' the speaker asks the luckless girl,

> And whither are you going, child
> Tonight along these lonesome ways?

But there is no question of imitation: such poems have a common source (from which 'The Little Girl Lost' also comes). A contrast with another Wordsworth poem

may be pointed if we remember that, though he writes as a religious poet, Blunden's grief finds no relief in faith—the child is 'alone': Wordsworth, on the other hand, in lamenting his son Thomas solaces himself with a bleak piety, reflecting the believer's distancing resignation rather than the father's nearness,

> Six months to six years added he remained
> Upon this sinful earth, by sin unstained:
> O blessed Lord! whose mercy then removed
> A child whom every eye that looked on loved;
> Support us, teach us calmly to resign
> What we possessed, and now is wholly thine!

The closing couplets of each poem point the contrast strikingly.[2]

To turn from '**To Joy**' to '**A First Impression (Tokyo)**' is to turn from the sparing completeness of utterance which compels the word 'universal' to an exercise in that deceptively loose mode, the 'conversation poem' which Blunden's lifelong favourite Coleridge brought to perfection. The poem is, aptly, in blank verse which allows the thought fluent movement and falls into three parts. The first fifteen lines place us with the poet beneath 'a strange roof' where, 'half round the swaying world', his dead baby's image comes with gentle insistence into his mind's eye. Perhaps she is in elysium, but he cannot come there and laments, 'would that earth's kind flowers / Might now be golden in your toddling path!' The second part of the poem moves naturally into 'musings' upon the living children all around him (if not his own), inspiring the consolatory,

> though one of these dear blooms
> Fall, still great childhood lords it all the way,
> And the whole earth may see and hear and glory.

A lesser poet might have ended here: lesser, because though the consolation is for Blunden a genuine one, one would not expect it to be enough for the man who suffers. And it must be admitted here that Blunden's touch is prone to waver where childhood at large is his theme. He shares with Wordsworth and Coleridge, notably, a nostalgia for 'great childhood' which leads him to force upon that state a heavier burden than children *as individuals* can support. The lax apostrophe quoted is a sign of overstrained feeling and a common inflexion of the Romantic voice, often betraying unconsciously the poet's urge to reject the cares of adult life. Here, it is only acceptable within the stream of the poem's feeling and is corrected (emotionally) by the purer tone of the closing, bare monosyllabic line: 'But still, I saw a ghost, and lacked one child.'

'**In a Country Churchyard**' at once suggests a comparison and a contrast with Gray's 'Elegy'. Gray's very regular iambic pentameter, with its alternating rhymes, creates a mood of reconciliation and acceptance. Blunden uses a similarly rhymed stanza, but varies the stresses to form an uneasy 4:2, 4:2 pattern; the result is hectic, urgent, restless:

> Earth is a quicksand; yon square tower
>   Would still seem bold,
> But its bleak flinty strength each hour
>   Is losing hold.
>
> Small sound of gasping undertow
>   In this green bed!
> Who shuts the gate will shut it slow,
>   Here sleep the dead:
>
> Here sleep, or slept; here, chance, they sleep,
>   Though still this soil
> As mad and clammed as shoals acreep
>   Around them boil.

These opening stanzas give a startling impression of the poet's agonized mind. 'Earth is a quicksand' establishes the feverish sense, disturbingly sustained by the diction that follows, of death as a relentless malevolent force; the very foundations of Gray's 'ivy-mantled tower' are undermined. This is indeed the most morbid of these poems, in which the poet's hopeful mind struggles for balance as if it were itself caught in a quicksand that 'not an instant stops / Its deadly flowing'. Anxiously he tries to stem this treacherous undertow with images of peace proper to churchyard rest or rapt rebirth in the heavens above, with 'sleep in the flux as on the breast', but these are borne down at last by the sad fate of what we know, or have known, which our future hopes, however strong, cannot dispel:

> But, joyous eyes,
> The deeps drag dull—
> O morning smile and song, so lies
> Thy tiny skull?

The strict stanzaic form the poet imposes upon **'In a Country Churchyard'**, albeit uneasy in effect, just holds together the tremulous feeling—which, in the naked reflections upon the fate of the 'tiny skull', is the least contained in these elegies and strikingly at variance with that developed in the earlier **'The Child's Grave'**.

The poems so far discussed were all written within three years of the child's death and focus, with varying intensity, upon painfully close memories of her. Either her fate is felt all too nearly, as in **'In a Country Churchyard'**, or the poet seeks consciously to control this by opposing death with life (**'A First Impression'**) or, in the finest, most universal view he distils in **'To Joy'** the essence of a tortured parent's loss. By 1925 the upper veins of grief had been worked; he does not return to Joy till twenty-four years later, in *After the Bombing* (1949), with **'Joy and Margaret'**. Though I do not count this poem among the elegies, a brief com-

ment will be relevant to the general theme. Joy is addressed directly and again with deep recollection of the distant suffering, as when he recalls how

> while you lay in that gray clutch
> You heard my step, you knew my touch,
> And looked cross wonder that I failed
> To shield you from the cold and heat.

Yet now another daughter—'a second self'—has been born with whom Joy may, in spirit, play and share delight, the living now keeping alive the happier thoughts of the dead child. Is this a special pleading of the poet's desire? This consolation differs markedly from the saving last lines of **'A First Impression'**— 'saving' in that there he pressed his feeling to what one feels is a truer point, no tidy ending. This, however, is dangerous ground: poetry often obeys mood and the mood is true enough.

It takes many years for painful memories to find their level in the mind, so that they become absorbed into the texture of maturing feeling, the personal being subsumed in the universal and yet retaining its potency for the individual. **'But at Last'**, published forty years after **'The Child's Grave'**, is the refined, perhaps final product of this process:

> These images of quiet, these I should not call
> Death's figures, quiet as are the shroud and pall.
> The millsail pauses, all so still
> On the knoll above the village; in its form
> A watchful will then bides its time,
> As in a clear sky a storm.
> And that engraved broad bell
> So silent in the dusky stony tower
> Is yet the vessel of the waiting chime.
> Today, this hour,
> That bell you see black on the sky, or climb
> And see, where the whole peal rests,
> Is nothing dead; nor is that battered lantern nor
> The crowbar on the belfry floor
> Past work and use.
> Begin; the peal's awake, what clang profuse!
> —This flower
> Upon your grave, golden child, is other
> Than death's wry token;
> Its slackened sense
> In its silence, fallen
> Is of a soul flown hence.
> The tears of the father and mother
> Are dry as these petals: let them make a copy
> For those who crest the tomb, a withered poppy.
> Our child could fall asleep long nights together.
> To slumber and to wither
> Must be some difference. Look, then: that millsail
>   strong
> Before long
> May become a sadder sign, its prompting spent,
> From quiet power turned failure,—next, evanishment:
> Forced by the serious enemy of light breath
> Motion and pulse, like her, once rosy innocent:
> Death's image at last, where quiet seemed immanent.

Readers may doubt whether this poem belongs to these elegies at all. If my supposition when I first read it, that it did, was correct, then the memory of Joy would here be implicit and perhaps hidden from the poet himself. When I suggested this to him, he replied: "**"But at Last"** was one of the dreamy pieces I wrote in Hong Kong, on an imaginary scene. . . . I suppose that the child Joy was back with me, a memory—only, lost.'

'But at Last' differs markedly from the other elegies in both form and intention. The manner is more typical of Edward Thomas's than of Blunden's poetry (though other examples exist in Blunden's work). As Thomas often does, Blunden began with images that carried strong personal resonance—the 'images of quiet'—and followed where their associations led him; there was no conscious attempt to recall the lost child. There is formal rhyme, as in Thomas, but the line lengths are subtly varied to suggest the turns, pauses, and breaks in the reverie. The process can hardly be unravelled and expressed in prose terms: such poetry is its own speech. The 'close reading' that follows is necessarily tentative.

The 'images of quiet', the millsail and the bell, are introduced as candidates for 'Death's figures' though the poet would not himself pass them as such. The millsail pauses, still, but will move on: its rest is delusory—'in its form / A watchful will then bides its time': if Death is the utter negation of life, the millsail and bell, only temporarily suspended, are not 'Death's figures'. Though both are delusory semblances of death, they have a contrasting effect: the 'will' behind the sail seems ominous, while the bell conceals the lively 'clang profuse'. A third image is now abruptly introduced, though not too abruptly, for there is a natural movement from the bell-tower to the graveyard below, the eye dropping from these figures of suspended life to a *true* figure of death—the flower upon the grave? Again, it is not, if death signifies total extinction: the life, 'the soul', has flown and the mind is prompted to reflect upon, not death, but higher life. Now comes a transition, again by association, to the tears of the parents, necessarily dry, the freshness of their mourning staled by time, as the flowers on the grave have withered (and not been replaced): let the dried petals, therefore, be a fitting mark of remembrance. Now follows 'Our child could fall asleep long nights together'; this introduces another ambiguous 'image of quiet', sleep, capable of being a traditional figure of death in a regenerative sense,

> To slumber and to wither
> Must be some difference

—this poses a crucial question: is sleep a 'truer' figure for death than the withered petal? It may appear that the poet has already answered this (ll. 26-8), where the 'slackened sense' signifies flight to a higher form bear-ing no relation to the earthly husk, but this seems to stand outside the main line of the poem as it develops.

With 'Look, then', the poet seemingly turns to explication, taking first the millsail image with 'slumber': both are, after all, signs of death in an absolute sense, the power they draw upon being only temporary—like that of the 'rosy innocent' stilled by 'the serious enemy of light breath'—and so, at last, will become 'death's image' in truth, no longer symbolic of quiet. Quiet had seemed immanent: in fact it was death, though at first the poet 'should not call it so'; the 'watchful will' that bided its time was, then, the 'immanent will'. Brooding through images of quiet, then, is always death: there are the false images and the true—the withered petals and, perhaps, the bell, bringing together the ideas of transcendence and its celebration, but this latter image is not carried through the poem and has no ultimate force.

Is any 'meaning' decipherable? The poet himself has written, 'It seems to me that the opposition of quiet and death is the "main line" of it all', and adds '"Immanent" is T. Hardy's word in the Immanent Will'—which can be inferred from relating l. 8 to ll. 46-7. In the Fore Scene of *The Dynasts* the Shade of the Earth asks, 'What of the Immanent Will and Its designs?' and the Spirit of the Years replies:

> It works unconsciously, as heretofore
> Eternal artistries in Circumstance,
> Whose patterns, wrought by rapt aesthetic rote,
> Seem in themselves Its single listless aim,
> And not their consequence.

Hardy's Will works through time regardless of 'consequence' to humanity in terms of its happiness or misery; it is the blind unmeaning progression of things. Is this then what emerges from the 'dreamy' musings of a religious poet? Evidently it is the poem's 'line': images of quiet are delusory figures, inconsequential patterns, there is no difference between sleep and withering, quiet shades into death and extinction and can be no mere symbol of it. 'Soul flown hence' may work against this impression, but not the sense of the whole: the hopeful element dims before a cooler vision which is, in its mood, life-centred yet resigned to death, leaving transcendence an open question. Outstanding amongst these elegies, 'But at Last' shares with 'To Joy' a vital freedom from the bonds of predetermined beliefs and patterns of presentation, and in these two poems feeling finds memorably its own 'true voice'.

Notes

1. *Poems of Many Years* (Collins, 1957), pp. 89, 110, 113, 117, and 119; *A Hong Kong House* is also published by Collins.

2. But compare *The Excursion,* Bk. III, ll. 636-49, where the Solitary's moving narrative of his shattering loss of two children 'with a short interval of time between' surely carries the transferred force of Wordsworth's own double bereavement in 1812.

J. E. Morpurgo (essay date October 1974)

SOURCE: Morpurgo, J. E. "Edmund Blunden: Poet of Community." *Contemporary Review* 225, no. 1305 (October 1974): 192-98.

[*In the following essay, Morpurgo discusses Blunden as a poet who attempted to maintain a connection to the poets of the past and to encourage those of the future.*]

In the months since Edmund Blunden died, men of great distinction have paid tribute to his genius as poet, critic, biographer, teacher, memorialist of a generation and, above all, to that quality which those of us who knew him prize beyond all knowledge of his artistry or all confidence in the durability of his literary reputation: his wondrous gift for friendship. They have spoken with eloquence, written with elegance—and always with affection and gratitude—for Britain, for Japan, for Hong Kong, for the whole corporation of letters.

The celebration of his connection with Christ's Hospital is seemingly a humbler duty but, because Blunden responded with such munificence to the inspiration that he drew from the tradition of the school in which he was educated, the domestic nature of this tribute is immediately enlarged and becomes in some measure an explanation of the writer, a reiteration of the purposes for which he worked and, even, a plea for the perpetuation of his services.

Individuals, places, institutions: to these Blunden gave loyalty and for him loyalty was never fettered by chronology. He was not so much traditionalist as apostle of continuity, no less active in the encouragement of the future than in the preservation or restoration of the past. He was above all things the poet of community and, though his devotion to Christ's Hospital was direct it was also symbolical; it was for him emphatic in a vast metaphor which embraced his total dedication to his task. By concentrating upon the intimate—be it Christ's Hospital, a country village or a platoon of infantrymen—he presented the universal, by dwelling upon the parochial he demonstrated the synoptic.

When, in 1909, Edmund Blunden entered Christ's Hospital and was listed among the boys joining the house named after Samuel Taylor Coleridge the gods on Parnassus must have congratulated themselves on their magnificent prescience. True, the odds were high that the fluttering hands of prophecy would contrive some link between the name of Blunden and the name of one or other of his great literary precursors. For three and a half centuries products of Edward VI's 'dede of pittie' had denied the poverty of their childhood origins by the richness of their adult achievements. Many had risen high in the service of State and Church; one, Edmund Campion, so high in the service of the 'wrong' church that he had been beatified by Rome. Others had won great wealth. Blues had been prominent among the pioneers who unrolled the maps of Canada, New Zealand, and Australia. The Indian Empire, the Russia of the Czars and the United States of the Founding Fathers all owed something to men who had once been Bluecoat boys. Yet, despite all this diversity of notability, when at about the time of Blunden's birth, Christ's Hospital planned the move from its ancient home in the heart of the City of London to the middle of the Sussex Weald and planned also to exchange austerely numbered 'wards' for the proud proclamation of residential houses named after the school's greatest sons the response to the especial genius of the Foundation was inevitable. Five of the eight houses were called after men of letters, a sixth was left without eponym, as if waiting upon the time when royal anger would fade and James Henry Leigh Hunt could be given his due.

Blunden was to devote much of his rare skill to the celebration of those who had come before him to Christ's Hospital. No critic did more than he to hold the fame of Charles Lamb against bustling changes in public taste. His devotion to the cause of Leigh Hunt was just as sturdy and had it not been for his advocacy it is doubtful if the reputation of that bold journalist and most perspicacious of editors could have survived the libels of Dickens and the persistent antagonism of the high priests of the Byron cult. (It was a coincidence but a coincidence much to Blunden's liking that he came eventually to Printing House Square where his sensitive ear could still catch echoes of the voice of yet another of the patronal Blues, Thomas Barnes, the editor who first put thunder into the tones of *The Times.*)

Despite these subsequent connections created out of affection and respect and honoured by his loving criticism the early conjunction of Blunden and Coleridge was even more apt than would have been an oracular hyphen between his name and that of Lamb, of Leigh Hunt or of Barnes.

Like Lamb, Blunden was born a Londoner but for him London could never be what it was for Elia, the centre and circumference of his spirit. ('These are thy pleasures, O London with-the-many-sins. For this may Keswick and her giant brood go hang!') Although he spent some of the happiest years of his life in the East, and is in Hong Kong and Japan remembered with admiration and love that comes close to reverence, Blunden never coveted and never achieved the cosmo-politanism which came to Leigh Hunt through American and West Indian parentage. Wherever he found himself, be it in London or Oxford, the Orient or even on the blood-soaked battlefields of Flanders, like Coleridge Blunden remained unshakeably and unmistakeably a son of the English countryside—he himself would have used the honourable, evocative and precise description: an English yeoman.

Blunden responded eagerly to that early prompting from the name of Coleridge: the very first book that he bought for himself was a collection of Coleridge's poems. His consciousness of affinity with the greatest of Blues was heightened when, in the last year of his schooldays, like Coleridge before him, he became head of the school, Senior Grecian. In his adult years Blunden was modest, almost to a fault. Not the Hawthornden Prize, not the frequent reprintings of **Undertones of War,** not even his election to the Chair of Poetry at Oxford could persuade him to become a public person-ality and, though his undramatic nature enhanced the affection in which he was held by his friends, it may be that his reticence denied to him a measure of prominence such as some of his contemporaries won too easily merely by becoming pundits. His braggart moments he reserved for the most part for reminiscences of cricket and even of these cherished performances when he presented a reprise it was always of himself as First Gravedigger to some far nobler Hamlet, as when he told of the time when he had fielded to the bowling of Percy Fender or of that even more glorious occasion when he had guarded the other end whilst Keith Miller scored a century. But that he had been Senior Grecian, for this grandeur in his youth there was no modesty and even forty years after he had left school he would allow himself the conceit that thus he had established his eternal seniority even over Lamb and Leigh Hunt who had been superannuated as mere Deputy Grecians. Almost it made him the equal of his superb predeces-sor.

There was pride but not vanity in Blunden's acceptance of his inheritance. He was too much an original—and too modest—to attempt imitation but the affinity with Samuel Taylor Coleridge is palpable in much of Blunden's verse and prose. Poet answered to poet, scholar to scholar, countryman to countryman, Blue to Blue. The genius that had gone before he honoured in lectures, essays, poems and innumerable allusions. Even, because Blunden was deeply conscious that to be an heir carries with it responsibilities to enlarge the heritage, he varied themes that echoed from Coleridge, resetting them according to the mode which reflected his own generally happier life. Thus in his essay *Sus-*

sex, Blunden, who entered Christ's Hospital after the move from London had made the Weald into the school's back-garden, holds in subtle reminiscence *Frost at Midnight:*

> "But O! how oft
> How oft, at school, with most believing mind,
> Presageful, have I gazed upon the bars."

and in his own delight at the close harmony between school and country turns a key to free a spirit 'pent mid cloisters dim':

> When I went to the Bluecoat School it had not long
> been newly built in a then sleepy corner of the country.
> It was, and is, fortunate in its neighbourhood. It lies in
> the lowland, yet with its near variety of wood and hill,
> its further prospects of heights and blue horizons . . .

The bars that had warded Coleridge against all things 'lovely but the sky and stars' Blunden magicked into the gates that stood, forever opened and unhindering, on the road that led to Shelley Wood and so on into the 'fairy wilderness'. And mischievously—by the use of a pun—the bells that long ago proclaimed only homesick-ness to the young Coleridge

> . . . as oft
> With unclosed lids, already have I dreamt
> Of my sweet birth-place, and the old church-tower,
> Whose bells, the poor man's only music, rang
> From morn to evening . . .

now in Blunden's prose are pealed again to proclaim across the Weald, not loneliness, separation and restric-tion, but freedom and a sense of communion between school and the world outside the gates:

> The chiming name of Chanctonbury was ever with us,
> and the ring often beckoned us southwards.

A full-length history, a pageant, several essays, a number of poems, allusions innumerable, and enthusias-tic and energetic collaboration in the compilation of the volume which celebrated the Christ's Hospital Quater-centenary—all this he contrived to present to his contemporaries and to pass on to subsequent genera-tions the useful ethos of Christ's Hospital; all this and his several books on Lamb and Leigh Hunt. It was a handsome return for the 'benefits that he had received in this place', the most prolific even in the record of a foundation that has so often drawn celebrative literature from its celebrated literary sons and assuredly the most generous that any author in the whole canon of English letters has given to the place of his education. But the task that he had set himself was never completed; the symmetry which he planned for his career was tragi-cally destroyed; his biography of Coleridge remained unfinished when the last illness struck.

Blunden's handsome interpretation of Christ's Hospital and his unselfish readiness to further the cause of com-munity and continuity persuaded him to cherish those who followed him through Christ's Hospital into the literary life with the same generosity that he had devoted to his predecessors. Encouragement was part of his art. There is in one of his letters to the poet Keith Douglas (a Blue and one of Blunden's pupils at Merton) a passage which illustrates both Blunden's conviction that (in the words of yet another literary Blue, John Middleton Murry) through Christ's Hospital 'we are endowed with ancestors' and also his zeal for encouraging his juniors.

> We have had some pretty good poets [he wrote to Douglas in 1940], Peele, Coleridge, Lamb, Hunt, but the line must be extended! and I think you can do it.

Many of us have reason to be grateful for Blunden's patronage. Too often he sacrificed his own opportunities to give us our chance but the readiness with which he thrust forward men younger and lesser than himself does help to explain the centrality of Blunden in the literary life of our times and, perhaps even more important, the manner in which this quiet, unassuming man became the creator and the heart of a great web of interlocking friendships which stretches out to all the continents.

Christ's Hospital was focal to his life and work, but his wisdom was too intense and his generosity too profuse to allow him to mistake symbol for totality. Others, less fortunate than us, he embraced into the community and often he would say of some friend, living or long-since dead when Blunden was born, 'He should be one of us', but his generosity was never soft and sometimes, for example, when told of an Old Blue who had denied his origins, he would spit out his distaste: 'We do not speak of him'—an echo of Leigh Hunt's dismissal of Edward Thornton:

> We have had an ambassador among us, but as he . . . is ashamed of us, we are hereby more ashamed of him, and accordingly omit him.

But malice—even when it was merited—did not come easily or often from Blunden. The enlargement of the community was more to his taste than the exclusion of offenders. There is logic in the circumstance that the first of his many acts of warm-hearted scholarship engineered a revival of the poetry of John Clare, for, like Blunden, Clare was a countryman and, though not a Blue, like all Blues he was born to deprivation. There is logic more immediate in Blunden's devotion to Shelley; even a rich aristocrat could be made 'one of us' if he was a neighbour, a man of Sussex, his properties an easy walk away, his mother's home, Stammerham, actually within the school estate—and he himself sponsored for the brotherhood by Leigh Hunt. And as with Shelley, so also with William Collins; literary neighbourliness that stretched out so comfortably to Warnham was with no great difficulty enlarged to take in a scholar of Chichester Cathedral School.

The conjunction of Christ's Hospital and Sussex was for Blunden a happy coincidence. Sussex was in his bones and, though he moved later to the far Orient and settled eventually in East Anglia, Sussex was for him the first, the natural and the most enduring enlargement of the Bluecoat community. The major poet of Sussex and her minor versifiers he held in affection, but in Sussex he identified that other inheritance which combined with ancestors provided by Christ's Hospital to give him both privilege and responsibility.

> Names are vanished save the few
> In the old brown Bible scrawled;
> These were men of pith and thew,
> Whom the city never called.

By his own powers he made poets and scribblers long dead into contemporaries; through his own generosity he extended the courtesy of shared generation to men much younger than himself; but a hideous alchemy not of his own devising added a dimension to his community with the nameless, the unidentifiable men of Sussex, and for him made those ordinary men extraordinary and all-important. Within months of leaving school he was hurled into the midst of the most vicious war that mankind has ever inflicted upon itself. He went into battle with men who were drawn, most of them, from this county and with officers who were, some of them, also Blues. The intimacy of background sharpened the tragedy but it also gave additional depth to his compassion. His countryman's delight in the fecundity of his own Sussex informed his sorrow as he watched the destruction of Flanders:

> I have seen a green country, useful to the race,
> Knocked silly with guns and mines, its villages
>   vanished,
> Even the last rat and kestrel banished—
> God bless us all, this was peculiar grace.

For him the guns were never silenced; over fifty years the bombardment of mind and spirit continued, yet, though protest and mourning were seldom absent from his conversation or from his writing, his reaction to war was of a different, and perhaps a nobler kind than that of most of his contemporary poets. Destruction, waste, futility, these things caused him pain, but above the discords he sang his lovely hymns. The grief was real but so was the optimism:

> O never dead! you live, your old songs yet
> Pass me each day, your faith still routs my dread,
> Your past and future are my parapet.

Blunden stayed for the rest of his days within earshot of Ypres and Hamel, 'haunted ever by war's agony'; he remained also for the rest of his days within the world-wide and timeless fraternity of soldiers. He had enlarged his community once more and when a second World War hurtled another generation into battle he served alongside that generation as if it were his own. He was by then too old to be a fighting man, though there are many who remember him, in uniform once again, teaching map-reading to Oxford undergraduates, but his care for my contemporaries was never distant. I have among my collection of Blunden letters one which reached me in Italy as we were battering our way through the Gothic Line. It came as reply to a note of mine thanking him for a copy of *Cricket Country* (and like all his correspondence for its exquisite calligraphy merits a place in an exhibition-gallery as for its elegant construction it could go into any anthology of the art of the letter).

> Your writing to me from the battlefield and its godless precincts is a delightful kindness and I value highly such praise for my book on or around Cricket. It was a book written in the hope that it would help some whom the damn'd war was holding at distance.

But his greatest service between 1939 and 1945 was happily just what he would have wished for himself: he helped to extend the line. Firm in his faith that 'the fighting man in this as in other wars is at least the only man whom truth really cares to meet' he had taught younger men to continue as artists even whilst they managed as well as they could their temporary role as soldiers. It is part of a tribute to Blunden that one can claim that two of the finest and most sensitive books about the Second War, Keith Douglas's *Alamein to Zem Zem* and Douglas Grant's *The Fuel of the Fire,* were by authors who had been his pupils at Merton and that Keith Douglas was also a Blue.

Those of us who remember the man will hold that memory among our treasures for the rest of our days. For me, clear in my recollection is that first time I saw him, in my house-master's study at Christ's Hospital, small, quiet-voiced and mild-seeming, almost lost in the depths of an armchair, but awesome as the greatest living Old Blue and indeed the greatest man that I had ever met. I know still my amazement and delight that the winner of the Hawthornden, the author of **Undertones of War** was not merely listening to my idiot ambitions to follow the craft of letters, he was actually supporting my lunacy. Twenty years later I see him, earnest and eager, when I had him once on the field captaining a side that contained no fewer than six Test players in the annual festival of his twin gods, Literature and Cricket. And I know that I share with a privileged few particular delight in a mental picture; Blunden, his C.B.E. and his M.C. safety-pinned most unsafely to his dinner-jacket, as he drank his pint of beer in a City pub which we had made our rendezvous before passing on to the opulence of the Mansion House for the Christ's Hospital Quatercentenary Banquet. Those who were there will forever hear him talking as he talked then, of some obscure literary Blue of the distant past whose poetry, by quotation and praise, Blunden made more memorable than it should be, and talking too, as he

talked then of one recently of our number whose batting was made even more elegant than it has ever been by Blunden's recounting.

The works that he added to the great tradition are for the centuries. The pride that comes with echoing—and enlarging—Blunden's phrase transcends the parochial. 'We have had some pretty good poets, Peele, Coleridge, Lamb, Hunt' . . . and Douglas. Edmund Blunden stands with the finest and his imperative to continuity cannot be silenced:

> But the line must be extended.

Miriam J. Benkovitz (essay date April 1980)

SOURCE: Benkovitz, Miriam J. "Edmund Blunden and the Incitements of Japan." *Books at Iowa,* no. 32 (April 1980): 15-24.

[*In the following essay, Benkovitz discusses the poetry Blunden wrote while teaching in Japan, particularly the verses in* Japanese Garland, *a collection she maintains firmly established Blunden as a romantic poet.*]

When Cyril Beaumont, bookseller and publisher, suggested to Edmund Blunden in the first year of his stay in Tokyo that he produce a "set of poems on Japan," Blunden disparaged the idea. He had found nothing there, after some five months, conducive to poetry. "Japan as presented here in Tokyo," he told Beaumont in a letter of November 17, 1924, "is far from inspiring one to poetry—to blasphemy is the direction!" Blunden conceded, however, that poetry on Japan was not entirely out of the question, and he promised Beaumont anything which "honesty & plainness need not disown." Blunden admitted that he might "be moved by the relics of the finer dynasties, Kyoto and so forth." He went on, "I can't say knowing that my power of poetry (whatever it is) depends on certain very sudden & subtle incitements."

Unlike so many English poets, Blunden did not enlarge on those incitements. For him there was no talk of imitation or amplification, no reference to Sir Philip Sidney's golden world or to Wordsworth's "emotion recollected in tranquillity." Indeed, if Blunden had contemplated those "sudden & subtle incitements" until he could analyze and explain them, he made no effort to do so in the five letters he wrote from Japan to Cyril Beaumont and another 45 to Richard Cobden-Sanderson, friend and publisher,[1] plus a few letters to one or two others, now in the Special Collections of the Library of The University of Iowa. Nevertheless, what provoked Blunden to poetry is apparent, at least in part, in the manuscript he eventually delivered to Beaumont, *Japanese Garland,* a book of poems having to do with Japan, even with Tokyo.

If the letters from Tokyo are an indication, Blunden's poetic impulse and indeed his extensive literary output in those Tokyo years came from a constant frustration and discontent. Even before he left his home at Stansfield near Clare in Suffolk, Blunden was troubled about going to Japan. Although he had referred to the possibility in late January and again a week later,[2] the first confirmation in these letters came in one addressed to Cobden-Sanderson on February 9, 1924: "I am projecting myself . . . into the bosom of the Japanese," Blunden wrote. "R. Nichols is leaving his English professorship at Tokyo, I was asked to take it, &, the salary being fair, I thought I would." But the decision was more momentous than Blunden's mild words imply. Mary Blunden, his wife of only six years, refused to go with him. "Mary is staying here, to my surprise," Blunden told Cobden-Sanderson, "but she prefers to do so, not visualizing Japan as the land of hope & glory which it now appears to me." And indeed it did appear so. England was racked by the strikes which culminated in the General Strike of 1926. Postwar malaise, which Blunden had tried hard to overcome, lingered with him. More immediately, returns for a man whose income was derived solely from writing were scant. By contrast, Japan offered a sure thing in the way of earnings as well as the allure of the remote East. Englishmen, including the bookish ones, had long gone to far places to earn their way, and Blunden meant to join their ranks. But before the date for his departure was set, his wife had lessened his enthusiasm by her refusal to go with him; and no protest or pleading moved her. He told Cobden-Sanderson that Mary would hear no argument, that for her Stansfield was enough, and she refused to budge.[3] Ten days later, to Beaumont, Blunden explained his delay in supplying a tardy manuscript by saying that he was "thrown . . . out of gear" by the anticipation of Japan.[4] However predictable a flurry of nerves at so strange and long a journey may be, Blunden was unduly agitated. He spoke of his coming "exile" and confessed that he was "getting worse & worse, a state of no state overwhelming" him.[5] He then decided he must delay completion of his life of Leigh Hunt owing to lack of research materials until he returned from Japan. Furthermore he had found a "sad misprint" in his edition of Christopher Smart's poems, and he urged the publisher to issue an erratum slip and insert it in the book.[6] All in all, these were mournful and harrowing "about-to-be exiled moments."

At last on Friday, March 28, 1924 at 4:10 P.M., Blunden left Liverpool Street Station, London, on the boat-train for Southampton, where he boarded the *S. S. Hakone Maru* to sail by way of Singapore and Hong Kong halfway round the "swaying" world to Japan. There he came ashore at Yokohama and was promptly "hurried along in the most amiable manner" to see the Maiko Conchological Cabinet. What acquaintance satisfied his own enthusiasm for the conchological in this way or

why is lost now, but Blunden never forgot the incident. After viewing the museum, he traveled to Tokyo by rail, a form of transportation in 1924 which had none of the swift, smooth comfort of present times in Japan. Blunden reached Tokyo on May 13, 1924,[7] and he did not like it.

He began by confessing to Beaumont that he was not precisely "enamoured" of Tokyo. That was early in his stay. But when Blunden had been in Tokyo almost a year, he still had only one good thing to say about his "Japanese experiment"; it was passing. "One day telleth another," he said. "I feel no striving, no new orientation; a few friends support me, and the rest is not silence, but a useless uproar, signifying nothing."[8] And before another year had gone, he lamented that he had ever signed his contract, and he was certain that England was the only place for him. An opportunity to go from Japan to America brought forth a quick determination to go from Japan "to England, if the Gods are good, & nowhere else."[9] In summer the heat "half melted" him and fleas and mosquitoes plagued him. When winter came, he complained of snow and ice. His asthma troubled him from time to time.

Blunden tried to shelter himself from his environment. Japanese speech seemed a nuisance to learn, and although he had a few phrases which he could "bring out" from time to time, he chose not to work at acquiring more. he asked Cobden-Sanderson, "Can I go through day after day in my present ignorant fashion, observing nothing peculiar in Japanese custom, adding no weird word to my vocabulary?" Blunden's answer to his own question read, "Probably I can."[10]

Of course he could not. The size and noise of Tokyo are formidable, but its special flavor is undeniable, and it was more pronounced in 1924 before street signs were posted in English, automobiles clogged the streets, and many people adopted Western dress. Blunden reported his tendence to "bow & scrape after the manner of the country" and an ability to wield chopsticks "well enough to face the future." In any case the food was acceptable. He said that eels and rice "went down well" and the feelers of cuttle fish were "much more Christian eating" than might be imagined. He missed English beer and whiskey, but while saké was "nothing extraordinary," a few cups created a "mildly oiled insouciance."[11] He hardly managed to disregard the small earth tremors, reminders of the massive earthquake of September 1923, which shook Tokyo at intervals. On August 15, he wrote of a minor quake at about two that morning, so "beautiful" that he considered getting out of bed—that bed spread so "reverently" by his "henchman" on the straw-matted floor and covered with a mosquito net which let in only the "more cunning mosquitoes."[12] Living conditions in general were difficult. He was more content with them, however, when he moved in January 1925 from 26 Kitoyamabushi-cho, Uchigome, to the Kikufuji Hotel, Hongo (the section of Tokyo in which the university is located). It was more expensive and it lacked a bar, but all in all it was an improvement on his first address. Still, his description of the place in a letter of November 1 was caustic:

> this Hotel is quite a variety, and has its own special features; the staff is constantly altered to suit the latest requirements (of the money-lender opposite), & the entrance has recently been enriched with a new set of lockers for the clogs of the guests; ping-pong may be indulged in downstairs, while, mingling with the mirth of the champions and their numerous advisers, the chimes of the two stately clocks fill the ear and suggest the time within half an hour either way. Oil stoves may be supplied by the guests; otherwise it is possible that they will be frozen, but the hotel is in touch with a garage stabling an admired motor hearse for the use of departing clients.

Blunden went on about his own room or "cell" as he called it: "The owner's three hats, (two punctured), hang symmetrically above his homely bed; a plate of bananas suggests the Last days of Pompeii . . . and three roses are blooming . . . in a ginger jar."[13]

And at length Blunden looked around him, and he grudgingly recorded something of Japan. The countryside, viewed on "excursions into the hills & down by the sea" in July 1924, roused his admiration. He admitted that it looked very nice, that the rural cottages had a "Rembrandtesque reminiscence" about them and that "bamboos and pines make very pleasant forests."[14] But when Cobden-Sanderson asked for a "vivid description" of Tokyo, Blunden replied with scorn, "What, of paper lanterns, open drains, flower-like ladies, naked brown labourers, grins and stares perpetual, the Imperial Hotel (about half a crown a minute), the cinematograph theatre . . . ?"[15] He half promised to send a long account of "Tokyanity" when autumn brought cooler weather; but even in the dead of winter he refused to write more about the city because he had "given up swearing." Only in the summer of 1926 did he set down anything about the "cries of 'Eels,' 'Bananas'; drums of exorcisers of devils, bells of newspaper boys," and then he lumped them together as the "usual monotony all round."[16]

That impatient, bored endurance colored his accounts of his teaching, too. Blunden approached it with irony, sometimes distaste. Each day was a chore and when it was done he still had to "contemplate a little more work another day." At last he decided that to "profess" was not his "track," although he had acquired a "strong professorial incrustation—a crabbed o'ergathering of dictatorial didacticism," which, however, he promised to shed.[17] But the "so-called University" did not measure up to his standards. It had no library "worth the name"

and the students were often obtuse and, in accord with their Japanese manners, too polite to admit that what he told them penetrated neither their habits of thought nor the language barrier. But to Blunden his students were men who "have ears & hear not." He cited as an example of the questions to which his "talents" were currently applied, "Sir, is the owner of a public house called a publisher?" and added that his reply did not matter; for "most of the J. don't believe an honest answer—they stick to their own interpretation."[18]

Yet, among the "150 unfortunate wretches" to whom he lectured and among his colleagues, Blunden found men to respect and like and work with. While staring "stonily at the horrid truth" of his commitment to Tokyo and recording his discontent with it in letter after letter, Blunden was endlessly busy with literary matters. He read proofs sent him from London, such as those for *The Actor* by the obscure eighteenth-century English poet Robert Lloyd, published at the Beaumont Press in 1926 with an introductory essay by Blunden. He attempted to find a Japanese publisher for Cyril Beaumont's *The Mysterious Toyshop*, which appeared in London in 1924. He recommended the work of colleagues at the Imperial University. He had been in Tokyo less than a year when in January 1925, he initiated English publication of "Master Ishii's little poetry book," a volume which appeared in January 1926, *Twelve Poems* by Haxon Ishii, and was duly reviewed in the *Times Literary Supplement*. Similarly Blunden suggested that Cobden-Sanderson consider a collection of verse by an associate, Sherard Vines, a "lively young poet of the Sitwellian tint" whose poems Blunden characterized as "modern & . . . masterly, full of novel poetic motives and splendid imaginations." Vines's book, *Triforium*, appeared, too, under Cobden-Sanderson's imprint.[19] Blunden's greatest enthusiasm, however, was for Takeshi Saito, both colleague and student and, according to Blunden, "scholar, gentleman, and Christian of the first quality." With Saito, Blunden prepared for publication a selection from *The Examiner*, a paper which in its day had carried essays by Leigh Hunt and Charles Lamb. This was sent to Cobden-Sanderson as was Saito's doctoral dissertation, an essay on Keats's view of poetry.[20] Blunden worried the book on Leigh Hunt, left unfinished for lack of the British Library; he commenced a collection of William Collins's poems; and he wrote an essay *On the Poems of Henry Vaughan*. An essay on John Clare delivered as a lecture to an audience of American, English, and Japanese women in October 1924, "by way of ending" his "29th year," was issued in Japan in April or May 1926 as a pamphlet limited to 20 copies.[21] And Blunden's verses began to appear in journals published in Japan. One called *Poetica*, made up primarily of materials written in Japanese, from time to time printed poems by Robert Nichols, Blunden's predecessor at the Imperial University, and by Blunden, in English, of course. His verses appeared in the *Oriental Literary Times,* an elusive periodical, whose existence is known partly because Blunden referred to it in writing to Cobden-Sanderson. In another of those recommendations of the work of his colleagues, Blunden wrote about Neville Whymant, philologist and linguist, who had two manuscripts in search of a publisher. In a letter of May 6, 1925, after presenting Whymant's merits as man and writer and asking the publisher to consider the two manuscripts by Whymant, Blunden added, "Lately he & I produced a little magazine together but we might have saved our trouble for it was not bought."[22] And when Blunden received a copy of the facsimile edition of Christopher Smart's "Song to David," issued by the Clarendon Press in 1926, he wrote the sonnet which begins,

> The Song itself! thus the majestic rhyme
> Before the secret-smiling author came;
> Thus stood the page where thus he wrote his name
> With instinct of his triumph over time.

Blunden might complain that Tokyo did not move him to poetry, but obviously those "sudden & subtle incitements" of which he spoke were not lacking. Indeed, by mid-June, hardly six weeks after his arrival, he told Cobden-Sanderson that he had written some verses. What verses they were, Blunden did not say, but among them may well have been the slightly flawed but very personal and moving lines of **"A 'First Impression' (Tokyo)."** Then Blunden's inclination to poetry, indeed to anything literary, began to slacken. In November, in a letter to Cobden-Sanderson, Blunden said, "Literature seems a curious dream in this Tokyo. I am always feeling my arm to make sure I yet subsist." He went on with the complaint usually voiced by the scholar-teacher: "Even reading seems to take hours longer than of old, and as for writing, I no sooner sit down to it than it's time for bed, or the university."[23] He managed, however, despite the "mortifying effect" of Tokyo, to maintain his "habit of versifying."

Some of this versifying produced the poetry which was published as a supplement to Blunden's account of his wartime experiences. He had tried to write such a book as early as 1918, but he abandoned it, an incomplete manuscript filled with false gaiety and unexamined detail.[24] In Tokyo, removed in time and place from the world of the war, Blunden worked at this book intermittently throughout most of his stay in Japan. He first mentioned it from there in a letter of September 6, 1924 as a "prose + verse work" which was "coming on." He added that he doubted its practicality as a publishing venture, but he meant to get it done and submit it to Cobden-Sanderson. In April of the next year, Blunden referred again to the poetry for the book. He had first planned to have it ready for the publisher in 1926, but not until 1927, well after it was finished, did he speak

of sending the manuscript. At that time Blunden named the book—a "large manuscript . . . called **'Undertones of War'**"—and described it—a "prose record with a supplement of some thirty poems." And even then the book needed corrections and additions from Blunden's journals, left in England.[25]

Other poetry writing was for a collection under preparation before Blunden left England. Since it was to include only poems written since *The Shepherd,* a book of his verse awarded the prestigious Hawthornden Prize in 1922, Blunden called it "New Verse." From Tokyo in late summer 1924, he remarked on his eagerness to get the manuscript of the book to Cobden-Sanderson and went on to talk about the job of selecting from the hundred or so poems already in hand. These included, Blunden said, "quite a strong detachment" of unpublished poems, pieces published in magazines, and pieces already given to Cyril Beaumont for other publication.[26]

The selections already in Beaumont's hands had been delivered early in March 1924. These were for a volume to be called *Masks of Time* and produced, as *To Nature* had been, in a limited edition. Six months after publication, the rights in the poems of *Masks of Time* returned to Blunden and thus became available for inclusion in whatever volume he chose. But no date could be set for reversion of rights and a second publication until *Masks of Time* appeared. As late as September 6, 1924, Blunden had heard nothing from Beaumont, and the proofs did not reach Tokyo until November 17.[27]

Nevertheless Blunden had made his selection for "New Poems" by mid-August 1924 and on September 6 he promised to send it at once.[28] Eight months later it was still in Tokyo, but he declared in a letter of May 5, 1925 that he was "posting by this post" the manuscript, now called *English Poems.*[29] With that title, it came out in January 1926.

Two pieces which first appeared in *English Poems* later introduced *Japanese Garland,* the "set of poems on Japan" for which Beaumont had asked. These two are **"A 'First Impression' (Tokyo)"** and **"The Daimyo's Pond."** That they serve both books helps to clarify the "sudden & subtle incitements" which Blunden maintained to be the source of his "power of poetry." Obviously it was not a question of place. In *Retreat,* his next volume of verse which he took with him in manuscript when he left Japan in 1927, Blunden carefully explained that no poems on "Japanese topics and impulses" appeared in that volume; he had set such pieces aside for "separate or subsequent presentation."[30] These were the heart of *Japanese Garland,* obviously composed mostly in Japan but not complete when he left there. He added to it well after his return to England. On January 4, 1928, from Cowlinge, Newmarket, Surrey, Blunden sent Beaumont a new poem to be included in *Japanese*

Garland and offered to send still another in a few days if there was room for it. In other words, Blunden could write about Japanese topics in Japan as he had about English ones in England. But he could also write about Japanese topics in England or vice versa. The sonnet about Christopher Smart's "Song to David," composed in December 1926[31] and indeed the whole of *Retreat* as well as *Japanese Garland* demonstrate the irrelevance of place.

Japanese Garland makes apparent not only the fact that for Blunden the incitement might occur anywhere but also that the "topics and impulses" were not the poem. They served as something to talk about *ostensibly*. Most of Blunden's poems are about his own emotions— **"The Daimyo's Pond"** about loneliness, **"A 'First Impression' (Tokyo)"** about his grief for a dead child and his joy in two living ones. Even **"The Author's Last Words to his Students"** is not about his students but about himself. In other words, *Japanese Garland* puts Blunden in the mainstream of English poets classified as romantic: Clare, Shelley, Keats. And his poetry, as Wordsworth, another romantic, defined it was the "spontaneous overflow of powerful feeling." That feeling was provoked by some object—a pond, a tempest, a walk in Nara—and the emotion was correlated with it so that his apparent incitement is the object and the real one the emotion which it produces and with which it correlates. Blunden himself recognized the fact when he spoke of the "inward sequence" of the poems in *Japanese Garland* and "the strong family likeness between all."[32]

Although Blunden had more to say about his reaction to Japan after a second visit in the 1940s, *Japanese Garland* is his final word about his stay there from May 1924 to August 1927. Contrary to his expectations, he found numerous incentives to poetry. He found them even in Tokyo, and while the sharp distaste for the city, so blatant in Blunden's letters, is missing from the poems, they imply no approval. **"Building the Library, Tokyo University Night Scene"** welcomes this "one more home" for the "great Muse"; but one of the more offensive qualities of Tokyo, a careless cruelty, is implicit in the title **"On A Small Dog, thrust out in a Tokyo street soon after his birth and rescued in vain."** The "vivid description" which he had derided to Cobden-Sanderson, Blunden supplied in **"Ornamentations"**:

> The curving cranes with serpent necks
>   Knotted on these enamelled streams,
> The gloating mouths thrust out to vex
>   The red-eyed war-god's frenzy dreams,
> The inscrutable and dog-like grin
> Of demi-lions lock me in!

That is a vivid first stanza. Perhaps more evocative of place and more typical of Blunden is the dark majesty he found outside Tokyo when he sailed the Inland Sea of Japan:

> Here in the moonlit sea,
>   While swift we fly, while tranced we gaze,
>   The fishers wind their ancient ways:
> Now like sea-lilies loom their luring sails,
> Or heaven's envoys walking fountained vales;
>   And now by one deflection dark,
>   Like waiting vultures of the night
> Each pirate blackness skulks, a murderous mark
>   Begotten by a thing of light,
> Like apprehension's baffling destiny.[33]

Notes

1. Letters which Blunden wrote to both men shortly before going to Japan and after his return are also at Iowa.

2. Edmund Blunden (hereafter referred to as EB) to Cyril Beaumont, Stansfield, Clare, Suffolk, January 28, 1924; EB to R. A. V. Morris, Stansfield, Clare, Suffolk, February 3, 1924.

3. Cf. EB to Richard Cobden-Sanderson, Stansfield, Clare, Suffolk, February 14, 1924. Blunden's wife, whom he had married in 1918, was Mary Daines Blunden.

4. February 24, 1924.

5. EB to Beaumont, Stansfield, Clare, Suffolk, March 2, 1924.

6. Cf. EB to Cobden-Sanderson, Stansfield, Clare, Suffolk, March 18, 1924, March 26, 1924; cf. Christopher Smart, *A Song to David with Other Poems*, ed. Edmund Blunden, London, 1924.

7. Cf. Edmund Blunden, *A Wanderer in Japan.* [Tokyo, 1949], p. 93; EB to Cobden-Sanderson, Stansfield, Clare, Suffolk, March 26, 1924.

8. EB to Cobden-Sanderson, Tokyo, April 3, 1925; cf. EB to Beaumont, Tokyo, July 22, 1924.

9. EB to Cobden-Sanderson, Tokyo, June 28, 1925; cf. EB to Cobden-Sanderson, Tokyo, April 24, 1926.

10. June 18, 1924; cf. EB to Cobden-Sanderson, Tokyo, May 5, 1925.

11. EB to Beaumont, Tokyo, July 22, 1924; EB to Cobden-Sanderson, Tokyo, July 14, 1924.

12. EB to Cobden-Sanderson, Tokyo, August 15, 1924.

13. EB to Cobden-Sanderson, Tokyo, November 1, 1925; cf. EB to Cobden-Sanderson, Tokyo, January 9 [1925].

14. EB to Cobden-Sanderson, Tokyo, July 14, 1924.

15. EB to Cobden-Sanderson, Tokyo, August 15, 1924.

16. EB to Cobden-Sanderson, Tokyo, July 6, 1926; cf. EB to Cobden-Sanderson, Tokyo, January 9 [1925].

17. EB to Cobden-Sanderson, Tokyo, May 19, 1927, March 8, 1927.

18. EB to Cobden-Sanderson, Tokyo, June 28, 1925.

19. EB to Cobden-Sanderson, Tokyo, June 3, 1925, August 28, 1925, January 18, 1925. Cf. Sherard Vines, *Triforium,* London, 1928; Cobden-Sanderson published Vines's *The Pyramid* with prefatory verses by Blunden and Yone Noguchi in 1926. For the review of Ishii's *Twelve Poems* see "New Books and Reprints" in *TLS* [*Times Literary Supplement*], March 11, 1926, p. 187. Cf. EB to Beaumont, Tokyo, July 22, 1924.

20. EB to Cobden-Sanderson, Tokyo, March 31, 1927; cf. EB to Cobden-Sanderson, Tokyo, May 19, 1927; Takeshi Saito, *Keats' View of Poetry [with] an essay on English Literature in Japan by Edmund Blunden,* London, 1929.

21. Cf. EB to Cobden-Sanderson, Tokyo, May 19, 1926, October 7, 1926, October 28, 1926, May 24, 1926, July 6, 1926, March 15, 1927.

22. EB to Cobden-Sanderson, Tokyo, May 6, 1925. The *Oriental Literary Times* appeared in six issues from January 15 to April 1, 1925. None of Neville Whymant's books was published by Cobden-Sanderson.

23. EB to Cobden-Sanderson, Tokyo, November 11, 1924; cf. EB to Cobden-Sanderson, Tokyo, June 18, 1924. See also the autograph signed copy of Blunden's sonnet "On receiving from the Clarendon Press the new Facsimile edition of Christopher Smart's 'Song to David'" dated from Tokyo, "Dec. 1926."

24. Cf. Edmund Blunden, "Preliminary" in *Undertones of War,* London, 1928; Miriam J. Benkovitz, "Edmund Blunden's Ghosts," in *Columbia Library Columns,* February 1978, pp. 14-22.

25. EB to Cobden-Sanderson, Tokyo, March 31, 1927; cf. EB to Cobden-Sanderson, Tokyo, April 3, 1925.

26. April 15, 1924.

27. Cf. EB to Beaumont, Tokyo, November 17, 1924.

28. Cf. EB to Cobden-Sanderson, Tokyo, September 6, 1924, August 15, 1924.

29. Cf. EB to Cobden-Sanderson, Tokyo, May 5, 1925.

30. Edmund Blunden, ["Author's Note"] in *Retreat,* London, 1928, p. [7].

31. Cf. EB to Beaumont, Cowlinge, Newmarket, Suffolk, January 4, 1928.

32. EB to Beaumont, Cowlinge, Newmarket, Suffolk, May 3, 1928.

33. Edmund Blunden, "Inland Sea," in *Japanese Garland,* London, 1928, p. 26.

Sumie Okada (essay date 1988)

SOURCE: Okada, Sumie. "Poetry in Love." In *Edmund Blunden and Japan: The History of a Relationship,* pp. 56-92. Houndmills, Basingstoke, Hampshire, England: Macmillan, 1988.

[*In the following excerpt, Okada explores the effect Blunden's clandestine relationship with Aki Hayashi had on his poetry.*]

Aki Hayashi undoubtedly had a considerable effect, directly and indirectly, on Blunden's writings and particularly on his poetry. The poetry he wrote in Japan, and on Japanese subjects after his return to England, is suffused with the particular sense of, and feeling for, Japan, which he had acquired from his relations with her. He could, and did, also confide to her his feelings about the First World War; and his letters to her often refer to it, sometimes associating Japanese landscapes with what he had seen in Flanders.

The scenery of Tohoku District which Blunden had passed on board the train to see Ralph Hodgson reminded him of Flanders.

> The journey was stuffy and uncomfortable but I enjoyed the snowstorm outside, and the appearance of the lonely places with groups of farm buildings, flat roads, ditches and short avenues of trees suited my war-book, resembling Flanders. I missed my glimpses of the sea, but no doubt they would have been very dull & imperfect ones.
>
> (21 March 1926)

In the summer of 1932 he visited 'the old country of the war', and sent a postcard to Aki describing the then peaceful sight of 'countless wild flowers' and 'clear sparkling streams'.

> Postcard Paris
>
> This is a half-way house for us, my dear A., on our wanderings; we first passed through the old country of the war, from Cassel to Béthune and to Amiens, and have been almost 2 days here. As the skies have been cloudy (not very different from London) the bright colours that this picture shows have not been obvi-

ous. . . . Have been very slack in writing letters & c., but not otherwise—we took some very long walks, two of them in the old battlefields of the La Bassée and the Beaumont Hamel one. Hardly any trace of war would meet your eye there now if you were not told what to watch for; and by Hamel the river valley is fresh and beautiful, with countless wild flowers and clear sparkling streams. . . . will write again in a few days, I expect from Perigueux in south-west France. We found my friends the Bonnerots at Amiens, saw them again here, and shall catch them up on the sea shore not too far from Perigueux.

(4 August 1932)

Blunden tried to 'transfer' these scenes into a novel on which he was collaborating with Sylva Norman.

Cleave's Yalding

There is something dear A which you can usefully do at once for me at the Museum. I want to have by me while writing my new book with Sylva Norman such passages from *Froissart's Chronicles* as may serve. It is a famous old book but I have no copy. The passages I shall need are those relating to the English in Périgord, and especially their wars and so on in these places: Domme, Brive, Sarlat, Périgueux, Rocamadour—all which we lately visited.

(8 September 1932)

War memories were brought back to him by small incidents, such as an article in a Sunday paper (28 May 1936), in which the Prince of Wales was reported to have recollected his narrow escape from arrest as a spy, and his encounter with Lieutenant Blunden. Yet Blunden himself could not recollect that incident and found the article strange, 'though Canal Bank in 1917 was enough to make one forget anything!'

Today a friend of Sylva's sent her a cutting from a *Sunday Pictorial*, in which the Prince of Wales is stated to have been nearly arrested as a spy on the Canal Bank, Ypres in 1917, and to have been brought to our Battalion H.Q. where Lieut. Edmund Blunden all alone received him! This is passing strange. I don't think I should have forgotten the episode, though Canal Bank in 1917 was enough to make one forget anything! Mr Mottram has published a new book on the Western Front in which he several times mentions me very handsomely.

(28 May 1936)

The volunteer service of Blunden's son John during the Second World War also evoked the memory of his own volunteering during the First World War. As a father he was concerned about his son's action.

Merton College, Oxford

My son writes that he has volunteered for the Air (as a pilot), though still under the age of conscription. It is all rather unhappy to me. I was a month or two older when I joined in 1915.

(1 February 1941)

The cloudy summer weather again brings another memory of the War—a fierce battle in the Passchendaele region.

Merton College, Oxford

We have cloudy weather and the summer seems to be breaking up—but so it was in 1917 at this date when like so many others I was about to attack the Germans in the Passchendaele region!

(29 July 1941)

About 16 years before this letter, in Japan, Blunden related the result of some battle:

Kikufuji Hotel, Hongo, Tokyo

Today, 9 years ago, my battalion attacked and captured a German trench; in which proceeding I played some, alas! too insignificant part, and experienced more in 48 hours than some old gentlemen in all their lives.

(21 October 1925)

Blunden seems to have desired that Aki too should share and understand his unforgettable memories.

No wonder Claire Poynting told a reporter that 'their lives were dominated by it (war), and that up until he died in 1974 no day passed in which he did not refer to that war'. In particular changes of weather used to fill him with memories.[1]

Blunden was not only obsessed by vivid memories of the war and driven to re-visit the old scenes of action, but was actually involved with service for the War Graves Commission.

9 Woodstock Close, Oxford

Perhaps you saw in Monday's newspaper that I have been called on to serve (no salary attached!) on the War Graves Commission. A sudden series of messages on Friday and Saturday, then a visit by Major-General Sir Fabian Ware—and the deed was done.

(4 March 1936)

Friendships developed during the war, which resulted in continued reunions of the old soldiers for a long period of time afterwards.

Went to Brighton on Saturday for our annual dinner of Old Soldiers, lots of beer was drunk and many stories were told once more.

(7 March 1939)

67 Pembury Road, Tonbridge

. . . On Saturday afternoon I go to Worthing, for the annual dinner of our old Royal Sussex battalions; will be back at Tonbridge on Sunday evening, & here as usual on Monday.

(12 March 1953)

Even in Hong Kong Blunden seems to have been unable to escape such ties. He had to send a message to the annual Dinner of his old Royal Sussex battalions, or was concerned about his old friends' state of health and 'youthfulness'.

> The University, Hong Kong
>
> . . . General Harrison writes quite often, as he has done since 1918, and tells me that my old companion Sergeant Worley of Worthing has had a troublesome operation. Alas, the years do make these changes in us. I can only be thankful that G. H. H. has kept so young, and some more of the old Royal Sussex. They had their annual Dinner at Worthing and I had sent a message which G. H. H. read out.
>
> (6 April 1954)

He was requested to write something for the fortieth anniversary of his battalions.

> The University, Hong Kong
>
> The Royal Sussex (South-down Battalions) are to celebrate their 40th anniversary at Bexhill & c. in September, and I am desired to write something for the 'souvenir programme.' I wish one of them would arrange a quiet seaside week for you by way of rewarding me.
>
> (15 June 1954)

Blunden was given 'a present, a 4-page letter from Dickens to Forster' from an old war friend:

> The University, Hong Kong
>
> . . . Lately a gentleman who was in the same Division as me in War I and read my book about it sent me as a present a 4-page letter from Dickens to Forster. I have not many such things here and this is accordingly a special Benefit.
>
> (26 April 1955)

His truest and most serious feeling, however, towards his fellow soldiers killed in the War is conveyed in the following passage, in which he says neither himself nor Sassoon would be pleased with the grand ceremony for the fallen—which he regards as a mere 'show-piece'.

> The University, Hong Kong
>
> On Sunday we must attend a show-piece—the unveiling of a War Graves Memorial; shall be happy when this is all over, the captains & the kings depart, and we can go peacefully home. It will no doubt be a stately ceremony, led by a famous General from England. My spirit like S. Sassoon's hardly rejoices in any such public performances concerning the fallen.
>
> (15 February 1955)

Meanwhile, his books on the First World War seemed to find increasing favour. A new edition of *Undertones of War* was to be published in the World's Classics Series and his pamphlet on the War Poets of 1914-18 in the British Council Series was published.

> The University, Hong Kong
>
> What else? There is to be a new edition of '**Undertones of War**' in the World's Classics series (Oxford Univ. Press.) I owe this to my friend D. Hudson of Merton College who is now I think in charge of that series. So I must before long get together a new Introduction & in it I shall have a chance of speaking about Philip Tomlinson. A great shame that he has not lived to see the new edition, and perhaps the introduction would have come from *his* pen.
>
> (7 July 1955)

> UNIVERSITY OF HONG KONG
> DEPARTMENT OF ENGLISH
>
> . . . When you are near B. M., call at 59 New Oxford Street,—Albion House—on Mʳ Brander, and he will give you a copy of my pamphlet in his British Council Series, on the War Poets of 1914-18. It will have been published when this reaches you. It is chiefly about Rupert Brooke, W. Owen and S. S. who is given an unusual photograph, from 1916, . . .
>
> (18 July 1958)

More than anything else, his mind always wandered back to his 'old Somme villages', which he would visit whenever he had the opportunity.

> Sylva leaves for Italy tonight and we may meet her in Rome early in June—as yet we have no address in Rome & we shall be a bit of a party—C., E., 4 girls 1 amah, 2 young ladies from the English Department. I was intending to visit Shelley's last home in Lerici, but have had to put the thought from me; alas.—One day perhaps. In July we may be in Paris awhile, & once more my desire is to return briefly to our old Somme villages, but it can hardly be fulfilled. In 1963, I tell myself, but nobody can be sure that way—. . .
>
> (25 April 1961)

When he returned to Oxford again after the First World War, Blunden seemed to be always looking for a sense of surety and certainty. His poem '**April Byeway**', published in *A Queen's College Miscellany* in 1921, conveys some of the despair and suffering he felt as a result of his fierce War experiences. Here he was looking for certainty and stability in a changing world—an 'unseen friend' who alone seems to represent such reality.

> But the old forge and mill are shut and done,
>   The tower is crumbling down, stone by stone falls;
> An ague doubt comes creeping in the sun.
>   The sun himself is shaken, the day appals,
>   The concourse of a thousand tempests sprawls
> Over the blue-lipped lakes and maddening groves,
>   Like agonies of gods the clouds are whirled,
> The stormwind like the demon huntsman roves—
>   Still stands my friend, though all's to chaos hurled.
>   The unseen friend, the one sure friend in all the world.[2]

This last stanza echoes Yeats's poems which are similar in tone and written in the same period.

The Second Coming

Turning and turning in the widening gyre
The falcon cannot hear the falconer;
Things fall apart; the centre cannot hold;
Mere anarchy is loosed upon the world,
The blood-dimmed tide is loosed, and everywhere
The ceremony of innocence is drowned;
The best lack all conviction, while the worst
Are full of passionate intensity.

Surely some revelation is at hand;
Surely the Second Coming is at hand.[3]

A Prayer for My Daughter

* * *

Considering that, all hatred driven hence,
The soul recovers radical innocence
And learns at last that it is self-delighting,
Self-appeasing, self-affrighting,

And will that its own sweet will is Heaven's will;
She can, though every face should scowl
And every windy quarter howl
Or every bellows burst, be happy still.[4]

Yeats treats the theme of 'despair and anarchy' in a larger historical context, associating it with the image of the Second Coming; and again in 'A Prayer for My Daughter', he hopes to see salvation and a new security coming from the sweet will of Heaven, with which his daughter's soul, recovering radical innocence, should be united. Blunden's hope lies in his friend, 'The unseen friend, the one sure friend in all the world', which is a much more personal response to the trauma than Yeats's universalism. Perhaps, this is one of the reasons why Blunden's poems have largely failed to appeal to the twentieth-century reader.

It was not long after this that Blunden was to find altogether new kinds of security—and insecurity—in Japan.

Turning to the poetry which Blunden wrote directly under the influence of Japan and his relations with Aki Hayashi, let us begin with two very moving examples: **'Lonely Love'** and **'Ainu Child'**.

'Lonely Love'

I love to see those loving and beloved
Whom Nature seems to have spited; unattractive,
Unnoticeable people, whose dry track
No honey-drop of praise, or understanding,
Or bare acknowledgement that they existed,
Perhaps yet moistened. Still, they make their world.

She with her arm in his—O Fate, be kind,
Though late, be kind; let her have never cause
To live outside her dream, nor unadore
This underling in body, mind and type,
Nor part from him what makes her dwarfish form

Take grace and fortune, envy's antitone.

I saw where through the plain a river and road
Ran quietly, and asked no more event
Than sun and rain and wind, and night and day,
Two walking—from what cruel show escaped?
Deformity, defect of mind their portion.
But I forget the rest of that free day of mine,
And in what flowerful coils, what airy music
It led me there and on; those two I see
Who, loving, walking slowly, saw not me,
But shared with me the strangest happiness.[5]

'Ainu Child'

On the straggling scanty hedge out there
We are shown the remnants of an unlucky bear,
And the hunter is proud.
Then the little crowd
Drifts back to the street; and the children share
A handful of sweets, and stare and stare.

In the sunshine, the grass is bright green; time half
    sleeps;
But the thought of dead bears like a cold shade creeps
On our minds, and the gloom
Of a race in a tomb,
Where old age itself no more harvest reaps
Than the bones of bears torn from their woodland
    deeps.

Among these small children one larger child waits,
Her eyes on the strange woman; contemplates;
And she has good eyes,
We begin to surmise
She implores that strange woman to challenge her
    fates,
And take her and break for her all the locked gates.[6]

'Lonely Love' is very 'un-Japanese'—it illustrates the great difference between Blunden's response to life and the Japanese one. He doesn't care about the *absence* of grace and beauty in the people and in the poem. He *loves* it! This would seem strange to a Japanese.

To love pathos and deprivation is characteristic of Blunden as it also is of Hardy and Larkin as poets.

> As Larkin has himself wryly remarked: 'Deprivation for me is what daffodils were for Wordsworth.' What is perfect as a poem is what is imperfect in life.[7]

In this respect the three poets are very similar. There seems no doubt that his feeling for Aki is reflected in **'Lonely Love'**. He also had affection for sad, deprived and unloved writers, as is shown by his interest in such poets as Lamb, Clare and Smart, and also in the First World War poet Ivor Gurney. On the other hand, some of Blunden's poems are very close to the Japanese. The 'meticulous' nature poems show not only his poet's eye for the country, but the influence of Aki's knowledge of Japanese poetry, which she imparted to him.

Another feature of his poetry is the seasonal description of nature, which is also evident in his letters. Blunden's descriptions result from his detailed observations and sharp senses, in both his poetry and his letters to Aki. Indeed he is opposed to the Modernist way of transforming things into symbols of the poet's psyche—represented by such a poet as T. S. Eliot—which, he declares, is not the sort of poetry he enjoys (19 October 1954). Blunden prefers to preserve nature in poetry in its purest and most natural form, as can be seen in his descriptions of the vivacity of nature—the living, growing, changing life of flowers, birds, light, wind and animals.

> At last the world of birds, flowers, bees, even worms thinks the spring is coming, and I expect you hear the early morning music much as here.
>
> (17 March 1942)

Blunden can be sharp enough to discern changes in the quality of birdsong:

> Easter Monday, but it does not feel much like a holiday, though some of the birds are holding a concert (rather sharp voices until the spring really brings forth the sweetest singers.)
>
> (6 April 1942)

> You must hear all the birds sing that you can the next week or two, for when the summer gets drowsy so do they; they are almost without music then until the autumn.
>
> (18 June 1931)

The dramatic power of transformation by light is described with a romantic touch:

> MERTON COLLEGE, OXFORD
>
> . . . Here it's a fine spring day, which I hope makes some sunshine for you also in London; a glorious rainbow here yesterday appeared to spring from the back of a sheep feeding in the meadow below my window, & in its light all the flock had a dark dusky gold fleece.
>
> (22 April 1932)

'Lonely Love' certainly shows Blunden's appreciation of Aki's solitude and his realisation of her position, as well as his tenderness for her. Undoubtedly Blunden came to feel, through her, emotions in his poetry he would not otherwise have had. In a similar vein Blunden's poems on Japan published in *Near and Far* record his first impressions of Japan, the shock he experienced in assimilating the different culture and sensibility, and above all, his clandestine love for Aki Hayashi. Many of them correspond well with his comments on Japan and its people written in his letters to Aki during this period. Indeed, the combination of the poems and the letters reveal much about his reactions to the different culture and to 'forbidden' love.

Near and Far, which was published in 1929, contains principally *Japanese Garland* and *Moods, Conjectures and Fancies.* As the flyleaf of the book explains, the poems here were written during his stay in Japan, and the two years immediately following his return to England in 1927; and would ideally reveal his emotions during this period.

> Several of the pieces in this new volume are on Japanese subjects. The rest are the work of the last two years. They offer some fresh melodies to those who still desire the music of verse. Inevitably, the note of English country life is expected from Mr Blunden's poetry, and will be heard here; but the spirit of man is his wider field.

Without dedicating *Japanese Garland* to Aki, Blunden presented her with a copy whose flyleaf bears in his own hand the tribute: 'To the best flower in any Japanese Garland, Aki Hayashi'. One of the reasons for his avoiding the form of a dedication may have been that his love for her had to be kept secret because he was still married to his wife Mary. He asks Aki in his letter to keep the matter secret.

> I hold you so fast in my love and honour, you must be my refuge if ever my friends forsake me. But it will help us, if we can keep a secret.
>
> (31 August 1925)

Perhaps in response to this effort to hide true emotions, the tone of most of the poems in *Near and Far* acquires a *haiku*-like quality, impressionistic and 'detached'—because of the frequent lack of specific cases. Often, the person(s) involved, or even the time and place, are only abstractly sketched, in the manner of the paintings of Turner or Japanese ink-paintings.

Indeed, Blunden himself seems to be well aware of this 'trick'. In his Prefatory Notes he indicates that he has made an effort to hide his true emotions—trying to disguise the Japanese scenes with allusions to England and vice versa. He apologises for this 'transformation', and tries to explain it away by saying that there is not much difference between cherry blossom and rose, rice and bread, and so on. In fact, though, his poems do not greatly disguise his 'true' feelings and reactions.

> Prefatory Note
>
> These poems are chiefly the product of the last two years. The Japanese pieces, however, are mainly reprinted from a volume issued by Mr C. W. Beaumont in 1927 in a limited and decorated edition. . . .
>
> It is not my habit to reply to my critics, who have been generous to me as a versifier for years. But, in respect of the Japanese pieces which I have written—and I hope to write more—I may be allowed a word. They were blamed here and there for their English tone, and their author was described as an incorrigible 'Briton'. Those, however, who go from England to Japan without succumbing first to Japanesery will find that there is no great gulf between the old experiences and the new. Substitute cherry-blossom for rose, and rice for bread,

and Alps for Chilterns—you do not thereby produce a mystical incomprehensibility. That is better (and worse) provided by avoiding Japan and the Japanese and just being 'Oriental'.

He also writes to Aki:

> I await news of my **English Poems,** which should have been issued last month in London; lately I wrote two pieces, one short & one long. The short one I will copy for Aki now. It is an English scene but it may resemble something here. My unalterable blessings and love, Eddie.
>
> (3 December 1925)

In a sense, it is also true that his 'difficulties' and sense of 'strangeness' were greatly mitigated by his gradual absorption into Japanese society, much assisted by Aki.

> I nowadays do not notice so keenly the points at which Japanese minds, manners and nerves entirely differ from ours.
>
> (23 October 1925)

But the effects of that absorption do not seem to penetrate far below the surface. In reality his poems implicitly disclose how deeply he *was* puzzled by the 'mystical incomprehensibility' and inscrutability of the Japanese culture and by his complex attraction to a Japanese woman.

His suppressed and secret love for Aki and its uneasy emotion and probable guilt are disclosed in his use of dark and passionate words in the poems—'steals away' and 'witch-like' in **'Far East'**; 'Defines the daemon's murderous work' in **'Eastern Tempest'**; 'luring sails', 'deflection dark', 'waiting vultures of the night', 'Each pirate blackness skulks', 'a murderous mark', 'apprehension's baffling destiny' in **'Inland Sea'**; 'sabred shades', 'black voice' of the bell, and 'dead man's eye' of Buddha in **'The Quick and the Dead'**; such lines as 'The murmur runs along their rugged lines, "What black ship waits the crash of our typhoon?"', 'jealous gods', 'Their mysteries luring that young seraph-cloud' in **'The Inviolate'**; 'nooks' in **'Building the Library, Tokyo University'**; 'ghost' of cherry-flowers, 'Blind eyes' of a small dog in **'On a small Dog, thrust out in a Tokyo Street soon after his birth, and rescued in vain'**; 'So by too harsh instrusion / Left colourless confusion', 'my gloomed perspective in strange mood', 'eyeless lethargy', 'My hobbling commonplaces', 'a frail guide' in **'The Author's Last Words to his Students'**. On the other hand, some of his phrases suggest a quest for the safety of a secure home—'binds' in **'Far East'** or 'And build them one more home . . . For the great Muse to come!' in **'Building the Library, Tokyo University—Night Scene'**.

> Fine fields, wide-lapped, whose loveliest-born
>   Day's first bright cohort finds,

And steals away; where lustier corn
And red-faced churl invades at morn
  And proud as Caesar binds—[8]

O swiftly serve thy quiet will,
  And build them one more home
Where nooks shall be most kind and still
  For the great Muse to come![9]

He also writes to Aki of his wish for a home.

> It is like your strong and active love to go to your Canadian friend's house & see how some things are done abroad. I shall not cause you a lot of trouble and difficulty, for I know you will do everything well. It will seem like liberty itself & delight with it to me, after almost two years of no-home—.
>
> (14 November 1925)

Under the spell of love, Blunden seemed to feel things around him more intensely than usual as if the 'dark' and 'mystical' undercurrents were moving and skulking like the 'waiting vultures of the night' whose 'murmur runs along'. In his calmer period, perhaps before meeting Aki in the summer of 1925, Blunden must have been a sober, rather lonely, and yet youthfully ambitious teacher who aspired to be a successful poet like Thomas Hardy. He longed to 'Enchant the live gems from the unknown abyss, / And make them seen, the strangely beautiful'.[10]

> I had a letter from Mrs Thomas Hardy, but nothing very definite in it except that Mr Hardy is publishing a volume of poems this autumn. So am I!! and curiously enough when T. H. published last, I did too, and the editor of the *London Mercury* honoured me by reviewing my pieces in the same column with Mr Hardy's.
>
> (23 October 1925)

The incantation of 'love' came to him swiftly and unexpectedly.

> But still how gentle and beautiful a love has awakened between you and me! I shall rely on it and live on it in many solitary hours. It is a charm to keep me going. I am most distressed that I cannot fulfil all that I ought to Autumn, as things stand now—but you have unselfish patience and a splendid courage. When I was with you, the cares of this hurried and bilious world ceased to touch me. I loved whatever gave me the chance to do some slight thing for you: and, as it has been, so it will continue to be.
>
> (29 August 1925)

The second poem of **Japanese Garland, 'Ornamentations'**, records the acute and powerful shock reactions of Blunden's western sensibility to its first encounter with the strange art of curving cranes, red-eyed war-gods and demi-lions. The poem begins in similar vein to Yeats's depiction of his slouching monster in 'The Second Coming'.

The curving cranes with serpent necks
     Knotted on these enamelled streams,
The gloating mouths thrust out to vex
     The red-eyed war-gods' frenzy dreams,
The inscrutable and dog-like grin
Of demi-lions lock me in!

With countless crafty manacles,
     Dead men's dexterity strives to bind,
Like some machine that all but feels,
     The amazed and apathizing mind.
Cornices, crannies, shape in shape,
Bud glittering eyes, defy escape.[11]

Again there is depicted a similar world to Yeats's 'Byzantium'—the craftsman's realm of art. Yeats writes:

A mouth that has no moisture and no breath
Breathless mouths may summon;
            . . . . .

Miracle, bird, or golden handiwork,
More miracles than bird or handiwork,
Planted on the star-lit golden bough.
            . . . . .

. . . The smithies break the flood,
The golden smithies of the Emperor!
Marbles of the dancing floor
Break bitter furies of complexity,
Those images that yet
Fresh images beget,
That dolphin-torn, that gong-tormented sea.

The difference lies in that Blunden's cranes do not scream or crow whereas Yeats's golden bird does and even 'scorns aloud'.

Can like the cocks of Hades crow,
Or, by the moon embittered, scorn aloud
In glory of changeless metal
Common bird or petal
And all complexities of mire or blood.

In other words, Yeats 'regards' or treats lifeless artifice as a living object, which is clearly indicated in his open declaration:

I hail the superhuman;
I call it death-in-life and life-in-death.[12]

Though they did not know each other, both Yeats and Blunden had a great interest in Japan and its art; but Blunden preferred a plainer and more straightforward expression of his feelings. Did Yeats borrow from Blunden? The similarity of 'images (ornamentations) and gongs (drum, knell, etc.)' is striking. Blunden's poem was published in 1928, two years before Yeats's 'Byzantium'.

Though tormented by the gloating mouths of the ornamental cranes and dog-like grin of demi-lions, he praised the craftsmen's dexterity in binding pieces together, and the glittering eyes of artifice. Yet, he feels the mind present in these ornamentations rather uncongenial and disagreeable—'The amazed and apathizing'. Blunden's sensibility had been so shaped by the aesthetic of gentleness and smoothness that he was taken aback by the oriental aesthetic of terror and 'monstrosity'. He much preferred to escape into the gentler and more peaceful world of 'roses and daffodils'.

Heavily hangs this haughty air,
     Drum, knell and drone commingling slow;
Claw-tendrils reach, man-monsters glare;
     The victim heart prepares to know
Art's terror, dragon genius—till
Thought spies one rose or daffodil.[13]

Thus Blunden conveys his culture-shock on a much less grand scale than Yeats would do—'till Thought *spies* one rose or daffodil'.

Here is the contrast between the 'feminine' sensibility of western art and culture and 'masculine' culture represented by Japanese art's 'terror'. Western culture reveres not only women's beauty but the gentle and peaceful gracefulness of Nature much more than its eastern counterpart, which can sometimes reflect an aesthetic of cruelty disguised as manly vigour and sustained by a male-dominated society. Blunden's poem **'The Match'** conveys that aspect of cruelty: he observes an 'ordinary scene' for any Japanese who loves baked eels—cooking eels alive in front of the shopper in order to capture the meat at its tastiest.

'The Match'

In a round cavern glass, in steely water
(None yet so comfortless appalled the day)
A man-eel poised, his lacquer-skin disparted
In desert reds and wharfy green; his eyes too
Burned like beads of venom.
Beyond the glass the torturer stood, with thrustings,
Passes, grimaces, toothy grins, warped oeillades.
To this black magic mania's eel retorted
With fierce yet futile muzzle, and lancing darted
In an electric rapine, against the wall
Of glass, or life: those disputants of nothing,
So acidly attracting, lovingly loathing,
Driven by cold radii, goblin lovers, seemed yet
The difficult dumb-show of my generation.[14]

Yet Blunden's western pacifist eyes reacted to the scene as nothing but a sign of barbarism. The trained cook of eels stood for a torturer. In a similar vein, what aggravated Blunden most in Japan was the prevailing social *apathy,* associated with his observation of the absence of a charitable mentality in Japan as I mentioned in the previous chapter in connection with the 'small dog' poem.

The apparently expressionless faces of the Japanese, sustained by their effort to hide emotions and feelings, have always been an enigma to western observers.

Those traits helped to create the famous image of inscrutable orientalism, and Blunden might at first have fallen victim to the cliché; also the initial language barrier probably contributed to his impression of Japanese 'apathy'—which was probably in fact the impact of Japanese stoicism.

Blunden recognised another apathy prevailing in the atmosphere of Tokyo University. He writes to Aki:

> Some letters are just in from England, with urgent command that I return; and indeed, for all the University deserves of me, I should not be wrong to do so, but there is more in question than the apathy and discourtesy of that 'Academic Body'.

(18 December 1925)

One of the benefits for Blunden of his direct contact with the opposite cultural sensibility to his own was to bring to his poems a 'masculine' touch—some strength and dynamism. He uses more pointed verbs like 'invade' or 'climb' (in **'Far East'**) together with emphatically masculine images, which are rarely perceivable traits in Blunden's early poems about English scenes such as **'The Waggoner'** or **'Almswoman'**.

For instance, **'Eastern Tempest'** conveys a vivid description of the blind rage of a storm which attacked the whole country in early September—the time of tempests. Blunden depicts the violence of the storm in the first part of the poem; but it passes quickly, and is replaced by a very fine blue sky and sun—the Japanese phrase 'after the typhoon' refers to the natural passing away of tumultuous disturbances:

> That flying angel's torrent cry
>
> . . . . .
>
> In Chance's eye what desperate deed?

The sudden transformation of the storm into a peaceful blue sky seems to the western eyes of Blunden like a merciful deed of a beneficent god.

> A kinder god discerns, replies,
> And stills the land's storm-shouts to sighs;
> The clouds in massy folds apart
> Disclose the day's bright bleeding heart,
>
> . . . . .
>
> From flame to flame the vision glows,
> Till all the pools of heaven unclose
> The lotus-light, the hue, the balm
> Of wisdom infinitely calm.[15]

Blunden again takes refuge in a 'kinder god (who) stills the land's storm-shouts to sighs' from the eastern 'daemon's murderous work', as he once had sheltered himself in the world of 'rose or daffodil' in response to the monstrous ornamentations.

Another 'charity-minded' poem, **'Sir William Treloar's Dinner for Crippled Children'** describes 'an ancient England in the new' where 'greatness and good-nature, still thrive', and where we hear Blunden's great sigh of relief after his traumatically hurtful experiences in Japan.

> This is an ancient England in the new;
> Hear how those thousand children leap and sing.
> Their dreams, their wonder and their pleasure ring
> Through England; young expectancy comes true,
> While Mayor and Alderman and Usher bright
> With robes and jewels out of a fairy story,
> And brighter hearts, wish them their heart's delight,
> And music shows them sudden streets of glory.
>
> Here walks the shade of Whittington in bliss;
> O greatness and good-nature, still you thrive.
> I thank my God, Charles Lamb is still alive
> In these new Londoners; they shall not miss
> The crown of life; here's Coram, Dickens, Hood,
> Christmas and Christ profoundly understood.[16]

To the same category of commonplace poems belong **'On a Biographical Dictionary'** which contains Blunden's celebration of the exclusive entry of 'men and women of great soul / Replying, singing to their genius' in the prestigious book.

> Proud is assembly, and the anthem proud
> That populous nave and aisle and gallery raise
> In conscious strength, till God in his bright cloud
> Seems hovering to that multitude of praise.
> Yet from this mild prosaic book, as loud,
> As strong, as various, from as many throats,
> I hear the Gloria of a golden crowd,
> And there the heavenly wing still brighter floats.
>
> I hear the trumpet and alarm of time
> Appeal, and men and women of great soul
> Replying, singing to their genius climb;
> Deep wisdoms hearten, organ-yearnings roll;
> Tried faith transfigures every imperfection
> Into one chant, one radiance and election.[17]

In **'The Quick and the Dead'**, Blunden finds much happiness in walking with friends in Nara—the most ancient city of Japan where the dead, including the huge Buddha, appeared to be more powerful than the living.

> Once we three in Nara walked
> Where pomp and fame look through the leaves;
> With sabred shades we walked and talked
> By lacquered gates and bow-like eaves,
> By pools where carp doze through their green
> Eternities, to lonelier shrines
> Where mossy courtyards lie serene
> Beneath some peasant-planted pines.
>
> Less of that giant, surly bell
> Whose black voice warned us at all hours
> My late remembrance likes to tell,
> Less of the Buddha as he lours

With thick curled skull and dead man's eye,
Of old wives' faithful groan of prayer,
Of fire-robed ritual trooping by,
Than the plain joy, three friends walked there.[18]

Blunden cares less for the giant bell and historic Buddha than for the company of his friends. Yet, if we replace the number three by two, the poem turns into a love poem, depicting Blunden enjoying Nara in the company of Aki—'the plain joy' of walking together. Indeed, one of his letters to Aki suggests he was very fond of that city.

> I wonder if another time we might not rather go to such a place as the Nara hotel or the Kyoto places; though it might be difficult for you to get away. This point too we must try to think over. In expense the Nara hotel w[d]. be considerably less, & it's very finely furnished & managed.
>
> (5 September 1925)

Despite Blunden's efforts to hide his love affair with Aki, this poem fails somehow to disguise the aura of secret joy. Another interesting point is Blunden's fondness for the images of 'walking' and 'passing'. **'The Lonely Love'** depicts such a scene—two deformed people in love pass Blunden without noticing him; yet the strange sensation created by seeing them inspired him to write the poem. Blunden *loved* feeling such unusual sensations, especially if private to himself—only a wasp could compare!

> . . . Here came my flitting thought,
> The only visitor of a sunny day,
> Except the half-mad wasp that fights with all, . . .[19]

The enchantment of the combination of 'unwanted' and the 'kind touch' of God or Nature is another recurrent image. **'The Kiln'** is a very good representative:

> Beside the creek where seldom oar or sail
> Adventures, and the gulls whistling like men
> Patrol the pasture of the falling tide,
> Like Timon's mansion stands the silent kiln.
> Half citadel, half temple, strong it stands
> With layered stones built into cavernous curves,
> The fire-vault now as cool as leaves and stones
> And dews can be. Here came my flitting thought,
> The only visitor of a sunny day,
> Except the half-mad wasp that fights with all,
> The leaping cricket in his apple-green,
> And emerald beetle with his golden helmet;
> While the south wind woke all the colony
> Of sorrels and sparse daisies, berried ivies
> And thorns bowed down with sloes, and brambles red
> Offering a feast that no child came to take.
>
> In these unwanted derelicts of man
> Nature has touched the picture with a smile
> Of more than usual mystery; the far heights
> With thunderous forest marshalled are her toil,
> But this her toy, her petty larceny,

> That pleased her, lurking like a gipsy girl,
> My thought came here with artfulness like hers
> To spy on her, and, though she fled, pursued
> To where on eastern islands, in the cells
> Of once grave seers, her iris woos the wind.[20]

Blunden was often thrilled by the movements of walking, passing and running (of streams and rivers); and **'Epitaph'** conveys the symbolism he wanted to embody in those images. There 'running stream' suggests the pathos of passing years and the never-static phases of human life; as a Japanese proverb says, 'Man can never stand in the same stream again': exactly the same thought as that expressed by the ancient Greek philosopher Heracleitus 'you cannot bathe twice in the same river'. The classic Greek and the classic Japanese have the same sadness and also, sometimes, the same cruelty. But Blunden's poetry is never cruel.

> Happily through my years this small stream ran;
> It charmed the boy, and purified the man;
> Its hollowed banks were my romantic caves,
> Its winter tumults made my ocean waves.[21]

Ironically, though ceaselessly moving, the stream is always in the same place, whereas a man might go abroad and change his abode. In fact, Blunden loved long walks and he wrote to Aki:

> Thank you so much for praising my poems, but I repeat you will like them more when you have spent some little time in the country which gave them life. It gave me life too, but a little too much asthma with it. Love, my love to you Edmund.
>
> (13 October 1925)

> . . . and I wish I could go for a walk with you even there or anywhere. . . . Every day & hour I think of you my very deeply loved Aki. It's wretched to find how slowly some days go by.
>
> (6 October 1925)

The second stanza envisages an Aki-like face mirrored in the stream among foxgloves. He brought her to England 'who was gone' (to London?), while Blunden sat and meditated on his life, talking to and counselling the running stream of Yalding; he was surrounded by the wealth and consolation of Nature, now in its 'English' colours.

> With all my years this pretty stream sang on.
> I brought one here to praise it; who is gone,
> Yet in that crystal soul her mirrored face
> With foxgloves looking in still finds a place.
> Even the Muse's 'melody unheard'
> For me is woven with this water's word,
> Since here I sat to read immortal song;
> The ripple played to that, nor answered wrong.
> All that deep-sighing elegy might mourn,
> Glad lyric hail, and sonnet-thought adorn,
> The changeful rivulet from stone to stone
> Enchanted into anthems of its own.

My travel then! my wealth, my dream, my love,
True Golden Treasury and Golden Grove!
Accept one weakness, let one pale shade cling
Where with so strong a life you run and sing.[22]

His adoration of 'running' seems to be related to his concern with the idea of passing Time. He mentions it in **'Summer Rainstorm'**:

Joy's masque and fashion of Time's Samson-passion
Deceives no lark that springs from weed and clod.
    Through their frank sight
    I feel the bright
Angel-event of sunset's fresh creation
And fields made lovely with the living God.[23]

In fact, Blunden dedicated to Aki a small fragment of a Shakespearean sonnet, using the image of Love's faith in his love letter.

A. H.   E. B.
28.8.1925

Love's not Time's fool, though rosy lips & cheeks
In compass of his bending sickle come;
Love changes not with his brief hours and weeks,
But bears it out e'en to the edge of Doom.

Comparing the English **'Summer Rainstorm'** with the **'Eastern Tempest'** reveals the much smaller scale of Nature's disturbance, seen as joyous and even merry—in the western isle.

Sweet conversations, woodland incantations
Are thrilling through the tides of gale and shower,
    Which now conceal,
    Now blue-reveal,
Across the fallow's russet undulations
A broken windmill and a silent tower.

And sometimes glancing through the top sprigs danc-
    ing
Elf-wings set out on visit and patrol.
    Though the full cloud
    Frowns monster-browed,
Those merry wild-folk chirruping and chancing
Know the kind truth; would I had such a soul!

Joy's masque and fashion of Time's Samson-passion
Deceives . . .[24]

Similarly, if we compare **'The Quick and the Dead'** with **'Epitaph'** as poems both suggesting Blunden's clandestine love, we can see how strongly the poem on Nara is imbued with *haiku*-like quantities.

A *haiku* is a 17-syllable verse form consisting of three metrical units of 5, 7 and 5 syllables respectively, and the focal point which the author wants to stress usually falls on the last metrical unit. Now the second stanza of **'The Quick and the Dead'** has a similar effect:

Less of that giant, surly bell
Whose black voice warned us at all hours

My late remembrance likes to tell,
Less of the Buddha as he lours
With thick curled skull and dead man's eye,
Of old wives' faithful groan of prayer,
Of fire-robed ritual trooping by,
Than the plain joy, three friends walked there.[25]

Not only does the main message of the poem come at the end—'the plain joy'—but we may see as equivalent to the first metrical unit of a *haiku*, the image of the bell, up to 'My late remembrance likes to tell', and as the second metrical unit ('Less of the Buddha . . . trooping by'), which concerns the fearsome godhead and the measured gestures of the devout.

On the whole, the poem written in England, **'Epitaph'**, carries much freer, richer, diversified and more direct emotions unrestricted by the influence of a confined use of syllables, the neat 'nothingness' of *haiku* poems.

A much deeper influence of the *haiku* may be traced in **'Inland Sea'** and **'The Inviolate'**—in both poems the surface messages are simple: 'in the moonlit sea, The fishers wind their ancient ways'; or 'on the white Pacific shore the pines still serve their jealous gods, . . . God-gates and temples glow with changeless noon'. All the remaining phrases are 'ornamentations' supporting the main message.

'Inland Sea'

Here in the moonlit sea,
While swift we fly, while tranced we gaze,
The fishers wind their ancient ways:
Now like sea-lilies loom their luring sails,
Or heaven's envoys walking fountained vales;
    And now by one deflection dark,
    Like waiting vultures of the night
Each pirate blackness skulks, a murderous mark
    Begotten by a thing of light,
Like apprehension's baffling destiny.[26]

'The Inviolate'

There on the white Pacific shore the pines
    Still serve their jealous gods, and late and soon
The murmur runs along their rugged lines,
    'What black ship[27] waits the crash of our typhoon?'

And in this vigil circled, calm and proud,
    God-gates and temples glow with changeless noon,
Their mysteries luring that young seraph-cloud
    Swan-like between the mountain and the moon.[28]

The *haiku* shares some features with Japanese forms of 'politeness'. Both tend to avoid self-imposing asser-tions; hence a poem's message is likely to be indirect, blurred and ambiguous leaving the final interpretation to the reader. Blunden seems to have followed this fashion in writing **'Inland Sea'** in which he tried to convey 'apprehension's baffling destiny' in association with the picturesque scene of 'the fishers wind[ing] their ancient ways in the moonlit sea'. Equally in **'The Inviolate'** there lies no explicit message. Blunden was impressed by the inviolate god-gates and temples seemingly formed by the trees on the shore which stood calm and proud despite the 'malicious' murmurs concerning the omen of the black ship; and their mysterious stance lured the swan-like cloud.

The expression not only of thought and emotion, but also of colour tends to be restricted in the *haiku*. The influence of this is especially marked in the above poems. Only 'darkness and light' are depicted in **'Inland Sea'**; in **'The Inviolate'**, the green of the pines and the 'red' of god-gates and temples are intentionally unmentioned, reflecting the poet's fear of disturbing the balance of black-and-white like in an ink-painting.

'The Deeper Friendship' confirms in a more open manner Blunden's reliance on 'one final hold'— *probably* suggesting Aki's love and support for him, though Blunden uses religious imagery: 'I know one hearth, one love that shine beyond fear'.

> Were all eyes changed, were even poetry cold,
> Were those long systems of hope that I tried to deploy
> Skeletons, still I should keep one final hold,
> Since clearer and clearer returns my first-found joy.
>
> I would go, once more, through the sunless autumn in
>   trouble;
> Thin and cold rain dripping down through branches
>   black,
> Streams hoarse-hurrying and pools spreading over the
>   stubble,
> And the waggoner leaving the hovel under his sack
>
> Would guide me along by the gate and deserted sid-
>   ing,
> The inn with the tattered arbour, the choking weir;
> And yet, security there would need small guiding.
> I know one hearth, one love that shine beyond fear.
>
> There, though the sharpest storm and flood were
>   abroad,
> And the last husk and leaf were stripped from the
>   tree,
> I would sue for peace where the rats and mice have
>   gnawed,
> And well content that Nature should bury me.[29]

After his return from Japan to Cowlinge in Suffolk and to Yalding—where his parents lived—in August 1927, Blunden had to endure the humiliation of his wife Mary's infidelity during his absence. Even his pent-up expectations concerning home-coming were despoiled by the rift with her—the way he felt she had deceived his trust and love. A number of poems truthfully convey his sadness and disappointment.

> I knew Seraphina; Nature gave her hue,
> Glance, sympathy, note, like one from Eden.

> I saw her smile warp, heard her lyric deaden;
>   She turned to harlotry;—this I took to be new.
>
> Say what you will, our God sees how they run.
> These disillusions are His curious proving
> That He loves humanity and will go on loving;
>   Over there are faith, life, virtue in the sun.[30]

In his plight nothing more seemed to console Blunden than Aki's devotion to him and assistance with his work; but he desperately tried to believe in the love of God— 'These disillusions are His curious proving / That He loves humanity and will go on loving'.

> The measureless houses of dreams,
> And the magic of hours within hours;
> And those who pass by like clear streams,
> Pass by us, on a journey not ours!
> The eyes that we know and we fear,
> As waters of Castaly clear,
> That gaze that should once have been sweet,
> Now a terror to meet!
> —Yet, both in one corridor narrowly led,
> Those steps in another intensity tread;
> There is space that convenes us, but holds us apart;
> Sunlight and sunlight, distinctly combined,
> As a wish with the wind
> And all heaven with one heart.[31]

This poem could be associated with Blunden's remark in a letter to Aki about a curious dream, in which he was on board a bus together with Aki and Mary:

> —Last night I dreamed that you were riding in a bus with me, when someone touched my shoulder, & it was Mrs M. Blunden, who made a 'scene'.
>
>   (27 January 1930)

He seems to be struggling with the problem of whether reconciliation was possible; he seems to have been torn, too: 'There is space that convenes us, but holds us apart'.

In these great difficulties Blunden took comfort in the support of his family.

>   . . . Come,
> And see how kindly all's at home.
> No sweeter things than these I rhyme,
> And this by much their sweetest time.[32]

The shadow of his loneliness became deeper, and his happy and optimistic familiarity with the Nature of the village sounds vain:

> **'Familiarity'**
>
> Dance not your spectral dance at me;
>   I know you well!
> Along this lane there lives no tree
>   But I can tell.
> I know each fall and rise and twist;

You—why, a wildflower in the mist,
    The moon, the mist.

Sound not that long alarm, gray tower,
    I know you well;
This is your habit at this hour,
    You and your bell!
If once, I heard a hundred times
Through evening's ambuscade your chimes—
    Dark tower, your chimes.

Enforce not that no-meaning so,
    Familiar stream;
Whether you tune it high or low,
    I know your theme;
A proud-fed but a puny rill,
A meadow brook, poured quick and shrill—
    Alone and shrill.

Sprawl not so monster-like, blind mist;
    I know not "seems";
I am too old a realist
    To take sea-dreams
From you, or think a great white Whale
Floats through our hawthorn-scented vale—
    This foam-cold vale.[33]

'War's People'

Through the tender amaranthine domes
Of angel-evenings echoing summer song,
    Through the black rock-tombs
Of winter, and where autumn floods prolong
    The midnight roar and tumbling thunder,
    Through spring's daisy-peeping wonder,
    Round and beyond and over and under,
        I see our homes.

                    . . . . .

From low-gorged lairs, which outshine Zion's towers,
Weak rags of walls, the forts of godlike powers.
    We went, returned,
But came with that far country learned;
Strange stars, and dream-like sounds, changed speech
    and law are ours.[34]

Confused and saddened, Blunden was disturbed by his awareness of other people's eyes upon him:

    In animation beautiful
    Returns your chance; now wander with
    The sparkle on the living seas,
    Nor fear that in these green estates
        Ambushed may lie
    The hooded serpent with the human eye . . .[35]

His troubled mind continued to suffer:

    Would understanding win herself my vote,
    Now, having known this crisis thirty years,
    She should decide me why it overwhelms
    My chart of time and history; should declare
    What in the spirit of a man long schooled
    To human concept and devotion dear,
    Upraised by sure example, undefiled

By misery and defeat, still in the sun—
What stirs in him, and finds its brother-self,
From that late sky. Again that sky, that tower,
These effigies and wizardries of chance,
Those soundless vollies of pale and distant birds
Have taken him, and from his whirring toils
Made him as far away, as unconcerned,
As consonant with the Power as its bare trees.[36]

Clearly he had to reassure himself many times that he would keep his own spirit intact—'undefiled / By misery and defeat' during his personal crisis. The carefree innocence of **'Inland Sea'** in Japan now turned into the sea of sighs—like Matthew Arnold's famous poem 'Dover Beach'.

    Hear on the shore too the sighed monotones
    Of waves that in weakness slip past the purled stones;
    The seethe of blown sand round the dry fractured hull,
    Salt-reeds and tusked fence; hear the struck gull
        With death in his bones.

    Slow comes the net in, that's filled with frustration;
    Night ends the day of thwart discreation;
    I would be your miracle-worker, sad friend,
    Bid a music for you and a new star ascends,—
        But I know isolation.[37]

Again, **'Return'** suggests there was no real relief for Blunden to enjoy at home, all the sadness of broken loves awaiting him:

    And Love, even Love, has dropped her lilies
        On the hot highroad; once she knew
    How columbines and daffadillies
        Created her own sun and dew.

    Return; how stands that man enchanted
        Who, after seas and mountains crossed,
    Finds his old threshold, so long scanted,
        With not a rose or robin lost!

    The wise, from passion now retreating
        To the hamlets of the mind,
    In every glance have claimed the greeting
        Of spirits infinitely kind.[38]

During this difficult period Blunden often met Aki who was living and working for him in London; and one such outing took place in Cambridge.

    Once again I have to tell you that I have been in a melancholy state and unable to attend to anything. I hope you got your train and reached home safely; it was a most happy afternoon in the air and in the church too, though as you know so well England is not at her best in the present mood. I cycled from Cambridge through the dark, & was somewhat troubled by the speed and glaring lamps of the motor-buses and cars, but got home in a little more than 2 hours. The next day we went to Felixstowe; it was a failure. M. said she would send you a present, & that was almost the only kind thing she said all day.

                                        (9 July 1928)

Blunden's poem **'A Quartet'** ('The Mikado' at Cambridge) tells of the production which he saw on a different occasion.

> Deep-moved I mark their choral master-piece,
> Their union in each swell and dying fall.[39]

He also wrote in his letter to Aki:

> No need to copy mere scraps and commonplace, but anything with real information or vivid interest. So much, my dear Aki, for work: I have no news, except that Plomer wrote & sent you his good wishes. . . . (Went to Cambridge last night saw 'The Mikado' which was very melodious and amusing, w^d. have made you laugh at the 'Japanese' girls & costumes.)
>
> (5 May 1928)

A connotative poem, **'Values'** concludes the book *Near and Far,* implying Blunden's high evaluation of English culture in which a kinder God and truth dominate. This was the precious rediscovery and re-appropriation of the ethos of his *own* country after his traumatic encounters with Eastern demi-gods, Buddha's dead eyes and ghoulish ornamentations in Japan—all appearing to him excessively implacable and intimidating. He also argues that Japanese value-judgements, which rigorously demand social standards of perfection, are wrong—and so also any other form of absolutism. In this context, the last poem of *Japanese Garland,* **'The Author's Last Words to his Students'**, well represents an aspect of Japanese sensibility—formalised modesty—which influenced Blunden.

'Values'

> Till darkness lays a hand on these gray eyes
> And out of man my ghost is sent alone,
> It is my chance to know that force and size
> Are nothing but by answered undertone.
> No beauty even of absolute perfection
> Dominates here—the glance, the pause, the guess
> Must be my amulets of resurrection;
> Raindrops may murder, lightnings may caress.
>
> There I was tortured, but I cannot grieve;
> There crowned and palaced—visibles deceive.
> That storm of belfried cities in my mind
> Leaves me my vespers cool and eglantined.
> From love's wide-flowering mountain-side I chose
> This sprig of green, in which an angel shows.[40]

In the sonnet **'Values'** Blunden embodies several of his conclusions concerning the differences in values and 'sensibilities' between England and Japan. The first is: 'It is my chance to know that force and size / Are nothing but by answered undertone'. 'Force and size' could imply an army or even the Buddha, and may refer to both his major historical experiences—the War, and Japan.

In the latter half of the octet ('No beauty . . .') he tries to make it clear that he values undertones much more than force and size; that he much prefers England where

'the glance, the pause, the guess' are appreciated more deeply than absolute beauty or perfection. In the poem: 'Raindrops may murder, lightnings may caress'.

The relevance of this message is two-fold; firstly to the sensibilities of his Japanese students and secondly to his relationship with Aki.

'The Author's Last Words to His Students'[41]

> Forgive what I, adventuring highest themes,
> Have spoiled and darkened, and the awkward hand
> That longed to point the moral of man's dreams
> And shut the wicket-gates of fairyland:
> So by too harsh intrusion
> Left colourless confusion.
>
> For even the glories that I most revered,
> Seen through my gloomed perspective in strange mood,
> Were not what to our British seers appeared;
> I spoke of peace, I made a solitude,
> Herding with deathless graces
> My hobbling commonplaces.
>
> Forgive that eyeless lethargy which chilled
> Your ardours and I fear dimmed much fine gold—
> What your bright passion, leaping ages, thrilled
> To find and claim, and I yet dared withhold;
> These and all chance offences
> Against your finer senses.
>
> And I will ever pray for your souls' health,
> Remembering how, deep-tasked yet eager-eyed,
> You loved imagination's commonwealth,
> Following with smiling wonder a frail guide
> Who hears beyond the ocean
> The voice of your devotion.[42]

From the beginning he sounds very apologetic, 'Forgive what I . . .'—which is a sure sign of Japanese influence in which absolute value dominates the rest; hence as perfection will be the *ultimate* goal, one has to be always apologetic for one's failure to attain it.

In the context of his relationship with Aki, Blunden mentions in a letter how much he misses her in his room adding 'even an imagination can hurt'. Such kinder, tender, sympathetic, lyrical concepts of life and Nature were in the background when he wrote that 'Raindrops (not even the army or eastern tempest) may murder, lightnings may caress'.

> My Autumn
>
> . . . I can see you too, but imagination is not the life itself, and hurts as much as it pleases.
>
> (31 August 1925)

These were the mixed feelings of his reaction to the prevailing Japanese reality he had experienced, in which the people had to suppress those aspects of their sensibilities which would enable them to understand the undertones of things—politeness, substituted for sympathy; they narrowly concerned themselves with the values of visible things—shape, force and size; in this sense one might compare the poem with Yeats's 'The Statues'.[43]

Lacking real encounters with Greek culture, Yeats's poem could be said to remain too general and abstract. The feminine sensibility at the base of western culture, which Blunden favoured, clashes interestingly in his poem with more masculine eastern sensitivity that could be fierce, brutal and less caring.

In the sestet, Blunden's message is simple, 'visibles deceive'. Thus he returns with relief to the womb-like protection of 'vespers cool and eglantined'. The couplet of the poem summarises:

> From love's wide-flowering mountain-side I chose
> This sprig of green, in which an angel shows.[44]

Thus he ultimately chose the 'sprig of green (Nature), in which an angel shows'. By thus closely associating Nature with the supernatural—like an angel or love—Blunden follows western mental patterns which place special value on the supernatural as a higher and more enlightened form than the natural world; whereas the Japanese value-judgement tends to terminate in the perfection of natural, hardly aspiring to supernatural existence in its true sense. This might be attributable to the different cultural concepts of God. Hence, he seems to have risen into love, not only his own personal love but a wider Christian love (cf. **'Deeper Friendship'**). The association of love and the angel, bearing in mind also the images of bells and drums in other poems, could direct us to the famous passage on love in I Corinthians: 13 in the Bible:

> I may speak in tongues of men or of angels, but if I am without love, I am a sounding gong or a clanging cymbal. I may have the gift of prophecy, and know every hidden truth; I may have faith strong enough to move mountains; but if I have not love I am nothing. . . . Love is patient, love is kind and envies no one.

Finally then, in his deferential way, Blunden seems to be hailing the triumph of Christian love over the unsympathetic gaze of Buddha's dead eye. This is perhaps his basic judgement on the Japanese culture which he had encountered; and if so, is a measure of the shock of that encounter.

Notes

1. Caroline Moorehead, 'The Poets We Nearly Forgot', in 'Women at War', *The Times*, 9 November 1981, p. 9. (The newspaper erroneously gives 1976 as the date of Blunden's death.)

2. *A Queen's College Miscellany* (1921) p. 20.

3. W. B. Yeats, *The Collected Poems of W. B. Yeats* (London: Macmillan, 1965) pp. 210-11.

4. Ibid., pp. 213-14.

5. Edmund Blunden, *An Elegy and Other Poems* (London: Cobden-Sanderson, 1937) p. 82.

6. Edmund Blunden, *A Wanderer in Japan: Sketches and Reflections in Prose and Verse* (Tokyo: Asahi Shimbunsha, 1950) p. 61.

7. John Bayley, *Selected Essays* (Cambridge: Cambridge University Press, 1984) p. 93.

8. Edmund Blunden, 'Far East' in *Near and Far: New Poems* (London: Cobden-Sanderson, 1929) p. 22. Subsequently referred to as *Near and Far*.

9. 'Building the Library, Tokyo University', ibid., p. 30.

10. Edmund Blunden, *Japanese Garland* (London: Beaumont Press, 1928) p. 14.

11. Blunden, *Near and Far*, p. 21.

12. *The Collected Poems of W. B. Yeats* (London: Macmillan, 1965) pp. 280-1.

13. Blunden, *Near and Far*, p. 21.

14. Edmund Blunden, *Retreat* (London: Cobden-Sanderson, 1928) p. 66.

15. Blunden, *Near and Far*, pp. 25-6.

16. 'Sir William Treloar's Dinner for Crippled Children', ibid., p. 65.

17. 'On a Biographical Dictionary', ibid., p. 61.

18. 'The Quick and the Dead', ibid., p. 28.

19. 'The Kiln', ibid., p. 50.

20. Ibid.

21. 'Epitaph', ibid., p. 59.

22. Ibid., pp. 59-60.

23. 'Summer Rainstorm', ibid., p. 49.

24. Ibid.

25. 'The Quick and the Dead', ibid., p. 28.

26. 'Inland Sea', ibid., p. 27.

27. A 'black ship' was a foreign warship such as those introduced by Commodore Matthew Calbraith Perry (1794-1858), a US naval officer who re-opened Japan to the Western world after more than 200 years.

28. 'The Inviolate', in Blunden, *Near and Far*, p. 29.

29. 'The Deeper Friendship', ibid., pp. 55-6.

30. 'Report on Experience', ibid., p. 58.

31. 'Dream Encounters', ibid., p. 43.

32. 'Autumn in the Weald', ibid., p. 52.

33. 'Familiarity', ibid., pp. 37-8.

34. 'War's People', ibid., pp. 41-2.

35. 'Fragment', ibid., p. 47.

36. 'The Correlation', ibid., p. 51.

37. 'The Blind Lead the Blind', ibid., p. 57.

38. 'Return', ibid., pp. 53-4.

39. 'A Quartet', ibid., p. 62.

40. 'Values', ibid., p. 67.

41. In the School of English Literature, Tokyo Imperial University, 1924-7.

42. Blunden, *Near and Far*, pp. 32-3.

43. The significance of shape and appearance is represented by such art forms as flower arrangements, the tea-ceremony, or Noh plays, or even the films of Kurosawa in which all movements and emotions tend to be stylised, and concentration put on intensity and aesthetic perfection.

44. Blunden, *Near and Far*, p. 67.

Thomas G. Bowie, Jr. (essay date fall/winter 1993)

SOURCE: Bowie, Jr., Thomas G. "An I for an Eye: Edmund Blunden's War." *War, Literature, and the Arts* (fall/winter 1993): 21-47.

[*In the following essay, Bowie discusses Blunden's* Undertones of War, *a volume that includes a prose narrative of his war experiences as well as a number of his war poems.*]

Many Great War personal narratives consciously situate themselves in a generic "no man's land," falling between historical memoir and literary autobiography, allowing considerable leeway in their interpretation. And when we attend to this generic conflict, when we use genre as a heuristic tool, we begin to fully appreciate the inexorable tension between the world of the war and the narrative construction of it. More specifically, by exploring the dialectical struggle in Edmund Blunden's rendering of the war—the struggle between raw experience and formed language—we can begin to understand why he insists upon personal narrative as *the* way to tell *his* story. In fact, his insistence on personal narrative as the most appropriate mode of

response to the war directs our attention to the intersection between personal and cultural modes of interpretation, exposing the power of narrative to both discover and create selves—individually, culturally, and ideologically. For we see in Blunden's attempt to fuse the partial vision of his individual perspective with the transcendent wholeness offered by narrative form an ongoing dialectical exchange between part and whole, between content and form, between individual and context, and between self-discovery and self-creation. First and last, this endlessly dynamic process is a narrative one: *the process of telling a story.*

During the war, Blunden was already painfully aware of the difficulty surrounding his ability to tell his story. In a letter he wrote home in January of 1917 he consciously reflected on the inadequacy of literary forms to capture his experience: "I wish I could weave together all the moods and manners that I see out here, and make the epic of the age. But chivalry is not the atmosphere. It is all routine, a business with plenty of paper credit." Although Edmund Blunden never attempted to write an epic of the Great War, his complex personal narrative of the conflict, **Undertones of War** (1928), does go a long way towards exposing the often conflicting moods and manners so characteristic of military experience on the Western Front. Moreover, as this early example of sensitivity to genre and style reminds us, the issue of how to interpret experience—how to tell his story—concerned Blunden for many years, perhaps becoming the inescapable preoccupation of his life. Given that he never could say "good-bye to all that," Blunden's post-war life became an extended, quiet struggle to locate an adequate mode of apprehension for his haunting ordeal. Introducing a volume called *Great Short Stories of the War* in 1930, Blunden comments that "the mind of the soldier on active service was continually beginning a new short story, which had almost always to be broken off without a conclusion" (ii).

Someplace in the daunting reality of war, there is a tellable truth. Somewhere in the range of forms available, in the matrix of potential war narratives, the soldier's story—however inconclusive—might be found. But the war writer faces an intimidating challenge because he must impose narrative closure on a story that has no proper ending, because "each circumstance of the British experience that is still with me has ceased for me to be big or little," in short, because war is a confusing, chaotic, and often contradictory experience (***Undertones,*** 200). Blunden outlines a few of the paradoxes a soldier confronts in war: "you are one of an army of millions—and you are alone; you are nothing, and everything; you press this piece of metal, and you may bring misery on a girl at the other end of the earth; you move an inch or two in a wrong direction, and—what then?" (*Stories,* ii). The war was full of such questions and dilemmas; but what if, as in Blunden's case, luck holds out and you survive the war? What then?

Edmund Blunden's answer is clear: *you tell your story.* His own tale of war is a crafted and consciously literary work in which Blunden struggles to (re)present the contradictions of his experience on the front. Despite the "peculiar difficulty" an artist encounters in selecting "the sights, words, incidents, which seem essential" to convey the war, Blunden argues that "the art is rather to collect them" (*Undertones,* 201). And so he does collect them, in all their kaleidoscopic variety and brilliance.

> The last few months have been a new world, of which the succession of sensations erratically occupies my mind; the bowed heads of working parties and reliefs moving up by 'trenches' made of sacking and brushwood; the bullets leaping angrily from old rafters shining in greenish flarelight; an old pump and a tiled floor in the moon; bedsteads and broken mattresses hanging over cracked and scarred walls; Germans seen as momentary shadows among wire hedges; tallowy, blood-dashed faces—oh, put back the blanket; a gate, opening into a battlefield; boys, treating the terror and torment with the philosophy of men; cheeky newspaper sellers passing the gunpits; stretcher bearers on the same road an hour after; the old labourer at his cottage door pointing out with awe and importance the eaves chipped by anti-aircraft shrapnel (the guns meanwhile thundering away on the next village). . . .
>
> (85)

Blunden immerses us in the tide of his narrative, sets us adrift in a vague and shadowy world. Although his narrative follows an orderly succession of chapters, the flow determined by chronology (embarking for France in the winter of 1916, returning home with frazzled nerves late in 1918), Blunden's deeply personal account often moves randomly amidst the ebb and flow of war. Moments of great natural beauty alternate with scenes of nature ravaged by war, and Blunden often displays "the tenacity of fancy amid 'grim reality'" (*Undertones,* 33). Perhaps no scene better characterizes Blunden's story than this description of patrolling:

> If one went patrolling, it was almost inevitable that one would soon creep round some hole or suspect heap, and then, suddenly, one no longer knew which was the German line, which our own. Puzzling dazzling lights flew up, fell in the grass beside and flared like bonfires; one heard movements, saw figures, conjectured distances, and all in that state of dilemma. Willow-trees seemed moving men. Compasses responded to old iron. At last by luck or some stroke of recognition one found one's self; but there was danger of not doing so; and the battalion which relieved us sent a patrol out, only to lose it that way. The patrol came against wire, and bombed with all its skill; the men behind the wire fired their Lewis gun with no less determination; and when the killed and wounded amounted to a dozen or more it was found that the patrol and the defenders were of the same battalion.
>
> (74)

Blunden finds himself in a world without direction, in a war where your worst enemy is often yourself, in an existential landscape illuminated by "puzzling dazzling lights" where his greatest hope is to find himself. *Undertones of War* seeks to interpret this world, to narrate its reality. Blunden's book asks its readers, quietly and simply, to hear its story.

In a 1925 essay titled "War and Peace," Blunden reflects on the war as an event that enlarged his "mortal franchise" and opened "a new sphere of consciousness" (17). Although the shadowy complexion of Blunden's war experience remains somewhat of a mystery even to himself, immersion in "the fierce electricity of an overwhelming tempest of forces and emotions" clearly has given him a profound appreciation of the "deep-lighted detail" of ordinary life, just as it inevitably provides a horizon against which to view subsequent life (18). Like a person emerging from a coma, Blunden leaves the war disoriented yet embracing life with new-found vigor. But henceforth nature and the "desperate drudgery" of war are inextricably bound together for him, their wartime fusion demanding "a more intense word than memories" to adequately convey their troubled union (15). Blunden knows well that this union can be mapped in a number of ways, each one more or less responsive to the complexly fused features of his war experience. Approaching his war narrative, then, we, too, need a more resonant word than "memories" to fully describe what it seeks to apprehend; we need a word more fully responsive to the equivocal dialogue of his text.

One of Blunden's most perceptive critics, Thomas Mallon, provides such a word, when he speaks of Blunden as "almost indisputably his generation's foremost poet of war-hauntedness." We might easily extend this claim to his generation's prose works as well.[1] Some would say that Siegfried Sassoon also has a legitimate claim to this dubious honor. His twenty-year struggle to come to terms with the paradoxes and elusiveness of his wartime experience strongly testifies to his own profound "war-hauntedness." But Blunden's custodial care of works of other war poets and the pervasive echoes of war in his poetry give us several important reasons to examine this feature of his work most closely. To be sure, Blunden's text often seems haunted by the very undertones he seeks to expose: ghostly features dot the narrative as it attempts to map the memories of Blunden's experience.[2] In a way, the "Preliminary" to his text provides a small scale version of this larger narrative map, significantly forecasting the confusing epistemological ground his text will then negotiate. Blunden invites readers to survey the terrain he has carefully and often painfully charted, to engage a dynamic text conspicuously in dialogue with itself and with other texts: one constantly modulating its narrative voice, one freely ranging over a field of generic tension, one exhibiting a subtle unease through its deceptive irony, yet one insistently attempting to remember, "to go over the ground again" (viii).

Blunden establishes an ambiguous tone from the very outset of his text, opening his "Preliminary" with an evasive rhetorical question: "Why should I not write it?" Importantly, the focus here is not on why he *should* write it, but rather on why he should *not*—the object "it" remaining vague and undefined throughout. In light of Blunden's own reluctance to define his narrative *it*, we too must be wary of prematurely limiting possible antecedents for the pronoun. Terms such as *memoir, autobiography,* or some other *it* recording the personal experience of war might close off the careful ambiguity Blunden seeks here.[3] He encourages us to approach *it* cautiously, to study *it* by turns for what *it* appears to be, as well as for what *it* seems not to be. He gradually asks us, with his studied and indirect rhetoric, to observe the quiet clash between his parade of excuses for not writing and a vague but guiding sense of responsibility.

Jousting with memory, perhaps fleeing certain ghosts, Blunden presents a litany of reasons why his war account should not be written: "I know that it is very local, limited, incoherent; that it is almost useless, in the sense that no one will read it who is not already aware of all the intimations and discoveries in it" (vii). Blunden knows that many in his audience in 1928 have made the same journey he has, and he pauses to observe that readers who have not shared this ordeal will fail, no doubt, to understand his narrative: "Neither will they understand—that will not be all my fault." Once again, *what* we will fail to understand remains, as yet, undefined. With these reservations we slowly begin to sense that the truth of his war experience might elude narrative apprehension—both his and ours—in important ways.

Blunden is painfully aware that too often, in the years since the war, various firsthand accounts purporting to represent trench warfare have disappointed; too often, they have not conveyed the whole truth of it; too often, in turn, audiences have failed to understand.[4] In his own text, while sketching a trench maintenance party, Blunden points directly to one previous failure. Recalling the scene, he observes that the men

> enjoyed this form of active service with pathetic delight—and what men were they? Willing, shy, mostly rather like invalids, thinking of their families. Barbusse would have "got them wrong," save in this: they were all doomed.
>
> (122)

Characteristically, getting it right or wrong is of the utmost importance to Blunden: he insists that war narratives must be measured against a horizon of experien-

tial truth, one capable of conveying a diversity and complexity of war experience—even if this means including willing, complacent soldiers in the narrative picture. Yet the horizon remains fluid and a bit indistinct for Blunden; it remains capable of accommodating the diversity of truths—such as Barbusse's inescapable fate and Blunden's willing workers—that frequently intersect in war experience.

So as we see here, Blunden typically sets his narrative in dialogue with other renderings of the war, consciously weighing the adequacy of their payments, consciously enfolding their mediations within his own. Reflecting on past failures, assessing various standards of truth, Blunden also probes his own abilities through the litany of excuses in his "Preliminary": "I know that memory has her little ways, and by now she has concealed precisely that look, that word, that coincidence of nature without and nature within which I long to remember" (vii). The possibility exists that he too might get it wrong, that memory might fail him. His textual dialogue includes both past and present selves, and it troubles their connection in the "little ways" of memory. Furthermore, the dual allegiance of memory—to both external and internal nature, to both the natural, public world and to an inner, private human nature—also hinders the process of narrative recall through its insistence upon their uncanny coincidence. At this point, facing an almost useless and impossible task, surely Blunden has presented sufficient reasons not to write. Yet the seductive force of memory, tellingly figured as a female muse who takes "a perverse pleasure in playing with her votaries," provokes a desire that draws Blunden on.[5]

Significantly, however, even this desire is quickly checked when he is "inclined to think that [memory's] playfulness has been growing rather more trying latterly: and perhaps I am gradually becoming colder in my enthusiasm to win a few gazes" (vii). Finally he answers the voices that encourage him not to write with an almost mournful resignation: "If these things are so, it is now or never for the rendering, however discoloured and lacunary, which I propose" (vii). At last, Blunden identifies the "it" he must write as a fatally inadequate "rendering." As an artistic rendering, the picture may be discolored by form or style; as an historical record, it may be riddled with gaps or muddled by time; as a personal account, it may conflate past and present selves in the ways of memory; yet, as we might infer from the letter home noted above, the idea of rendering also evokes a financial sense—he must pay a debt, settle an account, render the narrative obligation that is due for his enlarged "mortal franchise." And he must pay now—or never.

In part, as Blunden recalls this experience, he realizes that he must address the routine details it evokes—the abundant details and images that literary business frequently conveys by drawing on the paper credit of realism—and thus he proposes to render his work according to conventional realistic contracts and forms. Not only will he abide by these conditions, but he genuinely wishes to convey as much of his experience as possible through them. In addition, as Paul Fussell's close reading of *Undertones* explains, traces of the English pastoral tradition linger throughout Blunden's narrative, conveying a literary culture

> so ripe, so mellow and mature, that it is a surprise to recall that Blunden was only twenty-eight when he began writing [*Undertones*]. . . . He is already practiced in the old man's sense of memory as something like a ritual obligation.
>
> (259)

But the debt Blunden must pay far exceeds his obligation either to an arcadian tradition or to realistic forms of narrative. As this evasive preamble demonstrates, Blunden qualifies his project with reticence, with the notion of rendering an unpayable debt, with an awareness of the profound responsibility it entails and a sense of the radical otherness of the experience he seeks to communicate. Thus, at the same time he deploys conventional techniques and modes to convey the very real images of his past experience, the shadow of truth falls across his work, haunting the text and his imagination, demanding that he acknowledge the limitations of convention by attaching a release clause to his contract. *When* we fail to understand—not *if*—the blame will not all be his. As readers, he demands we too take responsibility for this conversation. We must engage in dialogue in order to approach the reality he (re)presents.

But the dialogue Blunden's text suggests here is far from simple and begs for an exegesis that truly recognizes the maze of undertones, the wealth of shadows, the variety of debts paid and incurred through it. It is a narrative that directly invites readers to converse with it, to hear its voices, to join its world. It is a narrative that insists upon a dynamic relation to the reality of the past it (re)presents.

In several of the poems Blunden appends to *Undertones*—especially in **"Another Journey From Bethune to Cuinchy"** where "I see you walking / . . . But that 'you' is I"—the dialogue and a certain confusion of selves is explicit, openly generating problems of "Who's who? you or I?" (335). The prose narrative often catches the same uncertainty and invites similar participation from the reader. The world of the war becomes Blunden's world, a world he leaves only infrequently and reluctantly, thus a world he places readers resolutely within. It is a complex world filled with irony and paradox, one spinning between scenes of horror and compassion, one oscillating between moments of personal disorientation and natural stability. The

dialogue Blunden proposes through his text enables us to recognize the reality of the experience he conveys—to touch its face and identify with it—and at the same time to admit the radical, haunted, evasive otherness of an ordeal that his narrative can only suggest but never capture. Alternating freely between the facts of experience and the conventions of art, between a desire to avoid writing and a need to write, between the past and the present, Blunden's narrative journey leads us through a world filled with contradictions; it invites us to hear the undertones of conflict and through the process of narrative mediation to comprehend its haunting dialogue.

Throughout *Undertones,* this process of mediation, this narrative dialogue mandates a dynamic interpretation of the text, an ongoing interaction with it. For example, in the closing paragraphs of the "Preliminary," Blunden casually admits that "I tried once before" (viii).[6] Even though this reference to a past attempt remains somewhat elusive, the metaphoric resonance of his present "rendering" quietly comments on the whole range of forms, strategies, conventions and techniques that will far exceed the "depressing forced gaiety" of his earlier version. Then he "misunderstood," he pulled at "Truth's nose"; now he sees truth's face more clearly. Then he wrote imitating a cheery "beanish" style; now he approaches with solemn reserve. This textual dialogue between past and present, between traditional styles and reflective undertones, between failed attempts and outstanding debts reveals a self-reflexive narrative commitment that clearly exceeds the narrow parameters of realistic history or pastoral elegy. To project faithfully the complexity his experience demands, he intentionally turns now to a dynamic form of personal narrative.

Although Blunden encourages us to hear many dialogues scarcely audible in the undertones of war, the conversation remains far from clear—even to him. Despite his maturing vision, he fears the inadequacy of his narrative payment. In his poetry, especially those poems directly concerned with specific battles such as **"Third Ypres,"** he has attempted another account of "the image and horror of it," yet these poems also resist firmly pinning *it* down (viii). Something in Blunden's experience on the Western Front seems to resolutely defy containment by conventional literary forms and language.

So despite his poetic efforts, Blunden acknowledges that "it was impossible not to look again, and to descry the ground, how thickly and innumerably yet it was strewn with the facts or notions of war experience. I must go over the ground again" (viii). And it is this dynamic process of going over the ground again, of picking up and conversing with the broken images, the facts and notions of war strewn in memory, that will constitute the most substantial "it" Blunden offers us. For **Undertones** is as much a conversation with memory and various narrative traditions as it is a record of the experience of war.[7] More directly, Blunden stages a conscious dialogue between the confident record of experience and the reluctant recall of memory. Early in the narrative, he admits that "whereas in my mind the order of events may be confused, no doubt a reference to the battalion records would right it; yet does it matter greatly? or are not pictures and evocations better than strict dates?" (22). He reminds us again that this is not empirical history, and that the truth manifested through his narrative requires negotiation: sometimes drawing upon the facts of war experience, sometimes catching only a reflection in "the mirror of time gone by" (23), other times admitting "It was all a ghost story" (50).

Blunden continually invites us to hear the many voices of his text, the muted undertones of war and memory:

A voice, perhaps not my own, answers within me. You will not go over the ground again, it says, until that hour when agony's clawed face softens into the smilingness of a young spring day; when you, like Hamlet, your prince of peaceful war makers, give the ghost a '*Hic et ubique?* then we'll change our ground,' and not this time in vain.

(viii-ix)

The ghostly voices within, the literary shadows of past warriors, the transfigured faces of war, and the actual ghosts of lost "companions like E. W. T., and W. J. C., and A. G. V., from whose recaptured gentleness no sign of death's astonishment or time's separation shall be imaginable" all haunt this text from its opening lines. Blunden insists on their importance; as we shall see, they make **Undertones** far more than mere "memories."[8]

* * *

THE NARRATIVE EYE

The Scotchman murmured to himself, "Only a boy— only a boy," and shed tears, while his mate grunted an angry sympathy. Then, "But you'll be all right, son— excuse me, won't you—you'll be all right."

—*Undertones* (3)

Readers of Blunden's text may miss the importance of this evasive, reticent, ghostly quality of **Undertones.** They may miss the dialogue, the questioning, the subtle and doubting *"won't you"* that interrupts a seemingly straightforward statement such as "But you'll be all right, son—excuse me, won't you—you'll be all right." Readers may fail to hear the rhetorical ring and invitation to participate in passages such as this: "for as yet, *you must know,* I was in a sense more afraid of our own guns than I was of the enemy's" (my italics, 51). Readers may overlook the quiet dialogue he carries on

between his past and present self, between his narrator and his readers, between his text and those by other war writers: they may miss his wish that

I could tell you half as intricately and spiritually [as H. M. Tomlinson did in *Waiting for Daylight*] the spell which made us haunt there [a library]; the cajoling ghostliness of the many printed papers and manuscript sermons which littered the floor of the priest's house and drifted into his garden; the sunny terror which dwelt in every dust grain on the road, in every leaf on the currant bushes near that churchyard, the clatter of guns, the coexistent extraordinary silence; the summer ripeness, the futility of it; the absence of farmyard and inn-parlour voices which yet you could hear.

(52-53)

We must not close off the "coexistent" and contradictory features of his text; we must neither ignore the undertones nor make his dialogue a monologue. Yet because Blunden packs his narrative with so many details and vivid images, telling a story of the education of an open and impressionable youth—a personal history that follows a direct line from his matriculation "under orders for France" to his merciful departure for home in 1918—the historical record of his text can easily be overemphasized (1). It is tempting to relate to the reality of his text exclusively through this historical lens, noting its identity with the events of the past, measuring its reenactment of the war.

Time after time, of course, Blunden does display the attentive eye of a reporter. For example, near the end of the narrative he remarks that "no stable invention of dreams could be more dizzily dreadful" than these glimpses of the forward area:

A view of Spoil Bank under these conditions is in my mind's eye—a hump of slimy soil, with low lurching frames of dugouts seen in some too gaudy glare; a swelling pool of dirty water beside it, among many pools not so big—the record shell hole; tree spikes, shells of wagons, bony spokes forking upward; lightnings east and west of it, dingy splashes; drivers on their seats, looking straight onward; gunners with electric torches finding their way; infantry silhouettes and shadows bowed and laden, and the plank road, tilted, breached, blocked, still stretching ahead.

(237)

The impressive word-painting Blunden displays here allows us to feel the slimy mud, to smell the putrid water, to sense the exhaustion and disorientation of the infantry soldiers. Blunden, the writer, places us within a chaotic and fragmented scene of war; he invites us to view events through his "mind's eye."

On one level, then, his work might well be called a memoir or reminiscence, might be seen primarily as a historical chronicle of war, might be read for its convincing reenactment of the past. The military historian Correlli Barnett values this aspect of Blunden's work:

. . . the reminiscences and the novels—the two often come to much the same thing—tell us just [what the Western Front was like]—and do so with all the awareness, imaginative insight, and skill of writers of first-class talent. Books like Blunden's *Undertones of War,* or Williamson's *Patriot's Progress,* or Frederic Manning's *Her Privates We* enable us to see, smell, feel, and touch the reality of life and battle on the Western Front. . . . I would simply like to point out that, carefully weighed, this evidence is of the highest value to the historian.

(2)

The crux, however, is *how* we ought to carefully weigh this historical evidence. What standards or categories apply? How should we relate to the objective reality it conveys? Barnett initially seems comfortable with distinctions similar to those Wayne Shumaker makes between typical modes of personal writing, especially between nonsubjective forms such as memoir and reminiscence and more directly subjective forms of autobiography. For Shumaker, in a memoir or reminiscence, "so far as the focus is kept steadily on an impersonal subject, the personality of the autobiographer (if we are willing to grant him the title) relinquishes centrality to something other than itself" (51). Clearly, Barnett begins by focusing on the impersonal historical evidence in Blunden's text, carefully avoiding his status as autobiographer. In light of Blunden's own reticence about the generic status of his work, does such a reading adequately interpret *Undertones*? Should we value Blunden's work chiefly for its objective history of the war? More generally, how useful or important are such generic distinctions?

Generic categories often cause more confusion than assistance when reading a text, so we need to consider the conventional labels critics attach to Blunden's "rendering" of "it."[9] Bernard Bergonzi calls Blunden a "consciously objective writer"—as opposed to a subjective author who offers his "own reflections" and shows the "war as it affected his own development"—noting that *Undertones of War* is much less than a full autobiography: it is a severely selective account of Blunden's experiences as a very young subaltern, on the Somme and at the Third Battle of Ypres" (147-150). To be sure, Blunden does restrict the scope of his narrative; his focus never leaves the war. Yet how much does such a distinction really tell us about *Undertones*? Having disqualified Blunden's text as autobiography, Bergonzi has left himself without a convenient label for a work that he calls Blunden's "attempt to make sense out of his own experiences, to trace a pattern in the scarifying events that had impinged on his formative years" (150). More importantly, his division between objective and subjective narratives seems both inadequate and reductive in even his own reading of Blunden. Moreover, any emplotting of events—any tracing of a pattern—necessarily interprets events, necessar-

ily offers individual reflections on them, necessarily blends objective and subjective modes.

Nevertheless, as we see with Barnett's and Bergonzi's readings, some critics do seem comfortable with an objective label such as memoir for *Undertones,* even with the limitations it necessarily implies.[10] Extending distinctions made by Roy Pascal and Wayne Shumaker to twentieth-century autobiography, Brian Finney suggests that both reminiscence and memoir "concentrate on the world outside the self"—on a public world often concerned with social, political and military history (150). Although such a division between public and private worlds may possibly be fair to the generals and statesmen we usually encounter through other modern "memoirs," it does seem grossly unjust to Blunden's work.

After all, he writes as an individual soldier caught in a clash of mass armies, as a private poet recording a public catastrophe, as an author seeking to pay both private and public debts. Blunden writes, in short, as a mediator between private and public spheres, fluctuating between a partial view of individual experience and a more collective narrative of general events in several ways. First, *Undertones* carefully blends Blunden's personal testimony with more distant third-person reflections. The quiet shift in the following passage from the general "one" to the personal "I" is typical: "One might sit, as I did, upon our parapet, and spend several minutes looking at the opposite line and the ruins and expensive cemetery of Villers Guislain, without any disaster" (270). Next, the tension of a term such as soldier-poet captures some of the duality of his work by yoking together his public commitments and private reactions. Although his wartime poetry was tame compared to that of Sassoon or Owen, Blunden's status as a poet in uniform definitely influenced his view of the front. In fact, following the publication of a book of his poems, he was transferred to battalion headquarters: the "book of verse had done its work; and the same evening I was at dinner in Harrison's presence, afraid of him and everyone else in high command, and marvelling at the fine glass which was in use there" (78). Though still a poet among soldiers, his new position placed him a distance from "worse places and cruder warfare," allowing him to play a new role as "Field Works Officer," a role that perhaps saved his life. In this position, he adds both "practical and (as the world was then constituted) some artistic touches" to the trenches, and views the workings of the brigade staff with "amazement and consternation" (79). Finally, we have only to reflect on the even greater paradox of his status as a soldier, both agent of destruction and victim of it—or on his role as protagonist in an autobiographical text, both participant in the events and narrator of them—to begin to appreciate the complex processes of mediation at work throughout Blunden's text. His awareness of his role as arbiter of these oppositions resembles Frederic Manning's insight in *The Middle Parts of Fortune*: "There was no man of them unaware of the mystery which encompassed him, for he was part of it; he could neither separate himself entirely from it, nor identify himself with it completely" (182). Whereas Manning turns the "myriad faces" of war on us, Blunden places us in the midst of a dialogue between the voices of war—voices both public and private.

As a dynamic and personal narrative, then, *Undertones* conducts a narrative dialogue between a historical chronicle of war experience and a personal interpretation of it. Blunden indisputably provides the eye of this text, yet he is also the "I" directing it. When the memories are too intense, he redirects them, turning the public eye away with private vision.

> But let us be getting out of this sector. It is too near Hulluch and the Hohenzollern. The listening posts are not anxious to go out far at night, and I am sure I agree with them; they have had too many pineapples and not enough sleep. . . . When we got away, it was a full moon, eternal and, so it happened, but little insulted by the war's hoarse croaking.
>
> (67)

Thus for all the historical force his narrative carries—as a public record of the war, as an objective account of events—its status as an artistically crafted "personal statement should remain equally significant" (Hardie, 5).

* * *

THE NARRATIVE "I"

"The mind swoons doubly burdened"

—**"Third Ypres"** (307)

Blunden intentionally keeps a number of modes of apprehension in suspension throughout his narrative dialogue, intentionally playing the voices of history and memoir against those of various autobiographical selves. Recall Blunden's description of the front quoted above: on the first level it does appear that his narrator relinquishes claim to an autobiographical personality in favor of detailed reporting of the war. Yet the dizzying, impressionistic quality of this description, with its muted lightning, surreal images, and shadowy soldiers begs for attention too. A specific point of view generates these impressions; they flow from a reticent but visible narrator. He is an educated officer, a budding poet from a middleclass background, a sensitive witness to a scene of appalling degradation. Blunden sets this scene—very specifically for his readers—in his "mind's eye," encouraging the reader's mind to swoon "doubly burdened" with the poet's. Although the descriptive richness of passages such as this one enables us to see

the war through his physical eye, through the seemingly transparent narrative record he presents, a controlling and configuring "I" always lurks behind the scene.

So rather than effacing his personality as in a memoir, the issue of a "mind's eye" and the "inner I" directing it become central to Blunden's understanding of the war. In other words, *Undertones* simultaneously records historical events and interprets them within the complex dialogue of a personal narrative. It dynamically fuses experience and the shaping forces of memory, admitting that only together can the sameness of events and the distancing otherness of art and memory begin to approximate the experience of war. Looking back, this point merely underscores the difficulty Blunden faced labeling his own work—a difficulty critics continue to labor with.[11] Of course it also encourages us to pursue the dynamic understanding his narrative invites, to locate his narrative within its appropriate contexts, to simultaneously read its various narrative registers.

One context almost totally overlooked for Blunden's work is the autobiographical tradition within which he writes. Frequently, critics concentrate on the sense of radical discontinuity that the war brought to participants, and on the corresponding inadequacy of available forms for literary presentation. But every author writes within a discernible tradition—inevitably invoking cultural narratives and reshaping available paradigms. Granting the difficulty of isolating the historical traits of a genre at any given point, nevertheless some generalizations regarding the Edwardian autobiographical tradition do seem particularly informative for Blunden's work.

Carl Dawson, in his study of Edwardian autobiography *Prophets of Past Time* (1988), focuses on "writers who worked in the new climate of the *fin de siècle,* who wrote with a self-consciousness that was as historical as it was personal" (xiii). As we have begun to see, this Edwardian blend of historical and personal self-consciousness clearly carries over into Blunden's postwar narrative as well. His reenactment of events remains as much a private story of coming of age—a narrative search for identity—as it does a public history of the front.

Blunden's youthful search for identity perhaps made him more vulnerable to inventing selves than other Great War writers; in any event, his narrative continually questions his ability to measure up to the various roles in military life. Without an established civilian identity, a socially inscribed role such as Siegfried Sassoon's fox hunting persona, Blunden struggles in his narrative to locate a self he can live with.

Perhaps this characteristic struggle to define a narrative self is the most important feature an understanding of Edwardian autobiography contributes to our interpretation of Blunden's work. Sharing a fundamental uncertainty with the major autobiographers of his time, Blunden offers his own particular emphasis to the tradition. Frequently wondering why "by good luck I escaped a piece of trouble" in this or that sector (81), or commenting on a "lucky jump" or a dud shell falling nearby, his proximity to random death continually hampers his efforts to locate an autobiographical self of some permanence. In a war situation more chaotic and uncertain than his literary predecessors faced, Blunden endured a perpetual and numbing onslaught:

> I remember that I was talking with somebody about one 'Charlie' Aston, an officer's servant, who had been running here and there to collect watches from German dead. He had just returned to his chosen shell hole, with several fine specimens, when a huge shell burst in the very place. But not much notice was taken, or elegy uttered, for everywhere the same destruction threatened.
>
> (222)

Yet, importantly, Blunden endured. In a land full of wastage and destruction, it must have been almost impossible not to question the integrity or permanence of the self. Still Blunden's text bears out Dawson's conclusion that although the "radical exploration of self in modern autobiography" may tend to threaten individual freedom or may seem to make constructions of the self unbearably vulnerable, these "autobiographies remain human documents however slippery their medium" (207-8).

It is just such a dialectical insistence on the resilience of an autobiographical self—or selves—in the face of the horrific events of the Western Front, and in its prominence in the narrative account of those events, that makes Blunden's work such a powerfully human document. The "harmless young shepherd in a soldier's coat" that closes the narrative often prompts critical attention (276), but this is only one role among many that Blunden assumes in the narrative. Whereas the humane shepherd tending his flock presents one possible metaphoric self for Blunden, at the beginning of his story we hear the voice of a young, naive man "not anxious to go," one who is filled with "an uncertain but unceasing disquiet" (1). Certainly these roles overlap in their essentially naive views of life, but the untried youth grimly facing the unknown challenges of a foreboding world lacks the pastoral immunity his arcadian counterpart offers. And although the young Blunden we first meet has yet to face the horrors of war, "there was something about France in those days which seemed to me, despite all journalistic enchanters, to be dangerous" (1). We have only to recall the chivalry and romance of the dispatches the journalist Philip Gibbs sent home in order to appreciate Blunden's scorn or to share his doubts: even sheltered in England, insulated by the Channel, undertones of war have

filtered in. So Blunden embarks for France already suspicious of general truths, already sensitive to the power of rhetoric and language, already blending the roles of naive youth and skeptical maturity. The legacy of Edwardian autobiography, combined with the retrospective situation he writes within, thus provides Blunden with both a mode of apprehending the unique events soon to follow as well as a way of configuring them for narrative presentation. Whether or not he did so consciously, his personal struggle to interpret his war experience clearly indicates a dialogue with this tradition.

* * *

"DARING THE HUGE DARK:" THE MIND'S EYE

> I might have known the war by this time, but I was still too young to know that depth of ironic cruelty.
>
> —*Undertones* (275)

In the next to last poem printed in *Undertones,* **"Flanders Now,"** Blunden sketches an image of the "flower of manhood, daring the huge dark," quietly directing our attention to those who "slept, and rose, and lived and died somehow—" (340-1). These same voices, of those who lived and died somehow, converse with us throughout his prose narrative as well, murmuring among the broken images and undertones of the text. Paul Fussell claims that Blunden, even at the end of the narrative, "despite the knowledge he has attained, especially at the pillboxes . . . is still innocent" (265). I disagree. The undertones may be muffled at times, the irony may be subtle, but our dialogue with the text must admit both. Perhaps in the "harmless shepherd in a soldier's coat" that closes **Undertones,** perhaps in what Fussell calls "that objective distancing, that tender withdrawing vision of a terribly vulnerable third-person," the pretense of innocence is maintained (267). But it is never more than a pretense. As we have seen, this is only one moment in the shifting counterpoint of this dynamic narrative. Just as Blunden can only apprehend the fullness of his war experience through an ongoing dialogue with several traditions, through a constant challenge of narrative eye by "I," so too our approach to the reality his text communicates must pass through successive filters of historical and literary interpretation.

In a way that ought to be appreciated, **Undertones** also looks forward to the works of the thirties—especially to those associated with the "Auden Generation." Samuel Hynes describes these works as "urging a kind of writing that would be affective, immediate, and concerned with ideas, moral not aesthetic in its central intention, and organized by that intention rather than by its correspondence to the observed world" (*Auden,* 13). Although Blunden's work anticipates rather than partakes of this tradition—he is concerned both with correspondence to the observed world of the war *and* with the moral intention of the work—Hynes' description catches a number of important features of Blunden's narrative. The enlargement of Blunden's mortal franchise has been purchased at great price; he revisits the war, tramps over the ground again, because he believes this journey can encourage action in the public world, because the journey has a moral purpose. Blunden shapes his text and draws upon various literary traditions from pastoral to autobiography. But for Blunden, the continually shifting center of consciousness of his narrative and the variety of roles he plays searching for self identity inevitably intersect with the debt he must pay to those who know fully the ironic cruelty of war. Haunted by "the huge dark," Blunden pays this debt; doing so, his work claims both personal and public authority through experience—not innocence.

At the beginning of the text, in his pastoral garb, Blunden shepherds a

> squad of men nominally recovered from wounds "back to the war, although" they hid [from him] what daily grew plain enough—the knowledge that the war had released them but for a few minutes, that the war would reclaim them, that the war was jealous war and a long-lasting. 1914, 1915, 1916. . . .
>
> (1-2)

His premonitions notwithstanding, as the god of war drew them gradually nearer, Blunden would occasionally "ask the silly questions of nonrealization; they in their tolerance pardoned, smiled, and hinted, knowing that I was learning, and should not escape the full lesson" (2). Thus, early in his text we encounter the sense that the truth of war is a lesson that can—and indeed must—be learned. Importantly, these lessons are taught without consideration of social position or educational status, and even "experience was nothing but a casual protection" (40). Here, ordinary soldiers often teach officers, and the voices of survivors—"shocked and sad"—echo quietly. Through the chapters that follow, from the early one titled "Trench Education" to the later "Coming of Age" to the penultimate "School Not At Wittenberg" Blunden gradually completes his and our education.

Blunden's opening chapter sets us on a journey with him, enrolling us in the school of the Western Front. Like all autobiographers, Blunden must play the dual role of student and teacher, of historical participant and transhistorical (re)presenter. His solution to this standard autobiographical dilemma is to position *us* in the midst of a narrative dialogue, to encourage *us* to recognize the complex narrative mingling of eye and I, the crossing between world and self, and the intertwining of nar-

rative history and personal story. Through the challenge of and commitment to narrative dialogue, Blunden reveals his truth of war.

Significantly, Dawson's study of the recollective process of autobiography ends demanding "a wholesale rethinking of generic boundaries," inviting us to understand autobiography as a process "which tests the self in the process of discovery. [Autobiography] also involves the wrestle between remembering and forgetting, that web and warp of memory which reminds its teller of paradox and mystery, of life lost and life found" (216). Blunden's own efforts to create his narrative—to define its generic range and his position as narrator within it—speak to us clearly of the tension Dawson outlines and underlines. Blunden's constant attempt "to understand the drift of the war," to record the recurring "hints" that often culminate in suffering, to come to grips with a dawning awareness that "It's a lie; we're a lie" (38, 65), reminds us that his is indeed a narrative of self-testing. The textual dialogue between various metaphors of the self—Blunden as pastoral innocent, as inexperienced soldier, as battalion poet, as enlightened skeptic—reveals an awareness that his narrative can only posit selfhood within a field of epistemological doubt. So it is a tentative narrative, one full of uncertainty and moments of disorientation.

But it is finally a narrative that allowed Blunden to reflect on the stark reality of the "huge dark" that haunts his memory, a narrative that enabled Blunden to tell the most important story of his life. He paid his debt; we can only pay ours by listening.

Notes

1. Mallon's book for the Twayne series, *Edmund Blunden* (1983), remains the fullest study of Blunden's work, as well as the most complete biography to date. Although Blunden may always be seen as a "minor" figure in twentieth-century literature, Mallon's careful analysis of his lifelong work provides a number of well-considered reasons for studying it. For specific comments on the influence of the Great War on Blunden, see the chapter "Born for This: Blunden's War" (52-70).

2. Alec Hardy quotes H. M. Tomlinson's 1930 review of *Undertones*: "Blunden's book, in fact, is by a ghost for other ghosts; some readers will not know what it is all about." Hardy then explains that the "uneasiness" we sense in *Undertones* "is more than the 'atmosphere' of the book; it is Blunden's method of disturbing his readers into understanding his undertones" (6). Paul Fussell speaks of Blunden's motif of cartography in *Undertones* as "an act of memory conceived as an act of military reconnaissance," where "the

'ground' is the past imaged as military terrain, spread out for visiting and mapping as his battalion front had been mapped by the younger Blunden only seven years earlier" (259-60).

3. In 1933, Blunden turned his historical talents directly to writing "A Battalion History" for the 11th Royal Sussex Regiment. Whereas *Undertones* sets out to be a complex blend of historical, autobiographical, narrative, and poetic writing, the battalion history clearly seeks to be read as a fairly direct chronicle of events. The flat descriptive prose of this history clearly contrasts with the rich dialogue characteristic of *Undertones.* The variety of intentions manifested in *Undertones,* revealed especially through the "Preliminary," sets his personal narrative apart from the more limited history. Interestingly, though, Blunden also presents this history—"with apologies"—as payment of a debt, as obliging a request from old friends. "Unfortunately," he writes, "it is shorter than they expected, but the war was also shorter than they expected" (*Mind's Eye,* 58-85). In this characteristic gesture of both identity with his friends and separation from them, we glimpse another example of Blunden's sensitivity to the difficulty of reclaiming the past.

4. In Robert Graves' review of *Undertones* (on December 15, 1928) he comments: "Blunden is about the first man I have read who has realized that the problem of writing about trench-warfare lies in the 'peculiar difficulty of selecting the sights, faces, words, incidents which characterized the times,' and that the solution is 'to collect them in their original form of incoherence,'" and notes that any two pages of Blunden's text are worth the whole of other accounts—"they have the real stuff in them" (*Nation,* 420).

5. The complex resonance of this feminine gendering might first be glossed by the biographical fact that when Blunden wrote this (1924) he was in Japan, alone, facing the imminent collapse of his first marriage to Mary Daines. Thus the seductive lure of the muse, and his cooling interest in her, both have individually explicable referents. Yet in larger social terms, the feminist criticism of Sandra M. Gilbert—especially "Soldier's Heart: Literary Men, Literary Women, and the Great War" (1983)—provides a convincing analysis of the complicated reworking of gender roles occasioned by the Great War. She argues that "as young men became increasingly alienated from their prewar selves, increasingly immured in the muck and blood of No Man's Land, women seemed to become, as if by some uncanny swing of history's pendulum, ever more powerful" (425). The control Blunden's muse exerts here then can be explained

in terms of a more general economic power and social authority as well.

6. Before the war even ended, Blunden attempted to write a version of his experience on the Western Front titled *De Bello Germanico: A Fragment of Trench History* (1918). Blunden's brother Gilbert published it in 1930, at Hawstead. Mallon remarks that Blunden's "description of it [in *Undertones*], although overly modest, is basically correct. The prose lacks the distinctive calm of that in *Undertones of War*" (118, note 76).

7. Thomas Mallon argues, rightly, I think, that "as the years passed, his grappling with the subject of war became the subject itself, he examined war-hauntedness as much as war, and the ramifications of this inquiry were felt in his nature and philosophic poetry as well" (62). However, as I will argue here, the intersection of war-memory and war itself as subjects was already of concern to Blunden when he wrote *Undertones.* Perhaps more importantly, the evolution of concern Mallon traces here may well indicate a deeper appreciation by Blunden—and/or by his critics—of the way war-hauntedness becomes hopelessly intertwined with war reality.

8. We must be cautious here, however, not to cripple Blunden's work by reducing it merely to a haunted text. Thomas Mallon also comments on the ghostly quality of the book, concluding that "while its gentle qualities make the book accessible to the unscarred reader, one senses that Blunden is speaking foremost to the dead and haunted"; and later, "the reader himself sometimes wonders at the selection of detail in *Undertones*; the presence of the dead often explains things" (65). On the contrary, as I shall show, Blunden's ghostly prose engages the epistemological quandary facing all writers who deal with this conflict; his prose directly enters the narrative discourse of mortality, enabling us to read his text as it speaks to a very real and living audience as well.

9. I do not pretend to offer anything more here than a provocative footnote to a very complex issue. In fact, the definition of what constitutes an autobiography, and how best to understand the many forms, acts, and sub-genres that gather under the autobiographical umbrella, has been the subject of several recent studies of the genre. From Roy Pascal's early study, *Design and Truth in Autobiography* (1960), including James Olney's *Metaphors of the Self* (1972) and Elizabeth Bruss' *Autobiographical Acts: The Changing Situation of a Literary Genre* (1976), to Philippe Lejeune's essay "The Autobiographical Contract" (1982), William C. Spengemann's historical study of *The Forms of Autobiography* (1980), and Brian Finney's survey of

twentieth-century British autobiography (*The Inner I*, 1985), critics of autobiography seem to agree with Bruss that "faulty or naive assumptions about the nature of a genre impair the criticism of autobiographical writing" (1). Needless to say, there is less agreement on how best to clarify these erroneous definitions. Nonetheless, as Adena Rosmarin convincingly argues in *The Power of Genre*, generic perception—particularly when genre is viewed heuristically rather than prescriptively—often can extend the boundaries of interpretation. Thus it is the limiting nature of labels such as memoir or reminiscence that I focus on here, asking for a heuristically enabling understanding of genre instead.

10. Fussell adopts the term memoir for the personal narratives of the Great War, but he wants to place additional pressure on the fictive or constructed nature of these texts. Although he certainly suggests the need for greater attentiveness to the richness of these works, all too often his own analysis truncates this same richness. In some ways, the critical label we attach to Blunden's work is of far greater relevance to contemporary readers (and makers of literary canons) than it is to the genesis of the work itself. But as we have already seen from the "Preliminary," and as we shall soon see through a discussion of Edwardian autobiography, Blunden was acutely aware of the literary forms and traditions (and their grounding assumptions) available when he wrote *Undertones*.

11. Paul Fussell initially seems attentive to the strain of conventional terms, calling Blunden's work an "extended pastoral elegy in prose," and later referring to it as "whatever it is" (254-55). But following his typical method, this ambiguity is only temporary. Once Fussell decides on a label for a work—even a hybrid term like pastoral elegy—he then closes off other dimensions of the text, other registers of meaning. Thus his one-dimensional reading of Blunden provides an illuminating discussion of Blunden's debt to the pastoral tradition, and almost no awareness of the autobiographical, or even historical, aspects of his text.

Works Cited

Barnett, Correlli. "A Military Historian's View of the Great War." *Essays by Divers Hands*. Vol. 36. Ed. Mary Stocks. London: Oxford UP, 1970.

Bergonzi, Bernard. *Heroes' Twilight: A Study of the Literature of the Great War*. 1965. London: Constable, 1980.

Blunden, Edmund. *Edmund Blunden: A Selection of his Poetry and Prose*. Selected by Kenneth Hopkins. London: Rupert Hart-Davis, 1950.

———, ed. *Great Short Stories of the War: England, France, Germany, America*. London: Eyre and Spottiswoode, 1930.

———. *The Mind's Eye*. 1934. Freeport, NY: Books for Library Press, 1967.

———. *Poems of Edmund Blunden, 1914-1930*. London: Cobden-Sanderson, 1930.

———. *Undertones of War*. 1928. Garden City: Doubleday, Doren, 1929.

———. *War Poets 1914-1918*. London: Longmans, Green, 1958.

Bruss, Elizabeth. *Autobiographical Acts: The Changing Situation of a Literary Genre*. Baltimore: Johns Hopkins UP, 1976.

Dawson, Carl. *Prophets of Past Time: Seven British Autobiographers, 1880-1914*. Baltimore: Johns Hopkins UP, 1988.

Eakin, Paul John. *Fictions in Autobiography: Studies in the Art of Self-Invention*. Princeton: Princeton UP, 1985.

Finney, Brian. *The Inner I: British Literary Autobiography of the Twentieth Century*. New York: Oxford UP, 1985.

Fussell, Paul. *The Great War and Modern Memory*. London: Oxford UP, 1975.

———. "Modernism, Adversary Culture and Edmund Blunden." *Sewanee Review*. 94.4 (Fall 1986): 583-601.

Gilbert, Sandra M. "Soldier's Heart: Literary Men, Literary Women, and the Great War." *Signs: Journal of Women in Culture and Society*. 8.3 (Spring 1983): 422-450.

Graham, Desmond. *The Truth of War: Owen, Blunden, Rosenberg*. Manchester: Carcanet Press, 1974. 79-131.

Hardie, Alec M. *Edmund Blunden*. 1958. Writers and Their Work Series 94. Burnt Mill, Harlow, Essex: Longmans Group, 1971.

Hynes, Samuel. *The Auden Generation: Literature and Politics in England in the 1930's*. London: Bodley Head, 1976.

Mallon, Thomas. *Edmund Blunden*. Twayne's English Author Series. Boston: Twayne, 1983.

Manning, Frederic. *The Middle Parts of Fortune: Somme and Ancre, 1916*. 1929. New York: St. Martin's, 1977.

Olney, James. "Autobiography: An Anatomy and a Taxonomy." *Neohelicon*. 13 (1986): 57-82.

———. *Metaphors of Self: The Meaning of Autobiography*. Princeton: Princeton UP, 1972.

————, ed. *Autobiography: Essays Theoretical and Critical*. Princeton: Princeton UP, 1980.

Pascal, Roy. *Design and Truth in Autobiography*. London: Routledge & Kegan Paul, 1960.

Shumaker, Wayne. *English Autobiography: Its Emergence, Materials and Forms*. Berkeley and Los Angeles: U of California P, 1954.

Spengemann, William C. *The Forms of Autobiography: Episodes in the History of a Literary Genre*. New Haven: Yale UP, 1979.

A. D. Burnett (essay date January 1994)

SOURCE: Burnett, A. D. "Crisis and Testament: Blunden and 'Values.'" *Durham University Journal* (January 1994): 105-18.

[*In the following essay, Burnett examines Blunden's 1929 poem "Values" in terms of its literary and biographical importance.*]

COMPOSITION AND PUBLICATION

The sonnet **'Values'** by Edmund Blunden (1896-1974) appeared in print in *The Observer* on 2 June 1929 and, shortly thereafter, was published in the collection ***Near and Far: New Poems*** in September 1929. A note to this collection states that the poems which it contains were written in Japan, where Blunden was resident from 1924 to 1927, and in the two years following his return to Britain, that is from 1927 to 1929. This poem (of which no manuscript is known to survive) may, therefore, have been written as early as 1924, although its oblique references to Japan and its late appearance in a journal may suggest that it was written in or nearer to 1929 than 1924. The probability that it was composed towards the end of this period is further suggested by the fact that a number of other poems concerning Japan were issued in ***Japanese Garland*** in September 1928 and that this sonnet was not included amongst those published in ***Retreat*** in May 1928.

Blunden clearly judged it of some importance since he placed it last in ***Near and Far*** and reprinted it both in ***The Poems*** of 1930 and in a late selection entitled ***Poems of Many Years*** in 1957 while he also included it amongst a dozen poems which he read aloud in a British Council recording of 1964. Others also have valued it since it appears as the last poem in a very brief anthology of Blunden's work entitled ***A Selection of the Shorter Poems*** which was issued in 1966 and in ***A Selection from the Poems*** in 1969, the latter certainly and the former apparently chosen by J. White.[1] The text was also printed with a very brief comment by A. M. Hardie in his useful introduction to Blunden in 1958.[2]

The poem was, moreover, read by his younger daughter at his funeral and it also concluded the memorial address of Sir Rupert Hart-Davis. Evidently, those who knew him well instinctively recognised its importance to him just as the mourners at the private service for Verdi spontaneously and without prompting sang together the slaves' chorus from *Nabucco*. (See Appendix for text of poem.)

PERSONAL BACKGROUND

The poem was written during a critical period in Blunden's life. In the late Twenties he had considered and recorded his experiences as a soldier on the Western Front in the First World War in ***Undertones of War*** (first published in November 1928) and he subsequently worked on revisions for this personal testament for the revised edition of 1930. In late August of 1927, moreover, he had returned to Britain after spending some three years as a Professor at Tokyo Imperial University. While there, he had in 1925 become the lover of Aki Hayashi, a school teacher from Nagoya, and he brought her with him as his secretary and copyist on his return to Britain. This is a relationship which has only recently been revealed and documented.[3] In 1928, moreover, he left his wife (who had also been unfaithful to him during his absence) and subsequently divorced her in 1931.

During the middle and late Twenties, therefore, Blunden sought to come to terms with his traumatic experiences on the Western Front and had not only to seek to accept and understand its hideous carnage but had also to reassess the idyllic rural peace and innocence and the apparently settled certainties which he had known as he grew up. In addition, he had to adjust from village life at his childhood home in Yalding to that of the modern metropolis, firstly in London and then in Tokyo. There was, furthermore, the fundamental contrast between western and eastern culture and society which he had to face in Britain and in Japan. He had, moreover, married and then loved another woman and he had then had to reconcile each of these fraught engagements as best he might. There were also, and not least, the existential stresses of poor health as a consequence of the war, of coping with his memories of trench warfare, of adjusting to the metropolis and then to a completely alien language, culture and society in Japan, of making a somewhat precarious and unsettled livelihood as a man of letters and then as a teacher and critic with diverse and conflicting responsibilities, and of coping with the death of his child, the infidelity and estrangement of his wife, and the not unreasonable demands of his Japanese lover. For Blunden, as for others, the war which had begun in 1914 did not end in 1918.

This period, in short, was for him a time of conflict, of a continuing war both with others and within himself, and between very different ways of life and their implicit values. There was in consequence a danger that he might collapse and fall apart, broken, divided, and alienated from others and from the world. That this did not happen is owing in large measure to himself and his response.

Significantly and valuably, he continued to read, study and express both in prose and poetry his deep love for the English countryside and its life; this was a sheet anchor to his spirit to which he held fast throughout his life and to which his scholarship and published work in the field of English literature also attest. He came, moreover, to terms with his suffering as a soldier and was able to articulate and both re-live and relieve his anguish in *Undertones of War.* Indeed, his departure for Japan was not only financially advantageous but also enabled him to distance himself from Europe and its horrors and thereby to secure more fully both some relief from his suffering and the detachment which he sought and needed so as to approach his experience more objectively. Japan offered material security and social position but also, and as importantly, another world which could offer escape, novelty and a wider perspective, a distance and a difference, in which he could rest, refresh and heal himself and take stock,—rather as for Lafcadio Hearn who had travelled to Japan in 1890, albeit in very different circumstances.

There was, therefore, during this period a deliberate attempt by Blunden to ponder life and its meaning and thereby to resolve his inner perplexities and suffering. This attempt to make sense of himself and his world, which one might expect in an older writer, was, in his circumstances, both necessary and desirable for one who, though so young, had lived so fully and intensely; as he remarked of the capture of a German trench in 1916 in a letter to Aki Hayashi of 21 October 1925[4] he had 'experienced more in 48 hours than some old gentlemen in all their lives',—and there were other trenches for him as well. The major testament to and resolution of this crisis were in *Undertones of War,* but the poems and—in their own way—the literary scholarship and engagement with English literature were also important. As he noted of himself in the introduction to his *Poems* of 1930, he had always suspected himself 'of some inclination to explore other subjects' than the rural and it is significant that the longest section in this substantial collection is entitled 'Experience and Soliloquy' (in which **'Values'** is included); it also contains another sonnet of chastened retrospection entitled **'Report on Experience'** which has been much anthologised.

His new vantage point in Japan, however, whatever its financial and personal advantages, had also a very different language, culture and society. As such, it inevitably estranged him and deepened his sense of alienation and crisis of identity. In his poems of this period he wrestled with the disorientation brought about by his new surroundings and attempted to find a meaning both in his new world and in himself. Many of these poems do, therefore, deal with Japan. They are, further, a celebration of a shared love of nature as well as evidence of a common spirit.

There is, moreover, a similar preference for indirect statement, for undertones (as in the title of his account of the war) and for suggestive hints and the discriminating nuance rather than for the explicit, emphatic and simplistic, as well as for a muted balance in response to life, not indifferent but not overly attached. Such a strategy of disengagement was, in part, innate since he was by nature gentle, undemonstrative and gracefully reticent and diffident, and it is also borne out by his absorption in poetry in the trenches and in his sustained detachment from the horrors of war,—a response very different from the passionate engagement and deep pity of Wilfred Owen. There were no doubt affinities between Blunden and Japan, but Japanese precept and practice enabled him to refine and shape his own response and work and thereby to resolve his personal predicament.

These new approaches can be seen both in **'Values'** and in other poems of this period. For example, in **'The Stone Garden (Kyoto)'**, he opposes 'modest' truths to 'mansoul in commotion' and affirms 'the soul which knows no wild extremes',—just as in a letter to Aki Hayashi of 29 September 1925 he likewise praises the 'Autumn equanimity of thing' (probably referring to her as well as to the season since her forename was a homonym of autumn and he regularly addressed her as such).[5] For Blunden, indeed, as for Hearn some thirty years before, his understanding of the country and its spirit was to be mediated and embodied by a woman and was not merely apprehended through talk and words.

There is, therefore, during the twenties a deliberate attempt by Blunden to come to terms with his experiences and with his response to and valuation of life. It is a development which was both stimulated and in some respects facilitated by his departure from Europe and his stay in Japan. It is a development, moreover, which was articulated in both his poetry and prose of this period and which was notably crystallised in *Undertones of War.* Amongst the poems of this period, the sonnet **'Values'** is also very significant. It is a poem which was forged from deep personal suffering as well as much experience of life at a crucial period which is perhaps best described as a prolonged crisis and which embodies a wealth of common human as well as of individual significance. It meant much to him and it was pointedly placed to conclude his collection *Near and Far* in 1929, a collection for which it serves as a summing up, as both epigraph and epitome. In view of its complexity, however, its interpretation presents problems which need to be considered in some detail.

PARAPHRASE OF TEXT

Blunden asserts in this poem that the valuation which we place upon the world, its people and events, springs from the individual and is not a necessary and inherent quality of the world itself: 'force and size / Are nothing but by answered undertone'; what is important is so only through our valuation of it as such. The individual may well be much less than what he or she perceives and the response in consequence no more than an 'undertone', but it is this which matters. As a corollary, moreover, no beauty (as opposed to brute force) 'even of absolute perfection' can dominate if one so chooses. [lines 3-6]

This insight, moreover, is brought about by 'chance', that is, the accidents of life and experience, rather than by conscious thought and ratiocination. It is, further, a view to which the author will cleave until death. It may be that death will revise or amplify his conviction, but until death this is his creed. [lines 1-2]

The author's own experience, moreover, confirms this position. Thus, even though he suffered deeply (presumably in the trenches during the First World War) he does not grieve and, equally, even though he was honoured and treated like a prince (presumably as a Professor in Japan after the war) he does not exult. It is his own response to his circumstances which matters and not his situation. Outward circumstances, in short, are deceptive—or, as he puts it, 'visibles deceive'— since one can rise above these. [lines 9-10]

The valuation which we place upon the world is, therefore, fundamental rather than the world itself. But what kind of values should one hold? How does one arrive at these? And how are they to be expressed? These questions also need to be resolved if the world is to be judged properly.

With regard to the first, they are evidently values independent of the world and also of conventional responses to the world. [lines 9-10] But they are free not only of attachment to suffering and happiness but also to worldly perfection as an ideal and source of pleasure and refuge: 'No beauty even of absolute perfection / Dominates here',—the place suggested presumably a place of the spirit rather than a particular country such as Britain or Japan, a state of being and understanding rather than of location in the phenomenal world. [lines 5-6] Worldly love, too, despite its abundance, is to be enjoyed in moderation. [lines 13-14]

With regard to the second question, how one is to arrive at these values, Blunden refers to 'the glance, the pause, the guess'. It is by these means that he expects

to secure his salvation and these will provide the 'amulets of resurrection', protecting him from evil and securing for him a new and better life as a charm protects the warrior and aids the lover. The sense is, of course, transferred and the metaphor implies that by these means he will be able to transform and renew his life so that he is, as it were, 'born again' or resurrected and will as a consequence be enabled to survive death. Little is said as to the means, but it is clear by implication that these do not involve rational thought and concentration—confirming the earlier reference to 'chance'—and are somewhat tangential and impressionistic ('glance'), arise from meditation or at least leisure from life's busyness ('pause') and are essentially provisional and imprecise in nature ('guess') as distinct from the clarity and certainty of logical thought and its constructs. [lines 6-7]

With regard to their expression, these may be either gentle or violent,—though, in accord with the philosophy of the poem, the consequences are not necessarily what one might expect since all depends upon the response of the individual; thus, raindrops may 'murder' while lightning may 'caress'. Both rain and lightning come from heaven and a religious significance is probably suggested, a relief from spiritual drought and the shock of profound illumination. But their force cannot be denied, just as rain can wear away stone or drown soldiers in trenches while lightning can and does illuminate but not ravage a landscape,—the one a gentle violence and the other a violent gentleness. [line 8]

As a consequence of his philosophy, the commotion, the 'storm', of the world leaves the author untouched and at ease, the more remarkably since he is apparently within it and free only 'in his mind'. Man and his cities (the characteristic and most substantial achievement of humanity) do not possess him nor do their belfries, the bell towers which adorn churches in the West and thereby symbolise human religions. Instead, he chooses and enjoys his 'vespers', not the world's business and busyness but evening prayers which are not only 'cool'—as one would expect in the evening after the heat of the day—but which are also flowery and therefore pleasant. This term denotes the penultimate canonical hour and service and, more particularly for Blunden, evensong in an Anglican church. This passage, moreover, not only suggests a close or ending but also a sense of 'calm of mind all passion spent', of trials passed and of gentle contemplation of the world and its flux and torments as well as its possibilities. [lines 11-12]

Finally, the poem turns to love, the central and abiding human need and preoccupation,—a 'wide-flowering mountain-side' indeed. As one might expect, however, from the philosophy of non-attachment already adumbrated, Blunden's response is not to seize this in all its splendour and variety but instead to choose merely a token, a sprig 'in which an angel shows': what he desires and what he bears as a witness to his belief is an emblem not of the flesh but rather of the spirit which manifests within it, a love that is without desire and which gives and does not wish to possess, Venus as Urania and not Pandemos. Ultimately, he accepts and includes love in his scheme of things and in his values, but it is not the love which the world knows (though this is recognised) but one which is without desire and cares not for itself,—a positive and not a negative non-attachment, caring for other sentient beings but free of their suffering. Further, as this statement concludes the poem, there is an implication that this is what matters above all. [lines 13-14]

Universal and Regional Significance

This poem like other works of art can be interpreted on different levels, each of which is valid and necessary to a full understanding and appreciation of its meaning. A Madonna and Child, for example, is, on one level, a depiction of a mother with her child, a concept of universal significance. It is also, however, a representation within and for a Christian culture of the Mother of God and of Christ as an infant and, as such, is of particular and distinct significance to Christians, particularly if it is also intended to symbolise God and the Church,—that is, Christ and humanity (as represented by his earthly mother). Yet it is also and inescapably a painting by a particular artist of a particular mother and child and as such reflects and is affected by the artist's skill, experience and circumstances of production as well as by his relationship to his sitters and his own attitudes to established beliefs.

Similarly, this poem can be interpreted both for its universal meaning and for its particular western meaning in addition as well as for its particular significance for its author. In this case, furthermore, it is necessary to emphasise the latter since this sonnet is primarily an expression of belief and one which is both diverse and complex because Blunden had lived both in the West and East. One should also note that what is universal and regional—whether of the West or of the East—is to a degree individual as well since it is apprehended and mediated by a particular individual, in this case the poet.

There are consequently, in the first place, certain statements in this poem which are, as it were, culture-free and can be understood and considered irrespective of the cultural background of a reader. There is, for example, the view that the valuation to be placed upon the world springs from the individual and that our values are better freed from conventional assumptions

and expectations and are enhanced by non-attachment to worldly love and beauty, however exceptional.

But there are also elements which are more fully understood by reference to western thought and its development. The emphasis upon moderation echoes the golden mean of the Greeks while the indifference to fate and to fortune's wheel recalls that of the classical Stoics. Likewise, the proposition of Protagoras that man is the measure of all things is also implied. Other elements, reinforced by Christian terms such as 'vespers' and 'belfries', refer to a Christian context and tradition, notably the preference for a higher love which can reasonably be interpreted in the light of passages in the Bible such as I Corinthians xiii. There are also in this context the emphasis upon meditation and retreat from the world (as in a monastery), the stress upon experience as against dogma and thought (a recurring strand in Christian thinking emphasised again and again by reformers in the West), and the rejection of the pleasures and joys of the flesh (as in the medieval *contemptus mundi*),—though Blunden's position is closer to Epicurus than Savonarola.

It should be noted, however, that the above elements are common, albeit with somewhat different emphasis and formulation, to other of the higher religions and are also to be found in Buddhism, with which Blunden had become acquainted in Japan. It does, therefore, seem reasonable to ascribe these elements both to the West and to the East as well, given what is known of the author and his circumstances at the time of this poem's composition. Indeed, some of the elements can be more fully understood in the light of eastern tradition and in particular Zen Buddhism in Japan, such as, for example, the strong emphasis upon experience rather than upon belief as the foundation of religious practice, the preference for non-attachment to the world rather than rejection of it, the indifference to dogma and logic (which has traditionally been privileged and subtly practised in the West, as by Aquinas and the medieval Schoolmen), the willingness to live with the uncertain and the provisional, and also perhaps the sudden, lightning-like illumination of satori (which may be alluded to in the eighth line). The non-pedagogic mode of the poem is also characteristic of teaching in this sect: as in a koan, there is a refusal to state precisely and clearly what should be valued, and there is a corresponding emphasis not only upon meditation and impression as a means to truth but also upon the necessity to ponder and resolve issues actively and independently rather than passively to receive ideas. Such approaches to the world are undoubtedly present in the West, but they are more explicitly articulated and accepted in Zen Buddhism and, to a degree, in other eastern religions. The poem has, therefore, much of universal significance, but this can and should be interpreted from both a western and an eastern perspective.

INDIVIDUAL SIGNIFICANCE

The poem should also be considered with reference to its creator and his circumstances. Blunden had lived very deeply, suffering much in the trenches, and had then moved to a completely different world and much better conditions in Japan. It was, therefore, natural that he should wish to reflect upon his experience in the way that a much older man would do,—and this poem is a testimony to this process of reflection. The enormous contrast in values between those of his youth and his experience of the trenches as well as those between Britain and Japan must also have forced him to ponder deeply upon how he should approach the world. A poem such as this which seeks to state his conclusions in this respect is, therefore, what one would expect. It is, moreover, not merely a testimony to his soul-searching but a testament as well on account of its complexity and fullness.

The poem, in stating his reflections, also refers to and draws upon his experience and cannot, therefore, be fully understood without understanding this as well. It opens with a statement of mortality. As a soldier he had been well aware that even in life we are in the presence of death and it is in this context significant that in considering his response to life he should begin with death, the more so as his health had been affected by his war service and he was, like Keats, conscious of his mortal frailty. The poem also refers, albeit indirectly and by implication, to the conflicts and contrasts in his own life, to peace and war, to East and West, to city and country, to extremes of suffering and prosperity, to brute force and exquisite beauty, and to love and physical desire. The somewhat imprecise location of the poem is also suggestive of a writer poised between East and West, between different professions, between women, uncertain of precisely where he is and should be and of his identity and purpose. There is some evidence, as has been noted above, that the poem was written after his return to Britain and this is also implied by the opposition between two references to 'there' which refer to the trenches in northern France and Belgium and Japan and 'here' which by contrast in the context of Blunden's life must refer to Britain. But the references are not clear and unambiguous so it is therefore probable that the location of the author was not intended to be precisely specified, no doubt so that the locus of the poem should be understood generally and also primarily as a state of being and of understanding, a place of the spirit rather than one in this world. Nonetheless, there is an underlying unease as to place which has a certain personal force and which can be better and more fully understood in the light of Blunden's own position at this time.

There is, furthermore, not only an assertion of but a felt need for peace and rural rest, for 'vespers cool and eglantined', which presumably articulates Blunden's own need for quiet and a retreat from personal conflict. Likewise, the references to death and resurrection as well as to a withdrawal from life and to a life of reflection rather than of action express his own experience of death and of new beginnings and a need to renew and re-shape himself: the killer of the trenches had to become a man of peace while the English country boy had to adjust to a new life in large cities and abroad. His stay in Japan, further, gave him leisure for reflection.

The strategy of the poem, moreover, its preference for muted suggestion, accords with Blunden's own undemonstrative and reticent temperament. More importantly, there is also an emphasis upon an oblique and gentle response to experience which is crystallised in the word 'undertone'. This would appear to refer to his approach to his suffering in the trenches where he 'was tortured' and thus also to his account of this which was published in 1928 as *Undertones of War,*—a work on whose revision he was engaged until 1930. The philosophy of the poem, moreover, its emphasis upon a personal and authentic response to the world, upon the need for detachment suffused with a higher and undemanding love, and of the acceptance of truths which are arrived at through experience rather than ratiocination and which are both provisional and imprecise, accords with Blunden's own views. One may also note that it is a natural and reasonable response for a young man whose sheltered upbringing had been savagely interrupted by years of violence and for whom book learning and its certainties were no longer sufficient.

There is, furthermore, in the final couplet of the poem a reference to love which is probably also of personal as well as of general significance. Blunden is well aware of the force and diversity of human love which he describes as a 'wide-flowering mountain-side'. This image for the world of love is probably derived from the similar and unusual image in Marlowe's 'The Passionate Shepherd to his Love', a poem which was—as will be shown below—familiar both to Blunden and his Japanese mistress and one in which the lover invites his mistress to prove all the pleasures 'That hills and valleys, dales and fields, / And all the craggy mountains yields.' There is also a reference here (as in Marlowe) to an abundance of flowers which are often used metaphorically to refer to the pleasures of love and, more particularly, the maidenhoods of virgins. In the preceding line, moreover, there is a reference in a religious context to the eglantine or sweetbriar, which has amorous associations, and in connection with which Blunden may also have recalled the 'dewy rosary on the eglantine' in the passionate elopement narrated by

Keats in his *Isabella* (stanza 24, line 188), a poem with which he would certainly have been familiar. The 'vespers cool' of the preceding line would also suggest the pleasures of the night, to which the late flowering eglantine is particularly appropriate and which Shelley describes as 'moon-unfolded' in the fragment 'Wine of the Fairies' ['I am drunk with the honey wine'].

The final two lines, therefore, are not only important on account of their position as the concluding couplet of a Shakespearean sonnet but also in their context and owing to their wealth of literary association. One may also note that these associations and this particular form of sonnet, to a degree from Shakespeare's own work, both relate to love.

The author, however, chooses not to explore and scale the mountain-side and to gather its abundance of flowers but instead to pluck a single sprig alone, a token and no more. He is also aware that the love chosen thus is essentially spiritual rather than earthly since it is one 'in which an angel shows': the physical presence of the beloved manifests a deeper and more beautiful and selfless love.

There is, undoubtedly, a general human truth in this passage, but there is probably in addition a particular application to Blunden himself. Quite apart from the evidence for such an application, one may note as a preliminary that this poem contains several references to Blunden's life and views so that it seems not unreasonable in this context to suppose that the concluding reference to love must have some personal significance as well. One possible incident to which he may refer is described in the following episode from **Undertones of War** during which he was resting in a cattle truck behind the front:

> There came along a girl of fourteen or so, with a small brother, and looked in. We talked, and—we fell in love. That 'I' may be still in love with her, Marie-Louise of course, so black-eyed, and serious, and early-old with the inheritance of peasant experience—I have seen her alone since in many a moment of escape and fantasy. Still she looks in on this life's sultry cattle-truck, halted awhile in some drab siding, and once again we kiss, innocent as petals in the breeze. With what sad resignation to the tyrannical moment, which she hardly credits to be true, lifting her slow hand doubtfully to wave farewell, does that child-love of only one day's courting watch me pass into the voluminous, angry, darkening distance: ah, Marie-Louise![6]

In the poem also, in a moment similarly of reverie and contemplation withdrawn from the battle of life, the author chooses to dwell upon a love which is innocent, slight and young—'a sprig of green, in which an angel shows.' Love, further, is characterised by its flowers as in the prose by petals. That Marie-Louise may indeed

lie behind this passage is further suggested by Blunden's remark that he had 'seen her alone since in many a moment of escape and fantasy'.

It is, however, also possible that this couplet draws upon Blunden's experience not of one girl but of another too and that it may refer both to an innocent child-woman and to a young and sexually inexperienced woman who was his mistress briefly and subsequently in Japan. It would not be surprising for the former to recur to him, as he himself admitted, and at the same time for the latter to press more forcefully upon his thoughts in view of their affair. That this may be the case is suggested by the fact that there is an emphasis upon choice and that there is also, as will be shown, some verbal evidence which alludes to his mistress.

Although the precise date of the composition of this poem is unknown, it was written during a period when he was, firstly, separated from his wife in Japan and, subsequently, re-united with but estranged and then separated from her prior to divorce. If there is here a personal and present reference, therefore, it is not to his first wife. However, during this period he also met in 1925 a schoolteacher in Japan, Aki Hayashi, and briefly became her lover. She was both chaste and unmarried and was presumably deflowered by him. He was, however, aware of her needs as a woman and of the 'suddenness and completeness' of her love for him, as he acknowledged in a letter to her of 3 September 1925,[7]—a response to which he may possibly refer in the phrase 'lightnings may caress'. In the same letter, nonetheless, he also recognised that, despite his pleasure in her, her affection was what mattered. Further, he recognised in a later letter to her of 24 September 1925[8] that her love was sacrificial and selfless in its nature and that she was, as he reaffirmed in a later letter of 7 March 1932 a 'pattern of courage and goodness'.[9]

The affair was, however, brief and his response to her affectionate and friendly rather than profoundly and permanently passionate. He employed her as his secretary and secured her return in 1927 to Britain where she acted as a valued research assistant, primarily in the British Museum Library, for many years thereafter. She had sought for a statement of his intentions towards her and he had promised in a note of 17 January 1927 that he would, if he were ever free to do so, probably marry her.[10] In the event, however, he divorced his first wife and married another woman in 1932.

The final two lines of the poem may, therefore, in addition to their general truth, refer to his relationship with Aki Hayashi and to his recognition of her selfless love for him at a time when he was deprived of affection and female company. In this connection it may also be significant, as has been noted above, that the poem is in the form of a Shakespearean sonnet since he had sent part of such a sonnet swearing eternal love to Aki Hayashi on 28 August 1925, very soon after they had first met and fallen in love.[11] It was, of course, a relationship which demanded discretion, notably with his wife, and this would account for the poem's veiled allusion. At the same time, it would be readily understood by his lover and would therefore serve also as a token of his affection for her and a recognition of her good and selfless nature. Such an interpretation is further suggested by a fragment subscribed by Blunden and dated 5 May 1926, whose text is as follows:

> Aki asks me to write,—
> That I would sooner live with her,
> And be her love,
> Than with anyone,
> If I was not already married.[12]

The wording in the second and third lines not only echoes the repeated phrase 'Come live with me and be my love' in Marlowe's 'The Passionate Shepherd to his Love' but also implies that this poem was familiar to each of them,—and was, indeed, raised with him by his lover. Yet, as has been noted above, it is an image of the world of love derived from that presented in this poem, of its 'hills' and 'mountains', which Blunden adopts in the final couplet of the sonnet to refer to love. It is, therefore, quite possible that in adopting this image for love Blunden intended to refer specifically to his love for Aki and to do so in a way which would be intelligible to her but not to others. It is a sense which may well have been lost to others close to him later in his life, even though they instinctively appreciated the importance of this poem for him. One should also note in this connection that Marlowe's poem, as Blunden was no doubt aware, is derived, like many others in English, from the *Vivamus, mea Lesbia, atque amemus* of Catullus and that it implies an irregular rather than a legitimate married union; as such, it would be particularly appropriate for Blunden and Aki Hayashi at this time.

It is, moreover, possible to speculate in the context of a shared and secret reference between lovers that a further meaning was present. Blunden not only refers to a 'sprig' but also adopts the past tense in his plucking of it. The implication is that in his view his affair with Aki is relatively unimportant and is at an end. In other words, he is rejecting an intimate physical relationship (which was, in any case, very brief) but is prepared to recognise and accept his lover's unselfish and undemanding—indeed, as he suggests, angelic—devotion to him. It is not clear, however, whether Blunden intended to put forward this view (albeit in veiled metaphorical terms) or whether he wrote more wisely than he knew. It is possible, in the latter case, that he was not consciously aware of the drift of his feelings and their outworking in the years ahead and was consciously only concerned at this juncture in the poem to empha-

sise the value of disinterested love in the world. On the other hand, it is possible that he was aware of a change in the nature of his relationship with Aki and sought in this passage to offer a delicate hint to her of his position; in view of her clear dissatisfaction with the development of their relationship after their arrival in Britain from Japan in 1927 such delicacy on Blunden's part would, of course, have been prudent as well as tactful. Such an interpretation posits a date of composition closer to 1929 than to 1925 (which must form the *terminus a quo*) since by then Aki's relationship with him was indeed one of friendship and intellectual assistance to Blunden's numerous literary and academic projects. As has been noted above, there is both internal and external evidence that the poem was indeed written at the later date. Without firm manuscript or other evidence for the dating of the text, however, this issue cannot be resolved, but it is possible that Blunden was aware of a change in his attitude towards Aki and wished discreetly to suggest this to her. There may also, on this interpretation, have been a further wish— whether conscious or not—to appeal to her better nature and to suggest to her that she should abandon her proper and reasonable needs as a woman and become an 'angel' who would not only unselfishly assist him but would also accept a platonic relationship without protest: disinterested devotion—by another rather than himself—could offer a means to reconcile her with becoming his assistant rather than his mistress. In this context, moreover, it is possible that one theme of the poem, the need for moderation and non-attachment, could also serve as a suggestion to her not to expect and wish too much from her relationship with him.

BLUNDEN AND JAPAN

The poem is also of interest as evidence of Blunden's relationship with Japan,—a significance which is both individual and yet also national. It is a complex relationship which needs to be approached with caution.

During the Twenties, Blunden spent some three years as a Professor in Tokyo and was much attracted to the Japanese people and their culture, returning again after the Second World War from 1947 to 1950 and thereafter for five shorter visits between 1955 and 1964. As with Lafcadio Hearn, his understanding was mediated and deepened by a woman, Aki Hayashi, with whom he fell in love and who was able to solace, support and instruct him in a very alien, as well as for him rather solitary, environment. One must note further that she not only helped him at a difficult time in his life and gave him a more profound and inward appreciation of her native country as well as an intimate relationship within it but that she also, both in Japan and—principally—on their arrival in Britain, acted as his research assistant for nearly forty years: like Dorothy Wordsworth, her loyal and sacrificial friendship and intellectual services were invaluable to him. Any assessment of Blunden's achievement must, therefore, also recognise that of his Japanese helpmeet and spiritual sister just as it must also take account of his affection and respect for Japanese culture and his repeated residence in Japan.

In addition, one must recognise that many of his poems and much occasional verse were written in or about Japan while some of his critical work was published in Japan and had a Japanese audience in view. During his first visit, moreover, Japan enabled him to distance himself from his traumatic experiences in the trenches and to approach these more objectively and come to terms with them in *Undertones of War,* a work which he began and which was largely written in Japan. Other poems, furthermore, allude to Japan and one of these, **'Values'**, refers both to his work there as a Professor and apparently, though discreetly, to his relationship with Aki Hayashi.

This poem, moreover, is not only important as a testament to his beliefs at a critical period in his life but is also interesting as a witness to attitudes with which he would have become familiar in Japan, particularly in Zen Buddhism, such as the emphasis upon lived experience rather than upon belief, the indifference to ratiocination and logic, the willingness to live with uncertainty and to accept imprecise or provisional knowledge, the sudden illumination of satori, and the emphasis upon non-attachment rather than rejection of the world. Such elements are, of course, also to be found in the West, but they are much more clearly articulated and correlated in Zen so that it seems reasonable to suggest that their presence and combination in this poem are owing in part to Japanese influence. The allusive strategy and the discreet, elliptical reticence and understatement of the poem (which are likewise characteristic and compelling in his memoir of the war) were probably also encouraged and refined by contact with Japanese literature and society in which such approaches are cultivated and much appreciated. It may be that in this respect he adopted in this poem the spirit rather than the terms and images of the Japanese, but their influence is nonetheless clear.

However, it would be unwise to ignore Blunden's western inheritance and upbringing and one must also recognise in this poem, for example, Protagoras, the Stoics, Jesus and St. Paul. There was, moreover, an affinity between Blunden's reserved and gentle temperament and love of nature with those of his hosts: Japan may have fostered his response but it did not create it. Further, Blunden was critical of certain aspects of Japanese life and culture as can be seen, for instance, in poems such as **'The Match'** and **'On a Small Dog Thrust Out in a Tokyo Street'**. **'Values'**, indeed, can

and should be interpreted not only as an acknowledgment of Japan but also as a response to it. It was a response both to the country and also to individuals within it.

As a country, Japan by its very difference forced Blunden to come to terms with the extraordinary diversity of the world so that the genesis of this poem is in part a response to the need to re-assess his beliefs and values in the face of a completely different language, culture and society. In this and in other poems, moreover, he responded to particular individuals in Japan. As has been noted above, **'Values'** may be in part addressed to and a response to Aki Hayashi; on this interpretation, their intimate relationship, he suggests, is at an end and he would prefer her to be—as he sees her—an 'angel' who can accept this alteration without anger and become his assistant and not his mistress. It may be, moreover, possible that the poem is also in part addressed to those whom he had taught or known in Japan, albeit much less explicitly than a poem such as **'The Author's Last Words to His Students'**. In his teaching at Tokyo, where unlike his predecessors he lived very modestly, Blunden had emphasised personal contacts and had refused to be regarded as an omniscient authority upon English literature and life. In this context and given, too, an audience in Japan as well as in the English-speaking world, it is significant that he emphasises impressions and, as a corollary, the provisional and disdains book learning and logic as a means to truth: the author, in short, is not a scholarly god but, on the contrary, a very fallible human being,— and one, moreover, relying upon 'amulets' for his success. It is also possible that his insistence upon an individual and authentic response to experience and upon a refusal of conventional certainties would have particular force and relevance in a society which placed—as to a degree it still does—much emphasis upon social conformity and deference to superiors both in thought and deed. Like Socrates in ancient Athens, his message (though salutary) is disturbing to the conformist and conventional, even though it is—as his Japanese audience would no doubt wish—quietly stated and enhanced by the tacit courtesy of his acknowledgment of attitudes to be found in Zen Buddhism.

EVALUATION

Exegesis is important, but a literary text such as a poem must finally be judged not merely on its meaning but also and primarily upon its presentation of this and upon its literary value. What this poem has to say is important and can and should be considered in its different levels of significance,—universal, regional (in this case in both East as well as West) and individual. But it is not merely a philosophical and human but also and primarily an aesthetic text and, like a painting or any other work of art in another medium, it must be judged as the work of art which it purports to be.

This particular poem is complex and embodies many ideas and references as well as much personal significance. It is, therefore, fitting that it adopts the form of a Shakespearean sonnet since it likewise seeks to offer a brief, complex and resonant personal statement.

The overt thrust and emphasis of the poem are in ideas. These are, however, not wholly clear, partly through extreme compression and partly through a rather rambling and disordered arrangement, which the paraphrase above with its line references indicates. The thoughts, moreover, are not original and have many precedents in the philosophical heritage of both the West and the East. Thus, although the ideas have the force of compression, they lack the necessary and more compelling force of clarity and order: they are, further, as Blunden remarks elsewhere of his own work, 'hobbling commonplaces'. The final two lines, moreover, which both as a conclusion and as the closing couplet of a Shakespearean sonnet, carry particular weight merely add to but do not sum up and reinforce the sense of the whole: the conclusion is, therefore, somewhat limp and lame and does not, indeed, sit altogether easily with the central theme of non-attachment, even though it does make sense in the context of Blunden's personal situation at this time.

It is, nonetheless, possible to make the commonplace memorable by fine expression so that, as Pope remarks, 'What oft was thought' is 'ne'er so well expressed.' However, the ideas are not brought to life by fine images nor by striking and original language. Thus, for example, death is imagined as a 'darkness' upon the eyes, 'amulets' avert evil and charm fortune, 'crowns' and 'palaces' symbolise worldly position, 'vespers' denote evening meditation, the bustle and busyness of cities are rendered as a 'storm', and a token of love is conceived as a 'sprig' plucked from Marlowe's mountain-side. The ideas, in short, are not freshly and forcefully realised as they must be if they are to work in a poem but are bodied forth by very familiar and hence rather lifeless images. Nor is the language original and effective. There are many ponderous latinate substantives while the few adjectives are either relatively imprecise (as 'cool') or derivative (as 'eglantined'): the verbal coin is worn and not freshly minted. It is true that in this poem he is addressing general ideas, but his imagination and sensibility are not as fully engaged as his mind.

There is, furthermore, a dichotomy between the overt content and the language and verse form. The expressed unconcern with worldly position and, indeed, the world itself as well as the emphasis upon understatement, impression and the provisional are expressed in the tight, formal structure of the sonnet with its intricate, precise and closely controlled rhyme scheme and in cerebral and allusive vocabulary with complex and broken syntax. A plea for an authentic and individual response to life untrammelled by book learning is, thus, made in a formal, learned and thoroughly conventional straitjacket: the poem is a triumph of restraint and fine writing but not of liberty and sincere feeling. It is as though he felt the need for the ark of form amidst the flux and flood of experience, for the assurance of the sonnet with its discipline and order in face of the centrifugal diversity of his life: here at least was a centre which would hold.

In part, no doubt, Blunden was the prisoner as well as the inheritor and interpreter of his literary upbringing and was subservient to received forms and conventional expressions because he was neither exceptionally original nor sufficiently independent to pour new wine into new bottles and integrate form and content successfully. In part, too, there was an inescapable but unresolved conflict between the poet and the philosopher: the effort to express ideas, albeit somewhat unclearly and disjointedly, has weakened their imaginative and linguistic expression. But the problem is not merely poetic but also and more profoundly personal.

It is clear that the poem has considerable personal significance and can be related to much of Blunden's experience at a time of prolonged conflict and crisis. There are present, for example, his awareness of his mortality, his uncertainty as to his place and purpose, his experiences in the trenches and in both East and West, his need for quiet and reflection as well as for renewal, and a temperamental reticence and understatement as well as, apparently, his love both for Marie-Louise and for Aki Hayashi. There is, further, a sense of closure and of endings throughout from the death in the first line to those of others either in the trenches or in the death in life of modern urban society as well as a spirit of contemplation which suggests a withdrawal from the world and the evening of life as of the day with a final nostalgic reminiscence of love's possibilities. It is, of course, a mood which tallies with and expresses his personal situation at this time, particularly after his departure from Japan and friends and colleagues there as well as his estrangement both from his wife and his mistress. In this poem, moreover, he was addressing not only his own problems and concerns but also, very probably, a woman he had loved and, possibly, his students and their society in Japan as well as a wider world. Such a dialogue and such a diverse and contrary complex and pressure of experience can be both lively and creative,—as, for instance, in Yeats or in the late sonnets of Hopkins in which the man of flesh and the man of God wrestle with each other. But the Blakean energy of contraries is here not released and realised and the spring does not flow from the rock. The author and his concerns are clearly present, but are distanced and the text remains not merely circumspect but also significantly impersonal and inert.

One can only speculate as to the reasons for this want of life, but there is a mismatch between the explicit text and a subversive and not fully recognised and realised sub-text which may well reflect a similar division in Blunden's life as well as in the poem. The uncertainty as to place is symptomatic. The poem was probably composed in Britain in the late 1920s and is ostensibly located there, but it is evidently intended to suggest a place of the spirit. Such a locus would, of course, be appropriate for the enunciation of general truths. But one suspects that the man was less securely placed than the persona which he adopts so that the poem elides the displacement and disorientation of the poet and his uncertainty as to his identity, role and purpose. The force of the contraries within him, moreover, is stated rather than fully engaged and only emerges forcibly and effectively in the line 'Raindrops may murder, lightnings may caress.'

The process of reflection, furthermore, is stated and is also implied, but achieves no satisfactory resolution since the values which are its fruits are only very sketchily suggested. Moreover, despite the claim to detachment and to 'vespers cool and eglantined', the writer was in fact as pressed as before: the repose of the poem is, therefore, desired rather than truly felt and known while the non-attachment to the world and its concerns is likewise willed rather than lived. (One may add further that if it were genuine it would not be necessary to withdraw from the world in order to stand apart from it.) There is a sense, indeed, that the disengagement—which he had sought earlier in the trenches with poetry—is an evasion rather than a true detachment. Nor is there renewal and regeneration; the need and the desire are undoubtedly present but not the new life which he seeks: there is an imagined retreat from the world but not a transformation of his response to it. The experience, in fact, is not fully realised in verse because it was not fully realised in himself. It was, indeed, only much later in his life that Blunden was to experience deep happiness and a lasting security with his third wife and in the English countryside which meant so much to him.

Love also enters, rather awkwardly, as an afterthought in the final couplet, but is not central as it was for the poet at this time. The coy discretion and the somewhat forlorn moderation in love which the poem affects are certainly untrue of the author. Further, although there is apparently a reference to his Japanese lover, the force and complexity of this relationship—let alone that with his first wife—are omitted. The poem is a triumph of good manners and restraint over the splendours and the miseries of life and love.

It is, thus, in this and the worst sense, a very English poem. The bridle has not mastered but displaced the horse and the tensions and energies of the man have been sacrificed to the discretion and restraint of society. In poetry unlike life, however, good intentions are not sufficient. Tact and consideration, nonetheless, are probably not wholly to be blamed. Important issues such as love are broached, but these are obliquely and not fully faced, the whole truth is not stated, and what is said is veiled, compressed, and rather disordered. As a consequence, a poem, which is—and is rightly considered to be—central to Blunden and which offers some valuable general truths, fails to be fully effective.

And yet the poem moves and matters. Highly wrought, rhetorical and contrived though it may be, it does address important issues which are still relevant and in it Blunden does seek to face the passion and contraries and the extraordinary diversity of his lived experience, to integrate these, to establish his identity, and to renew and to state his response to the world. The testament is not fully equal to its occasion, but one honours the attempt. The poem has, moreover, a right to be considered in terms of its tradition of shaped art and discourse, a tradition which is not sufficiently valued today. The practice of poetry, moreover, implies values, and theories founded upon poetry likewise: every poetic, indeed, as Steiner has suggested, predicates an ethic. In this poem a commitment to and an engagement with shared discourse and a traditional, intricate and tightly controlled form witness to a society which accepts both order and inherited patterns of behaviour and also a compact between word and world and between individuals. Formally, it affirms and exemplifies the societal restraints and relationships of which it speaks. Its sense, furthermore, is by no means simple and straightforward; its reading, indeed, demands not only a wide knowledge of life and literature but also a speculative and tentative response, a willingness to live with uncertainty, such as Blunden himself seeks: its meaning is its reading too. There is, too, a sub-text, albeit not fully explicit and realised and in some respects subversive, which enhances the force and complexity of the poem. There are also a sense of endings and a plangent tone which are truly felt and these are linked to a pervading spirit of weariness which the outworn metaphors and language embody and reinforce. There is, further, a mood of uncertainty and estrangement, of doubt and difficulty, with a corresponding longing for peace and for release, which are likewise deeply felt. Moreover, the very restraint of the poem, which the self-denying discipline of the form affirms, suggests one root and aspect of the detachment which it seeks while the honesty, the sense of statements rooted in experience, convinces too. It is not a great poem, but it is interesting, complex and important, a poem of many presences, between selves and between worlds as well.

CONCLUSION

'**Values**' is a sonnet which Blunden and others who knew him and his work judged important. Evidence, both internal and external, as to its composition suggests that it was written in Britain in the late 1920s after his return from Japan. It was, thus, written at a critical period in his life, at a time of conflict within himself and with others and between very different ways of life and their values. During this prolonged personal crisis of identity and purpose he sought to reconsider and master his experience and to come to terms with the violence and diversity of the world, notably in **Undertones of War.** This poem is also, however, a significant testimony to his life and a testament of his beliefs.

Its exegesis presents difficulties on account of the complexity and compression of the ideas and references both to himself and others which it contains. The primary emphasis is upon an insistence that man is the measure of all things and that, as a corollary, each individual should find a personal and authentic response to the world. Balance and moderation are also desirable with regard to suffering, love and beauty as, too, is an indifference to the world and its affairs. A spiritual and unselfish love is also desirable. This philosophy of benign detachment and quiet reflection is, moreover, founded upon personal and chance experience and impressions and eschews the precise certainties of dogma and logical thought.

The poem embodies important general and abiding truths, but these can also be more fully understood by reference to the philosophical heritage not only of Europe but also of the East, in particular Zen Buddhism as it has evolved in Japan. The insistence upon experience rather than upon dogma, the preference for non-attachment to the world rather than rejection of it, the indifference to logic, and the non-pedagogic mode as well as, possibly, the sudden illumination of satori are all not only emphasised but correlated in Zen as they are in this poem.

This sonnet has also much personal significance for Blunden since it is not only a testament to his beliefs but also refers to and reflects upon his experiences both in the trenches and in Japan as well as in the West. In addition, it appears to allude to his shared love with Aki Hayashi and would also appear both to recognise her sincere and sacrificial love for him and also to suggest that his feelings towards her had changed. In this respect, moreover, it provides further evidence of Blunden's complex and diverse relationship with Japan, a society and culture which this poem in part addresses, responds to, and acknowledges.

As a poem, however, **'Values'**, though highly wrought and literary, is both impersonal and inert. The pressure and charged complex of diverse and contrary experience which undoubtedly lie behind the poem have not been imaginatively realised and the assertions of detachment, of repose and of moderation in love are willed rather than lived and convincingly alive. Despite its complexity and considerable compression, therefore, the poem does not fully succeed. Failure can, however, be more interesting and instructive than success. In this case, various factors are probably responsible, such as the emphasis upon ideas rather than upon feeling and imagination, the need for tact and restraint by Blunden in referring to certain aspects of his life, and a want of creative independence and of major poetic talent. But there is also a sense that his response is *voulu,* willed rather than attained: detachment is, indeed, desired but not achieved and appears rather as an evasion of than a disengagement from opposites; repose likewise is a wish rather than a fact, while the force and passion of human love are merely hinted at and refused. The man and the poet are at odds and it is the poetry which suffers. The poem is, indeed, characteristic of much else in Blunden's poetry which is likewise discursive and sententious (as he frankly recognised) but also too often occasional and superficial, a courteous and diplomatic response to a person or place but also a refusal of their full truth. What is socially acceptable and welcome—as much of his fluent and facile *vers d'occasion* undoubtedly was—is nonetheless without the disturbing and awkward challenge of great art which is, at bottom, to look fully at ourselves and others. Discretion is a social virtue but a bad habit for the artist; as Picabia remarked, 'There is only one way to save your life: sacrifice your reputation.' For the artist, it is not the social lie but truth which must be absolute. In this poem, therefore, Blunden holds up but does not fully display or face a mirror to himself and his world. Perhaps in such a cruelly confining compass he could not. That he could do so, memorably and unchallengeably, is exemplified by **Undertones of War,** a shield of Perseus whose terrors be resolutely braved. Here too, significantly and abundantly, is the 'objectification necessary to art' which MacDiarmid desired and praised.

The attempt, however, matters as well as success. What Blunden faced as an individual, stoutly and resourcefully, in the second and third decades of this century and what he tried to sum up and resolve in this poem is what many of his contemporaries had to face and what the modern world in its own circumstances must also face. Just as in his memoir of the war he faced and memorably stated the suffering and waste of violence, so in this poem he sought to express and resolve a personal crisis which is now universal and to offer a testimony which is a testament not only to the violence but also to the extraordinary diversity of human culture, behaviour and belief. Is it possible, given these, to ascertain and establish precise, certain and unalterable truths and values behind the manifold flux of phenomena as a guide to action and as an assurance of identity and purpose or is it not possible? If it is, can one then avoid the dogma, the narrow and disabling sectarianism, the intolerance, and the denial and persecution of perceived error which too often spring from such certainties? If not, is one inescapably doomed to scepticism, confusion, aimless insecurity and uncertainty, a nihilistic relativism or—at best—a spineless pluralism, in a world in which all appears to be opinion and sensation and the phenomenal is all? Is a sense of absurdity, exacerbated by the increasing specialisation and fragmentation of modern life, inescapable? It is, for our age and in our own terms, the quarrel of Socrates with Gorgias, the perennial dispute between an enlightened and a fundamental scepticism. Blunden's dilemma is ours as well and his response, even though it is not wholly convincingly realised in this poem, is salutary and pertinent. The world is extraordinarily diverse and it is difficult to ascertain its full meaning and purpose, but there are attitudes and values which include love and which also favour a withdrawal from and a benign non-attachment to the world. Values, moreover, matter since we must not only seek to understand, however imperfectly, but also to assess. These values, nonetheless, must be apprehended and can only be validated by the individual rather than society and cannot be fully and precisely known and stated so that each one must not only accept personal responsibility but also be willing to live with uncertainty: for Blunden, as for Socrates, the beginning of wisdom is in the knowledge and acceptance of our ignorance. It is an uncertainty which is both inevitable and desirable and which is, in fact, not a weakness but a strength. Further, his pragmatism and restraint as well as the implicit and characteristic respect for others which his values predicate are, in the best sense, his Englishness.

APPENDIX

'Values'

Till darkness lays a hand on these gray eyes
And out of man my ghost is sent alone,
It is my chance to know that force and size
Are nothing but by answered undertone.
No beauty even of absolute perfection
Dominates here—the glance, the pause, the guess
Must be my amulets of resurrection;
Raindrops may murder, lightnings may caress.

There I was tortured, but I cannot grieve;
There crowned and palaced—visibles deceive.
That storm of belfried cities in my mind
Leaves me my vespers cool and eglantined.
From love's wide-flowering mountain-side I chose
This sprig of green, in which an angel shows.

Notes

1. Information in this paragraph is derived from the following work: Kirkpatrick, B. J. *A Bibliography of Edmund Blunden* (The Soho Bibliographies, 20—Oxford: Clarendon Press, 1979).

2. Hardie, A. M. *Edmund Blunden* (Writers and Their Work, 94—Harlow: Longman, 1958, rev. 1971), pp. 24-25.

3. Okada, S. *Edmund Blunden and Japan: The History of a Relationship* (London: Macmillan, 1988).

4. Op. cit., p. 58.

5. Op. cit., p. 106.

6. Blunden, E. C. *Undertones of War* (Rev. ed. London: Cobden-Sanderson, 1930), pp. 208-9.

7. Okada, p. 13.

8. Op. cit., p. 105.

9. Op. cit., p. 28.

10. Op. cit., p. 21.

11. Op. cit., p. 10.

12. Op. cit., pp. 20-21 and 126.

Bernard Schweizer (essay date summer 1995)

SOURCE: Schweizer, Bernard. "Blunden's 'Two Voices' and 'Preparations for Victory.'" *Explicator* 53, no. 4 (summer 1995): 226-30.

[*In the following essay, Schweizer discusses sense perceptions highlighted in two of Blunden's war poems, contending that "Two Voices" privileges auditory sensations, while "Preparations for Victory" foregrounds visual perception.*]

Some of Edmund Blunden's best war poems deal with the experience of battle by exclusively invoking one particular kind of sense perception. Hearing is foregrounded in the poem entitled **"Two Voices,"** whereas in **"Preparations for Victory"** visual perception is predominant. Both poems render the horrors of the war very authentically, however, and the limitation to one particular kind of perception does not impede the overall artistic quality of the poems. I will deal here with questions related to Blunden's deliberate concentration on hearing or seeing, trying to analyze the general implications as well as the specific poetic effects of such a presentation.

"Two Voices" portrays a group of soldiers huddled together in a small hut near the front line in France. The poem's title refers to two quoted statements spoken by a military officer: "'There's something in the air,'"[1] and "'We're going South, man'" (line 7). Ironically, both sentences appear perfectly innocuous taken out of their context. On closer inspection, however, the first statement turns out to be a euphemism for saying that an attack from the enemy seems imminent, and the second is the order to march toward the enemy lines, anticipating suffering and death. The incoherence between the seeming innocence of the two statements and their dire consequence from the point of view of the soldier invites the reader to listen to the overtones or implied associations of "plain words" (3). But Blunden does more than pointing out the euphemistic, evasive nature of human communication on the battleground: in fact, he addresses the function of auditory perception in general. Throughout the poem, sounds other than language are described, and they all point to the recognition that hearing and death are inextricably intertwined for the soldier whose plight it is to perish "in silence" (4).

The majority of the poem's verb phrases concern hearing or speaking: "said," "left the phrase," "ordered," "bade," "spoke," "racked," "broke the news," "sang," "humming," "hear." Only six verbs (not counting auxiliary verbs) deal with matters other than sound: "bred," "waited," "took," "withdraws," "wrecked," "shrouds." Moreover, a number of nouns also denote sound or noise: "tumult," "huge ping-bang," "roaring night," and "voices." This lexical enumeration demonstrates that the poem's main emphasis is indeed on elements of auditory perception. But a sharp line is drawn between listening and speaking. Blunden reduces the soldiers to listeners who must hear the orders foreboding death as well as the various noises of war, such as the sound of the howitzer. Theirs must be a mute acceptance of the "death-news" implicit in the commander's "plain words," which in his soldiers "bred a tumult" (3-4). The soldier's voice is muted: the internal tumult of despair remains inaudible. Throughout the poem only the officer's voice is heard, making it plain that the war gives a voice only to those who are in a position to give orders. For the soldier, the implications of the commander's voice are no less deadly than the noises of weaponry. Therefore, throughout the poem, only the commanding officer can step out of the destructive implications of hearing to immerse himself in the visual realm, as he walks complacently "among the apple-trees all bloom and scent" (12). The deadly associations of sound have only a limited significance for him. Thus **"Two Voices"** offers an impression of the war from the perspective of the soldier for whom sound indiscriminately connotes death.

However, sound also distorts the potentially redemptive scene of pastoral tranquility associated with the commander. Indeed, an element of absurdity enters the poem in the second stanza, as the officer's death news is accompanied by the most pastoral of sounds—the skylark: "as thus he broke / The death-news, bright the skylarks sang" (9-10). The contrast is heightened by the close proximity of the onomatopoeic "ping-bang" (8), representing weaponry, and the song of the skylark (10). Again, we realize that the soldier, for whom the pastoral

is an elusive phantom, is reduced to silence, as marching orders, gunfire, and birds' song melt into one ominous noise foreboding death. At the end of the poem, the "roaring night / Which wrecked our flower" (13-14) epitomizes the relationship between sound and death—the flower of life is crushed by the reverberations of the sounds (both human and nonhuman) that preoccupy the soldier's perception.

In **"Preparations for Victory,"** the visual sense dominates the perceptual focus of the poem. Although auditory perception plays a certain role, for instance in the line "these great shouting smokes and snarling jags,"[2] the main emphasis is now on the association of vision and light with the devastations of war. The poem is structured as a dialogue between the I-narrator and his soul; the tone is ironic, as the narrator commands his soul to do the very things that common sense forbids, namely not to "dread . . . the pestilence that hags / The valley" (1-2) and not to flinch "at these great shouting smokes and snarling jags" (3). After commanding his soul to perform such humanly impossible tasks, the narrator's self then summons his soul to look at a pastoral image of "gardens, [where] mossed boughs are hung / With apples whose bright cheeks none might excel" (7-8). Paradoxically, as we learn a little later, the war has taken away from the poet the possibility of a visual retreat into such pastoral idylls. Now the sights of rural beauty become ironically undermined the minute they are invoked. The suggested contemplation of nature's beauty in juxtaposition with the "great shouting smokes" or the "ruin" of battle acquires an ironic undertone, which turns into plain sarcasm when the word "excel," associated with pastoral tranquillity, is rhymed brutally with "shell." At this point one begins to wonder if the suggestion to "look" at the gardens is not in fact a sad reminiscence of the time when seeing and knowing could still inform one another, before they were irrevocably sundered by life's exposure to the horrors and inconsistencies of war. The visual details that we encounter in both **"Two Voices"** and **"Preparations for Victory"** appear strained and somewhat affected, self-consciously so, as Jon Silkin affirms, since for Blunden "the pastoral framework has been shattered by contemporary experience."[3]

Although the eye is yearning for relief from the burden of perception in times of war, the impact of pastoral images is doubly taunting: on the one hand, the "supply" of scenes holding the promise of such relief is quickly running out: "there's a house *as yet* unshattered by a shell"; "mark the *yet* unmurdered tree" (my emphasis). Besides Blunden's concern for the ever-diminishing store of pastoral sights (and sites), the objects of beauty are irrevocably contaminated by the bane of war: "The tokens of dear homes that court the eye, / And yet I see them not as I would see" (12-13). The eye, used to the devastations of war, is no longer capable of perceiving the innocence of unviolated objects. The enemy (which seems to be anyone who would cause the war to go on) not only threatens one's life, but also "sickens the light" by which one sees, thus rendering the contemplation of beauty impossible in the first place. Pastoral enclaves, those "tokens of dear homes that court the eye" (12), can offer no relief from the overall scene of horror, manifest in ruins, shattered houses, and "murdered" trees. On the contrary, the fruitless appeal to vision actually sharpens the pain of seeing an actuality that contradicts all precepts of humanity.

The invitation to "look, here are gardens" (7) sounds perfectly cynical when the narrator in the fourth but last line invokes the sense of sight once more, this time, however, spelling doom for the soldiers: "Look, we lose." Significantly, here the invitation to look is coupled with the going of light ("The sky is gone, the lightless, drenching haze" [25]), leading up the final association of death with absolute loss of sight: "The black fiend leaps brick-red as life's last picture goes" (27). Whereas in **"Two Voices"** death and destruction issue from sounds, in **"Preparations for Victory"** death assures its grip on the soldier's consciousness through images of daunting ambivalence. In both poems, sensual perception (either listening or seeing) is shown to be an extension of the forces that operate in the war; at the same time, it is perceived as a function of the military hierarchy, as higher ranking officers are shown to be less affected by the visual and auditory oppression to which the lower ranking individuals are exposed. Even though Blunden himself belonged to the more privileged caste of officers, he seems to have deeply sympathized with the plight of the soldier, whose victimization he rendered vividly by depicting their subjection to sensory perception. Since listening and hearing are sensations that man is unable to "turn off," the two poems discussed here show the soldier in the fullness of his predicament, as the war subverts the means by which beauty can enter the human mind. Thus, sense perception becomes an accessory of man's own mental entrapment and, finally, of physical death.

Both poems under discussion here represent a different aspect of the soldier's experience in World War I, and both poems describe sensory perception to be in close relationship with death. With this choice Blunden demonstrates how powerful and, at the same time, how utterly fragmenting the impressions of war are, making it impossible for the poet to render a complete picture of the horrors he encounters. Blunden saw fit to deal with the auditory and the visual aspect of war separately, each time, however, presenting a perfectly gruesome and ultimately convincing picture of the experience. A fundamental irony is apparent, of course, in the fact that both poems, while describing the morbid implications of sound and sight, use those very elements to create

poetic form. The rhyme schemes are perfectly regular, the sounds are melodious, and the verbal images (especially in **"Preparations for Victory"**), in spite of their sinister implications and ironic intent, possess a beauty of their own. This suggests, on the one hand, that Blunden recognized the importance of art to recapture a notion of beauty that has been obliterated by the war. On the other hand, it signifies that the interplay between form and content is precisely what is missing in the war, as the experience of shocking violence makes it impossible to attribute any reasonable meaning or content to the horrendous sounds and views that assault the human consciousness. By deliberately reducing perception to a selective process of association, the poet manages to restore a sense of wholeness to the world—a paradoxical property of Blunden's work that testifies to the poet's skill in overcoming the fragmentation and alienation that individuals encounter on the battleground.

Notes

1. Edmund Blunden, *Selected Poems,* ed. Robin Marsack (Great Britain: Carcanet Press Ltd., 1982) 48, line 1. All subsequent references are to this text.

2. *Ibid.* 48-49, line 3.

3. Jon Silkin, *Out of Battle: The Poetry of the Great War* (Oxford: Oxford U P, 1972) 120.

Peter Scupham (essay date January-February 1999)

SOURCE: Scupham, Peter. "Shelf Lives: 3: Edmund Blunden." *P. N. Review* 25, no. 3 (January-February 1999): 59-61.

[*In the following essay, Scupham examines several of Blunden's war poems.*]

> Yes, I still remember
>   The whole thing in a way;
> Edge and exactitude
>   Depend on the day.

I am writing this piece over those few November days which the Great War claims back from us, its heirs and successors, whether we know or care. In the still, drenching rain which seems appropriate to Remembrance Sunday I am surrounded by echoes and emblems: a piece of glass from Ypres Cathedral, a newspaper article which ends with a roll-call, a special litany which gives the 300 odd names of the known British survivors, a photograph of my father in his cadet's uniform: a touching pastiche of his brother Tommy, on leave from the Western front, who sits easily beside him, bandoliered, immaculate, affectionate. In our tiny church we have sung the appropriate hymns and heard one more proper name read aloud for his once-a-year resurrection—the only man from this scattered hamlet killed in action some eighty years ago. We have kept two minutes' silence, And for these few days, while we have been given by the media a newly-discovered poem by Sassoon, a draft version of Owen's 'Anthem for Doomed Youth', I have been returning to the poems of Edmund Blunden, and particularly those poems which seem to me to display best his unobtrusive and singularly English gift for elegy; that intense keening for the dead, those memorials to the intensity of living he found serving with the Royal Sussex in France and Flanders.

Such a copious career: the literary work as poet, essayist and biographer, the celebrant of cricket, the rediscoverer of Collins, Clare and Kirke White, the lecturer and teacher bridge-building between West and East with his work in Japan. Out of a tangled and haunted life, disciplined by a prodigious work-load, Blunden gave and called out great affection—and perhaps one of the things that made this possible was his instinctive feeling for loyalties. That sense of sharp individuality which led Harold Owen to think always of his brother Wilfred as the 'Old Wolf', the distancing, self-protecting habits which are natural to most makers seem absent. Blunden understood *participation mystique*, the strength of tradition in a school, a regiment. His loyalties to Christ's Hospital and its Old Blues—whom to his delight included Charles Lamb, Leigh Hunt and Coleridge—to his students in Japan, to the Royal Sussex were indissoluble. It would have been impossible for him to feel that violent dissonance between loyalty and hatred which runs through Robert Graves' *Goodbye to All That*. 'You damned snobs, I'll survive you all. There'll come a time when there won't be one of you left to remember battalion mess at Laventie' is *not* a Blunden sentiment. He likes the words 'our' and 'we'; he is a poet of community and fellowship whose passion for cricket as player, observer and meditative memorialist comes as no surprise.

Tensions, though, are productive. 'Edge and exactitude' are a good recipe, but not always one taken by this poet who closes ***Undertones of War*** with a sentence often seen as a hostage to literary fortune. He leaves his battalion, which will suffer further slaughter in a yet unravaged landscape, with the words: 'No destined anguish lifted its snaky head to poison a harmless young shepherd in a soldier's coat.' The harmless shepherd with a Military Cross! That image of the shepherd links Blunden the celebrant of the natural world and the peasant past with Blunden the platoon commander. I think of Herbert Read's 'My Company':

> I know that I'll wander with a cry:
> 'O beautiful men, O men I loved,
> O whither are you gone, my company?'

First the caveats, then the admiration. Blunden, as Read in 'My Company', is caught between two dictions: one dead, the other powerless to be born—except that other dictions and strategies are being born, which Blunden will largely ignore. Where Edward Thomas freed himself from the bindweed, or Chinese Moon Flower tangle of his prose, Blunden's country sentiments rarely come clean in the Thomas way, and despite his allegiance to Clare, the edge and exactitude of Clare have drowsed off. Blunden's own 'Shepherd' 'With untrimmed staff, smock stitched like honeycomb, / With great-tongued boots, and buskins to the thigh' stalks through sonorous iambics in his patriarchal mode as if he had stepped straight from one of Palmer's etchings or Blake's woodcuts for Thornton's *Virgil,* accompanied by barn, kiln, windmill, sheep-bells and leaping firelight. And, unfortunately, there is a deal of slumber and lotus-eating in the body of Blunden's poetry, a deal of theeing and thouing, and a vocabulary—kisks, dripple, elmin, stolchy—which reminds me of the story of Hardy hunting a precedent for a usage in the OED and finding the word had only been used in literature once, by Thomas Hardy, in *Far from the Madding Crowd*. Not to mention elves, which are, regrettably, more frequent visitors to Blunden's poems than they are to the landscapes round here. These inveterate habits of peopling landscape with literature, which call out a smiling affection in me, die hard. Take **'Premature Rejoicing'**:

> What's that over there?
>   Thiepval Wood.
> Take a steady look at it; it'll do you good.
> Here, these glasses will help you. See any flowers?
> There sleeps Titania (correct—the Wood is ours);
> There sleeps Titania in a deep dug-out,
> Waking, she wonders what all the din's about . . .

and that brings me to the poems of war-experience, which seem to me to have some singular and special virtues. Whatever the myth of England that village boy from Yalding, that schoolboy from Christ's Hospital took with him to the trenches, it was a deep and sustaining one. 'There lives the dearest freshness deep down things', Hopkins wrote, in 'God's Grandeur', and this 'dearest freshness' ancient, always renewed, a pre-industrial continuity Blunden could not see failing, runs as a kind of life-giving ground-bass to his war poems, as in **'At Senlis Once'**:

> Clad so cleanly this remnant of poor wretches
> Picked up life like the hens in orchard ditches.
>   Gazed on the mill-sails, heard the church-bell,
>   Found an honest glass all manner of riches.
>
> How they crowded the barn with lusty laughter,
> Hailed the pierrots and shook each shadowy rafter,
>   Even could ridicule their own sufferings,
>   Sang as though nothing but joy came after!

It is fellowship again, that bedrock of something solid, kind, transitory yet timeless that Blunden returns to: a fellowship ultimately undisturbed by death, as in the 1932 pamphlet *Fall In, Ghosts: An Essay on a Battalion Reunion.* The living and the dead are interchangeable at this Feast of All Souls: 'Will there be chairs enough for all of us, as the troops return to the tables to listen forgivingly to this rhetoric? At what point do we separate from those other listeners I named? Are we not all in the same boat? Fall in, ghosts!' Edmund Blunden was born in 1896, yet by the time he was in his thirties, writing such poems as **'Their Very Memory'**, the weight of the dead and the responsibility he feels to carry them back to the light force him to write like an old man:

> When they smiled
> Earth's inferno changed and melted
>   Greenwood mild;
> Every village where they halted
>   Shone with them through square and alley.
>
>   Now my mind
> Faint and few records their showings,
>   Brave, strong, kind—
> I'd unlock you all their doings
>   But the keys are locked and twisted.

Paul Fussell, in his fascinating book *The Great War and Modern Memory,* talks of rural, pre-industrial England as being the repository of those values against which Blunden can measure the spoliations of the Great War; for Fussell 'Blunden's style is his critique', which seems exactly right. And yet, and yet . . . It is hard to disentangle rural fact from rural fiction, literary perceptions from literary artifice. Edwardian country children could live, as my parents did, in a richness compounded by the richness of the books they read. 'I shan't write my autobiography,' my father said. 'It's all in Wordsworth and Vaughan.' Blunden's poems have less to say of the incorrigible harshness of country life, of a Tess stone-picking at Flintcombe Ash, of eviction, ignorance and the *insanitary* picturesque. Still, other pens have dwelt on that, and we all need our certifying myths, our good places. Richard Jefferies told us truths in *Bevis* not contradicted by those in *Hodge and His Masters,* and Blunden served with the Royal Sussex, not the Accrington Pals. Blunden's **'At Rugmer'**, a revisiting of the battlefield after the Armistice, makes an identification with a natural process explicit in a happily unencumbered poem quoted in its entirety . . .

> Among sequestered farms and where brown orchards
> Weave in the thin and coiling wind, and where
> The pale cold river ripples still as moorhens
> Work their restless crossing,
> Among such places, when October warnings
> Sound from each kex and thorn and shifting leaf,
> We well might wander, and renew some stories
> Of a dim time when we were kex and thorn,
> Sere leaf, ready to hear a hissing wind

> Whip down and wipe us out; our season seemed
> At any second closing.
> So, we were wrong. But we have lived this landscape,
> And have an understanding with these shades.

Blunden had an understanding with those shades all his life; they may be transposed into kex and thorn, hens, sere leaves, but they are first and foremost his companions-in-arms. A self-effacing, undramatic love for them shines through his diction and in a curious way calms and balances the cataclysmic events of 1914-1918 in a way no other poet quite does for me. It is, perhaps, a pity that the quiet conversational ease of a poem like **'At Rugmer'** wasn't practised more frequently; one might say the same of Kipling's 'The Way through the Woods', which seems something of a sport among Kipling's poems of rhythmic verve and brio. But Blunden has his odd surprises, his forward gestures, such as **'Into the Salient'**:

> There is a cellar, or was just now.
> If the wreck isn't knocked in on us all,
> We may emerge past the two Belgian policemen,
> The owner's representatives,
> Standing in their capes on the steps of the hollow
>   estaminet
>
> Open at all hours to the winds
> At the Poperinghe end of Ypres.
> O if we do, if time will pass in time,
> We will march
> With rifles butt-upwards, in our teeth, any way you
>   like,
> Into seven days of country where you come out any
>   door.

The limitations of Blunden pace equally with his strengths. We come back always to the localities of brotherhood, loyalties to those specifics of place and person which matter so much to him. The more universal range of Owen and the generalisations of Sassoon's critiques are foreign to Blunden; I think his nearest equivalent in human sympathies is Ivor Gurney, with music and Gloucestershire as his benchmarks. A Gurney poem can catch the breath in an odd amazement with its drag-jolt metres and quirks of phrasing—'Butchers and Tombs', where the book falls open, will do:

> And so the disregarders of blister on heel,
> Pack on shoulder, barrage and work at the wires,
> One wooden cross had for ensign of honour and life
>   gone—
>
> Save when the Gloucesters turning sudden to tell to
>   one
> Some joke, would remember and say 'That joke is
>   done,'
> Since he who would understand was so cold he could
>   not feel,
> And clay binds hard, and sandbags get rotten and
>   crumble.

Blunden seems in a curious conspiracy with time, preternaturally sagacious, conscious of his future role as spokesman and memorialist. The still young Blunden can dedicate **'The Veteran'** to his Colonel, Colonel Harrison, as if to charm his admired Commanding Officer into a deserved happiness, the first line 'He stumbles silver-haired among his bees' immediately linking the centuries, with its conflated echo of Peele's 'His golden locks time hath to silver turned' and 'His helmet now shall make a hive for bees'. The war, though, is not seen as bringing about an irretrievable situation, the civilization Blunden cares for is not Pound's 'old bitch gone in the teeth'; the 'green country, useful to the race, / Knocked silly with guns and mines, its villages vanished' will recover, though the 'bright bewildering green' of **'The Sunlit Vale'** will not deceive him. He will somehow re-group the unfashionable words beauty, companion, innocence, joy—and Joy was the name of his lost daughter, who died in 1919 when only a month or so old. Over and over individuality textures the poems; trench names, place names, the names of soldiers—Worley, Daniells, Ashford—peg the poems down, defining Blunden as the survivor who best evokes for us the presence of war in the company of the loved at particular times in particular places. I read Blunden as that voice which against all the odds, the limitations of his diction, his metrics, his literary luggage, can still move one into understanding something of the good that flourished in those fields. It is Blunden who can move me to tears.

Blunden died in 1974. Another final sentence, this time from Barry Webb's *Edmund Blunden, a Biography*: 'Among the group standing by the side of the grave was a small unobtrusive figure: he was Private A. E. Beeney of the 11th Royal Sussex Regiment, who had been Edmund's runner at Ypres and Passchendaele. Stepping forward he let fall from his hand a wreath of Flanders poppies which fluttered down on the coffin in fond and final salute.' In **'War Cemetery'** the dead watch life:

> They smile a little. 'As the thing began
> It ended; only, as you see, we boys
> Have copped unlucky, and the C.O. too,

> But he'd just had *his* leave; well, all that noise,
> And all us millions as they say *napu*.'
>   Thus a dim music every step I tread
>   Connotes the living purpose of these dead.

And now, only some three hundred soldiers are left to die—a skirmish—before knowledge felt on the pulse becomes the coded, ambivalent message of history.

FURTHER READING

Biographies

Hardie, Alec M. *Edmund Blunden*. London: Longmans, Green & Co. Ltd., 1958, 43 p.
    Brief account of Blunden's life and career as a poet.

Webb, Barry. *Edmund Blunden: A Biography*. New Haven, Conn.: Yale University Press, 1990, 360 p.
    Comprehensive coverage of Blunden's life and writing career.

Criticism

Benkovitz, Miriam J. "Edmund Blunden's Ghosts." *Columbia Library Columns* 27, no. 2 (February 1978): 14-22.
    Discussion of Blunden's *Undertones of War*, a narrative of his wartime experiences that proved far more difficult for him to write than his poems about the war.

Fussell, Paul. "Modernism, Adversary Culture, and Edmund Blunden." *Sewanee Review* 94, no. 4 (fall 1986): 583-601.
    Explores Blunden's work within the context of Modernism.

Studley, John. "Motion and Stillness: Antithetical Imagery in Edmund Blunden's Early Poetry." *Four Decades of Poetry 1890-1930* 1, no. 2 (July 1976): 93-108.
    Studies the nature poems of Blunden's early career, finding that his poetry of the countryside also includes serious commentary on culture and morality.

Additional coverage of Blunden's life and career is contained in the following sources published by Thomson Gale: *British Writers*, Vol. 6; *Contemporary Authors*, Vols. 17-18; *Contemporary Authors New Revision Series*, Vol. 54; *Contemporary Authors—Obituary*, Vols. 45-48; *Contemporary Authors Permanent Series*, Vol. 2; *Contemporary Literary Criticism*, Vols. 2 and 56; *Dictionary of Literary Biography*, Vols. 20, 100 and 155; *Literature Resource Center*; *Major 20th-Century Writers*, Ed. 1; and *Poets: American and British*.

Carolyn Kizer
1925-

American poet, translator, essayist, and editor.

INTRODUCTION

Kizer is an award-winning poet whose work is greatly influenced by her commitment to feminism and other social issues, by her lifelong interest in China and Chinese poetry, and by her devotion to the Pacific Northwest, where she was born.

BIOGRAPHICAL INFORMATION

Born in Spokane, Washington, on December 10, 1925, Kizer was the only child of Mabel Ashley and Benjamin Hamilton Kizer. Her mother studied philosophy and art at Harvard and earned a Ph.D. in biology from Stanford and her father was an attorney. Both were active in a variety of liberal social causes, and Kizer was raised in a household frequented by intellectuals from all over the world. She attended Sarah Lawrence College where she earned a B.A. in 1945. She did graduate work at Columbia University, where she received a Chinese Cultural Fellowship in Comparative Literature, and at the University of Washington in Seattle, where she studied under Theodore Roethke. In 1948 Kizer married Charles Stimson Bullitt, with whom she had three children, two girls and a boy. The couple divorced in 1954. In 1975 Kizer married John Marshall Woodbridge, an architect.

In 1959 Kizer founded the journal *Poetry Northwest,* which she also edited from 1959 until 1965. She has held a wide variety of academic posts, among them poet-in-residence at the University of North Carolina, Hurst Professor at Washington University in St. Louis, and acting director of the graduate writing program at Columbia University. She has served as a lecturer at Barnard College and Ohio University, as professor of poetry in the Iowa Writers Workshop, and as senior fellow in humanities at Princeton University. Her awards include the 1985 Pulitzer Prize for *Yin: New Poems* (1984) and the Theodore Roethke Memorial Foundation Poetry Award (1988). Kizer lives in Sonoma, California.

MAJOR WORKS

Kizer's early work deals with universal themes and often employs grotesque imagery. Her first collection, *The Ungrateful Garden,* appeared in 1961 and examines

the relationship between humankind and nature, often undercutting the notion that nature is capable of providing comfort and consolation. In Kizer's poetry, nature is not necessarily evil or threatening, but neither is it beneficent—it is simply indifferent to humanity. Included in this collection is one of Kizer's best-known individual poems, "The Great Blue Heron"—a bird which, for Kizer, serves as a harbinger of death. Several other poems in the book deal with the dehumanizing aspects of government.

Kizer's second book, *Knock upon Silence* (1965), is divided into four sections and deals with both Eastern and Western cultures. "Pro Femina," one of her most frequently cited individual poems, and "A Month in Summer" represent the Western segment of the collection, while her "Chinese Imitations" and a number of translations of the poetry of Tu Fu make up the Eastern portion. The satiric "Pro Femina" tells the story of Robert Louis Stevenson's last days in Samoa, narrated in the first person by his wife, Fanny Stevenson, who serves as her husband's nurse and provider. *Midnight Was My Cry: New and Selected Poems* (1971) contains selections from Kizer's first two volumes, as well as sixteen new poems dealing with such social and political issues as the Vietnam War and the civil rights movement.

Kizer published no new poetry volumes until 1984, when both *Yin: New Poems* and *Mermaids in the Basement: Poems for Women* appeared. The latter contains selections from her earlier volumes of poetry, as does *The Nearness of You* (1986), which also includes "poems for men," making it a companion piece of sorts to *Mermaids*. The new poetry of *Yin* exhibits a marked difference from Kizer's earlier work in that it features poetry more personal than any she had written before; the collection earned the Pulitzer Prize in 1985.

In 1988 Kizer produced a book of translations from the works of several poets in a variety of languages, *Carrying Over: Poems from the Chinese, Urdu, Macedonian, Yiddish, and French African*. She has also written two volumes of essays and edited a collection of poetry by women.

CRITICAL RECEPTION

Although Kizer has not been an especially prolific poet, she has been acclaimed for her technical mastery and her tough, unsentimental subject matter. Her view of nature as a disinterested force in the lives of human beings is a departure from the usual representation of nature in poetry, as many critics have pointed out. Derek T. Leuenberger, for example, has analyzed "The Great Blue Heron" and finds that "rather than a depiction of nature as an idealized, benevolent entity, Kizer's heron is a baleful image presaging her mother's approaching death." Yet Kizer does not seem to see nature as evil or threatening; rather, it is simply indifferent to human problems and cannot, therefore, be the consoling and comforting force that many poets claim it is.

Kizer's commitment to political causes and to feminism is examined in the criticism of Ruth Salvaggio, who suggests that Kizer is instrumental in formulating a feminist poetics. According to Salvaggio, "Kizer shows us that women poets can do more than remain caught in romantic reverie. They can, and must, become part of a social world desperately in need of change." Judith Emlyn Johnson also praises Kizer's contributions to a feminist poetics, more specifically to what she calls a "poetics of generosity." Both critics laud Kizer for granting power and agency to female voices, for associating women with action and change, and for abandoning objectivity in favor of subjectivity.

Dominic Cheung has studied the sources for Kizer's "Chinese Imitations," noting the inaccuracies in the Arthur Waley translations of Chinese poems that provide the basis for her poems "Summer near the River" and "Hiding Our Love." Despite such imprecise translations, however, Cheung finds that Kizer "has effectively captured the subtlest nuances of the Chinese works while often bringing latent connotations to full and precise imagistic expression." Kizer often interjects her own poetry into sections of the Chinese poems that contain untranslatable allusions and Cheung praises the "balance she has struck between her vision and that which is inherent in the Chinese poems."

PRINCIPAL WORKS

Poetry

The Ungrateful Garden 1961
Knock upon Silence 1965
Midnight Was My Cry: New and Selected Poems 1971
Mermaids in the Basement: Poems for Women 1984
Yin: New Poems 1984
The Nearness of You 1986
Carrying Over: Poems from the Chinese, Urdu, Macedonian, Yiddish, and French African [translator] 1988
A Splintered Mirror: Chinese Poetry from the Democracy Movement [translator, with Donald Finkel] 1991
Harping On: Poems 1985-1995 1996
Cool, Calm, & Collected: Poems 1960-2000 2001

Other Major Works

Proses: On Poems and Poets (autobiographical prose, essays) 1993
100 Great Poems by Women [editor] (poetry) 1995
Picking and Choosing: Essays on Prose (essays) 1995

CRITICISM

Derek T. Leuenberger (essay date winter 1999)

SOURCE: Leuenberger, Derek T. "Kizer's 'The Great Blue Heron.'" *Explicator* 57, no. 2 (winter 1999): 115-18.

[*In the following essay, Leuenberger discusses Kizer's view of the relationship between humankind and nature as well as her use of the heron as a harbinger of death.*]

In her poem **"The Great Blue Heron,"** from the collection ***Mermaids in the Basement,*** Carolyn Kizer deliberately eschews the somewhat typical poetic view of nature as the vibrant, richly spiritual partner of humanity.[1] Rather than a depiction of nature as an idealized, benevolent entity, Kizer's heron is a baleful image presaging her mother's approaching death. Kizer's choice of imagery sketches an account of a disinterested nature, taking a form dictated only by the narrator's memory.

As Kizer's child persona stands on a deserted beach watching the heron, her physical description of the bird is telling. In the first stanza, she calls attention to the bird's "tattered wings / He wore as a hunchback's coat." Later, Kizer describes the heron as it flies away, calling attention to the wings as "ashen things," "grounded, unwieldy, ragged," and "[a] pair of broken arms / That were not made for flight" (26-29). Rather than the more archetypal image of freedom and natural grandeur, Kizer gives the heron the bearing of a carrion bird. Kizer's unflattering adjectives are surprising when used in reference to a bird often thought of as elegant and graceful, but the portrayal is fitting. As she stands in the "dusty light" of summer, the narrator's remembrance of the day, and the correlative image of the heron, is darkened in memory; unknown to the child, but recognized by the adult, her mother is approaching death.

A sense of death and finality hangs over the poem as the heron is described in ghostly terms. The heron is a "spectral bird (22)," a "shadow without a shadow" (5). We sense that the heron is a herald of the future, a ghost of Kizer's coming loss. As she observes the bird, she asks, "Heron, whose ghost are you?" (15). The child is incognizant of what the bird represents. Her "mother knew what he was" (32), however: the Angel of Death, foreshadowing the end. The gaunt, ghostly heron is a macabre image of nature in an unaccustomed role, harbinger of death.

Augmenting the poem's morbid tenor as embodied by the heron, the portrayal of the natural setting furthers the tone of desolation. The child stands alone on a "bare strip of shore" (41) marking the location of a "long-decayed resort" (11). Kizer mentions only a few distant pines in addition to herself, her mother, and the heron, but no other animals or vegetation, no water, little suggestive of life. It is a "canvas day" (7), a painting, unreal and lifeless. Kizer's natural world is a realm of emptiness.

Rather than nature as green and vibrant, Kizer invokes the images of fire, ashes, and smoke. The "ashen" wings of the heron, the burned summer house, "[s]o many smokes and fires" (36) gradually darken Kizer's view of the world. It is nature in the aftermath of catastrophe: charred, sterile, and forlorn. The child stands on the beach, "[i]n the sudden chill of the burned" (17), sensing the ominous future in this barren place. In the last lines, Kizer acknowledges her mother's fate:

> When, like gray smoke, a vapor
> Floating into the sky,
> A handful of paper ashes,
> My mother would drift away.

(15)

Here Kizer refers to her mother's soon-realized death and subsequent cremation.[2] The fire and ash imagery brings to mind the phoenix myth. In Kizer's version, however, there is no rebirth. There is no tone of redemption or hope. Instead, Kizer can impart only resignation; the end is known, and reflection brings little comfort.

Although **"The Great Blue Heron"** is certainly portentous and stark, it is important to note that the poem's emotional climate does not indicate a sense of anger or injustice. Elizabeth House points out that Kizer "never suggests that the bird is evil. As part of nature, he merely reflects the cycle of life and death that time imposes on all living creatures" (403). Instead, in the final stanza, Kizer describes the heron as "heavy upon my eye" and "denser than my repose," never as evil or malevolent. Kizer pointedly portrays nature as the message bearer, not the agent, of death; she recounts the heron's appearance only in terms of her own emotions.

However, Kizer's portrayal of the heron's role within the natural cycle does not indicate a harmonious coexistence with her narrator. After "fifteen summers and snows" (48), the narrator, now a grown woman, asks, "Why have you followed me here, / Heavy and far away?" (45-46). Kizer's persona still has not fully reconciled herself with the heron's message. The cycle continues, perpetuating the uncomfortable relationship between individual and nature.

The natural world Kizer writes of is not the serene, benevolent world of Wordsworth. Nor is it the darkly beautiful world of W. S. Merwin, resplendent even at the moment of its destruction, and at its worst, exacting retribution from humankind.[3] Rather, Kizer leaves us with the sense that nature is in itself dispassionate. Neither benevolent nor malevolent, nature can only reflect; it gives form to perception and is molded by the passage of time.

Notes

1. The Romantics, as the clearest example of this view, paradigmatically portrayed nature as a setting of spirituality, conveying a harmonious and complimentary relationship with humanity. William Wordsworth, in the preface to the second edition of *Lyrical Ballads,* states that the poet "considers man and nature as essentially adapted

to one another, and the mind of man as naturally the mirror of the fairest and most interesting qualities of nature" (76).

2. Disclosed in the poem "The Blessing," *Mermaids* 16-19.

3. Hank Lazer calls *The Lice* "an extended myth of uncreation, the story of the disappearance of the animal world because of man's arrogance and shortsightedness" (262). See "The Last One" and "For a Coming Extinction" from *The Lice* as characteristic examples of Merwin's treatment of nature (10-12, 68-69).

Works Cited

House, Elizabeth. "Carolyn Kizer." *Dictionary of Literary Biography.* Ed. Donald J. Greiner. Vol. 5. Pt. 1. Detroit: Gale Research, 1980. 402-05.

Kizer, Carolyn. *Mermaids in the Basement: Poems for Women.* Port Townsend: Copper Canyon, 1984. 14-15.

Lazer, Hank. "For a Coming Extinction: A Reading of W. S. Merwin's *The Lice.*" *ELH* 49.1 (1982): 262-85.

Merwin, W. S. *The Lice.* New York: Atheneum, 1967.

Wordsworth, William. Preface. *Lyrical Ballads.* 1802. Ed. Michael Mason. Longman Annotated Texts. New York: Longman, 1992.

Ruth Salvaggio (essay date 2001)

SOURCE: Salvaggio, Ruth. "Kizer's Politics: Poetry and Feminism." In *Carolyn Kizer: Perspectives on Her Life and Work,* edited by Annie Finch, Johanna Keller, and Candace McClelland, pp. 55-70. Fort Lee, N.J.: CavanKerry Press, 2001.

[*In the following essay, Salvaggio examines the connections between Kizer's political beliefs, her commitment to feminism, and her poetry.*]

Carolyn Kizer tells us that she grew up in "an intensely political household." Her mother was a social activist who, among other things, "ran the first federally sponsored drug clinic in New York City" and was "an organizer for the I.W.W." "Politically," Kizer says of her mother, "she was a radical. . . ." Her father, a more distant influence on Kizer's life, was a lawyer with his own kind of "war chant: truth, justice, equity, freedom, and law."[1] No surprise, then, that Kizer herself has been intensely involved in politics and that politics has infused her poetry. As Director of Literary Programs for the NEA, for instance, the anti-war Kizer accepted funding from a pro-Vietnam war administration, reasoning that "the worse things are politically in a country,

the more you need a strong arts program."[2] And she openly identifies herself as a feminist, dedicating her collection *Mermaids in the Basement* to "my dear friends everywhere, feminists all."

The connection between Kizer's politics and feminism, I believe, is a crucial one. It not only helps explain the social aspect of Kizer's poetry as being much more than traditionally "public" or "classical." Even more important, it helps us understand how women poets are mixing aesthetics and politics—and how the political movement of feminism is at last finding expression in the voices of women poets. This is good news for feminism. It may even be better news for poetry, which has long served as a vehicle for the expression not only of individual feeling, but more precisely of the subjective feelings of men. Women poets, of course, must also write their subjectivity, and in fact the recent emergence of women's voices in poetry has involved just that kind of expression—what Kizer herself calls "the world's best-kept secret: / Merely the private lives of one-half of humanity."[3] But in addition to speaking for themselves, women poets are also speaking for others. They are reminding us that neither feminism nor poetry can remain isolated from a world in which otherness has too often been ignored and even suppressed. Writing both *as* other and *for* others, they open poetry to multiple voices. And they do this in different ways. Muriel Rukeyser leaps directly into political subjects in her poetry. Adrienne Rich, in her recent collection, *Your Native Land, Your Life,* speaks through the experience of diverse others. And a growing number of African American, Hispanic, Native American, and international women poets, especially from Third World countries, are expressing their social experience in strikingly political contexts—poets such as Paula Gunn Allen, Audre Lorde, Rosario Castellanos, Cherri Moraga, and Nellie Wong.

Carolyn Kizer joins in with these multiple voices by making both women and poetry into large subjects. I take the word "large" from Kizer's poem **"Dream of a Large Lady,"**[4] for here we find just that engagement with otherness that underlies both her politics and feminism. The poem opens with a woman climbing down a ladder from a gun emplacement. Unable to dislodge the gun, this large lady unpacks her lunch, and consumes "a single / hard-boiled egg / leaving the shell / not as litter but as symbolism / on the sullen gun / in its grey rotunda." She then meets another woman, this one with orange hair, who likes the large lady's poetry and invites her in for tea. The large lady accepts, and in this mood of acceptance and reconciliation, Kizer ends her poem describing the large lady's vision:

> With a sigh, she puts aside the memory
> of the grey gun she could only decorate
> but not destroy.

> Though clear in her eye she holds a vision:
>   the thin, ceremonious shell
>   of her eaten egg
>
> painted by the sun against the sky.

I see this "large lady" as Kizer herself, a woman poet who tries to "damage the gun," to buck the controlling powers—military, capitalist, patriarchal. At the same time, I also see Kizer reflected in the "orange lady," a woman who admires poesy and sips tea. Each engages the experience of the other. But particularly the large lady, who wants at once "to contemplate / the blue view / and to damage the gun," epitomizes what I take to be Kizer's own vision of largeness—an expansive vision that allows both the aesthetic and the political a place in poetry. There is a quiet aesthetic moment. But there is something else, that almost incongruous vision of the egg shell and the fun. "Clear in her eye" the large lady sees the world aesthetically, but she also sees it with what Lillian Robinson calls "the keen eye of politics."

This vision is surely part of a "poetics of generosity," a poetics described by Judith Johnson as Kizer's full engagement with a "multiplicity of energies" that signals the re-emergence of woman's subjectivity in poetry. Johnson argues that such a poetics is "central to feminism," for it not only reconstitutes the lost voice of woman as poet, but shows women—and Kizer herself—to be fully engaged in "life's furious contradictions."[5] Recovering her voice, the woman poet refuses to partake in the controlling discourse of a masculine poetic tradition, refuses to assume the role of speaking subject who controls the discursive object. She splits the subject-object dichotomy, and opens poetry to multiplicity.

Kizer's "large lady," it seems to me, shows us the essential political dimension of this generosity and engagement. For this lady not only speaks, she acts. And through this lady, Kizer has infused herself into the poem's action. It is, of course, not real political action, since the lady cannot really dislodge the gun. Nor is it descriptive of some actual political event. But what does happen here is something very important: Kizer is bringing together women and poetry, poetry and politics. The "orange lady" and "large lady," I would suggest, represent the very aesthetic and political merger that is taking place. Their drinking of tea mixes the two forms of experience that have long remained antithetical in poetic tradition, and that are now coming closer and closer together in an emerging feminist poetics. For even if the large lady "could only decorate / but not destroy" the gun, there remains the final vision of the "ceremonious shell" in the "grey rotunda." Here is the sign, the emblem, of Kizer's political aesthetics.

But politics is always more than a sign, and Kizer is no mere sign-carrier. What distinguishes her political vision—what marks it as "feminist," as I will be explain-

ing later—is that she herself becomes part of the action. Never divorced from the object of her writing, Kizer is a subject intensely involved in her poetic politics. She does not comment from a safe distance, but always infuses herself in the experience. In **"Race Relations,"** for instance, she sings in her "white oasis" while an unnamed other works and bleeds. Unable to change this very situation which is the object of her description, she becomes part of it—"sentenced to wait" through "our love-hate duet."[6] In **"Poem, Small and Delible,"** she describes a group "picketing Woolworth's," holding signs with words as "baffling, as arcane / As poems." Kizer stands here in the poem, the woman who asked the question, "Who cares, lady?" She stands here as poet and activist, reflecting on the questions, thinking of Gandhi. "They will know who *he* was," she says, "And that Art and Action, mostly incompatible, / Could support each other now and then."[7]

This political vision, intricately linked to the generosity of Kizer's poetry, is also central to feminism. What's more important is that it shows the crucial role Carolyn Kizer plays in shaping a feminist political poetics. This task is a vitally important one—not only for the feminist movement, which has been seeking poetry that voices its political agenda, but for poetry itself, which has long needed to recapture its lost social imperative. In 1978, Lillian Robinson borrowed a phrase from an anonymous woman poet, "the keen eye of politics," to write about "Poetry and the Feminist Movement." Exploring a diversity of poems by women, she identifies the "new voice," the "new set of concerns and preoccupations" that characterize women's poetry.[8] Yet while celebrating the emergence of this new consciousness, she is troubled by the absence of a strong social and political voice, claiming that "the personal aspect is the only dimension of the question that feminist poetry has been able to reach at all." Her summary of what is lacking in women's poetry leads me directly to a discussion of what Carolyn Kizer offers. Robinson explains:

> The poetry of the women's movement has failed to challenge a charter assumption of bourgeois literature: the notion that literature in general and poetry in particular exist for the expression of the private, individual, and subjective element in supposedly universal human experience. . . . But ours is a movement that is only half certain where it is marching, and poetry is more often relegated to the "cultural events" . . . the thing we drop into when the real political work is over. It needs to be more than that.[9]

Kizer's poetry is more. It is, like the lady she describes, "large." It not only encompasses the political, but places women in the feminist political world, and in so doing re-places poetry in its political context.

But why insist, as I do, that Kizer's poetic politics is a "feminist" politics? For clearly she writes on a variety of political subjects, and though she describes herself as a feminist, her concerns would seem to exceed those specifically relevant to women. My reason for identifying such a politics as feminist also has to do with the "largeness" of Kizer's lady, for the most important thing about this "large lady" is that she is a woman—a woman activist and poet who brings her vision *as a woman* to what she says and does. In suggesting this, I am also insisting on the "largeness" of feminism itself, a movement which does not restrict itself to the oppression of women (as if that were not enough), but which sees any form of oppression as intricately linked to patriarchal systems of dominance and control.

This is why it is so necessary to see Kizer's "poetics of generosity" connected to her political poetics. For if her generous poetics is what allows her to split the subject-object dynamics in which male poets have controlled the feminine object of their description, it is Kizer's political poetics that allows her to infuse women's new subjectivity with energy and make the woman poet herself as agent of both "Art and Action." Interestingly, Kizer's poetry is often described as "public" or "classical," and she herself looks to such public poets as Homer and Pope for her heritage.[10] And yet I believe that she is political in a way that these men never could be, for like Sappho—the other classical poet she claims—she writes from the other side of oppression, from the position of woman. She necessarily opens poetry to the voice of the confiscated object, transforms that object in the fury of action where she can not only find her lost voice but also change the world.

Consider, for instance, the way Kizer and Pope deal differently with the politics of writing. From his early *Essay on Criticism* on through the *Dunciad,* Pope shows a special fondness for making fun of bad writers. As a defender of standards and propriety, he never lost the opportunity to demean and belittle his opposition. His life was a constant warfare between those who ridiculed him, and his devastating return of that ridicule. Now look at Kizer's poem **"Promising Author,"**[11] in which she recalls her time with a writer who is clearly obnoxious—who curled his lip as he "ran down every writer in the place," who "sneered" at his "shabby friends" who lent him money, who "became glib as any Grub Street hack,"

> Then demanded help
> To write the novel you would never write:
> As I turned you from the door
> You cursed me, and I cursed you back.

Pope would leave it there. Content to describe the scene from his objective perch, he rarely entered into, never imagined what it might be like to be that person. But listen to the end of Kizer's poem:

> Once I believed you were the great white shark,
> Slick predator, with tough scarred hide.

> But now I know you were a small sea-lion,
> Vulnerable, whiskery, afraid,
> Who wept for mercy as you died.

Kizer is generous through engagement, enters the mind and body of this "hack," becomes part of the politics of writing. I wonder if only a woman could do this, could know what it's like to be on the other side of propriety, and therefore sympathize. To her, this "promising author" turns out to be no monster, but only a "beat-up scarecrow out of Oz," a man whose bravado can only be tamed by our understanding. Is such understanding "feminist"? I say that, there, it is—that it defines what the woman poet does when she finds her voice and brings that voice to the social arena. She changes the way we think about each other, the way we relate to each other. She enters into the world to change it.

To make generosity political, one must—to use a phrase from Cynthia Ozick—"leap into otherness." The poet cannot be content to find her own voice, essential as that endeavor is. She must do more. She must mix her voice with that of others, bring it into the social chorus. Kizer herself is uncomfortable with the term "public poetry." "I'm not sure I like that term," she says, and then suggests, "Social poetry?"[12] I wonder if her reason may be that "public poetry" carries with it the notion of oratorical speech, of speaking from the privileged position to some uninformed mass in need of edification. "Social poetry," the term she suggests instead, would seem to be more engaging, more caught up in the process of exchange and interchange. So much of Kizer's poetry has involved that kind of interchange, that "leap into otherness." And I believe this is exactly what makes her poetry political. Whether she is in the group picketing at Woolworth's, or participating in a "love-hate duet," or leaving an egg shell on top of a gun and then sipping tea with an "orange lady," Kizer shows us that women poets can do more than remain caught in romantic reverie. They can, and must, become part of a social world desperately in need of change.

And Kizer's world is strikingly social. She describes herself as being in the "Roman" line—with Catullus, Juvenal, and Pope.[13] And yet, to me, she is much more generous than these men. She has their wit and flair, to be sure, and her language is often as crisp and controlled. Yet when she writes in the tradition, even following their forms, the result strikes me as something very different—different because she makes a public situation personal, because she becomes part of a world which they have been largely content to mock from their distanced positions. **"Tying One On in Vienna"**[14] is a perfect example of what I mean. It has all the exuberance of Juvenal and Pope, all the drunken madness of classical satire. Except that right there in the middle of the poem is Kizer herself, drinking away, "tying one on." If Juvenal and Pope have as their political agenda an exposition of a world gone mad, then Kizer does too—but she not only sees herself as part of that madness, she willingly joins in. There is generosity here, to be sure. But I want to insist that this is *political* generosity—a personal and political engagement with empires gone mad, empires we can only understand when we ourselves are mad, excessive, in love:

> Turks and Hellenes, Mongols, Shakespearean schol-
> ars—Hegel!
> Continuity is all!
> Changing the petticoat guard at the palace of Paul;
> Orange groves, All Souls' Day, 4th of July parades;
> Vienna, Spokane, Los Angeles County—even Ham-
> burg. . . .
> And over all others, the face of my lover,
> A man with the brain of an angel!

The phrase repeated in the poem is "an excess of feeling." This is what allows Kizer—drinking, weeping, celebrating—to understand both the personal and the political. The world may be mad, but she is part of it, as we all are. Her "excess of feeling" makes it all tolerable, even joyous. She can "drink to the health of my ex-husband / And other enemies, known and unknown." She can "FORGIVE ALL LOUSY POETS / AS THEY SHALL FORGIVE ME." (Can we imagine this coming from Pope?) And there in Vienna, even political aggression can be forgiven. For Kizer herself is there, in the room, where it happened:

> Even the rathskeller door, with its broken hinges
> Since the Russian troops hammered it down, looking
>   for girls,
> Even the old door, wounded with bayonet marks,
> Dances and reels, and my soul staggers for joy,
> And we are healed together, noble Viennese landlord!

It is here, too, that we find what Kizer's politics is all about. It is a politics of love. It is a woman's politics—built on engagement, interchange, understanding. On a wonderful personal level, Kizer describes herself as plunging her nose into her lover's navel: "Oh, what a heavenly odor! / Landlord, hold me up by the hair / Before I drown." The poem ends with Kizer bringing this personal love to the world:

> The soul of the world is a nose,
> A nose in a navel. The red sun sets in the navel of
>   heaven.
> God save a disorderly world, and the wild United Na-
>   tions! . . .
> And save us all: poets, Mongolians, landlords &
>   ladies, mad musicians.

No matter what the subject of her poem—reeling exuberance or tragic circumstance—we need to understand the willing engagement and pure love that fuels Kizer's politics. That we should discover this in a woman poet seems to me no accident. For women have long been the ones who empathize with others, who

"leap into otherness," in a culture where men assume positions of distance and control. If anyone can bring politics back to poetry, can transform the political so that it becomes personal, it is the woman poet whose subjectivity is already defined by otherness. In her poem **"The Death of the Public Servant,"**[15] which has all the trappings of a classical panegyric, Kizer transforms an unknown public figure into a personal friend. She speaks to this Canadian ambassador who committed suicide because of charges that he was a communist. She brings the political tragedy close to her, and close to us. "This is the day when good men die from windows," she says, and then addresses him directly— "Now you, in Cairo." Her public commentary echoes out beyond the personal:

> Once there was a place for gentle heroes.
> Now they are madmen who, scuttling down corridors,
> Eluding guards, climb lavatory walls
> And squeeze through air-vents to their liberation. . . .

But Kizer's public message is never far from her personal voice, the voice that makes it all meaningful for her, for us, for the rooms and worlds we live in far away from Cairo:

> I mark the fourth of April on this page,
> When the sun came up and glittered on the windows
> As you fell away from daylight into heaven:
> The muck of Cairo, and a world silenced forever.
> A poet, to whom no one cruel or imposing listens,
> Disdained by senates, whispers to your dust;
> Though you escape from words, whom words pursued,
> Take these to your shade: of rage, of grief, of love.

The message is again one of love. Without that, there's no place for politics in poetry. There's no place for politics at all, unless we believe that all public actions take place in a world of suspicion, hatred, death. If the poet does not leap into the political, then she is doomed to the position of outsider, mocking and criticizing a world which poetry shuns.

Kizer does not do that. Sending **"Lines to Accompany Flowers for Eve,"**[16] a woman "who took heroin, then sleeping pills / and who lies in a New York hospital," Kizer now makes the personal political, forcing us to merge these two experiences which are both at the heart of this tragedy:

> But what has flung you here for salvaging
> From a city's dereliction, this New York?
> A world against whose finger-and-breath marked
>   windows
> These weak flares may be set.

The question is addressed to Eve, for we want to know why she took the drugs, the pills. But the question is also addressed to all of us, who make our marks on the same kind of windows, seek the same kinds of escape.

For we all need to answer such questions if we are ever to understand why. Just as surely as Kizer has entered this poem, we are all implicated in its politics. Closeness matters here in the poem, bringing us into the world of Cairo, New York—or a different New York where Kizer dreams of her friend Nicanor lost in Chile, and of her friend Barbara in Barcelona seeking the right revolution, the right solution. In **"October, 1973"**[17] this dream vaults Kizer into the world of the lost—where politics becomes so intermixed with the personal loss that she can only dream of telephone connections, revolutions, reunions. Kizer is there again, inside the poem, picking up the phone to hear the personal voice:

> "Dear Carolyn . . ." It *is* Nicanor!
> And the connection is broken, because when I wake up,
> in this white room, in this white silence,
>   in this backwater of silence
> on this Isla Blanca:
>   Nicanor, Nicanor,
> are you, too, silent under the earth,
>   Brother? Brother?

The political is not only personal, it is familial. And how can it be otherwise? Unless we see ourselves intimately related to these experiences, then the world will always remain at a distance from the self. Such a situation has not only been tragic for women—keeping them outside the realm of what "counts" as human events and history. It has been just as damaging for poetry itself—separating it from the whirl of social activity in which the lives of women and men take on meaning and value.

Since I have been arguing that Kizer's political aesthetics—her engagement with otherness and with others, her insistence on mixing together the personal and the social—is a feminist act, it only seems natural that the poem I consider crucial for an understanding of her feminist politics is **"Pro Femina."**[18] It is crucial in two ways: first, for the way in which parts one, two, and three unfold as a powerful social statement expressed in traditional poetic form; and second, for the way in which part four, "Fanny," merges the personal and political in recreating "one of the world's best-kept secrets"—the life of Fanny Osbourne Stevenson while she lived under the shadow of her husband.

There is something about the first three sections of **"Pro Femina"** that reminds me of the spirit and tone of **"Tying One On in Vienna."** Both poems are filled with wit and exuberance. Both contain powerful social commentary. And Kizer herself is so much a part of both of them. If Kizer can learn how to love the world and all its crazy empires in **"Tying One On in Vienna,"** then what she learns—and teaches us—in **"Pro Femina"** is that we can also love ourselves as women, "I mean real women, like *you* and like *me*." Using and at the same time abusing the form of traditional satires directed against women, instead of speaking about women from the privileged position of the male poet, she speaks directly to them and with them—"losing our lipsticks, you, me, / In ephemeral stockings, clutching our handbags and packages." Infused in this feminine world, Kizer doesn't scowl from without or within, but celebrates and forgives. This is a "large" love poem, a love poem in the best social sense.

Of course there's a healthy dose of anger in this poem, an awareness of the "millions / Of mutes for every Saint Joan or sainted Jane Austen, / Who, vague-eyed and acquiescent, worshiped God as a man," or of "Our masks, always in peril of smearing or cracking, / In need of continuous check in the mirror of silverware. . . ." But for all this, the "fate" of women—much like the mad world Kizer contemplates in Vienna—is exuberantly crazy. "We *are* hyenas. Yes, we admit it," Kizer boasts. And with that boast comes just the kind of vibrant engagement that allows us to celebrate rather than shun this feminine world. It is crazy to think that millions of women have worshiped God as a man. It is crazy that we "primp, preen, prink, pluck and prize" our flesh for men who cover their "chicken wrists or meek shoulders" with "a formal, hard-fibered assurance." Once we see ourselves as part of all this, instead of outside and distanced, then and only then can we become involved in the process of transformation. To be political is to be part of, engaged in, the world in motion:

> Give us a few decades
> Of grace, to encourage the fine art of acquiescence
> And we might save the race. Meanwhile, observe our
>   creative chaos,
> Flux, efflorescence—whatever you care to call it!

It is this sense of "creative chaos" and "flux" that is at the heart of Kizer's political engagement. Writing in the tradition of political satires on women, she makes women come alive in the politics of her poem. For all of Kizer's admiration of Juvenal and Pope, her poetry is decidedly different. They criticize from a distance, she celebrates from within. They shun the otherness of woman, she leaps into it. The chaos they condemn is feminine, the feminine chaos she praises "might save the race." Perhaps Kizer's finest accomplishment as a social poet is that she has redirected the energies of classical verse. Bucking the misogynist tradition, yet all the while embracing its wit and liveliness, she brings women to life in the poetic domain. No longer the object of description and figuration, women become subjects of action and change—subjects who can create.

How can women create if they are confined within the dynamics of objectification? "I've been fascinated for many years," Kizer says, "about what women who are the support or nourishment of fathers, brothers, husbands, sons, do. What do these women—Wordsworth's sister, Lizst's sister, Alice James, etc., you name it—what do they do with their creativity if they're terribly creative people, as Fanny Osbourne Stevenson was?"[19] Kizer claims that the poem **"Fanny,"** which she eventually attached to **"Pro Femina,"** was the central part of her collection *Yin.* "I worked on that poem for many years, and I know that it was the focus of that book, the linchpin. . . . Whenever I was pregnant, I always wanted to stay pregnant as long as possible because I enjoyed it. In a sense I think that's true with poems, with the big poem."[20] It is curious, and I think very meaningful, that Kizer should link the issues of women's creativity with her own pregnant engagement with the poem **"Fanny"**—and that both of these issues would finally be linked in **"Pro Femina."** For it seems to me that Kizer's concern with women's creativity— "our creative chaos, / Flux, efflorescence"—is exactly what defines her feminist politics. Pregnancy means transformation and birth. To write the story of Fanny Osbourne Stevenson as though the writing itself were a kind of pregnancy is to give birth to this woman and her creativity—to the woman herself and to the work she does. And this, I suggest, is intensely political.

"Pro Femina" ends not simply with the story of a woman, but the story of her creativity, her work. "The curious thing about English feminism," Kizer says, "the interesting thing is, where's the work? I think the class system and masculine dominance is still so prevalent that everybody's still under it. I can't think of any other reason. But it's interesting that in a country like Nicaragua, for example, Ortega's wife is one of the most widely read poets in the country—Rosario."[21] Kizer's remarks are very similar to those of Lillian Robinson who, in putting together a collection of literature by and about working women, found "that the modern literary tradition is remote from the meanings of work in human life, and that poetry is particularly alienated from it." Such observations force Robinson to the conclusion that "feminist poetry's emphasis on the inwardness of individuals distorts the movement's basic perception that 'the personal is political'. . . ."[22] True enough, the personal is political. And yet, as Robinson insists, the political is also personal—and this is especially so for women who suffer the effects of legislation and social policy on such matters as divorce, property rights, and abortion. To keep these issues out of poetry is to keep the world of politics safely distanced from the personal lives of the very women affected by politics.

Fanny Osbourne Stevenson worked continually in Samoa, but it is only the work and writing of her husband, Robert Louis Stevenson, that is remembered or even acknowledged as work. The subject here is Fanny's personal life, but the larger issue is political. It concerns no less than the systematic, historical suppression of what women do and how they create. What did Fanny do? Kizer tells us: "what she did was plant." Asked if "planting" could be regarded as a central image in her poetry, Kizer responds "Oh, absolutely! Of course it's an intensely feminine thing."[23] Allowing Fanny to speak her experience, Kizer gives voice to this suppression:

> Louis has called me a peasant. How I brooded!
> Confided it to you, diary, then crossed it out.
> Peasant because I delve in earth, the earth I won.
> Confiding my seed and root—I too a creator?

If this poem is a tribute to Fanny's creativity, it is a savage indictment of male achievements that constitute the stuff of history. "No one else works much," Fanny says, and then adds, "Of course, RLS is not idle; he is writing *A Footnote to History*: / How the great powers combine to carve up these islands." Fanny, too, is a part of this colonial carving, regarded as a "peasant" by her husband—"Though Louis says he finds the peasant class 'interesting.'"

Through the description of Fanny's planting—the catalogue of potatoes, artichokes, corn, peas, onions, mint root, mangoes, rhubarb, asparagus, coffee, melons, cacao, rubber, sunflower, massio, citron, vanilla, gum, peanuts, grenadilla, ylang-ylang, pineapple—we get a sense of a creation far richer than anything history could record. The contrast between woman's and man's domain is all too clear: "Louis writes to *The Times* / Of 'the foul colonial politics.' I send to New York for seeds. . . . Louis' own seed, / *David Balfour,* is growing. I wrote nothing / From June till the end of this year; too busy planting." The planting, it would seem, is a mixed blessing: at once the source and productivity of her creativity, it is also her prison—like wild tropical growth caging her in. Of her diary, she says, "I stopped writing this. Too hysterical with migraine. / Also, people find where I hide it, and strike things out."

It is only after Louis' death that Fanny can understand what her planting was all about—"an intensely feminine thing," as Kizer would say, but an experience that consumed her in the nourishment of her husband's work. "I will leave here," Fanny says,

> I will live like a gipsy
> In my wild, ragged clothes, until I am old, old.
> I will have pretty gardens wherever I am,
> But never breadfruit, custard apples, grenadillas,
>   cacao,
> Pineapple, ylang-ylang, citron, mango, cacao,
> Never again succumb to the fever of planting.

If planting is Fanny's life and work, the "fever of planting" is her fate as a woman whose work is devalued— despite its richness, its nourishment, its creative energy.

This is not Fanny Osbourne Stevenson's personal problem. This is a problem that twists and blocks the creativity of every woman whose labor is regarded as peasant's work. Fanny is "wild" and will "live like a gipsy." She joins the ranks of Kizer's crazy women, "hyenas," who are beginning to know what their hysteria is all about. It *is* crazy that the most fertile work in the world—the work of women and peasants, the work of pregnancy, planting, and birth—is the very work that has been dismissed and ignored.

Kizer doesn't stand outside Fanny's personal world. Nor does she stand outside its politics, safely taking a position pro or con. She puts herself inside it. She makes women's poetry "large"—large in the same way that women's lives are far bigger and richer than any description of their personal plight can convey. Not content to find her own poetic voice, she leaps into the experience of others, takes on the world through a sympathetic, sometimes angry, often joyous engagement. In her poem **"Singing Aloud,"**[24] she describes her giving way, as she grows older, to singing—in the open, in public. The animals join her, squirrels and rabbits and birds. Song enlarges the world.

> When I go to the zoo, the primates and I, in communion
> Hoot at each other, or signal with earthy gestures.
> We must move further out of town, we musical birds and animals
> Or they'll lock us up like the apes, and control us forever.

Song enlarges the world. And so does poetry. We can't keep it to ourselves, Kizer says, as a poet and a woman. She "can't get rid of the tempting tic of pentameter, / Of the urge to impose form on what I can't understand, / Or that which I have to transform because it's too grim as it is."

That urge to write and to transform—that is what makes Kizer's poetry creative, generous, political. In **"A Muse of Water,"**[25] she takes back water from the "Masters of Civilization" and returns it to women, to the "water-carriers of our young / Till waters burst, and white streams flow / Artesian, from the lifted breast." Transforming this maternal act into public manifesto, she urges women:

> Fasten the blouse, and mount the steps
> From the kitchen taps to Royal Barge,
> Assume the trident, don the crown. . . .

The message is as personal as childbirth, as political as the crown. "Rejoice," she tells us, "when a faint music rises / Out of a brackish clump of weeds." This music, flowing from women like water, enlarges the world. And Carolyn Kizer is the "large lady" singing this music.

Notes

1. *The Nearness of You,* pp. 64-65, 70; *Yin,* p. 37.

2. Barbato, p. 58.

3. *Mermaids,* p. 44.

4. *Yin,* reprinted in *Mermaids,* p. 101-102.

5. See Johnson, this volume, pp. 97, 120.

6. *Yin,* pp. 26-27.

7. *Midnight,* pp. 66-67.

8. Robinson, p. 262.

9. *Ibid.*

10. Kizer, "Alexander Pope: Clearing the Air Around a Giant," p. 22.

11. *The Nearness of You,* pp. 19-20.

12. Rigsbee, p. 135.

13. *Ibid.*

14. *The Ungrateful Garden,* reprinted in *The Nearness of You,* pp. 29-32.

15. *Ibid.,* pp. 23-24

16. *Midnight,* reprinted in *Mermaids,* pp. 36-37.

17. *Yin,* pp. 53-54.

18. Pts. I-III in *Knock Upon Silence,* pt. IV ("Fanny") in *Yin,* reprinted in *Mermaids,* pp. 41-51.

19. Rigsbee, p. 133.

20. *Ibid.*

21. *Ibid.*

22. Robinson, pp. 296, 301.

23. Rigsbee, p. 133.

24. *Midnight,* pp. 10-11.

25. *The Ungrateful Garden,* reprinted in *Mermaids,* pp. 104-105.

Texts Cited

Barbato, Joseph. "'Going Through Life with a Pencil': Carolyn Kizer." *Small Press,* 3 (November-December, 1985): pp. 54-58.

Johnson, Judith Emlyn. "Re/Membering the Goddess: Carolyn Kizer and the Poetics of Generosity" [in this volume].

Kizer, Carolyn. "Alexander Pope: Clearing the Air Around a Giant." *San Jose Mercury News* (August 17, 1986): pp. 21-23.

———. *Midnight Was My Cry,* (Garden City, New York: Doubleday & Company, 1971).

———. *Yin,* (Brockport, New York: BOA Editions, Ltd., 1984).

———. *Mermaids in the Basement,* (Port Townsend: Copper Canyon Press, 1984).

———. *The Nearness of You,* (Port Townsend: Copper Canyon Press, 1986).

Ozick, Cynthia. "The Moral Necessity of Metaphor: Rooting History in a Figure of Speech." *Harper's* 272 (May 1986): pp. 62-68.

Rigsbee, David and Steven Ford Brown. "Not Their History but Our Myth: An Interview with Carolyn Kizer." *An Answering Music: On the Poetry of Carolyn Kizer,* (David Rigsbee, ed. Boston: Ford-Brown & Company, 1990): pp. 126-147.

Robinson, Lillian S. "The Keen Eye. . . . Watching: Poetry and the Feminist Movement" in *Sex, Class, & Culture,* (New York: Methuen, 1978): pp. 254-309.

Judith Emlyn Johnson (essay date 2001)

SOURCE: Johnson, Judith Emlyn. "Re/Membering the Goddess: Carolyn Kizer and the Poetics of Generosity." In *Carolyn Kizer: Perspectives on Her Life and Work,* edited by Annie Finch, Johanna Keller, and Candace McClelland, pp. 97-125. Fort Lee, N.J.: CavanKerry Press, 2001.

[*In the following essay, Johnson praises Kizer for her pioneering work in an emerging style of feminist poetics associated with generosity.*]

Since the late 1960s I have been slowly feeling my way towards some definition or description of a poetics of generosity, to be to our apparent poetics of parsimony, as an economics of generosity might be to our present economics of scarcity. For this search, Carolyn Kizer has been both moon and polar star, both illumination and guide. In this essay I celebrate not only a prophetic feminist poet, but a leader and foremost exemplar of this newly reemergent poetics, a poetics which is, I shall argue, although not exclusively feminist, central to feminism.[1]

Carolyn Kizer said in 1971 of her own work, "I am a premature Women's Liberationist. I was writing poems on the subject ten years before it became fashionable."[2] She is also a fine crafter of traditional western poetic forms, of haiku, and of the more contemporary open forms. She is a translator, a satirist, a lyric poet, and, as founding editor of *Poetry Northwest* and as the first director of the Literature Program of the National Endowment for the Arts, has strongly influenced the course of contemporary American poetry. Here, without wishing to limit her to the feminism so strong in both the form and the substance of her work, I consider her primarily from the vantage point of my own feminist stance.

The first I knew of Carolyn,[3] some time in the late 1960s, she was the author of a volume of poetry suffused with energy and marked by precision, delicacy, and strength of lyrical feeling. This was a poet who addressed a wide range of cultural contexts and associations and who was willing to tackle great and difficult subjects and to write unfashionable poems. At a time, for example, when the elegantly savage style of Augustan satire had maybe reached its nadir, this poet wrote **"Pro Femina,"** which took the risk of talking about the condition of women long before that was an acceptable contemporary theme, and doing so in a style that for verve, wit, and polished outrage, not to say occasional venom, had not been heard since the satires of Pope. Both the lyricism and the wit, furthermore, struck me as those of a poet confident of her own powers and generous in her trust of her readers and of the poems themselves. This confidence made it unnecessary for her to hide behind either the careful construct of her irony or the pretense of a neuter voice, the first of which seemed obligatory for all poets who came of age in the 1950s and early 1960s, and the second obligatory for women writing at that time, as it had been for the generation that had preceded us.[4]

This forthrightly woman-centered voice and wholehearted commitment to the immediacy of the poem may have caused occasional misreadings of Carolyn's work. More often, however, reviewers made sensitive attempts to formulate accurate reactions to poems for which the feminist critical context and vocabulary either did not yet exist or were not yet widely understood. Hence one reviewer's courtly characterization of her as "Roman Matron and . . . Oriental Courtesan together."[5] Clearly it is possible, and even somewhat obvious, to read this as an unintentional put-down.[6] Such a reading fails to allow for the effect of characterizing an archetypal, a larger-than-life, a heroically mythic quality of the persona her poems construct. Yes, at times this persona speaks as matron, not simply as ordinary, everyday matron, but as legendary Matron, not housewife but incarnation of The Household, the archetypal character of Matron speaking with the weight of history and of generations of "the private lives of one-half of humanity."[7] At times she speaks as courtesan, not woman up for grabs but woman of erotic power and skill, who avowedly loves men, likes to court and please them, and who expects them to court and please her, too. At times she speaks as quintessential mother, as daughter, as wife (even somewhat balefully as ex-wife), and as friend. At times she speaks clearly and powerfully as citizen of the international community of poets, in the tone and with the authority of a poet who knows herself to have every right to first-class citizenship. And, in many of the poems, she speaks as Goddess, the role that can contain and engender all the other roles. This insistence on woman's centrality both in public and in personal contexts creates a vision of woman as herself a primary rather than a derivative incarnation of Blake's "human form divine," having, like Sir Thomas Browne, her own "peece of divinity in [her]."[8] Such a vision is central to the current feminist enterprise.

Contemporary feminist poetry has been equally concerned with asserting the woman poet's right to write,[9] with reclaiming a lost or obscured tradition of women's poetry, with appropriating and subverting those aspects of the predominantly male literary discourses we find useful,[10] and with negating, de/fusing or re/fusing those aspects hostile to us. Thus, the feminist enterprise has not been restricted to expressions of rage and opposition to oppressive social arrangements. It has certainly included such expressions, but the rage has, in my reading, been secondary, the means to an end and not the end itself. The major enterprise has not been destructive but creative: the task of recapturing, rebuilding, retrieving, remembering, or inventing, if necessary, women's dismembered or disremembered knowledge of empowerment; the knowledge of being self and not other, author and not mirror, subject and not object. This many-sided project has caused us to propose radical re/vision of the art we inherited: of the forms, the techniques, the conventions, the nature of the language, the themes, the inherited canon itself, the very idea of a canon, the classifications within that canon, the divisions of poets or themes into major and minor, and the position of poet in relation to audience, to poem, and to herself. Although not a radical feminist in the sense of advocating feminist separatism or radical disruptions of conventional biological or linguistic arrangements, Carolyn Kizer has dealt with the basic questions at the root of feminist poetry: how to use the tradition that we learned to love and then found either hated or ignored us, how to re/claim the lost Goddess of poetry and of civilization for our own. In exploring these questions her work proposes extremely useful integrations of western and eastern traditions and re/creates a new, woman-centered vision of woman as myth and archetype of her own subjectivity.

As many recent feminist literary critics have pointed out, male poets take for granted their entitlement to a tradition and a locus for the subjectivity of their voices as female poets cannot.[11] The woman poet, typically, even aside from institutionalized denigration, has experienced literary tradition as the presence of an assumed male speaker and as her own absence from a speaking role. She has experienced not only her own absence but the weight of absence as it is incarnated in

an entire obliterated tradition of voices that do not speak, voices unnamed, unrecorded. This is absence doubled and redoubled, absence squared and cubed, absence that cannot teach her the forms of her own subjectivity. When she looks for a voice to model her own voice upon, she finds nothing but male subjectivity, male presentation of woman in the role of object. Lacking such models, the woman poet, a dismembered female Orpheus, tries to build her voice out of fragments.[12] Some of these are fragments of the male tradition she can use or alter to her purpose. Some are fragments of the image of herself she constructs from piecing together the less gynophobic aspects of traditional male visions of Woman. Some are the threads of connection that she weaves with her female contemporaries. As many critics have noted, these connections must be woven anew each generation, because the woman writers of each generation have more often than not been obscured or obliterated from the literary canon before their female successors could make use of them.[13]

Anthropologically and historically, this task of reconstructing a tradition of female empowerment has sometimes involved assuming a prehistoric matriarchy. Theologically it has involved the hypotheses that Goddess worship preceded God worship, that the powers and experiences historically attributed to male deities were prehistorically attributed to female ones, and that female potentiality, immanence, or becoming is as potent as male actuality, presence, or being.[14] Poetically, it has involved using any or all of these approaches to construct a voice that can embody women's power as subject.

Carolyn's process of constructing an empowered voice began, as did that of her contemporary, Adrienne Rich, with an obvious lyric gift, technical "mastery,"[15] and the ability to internalize the voice of the part of the tradition admired in what we might call the Age of Auden. It also began with quiet efforts to subvert this voice. The title poem of *The Ungrateful Garden* (1961),[16] recycles the myth of Midas and the Golden Touch in impeccably neat quatrains. The stanzas are heavily marked with antithesis, repetition of vowel sounds, and alliteration: "*hugg*ed his *a*gues, *lo*ved his *lu*st, / But *d*amned to *h*ell the out-of-*d*oors . . ." (emphases mine). One might note as Audenesque not only the control of parallel structures, alliteration, and consonance in the first of these two lines, but the shift from the ornately rhetorical to the colloquial in the second. Similar constructions are at work in stanza three ("Th*is gif*t, he'*d* thought, would *gil*d his joys, / *Sil*t up the w*a*ters of his grie*f*; / H*is law*ns a *wild*erness of noise, / The heavy c*lang* of *leaf* on *leaf*."). And the tone of the final stanza ("Dazzled with wounds, he limped away / To climb into his golden bed. / Roses, roses can betray. / 'Nature is evil,' Midas said.") may also carry an echo of Auden or of Eliot, although the particular quality of ironic fury is characteristic of one stream in Carolyn's work, and the use of classical mythology to embody personal concerns derives as much from Louise Bogan as from Auden.

This is, in all its strength, a literary poem.[17] The literary poem has been marked by the use of traditional, frequently classical themes and traditional rhetoric. Modernist poets[18] have typically used the literary poem semiparodically, in tones varying from gentle irony to the most savage contempt, whether for the lexicon itself or for the contemporary culture they could assault by means of it: "Death and the Raven drift above, / and Sweeney guards the horned gate. . . ." or "I'll love you till the ocean / Is folded and hung up to dry."[19] For the woman poet bathed in this lexicon however, there is an additional usefulness in a parodic approach, quite aside from the Modernist agenda. Part of her task is, after all, to define herself as woman and not as neuter or pseudo-man, to separate herself from the tradition which already simultaneously defines her as separate and requires her to obliterate her identity in order to end or at least ameliorate the separation. Here, therefore, the classical themes and rhetoric are used to challenge traditional sets of positions: nature against artifact, flesh against spirit, generosity against greed, "outside" against "within." Thus, the argument moves from Midas's own masochistic cherishing of his "streaming sores" to his final, traditional, and drastically erroneous attribution of his inward and outward condition to the evil in Nature rather than to an evil in himself.

Similarly, in **"Streets of Pearl and Gold"**[20] the poet gives us the context with an epigraph from Andrew Marvell's "Upon Appleton House," one of the great poems on order and the nature of civilization. She then creates a detailed counterpoint to Marvell's imagery in order to characterize the progress to chaos and heartlessness in our world, and the process by which we use art to restore order ("Not rats or roaches in the wainscot / Nor the old staled odors of man's functioning / But that they were chalice of our history. . . ." and "Paint out the day and you will keep the time. . . .").

Midas' final recourse to his "golden bed" for comfort, even while insisting that "Nature is evil," reads as a flight back to a Nature (and possibly also to Woman as Nature's presence in that bed) he himself has made hostile. The ending of **"Streets of Pearl and Gold,"** with its elaborate play on the Cross and "X of loss" ends in similar comment on the tradition's recourse to woman as nature's surrogate: "So stamp your canvas with the X of loss, / Art mutilated, stained with abuse and rage. / But mark it also as the cross of love / Who hold this woman-flesh, touch it alive, / As I try to keep us, here upon the page." The speaker, however, here involves herself in the effort to fix—both hold and repair—the world in art "here upon the page." And careful readers may note that a reversal of roles has taken place. The male artist/lover who, throughout the poem, has been creating "art mutilated . . . with abuse and rage," flees, like Midas fleeing to his bed, to the "woman-flesh" outside his construction, hoping to "touch it alive." But meanwhile the speaker, attempting her own construction, must "try to keep us, here upon the page." Among its other appropriations and reversals, then, this later poem shows the subjectivity and enterprise of art moving away from its traditional male centers to the female artist, the poet herself.

Not only the treatments of theme in these two poems but their elaborate formal structures challenge the very formal structures they use. The more elaborate the formal rhetoric of each poem, the more it turns on itself, forcing the reader to question what can be attributed to nature, and what to art in the poem itself. Within the poem's formally constricted style and the weight of allusion to prior tradition, after all, be-ringed with artifice, as far from natural spontaneity as it can get, what side is the poet herself on, given that she has chosen to write within such strictures?

It seems clear to me that in these early, formally constricted poems, the poet is following more than the Modernist agenda of contrasting this century's sordid reality with classical myths of transcendence. Although they do so subtly, courteously, gently, even lovingly, these poems of the 1960s deal, without in fact making a big deal of it, in prophetically feminist ways, with the literary tradition and its formal constrictions as specifically male constructions. The use, for example, of formal antithesis in **"The Ungrateful Garden"** constitutes a challenge to Midas's, and by extension to the tradition's, uses of antithetical modes to structure reality. By parodying and exaggerating these constructions the poem both appropriates and subverts them. That is to say, it lays a claim to a mode that, rather than allowing to exclude it, it will ultimately reject. Midas's misplaced insistence, central to our entire literary tradition, on seeing the world in terms of oppositions rather than of complementarities, of Nature versus Art, rather than of Nature embodied in Art, or of Art in Nature, were later to become central targets of contemporary feminist challenge. The poem implies that the actual evil in Midas consists of both his construction of mutually exclusive opposites and his projection of his own nature outward onto Nature herself. This study of Midas's love of gold and of artifice, his anality (in Freudian terms), and his love-hate relationship with his own earthly body (his sores), and this refusal to endorse his projection of his own inner evil outward onto nature are thus prophetic of later feminist analyses of precisely these cultural constructions and constrictions. And the poem, while making its own uses of a classical theme and technique, wryly challenges and subverts both.

In this light, we can see that even the elegance of the poem's sound constructions subverts traditional uses of such elegance. For example, in stanza three of **"The Ungrateful Garden"** ("Th*is gift*, he'*d* thought, would *gild* his joys, / *Sil*t up the *w*aters of his grie*f;* / H*is* la*w*ns a *wild*erness of noise, / The hea*vy* c*l*ang of *leaf* on *leaf*."), we can see how much of the consonance and alliteration are in fact analyzed, deconstructed or disassembled rather than exactly repeated configurations. "*Gift*" is taken apart, with its vowel going one way to be recycled in "*gild*," and "*silt*," "Wilderness," and its consonants reappearing separated by a different although related vowel in "grie*f*." The "wa" from "waters" is reversed and combined with the "I" from "gild" and "silt" to make "lawns," then reconstituted in its original order but with the vowel from "gild" and "silt" to make "wilderness." I leave it to the reader to follow similar permutations of other sounds I've italicized. The effect of this is to make us hear how the tight artifice that Midas wants to freeze into those very same metallic constructions that will constrict him is constantly slipping, changing, and recycling, even as Nature itself recycles, the sounds the poem's rigid structure pretends to hold changeless. An appearance of rigidity is being used to disassemble, to dismember, to dis/remember rigidity, and thereby to comment ironically not merely on the content of male-centered classical mythology but on the rhetorical forms by which that mythology perpetuates itself. This use of analyzed or disassembled patterns of sound and language is likewise consonant with one vein of feminist subversion of language and thought patterns, deriving originally from Dickinson, and now tending, in one group, toward radical language dislocations and non-linear structures.[21]

One of the ways to subvert or contravene a constricting tradition, of course, is to go outside it, to seek models in another country or another age. The traditions of Chinese and Japanese poetry have been particularly fertile in Carolyn's construction of her voice as both poet and woman poet, partly for their avoidance of abstraction and bombast and for their grounding in the intimate, the daily, and the personal, and partly because they provide her with a method to "refuse rather than cultivate formal distance."[22] **"Singing Aloud"**[23] is both an example of and a comment on this process. It begins with fine informality: "We all have our faults. Mine is trying to write poems. / New scenery, someone I like, anything sets me off! / I hear my own voice going on, like a god or an oracle, / That cello-tone, intuition. That bell-note of wisdom." The tone is both exuberant and self-mocking; the speaker does not entirely regret her ability to let "anything set her off." But already we hear a note of discomfort with the shaping force of the tradition: she does not feel entirely comfortable with the sound of her voice, in the traditional tones of poetry, "going on like a god or an oracle." She has tried and failed, she confesses, to "get rid of the tempting tic of pentameter, / Of the urge to impose a form on what I don't understand. . . ." In contrast to these traditional

vices, age, she suggests, begins to bring her some new virtues. She flees to the actual. Instead of reading her new poems to friends, she shakes branches over herself in the park "so I am covered with petals, / Each petal a metaphor." The image and mood here seem drawn very directly from the vocabularies both of Chinese and of Japanese poetry, particularly in the concreteness with which obliteration of the speaker's former romantic-egotistical stance is suggested by her being covered with petals. Along with the ego of the romantic tradition, she also abandons her dignity. She sings aloud and cavorts, indulging in "innocent folly," accompanied by "squirrels and rabbits . . . with inaudible voices." At the very last, the speaker exuberantly heads for the zoo, where "the primates and I, in communion, / Hoot at each other, or signal with earthy gestures."

This poem is on one level a comment on the poet's own earlier work, on another a successful attempt to remake her own voice, as Yeats did when he turned away from the successes of his earlier style to forge what he called "a poem maybe as cold / and passionate as the dawn."[24] The lush rhetoric, the tight elegance of the earlier meters is gone. The dominant metaphor is not dignified and high-toned, as is even the most sordid element in **"Streets of Pearl and Gold,"** but exuberantly low. Instead of poetic communication pouring from cups of gold it bounds about at the zoo with poet and primate making "earthy gestures," which may well include a few gross ones. The resulting lyric communication is "hooting" instead of speech or song. This new poetic voice is still that of a satirist and a student of myth and history. It is, however, an irreverent and informal voice, sophisticated and confident enough of its control to laugh at its great subjects—history, poetry, and love—and yet serious enough to go beyond laughter. And the elements of the transformation, what one might think of as the theoretical stations of the journey, are the ones contemporary women poets have consistently chosen: forsaking the seductive high tone and rhetoric of the inherited tradition; getting back down to earth and away from abstraction; reclaiming the personal, the trivial, the intimate, the daily, the "primate" concerns as the proper concerns of poetry; exploring not our difference from other animals but our connection with them.[25] In addition, the speaker's characterization of her speech as a "hoot" anticipates and thus defuses possible male denigration of her poetry in precisely these terms.

This corrective orientalization of Carolyn's technique reached its most extended treatment in the long poem **"A Month in Summer."**[26] The poem, which incorporates attitudes, techniques, and fragments or imitations of Japanese poetry, combines the forms of the prose journal and the haiku. This allows the poet one solution of that traditional problem of the long poem: how to achieve moments of higher intensity and yet vary the tone so that the whole poem is not on the same plane; or conversely, how to allow for transitional passages, or passages of varied intensity, without letting the more relaxed sections seem thin by contrast. In this poem about the slow disintegration of a love affair, the haiku work to focus, to draw together, to construct figures for moments of feeling or intellectual perception, while the journal provides the field, the setting, the ground, from which the polished figures stand out. The net effect of this prose/poem alternation, paradoxically, is to devalorize the self-consciously "poetic" moments and to re-valorize the dailiness of life by restoring the moments of perception to their place in the suspended and equal flow of consciousness. This approach, in other words, simultaneously domesticates the archetypal themes of love and loss and heightens or glamorizes the everyday context in which they take place.

For example, the disarming section "Nineteenth Day" wryly admits to "Inertia. / One of the profound consolations in reading the works of Japanese men of letters is their frank acknowledgement of neurotic sloth." Promptly, however, it converts this admission to a statement of pain: "Or the overwhelming impulse, when faced with hurt or conflict, to stay in bed under the covers!" The poet intends us to understand that the speaker is "faced with hurt or conflict" at that moment and is reacting to it like a Japanese man of letters. Because of our cultural assumptions about male and female behavior in the face of grief, this confession both valorizes, by masculinizing, the speaker's behavior and feminizes that of the Japanese men. It also, of course, makes the speaker, however isolated during her separation from her departing lover, part of an international community of letters. By the "Twenty-First Day," the speaker, pursuing gender questions further, asks, "Is it suffering which defeminizes?" She follows this with a haiku in which she describes herself as "neutered and wistful."

The question she has put to herself and us is not merely rhetorical. The suggestion that, far from her suffering making the poet more womanly, it makes her less so, is a radical reversal of the convention that women must suffer to be beautiful.[27] Furthermore, this question of what is woman, what is feminine, has been a constant theme in Carolyn's work, repeated both in traditional and open form poems. **"The Dying Goddess," "The Copulating Gods," "Columns and Caryatids," "A Muse of Water,"** and many more, are not mere exercises in classicism and not merely re/visions of the classical tradition, as discussed above. They are all, in their various aspects, examinations of woman as Figure: as muse, goddess, archetype, idea, object, subject in the process of becoming subject; woman in relation both to the view the traditional, male-dominated culture has taken of her and to the view she must take of herself. Many of these examinations of the Idea of Woman, or

of her Idea of Her Self, take place in poems on friendship, for example, the poems to or about Jan. Many take place in mother-daughter poems, involving both the poet's own mother and her daughters. The most elaborate of these is the long prose memoir of the poet's mother in *Yin,* significantly entitled **"A Muse."** In the remainder of this essay, however, I am going to limit my discussion to the theme of Woman as Goddess, because it both appropriates and challenges the traditional male reifications of Woman.

In a poem that looks at the subject vs. object theme, **"The Copulating Gods,"**[28] the poet writes of what she seems to treat as a human rather than a specifically female predicament. With her typical combination of humor and gravity, she begins by establishing both the speaker and her lover as archetypal and immortal: "Brushing back the curls from your famous brow, / Lingering over the prominent temple vein, / . . . I ponder how self-consciously / the gods must fornicate." Here the speaker allows her male companion to share the traditional female predicament of being the object of another's contemplation. That is, of course, true of him in his roles as God and as public figure, possibly famous man or well-known fellow poet, possibly target of admiring groupies at poetry readings. It is also true of him in his role as her lover and the object of her thought, doubly true because in this poem, he rather than she is enacting the role of object: she is writing this poem about him rather than he about her.

Yet, significantly, the man to whom this poem is addressed is not in fact object rather than subject, or not more object or less subject than the speaker herself. Not "You" or "I" but "*We* were their religion before they were born. . . ." Although this objectification of lovers or of famous personalities is presented by the deliberate choice of conventional, gendered language as a male activity, both man and woman are equally its victims: "*Men* continue to invent *our* histories, / Deny *our equal* pleasure in *each other.* Clubfoot, nymphomaniac, they dub *us.* . . ." (emphases mine). The poem ends with the speaker's provisional acceptance of this objectification, this subtraction of their positions as subject of their own story: "I know we are not our history but their myth." She then invites her lover to transcend their condition in the traditional way in her arms: "Come, kiss! / Come, swoon again, we who invented dying / And the whole alchemy of resurrection. / They will concoct a scripture explaining this." The lovers swoon into their state as public myth rather than private history; they accept their condition as object or icon, with the concomitant death of their subjectivity. But, by the alchemy of resurrection, the speaker suggests, they will nonetheless be reborn into a transcendent and mythic selfhood as scriptural figures, perhaps as poets, although this mythic selfhood is presented, mockingly, as "concoct[ed]."

It is possible to read this poem as a treatment of the loss of self involved in public life, with particular reference to such figures as The Poet. Clearly, the speaker considers both herself and her companion in those roles. It may also be read as a dialogue with poems like Donne's "The Canonization," in which, likewise, the lovers die out of ego and personhood to be resurrected as exemplars of holy love: "We can dy by it, if not live by love. / And if unfit for tombes and hearse / Our legend bee, it will be fit for verse." Read this way, the poem enters the long tradition of poetry on love, transcendence, and the death of the ego, and on lovers as supra-personal icons for the world, who "did all to you epitomize, / Countries, Townes, Courts. . . . / A Patterne of your love!"[29] Donne's "patterne" becomes Carolyn's "scriptures."[30] And the word "scriptures" itself, it seems to me, is used here precisely to invoke for the reader the intermingling of sacred and profane love characteristics of this strand in the tradition. In both kinds of love, the dying of the ego is never an unmixed blessing. In neither is the transformation from subject of one's own life to object of another's contemplation painless.

The poem has, however, an additional richness if read as arising out of the female speaker's specific experience of a specific female condition: "not our history but their myth." Here the speaker generously insists on using that experience as a bridge to her male companion. Rather than exclude him as the adversarial instrument of her reification, the negation of her subjectivity, she includes him as fellow victim in the reification and fellow icon in her later transcendence.

The inclusive stance and complex tone, both amused and serious, both passionate and ironic, in which wit and irony do not diminish the speaker's commitment to the emotion of the poem, look forward to the more developed aesthetic stance of later work. This is a poetry which refuses to be limited to a single, traditional stance, whether of ironic commentator outside of and distrustful of passion, or of impassioned participant. By taking both positions, it simultaneously engages, subverts, and revises the traditions involving the lover as subject/object. It also, in this and in the range of readings it opens to us, exemplifies the poetics of generosity. This poetics neither assumes any scarcity of means for focusing the poem and holding the reader, nor insists on any need for an exorbitant and tight-lipped economy in the construction or field of reference of the poem. Instead this aesthetic assumes an infinity of plentitude in art, as well as the reader's generous willingness to trust the poem and experience it in all its scope, its simultaneity of effects.[31] As a feminist technique it both embodies and goes beyond the less inclusive stances of irony, of looking askance, "looking out of the corners of one's eyes," at the tradition and at women's objectification within it.[32]

A more direct examination of the reification of the Goddess as muse is the subject of "A Muse of Water."[33] The poem is addressed, like "The Copulating Gods," to a male listener. Since women have traditionally played the role of muse to male artists, the listener may be a male poet. The poem may perhaps be seen as the poet's *apologia pro sua vita* for daring to be artist rather than or as well as muse. The poem begins by establishing the speaker as a poet without any nurturing presence but her own. She has, however, a sense of her connection to other women: it is not I but "*We* who must act as handmaidens / To our own goddess . . ." as we strive to "glimpse the muse." Already the traditional terms are being reversed; women poets are seeking our own muse rather than accepting roles as muses to men. True, our search for selfhood makes us "Narcissists by necessity," the traditional condemnation of women, that men, no mean narcissists themselves, have traditionally offered as indictment, without the examination of the historical context.[34]

Probably, in the context of the poem, the speaker assumes that her male listener endorses this traditional indictment of women's narcissism. She therefore presents for his contemplation women in the varied roles of muses, guardians, nurturers, or even governors and "Virgin Queens," not subjects of our own reveries but objects in men's constructs, in the damaged world "your civilizing lusts have made." The lusts are civilizing both because they create the civilization we now have and because the need to civilize as Man has experienced it indeed comes from lust rather than love for the natural world. The speaker compares this process to the "Water Music . . . / That men bestow on Virgin Queens" and that the Queen commands to be played on the royal barge. The Queen, we are surely intended to remember, has not composed this music herself, but invokes the work of a male composer, which he "bestows" on her. In this commanded music, therefore, her purported power is not her own but a reflection of his.

By the end of the poem, however, the water music the speaker seeks and commands her male contemporaries to hear is no longer a male creation on a constructed barge. Spontaneously, it "rises / Out of a brackish clump of weeds, / Out of the marsh at ocean-side, / Out of the oil-stained river's gleam." It is no longer the music of men's art but the music of women's nature. Indeed, from the speaker's tone, man seems singularly and perhaps restfully absent: "Discover the deserted beach / Where ghosts of curlews safely wade: / Here the warm shallows lave your feet / Like tawny hair of magdalens." The beach is deserted, and thus, the ghosts of curlews may "safely wade," free from fear of predators. This safety is, on one level, ironic and illusory. That the curlews are ghosts implies both that they have already fallen prey to some violation of whatever natural safety they might have expected, and that it is the memory of a state of safety rather than its actuality the poet has summoned.

In the references to religious ritual and to redemption, the shallows that "lave your feet / Like tawny hair of magdalens," both enact and reverse the conventional roles of the Magdalen and the Messiah. This magdalen, significantly non-hierarchal and lower-case, whose name is by this be/heading and de/capitalization demoted from the name of a person to the name of a condition of servitude, lacks, as the first stanza pointed out, her own handmaiden. The concept of a handmaiden for the magdalen is itself a paradoxical reversal of the norm. Forced by this lack to act as "handmaiden to [her] own goddess," the magdalen laves the feet of a male figure now occupying, precisely because she laves his feet, the traditional role of the messiah. The implications of this act are multiple. Because she is "forced to act as handmaiden to her own goddess," and now acts as handmaiden to him, he is "forced to act" as goddess to her. He, through these language constructions, performs the role of muse and inspiration for her while also co-opting the goddess herself in that role. Furthermore, it is her service to him that creates, signifies, and validates his function as messiah.

Thus, indeed she performs woman's traditional service to man, echo and magdalen, both nurturing and validating him, at enormous cost to herself. Her nurturance allows him to replace the Goddess as her muse and establishes him as her messiah. But her nurturance, although it does lead to the traditional death, both does and does not lead to the traditional resurrection and redemption: "Here, if you care, and lie full-length, / Is water deep enough to drown." Is this tender promise one of erotic joy, regretful prophecy, or ironic threat? The tone indeed promises him both a crucifixion and a redemption. The drowning of the self may function, for the male poet, both as death and as baptism into renewed innocence. It is also, in this poem, the death by water of the male ego and of its central place in the female literary tradition. This redeemer, in fact, does not redeem but is redeemed by the magdalen's service to him. Furthermore, this ending is both a return to the original myth of Narcissus with which, we may remember, the poem started, and a reversal of men's traditional use of it against women. In this simultaneous baptism and crucifixion, it is he, not she, who enacts the conventional role of Narcissus, drowned in his reflection of and on himself. Nor is she relegated to the conventional position as his echo; as in **"The Copulating Gods,"** the subject/object relationship is changed by the fact that she, not he, has written the poem and has taken for herself, however gently, the power of the gaze and voice.

The satires and the mixed satire-and-narrative-lyric poems adopt the aesthetic of generosity from a different

stance. Like **"The Copulating Gods,"** they function both by including the speaker in the injustices she attacks and by including the enactors of injustice as fellow victims. Thus, **"Pro Femina,"** in its first three sections, forsakes the leisurely, worldly, meditative tone of gentle laughter at and participation in history's errors to adopt a more concentrated tone of satirical exasperation. The first stanza of section one raises again the question of what is womanly or unwomanly, while establishing the speaker in a women's tradition (Sappho) and in opposition to a men's tradition (Juvenal): "From Sappho to myself, consider the fate of women. / How unwomanly to discuss it! Like a noose or an albatross necktie. / The clinical sobriquet hangs us: cod-piece coveters . . . / Juvenal set us apart in denouncing our vices / Which had grown, in part, from having been set apart. . . ." But the poem itself does not adopt and emulate the Sapphic lyric, as, for example, H. D.'s poems did. Instead it appropriates and subverts Juvenalian satire. It does this by accepting the traditional Juvenalian indictments of women and then turning them into both an indictment of men for making them and a boast of women's heroic qualities in enduring them. After disarming the conventional criticisms by doing them much better than they are usually done, the poet can then go on to state her case as a woman and a free intellect. But even this strategy allows due place to the conventional attacks. For example, the line "While men have politely debated free will, we have howled for it . . . ," accepts the conventional role of woman as howling termagant, then throws it back in man's face as being forced on her by his denial of her free will. And the poem, while rushing energetically through its indictment of sexism and its concurrent promise to revalue women's "well known / Respect for life because it hurts so much to come out with it," nonetheless includes its male readers in its promise of charity and redemption. "Relax, and let us absorb you," the speaker soothingly offers, comparing herself in passing to the entire nation of China as it absorbed successive waves of barbarian invaders, and slyly aware of how little she is flattering him by his part in the comparison. "You can learn temperance in a more temperate climate." Like the redemption through drowning of the ego in the previous poem, redemption through absorption is probably pretty far from what the male listener had in mind. It may also be what, traditionally, we should assume him to have feared most from women. To offer it to him, then, whether as promise or threat, is, again, both to accept and to claim as a right a female power men have traditionally seen as evil.

This is a satire about history and culture, and about what gynophobia does to history and culture. As a satire about history and culture it is in the mainstream of literary tradition. What transforms and transfuses it is its doubleness, the inclusiveness of the poet's vision, as well as its immediate and energetic tone of personal presence. We can see the effects of close study of Pope, Juvenal, and other satirists. The use of such epithets as "indigo intellectuals" or such linkages as "toast and Teasdales," for example, is unkind enough to remind us of similar constructions in *The Dunciad.* The poet, however, unlike Pope, does not adopt the third person, nor the externalized and noncomplicitous tone of exasperated cultural arbiter outside the evils under attack.[35] Instead, she is right there in the center of her poem, not isolated from but a member of the community of women, involved in both the attack and the defense. She refuses to be contained by the prior satiric structures of abstraction or generalization. Resisting stricture and constriction at every turn, inextricably a part of everything she attacks, she rushes off to "get back to the meeting" in every sense. The meeting of roles traditionally separated in satire is precisely what she insists on enacting.

"Fanny,"[36] the fourth section of **"Pro Femina,"** written much later than the other three, engages in an even more drastic subversion of the traditional framework of satire. Reversing the normal structure of Greek dramatic presentations, three tragedies followed by a satyr play, **"Pro Femina,"** in the version printed in *Mermaids in the Basement,* presents the final days of Robert Louis Stevenson in Samoa, from the point of view of Fanny Stevenson, as she nurses him, "[keeps] him alive for eight more years," and frantically tries to counter his impending death with the nurturing force of her gardening. His illness thus becomes the object of her heroic struggle against death rather than the subject of his own tragedy. The use of the first person narrator in this, as in other works discussed above, keeps the subjectivity and selfhood of the speaker firmly before us at all times. The poem both does and does not present Fanny in the conventional female role of nurturer of male genius. We see comparatively little of Louis's struggle for life, or even of Fanny nurturing him. Instead we see her buying seeds, planting them, cultivating the stubborn earth, interacting with "the Reverend Mr. Claxton," with "Mr. Carruthers, the island solicitor," and with "a young thief" who brings her pineapple plants. Louis belittles her efforts, telling her she has "the soul of a peasant," but she continues to assert her own subjectivity as the heroic figure of her own mythology. Although she is far from uncaring towards Louis and functions toward him as earth mother and Goddess, she seems not to do so exclusively for his benefit. The poem's relentless piling up of seasonal and gardening detail creates a displacement of Louis from the center to the periphery both of our consciousness and of Fanny's, so that what this earth mother nurtures is the earth itself rather than any one of earth's children. In fact, the displacement of Louis from the center of her attention represents, on one level, her flight from her role as his nurse and nurturer. This section of **"Pro Femina,"** therefore, while presenting woman in her traditional role as nurturer,

removes man from the center of her attention, removes her from the House, and places her firmly outside domesticity and inside the performance of History. Fanny and not Louis seems to enact the traditional colonizing role in Samoa. While Louis "writes to *The Times* / Of 'the foul colonial politics.' I send to New York for seeds." He complains; she acts. It is her action that brings European seedlings to the island, and it is she who in the end bears the historical responsibility for seedtime and harvest, the Biblical symbols of earth's continuation and renewal.

A similar commingling of venom, outrage, and participation in responsibility for injustice occupies the center of **"Running Away from Home."**[37] This poem begins as a catalog of the small town repressions and hypocrisies of such characters as: "Dear Phil . . . / Whose car had a detachable steering wheel; / He'd hand it to his scared, protesting girl, / Saying, 'Okay, *you* drive'— steering with his knees. . . ." and "Dear Sally . . . / [who] Knelt on cold stone, with chilblained knees, to pray, / 'Dear God, Dear Christ! Don't let him go All The Way!'" Much of this indictment is focused specifically on the role of repressive religious practices in distorting society, "Spooked by plaster madonnas, switched by sadistic nuns, / Given sex instruction by dirty old men in skirts." But this poem is not merely a hilarious letter of attack on Dear Phil, Dear Sally, the nuns, and the dirty old men, or even the rest of its dramatis personae: the "crazed rednecks" from Idaho, the "mad orphans" from Oregon, the "insane salesman" from Spokane, and the "people from Montana [who] are put away." The speaker, furious with grief at the constricted and wrecked lives she contemplates, involves herself, acknowledging fiercely and complicitously, "I know your secrets." Furthermore, the moments of fiery wit are set in a framework of tag ends of literary quotation torn from a literature and a culture in disarray. The mad poets and artists the speaker claims to know flounder both ridiculously and tragically, "in my craft and sullen ebbing," in a wild conjunction of Kraft-Ebbing's science and Dylan Thomas's "craft and sullen art." Like drunken, suicidal, creatively inept, and sexually tormented Shelleys, they "squint at the light / Staining the white radiance of O'Leary's cell." Compassion is tragically missing. All this savagery is funny, but it is also dead serious: "After Spokane," the poet snarls, after having established herself as having been at one point part of the Spokane scene (and possibly, by implication, one of Spokane's "insane salesmen"), "what horrors lurk in Hell?"

With savage indignation this poem holds up a civilization and its cultural and literary constructs for us to laugh and weep at. But the poet is not merely attacking derivative or meaningless art, cramped imaginations, and science wildly out of control—"Mondrian O'Leary" and the "seven-humped, mutated radioactive Chinook salmon," that "stain the white radiance of O'Leary's brain." She is lamenting the wreckage of lives. The people she shows us are cracking up both in cars and in madhouses. Their fates become not merely the casualties but the amusements of a society that has itself gone mad. The culminating vision of the inmates of "mad Medical Lake" who become the source of laughter for weekend visitors is both horrifyingly grotesque and surreal, but it is not unreal. And the poem itself acknowledges by implication that it has been doing exactly what it accuses the visitors of doing. It too, after all, has toured the hospital with us, ridiculing "Mrs. Hurley, somebody's grandma, / Eating gravy with her bare hands." Our bitter laughter throughout the poem is the sign not only of the speaker's but of the readers' participation in the mockery. The visitors' reaction of "Just animals, Rosetta. / She's not *your* mother. Don't let it get you" is implicitly that of both readers and poet, until the moment when the poem has implicated us so strongly that we see it for what it is and reject it. The vision of "mad Medical Lake" and its "white ruin of muscular men / Twisting bars like Gargantua" is not very far as image from that earlier, more tolerant vision of the poet and the primate hooting earthily at each other in the zoo. The total stance and vision of the two poems, however, are worlds apart. **"Singing Aloud"** is a sunny view of the poetic ego deflating itself that ends with a moment of ludicrous but friendly communication with nature. **"Running Away from Home"** is a denunciation of a mad world that ends with poet's and reader's anguished complicity in the madness.

A similar transformation of focus and expectations, with a similar reciprocity of poet and subject, occurs in **"Food of Love."**[38] At first we read the poem as a gleefully violent, half-joking, half-serious treatment of the mutual destructiveness of lovers. The speaker first devours her lover, then turns him into a Sahara, then swells to fill his entire field of vision until he has no choice but to let her absorb and renew him, gigantic desert though he may be. The central trope is the conventional figure of speech—"I love you so much I could eat you up"—here transformed into a literal situation and then developed, as the epigraph warns, "to the bitter end" as if it were an actual event. The original cliché is expanded to "I'm going to murder you with love. . . . / I'm going to hug you, bone by bone, / Till you're dead all over. / Then I will dine on your delectable marrow." This transformation and elaboration of the traditional play in love poetry on "dying," already seen in **"The Copulating Gods,"** places the poem, once again, in a revisionary women's tradition.

In this version of love's mythic death and rebirth, the woman again refuses her traditional role of passive victim. Instead, she accepts, indeed triumphantly boasts of, her role as castrator: "with my female blade I'll carve my name / In your most aspiring palm / Before I chop it down." In the field of sexual combat, she is marking him as her property, her trophy, rather than the other way around. Biologically, this trope refers to her role as depletor of his sexual energy. Socially it refers to her sexual assertiveness, which seems to her lover like a phallic claim ("my female blade"). Culturally it refers to the charged epithets customarily applied to female sexual assertiveness. This assertiveness, as men have traditionally feared, ends by demolishing the lover. He becomes the speaker's "host, my final supper on earth." The word "host" here is richly charged: the lover is the host who entertains the speaker at a dinner party at which he is the meal, the host who allows a parasite to occupy and devour his body. He is, obviously, also the Host as agent of sacrifice and redemption, clearly spelled out in the reference to the Last Supper. The poem, in what looks at first like an atmosphere of exuberant joking, of earthy hyperbole, has ended by revising from a woman's point of view, not only the conventional attitude towards the physiology of sex, but its relationship to that whole deep and concealed process by which, as Wilde put it, "each man kills the thing he loves."[39] And by calling the lover the "Host" the speaker makes him as much the agent of her rebirth and redemption as she is of his when she resurrects him. The relationship, in spite of its apparent inequity, is at least reciprocal, although men might complain, as women do of similar inequitable but reciprocal relationships, that such reciprocity is not much comfort when survival is at issue. It should, furthermore, be pointed out that the interaction remains as double-edged at the end as it was at the beginning. The lover, after his resurrection, will "begin to die again." While on one level this is a promise of blisses yet to come, on another it sounds like a threat.

The culminating poem in this body of work is **"Semele Recycled."**[40] Here the dis/membered and dis/remembered Goddess speaks again in that energetically human voice we have come to recognize. This time she has been dismembered, not, as in the recorded form of the myth, by her lover's divine radiance, but more realistically, by his departure.[41] "When you left me I was all broken up" or "I went to pieces" or "I fell apart," ordinary figures of speech, becomes, "After you left me forever, / I was broken into pieces, / and all the pieces flung into the river." The speaker narrates this process of dismemberment not through one but through two cycles of rebirth. In the first cycle, every individual part, instead of decaying, is put to some temporary and specialized use by the people who find it, exactly the way a woman may serve as a wife in one context; a waitress, secretary, or a model in another; a mother in still another; a lover or a goddess, a teacher, a housekeeper, an oracle, in still others. She is no longer a whole human being. She has been broken down and objectified by the uses others find for her.

These partial uses are painful to her. Some of them exploit or violate her sexuality; they leave a "trail of blood . . . [that] attracted the carp and eels, and the river turtle / easily landed, dazed by my tasty red." They are also not entirely harmless to the users. The goddess's eyes, when placed in a diadem by a prospective bride, scare away the bridegroom. This image may suggest both his terror at the thought of his bride's awakening subjectivity (her "I's"), and his willingness to let her learn anything from prior women's experience, particularly since she has overdone things a bit and become "all eyes," perhaps through too much insistence on her Self. Her being "all eyes," however, also suggests the bride's untutored effort at connection, however inappropriate and posthumous, with other women. Even in trying to don the consciousness of another woman she has become a thing, a partial creature and not a person, like the speaker, whose eyes she has put on and whose consciousness she has thus partially adopted. Finally the image suggests the awful effect her encircled innocence, lack of eyes, ego, and connection with other women, has on both bride and groom. Similarly, the speaker's genitals, when they are tossed into a trough, have a "radiance" that so maddens the sows that they trample each other in their haste to escape. This may suggest both woman's terror at the consequences of her own sexuality and our traditional socially conditioned failures at solidarity with each other. The sows, in their "greed," see the goddess's sexual parts as a threat rather than as a sign of what they and she have in common. In a bitter acknowledgment of the denial of women's sexuality, the speaker tells us that eventually these parts were discarded upon a compost heap. And, although in this poem the speaker, unlike the earlier speaker in **"Singing Aloud,"** accepts her traditional poetic role as divine oracle, she has no sense of intent. "The breeze wound through my mouth and empty sockets / so my lungs would sigh and my dead tongue mutter," but she herself says nothing. Her sockets are empty; no self resides there. Without her consciousness and her wholeness, she is an empty oracle and her words have no meaning. She is not a whole person but only a bundle of functions and symptoms. Reduced to her complaints, she becomes no more than an occasion for seers, whether medical, psychiatric, or sociological, to find "occupation, interpreting [her] sighs." These, we are probably meant to remember, they interpret as signs of *her* illness, neurosis, or deficiency, as they try to solve their self-created riddle: what do women want.

All this false, uncomfortable, and partial rebirth, this fragmented and exploitative use of the Goddess, is undone when the one worshipper who loves her as a complete being instead of as a scattering of functions recalls her. He remembers her, having previously forgotten and left her; he also literally recalls both the Goddess and her sexual subjectivity: "but then your great voice rang out under the skies / my name! and all those private names / for the parts and places that had loved you best." Her "parts and places" love him; he is the object, she the subject, however reduced to her functions. Yet, she allows him his traditional subjectivity, too: he does the calling and the naming. At this summons, the Goddess's parts, in a typically farcical frenzy, scurry madly from "their various places and helpful functions" to reassemble themselves, including the sexual parts reclaimed from the compost. Pursued by the people who still want to use her varied services, the Goddess and her lover "fell in a heap on the compost heap / and all our loving parts made love at once." So in this second, true rebirth, the Goddess's parts return to their proper uses, their uses as elements of her subjective and purposeful life rather than as objects of other people's consumption. The people who have, like the readers of love's scriptures in **"The Copulating Gods,"** watched this copulation (including, of course, those of us who have just been reading the poem), disperse and go "decently about their [our] business."

This second rebirth, however, is not an unmixed blessing, even though it takes place through and for love, and restores the Goddess to her personhood. First of all, a "recycling" is not the same as a "rebirth." It implies an inescapable use by others rather than the Goddess's centrality to and use of her own life. In this narrative, it is "passion" that has suffered the "birth and rebirth and decay." The Goddess has simply been "recycled." And even though lover and Goddess are purified, having "bathed in the river" and become "sweet and wholesome again," even though they "worship each other in whispers" and in perfect reciprocity, this rebirth is not permanent but cyclical. Not the Goddess as a whole person, but, once again, "The inner parts remember fermenting hay, / the comfortable odor of dung, the animal incense, / and passion, its bloody labor, / its birth and rebirth and decay."

This rich and complex poem can be read as a feminist allegory of the loss and rebirth of women's subjectivity and sexuality, of the fragility of our relationship with man, and of the recovery of a woman-centered mythic imagery for the notions of death and redemption. It can also be read as an allegory of women's recovery of our own dis/membered histories and mythologies. It can be read, like **"Food of Love,"** as a double-edged celebration of the cycles of love and of nature. It can be read as a very great love poem, unique in its lack of complaint, rage, or indictment of the lover (whose periodic departures relegate the Goddess to the compost heap), honest in its speaker's confession that the loss of love feels like the loss of self, and beautifully direct in its celebration of the physicality of love and of woman's own physicality ("my sacred slit / Which loved you best of all").

On one level, this poem reverses the many myths about the tearing apart and rebirth of a male God or mythic figure, whether Orpheus, Dionysus, or Osiris, and of the Goddess who mourns him, reassembles him, or recycles him. Read thus, it joins contemporary revisionist feminism in proclaiming that the men got it all wrong, that not the man but the woman gets torn apart and used in bits and pieces and recycled: it is Woman whose constant death and rebirth in the world's endless uses of us makes the corn grow and the rain fall; it is not the falling down and the rising up of the phallus but our own hard work and loss of ourselves that has kept things going. Yet to reduce the poem to this and to this alone would falsify it. This Goddess is still in love with men, however aware she may be of their misuse of her and of their hostility to her power. She cannot imagine herself without them, however double-edged her love and theirs may be.

This richness, this generosity of effect and of intent, extends into the management of the poem, the effortless transitions from high seriousness to the mordantly witty hyperbole with which the central metaphor of woman's fragmentation is worked out. The accuracy of the allusion to the "trail of blood" of the speaker's sexual flow gives way to the speaker's bitterly boastful description of her "tasty red" and its usefulness for entrapping turtles (entrapment, of course, being one of the conventional charges against both women and goddesses). This leads to the wild farce of such moments as those when the bridegroom runs away from the girl who has become "all eyes." The grim vision of the Goddess's head, speaking "oracles" with the breeze winding through the mouth and empty eyes, the wind-filled lungs sighing and the dead tongue muttering, create simultaneously a tragic and a comic view of the poet's role. From such moments of grim humor or of farce the poem shifts, with no cracking apart at the seams, however much the speaker herself has cracked apart, to the joyful lyricism of such stanzas as those in which the Goddess gets herself together again (another logically literal and comic reenactment of a figure of speech). Even when farcical, the poem is serious, and its highest lyrical moments are likely to shift to farce, then to burlesque stunts, then to expansive transcendence and quiet peacefulness in the final stanza. Nothing is forgotten or undone in this resolution. The Goddess has gotten herself together, but she has kept the terrifying vision of her death and her decay. Clearly the aesthetic behind this poem is not an aesthetic of economy, of parsimony, of the single perception or the unified creation of an effect. This poem works, not out of scarcity, but out of "amplitude [and] awe,"[42] the precise qualities Dickinson complained leaked out of women's lives when they surrendered their autonomy to men. Although every prop, every image, every tonal shift in the poem contributes to a kind of economy by finding a use for itself, like the various parts of the Goddess employed in their "helpful functions," there is more than a minimum, and more than enough, more than contemporary parsimony could find a use for. The poem radiates, glories, triumphs in and through its massive abundance.

Traditionally, our culture has represented life as a series of mutually exclusive polarities: man vs. woman, life vs. death, love vs. hate, destruction vs. creation, enough vs. too much, tragedy vs. farce. The newly emerging woman's tradition exemplified in the work of such poets as Carolyn Kizer and Muriel Rukeyser, without in any way denying or refusing these polarities, re/fuses them, absorbs them, redefines them, reassembles them. In the aesthetic of generosity, life's furious contradictions become neither harmony nor counterpoint, but something for which we have not yet made an accurate technical term. They are not harmony because harmony has heretofore implied subordination of an accompaniment to a melodic line or of the notes played in the construction, deprived of equal autonomy, to the harmonic whole. They are not counterpoint because the strains work not "against" but in balanced junction "with" each other. So it is with the balance of meanings, tones, and methods in Carolyn's poems. One does not negate another. A new approach does not imply the abandonment of a former approach. Early poems and methods stand in happy juxtaposition to more recent ones, the poet's earlier stances recycled throughout the recent collections. Changes of voice are not rejections but true changes of mind, new aspects, costumes, expansions. They do not "counter" or undercut each other as the irony characteristic of this century's poetry in our decades has typically worked to counter or undercut emotion. Instead they balance, reciprocate, mirror, and fuse with each other, allowing each poem the full force of its multiplicity of energies, even when we cannot imagine such materials co-existing in such balance, such full and whole-heartedly enthusiastic correlationship. These are the fragments of woman-centered tradition re/membered and restored to power and wholeness.

The poetics of generosity commits itself to the passions of the poem rather than retreating from them. It trusts the poem's energy. Above all, it trusts the reader, knowing her to be no adversary but a co-creator of the poem's force and as generous in her welcome of the poem as the poet herself. A poetics built on generosity is a poetics built on inclusiveness, on force of feeling and intellect, on trust, and on the will to change and to offer change. This generosity we find in Whitman's democratic fervor, in Dickinson's constantly shifting meanings and in her equation of poetry with possibility, in Hopkins' exuberant orgies of language, in Rukeyser's splendid inclusiveness of the political, the erotic, and the transcendental. In this part of the century we find it in Carolyn Kizer's Goddesses, lovers, muses, and large-spirited voice.

Notes

1. To accept plentitude rather than parsimony, emotion rather than unearned irony functioning as denial of emotion, has, of course, been the task of poets as different from each other as Allen Ginsberg and Adrienne Rich. Feminists may need, however, to formulate the aesthetic as a basic condition of our creativity.

2. Carolyn Kizer, in jacket copy for *Midnight Was My Cry.*

3. Since 1970 I have been a friend of Carolyn Kizer's. I am not going to create a false appearance of academic objectivity by referring to her by her surname. The value often placed on objectivity is counter-productive. Objectivity unmediated by personal involvement falsifies as much as unacknowledged or dishonest subjectivity. In any event, an involvement, a stake in something, whether or not it is acknowledged, always exists. One of my assets as a reader of Carolyn's poetry is precisely my lack of objectivity, my personal involvement, my immersion in her work. I suspect it would be hard to find a poet of her and my generation who had somehow managed to avoid knowing and having a personal involvement with her. Poets become friends much of the time because we feel affinities for each other's work. Those affinities lead to informed readings and then to close friendships.

4. On this subject, Juhasz in *Naked and Fiery Forms* is particularly useful. See her discussion of Marianne Moore, for example.

5. Richard Howard, in a review in *Tri-Quarterly,* reprinted on the dust jacket of *Midnight Was My Cry.*

6. Would this writer, or any, have characterized, for example, a poet like James Dickey as "Southern redneck and all-purpose stud?" If he had attempted such an irrelevancy, would he or Dickey's publisher have felt that the presence of such a comment on a book jacket might tend to sell books?

7. Carolyn Kizer, "Pro Femina: Part Three," *Mermaids in the Basement,* p. 44.

8. William Blake, "The Divine Image"; Sir Thomas Browne, *Religio Medici.*

9. Gilbert and Gubar in their opening chapter, Rich in "When We Dead Awaken," and Juhasz, in her chapter on "The Double Bind of the Woman Writer," have laid the groundwork for all future discussions of this situation.

10. Ostriker. The title of her book tells the story; the book documents it.

11. Juhasz, Gilbert and Gubar, and Moers all deal with this.

12. I have dealt in more detail with the woman poet's use of the Orpheus myth as a focus for her efforts to form a public voice for herself in a paper on Muriel Rukeyser's Orpheus poems at the MLA, and in two papers on the artist Ethel Schwabacher delivered at conferences on Schwabacher's art and journals. My papers examine two related questions: how does the woman artist deal with her fragmentation, and how does her work change when her vision of her public voice changes from identification with Orpheus to identification with Eurydice.

13. Moers, Juhasz, Gilbert & Gubar.

14. Daly.

15. I use this term here deliberately to carry overtones of purposeful control of male traditional poetic forms.

16. *The Ungrateful Garden,* 1961, reprinted in *The Nearness of You,* 1986, p. 18.

17. I don't use the word literary pejoratively but for characterization.

18. Perhaps eccentrically, I refuse to use the term "Modern" to describe a movement of formative poems which were written in the first half of this century, and all the major figures of which are dead. T. S. Eliot et al. are no longer modern in the strict sense. We who write now in this modern time are the moderns, whether or not we follow aesthetics that were modern in earlier decades. "Modernist" is not accurate either, but at least it suggests an attitude associated with a movement in art, rather than asserting a contemporary quality to work no longer contemporary in its origins. Until somebody coins a term that accurately describes the Modernist movement's approach to poetics, I use this term *faute de mieux.*

19. T. S. Eliot, "Sweeney Among the Nightingales"; W. H. Auden, "As I Went Out One Evening." To both poems, I would guess, Carolyn's poem owes something both in tone and in rhetoric, as, in its general use of classical themes, it owes much to Louise Bogan.

20. *The Ungrateful Garden,* reprinted in *The Nearness of You,* p. 53.

21. Women's challenges in this century to the nature of traditional language and linearity were prefigured in early, radical linguistic dismantling by such figures as Gertrude Stein. The current generation of women involved in radical linguistic experimentation includes Susan Howe, Kathleen

Fraser, and Lyn Hejinian. This is also an important part of the agenda of an influential group of male poets, but arising out of a different experience of and relationship to language.

22. Ostriker, commenting on Kizer and other poets, p. 12.

23. *Midnight Was My Cry,* p. 10.

24. William Butler Yeats, "The Fisherman."

25. This is not to suggest that contemporary male poets have not also used some of the same correctives; the entire range of so-called "Post-Modern" poetry in this country has been nourished by them. I am suggesting, however, that this correction or shaking of the prior tradition has a particular and specific force, different from its force in men's work, when women do it, because the need is greater in degree and different in kind. To some extent we might argue that the men writing recently may have consciously or unconsciously adopted or converged with parts of the feminist literary agenda.

26. *Knock Upon Silence,* 1965, reprinted in *Mermaids in the Basement,* p. 20.

27. See, for example, Yeats, "Adam's Curse," which, when it deals with Eve's curse, equates suffering with labor, and has the "beautiful wild woman" lament that she "must labor to be beautiful."

28. Reprinted from earlier volumes in *Yin,* p. 20.

29. John Donne, "The Canonization."

30. For a feminist point of view on the drawbacks of this transcendence, some readers may find it useful to read the sections on Clarissa as "exemplar of her sex" and on Sir Willoughby Patterne in Brownstein.

31. Rich, in "When We Dead Awaken," written in 1971, spoke of a "deep fatalistic pessimism" in the poetry of her male contemporaries. At about the time her essay was first published, I attended a literary conference at which a distinguished poet and friend of mine spoke of his resistance to poems that attempted to "overwhelm" him, giving such examples as Hopkins' *The Wreck of the Deutschland,* Thompson's "The Hound of Heaven," and almost anything by Dylan Thomas and Whitman. I thought of Donne's "Batter my heart, three-person'd God. . . ." and wondered why this successful man's ego seemed so fragile that he had to protect it carefully not only from the great and generous force of language, but from everything he perceived as most sacred. The pessimism Rich noticed and the self-protective shrinking back from emotion I found so pitiful seemed to me directly

related. Subsequent thought has convinced me that the irony and complexity that, at their most exuberant in the early part of the century, embodied generosity by welcoming all the intertwined passion and range of possible interactions of a text, have somehow become confused, in a dominant aesthetic of our generation, with a fear to commit oneself to passion or range for fear of being judged sentimental. But, if sentimentality is unearned emotion, then this petty and self-protective pseudo-irony, this withholding of justified passion, is the sentimentality of our age. This recognition may have something to do with why June Jordan entitled a recent book of poems *Passion.*

Muriel Rukeyser, in *The Life of Poetry* (New York: William Morrow & Company, 1974), first published in 1949, analyzes a deeper level of the fear of poetry, and grounds this fear less in a fear of sentimentality than in a desperate fear of emotion and of giving due force to the unconscious life within us. If she is right, then the poetics of parsimony is based upon a basic fear of surrender, a fear of poetry itself.

32. Sigrid Weigl, "Double Focus," in *Feminist Aesthetics,* p. 80.

33. From an earlier volume, reprinted as the closing poem of *Mermaids in the Basement,* p. 104.

34. A useful discussion of this dilemma as it involves visual art and the problem of the gaze may be found in Elizabeth Lenk, "The Self-Reflecting Woman," *Feminist Aesthetics,* p. 51.

35. Pope does use the first person in *The Dunciad,* but in formalized invocations to the muse or similar set pieces. He presents his narrative and his envenomed character sketches as if they were somehow externalized statements of fact rather than personal expressions of rage. Only the language (what an only!) shows him to be personally involved.

36. Parts one, two, and three of "Pro Femina" first appeared in book form in *Knock Upon Silence.* In *Yin,* those three parts are not reprinted, and "Fanny" makes her first appearance in book form as a poem in a section entitled "Fanny and the Affections." In *Mermaids in the Basement,* published the same year as *Yin,* "Pro Femina" has four sections, labeled "Part One," "Part Two," "Part Three," and "Part Four: Fanny." This, most probably, represents the poet's most recent organization of this material, and the one most useful to me to examine in the context of my argument. There is, of course, no reason why the poet should not continue to present her work in multiple ver-

sions, arranged as the context dictates. That constant changing and rejuxtaposition of the lineup from one volume to the next, is, in fact, a basic organizing principle of her work, and signifies a denial of linearity and a refusal of the later self to reject any of the earlier self's modes. [Editors' note: "Pro Femina" was published with a new fifth section as a chapbook in 2000, and the full text is included in *Cool, Calm, & Collected: Poems 1960-2000,* published in 2001.]

37. *Yin,* p. 29.

38. *Yin,* p. 28.

39. Oscar Wilde, "The Ballad of Reading Gaol."

40. *Yin,* p. 13.

41. In the traditional form of the myth, Semele was a human woman Zeus adopted human form to court. She asked him to appear to her in his divine glory. When he consented to do so, his blaze of heat consumed her to ashes. Before she was totally consumed, Zeus tore her unborn infant, Dionysus, out of her body, and concealed the baby in his thigh until the proper moment for birth (another of those mythical reversals of the actual biology of birth, like the birth of Athene from Zeus's head, Eve from Adam's rib, and the practice of couvade). When Dionysus himself became a god, he restored Semele to life and promoted her to Goddesshood. Semele, in her traditional form, is thus a highly ambiguous Goddess for this poet to re/member. This recycling of the myth, in the form she gives it, constitutes a revisionary proposition that the recorded form of the myth is an error, and an assertion that Semele was not a victim of her own vanity but another form of the resurrected deity of renewal.

42. Emily Dickinson, #732 "She rose to his requirement."

Texts Cited

I. Carolyn Kizer's poems have been reprinted in later collections and in varying arrangements as earlier ones went out of print. My notes will cite the earliest book publication and the most recent, and give page numbers for the most recent.

Kizer, Carolyn. *Knock Upon Silence.* Seattle: University of Washington Press, 1968.

———. *Mermaids in the Basement: Poems for Women.* Port Townsend, Washington: Copper Canyon Press, 1984.

———. *The Nearness of You.* Port Townsend, Washington: Copper Canyon Press, 1986.

———. *The Ungrateful Garden.* Bloomington: Indiana University Press, 1961.

———. *Yin.* Brockport, New York: BOA Editions, 1984.

II. When I quote directly from widely available examples of our inherited literary tradition, I will cite author and poem title, but not book, edition, or page number.

III. Texts I find indispensable for the consideration of feminist literary theory as it relates to this essay are:

Brownstein, Rachel. *Becoming a Heroine: Reading About Women in Novels.* New York: The Viking Press, 1982.

Daly, Mary. *Beyond God the Father: Toward a Philosophy of Women's Liberation.* Boston: Beacon Press, 1973.

Ecker, Gisela, ed. *Feminist Aesthetics.* Boston: Beacon Press, 1986.

Gilbert, Sandra and Gubar, Susan. *The Madwoman in the Attic: The Woman Writer and the Nineteenth Century Literary Imagination.* New Haven: Yale University Press, 1979.

Juhasz, Susanne. *Naked and Fiery Forms: Modern American Poetry by Women, a New Tradition.* New York: Harper and Row, 1976.

Moers, Ellen. *Literary Women.* Garden City, New York: Doubleday & Company, 1977.

Ostriker, Alicia Suskin. *Stealing the Language: An Emergence of Women's Poetry in America.* Boston: Beacon Press, 1986.

Rich, Adrienne. *On Lies, Secrets, and Silence: Selected Prose 1966-1978.* New York: W. W. Norton & Company, 1979.

Rukeyser, Muriel. *The Life of Poetry.* New York: William Morrow & Company, 1974.

FURTHER READING

Criticism

Cheung, Dominic. "Carolyn Kizer and Her Chinese Imitations." *New Asia Academic Bulletin* 1 (1978): 77-84.

> Examines the sources for Kizer's imitations of Arthur Waley's early-twentieth-century translations of Chinese poetry.

Malkoff, Karl. "Kizer, Carolyn." *Crowell's Handbook of Contemporary American Poetry,* pp. 162-64. New York: Thomas Y. Crowell Company, 1973.

> Brief entry on Kizer's work, highlighting the poems "The Great Blue Heron" and "Pro Femina."

Montague, John. "Kizer, Carolyn (Ashley)." In *Contemporary Poets,* edited by James Vinson and D. L. Kirkpatrick, pp. 458-59. New York: St. Martin's Press, 1985.

> Brief discussion of Kizer's life and career, with commentary on "A Muse of Water" and "A Widow in Wintertime."

Skelton, Robin. Introduction to *Five Poets of the Pacific Northwest,* edited by Robin Skelton, pp. xv-xxv. Seattle, Wash.: University of Washington Press, 1964.

> Brief discussion of "Pro Femina," "The Great Blue Heron," and "Summer Near the River."

Additional coverage of Kizer's life and career is contained in the following sources published by Thomson Gale: *Contemporary Authors,* **Vols. 65-68;** *Contemporary Authors Autobiography Series,* **Vol. 5;** *Contemporary Authors New Revision Series,* **Vols. 24, 70, and 134;** *Contemporary Literary Criticism,* **Vols. 15, 39, and 80;** *Contemporary Poets,* **Ed. 7;** *Contemporary Women Poets; Dictionary of Literary Biography,* **Vols. 5 and 169;** *DISCovering Authors Modules***: Poets;** *Encyclopedia of World Literature in the 20th Century,* **Ed. 3;** *Literature Resource Center; Major 20th-Century Writers,* **Ed. 2;** *Major 21st-Century Writers* **(e-book), 2005;** *Poetry for Students,* **Vol. 18; and** *Twayne's Companion to Contemporary Literature in English,* **Ed. 1:1.**

George Seferis
1900-1971

(Pseudonym of Giorgos Stylianou Seferiádes) Greek poet, essayist, novelist, and critic.

INTRODUCTION

The first Greek writer to win the Nobel Prize in Literature, Seferis was a celebrated poet who combined elements of ancient Greek mythology and modern historical events in his writing.

BIOGRAPHICAL INFORMATION

Seferis was born Giorgos Stylianou Seferiádes in Smyrna, Turkey, on March 13, 1900, into a prosperous family. He was the eldest son of Dhespo Tenekidhis, the daughter of a wealthy landowner, and Stélios P. Seferiádes, a lawyer who demanded that his son study law and pursue a career in diplomacy, despite Seferis's desire to study literature and write poetry. He had one sister, Ioánna, who would later serve as her brother's biographer. In 1914, at the beginning of World War I, the family left Smyrna for Athens, where Seferis attended the First Classical Gymnasium, graduating in 1917. A year later the family moved to Paris, where his father established a law practice and Seferis began studying at the Sorbonne. He received his law degree in 1924. From there he went to London, intent on learning English, which would help him in his later career as a diplomat. In 1922 the Turks had retaken Smyrna and the city's Greek community was completely destroyed; although Seferis and his family were not in the city at the time, they lost a substantial part of their fortune. The fact that he could never return to the city of his birth contributed to Seferis's lifelong feeling of exile and to his decision to enter the diplomatic corps. In 1931 he began serving in the Greek consulate in London, where he stayed for three years. There he discovered the poetry of T. S. Eliot, a poet with whom he is often compared. Over the years he served in a variety of diplomatic positions in Athens, Albania, South Africa, Egypt, Palestine, and Italy. In 1941 Seferis married Marie Zannos; the couple had no children. In the 1950s he served as minister to Syria, Iraq, and Jordan, and as ambassador to Lebanon, the United Nations, and Great Britain. Seferis retired from government service in 1962 and devoted himself to his writ-

ing; a year later he became the first Greek to win the Nobel Prize for Literature. Seferis died on September 20, 1971, in Athens.

MAJOR WORKS

Seferis's first volume of verse, *Strophe* or *Turning Point,* produced in 1931, includes the highly-acclaimed "Erotikos Logos," based on the seventeenth-century Greek epic romance *Erotokritos.* In 1932, he published *I Sterna* (*The Cistern*), a collection of verse that expresses the pain and suffering caused by the ravages of time, not only to individuals, but to entire populations as well. In 1935 he published a collection of twenty-four poems entitled *Mythistorema* (*Mythical Story*), his attempt to connect the mythology of the ancient Greeks to modern historical events. It is often considered his masterpiece. *Gymnopaidia* appeared a year later, containing the individual poems "Santorini" and "Mycenae." *The Book of Exercises* (1940), containing a sequence of poems grouped under the name "Strates Thalassinos," features a modern Odysseus as the narrator.

On the eve of World War II, Seferis wrote his most critically-acclaimed individual poem, "The King of Asine" referencing Homer's *Odyssey* and commenting on the allusive quality of heroism and past glory in the face of almost certain annihilation. Seferis's longest poem is "The Thrush" (1947), divided into three parts and apparently inspired by the wreck of a small boat, the *Thrush,* in the waters off the island of Poros, which the poet visited in 1946. The work draws heavily on the story of Odysseus and features Elpenor, one of Homer's minor characters that Seferis used repeatedly in his verse. "The Thrush" is considered one of the poet's most autobiographical poems.

CRITICAL RECEPTION

Most critics have emphasized the importance of Greek myth, history, and tradition in Seferis's poetry. Andonis Decavalles finds that Seferis was "deeply involved, deeply familiar with and painfully aware of the crushing weight of a cultural inheritance." At the same time, however, he was well acquainted with the languages and cultures of several European and Middle-Eastern countries, and according to Decavalles, was "well-versed in the prevalent modern literary trends abroad." The result was a poetry that looked both to the past and to the future. G. Georgiades Arnakis also notes the importance of Greece in Seferis's work, contending that the poet's many years abroad left him with a profound nostalgia for his country and a sense of tragedy for the sufferings of the Greek people. Nonetheless, reports Arnakis, "his sense of the tragic clearly transcends the bounds of Greece and embraces the whole world." The tragic element in Seferis's poetry is also highlighted by Anthony N. Zahareas, who contends that "no Greek poet is more intensely aware of the abyss between a great past and a dismal present than George Seferis." For Roderick Beaton, Seferis's interest in the past can be simply explained by his distaste for the present. However, Beaton insists that Seferis was not "merely seeking refuge from the modern world among the myths and statues of the past," since his poetry is filled with allusions to modern Greek history and politics.

Most of Seferis's poems relate the past to the present, or more specifically, ancient Greek myth to modern Greek history; Edmund Keeley and Philip Sherrard, who have translated many of Seferis's poems into English, have commented on the skill with which the poet combined these elements. According to Keeley and Sherrard, "before he attempts to carry the reader to the level of myth, he earns his sympathy and belief by convincingly representing the present reality sustaining

his myth—and it is a contemporary, Greek reality always." Dimitris Dimiroulis suggests that Seferis's success as a poet can be traced in part to his ability in "carefully grafting some concepts and practices of European modernism onto the legacy of Greek tradition."

Kostas Myrsiades has studied Seferis's use of the figure of Odysseus and concluded that the poet transformed Homer's character "into an exile, a fatherly sea captain, a pilgrim" who is unable to return to his homeland, thus making him "a pathetic sufferer who bends to his fate, unlike his ancestor." Homeric elements also play an important role in "The Thrush," whose narrator is again a modern-day Odysseus. At the same time, however, the poem has strong connections to the poet's life, according to Eva P. Lester and Dmitri Kyriazis, who note "the interplay of verses with the thoughts and dream imagery from the poet's diary." Seferis's perception of himself as a permanent exile from his homeland shows up in much of his work, such as the poems of *Logbook I* (1940), written on the eve of World War II. C. Capri-Karka believes the title refers to a "narrator who feels unsettled, living in a place where he does not belong, on a temporary basis." Capri-Karka finds a similar theme in "The Return of the Exile" from *Mythistorema,* whose narrator can never return to his homeland because it has been destroyed.

Seferis's poetry is known for the complexity of its imagery and symbolism. Lester and Kyriazis call him "a visual poet dominated by powerful images carrying crucial ideas and determining the flow of the poem." Decavalles sees him as "not an easy poet" and describes Seferis's use of a volcanic island as "a symbol for lost lands, lost worlds, lost hopes." Rachel Hadas discusses Seferis's use of sea imagery, observing the poet often focuses on the negative qualities of the sea rather than its beauties, and the depths of the sea rather than its surface. In addition, according to Hadas, he almost always employs classical references to the sea from Homer and Aeschylus, and as a result his poetry avoids monotony and offers a fresh perspective on an apparently timeless natural element.

PRINCIPAL WORKS

Poetry

Strophe [*Turning Point*] 1931
I Sterna [*The Cistern*] 1932
Mythistorema [*Mythical Story*] 1935
Gymnopaidia 1936

The Book of Exercises 1940
Logbook I 1940
Logbook II 1944
Collected Poems, 1924-1946 1950
Logbook III 1955
Poems 1960
Collected Poems, 1924-1955 1967
Tria Krilka Poema [*Three Secret Poems*] 1967
The Book of Exercises II 1976

Other Major Works

A Dialogue on Poetry (essay) 1939
Dokimes (criticism) 1944
*On the Greek Style: Selected Essays in Poetry and Hel-
   lenism* [translated by Warner and T. Frangopoulos]
   (essays) 1966
Days of 1945-1951: A Poet's Journal (journal) 1974
Six Nights on the Acropolis (novel) 1974
Meres 20 Aprili 1951-4 Avgoustou 1956 (journal) 1986

CRITICISM

Andonis Decavalles (essay date spring 1964)

SOURCE: Decavalles, Andonis. "The Nobel Prize for
Literature: Ghiorgos Seferis." *Charioteer,* no. 6 (spring
1964): 7-12.

[*In the following essay, Decavalles discusses the literary accomplishments that earned Seferis the Nobel
Prize.*]

The Charioteer rejoices over the news that the Nobel
Prize for Literature this year was awarded to Ghiorgos
Seferis, the greatest of the living Greek poets, "for his
eminent lyrical writings inspired by a deep feeling for
the Hellenic world of culture." His poetry carries on the
"classical heritage" with "its unique thought and style
and its beauty of language." The Swedish Academy
significantly added that this prize was a "tribute to the
Greece of today whose wealth of literature has perhaps
waited too long for its laurel wreath."

Those who admire Seferis and who love Greece must
have been deeply touched by the poet's dignified humility when he learned the news. "Greece," he said, "could
have won this prize earlier, with other poets." Tears
were in his eyes when he expressed the wish that the
congratulations of the Academy should go "to Greece."

In little more than eighty years after her Phoenix-like
rebirth from the ashes, from four hundred years of dark
slavery, Greece could stand proud of her literary accomplishments. The poetry of Kostes Palamas and Con-
stantinos Cavafis, and later of Anghelos Sikelianos and
Nikos Kazantzakis, easily ranks among the best in
Western literature. The Greek language, however, which
was once the imperial road of international culture, has
long been a barrier to their wider recognition. Cavafis,
after his death, slowly but certainly—though much of
his original music remains obstinately untranslatable—
has won his deserved place among the foremost lyrical
poets of our century. It is a strange, regrettable fact that
Kazantzakis, despite his international acclaim, has not
been awarded the supreme laurel.

The above comment is meant to enhance, not to diminish, the glory of the present award. The laurel that went
now to Seferis is thoroughly deserved. It is to the special
credit of the Swedish Academy that they awarded a
poet who is undoubtedly great but not "popular." A full
appreciation of his work is not to be expected from the
average reader.

Seferis is not an easy poet, especially in his major accomplishments. From the beginning, he was a pioneer
in poetic expression, an experimenter with language,
and, in certain respects, a "cryptic" poet. He is the poet
of subtly refined vision and deep sensitivity, a master of
economy, of the "right word," of suggestiveness and
controlled emotion, a master of the unspoken, of the
haunted silence that is one of the prime elements of
poetry. What cannot be rationally grasped in his verse
can always be felt and felt deeply, especially by those
who have lived the tragedy of our modern world.

It cannot, however, be emphasized too much that Seferis, a Greek by descent, birth, upbringing and experience, is best understood in relation to Greek culture,
Greek myth, literature, tradition and the age-old historical adventure of Greece. His voice is, above all, that of
a modern Greek conscience deeply involved, deeply
familiar with and painfully aware of the crushing weight
of a cultural inheritance. The poet's major aim has been
to recognize, define and weigh the elements of that
conscience, as they have acted in the destiny of Greece.

The development of his art dates from the early thirties.
He always felt himself to be a "refugee," an "exile," for
he came to Athens from his native Smyrna, that prosperous and *fourmillante citée* of ancient Ionia, at the age of
fourteen, about eight years before that Ionian world was
lost for Greece in the catastrophe of 1922. He studied
law and letters in Athens and later in France. Soon
afterwards, he joined the Greek diplomatic service. His
assignments brought him in direct contact with the critical developments of modern world history. They seem
also to have emphasized in him his original feeling of

being an exile and a refugee, particularly when, during the Nazi occupation of Greece, he had to move with the other Greek officials from Egypt to South Africa and then to Italy, waiting for the day of liberation.

Seferis spent several years in London, first as Proconsul and Director of the General Consulate (1931-34), then as Minister-Counselor to the Embassy (1951-53), and finally as Royal Greek Ambassador (1957-62). In London he made a discovery that proved decisive to the development of his art. In an Oxford Street bookshop, he came across a little volume of T. S. Eliot's verse, at a time, 1931, when Eliot was still comparatively unknown. Eliot's verse was a sudden revelation to Seferis. He heard in Eliot that poetic voice that helped him to discover his own.

Seferis first appeared in Greek letters with the volume *Strophe* (*Turning Point*) in 1931, at a time when Greek verse had reached the point of exhaustion in following either the major tone, rhetorical and philosophic, of the Palamas-Sikelianos tradition, or the minor tone of post-romantic lyricism, idyllic, parnassian, escapist and pessimistic. The most advanced voices were experimenting with symbolism and *poésie pure*. Springing from this latter climate, and well-versed in the prevalent modern literary trends abroad, Seferis mastered a pure poetry that brought Greek verse into a new dawn. Simplicity, economy of expression, avoidance of adjectives and other ornaments, idiomatic language, crisp imagery, fresh, even bold, metaphor and an exquisite music were the qualities of his work.

Strophe was a collection of lyrics, expressing moments of sensibility, instant impressions, where several new elements were tried in the older molds. The poet tried to grasp in a non-traditional manner the peculiar quality and individuality of a feeling, to express an emotional quintessence through tangible particulars. A longer poem, **"Erotikos Logos,"** in this collection, is already an achievement wherein the traditional framework of the alternating fifteen and fourteen syllable lines, the old and the new are perfectly blended. In this **"Song of Love,"** which has in it ample echoes of the demotic song, the experience of physical love is lyrically recollected in its wider significance. Mr. Sherrard has already remarked that the woman here, as well as in other poems of Seferis, is not only a physical creature of beauty and pleasure but is also an emblem, an embodiment of fate, an initiator and a priestess of the mysteries. Through the physical experience of love with woman "man becomes aware of a new level of reality." Pandemos Aphrodite leads to Urania Aphrodite, not, however, in a religious, purely spiritual or metaphysical sense. True to his Greek temperament, Seferis excluded from his vision a reality that would not be human and earthly. His timelessness lies within the dimensions of time.

In *Sterna* (*The Cistern*), his second book of verse, 1935, the area of experience becomes deeper and wider. The form of the poem is still traditional, but a painful awareness of the ravages of time, of human suffering, the role of memory, the feeling of participating with others, of sharing with them in the destiny of a race and of humankind, introduce the tone of his later verse. Always choosing to waver between the subjective and the objective, his voice blends the personal with the impersonal. The "we" makes his poems move on three concurrent levels: the personal, the racial, and the human.

The "cistern" is a symbol of our deeper, intimate, secret self, of our conscience apart from the surrounding reality, as it gathers the experience of our losses. The world of the sun and the sea, of love and beauty, is clouded by the haunting darkness of departures, of memories, of unfulfilled dreams and longings. However, no matter how successfully it carries the connotation that the poet intends it to carry as a familiar feature of Greek reality, the cistern is still a limited, private symbol.

The poet's growing vision and his deepening sense of universality required more solid elements to materialize. Seferis did not have far to go for such elements. The roots were there, in himself as well as in his land and its history. The perennial battle of racial and cultural survival made Greece a place where all the ages and stages of her development, from the mythic and the Homeric times to the present, have been kept necessarily alive, actively alive. Indeed, the shield of Achilles, the shield of the fullness of life as against an always impending, an always overcome death, could be symbolic of nothing more than the Greek conscience itself in its struggle against the calamities which history has brought upon her.

In his next volume, *Mythistorema* (*Mythical Story*), 1935, which is considered to be the poet's masterpiece and which was chosen by the Swedish Academy for the award, Seferis's vision embraces myth and history. A past that has never died, that haunts the Greek conscience wherever it wanders in the Greek land and sea or beyond, with the visible testimonies, the ruins and statues, the sites of great events, even nature itself, enriches the present reality. The elemental symbols of Greek life—the ships, oars, masts, anchors, rocks, headlands, pines, olives, wild herbs, blue skies, whimsical winds, the barren soil, the mountains, the frugality of conditions, and the traces of human toil—these and the remnants of achievements and catastrophes, ancient, Byzantine, and modern, bring all time together. The present reality constantly causes the poet to dwell in memories and introspection about man's predicament and the peripety of human values.

In this mixture of past and present, the dead are not really dead. They are still part of the life of the living.

They are constantly summoned by memory and bring undecipherable, taunting messages. The dead give no solution to our problems, no real solace to our despair, no escape to our anxiety, but they reveal certain patterns in their experiences which have also been our own. In another sense and dimension, beauty, whatever that beauty was in their lives, challenges us, increases the feeling of our responsibility, rests heavily upon us, and we struggle not to sink under its burden.

Seferis's approach to the past is not romantic and it is not literary. It is genuine and emotional. An always controlled emotion is powerfully and dramatically sustained through the poet's identification with the legendary figures, the land and its people. Of course, no other figure out of the legendary past could be more comprehensively and more deeply expressive of the Greek temperament, of the Greek historical and psychical experience, than that of the great traveler, the great exile, the great lover of life and its wisdom, and of his native soil—Odysseus. Odysseus was bound to become Seferis's most meaningful *persona,* and his wanderings are the poet's major pattern of emotional experience.

Mythistorema, a collection of fifteen lyrical, dramatic monologues of varying length, mostly free verse, gives—in a variety of images and circumstances—the wandering of a personified Greek conscience, predominantly the poet's own, through a world of lost values. This world is haunted everywhere by the presence of the past and by a desperate longing for revelation, for self-recovery and fulfillment, for justice and for freedom. There is in these poems an interplay of sense and memory, of struggle and fatality. A miracle that is expected never comes. We are left with the memories and illusions, with the broken oars, the remnants of the unaccomplished trips to the islands of the blessed. The companions perish, Elpenor among them, sinking into the flux of things, the stream of everyday reality, but the Ulyssean self continues its anxious quest and strives also to save the others against the blows of reality.

Among Seferis's later books, *Gymnopaidia,* 1936, comprised two significant poems on the same theme and in the same emotional atmosphere. In **"Santorini,"** the volcanic island, with its sinking and reappearing islets, becomes a symbol for lost lands, lost worlds, lost hopes, a symbol of the undecipherable pattern of our experience, of the contrast between justice and injustice. In **"Mycenae,"** the voices of past racial experience, as they come from the dark stones, make the present wanderer sink under their weight and cause him to call desperately for a helping hand.

The Book of Exercises, 1940, is mostly a selection of older and more recent experiments with matter and form in a wide range of moods. The Odyssean theme is again in the group of poems called *Strates Thalassinos (Sea Paths* or *Sea Traveler).* The creation of this new Odyssean *persona* carries more positively into the present the old myth of wandering. The voice of Strates Thalassinos, the later mouthpiece of the poet, is what we mostly hear in *Log Books A, B,* and *C,* which came out in 1940, 1944 and 1955. At the end of *Log Book A* is **"The King of Assine,"** deemed by many readers to be Seferis's best poem.

Log Book B contains some of the poet's most significant works. It is a series of dramatic accounts of Seferis's emotional experiences as an exile in foreign lands during the Nazi occupation of Greece, and it reaches its climax in **"The Last Stop,"** written in Cava dei Tirreni, October 1944.

Before his latest book of poems, *Log Book C,* inspired by the Cypriot struggle for liberation and reunion with Greece, Seferis published **"The Thrush,"** 1947, a poem in three parts, or rather three movements corresponding to those of a sonata. "Thrush" was the name of a ship sunk during the war off the shores of the island of Poros and symbolises that black ship on which Odysseus sailed to Hades. In the poem we first find the traveler in the luxurious palace of Crete, longing for his home. Then we see Elpenor, shortly before his fatal fall, trying unsuccessfully to entice Circe into a love embrace. Nekuia follows where Odysseus is metamorphosed into Oedipus, the Oedipus at Kolonos, a more suitable figure for the element of transcendence that the poet wishes to introduce in this poem. The experience of death effects another significant transformation. The finally ascending spirit, rising into the world of light and of justice, as a symbol of self-integration, is not that of Oedipus but of his daughter Antigone, who with her indomitable action reconciled the world of the dead with the world of the living.

There may be similarities or correspondences between the technique of this poem and that of the *Four Quartets.* Thematically, however, there are significant differences. In both poems the theme is that of transcendence, of teleology, of the destiny of the soul. But whereas Eliot builds his vision with elements of traditional Christianity, Seferis stays entirely within his Greek tradition, where Heaven is only a projection, a quintessence of the earth, of human reality and the divinity of man.

G. Georgiades Arnakis (essay date spring 1964)

SOURCE: Arnakis, G. Georgiades. "The Tragedy of Man in the Poetry of George Seféris." *Texas Quarterly* 7, no. 1 (spring 1964): 55-67.

[*In the following essay, Arnakis explores the elements of tragedy and despair in Seferis's poetry.*]

In contemporary Greece, George Seféris (pen name for George Seferiádes), Nobel Prize winner for poetry in 1963, is a leading representative of the so-called "generation of 1930," which includes the novelists Ilías Venézis, George Theotokás, Strátis Myrivílis—to mention only those whose books have been translated into English[1]—and the poet Nikephóros Vrettákos. The poets and prose writers, some twenty in all, who made their appearance in or about the year 1930, offered a rich contribution to Modern Greece's literary renaissance, thereby supplementing the very significant work of Costís Palamás, George Drosínis, Ángelos Sikelianós, Níkos Kazandjákis, Yiánnis Psycháris, and Gregórios Xenópoulos. These six writers, who died between 1929 and 1957—the first three poets, the last three mainly novelists—were Greece's most eligible candidates for the Nobel Prize in Literature in the years preceding the Second World War, while two of the group, Sikelianós and Kazandjákis, who died in 1951 and 1957 respectively, hoped to win the coveted distinction in the postwar period. Constantine Caváfis (C. P. Cavafy), living in Alexandria, Egypt, and isolated from the Greek scene, was not seriously discussed as a Nobel aspirant, though he had begun to attract attention outside Greece in the 1920s. It was only after his death in 1933 that he was acclaimed as the T. S. Eliot of Modern Greece and recognized as a poet of talent and originality, if not a genius. The beginnings of his poetry antedate Eliot's by nearly two decades. Of Seféris' contemporaries and fellow poets, Vrettákos, whose verse is inspired by humanistic and cosmopolitan themes and has a genuine lyric quality, is almost entirely unknown outside the Greek-speaking area. Cóstas Várnalis, another leading Greek poet, belongs to the earlier generation and has been a controversial figure on account of his leftist views. Vrettákos, too, was critical of the postwar governments in Greece, yet in 1956 he received the State Prize for Poetry. Seféris, on the other hand, has always been described as a nationalist and was loyal to the government by virtue of his position in the diplomatic service.

The work of Seféris is not quite so voluminous as that of the other Greek writers who have been mentioned in connection with the Nobel Prize. Nor is his life particularly versatile or exciting (for a Greek). He was born in Smyrna in 1900, the son of a prosperous family of professional men and merchants. His father Stélios Seferiádes, who wrote poetry and translated Byron into Greek, was a lawyer. Later he became professor of international law at the University of Athens and a judge at the International Court of the Hague. The important event in the life of the Seferiádes family was the destruction of the flourishing Greek community of Smyrna and the exodus of the Greeks of Asia Minor during and after the victory of the Nationalist Turks (1922). The Seferiádes' lost their fortune, though they never suffered any privations as displaced persons in Greece. In fact, the poet and his parents were away from Smyrna at the time of the disaster. Like his father, George Seféris studied law in Paris. In 1926 he entered the diplomatic service of his country.

As a career diplomat, the poet lived in various places—France, England, Albania, Palestine, Syria, Egypt, South Africa, Italy—before and during the war. In 1945-46 he was political councilor to the regent of Greece, Archbishop Damaskenós, and his last diplomatic post was that of Greek ambassador in London.

Seféris' long residence outside Greece no doubt influenced his spiritual life. His nostalgic recollection of the mother country led him into an unreal world—a world that is essentially tragic—in which Greece symbolizes eternity and the Greek view is identified with a panhuman scope. The sufferings of the Greek people, highlighted by the Asia Minor disaster, the two civil wars (1944 and 1946-49), and the futile struggle of Cyprus (1955-59), have doubtless had an impact on the soul of the diplomat-poet. At the same time, his sense of the tragic clearly transcends the bounds of Greece and embraces the whole world. Greece's tragedy is only the microcosm of a bewildered universe.

If one were to judge Seféris from his external appearance, the impression he would have would be that of an austere, lonely man, a man for whom one could feel respect, perhaps admiration—rarely affection. As political councilor to the regent at a very critical time, Seféris was often attacked (not only by his opponents), but he never bothered to defend himself. Pedestrians in the streets of postwar Athens remember him as he walked out of the regent's mansion at noon, a dignified gentleman, dressed usually in black, his head erect, apparently indifferent to the world around him, while the stench of the corpses that the municipality workmen were digging out of the Royal Garden across the boulevard filled the air to suffocation and compelled everybody to hurry on as fast as his feet could take him. The corpses were those of the victims of the civil war; the pedestrians were the survivors of the famine that had decimated Athens during the Axis Occupation. In his capacity as political mentor to the old archbishop, Seféris lived in Athens for a longer period of time than he had ever done in his mature years. Thus he witnessed another tragic chapter of Modern Greek history.

His immediate circle consisted of his family, all of whom had intellectual and artistic interests—his wife, since his marriage in 1941; his cousins; his sister, the gifted and dynamic Mme Ioánna Tsátsou, socially prominent and the archbishop's chief assistant in relief work during the famine; and his brother-in-law Constantine Tsátsos, an Athenian, who taught philosophy of law at the University of Athens, held three ministerial portfolios in the cabinet appointed by the regent, and was perhaps the most articulate intellectual in favor of Greece's unreserved alignment with the West in the crucial year 1945.

Outside his family circle, during and after the war, Seféris had friendships with some of the Greek authors of his generation and with a few French, English, and Americans who were in Greece in 1940 or in 1945. The literary members of the foreign group were Robert Levesque, his French translator,[2] Lawrence Durrell, who collaborated in an English translation of Seféris' poems,[3] Robert Liddell, who studied Seféris' poetry in the original as part of his Greek training, and Henry Miller, enthusiastic admirer of Greek achievement (*The Colossus of Maroussi*, 1941). What the entire circle had in common, in the eyes of an outsider, was a special love for the poetry of T. S. Eliot. Seféris had translated *The Waste Land* into Greek (published in Athens, 1936) and the others agreed on recognizing him as a pioneer in Greek poetry—in a very real sense the Eliot of Greece. Later, in England, Seféris widened his circle of literary friends. He received the Foyle Prize for Poetry and an honorary doctorate at Cambridge University.

Seféris began publishing his poetry five years before the translation of *The Waste Land*. His first volume, entitled *Strophē* (Turn), came out in 1931. It was followed by **"Erotikós Lógos"** (Discourse on Love) and *É Stérna* (The Cistern) in 1932; *Mythistórēma* (Mythical Story) in 1935; and *Gymnopaedía* (Athletic Exercises) in 1936. *Mythistórēma* is a collection of poems, about thirty pages in all—that is, somewhat larger than *Strophē*—while the others are even shorter.

During and immediately after the war, Seféris continued writing poetry, which came out in four thin volumes, whose titles can be translated into English as follows: *Exercise Book* (published in 1940), *Journal on Deck, I* (1940), *Journal on Deck, II* (1944 and 1945), and **"Thrush"** (*Kichlē*, name of a ship, 1947).

All of Seféris' poetical works were published again in 1950 in one volume entitled *Poems, 1924-1946.* This book of 248 pages contained the entire poetic production of Seféris until that time. The 56-page book that was published in 1955, inspired by the Hellenism of Cyprus, is anticlimactic from the point of view of lyric quality. It bears the Classical title *Kypron, hou m'ethespisen . . . (Cyprus, to which [Apollo] Assigned Me . . .).* In the latest (1962) edition of Seféris' complete poetical works the Cyprus verses appeared under the title *Journal on Deck, III.*

Seféris' prose work consists of essays. They deal with a variety of subjects—T. S. Eliot, C. P. Caváfis, Palamás, Sikelianós, the origin and character of art, *Erotócritos* (Cretan romance written in the seventeenth century), Andréas Cálvos (Greek poet living in England in the early reign of Queen Victoria), Makriyiánnis (general in the Greek Revolution and author of interesting memoirs), and a description of the rock churches of Cappadocia, among which he spent three days when he served at the Greek embassy of Ankara, Turkey, in 1950. Except for the last, these essays were collected in one volume and were published in Athens in 1962.

In discussing modern subjects Seféris tends to look for similarities and points of contact with Classical Greece. Once he finds a path leading to Classical Greece he feels he is secure enough to survey the world, as if from a high mountain. However, his is not the cold eye of the neutral observer, or the serene vision of the classicist, but the warm look of a Christ gazing on the multitude from the hillside. Indeed, his poems reveal a personality that is totally alien to our first impression of Seféris.

Seféris the poet is profoundly aware of an all-pervading, omnipotent death, under whose shadow man wages a foredoomed struggle for the integration of his personality, the merging of kindred souls, or a full experience of life. Instead of amalgamation and fulfillment, man knows only disintegration and a void, the helplessness of the soul that is tormented because it is cut into numberless particles. To use Robert Browning's phrase, his is a world of broken arcs. There can never be a "perfect round," not even in heaven. The poet has no vision of heaven. Hellenism, in the cultural and humanistic sense, offers no remedy to the struggling soul. Neither does Byzantine Christianity that so often provides a haven for the Modern Greek thinker. Seféris is the exact opposite of Phótis Kóndoglou, the leader of Neo-Byzantinism in Greece, who has produced both painting and literature. While Kóndoglou thirsts for a mystic union with God, almost like the hesychasts of the fourteenth century, or feels secure in his own "Polis of the Pan-Basileus" (the Byzantine Holy City of an earlier day), Seféris utters notes of despair, not passionate but subdued. Resigned pessimism, Euripidean but not revolutionary, is the main content of Seféris' poetry.

Greece is the origin and the central theme of his pessimism. "No matter where I travel," he says, "Greece causes me pain."

> Ships blow their whistles now that night falls on the
>   Piraeus
> They whistle constantly but no capstan moves
> No chain has glittered wet in the last light of sunset
> The captain stands turned into marble, dressed in white
>   and gold.
>
> No matter where I travel, Greece causes me pain;
> Curtains of mountains seas bare granite.
> The ship that sails is called AGONY 937.[4]
>
> *Exercise Book*

Out of the mist of London, which for Seféris, as for Eliot, "has the acrid taste of death," the poet remembers the country that has cisterns and rivers without water; temples and houses in ruins; mutilated statues; broken columns; skeleton ships forgotten on the beaches; cracked oars from voyages unfinished; barren mountains; and "bodies that know not how to love" (***Mythical Story,*** x, xii). These are the pictures that haunt him wherever he goes.

Very often the Greek landscape has a personal, mystic and symbolic, character. So does Greek mythology, though perhaps in a less esoteric manner. The well known figures of Greek drama appear on the modern scene as eternal symbols of the various aspects of human tragedy. Agamemnon, murdered by his wife's lover Aegisthus, is haunted by nightmares and will not die.

> I woke up with this marble head in my hands
> It tires my elbows, I don't know where to put it.
> It fell down in my dream as I was coming out of a
>   dream
> Our life was so united, it will be hard to keep it apart.
>
> *Mythical Story,* III

The hero finds no peace in death. Even worse is the fate of his son, Orestes, the Avenger. Orestes hears the warning:

> The sea . . . you cannot reach no matter how hard
>   you run
> No matter how you turn in front of the black Furies
>   heavy with boredom
> Yet unrelenting.
>
> *Mythical Story,* XVI

In verses reminiscent of Eliot's pessimism, Seféris tells us that man (more specifically the Greek) has something in common with the destiny of Agamemnon and Orestes.

> The strange visions we saw . . .
> Pass and disappear in the motionless foliage of a pep-
>   per tree . . .
> For we have known this fate of ours so well
> Twisting around between broken stones, three or six
>   thousand years
> Searching for buildings ruined, where may have been
>   our home
> Trying to recall dates and heroic deeds . . .
> Shall we be able to die normally?
>
> *Mythical Story,* XXII

There is something that the poet can envy in the seclusion and stability of a cistern. Like his soul, it is dark and full of the element of death. But it is not tormented like his soul. The Cistern symbolizes a peaceful world.

> The stars
> Don't touch its heart. Each day
> Lengthens, opens and shuts, but doesn't touch it . . .
> On its towering vault of a merciless night
> Cares trod and joys pass by

> With the lively castanet rhythm of fate
> Faces light up, glimmer for a moment
> And fade out in ebony blackness.
>
> Shapes that depart: Bunches of eyes
> Roll down in a furrow of sadness
> And the signals of the great day
> Lead them on and bring them closer
> To the black earth that asks for no ransom.
>
> The body of man bends down to the earth
> And only a thirsty love remains;
> Turned into marble at the touch of time
> The statue reclines nude on the broad
> Breast, which softens it little by little.
>
> The thirst of love longs for tears
> The roses droop—our soul
> The heart-throbs of the universe are heard on the
>   leaves
> Dusk creeps in like a way-worn traveller
> Then comes night and then the grave.
>
> Yet here in the earth a Cistern has been built
> Secret lonely warm, which hoards
> The muttering of every being in the open air
> The struggle with the night with the day
> The world grows in numbers, passes, doesn't touch it
> . . .
>
> But night has no faith in the dawn
> And love survives to weave the cloak of death
> Just like the soul that is free,
> A Cistern that teaches silence
> Within the city that is burning.
>
> *The Cistern*

Hamlet contemplates suicide but lacks the will power to commit it and turns his energy into staging a play. The poet, too, fully aware of death, walks on the paths of life. While life lasts, the quest continues—we are not sure we know for what. We travel in strange seas, "huddled up, together with yellow women and crying babies."

> What do our souls want traveling
> On rotten sea planks
> From port to port?
>
> Pushing aside broken rocks, breathing
> The cool scent of the pine tree every day with greater
>   difficulty,
> Swimming in the waters of this sea
> Or of that sea,
> With no sense of touch
> No human beings
> In a country which is no longer ours
> Nor yours.
>
> We had known that the islands were beautiful
> Somewhere near here, where we are searching,
> Perhaps a little higher or a little lower
> Only a short distance away.
>
> *Mythical Story,* VIII

The eternal traveller, condemned to perpetual disappointment, remains an eternal refugee. At times life seems to be a quest for the long-forgotten kingdom of Asinē.

> No living being, the wild pigeons were gone,
> And the king of Asinē, whom we have been trying to
>   find the last two years,
> Unknown, forgotten by all, even by Homer;
> Only one word in the Iliad and that uncertain
> Thrown here like a golden death mask.
> Did you touch it, do you remember its sound? hollow
>   in the light of day
> Like a dry water jug in the dug-up earth;
> The same sound of the sea with our oars.
> The king of Asinē a void under the mask
> Everywhere with us everywhere with us, under no
>   more than a name:
> *"Asinēn te. . . . Asinēn te . . ."*[5]
>
> **Journal on Deck, I: "The King of Asinē"**

The only element that is attainable and constant (as constant as anything can be) is the sea—infinite and inscrutable. It symbolizes death. Its rocks and islands are the multifarious aspects of man's life, or his destiny.

> No one can escape, what is the use of power? You
>   cannot
> Escape the sea, your cradle, which you seek
> At this hour of the contest, enveloped by the breath of
>   horses,
> With flutes which sang of autumn in a Lydian mode
> . . .
>
> **Mythical Story, XVI**

The rocks and islands, whatever their appearance, forbode nothing good.

> In the place which has disintegrated, which no longer
>   exists,
> The place which was ours once upon a time,
> The islands sink—rust and ashes.
>
> **Gymnopaedia**

The refugee traveller stops at various ports for shorter or longer visits. These ports are, of course, the various phases of the poet's life in the categories of space and time. The autobiographical element is held down by Classical discipline and stays inside the basic theme—that of Life (with a capital L and with an extrapersonal, extranational scope). It is true that at times Seféris will write verses like these:

> They took my houses away from me. Those happened
> To be years of disaster—war devastation exile;
> The hunter sometimes finds migratory birds
> Sometimes he doesn't find them; the hunt
> Was rich in my years; the shot carried away large
>   numbers;
> Others come back or lose their minds in the shelters.
>
> **"Thrush," I**

But he is ready to affirm (for example in the Preface to Levesque's translation) that so far as he can see such events as the destruction of the Greek quarter of Smyrna have had no appreciable influence on his philosophy of life. He was, it will be recalled, twenty-two years old at that time and away from the scene of the tragedy.

Nevertheless, there are clear references to places that Seféris visited later in life and they seem to exert a noticeable influence on his thought. Places evoke spirits, and events teach their lessons. The fall of the Republic of Czechoslovakia; London fog "with the taste of death"; Albania's poverty and bare monotony ("Tall Ghegs[6] and short Tosks[7] / Sickles in the summer and axes in the winter"); the Nile's languid waters that have known no change; Jerusalem, holy city crowded with miserable refugees; South Africa, with the sharpness of a new arrival; pagan temples and Christian monasteries on the island of Cyprus; and battlefields in Southern Italy. In many cases there is a subtle harmony between the external world and the yearnings of the poet's soul. Somewhat in the style of Pindar, nature sets the stage for the exposition of ideas, and the transient gives its place to the eternal.

As he watches the Nile—"An Old Man on the Bank of the River"—the poet grasps the significance of what he calls "a permanent orientation."

> We must reckon which way we are going,
> Not such as our pain calls for and our hungry children
> And the void of the invitation of comrades from the
>   opposite shore;
> Nor such as the darkened light whispers in the
>   emergency ward,
> The pharmaceutical splendor on the pillow of the lad
>   who had an operation this noon;
> But in some other way, perhaps I mean the way
> The long river, coming out of the lakes secluded deep
>   in Africa,
> He who once was a god and then became a passage, a
>   benefactor, a judge, a delta,
> He who is never the same, as wise men of yesteryear
>   taught us,
> And yet always remains the same body, the same bed,
>   the same Signal
> The same orientation.
>
> **Journal on Deck, II**

Man's failure to attain security, the indolence and stupidity of a confused generation, is presented dramatically, after an opening stanza with allusions to "spring . . . light colors . . . blossoms and roses."

> When the new roses were in bud
> The elders blundered
> And they gave up all
> Grandchildren and great-grandchildren
> And the deeply ploughed fields
> And the green mountains
> And love and fortune

Kindness and roof
And rivers and sea.

Journal on Deck, II: **"Spring, A. D."**

The references to blossoming almond trees and blue skies are repeated shortly before the poet mentions "the martyr . . . the amphitheater . . . the executioner" when

There was a lake of seclusion
A lake of privation
Untouched and unmarked.

The allusion is not only to Czechoslovakia in the spring of 1939 but also to the fate of the Jews and to all the victims of Nazi oppression in wartime Europe.

There were, of course, hopes that at the end of the war there would be no more hungry children, sordid refugee camps, blackouts, and air raids. Possibly with such hopes in his heart the poet returned to Greece, "to the country of light," where "man can be reborn." He yearned for such a rebirth. But he was soon to discover that in the timeless conflict between light and darkness, man has a propensity towards darkness. The new phase of his agony finds expression in the great question: "Why shouldn't life merge with absolute light but bends downwards, towards darkness?"

For a few days the poet vacations on the idyllic island of Poros, on the opposite shore of the Saronic Gulf. In the harbor lies a small ship called *Kichlē* (Thrush), sunk there by enemy aircraft in 1941. Its smokestack and masts are discernible from "The House by the Sea," where the poet spends his days. Around him extends the transparency of the Grecian landscape; in front of him the shipwreck. There is much that the shipwreck has in common with the poet. He, too, is helpless, rejected, a sad relic of the war. Voices from the deep speak to his soul of things that, in the language of Euripides, "it would have been better, had they remained untold." But the poet must let the voice of tragedy be heard. In a Classical land he contemplates the statues and how they live. They live in death; they are dead in life. They symbolize the perennial struggle between light and darkness. "We are the statues," says Elpenor to the Woman (Kirkē). Elpenor, whose personality is antipodal to that of Ulysses ("poor, idiotic Elpenor"), is confused and the companionship of the Woman can give him no sense of fulfillment. Yet his intuitive image-world is far broader than her consciousness of reality. The dialogue is drowned in the din of daily existence—a radio broadcasting a parting song, scraps of a disjointed life, a reference to nightfall, and fragments of news dispatches from the war. The cryptic word PSYCHAMOI-BOS (applicable, perhaps, to Hermes-who-escorts-the-dead or to Ares the consumer of mortals) brings the confusion to an end.

But let us hear the words of Elpenor as he ponders on the life of statues:

"Listen to this, too. In the moonlight
Statues sometimes bend like the reed
In the midst of living fruit—the statues;
Flame becomes cool like oleander,
I mean the flame that consumes man."

"It is some reflection of light—shadows in the dark."

"Perhaps it's the dark which opened, like a blue
   pomegranate,
A dark breast, and filled you with stars
Interrupting the course of time.

And yet statues
Bend sometimes, splitting desire
Into two, like a ripe peach; and the flame
Becomes a kiss on the limbs and a sob
And then a cool leaf that the wind blows away;
They bend; they grow light with a human weight.
You don't forget it."

"The statues are in the museum."

"No, they haunt you—how come you don't see it?
I mean to say—with their broken limbs,
With their erstwhile features which you never saw
And yet you know.

Just as when
You fall in love at the end of your youth
With a woman who has kept her beauty, you are afraid,
While you hold her naked at noon,
Of the memory that wakes up in your bosom;
You are afraid that your kiss may betray you
Into other beds now belonging to your past
Beds which can perhaps become specters
So easily so easily and bring to life
Images in the mirror, bodies that once were:
Their pleasure.

Just as when
You come back from abroad and you chance to open
An old chest locked up long ago
And you find rags that were the clothes you had on
During beautiful hours, festivals with lights
Of many colors, mirrored, now becoming dim
And all that remains is the perfume of the absence
Of a young face.

Truly, those statues
Are not ruins; it's you that are a ruin;
They haunt you with a strange virginity
In the house in the office in the receptions
Of princes, in the unconfessed fear of sleep;
They speak of incidents you wish had never occurred
Or might have occurred after your death,
And this is hard because—"
          "Statues are in the museum. Good night."

          "Because statues are no ruins any more,
We are ruins. Statues bend softly. Good night."

                                        "Thrush," II

Other visions, too, haunt the poet on the island of Poros that keep him awake to the struggle between life and death. As he watches the spider spin its web at dusk he has a premonition that "someone will come to bid him goodbye."

> . . . they are dressing him up
> In white and black clothes with jewelry of many colors
> And venerable dames with grey hair and black lace
> Are whispering around him.
>
> **"Thrush,"** I

At the same time

> A woman . . . returning from southern ports
> Smyrna Rhodes Syracuse Alexandria,
> From closed cities that are like warm window shut-
>   ters,
> Comes up the steps without noticing
> Those who fell asleep under the staircase.
>
> **"Thrush,"** I

They are the dead—ancestors and contemporaries, heroes and victims of "the world's wrong."

From the crowd of heroes, two stand out. They are both condemned men as they enter the poet's image-world: Oedipus and Socrates. The former, a victim of whimsical gods, is the Suppliant that we have known in Sophocles' *Oedipus at Colonus.* As in the opening scene of the play, Oedipus addresses his daughter Antigone, his guide and companion, in a pleading voice which in Seféris' verse sounds more passionate than in the classic.

> Angelic and black, light,
> Laughter of the waves on the highways of the sea,
> Tearful laughter,
> The old man, the suppliant, sees you
> As he drags his feet on the unseen slabs
> Sees you reflected in his blood
> That fathered Eteocles and Polyneices.
> Angelic and black, day;
> The acrid taste of woman that poisons the prisoner
> Comes from a refreshing wave, a branch strewn with
>   dewdrops.
> Sing, little Antigone, sing, sing . . .
> Let me not talk to you of the past, let me talk about
>   love;
> Adorn your hair with the thorns of the sun,
> Maiden of the black fate;
> The heart of the Scorpion has ended its reign,
> The tyrant has abandoned the man,
> And all the daughters of the sea, Nereids and Graeae,
> Rush to the translucence of the Rising Venus;
> Whoever did not love will love no more,
> In the light.
>
>   You are
> In a large house with many windows open
> You come running from room to room, not knowing
>   from which to look out first,

> You know that the pine trees will be gone, together
>   with the reflected mountains and the chirping of the
>   birds,
> The sea will dry up, a shattered vase, from north to
>   south,
> Your eyes will empty out the light of day
> How suddenly the cicadas stop all at once.
>
> **"Thrush,"** III

Mankind courts disaster, often through no fault of its own; man is weak; and Oedipus can have no hope that love will prevail. Nevertheless, he is a product of the remote, heroic age, which was accustomed to extremes. Socrates, who lived to see the greatest masterpieces of the Periclean age; who came close to the perfect *metron* in Athenian humanism; and who placed the voice of the god-within-him above expediency—drank the hemlock. The poet sees him yearning for a drop of blood, the life-giving element that may restore him to the upper regions. Seféris lodges an undying complaint against Athens, the country of Greece, and the whole of mankind:

> Lands of the sun, you cannot face the sun.
> Lands of man, you cannot face man.
>
> **"Thrush,"** III

It is natural for the poet "who has known the fate of man" to see the all-devouring death everywhere, even in the country of light and rebirth. Here is the climax of his pessimism: As he sees Greek youths, the new Athenian *epheboi,* the hope of the future, diving in the waters of the blue Aegean from the masts of a sailing boat on a summer afternoon, his mind goes back to the dead ancestors, descending to the Acherusian Lake. The youths are unaware of their destiny just as the woman, whom we saw coming up, was unaware of those "who fell asleep under the staircase."

> With a coin between their teeth,[8] still swimming,
> While the sun sews with golden stitches
> Sails and wet boards and marine colors;
> Even now descending, tilted to one side,
> To reach the pebbles of the bottom,
> White funeral vases.[9]
>
> **"Thrush,"** III

The sea, with the silence of death, absorbs all, yet the brawny youths will continue diving in the waters of the Aegean and warm-hearted women will ever climb staircases, ignoring those who sleep underneath. This, no doubt, is the nature of life and it is also the essence of tragedy in the poetry of Seféris.

Notes

1. Venézis, *Beyond the Aegean* (New York, n.d.). *Aeolia* in the English edition (1949). Theotokás, *Argo* (London, 1951). Myrivílis, *The Mermaid Madonna* (New York, 1960). Excerpts from the

works of these and other authors have been published in English translation in *The Charioteer—A Quarterly Review of Modern Greek Culture* (New York, 1960 ff.). Number One contains translations from Níkos Kazandjákis, Pandelís Prevelákis, Sikelianós, Myrivílis, and Vrettákos; Number Two, from Odysseus Elýtis and Venézis; Number Three, from Tákis Papatzónis and I. M. Panayiotópoulos; Number Four, from Ángelos Terzákis; and Number Five, from George Theotokás and Phótis Kóndoglou. Prevelákis, Panayiotópoulos, and Terzákis are three great novelists whose novels have not been translated into English. On the whole, Modern Greek literature has failed to win the recognition it deserves because few of its masterpieces have been translated into the more widely known languages.

2. *Séféris—Choix de poèmes traduits et accompagnés du texte grec* (Athens, 1945).

3. *The King of Asinē and Other Poems by George Seferis,* translated from the Greek by Nanos Valaoritis, Bernard Spencer, and Lawrence Durrell (London, 1948). Durrell kept up his interest in Modern Greek poetry and published another translation—*Six Poems from the Greek of Sikelianos and Seferis* (London, 1946).

4. All translations in this article are by the writer. The punctuation, whenever feasible, is that of the poet. So is the arrangement of the verses.

5. "And Asinē . . . and Asinē." *Iliad,* II, 560.

6. Northern Albanians.

7. Southern Albanians.

8. According to Greek mythology, Charon's fee for ferrying the dead across the lake of the Underworld.

9. *Lēkythoi* in the original.

Edmund Keeley and Philip Sherrard (essay date 1967)

SOURCE: Keeley, Edmund, and Philip Sherrard. "Foreword." In *George Seferis: Collected Poems 1924-1955,* translated, edited, and introduced by Edmund Keeley and Philip Sherrard, pp. v-xiii. Princeton, N.J.: Princeton University Press, 1967.

[*In the following foreword to their edition of Seferis's poetry, Keeley and Sherrard discuss the poet's participation in the revival of classical Greek literature in the nineteenth and twentieth centuries, as well as Seferis's use of sources from the Greek folk tradition dating back to the Byzantine period.*]

The poetry of George Seferis, whatever relation it may have to the literature of other countries, stems first of all from a tradition that is eminently Greek. This means that it not only shares in the modern revival which has produced, during the last hundred and fifty years or so, such distinguished Greek poets as Solomos, Kalvos, Palamas, Sikelianos, and Cavafy; it also proceeds, like most of the poetry that belongs to this revival, from earlier sources. One of these is the long tradition of Greek ballads and folk songs. Both the spirit of Greek folk literature and its dominant form, the "dekapentasyllavos,"[1] can be traced back directly at least to the Byzantine period, and both have been consistently influential since that time, though the form has naturally been modified in keeping with new needs. Seferis's early poem, **"Erotikos Logos"** (1930), is a major example of such modification: a successful attempt to adapt the dekapentasyllavos line to the expression of a contemporary sensibility. Another area of the postmedieval poetic tradition that has remained equally influential is the more complex and sophisticated literature which developed on the island of Crete during the sixteenth and seventeenth centuries. The dramatic literature of Crete includes plays such as *Abraham's Sacrifice,* a religious work, and the *Erophile,* a bloodthirsty tragedy in which all the main characters are killed or kill themselves; but the masterpiece of this more complex (and, in contrast with the folk ballads, more introspective) tradition is the epic romance, the *Erotokritos,* by Vitzentzos Kornaros, a work of 10,052 verses telling of the love of Aretousa, daughter of the king of Athens, and the valiant Erotokritos, son of one of the leading court families. This epic became immensely popular throughout the Greek world, great sections—and sometimes even the whole of it—being recited by heart as though an ordinary folk epic: the kind of recitation that haunts Seferis's persona in **"Upon a Foreign Verse,"** where he speaks of

> . . . certain old sailors of my childhood who, leaning on their nets with winter coming on and the wind angering
> used to recite, with tears in their eyes, the song of Erotokritos;
> it was then I would shudder in my sleep at the unjust fate of Aretousa descending the marble stairs.

Seferis has written the best Greek critical commentary on the *Erotokritos,*[2] and its influence, as a monument to the poetic possibilities of the demotic Greek language,[3] is apparent from the use he makes of it in his **"Erotikos Logos,"** where he introduces actual phrases from the epic into the text of his poem in order to establish an analogy between his diction and that of another vital, relevant moment in his nation's literary past.

Cretan literature of the sixteenth and seventeenth centuries and the folk tradition are, then, among the more important local sources of Seferis's art, particularly because of their creative exploitation of the Greek language; at the same time, however, the poetry of Seferis and that of his immediate predecessors differs in an important respect from the poetry of both these literatures: in the use made of images, characters, and myths that derive from ancient Greece. Whether it is Palamas contrasting the "people of relics"—who reign among the temples and olive groves of the Attic landscape—with the modern crowd crawling along sluggishly, like a caterpillar over a white flower (in *Life Immovable*); or Cavafy evoking—perhaps ironically, perhaps erotically—some scene out of his poetic world of Hellenistic Alexandria; or Sikelianos endeavoring to resurrect the whole pantheon of the ancient gods and to be a hierophant to their mysteries; or Seferis searching for the archaic king of Asine—the substantial man who fought with heroes—and finding only the unsubstantial void of contemporary existence; whichever it is, the ancient world in all its aspects preoccupies the imagination of these poets constantly. This preoccupation is only natural in a country which, like Greece, remains full of the physical remnants of antiquity; everywhere reminders of the ancient past leap to the eye and stimulate the mind:

> Scattered drums of a Doric column
> Razed to the ground
> By unexpected earthquakes

as Sikelianos puts it in *The Conscience of Personal Creativeness,* or to quote Seferis himself: "fragments of a life which was once complete, disturbing fragments, close to us, ours for one moment, and then mysterious and unapproachable as the lines of a stone licked smooth by the wave or of a shell in the sea's depths."[4] This means that the Greek poet who draws on classical mythology in shaping the drama of his verse enjoys a large advantage over his similarly disposed contemporaries in England or America: he can evoke characters and settings that have mythological overtones with less danger of being merely literary in doing so, with less danger of arbitrarily imposing gods and heroes on an alien landscape—Tiresias on the Thames or Prometheus in Pennsylvania, for example—since his own natural landscape is that to which these gods and heroes themselves once belonged and in which they still confront the mind's eye plausibly.

Seferis, like most other poets of modern Greece, has fully exploited this advantage. His secret (in addition to his advantage) is that he always offers an appropriate setting—a poetically realistic setting—before he allows any legendary figures to appear on his stage; before he attempts to carry the reader to the level of myth, he earns his sympathy and belief by convincingly representing the present reality sustaining his myth—and it is a contemporary, Greek reality always. In this way the myth comes to life fully, the ancient and modern worlds meet in a metaphor without strain or contrivance as we find the legendary figures moving anachronistically onto the contemporary stage that the poet has set before our eyes. The anachronism is, of course, very much to the point: in one sense, what was then is now, but in another sense, what is now was then; the modern voyager, for instance, shares something of Odysseus's fate, while Odysseus finds a symbolic representation of his fate in the modern setting that the poet has him confront: the deserted, arid, repetitious land and the calm, embittering sea so frequently encountered in Seferis's poetry are symbolic of Odysseus's frustrating voyage, of his failure to realize the island paradise he longs for. And his fate is that of every wanderer seeking a final harbor, a spiritual fulfillment, that he can't seem to reach. The frustrations of the wanderer are perennial; as Seferis puts it in an illuminating commentary on the role of mythic characters in his verse: ". . . men of inconstancy, of wanderings and of wars, though they differ and may change in terms of greatness and value . . . always move among the same monsters and the same longings. So we keep the symbols and the names that the myth has brought down to us, realizing as we do so that the typical characters have changed in keeping with the passing of time and the different conditions of our world—which are none other than the conditions of everyone who seeks expression."[5]

The mythology of the ancient world thus plays a crucial role in Seferis, but it would be a mistake to regard this source in isolation, since all the various threads of the Greek tradition that we have mentioned here—folk, literary, and mythic—are tightly woven together in his work; one senses really the whole of the Greek past, as it is represented in poetry from the age of Homer down to the contemporary period, behind Seferis's maturest verse, giving it overtones and undertones sometimes too subtle for the non-Greek ear to catch (especially when they have to be caught in a language foreign to the text). But even as one does catch the sound of a richly traditional voice, a voice learned in the best poetry of previous ages, one is also aware that the voice is very much of the present age and that the poet's sensibility couldn't be farther from that of an antiquarian delving nostalgically into the past in order to escape from the bewilderments and afflictions of modern life: the past is always there to shape and illuminate an image of the present. And if this image seems inevitably to have its sorrow—that "καημός της Ρωμιοσύνης" which is so specifically Greek that Seferis rightly regards any translation of the phrase a distortion—one can take it simply for an index of the image's veracity, since a mature consciousness in the Greek world cannot but be aware of how much this world has achieved only to find everything suddenly ruined by the "war, destruction, exile" of constantly unpropitious times, as Seferis's persona puts it in **"Thrush"**—aware of how much and how little individual creative effort signifies in a world so vulnerable. It is the depth of this awareness, so often incomprehensible to nations with shorter and less tragic histories or with more superficial memories, that serves him for protection against those too-easily won positions, that too-readily assumed despair, from which much modern poetry issues.

If Seferis's sensibility has always been too specifically Greek to allow the easy sharing of what he himself has called "the 'Waste Land' feeling" that was common to Anglo-American and European poets after World War I,[6] his expression of this sensibility has been influenced by the example of several poets outside the Greek tradition. There is no doubt, for instance, that in the early phase of his career Seferis was keenly interested in the tonal and stylistic experiments of his French contemporaries, and, indeed, often seemed to be striving for a "pure" poetry in the manner of Valéry. With the appearance of *Mythistorema* in 1935, a distinct change in style became evident, in part the consequence of the poet's sympathetic reading of Eliot and Pound during the early thirties and in part the last phase of a personal stylistic catharsis that had already begun to show in *The Cistern* (1932). With *Mythistorema,* Seferis abandoned the relatively formal mode of his earlier volumes in favor of the much freer and more natural mode that is characteristic of all his mature poetry,[7] where we inevitably find a precisely controlled style, undecorated by embellishment, the coloring always primary and the imagery sparse. In this mature poetry Seferis also combines the modes of everyday speech with the forms and rhythms of traditional usage in a way that creates the effect of both density and economy—an effect almost impossible to reproduce in English, however carefully one may attempt to duplicate the particular character of the poet's style.

But if one discerns the influence of foreign sources in Seferis's stylistic development, one also discerns that the substance of his poetry has remained consistently individual since the start: in the finest poems of each of his volumes (often those least accessible to the Western reader because the least mythological or "classicist"), there is always that tragic sense of life which comes most forcefully out of a direct, personal experience of history—out of a poet *engagé* responding to what he has known and felt of human suffering, or at least what he has clearly seen of it at close quarters. This is not merely to repeat the frequently suggested relationship, for example, between Seferis's poetic representation of exile and his actual exile after the loss of his childhood home in the Asia Minor disaster of 1922 and during his many years away from Greece in his country's diplomatic service, valid though this relationship may be in some respects; more important, perhaps, than his capacity to make the personal poetic in this way is his capacity to capture the metaphoric significance of some event that has moved him, his capacity to transform a personal

experience or insight into a metaphor that defines the character of our times: for example, the metaphor of that "presentable and quiet" man who walks along weeping in **"Narration,"** the "instrument of a boundless pain / that's finally lost all significance"; or the couple at the end of **"The Last Day"** who go home to turn on the light because they are sick of walking in the dusk; or the messengers in **"Our Sun"** who arrive, dirty and breathless, to die with only one intelligible sentence on their lips: "We don't have time" (all of these poems written, incidentally, either just before or just after the outbreak of World War II in Europe). These are the kind of metaphors that project Seferis's vision beyond any strictly local or strictly personal history and that bring to the mind's eye images as definitive, as universal, as any offered by the poetry of Seferis's contemporaries in Europe and America.

There are also moments when an event that would seem to be only of local or personal significance becomes the occasion for a simple statement of truth about the modern experience—a statement more direct, and sometimes more precise, than the poet's metaphoric mode allows: the second stanza of **"The Last Stop"** (p. 305), written on the eve of Seferis's return to Greece at the end of World War II, is an occasion of this kind, as is the conclusion of **"Helen"** (pp. 53ff.), written during the Cyprus conflict of the early 1950's. It is moments such as these, when the poet describes the corruption of war in a voice made wise and simple by the clearest vision, that raise his poems about specific historical events far above the level of political comment or propaganda and that show him to have sustained—through his poems about World War II and his volume dedicated to the people of Cyprus—the same universalizing sensibility that has shaped his image of contemporary history since *Mythistorema* and several earlier poems that anticipate it. The distinguishing attribute of Seferis's genius—one that he shares with Yeats and Eliot—has always been his ability to make out of a local politics, out of a personal history or mythology, some sort of general statement or metaphor; his long Odyssean voyage on rotten timbers to those islands ever slightly out of reach has the same force of definitive, general insight that we find in Yeats's voyage to Byzantium or Eliot's journey over desert country to a fragmentary salvation. Seferis's politics are never simply the restricted politics of a nationalist—though he is very much a "national" poet in his choice of themes, and though his vision is often rendered in those terms that best characterize his nation: its landscape, its literature, its historical and mythic past. His politics are those of the poet with an especially acute sensitivity to the larger implications of contemporary history. Though he is preoccupied with his tradition as few other poets of the same generation are with theirs, and though he has long been engaged, directly and actively, in the immediate political aspirations of his nation, his value as a poet lies in what he has made of this preoccupation and this engagement in fashioning a broad poetic vision—in offering insights that carry with them the weight of universal truths and that thus serve to reveal the deeper meaning of our times. This collected edition will, it is hoped, both illustrate the full range of Seferis's vision and demonstrate how consistently penetrating his insights have remained throughout his mature years.

Notes

1. A line of fifteen syllables, with a caesura after the eighth syllable and two main accents, one on the sixth or eighth syllable and one on the fourteenth.

2. Included in Δοκιμές (see Bibliographical Note).

3. Demotic Greek, as opposed to purist Greek (known as "katharevousa") is now the literary language of modern Greece, though it was not generally accepted as such until this century.

4. From *Delphi* (see Bibliographical Note).

5. From "'Ένα γράμμα γιὰ τὴν <Κίχλη" [A Letter on "Thrush"], 'Αγγλοελληνικὴ 'Επιθεώρηση, ιv (July-August 1950), 501-506.

6. In "Letter to a Foreign Friend" (included in Rex Warner's translation of Seferis's essays, *On the Greek Style*; see Bibliographical Note).

7. We have chosen to open this collected edition with the poem in which Seferis's mature voice is first heard rather than with the poems of his less characteristic—and less translatable—early phase (see note to "Rhymed Poems," p. 487).

Bibliographical Note

In this note we do not attempt to cite all possible sources that would be relevant to a thorough study of Seferis's poetry, a purpose better served (for works before 1962) by G. K. Katsimbalis' Βιβλιογραφία Γιώργου σεφέρη (Athens 1961), which also appeared in Γιὰ τὸν σεφέρη (see below). We offer here only a list of the first Greek editions of the various volumes that constitute Seferis's collected poems, his own principal prose works and translations, and, in addition, the most important works devoted to his poetry in English, Greek, and other languages.

I. First editions of Seferis's poems (published as volumes)

Στροφή [*Turning Point*] (Athens, 1931)

'Η Στέρνα [*The Cistern*] (Athens, 1932)

Μυθιστόρημα [*Mythistorema*] (Athens, 1935)

Τετράδιο Γυμνασμάτων [*Book of Exercises*] (Athens, 1940)

'Ημερολόγιο Καταστρώματος [*Logbook I*] (Athens, 1940)

'Ημερολόγιο Καταστρώματος, Β [*Logbook II*] (Alexandria, 1944)

«Κίχλη» ["Thrush"] (Athens, 1947)

'Ημερολόγιο Καταστρώματος, Γ [*Logbook III*] (Athens, 1955), originally published as . . . Κύπρον, οὗ μ'ἐθέσπισεν . . . Τρία Κρυφὰ Ποιήματα [*Three Secret Poems*] (Athens, 1966). This short volume appeared in December, 1966, too late to be included in this English edition.

II. Seferis's principal prose works

Τρεῖς μέρες στὰ μοναστήρια τῆς Καππαδοκίας [Three Days at the Monasteries of Kappadokia] (Athens, 1953). Also in French: Institut Français, Athens, 1953.

Δοκιμές [Essays], 2nd ed. (Athens, 1962)

Delphi (Munich and Ahrback/Hanover, 1963). Reprint from the Greek text in 'Ο Ταχυδρόμος, Athens, 1962.

Discours de Stockholm (Athens, 1964)

'Η Γλῶσσα στὴν Ποίησή μας (Thessaloniki, 1965)

III. Seferis's principal translations

Θ. Σ. ''Ελιοτ: 'Η ''Ερημη Χώρα καὶ ἄλλα ποιήματα [The Waste Land and Other Poems], 3rd ed. (Athens, 1965)

Θ. Σ. ''Ελιοτ: Δολοφονία στὴν 'Εκκλησία [Murder in the Cathedral], 2nd ed. (Athens, 1965)

'Αντιγραφές [Copies] (Athens, 1965)

''Ασμα ἀσμάτων [The Song of Songs] (Athens, 1966)

'Η 'Αποκάλυψη τοῦ 'Ιωάννη [The Apocalypse of St. John] (Athens, 1966)

IV. Selected translations of Seferis into English and other major languages

Robert Levesque, *Séféris* (Athens, 1945). French, with Introduction by the translator.

Bernard Spencer, Nanos Valaoritis, Lawrence Durrell, *The King of Asine* and *Other Poems* (London, 1948). Introduction by Rex Warner.

Edmund Keeley and Philip Sherrard, *Six Poets of Modern Greece* (London, 1960). Introduction and Notes by the translators. Also published in an American edition (New York, 1961).

Rex Warner, *Poems* (London, 1960). Introduction and Notes by the translator. Also published in an American edition (Boston, 1961).

Christian Enzensberger, *Poesie* (Frankfurt am Main, 1962)

Filippo Maria Pontani, *Poesie* (Milan, 1963). Introduction and Notes by translator, Greek text *en face*.

Filippo Maria Pontani, *Le Parole E I Marmi* (Milan, 1963). A collection of essays from *Dokimes*.

Börje Knös and Johannes Edfelt, *Dikter* (Stockholm, 1963)

Hjalmar Gullberg, *Stenarnas Dictare Tolkningar* (Stockholm, 1963)

Jacques Lacarrière, *Poèmes* (Paris, 1964). Introduction by Ives Bonnefoy; Preface by Gaetan Picon.

Sture Linner, *T. S. Eliot and C. P. Cavafy* (Stockholm, 1965). Accompanying a translation of Cavafy's poems. See also, by the same author, *Giorgos Seferis: en Introduktion* (Stockholm, 1963).

Lysandro Z. D. Galtier, *"El Zorzal" y ostros Poemas* ["Thrush" and other Poems] (Buenos Aires, 1966)

Rex Warner, *On the Greek Style* (Boston, 1966). Selected essays from Δοκιμές.

V. CRITICAL BOOKS ON SEFERIS

Andreas Karandonis, 'Ο ποιητὴς Γιῶργος Σεφέρης (Athens, 1957)

Γιὰ τὸν Σεφέρη, ed. G. P. Savidis (Athens, 1961). A collection of essays on Seferis in Greek by many hands, commemorating the thirtieth anniversary of the publication of Seferis's first volume, Στροφὴ [*Turning Point.*]

VI. CRITICAL ARTICLES IN ENGLISH ON SEFERIS

S. Baud-Bovy, "A Greek Poet (G. Seferis)," *The Link*, Oxford, June 1938, pp. 1-6.

Nicholas Bachtin, "English Poetry in Greek (Notes on a comparative study of poetic idioms)" Parts 1 and 2, *The Link*, Oxford, June 1938, pp. 77-84, and June 1939, pp. 49-63. Commentary on Seferis's translation of Eliot (see especially Part 1).

W. B. Stanford, *The Ulysses Theme*, Chapter XIV (Oxford, 1954), pp. 176-78.

Edmund Keeley, "T. S. Eliot and the Poetry of George Seferis," *Comparative Literature*, Summer 1956, pp. 214-26.

Edmund Keeley, "George Seferis and Stratis the Mariner," *Accent*, Summer 1956, pp. 153-57.

Philip Sherrard, "George Seferis" in *The Marble Threshing Floor: Studies in Modern Greek Poetry* (London, 1956), pp. 185-231.

Kimon Friar, "George Seferis: The Greek Poet Who Won the Nobel Prize," *Saturday Review,* Nov. 30, 1963, pp. 16-20.

G. Georgiades Arnakis, "The Tragedy of Man in the Poetry of George Seferis," *The Texas Quarterly*, Spring 1964, pp. 55-67.

Edmund Keeley, "Seferis's Elpenor: A Man of No Fortune," *The Kenyon Review,* Summer 1966, pp. 378-390.

Thomas Doulis (essay date winter 1968)

SOURCE: Doulis, Thomas. "The Strategy of George Seferis: The Individual Poet and the Greek Tradition." *Texas Quarterly* 11, no. 4 (winter 1968): 72-88.

[*In the following essay, Doulis explores Seferis's place within the tradition of Greek poetry.*]

In a lecture on the Greek primitive painter Theophilos, delivered to the British Institute of Athens in 1947, George Seferis discussed a topic that had preoccupied him in the decade before the Second World War. It was two years after a brutal four year occupation, preceded by a crippling war, and during a civil war whose effects on Greece would be far-reaching. Yet it was, as well, an appropriate time to discuss his thoughts on art: Greece was relatively free after a decade of repressive government, not only of the German Nazi and Italian Fascist variety, but of the Greek Fascist variety as well, since the dictatorial regime of General Metaxas attempted to impose certain of its attitudes on Greek art and history on the contemporary consciousness.

For the little more than four years of the Metaxas regime (between August 4, 1936, when the General took over, and October 28, 1940, when Greece was attacked by Fascist Italy), the Greeks were a nation subjected to the moral edification and patriotic self-consciousness that appear to be inseparable from the genteel puritanism of middle-class dictatorships. For Greece this meant, among other things, that the normally inflexible demand that all formal occasions be marked by the use of the *katharevousa,* or the purist form of the Greek language, became even more repressive. Rallies, school assemblies, the government-controlled radio, all official organs, in fact, stressed a safe Hellenic "purity" that tended to elevate current Greece from her immediate past and locate her back among the ancients, before the Slavs and Turks, before the demeaning present, back when Greece was the center of thought and not a minor, Balkan nation on the edge of Europe.

The place of the individual talent within the tradition, a theme that had presented itself to T. S. Eliot, had never ceased to challenge Seferis since the publication of his first collection, **Strophe (*Turning Point*)** in 1931. During this significant Theophilos lecture delivered two years after his return from the Middle East and Africa, where he had served with the Greek Government-in-Exile, Seferis expressed many of the thoughts on the Modern Greek cultural tradition that had matured in him during the long remove from Nazi-occupied Hellas.

Seferis' political credentials were impeccable, his language was a clear, supple demotic (the language struggle in democratic Greece had ceased to exist) and the subject matter of his lecture—Theophilos Hadjimichael—could easily have been employed by another man to prove a political point irrelevant or antithetical to that of George Seferis.

The Greek folk-painter Theophilos was born in Mytilene around 1860 and died there in 1934. He lived in Volos and Pelion from 1895 to 1925, working as a painter; it is probable, however, that he lived in Smyrna as well, for he refers to himself as a "sometime guard commander and gate-keeper" there, most probably at the Greek consulate. Extreme poverty compelled him to earn his living by manual labor and he sold his paintings (whose subject matter ranged from the Greek myths to scenes of *The Iliad,* of the Cretan epic *Erotokritos,* of the Greek War of Independence, and of folk scenes and landscapes) for very little. Theophilos was achieving fame when Seferis lectured on him (his canvases were hung in the Louvre), a fame that culminated in the inauguration in 1965 of the Theophilos Museum on the Island of Mytilene (Lesbos).

But what does George Seferis, a poet of European stature and classical cultivation, have in common with an unlettered "primitive" painter who wore a traditional *foustanella*—a warrior's skirt—and was looked upon as an eccentric and harmless sentimentalist? As Seferis said in his lecture:

> The Greek cultural heritage is so vast that no one really knows who is going to be called to carry out its designs in practice. There are times when this heritage is in the hands of the most famous men in the history of the world, and there are other times when it goes into hiding among the nameless, waiting for the reappearance of the great names. Anyone who takes the trouble to look into this endless adventure will learn a lesson of great value. Our folk song can, in the sensitivity of one and the same person, throw fresh light on Homer and fill in the meaning of Aeschylus. This is no small thing, and it is a thing that could only happen in Greece.
>
> (Seferis, *On the Greek Style: Selected Essays in Poetry and Hellenism.*)

Theophilos, it appears from the lecture, is one of the "nameless" in whom the heritage had found a dwelling, one of the anonymous in whom the vast Greek tradition had chosen to carry out its designate designs. General Makriyannis is a similar figure, a great warrior in the struggle for Greek Independence who learned to read and write late in life so that he could write the *Memoirs,* a book considered by Seferis and many other Greek intellectuals as a landmark in modern Hellenic literature.

But Seferis is afraid of being misunderstood; he has not "the least wish to exalt the uneducated at the expense of the educated, or to suggest that there is anything

harmful in disciplined training and in knowledge," particularly since Seferis is to be numbered among the most cultivated and erudite of Greek poets. But if "education and knowledge are a training in life" men can learn much from people like Theophilos and Makriyannis "who have worked in the dark but found their way searching along dark passages of what is . . . a very cultivated collective soul—the soul of our people."

Theophilos, who learned from penny leaflets or worn out school texts, whose gallery was composed of "post cards and cheap chromos," succeeded in achieving a greatness that is more and more being recognized. Seferis eventually compares him to Vincenzos Kornaros, the Cretan poet of the seventeenth century and author of the love epic *Erotokritos,* a work modelled on a French romance, *Paris et Vienne,* "a sort of chromo of his time."

Theophilos, Makriyannis, Kornaros: three major figures in modern Greek culture; three men whose lack of formal education and technical training and whose unself-consciousness as artists would tend to make them polar opposites of Seferis become, instead, his mentors and supports.

> Since 1926, when I first held in my hands *The Memoirs of General Makriyannis* down to this very day, no month has passed without my reading some of its pages, no week without my thinking of some exquisitely vital passages which I have found there. These pages have been my companions through voyages and peregrinations; in joys and sorrows they have been sources of illumination and of consolation. In this country of ours, where we are sometimes so cruelly self-taught, Makriyannis has been the humblest and also the steadiest of my teachers.

Later in the same essay, "Makriyannis" (also delivered first as a lecture, in the war-time Alexandria and Cairo of 1940), Seferis calls Makriyannis "the most significant writer of prose in modern Greek literature" not only because of the "purity" of his language, but because he carried within him certain racial characteristics that placed him directly in the tradition of the ancients.

> At the beginning of the Revolution, in Arta, Makriyannis overhears one of the local beys speaking to his friends. He is careful to note the words:
>
> "Pashas and beys, we shall be destroyed, destroyed! For this war is not with Moscow nor the French. We have wronged the Greek infidel and taken away his wealth and honor. And this darkened his eyes and he rose up in arms. And this Sultan, this beast of burden, does not know what is happening. He is deceived by those around him."
>
> The cause of the Greek Revolution and of the ruin of the Turks is expressed by Makriyannis in one sentence which he puts into the mouth of an enemy. It is just as

when Aeschylus makes the enemy speak of their rout at Salamis: "We shall be destroyed, because we did wrong." *If we want to understand the ancient Greeks, it is always into the soul of our own people that we should look.* (Italics mine)

Makriyannis is "a branch of that 'stalwart tree' that gave to Greek culture a number of works, among which are included *Erotokritos, The Sacrifice of Abraham* (a Cretan religious drama), the splendid Greek folk song, and "the greatest artist we have produced since the ancient Greeks, Domenicos Theotocopoulos—El Greco."

A strange mixture, one would say at first glance. But it is strange only when one is unconscious of the criterion he uses to judge Greek art—the canon of the academic Greek tradition. Much has been written about the Greek tradition and the Greek "spirit" in art that is invalid because most students conveniently compartmentalize the idea of what is "Greek" on the far side of the Great Alexander's giant corpse. Whatever comes after that, the logic goes, is not "Hellenic" at all but "Hellenistic," and the Hellenistic period was marked, as everyone knows, by the political subjugation of the Greeks and by the genetic mixture of other races with the Greek (as if this were something disreputable in itself and something that had never happened to the race, that the Greek people were, in other words, *pure*; recent anthropological investigation has substantiated the claim that the "hellenes" of Periclean times were the results of the fusion of the Hellenes and the Pelasgian peoples). From the Hellenistic times onward, to follow the reasoning, the Greeks went into one unending retrogression, going from a sterile paganism, to what was even worse, a fervent and oriental Christianity—Byzantium—and finally, culminating in the deep-freeze of four centuries' duration, the Turkish domination.

During the long "death throes" of the race only one beacon existed for those semibarbaric brigands and pirates, and the merchants of the Levant who insisted, pathetically, that they were the descendants of both the ancient Greeks and the Byzantines (anyone who would couple the two was obviously raving): the hope of national liberation.

Certainly the many years of subordination to foreign conquerors had caused irreparable damage to the Greek political and ecclesiastical institutions, but language—the medium of culture—was itself changed in a number of ways. From the time the Turks subjugated Greece, by and large, they permitted no instruction in the Greek language that was not primarily ecclesiastical in nature. This tended to polarize Greek into two forms, the academic or ecclesiastical Greek and the Romaic or vernacular of the peoples of the Eastern Roman Empire—a polarity to which Greek had been liable for

centuries but which had always corrected itself since it was a living language used by citizens in their ordinary daily functions. In the highly fragmented and artificial existence of the Greeks during the four hundred years of subjugation to the Turks, the organic unity of the Greek language was broken and a chasm yawned between an increasingly artificial language of the church and literary documents, the *katharevousa,* and the steadily corrupted vernacular of everyday life, the *demotiki.*

In searching for a guide to what the Greek cultural tradition is, therefore, one tended—particularly in the Greece of the 1930s—to bypass the recent centuries, those chronicles of shame and decline, and to search for a Greek canon or a cultural identity either in Byzantium, in Alexandria, or in Periclean Athens. Not many cultures possess such a wealth and complexity in their past, but the cost of such richness is great; the Greek cultural heritage is one of the most fragmented, recording as it does the vast, barometric swings of the human temperament.

Seferis, in "Cavafy and Eliot—A Comparison," states:

> . . . According to the general view of foreigners, and no doubt of many Greeks, too, classical Greece, Byzantine Greece and modern Greece are disconnected and independent countries; and everyone confines himself to his special subject. It is not till about the time of the beginning of the last war that we begin to observe the formation of a rather hazy consciousness that Greece is indeed a whole and that we find young people from foreign countries becoming interested in Greek poetry, not as some kind of study in linguistics but as a living art which is part of a living tradition.

This fragmentation has occurred because the Greek tradition has been conceived of primarily as a learned tradition, something established by scholars and comprising texts and works of art. To Hellenists, i.e., classical scholars, this means "secular" art usually, thus disqualifying icons, murals, mosaics, church architecture, anything in the Christian tradition because "Greek" obviously means "pagan" whereas Byzantine (a word often used in the pejorative) means Christian.

> About twenty centuries have elapsed from the time the Gospels were written, or, if we wish, from the time the last Alexandrian craftsmen of the word were silenced. And this long period presents certain important characteristics to the student of Greek literature. First, there is no interruption or variation or reorientation—the road is straight. We have never known a "Renaissance" of the sort the European peoples of the West knew, nor such a decline or nadir. Second and more important: these endless millennia are covered by a profound silence. I am using the perspective of poetry at its most general, the aspect of that art that, using the word as its medium, struggles to express, to correct, and to communicate feelings. But the people of those

times had blood that throbbed in their veins, they had hands for embracing and for killing. Their feelings, however, are forever lost to us. Lost in the way that those of the people of Homer's time, of Dante's time, and of Shakespeare's time are not. But Greek had never ceased to be written. On the contrary, the Greek learned tradition is one of the oldest and least interrupted in the world. What is the matter? What has happened is that from the time of the Gospels until the years that preceded Palamas [Kostis Palamas, poet, 1858-1943], that is, until the years that the enslaved Nation begins to waken, the Greek texts do not express or create—they describe. We have the impression while reading them that we are circling a closed castle, one that will never open. They are dead and their language is dead. They "atticize." They are artificial. They are proudly independent and solitary—an endless shroud. And this shroud does not cover the living.

(Seferis, *Dokimes*)

To limit the Greek tradition to the tradition of the learned, therefore, is to see the Greek past not as one continuing expression of a people throughout their long history, but as a series of separate, highly differing, and virtually contradictory cultures bound together rather loosely by the use of the same language—in various stages of "corruption." To broaden the meaning of the Greek tradition to include the expression of the Greek people would provide a worthy and rich continuity.

This "endless shroud" of dead language is occasionally pierced by folk expression; Seferis frequently mentions the folk tradition he will use to counter that of the learned: ". . . the songs of the Akritic cycle, the popular verses of Constantinople, the Cretan Theater, *Erotokritos*." With the Turkish conquest of Byzantium and the Greek lands, though, the only living expression of Greek occurs among the people.

We may make many bitter comments about the abyss that may sometimes divide the learned and cultivated from the voice of life when we think that for many centuries the only true poet of the race was the anonymous and unlettered folk and that the only significant prose writer of whom I am aware is again one of the humble—a man who learned to read and write when in his thirties—Makriyannis. *And the strangest fact is that the unlettered folk bear with them Much more faithfully the ancient Greek spirit than does the vast rhetorical tradition of the purists . . . which is nothing more than an unbroken gag.*

It is this folk tradition that has constantly been misunderstood by the learned, who considered *Erotokritos* beneath the interest of the serious, fit reading matter for "servant girls," as Korais—the Paris-based classicist and grammarian—termed it. But Kornaros, Seferis claims, exulted in language, and the effortless diction of *Erotokritos* is a proof that during the Cretan Renaissance the resources of the poet's language and his sensibility were not at odds. This creative epoch, when

Crete was under the Venetians, whose hegemony also provided the environment for El Greco, was to end with the Turkish conquest of the island in 1699. After this, the Greek language ceased to flourish. Dionysios, Count Solomos (1798-1857), the national poet of Greece,

. . . guided by the Cretan poems and the folk songs, pursued his career, leaving us the bright fragments of the work he had dreamed about. But we will not re-encounter the ease with which the poet of *Erotokritos* wrote. On the contrary, we will notice that Solomos had a poetic sensibility developed disproportionately for the language of his time, which had greatly declined from the time of the Cretan Renaissance. We see that the language of Solomos can follow him only with difficulty and fragmentation. Only a small part of his sensibility can be communicated. The other, the unexpressed, is the "hoarseness" that tortures him. This is his struggle and even the emblem of his worth. He did not deign to compromise by employing words that approximated his meaning. Solomos confronted language with the precise conscience that—with Baudelaire and Mallarme—we encounter only later in Europe.

The language, as the poetry of Solomos and Kalvos will testify, had suffered after the fall of Crete to the Turks. Literature flourished only in those Greek lands where the Turks had not set foot. In the mainland, most Aegean Islands, Constantinople, and the other cities of Asia Minor, where Greek life was dominated politically by the Turks, the Orthodox Church was the sole unifying force of Hellenism as such, and poetic expression—barring folk poetry—tended to be in *purist* Greek.

Of the four genuinely great Greek poets, only Palamas used Greek with the power of a man whose language was the adequate vehicle for his sensibility. "Solomos, Kalvos, and Cavafy," Seferis writes several times, "(are) three great Greek poets who did not know Greek."

None of them took to Greek naturally. Each struggled with it in his own way, and only Cavafy was fortunate enough to be able to mould the Greek language to his own demands, for Solomos and Kalvos both foundered. The toll was vast in the estrangement between the unlettered Greeks who loved the monuments of their folk tradition and the learned who kept harking back to a classic past they did not fully understand, a Parnassian ideal they saw reflected through the Italian Renaissance, the French Enlightenment, and the Romantic Movement, cultivating a language so removed from the speech of the people that it was doomed to be forgotten.

The learned have contempt for the folk and they, in turn, look at the learned as though they are colorful birds of paradise. The bridges are down and everyone follows the river from his own side. On one bank they sing and speak like human beings, like Makriyannis. On the other they "compose" or speechify. This is how, in other words, we have gone on our way until at the end of the 18th century the river seems to narrow and it appears that the two processions will meet: Solomos.

But the linguistic position taken explicitly by Seferis in the above passage has been accepted by virtually every serious Greek poet of the twentieth century. To the hasty observer, therefore, it would seem that the conflict between the learned and the folk tradition can have been smoothed over easily by a language compromise. This is not the case, however, since the dichotomy manifests itself anew in a debate between Seferis and Constantine Tsatsos, then professor of philosophy at the University of Athens, now President of the Greek Academy.

Roughly, the thesis is whether modern poetry is antithetical to the Greek tradition. Tsatsos, a worthy representative of the founder of the Greek learned tradition, Plato, claims it is, since the "Tradition" has always exalted the "rational" over the "irrational."

> Although poetry by its nature differs from the rational, coherent expression, this difference cannot go beyond a certain degree without destroying poetry itself. The new movement (of poetry) either extends this degree more than it should, giving the irrational greater importance than it can aesthetically assume, or it rejects this distinction completely. A rejection like this of the rational and the coherent in poetry goes against the deepest sources of the Greek spirit and Greek beauty; it is, moreover, antithetical to every strong perception of the beautiful.

The direct and personal involvement of Seferis must not be underestimated. By this time—1938—he had already published The *Turning Point* (1931), *The Cistern* (1932), *Myth-History* (1935), and *Gymnopaedia* (1936). His poetic career is accused of falling outside the canons of traditional Greek beauty; for a man whose sense of "Greekness" is as intense as Seferis' this accusation is a serious one. Beyond concern for his personal career, however, the position of Dr. Tsatsos threatens to place most "modern" art outside the established Greek canon: surrealism, atonal music, nearly every one of the century's expressions, and by extension one of its "discoveries," primitive art, would be condemned by Dr. Tsatsos as "irrational" in conception, "incoherent" or "nonsequential" in execution, and thus outside the canon of Greek beauty, which stresses the rational, the symmetrical, and the harmonious.

"The dilemma is inexorable," Seferis says:

> Either we will face Western civilization, which is in great part our own, studying with seriousness and with sober courage its living sources (and I cannot see how this will occur unless we draw up the strength from our own roots and without a systematic labor for our own tradition) or we will . . . ignore it, allowing it to undermine us . . . with the mass culture and vulgarity, the worst form of its influence.

Seferis conceives of this dilemma, therefore, not solely in Greek terms, i.e., the standards of modern poetry are contrary to the standards maintained not just by the Greek tradition, but by the European as well. In this he is followed by his opponent, Dr. Tsatsos. Something unique has happened in European art in the twentieth century, something that separates "modern" art not only from the art of the past but from the art that has continued to be produced by artists alive and functioning at this time, whose values are basically still those of the "tradition."

If the Greek artist is compelled by the logic of his tradition to eschew newer forms of expression, then his tradition has not "logic" to combat but "rigidity" and the tradition must be either rejected (which to a thoughtful and serious man is unthinkable) or re-evaluated.

The dilemma, therefore, is not solely that of his culture but that of the poet, Seferis, himself as well. He can make a clean break as did Yannis Papadiamandopoulos, who called himself Jean Moreas, wrote in French, and helped form the Symbolist school in France, or he can continue writing in Greek and search through the vast Greek cultural heritage, not knowing "who is going to be called to carry out its designs in practice," hoping in this "endless adventure . . . to learn a lesson of great value." If he chooses the latter course, however, he must meet the thrust of his friend Constantine Tsatsos who reminds him, with the force of the tradition, of something a serious man must not dismiss; great value has in the past been placed on the precision of expression. What standard other than that of skill do we have for distinguishing the fussy from the suggestive, the chaotic from the complex, the pretentious from the profound?

Dr. Tsatsos discerns in the heart of the "modern" movement the possibility of an eventual breakdown in the traditional valuation of poetic skill. When that is gone, what other canon do we have for evaluating the work of artists.

> The intention of this modern movement is to transpose poetry to an area where the sequence (of thought) is loosened . . . where the aesthetic meaning and the rational meaning of the poetic expression do not only differ while maintaining some connection, which has always happened in poetry until today, but tend to divide fundamentally so that rational meaning becomes non-existent. It is through this that an element of intellectual obscurity intrudes, which demands from every reader a personal task of supplementing the poetry according to his own leaning and thus prompts—with the few allusions which the specific word promotes—a completely subjective and for that reason frequently dangerous and false aesthetic impression.

After cautioning that this antithesis between the "rational" and "irrational" elements in poetry may not be actual, merely a result of our displeasure in the work or our inability to understand it, Seferis questions the foundations of Dr. Tsatsos' critical position. The rational, the symmetrical, and the harmonious are "Greek" standards of beauty only because they were canonized by the scholarly tradition.

What can be more purely "Greek" than that most Greek of Greek arts, the folk song, a creation of the people, the art of the nameless, whose expression can be found not only in the lays of Homer, but in the songs of the dramatists as well, whose view of life is carried into the modern era essentially unchanged by this anonymous folk. According to Seferis' line of reasoning, Fauriel, the first gatherer of the Greek folk songs, and Polites, founder of the Greek Folklore Society, would not at all agree with Dr. Tsatsos when he says that the deepest springs of Greek art aim toward the rational expression. To illustrate this he quotes from a folk song collected by Nicholas Polites in *Selections from the Songs of the Greek People.*

> I kissed red lips and my own lips were dyed red.
> I wiped them with my handkerchief and it was dyed red.
> I washed it in the river and the river was dyed red.
> The shores were dyed red and the great sea.
> An eagle flew down to drink the water and his feathers were dyed red.
> Dyed red was half the sun and the full moon.

If we had not been accustomed to folk poetry and were given a poem like this by an unknown poet, Seferis continues, we would consider it "illogical" although its imagery adheres to a clear design. We would consider this folk song antithetical to the "deepest springs of the Greek spirit" and a violation of what we think of as "Greek beauty."

If the avant-garde school can possibly be criticized for loosening the standard of precision in poetic expression, it is also responsible, according to Dr. Tsatsos, for a decline in the sense of the "Greekness" of the work. Older poets and writers were more ethnocentric, more concerned with expressing poetic sentiments, chronicling the sufferings of the Greek people, studying the customs of the folk, work in the fields and on the sea, church festivities, folklore, the beauties of the countryside. Their duty was a great one, national in scope. They struggled to celebrate what was unique in the Greek, what distinguished the Hellenes from their neighbors, what related them to their resplendent past.

> Our older writers were extraordinarily vigorous and sometimes exclusive to the extreme in their attempts to express the Greek spirit, its land and its history. Along with this, they cultivated and enriched the language, making it precise by their attention and their love. Their rhythm, their modes of expression were molded by the intensive exploitation of the treasures to be found in our folklore. The activities of the avant-garde are contrary to this. . . .

It is a "great and beautiful" thing, Seferis admits, to speak of "Greekness" in an art, but this *Hellenikotita* is

also difficult and dangerous. The poets who used the *katharevousa* tried to achieve nothing else but "Greekness," a purity they would have achieved, they thought, only when they rid themselves and their people of the "stigmata of barbarism" and attained the purity of language and art of Sophocles and Plato. "And their reward was what might have been expected—a destruction and a drying up of Hellenism's fairest and truests streams."

Instead of achieving "Greekness," they misunderstood *Erotokritos,* one of the great monuments of modern Greek literature. So involved were they with content rather than style, that they ignored the knowledgeability of Kornaros, the poet of *Erotokritos,* his confidence in the use of language, his line-by-line coherence, his verbal economy, his development of a "recitative"— what Seferis calls the "pacing" through the necessarily dry and undramatic passages in the epic, his sensibility, and his sanity. They did not see that Kornaros was free of the flights of romanticism. In fact, Seferis claims that if he ever wanted to translate Racine into Greek, he would use the style and diction of *Erotokritos.*

Moreover, there is a difference, Seferis claims, between "slavish imitation" and "influence." Just as Dante used the scheme of an Arab poet and mystic Racine borrowed tragic plots from Euripides, and Shakespeare took the story of *Timon of Athens,* among others, from Plutarch, so Kornaros employed the story of Pierre de la Cypede, *The Romance of Paris and Vienne* for his epic. Each poet borrows what he likes but turns it into something personal, something that represents—not the original influence—but the poet's own sensibility and the temper of his age and culture.

> And no one imprisons himself within himself for fear that he would lose his uniqueness. His originality is his strength and he believes in it. That is why it is not at all strange that during this time, which exhibits an overwhelming cross-fertilization of intellectual currents between ages and lands, is precisely the era when the foundations of the great national literatures of the European peoples are established.

That a work of art is "Hellenic" or not is confused by certain historical factors. Alexander the Great bore Hellenism with his armies and this major cultural diaspora made Greek culture available to many differing temperaments and traditions until the Renaissance, when coincidentally the Greek people were subjugated by the Turks. Certainly Byzantine scholars saved the ancient treasures of Hellas by bringing them to the West, but they were not the *cause* of the Renaissance. Nor did any Greeks (aside from Dominicos Theotocopoulos) participate in the Renaissance of Western culture until the "reawakening" of the Greek people during the Revolutionary struggle against the Ottomans. Then, the best of the artists went to the West and tried to bring back to liberated Greece the heritage that had left our country in order to be preserved. But this heritage was not a matter of lifeless gold; it was a living thing that had fertilized its surroundings and taken root and borne fruit. And through these functions it gradually came to be a general and abstract framework inside which many powerful intelligences came to find their places, each completely different from the others and more consonant with their own selves than with anything else. Dante's Ulysses, Shakespeare's Venus and Adonis, Racine's Phaedre and Holderlin's Hyperion, apart from their worldwide significance and value, belong basically to the times and the races of their creators; their Hellenic subject matter is, as motivation, something external and superficial. We, however, with the most legitimate and commendable motives, burning, as we were, with the desire to bring back to Greece everything that was Hellenic and seeing signs of Hellenism everywhere, brought back, without looking more deeply into the matter, countless foreign values which in fact had nothing to do with our own land at all.

But must the values of the past be dismissed? If every era has its own aesthetic canons and only the works created at that time satisfy the people alive then, how can a tradition—in this sense—have any validity? If the values of the past can be dismissed by every generation, Dr. Tsatsos asks, how can we develop the critical apparatus independent of time that will help us study the works of the past, evaluate them, and "rescue" them, finally, from the maelstrom of history?

> Either, it would seem, the work of the past remains alive and equal to the newest works, and then the attempt to find new modes of form and new "schools" becomes pointless; or else we are aesthetically more profoundly and more genuinely moved by the new works of art, in which case the old masterpieces, seen as an aesthetic "good," are losing their value.

Seferis does not accept this, seeing no antinomy between the works of the past and the present. In fact, he claims that the newer works clarify, lighten, and enrich our understanding of the older. "It is well known," he answers Dr. Tsatsos, "how our understanding of Villon and Shakespeare has been enlarged by the romantic movement, which was itself a 'new school' attempting 'newer forms on art.'"

There is no disagreement between them, Seferis claims, when Dr. Tsatsos urges: "Read, gentlemen, your classics; you can never read them enough," but he would like to distinguish, not between classic and nonclassic, but between great poets and their imitators, the bad artists. "The lesser, the ignorant, those who cannot stand on their own, either imitate Pindar or Goethe or Baudelaire or Kostis Palamas or surrealism. . . ."

It is not solely imitation that is to be feared in the judgment of a work in the past; we must be on our guard against permitting our judgment to be influenced by the

very *age* of a work. We must, therefore, try to distinguish between the reverence we may have for a work of art—the Parthenon, for example—which is irrelevant to its artistic value, though intimately involved with its historical past, and the aesthetic confrontation with that particular work.

There is, moreover, a danger in thinking of certain works as "eternal." It would be more precise, Seferis feels, to call them "long-lived," removing from the adjective, however, whatever connotation it may have of preference or value. The word "eternal" is suspect because it begs the question. It is "eternal" because it has survived and it has survived because it is "eternal." The critic of the present, in other words, must form an hierarchy of the works of art rescued from the past, but neither he nor any other rational being has control over what is to survive.

> Once we agree that the judgment of time is worthless, since it condemns to the abyss a tragedy by Aeschylus although it saves, like a valued heirloom, a worthless epigram of the Palatine Anthology; once we accept, then, that the works which are for us unbelievable in their mediocrity may have provided past generations with a powerful poetic sentiment, we are left to assign our own values to the questions posed by the works that have survived until our times, and they are the questions of our era: pressing and contemporary questions. This is an important matter because from our answer depends our stance in the world of art.

In assigning hierarchical value to works of art, however, we may become influenced by our religious, political, metaphysical, philosophical, or sociological beliefs. This conflict between our other attitudes and the aesthetic values may becloud the issue of whether a poem is great or not. This has happened throughout history from Plato's ban on poets in his *Republic,* through the Inquisition, to our politically oriented times. There would be little difficulty, though, if the proponents of a philosophy, a religion, or a political belief were to admit that their dogmas were more important than aesthetics. When the values are allowed to become confused we find ourselves confronted by fanatics who destroy works of art because they happen to contradict their dogmas but try to justify their actions by saying that these works violate somehow laws of art which they assure us are unchanging.

Plato is consistent, and according to Seferis, his is "the only logical and honorable position," since, realizing that poetry is a "bad opponent" of philosophy and contests with her for the soul of the citizen, he decided to exile poetry from his *Republic* and this although he had loved Homer from his youth. But, as Plato claims, we must honor truth first and must restrain for her sake our feelings and our love for human beings.

> When we realize that Plato was, in his way, one of the greatest poets of the world, and when we remember

how deep was his feeling for poetry, we can comprehend how great the cost can be of a submission to
philosophical duty.

The poet differs from the mystic and the scientist in
that he cannot be convinced that what he is searching
for is absolute. A mystic wishes to be in communion
with God and does not trouble himself overmuch if he
is or is not in communion with man, while the scientist
discovers laws that exist and function whether or not
there are "beings on this earth or Mars." We can claim
that the music of Bach or the tragedies of Aeschylus are
independent of time and would exist eternally even in
the event of the destruction of the earth, but we cannot
claim this with the same meaning that the geometrician
states one of his theorems.

Art is involved in the human condition. Even though
there may be analogies and relations in their creativity,
the poet differs from the mystic in that he fails if he
does not speak to man. "It may be," Seferis states, "that
our communion with the eternal is a goal of art . . .
but it is unfounded to say that the eternal dictates rules
as to the method of creating good or bad poetry."

But in all of this Seferis does not mean to downgrade
the importance of the critic, whom he considers more
than an interpreter. The able critic, he continues, shows
us how to experience and evaluate the art that exists
about us. Since we are creatures of the art we have assimilated in the past, however, the judgments that we
make are not made by us but by the values that we,
consciously or unconsciously, carry within us. New art,
therefore, demands from us a sacrifice of those things
that we have valued in the past. Seferis essays an analogy: the role of the critic is to be like a water-diviner
who uncovers within us new sources of feeling, using
as an instrument not abstract thought but the art of his
time. This analogy he supports with a quotation from
Kostis Palamas:

> There exists no work of the human spirit, as fragmented
> and as unconnected as it may initially appear, which
> cannot be traced to a primary source . . . and which
> cannot be assigned to a creative idea. The intellect
> manifests itself as a unity and an activity, and it is
> enough for us to examine closely and patiently, until
> we can comprehend the complete uniqueness of every
> intellectual source and the development that is deter-
> mined from this uniqueness. Wherever we want to
> understand an intellectual impulse, a personality (by
> which I do not mean to signify the existence of an
> historical being but of an objective work), we must
> confront it as a self-existent, organic, and meaningful
> whole which is governed by its own laws. Reports
> about its general meaning, comparisons, and analogies
> (as aids) for the comprehension are not valid here.
> They are even dangerous. . . . We must encounter
> directly the idiomorphic and unique, that which is
> similar to nothing else, and to find the convincing judg-
> ment that will crystallize and conceptualize whatever is
> totally new. . . .

The critic's role, therefore, is not merely to compare a
work of art with an inflexible standard gained from the
achievements of the past, a past that can be misinter-
preted, moreover, because much of what has survived is
the product of blind fate and human folly as well as its
"intrinsic" value, but to "comprehend" a work of art, to
enter into its own logic, not to compare or to judge it
before he has grasped the work in all its uniqueness.

It is too easy to call poetry "dark" and "obscure" and to
dismiss it, Seferis claims. The attack on "irrational"
poetry by philosophers is not a new phenomenon, but
goes back to the *Republic*. It is revealing that Plato
would launch an attack on poetry, calling it "fiction,"
"false invention," and "foolish error" at the very time
that Homer and Sophocles represented poetry to the
ancient Greeks. Since "darkness" and "obscurity" have
been considered qualities of poetry from the beginning
of the "tradition," it would seem that critics who are
hostile to poetry are saying nothing particularly new.
This is not so, however, since poets nowadays are being
accused of wanting to be obscure.

The truth is otherwise, though. "In a world that is
emotionally fragmented and anarchic it is not art alone
that becomes 'difficult' and falls into an impasse, but
politics and love and the salvation of man." It seems to
be a maxim borne out by history that the more agreement people have amongst themselves, the more poetry
can become objective. But the modern world lacks the
unity of belief that the ancient Greeks and Chinese had.
Since this bond of tradition has loosened and art has
become subjective, the poet's only hope of being
understood is not in his emphasis and use of a common
and cherished past, but in the sensitivity and acuteness
of his audience's perceptions.

If we study modern poets carefully, Seferis suggests,
we will discover that they are more "logically organized" than their predecessors. It is only because their
poetry is denser, more elliptical, and more difficult that
they are considered "obscure." The reader, however, is
not fulfilling his duty if he rejects, without attempting
to understand, the poetry of his time. We must recall,
Seferis chides his Greek reader, that the poetry of Palamas, of Gryparis, and of Cavafy was not immediately
recognized, that—on the contrary—it was considered
displeasing at first. The Anglo-American reader will accept the justice of the remark and be able to cite several
like cases without too much effort.

We are free to make our own judgments of the values
of works of art, whether of the past or of the present.
We are committed if we wish to fulfill the functions of
the genuine critic to search among the contemporary
works of art that initially repel, displease, or disorient
us for their own rules of creation, not demanding that
they submit to the rules of past creations. The Greek

artist must, therefore, submit to his duty of expressing himself without fear that he will be judged an apostate from the past of his people.

Besides being free to choose modernity, the Greek poet's choice is even greater once he has recognized the legitimacy of his immediate parentage, the folk tradition, and ceased yearning for a lineage that is exclusively imperial. The Greek tradition is a fusion of the learned and the folk past and the selection of only one will result in the impoverishment of the complexity, the resonance, and the importance of a poet's work. To reject the works of the folk would be to reject the demotic song and even *Erotokritos*; to reject the learned tradition would be to lose the works of Cavafy. To do either would be to lessen something of the greatness of the tradition.

> For this tradition is not, as some see it, an affair of isolated promontories, some great names, some illuminating texts; instead it is like what others of us see and feel in the little mosaics of a humble Byzantine church—the Ionian philosophers, the popular verses of the period of the Comneni, the epigrams of the Anthology, Greek folk song, Aeschylus, Palamas, Solomos, Sikelianos, Kalvos, Cavafy, the Parthenon, Homer, all living in a moment of time, in this Europe of today and looking at our devastated homes.

"The Greek tradition is full of contrasts," Seferis says in another context, "which great men harmonize." This statement he meant of Angelos Sikelianos, but it fits Seferis as well. Besides the body of his poetry, which was not in the province of this essay, but which reveals him to belong firmly in the tradition, his prose has emphasized the necessity for a restudy and realignment of the Greek past, one that will deepen and clarify the meaning of Hellenism.

Anthony N. Zahareas (essay date spring 1968)

SOURCE: Zahareas, Anthony N. "George Seferis: Myth and History." *Books Abroad* 42, no. 2 (spring 1968): 190-98.

[*In the following essay, Zahareas examines Seferis's incorporation of both classical mythology and the modern history of the Greek people in his poetry.*]

No Greek poet is more intensely aware of the abyss between a great past and a dismal present than George Seferis, winner of the Nobel Prize for Literature in 1963.[1] "Wherever I travel, Greece wounds me still," the poet laments as he peers into Greek realities and recoils in agony at what he finds there. In his speech of acceptance on receiving the prize at Stockholm, George Seferis expressed above all the dilemma of being Greek:

> I belong to a small country. It is a rocky projection in the Mediterranean that has in its favor only the effort of its people, the sea and the light of its bright sun. It *is* a small country, but its tradition is immense.

The attraction of George Seferis for American readers may lie therefore in his poetic concern with Greece, just as the attraction of William Faulkner for foreign readers lies partly in his commitment to the Deep South. The circumstances of the Deep South and Greece, the matrixes of Faulkner's prose and Seferis' verse, define tragic moments in history when a frustrated region lives in the shadow of its legendary past and, inevitably, traditional values lose their power to comfort or sustain.

The Swedish Academy cited Seferis' treatment of the Greek landscape and especially his concentration on the deep mystery of stones, marble fragments, and silent smiling statues. These grounds littered with ruins, ancient marine kingdoms, empty harbors, the trail of arid mountains, slow-moving ships, abandoned homesites, together with the Aegean sea, the bright sun, and the maddening wind are woven into a symbolic net, the tangled web of the Hellenic experience. Moreover, the Hellenic experience embraces the moral conflicts and existential doubts that characterize much of the problematic literature of our times. The poet usually gazes at stone images and searches for some identity with past values, but statues do not always reveal their hidden truths and man must face the mystery alone, maimed, as it were:

> I woke with this marble head in my hands
> which exhausts my elbows and I don't know where to
>   prop it.
> It was falling into the dream as I was coming out of
>   the dream
>
> so our lives joined and it'll be hard to part again.
>
> I look into the eyes; neither shut nor open,
> I speak to the mouth which always strives to speak,
> I hold the cheeks which have grown beyond the skin.
> I can do no more;
>
> my hands vanish and then approach me
> mutilated.

The irresoluble contrast between man and statue accents the yearning for some answers to our existence and symbolizes the predicament of man trapped by his past. "He sinks who lifts the great stones" is the refrain of **"Santorin"** and **"Mycenae."** Yet man, somehow, accepts the burden for he needs the kinship with his historical and legendary past: "These stones I have lifted as long as I was able, / these stones I have loved as long as I was able, / these stones, my fate." Thus through broken stones, marble fragments, or confined spaces, indigenous sights of the Greek ambience, the dispersement, alienation, or the flow of time, typical motifs of contemporary literature, stand out. The search amidst ruins and the tormenting self-questioning, together, form a permanent backdrop of Seferis' verse and are a steady reminder of the tragic predicament of finding a way to be and a way to die:

> Because we have known so well this fate of ours,
> wandering through broken stones, three or six
>   thousand years,
>
> shall we be able?
>
> Because we have been bound, because we have been
>   scattered,
> and have struggled with unreal difficulties, as they put
>   it
>
> shall we be able to die according to the rules?

Whether the answer is yes or no, whether the gap between heroic memories and present breakdowns can ever be bridged, what stands out in the poetry of Seferis is the painful trial of man who by seeking, asking, wandering, and enduring, tries to find his center, to come to terms with some viable truth among the heaps of uncertainty.

George Seferis was a career diplomat and he has said, half serious, half tongue-in-cheek, that he never regrets having chosen a profession that is totally divorced from poetry. And we must see him under this double aspect—a sensitive poet attracted by myths but also a commonsensical man of affairs grounded in history. The biographical facts are significant. He was born George Seferiadhis in 1900 in Smyrna and spent his childhood on the Asiatic seacoast where the Greeks, despite a long Turkish rule, had kept their language, their religion, and their traditions. In 1914 he left because of the war, and in 1922 the Greeks were ousted from Asia Minor, Smyrna was destroyed, and Seferis was never to see his birthplace again. The shock of the disaster, the pain of exile, and the general disillusion became strong shaping influences upon his poetry. And his professional duties enabled him to assess with objectivity the problem of a country more and more isolated in the world.

The situation of Seferis as poet only bears out his experience as diplomat. He opened his acceptance speech at Stockholm, delivered ironically in French, with an acute and poignant statement of a Greek writer's frustration:

> At this moment I feel that I am a contradiction. The Swedish Academy has, in fact, decided that my efforts within a language famous for many centuries but of little if any extension in its present form, were worthy of this high distinction. The Academy wished to honor my native language, yet here I am thanking you for the honor in a foreign tongue. Please accept the excuses that I must also make for myself.

Seferis is both a spokesman and a symptom of the Greek condition. Unlike other Nobel winners who elaborated universal problems, he discussed the development and importance of modern Greek poetry. It was an act of solidarity: "I need this solidarity," he concluded in Stockholm, "because if I do not understand my own people, with all their virtues and their vices, I feel that I shall not be able to understand the other people of this big world." Thus the first Greek ever to win the Nobel Prize happens to embody most purely and persuasively the Greek sense of acceptance and fellowship—crystallized in the tragic myth of Oedipus and the tragic history of Socrates.

I

Seferis is an unusual Greek in that he is not a prolific writer. In three decades, he has written one volume of poetry, one of critical essays, and one of translations.[2] His style is economical and simple: "I want nothing more but to speak simply; may I be given this grace. / Because we load the song with so much music that little by little it is sinking." His poetic expression is deliberately condensed and gnomic, and consequently his simple phrases carry a weight beyond their ostensible meaning; each poem is pure, the result of a careful, conscious word-for-word technique that makes heavy demands upon the reader.

His first book of poems, *Strophé,* was published in 1931; the title means stanza but also *Turning Point,* a prophetic term since the collection opened new directions for Greek poetry. Seferis initiates here themes like the passing of time, the anxiety of death, sensuality and sterility. In **"Rima,"** for example, he juxtaposes life's vital activities with the consideration that man dies a little every day until he dies for good: "'T is the time when dusk is drowned / and I tire searching in darkness . . . / (Our life diminishes a little every day)." Recollection of past activities (loving, hunting, sun-bathing) leads to a meditation on the preciousness of experience now reluctantly surrendered. The only long poem in the first collection, **"Song of Love"** (**"Erotikós Logos"**), is an account of passion in time: the poet evokes something beloved and is briefly in an intoxicated state of expectancy but eventually realizes that the changes of time are final.

> . . . Red rose of wind and fate
> you only remained in memory, a heavy cadence,
> rose of the night you passed by, a purpureal tempest,
> a tempest of the sea . . . And the world, it is simple.

Recalled experience is maddeningly incomplete because something lost cannot be summoned up again in its dazzling actuality. As with Proust, spots of time (here "corals of memory" or "dense flutterings") overcome temporarily the ravages of oblivion and bring about the miracle of identity with one's past. The psychological development of exaltation and letdown ends in the matter-of-fact acceptance that the world is simple after all. The implication is that man outgrows his dreams. Seferis brings to the retrospective meaning of time a gentle and somber resignation which will become central in his later poetry.

The anxieties of *Strophé* and **"Song of Love"** assume by 1932 a tragic vision in *Cistern* (*Sterna*): "Here on the ground taking roots, a cistern, / a cave of hidden water collecting treasures." The underground, sealed reservoir is like man's sleepless consciousness; above, one hears footsteps of crowds marching silently, blindly through a mysteriously unreal, hell-like atmosphere of "ebony darkness." If we could only forget and "let roses blossom in the blood of our wound." The poet recalls anxiously pleasure, fertility, blooming lemon trees, and suddenly envisions a spring procession: "Mournful shadows upon dead wreaths / footsteps . . . footsteps . . . the slow bell / unwinds a dark chain." The spectacle is Christ's funeral as recreated in Athens every year two days before Easter. Crowds move slowly holding candles and singing laments which, nevertheless, betray the hope of redemption. And all the while, the cortege has been passing, ironically, under the Acropolis:

> "We are dying! Our gods are dying! . . ."
> And the marbles know it as they gaze
> like a white down upon the victim,
> strange to us, full of eyelids, broken pieces,
> as the crowds of death wind by.

Visually, a telling scene: the Parthenon columns gaze silently upon this mournful march toward Resurrection; as the wise silence of pagan stones makes clear, there is no Resurrection. Footsteps are both those of the cortege and the ones that echo over the cistern which patiently bides its time: "'T is a cistern that teaches silence / inside the lighted city." The crisis before the cistern, that is, the moment before man crosses the ultimate frontier of life on to death, is here magnified into a majestic awareness of the pattern of history, balancing the hope of Christianity with the finality of paganism.

Seferis undercuts rhetoric or patriotic bombast while his simplicity deflates exaggerated notions of Greece's "destiny" and heroic grandeur. He offers an anti-heroic vision of life, a skeptical appraisal of rampant heroism, and a concern more about the predicament of the Greeks than their heroism. This explains why Seferis did not plunge into partisan commentary upon the political, social, and literary conflicts of contemporary Greece, an extraordinary feat considering the temptations and pressures for involvement. He distrusts easy commitment and concentrates on the anonymous participants that few care to remember: "Again and again the same things, you will tell me, friend. / Yet the thought of the exile, the thought of the prisoner, the thought / of man

become mere commodity / try and change that, you cannot." And I suspect that his concern for the young of Greece (he considers his Nobel award one of their few victories) is part of his commitment to those who are ground to oblivion by history, to the anonymous and the insignificant.

II

Following his first poems, Seferis abandons rhyme, eliminates whatever smacks of tour de force, and concentrates on simple, dense, subtle musical expressions. The combination of austere form and the Greek circumstance leads in 1935 to the famous *Mithistórema.* The work consists of twenty-four poems complete in themselves but also part of a unified whole. The title is ambiguous, meaning, variously, myth and history, myth of history, mythical story, novel, or romance. Perhaps "legend" is more appropriate, that is, a true or fictional account that comes down from the past. "The immemorial drama" that is to "begin once more" is a trying journey while the actors are voyagers who suffer physical deprivations and hopeless yearning. Each poem is about a visited spot, a relic found, a misadventure, a recollection, an observation, a lament. The characters are ancient or modern Argonauts "sweating at the oars," exiles "tasting the bitter bread," pilgrims "in aimless pilgrimages," harassed Orestes circling "onto the track," expectant Odysseus, refugees, and several others. The narrator speaks as "I" or "we" and this compound voice of multiple identities moves back and forth in time until the borderline between past and present is completely blurred. Thus the voyage is also an act of self-examination and a meditation upon the human condition by straddling, as it were, the diverse times of civilization, by wandering among the various mirrors of myth and reality.

Mithistórema stands to an epic as an oratorio to opera. There are no glorious action and no glamorous figures but rather silent sufferers ("They did not complain / because of weariness or because of thirst or because of frost") not recorded in history and referred to only in passing in the legends about Jason and Odysseus.

> They had the bearing of trees and waves
> that accept the wind and the rain,
> accept the night and the sun,
> without changing in the midst of change.

The "mythistorical" voyager is the common man found anywhere in all times of Greek history, who endures through time and survives the changes in political, social, and religious philosophies because he lives, necessarily, by a basic philosophy which is a law of life—one lives as one can. The Argonauts toil submissively, endure all humbly, die a death that is, justly, forgotten:

The companions expired, one after the other
with downcast eyes. Their oars
indicate the places where they sleep on the shore.

And no one remembers them. Justice.

We remember Jason or Odysseus but not the lads who followed them. The last word, *justice,* is the awareness that these are after all the rules of the game but it is also a questioning of the fairness of these rules. Justice and injustice are here inextricably mingled as in all Greek tragedies.

The title indicates the poetic structure because myth and history are juxtaposed so that they make their own comment on each other. There is an oscillation between modern Greece where seamen live in a concrete world and ancient Greece where Argonauts live in a legendary world. The condition of modern seamen and ancient Argonauts is alike in that it is a tragic condition but their reality differs in that one is real and the other fabricated in the mind of some poet. Seferis presses this boundary situation of history and myth for its total yield. In the invented world of myth, the Argonaut is anonymous, and his is the fiction of a non-existent character; in the real world of history, the anonymous Argonaut is only a shadow of reality, he is only a myth; but also in the world of history, the anonymous Argonaut, as a tragic spirit, exists—he endures beyond myth and belongs to the world in which the common Greek seaman exists. Each one suffers and endures anonymously like the other, that is, the tragic pattern of anonymous toil, effort, and death give unity to myth and history. The Argonaut or the modern Greek, "we," are all such stuff as myths are made on even if our life is surrounded by history. Our legendary past casts light on our tragedy just as our history substantiates the tragic stuff of past myths. Tragic fellowship is the bridge that Seferis constructs so that one can cross the abyss between myth and history.

After being led slowly but remorselessly toward the meaning of the ancient dead who "smile in a strange silence" and after being confronted with the tantalizing question whether one can die according to the rules, *Mithistórema* ends with two poems that balance each other:

Only a little more
And we shall see the almond trees in bloom
the marbles shining in the sun
the sea rippling

only a little more,
let us rise a little higher.

For, finally, lucidity is comforting and painful awareness is a movement toward recovery, a turning toward acceptance where consolation is not completely shut out. We are made to take a glimpse at the abyss but also at the possibilities of acceptance and hope. The vision of *Mithistórema* is thus neither of total despair nor of total redemption but, as with Greek tragedies, of something tantalizingly, precariously in between. The end is deliberately one of an ambiguous calm:

Here come to an end the works of the sea, the works
    of love.
Those who some day shall live here where we end,
if by chance the blood should darken in their memory
    and overflows
let them not forget us, the feeble souls among the as-
    phodels.
Let them turn the victim head toward the weird dark-
    ness:

we who had nothing shall teach them peace.

The calm melancholy of leave-taking seals *Mithistórema* with a new sense of contact between life and death. The peace offered is that of "strange silence," a reminder of the mystery of our lot. The Greeks saw the human predicament "shining in the sun" as part of the order of things. The choice involves finality and hope in an unclear mixture and leads to the awareness that there is some principle of order within the haphazard scheme of things.

Mithistórema is, despite "purity" and "modern" techniques, circumstantial poetry. For Seferis is committed to Greece as Antonio Machado was committed to Spain and W. B. Yeats to Ireland. In all three there is a strong sense of the regional particularity. Spain, Ireland, and Greece are, to paraphrase Hawthorne, quite as large a lump of earth as the heart can really take in. When a Greek poet journeys on a little steamship from port to port and sees the "curtains of mountains, archipelagoes, naked granite," observes "the bitterness of the harbor once all the ships are gone," overhears social trivialities and feels the banality, waste, sterility, frustration, and misery of provincial Greece, naturally Greece wounds him and "They call the ship that travels, AGONY 937," that is, the poet always mingles in "agony" the private world, the Greek world, and the big world. The combination of regionalism and universality makes his poems engrossing, utterly faithful to their own terms. Seferis invents a mythical Aegean world complete and living in all its details and his journeys into the Aegean Sea stand as a parable or legend of Greek history and man's history.

III

Seferis strove constantly to make his poems move upon several planes, and in **"The King of Asine,"** his acknowledged masterpiece written on the eve of World War II, he perfects the technique of transition from one plane to another. The poet searches around a ruined

fortress in the small sea kingdom of Asine near Nau-
plion for its old king, "unknown, forgotten by all, even
by Homer / just one word in the *Iliad* and that
uncertain." The allusion is to "Asinen té" in Homer's
list of those heroes who came to fight against Troy. It
means "and Asine," that is, let me tell you of one more
king who took part in battle. The search underlines the
changes: ruins in place of a fortress, a name for a king
and a bat, symbol of uninhabitedness, in place of the
kingdom's activity. Seferis constructs his modern Greek
poem around the ancient Greek phrase "Asinen té":

> The king of Asine a void under the mask,
> everywhere with us, everywhere with us, under a
> name:
> 'Asinen té . . . Asinen té . . .'

Seferis converts Homer's line into a refrain and skillfully grafts it into a modernized elegy. The effect is
striking and the Homeric affirmation "and of another
hero" reads as an ambiguous lamentory query, "What of
Asine, the hero hardly mentioned by Homer?" The lament for the king leads to a question about the tangible
and intangible realities that vanish, recalling François
Villon's "But where are the snows of yesteryear?"

> Do they exist, the movement of the face the form of
> affection
> of those who dwindled so strangely in our life,
> of those who remained wave-shadows and thoughts
> like the endless sea?

The recollection of past splendor is a reminder that, in
the face of death and annihilation, all pretensions of
glory are puny and futile. And the refrain "Asinen té"
is so placed that it draws all the attention and infuses an
ironic reality both into Villon's elegiac motif and into
the Homeric epic formula.

> Asinen té . . . Asinen té . . .
> Could this have been the king of Asine
> for whom we search so carefully about the acropolis
> feeling sometimes with our fingers his very touch upon
> the stones?

Echoes from *Macbeth*: Asine was but a walking shadow
after all, one more player in a big play who appeared
briefly upon the stage and then was heard no more. And
heroism is one more illusion. Asine was listed and
sought out as a great king, but Asine is in fact a shadow
of a king, a shadow of a hero—"a void under the
mask"—with only one phrase in an epic, no more, for
his heroic identity.

"The Thrush" is Seferis' best-known work after the
war. It is a very dense poem where everything can be
read as an account of postwar experience or as an
extensive structure of existence, and is held together by
a whole network of real and symbolic references. Its
literary and contemporary allusions, something like

Joyce's *Ulysses,* will be resolved only with the passing
of years. The setting is the picturesque island of Poros
(Seferis spends most of his summers there) where one
could still see after the war the hull of a small ship, the
Thrush, sunk by the Germans in 1941. The half-
submerged boat punctuates the waste and bitter
memories of the war as well as man's precarious position. The narrator is here a mature Ulysses back from
the war, the witness to many absurdities and to many
bitter experiences, now skeptical, stoical, tolerant. The
surroundings provide a canvas for his inner conflicts
and his meditations on the human condition: a house
near the sea focuses on the idea of stability and emptiness; a conversation between a young war companion
who recalls Elpenor in Homer's *Odyssey* and a capri-
cious woman who recalls Circe dramatizes the irony of
physical proximity and spiritual distance; a radio by the
beach is a reminder of inanities and mechanized
conventionalities; the wreck of the *Thrush* points to the
imminence of death; finally, a little girl on the beach,
called Antigone, symbolizes the hope for regeneration.
The older Ulysses is mature but unable to indulge in
life as before; in short, the restless seeker is now rest-
lessly remembering and everything in his mind turns
into a network of symbols as in the works of Aeschylus. Life and death, past and present, war and peace,
myth and reality, time and eternity, memory and
oblivion, passion and inadequacy, and many more
universal themes are perfectly integrated, somehow, and
viewed in terms of Greek symbols, Greek landscape,
and Greek traditions.

As the poet observes the sunken *Thrush* he hears voices
coming from the bottom of the boat as if from Hades.
He is especially drawn by one "calm, changeless, still"
voice:

> And if you sentence me to drink poison, I thank you;
> your law shall be my law; for where should I go
> wandering about in foreign lands, a rolling stone.
> I choose death rather.

He recognizes Socrates, the wronged one. The implications of injustice, exile, and death lead to introspection
and in a moving review of his past we see all the echoes
of existential anguish:

> As the years go by
> so increase in number the judges who condemn you;
> as the years go by and you converse with fewer voices,
> you gaze with other eyes upon the sun.

The poet sees clearly malevolence, frauds, privations,
the sting of criticism, the mockery of friends. But the
personal drama is superseded by the awesome drama of
the war.

What conclusion can result from this abyss of private
and general catastrophes? The poem is resolved in a
series of dualities:

> Angelic and black light,
> daughter of waves on playgrounds of the sea,
> tearful laughter,
> the old man looks on you, suppliant
> ready to make his way over invisible slabs,
> light mirrored in his blood
> that gave birth to Eteocles and Polynikes.
> Angelic and black day. . . .

Light and darkness are symbolic of the circle of man's life. The old man is Oedipus who in darkness saw light, who has just begun on the hard road to understand the true meaning of his answer, *man,* to the riddle of the Sphinx. The poet next addresses Antigone, a little girl on the beach as well as a figure of tragic ambivalence:

> O sing, little Antigone, sing O sing . . .
> I do not speak of things past, I speak of love;
> crown your hair with thorns of the sun,
> dark girl.
>   . . . . .
> he who has never loved shall love,
> in the light. . . .

Antigone carries within her the two worlds of man, the two brothers Eteocles and Polynikes, the angelic and the black light. "The Tyrant inside man has left" and there is time for one to love in these difficult days. But this is not an easily accessible love for one must experience the light, that is, the total awareness of our lot with its vulnerabilities and all its direness. Seferis provides that satisfying and perfected embodiment of a long-sought truth which gives at once the impression of recognition and discovery. The sustained quest of the poet-Ulysses and the appearance of Antigone set everything in the light of Greek tragedy: man's sorry lot and his capacity to learn, to "see in his blood" as Oedipus the angelic and the black light. The resolution emerges in a kind of dark luminousness, the characteristic half-light of Greek tragedy.

After many years of self-search and a terrible war, **"The Thrush"** seems to be both a comment and an answer to the question raised by *Mithistórema.* Man can die according to the rules, of course, but the road is difficult, full of fragmentary, tentative, and precarious truths. Suffering will not be avoided, but suffering can lead to light, to the knowledge of what one is and what it means to be.

No single work sums up Seferis better than "Makriyanis, one Greek," an essay about a hero in the struggle for independence of the 1820's. John Makriyanis was an illiterate who, somehow, left behind a remarkable book of memoirs: "And whatever I mark down here," he explains, "I mark down because I cannot stand to see injustice choke what is just. For this reason I learned letters in my old days and I jot these notes here gross and raw because as a child there was no way for me to learn." Seferis is awed by the sheer will of this illiterate

fighter to express himself and by the literary quality of the memoirs written under personal limitations, historical conditions, and private dangers that would have reduced any lesser man to silence. Makriyanis' passionate need for expression is for Seferis like "these stubborn plants that, once their roots take hold, go on overcoming walls, stones and graveyards."

Makriyanis was in later years persecuted by his liberated countrymen, and Seferis sees in this ironic twist of fate the makings of a significant, tragic action as in ancient drama—not because of the lamentable blows that fell upon a heroic figure but because of his counter-thrust that makes for authentic drama. This counter-thrust can be seen in Makriyanis' lifelong, innocent conversations with God which he records in the memoirs whenever he encounters difficulties. In one such confrontation with God, he comes face to face with his destiny and strikes back, as in a play, with words. The harassed national hero addresses God pitifully but also firmly: "And you don't hear us and you don't see us . . . And me groaning night and day with my wounds. And I have to see my miserable family and my children choking in tears and without shoes. And six months jailed in a cramped dungeon. And unable to see a doctor, and they don't let anyone come near us or see us. All wish that we should perish. They question all of us, they search our houses, our basements, our roofs, our boxes . . . even your own icons. . . ." Makriyanis was no longer able to come to an understanding with God. The times had changed. The national hero was now imprisoned, beaten, tried and convicted but he stood his ground, in the words of Seferis, "a man reaching the heights of man." He is for Seferis the image of Greece. For Makriyanis finds out, like the "companions" of myth and history, that the world is not always reasonable and not always just. But unjustified suffering must be endured and accepted as part of the mystery, and Makriyanis—a sort of Oedipus and Job put into one modern dress—can do no more than persevere in the pride of his convictions, and to understand. For in his appeal to God against God, in seeing the "angelic and black light" of his lot he has learned, like Greece, to live and to die according to the rules.

Notes

1. See "Seferis," by John E. Rexine, *Books Abroad* 41:1, pp. 37-38.

2. Seferis' poems are available in English: *Poems,* Rex Warner, tr., Atlantic-Little, Brown (Boston, 1964); and *Collected Poems 1924-1955,* E. Keeley, P. Sherrard, trs., Princeton University Press (Princeton, N. J., 1967); see this issue for review p. 335. A selection from Seferis' essays, among them the one on Makriyanis, has been published with the title *On the Greek Style,* R. Warner, Th.

Frangopoulos, trs., Atlantic-Little, Brown (Boston, 1966). For a review of *Tría Krifá Piïmata,* Seferis' latest work, which came out too late to be included in *Collected Poems* (see above) or in this article, see this issue, p. 320.

Stavros Deligiorgis (review date spring/summer 1975)

SOURCE: Deligiorgis, Stavros. "Greek Light." *Parnassus: Poetry in Review* 3, no. 2 (spring/summer 1975): 113-20.

[*In the following review of* Days of 1945-1951: A Poet's Journal, *Deligiorgis examines Seferis's reaction, in his writing, to world events in the years immediately following World War II.*]

I: CAUDAL PROCESSUS

Quiet but powerful descent. We hear Marcus Aurelius in Seferis' acknowledgment of his masters; we hear Montaigne, also, in the awareness of other cultures and the inability to resist comparison. All the French meditators are there also, from Stendhal to Valéry, who wrote about writing. And all the unacknowledged ancient epistolographers who ever condescended to write about moving from town to country and then back to town, about the health of a relative, the death of an animal, the life of a prostitute. The culmination in the *Greek Anthology* is well known: the poetry by talking about actors, suicides, slaves, freaks, merchants, schools did not merely expand the stylizations of New Comedy, it showed the wild range of the world great ideas historians left untouched, showing perhaps better than the historians how those centuries of world empires, sick troikas, and religions like tropical diseases happened. This is a volume to place, necessarily, next to the **Collected Poems** that Sherrard and Keeley translated a few years ago. It is a book, like the *Greek Anthology,* that shows its making, but also the poet's making at the same time.

Seferis' prose feels, thumbs through, and listens: Paul Eluard reading good poems at the French Institute in Athens, but repeating, and repeating himself, and never asking a question; the Bikini bomb called "Gilda," anabolizing Hollywood (and Doctor Strangelove, *ante litteram*), but catabolizing Europe which started it all; Kazantzakis and Sikelianos—an author about as famous as Kazantzakis—about to propose to the Nobel Committee that it divide the prize it had not yet awarded between the two of them; the record of a dream of Gide in drag and in gay company; one and a half women fainting at a lecture by Seferis on Cavafy and Eliot; Henri Michaux' idea of lecturing: "Look at the audi-

ence, pick someone out, and say '*Toi, mon vieux . . .* I must put certain things in your head'"; Jean Cocteau's platitudes in Ankara, about Ankara sprung "like Minerva . . . from the head of Zeus," Zeus understood by Seferis to mean Kemal Ataturk; Michael James (grandson of William and grandnephew of Henry James) cleaning mosaics at an excavation in Constantinople; the relevance of Bergson and Proust to his reading of Cavafy; S. Bey, the Smyrniot currant merchant, angry at Eliot's reference to Mr. Eugenides, but, then, turning into an Eliot fan, the city of Smyrna, all the while, carrying on a perpetual census! Naturally. Seferis, who was born and raised there, returns a grown man to see the remnant of the slaughterhouse it became in the early Twenties. The waves of indifference, the strangeness, the family haunts, the reality that he had started his journal at the age of twelve in Smyrna amount to a delirium that he can barely stand. He knows he is manhandled into the world of the dead.

II: TECTOPONTINE FIBER

No writing can prepare you for that. Seferis recoils from "literature." Literature does not deal with the desecration of churches by Turks, or mosques by Greeks (he wishes both demolished them), nor with the U. S. Army interests in chemical and biological warfare, nor with broadcasts during the Second World War proclaiming the Germans—poised for the bludgeoning that broke half the living body of Greece—a people free of original sin. The difficulty of "writing," the moral point of it, Seferis' recording weeks of sensing, seeing silence, are all part of the humility, the involvement, and the intense understanding of this document. He wonders if a diaspora couldn't be the basis of decency in creativity. Which is the context, of course, of Seferis' concern with Cavafy, for whom the barbarians would have been a kind of solution, the journey to Ithaca had better have no end, and the Thermopylae in our lives properly guarded by the very resolute few who have clear knowledge that Ephialtes will come and that the Persians will finally go through. This is not fatalism; just the guarantee of perpetual upheaval, the poet in the midst of it unable to moralize, unable to be a poet. Here are a few verses from **"L'Angolo Franciscano"**:

. . . . .

and everywhere the leaves hold hands and hem you
  in.
Among these mountains with color beyond life,
in these wildernesses, dry depths
from seas you might once have sailed,
in the small garden, here, the fruits,
here the children of religion;
unripe offerings ripe offerings rotten offerings.
"How did we become like this?"
Better to ask
the wizards the jugglers and the villains. . . .

The public scene between 1945 and 1951 meant the years of "aid" from the two super-sides (in money, advisors, arms), and a war that showed the Greeks' readiness to die for a cause and against one another. Also Greek meretriciousness, depending on the side. They were years of corruption, international fairs, arts festivals, fatter tourism, worsening Cyprus, earthquakes, richer ship-owners riding the infamous cold war, and, everywhere the offal of rhetoric, the floating of conscience. When the Greeks were not preying on each other, they were on the move. Large numbers coming to the mainland from Romania, the USSR, and Egypt; large numbers then emigrating to New Zealand, South America, and Canada; Communists settling in Eastern European countries (visited and interviewed by Vassilis Vassilikos in the Sixties). Seferis the political animal is sniffing, clawing, ruminating, licking wounds, and getting new wounds:

> I said once, blood
> brings blood and more blood—
> they thought it a mountebank's act,
> old fairy tales.
> Still I whispered. . . .

> At noon on the American warship Providence. . . . As soon as I went aboard I felt like a captive in the hands of doctors and nurses preparing to operate. . . . "Like a cannon," explained the admiral, "they launch the plane at an initial speed of sixty miles per hour." "And the pilot's head?" someone asked. "It would get crushed, of course," said the admiral casually, "but there is a special apparatus." Later they opened the hold where the storageroom and workshop are. A chamber of scientific destruction.

Only victims have his kind of astonishment. His fellow-countrymen, like the survivors on a raft, cannibalizing one another; the ministry where he was working giving off the smells of a hospital; the hospital where he is operated, where he begs for a bowl of water to wash, reminding him of Jerusalem, or Delphi! (Athens?); the power games looking more and more like *grand guignol,* with everybody cowardly murderous and self-righteous. There is no need to ask. Calumny, speculation, inhumanity are within each one of us. Poetry, when it happens, is truly like building on the wide open sea:

> There is a drama of blood much deeper, much more organic . . . which may become apparent to whoever perceives that behind the gray and golden weft of the Attic summer exists a frightful black. The stories we read about the . . . Atreids or Labdacids show in some way what I feel. Attic tragedy, the highest poetic image of this hemmed in world, constantly striving to live and breathe upon this narrow golden strip of land . . . with little hope of being saved from sinking to the bottom. This creates its humaneness.

III: ALBUM PROFUNDUM

Seferis is shifting. We catch a glimpse of the submerged, and weightiest, side. Like those floating masses of solidified fresh water, hundreds of miles long, we can-

not encompass the caves, the blue crags, the resonant chasms all at once. Seferis is a man who entrusts you with his dreams; he entrusts you with his youth. Between the notes for a poem that comes slowly he constructs a little doll of acorns and nuts; her name is Mrs. Zen.

> "Contra tempo senza brio"

> . . . my thoughts
> descended, descended
> toward the seashells,
> the curved lips,
> the closed-in music;

> and these odds and ends
> that I put together
> with my fingers, kept
> slipping away from me,
> leaving nothing behind
> but a little poison
> and this tiny person
> I call Mrs. Zen.

> (**"Mrs. Zen"**)

The true Seferis prays to be rid of the dross of effort. He frees himself through a long progression of "Zen problems," as he calls them, sown across every one of his perceptions, associations, and fears. He gives us a good record, and the good word. T. S. Eliot's *Four Quartets,* St.-J. Perse's *Anabase,* W. H. Auden's "Spain," Jules Laforgue's poems, B[owra?], the last European, who knew his classics and could converse on anything "from Lorca to Pasternak," all are periphery by comparison to the calm centering Richards' *Mencius on the Mind* gives him. Basho is very much with him; yet he avoids the jargon of the Koan, as he avoids the term Tanka, but we sense his vision, the circle of transcendence. We cannot speak of Orientalism, however, for just as often we will hear of the Cappadocian fathers, of the apocryphal Protevangelium Jacobi, of the Studites, of St. John of Patmos. But that's not all. The inhospitable plateau of Anatolia affects him to the point of physical distress, yet he hears, right on time, that it is only the radioactivity of the terrain. As he leaves the anguished birthplace he wonders if he will "miss the protection of the Anatolian steppe."

This is the master's second blast. The shock to the Greeks to know themselves really known for what they are; and a shock to know what manner of man Seferis was.

> I imagine that the Argonauts, as they went along, now and then uttered foolish cries. Like the rhythm of the chorale, which is such a voyage.
> Foolish cries, but definite. I remember those days on Poros and my impatience when I heard: "How beautiful!
> What a marvel! What magic!" In the evening I read the

newspaper as if I were uncovering a miserable wound.
This light and this wound; this coming and going
 between
the light of day and man's tragedy that tests your
entrails: the marriage of heaven and hell, that's the
passion of a beautiful day. You must be very alive and
have crushed your ribs on many Clashing Rocks to
 retain
this passion. You must have loved life like a man who
 has
retained within him, throughout all his ages, the child
he once was.

Empedocles had already asked this question, in a slightly different way. Seferis might easily be satisfied with the appeal in the *Arabian Nights* which he translates:

Let the houses become habitations of the dead;
you will find different lands, other cities,
but you will find no other soul like your own.

A prayer he postpones from the beginning of the journal burst forth as a *Canzona,* at five in the morning.

Figure of sunken sanctuaries

. . . . .

land of the living

. . . . .

in cities shriveled within their walls;
down in the plains of the enemies,
stand by us.

And among our brothers spinning
the two branched blood in their veins,
in the wild fear of love,
in the tenderness of hate,
in the downhill of darkness,
help us.

The sum of it? A snatch of prose and the ending of a poem ought to show.

There's been no electricity since the day before yesterday; the fuses are burnt out. Today we tell Evangelia about the mishap. She replies: "In my sleep I saw you distressed; this must be it." It's natural that the language of dreams pertains even to trifles; messengers condescending even to humble errands. The intellectuals have made them speak only with the trumpet of Jericho or with bagpipes.

And all together sway at the edge of the abyss,
without coherence, without ego, and the mountain
 peaks
that woke up so jagged, and your brackish body

dancing, dying, dancing again,
and the reeds nailed to the angry delta
Stut-ter-ring th-read hea-vy to-orch la-lab-la
byrinth; alpha, beta, gamma, delta . . .

C. Capri-Karka (essay date 1982)

SOURCE: Capri-Karka, C. "Turning Point." In *Love and the Symbolic Journey in the Poetry of Cavafy, Eliot, and Seferis,* pp. 157-84. New York: Pella Publishing Company, 1982.

[*In the following excerpt, Capri-Karka provides a reading of the poems in Seferis's collection* Turning Point, *many of which express a sense of disillusionment and decay.*]

Turning Point is Seferis' first collection of poems. Even in this early work, published in 1931, one can find signs of his profound consciousness of the classical Greek tradition and at the same time of his thorough assimilation of the Greek and European poetic techniques of the time, most notably of the French symbolists. It is all written in rhyme and, although not as fine in form as his later work, it employs the same complex imagery and symbolism encountered in the collections that followed. Some of the recurrent motifs in his work appear for the first time here, providing the basis for further variation and development in his later poetry of certain essential themes which he keeps reiterating.

The collection opens with the poem **"Turning Point,"** which has the same title as the whole collection. It refers to the persona's change of attitude toward life, presumably as a result of a betrayal in love. This change is also implied in the epigraph of *Turning Point,*[1] and it is also referred to in the poem **"Denial"** of the same collection. A moment of terror comes to the protagonist, and the delightful journey of love becomes abortive, as betrayal poisons, like a snake, the heavenly garden.

"TURNING POINT"

Although the poem **"Turning Point"** refers to a very important moment in the protagonist's life, as far as time is concerned it represented a mere "grain of sand" in the hourglass. The protagonist does not spell out exactly what the moment was. He says only that it was ominous: it reached him "like a black pigeon" and it was comparable to seeing "the Hydra / in the heavenly garden."[2] Although the poet alludes here to the snake in paradise, the fact that Hydra is also a constellation suggests another way in which the protagonist saw "the Hydra" in the heavenly garden. In terms of the symbolic journey, the "return to a lost paradise," as Seferis puts it,[3] is frustrated.

The protagonist also tells us that this moment reached him "at the close of a last supper," which implies the anticipation of a betrayal and a crucifixion. This same ominous moment, again referred to as a tiny "grain of sand," appears once more in a later poem, **"Stratis the Sailor Describes a Man."** Here again the nature of this terrible experience is not made clear but it is obvious that it was a catastrophe of some magnitude. This poem will be discussed later, but it should be pointed out here that in it he picks up the same idea he left off from in the **"Turning Point."** After the "last supper" and the implied crucifixion, in **"Stratis the Sailor Describes a Man"** he suggests that he does not believe in the miracle of resurrection.

Using the metaphor of the hourglass in **"Turning Point,"** the protagonist refers to his life as a "tragic clepsydra" and he dramatizes the terrible moment as a tiny "grain of sand" which "kept the whole / tragic clepsydra dumb." Thus, he isolates the important moment but avoids any specific explanation of it. The tremendous consequences of this moment in the protagonist's life are also evident in the two lines from the seventeenth-century Greek romance *Erotokritos,* which are used as an epigraph for the collection *Turning Point.*

> But everything went wrong for me and upside down,
> the nature of things was reborn for me.

He is even more specific in his *Journals.* written at about the same time, where he says that "one grain of sand can change a whole life."[4] This grain of sand in **"Turning Point,"** and in the section **"Man"** of **"Stratis the Sailor Describes a Man,"** is also a symbol of sterile love.

"SLOWLY YOU SPOKE"

The abrupt disappearance of love due to an unexplained change forms the substance of the second poem of this collection. How intense this love must have been and how important to the poet we are told both directly and indirectly: the poet tells us that this woman used to be his "fate's woof," and he contrasts the sunshine, which was bright when she spoke, to the darkness which has fallen upon the world now that love has gone. He wonders with surprise what happened to the whole universe within "five moments."[5] A metamorphosis seems to have taken place, something that appears again and again in Seferis' work. For instance, in his novel *Six Nights on the Acropolis,* his hero Stratis, alone in his room, is thinking: "And you are only watching: a coat that has become unwearable since yesterday; a wrinkle that was invisible this morning, a love that was still eternal a moment ago."[6] In this poem, the metamorphosis "rubbed out" his love after a very brief existence. This rubbing out is similar to the situation described in another more complex poem, **"Denial"**:

> On the golden sand
> we wrote her name;
> but the sea-breeze blew
> and the writing vanished.

The absence of love and the feeling of emptiness and sterility that goes with it is symbolized by a "dry pitcher." Seferis uses this symbol several times in similar situations, as for instance in **"The King of Asine,"** where he even extends the image by describing the hollow sound given off by the empty pitcher:

> . . . remember its sound? Hollow in the light
> like a dry jar in dug earth.[7]

Also, in poem **"10"** of the *Mythistorema* sequence, the lack of love is symbolized by the empty cisterns with a hollow sound:

> Only some cisterns, empty; they ring and are to us
> Objects of worship.
> A sound stagnant, hollow like our solitude,
> Like our love and like our bodies.

In the last stanza of **"Slowly You Spoke"** there is again the darkness that is usually associated with the absence of love. The question "Where is the place" is best understood by reference to a sentence that appears twice in Seferis' novel *Six Nights on the Acropolis.* There a young woman tells the protagonist: "I am not the place where your body exists," and on another occasion the hero himself asks, "Which is the place where our body exists?"[8] Also, in the *Three Secret Poems* the voice of Proteus is heard saying:

> I am your land;
> perhaps I am no one,
> yet I can become what you wish.[9]

With this in mind, we realize that the question in the poem, "Where is the place," does not mean that he cannot locate the actual place where he once was happy but that without love he feels as though his body has lost its place. Another reference very relevant to the next line, "and your nakedness to the waist," is found in the poem **"Memory II"**:

> Our life itself, yet different, just as when
> Woman's nakedness is revealed and her face changes
> And yet is the same face. Those who have loved
> Know this. The world, in the light of other people,
> Withers away. But this you must remember:
> Hades and Dionysus are the same.

Love fades after its consummation and a woman's face appears less attractive after she strips naked. In **"Slowly You Spoke"** the poet carefully specifies that the nakedness is "to the waist"; in other words, he recalls, in his wonder and despair, the happy moments of expectation, before the illusion had vanished, when she excited his imagination. Now his tragedy is that he no longer sees a "style" in the woman's "soul," as he did before. She is now like every other woman.

As far as the symbolic journey is concerned, it has come to an abrupt end here with the sudden disappearance of love. Love is so ephemeral ("An unwritten love rubbed out") that it is almost absurd, and for the bewildered protagonist, who wonders "what's happened" in "Five seconds," the voyage seems to have been interrupted rather than having come to an end.

"The Sorrowing Girl"

In **"The Sorrowing Girl"** the poet describes the suffering of a young woman in love and he is moved by her emotional restraint.

The girl appears "On the stone of patience," but, as the images that follow indicate, this patience is actually a slow torment. The black of her eye reveals her pain, and on her lips there is a line "that's naked and trembles."

The description moves inward to her mind, where there is a "music from which the tear starts."[10] Her body, on the other hand, "returns from the [edge] to the [fruit]." Fruit in Seferis has rich symbolic connotations; "to reap the fruit" usually means erotic fulfilment.[11] Thus, this image, although ambiguous, must imply that she is not only a romantic person but a passionate woman with sensual desires. And yet, as the last stanza indicates, her anguish is "unmoaning"; she is suffering in a discreet, restrained manner. In this stanza Seferis brings together two very different ideas, the unmoaning anguish of the heart and the starfilled sky:

> but your heart's anguish
> was unmoaning, became
> what a starfilled sky
> gives to the world.[12]

The starfilled sky gives to the world a feeling of harmony and balance, and this is also what the restraint of the sorrowing girl inspires.

Looking at the poem as a whole, we can see that the poet values her restraint very highly. He is touched by the dignity she shows in her unhappiness. It is evident that there must have been an erotic involvement between the girl and the narrator which has come to an end. He could now be indifferent or cynical. The fact that he values the girl's silent suffering as well as her capacity for love reveals something about the narrator's own problem. As in some of Seferis' other poems, such as **"Comments," "Rocket," "Automobile"** and **"In Memoriam,"** the persona is unhappy because he remains detached. Of course, if one examines his poetry as a whole, the poet's attitude toward love is much more complicated than that.

In terms of the symbolic journey, one can say that the journey of both the unhappy girl whose love was unrequited and of the detached lover remains unfinished, very far from Ithaca.

"Automobile"

"Automobile" describes a journey, both literal and symbolic. It conveys the emptiness and the tedium following an erotic encounter. The two lovers are leaving together in a car. They feel remote and separate. It is interesting that in order to emphasize this separation, Seferis uses the image of a pair of compasses, the same image that was used by Donne for exactly the opposite effect.[13] What is stressed in Donne's poem is the connection between the two feet of the compass, which makes them interdependent. Seferis, on the contrary, sees the two feet of the compass as parallel but separate; he compares them to a highway separated in the middle by a line, and he tells us, in the last stanza, that the hearts of the two lovers travel separately, one on the left side of the road and the other on the right.

The first stanza has a light tone. The idea of speed is conveyed by the two original images:

> fingers of wind in the hair
> and miles in the belly.

But with the first line of the second stanza the feeling of emptiness is introduced:

> the two of us were leaving, empty,
> whiplash for the mild gaze;
> the mind make up, the blood make up
> naked, naked, naked!

The protagonist feels that the beautiful illusion created by the mind before the erotic encounter is like maquillage covering up reality. Also, the blood's radiance was "make-up" and has worn off, leaving them "naked." The repetition of this word three times in the last line emphasizes the fact that the protagonists feel empty, stripped of any meaning. Seferis is more explicit on this point in another poem, **"The Thrush,"** where he says:

> Flesh's delirium, the lovely dance
> That ends in nakedness.

What he was writing in his *Journals* at about the same time is also characteristic: "This feeling of the ephemeral freezes me and paralyzes my strength. I know that this feeling was (and is now) probably my worst enemy."[14]

The next stanza, as emphasized by the use of italics, is a flashback to the erotic moments. The sensuous handling of this transient experience makes the contrast between this scene and the tedium that follows it more intense. The elevated feeling conveyed by the dizziness suggests a complete abandonment to the senses. The transient nature of this feeling is conveyed by the image of a fish slipping away in the sea. Both the fish and the sea are symbols very often connected with an erotic experience in Seferis' poetry. Here the protagonist is sunk in the light and transparent element of water, midway between illusion and reality.

As far as the journey is concerned, on the literal level it continues, while on the symbolic level it has reached a dead end.

"DENIAL"

"Denial" is an important poem, which deals with what Seferis has called in Greek "Καημὸς τοῦ αἰσθησιασμοῦ" (the sorrow and longing of sensuality).[15] It is one of the very few poems about which the poet wrote some comments. The protagonists are Elpenors,[16] a character who appears often in his poetry. In an essay, referring to another poem of this collection, the **"Companions in Hades,"** Seferis wrote: "The unaware and the satiated who have eaten the oxen of the sun are Elpenors. The same thing I would say about the patient people of **'Denial.'"**[17]

In the first stanza, the Elpenors appear on a "secret seashore"; they are thirsty but the water is brackish.[18] The unpleasant taste of the water suggests that the erotic experience was unsatisfying; love was spoiled. In terms of the symbolism of the journey, the destination was not reached.

In the next stanza a different experience follows the first, as they write a woman's name on the sand but the sea-breeze blows and erases the writing. The implication here is that this love was ephemeral. The sand is also a symbol of barrenness. Like "a castle built on the sand," this love could not endure, as it probably would have if the protagonist had carved the name on a tree or a stone. Again, there is no fulfilment.

The last stanza is a recapitulation followed by the decision to deny passion:

> With what spirit, what heart,
> what desire and passion
> we lived our life: a mistake!
> So we changed our life.

The Elpenors realize that although these loves are superficial and ephemeral, they can become an obsession. This vulnerability to passion may be fatal. They become "patient," as Seferis tells us, and this change in direction is in line with the title of the collection *Turning Point.*

"THE COMPANIONS IN HADES"

The epigraph of this poem comes from the opening passage of the *Odyssey*:

> fools, who ate the cattle of Helios Hyperion;
> but he deprived them of the day of their return.[19]

It is of particular significance that Homer, from the very beginning, singles out this sacrilege, attributing to it the failure of Odysseus' companions to return home. In an essay, "A Staging for **'The Thrush,'**" Seferis writes that the "unaware and satiated" who ate the oxen of the sun in the **"Companions in Hades"** are Elpenors.[20] The Homeric Elpenor had died before his companions ate the oxen of the sun, but here Seferis refers to the more generalized character of modern Elpenor, who plays a central role in his poetry.[21] Because of their uncontrolled sensuality, their inability to curb their animal appetites, they violated the sacred law and were deprived of access to the lost paradise.

Seferis makes a special point in his commentary about Homer's Tiresias warning Odysseus and his companions to respect the oxen of the sun as a condition for their return. Tiresias talks to Odysseus about the light and the sun. Seferis adds:

> The whole question is how one can honor the oxen of the sun, how one can honor the light of every day that God gives one. The companions did not respect them, they devoured them, the fools, and they were lost . . . Scattered, wasted, they can no longer face either the sun or man:
>
> > Lands of sun, where you cannot face the sun.
> > Lands of man, where you cannot face the man.[22]

The meaning of Seferis' words "how one can honor the light of every day that God gives one" becomes clearer if one bears in mind that light is used by the poet as a complex symbol meaning, among other things, love.[23] When he writes that the companions did not honor the light, did not respect the oxen of the sun,[24] he implies that they committed a sacrilege, they spoiled love.

In the first stanza, the modern Elpenors confess that they have eaten the cattle of the sun, not because they did not have anything else to eat—they had "some hardtack"—but out of mere "stupidity." They blame themselves for this thoughtless act.

In the second stanza, they compare each ox to a castle. In order to understand this unusual simile it is necessary to refer to a sentence in Seferis' novel *Six Nights on the Acropolis,* attributed to one of the leaders of the Greek War of Independence, Makriyannis, whom the poet considered the embodiment of the "just man": "The fortress [Acropolis] now wants to destroy those who wanted to destroy it." Makriyannis, who was defending the Acropolis—which was a fortress at that time—against the Turks, saw this act, this attempt to conquer the fortress, as an injustice that would lead to punishment.[25] In this sense, eating the sacred oxen is as unjust as conquering a fortress, and in both cases one becomes "a hero and a star," an ironic way of saying that one loses his life.

In the third stanza, the poet returns to the story in a sort of flashback and narrates what happened:

> On the earth's back we hungered,
> but when we'd eaten well
> we fell to these lower regions
> [unaware] and [satiated].

Thus, the companions end in the underworld, with no hope of return. They fail to complete their journey.

An important element, which comes out of this description, is that these modern Elpenors committed consciously the hubris which cost their lives, just as Odysseus' companions did in Homer, ignoring Tiresias' warning. Thus, their fall from grace—to the "lower regions"—is the result of conscious defiance. The word "unaware" in the last line of the poem refers to the fact that they do not know how serious the punishment for their act will be.

There is some similarity between the **"Companions in Hades"** and T. S. Eliot's "Marina," although the central idea is different. Eliot's lines:

> Those who sit in the stye of contentment, meaning Death
> Those who suffer the ecstasy of the animals, meaning Death,

convey the same idea of the fatal inability to control animal appetites. However, Seferis refers to the punishment of excess, while Eliot's attitude toward sensual pleasure in general is critical.

There is also a similarity in technique between the two poems. Seferis is using here what Eliot called the "mythical method," the establishment of a continuous parallel between a myth and a contemporary situation. As Edmund Keeley comments, however, Seferis wrote the **"Companions in Hades"** before he became acquainted with T. S. Eliot's poetry.[26]

"Fog"

The seventh poem in this collection, **"Fog,"** is probably the first poem Seferis wrote, at least among the first that he published. Here again the symbolic journey is not realized and the persona chooses a life "cold as a fish" after rejecting both alternatives presented to him: to start an affair with a woman who obviously does not inspire him, or to yield to the dangerous temptation of a paradise, offered by an "angel," which would eventually lead him to disaster. In contrast to their traditional meaning, angels in Seferis' poetry are usually—but not always—dangerous. There is a similarity in this respect between Seferis and Rainer Maria Rilke, who also presents angels, especially in his *Duino Elegies,* as sometimes austere, aloof and perilous[27] and sometimes "affirmative."[28]

The poem opens with a fragment of an English song,[29] which urges a young man to confess his love to a girl.

> "Say it with a ukulele . . ."
> grumbles some gramophone.[30]

The protagonist's response to the urging of the song leaves no doubt that he is absolutely incapable of loving the young woman:

> Christ, tell me what to say to her
> now that I am used to my loneliness?

Following the stream of consciousness, he is led from this song to some other, rather similar songs played by beggars in the streets, on their accordions, calling on the angels of a supposed paradise:

> And the angels opened their wings
> but below the mists condensed.

The protagonist, however, is grateful for the fog, because without it those angels who "are hell" would trap him and catch his poor soul as though it were a thrush.

The poem continues with an imaginary dialogue. "And life's cold as a fish"; but the persona says flatly that he prefers it this way. To the question "Is that how you live?" he answers "Yes," and he justifies his way of life by pointing out that

> So many are the drowned
> down on the sea's bed.

They are, presumably, those who sought the paradise of the "angels" and whose promised happiness ended in disaster. Love appears as some sort of hunt, and many are caught in its trap, like thrushes—an image that appears again and again in Seferis.

The motif "Say it with a ukulele" is repeated, and this time the protagonist makes an appeal for real love instead of shallow talk:

> Words for words, and more words?
> Love, where's your church,
> I'm tired of this hermitage.[31]

We learn here, in contrast to the fourth stanza, that the protagonist longs for a genuine love and is not made for a life as "cold as a fish," which he is now leading. The stream of consciousness brings him now to consider his whole life, wishing that it were "straight":

> Ah, were life but straight
> how we'd live it then!
> But it's fated otherwise,
> you have to turn in a small corner.

This ties in with the first poem of the collection, **"Turning Point,"** when he saw the snake in the heavenly garden. He does not seem to know where this compulsory turn will lead him. This idea of a life which is "straight," "right," "whole," etc., is very important to Seferis. It is met again in the poem **"An Old Man on the River Bank"**:

> Not like us . . .
> Caught in the gaudy nets of a life which was right and
>   turned to dust and sank into the sand.

What Seferis obviously has in mind when he speaks of a "straight" or "right" life is the Aeschylean idea that any excess constitutes a hubris that is to be punished.

The poem ends in a very low mood, as the persona is searching in despair for some consolation. The same fragment of the song haunts him:

> "Say it with a ukulele . . ."
> I see her red nails—
> how they must glow in firelight—
> and I recall her coughing.[32]

The protagonist does not hide his uneasy feelings toward this woman, since the only things he mentions about her are her red nails[33]—suggesting a kind of sensual danger—and her unpleasant cough. The poet uses this image of coughing later in the poem **"The Thrush,"** pointing out how changeable a love is:

> The golden barrel is done
> And a rag is what was the sun,
> A rag on the neck of a woman in middle age
> Who coughs and who never stops coughing.

"The Mood of a Day"

The memory of a lost paradise is conveyed by the first four lines of **"The Mood of a Day,"** while the rest of the poem refers to an absurd present, a meaningless life from which love is absent. This life is symbolized in the last part of the poem by a ghost-ship which continues its journey while all its passengers are doomed never to reach their destination, since they are already dead.

The first stanza starts with the "mood of a day," which the protagonist lived ten years ago in a foreign country, and also with a unique moment that "took on wings and vanished like an angel of the Lord"—imagery related to a lost paradise.

Seferis presents here in quick succession the "mood of a day," "the airy spirit of a moment," "the voice of a woman" hard to forget and "an end inconsolable, the marble setting of some September." Although one cannot be sure that the four lines are connected and refer to the same event, it seems probable that the poet is trying here to convey the feeling of a separation. He is intentionally ambiguous in this stanza, which brings to mind his admission in his *Journals,* "I write in order to

postpone a confession."[34] The return to a lost paradise is the purpose of the journey in Seferis' symbolism. But the return is not realized in this poem, any more than it is in most of his other poems. The lost paradise is only a source of despair, as he wrote in his *Journals* at about the same time the poem was written: "I can discern at certain times of unbelievable solitude an unexpected lost paradise that has left its traces on us only to torture us without leading us anywhere."[35]

Seferis is not clear in this poem about whether the loss of the paradise was the result of death or of a separation or occurred for some other reason. The woman was forgotten "with such care" (the Greek word is "prudence," which usually has an unpleasant ring in Seferis), representing a contradictory mood, suggesting that the "inconsolable end" was the result of a decision rather than of death. However, Seferis has warned us in his *Journals* that one should not try to "attribute everything to a separation."[36] It is possible that the loss of the paradise was a consequence of seeing in it the snake that was mentioned in the first poem of this collection, **"Turning Point."**

Whatever the reasons may be, one can see the disastrous consequences of the loss of paradise in the description of the dreary present, which follows in the next few lines. New but strange houses, dusty clinics, coffin shops, the suffering of a sensitive pharmacist on night duty and the disorder of the protagonist's room reflect his inner chaos. Sickness permeates the whole scene; the protagonist is fatigued and lost, unable to face reality. Life has become a disjunctive series of absurd words and empty gestures, and the persona asks:

> Where is love that with one stroke cuts time in two
>   and stuns it?

This takes us back to the beginning of the poem, as if life had stopped ten years ago, leaving the memory of a lost happiness.

The poem ends with the image of a ghost-ship,[37] which continues its voyage although not a soul is alive in it— the symbol of a life that goes on while one feels dead inside.

"Comments"

The poem **"Comments,"** which was omitted from the translation of Seferis' *Collected Poems,* is another expression of the same psychological climate that characterizes most of the poems in this collection.[38] The symbolic journey toward fulfilment is terribly frustrated because the effort at communication between the protagonist and the woman fails. Deep in their hearts a confession of love is hidden, but it remains suspended; their lips move but pronounce the wrong words. The only hope is the response of the body, which they expect as a blessing. But the miracle does not take place. The angel who would bring it about never approaches. The poet remembers such an angel from a lost paradise in his past. In contrast to **"Fog,"** where the angels were threatening, here the angel would bring happiness. In Seferis, as mentioned before, the angels are sometimes good, sometimes evil. Here, had the angel appeared, the "quick rings," like concentric waves on the surface of the water, would have opened up and the noose would have loosened.[39] The communication is not realized. The woman is very attractive but remains "a stranger to [his] soul." The protagonist feels empty; he finds the evening absurd.

In the last stanza he reverts to the darkness of loneliness. The black color of her eyes is now associated with the horror of the dark night—although the poet leaves the point a bit ambiguous since he simply places the two images in juxtaposition and does not connect them explicitly. He had hoped for some communication, which would have cut his silence like a blade, but now this hope has proved to be an illusion, a "chimera," and the blade goes back into the sheath. A blade going into a sheath usually connotes sexual intercourse; here, however, the whole context suggests that the return of the blade into the sheath signifies the decision not to proceed with sexual intercourse. There is a certain similarity between this poem and "The Love Song of J. Alfred Prufrock," although **"Comments"** concerns both partners. The impulse of the lovers to reach out for one another is frustrated by a psychological block at the outset. The difference, however, is that in **"Comments"** this block is due more to some kind of subconscious reluctance of the protagonist, who finds the evening senseless and foolish, whereas in Eliot's poem it is due more to a lack of daring, a maimed virility.

"Rocket"

This poem was published in 1931, at a time when the only rockets widely known were fireworks, which travel with great speed, leaving a trail of light and culminating in a brilliant display of stars and golden lines illuminating the sky. This display lasts a very short time, as the scattered stars and bright lines are quickly extinguished.

Seferis uses the rocket as a symbol of the phantasmagoria created by an intense and ephemeral love that momentarily elevates the protagonist above the sphere of everyday life. The magic is described with such images as "the blue light on our fingers" and the "thousand antennae" that "grope giddily to find the sky." The culmination is reached in the stanza:

> there was a deer
> yellow as sulphur
> there was a tower
> built of gold.

Seferis uses the image of a deer or antelope to describe a slender young body in other poems as well, for instance in **"Stratis the Sailor Describes a Man"** ("a young woman whose transparent dress revealed the lines of her body, slim and full of spirit, like a gazelle's") and in an unpublished poem.[40] The bright color "yellow as sulphur" that the poet ascribes to the deer represents the impression one gets when one walks in a wood and sees this delicate animal, while at the same time it is also related to the rocket, since sulphur is one of the inflammable chemicals used in manufacturing rockets. The critic Minas Demakis characterizes **"Rocket"** as "a modern erotic poem" and explains: "love is here like a rocket; it has the same transient quality—which reaches the sphere of the soul and illuminates the heavens."[41] He then points out that the view of love at its prime, when it was "a tower / built of gold," lasts only for a moment and then shifts immediately to the time of decline, when "lilies whitened / the beloved's hair."

In the fifth stanza we come to the point where the fireworks are extinguished, when the spell of love dies. Five black crows, symbols of death, quarrel and scatter in five directions after they had "counted their years," which implies aging and decay. Their black color is the color of the smoke that remains after the fireworks are extinguished.

The emphasis in this poem is on the speed of the rocket and on the abrupt disappearance of the magic. The "red carnation" (a symbol of love) is quickly replaced by the white lilies that cover the woman's hair, suggesting abrupt aging. The protagonist finds himself in the sad position of writing books about the "beautiful woman's body,"[42] and he ends by complaining that he is tired of living "only with peacocks"—in other words, with the abstract beauty of art—and traveling "always / in the mermaid's eyes." George Savidis feels that the sixth stanza is "one of the few direct references Seferis makes to his art; most of them are associated with a sense of futility and of doubt about the fruitfulness of the poetic act."[43] As for the reference to the mermaid, which appears often in Seferis' poetry, the poet has written in his novel that he considers her "half woman, half myth."[44] In another part of the *Journals* he asks "will the body of the mermaid ever come to life?"[45]—a question which shows that traveling always "in the mermaid's eyes" one never reaches his destination, a fulfilment. This aimless wandering, which fascinates Cavafy, Seferis finds dreadful. As he says in the passage of his *Journals* quoted before, "the ephemeral makes me freeze";[46] and poems like **"Automobile"** and **"Rocket"** express his frustration at not being able to feel real love for these women. "At my age," he writes in his *Journals*. "I am ashamed to write it, I have nothing else besides instincts,"[47] and in another instance, "How many women promised you the same kingdom?"[48] This kingdom, this paradise, is what the protagonist has in mind: real communication. The ephemeral affair of which the **"Rocket"** is a symbol usually takes one out of the sphere of communication. The continuous transfers and traveling associated with Seferis' profession played a serious role in this respect, preventing him (until he was in his late thirties) from relating to people and environments. But this was not the whole problem. As he himself wrote in his *Journals* in 1931:

> I don't like to delude myself or to deceive others. It would be simpler, and I think this is what all people do with a little compromise, to attribute everything to separations.[49]

It is also interesting to note the context in which Seferis uses the word "rocket" in his novel *Six Nights on the Acropolis*. In it a character says:

> I have been driving a streetcar for so many years now. Patissia—Ampelokipi, Ampelokipi—Patissia; a bell to start, a bell to stop; and all over again. What has my life been? A wheel! Have I known anything else? The other day my streetcar stalled and I got down. Behind us another streetcar was coming. I saw it climbing up the rails, coming up fast, how can I say it, like a rocket. Since then, I think that maybe I am also coming up fast like that . . .
>
> "Watch out that you don't get any crazy ideas!" Visani-aris said. "I had a colleague who was, like me, making the rounds with a gramophone; one day he told me, 'I am a noble man and sympathetic too. I am not like you, like some hashish addicts, some bums who run around with the gramophones; I am a musician, I have dignity. I play at the Tuberculosis Hospital. The records that the tuberculosis patients ask for, the Traviatas, the Toscas, are inexpensive. I make good money.' In the end he caught the Traviata and passed away."[50]

The gramophone player is a typical case of a man overstepping his bounds and paying the price for it. And the friend of the streetcar driver uses the incident to warn him that the excessive speed of the rocket is dangerous. Although the conversation sounds simple-minded, the Aeschylean overtones cannot be missed.

"Rhyme"

"Rhyme" is written in the same mood as most of the poems in the collection *Turning Point* (the **"Automobile,"** the **"Rocket," "Slowly You Spoke,"** the **"Sorrowing Girl"**), whose main theme is a love that fades away, leaving the protagonist with a feeling of emptiness.

From the beginning the protagonist remembers the lips of the beloved person as "guardians" of love, but he immediately undercuts this idea with the words "that was to fade," which suggest the futility of the effort and

imply a strange tendency to escape on his part. This tendency appears more clearly in the next poem of the collection, **"In Memoriam."**[51] The same sense of futility is conveyed by the second line of **"Rhyme"**: "hands, bonds of my youth that was to go." Here again the hands of the beloved person that could have held him and saved him from aging fail to do so. If one recalls that Seferis wrote this poem when he was only twenty-nine, one realizes that he speaks here in symbolic terms: love, which could have prevented him from decay, is gone. In his *Journals* the poet wrote a few lines which are very relevant in this context.

> This distress appears in the form of a dim river that flows unimpeded and dominating. Et de ce fleuve de mains fugitives qui se perd dans le calme de la mer—as your friend Stratis the Sailor would say. I feel an unbearable need for love, physical love, because it holds me and takes me out of this condition. It is the only thing that can keep me out of this confusion and of this flight.[52]

The "fugitive hands" in this case are the thousands of wild hands that are trying to carry him away and not the hands of love that could save him. But the overall picture is the same: he is going down a river and physical love is the only thing he can hold on to. This is also the meaning of his dramatic appeal in the poem **"Mycenae"**: "Give me your hands, give me your hands, give me your hands," and of several other references to the hands of beloved persons in his writings.

In this case, however, the hands could not save him, presumably because love faded away. This idea of the disappearance of love is reinforced by the third line, "color of a face lost in nature somewhere," while in the fourth, "trees . . . birds . . . hunting . . ." we see something very often encountered in Seferis: love presented with images of hunting or trapping. George Savidis refers to several places in the poet's work where the senses are compared to nets in which man can be trapped,[53] as has already been mentioned in discussing the poem **"Fog."**

The second stanza starts with a strong sensuous image, as the protagonist addresses his body:

> Body black in the sun's heat like a grape
> body, my rich ship, where are you traveling?

However, the stanza as a whole contains an antithesis because, the "rich ship" is on a voyage with no direction, and this hopeless wandering conveys a sense of waste.

George Savidis suggests that the question the protagonist asks is "rhetorical" at a time when he "believed in the omnipotence of the body."[54] In my view, the poet no longer believed in the omnipotence of the body when he wrote this poem. He did believe in it at an earlier period, before the crucial moment he describes in the **"Turning Point,"** the very first of his published poems, where he says that he saw "the Hydra / in the heavenly garden." Here there is fatigue and psychological deterioration. The persona confesses that "twilight drowns" and that he is tired searching for love in the darkness. This is an agonizing search, and there is no fulfilment in sight—hardly what one would have expected from someone believing in the omnipotence of the body. The question is not rhetorical, and it implies an aimless wandering. This rich ship is not essentially very different from the ship of the **"Mood of a Day."** The crew there is already dead, but here also "Our life [keeps shrinking] every day."

"In Memoriam"

The symbolic journey in this poem is an escape without a destination; an escape from a love that seemed near perfect for the fastidious protagonist.[55]

Addressing the woman he loved, the persona tells her that she was "the divine silence." In Seferis' *Journals* we find some passages that help us understand the meaning this divine silence had for the poet. On February 8, 1933, he wrote:

> . . . Like the insistent memory of this act, many years later, when a man has seen a lot, and is slowly returning from the bitter journey that is called love; when he has learned that love is not moonlight and little cries— except only for the cats—but silence, sometimes unbearable silence, and a rock exposed to the sun at high noon.[56]

Earlier, on July 31, 1930, in another passage which is also interesting because of its treatment of love as a journey, he wrote:

> Such was our silent fate, even before, in the good days, when a glance, an embrace, made us taste the gifts of God. We saw each other seldom, once a week, once in ten days because such was the social order. Two or three hours. And then we forgot. We forgot our troubles and with them the images and ornaments which our souls had separately gathered on the surface of the world. Do you remember how much we were afraid of words? We did not know where they would lead us. Once or twice, in the beginning, we did speak, and after we said whatever we didn't want to say—mostly that—we embraced each other. Since that time, no confession, no complaint stirred the hours that we were given to live together. We spent two or three years of a secret and silent love, and I can't really say how long the magic lasted. When I look back at those hours, our hours, I see them outside the passing of time, like a ghost-ship that would travel on the river of change, and that we had boarded and unboarded without explanation. This is how I imagine eternal life, like that journey.[57]

We can see, then, that the woman he calls "divine silence" must have responded to his deepest longing; yet, the protagonist felt "the shivering for flight." And it is not an escape which brings relief, but, as he says in the second stanza, addressing himself this time, it is as if he were carried away by a vortex that left him with a bitter feeling of abandonment and dejection. A similar vortex appears in a poem with the tentative title **"Journey,"** which was published only in Seferis' *Journals* (January 18, 1931).

> Aeolus' island, I returned with the winds
> that your master gave me, closed in a sack.
> My companions cut the silver strings
> cut short my sleep, cut short the sleep of the sea
> and let me loose at the root of the vortex
> alone with my exhaustion and my dejection . . .[58]

This vortex is also reminiscent of the whirlpool in which Phlebas was drowned in T. S. Eliot's *Waste Land*.[59]

Thus, the symbolic journey in **"In Memoriam"** again has no end. It is the protagonist's constant tendency for escape, described later in more detail in the poem **"Flight,"** the reason for which is implied in the title **"In Memoriam"** and in the last two lines of the poem:

> When night falls I see in the foliage
> the eyes of our friends, closed.

The same image of the eyes in the foliage was used by Seferis in another poem, **"For One Available Rose,"** which appeared in the collection *Book of Exercises II*:

> What weighs heavily upon us is the thirst of the others the altered ones
> we bring them flowers in the morning fooling ourselves
> what use are the flowers to them? And they breathe the cypress trees
> with those lips, and at night the eyes in the foliage
> . . .

In a later poem, **"The Last Stop,"** he wrote: "Our mind is a virgin forest of murdered friends." The memory of those dead friends, together with the traumatic experience of the destruction of his hometown Smyrna, played a crucial role in the poet's inner life, although it was not the only source of his unhappiness.

"Erotikos Logos" (1930)

The collection *Turning Point* ends with the long poem **"Erotikos Logos"** (**"Love Song"**). In this poem, as in most of this collection, the symbolic journey of love does not reach Ithaca because the return is blocked by the memory of a past erotic experience. In spite of its overwhelming passion, this experience, conveyed by the allusion of two snakes making love, may have been associated with a betrayal or a violation. This impression is supported by the fact that in it the poet uses the snake imagery, as he does with the Hydra in the opening poem of this collection.

The first part of the poem starts with the protagonist expressing a complaint to the "Rose of fate" which deliberately wounded him. The rose is a symbol of love, but the addition of the words "fate" and "wound" and the whole context of the first stanza suggest that the course of this love was predetermined, as if a secret law of nature had to be followed. The woman was simply an agent delivering a "command" which originated somewhere else: "and the command you [agreed] to give us was beautiful." Her smile was like a "ready sword"—another indication that this was going to be a painful experience.

The second stanza is euphoric, describing the phantasmagoria created by the approaching love and culminating in the optimistic statement, "the world was easy: a simple pulsation." Since we already know from the first stanza what is to follow, we realize that this is a bitter irony.

In part II, the poet uses another symbol for love, the sea. Although there is an optimistic surface again as he assures us that

> The secrets of the sea are forgotten on the shores
> the darkness of the depths are forgotten on the surf,

this awareness of the existence of secrets and dark depths creates a sense of vague danger. Suddenly the "purple" "corals of memory" shine bright. This must be the memory of a lost paradise. The protagonist remains motionless, hoping that the mysterious process will start again, like magic. He will touch again "the tree with the apples" and experience again the paradise of his memory, toward which a thread is guiding him. The sensuous experience, which he describes as a "dark shivering in the root and the leaves,"[60] works here as an invocation, a wish and a longing for "the forgotten dawn." The wish is expanded in the whole next stanza, which presents a picture of anticipated harmony and happiness.

> May lilies blossom again on the meadow of separation
> may days open mature, the embrace of the heavens,[61]
> may those eyes alone shine in the glare
> the pure soul be outlined like the song of a flute.

But this euphoria does not last long. The symbolic night falls, the eyes that shone bright are closed and only ashes remain. Instead of "the song of a flute" he hears a "choked hum" and a "dense fluttering," as if something he cannot see were flying away. The poet is left with the same taste of decay he described in several poems of this collection (**"Turning Point," "Automobile," "Slowly You Spoke," "Comments"**) and in his *Journals*. Love disappears, leaving behind only ashes, just at the moment he had hoped that the "bridges" would be built and a more complete communication would be established.

Part III starts with a repetition of the line "O dark shivering in the root and the leaves" and continues with a new invocation to the woman and her sensuous beauty:

> and let your desire, deep like the shade of a walnut
>   tree, bend
> and flood us with your lavish hair
> from the down of the kiss to the leaves of the heart.

What he longs for is to experience again the unique sensation and return to the lost paradise. The key word here is "again"; he wants to hear the same words he heard in a similar situation from someone else in the past.

As she speaks about the way she feels, she uses words and images that remind one of a heavenly garden. The passing of time has become "soft and unworldly," "scented shrubs"[62] are around them, "a flock of doves" descends and the stars are a human touch on her breast.[63] As far as she is concerned, everything seems ideal. She feels resurrected,[64] because her past was lifeless without love.

With the end of the quotation, however, we return to the disillusionment.

> The broken sunset declined and was gone
> and it seemed a delusion to ask for the gifts of the
>   sky.

The dawn is replaced by the "moon's thorn" and the "mountain's shadows."

The last stanza in part III is in italics, as if it were not a continuation of the preceding but a quotation from something else, interjected here. It is not the voice of the narrator but an inner voice.

> *. . . In the mirror how our love diminishes*
> *in sleep the dreams, school of forgetfulness*
> *in the depths of time, how the heart contracts*
> *and vanishes in the rocking of a foreign embrace.*

Seen in the light of this passage, the line "In the mirror how our love diminishes" becomes clear: other images and persons intervene and little by little he drifts apart from her. His dreams also teach him to forget her. As the next line indicates, those images and dreams come from "the depths of time," from his past. A "foreign embrace"—foreign in relation to the present one, most probably the love he experienced in the lost paradise—comes slowly back and makes his heart contract and the present love disappear. In other words, his subconscious, which is awake while he is asleep, suggests the idea of forgetfulness.

The next part (IV) refers, in my view, to this past experience. The poet presents two serpents, which are separated and which crawl in a dark forest in search of each other for "a secret love in hidden retreats." Their longing is so strong that they do not sleep, do not drink, do not eat.

There is some ambiguity in the choice of the snakes to represent the two lovers. There are two references to the snakes of **"Erotikos Logos"** in the poet's *Journals.* At one point it is suggested that the two snakes were actually one and at another that there are ten snakes.[65] The snake is a symbol of evil and betrayal, and Seferis has used it in this sense in his poetry. In the first poem of this collection, **"Turning Point,"** the crucial moment he describes kept "the whole / tragic clepsydra dumb, / as though it had seen the Hydra [the snake] / in the heavenly garden." Although he avoided any specific explanation of it, there is no doubt that it was an ominous moment. Also, when Seferis does not use biblical symbolism but the Aeschylean idea of hubris, as in the poem **"Mycenae,"** the snake is again connected with evil. The perpetuation of crime is evident in the following passage from **"Mycenae,"** in which the protagonist identifies with the Atridae. There is most probably a connection here with Clytemnestra's vision in Aeschylus' *Libation Bearers.* She dreamed that she gave birth to a serpent and that she suckled it as if it had been a baby; but together with the milk the serpent drew dotted blood from her breast. The dream was an omen anticipating Clytemnestra's slaying by Orestes.

> Tortured by my own garment
> Condemned by my own gods,
>
> . . . . .
>   I
> Who have so often followed
> The path that leads from murderer to victim
> From victim to the punishment
> And from the punishment up to another murder;
> Groping my way
> Over the purple welling inexhaustible
> That night of the return
> When the whistling began
> Of Furies in the scanty grass—
> I have seen snakes crossed with vipers
> Knotted about the accursed generation
> Our fate.[66]

Thus, by choosing the snakes as symbols of the lovers in the lost paradise, Seferis certainly wanted to imply something—most probably that their love, in spite of its overwhelming passion and ecstasy, was related to a betrayal or a violation.

The erotic encounter of the two lovers is described in very sensuous terms:

> Circling, twisting, their insatiable intent
> spins, multiplies, turns, spreads rings on the body
> which the laws of the starry dome silently govern,
> stirring its hot, irrepressible frenzy.[67]

The erotic moments fall like magic drops of water in the silver cup of silence. Their echoes are like those of a chisel curving the lines of a statue. Then,

> The statue suddenly dawns. But the bodies have vanished
> in the sea in the wind in the sun in the rain.

The image of the statue is rather enigmatic. Three passages from Seferis' writings throw some light on the meaning of the symbol of the statue. The poet himself has suggested[68] that the first of them is parallel to the above lines of **"Erotikos Logos."**

> Oh it is true the fragments
> Are not the statues. You are yourself the remains
> They haunt you with their strange virginity.[69]

> The statues symbolize nothing else but the human bodies which have been hardened by insensitivity, are bent by love or are mutilated by the waste of time.[70]

> Look how our gestures, our movements, our acts, our emotions, our thoughts turn instantaneously into marble as soon as they enter the past, as if they had sunk in "liquified" air. And all these remain motionless there, for ever; nothing can change their pose. We give birth to statues every passing moment. This struck me like a sudden vision three days ago. Since then I have been following this process with anxiety.[71]

These passages help to illuminate to a certain extent the symbolic meaning of the statues, which appear often and are very significant in Seferis' poetry. Some ambiguity, however, still remains. In the case of the two lovers of **"Erotikos Logos,"** for instance, the question remains why instead of the dawn the protagonist was wishing for ("if it were but you who would bring the forgotten dawn") it is "the statue [that] dawns," while "the bodies have vanished." It is true that the next two lines,

> So the beauties nature grants us are born
> but who knows if a soul hasn't died in the world,

suggest the creation of a work of art, at the cost of the artist's soul.[72] But this is only part of the explanation. In my view, the reason why at the end of sensual pleasure the protagonist of **"Erotikos Logos"** finds, not fulfilment, but the body's transformation into marble, must lie in the fact that in his imagination the two separated snakes return, as we see in the next stanza:

> The parted snakes must have returned[73] in fantasy
> (the forest glitters with birds, shoots, blossoms)
> their wavy searching still remains,
> like the turnings of the cycle that bring sorrow.

This is the memory of a lost paradise, as the description in parentheses above indicates. The mutual longing of the two snakes "still remains" and becomes a source of sorrow. And the poet, haunted by this memory, cannot reach fulfilment in the present.

The last part (V) starts with an insistently nostalgic tone:

> Where is the double-edged day that had changed everything?

he wonders, in despair, although he has just failed to revive the paradise of his youth.

In his essay "A Staging for **'The Thrush'**" Seferis himself refers to some poems where this unique moment of love is described.[74]

> Where is love that with one stroke cuts time in two and stuns it?
>
> **("The Mood of A Day")**

> The night perhaps: which opened, a blue pomegranate,
> Dark breasts, filling you full of stars,
> Cutting down time.
>
> **("The Thrush")**

Part V continues with the poet expressing himself in terms of a symbolic journey and using a direct reference to the Homeric myth.

> Won't there be a navigable river for us?
> Won't there be a sky to drop dew
> for the soul benumbed and nourished by the lotus?

This exotic and dangerous fruit deprived some of Odysseus' companions of their day of return. By confessing here that his soul was "nourished"[75] by this fruit, the poet implies that there is no hope for him either. He is probably referring here to the time in his life when he "believed in the omnipotence of the body" and his senses had benumbed his soul. Now he is longing for "the dawn of heaven," which remains unforgettable in his memory, but he realizes that there is no return to Ithaca. The question "Won't there be a navigable river for us?" is rhetorical. Only a "miracle" could save him. He waits for the messenger[76] "On the stone of patience," but miracles do not happen often.

As the poem ends, he addresses again—as he did in the beginning—the "red rose of the wind and fate," admitting with fatigue that the only thing that remains from it in his memory is a "heavy rhythm" like an undulation of the sea.

> Red rose of the wind and of fate
> you remained in memory only, a heavy rhythm
> rose of the night, you passed, undulating purple
> undulation of the sea . . . The world is simple.

The "undulating purple" represents the reflection of the red rose on the water, and since in the beginning of the poem the rose was about to wound the protagonist, this purple, on the symbolic level, is the pain and the blood of this love.[77]

The ending of the poem, "The world is simple," can only be seen as a tragic irony. The Italian critic Lucia Marcheselli, in a discussion with the poet, asked him specifically whether this statement about the simplicity of the world was indeed ironic. Seferis asserted that this was his intention by the comment: "But isn't there καημός [deep sorrow] in sarcasm?"[78]

Notes

1. But everything went wrong for me and upside down, the nature of things was reborn for me.

2. Hydra was a poisonous water snake with nine heads that grew in number when severed—unless cauterized, as Hercules proved in destroying it. It is also a southern constellation, represented as a snake on maps of the heavens.

3. *Essays,* 2:49.

4. *Journal A,* 135.

5. The more exact meaning of the word Seferis uses in the Greek text is "moments," not "seconds."

6. George Seferis, Έξη νύχτες στὴν ᾽Ακρόπολη [*Six Nights on the Acropolis*] (Athens: Hermes, 1974) 100.

7. Keeley and Sherrard's translation is used here, because the word "sound" brings out better the point I wish to make.

8. *Six Nights on the Acropolis,* 117, 111.

9. *Three Secret Poems,* 27. Although the word "land" appears here instead of "place," the original Greek word is again τόπος, as in the other two quotations.

10. Keeley and Sherrard translate this phrase as "the motive / that starts tears." The word σκοπὸς used here usually means "purpose" or "motive," but often refers also to a musical line or tune. In my view, the latter meaning is what the poet had in mind here.

11. See, for instance, the words of Logomanos in *Six Nights on the Acropolis*: "The time will come when I'll initiate her, and we'll reap together the gentle fruit" (124).

12. The word order has been changed here, because as it stands in the published translation the impression is created that the starfilled sky is given to the world, which is not what the Greek original says. A word-by-word translation would be: "became the meaning given to the world by a starfilled sky." Seferis refers to this meaning of the starfilled sky in one of his *Journals.* Speaking about "this special element of Hellenism," which

is difficult to define but can only be felt, he gives a series of persons, places or things that can help us follow its direction: "Homer, Aeschylus, Herodotus—and Bach, Shakespeare and all the other great ones—and Attica, the waves of the Aegean and the starfilled sky." "Because," he concludes, "among other things, Hellenism means humanism" (*Journal D,* 134).

13. "A Valediction: Forbidding Mourning."

14. *Journal A,* 10.

15. "A Staging for 'The Thrush,'" *Essays,* 2:36.

16. In a later poem, "The Thrush," Seferis calls this character "lustful Elpenor." As will be discussed in connection with the "Companions in Hades" and also with "The Thrush," Seferis borrows this character from Homer but modifies him. In Homer, Elpenor is presented as drunk, while in Seferis he is a more general symbol of the sensualist. The common characteristic, however, is a weakness, an inability to control their impulses.

17. "A Staging for 'The Thrush,'" *Essays,* 2:38.

18. Compare the phrase in *Six Nights on the Acropolis*: "the brackish taste of uncertainty" (15).

19. *The Odyssey,* I. 8-9.

20. *Essays,* 2:38.

21. Edmund Keeley, in his essay "Seferis' Elpenor," discusses this subject extensively, emphasizing that "the hedonistic violation of the just order of things literally precludes the return of these modern Elpenors to a lost Paradise. The implication is that no man can aspire toward spiritual liberation until he learns to control his animal appetites, the beast in him that Homer's Circe exploited so cruelly." *The Kenyon Review* (Summer 1966) 389.

22. "A Staging for 'The Thrush,'" *Essays,* 2:52.

23. The identification of light with love is more explicit in a later poem, "The Thrush."

24. The sun, according to C. G. Jung, is considered "a fructifier and creator." *Symbols of Transformation* (Princeton, N.J.: Princeton University Press, 1967) 100.

25. *Six Nights,* 137. Also in the essay about Makriyannis, Seferis mentions the hubris committed by the Persian King Xerxes, who whipped the sea, as a consequence of which his fleet was destroyed and all hands perished in it. Similarly, Seferis here implies that as Aeschylus used a personification of the sea, which punishes Xerxes' hubris, Makriyannis (without knowing about Aeschylus because he was uneducated) uses the personification of the fortress which destroys those who attack it. *Essays,* 1:257.

26. Edmund Keeley, "T. S. Eliot and the Poetry of George Seferis," *Comparative Literature* (Summer 1956) 216.

27.   If the dangerous archangel
            took one step now
                 down toward us
         from behind the stars
            our heartbeats
                 rising like thunder
         would kill us.

                                            ("The Second Elegy")

Duino Elegies, tr. David Young (New York: W. W. Norton, 1978) 27.

28. "Sing out jubilation and praise to affirmative angels" ("The Tenth Elegy"). *Duino Elegies,* tr. C. F. MacIntyre (Berkeley and Los Angeles: University of California Press, 1961) 75.

29. In early editions, the epigraph of this poem, "Say it with a ukelele," was followed by the explanation "English Song."

30. In a later poem, "In the Kyrenia District," the same song appears, sung this time by a person who later dies. The motif of a dead friend whose voice returns from the past appears often in Seferis' poetry as a tyrannical memory, as for instance in the Haiku:

         Is this the voice
         of our dead friends
         or of the gramophone?

31. The Greek word used here, μετόχια, is not fully conveyed by the term "hermitage." Μετόχι is an outlying farm or estate run by a monastery, i.e., a place away from the center of worship. The protagonist does not complain that he is tired of living in solitude, as the word hermitage suggests, but of experiencing many ephemeral affairs, as implied by the fact that μετόχια is in the plural.

32. The correct translation should have the *woman* coughing in the past.

33. Even when describing a very attractive, sensual woman later in his *Journals,* a "half negress with black curled hair like a fur cap," he mentions that her nails—she was apparently wearing red nail polish—were "bloodthirsty." He then adds that she was "a kind of Salome without decapitations, a kind of castrated Semiramis." *Journal B,* 104.

34. *Journal A,* 76.

35. The whole passage in which this sentence appears is somewhat more revealing, because in its context the lost paradise is connected with the memory of the poet's dead friends. The first sentence of this passage appeared also, slightly modified, in a haiku:

Is this the voice
of our dead friends
or the gramophone?

The passage, dated Sunday, September 30, 1931, is as follows:

Is it the voice of our dead friends?—the gramophones insist. One of them in every room, they serve on their black trays [δίσ‌κos in Greek means both "tray" and "record"—C. K.] Spanish or Negro nostalgias. I feel that I am subjected to a systematic mechanical process which brings me successively from the lower to the upper world, and I have the impression that this will continue forever. Where have our own soft, human lines gone? Now I think of the lines without the human beings. I can discern at certain times of unbelievable solitude an unexplained lost paradise that has left its traces on us only to torture us without leading us anywhere.

On the other hand, in another poem, "Stratis the Sailor Describes a Man," the lost paradise is related to the memory of a dead woman: "You know, I love a woman who's gone away perhaps / to the other world."

36. *Journal B,* 13.

37. As the epigraph of this poem indicates, it is the ship met by Arthur Gordon Pym, the hero of Edgar Allen Poe's story *The Narrative of Arthur Gordon Pym.*

38. The following literal translation of the poem is presented here, to help the reader follow the discussion:

"Comments"

Darkness had fallen upon the veranda / something flew by in a hurry / a suppressed confession / was nested in our hearts.

The voice withered, fruitless; / on our lips a flock of wrong words / and only from the depths of the body / O Lord, we expected a blessing.

Darkness hummed inside the house / and from the light of the evening star / to the magnet of your hair / remember the unapproachable angel.

With the rapid rings / fallen suddenly two fans / to the thought which we read / like a prayer from a gospel book.

Woman stranger to my soul / your surprise is what I am left with / beautiful, beloved woman / this senseless evening.

And the black rings of your eyes / and the airy horror of the night . . . / Bend and get back into the sheath / Blade of my silence, chimera.

39. This process is described in more detail in one of the three versions of a never-published poem included in Seferis' *Journal A* (114), from about the same time that *Turning Point* was written:

Set your ear and listen to the sounds
that buzz in a house full of darkness
. . . . .

Let your sense of touch and hearing
fall on the skin of the black drum
drop them like a plumbline in the ocean and hold your breath
cling to the darkness which creates rings like the circles of a target
and loosens the tightness of the noose.

40.   And yet you loved the comrade whom you left
to take the dark path
As you stretch your hands
as you fix your eyes
as you don't know anything, walking along
his hands follow you
his eyes follow you
his loss follows you like a shadow
with that grace of a gazelle he had in the sun.

(*Journal C,* 34)

41. Minas Demakis, "Μία ἀντιπροσωπευτικὴ φωνὴ τῶν χρόνων μας" ["A Representative Voice of our Times"], *Nea Hestia* 92 (1972) 1427.

42. The original Greek word used here, ὄμορφη, means "beautiful," not "beloved."

43. George Savidis, "Μιὰ Περιδιάβαση" ["A Wandering"], Γιὰ τὸν σεφέρη [*For Seferis*] (Athens, 1961) 386.

44. *Six Nights,* 41.

45. *Journal B,* 31.

46. *Journal A,* 10.

47. *Journal A,* 47.

48. *Journal A,* 112.

49. *Journal B,* 13.

50. *Six Nights,* 83. The novel was written at the same time as "Rocket" and revised many years later. The expression "caught the Traviata" means contracted tuberculosis, the disease that causes the death of the heroine in the opera.

51. This poem was not included in the *Collected Poems.* See below, note 55, for my literal translation.

52. *Journal B,* 96. The phrase in French, "Et de ce fleuve . . ." is from a small poem in French, "Etude," which appeared in Seferis' *Journal B* a few months before the quoted passage (69-70).

53. *For Seferis,* 401-2.

54. *For Seferis,* 324.

55. This poem was also omitted from the *Collected Poems.* The following is my literal translation of this difficult poem, which will help the reader follow the discussion:

"In Memoriam"

You were the divine silence / and as white as rice / but the shivering for flight / always keeps coming back.

You got into the whirlpool / centrifugal soul / that leaves us / in a remote bitterness.

When night falls, I see in the foliage / the eyes of our friends, closed.

56. *Journal B,* 104.

57. *Journal A,* 122.

58. In Seferis' draft (*Journal A,* 134) a question mark appears after the title "Journey."

59. Seferis had not yet read the *Waste Land* when he wrote these lines.

60. The word "root" is used here in the singular, because the original Greek ρίζα is in the singular. Seferis refers to the human body as if it were a plant or a tree—an imagery that he uses very often and in various contexts.

61. The image is from the seventeenth-century romance *Erotokritos.*

62. In his essay "A Staging for 'The Thrush,'" Seferis, referring to a similar expression in "The Thrush," writes: "the cool leaf, the leaf that respires, in the sense of fulfilment of desire," and then cites as another example the "scented shrubs" of "Erotikos Logos." *Essays,* 2:42.

63. As Walter Kaiser remarks in his Introduction to the *Three Secret Poems,* this kind of image "although comprehensible, achieves its full impact only for someone who has experienced the palpable closeness of stars in those Mediterranean latitudes" (xi).

64. The term "resurrected" is a more precise equivalent of the Greek ἀναστηθεῖ, which is used here.

65. *Journal B,* 90.

66. Cassandra, in *Agamemnon,* referring to the boldness of Clytemnestra in slaying her husband, says: "What odious monster shall I fitly call her? an amphisbaena?" (a fabulous snake which moves both backward and forward, ll. 1230-3).

67. The Greek word αφορμή, which is rendered here as "frenzy," literally translated means "primary cause," "motive" or "origin."

68. *Essays,* 2:43.

69. From "The Thrush."

70. From a letter to his French translator, Robert Levesque (*For Seferis,* 268).

71. *Journal A,* 75.

72. See also Robert Levesque's Introduction to his French translation of Seferis' poems, *Séféris: Choix de Poèmes traduits et accompagnés du texte grec avec une préface* (Athens: Ikaros, 1945).

73. The Greek γύριζαν means both "circle" and "return." For my interpretation of the poem it is crucial to render it here as "return."

74. *Essays,* 2:42.

75. The Greek word ἀνάθρεψε, which Seferis uses here, literally translates as "reared."

76. The word used by Seferis here, ἄγγελος, means "messenger" in ancient Greek and "angel" in modern Greek. Seferis very effectively combines the two meanings here, in a manner reminiscent of the mysterious messengers in *Waiting for Godot.*

77. Compare, for instance, Odysseus Elytis' phrase, "The blood of love has robed me in purple." *The Axion Esti,* trs. Edmund Keeley and George Savidis (Pittsburgh: University of Pittsburgh Press, 1974) 97.

78. I am indebted to Lucia Marcheselli for this information.

Bibliography

Demakis, Minas. "Μια ἀντιπροσωπευτικὴ φωνὴ τῶν χρόνων μας" ["A Representative Voice of our Times"]. *Nea Hestia* 92 (1972) 1420-1449.

Elytis, Odysseus. *The Axion Esti.* Trs. Edmund Keeley and George Savidis. Pittsburgh: University of Pittsburgh Press, 1974.

Jung, C. G. *Symbols of Transformation.* Tr. R. F. C. Hull. 2d ed. Princeton, N.J.: Princeton University Press, 1967.

Keeley, Edmund. "T. S. Eliot and the Poetry of George Seferis." *Comparative Literature* (Summer 1956) 214-26.

———. "Seferis' Elpenor: A Man of No Fortune." *The Kenyon Review* (Summer 1966) 378-90.

Levesque, Robert. *Séféris: Choix de Poèmes traduits et accompagnés du texte grec avec une préface.* Athens: Ikaros, 1945.

Rilke, Rainer Maria. *Duino Elegies.* Tr. C. F. MacIntyre. Berkeley and Los Angeles: University of California Press, 1961.

———. *Duino Elegies.* Tr. David Young. New York: W. W. Norton, 1978.

Savidis, George. "Μια Περιδιάβαση" ["A Wandering"]. In Γιὰ τὸν σεφέρη [*For Seferis*], eds. Leonidas Zenakos and George Savidis, 304-408. Athens: n.p., 1961.

———. Πάνω Νερὰ [*Upper Waters*]. Athens: Hermes, 1973.

Seferis, George. *Poems.* Tr. Rex Warner. Boston: Little, Brown & Co., 1964.

———. *Collected Poems 1924-1955.* Trs. Edmund Keeley and Philip Sherrard. Princeton, N.J.: Princeton University Press, 1967.

———. *Three Secret Poems.* Tr. Walter Kaiser. Cambridge, Mass.: Harvard University Press, 1969.

———. *The King of Asine and Other Poems.* Trs. Bernard Spencer, Nanos Valaoritis and Lawrence Durrell. London: John Lehman, 1948.

———. Δοℵιμὲς [*Essays*]. 3d ed. 2 vols. Athens: Ikaros, 1974.

———. Ποιήματα [*Poems*]. 11th ed. Ed. George Savidis. Athens: Ikaros, 1977.

———. Ἕξη νύχτες στὴν Ἀℵρόπολη [*Six Nights on the Acropolis*]. Athens: Hermes, 1974.

———. Μέρες [*Days*]. 5 vols. Athens: Ikaros. Vol. *A* (February 16, 1925-August 17, 1931), 1975; vol. *B* (August 24, 1931-February 12, 1934), 1975; vol. *C* (April 16, 1934-December 14, 1940), 1977; vol. *D* (January 1, 1941-December 31, 1944), 1977; vol. *E* (January 1, 1945-April 19, 1951), 1973.

———. *A Poet's Journal: Days of 1945-1951.* Tr. Athan Anagnostopoulos. Cambridge, Mass.: Harvard University Press, 1974.

———. Τετράδιο Γυμνασμάτων, Β' [*Book of Exercises B*]. Ed. George Savidis. Athens: Ikaros, 1976.

Eva P. Lester and Dmitri Kyriazis (essay date summer 1984)

SOURCE: Lester, Eva P., and Dmitri Kyriazis. "George Seferis's Poetic Insight." *American Imago* 41, no. 2 (summer 1984): 129-54.

[*In the following essay, Lester and Kyriazis explore the relationship between events in Seferis's life and his 1946 poem "The Thrush."*]

"Thrush" is the longest and, possibly, the most significant poem of George Seferis, the Greek poet and diplomat (Nobel Prize 1963).[1] The poem is of particular value to the psychoanalytic exploration of the creative process as we have rich biographical and autobiographical material pertaining to the poet's life experiences in general and to events closely related to the writing of the poem in particular. The poet's diaries, the dreams he reported at the time, and the dense symbolism of the poem contain elements of a profound personal crisis, while the dénouement of the poem carries with it the resolution of the crisis.

Seferis wrote the poem within two weeks in October 1946, but exercises and full verses are found in his diary several months before the actual writing. The fall of 1946 marked a turning point in Seferis' life, the end of a long period of stagnation and self-doubt and the restoration of the poet's creative thrust. Several years of private anguish and search for a personal space left him with a profound sense of despair and disgust. The war years spent in "bitter exile" (Egypt and South Africa) were followed by the return to Greece, a homeland devastated by the war and seething with violent political passions. These passions, which culminated in a short but fierce civil war in December of 1944, left the poet with deep psychic scars. In the spring of 1945 he wrote:

> I can't remember another year as bad as this last one; nothing as horrible as the last two months . . . all these days nothing but a lamentable monotony and a barbaric obsession for destruction.
>
> (1973, p. 11)

From a vast cultural heritage which he has used with mastery in his work, Seferis chose as the central idea to the poem the concept of "nekya," the ritual offering of sacrifice to the dead souls for their counsel. **"Thrush"** is the poet's personal descent into Hades and the search into his own depths. Equally, the poem is his acceptance of the fateful answer, the inexorable truth without which the poet cannot restore his battered self.

In a short essay (1974), Seferis presents the poem as an allegory of the last part of Odysseus' long voyage to Ithaca. He explains that the "I" in the poem is that of another, a present-day, Odysseus. The poem allegorically extends from the moment he is setting foot to Circe's island until the very end of his descent to Hades when he exchanges the last words with the soul of his dead mother.

Seferis is a visual poet dominated by powerful images carrying crucial ideas and determining the flow of the poem. In **"Thrush,"** the musical rhythmical parts are the weakest passages; the return of the image usually signals a turning point and a fresh creative impulse. Significantly, Seferis himself, in his attempt to explain the poem, invites the reader to follow him into a theatrical set. ". . . [W]ith this [set] it is not all that improbable that the poem could be made into a movie" (1974, p. 30). The poet "sees" his poem and invites us to "see" it with him.

The Poet

There is no official biography of the poet. But his own published diaries, a volume of correspondence and the biographical study *My Brother, George Seferis* (Tsatsou, 1973) based mostly on the 1919-1925 letters to his sister Joanna, give adequate information about the person and his life.

The eldest son of a prominent Greek family from Smyrna, the poet, born in 1900, grew up with a strong sense of destiny. His father, a professor of law and a poet himself, was a strict authoritarian who made great demands on his first son. The sister writes: "As the years went by, father's autocratic nature oppressed us all but mostly G. It was mostly from him that he demanded absolute perfection in everything. He supervised his studies, personally sitting next to him till the small hours of the night. I could feel G's anguish, I was always so sorry for him" (p.19). The father himself chose the son's career, law and diplomacy, against his own wishes to study literature and become a poet. Not daring to disobey paternal dictates, he pursued law with tremendous conscious and unconscious bitterness and resistance. One of the recurring themes in the poet's diaries is his struggle within the inevitable duality imposed on his life: the private contemplative individual in need of intense personal experience and total concentration, and the professional man, exclusively social, political and public; the poet, viewing and sensing life indirectly through his emotions and abstracted word symbols, and the administrator and policy maker, the man of action asked to perform and to manipulate people and events.

In September, 1942 Seferis writes:

> I am thinking of this devastation of the self. My life often seems to me like a candle, lighted and forgotten inside an empty room. It consumes itself for no reason or purpose.
>
> (1977, p. 249)

In August, 1944:

> As I watch the people of my generation I feel at times such a very deep bitterness. It exhausts me that I cannot lock myself away from everybody.
>
> (1973, p. 347)

This personal contradiction extends to another duality, a vertical split in his ego, apparent in the contrast between the restraint, placid, staid exterior and the internal turbulence, always contained for fear of explosion.

In March, 1943 he writes:

> This morning I finished the first literary pages I wrote since last July. Always in a hurry, on my knees as it were, like everything I am doing here. This morning as I was writing on this narrow miserable little table I burst into sobs and cried without being able to stop. I have to keep my emotions tightly bottled up because if I let them out I will drown in a storm of intense feeling.
>
> (1977, p. 285)

In 1914, the family moved to Athens and in 1918 to Paris where the father was heading a Greek delegation for the post-war peace negotiations. The following year,

the mother and two young children returned to Smyrna and then sensing the approaching Turkish uprising, they left the homeland for good, settling in Athens. From then on, the family seemed to break down. Seferis and his father remained in Paris but lived separate lives. In 1924, Seferis obtained his law degree and returned to Athens; the father, estranged but never quite separated from his wife, stayed in Paris. In 1926, the poet entered the foreign service, and the same year his mother died. His first book of poetry was published in 1931. In 1941, with his bride (he married at 41 and had no children) he followed the Greek government in its flight to Africa. In 1962, Seferis was appointed ambassador to London, and in 1963 he received the Nobel Prize for literature. The poet died in 1971 from a peptic ulcer.

THE POEM

The caption, taken from Plutarch, introduces the reader to the ominous truths contained in the poem.

"Ephemeral progeny of a vicious demon and a harsh fate, why do you force me to speak of things that it would be better for you not to know?"

The poem is divided into three parts. In the first two, the poet remembers, sums up and sets the stage, bringing in one by one the archetypal images, the echoes from the past and the loud vulgar noises of the present. The set is then ready for the third and climactic part, the *nekya*, the symbolic descent to Hades, where he will receive an oracle. The poet, like Odysseus—the identity which as he says overrides all other identities in the Greek character—knows he cannot find counsel in the "upper" world, the world of reason and immediate perception. He must make the difficult voyage and descend into the depths of the self. Once there, however, unlike Odysseus, the poet will turn not to the blind prophet, Tiresias, but to the philosopher Socrates for the final resolution.

PART I: "THE HOUSE NEAR THE SEA"

The first six verses introduce the perception of the self as a tragic man living in a tragic era.

> The houses I had they took away from me. The times happened to be unpropitious: war, destruction, exile; sometimes the hunter hits the migratory birds, sometimes he doesn't hit them. Hunting was good in my time, many felt the pellet; the rest circle aimlessly or go mad in the shelters.

Man is destined to loss and suffering. The houses, like the empty shells of the self, reflect the ravages of war, the loss of dreams, the savagery of men. The allegory of the verses keeps the imagery dim and vague.

> I don't know much about houses.
> I know they have their own nature, nothing else.

When the architect's finished, they change,
they frown or smile or even grow stubborn
with those who stayed behind, with those who went
    away
with others who'd come back if they could
or others who disappeared, now that the world's
    become
a limitless hotel.

The poet has turned to the houses of his past, especially the beloved house of Scala, the "house by the sea" of his childhood. In December 1942, while living in Pretoria, he recorded the following dream:

I am in Scala, I cast my eyes around greedily like powerful lenses. It is a world with a sky close to me, a finite and familiar sky. Everything, the house, the objects all were faithful to me; I had the burning feeling they were all mine, almost part of me, as if I were a child and they were my toys.

(1977, p. 250)

This wish of oneness with the house and the sky in the dream, this bliss of union with past objects, represents the restoration of a lost narcissistic perfection, in sharp contrast with the real state of the impoverished self at the time, the self of the "exiled," living in an "open world without sky." At another point during the same period he talked of houses, how

we use them like clothing to wrap ourselves with . . . All these strange costumes (all these houses since we left Crete) make me think we have nothing left but our naked bodies (abandoned) in this or that land, a land without a sky.

(1977, p. 175)

In the poem, the memories surge in, together with the awareness of his own "waste land", a world that has become "a limitless hotel."[2] But he refuses admittance to his lost paradise: The childhood houses are now sealed holding their memories stubbornly in their dark spaces.

I don't know much about houses,
I remember their joy and their sorrow.

The poet, like the much-travelled Odysseus, has finally reached shore and is ready to abandon the dream of the lost Scala and deal with the present. For the Homeric hero, this present was Circe and her power over him and his companions. The poet, however, leaves the immediacy of this encounter with the sorceress for the second part of the poem and, at this point, in a dream-like fashion, he returns briefly to his own memories and draws from his personal past. A powerful image enters the poet's awareness, ushering in an old death fantasy. It seems to be an echo from the poet's painful years in Paris when, separated from his mother and without the security of the beloved Scala, he felt a double exile. Alone and forced to study law which he detested, Sef-

eris developed a severe depression, and the long almost daily letters to his sister are replete with ideas of suicide. "I would like to use my blood as ink today. This evening, 'the man who committed suicide' as you call him, was here with me . . . he will die uttering wordless sounds." Immediately following is the fantasy of the sensuous woman. In the poet's personal mythology, but also in the popular folklore from which he draws heavily, death and sensuality are often interwoven. In the same letter to his sister, referring to the young woman he is sexually attracted to but suspects and fears as a seductress, he writes: "I wonder at times whether the look of a woman who claims she loves you is much different from that of Salome turned to the head of Johanaan" (Tsatsou, 1973, p. 103).

[S]ometimes, near the sea, in naked rooms with a single iron bed and nothing of my own watching the evening spider, I imagine that someone is getting ready to come, that they dress him up;

that he is getting ready to come and say goodbye to me; or that a woman—eyelashes curled, high-girdled, climbs the stairs without seeing those who've fallen asleep under the stairs.

Houses, you know, grow stubborn easily when you strip them bare.

At this point, the first part of the poem ends.

Part II: "Sensual Elpenor"

In this part, Seferis returns to Circe. He never mentions her directly but the references are unmistakable. This part is in the form of a dialogue between Circe and Elpenor. The third person in this passage is the poet or the reader, our awareness, our condemnation and sympathy for what we are witnessing.

Psychologically, this part refers to the sexual experience in its fragmentation, and to the poet's defensive dissociation and flight from sensuality. Beyond this, it deals with man's attempt to transcend the dichotomy of body and soul, and accept a transformed ("carved") body as the one and only reality, the only enduring self.

Seferis uses Elpenor, a minor Homeric character, in several of his poems (Keeley, 1966). Elpenor was the young soldier ("a youth who never distinguished himself in the war and whose mind wasn't very sharp" [*Odyssey*, 1976, p. 146]) who, the morning of the departure from the island of Circe, still drowsy from sleep and drink, blundered from the terrace of the palace and smashed himself on the ground, and "his soul descended directly to the Hades."

Seferis' Elpenor, like the Homeric youth, is "nice, sentimental, average, wasted" (1974, p. 29).

These people, the tender ordinary men, tend to become the most popular of all my characters. At times I feel compassion for his likes but more often than not I feel a strong animosity against the softness he represents, all that which we sense around us as stagnant waters.

(1974, p. 41)

Above all, Elpenor is a poorly assimilated identity within the poet, a self-representation split off and disavowed from the poet's personality. From his biography, we suspect that, consciously, Elpenor may have represented the poet's brother, A., a constant source of anxious concern and scorn for Seferis. The youngest of the three, A. grew up under the shadow of his father and Seferis but, unlike the latter, whose resistance to his father led him to the creation of two lives, as a poet and a diplomat, thus accepting the paternal dictate and transcending it, A. defied the father's decision at first and then gave in, never finding a clear path in life. He practiced law for awhile and wrote poems, but only a slim volume was published posthumously and this through Seferis' own efforts. In 1946, estranged from his wife and son, A. emigrated to the U.S. where he died in 1951 in total isolation. The causes of his death remain unclear; there is a strong possibility that he committed suicide.

> I saw him yesterday standing by the door
> below my window; it was about
> seven o'clock; there was a woman with him.
>
> He was speaking fast, and she
> was gazing absently towards the gramophones;
>   . . . . .
>
> Listen to this also. In the moonlight
> the statues sometimes bend like reeds
> in the midst of ripe fruit—the statues;
> and the flame becomes a cool oleander,
> the flame that burns man, I mean.
>
> It's just the light . . . shadows of the night.
>   . . . . .
>
>   —And yet the statues
> bend sometimes, dividing desire in two,
> like a peach; and the flame
> becomes a kiss on the limbs, a sobbing,
> and then a cool leaf carried off by the wind;
> they bend; they become light with a human weight.
> You don't forget it.

The statue holds a single place in the mythology of the poet. It is more than a symbol of the human body; it contains the essence of the body, its mystic presence. In a previous poem Seferis wrote:

> I woke up with the marble head in my hands.
> It is exhausting my arms and I don't know
> where to let it rest.
>
> It was falling into the dream as I was coming
> out of the dream.

So our life became one and it will be difficult,
for it to separate again.

(Keeley 1967, p. 5)

It is Orestes speaking there about his murdered father. To a friend, Seferis remarked:

> The statues represent nothing but the human bodies ossified by insensitivity, bending by sexual love and mutilated by the ravages of age.

Elpenor is talking of his renounced desires, the memories of these desires and the memories of his frustrated ("ossified") sexual impulse. Indirectly, he is appealing to the woman to revive the desire, to spark in him the old flame. In this "lustful" island, as he describes Poros, the poet experiences a surge of sensuality which, as we see in his diaries, surprises him. He is uneasy, unsure of how to handle the awakening of a body he had believed static like marble. This preoccupation with his own sensuality is brought more into the open in the last part of the poem. Characteristically, the poet introduces the subject through Elpenor and his confrontation with Circe, first in an attempt to distance and dissociate himself from the immediacy of his desire and to "transform" (sublimate) his own fantasy about Circe.

In the poem, the woman remains indifferent to Elpenor's pleas:

>   —"The statues are in the museum".
> No, they pursue you, why can't you see it?
> I mean with their broken limbs,
> with their shape from another time, a shape you don't
>   yet know.

The woman remains distant, herself untouched by the desire she stimulates in the man, by the sexual impulse which overwhelms and fragments the male self. She is remote, inaccessible and eternal. The following dream, recorded in December, 1945, points to the fantasy of the woman as malevolent, devouring, insatiable but also prey to her own instincts and herself a victim of fate.

> In a room with two windows facing the sea. The house was crumbling, thin, as if made of cardboard—like theatrical sets painted naively. Something confusing about the whole thing, X in a good mood, in a sexual mood. Behind me there was another room in the back, a familiar room with familiar furniture; maybe the house in Scala. I am sitting at a table and I open a book, I turn the pages. An art book or a family album. X is sitting next to me and looks at me tenderly. Suddenly the ghost of his former wife wrapped in a grey gauze appears like the young woman in "Blithe Spirit" which I saw in Cairo. I know it is her but her face looks strange, the heavy makeup fading and peeling off. Angry and tortured she says, "In the bordello where you locked me up I ate pounds and pounds of arab

meat." In the dream I have a strong oppressive sensation of a continuous orgasm. A mob of arabs in long robes and fezes appears. They scream and gesture, horribly obscene gestures with their hands. Here I wake up.

                                                            (1973, p. 22)

The dream, replete with familiar symbols, deals partly with the oedipal triangle and Seferis' inability to maintain any tenderness with the father or a paternal object, when the latter turns to the sexual woman. (The poet always conceals the identities of people in his diaries by giving them mythical names or X, Y, Z letters.) The answer is to lock the woman away, remove her from the scene. The woman in the bordello seems to represent the renounced sexual impulse fused with devouring, oral aggressive urges. The feeling of being in a "set" points again to the poet's difficulty to withstand the full impact of the sexual desire. Dissociation sets in—the body, like a statue, bends and the self becomes fragmented. But the woman returns, the memories of lost or abandoned objects, the memory of discarded self-identities always come back and the sadistic impulses against the woman return as a superego haunting reminder. At the end, the poet affirms, nothing remains except our memories and fantasies which, emptied of their original emotion, resemble fragments of statues locked in museums. Throughout his life, Seferis is haunted by what is lost and what remains of the past. In another poem, **"The King of Asine,"** he writes:

> And the poet lingers, looking at the stones, and asks
>   himself
> does there really exist
> among these ruined lines, edges, points, hollows and
>   curves
> does there really exist
> here where one meets the path of rain, wind and ruin
> does there exist the movement of the face, shape of
>   the tenderness
> of those who've shrunk so strangely in our lives,
>   . . . . .
> or perhaps no, nothing is left but the weight
> the nostalgia for the weight of a living existence
> there where we now remain unsubstantial. . . .
>   . . . . .
> image of a form that the sentence to everlasting bitter-
>   ness
> has turned to marble:
> the poet a void.

Back to **"The Thrush,"** where the poet ponders the same question of how time and loss affect man and man's image of himself.

> It's as though
> at the end of your youth you love
> a woman who stayed beautiful,
> and you're constantly afraid,
> while you hold her naked at noon,
> of the memory that wakens in your embrace;

> It's as though
> returning home from some foreign country you hap-
>   pen to open
> an old trunk that's been locked up a long time
> and find the tatters of clothes you used to wear
> on happy occasions, at festivals with many-colored
>   lights,
> mirrored, now becoming dim.

> Really, those statues are not
> the fragments. You yourself are the relic;
> they haunt you with a strange virginity
> at home, at the office, at receptions for the celebrated,
> in the unconfessed terror of sleep;
> they speak of things you wish didn't exist
> or would exist years after your death,
> and that's difficult because
>   . . . . .
>   —"The statues are in the museum.
> Good night".
> —". . . because the statues are no longer
> fragments. We are. The statues bend lightly . . . Good
>   night".

At this point, they separate. Elpenor takes the road leading uphill and the woman moves on towards the beach "where the waves are drowned in the noise from the radio." The sub-heading "The radio" follows—a repetition and a resonance of the same material. This part is rhythmic, the verses are short, rhyming, and the mood derisive. It is a lamentation for the passage of time and youth, leaving the woman (and the weak impulsive drifting self) "senseless, blind and dumb." The only defense is to lock oneself in one's house and ignore all knocks at the door.

> and don't open, knock how they may:
> They shout but have nothing to say

It is a reference to the poet's own attempt during the past few years to isolate himself from others, to withdraw into a private existence where the only admitted reality was that of his poetry. But at the end of this part, he cannot shut the radio off, blaring news of the war. Ominous news of events culminating in a crisis: "The war . . . the merchant of souls" is the last verse of the second part of the poem.

PART III: THE WRECK "THRUSH"

At the end of the second part, the poet has kept his door locked but he could not shut out echoes of destruction. He is anguished and must search for another answer. The first year after his return to Greece, he remains depressed and aimless. In his diary, the poet realizes he can only search inside "within my own depths": "The subject of the poet is only one—his own body." "For days now I have been carving myself to make one verse" (1977, p. 132). But he feels alienated from his body, divided within himself and estranged from others. He cannot get a hold on any internal or external reality as a starting point. He has no orienting sign for his search. The war has been over for more than a year, his long "exile" is now a thing of the past, but the poet continues to feel empty, undecided. On April 4, 1946 he writes:

> Today was the first day of the approaching summer but it is of no use to me. April has brought violets and lilacs but I feel nothing, for me it has snowed all night.
>
> (1973, p. 31)

And then suddenly, on a short trip to a monastery, he is struck by the "immense" beauty of the countryside. A few days later he writes:

> This unexplained spell of the sea, how it begets such an immediate change in me: it is a mystery, a deep puzzle which I feel in my bones. I cannot comprehend it, I cannot come close, to reach the dividing line and cross over to the other world.
>
> (1973, p. 32)

A few weeks later:

> Since the beginning of this spring I feel an indescribable sensibility and enthrallment. It is like a dialogue between myself and the other (or God), this unending barter between myself and the sea, the mountains, the light and the air. Those mountains, one next to the other, like bodies embracing one another dissolving into one another then moving towards you to complete you. This extraordinary process does take place; I cannot articulate better this sudden revelation; from this point on it makes no difference who you are because actually you are not within yourself anymore, you are over there and once there you have committed a religious act.
>
> (1973, p. 37)

> My being is expanding in this other world. A frightful abyss is in my feet. Unbearable painful silence, dizziness. I feel inside the abyss in the womb of a woman, the womb of a stranger woman, the womb of the earth. A black and shining day.
>
> (p. 38)

For a long time, he struggles to understand the limits of light, the essence of light, the sudden blindness he feels in this cataclysm of sunshine. He struggles to understand the relationship of movement and stillness, the meaning of the "dance of mountains in their perfect immobility." Above all, he wants to grasp this oceanic feeling this

> fusion between nature and this mere human body. This simple insignificant and yet extraordinary, superhuman happening.
>
> (p. 39)

Seferis senses that he has hit upon something substantial, but he is still groping: he recalls the sentence "and you see the sun-light" and is pondering over its meaning:

> I could probe into these words and reach down to the depths of love. But I need a new language in order to talk about all this. A new language which I will have to nourish for years, working it with all that I loved and all that I lost, never to find again.
>
> (p. 40)

Seferis has the intuitive knowledge that he needs to reconstruct this internal world in order to accept the awesome truth contained in this simple sentence "I see the sunlight": Seeing the sunlight implies its opposite, the state of not seeing the sunlight; in other words, light always contains darkness, life always contains death. To accept life, one has to give up life and accept death:

> There is a primordial drama, a deep organic drama involving our blood and body and soul. You only begin seeing this when you sense that behind the golden tapestry of the summer there is a terrifying darkness and all of us are simply pawns to this darkness. The Greek tragedy is only the poetic image of this enclosed world struggling to survive and breathe in this narrow golden band knowing of the impending disappearance into the darkness, and it is this knowledge that gives this world its humanity.
>
> (p. 42)

In August, 1946, Seferis takes a short vacation to the island Poros and then, in September, he obtains a leave of absence and returns to the same island. Already on his first trip, he notices the wreck *Thrush,* a small boat "seen very clearly with its broken masts" inside the water. The leave of absence is the freedom from public life he needs to complete his merger with the sea and mountains and to continue his probing:

> I carry with me all this accumulated filth that I need to wash off and I must keep in mind that my years are committed from now on. I don't have the limitless bounds of youth anymore.
>
> (p. 52)

In the third passage of the poem, Seferis is ready for the internal voyage. The wreck *Thrush* will take him into Hades where the dead objects are waiting to be "rescued" and given up. His language is personal but also universal; it is the language of the poet as a man and of the poet as a people with a long historical and poetic past. Unlike the Homeric descent into Hades which, told in the third person, is the externalization of the fantasy, i.e., a story projected to the outside world (in the sense that the myth is projected), the poet's descent is an intrapsychic event: He hears the first voice from Hades while he is still contemplating the voyage. Here again, we have a flash of his deep insight into how the unconscious wish may surge into consciousness to illuminate and hasten the ego's measures to satisfy such a wish. The voice is that of Elpenor, his alter ego, the weak undifferentiated, repressed self. The envied and despised brother is now making his last gesture to the poet, a gesture of forgiveness before he will move into darkness forever.

> This wood that cooled my forehead
> at times when the noon burned my veins
> will flower in other hands. Take it, I'm giving it to you;
> look, it's wood from a lemon tree . . .
>   I heard the voice
> as I was gazing at the sea trying to make out
> a ship they'd sunk there years ago;
> it was called "Thrush," a small wreck; the masts,
> broken, swayed at odd angles deep underwater, like tentacles,
> or the memory of dreams, marking the hull:
> vague mouth of some huge dead sea-monster
> extinguished in the water. Calm spread all around.

In the Homeric text, Elpenor, still "un-mourned" and "unburied," explains his tragic death to Odysseus and begs him to bury his body so that his soul may find its rightful place among the dead. As a last request, he asks Odysseus to plant "an oar from his boat" on his tomb. The phallic symbolism is unmistakable in both passages, but in **"Thrush,"** Elpenor's gesture of handing the poet the branch of a lemon tree takes the added meaning of the poet's profoundly felt duty to his brother and his people: He is given (by Fate?) the brother's gift and he now must bring the lemon wood into full bloom.

> And in turn other voices
> slowly followed; whispers thin and thirsty
> emerging from the other side of the sun, the dark side;
> one would say they longed for a drop of blood to drink;
> familiar voices, but I couldn't distinguish one from the other.
> And then the voice of the old man reached me; I felt it
> quietly falling into the heart of day,
> as though motionless:
> And if you condemn me to drink poison, I thank you.
> Your law will be my law; how can I go
> wandering from one foreign country to another, a rolling stone.
> I prefer death.
> Who'll come out best only God knows.

At this point, ready to make the last significant choice of his life, Seferis unexpectedly turns to Socrates the philosopher, pronouncing the last words of his Apology to the Judges (Plato, 1970, p. 101). In the *Odyssey* the counsel came from the blind prophet Tiresias: Odysseus must respect the Sun's Cattle so that he may return to Ithaca. This counsel implies that life is predetermined and in the hands of the gods. The fate of Odysseus was already contained in his origins: As the grandson of Autocletos, he had inherited the seed of defiance against divine wish, the hubris that caused him a life of endless drifting. Through his suffering, however, Odysseus finally atoned, but also burned out the narcissistic arrogance of the wanderer and is now ready to return home to the generative years of middle life.

Seferis, a wanderer himself, does not feel his decision is predetermined and in the hands of the gods. Like Socrates, he accepts the right of the individual to make a choice and the power of the intellect to impose order in his world at least in a temporary and incomplete way. Like Socrates, Seferis proclaims the strength and the will to overcome personal narcissistic hurts to accommodate the interests of social necessity. But beyond these moral and ethical imperatives, in Seferis' identification with Socrates, there is the awareness of his destiny as a poet: Above all he feels he is a man of the Word (Logos). It is this commanding pole of his ego ideal which directs him to Socrates, another man of the Word. A dream that Seferis records on October 13, the exact time of the writing of the poem, is very revealing on this point. He prefaces the dream with the following statement:

> I woke up for the first time in years with a
> dream which gave me a great amount of joy.
>
>   (1973, p. 60)

The dream is very long and the scarce associative material in the diary makes it impossible to analyze it fully. However, its movement and final resolution, accompanied by an intense affective release, make it a critical document in our analysis.

> In a foreign city, Paris or London. Evening. I am having a conversation with a tobacconist. The store is lighted with a white light. *Feeling* that I have with me a friend for whom I am looking to find a room. The tobacconist is a Greek "compatriot," nice and friendly. Impossible to get any useful information for the room I am looking for. "Really," I tell him, "can't one find a room to rent by the hour?" "If it is by the hour," he says "myself . . ." We separate, laughing. I am walking on the wide sidewalk. I see (impossible to be sure of the face of the friend who is with me) a car driven by American soldiers or workers. We are impressed by the ease by which the front wheels are moving as if they are unscrewed. "It must be the new Ford model," I remark. In front of the car, when it stops, a bus, similar to those on the Kifissia route—not the yellow ones. The bus doesn't move; the Americans get out; loud argument. Any moment they will start a fistfight. A crowd gathers around. At the critical moment a tramway stops in front of the crowd. However the street is not in Athens; it reminds me of Boulevard Malesherbes in Paris. The tramway driver gets out with a wrench in his hand, very determined. He decides to straighten out their differences. The Americans, the bus driver and the tramway driver break through the crowd and come to a Gothic style house. They enter the house and suddenly I see them seated on shelves attached to the front of the house. From this position they discuss their differences very calmly. The crowd and myself among this crowd look idly but with some amazement. (I recall that a little while ago I had sat out on the balcony at

our house; I felt dizzy from being so high up and I called Maro to hold me. I recalled this incident and thought to myself: Look at them, I got dizzy just getting on the balcony and they are up there discussing something, so totally unconcerned.) After a while the disputation has been resolved, the three of them come down, crowds and vehicles are dispersed and I find myself on the shore of the Thames or in Venice in the company of actors dressed in colorful costumes (green, red and white); they are going down to the water as if to *board a boat in great mirth and merriment.* An indescribable relief rushes through my heart. I wake up with the words: Finally, I find myself in the world of Shakespeare.

In its manifest dimensions, the dream seems to be divided into three parts.

1. *In the first part,* the presence of the friend seems to be the dominant element. A friend who is so close, the dreamer *feels* his presence but cannot make out his face. A friend who most probably represents an important part of the poet himself. In his diary entry on the previous day Seferis mentions T. S. Eliot and C. Cavafy, the two poets who he admits had influenced him the most. The search for "a room to rent by the hour" in the dream may be associated to Cavafy's many poems with references to rooms where he had "rejoiced" his illicit (homosexual) love. In the same diary entry Seferis had copied some verses from T. S. Eliot's "East Coker" which he had read for the first time. He remarked, "If I knew them before I would have used them as a caption for *Mythistorema* [an earlier book of poems]":

> As we grow older
> The world becomes stranger, the pattern more compli-
>   cated
> Of dead and living. Not the intense moment
> Isolated, with no before and after,
> But a life time burning in every moment
> And not the lifetime of one man only
> But of old stones that cannot be deciphered.

In the verses that follow, from **"Thrush,"** we find his language overlapping and echoing Eliot's, but also recognize the cadence of Cavafy and the melancholy of what is no longer there expressed so well by the Alexandrian poet:

> It wouldn't have lasted long anyway
> years of experience make that clear.[3]

2. The second part of the dream is about the fight. Here, the "dream population" (Erikson, 1954) is likely to represent the immediate past, the war years and the poet's endless frustration and unexpressed rage against the "swindlers, psychopaths and moral cripples," as he describes many of the people he encountered in his public life (1977, p. 215). However, the reference to "Boulevard Malesherbes" in Paris permits another pos-sible linkage with a remote past, his student years in Paris, and his despair and rage during those times. The rage and hate for the powerful father condensed with more recent emotions is projected onto the tramway driver appearing with a wrench in his hand. But as we have seen, in the past months, the poet had struggled with his hates and had began to renounce hate. The communion with the land and the immersion into his rich cultural past (while in Poros, as he mentions in his diary, he committed himself to read one hundred verses from the *Illiad* each morning [1973, pp. 57]) offers the dreamer a resolution other than the use of brutal force. The adversaries sit and discuss calmly and reach agreement. The three men who in the dream "come down from their elevated posts to disperse the crowds" may refer to the poet's desire that the three males in the family engaged in bitter but covered struggle during most of Seferis' life be reconciled. The reference to the dizziness in high places and to his being assisted by his wife may reflect the poet's conflict between the weak dependent (on mother and sister) self and the strong, fearless, independent part, identified with the father.

3. *The last part of the dream* integrates and completes affective relief. The dreamer, free from crippling rage and conflict, may now join the group of actors, *ready to board a boat with incredible mirth and merriment.* Here two elements indicate that, however significant this resolution, it leaves the poet with a sense of loss: (a) He joins a group of actors, i.e. he is removing himself from life itself, he can only participate as if in a play. (b) The emphasis on the sentence "ready to board a boat with incredible mirth and merriment" may contain a reversal and a denial. In the last several months the poet had been "boarding the boat" to the depths of the self throughout his ceaseless search into his inner world and *knows* the search is painful. In the dream, the pain and loss are denied yet allow its conclusion. Pain and loss linger on and are replayed in the poem where the acceptance of the human dilemma ultimately becomes the truth of the poem.

In what follows, the poet looks closer at himself, at lost youth and old age, at the closeness of life and death.

> As the years go by
> the judges who condemn you grow in number;
> as the years go by and you converse with fewer voices,
> you see the sun with different eyes:
> you know that those who stayed behind
> were deceiving you
> the delirium of flesh, the lovely dance
> that ends in nakedness.
> You gaze at the sun, then you're lost in darkness.
> The doric chiton
> that swayed like the mountains when your fingers
>   touched it
> is a marble figure in the light,
> but its head is in darkness.

The poet goes on to grieve for the brave and the unheroic, for all those lost in the many battles of life.

> You see them in the sun behind the sun.

They are alive in oneself and their death is still so real:

> naked bodies plunging into black light
> with a coin between the teeth, swimming still,
> while the sun with golden needles sews
> sails and wet wood and colors of the sea;
> still now they're going down obliquely,
> the white lekythoi,
> towards the pebbles on the sea floor.

From this point on, the pace of the poem quickens as it is approaching the high drama of love and death. The poet again dips into the "collective consciousness" of his people, his "vast innerland of a poet" to find the archetypes for the eternal affections and afflictions besetting humans. As we read the poem, the image of Oedipus passes by, caught in his dilemma between "knowing, seeing and understanding and their interplay with ignorance, blindness and misunderstanding" (Simon, p. 92).

> Light, angelic and black,
> laughter of waves on the sea's highways,
> tear-stained laughter,
> the old suppliant sees you
> as he moves to cross the invisible fields—
> light mirrored in his blood,
> the blood that gave birth to Eteocles and Polynices.
> Day, angelic and black;

It is not the battles of impersonal war that cause darkness but "light mirrored in your blood," the beat of our hearts, the desires and the meanings of desires which push us continuously to the verge of the abyss. The poet continues, trying to find his way through the rush of images in his racing mind stirred up by the "old suppliant."

> the brackish taste of woman that poisons the prisoner
> emerges from the wave a cool branch adorned with
>   drops.
> Sing little Antigone, sing, O sing. . . .
> I'm not speaking to you about things past, I'm speak-
>   ing about love;
> decorate your hair with the sun's thorns,
> dark girl;

> the heart of the Scorpion has set,
> the tyrant in man has fled,
> and all the daughters of the sea, Nereids, Graeae,
> hurry to the radiance of the rising goddess:
> whoever has never loved will love,
> in the light.

In these two passages, several levels of meanings and multiple identifications are played out. The reference to Oedipus is from Antigone's address to the Chorus

(*Oedipus in Colonus*) telling them how her father was taken away (swallowed) by the "invisible fields" as "he was heading to a hidden death." The poet identifies with Antigone and mourns his own youth spent in the dark without the flame of sensual love. Like Antigone he feels he wasted several of his best years in despair and silence, a taciturn follower of a tyrant's will. But in this "lush," lustful island, he discovers that his body is not yet dead, but feels suspended. On October 25, he writes a short light poem which he calls **"Mrs. Zen"** (p. 71). He copies it in his diary but never publishes it, aware of its meagerness. It is essentially his obsession with physical love. On October 28, he is more explicit.

> I am writing in my room full of the ghosts I left there
> as I was fluttering like a bat entangled in desire and
> thoughts on the problem Zen. It is strange to find
> myself like a bag full of intense feelings, a bag sud-
> denly open and the whirling winds rushing out making
> me feel mad. All that was securely blocked in, is now
> released with the thrust of a violent spring in a Northern
> land. When will these feelings make contact with the
> other self, the self who can express it all. . . . It is this
> island (Poros), this island of Circe. I must decide soon,
> it is time to leave, it is time for the rocks of Ithaca.
>
> (p. 74)

The last verses of the long poem bear this sense of return to the rocks of Ithaca. They affirm the sense of release and relief, and the ineffable calm of the poet who finally seems able to accept and express the presence of death as the inextricable part of life and understand silence as contained in the words themselves, and darkness as the eternal question of our restless spirit.

> and you find yourself
> in a large house with many windows open
> running from room to room, not knowing from where
>   to look out first,
> because the pine trees will vanish, and the mirrored
>   mountains,
> and the chirping of birds
> the sea will drain dry, shattered glass, from north and
>   south
> your eyes will empty of the light of day—
> how suddenly and all together the cicadas stop.

The interplay of verses with the thoughts and dream imagery from the poet's diary leave little doubt that the resolution of the crisis is woven into the magic of the poem. Although it has many features of a middle life crisis, its loud echoes were already heard during the poet's youth. Seferis' whole life was lived as a slowly tightening drama reaching towards an end that always seemed elusive. At the age of forty-six, through his "cosmic emotional relationship" with the symbolic and physical objects of his world, he is able to take the final step in renouncing part of the self so that he may restore his sense of wholeness and endurance.

In the entry of October 31, Seferis writes in his diary:

These last few days I feel so strongly that I am wasting myself with the kind of life I live in Athens. Yesterday and today I have the intense desire to resign my post at the Ministry; not so much because I want to be a writer but because I want to grow and become a whole person before I die. Evening: I cut wood all afternoon. Came home drenched in sweat, hands full of resin. Took a bath and sat at my desk. I finished the poem. Title: **"Thrush."** I don't know how good it is; all I know is that it is finished.

(1973, p. 75)

On November 2:

It is hard to break away from a finished poem; hard to break off all the little threads. All day long today I was *touching* it; shining it, correcting it, adding a comma. I still feel bruised from this poem. It assimilated a great deal of my life of the last few years.

(pp. 77-78)

On December 2, the day of his departure from Poros:

I am leaving Poros heading for the unknown. The great peacefulness I have experienced here these last mornings I don't know whether I will find it again.

I am leaving with certain ideas about the *light*. It is my most significant "discovery" since I entered the Greek waters on my return home. [October 1944] this idea is expressed in **"The King of Assini"** and it is expressed in the **"Thrush."** I don't know whether I will be able to express it the way I feel about it, so very basic, the very foundation of life. I know I have to live with the (idea of) the light. From there on I am not sure . . . But there is one thing that I have fully understood here: no problem will be solved with slow hesitant movements; you either march ahead or you break down.

(p. 88)

The poet's work in the following years as a diplomat reaching the top, and as a poet publishing some of his best poems, indicate his continuing growth. Above all, Seferis' courageous stand against the political repression in Greece following the military coup of 1967 bears testimony to the enduring transformation in his character and to his ability to go on living "with the light."

Notes

1. For the poems, we are using Keeley's excellent translation to English; for all other texts we translate directly from Greek.

2. In 1936, Seferis published a translation in Greek of T. S. Eliot's *The Waste Land and Other Poems.* A long essay on T. S. Eliot's poetry is offered as an introduction to the poems.

3. "In the Evening," by C. Cavafy. Trans. E. Keeley and P. Sherrard, in *C. P. Cavafy. Collected Poems,* ed. G. Savidis, Princeton Univ. Press, 1975, pp. 137.

References

Erikson, E. H. (1954) "The Dream Specimen of Psychoanalysis," *J[ournal of the] Am[erican] Psychoan[alytic] Assoc[iation], 2*: 5-56.

Freud, S. (1930) *Civilization and Its Discontents. St. Ed., 21*: 57-146.

Greenacre Phyllis (1958) "The Family Romance of the Artist," *The Psychoanalytic Study of the Child 13*: 521-540.

Harrisson, I. B. (1979) "On Freud's View of the Infant-Mother Relationship and of the Oceanic Feeling—Some Subjective Influences," *J. Am. Psychoan. Assoc., 27*: 399-423.

Keeley, E. (1966) "Seferis' *Elpenor*: A man of no fortune," *Kenyon Rev[iew] 28*: 378-390.

Keeley, E., Sheppard Ph, (1967) *George Seferis. Collected Poems* (1924-1955) Princeton, Princeton Univ. Press.

"The Methodology of Psychoanalytic Biography" (1972) Gedo, J. E., reporter, *J. Am. Psychoan. Assoc. 20*: 638-650.

Odyssey (1976) Kazantzakis, N. and Kakridi, I., translators, Athens, Rodi.

Plato, *Socrates' Apology* (1970) Kouravelos, K. translator, Athens, Zacharopoulos.

Seferis, G. (1973) *Days 1945-1951,* Athens, Icaros.

Seferis, G. (1974) "A Set for "Thrush" in *Essays* Volume B, Athens, Icaros.

Seferis, G. (1977) *Days 1941-1944,* Athens, Icaros.

Simon, B. (1978) *Mind and Madness in Ancient Greece.* Cornell University Press, Ithaca.

Tsatsou, T. (1973) *My Brother George Seferis,* Athens, Estia Press.

Werman, D. (1979) "Methodological Problems in the Psychoanalytic Interpretation of Literature. A Review of Studies on Sophocles' *Antigone,*" *J. Am. Psychoan. Assoc. 27*: 451-478.

Rachel Hadas (essay date 1985)

SOURCE: Hadas, Rachel. "Trees, Gardens, Sea." In *Form, Cycle, Infinity: Landscape Imagery in the Poetry of Robert Frost and George Seferis,* pp. 90-151. Lewisburg, Penn.: Bucknell University Press, 1985.

[*In the following excerpt, Hadas examines Seferis's use of sea imagery in his poetry.*]

2. Seferis: The Sea

As Frost's titles often show fascination with nature and the seasons, so those of Seferis bespeak the Greek poet's preoccupation with the sea and voyaging. For Seferis, much in life and literature can be expressed through the figure of a sea journey. The epigraph to *Logbook I,* for example—"we remain in this position awaiting orders"—indicates both political and aesthetic uncertainty. But rich and flexible though the sea as symbol is, as poetic subject it is not without difficulties. Its very multitudinousness can lead to monotony, a kind of becalmed imagination embarrassed by too many riches.

For Seferis, as for most of his countrymen, the sea is of an importance that can scarcely be exaggerated. It represents at once the familiar and the beautiful; nostalgia for the lost, magical world of childhood; adventure and romance; history and tradition; and a linkage with the body of Greek myths. Its protean quality would seem to make the sea a poetic symbol par excellence, evocative yet amorphous, needing a distinctive imagination to shape it into significance. Without such an imaginative treatment, the danger is that the sea will signify everything in general and nothing in particular.

The boundless, hard-to-pin-down character of a sea which is nevertheless intensely loved is well shown in an essay by G.-A. Mangakis on Greek landscape. Mangakis calls the sea

> . . . an uninterrupted, ever-changing element with its radiant beauty and incessant motion, the endless open sea ever travelling with the wind . . . limitless, determined by a power unseen but strongly felt, which derives from boundlessness. . . . Thus, the first image of Greece is illuminated in a child's soul, as something so real it overflows all sensation and floods the heart to the brim, but at the same time as something intangible, sibylline, something passionately yearned for throughout life . . . yet never grasped in its definite shape, its true form.—This is the first experience: *the sea*.[1]

I quote this passage because it illustrates so well the splendors and miseries of the sea as a poetic subject. Like the experience it tries to describe, the language is charged with feeling yet oddly lacking in individuality, whether because the feeling for the sea the essayist is describing is so universal among his Greek readers that no definition is needed, or because the nature of the sea is to elude sharp evocation. A similar rhapsodic quality sometimes marks the passages in Seferis's journal which concern the sea, though the poet is less rhetorical than Mangakis:

> Inexplicable sorcery of the sea. How it changes me all at once: astonishment, deep amazement down to my bones. I can't understand. To go closer, to cross this line of separation for another world. . . . How is it possible to be the same man who was swimming in the water and who now is reading the newspaper? Here is something which is absolutely inconceivable to me.[2]

Amidst the yearning, however, a central idea is discernible: emphasis on the metamorphic power of the sea, its particular properties of cleansing and renewal, is more important in the passage than a raptly intangible boundlessness.

Moreover, the passage is in prose. Seferis rarely lost his sense of the difference between journalistic (if sincere) rhapsodizing about the sorcery of the sea and the sea-change which had to be wrought by the sorcery of poetry. He seems to have been wary of writing directly, *in his poetry,* about the wonders of the sea; and as a result his poems about the sea avoid monotony and shapelessness to a remarkable extent. Seferis accomplishes this feat by different means. First, many of the poems, especially earlier ones, treat times and places whence the sea is inaccessible or barely visible, an expanse glimpsed out of the corner of the eye. Another version of the sea perceives it as present but unsatisfactory: polluted or puzzling, becalmed, endless. A third approach penetrates the sea's surface and heads for the depths. Finally (and this method also touches almost every other use of the sea in his work) Seferis avails himself of classical references to the sea, above all the *Odyssey* and Aeschylus's *Agamemnon.* The use of myth bestows richness of perspective on an element whose nature is to appear flat and timeless. To write about statues, stones, inscriptions . . . is to ponder some of the most obvious remnants of the Greek past. To write about the sea means that the poet risks floating out of time (note Mangakis's use of words like "limitless" and "boundless" to evoke the unfettered quality, both temporally and spatially, of voyaging). By referring to the companions of Odysseus or to the Argonauts, Seferis makes the Aegean into a continuum.

I *The mermaid at the prow*

In Seferis's first volume of poems, *Turning Point,* the sea is at its most fugitive. One indication that the young poet is still finding his voice and subject is the paucity, in this volume, of the sense of place, whether the place is Greece or anywhere else. The poems exist in a brittle, tenuous, and sparsely imagined world. When the sea does appear in *Turning Point* it has a Laforguesque air of urbanity; it is not the Aegean but a French Symbolist sea.

> And life's cold as a fish
> —Is that how you live?—Yes, how else?
> So many are the drowned
> down on the sea's bed.
>
> Trees are like corals

their color gone,
carts are like ships
sunken and lonely . . .[3]

                          ("Fog")

As Nasos Vayenas points out, the chief function of this submarine vignette is to cast a despairing light onto the life up above. **"Fog"** moves away from the depths; its last stanza shows us firelight, red fingernails, someone coughing (a juxtaposition that recalls several such in *The Waste Land,* which Seferis had not yet read). The following poem in ***Turning Point,* "The Mood of a Day,"** in contrast to **"Fog"** moves *toward* the sea. As the epigraph from *Arthur Gordon Pym* suggests, both the cityscape and the ship in **"The Mood of a Day"** have a nightmarish air; the ship is full of dead people. Yet the movement from the third to the final stanza—from city to sea—is one of overwhelming relief, as of motion after long stalling, open air after claustrophobia.

Part of the relief is perhaps the reader's at hearing a true Seferic tone:

> He worries: if they knock at the door who will open it? If he opens a book whom will he look at? If he opens his soul who will look? Chain.
> Where is love that with one stroke cuts time in two and stuns it?
> Words only and gestures. A monotonous monologue in front of a mirror under a wrinkle.
> Like a drop of ink on a handkerchief, the boredom spreads.
>
> Everyone in the ship is dead, but the ship keeps going the way it was heading when it put out from the harbor
> how the captain's nails grew . . . and the boatswain, who had three mistresses in every port, unshaven . . .
> The ship swells slowly, the rigging fills with pride, and the day is turning mild.
> Three dolphins flash black, glistening; the mermaid smiles, and a forgotten sailor waves astride the yardarm.

The ship which moves purposefully out of the harbor whether its crew are dead or not is an image, compounded of hope and despair, of a tradition both moribund and hardy. The same paradox makes nails grow on a corpse. The question at this point in Seferis's work is where the ship is going—but it does seem to be going somewhere. The smiling mermaid and waving sailor seem to be responding to something, sending out some signal of recognition, unlike the narcissistic mirror-monologue in the preceding stanza.

It is characteristic of the stylistic veerings in ***Turning Point*** that **"The Mood of a Day"** is followed by **"Rocket,"** a poem which begins "It isn't the sea" and ends

> I can't live
> only with peacocks,
> nor travel always
> in the mermaid's eyes.

"Rocket" expresses impatience with the exotic trappings of symbolism, in the light of which (an elusive light which is neither the sea nor the world) the mermaid is doubly unsatisfactory. Like a peacock she is exotic, ornate; like the "monotonous monologue in front of a mirror" in **"The Mood of a Day"** she represents a self-communing gaze which narcissistically reflects itself alone. After ***Turning Point,*** Seferis did indeed avoid traveling "in the mermaid's eyes." The hall of mirrors, peacock, and pentacle of the first volume do not reappear, and the mermaid becomes rather a representative of the sea than a mode of consciousness.

The poems Seferis wrote in London after the publication of ***Turning Point*** are stylistically simpler and more uniform than before. Both these qualities are related to the persona of Stratis Thalassinos (Stratis the Mariner). Through the eyes of the nostalgic sailor, a poem like **"Hampstead"** expresses homesickness for the Mediterranean. But the work is cautious. Just as Seferis wears the mask of the seafarer, **"Hampstead"** approaches the sea gingerly, transforming the wished-for expanse of blue into a theatrical scrim. In fact Stratis just wants a *symbol* of the sea.[4]

> Now I long for a little quiet
> all I want is a hut on a hill
> or near a seashore
> all I want in front of my window
> is a sheet immersed in bluing
> spread there like the sea. . . .

With the sequence **"Mr. Stratis Thalassinos Describes a Man,"** Seferis moves a little closer to the water. The accessibility or forbidding quality of the sea is presented in terms of the psychological development of "a man," and vice versa: with the advent of puberty, the young man moves instinctively toward the sea. The following passage combines archetypal imagery with a kind of sea-yarn. It also reinforces the sense we have already gotten from the sparse references to the sea so far in Seferis that the sea is difficult of access, both attractive and forbidding but hard to reach.

> In the summer of my sixteenth year a strange voice sang in my ears;
> it was, I remember, at the sea's edge, among the red nets and a boat abandoned on the sand, a skeleton
> I tried to get closer to that voice by laying my ear to the sand
> the voice disappeared
> but there was a shooting star
> as though I were seeing a shooting star for the first time
> and on my lips the salt taste of waves.
> From that night the roots of the trees no longer came to me.

The next day a journey opened in my mind and closed
  again, like a picture book;
I thought of going down to the shore every evening
first to learn about the shore and then to go to sea;
the third day I fell in love with a girl on a hill. . . .

("**Adolescent**")

(Compare this passage to the later "**Stratis Thalassinos among the Agapanthi**," which links sea-voyaging and sexuality:

The first thing God made is love
then comes blood
and the thirst for blood
roused by
the body's sperm as by salt.
The first thing God made is the long journey. . . .)

In "**Mr. Stratis Thalassinos Describes a Man**," the linking of sex and the sea begins by being negative. After the failure of love on a hill, "I left and went back to sea," but the sea grows mellower. With the opening of "**Young Man**," Seferis's work advances simultaneously along several different fronts. The simple, colloquial language spans a synchronicity that can accommodate Aghia Sophia, a mermaid, "Captain" Odysseus, and an easy narrative mode:

I sailed for a year with Captain Odysseus
I was fine
in fair weather I made myself comfortable in the prow
  beside the mermaid
I sang of her red lips as I gazed at the flying-fish,
in storms I took refuge in a corner of the hold with
  the ship's dog who kept me warm.
One morning at the end of the year I saw minarets
the mate told me:
"That's Saint Sophia, tonight I'll take you to the
  women."

Like the logo he chose for his books, a two-tailed mermaid, the mermaid figurehead on the prow in "**Young Man**" links the various stages of Seferis's vision. Half-human, half-monstrous, and a fairytale creation associated with art and magic, she is surely the same apparition who smiled from the deck at the end of the "**Mood of a Day**." Barely glimpsed as long as the poems barely dare approach the sea, she is cuddly and companionable in "**Young Man**" for the hero, who is no longer an onlooker but a voyager himself. Disappearing in "**The Mood of a Day**," rejected in "**Rocket**," welcoming in "**Young Man**," the mermaid mirrors the poet's feeling for the sea. (To turn back for a minute to Mangakis's essay: "Thus Greece becomes danger . . . it appears, this danger, with the blue body of the sea, clothed in golden scales, and like the lovely mermaids of the fairy tale, summons you to a fatal, alluring adventure. . . ."[5])

The Stratis Thalassinos poems fall midway between *Turning Point* and the mature, characteristic voice Seferis found in *Mythical History*. Also in this transitional

group are "**Syngrou Avenue 1930**" and "**Foreign Verse**," two poems which have in common the appearance of a mermaid at their close. "**Syngrou Avenue**" uses marine metaphors to describe the Acropolis and its surroundings; though less artificial than that in "**Fog**," the effect is labored when the Acropolis is called "the petrified ship traveling with broken rigging toward the depths." (The Acropolis "travels" for the same reason that in "**In the Manner of G. S.**" Greece itself travels, so basic is the trope of a voyage in Seferis.) But the marine mode is more appropriate, naturally, when Phaleron and the sea are glimpsed at the end:

Break Ariadne's thread and look!
The blue body of the mermaid.

Again, the mermaid/sea is precariously located at the tail end (so to speak) of the poem, just appearing or vanishing. She may seem like a habitual means to poetic closure by now; but a variation on the image distinguishes a much greater poem than "**Syngrou**," "**Reflections on a Foreign Line of Verse**."

Dated Christmas 1931, "**Foreign Verse**" was written at around the same time as the Stratis Thalassinos series I have discussed. Rather than using a persona, the poem focuses on a single intensely imagined presence who is to pervade the rest of Seferis's work in a more muted way—the figure of Odysseus. Since the native habitat of Odysseus is marine, the sea functions structurally in "**Foreign Verse**" as a thing experienced rather than a hastily glimpsed streak of blue. The reference to Odysseus is not straightforward; Seferis takes his first line from the sonnet "Heureux qui comme Ulysse" by Joachim du Bellay, who was himself looking back longingly at the Odysseus archetype.[6] But far from being hobbled by complexities of literary reference, the poem is unencumberedly eloquent in a way new for Seferis.

"**Foreign Verse**" is partly about language and tradition.[7] But, like the language and tradition which were Seferis's heritage, it never gets far from, and incessantly returns to, the sea, since even emotion is expressed in terms of a voyage: "Fortunate if on setting out he's felt the rigging of a love strong in his body, spreading there like veins where the blood throbs." And Odysseus has been battered and shaped by the sea. We have progressed a long way from hanging up a sheet "immersed in bluing" before the window.

And again and again the shade of Odysseus appears
  before me, his eyes red from the waves' salt,
from his ripe longing to see once more the smoke
  ascending from his warm hearth and the dog grown
  old waiting by the door.

A large man, whispering through his whitened beard
  words in our language spoken as it was three
  thousand years ago.

> He extends a palm calloused by the ropes and the
> tiller, his skin weathered by the dry north wind, by
> heat and snow.

Odysseus is clearly the most important representative of the sea in this poem; it is as if he carries it with him wherever he goes. Yet the other emblem of the sea—the mermaid—appears in **"Foreign Verse"** as well, in the same place we found her in **"Mood of a Day"** or **"Syngrou"**—at the end, vanishing from sight.

> He speaks . . . I still see his hands that knew how to
> judge the carving of the mermaid at the prow
> presenting me the waveless blue sea in the heart of
> winter.

Like almost every other object in the poem, the mermaid becomes a measure of Odysseus's wisdom and experience. As a carved figure whose craftsmanship is judged by his skilled hands, she signifies art which is subject to scrutiny by those who are learned in its tradition. The mermaid is plastic art, of course, like the "carved reliefs of a humble art" we meet with in the first part of **Mythical History.** But since so much of **"Foreign Verse"** is about language, the verbal heritage passed on by Odysseus-like figures ("certain old sailors of my childhood who . . . used to recite, with tears in their eyes, the song of Erotocritos"), the mermaid can also be seen as the art that can be made of the sea: its timeless lyric aspect, whereas Odysseus is the grizzled epic narrator. Some kind of tradition in the etymological sense of *handing down* is going on at the end of the poem. Odysseus's wise hands (which we have already been told are callused) are shown "presenting me" [the speaker] with that sea of which the mermaid is an emblem. Such a transaction shows how much bigger Odysseus is than the mermaid who in other poems (though not here) has been equated with that waveless blue sea. Odysseus can judge the mermaid; she cannot judge him. She embodies the sea, but he travels on it. He, in fact, is human; she is not, though both here have a kind of immortality.

Seferis's early visions of the sea are tantalizingly fraught with significance but hard to grasp, like a dream which ends before its point is reached. In **"Foreign Verse"** for the first time the alluring but inscrutable mermaid is juxtaposed with the symbol par excellence in Western literature of hard daily experience of salt water.

II The sea that embittered us

Mythical History, a 24-part sequence written in 1933-34, presents a vision of the sea almost directly opposed to that epitomized by the attractive but fugitive mermaid. In **Mythical History** the sea is often present; the problem becomes how to escape it, or at least how to impose various kinds of limitation on its expanse. Without such markers the voyage might be endless. I want to consider especially sections 4, 8, 10, and 12.

In section 4 *(Argonauts)*:

> We went past many capes many islands the sea
> leading to another sea, gulls and seals.
> Sometimes unfortunate women wept
> lamenting their lost children
> and others raging sought Alexander the Great
> and glories buried in the heart of Asia.
> We moored on shores full of night-scents
> with birds singing, waters that left on the hands
> the memory of great happiness.
> But the voyages did not end.
> Their souls became one with the oars and the oarlocks
> with the solemn face of the prow
> with the rudder's wake
> with the water that shattered their image.
> The companions died one by one,
> with lowered eyes. Their oars
> mark the place where they sleep on the shore.
>
> No one remembers them. Justice.

The note is monotony and weariness that end in oblivion. Loveliness is located now on land, where scents and sounds recall happiness. Water seems to be inimical to memory: "the water . . . shattered their image. . . . No one remembers them." The same sea that shaped Odysseus in **"Foreign Verse"** has weathered these Argonauts into indistinguishability. In section 8 they or people very like them do the talking (Seferis constantly switches persons in **Mythical History**), questioning the purpose of their continuing voyage in lines that effortlessly encompass broader meanings about quests and goals. One of the most representative sections of the sequence, the section is worth quoting in full.

> What are they after, our souls, traveling
> on the decks of decayed ships
> crowded in with sallow women and crying babies
> unable to forget themselves either with the flying fish
> or with the stars that the masts point out at their tips?
> Grated by gramophone records
> committed to non-existent pilgrimages unwillingly,
> murmuring broken thoughts from foreign languages.
>
> What are they after, our souls, traveling
> on rotten brine-soaked timbers
> from harbor to harbor?
>
> Shifting broken stones, breathing in
> the pine's coolness with greater difficulty each day
> swimming in the waters of this sea
> and of that sea,
> without the sense of touch
> without men
> in a country that is no longer ours
> nor yours.
>
> We knew that the islands were beautiful
> somewhere round about here where we are groping—
> a little lower or a little higher,
> the slightest distance.

As if in search of something tangible, the poem moves from the decayed ship to the more palpable brine-soaked timbers and finally into the water. Surely the sea is neither nonexistent nor foreign. Yet the sensation of being in the water is also disappointing; the senses seem to fail, the power to distinguish gets lost, and finally the islands (which are revealed at the end to be one goal of the journey) cannot be located. The boundlessness and freedom from limitation which look so attractive from shore when the mermaid smiles prove to be a frightening expanse of anonymity.

Section 10 takes place back on land—a dry, shut-in land.

> Our country is closed in, all mountains
> that day and night have the low sky as their roof
> We have no rivers, we have no wells, we have no
>   springs,
> only a few cisterns—and these empty—that echo, and
>   that
> we worship.

Such a country might well make one long for the sea again. The world of **Mythical History** takes shape as one where voyages are wearisome shuttlings between the harsh alternatives ("two black Symplegades," they are called here) of boundless sea or arid land where dryness and sterility have invaded the people as well as the soil. Between these alternatives a dialectic rhythm prevails. If the poems are located on land, as 10 is, there is a longing for the sea's openness ("we go down / to the harbors on Sunday to breathe"). Section 5 also shows the tug of the sea:

> Dawn finds us beside the tired lamp
> drawing on paper, awkwardly, with effort,
> ships mermaids or sea-shells;
> at dusk we go down to the river
> because it shows us the way to the sea;
> and we spend the nights in cellars that smell of tar.

Yet that magically alluring sea, once you have set out on it, spells exhaustion, confusion, endless voyaging. Approaching either pole—either of the clashing rocks—Seferis's imagination recoils. The effect is gloomily paradoxical, as in section 16 where the sea can be neither escaped nor reached by the runner Orestes; but this gloomy paradox is the device that keeps **Mythical History** afloat and moving.

Section 12's two stanzas are about land and sea respectively and are bracketed by a one-line epigraph, "Bottle in the Sea," and a final closing line.

> "Bottle in the Sea"
>
> Three rocks, a few burnt pines, a solitary chapel
> and farther above
> the same landscape repeated starts again:
> three rocks in the shape of a gate-way, rusted,

> a few burnt pines, black and yellow,
> and a square hut buried in whitewash;
> and still farther above, many times over,
> the same landscape recurs level after level
> to the horizon, to the twilight sky.
>
> Here we moored the ship to splice the broken oars,
> to drink water and to sleep.
> The sea that embittered us is deep and unexplored
> and unfolds a boundless calm.
> Here among the pebbles we found a coin
> and threw dice for it.
> The youngest won it and disappeared.
>
> We set out again with our broken oars.

Rusted, burnt, dried, buried—the land is depicted in repeated images of desiccation. The sea, while more mysterious, is not very positively seen either; it has "embittered" us. Yet since it is unexplored it still, unlike the land, has secrets and can draw the voyagers on. The poem is in fact a brief rest before they reembark. Like salty quotation marks, the epigraph and last line enclose the utterance within a marine world; indeed, the epigraph turns the poem into a message which the last line hints may be all that remains of a shipwreck. (It is fair to add that Mrs. Tsatsou says the last line became a Seferis family slogan for perseverance under difficult circumstances.)[8]

Occurring at the dead center of a 24-part sequence, section 12 epitomizes the dialectic between sea and land, inwardness and outwardness, venture and retreat (and one could multiply categories like wet and dry) which shapes the entire sequence, taking on the task of narrative. Frost was quoted earlier as having said, "Narrative is a fearfully safe place to spend your time. Having ideas that are neither pro nor con is the happy thing."[9] Frost goes on to envision a series of dialectical oppositions above which the thinker can remain suspended. Both opposition and suspension characterize the motion of **Mythical History.** The sea's alternations of attractiveness and repulsion propel a continued movement but also a kind of removal, a complex disenchantment.[10]

Discussing the pessimism of **Mythical History** in historical and mythological terms, a Greek critic writes about the prototypical voyages to which the poem constantly refers.

> Both [the voyage of the Argonauts and that of Odysseus] had tragedy for their climate. Thus mention of them constitutes a continual reminder of the role of the voyage as an element in our history and of the tragedy of that history. For the age when Seferis is writing, however, the voyage is no longer a campaign or a triumphant war; it is a shipwreck . . . it is endless vicissitudes, it is loss, or it is simply myth, an unfulfilled longing, for no one has the strength—or has the strength remaining—to undertake such a venture. None of those on board wished for this adventure; they

are victims of fate and playthings of history. They have neither set out, like Argonauts, on an expedition, nor are they, like the companions of Odysseus, on their way home from a war which they sought out.[11]

The "endless vicissitudes" Karapanayiotis mentions translate structurally into the ambivalent pattern of longing/disappointment which accompanies and shapes the image of the sea in *Mythical History*—a pattern which is perceptible whether or not we link the poem to any particular mythology or history.

Another way of describing the uneasy dialectic which pervades *Mythical History* is as a succession of approaches to and retreats from edges (shores). To call such edges historical or ethical (i.e., to interpret them as decisions or victories, references to particular moments) is possible; but what is basic to the poem is the pattern of advance and retreat. The unsatisfactory nature of the sea in *Mythical History* is illuminated, I think, by Bachelard's account in *The Poetics of Space* of an equivalent dialectic.

> Outside and inside form a dialectic of division, the obvious geometry of which blinds us as soon as we bring it into play in metaphorical domains. It has the sharpness of the dialectics of *yes* and *no,* which decides everything. Unless one is careful, it is made into a basis of images that govern all thoughts of positive and negative. . . . Being is alternately condensation that disperses with a burst, and dispersion that flows back toward a center. Outside and inside are both intimate— they are always ready to be reversed, to exchange their hostility. If there exists a border-line surface between such an inside and outside, this surface is painful on both sides . . .
>
> In this drama of intimate geometry, where should one live?[12]

Or in Seferis's terms, "What are they after, our souls, traveling . . . ?"

III FREE YOURSELF FROM UNFAITHFUL TIME AND SINK

Neither the fugitive mermaid nor the frustrating expanse image of the sea gets beneath the surface of the water. Occasionally, though, Seferis ventures below the beautiful blue surface. The imaginative effort to penetrate the depths constitutes a third perspective of the sea.

The Cistern (1932) deserves mention but it is a special case. Personally I find the poem nearly impossible to read or discuss because overluxuriant language chokes the meaning like an unpruned vine. Beneath the richness of the poem's linguistic surface, which Seferis labored over for years, consistency of thought is hard to find. So far as one can tell, the cistern contains fresh water. This, and the fact that it is underground, make the cistern's nature as different as possible from the exposed breadth of the sea. The hiddenness of the water

means that its symbol, its message, is a secret one—and this hiddenness sorts well with the style of the poem. Also the cistern seems not to change, since it is beyond the reach of the other elements:

> Here in the earth a cistern has taken root
> den of secret water that gathers there.
> Its roof, resounding steps. The stars
> don't blend with its heart. Each day
> grows, opens, shuts, doesn't touch it.
> . . . . .
>
> But here in the earth a cistern has taken root
> warm, secret den that hoards
> the groan of each body in the air
> the battle with night, with day
> the world grows, passes, does not touch it.
>
> Time goes by, suns and moons,
> but the water has hardened like a mirror. . . .

Finally the cistern is said to "teach silence / in the flaming city." The image of patient, timeless subterranean waters quenching the flames of the upper world leaves one with contradictory senses of doom and consolation.[13] Such contradictions as organic ("taken root") yet unchanging; secret yet teaching; warm quenching— perhaps these are what the poem has to teach us about the depths.

Certainly *The Cistern* associates water and verticality. In *Gymnopaidia* Seferis further explores this association, this time in the clear, spare, yet hermetic style of *Mythical History* (*Gymnopaidia* was written in 1935). Like *Mythical History, Gymnopaidia* moves not by narrative but by a dialectic of opposition, though on a much smaller scale, since *Gymnopaidia* consists of only two poems. Where the longer sequence, with its stoppings and startings, pauses and renewals, departures and arrivals, is generally horizontal in movement, the direction of *Gymnopaidia* is not over the sea but into it. Islands rise, bodies sink; a shell is flung into the sea so that it sinks; "whoever raises the great stones" sinks. Seferis has taken the image of sinking from the description of Santorini in the Guide to Greece quoted in the epigraph of *Gymnopaidia,* endowing a neutral geological fact with poetic richness.

The sinking that fills *Gymnopaidia* is presumably a sinking into the sea. But this sea is quite a different sea from that in *Mythical History.* Instead of oblivion and mystery it offers an escape from time: "Free yourself from unfaithful time and sink." An escape from time may be an escape into death, but not any usual kind of death, since what sinks in this poem seems destined to rise again. The sea is mystically envisioned in *Gymnopaidia* above all as *otherness*—an alternative to the world above the surface, an alternative which, however enigmatic when seen from our standpoint, can nevertheless (with a little courage) be entered and experienced.

It would be a falsification for any account of *Gymnopaidia* to clarify what is obscure in the poem, which may be Seferis's most hermetic. No easy revelation awaits us; in the first line of **"Santorini"** we are told to "Bend if you can to the dark sea," and after many perusals the poems remain dark. But the darkness belongs to the depths, not the surface.

These depths of *Gymnopaidia,* with their paradoxical life/death/escape from time, recall Emily Vermeule's evocation of the ambivalent attitude of early Greeks to the sea.

> Because the Greeks were interested in unseen possibilities, the horizon between what they knew and what they imagined was easily represented for them by the water surface, which provoked a kind of double vision. Painters and poets were both attracted by the two realms which were mutually invisible . . . The sea makes a double viewpoint easy, as in the famous simile of the dead suitors in the Odyssey (xxii.384 ff.) . . . the shape of the sea gives the fisherman's viewpoint; the feelings of being at home in the dark and vulnerable to the sun belong to the fish, as though man's world and the sea's world were in mirror image, sometimes inimical, sometimes sympathetically linked, like men and gods.[14]

But such a mirror can only be envisioned if one is curious about what goes on beneath the surface. Some of the opacity of *Gymnopaidia* results from the opacity of the medium. Seferis refuses to make clear what is obscure by nature, and the poetic result is a prophetic blend of authority and vagueness.

> Voices out of stone out of sleep
> deeper here where the world darkens,
> memory of toil rooted in the rhythm
> beaten upon the earth by feet
> forgotten.
> Bodies sunk into the foundations
> of the other time, naked. Eyes
> fixed, fixed on a point
> that you can't make out, as much as you want to:
> the soul
> struggling to become your own soul. . . .[15]

In **"Thrush"** (1947) the plumbing of depths is a more luminous process. The very name of the poem points to at least some clarity as to what lies beneath the surface of the sea; "Thrush" was a small craft that had been sunk off Poros, the island where Seferis was staying at the time he wrote the poem. The poem is in three sections of which the third is the longest, in some ways the most obscure, and the most powerful; it is also the section closest to the sea. The first part of this section is entitled *"The wreck 'Thrush'";* the poet is trying to discern what is barely visible under the water.

> I heard the voice
> as I was gazing at the sea trying to make out
> a ship they'd sunk there years ago;

> it was called "Thrush," a small wreck; the masts,
> broken, swayed at odd angles deep underwater, like
>   tentacles,
> or the memory of dreams, marking the hull:
> vague mouth of some huge dead sea-monster
> extinguished in the water. Calm spread all around.

This wreckage, this vague monster, is given a voice in the passage that follows, if we take the necessary step of equating the submarine darkness with the darkness of Erebus, the ghost-filled underworld whence the voices come.

> And gradually, in turn, other voices followed,
> whispers thin and thirsty
> emerging from the other side of the sun, the dark side;
> you might say they longed for a drop of blood to
>   drink;
> familiar voices, but I couldn't distinguish one from
>   the
> other.

Without the lines devoted to the wrecked ship, these "other voices" would seem to be coming from a Homeric world of blood-sipping ghosts such as also appears in *Mythical History* 24 and **"Stratis Thalassinos among the Agapanthi."** But the sight of the fairly recent wreckage mediates the classical vision by filtering it through the depths of a sea that is at once contemporary and timeless. The wreck is familiar; the poet knows its provenance and name. Yet like the "bodies sunk into the foundations / of the other time, naked" in **"Mycenae,"** the fact that the wreck is sunken signifies the *otherness,* "sometimes inimical, sometimes sympathetically linked, like men and gods," mentioned by Vermeule.

In **"The King of Asine"** Seferis gives the act of searching for "ancient remains" a significance that transcends archaeology. Similarly, the act of peering at sunken wreckage here is a richly emblematic one. Peering beneath the surface of water to make out indistinct shapes is a symbol of understanding the past, the unconscious, and their artistic blend in poetry. It is probably with the above passage from **"Thrush"** in mind that Mrs. Tsatsou writes about her brother:

> . . . I have his soul before me, outwardly liquid and translucent, and in its depths, a black monster is swimming! The suffering of the race. Sometimes we see its shadow, sometimes its wings, sometimes, beneath the trembling of the water, whirlpools, hollows, humps, sometimes other signs.

> How he struggled to kill his emotional nature. He ironized events, above all himself. But did he indeed kill it? He covered it with stones and seaweed.[16]

The other underwater passage in **"Thrush"** is concerned with movement toward the depths rather than scrutiny of them from a distance. The repetition of "still" emphasizes the continued presentness of the downward thrust.

And the boys who dived from the bow-sprits
go like spindles twisting still,
naked bodies plunging into black light
with a coin between the teeth, swimming still,
while the sun with golden needles sews
sails and wet wood and colors of the sea;
still they're going down obliquely,
the white lekythoi,
toward the pebbles on the sea floor.

This passages transforms boys into vases—a metamorphosis of life into art which we can actually witness rather than guessing at it (as in the sinkings in *Gymnopaidia*). Such a metamorphosis is surely the key to escaping from "unfaithful time." Metamorphosis, sea-change, is the characteristic gift of Proteus, the Old Man of the Sea who is the master of transformations in *Odyssey* 4 and who recurs in Seferis's work. For example, in **"On Stage,"** the second of Seferis's *Three Secret Poems* (1966), the image of diving and of pebbles on the sea floor we have seen in **"Thrush"** recurs with the addition of Proteus.

Yet the sea was sweet
where I plunged in and swam as a child,
and later, as a young man,
while searching for shapes in the pebbles,
trying to discover rhythms,
the Old Sea-god said to me:
"I am the place you belong to;
I may be nobody,
but I can become whatever you want."

The "boys who dived from the bow-sprits" embody the poet who seeks knowledge of the depths, looks for patterns in pebbles; they also represent that transformation of life into art which is finally the only way of escaping from time. The sea-change of life into art, the present into the aorist, cannot be accomplished if the voyager is content to remain on the surface. One answer to the question posed in *Mythical History* 8 ("What are they after, our souls?") and a solution to that aporia may be: *the depths.*

IV AND WHO SHALL DRAIN IT DRY?

Edmund Keeley has written that Seferis uses "myth and symbol to shape the formless present."[17] For *present* we may substitute *sea* without the observation's losing its truth. The sea may be glimpsed, traveled over, plunged into—but who or what *is* it? In order to give the sea a shape Seferis often personifies it; we have already seen the mermaid and the figure of Odysseus as the latter appears in **"Foreign Verse."** Insofar as Odysseus is the prototype of a voyager, he is also present in the Stratis Thalassinos poems, in *Mythical History,* and in **"Thrush"**—that is, all Seferis's major work. Whether we call the effect synchronic or anachronistic, figures with classical names and attributes fit into Seferis's world with remarkable ease. We do not protest when

we find the Argonauts and Alexander the Great or the Symplegades and Sunday or Adonis and a cannon cohabiting the same poem. Elpenor's cigarette in Part II of **"Thrush"** hardly gives us pause. The poetic sleight of hand that makes these juxtapositions so acceptable is not in question, but it is explained by two critics in ways that are diametrically opposed.

"Seferis's secret," writes Keeley,

> is that he always offers an appropriate setting—a poetically realistic setting—before he allows any ghosts to appear on his stage; before he attempts to carry the reader to the level of myth, the level of timeless universalities, he wins his sympathy and belief by convincingly representing the present reality sustaining his myth—a contemporary, Greek reality always.[18]

According to Walter Kaiser, on the other hand, Seferis moves from mythic generality to contemporary particularity—at least for the non-Greek reader:

> Whereas normally in poetry of such classicism we perceive the particular and move on from there to the universal, in this case the process is curiously reversed. Most probably, it is the general applicability of Seferis' message which reaches us first, as these poems become almost instantaneously *our* poems and we relate them to our own experience of the world. To see how they are also *his* poems, to comprehend, that is, how they grow out of the personal and specific experiences of an individual Greek—this is what poses a greater difficulty for a foreigner. What is universal in his poetry we can test on our very pulse; what is personal and local we can, at best, only experience vicariously.[19]

It should be borne in mind that Keeley is writing about Seferis's middle period and Kaiser chiefly about *Three Secret Poems*; also that some of the difficulties of grasping the "personal and local" are owing to the language gap to which Kaiser frequently (and rightly) refers in his introduction to his translations of Seferis. In saying that Seferis's poems "grow out of the personal and specific experiences of an individual Greek," Kaiser is essentially repeating Keeley's point about "present reality."

Nevertheless, there is an interesting opposition in these two fine critics' perceptions of how the poetry works. For one, Seferis uses "present reality" to win sympathy and belief for the "timeless universality" which, it is implied, is the poet's real interest. For the other, it is the "general applicability" of Seferis's "universal" message which—regardless of the poet's intention—first becomes available to the reader and which then earns that reader's sympathy for the "personal and local."

I propose another way of looking at the problem. Instead of regarding personal and local detail as a sort of sugar coating for the pill of universality and myth, or vice versa, we might imagine Seferis as perceiving no distinction between these categories. The same quality of mind that gave the poet a synchronic view of Greek tradition, in the prose passage quoted below, made it possible for him to write the poetry quoted after that. In both, various eras huddle side by side in a happy disregard for chronology and history.

Writing about Cavafy's "basic characteristic, his unity," Seferis moves on to the larger and related unity of Greek culture (and not merely literary culture) as a whole:

> . . . we might attempt to place him and to feel him within the framework of the Greek tradition, the whole tradition, indivisible as it is. For this tradition is not, as some see it, an affair of isolated promontories, some great names, some illuminating texts; instead it is like what others of us see and feel in the little mosaics of a humble Byzantine church—the Ionian philosophers, the popular verses of the period of the Comneni, the epigrams of the Anthology, Greek folk song, Aeschylus, Palamas, Solomos, Sikelianos, Calvos, Cavafy, the Parthenon, Homer, *all living in a moment of time,* in this Europe of today and looking at our devastated homes. With this point of view Cavafy will not seem to us alien. . . .[20]

(Italics mine.)

In the light of such a passage as this, it seems beside the point to read **"Stratis Thalassinos among the Agapanthi"** as a battleground of past and present, universal and particular. Seferis needs past voices, names, and images in order to say what he is saying in the present.

> The first thing God made is love
> then comes blood
> and the thirst for blood
> roused by
> the body's sperm as by salt.
> The first thing God made is the long journey;
> that house there is waiting
> with its blue smoke
> with its aged dog
> waiting for the homecoming so that it can die.
> But the dead must guide me;
> it is the agapanthi that keep them from speaking,
> like the depths of the sea or the water in a glass.
> And the companions stay on in the palaces of Circe:
> my dear Elpenor! My poor, foolish Elpenor!
> Or don't you see them
> —"Oh help us!"—
> on the blackened ridge of Psara?

This poem was written in South Africa in 1942; Seferis was serving with the Greek government in exile. The sense of exile from home and the need of guidance recall the *Odyssey*; the war for freedom recalls Solomos's famous elegy of 1825, "The Destruction of Psara."[21] To non-Greek readers the second reference in particular may be obscure; but I see no way of separating the universal from the local in what Seferis is saying about war.

The references to incidents and a character from the *Odyssey,* and the use of Solomos's actual words, accomplish two things. First, Seferis avoids the kind of nonspecific, ultimately bland expression of feeling we saw in Mangakis's essay. Secondly, the presence of other voices gives an appropriate timelessness to the timeless theme of war. In exile, feeling cut off from Hellenism, Seferis reaches back to the Greek tradition—a reaching which is the real subject of **"Stratis Thalassinos among the Agapanthi"**; as well as much of his other work.[22]

> It's painful and difficult, the living are not enough for me
> first because they do not speak, and then
> because I have to ask the dead
> in order to go on farther.

Talking to the dead is Seferis's most striking use of myth in poetry, his strongest means of showing that Elpenor and the Independence Fighters of 1821 exist "in a moment of time." His use of quotation from ancient sources is far more interesting as a shaping device than the mere use of ancient names for timeless figures; it is also one of the most interesting ways Seferis approaches the sea. Proteus is Proteus, the same in Seferis as in the *Odyssey*; but a more distinctive proof of the multitudinousness (in fact the protean quality) of the sea can be found in the changes Seferis rings on line 958 of the *Agamemnon,* "There is the sea—and who will drain it dry?"

"The dead must guide me," says the mariner in **"Stratis Thalassinos among the Agapanthi"** "the living are not enough for me . . . I have to ask the dead / in order to go on farther." The quotation from Solomos at the end of that poem is an example of such guidance in a difficult moment. What kind of guidance does Aeschylus's line and its context provide? It appears—with variations—twice in **"Notes for a Week,"** once in *Mythical History,* and at the close of **"Thrush."** Comparing these different uses of the line ought to show some of the ways Seferis uses myth and dead voices to shape and dramatize the sea.

Even in its Aeschylean context, the line has a Delphic quality. Its enigmatic character is of course appropriate in that the line is spoken by that rhetorical riddler Clytemnestra as she welcomes Agamemnon home and tempts him to walk on the purple carpet. I use the Fagles translation.

AG.

> . . . And now,
> Since you have brought me down with your insistence,
> Just this once I enter my father's house,
> trampling royal crimson as I go.

CLYT.

> There is the sea
> *and who will drain it dry?* Precious as silver,
> inexhaustible, ever-new, it breeds the more we reap
> it—
> tides on tides of crimson dye our robes blood-red.
> Our lives are based on wealth, my king,
> the gods have seen to that.
> Destitution, our house has never heard the word.[23]

The image is deeply ironic and full of double-edged truth. It extends into the past and future as the purple fabric ripples beneath Agamemnon's feet. Clytemnestra boasts of the sea as proudly as if she owned it; indeed, she goes on to say that the Atreid house, reaping continual wealth from the red dye of the sea, *does* as good as own it. The speech beginning "There is the sea" is thus both outrageously arrogant and outrageously reasonable.

> The sea is both the reservoir of their riches and the incarnation of their never-ending strife, a harvest and a grisly reaping both. Thus the sea reflects the tapestries and Clytemnestra's victim, the deadliness beneath the surface grandeur of the fabrics and the man. The sinuous red line they form is in the vein of Agamemnon— they fuse his slaughters and his bloodline, his will and his hereditary guilt. And at every step he takes upon them he exceeds his limits and retraces his descent: an Olympian outrage to be punished by the forces of the Earth. For as he tramples on the gods he re-enacts his trampling on the innocents of Troy and on his daughter—just as his forebear trampled on the banquet of his children—and so the king reactivates the curse. As if caught in a slow-motion camera, all his murderous acts dissolve into a single act, deliberate and majestic and profane, that accelerates toward the murder that awaits him.
>
> An entire history of violence marches toward its violent but valid retribution.[24]

Fagles's and Stanford's vivid and poetic reading of the image unfolds like a brilliantly successful synecdoche from the sea to an entire history which we realize retrospectively is encapsulated in the line which begins the speech. The richness of association is more than poetic in its evocations; it is moral, historical, religious if we are aware of the family story Clytemnestra has in mind (and she knows that Agamemnon *is* aware of it, as Aeschylus knew his listeners were).

If then we read Seferis's variations on the line as references to the whole of Clytemnestra's speech and thus to the whole moral problem of the house of Atreus, it is clear that he could hardly have chosen a more humanly and complexly charged image of the sea. And if the reference escapes the reader? Seferis wrote of a comparable Aeschylean adaptation in **"Thrush,"** "I don't think that I'm unjustified in considering these things [Aeschylus; tragedy; ancient Greek; Greek

culture] as the common possession of us all; if they are not, so much the worse for us."[25] Unfortunately things *are* the worse for us; most of us now need notes to explain the line's provenance, let alone its larger context and suggestiveness.

If we are unaware of the Aeschylean reference, much of the effectiveness of the line is inevitably lost. But Seferis has preserved some of the dramatic quality of the original context of Clytemnestra's (largely rhetorical) question by emphasizing the line's interrogative tone in most of its recurrences. Whatever we take the sea to mean, it is often an open question in Seferis whether it can or will be or has been drained dry or not—and beyond this uncertainty, whether or not it ought to be. The answer to that question of course depends on how we interpret the sea. Recall in Aeschylus its double burden of riches and guilt, self-renewal and pollution. The sea is a synecdoche for both wealth and blood; beyond that, for a royal house and its violent past. If we know nothing of the house of Atreus or Clytemnestra's speech, the line as Seferis uses it still pulsates with ambivalence; it is a question to which there is no easy answer. Feeling that, we feel (I here agree with [Walter] Kaiser) the "general applicability" of the line before we sense its specific import. But it is questionable how specific the import ever becomes in the quotations that follow; the question of the sea is nearly always bigger than its context.

In **"Notes for a Week,"** some of the poems written in London in the early thirties, both **"Monday"** and **"Wednesday"** refer to the line.

> the river doesn't roll, it has forgotten the sea
> and yet there is the sea and who will drain it dry? . . .
> I look at the river
> sudden light puffs of wind pass under the impotent
> sun
> nothing else, the river waits;
> pity those who wait.
>
> **("Monday")**

> Brothers, we've shared our bread and our pain.
> No one hungers any longer, no one suffers
> and all of us have the same stature. Look at us!
> We look at you. We too. We too. We too.
> There is nothing beyond.
> —But the sea:
> I don't know why they've drained it dry.
>
> **("Wednesday")**

In both these poems, written far from home and imbued with the same nostalgia as **"Hampstead,"** the sea is desired but out of reach and out of sight. It is not quite certain that the sea exists at all; it has been forgotten by the river, it has perhaps been drained dry. The sea-less world is also a world without heroism, a world where the sun is "impotent" (as of course English sun is in comparison to Greek), where no one is greater than anyone else and there is no other life, no escape from unfaithful time: "nothing beyond." The violence that in Aeschylus makes the sea run red is absent from these pale poems, but so is its splendor and ability to renew itself.

In **Mythical History** 20, subtitled *Andromeda* in the Greek edition, the speaker is closer to the sea and senses it as a real thing: threat? escape? Both the first and second lines of this passage can be read as either fearful or yearning:

> These stones sinking into time, how far will they drag
> me with them?
> The sea, the sea, who will be able to drain it dry?
> I see the hands beckon each dawn to the vulture and
> the hawk
> bound as I am to the rock that suffering has made
> mine,
> I see the trees breathing the black serenity of the dead
> and then the smiles, so static, of the statues.

A kind of transcendent sublimity as splendid in its way as Clytemnestra's arrogance raises the tone of these lines above the usual human hopes and apprehensions. Andromeda, or a nameless consciousness, is able to perceive on a geological scale the processes of nature such as stones moving, trees breathing, the sea being (or not being) slowly depleted. What becomes of the sea is of vital but not personal importance to this consciousness, rather as in the opening of *Prometheus Bound*.

In the close of **"Thrush"** for the only time, the sea *does* drain dry.

> and you find yourself
> in a large house with many windows open
> running from room to room, not knowing from where
> to look out first,
> because the pine-trees will vanish, and the mirrored
> mountains, and the chirping of birds
> the sea will drain dry, shattered glass, from north and
> south
> your eyes will empty of daylight
> the way the cicadas suddenly, all together, fall silent.

Emptiness and cessation are presented with a light-hearted, almost rapturous rhythm and tone; Seferis himself called this section the *allegro* of **"Thrush."**[26] Silence, darkness, emptiness do not preclude an apocalyptic radiance; the silence seems to herald a new beginning, as does the cessation in **"Engomi,"** another transcendent moment. . . . But **"Engomi"** returns at its close to a world of sparse grass where "they take a long time to die"; here death is simply the stoppage of the poem on a note of paradoxical exultation.

Seferis has made extraordinarily varied, though consistently mysterious, uses of Aeschylus's line. The earlier work, emphasizing the life-giving quality of the sea, uses its possible draining as a source of apprehension, a sign of alienation consonant with the alienation of being in London. **Mythical History** moves closer to the world of Greek myth and Greek landscape, with its sinking stones, vulture, and statues; but with the dialectic familiar from our earlier discussion of this sequence, the sea is not necessarily more precious as it is more closely approached. Here it is inscrutable, perhaps dangerous, perhaps life-saving.

The actual draining of the sea at the end of **"Thrush"** sends us back to Aeschylus. What would such an exhaustion of resources mean in Clytemnestra's terms? Her sea is "inexhaustible, ever-new"; "Our lives are based on" the wealth it produces and do not understand deprivation. For that inexhaustible sea to dry up is unheard of, terrifying, and ultimately cleansing, even if it means death. Seferis is suggesting the end of a rich tradition with its wealth, for the poet, of history and legend; a final freeing, both exhilarating and dreadful, from the bond of the past. Instead of peering underwater in order to decipher the past, the poet can now run from room to room of unfulfilled potential. It is hard to know what kind of resource will replace Clytemnestra's rich and bloody sea; **"Thrush"** ends at this point, and so does the great majority of Seferis's best work. In **Logbook III** (1955) he turned to Cypriot legend and myth, and in **Three Secret Poems** language and continuity sometimes seem tenuous, the work of a tired man. Yet it is in **"On Stage,"** the second of these three poems, that Seferis comes closest to confronting Clytemnestra in all her sinister splendor—that Clytemnestra who remains in the background in all the changes run on her great line. In some kind of theatrical performance, a female figure appears on stage, unnamed but "Leaving the sheets to grow cold / and the avenging baths." Has Agamemnon already been murdered; is this *The Libation Bearers*? All we are shown is the figure's courage in the face of nameless attackers.

> They drew the knives from the sheaths,
> looked for a place to stab you.
> Only then did you cry out:
> "Let anyone come and sleep with me
> who wants to:
> am I not the sea?"

Arrogant, unanswerable, finally mysterious, this question is perhaps Seferis's final version of *Agamemnon* 958 and his final vision of the sea, as if the cleansed quality of the end of **"Thrush"** had to give way to the familiar elemental and mythological forces of tradition. In the following section, . . . Seferis is questioning his own vision, the use he has made of myth and symbol. "The sea: how did it become so, the sea?" To which the only answer is that given by Proteus: "I may be nobody, / but I can become whatever you want." In other words, *know thyself.*

Proteus is a reminder that the most constant thing about this changeable element is its truthfulness. As Emily Vermeule points out, sea-prophets like Proteus may be hard to catch, but, once caught, they never lie.[27] Vermeule also observes (what we have already seen in the line about the sea draining) that the sea is "double-faced and changeable, sometimes the way to paradise and sometimes the jaws of death, but never predictable." Life-giving and death-giving, the sea is the emblem of dialectic, and any symbol of it must be contradictory or incomplete. Yet in its formlessness it must be symbolized; it cries out for poetic treatment and challenges the poet's control over his own tradition. What Seferis says of the sea in his Makriyannis essay is true as well of his own struggle for equilibrium, his attempt to maintain a synchronic sense of Greek tradition and his place in it: "this element that, although always tormented, never stops striving towards a balance, towards a 'measure.'" Writing about the sea was a harsh test for Seferis: could he both be original and tell the truth? In his different ways of viewing the sea and especially his heed of "the dead" for guidance, Seferis managed to hold his own against the formlessness of the element as timeless as Homer, Aeschylus, Solomos.

I said [earlier] that the power of the imagination turns inanimate rock into "a mirror in which to dwell." Trees and the sea, of course, are mirrorlike in much more obvious ways. They reflect not only the constantly changing faces of nature but also ourselves—reflect, finally, the sense of life or death, hope or despair, we bring to a contemplation of natural metamorphosis. In Frost and Seferis gardens are blossom or decay; the sea is renewal or disappearance.

As if occasionally weary of the protean character of some of their preferred emblems, Frost and Seferis sometimes conjure them out of existence. In "After Apple-Picking" the world is perhaps no more than a dreamlike apparition; in Seferis's variations on the Aeschylean line about the sea, the sea itself vanishes. A powerful ambivalence about the beloved landscapes with which they are so familiar underlies such exorcisms; it is an ambivalence that will reappear more strongly when the poets turn from earthly landscapes toward the inaccessibilities of stars and light and their human mirrorings.

Notes

1. Georgios-Alexandros Mangakis, "My Greece," trans. Rachel Hadas, *The Charioteer,* No. 19 (1977): 66-67 (first appearance in *Eighteen Articles,* Athens, 1972).

2. Seferis, *Days,* journal entries for 12 May and 14 August 1946 (my translation).

3. On the influence of Verlaine and Laforgue on the early Seferis, see Naso Vayenas, *The Poet and the Dancer* (Athens: Kedros, 1979), 118-20. Vayenas derives "Fog" from Laforgue's "Complainte de l'automne monotone" and quotes:

> Nuits sous-marines!
> Pourpres forêts,
> Torrents de frais,
> Bancs en gésines.

To be sure [writes Vayenas] the meaning of the images in the two poets is not the same. For Laforgue the submarine world is the symbol of nirvana, of a vegetable, unorganized life, relieved of every human anxiety. Seferis remains on the first level of the comparison, suggesting the essential futility and inertia of human existence. (Translation mine.)

4. See also Vayenas, *Poet and Dancer,* on the possible derivation of "Hampstead" from Sikelianos's poem, pp. 197-200.

5. "My Greece," 66-67.

6. See W. B. Stanford, *The Ulysses Theme.*

7. See my paper "Upon a Foreign Verse: Translation and Tradition," *Translation Review,* no. 11 (1983): 31-36.

8. For the graffito-like aspect of Seferis's work, see Chapter I. The Tsatsou reference is from *My Brother George Seferis* (Athens: Hestia, 1973).

9. Robert Frost, quoted in Lawrence Thompson, *Robert Frost: The Years of Triumph,* 290.

10. See John Vernon, *The Garden and the Map,* 145:

> It is insufficient to talk simply about spatial cross-references . . . The point of repeated images, of cross-references, is that the image accumulates new meaning with each new appearance, since it is arrived at in the act of reading, in time; it therefore possesses not only its first appearance but a whole intermediary part of the poem or novel, as the part that constitutes its presence.

11. L. B. Karapanayiotis, "Mythistorema '61," in G. P. Savidis, ed., *For Seferis* (Athens: Ikaros, 1961), 225.

12. *Poetics of Space,* 211, 217.

13. On the confused and contradictory images in *The Cistern,* see also *Poet and Dancer,* 129-32.

14. Emily Vermeule, *Aspects of Death in Early Greek Art and Poetry* (Berkeley: University of California Press, 1979), 180.

15. Compare this passage with the opening of Section 4 of *Mythical History,* itself in turn a quotation from Plato's *Alcibiades,* p. 133B.

> And if the soul
> is to know itself

        it must look
        into a soul:
        the stranger and the enemy, we've seen him in the
            mirror.

16. *My Brother GS,* 190, 269.

17. Edmund Keeley, "T. S. Eliot and the Poetry of Seferis," *Comparative Literature* 8 (Summer 1965): 225.

18. Edmund Keeley, "Seferis' Elpenor: A Man of No Fortune," *Kenyon Review* 28 (June 1966): 378-79.

19. Walter Kaiser, trans. *Three Secret Poems by George Seferis,* Cambridge, Mass.: Harvard University Press, 1969), ix-x.

20. Seferis, "Cavafy and Eliot—a Comparison," in Rex Warner, editor and translator, *Seferis on the Greek Style* (London: Bodley Head, 1966), 161.

21. "On the blackened ridge of Psara":

    This line is from Solomos's "The Destruction of Psara" (1825). The island of Psara was razed and its people massacred during the Greek War of Independence (1821-1829). The complete poem is among the more famous in modern Greece. . . .

    Keeley and Sherrard, "Notes" to *George Seferis: Collected Poems (1924-1955)* (Princeton, N.J.: Princeton University Press, 1971), 265.

22. See my unpublished paper, "Talking to the Dead: Seferis and Tradition" (delivered at the MLA, Houston, Texas, 12/28/80).

23. Aeschylus, *The Oresteia,* trans. Robert Fagles (New York: Bantam Edition, 1977), 145.

24. Robert Fagles and W. B. Stanford, "A Reading of the Oresteia: The Serpent and the Eagle," *The Oresteia,* 27.

25. Seferis, "Letter on 'Thrush,'" *English-Greek Review.*

26. Seferis, quoted in *Poet and Dancer,* 278-79.

27. Vermeule, *Aspects of Death,* 190-91.

Bibliography

Antzaka, Sophia. *The Other Life in the Poetry of Seferis.* Athens, 1974.

Karantonis, Andreas. *The Poet George Seferis.* Athens: Hestia, 1957.

Keeley, Edmund, and Warren Wallace. "On Greek Poetry." Unpublished interview, 1979-80.

Lorentzatos, Zissimos. *The Lost Center and Other Essays.* Princeton, N.J.: Princeton University Press, 1980.

Pherentinou, Ariana. *Aeschylus in the Poetry of Seferis.* Athens: O.D.E.V., 1976.

Savidis, Giorgos, ed. *For Seferis: Festschrift.* Athens: Ikaros, 1961.

Seferis, George. *Six Nights on the Acropolis.* Athens: Hermes, 1978.

———. *Poems.* Athens: Ikaros, 11th printing, 1977.

———. *Days* (5 volumes):

Volume 1: 16 February 1925-17 August 1931. Athens: Ikaros, 1975.

Volume 2: 24 August 1931-12 February 1934. Athens: Ikaros, 1975.

Volume 3: 16 April 1934-14 December 1940. Athens: Ikaros, 1977.

Volume 4: 1 February 1941-31 December 1944. Athens: Ikaros, 1977.

Volume 5: 1 January 1945-19 April 1951. Athens: Ikaros, 1977.

———. "The Art of Poetry, XIII." *Paris Review,* no. 50 (Fall 1970): 56-93. (Interview by Edmund Keeley.)

———. *Three Secret Poems.* Translated by Walter Kaiser. Cambridge: Harvard University Press, 1969.

———. *Collected Poems* (expanded edition). Translated by Edmund Keeley and Philip Sherrard. Princeton, N.J.: Princeton University Press, 1981.

———. *Seferis on the Greek Style: Selected Essays on Poetry and Hellenism.* London: Bodley Head, 1966.

Thaniel, George. "George Seferis's 'Thrush' and T. S. Eliot's 'Four Quartets.'" *Neohelicon* 4, nos. 3-4 (1976): 261-82.

Tsatsou, Ioanna. *My Brother George Seferis.* Athens: Hestia, 1973.

Vayenas, Nasos. *The Poet and the Dancer: An Examination of the Poetics and Poetry of Seferis.* Athens: Kedros, 1979.

Vitti, Mario. *Corruption and the Logos: Introduction to the Poetry of George Seferis.* Athens: Hestia, 1978.

Dimitris Dimiroulis (essay date 1985)

SOURCE: Dimiroulis, Dimitris. "The 'Humble Art' and the Exquisite Rhetoric: Tropes in the Manner of George Seferis." In *The Text and Its Margins: Post-Structuralist Approaches to Twentieth-Century Greek Literature,* edited by Margaret Alexiou and Vassilis Lambropoulos, pp. 59-84. New York: Pella Publishing Company, 1985.

[In the following essay, Dimiroulis discusses the way Seferis handles tradition and language in his writing, maintaining that the poet skillfully infuses his work with the values and spirit of his homeland.]

The poetry of George Seferis has already been established as a major work of art in the corpus of modern Greek literature, and has even acquired the status of an exceptionally influential poetic discourse tantamount, in its prestige and authority, to the indisputable literary preeminence of the works of Solomos, Kalvos, Palamas and Cavafy. It is worth noticing that in the last twenty years we have not only witnessed a ceaselessly increasing concern for Seferis' poetry, but also a manifold proliferation of poetic styles and imagery emanating from the appeal of his artistry to a new generation of poets.

Equally impressive is his avowed *auctoritas,* exerted on literary criticism and historiography by means of an elaborate essayistic language and a powerful historical insight. Moreover, his fame has been ensured by the award of the Nobel Prize in 1963 and by the posthumous publication (still in progress) of many works, among which the most prominent are a novel, a volume of poems and his political and literary diaries.

It can be said that Seferis' continuing domination over the most significant issues in contemporary Greek literature and thought owes its strength and its lasting vigor to his perspicacity and adroitness in appropriating, modifying and exploiting ideas and beliefs of his time as well as in carefully grafting some concepts and practices of European modernism onto the legacy of Greek tradition. He developed, either in prose or in verse, a new artistic ideal, comprising mainly myths, symbols, historical images, national sensitivities and rhetorical techniques that enabled him to present himself as the last sonorous bard of a decaying Hellenism. Seferis alone of his contemporaries has been able to set himself up as a "national" poet by avoiding becoming entrapped in an excessive modernism and by having a poetic vision that encompassed a historical symbolism, a national mythology and a lyric idiom of great leverage.

It is not surprising, then, that his work has been and is constantly analyzed, interpreted and translated. Besides, it is considered very "Greek"[1] (whatever this adjective might mean for critical discourse), as the embodiment of a spirit and a past undeniably Hellenic, and it is identified with a certain notion of "Greekness" as a *modus vivendi* that has inspired the efforts of many Greek writers and intellectuals to build up a national ideology.

Seferis' literary stature derives its authority precisely from that dexterous infusion of national "values" into a modern poetic diction and from his admirable critical clairvoyance, whose importance lies mainly in its thematic persistency and consistency. By focusing his attention on the topics of tradition and language he touched upon two of the most serious and haunting is-

sues in Greek society and literature, closely related to the crucial question of national identity. In dealing with them he has been able to offer both a new historical perspective and a new literary style. This partly explains why his work, in spite of its difficulties, is being regarded as an exemplary manifestation of national consciousness and as a unique achievement in terms of language-ethos and moral vocation in general. It is rather evident that he is the father figure, the patriarch of contemporary Greek literature, whose shadow looms large in the minds of the descendants and in whose literary garden vegetate numerous docile acolytes.

To a great extent the critics of Seferis' work have been mesmerized by the luster and lure of his style and patronized by his authoritative omnipresence in almost every domain of literary discourse. This by no means implies that they confined themselves exclusively to the passive role of either reproducing and perpetuating his ideas or guaranteeing and defending his master-image of an ingenious and charismatic poet. Although the predominant tendency has been by and large one of advocating the idolization of the poet and the mystification of his writings, it did not prevent the development of alternative readings and interpretations. But even in these cases most of the critics accommodated and comforted themselves by virtually remaining in the old premises of criticism and abiding by established methods and ideas. The scenery is all too well known: biographical excavations as a widely recognized practice of supplying "true" information for understanding poetry; thorough investigations for the detection of sources, influences, similarities and plagiarisms; historical commentaries assuming a palpable and immediate correlation between poetry and history; procrustean paraphrases and inflated descriptions in the disguise of systematic interpretations; stylistic analyses amounting to picturesque accounts of the poet's outstanding inventiveness, and so forth.

However, the conformity to the prevailing norms of critical discourse has not always been unchallenged. We can notice here and there some slight alterations, some deviations and aberrations on a small scale, but they are, as it were, marginal resistances, insufficient for changing the whole picture. Even a few endeavors to provide new methods of analysis resulted in no more than their own isolation as noticeable but fruitless exceptions.[2] Seferis' poetry therefore is still being studied through either an old-fashioned empiricism embedded in received prejudices and preconceptions about history, society and culture or an idealistic grandiloquence assuredly invoking the timelessness of aesthetic values, the transparency of language and the sublimated presence of the poet's voice.

At any rate, it is not my intention to examine the character of this critical discourse in all its complexity, that is, to give an account of critical responses to Seferis' poetry, nor to challenge directly the validity of concrete critiques and militate against specific strategies, ideologies and policies reigning in the field. On the other hand, what has prompted me to engage myself in this detour on Seferis' poetry is precisely the conviction that traditional criticism has been caught in the web of its own pedantry and, furthermore, has been emasculated by its arrogant refusal to put its criteria and principles under systematic scrutiny and doubt. So it may well be that this paper implicates a polemic, though it has not been designed as such but rather as a preliminary reading that has apparently originated in preexisting oppositions without placing them in the center of its problematics; its objections to other readings is a point of departure, rather than of antagonistic coexistence.

More specifically, what I am going to propose is not a "definitive" interpretation or a "true" analysis but something quite different, which might be perceived as a "test-reading" in the sense that it connotes experimentation aiming, as far as Seferis' poetry is concerned, at delineating a virgin reading territory and opening up a new space of interpretative possibilities. As the title suggests, the approach of this reading is designated by rhetorical considerations and not by thematic or referential ones. What is at stake here is not the "proper" or "literal" meaning of the poems but their rhetorical status, the all-embracing figurality of their language and the tropological function of their "representation." Thus, the pivotal question is "whether a literary text is about that which it describes, represents or states" (de Man, 1979:57) and, consequently, whether the "reading is truly problematic" (58) or not. If meaning follows a secure path leading to the convergence of "the meaning read with the meaning stated" (57) in and by the text, then there would be no difficulty in finding it. This latter conjecture characterizes in fact a critical approach favoring the priority and uniformity of meaning, whereas the rhetorical one (to which this paper is primarily subscribed) interrogates both the production of meaning through a game of tropes and the conditions of its own problematic form.

This kind of reading which I am pursuing is therefore based on the assumption that the text, far from being an ontologically distinctive "entity," is a rhetorical construction never achieving its completion since its function is interminably deconstructive in that it "simultaneously asserts and denies the authority of its own rhetorical mode" (17). Yet such a reading should not be understood as a realization of a systematic theory about literature and language, for it does not employ a rigid method or a definite set of rules but stems from the intention to enliven the critical game with a proliferation of discursive practices. To a certain extent I adopt some of Paul de Man's views as they are illustrated in his version of rhetoric (which implies a "re-

coinage" of terms) and, particularly, as they are exemplified in his readings of Rilke, Nietzsche, Proust and Rousseau (de Man, 1979). This does not entail an unconditional approval of his deconstructive techniques or rhetorical devices, since I am not using his texts as a model but as a pre-text, as a starting point for a tentative reading. Therefore, modifications and digressions are not altogether excluded.

My purpose is neither to put Seferis' poetry under "the terrors of tropology" (Eagleton, 1982:22) nor to succumb to the "imperialism of rhetoric" (Kellner, 1981:15) but, to use a milder metaphor, to challenge the authenticity of poetic meaning by deploying tropological techniques devoid of any claim to originality, immediacy or innocence.

This essay could be labeled a "working paper" in the sense that it is enveloped in its own rhetorical mode, and as such it "intends to elicit from those to whom it is addressed a deepening rejoinder and continuation" (Steiner, 1980:ix).

* * *

After Palamas—the poet who marked with his imposing presence the whole field of Greek literature in the first half of this century—Seferis is perhaps the only poet who followed his example in exercising literary criticism not as a *parergon* but as a high-valued *ergon*. Throughout his life he had shown a keen interest in bringing together criticism and poetry and directing them toward a common ideal—an attempt that can also be seen in connection with the pattern used by poets like Valery and Eliot, whose works Seferis knew and admired.

Among the themes that recur both in his poetry and in his prose we can trace those that bear witness to an all-pervasive ambition for an art vigilant and self-aware: thus, he never ceases to be a poet in his literary criticism and a critic in his poetry. Some of the most privileged themes in his work refer to subjects like language, tradition, literary history, national spirit and artistic morality, and affirm his aspirations to proffer to his nation a new poetic mythology. With enviable skill and erudition, Seferis unfolds his vision for a poetry requiring of the poet a professional knowledge of and a mastery over his material regardless of the price he has to pay in order to get hold of them. For the poet "who does not strive for mastership over his material is not an artisan and his sensibility is imperfect" (1976:13). The acquisition of craftsmanship must reach so high a level that it will be impossible for the reader to single out the artificial elements of the poem.[3] By perceiving the poem as an organic unity containing "elements of the outside and inside world" (41) Seferis thinks of the poet as a conscientious *bricoleur* whose task is to provide the poetic meaning with a seamless, nearly invisible form. The *ousia* of the poem coincides with the *morphe*[4] because the poet smooths the rough edges of the material, and by so doing he facilitates the hidden meaning's ascent to the surface, leaving the dark depths of nature and human soul. Yet for this ideal unity to be achieved, the poet's skillfulness and grand technique do not suffice; what is further required is a strong dislike for ornamentation, embellishment and exaggeration, which strip the poem of its original purity, structural balance and harmony. In this sense poetry is neither a complex rhetorical device nor a rhetorical construct of a rich imagination but something similar to a natural object wisely carved and perfected by a humble craftsman—the poet as creator has almost disappeared behind the mask of an ordinary man. This metaphor, a prevalent one in Seferis, illustrates succinctly his determination to inaugurate a poetic idiom different in its tropological economy from contemporary or preceding ones and powerful enough to lay claim upon the future of the national poetry. For a better understanding of this strategy we can turn our attention to one of his poems, bearing in mind that what matters here is not Seferis' "real" intention but our encounter with an "orphaned" poem that "turns back upon itself in a manner that puts the authority of its own affirmations in doubt, especially when these affirmations refer to modes of writing that it advocates" (de Man, 1979:26-7).

In the poem **"An Old Man on the River Bank"** (1969:285), written in 1942, we have a stanza located at the very center of the text that divides it into two equal parts or, to put it differently, links the first and the second part in a very curious way, since it seems that it has nothing in common with them. The importance of this stanza has been stressed by many critics, who considered it a synopsis of Seferis' poetics, a straightforward statement about his artistic intentions. The presence of a speaking subject, presumably that of the poet, and the apocalyptic tone of its voice create so compelling an illusion that inevitably they have been taken as proofs of a *de profundis* confession:

> I want no more than to speak simply, to be granted that grace.
> Because we've loaded even our songs with so much music that they're slowly sinking
> and we've decorated our art so much that its features have been eaten away by gold
> and it's time to say our few words because tomorrow the soul sets sail.

If, instead of looking for the meaning of the text, we try to observe *how* it means, the horizon of our reading would be entirely different. Such a reorientation of the interpretative act would not only separate the means of the text from its meaning but would also underscore the absolute indeterminacy of the latter and its dependence on the rhetoricity of language.

All the same, the presence of that "I" in the first line attracts our attention by conveying a desire for speaking, that is, by addressing to us a "voice" that we cannot ignore: *"I want no more than to speak simply."* But instantly, at the very moment of its "eventuation," the "I" disappears and gives way to the general "we," the predominant collective subject of the text. In fact, this is the one of the two instances in the whole poem in which the first person singular is foregrounded, alluding to a strong impulse on the part of the poet to make, even momentarily, his presence to be felt and his voice to be heard. Yet its disappearance is not a "real" one, since it has never existed in the first place as *the* "true" subject but only as a figure among many others; its figurative significance is established by virtue of place and function, rather than of truth and essence, because it is nothing but a grammatical "entity" emerging from the intratextual nexus. Its disappearance, therefore, should be understood as a grammatical transformation resulting in the revalorization of the rhetorical relationships in the text.

Inasmuch as the "subject" is identified with an intention to speak it takes the form of an explicit and diaphanous "I," but when it proceeds to a retrospective justification of its claims it slips into an abstract and vague "we." The transition indicates, as it were, a dislocation of the voice due to the oscillation of the subject between a desire for immediate speech and a need for self-assurance. The resort to the collective subject reveals both a complicity in the distortion of the poetic language (as if there existed a common guilt for what has happened) and a reaffirmation of the willingness to save the purity and originality of speech. The mode of this movement is a synecdochical one, for it permits the substitution of whole for part and part for whole. The subject is no longer a concrete and unified center, a promise for salvation from the sin of language, a universal voice annunciating the paradise of art, but the last subterfuge of the trope, the ultimate synecdoche of writing, a mask behind a mask. The inequality between "I" and "we" is not literal but figurative, and what seems to be a linear grammatical transformation or miraculous metamorphosis of meaning is counterfeited by the elusiveness of the synecdoche and its endlessly reciprocating motion. The subject remains suspended, never achieving a full identity—a mere incident of the trope. Thus, we can, for instance, substitute the "I" for something more general and abstract and, by the same token, we can reduce the "we" to the singularity of a personal voice or intention without ever managing to pinpoint an extratextual presence, since the inexorable evasiveness of the trope renders the "meaning" inexhaustible. The interaction of what is written with what is read produces an infinite play of substitutions in which there is no likelihood for a stable meaning, and hence neither the "I" nor the "we" can escape from their tropological indeterminacy. Synecdoche in this case could be designated as "one of the borderline figures that create an ambivalent zone between metaphor and metonymy and that, by its spatial nature, creates the illusion of a synthesis by totalization" (de Man, 1979:63). In this sense, the "I" in the first line appears to be absorbed by the following "we" in a metaphorical rather than metonymic manner. Yet the looseness of the metaphorical link renders possible a metonymic contingency. It is because of this discrepancy in the behavior of the trope that the subject is always deferred: its presence is subverted by the figurality of language and the immanent ambiguity of its signifiers. And it is for this reason that we cannot take it for granted that the "voice" behind the "I" is the "voice" of the poet.

It can be said then that the stanza under discussion does not constitute a more reliable statement for Seferis' poetics than any other of his poems. The presence of the "I" and its filiation to "we" do not guarantee any clarity, honesty and unmediatedness, for both of them partake of the rhetorical game and operate as one more ruse through which the poem pretends to be speaking or intending to speak its master's voice in order to make its writing neutral and invisible.

We can pursue the argument in the same direction and within the same context by exploring the following plethora of tropes. The disapproval of the decorated art and the longing for an unmediated "simplicity" are expressed in spectacular metaphors arrayed in a complex system of substitutions and transformations. First we have the classical analogy poem/song, again a synecdoche of metaphorical nature (since any metonymic contiguity has been enfeebled in the historical course of the two words), which in its turn becomes the vehicle of another metaphor, that of the association of the song to an object we can "load." Similar metaphorical correspondences are obvious in utterances like "We've loaded . . . with so much music" and "they are slowly sinking." All these intertwined tropes are used to emphasize the assertion that the excessive decoration of the poem ("so much music") results in its disappearance: it lapses into silence not because it is short of language but because it has an enormous figurative surplus; its presence is almost nullified by its inability to control the inflation of tropes. The paradox here is that this dismissive assertion is itself overdecorated, and thereby the poem falls prey to the same rhetorical extravagance it had so rigorously denounced.

The rhetorical feast continues its unrestrained transfigurations in the following emphatic prosopopeia, by means of which a new series of metaphors comes into being. The "face" of art fades away at the very moment of its

glorification; the "gold" of language, the prosperity and propitiousness of the signifier, instead of adding to the aesthetic integrity and unity, deprives art of its voiced presence; behind the dazzling facade the corrosive accumulation of tropes accelerates the collapse of the entire poetic edifice. The "disfiguring power of figuration" (de Man, 1978:29) exposes the void lurking in the verbal overflow, but at the same time evinces the attachment of the poem to the very language it tries to escape from: the void, like silence, is no more than another rhetorical trick. When it is named as such, it ceases automatically to be a "real" void and when, conversely, it remains anonymous it does not exist as such. Every time the poem finds a way out of the impasse, it is confronted by the insurmountable density and impenetrability of its own language and is thus forced into a never-ending "inscape": in the end of any "end" a detritus of "tropes troping themselves" (Kellner, 1981:28) promises a new advent of the poem. The "few words" that must be said for the sake of salvation are condemned to a perpetual deferment, lost in the delusory quest of a "voice" and irredeemably estranged from their origin.

The initial desire for a pellucid and unadulterated language, for an art without semantic scruples or figurative complexities, for a representation saturated by complete meaning and for an accurate (i.e., "honest") expression of simple, unadorned experiences is destined to remain unfulfilled. There is no place for the poem outside figurality, that is, there is no possibility to disambiguate language, to overcome its inherent arbitrariness and conventionality. Within the infinite play of signifiers the poem never acquires the status of a concrete and tangible object but is always in progress, always in becoming—never in being. Yet, although it is bound up with this figurative rotation, it never refrains from seeking *plenitude, totality* and *literalness*: its contradictory structuration generates the constitutive *aporia* that accompanies its "existence" and engenders its "meaning." Even when it is aware of its powerlessness to dissolve the ambivalence of its inscription and to come to terms with its aporetic language, the poem insists on exploring the tropological labyrinth and questioning the impossibility of unequivocal signification.

When Seferis envisages a poetic language sheltered from the eroding effects of verbal alchemy, pure in its meaning and simple in its form, the tropology of his writing is anchored on metonymic ground, or, at least, it aspires to a comprehensive discourse articulated by contiguity and intended to regulate the representational lopsidedness of the signifier. In adumbrating such a mode of writing the text itself invokes the authority of speech ("I want . . . to speak," "it's time to say") and blurs the boundaries between speaking and writing by inseminating the familiarity of the former into the ambiguity of the latter; in order to enact the play of communication the poem tends to prefigure its own reading. Nevertheless, this process never takes place *in* the poem but is described *by* it as a desirable development and is echoed in an imagined poetic form. The writing of the poem is about the originality and uniqueness of its future and is realized as the narration of its postponement: the absence of the poem as *being* "constitutes" the presence of the poem as *reading.* In so far as the poem has to write whatever it intends to say, envision and dream, it cannot naturalize language or neutralize discourse, and therefore, when it renounces figuration and, especially, metaphor, it does so by means of a "tropological defiguration" (de Man, 1978:22) imbued with elaborate allegories, and when it tries to achieve the immediacy of speech, by disavowing the authority of written signs, it is always already locked up in the duplicitous function of writing.

It seems as if the poem is helplessly enclosed in a vicious circle of rhetorical devices, severed from its subject, voice and literal meaning and deconstructed by its own textuality. But does this mean that there is nothing beyond the spurious propositions of rhetoric and the treacherous equivocations of tropes? Could we say that the poem is definitely wrapped up in its aporia and enfolded in its inwardness? There is no easy answer to these questions but, even provisionally, I would suggest that the tropological mode of a poem appears as a response to other analogous modes within an intertextual framework and, perhaps, the interaction of different discourses brings the poem out of the abyss of rhetoric to the circumstantiality of history and society and, especially, to their discursive antinomies and antagonisms.

In Seferis' stanza (and generally in his poetry) we can ascertain a refutation of a certain tradition of poetic writing, a disapproval of recognized rhetorical techniques and, subsequently, we can assume that the signifiers, far from being whirled into the void, spring out from an act of reading whereby they enter into the realm of history. The difficulty arises when we realize that Seferis' venture to undermine tradition, by initiating a new poetic model that proclaims its emancipation from tropology, is beset with the same rhetorical figures it had been designed to oppose and, finally, to eliminate. This contradiction does not prove the subjugation of history to rhetoric but rather outlines their complementary *antithesis,* which generates the fundamental paradox of a language (and an art) in constant *crisis.* In this sense, Seferis' poetry is governed simultaneously by an ineluctable rhetorical repetitiveness and an eager interest in displacing, deflecting and differentiating a strong tradition within its own omnivorous diction; his poetic idiom could be classified as modernistic, despite its hesitancy to take great risks—if modernity is to be understood as a phenomenon inextricably woven with

both history and rhetoric. All the same, as de Man has pointed out, "assertions of literary modernity often end up by putting the possibility of being modern seriously into question. But precisely because this discovery goes against an original commitment that cannot be dismissed as erroneous, it never gets stated outright, but hides instead behind rhetorical devices of language that disguise and distort what the writer is actually saying, perhaps in contrast to what he meant to say" (1971:152). Similar is Seferis' commitment to modernity. By employing a double strategy he revalorizes traditional values and concepts and appropriates a considerable number of discursive techniques, but at the same time he obliterates the historical traces through an eloquent rhetoric; his writing shuttles histrionically between "I" and "we," metonymy and metaphor, presence and absence, voice and silence, tradition and modernity. These putative dichotomies perhaps explain why he so often resorts to catachresis, hyperbole and allegory as a means to provide his poetry with a seemingly unified and flawless mythology, though behind the consistent rhetoric the tropes never cease, by means of their deconstructive impetus, to unveil the hidden or translucent discrepancies. As for his poetics, there may well be no other apparent gain in my reading than the suspicion that beyond what is "literally" said or meant there is always another "story" in abeyance, which is never the last one but "simply" one more in the succession of rhetorical games.

For reasons of expediency I found it preferable to limit the reading to only one stanza, which has been chosen as an exemplar for looking at some of Seferis' poetic strategems. However, we can approach the whole poem quite effectively, if we are interested in the rhetorical interplay, without changing perspective.

* * *

Seferis' poetic work is in many respects permeated by images of silence, voidness, doom, fragmentation and belatedness. The poet is represented as a suffering artist on the verge of destruction and oblivion, as a lonely and desperate prophet who witnesses hopelessly to the degeneration of civilization and foresees the precipitating ruination of the humanistic tradition. He resembles an old man who has endured much and felt the sorrow and bitterness of experiencing the decline of a world in which he had invested the dreams and the hopes of his adolescence. Art is frequently conceived of as a fairy tale, efficacious in healing the wounds of a life full of losses, separations, disillusionments and betrayals. It tells the painful story of national misfortunes and personal frustrations in a calm, thoughtful and wistful language; its tone is that of melancholy, nostalgia and restrained emotion and could be likened to a slow-going and rhetorically embroidered narrative.

In the poem **"An Old Man on the River Bank"** we can locate such a narrative, told, as the title indicates, by an old man and intended to rhapsodize the predicament of a community with which the speaking subject shares an unpredictable future. It is a prolonged and ramified narration that seems to be the final stage of a larger but unknown story, the conclusion of an unwritten adventure that can be only partly reconstructed by the poem. In the opening lines a need for radical consideration of the future and for determination in making the necessary decisions in life is expressed directly by means of an almost unaffected language, while instantaneously a torrent of figures emphasizes the urgency to escape from the agonies and torments inflicted on the community by the historical milieu:

> And yet we should consider how we go forward.
> To feel is not enough, nor to think, nor to move
> nor to put your body in danger in front of an old
>   loophole
> when scalding oil and molten lead furrow the walls.
>
> And yet we should consider towards what we go
>   forward,
> not as our pain would have it, and our hungry children
> and the chasm between us and the companions calling
>   from the opposite shore;
> Nor the whispering of the bluish light in an improvised
>   hospital,
> the pharmaceutic glimmer on the pillow of the youth
>   operated upon at noon.

On the rhetorical level the fabric of the narration again sets off a desire (here presented as a necessity) to bypass the dramatization of language by reiterating the syntax of a moral imperative. The text, through successive negations of figuratively reflected experiences, points to a revision of history that would not take into account the rhetoric of struggle and pain. To the indirect questions "how we go forward" and "towards what we go forward" it does not provide an outright answer but, by means of a negative logic, it triggers a chain of metaphors meant to prevent a further proliferation of the trope. The movement forward presupposes a clearing of the ground, a transmission to a more contiguous grammar freed from the bonds of a disturbing rhetoric. But, while the text alludes to a grammar not yet found, the narration itself flows amid static metaphors that turn out to be, in a curious way, the only movement forward in terms of textual space and time. What the text tries to forget reemerges from its own writing, and the language it aspires to erase proves, though in a superficially negative manner, the impossibility of such an erasure. On the other hand, as the story proceeds, the agglomeration of tropes creates the impression that what will follow should be a kind of linguistic compensation, a positive answer to the rhetoric of suffering, the "real" movement forward. These expectations, far from being fulfilled, are being met with another figurative transformation, this time an absolute one with regard to the construction of the text:

> but it should be in some other way, I would say like
> the long river that emerges from the great lakes
>   enclosed deep in Africa,
> that was once a god and then became a road and a
>   benefactor, a judge and a delta;
> that is never the same, as the ancient wise men taught,
> and yet always remains the same body, the same bed,
>   and the same Sign,
> the same orientation.

Unexpectedly, the language of the poem becomes the main subject of the story, for instead of corresponding to the question of "literal" meaning ("how" and "towards what") it plunges into figurative repetition and consents to be carried away by the stream of metaphors. The movement forward does not bring the narration to the next logical stage of syntactic contiguity but disperses it to the metaphorical similarities.

The image of the "river" represents here the absolute metaphor that seems to have absorbed any other secondary trope and to have set the pace of the story. In fact there is no story any more, since this super-metaphor has reduced everything to mere incidents of its function and the only thing that is still being narrated coincides with the trope itself: the text eventually consists of a metaphor about metaphor, of an allegorical reading of the metaphorical movement toward its own reiteration. Moreover, the self-referential character of the trope unravels as a figure never changing and yet never the same, static and yet always in motion. Like the "river," which keeps its identity undivided in spite of its various metamorphoses, the trope remains unaffected by its persistent transfigurations. The allegory thereby not only thematizes the modalities of metaphor but, by affirming the ambiguity of the signifier, brings forward the immanent heterogeneity of all language, so much so as it assigns to the symbol of the "river" the status of a sign in which the Same and the Other seem to converge.

Thus, a narration that started searching for a language appropriate to its arcane purposes ends up by putting into question the very notion of language and by disclosing its differential sameness—its own unstable, elusive and ambivalent signs. The text, after this tropological self-examination, can no longer maintain its linguistic coherency and prevent its total deconstruction. The poet has potentially two interchangeable possibilities: either to leave his work "unfinished" in order to accentuate its problematic language or to carry on determined to accept the consequences and thus to participate in the ambiguous game of signs. Each of these possibilities would require a particular sense of irony (as a rhetorical mode) and a deep-rooted suspicion of poetic conventions (a suspicion exceeding the thematic and formal aspects of writing)—attributes rather rare in Seferis' work. However, he opts out of both possibilities and, as if in a state of anxiety and uncertainty, retreats immediately to a safer and more familiar area from where he strives to ensure that the subject, language and mythology of the poem remain intact. We have seen how his attempt had been subverted by what he tried in vain to surpass, namely by the very figurality of language; but even so the stanza that follows this first part of the poem underlies a desire to save the text from the unpredictability of figuration by inserting the authoritative voice of the "creator."

Furthermore, in an effort to mitigate this temporal deviation from the language and thematic congruity of the text, Seferis returns, in the second part of the poem, to the abandoned metaphor of the "river" ("that symbol which moves forward") and resumes his narration as if nothing has happened in the meantime, as if no change had taken place in the text. And this time he manages to handle the trope ably and aptly as to its figurative entropy by converting it into a long series of new metaphors that offset the disturbing rhetorical antinomies. Like the "river," which by moving forward disappears into exotic linguistic landscapes, the self-reflexive trope is stripped of its allegorical power and stands bereft of its critical efficacy. Thus, the poem finds itself at the point of its departure, harboring all the images and symbols it tried to depart from, facing the same historical impasse it hoped to escape, and holding the frail metaphors of its failure to tell a story without, in the process, breaking it. But even these metaphors, with their consoling symbolism, do not suffice for retaining the unity of the text; the loose connection among the three main parts of the poem reintroduces a forgotten but still acting metonymy that achieves an ostensible totalization by contiguity.

Seferis's language favors metaphor, although sometimes he declares the opposite. Indeed, the more spectacular the metaphorical inventions are, the more vulnerable the poem becomes to the gaps and discontinuities of its contiguous "meaning." When the poem we are dealing with approaches its end, we find ourselves stranded again in a language "with so much music" that even the familiarity of the interpersonal "we" is not enough to shorten the distance between lyricism and verbosity:

> . . . we the patient dough of a world that
> throws us out and kneads us,
> caught in the embroidered nets of a life that was a
> whole and then became dust and sank into the sands
> leaving behind it only that vague dizzying sway of a
> tall palm-tree.

The whole poem, as it unfolds its movements of tropes, as it takes the shape of a river both always identical to itself and never the same, alludes to a totality as much desirable as it is unattainable. And it is in the middle of

this purposeless movement that the poet feels obliged to appear, leaving its hiding place and declaring his intentions in an effort to create a solid ground of reference and to reinstate his absolute authority, which has momentarily been lost in its own labyrinth. It is, at the same time, an attempt to dissociate himself from the uncontrolled proliferation of tropes, to disengage himself of a language emblazoned by the old insignia of poetic nobility, and to save the poem from its discursive inflation by interposing the assertive "I" of a responsible and knowing subject. The central stanza reveals a desire for directly addressing the voice of this subject to itself and to the reader—a gesture of self-assurance and warning. But it is precisely the centrality of this double assertion that makes the two long parts of the poem seem irrevocably broken; the cleavage caused by the intrusion of the subject appears to inform an unbridgeable void at the heart of the figurative movement. Within this void the subject denies what it continues to perform—namely, the excessive play of writing. When it renounces the overproduction of signifying structures and advocates an *economy* of written signs, it is already inseparably tied to the most exquisite rhetoric, a rhetoric that avoids the void by reintegrating the appearance of the self into the anonymous prolixity of figurality. The void, as an interruption of ornamental representation, is inhabited by the ghosts of language; it offers what it destroys, it becomes what it was never thought to be: "The representation of a rhetorical structure which, as such, escapes the control of the self" only in order "to reintroduce the authority of a self at the far end of the most radical negation" (de Man, 1979:172).

Whatever its discrepancies, contradictions and illusions, however self-critical or self-doubting, with all its hesitations, interrogations and expectations, Seferis' poetic language represents a compact idiom rooted to the tradition more than the poet is prepared to recognize in his writing. The occasional evocation of themes, sentiments and anxieties belonging to modernism remains marginal or is effaced by the innermost realization of historical priorities. What he negates is not a worn-out language but the main preoccupations of modernism: the violence of writing and the writing of violence, the torturing exile of the subject, the explosion of the signs, the reduction of nationalism and the unrestrained passion for extremities both in life and in art. Confronted with the void Seferis, like the old man on the river bank, wants only to speak "simply," recalls nostalgically the lost vocation of the poet-craftsman, longs for the few words necessary to justify death, to surpass death through the lesser language of language. But, as he is fascinated by his own yearning, surrendered to his dream of a poetry returning to the simplicity and purity of nature, he keeps forgetting that he is still speaking the harmful language of art. Seferis' dream is an old dream—it reflects the guilt for the separation from an original harmony, immediacy and identity. He is like those old men who fall half-asleep when reciting a story but, despite their apparent lack of articulation, continue the narration without realizing the dividing line that separates dream from reality. And the "reality" is that they never ceased speaking—that is, writing—inside and outside the dream. These old men are very fond of their childhood, which they strive to recover either in language or in a community with which they share their oddities.

If Seferis can be regarded as a modern poet it is only insofar as he circumscribes modernism in the horizon of his poetry, at the periphery of his symbolic rhetoric. In his poetry the poet, the subject, the notion of Greekness represent the impossibility of being modern, since there is always a memory that compensates by being ever present. Even when this presence consists of mutilated statues, dead or lost companions, ruins of a glorious past, empty symbols, historical catastrophes and existential voids, in general of significant absences, what is present in and of the absent and absent in and of the present constitutes a mythology that turns modernity into unaccomplished history. To say this means that one does not take Seferis' language at face value, that is, as conveying a "truth," a "reality" or an "inner thought." Rhetoric and history (or rather rhetoric in and of history) in Seferis supplement the desire for artistic innocence and linguistic deflation with an overflow of signs. It is through this necessity of the written word that the poet envisages an economy of signs, an impossible language that approaches the materiality of things in order to disappear in the literal world of essential needs. The only truth of such an endeavor is that "truth" remains constantly deferred or, more precisely, it gives in to what it tries to defeat, that is, to the falsity, deceptiveness and inauthenticity of poetic language. The humanist Seferis seems to be afraid of his modernity, which he tries to keep under control by resorting to the dreams of an unbroken, though misunderstood, tradition. His relation to European modernism is eventually transformed into a passion for an ideal *topos* (Greece) and an ideal medium (Greek language).

It is by no means surprising then (especially if we take into account the present state of Greek criticism) that most of his critics share with him the same values and ideas. Thus, for instance, two of them, commenting on the central stanza of the above poem, note:

> His relation to the concrete, which is mainly an artistic characteristic, may be one of the motives that prompted him to look for simplicity, a simplicity which is the substance of the object . . . without which the function of the existence is inconceivable. All he asks for is this

simplicity . . . because only this can save him from formlessness, schematization, and aimless versification [*stichographia*] . . . Seferis has indeed this grace of simplicity.

(Karandonis, 1963:215-6)

> Poetry and poetics together are this turn [in Seferis' writing]. And I hope that we agree that here Seferis accepts unreservedly the need for clarity and simplicity in expression and, particularly, in poetic language.

(Sinopoulos, 1972:52)

This longing for an original and thus pure art, for an Apollonian order within the expressive nature of language and for an economizing wisdom over death marks the concept of "Greekness" in Seferis. In this sense, to be Greek and modern is to experience a profound antinomy or, in other words, to make your modernity the touchstone of a transcendental "Greekness." Finally, to be Greek is to keep your modernity in constant exile. In fact, such a dichotomy offers a *via negativa* to confer "Greekness" upon modernity, to subsume the latter under the former.

* * *

The aspiration for a "simple" language, as it is expressed in the poem we have just analyzed, is closely related to another theme that prevails in his poetry—that of the "humble art." The ideal function of the poetic language consists in abandoning its elitist ambitions, its predisposition to exaggeration and arrogance. The poet is no more than a humble craftsman, a wordsmith by trade who manages, through hard work, to deliver his message; his skill is acknowledged only if he is able to say more without intensifying the complexity and density of the language, in other words, if he possesses the knowledge of being "simple" and "humble." The former indicates a restrictive economy of expression while the latter alludes to a moral consciousness that favors an aesthetics of poverty and guilt, a style that refrains from posing as such. As early as 1934 Seferis introduced the rhetoric of an unaffected style, of a style devoid of stylization:

> We brought back
> these carved reliefs of a humble art.

(*Mythistorema*, 1)

The poet seeks to recover an art not yet evicted from the paradise of things, an art without "so many charms and so many symbols" ("Siroco 7 Levante"). This utopic land does not know the difference between words and things, thought and action, nature and culture: it is a land where everything happens in its "natural" order. Reading (and by implication writing) do not disturb the unity of life and the poet's happy consciousness, for there is no artificial light to break the darkness and the silence of the night:

The evening would fall
the flocks would echo descending to their fold
like some quite simple happy thought
and I would lie down to sleep
because I wouldn't have
even a candle to light,
light,
to read.

("**Five Poems by Mr. S. Thalassinos**"; I. "**Hampstead**")

Seferis presents the poet as an individual who experiences the antinomies of a divided self. All his attempts toward purification and originality are doomed to failure: his companions bear their own destiny, "their oars / mark the place where they sleep on the shore. / No one remembers them. Justice" (**Mythistorema,** 4). His people are the anonymous mob of the poems, the cause of his loneliness and misery, a threatening chorus, ignorant of the enacted drama; his images of human life, of nature and of happiness are distorted by the sinful mediation of language. Yet, in spite of this awareness, the poet retains his hope for a collective redemption, for a communal justification, for a return to nature. Seferis is the modern poet, the educated European, who sacrifices his cosmopolitanism in order to secure a privileged place that would enable him to provide a tradition, a mythology and a utopia to an imaginary people. For this purpose he resorts to a poetics of popular themes and stereotypes while, at the same time, he tries to establish his modern idiom as a common language. The tension between these two contradictory aims of his poetics undermines constantly the effort to reach an ultimate affirmation of his Rousseauistic dreams. Seferis, the poet who "speaks humbly and calmly" ("**Upon a Foreign Verse**"), is very anxious about the future of his writing: the "humble art" is by no means inferior to its rivals—on the contrary, it is precisely through that "humbleness" that it pursues its glorification. Such an art is an art of memory that makes recourse to a lost originality, aiming at a reconciliation between life and writing; its target is to recuperate what has been consumed or dissimulated by writing. Nevertheless, this memory is bound to rediscover its past within its most artful future:

I imagine that he who'll rediscover life in spite of so
     much
paper, so many emotions, so many debates and so
     much
teaching, will be someone like us, only with a slightly
tougher memory. We ourselves can't help still
     remembering
what we've given. He'll remember only what he's
     gained
from each of his offerings.

("**Mr. Stratis Thalassinos Describes a Man**"; 5. "**Man**")

The future that Seferis envisions moves retrospectively in an effort to restore life and reality as the original sources of an art spontaneous and simple: a commodity of the real life. Or, in his metaphorical language:

I prefer a drop of blood to a glass of ink.

("**Notes For A Week**"; "**Sunday**")

Writing for him is an act of suffering, the difficult task of confronting "a blank piece of paper which he must overcome" (1976:56), a desperate attempt to become the servant of life:

Dawn finds us beside the tired lamp
drawing on paper, awkwardly, with effort,
ships mermaids or sea-shells;

(**Mythistorema,** 5)

It is this melancholic nostalgia of the artist who has no other choice than to write even when he is suspicious of writing that makes Seferis unhappy: he has no other alternative than "to draw up idols and ornaments" (ibid., 2) in spite of the menacing void he has invented as a point of silent happiness. It is somewhere here that we can trace the root of the anti-intellectualism of the most intellectual of contemporary Greek poets:

Life has ruined us, along with Attic skies and the
intellectuals clambering up their own heads.

("**Letter of Mathios Paskalis**")

The "humble art"[5] is Seferis' escape from modernism, an escape toward an illusory nation, society and culture. But if he failed to become the craftsman he was dreaming of, he succeeded in becoming the only possible modern poet for a nation that has never recovered from its failure to understand history as such, a nation still searching "for the other life / beyond the statues" (**Mythistorema,** 5).

Seferis' poetic mythology then, which, in the form of a fairy tale, would offer to the national community a didactic narration of past glories and hardships (the dream of the never-never land of Hellas) should be considered not as a literal statement of a suffering individual, but as an elaborate poetic strategy that bestows on his poems an exquisite, though somehow monotonous, rhetoric. His work thereby should be regarded neither as a monument for national admiration nor as a masterpiece for critical servility, but as an opportunity for varied interpretative games that would invigorate the act of reading and liberate meaning from its closure: "The act of understanding is a temporal act that has its own history, but this history forever eludes totalization" (de Man, 1971: 32).

Without taking into account the irreversibly lost intentions of the poet, the enfeebled authority of his name and the irretrievably dissipated meaning of his language, the rhetorical reading opens a new space within which the poem is adopted by the critical praxis and thus is endlessly recreated by new modes of signification.

From this perspective, Seferis' poems cannot be considered as "offering insights that carry with them the weight of universal truths" or as serving "to retreat the deeper meaning of our times" (Keeley and Sherrard, 1969: xiii), but rather as rhetorical constructions amenable to change and exploitation. Defined in this way, poetry is liable to perpetual deconstruction—and, of course, so is criticism. According to de Man:

> The critical function of deconstruction is not to blur distinctions but to identify the power of linguistic figuration as it transforms differences into oppositions, analogies, contiguities, reversals, crossings, and any other of the relationships that articulate the textual field of tropes and of discourse. Hence the distinctively critical . . . function of texts, literary or other, with regard to aesthetic, ethical, epistemological, and practical judgements they are bound to generate."
>
> (1982: 510-1)

If such a rhetorical reading, as practiced here, seems incompatible with Seferis' poetry, it is appropriate to answer by invoking the poet himself: "There is no artist who has given the authentic interpretation of his work. Because even if there was one, he would have been able to prevent nothing" (1976:57).

To conclude: we cannot deprive writing of its future and authorize interpreters for our intentions; moreover, we do not have the power to eternalize meaning by incriminating the language. Let therefore rhetoric be the name for an interpretive expedition: at the end of the journey we realize, once more, that the fearful white whale of meaning is nothing but a figure of writing traveling through the centuries in different texts and encountering, in various disguises, its persistent hunters.

Notes

1. "The poetry of George Seferis, whatever it may have to the literature of other countries, stems first of all from a tradition that is eminently Greek" (Keeley and Sherrard, 1969: v).

2. See, for instance, the structuralist analysis of Seferis' poetry proposed by Kapsomenos (1975); a work which, in spite of its shortcomings, could have been fruitful, if Greek criticism was not so indifferently provincial.

3. "The artificial that gives us the impression of the artificial is . . . bad art" (1976: 67).

4. ". . . there is no distinction between form and essence in art" (1976: 201).

5. In a naive comment on this concept in Seferis' poetry, one of his critics writes: "For Seferis' poetic logic the expression of a *humble art* has the meaning of an art made by humble people" (Argyriou, 1980: 39-40).

References

ARGYRIOU, ALEXANDROS (1980). "Giorgos Seferes: Poietike Techne ke Istoria," in *Kyklos Sefere* (Athens: Etaireia Spoudon Moraiti) 9-102.

DE MAN, PAUL (1971). *Blindness and Insight: Essays in the Rhetoric of Contemporary Criticism* (New York: Oxford University Press).

———(1978). "The Epistemology of Metaphor," *Critical Inquiry* 5:1, 13-30.

———(1979). *Allegories of Reading* (New Haven: Yale University Press).

———(1982). "A Letter from Paul de Man," *Critical Inquiry* 8:3, 509-13.

EAGLETON, TERRY (1982). "Frederic Jameson: The Politics of Style," *Diacritics* 12:3, 14-22.

KAPSOMENOS, E. G. (1975). *E Syntaktike Dome tes Poietikes Glossas tou Sefere* (Salonica).

KARANDONIS, ANDREAS (1963). *O Poietes Giorgos Seferes* (Athens: Galaxias).

KEELEY, EDMUND, and SHERRARD, PHILIP (1969). "Foreword," in *George Seferis: Collected Poems, 1924-1955* (London: Jonathan Cape) v-xiii.

KELLNER, HANS (1981). "The Inflatable Trope as Narrative Theory: Structure or Allegory?" *Diacritics* 11:1, 14-28.

SEFERIS, GEORGE (1969). *Collected Poems, 1924-1955,* trs. E. Keeley and P. Sherrard (London: Jonathan Cape).

———(1976). *Dokimes,* vol. 1 (Athens: Ikaros).

SINOPOULOS, TAKIS (1972). "To 'kleisto' ke to 'anoichto' poiema ston Sefere," in *Vradia Sefere* (Athens: Kedros) 42-55.

STEINER, GEORGE (1980). "Preface," in *On Difficulty and Other Essays* (Oxford: Oxford University Press) ix-xi.

C. Capri-Karka (essay date 1985)

SOURCE: Capri-Karka, C. "*Logbook I.*" In *War in the Poetry of George Seferis: A Poem-by-Poem Analysis,* pp. 81-104. New York: Pella Publishing Company, 1985.

[*In the following excerpt, Capri-Karka examines the poems of Seferis's* Logbook I, *written just before World War II and dealing with the poet's feelings of foreboding regarding the coming war.*]

Unlike *Logbook II* and *Logbook III,* which were actually written outside of Greece and thus their title is appropriate on the literal level, most of the poems of *Log-*

book I were written in Greece in the years 1937-1940—with the exception of the first two or three poems of the collection, which were written in Korytsa, Albania, where Seferis was serving as a Greek consul. Thus, the title must refer to a metaphorical journey, the psychological wandering of the narrator who feels unsettled, living in a place where he does not belong, on a temporary basis, always in suspense. In this sense, *Logbook I* is a continuation of *Mythistorema,* which was permeated by a similar feeling. The difficulty of adjusting to a new environment, especially when one knows that his homeland has been completely destroyed and it will never be possible to return to it, is conveyed in one of the poems of this collection, **"The Return of the Exile,"** which was mentioned before.[1]

There is, however, another reason for suspense during this period, which concerns the future rather than the past—the approach of World War II. There is only a hint of this suspense in the epigraph of the collection, "'Hove-to. Awaiting instructions.' *Log Books,* passim," but the shadow of the war is unmistakably present in several of the poems of *Logbook I,*[2] especially in **"Our own Sun"** and **"The Last Day."** There is also a hint in **"Morning,"** where the perspective is dark, the horizon being covered with a black cloth although nature is in bloom. In his *Journals* of the same period, he refers to the Greeks of his time as "the generation of darkness"[3] and describes quite explicitly his thoughts on the subject of the impending war. As early as 1935 he speaks of "the other war that is coming"[4] as a certainty and the references become more frequent every year, as the beginning of World War II draws nearer.

The last three poems of *Logbook I* were written after World War II had started in Europe but before it had reached Greece. In two of them, in addition to the personal level, there are references to war: **"Les anges sont blancs"** expresses an unusual attitude toward the war, probably originating from a discussion of the poet with Henry Miller, while the **"Decision to Forget"** includes a prophetic image of the Aryan invasion of Greece.

"Our Own Sun" (1938)

In some of the poems written in the late thirties we see unmistakable signs of the approach of the Second World War. An important and, in a way, prophetic poem of this period is **"Our Own Sun,"** in which the themes of love and war are blended; Seferis presents war as the other side of the sun. In his symbolic language the sun has two sides: one is the light, which represents life, love and peace, but behind the light, on the other side, lurks darkness, death, war.

The relation of love and war is presented differently in every stanza of the poem. In the beginning there are parallel images that gradually converge and finally merge at the end of the poem.

In the first stanza, life has a bright side, the two people who share the sun, share love, are happy and do not suspect the dark side of the sun.

> This sun was mine and it was yours: we shared it.
> Who is in pain behind the golden curtain? Who is dy-
>   ing?
> A women cried out, beating her dry breasts: "Cowards,
> They have taken my children and torn them into
>   pieces.
>
> You killed them, looking in the evening at the fire-
>   flies
> With that strange look, lost in blind contemplation."
> Green light of a tree on a hand where blood was dry-
>   ing;
> A sleeping warrior grasping a lance that flared against
>   his side.

The image of the "Green light of a tree on a hand where blood was drying" suggests the continuity of life, which follows the laws of transformation. Nature goes on, indifferent, and is renewed regardless of individual deaths. The point Seferis wants to make here is the contrast between a man who is dying a senseless violent death and nature, which keeps on blooming around him. The woman accusing the men personifies the creative power that gives life; she reproaches men as warriors who take lives.

In the second stanza, the messengers arrive breathless and dirty, bringing the news about the impending catastrophe. They have been traveling for "Twenty days and nights" without stop; but the two lovers do not understand them. The message is for them "unintelligible words."

> This sun was ours. We saw nothing behind the gold
>   embroidery.
>
> Later the messengers came, breathless and dirty,
> Stammering out unintelligible words.

There is a prophetic tone in the warning of the messengers "We have no time," if one considers that these lines were written in the late thirties, when time was running short for peace in Europe and the menace of World War II was approaching.

> You told them to rest first and talk afterwards;
> The light had blinded you.
> They died saying "We have no time"; some rays of
>   sun they touched.
> You had forgotten that no one ever rests.

They don't have time because war is near, death is approaching. They die touching "some rays of the sun," trying to grasp, for a brief moment, life and love. The line "You had forgotten that no one ever rests" is very crucial because what it implies epitomizes the whole meaning of the poem: catastrophe and death can strike at any time, but people are unaware of it until they face it. The stanza

A woman howled "Cowards!" Like a dog in the night.
She must have once been beautiful as you,
With moist lips, living veins beneath the skin,
With love—

makes the same point in a different manner, by hinting at the fact that the unhappy mother crying for her slaughtered children was also a beautiful woman in love a little earlier and now she has been struck by disaster—as the happy lover may be some day. This brings in echoes of Cavafy's "Theodotos," where Pompeius' slaughter is presented not as a rare or unique event but as the kind of tragedy that can strike anyone at any time:

> And don't be too sure that in your life—
> restricted, regulated, prosaic—
> spectacular and horrible things like that don't happen.

Catastrophe lurks everywhere and love and happiness can suddenly be wiped out by death and war.

In the last stanza of the poem the polarity of love and war becomes explicit.

> This sun was ours; you kept it all; you did not want to
>   follow me.
> And then I learned these things behind the golden
>   curtain.
> We have no time. The messengers were right.

The protagonist becomes aware of the dark side of life when the person whom he loves abandons him. The relation between the two people changes. The one lover "keeps the sun" and does not want to share love anymore; he becomes a tormentor. There is a usurper and a victim in love, just as in war. Only when struck by disaster does the protagonist remember the words of the messengers: "we have no time."

The idea of a messenger "stammering out" "unintelligible" words—an ominous warning whose meaning is understood only when it is too late—is found, in a more explicit form, in the poet's *Journals*. In a comment about Cavafy, Seferis suggests that the Alexandrian poet was such a messenger whose warnings, had Hitler listened to him, could have prevented some of the catastrophes of World War II.

> He departed from our world at a time when the last act of our drama had ended: catastrophe was upon us. He was an exhausted, bent old man, mumbling about images he used to see in Alexandria. Very few listened to him and fewer understood his unintelligible muttering. What else but muttering, amid the massive hubbub of autarchical Europe, could the broadsides, which he printed at Kasimatis' and Ionas' printing shop be? It is not surprising that no one heard him. Great men vanished amidst those vociferations. He was a messenger, however. Had Hitler listened to him, what the Chancellery of Berlin saw in the last days of April 1945 would not have taken place. But what Caesar reads the writings of Artemidorus the Grammarian?[5]

The reference to Artemidoros the Grammarian is an allusion to Cavafy's "The Ides of March,"[6] which is very relevant to the context of this passage. Artemidoros tried to warn Caesar about the assassination plot against him, but Caesar did not realize the urgency of his message. Seferis pays a high tribute to Cavafy by suggesting that the wisdom of history conveyed in his poetry could have influenced the most powerful man in Europe of that time.

"The Last Day" (1939)

"The Last Day," with its gloomy atmosphere, conveys epigrammatically the agony and the depressing feeling of the approach of the Second World War. The title itself implies the sense of an imminent loss; it is the last day of happiness, the termination of a way of life, the end of the times of peace. The poem was not included in the original edition of *Logbook I*; Seferis added it in a later edition, with the date "February 1939." As he explains in his *Journals* he couldn't include it in the collection "because of the censorship."[7] It should be remembered that at that time, Greece, like Germany and Italy, was under a dictatorship.

The atmosphere of gloom and death is established from the opening lines, "The day was cloudy"; the sea was grey and the landscape was dominated by "A few slim cypresses nailed on the slope." Cypress is the traditional tree of Greek cemeteries and usually symbolizes death. "A funeral march moved by in the thin rain." Among all this "The troops were presenting arms as it started to drizzle." The presentation of arms is symbolic of the coming war. Seferis repeats three times (in the Greek original) that no one could come to a decision. This indecision is characteristic of the depressing feeling created by the approach of the war, which nobody seems to be able to stop. It also reveals a lot about the people waiting for the war. They are not making plans for attack or defense—they are overwhelmed by the events and unable to react to them. They know that the day after this "last day" the war is going to start, but they just sit idle, talking about the wind.

> "The wind is not north-east; it is south-east—";
> That was the only definite thing that was heard.
> And yet we knew that tomorrow there would be left
>   to us
> Nothing at all, not even the woman beside us drinking
>   sleep,
> Not even the memory that once we were men,
> By tomorrow's dawn nothing at all any more. . . .
>
> Tomorrow there would be left to us nothing at all,—
> Everything surrendered, . . .

The use of the wind in the first lines of the poem may have symbolic connotations. In Greece a wind from the north is usually violent and destructive while the south wind is warmer and milder. During the days before the onset of World War II, people and even government officials in Greece were trying to guess whether some minor event or gesture in the European political scene would have favorable or unfavorable implications for the country's possible involvement. Thus, on the symbolic level the guessing about the wind corresponds to a decision on whether the storm of the war (the strong north wind) was indeed approaching or not. What Seferis is suggesting here is that the decision that the wind was southeast—and therefore favorable—was wrong, since the war was unavoidable and catastrophe imminent. This attitude of unjustified optimism, which Seferis often refers to as "ostrich tactics,"[8] is a natural reaction of people in difficult times, but it was also characteristic of the government circles in Greece in those days. They did not want to believe that Greece would be dragged into the approaching war, although for Seferis and other far-sighted people this seemed inevitable.

This interpretation of the symbolic meaning of the wind in this poem is reinforced by the repetition of the motif in the poem **"Ayianapa II,"** subtitled "Spring 1156," where the wind is again a wind of war and destruction:

> This is no Palm Sunday wind
> no wind of Resurrection
> but a wind of fire, a wind of smoke,
> a wind of joyless life.[9]

The motif of the "favorable" wind continues in the second stanza of the **"Last Day,"** where a woman says that the wind "reminds" her of the spring, which in symbolic terms implies that she is optimistic, although she is obviously wrong. The same woman appears again near the end of the poem singing a song that refers to the spring:

> The light was sinking from the clouded day. No one
>   made up his mind.
> Tomorrow there would be left to us nothing at all,—
> Everything surrendered,—not even our hands,
> And our women working for strangers at the water
>   springs,
> Our children at the quarries.[10]
> My friend, walking beside me, was singing a snatch
>   of song
> "In spring, in summer, slaves . . ."

This fragment, "In spring, in summer, slaves . . ." is sufficient for any Greek reader to recognize the song. It is a song that the Greeks used to sing before the War of Independence of 1821 in order to overcome the despair of slavery: "Only this one more spring, this summer, will we be slaves, and then Russia will come, with its armies . . ." For many decades the nation was nurturing the unrealistic belief that the great Christian power would help them liberate themselves from the Turks. In the context of the **"Last Day"** the song suggests again

the perpetuation of false hopes. The allusion to slavery and liberation in this song fragment at a time of dictatorship and on the eve of a hopeless war has some ironic overtones. In times of hardship people often are under the illusion that very soon, the following spring, their ordeal will be over. Yet, as Seferis suggests in the very next poem, **"Spring A.D."** which starts with the line "Again with the spring," the conflict between the aggressor and the victim is always the prevailing pattern.[11]

After presenting in the beginning of the poem how people try to repress the thought of war or think about it with a paralyzing indecision, the poet raises a simple question in protest against the fatalistic acceptance of war as an inevitable fact:

> How does a man die? Strange that no one thought of
>   this.
> Or if one did, it was as a recollection from ancient
>   chronicles,
> The Crusades, perhaps, or the sea-battle fought at
>   Salamis.
> And yet death is a thing that happens. How does a
>   man die?

War is such a common and frequent event in human history that people tend to think it cannot be avoided, and they overlook how terribly it can affect their lives. By the simple words "And yet death is a thing that happens. How does a man die?" the poet reacts against this fatalistic attitude. He is making an appeal: he is asking people to think seriously about death, not as an abstract idea—"a recollection from ancient chronicles"—but as an overwhelming reality. Only by considering the horror of an individual death might one be led to realize that war is absurd and that it should not be accepted passively as something inevitable.

The first mention of the subject of one's death is in the second stanza when the woman asks the question "How shall we die?" The way one dies is a recurring motif in Seferis' poems and *Journals*. It appears in **"Santorin"**:

> When there is no longer any choice
> Of the death you wanted as your own.

In the **"Last Day"** it appears again in the third stanza:

> And yet one wins one's death, which is one's own
>   and nobody else's,
> And this kind of game is life.

The meaning of this choice of the way one dies becomes clearer when this passage is compared to a variation of the poem that appears as a fragment in the poet's *Journals* written a little earlier.

> And suddenly the moment comes for you to choose
>   this or that
> and suddenly the spring comes and then again in the
>   summer

we are slaves, breathing in the dusk with incoherent
    dreams in our heads
as our women work for strangers at the water springs.[12]

The implications of these passages are wider than the death of a simple individual and may refer also to the nation as a whole.[13] At the time the poem was written it appeared almost certain that the Axis would eventually occupy Greece, and the question in Seferis' mind was whether his country would simply surrender or try to defend itself as long as it could. As Greece was under a dictatorial regime, many—and Seferis among them—feared that this regime would not choose to fight a takeover by the forces of the Axis and especially Germany. This would be equivalent to a disgraceful death, whereas occupation after a courageous resistance would be an honorable one—and this is most probably the choice of death the poet had in mind.

The atmosphere that Seferis created from the beginning of the poem, by depicting the eve of the war as a cloudy, rainy day and with the funeral march and the cypresses foretelling a catastrophe, becomes even more depressing in the last three lines, in which the darkness of night is falling, symbolizing again the approach of the war.

A couple passed us, talking,
"I am sick and tired of the dusk, Let's go.
Let us go home now and turn on the light."

In these lines he has captured the prevailing mood among so many sensitive Europeans of that period: a despair over the gloomy outlook of the external world and, as a reaction, a tendency to withdraw—in other words, what was later to be known as alienation.

"Les Anges Sont Blancs" (1939)

War is only one of the themes of **"Les anges sont blancs,"** blended with those of love and artistic creation. The treatment of war is rather unusual, one might even say paradoxical, because it is not presented as a conflict of interests or of violent passions but rather as the result of a gradual deterioration of life to the point where people do not care about anything and kill each other indifferently, without emotion.

The poem is dedicated to Henry Miller and has as an epigraph a line from Balzac's autobiographical novel *Louis Lambert.* The connection between Miller and Balzac in Seferis' mind can be better understood by reference to his *Journals,* where the poet, who knew the American writer personally, quotes a passage from Miller's notes about Balzac.[14] Certain parts of this passage, Seferis suggests, should be compared with the *Tropic of Cancer.*[15] The passage refers to the decay of the "Parisian civilization" that Louis Lambert observed; Miller adds that "the death and disintegration Balzac

sensed over a century ago, has only heightened since then." Miller also writes that "Today every great city of the world stinks to high heaven and it is from this death of the world that an artist is obliged to draw his inspiration."[16] Thus, the common element is that both Balzac and Miller experienced and wrote about the disintegration of life.

Seferis starts the poem with the image of his protagonist, who "Like a sailor in the shrouds . . . slipped over the tropic of Cancer and the tropic of Capricorn." This allusion to Miller suggests a similarity with his persona in the two "Tropic" books; it implies a chaotic wandering amidst the deterioration and decay of the big cities (Paris in "Cancer" and New York in "Capricorn") and a loss of equilibrium. Seferis' protagonist cannot stand "at a man's height" but constantly alternates between two extreme levels, "from the height of a fire-fly" to the "height of a pine tree" or from "the dew of the stars" to the "dust of the earth." The presence of the "Naked women" surrounding the protagonist seems to suggest that this loss of balance, as in the case of Miller's persona, is not unrelated to his obsession with sex.[17] Also, the mention of the Centaurs (half-human, half-animals) alludes, most probably, to the grotesque way in which Miller often approaches sexuality.[18]

The surrealistic image that follows a few lines later, when the narrator says that the protagonist "greeted us / taking his head off and placing it on the iron table," implies man's disintegration. The narrator places the scene at about the time "the shape of Poland changed like ink drunk by blotting-paper," in other words the beginning of World War II.

The poem continues with an image of people killing each other as if they were sleepwalking, and this is followed by an identification of sleep with death and an emphasis on silence.

and the whole sky, empty and white, was a pigeon's
    huge wing beating with a rhythm of silence
and dolphins beneath the colored water turned dark
    quickly like the soul's movements
like movements of the imagination and the hands of
    men who grope and kill [each other] in sleep
in the huge unbroken rind of sleep that wraps around
    us, common to all of us, our common grave
                    . . . . .

And yet everything was white because the great sleep
    is white and the great death
calm and serene and isolated in an endless silence.
And the cackling of the guinea-hen at dawn and the
    cock that crowed falling into a deep well.[19]

This image of war between sleepwalkers makes more sense when one reads in Seferis' *Journals* the poet's discussion with Miller when the American writer visited Greece in 1939. Seferis writes that one night they started talking about the war, and he himself mentioned "the feeling one sometimes has that everything is happening as if in sleep, as if we were sleepwalkers." "Yes, it is curious," Miller answered. "In Paris some years ago, noticing how life every day becomes more abstract, we were saying with a friend: People will end up killing each other without realizing it. This is what is happening now."[20]

This idea of war as a fight between sleepwalkers appears again in one of Seferis' essays about a book by Artemidorus (second century A.D.) on dream interpretation. He writes that the most profound oneirocritic comment he knows is one by Heraclitus, quoted by Marcus Aurelius (6:42): "I think Heraclitus says that even sleepers are workers and cooperators in the things that take place in the world"; and Seferis continues:

> I always kept in mind these words; at the time slaughter was being prepared; and at the time of the great crisis—I don't know if it is over. I kept seeing those "sleepers," armed with the most infernal means, eliminate each other without waking up and . . .
>
> [Men's] hands groping and killing [each other] in their sleep
> inside the huge rind of sleep . . .
>
> as I was writing at that time. And I kept wondering, persistently, with how much waking and how much sleepwalking does humankind handle what takes place in the world. I found the sleepwalking to be a lot and the waking little. It is in this small part of our life, the waking dreams, that our nightmares have been transposed.[21]

The image of war is followed by another image, that of the protagonist lying in bed with fever, hallucinating or dreaming of people fighting and striking each other with axes and with their nails, without bleeding. This lack of blood implies a blunted sensitivity but also the kind of sterility Eliot alludes to in *The Waste Land*. The protagonist tortures himself with memories of the past when he sees his friends deep in the bottom of the sea; they are locked behind a door that does not open and they knock loudly, in great despair, and he sees himself as being with them.

> knowing nothing any longer among the white eyeballs of the blind and the sheets
> that you unfolded in fever to cover the daily procession
> of people who fail to bleed even when they strike [each other] with axes and nails;
> they were things isolated, put somewhere else, and the steps of whitewash
> descended to the threshold of the past and found silence and the door didn't open
> and it was as if your friends, in great despair, knocked loudly and you were with them
> but you heard nothing and dolphins rose around you dumbly in the seaweed.

The poem ends with the words of a man with "the teeth-marks of the tropics in his skin," which by allusion again to Miller's two books must be the wounds of a hedonist, who was "putting on his dark glasses as if he were going to work with a blowlamp"—an implication of the spectacle of the flaming angels he is about to introduce. Seferis starts the last section of the poem with the line "The angels are white," which brings into the poem Louis Lambert's dream-like situation, a state of catalepsy induced by the sight of the angels. In order to understand the implications of this sentence, which is of great importance for the poem since it is part of the epigraph—and also, in its original French version, the title of the poem—one must refer to Balzac's novel and the circumstances under which these words were uttered by its protagonist.

Louis Lambert is a young man with a rare and powerful mind who, from a very early age, detached himself from the world of everyday pursuits, searching out mysterious regions of abstract thought. When he falls in love with a young woman and is about to marry her he goes mad. He first falls into a state of catalepsy for three days; when he recovers, he is terrified and profoundly melancholic—he believes himself impotent and considers self-mutilation. The doctors pronounce his condition incurable and he dies a few years later. He spends the last years of his life under the care of the woman he loved, not recognizing anyone and speaking incoherently, except for some brief intervals of lucidity. His companion writes down some of his thoughts, which are appended to the novel as "Fragments." When the narrator, his childhood friend, visits Lambert after several years of separation, he finds him silent, mechanically rubbing his legs against each other. Suddenly, however, he stops this movement and says only: "Les anges sont blancs."

In his *Journals,* Seferis, right after the quotation from Miller's notes, quotes a line from *Louis Lambert* that provides us with a clue as to the meaning of the poem's ending, and this in turn throws some light on the whole poem. The line he quotes is "Cet X où je me suis autrefois heurté," taken from passage 8 of the fragments at the end of the novel, which are supposed to be the summing up of Lambert's studies and thoughts. In this passage, Louis Lambert writes that man is composed of thought and will, but then he adds that "there is in man a primal and controlling phenomenon which admits of no analysis. Decompose man," he writes, "to the utmost, and we may perhaps discover the elements of Thought and of Will, but we shall also find, without being able to solve it, the unknown quantity, that X against which I vainly flung myself in earlier days. This X is the LOGOS whose touch burns and destroys all such as are not prepared to receive it. It ceaselessly engenders SUBSTANCE."[22]

In view of this fragment, and especially of the line quoted by Seferis in his *Journals,* one can come to the conclusion that when he writes "The angels are white," adding that at the sight of the angels one's eye shrivels and he then turns into stone, he alludes to Lambert's disintegration in the face of love. What destroyed Lambert was the lack of the "factor X," the Logos. In its absence there could be no balance and "the life of the soul had annihilated the life of the body."[23] A similar lack of balance[24] can be seen in Miller's persona, who counteracted a traumatic erotic experience with a relentless pursuit of loveless sexual encounters. In Miller's own words, "Whoever, through too great love, which is monstrous after all, dies in his misery, is born again to know neither love nor hate, but to enjoy. And this joy of living, because it is unnaturally acquired, is a poison which eventually vitiates the whole world. Whatever is created beyond the normal limits of human suffering, acts as a boomerang and brings about destruction."[25]

The reference to the angels applies not only to Lambert's situation in Balzac's novel and indirectly to Miller's conception of love, but also to Seferis' persona. In order to appreciate this aspect it is necessary to trace the motif of angels throughout his poetry. Angels in Seferis are almost always associated with love, but while sometimes they are good, more often they are evil. In Greek the word "ἄγγελος" means both angel and messenger, and the word is sometimes used with dual meaning, especially in some of the early poems. Angels are often mentioned in connection with a "miracle" or the "Second Coming," but these terms are used in a secular sense.

In one of the earliest poems, **"Fog,"** angels are invoked in love songs and cause suffering while the protagonist sees their love as a trap he is happy to avoid. In **"Comments,"** the protagonist is attracted by a woman and wonders, in despair, why the miracle of love cannot take place and the angel that would bring it about never approaches. In the **"Mood of a Day,"** a happy erotic moment vanishes "like an angel of the Lord." Near the end of **"Erotikos Logos"** (**"Love Song"**), the protagonist waits "On the stone of patience" for the miracle that would "open the heavens"; he waits "for the [angel] as in the ancient drama." In the poem **"Hampstead,"** on the other hand, the phantasmagoria of love does not last and the metamorphosis of three thousand dancing angels "naked as steel" into a forgotten dog searching "for its master / or the Second Coming / or a bone" suggests a tyrannical love. In "Man," the last section of **"Stratis the Sailor Describes a Man,"** the protagonist gives up any hope for a miracle or "Second Coming" associated with love. And in the section **"Monday"** of the **"Notes for a Week,"** there is again a suggestion of a tyrannical relation as the angels, like vampires, run naked in the veins of the sleeping protagonists, "drink their blood and make them prudent." The Second Com-

ing is invoked again in **"Raven,"** this time by "suspended passions." This emphasis on passions rather than a person implies that love has permeated all existence and has become a torment. A similar situation revealing a destructive passion is suggested in the poem **"Interval of Joy,"** at the end of which an archangel is seen "exercising with a fiery sword" while one of the lovers watching him comments that the whole thing is inexplicable; he finds "people impossible to understand. / Play with the colours as they will, they all are black,"[26] implying the dark forces hidden inside man.

Finally, another dangerous angel appears in the short poem **"We Got out of the Walls,"**[27] written later than those mentioned above, which alludes to Cavafy's "Trojans." Unlike Cavafy's persona in that poem, Seferis' protagonist has overcome his fears and gotten out of the walls. However, in Seferis' poem the angel is the potential enemy outside, as in the "Trojans" it was Achilles. The fact that the "angel with the golden heels" dressed his nakedness with a blue flutter of wings implies that, in this case, for Seferis' protagonist the temptation has ceased to exist.

One can see from this very brief account of the way angels appear in Seferis' poetry that the poet's attitude—although ambivalent, to some extent, from the very beginning—reveals a gradual shift from the expectation or at least the possibility of a "miracle" brought about by the angels to an ominous situation where the angels are threatening, trapping and torturing man, and the "miracle" is impossible without a destruction, without the "scattering" of one's "blood to the eight points of the wind."

> "The angels are white flaming white and the eye that
>   would confront them shrivels
> and there's no other way you've got to become like
>   stone if you want their company
> and when you look for the miracle you've got to scatter your blood to the eight points of the wind
> because the miracle is nowhere but circulating in the
>   veins of man."

The miracle itself has undergone a transformation. In the earlier poems it was associated with love, while in **"Les anges sont blancs"** love burns and destroys those who are not ready to receive it and, ironically, the only miracle left is the artistic creation that can come from the disintegration of the artist's life.[28] Here again Miller's notes, quoted by Seferis, refer explicitly to this process: after writing that "from this death of the world the artist is obliged to draw his inspiration," Miller quotes a passage from Whitman's "Democratic Vistas":

> America has yet morally and artistically originated nothing . . . In the future of these states must arise poets immense far, and make great *poems of death.* The poems of life are great, but there must be the poems of the purport of life, not only in itself, but beyond itself . . .[29]

It is right after this quotation that Seferis inserts in his *Journals* the line from *Louis Lambert* mentioned earlier about the factor X, Logos, implying that this Logos is "the purport of life" to which Whitman refers. This is a very crucial point for the explication of the poem.

Thus, what Seferis is trying to do in **"Les anges sont blancs"** is to draw a parallel between the situation of the people who kill each other in war like sleepwalkers, the torpor of the protagonist who lives in a state of psychological arrest, obsessed with memories of the past, and the state of catalepsy of those who, like Lambert, have lost their balance, in order to suggest that life declines and disintegrates in all three of these situations because of the absence of the Logos.

The "Decision to Forget" (1939)

In the **"Decision to Forget,"** one of his most enigmatic symbolic poems, Seferis employs an unusual technique in order to convey human conflict and the horror of war. A serene landscape of a lake in which white swans glide changes suddenly to a sinister image of birds slaughtering people.

The main symbol of the poem is the swan. The motif of the swan has been used by Seferis in other poems, such as *Mythistorema,* **"Helen,"** **"Stratis the Sailor Describes a Man"** and *Three Secret Poems,* but it receives a more extensive treatment here. As in the case of several other recurring symbols in Seferis' poetry— the light, the sun, the sea—there is a dual quality also in the swan. He uses it as a symbol of beauty but also of destructiveness.

In his *Journals* Seferis specifically mentions that he uses the swan as a cruel being.[30] There are certain precedents in ancient Greek mythology and tragedy for this treatment of the swan. According to the myth, Cygnus (swan) was the son of Mars, the god of war; he was the King of Amphanae and used to kill passing strangers by forcing them into a duel that he always won, until he was himself defeated and killed by Hercules. It has been suggested that underlying this myth is the practice of human sacrifices in prehistoric Thessaly, which was discontinued with the spread of the worship of Apollo.[31] Another legend, which is mentioned in Aeschylus' *Prometheus Bound,* is that of the swan-shaped monsters Forcys,[32] sisters of the snake-haired Gorgons.

Seferis is making use of the dual meaning of the swan to suggest a connection between beauty and love on the one hand and destructiveness and war on the other. Zeus was metamorphosed into a beautiful swan to make love to Leda; Helen, who was born from this union, became the cause of war and of the destruction of Troy. Yeats in his "Leda and the Swan" parallels the ravishing of Leda to the destruction of Troy. The subject is discussed more in connection with the poem **"Helen."**

In the **"Decision to Forget"** both sides of the swan, the beautiful and the destructive, are presented. In the first three stanzas the beautiful predominates: a still lake, the swans "all white" with "still wings" gliding on its surface as if they don't even touch it. Yet this beauty is blended with the stillness of death.[33] There are also a few hints of the ominous to follow, like the fact that the swans are gliding "on a thin blade" or the line "as the stony eyes of the lions stare at you," which suggests an imminent danger.[34]

The picture of serenity changes suddenly to one of horror and destruction in the fourth and fifth stanzas.

> And yet the birds that slaughtered the village girls
>   were none other than these
> the blood reddened the milk on the flagstones
> and their horses cast noiselessly like molten lead
> illegible shapes into the troughs.
>
> And night suddenly tightened around their arched
>   necks
> which didn't sing because there was no way to die
> but beat, threshing men's bones blindly.
> And their wings cooled the horror.

It is quite evident that Seferis in the fourth stanza is no longer speaking about the swans as birds, but about the symbolic counterparts of their destructive side, some unspecified human invaders, slaughtering innocent village girls. In the fifth stanza he returns to the birds, speaking of their necks and their wings, but what they do, "threshing men's bones," could hardly be attributed to real birds.

The metamorphosis of the swans is so sudden and so horrible that their symbolic meaning is not easy to decipher. On the personal level, which predominates in this poem, the invaders are most probably the hunters in the hunter-victim situation that Seferis sees often in human relationships. On a more general level, there is another interpretation first proposed by the critic Nora Anagnostaki in an essay devoted primarily to this poem.[35] She suggests that the beautiful but cruel swans, with their arched necks turned to sickles threshing men's bones, represent the Aryan race, the Germans who had at that time started to invade the rest of Europe. The poem was published in December 1939 and was therefore written at a time when "the shape of Poland changed like ink drunk by blotting-paper," as Seferis writes in another poem.[36] War had not yet reached Greece, but in retrospect this horrible image is prophetic of what was to come. The swans would be an ideal symbol for the arrogant Aryan race. The landscape of the lake with the swans has something that brings to mind northern European mythology.

Swans are birds of the north, and Seferis has written in another poem that on a journey to the north the "immaculate wings of swans . . . wounded us."[37] The transformation of people into swans is part of German folk tales,[38] where swan-knights and swan-maidens appear very often; Lohengrin, the hero of one of the oldest and most widely known medieval legends, is known as the "knight of the swan." Thus, it is not unlikely that Seferis, who as a diplomat must have sensed quite early what Nazi Germany meant for Europe, used these handsome but cruel creatures to symbolize the German invaders, at least on one level of this poem.

As far as the central idea of the poem, as expressed in the title of the poem, is concerned, the motif of forgetting or rather of trying to repress a memory is repeated in a number of Seferis' poems, but in the **"Decision to Forget"** it finds its most extensive treatment. The epigraph of the poem, "who will reckon up our decision to forget," comes from poem "7" of **Mythistorema,** where it is implied that forgetting the painful memories of the war is almost impossible. A similar view is expressed in **"Stratis the Sailor Describes a Man,"** in which the protagonist, summing up his life, says that he has "reached the end" because he cannot help remembering what he has been through. On the other hand, when at the end of **"Salamis in Cyprus"** a voice suggests that "Now among these pebbles, it is better to forget,"[39] the protagonist's answer implies that retribution is inevitable because justice never forgets. Thus, as Savidis has suggested in connection with **"Salamis in Cyprus,"** "'The decision to forget' leads to injustice,"[40] which is what this poem is about, at least on the general level—referring to man's tendency to forget the horror of the war, once it is over. The poem suggests that by repressing the painful memory of the terrible moments he experienced, man is unable to put an end to the repeated aggressor-victim relationship that perpetuates war and slaughter.

Notes

1. See p. 52.

2. Savidis writes: "in *Logbook I,* I see no other thread than the monologue of the poet under the shadow of war." (*For Seferis,* 312)

3. *Journal C,* 28.

4. *Journal C,* 28.

5. *A Poet's Journal,* 136-7.

6.   My soul, guard against pomp and glory.
       And if you can't curb your ambitions,
       at least pursue them hesitantly, cautiously . . .

       And when you reach your summit, Caesar at last—
       when you assume the role of someone that famous—
       then be specially careful as you go out into the street,
       a conspicuous man of power with your retinue;
       and should a certain Artemidoros
       come up to you out of the crowd, bringing a letter,

and say hurriedly: "Read this right away.
There are important things in it concerning you"
be sure to stop; be sure to postpone
all talk of business . . .

                    . . . let even
the Senate itself wait—and find out at once
what important message Artemidoros has for you.

Translated by E. Keeley and P. Sherrard, *C. P. Cavafy: Collected Poems* (Princeton, N.J.: Princeton University Press, 1975) 55.

7. *Journal D,* 348.

8. "If we had at the helm people who could see the horizon and not ostriches who could hardly see one or two degrees of the cycle, we would certainly have a different way of thinking about the direction of the war." (Χειρόγραφο, Σεπτ. '41 [*Manuscript: September '41*], Athens: Ikaros, 1972, p. 54)

9. "Ayianapa II," as suggested by the subtitle, refers to the invasion of Cyprus by the Crusaders in A.D. 1156. See p. 188.

10. As mentioned by Seferis in his notes (*Collected Poems,* 482), this alludes to Thucydides, 7:87. This passage refers to the Athenians taken prisoner by the Syracusans in 413 B.C.

11. It is worth noting that in the poem "Spring A.D.," which follows "The Last Day," the motif of the spring is repeated and provides the central idea of the poem. After the birth of Christ people do not live peacefully, sharing love, but continue to suffer in a violent world of torture and deprivation, in which the pattern of the aggressor and the victim prevails. Life is offered to mankind every spring like a beautiful woman—a symbol of love—but it is wasted, as man is tortured by his fellow man. This symbolic woman opens windows in the sky but then vanishes, like the martyr who, tormented by his executioner, feels that he ascends to the sky, untouched, in apotheosis.

12. *Journal C,* 63.

13. Just as it does in *Mythistorema,* poem "22" where the poet asks:

    Because we have been bound, because we have been scattered,
    And have struggled with difficulties described as non-existent,
    Lost, then finding again a road full of blind battalions,
    Sinking in marshes and in the lake of Marathon,
    Shall we be able to die in a normal way?

14. *Journal C,* 146. Later, Miller wrote an essay, "Balzac and his Double," based presumably on these notes.

15. What Seferis had in mind when suggesting this comparison must have been recurring images in the *Tropic of Cancer* related to cancer, such as those on pp. 1, 2, 4, 53 and 167, from which the following quotation can serve as an example: "Wherever there are walls, there are posters with bright venomous crabs heralding the approach of cancer. No matter where you go, no matter what you touch, there is cancer and syphilis. It is written in the sky; in flames and dances like an evil portent. It has eaten into our souls and we are nothing but a dead thing like the moon." (*Tropic of Cancer,* New York: Grove Press, 1961)

16. *Journal C,* 146.

17. Miller writes that the *Tropics* are about "the Dionysian theme which . . . must be the theme for the writers to come—the only theme permissible or possible." Quoted by Allan Friedman from a letter of Miller to Lawrence Durrell ("The Pitching of Love's Mansion in the *Tropics,*" in *Henry Miller: Three Decades of Criticism,* ed. Edward Mitchell, New York: New York University Press, 1971, p. 152). Miller chose his titles very carefully; as he wrote upon seeing the title "A Man Cut to Slices," "we are all dead or dying or about to die. We need good titles" (*Tropic of Cancer,* p. 36). The title *Tropic of Cancer* has symbolic connotations connected either with astrology or with malignancy. About the zodiacal sign of the crab Miller writes: "I am Chancre, the crab, which moves sideways and backwards and forwards at will. I move in strange tropics and deal in high explosives . . . Because of Uranus which crosses my longitudinal I am inordinately fond of c——, hot chitterlings and water bottles" (*Black Spring,* New York: Grove Press, 1963, p. 29). The "tropic" of the title refers to "the meridian that separates the hemispheres of life and death" (*Tropic of Cancer,* 241). On the other hand, the recurring images of cancer, syphilis, decay and corruption suggest that the title refers to Paris as a symbol of a malignant megalopolis reflecting the decline of the Western world. (See Kingsley Widmer, *Henry Miller,* New York: Twayne Publishers, 1963, p. 26).

18. According to the *Encyclopaedia Britannica* (1971 ed., 5:170) the Centaurs were "wild, lawless and inhospitable beings, the slaves of their animal passions." Miller himself characterizes them as "monstrous" beings that "have upset the norm, the balance" ("The Time of the Assassins," *Selected Prose,* 2, London: MacGibbon & Kee, 1965, p. 86). In another essay, he writes: "At the bottom of everything there's some animal: that's our deepest obsession. When I see human beings squirming up toward the light like wilted sunflowers, I say to myself: 'Squirm, you bastards, and pretend all you like, but at bottom you're a turtle or a guinea pig.' Greece was mad about horses and if they had had the wisdom to remain half horse instead of playing the Titan—well, we might have been spared a great many mythological pains" ("The Angel is my Watermark!" *Black Spring,* 71).

19. The crowing of the cock is not a sign of vitality here since the cock is drowning in the well, which could be seen as symbolic of the death of love. In a passage of his *Journals* written on the island of Hydra, where "Les anges sont blancs" was also written, Seferis notes: "Even the cries of the animals seem to be born out of silence: the cock that crowed down in the village . . ." *Journal C,* 143.

20. *Journal C,* 142.

21. *Essays* 2:330-31.

22. H. De Balzac, *Louis Lambert,* trans. K. F. Wormeley (Boston: Roberts Brothers, n.d.) 140.

23. *Louis Lambert,* 135.

24. In the *Tropic of Capricorn,* Miller repudiates the Logos and confesses his fascination with the "object." "Only the object haunted me," he writes, "the separate, detached, insignificant thing," even "the worthless thing," which, he believes, contains "the secret of [his] own regeneration" (New York: Grove Press, 1961) 53-4.

25. *Tropic of Capricorn,* 67-8.

26. In contrast to the rest of the poems mentioned above in relation to the angel motif—which have been discussed in some detail in *Love and the Symbolic Journey in the Poetry of Cavafy, Eliot and Seferis* [C. Capri-Karka. New York: Pella Publishing, 1982]—no such analysis is available for the "Interval of Joy." For this reason, a short discussion is given here to help the reader see the motif in its context.

The "Interval of Joy" refers to the joy of an uninhibited erotic life in which the Dionysian element predominates but which does not last long and is followed by an awareness of the dangers lurking behind it. The poem, in the beginning, conveys the euphoria of a radiant morning, when the protagonist feels happy and free of care. However, after the first few lines, some symbols appear that, as the description goes on, become more and more ominous. The enormous sun is "all thorns," but they are "so high up in the sky" that one might hope that the danger they represent is very remote—although the way the poem ends proves the opposite. Also, the "wood of Judas trees" is a symbol associated with betrayal; and although in this scenery "Young Loves and satyrs sported there and sang," one could catch through the "black laurel leaves" (another ominous symbol) "the rosy gleam / Of little children's limbs." The scenery depicts the wild life of satyrs, fauns and nymphs, while later in the poem a dangerous angel appears. Satyrs and fauns, being associated with Dionysus, are creatures of the wild, part men and part beasts in which the erotic and the destructive element coexist. The rosy gleam of little children's limbs through the leaves hints at this destructiveness. The ominous overtones of this image, clearly discernible in the Greek original, "κι' ἔϐλεπες ρόδινα μέλη μέσα στὶς μαῦρες δάφνες/σάρκες μικρῶν παιδιῶν," are not fully conveyed in any of the published English translations; "σάρκες" is the plural of "σάρκα" ("flesh") and cannot be rendered literally.

The feeling of joy the protagonist expresses in most of the poem does not seem to anticipate the change that follows; the ominous overtones are suggested only by the scenery. Only later, toward the end of the poem, does the protagonist hint to the abyss hidden below the beautiful scenery and, in a way, the beat of the "tender foot of an infant faun" is connected, symbolically speaking, with the opening of the closed well revealing the abyss. The protagonist tells his companion about the faun: "Do you remember his laugh? How full of joy" we were; but what follows is a quick change of scenery, the appearance of clouds in the sky, rain and the dampness of the earth. The protagonist recalls how his companion, lying down in the hut, had stopped laughing when looking upon the archangel "exercising with a fiery sword." He hears his companion wonder why people, although "play[ing] with colors as they will, they all are black." Thus, the interval of joy does not last as the poet returns, in the last line, to the dark forces man hides inside himself.

27.   We got out of the walls. Who was terrifying us?
         No one out here; dark blue colors on the earth, dark
         blue birds.
         Here and there huge rocks, glittering like mirrors
         and the angel with golden heels
         dressed his nakedness with a blue flutter of wings.

Like several other poems, "We Got out of the Walls" was not included in a collection by the poet himself. It appeared posthumously in the *Journals* (*E*, 180) and was included in the *Book of Exercises II*, 33.

28. On the connection between artistic creation and the life of the poet Miller writes:

> In our society the artist is not encouraged, not lauded, not rewarded, unless he makes use of a weapon more powerful than those employed by his adversaries. Such

a weapon is not to be found in shops or arsenals: it has to be forged by the artist himself out of his own tissue. When he releases it, he also destroys himself. It is the only method he has found to preserve his own kind . . . He must create, by the sacrifice of his own being, the awareness of a value and a dignity which the word human once connoted.

> *Patchen Man of Anger and Light* (New York: Padell, 1946) 11-12

29. *Journal C,* 146.

30. *Journal C,* 180. This is actually not very far from reality: according to the *Encyclopaedia Britannica* (1971 ed., 21:478), wild swans "because of their pugnacious disposition and voraciousness pose a threat to other waterfowl."

31. *Encyclopaedic Lexicon,* 8:288.

32. In *Prometheus Bound,* where the hero warns Io to guard against them, the Phorcys are described as three swan-shaped maidens, old women from birth, possessing one eye amongst them and a single tooth (ll. 794-6). Aeschylus also wrote a play *The Phorcides,* mentioned by Aristotle in his *Poetics* (18:1456a, 2), of which only a small fragment has been preserved (*Aeschylus* II, Loeb, 469-70).

33. Wing imagery in Seferis is associated with love but also with trapping. The white wings of the angels very often symbolize both beauty and destruction, as in the poems "Fog," "Monday" of the sequence "Notes for a Week" and poem "1" of *Mythistorema.*

34. In his *Journals,* Seferis compares one's fate to a lion that suddenly pounces and destroys everything. He writes "Sometimes I see fate as a young lion (or something like it) that might live with us. For years we try to win it over; we finally think that we have tamed it. All of a sudden it remembers its ancient blood. I started learning to look it in the eyes. They are wide open, calm, sometimes a sudden spark is seen in the pupil; it moves quickly around in a circle and disappears. I get the impression that the spark confirms a tragic certainty—we will see." (*Journal B,* 75)

35. *For Seferis,* p. 239-41.

36. "Les anges sont blancs," immediately preceding the "Decision to Forget" in the Greek editions and Keeley and Sherrard's translation.

37. Poem "1" of *Mythistorema.*

38. Kurt Ranke, ed., *Folk Tales of Germany,* transl. L. Baumann (Chicago: The University of Chicago Press, 1966).

39. —Now among these pebbles, it is better to forget;

It does no good to speak.
What the powerful have determined, who can change it?

40. *For Seferis,* 397.

Bibliography

Balzac, Honoré D. *Louis Lambert,* trans. K. F. Wormeley. Boston: Roberts Bros., n.d.

Cavafy, C. P. *Collected Poems.* Trs. Edmund Keeley and Philip Sherrard. Princeton, N.J.: Princeton University Press, 1975.

Ἐγͷκͷκλοπαιδικὸν Λεξικὸν [*Encyclopedic Lexicon*]. 12 vols. Athens: Eleftheroudakis, 1929.

Savidis, George. "Μιὰ Περιδιάβαση" ["A Wandering"]. In Γιὰ τὸν σεφέρη [*For Seferis*], eds. Leonidas Zenakos and George Savidis, 304-408. Athens: n.p., 1961.

Seferis, George. *Poems.* Tr. Rex Warner. Boston: Little, Brown & Co., 1964.

———. *Collected Poems 1924-1955.* Trs. Edmund Keeley and Philip Sherrard. Princeton, N.J.: Princeton University Press, 1967.

———. *Three Secret Poems.* Tr. Walter Kaiser. Cambridge, Mass.: Harvard University Press, 1969.

———. *The King of Asine and Other Poems.* Trs. Bernard Spencer, Nanos Valaoritis and Lawrence Durrell. London: John Lehman, 1948.

———. Δοκιμὲς [*Essays*]. 3d ed. 2 vols. Athens: Ikaros, 1974.

———. Ποιήματα [*Poems*]. 11th ed. Ed. George Savidis. Athens: Ikaros, 1977.

———. *On the Greek Style.* Trs. Rex Warner and Th.D. Frangopoulos. Boston: Little, Brown & Co., 1966.

———. Ἕξη νύχτες στὴν Ἀκρόπολη [*Six Nights on the Acropolis*]. Athens: Hermes, 1974.

———, tr. Θ.σ. Ἔλιοτ: Ἡ Ἔρημη Χώρα και ἄλλα ποιήματα [*T. S. Eliot: The Waste Land and Other Poems*]. 4th ed. Athens: Ikaros, 1967.

———. Μέρες [*Days*]. 5 vols. Athens: Ikaros. Vol. *A* (February 16, 1925-August 17, 1931), 1975; vol. *B* (August 24, 1931-February 12, 1934), 1975; vol. *C* (April 16, 1934-December 14, 1940), 1977; vol. *D* (January 1, 1941-December 31, 1944), 1977; vol. *E* (January 1, 1945-April 19, 1951), 1973.

———. *A Poet's Journal: Days of 1945-1951.* Tr. Athan Anagnostopoulos. Cambridge, Mass.: Harvard University Press, 1974.

———. Πολιτικὸ Ἡμερολόγιο Α', 1935-1944 [*Political Diary A: 1935-1944*]. Athens: Ikaros, 1979.

———. Τετράδιο Γυμνασμάτων, Β' [*Book of Exercises II*]. Ed. George Savidis. Athens: Ikaros, 1976.

———. Χειρόγραφο σεπ. '41 [*Manuscript Sept. '41*]. Athens: Ikaros, 1972.

Henry Gifford (essay date winter 1986)

SOURCE: Gifford, Henry. "George Seferis during the War." *Grand Street* 5, no. 2 (winter 1986): 175-86.

[*In the following essay, Gifford describes the poetry Seferis wrote during his years of exile from Greece during World War II.*]

There is an epigram by Cavafy entitled "Those Who Fought for the Achaian League":

> Brave are you who fought and fell gloriously:
> having no fear of those who conquered everywhere.
> You are blameless, if Diaios and Kritolaos were at
>   fault.
> "Our nation produces men like these," they will say
> about you. So marvelous will be your praise.
>
> Written in Alexandria by an Achaian;
> the seventh year of Ptolemy, Lathyros.

Diaios and Kritolaos were the incompetent generals who led the Achaian League to defeat by the Romans in 146 B.C. The seventh year of Ptolemy IX—Lathyros means "chickpea"—was 109 B.C.

These were the lines that George Seferis found himself repeating "one evening, in blacked-out Alexandria, a few days after the Battle of Crete." That would have been in June 1941, when the poem was, he says, "tragically to the point." It occurred to him for the first time that the real date on which the poem had been written, 1922, was significant. In that year the Greeks had undergone the "Asia Minor disaster," involving the loss of Smyrna and the end after so many centuries of the Greek presence in Anatolia. "Almost unconsciously" Seferis changed the ending of the poem:

> Written in Alexandria by an Achaian;
> the year the Nation met with disaster.

Later he added a second version:

> Whispered by an Achaian in Alexandria;
> when the Teutons had scorched Crete.

He was now at the beginning of an exile which lasted three and a half years to the day, from April 22, 1941, when he was evacuated from Peiraios as an official of the Greek government, until October 22, 1944, when he sighted the Acropolis from the deck of the ship carrying him home. This would prove to be for Seferis a time of exceptional strain and weariness of spirit. There was a minor consolation in being able to slip across from Cairo, which he abominated with its dust and stink and the "leprous houses" in narrow streets, to Alexandria and the Greek community there. Later, when he was transported with the government-in-exile to South Africa, even that consolation was lost. In June 1942 he contrived to return to the Middle East, only to find Cairo in a state of apprehension which reminded him of Athens before it fell. The years away from Greece were a torment to him. News of what was happening on the mainland came through slowly, and it added to his sense of futility. In Athens people were dying of starvation in their thousands; the German hand upon Greece was harshly repressive; there was no limit to the nation's suffering. When the resistance began to take shape, after one successful action by its opposing parties of left and right in which they together destroyed the Gorgopotamos viaduct, unity came to an end and the road to civil war lay open.

The record of what Seferis felt and thought over these years is moving to read and important to understand. He was put to the test in a way that had much in common with the experience of poets in Eastern Europe who had to endure catastrophe at first hand, and although Seferis was not in fear for his life, he could easily have despaired of the future. Only a dispossessed fugitive like himself could realize with the same anguish how ineffectual, until the tide turned at Alamein, was, by and large, the British command. The modern counterparts of Diaios and Kritolaos, or so they seemed to him, came and went; there appeared to be no sense of urgency, and he wondered whether the war was real to his allies as it had been to the Greek soldiers in 1940-41 when they drove the invading Italians back to the sea.

It is often remarked that Russians find exile from their country very hard to accept. The Greek diaspora goes far back into history, and in the last hundred years there have been large Greek communities all over the world. But Seferis seems to have been emotionally bound to Greece itself as much as any Russian to his native soil. This fact would make him, if nothing else did, the very opposite of Cavafy. A little poem he wrote in August 1943 when in Cairo speaks of "a music" that "crosses the sand, / crosses the sea":

> High mountains, don't you hear us!
> Help! Help!
> High mountains, we shall wear away,
>   dead among the dead.

Cavafy knew himself to be a decadent poet, and his interests lay mostly in the sub-history, as one might call it, of Hellenistic and Byzantine chronicles, when struggles and reverses took place for Greeks scattered over territory today no longer theirs, and the rulers of little states lived out their hours of hollow glory. Cavafy's view of history was deeply ironical; he wrote with a sense of *fin de siècle* more absolute than any his West European contemporaries (unless we include Eliot) may have professed. Seferis had not been much attracted to his work, until he came to know the later poems from the edition of 1935; their differences were too manifest. However, he was to occupy himself a good deal with Cavafy during his exile, copying out the poems and slowly adding a commentary. Cavafy's place in modern Greek poetry is anomalous, looming large and yet to one side of it. There was much in his work for Seferis to find alien. What he clung to for moral support during those years was the volume of Aeschylus he had with him, and also the memoirs of Makriyannis, the simple hero of Greek liberation in the campaign supported by Byron and the philhellenes of his day. Seferis's meditation on Cavafy was necessary to deepen and extend his awareness of the Greek tradition and its particular meaning for himself in the actual crisis.

He had been prepared at least subconsciously for exile, a theme that quite often recurs in his poetry before the war. Displaced himself by the loss of Smyrna, near which he had been born in 1900, he felt, like others of his generation too, ill at ease with the society in which he lived. Hence the appeal of Eliot, who seemed to have found expression for the sensibility of all his contemporaries in *The Waste Land,* "The Hollow Men" and "Difficulties of a Statesman," three poems that Seferis translated. After the war Seferis was to point out the parallels between Eliot and Cavafy, the first of whom had deeply influenced his own verse and his critical thought, while the second he tended to approach with the attitude of Hopkins, to "admire and do otherwise." Both Eliot and Cavafy, as he notes, were much concerned with tradition—Eliot needing to work for it, Cavafy to hold up under its weight. The problem took yet a third form for Seferis himself: to identify rightly the Hellenic tradition was an urgent task for a patriot wanting to recover a future for his country. And Seferis looked for continuity where Cavafy had never suspected it, among the mass of the Greek people, the illiterates, as they mainly were, who had kept alive the genius of the language and the essential tones of the Greek voice. Cavafy represented in the eyes of Seferis a striking anomaly: he was a Greek from the flat land of Egypt, with no knowledge of the mountains or of the sea except where it washed against the quays of Alexandria. For Seferis, without the high mountains, in the Egyptian "swamp," there was no alternative to wearing away, "dead among the dead."

The experience of the war years supported his steps in the right direction. Crete had been the birthplace of the Hellenic renaissance in the early seventeenth century; it had also sent into the western world Dominikos The-otokopoulos, El Greco, whose art would seem to have derived its specifically Greek qualities from the icon-painting of his older contemporary Damaskinos. When Seferis was briefly in Crete, on his way eventually to Egypt and then South Africa with the government-in-exile, his sense of that tradition had been enlivened. On May 13, 1941, he notes in his journal: "Heavy German raid at 04.30'. We went down to the garden. Clouds and the moon: a sky of Theotokopoulos'." In the same garden, again under the moon during an air raid, he quoted to the Cretan Manoli lying beside him a couple of lines from the seventeenth-century epic *Erotokritos* on the honest hand-to-hand fighting of previous un-mechanized wars, to which Manoli replied by continu-ing the quotation. Patrick Leigh Fermor had told how old shepherds keeping watch in the mountains during the partisan war with the Germans could recite hundreds of lines from the poem. The *Erotokritos* is a main source for the vigorous demotic tradition that Seferis prized. And the tradition was inseparable from those who had preserved it. "The heroes," he said, "who came down from the mountains are another race." One of them "with a great spreading beard, and full of wrinkles like an olive tree," had inspired Seferis with "an inconceiv-able longing to live here," in Crete. "These unknown men," he observed, "are the best thing our country has."

Their great predecessor, for Seferis, was Makriyannis, whose memoirs he regarded as a foundation work of modern Greek prose, though Makriyannis had been il-literate until at the age of thirty he taught himself letters to write them. With Makriyannis he associated the primitive painter Theophilos, once a doorkeeper in Smyrna. Both these men exemplified for him a truly educated mind, with shrewdness of observation, a sane simplicity, and a natural gift for expressing themselves. Makriyannis he called "the conscience of a whole people," and his own "humblest but most constant teacher."

This he said in a lecture of May 1943, given to a Greek audience first in Alexandria and then in Cairo. The criti-cal writings of Seferis during his exile—beginning with an address to Alexandrian schoolboys in June 1941 on two younger poets, Antoniou and Elytis, and also including a critique of a forerunner in the demotic verse tradition, Kalvos, and a memorial tribute to his own most important senior contemporary, Palamas—are all, like the notes on Cavafy, what he intended to signify when calling the collection of his critical pieces *Dokimes*. That is, they are "essays" in the tentative sense that Montaigne implied, attempts to clarify the values by which modern Greece could find its salva-tion.

The contrast in Seferis's mind throughout these years is a familiar one from the nineteenth century, between the unspoilt people on one side and their effete or unscrupu-lous countrymen in the ruling class who have lost altogether the common touch. This contrast was still very much alive in the 1930s, and reinforced by the war. If today we feel more doubts of its validity, that is because the nature of the people has changed in our increasingly urbanized world. Seferis was neither an in-nocent nor a sentimentalist, and his instinct was absolutely right in guiding him to the examples of Makriyannis and Theophilos, the *Erotokritos* and the oral ballads dating far back into Byzantine times and preserved by the people. He had the contemporary intel-lectual's perception of the waste land, which his impres-sions of Egypt, in its overripeness and decay, kept alive. This caused him all the more passionately to long for a return to Greek soil. There is no more poignant passage in his diary than that which describes his despair on the ship carrying him south of the line, away from the known constellations, from "what I have loved, the Hellenic world, Europe." He recognizes that he has become "utterly an orphan." Almost equal in poignancy is the entry made on Sunday, October 22, 1944, once more aboard a British ship, where he describes the mo-ment when he sighted the Acropolis. "All, foreigners and ourselves, soldiers and senior officers, the whole crew, from one end of the ship to the other, were ar-rested in an absolute silence, as when the conductor raps his baton on the desk in a concert hall." He records this as "the most beautiful, the most uplifting day in the world." The entry for the following day consists of the single word "Home."

It was appropriate that both these experiences should have happened at sea. He saw himself, in contrast to the housebound Cavafy in his half-lit library, as a man of the sea; and a figure that recurs in his poetry as a persona for Seferis is that of Stratis Thalassinos, Stratis the Seafarer. The volume of poetry he published just before his exile ended is called *Logbook II.* Its predecessor *Logbook I* had appeared in 1940; and in 1955 he would produce *Logbook III,* dedicated to the people of Cyprus, about whose predicament he had strong feelings. Each "logbook" is called in the Greek *Imerologio Katastromatos,* the latter word meaning "deck." Another poet to whom he explained his choice of this title had published a book called *Roses of a Room,* and Seferis seized on that image to explain their differences.

> The room is a "domain" of your own, as you say; the deck is not my own, completely my own, it is a mov-ing square which I have crossed and many people beside, and the wind, and the rain, and human bodies
> . . .

He goes on to explain that the event to have taken hold of him most strongly had been "the Asia Minor disaster" and after it "this war and the suffering of my country and of my people under this storm." Seferis writes not only of his personal fortunes, but of a national, or rather a world crisis, in which he has to participate. It was very clear to him that Hellenism meant the same thing as humanism, and the survival of Hellenism was inseparable from that of civilization as he understood it.

Such is the background to the thirteen poems that make up *Logbook II*. It begins with **"Days of June '41,"** and the opening image brings to mind that which Coleridge took from "The Ballad of Sir Patrick Spens" as the epigraph to "Dejection: an Ode":

> The new moon came out in Alexandria
> having the old one in its embrace.

"Dejection" is about the forfeiture of joy and the creative impulse:

> My genial spirits fail;
> And what can these avail
> To lift the smothering weight from off my breast?

How far Seferis had Coleridge's poem in mind it is impossible to say; the only reference to Coleridge in the two volumes of his *Essays* comes indirectly, through a quotation from E. M. Forster on "Anonymity" in *Two Cheers for Democracy,* not published until 1951. But the comparison, however insecurely based, is revealing. Seferis, like Coleridge, is painfully aware of what the latter had called in the poem "reality's dark dream," and reality was to become darker still, threatening him with sterility as a poet, once he had arrived in South Africa.

> And now the new moon has come out embracing
> the old; and the lovely island bleeding
> wounded; the serene island, the strong island, the in-
> nocent.

The poet walks with two friends "in the darkness of the heart" towards the Gate of the Sun, dark too, and their "thirst . . . / . . . keeps guard / exiled somewhere around here / near the tomb of Alexander the Great."

In the following poem, of September 1941, Alexander's tomb lies in another hemisphere. He is an orphan indeed:

> Lord, not with these men . . .

> Thine is the sea and the wind
> with a star hung in the firmament.
> Lord, they know not that we are
> what we are able to be
> healing our wounds with herbs
> that we find on the green slopes . . .

But now his "little prayer at each dawn" has to cross "the chasms of memory." The poet has become separated from his own kind. Like the friend whom he addresses in the next poem (October 1941), he has been deprived "of the light, of the sea, of bread":

> How did we fall, friend, into the drain of fear?
> It was not your fate, nor was it written to be mine,
> we never bought or sold such merchandise . . .

Blood like "Saint George on horseback . . ." will "nail with a spear to the ground the dragon" (an image Pasternak was to use in one of the poems attributed by him to Zhivago, with the same implications of an escape from tyranny). But this is only a hope, though urgently needed to face the nightmare, and the poem that follows next but one, **"Stratis the Seafarer among the Agapanthi,"** ends with a desperate call for help, now that his companions, like those of Odysseus, "remain in the palaces of Circe."

The agapanthi are African lilies, in spite of their Greek name, "love-flowers." But love itself has become suspect:

> The first thing that God made is love
> then comes blood
> and the thirst for blood . . .

Then he turns the thought another way:

> The first thing God made is the long journey;
> the house there waits
> with blue smoke
> with a dog grown old
> waiting so he may die for the return . . .

This recollection of the Odyssey had already appeared in a poem of 1931, **"On a Foreign Verse,"** the celebrated line of Du Bellay's with which Seferis began that poem:

> Happy is he who like Ulysses has made a good
> journey

—happy because he can return home to rest "full of experience and wisdom" (*plein d'usage et raison*). But Stratis the Seafarer is helpless in this alien landscape:

> There are no asphodels, violets, nor hyacinths:
> how can you speak to the dead . . .

Unless he can speak to the dead, there is no way forward; the living do not suffice for him; and

> the agapanthi order silence
> raising the little hand of a dark Arab child
> or even the steps of a goose in the air.

These flowers are "the asphodels of the blacks," and he asks: "How shall I get to know this religion?"

Seferis was not impressed by South Africa and what he regarded as its very thin and extraneous colonial culture. "The real people," he noted in March 1942, "are the Blacks, the proper natives." Even in their ragged European clothes they drew his attention by the "regal air" they had. However, from them and from the op-pressive electricity-laden sky above, he had to escape: "otherwise you fall, it is death." Having returned to Cairo, he writes in June 1942 **"An Old Man on the River Bank,"** about the problem of "how we go forward." Eliot had published *The Dry Salvages* in 1941, and Seferis "read it one afternoon in Capetown." The image there of "the lonely prow that goes forward slowly"—it recurs as he noted in "Marina," also translated by him—was "engraved on his mind." The "long river" in his poem that comes out of Africa is like Eliot's Mississippi,

> it was once a god and then became a road and a
> donor and a judge and a delta

and "is never the same." But if Eliot's example gave him encouragement here, a poem of the next month, **"Stratis Thalassinos on the Dead Sea,"** written after a visit to Palestine, has brought Seferis back to *The Waste Land*: Jerusalem is "a city without a helmsman," and

> In the Dead Sea
> there are no fish
> there is no seaweed
> nor sea-urchins
> there is no life.

The refrain, THIS IS THE PLACE, GENTLEMEN! (from a notice marking the alleged site of Christ's temptation in the wilderness) matches the insistence of HURRY UP PLEASE ITS TIME. The poet and his companions

> continue our journey
> many fathoms below the level of the Aegean.

A year later, in **"Days of April '43,"** he is still in Cairo, with its "rubbish, dung, stench and slander," trying not to slip on the melon rinds thrown by Arabs or refugee politicians. The volume, as published in Alexandria dur-ing the summer of 1944, ended with **"Here Among the Bones"** and its appeal to the high mountains that seem not to listen.

However, a thirteenth poem, written in early October, was added for the Athens edition of 1945. This is **"Last Stop,"** from Cava dei Tirreni, the "Etruscan village, behind the sea of Salerno," where Seferis and his wife were awaiting the return to Greece. Just as **"The King of Asine"** had marked a halt before the experience of *Logbook II,* so **"Last Stop"** prepares for **"Thrush,"** and *Logbook III,* the final stage of his poetry that looks back on the war and faces new difficulties, the betrayal of its ideals, over Cyprus.

As the moon turns the houses on the farther slope to bright enamel, he reflects that few moonlit nights have been to his liking. They recall before anything "islands,

the colour of a grieving Virgin, late in the waning," the Crete that had remained an open wound for him. But now the reckoning is due as the exiles return, and his-tory will collect from them its debt. The problem for Seferis was that of the refugee who has been excluded from the great drama in which his country is involved, and who must, like all exiles, he believes, have become a pettier and even a corrupted man. He had noticed how quickly those who arrived from Greece changed for the worse. Cavafy would appear to have given him the wide perspective to see what he had described in a note of February 1944 as "the fearful tragedy of the modern Greeks" (*Romiosyni*) and of Greeks throughout history:

> We come from Arabia, from Egypt, Palestine, Syria;
> the little state
> of Kommagene that went out like a small lamp
> many times returns to our mind,
> and great cities that lived for thousands of years
> and then become a place for pasture . . .

Cavafy had written two poems about "the little state of Kommagene" (his actual phrase), and perhaps the sense here of a people scattered in communities that rise and fall to decay is derived from him. Seferis finds those returning to be "souls shriveled by public sins":

> The rainy autumn in this hollow place
> festers the wound of each one of us . . .
>
> Man is easily worn down in the wars,
> man is soft, a bundle of grass.

Moreover, man is "thirsty" and "insatiable as grass":

> when the harvest comes
> he prefers that the scythes should whistle in another
>   field . . .

This may be, the poet admits, "the thinking of a refugee" and no doubt he is saying "the same things on and on." But rooted in his mind is the image of the suf-fering country, planting there "a virgin forest of slaughtered friends."

In this finely conclusive poem one hears the note, distantly, of Cavafy, and more distinctly present the note of Eliot. But Seferis has also caught the very ac-cent of Greek tragedy, the voice of the chorus in the plays of Aeschylus which embodied for him the moral sense of the Greek people, their innate feeling for justice. The last paragraph of the poem presents an unknown hero of the people, Michalis, "who left the hospital with open wounds" to continue the fight. Through the ordinary Greeks of his own time it was possible to communicate with Aeschylus, and under such guidance Seferis, also with his "open wounds," was ready to "move forward in the dark."

George Thaniel (essay date May 1987)

SOURCE: Thaniel, George. "Seferis and England: A Greek Poet in an English Landscape." *Journal of Modern Greek Studies* 5, no. 1 (May 1987): 85-109.

[*In the following essay, Thaniel discusses Seferis's association with England and T. S. Eliot and its effect on his writing.*]

The special relationship which George Seferis (1900-71) developed in the last 40 or so years of his life with Britain is obvious even to the casual observer of his life and his work. He started and finished the foreign part of his diplomatic career in London, and on various other occasions, before, during and after the Second World War, he had to deal with British politicians, diplomats, and military officers. Seferis developed a close tie with T. S. Eliot, but he had many connections with other influential English writers as well. It would be fair to say that without the publicity which these writers provided for his literary work and the honors which he received in Britain towards the end of his career (1960-62), the Swedish Academy could not have known enough about Seferis to consider him a candidate for the Nobel Prize for literature and finally to award it to him in 1963, the first Greek writer to have received it.

The connections of Seferis with England and the English intelligentsia were celebrated, after his death, by exhibitions held in Athens and London, the eulogies which British friends published on his behalf, and the scholarship which his poetry and essays generated in the English-speaking world. One might add that the associations of Seferis with North American intellectuals and institutions seem really to postdate the awarding of the Nobel prize and may be seen as extensions of his longer-standing ones with Britain.

These facts are fairly well known; yet, apart from Seferis' association with the poetry and critical thought of Eliot, there has never been an attempt, beyond generalities, to explore them. The topic has many ramifications and should be meaningful to comparatists as well as English and Greek specialists. I propose to investigate it, taking as my base Seferis' own work: poetry, essays, diaries, correspondence, and other relevant material. I begin with the question of Seferis' reactions to the natural and human landscape of Britain in the formative years of 1931-34, when he served his country as acting Consul General in London, as well as in the summer of 1944, when Seferis flew to England from Egypt, carrying certain messages to the British Government from the Greek Government in exile. The recently published *Meres F,* which covers Seferis' second extended stay (1951-52) in England, mirrors his associations with a number of well-known English writers and other intellectual men rather than his reactions to the natural and human landscape of Britain. Seferis' *Meres G,* which covers the years 1957-62 (when Seferis served as Greek Ambassador in Britain) is not available yet, with the exception of a few entries which have been printed in magazines.

* * *

Seferis was born at Smyrna, in Asia Minor. He was raised both there and subsequently in Athens, and, for the rest of his life, he remained an emotional captive of the Greek landscape with its frequent views of the sea. Astrology-minded persons might see a significance in that Seferis was born under the sign of Pisces, on 29 February, by the old Greek Calendar (13 March, by the new), in 1900. Many of the happier notes in his poetry are related to the sea. The diaries reflect this fascination with the sea more directly: "My second swim, at Vouliagmeni. *Magic* of the sea hard to explain. How it changes me all at once: my wonder, a wonder deep to the bone. I cannot understand. I should go closer, I should try to cross that borderline into another world" (*Meres E* 1973: 33).

Between 1918 and 1924 Seferis studied in Paris and, although he sometimes felt emotionally alienated, he loved the city and its rich cultural atmosphere. "I spent six and a half years in Paris," Seferis noted in his diary. "I lived fully and wholeheartedly, loving each moment, each corner of the city and each stone" (*Meres B* 1975: 80). In the second half of 1924, after he had received his diploma in law, Seferis traveled to London with the purpose of learning English, in view of the fact that his family wanted him to make a career as a diplomat. His earliest poem, **"Fog"** (*sic* in the original), dates from those days. The younger sister of Seferis, Ioanna, had already received from him letters with descriptions of foggy days in Paris (Tsatsos 1982: *passim*), but it was London, on Christmas Day, 1924 (hence, probably, the caricature of angels in the second and third stanzas) that inspired Seferis with a poem on the subject of fog, a meteorological phenomenon strange for a Greek.

"Fog"

say it with a ukulele

"Say it with a ukulele . . ."
grumbles some gramophone;
Christ, tell me what to say to her
now that I'm used to my loneliness?

With accordions squeezed
by well-dressed beggars
they call on the angels
and their angels are hell.

And the angels opened their wings
but, below, the mists condensed,
thank God, for otherwise they'd catch
our poor souls like thrushes.

And life's cold as a fish
—Is that how you live?—Yes, how else?
So many are the drowned
down on the sea's bed.

Trees are like corals
their color gone,
carts are like ships
sunken and lonely . . .

"Say it with a ukulele . . ."
Words for words, and more words?
Love, where's your church,
I'm tired of this hermitage.

Ah, were life but straight
how we'd live it then!
But it's fated otherwise,
you have to turn in a small corner.

And what corner is it? Who knows?
Lights shine on lights
pallidly, the hoarfrosts are dumb,
and our soul's in our teeth.

Will we find consolation?
Day put on night—
everything is night, everything is night—
we'll find something, if we search . . .

"Say it with a ukulele . . ."
I see her red nails—
how they must glow in firelight—
and I remember her with her cough.

This poem, which partly rhymes in the original (the second and fourth lines of each stanza end on similar sounds) and has naturally lost part of its charm in the free verse translation, well suggests, *à la manière de* Corbière and Laforgue, the young poet's relation to London in winter, and also reflects an attitude which Seferis continued to express, with variations of tone and color, in the remainder of his work. It is a critical attitude towards life. The tone in **"Fog"** is mordant and self-deprecating but not as yet tragic.

Six years passed before Seferis saw London again. In 1931 he was posted to England, to serve in the Greek consulate. He sailed to Marseilles, toured Southern France in a French colleague's automobile, took the train to Paris, where he saw a performance of dances from Indochina (part of the Colonial Exhibition of '31), and proceeded to London, arriving on Monday, 17 August. "Green grass and smells of bacon," he noted in his diary (24 August), "I have the impression of spending the night locked in a room filled with flowers. I cannot breathe very well." The frequent rain depressed him. "In the room next to mine a phonograph is heard. The panes in my window where the rain is beating, are startled every so many minutes by the subway" (12 September). "*Is it the voices of our dead friends?*"[1] The phonographs persist. Each room here seems to have a phonograph which serves, on black disks,[2] Spanish and Negro tunes" (20 September). Three months later, Seferis, too, procured himself such an instrument in order to hear his favorite music, Franck, Debussy, Stravinsky, and—one presumes—jazz, which he also liked very much. "He [Seferis] knew every [jazz] virtuoso of any account; he was a subscriber to 'Le Jazz Hot' I soon discovered," Henry Miller has written (1941: 107). Miller met Seferis in Athens, in 1939, but the craze of Seferis for jazz dated from his London days, as he himself has informed us in "Conversation with Seferis" (Keeley 1983: 201).

Soon after his arrival, Seferis moved to Hampstead, a district of London, as boarder of an old widow and her chain-smoking and ever-coughing daughter. He took care to describe his new surroundings and daily routine in letters to Greece. He spent many hours every day at his desk, alone, reading and writing. What he saw from his window is sometimes described in terms worthy of Evelyn Waugh: "A feeble sunshine touches my desk. A few minutes ago as I was putting on my clothes, I could see through my bedroom window two plump Amaltheias playing tennis. Two mobile castles. The little ball was Ariel: light, agile, it made fun of them" (28 May 1932). By "Amaltheias" Seferis meant of course "she-goats"—in Greek myth, Amaltheia was a female goat who nursed the infant Zeus. Seferis used the animal image again, 20 days later, in a different context: "It has not stopped raining for the last fifteen days. If the theory about the environment is true, then the English should be frogs" (28 May 1932).

The image of a different world often entered Seferis' mind: "A small house among the pines, basil plants in the pots, and white-washed walls, and at the foot of the hill the great world open to all directions" (20 September 1931).[3] Later, when he woke up one December morning and felt trapped by the solid cold, he was hallucinated by a blazing noontime sun in Athens, concrete "like a piece of bread." But Greece, in general, was also on his mind. Before leaving for England, Seferis had published in Athens his first book, *Turning Point,* and was ruminating on the reactions of critics and friends, several of them negative. Imagery from those poems came to haunt his new impressions from London: "Today, Sunday, I stayed indoors for the whole day. The air outside was filled with fog: you could not see two yards before you. Now, in the evening, the street lamp looks totally alienated—like that ship of Arthur Gordon Pym.[4] I understand the Spaniard who took such a lamp inside his room to give it protection" (29 November 1931). The Spaniard was Ramon Gomez de la Serna, a surrealist about whom we hear in *Meres D* (1977: 283).[5]

Seferis was still under the spell of French culture. He listened mostly to French music, read French writers, spiced his letters with French quotes, and thought that if he had good company he would have liked to spend New Year's Day in Paris. The river Thames was inevitably compared with the Seine:

> This afternoon, about 3:30, I walked down to the river. It is the only area which I like unreservedly, and I am sorry that its embankments are not longer, as in Paris, so that I could follow them for two hours on foot. This would have given me a big rest. The river does not look at all like the Seine; it is much wider and succeeds in giving you the impression of being part of the sea which is nearby. The bridges are enormous and shake in the centre, the current looks swifter and more in tune with the sky, which it carresses, in the evening (for this is the impression I get). If I were not a little nervous, I could have stood for hours, looking at the illuminated ads that puncture the fog or, further down, the tug boats which look from the distance like a black island, an ungoverned mass. You must have seen paintings of Whistler or Turner. Add a note of Bach and you will be able to visualize the scene I am describing.

(16 December 1931)

Here is a man who has seen many works by the Impressionists in Paris (Manet, Monet, Renoir) and some in London and who does not overstate his description of landscape. A poem which Seferis wrote about the same time shows his love of economy and precision more fully:

"Hampstead"

> Like a bird with broken wing
> that had traveled through wind for years
> like a bird unable to endure
> tempest and wind
> the evening falls.
> On the green grass
> three thousand angels had danced the day long
> naked as steel
> the pale evening falls;
> the three thousand angels
> gathered in their wings, became
> a god
> forgotten
> that barks
> alone
> and searches for its master
> or the Second Coming
> or a bone.
> Now I long for a little quiet
> all I want is a hut on a hill
> or near a seashore
> all I want in front of my window
> is a sheet immersed in bluing
> spread there like the sea
> all I want in my vase
> is even a false carnation
> red paper wound on wire
> so that the wind
> the wind can control it easily
> as much as it wants to.
> The evening would fall

> the flocks would echo descending to their fold
> like some quite simple happy thought
> and I would lie down to sleep
> because I wouldn't have
> even a candle to light,
> light,
> to read.

"Hampstead" is a remarkable poem which, as Vayenas (1979: 123) has aptly observed, combines realism and symbolism in equal amounts. This combination was made possible, in part, because the English landscape which Seferis is describing was less familiar to him and he felt the need to be accurate in its description. On the other hand, his recollections of the Greek scenery did not relate to a specific locale but to a hypothetical one. The balancing of two different landscapes against each other accords the poem a certain pleasant rhythm.[6]

Seferis' need to escape the London air, however, involved much more than hypothetical Greek landscapes. Listening to Stravinsky's *Rite of Spring,* Seferis remembered Nijinski, who had danced it, and composed a long poem in prose, **"Nijinski,"** describing a dream in which he had seen the famous dancer go through a symbolic ritual. **"Hampstead"** and **"Nijinski"** and other poems of this period belong in a series of poems supposedly written by Stratis Thalassinos (Stratis the Mariner, or Sailor), a persona which Seferis had used to represent a more adventurous, aggressive, and realistic part of his personality, his Odyssean self, so to speak. The name may have been "given" to Seferis by *The Arabian Nights* on the analogy of Sinbad the Sailor. Seferis' other, more self-conscious self, was composing, or at least trying to finish a more lyrical, rhymed poem, *The Cistern,* which he had sketched while in Greece and which, when finally published in 1932, was thought by critics a Greek equivalent of Valéry's *Le Cimetière Marin,* just as Seferis' **"Erotikos Logos"** (part of his collection *Turning Point*) had been taken to be a Greek analogue of Valéry's *La Jeune Parque.*

The problems which Seferis experienced in his effort to secure the uniform tone of a symbolist, typical of Mallarmé or Valéry, in *The Cistern,* remind us of the epigraph from Pindar: "There is a most vain class among men which, despising ordinary things, fixes its eyes on distant things, pursuing empty air with idle hopes. . . ." (*Pythian Odes,* 3, 21-23), which Seferis had attached to his **"Erotikos Logos."** The suspicion which Seferis had when attaching this, namely that he was pursuing something out of tune with his time and everyday experience, grew stronger as he tried to rework and polish *The Cistern* in London. He had changed, or at least his perception of things had changed, and in a very human way he blamed the environment: "Pure lyrical poetry does not go well with London: I cannot sing: I have no tune, if you like" (28 May 1932). His discomfiture had to do with the daily habits of his landladies:

182

I was awakened at 8 by the phonograph of my houseladies and then kept on edge by the vacuum cleaner. It sounds like a street drill. Every morning the same old story. The phonograph is a new problem. About a fortnight ago, the ladies obtained the recording of a song from a musical review and now they suck at it like candy. The old lady wakes up in the morning on that and the daughter goes to bed in the evening on the same. I am trying to come to terms with their perception of music. They consider me a fool for the music I buy, I mean the simpler works like Franck's *Symphony* and Granados' *Dances;* they find them *most unusual.* (Naturally, when I am to play [Stravinsky's] *Rite of Spring* or Satie's *Gymnopédies,* I double lock myself in).

(8 May 1932)

Seferis was making a resolute effort, at this time, to update himself musically, by going to concerts and writing subtle analyses of what he heard in letters he sent to a female friend well versed in music. Several of Seferis' poems had their origin in his favorite musical pieces, and R. Beaton may be right in suggesting that in a 1931 entry of *Meres B,* where Seferis recounts an idea of a piece of music, "The Watch and the Expedition of the Argonauts," we have a foreshadowing, in musical terms, of what later became the poem-sequence *Mythistorima.*[7] Many years later, he became friends with Igor Stravinsky, a composer he had always admired, and wrote a fine introduction to Stravinsky's *Poetics of Music,* a reprint of the Charles Eliot Norton Lectures which the Russian composer had given at Harvard before the Second World War.[8]

In the middle of May 1932 Seferis was overwhelmed by the torrential English spring which he could not help comparing with the leaner spring of Attica. Again his descriptions of the nature around him are impressionistic and studded with felicitous similes:

In the morning I took a long walk in Regent's [Park]. You felt the invisible sun pressing upon the clouds which, in their turn, were weighing upon the people. On the living grass, children, dressed in bright colors, looked like wooden toys. One child pretended to be dead while the others threw on his body handfulls of grass and earth, until some rogue of a child picked up a brick which he dropped on the belly of the dead child, who was resurrected at once with tears. Further down, a small white-clad Japanese girl was hopping like a chickpea; alone, like an exiled haiku.

(12 June 1932)[9]

In July 1932 Seferis moved his residence from Hampstead to an apartment attached to the Greek consulate where he now had increased responsibilities. To combat boredom and give at least verbal form to things which concerned him, he composed haiku:

When the haiku came out all right, I felt relieved, as if all those spiders, labyrinths, and 'the ineffable' things of a blind life were transformed, for a moment, into

something real—a pine needle or a beach pebble, let us say, into seventeen syllables. I dare tell myself that the problem [of life] is not harder than the problem of a haiku.

(23 July 1932)[10]

On his first anniversary in England, Seferis counted the pros and cons of the year:

[I am left] with two things: the flame and the river. . . . Here I set about trying to know this country better, to learn the language at least. I heard the best music of Europe. I visited superb museums. Books can be read anywhere. But I missed the company of people, the freshness and stimulation of human contact. I came to know the ordinary people, but I was not able to know the better ones. My type of work does not offer any intellectual environment and indiscretion is not my forte. After all, the best artists here are thought of as silly or scandalous, and those interested in them "highbrow"—an untranslatable and forbidding word. I happened to scandalize some decent gentleman by referring (in passing) to Byron! You would not dare to say anything about Lawrence or Joyce, who wrote books now forbidden. Well, the big city; that is something. To learn a language; that is also something. And to earn your living without being a burden to someone; that is certainly something. There is my balance.

(23 July 1932)

The passage is straightforward and speaks for itself. As for the "flame and the river," we should think back to the poem **"Nijinski,"** which Seferis was inspired to write by contemplating the flames of his fire at Hampstead, and to his description of the river Thames. The "flame" and the "river" are also symbols which Seferis found in the poetry of Eliot, and which he used in his own way more than once. In fact, one could see in this oracular summing up of Seferis' gains from his first year in England, an allusion to Eliot, who is not named in the diary entries of 1932, although verses from Eliot's *Ash Wednesday* were quoted once (18 September 1932), after the laconic introduction: "When I returned home, I read some English poems."

From other sources, Ioanna Tsatsos' *My Brother George Seferis,* and the correspondence between Seferis and George Theotokas, we know that Seferis was preoccupied with Eliot throughout 1932, and in an essay which he wrote many years later, "Letter to a Foreign Friend," (*On the Greek style* 1966: 166) we learn the circumstances of his first coming upon Eliot's poetry shortly before Christmas 1931. The question is why such a capital event did not find its way into Seferis' diary. There are possibly two answers. The first is given by Seferis himself in his *Meres C* (1977: 178) where he states that a diary is hardly all our moments, or the essence of our life, but merely the trace, almost accidental, of any given moment, now and then, and not always of the most significant moment" (3 March 1940). The second is that for many months, perhaps for more than a year, Seferis was not exactly sure of the significance of his discovery and the impact it was going to have on his own work. The present writer believes that it was Eliot's essays, in which Seferis found many of his own thoughts on poetry clarified, that attracted Seferis first.[11] The poet Eliot's dramatic manner of expression and stylistic innovations took more time to work their influence on the Greek poet.

When Seferis writes to George Theotokas on 20 August 1932 (1975: 116-117), he quotes some lines from Eliot's *The Hollow Men* but does so for emphasis. His mind is still preoccupied with what we may guess to be the two series of poems he wanted to complete and publish after *The Cistern.* We have already referred to these poems, starting from **"Hampstead,"** first in the series **"Five Poems by Mr. Stratis the Mariner,"** and **"Nijinski,"** last in the series **"Mr. Stratis the Mariner Describes a Man."** Seferis says to Theotokas:

> I have also started something. It has been dragging along since last October. . . . If it materializes, I will feel much relieved. But I do not dare to think about what is going to happen with the public and the critics. If it does not materialize, I will be very unhappy, mon cher chevalier.
>
> Between the conception
> And the creation
> Between the emotion
> And the purpose
> Falls the shadow
>
> says Eliot.

Moreover, the incompatibility which Seferis still found, towards the end of 1932, between himself and the English environment, is evident in the humorous entry for 17 October, the last substantial entry for the year.

> Stratis the Mariner . . . came up to tell me:
>
> —You know, I have found one of the serpents of *Erotikos Logos.*[12]
>
> He opened a newspaper and read: "10 snakes free." Then, in the same manner:
>
> —And the important thing is that it spoke to me. Yes, Sir, it spoke: "*Erotikos Logos* is lying; it was not two serpents; it was a single one, I!" I begged him not to bother me. He left whispering:
>
> —O.K., O.K., goodbye! If you do not believe me go and find out for yourself. But you must hurry, I am not sure you are going to catch it in time. In the paper which he threw on the table I read:
>
> "They say that it cannot live for long in the cold night air and that *although it is strong enough to kill a goat in its native country it has no future in England.*"[13]

And yet, it had, if we take the "serpent" to be Seferis himself, who took time to acclimatize himself in England. If, however, we take the "serpent" to be an al-

lusion to the erotic self of the poet, it is another story. In any case, towards the end of 1932, Seferis is still concerned with his published work and feels a stranger in England.

* * *

Before we consider the seminal year of 1933, in December of which Seferis started writing his first major work, *Mythistorima,* we should look again at those poems, in his collection *Book of Exercises* (published in 1940), which were "given" to the poet before 1933. **"Reflections on a Foreign Line of Verse"** takes its cue from Joachim du Bellay's poem "Les Regrets," especially its first line: "Heureux qui comme Ulysse a fait un beau voyage." On first view, this poem would suggest the use of the "mythical method" which Seferis had already used, if unconsciously, in an earlier poem, **"The Companions in Hell"** (in *Turning Point*).[14] But the "mythical method"—which, as the present writer believes, Seferis consciously adopted only after he had observed it in Eliot—works here only to a degree, since the bond between the hero, Ulysses, and the modern poet, who sees his life unfolding along Ulyssean lines, is not a complete identification but a mere correspondence. On the other hand, the influence of the English environment on the poem is indirect, and we may see it, for instance, behind lines such as "sometimes when I sit surrounded by exile I hear its distant murmur like the sound of sea struck by an inexplicable hurricane," where "its" refers to the love or lust for life which the hero possesses when he sets out on his long voyage. The Ulysses who appears to comfort the despairing narrator of the poem is not Cavafy's compulsive traveler and refined hedonist (poem "Ithaki"), but an old, seasoned man with a white beard and hands "calloused by the ropes and the tiller, his skin weathered by the dry north wind, by heat and snow," and has come to tell the narrator (who is to be identified with the poet) how he may build his own wooden horse to capture his own Troy. This poem, which was noticed and discussed by W. B. Stanford (1954: 177-178), is quite removed from the playful and fantaisist poems of *Turning Point* and may be said to prefigure, particularly with its last lines, the somber imagery of much of Seferis' later poetry. The new, realistic and dramatic mode which Seferis developed while in England is evident, to a degree, in this poem.

Considering the 16 haiku printed in *Book of Exercises,* we stop at this one:

> Is it the voice
> of our dead friends or
> the gramophone

which was "given" to Seferis by a popular English song, as his diary suggests;[15] and the following, specially titled **"In the Museum Gardens"**:

Empty chairs:
the statues have gone back
in the other museum

where the museum alluded to might be in London or anywhere. What is more remarkable here is the use of "statues" in the sense of the "living dead," an image which recurs in Seferis' poetry.

"Hampstead," first in the Stratis the Mariner series, was discussed earlier. The second, brief piece in the series may be an autobiographical sketch of Seferis the acting Consul General:

"Psychology"

This gentleman
takes his bath each morning
in the waters of the Dead Sea
then dons a bitter smile
for business and clients.

The image of "flame-gazing," found in the poem **"Nijinski,"** seems to start the other Stratis the Mariner poems, also in *Book of Exercises,* the series **"Stratis the Mariner Describes a Man."** The man who sits, every afternoon, "staring at a flame," and is now confiding to Stratis the Mariner, is of course Seferis' other, more intimate self, who reviews his life starting with his childhood. But this is not strictly an autobiographical poem in spite of its personal tone. The speaker and confessant is rather a composite representative of a whole generation of Greeks who grew up along with Seferis and had to face the same disillusionments and withstand similar pressures. The speaker is a sensitive and exacting individual who has tried to secure a foothold in the quicksands of modern history. This desirable and finally identifiable *pied d'appui* is the "flame," a symbol of balance between memory and forgetfulness:

What can a flame remember? If it remembers a little
less than is necessary, it goes out; if it remembers a
little more than is necessary, it goes out. If only it
could teach us, while it burns, to remember correctly.

(5. **"Man"**)

In the beginning of 1933 Seferis' morale was rather low, if we judge from his diary. He was not amused even by a letter which he received, as consul, in which the writer, unknown to him, wanted to be informed why a column of the Olympian Zeus temple in Athens had collapsed sometime in the last century, while the others were still standing, and inquired whether he could obtain a photo of the fallen column.[16] The diary entries and letters, which Seferis sent to Greece during this period, are nervous and, at times, delirious. As he said, he missed companions and human affection. We also suspect that Seferis was disappointed by the reactions of critics and friends in Greece to *The Cistern* and uncertain about his poetics, finding himself at a

crossroad, between *poésie pure,* represented by his poems **"Erotikos Logos"** and *The Cistern,* and realism which at this time was reflected in the Stratis the Mariner poems. Seferis agonized *à la* Mallarmé ("le papier vide que la blancheur défend") over the blank paper: "Midnight. Early in the afternoon, it was snowing heavily; the roads were slippery. The paper is now for me like the glass which fishermen use to scan the depths of the sea" (23 February).

But a bell had rung. Seferis was reading Eliot's poetry and essays more and more, finding many of his deeper concerns and aspirations spelled out in Eliot's work, all the time resisting Eliot's religious mysticism. He wanted to meet Eliot and asked a Greek friend, who knew the English poet, to write a letter of introduction on his behalf. But Eliot was away in America for the Charles Eliot Norton Lectures at Harvard. The two men finally met as late as 1951, and many years later, in 1967, Seferis himself was asked to deliver the same prestigious series of lectures for 1969. He declined, however, on the argument that it would not be proper for him to lecture and teach outside Greece, when many other men of letters were not allowed to do the same inside Greece (which, at the time, was under the dictatorial regime of the Colonels).

Seferis' interest in Eliot was made evident in the 15 April 1933 entry of his diary, an entry pregnant with facts and ideas that would find fruition in verse as well as critical essays in years to come:

Yesterday I listened to Händel's *Messiah.* I also read a
lot of Eliot and thought about him. I should start an essay on Eliot. I would touch upon the issues that interest
me, although I regret that my knowledge of the English
language and literature is inadequate. I know things
which nobody else in Greece knows, and this man
interests me. Last year I thought that he was the first
poet whom I have influenced! I could not explain this
similarity in our inclinations and quests in any other
way. The truth is that we both had the same teachers in
a period which counts: Laforgue, Corbière, etc. . . .
Last night, I threw on paper about thirty lines of *The
Waste Land* in [Greek] translation. It would be a tour
de force for someone to translate such a work. But I
will pursue it.

The relationship of Seferis to Eliot has been a prominent issue with Greek critics and has been discussed from various angles, with or without apparent bias. Some British and American scholars have also contributed fairly sober thoughts on the issue. The present writer intends eventually to give his own position, but in the proper context. For the time being, let in suffice to say that sometime *nel mezzo del camino* of his life and in an alien environment, Seferis was able to see beyond his personal problems and beyond the English landscape itself, natural and human, into areas as yet half-realized in his mind. He did so with Eliot as his guide, just as

Dante had done something similar many centuries earlier, with the help of another poet, Vergil:

> I spent three entire days alone in the [Easter] holidays. I did not feel bored, although I went out very little. Something is being fermented inside me. I may be deceiving myself. Anyway, the wind has changed direction, from denial to affirmation.
>
> (17 April 1933)

Two weeks later, Seferis sailed upstream on the Thames, to Hampton Court, but bothered by the large crowds of people, returned almost immediately, looking at the green banks of the river and the other boats sailing by. He liked what he saw and remembered some of Spenser quoted by Eliot in *The Waste Land*: "Sweet Thames, run softly till I end my song, / Sweet Thames, run softly, for I speak not loud or long." He noted that he had seen Eliot in a dream the previous night.

Eliot does not reappear in the few remaining entries of Seferis' 1931-34 diary, which ends with Seferis' return to Athens, by ship, in February 1934. The few entries mirror a familiar Seferis who goes to theatres and concert halls and describes, in minute and often picturesque details, both the ambiance and the performance—he particularly liked an evening of Indian music and dancing, while he felt uneasy about Wagner—, and who takes solitary but equally observant walks in parks and around the historical areas of London, such as Chelsea, commenting on the old houses of eminent writers and artists of the past, watching the anonymous crowds act out various parts in the tragic comedy of life:

> How to go about liking this city? It lacks shape. Sometimes, however, it grows into a music of architectural bulk, strength of buildings and hospitals. The river holds the line of the melody.
>
> (22 November 1933)

There are poems written during this period which compensate for the scarcity of the diary entries and which, moreover, suggest the ways in which Eliot's influence was skillfully woven into the fabric of Seferis' art. The series of poems **"Notes For A Week,"** written in the summer of 1933 and subtitled "British grown daffodils," are in terms of articulation and imagery Eliotic, in contrast to the Stratis the Mariner poems where no Eliotic influence is apparent. The new series, also in ***Book of Exercises,*** has been given scanty attention by critics probably because for many years the series was not known in its complete form,[17] and because of the intensely private character of these poems, hard to understand without some explanatory notes. More than any other poems of Seferis, **"Notes For A Week"** are products of the English environment with which Seferis was gradually coming to terms in 1933. In **"Monday,"** the initial image of the "blind"

sleeping "among the bending asphodels" is developed around a parenthesis: ("I remember the paphiopedilums of another winter / enclosed in the hothouse heat. Enough of Life":),[18] which exploits part of the diary entry of 13 March 1933:

> Yesterday I went to Kew. The spring, what they call here "crocus time", was beautiful. . . . I tried to get into the small enclosure of the paphiopedilums, but the huge crowd and the stench together with the heavy air of the hothouse made me giddy.

We could also compare the following entry from the diary:

> It is eight in the evening; there is still some light outside. I drew my curtains apart, as far as they could go. I have just turned on the light. From my window I see, across from me, a most classical-looking pediment, colour of a dove breast. Paintings of De Chirico.
>
> (17 June 1933)

with its compression in these verses from **"Sunday"**:

> Soon it'll be dark; I see a pediment of amputated statues still looking at me. What do statues weigh?

The pictorial impression of the diary entry has become here a haunting image with overtones of tragedy and double entendre. The broken statues symbolize a dead and useless past, on the one hand, and the living dead of today, those whom Seferis saw in his walks in the streets of London and in the subway and whom he found walking across the London bridges in Eliot's *The Waste Land*.

One whole poem from the series reveals, better, Seferis' new and freer technique:

"Thursday"

> I saw her die many times
> sometimes crying in my arms
> sometimes in a stranger's arms
> sometimes alone, naked;
> so she lived near me.
> Now at last I know there's nothing further
> and I wait.
> If I'm sorry, it's a private matter
> like the feeling for things so simple
> that, as they say, one's passed beyond them;
> and yet I'm sorry still because
> I too didn't become (as I would have wished)
> like the grass I heard sprouting
> one night near a pine-tree;
> because I didn't follow the sea
> another night when the waters were withdrawing
> gently drinking their own bitterness,
> and I didn't even understand, as I groped in the damp
>   seaweed,
> how much honor remains in the hands of men.
> All this passed by slowly and conclusively
> like the barges with faded names:

HELEN OF SPARTA, TYRANNUS, GLORIA
 MUNDI
they passed under the bridges beyond the chimneys
with two stooping men at the prow and stern
naked to the waist;
they passed, I can't distinguish anything, in the morning fog
the sheep, curled, ruminating, barely stand out
nor does the moon stand out above
the waiting river;
only seven lances plunged in the water
stagnant, bloodless
and sometimes on the flagstones, sadly lit
under the squint-eyed castle,
drawn with red and yellow pencil:
the Nazarene, showing his wound.
"Don't throw your heart to the dogs.
Don't throw your heart to the dogs."
Her voice sinks as the clock strikes;
your will, I sought your will.

"Mixing memory with observation"—to paraphrase Eliot—Seferis has brought together, here, material of varied provenance, following a method of free associations, enlarging the scope of the poem from the personal to the universal as he allows images from the Greek and the British landscapes to creep into his poem. "Don't throw your heart to the dogs. / Don't throw your heart to the dogs" may be the exhortation of a preacher whom Seferis encountered in a London street. This is also a variation of a Gospel passage: "Give not that which is holy unto the dogs" (Matt. 7:6). As for the picture with the Nazarene, it is the reflection of an incident which Seferis has related elsewhere.[19] The last line also has unmistakable biblical overtones, and we may further recall that Thursday, in the Greek orthodox tradition, is the day of Christ's crucifixion.

In **"Notes For A Week,"** Seferis does not borrow any unassimilated imagery from Eliot (he was too intelligent for that). He was simply encouraged, by the example of Eliot's poetry, to mix together what we could call his older "baggage of images" (from the Greek and French cultures) with the new impressions he obtained from the London, and more broadly, English environment, and to follow a stream-of-consciousness technique, which is more evident as such than in his previous poetry. In the title, the word *"Week"* is intentionally put in quotes to distract us from the idea that we have, here, to do with seven poems, each one written on a different day of a particular week. **"Notes For A Week"** is, on the whole, a transitional piece of work for Seferis, on his way to conceiving and writing his first really mature work, the 24 piece *Mythistorima.*

The two and a half years which George Seferis spent in England, between 1931 and 1934, were definitely for him a formative period. He even came to like London, at least partially, in the few months that preceded his return to Athens. He seems to have enjoyed the spring

of 1933 and the contemporary London scene and felt depressed when, for a while, he was in danger of being posted to Cardiff. "I did not enter the Diplomatic Service in order to be a Harbour Master for four years," he wrote, somewhat bitterly, to his sister (Tsatsos 1982: 212), and it is probably this problem, among others, which prompted him to make to George Theotokas the following comment on some Athenian critic's pseudo-grand utterance ("je suis un homme en proie au temps et au problème total"): "Moi," Seferis said, "je suis un homme en proie au mauvais temps (I am in London, after all) et aux problèmes partiels" (1975: 126).

The second half of this period is quite removed from the time of Seferis' early lyrics—this, in fact, he admits to his sister (Tsatsos 1982: 211)—but it is also removed even from the beginning of his stay in London, when he was trying to translate Valéry's essay *Propos sur la poésie* (*Ibid.*: 197). Self-absorption is prominent in the diary entries, although we know from other sources (letters to his sister, brother-in-law and Theotokas) that Seferis was also concerned at this time with the political and economic crisis in his native Greece (a reflection of the international monetary crisis after the depression in America). He also had thoughts about others, like his baby niece for whom he translated, in rhyming Greek, verses of D. H. Lawrence. His homesickness was expressed variously. For Theotokas' name day, he sent a card with the bust of Homer at the British museum and in "Letter to a Foreign Friend" (*On the Greek Style* 1966: 165-166) he relates how he used to find temporary "shelter" in the aforesaid museum and the National Gallery:

> I remember the time—it now seems so long ago—when I was making my first faltering discovery of London, which I thought of as a gigantic seaport, and of the English language, whose music sounded so much more fluid than that of our own tongue. Also, the shock I experienced at the sour taste of death in the fog, and the intensified circulation of fear in the arteries of the great city. . . . I carried with me a great nostalgia, which was awakened on many occasions by the kind of formless sensitivity and patient, really cold politeness with which I was surrounded. I had no friends in England then. My only acquaintances were the crowds in the streets and the museums. . . . I often had to rush out of my house to see again a fragment of the Greek marbles. . . . or a small portrait by El Greco at the National Gallery.

* * *

When Seferis left England in February 1934, he could not foresee the circumstances under which he was to set foot in that country again. It was ten years later and during the last worst air raids on London that Seferis accompanied a Greek politician on an official mission to England and flew there from Cairo via Morocco. It was a very difficult time for him, for apart from the general uncertainty of the political situation and the troubles of exile, Seferis felt victimized by his own people, object of intrigues and petty jealousies. The book he read during the flight was characteristic of his feelings at the time, Kafka's *The Castle,* "a book that reflects well enough," he noted on the margin, "my present situation: this man who tries to enter an impenetrable castle, high on the hill, and becomes entangled, everytime, in endless nets . . . like a fish out of the water" (14 July 1944) (*Meres D* 1977: 334).

When the plane finally landed in England (Swinton), the greenness of the landscape struck Seferis just as it had struck him in 1931: "I think I remember these houses with their thatched roofs and the small quiet windows, and all that green colour which I missed so much in Egypt and which my eyes absorb now, like water. I think I have strolled about here ten or twelve years ago." And a little later, he wrote "Fields of England, strange workings of memory. In the last ten years I have not recalled them more than four or five times, remotely, abstractly. Now, it is as though I left them asleep, like that, last Sunday" (15 July 1944).

Two weeks later, Seferis was a guest at the country estate of David Wallace, an English officer with whom he had worked in Greece and Egypt.

> In the afternoon, we took a walk on the green hills and through wooded paths. Many aeroplanes in the sky. Only those remind you of the war. We had supper at Beechwood [one of the houses on the estate]. Good wines. Nine rooms, remnants of a time when they hosted twenty or thirty people during week-ends. When we went upstairs to sleep, the servant had emptied our poor little suitcases and arranged everything neatly. Through the window, I could see sheep ruminating calmly, almost at the same level with where I sat in the armchair. Slow and quiet end of the day, that darkening which seems never ending at this time in England. The room which they gave us is entirely painted in white and lead colors. Pictures of plants all around the walls: Calanthe Vestita, Oncidium Sarcodes, Cymbidium Eburneum. I feel sleep pressing on my eyelids as I take these names down. . . .

> (24 July 1944)

The man who used to copy in his notebook the exotic names of plants which he found in the parks of London, during the peaceful years of 1931-34, still does so, during the critical days of 1944. He has a sensual feeling for language, and the ruins of the war elicit a similar response from his eyes. His descriptions are frugal but also sensitive: "As we were entering the park from Bayswater, across from a house that had been hit, the trees were bare, without a single leaf, as if you had skinned them with a knife" (19 July 1944). In the many ruins around Saint Paul's, Seferis noted the violet flowers that grew where there used to be high buildings. He witnessed the evacuation of women and children from

London because of the "robots." In the 1930s Seferis had recorded in his diary fleeting impressions from the anonymous, often miserable crowds, which he saw in the streets of the English capital, the unemployed and the drunk. In his brief 1944 visit, he felt deep sympathy for all of those, regardless of their social status, who were paying a big price to the war, above all for the old and the very young whom he saw sleeping in the subway stations (scenes immortalized in the drawings of Henry Moore):

> In the tube. Wooden scaffolds filled with people. Others are lying on the pavement. Your eyes stop on the faces of the old and the children; a little girl with blond hair, or tired, fixed eyes on heavily wrinkled faces. You would say that they are asleep like that, with eyelids open as if they were dead, while the trains come and go.

> (26 July 1944)

In the early hours of 19 July, Seferis was kept awake by the persistent bombings around the "Ritz," where he and his Greek companion were staying. By 2:20 a.m. he had counted six explosions and described the process of an explosion as he caught it by ear. Exhausted, he fell asleep while the bombings went on. "One of the worst nights since the war began," the waiter, who brought them breakfast, said in the morning. Several days later, Seferis visited a Greek acquaintance at her estate in Frimley where he saw and admired a huge, strong and calm bull, who (as they informed him) had been recently deprived of one of his five heifers, when a doodlebug killed her. Seferis could not miss recording the graphic detail.

But how more concrete had the human landscape of England become for Seferis by 1944? Much more concrete. T. S. Eliot, whom Seferis had translated and published in 1936 with copious notes, had not as yet been met; but, in his capacity as foreign press officer in the Greek Ministry of Press and Information since 1938, Seferis had the opportunity to work with several Englishmen. These contacts continued and even increased during the war years in view of the common war effort between Greece and England. All these associations and their echoes, if any, in the poetry, the critical and confessional prose of Seferis deserve separate treatment. Here, it may suffice to suggest Seferis' fair and independent mind vis-à-vis the British men he met and worked with during these years by considering part of a 1944 entry in his diary, precisely from the period of his brief visit to England in war which we have been discussing above:

> In the station, P. with his [Greek] shepherd's staff, waiting to travel to London. He is a fair-haired Scot, not quite thirty perhaps. Before the war, he used to make beer and whiskey. Now, he is a lieutenant-colonel and link with the resistance in the Peloponnese. He has

learned Greek. He is going to see his wife for a few days, after two years. Should he phone her first, or not? This is his big question. . . . [On the train] "England never changes. England is always Sleepy" *(sic)*, P. says, as if he was singing his deeper yearning. Which yearning? That for his wife? For his adventures in Greece? His feelings about the destiny of the war? He is reading Tolstoy's *War and Peace.* We exchange bitter-sweet jokes about Greece. He observes: "I do not trust the Greeks who speak good English."—"You are right," I say, "I have the same feeling about the British who know our language well." An old breed they are, these young men (I mean the better ones, not the levantine kind) who begin their political career with adventures in our land. The type strikes me as half intellectual and half corsair of the Drake period. As an individual, you can't help liking them. It is another story that they have turned us upside down while being trained on how to crop the scanty hair on our poor heads. After all, however high their social status is, they pay like the others.

(15 July 1944)

Literature could not be very much in Seferis' mind during those critical days of 1944. However, four days before flying back to Cairo, Seferis records meeting Cyril Connolly in the lobby of the "Ritz," without giving any other details, while several days earlier he had asked Leonard Russell, editor of the literary page of *The Sunday Times,* to name some of the better books that had appeared in England during the war period. "This is a difficult question," was Russell's only answer.

No poems of Seferis seem to have originated directly in the impressions of his month-long official visit in the England of 1944. But there is a poem from his Egypt days, **"An Old Man on the River Bank,"** in which the image of the Nile seems to overlap with the vision of the Thames, as Seferis had it in the 1930s as well as the motif of the river which he had found in Eliot's *Four Quartets.* In this poem, Seferis considers the fortuities of his life and the accidents of the war, the "hungry children and the chasm between" himself and his companions "and the companions calling from the opposite shore" (that is, occupied Greece), the "bluish light" of the hospital and the "glimmer on the pillow of the youth" who had undergone surgery, all these implacable urgencies and fatalities. He feels that he should still go forward "like / the long river that emerges from the great lakes enclosed deep in Africa, / that was once a god and then became a road and a benefactor, a judge and a delta: / that is never the same, as the ancient wise men taught, / and yet always remains the same body, the same bed, and the same Sign, / the same orientation." (lines 5-15). The central river motif of the poem is further elaborated and brought into connection with the fluid yet persistent ways of the human psyche in the following passage:

If pain is human we are not human beings merely to
   suffer pain;

that's why I think so much these days about the great
   river,
that symbol which moves forward among herbs and
   greenery
and beasts that graze and drink, men who sow and
   harvest,
great tombs even and small habitations of the dead.
That current which goes its way and which is not so
   different from the blood of men.

(lines 20-25)

* * *

Seferis was a reserved and often self-conscious man, one who "se voyait voir"—to remember Valéry's *La Soirée avec Monsieur Teste,* which Seferis translated into Greek. But he was also a man with a sensual feeling for his surroundings, both natural and man-made, including art. George Braque has written that it is not enough for an artist to make the others see what he paints, he must make them feel it as well.[20] Seferis quoted this statement of Braque with obvious approval, while commenting on the work of the Cypriot painter Diamantis.[21] For Seferis the aesthetic was an extension of the sensual. We thus understand his impulsive visits to the London museums to look at his favorite exhibits and the ways in which he tried to salvage from the English landscape whatever could compensate for his being away from Greece. A loner though he was, he needed human companionship and this he missed during his first stay in England. Again, the substitute was found in the arts, music which Seferis heard with great concentration, poetry which he wrote with even greater attention, eventually with encouragement from Eliot's work. The England-based Seferis of 1931-34 and of July-August 1944 was a Greek poet, conscious of his heritage and eager to honor and continue the literary tradition of his land, but also ready to learn from other places, other traditions, and creatively to "steal" from other contemporary writers, true to his belief, variously expressed in his essays, that there is no parthenogenesis in art. In patent or latent ways, creation is ultimately a collective business.

Notes

The paper was researched and written in Athens, Greece, and in Toronto, Canada, and is part of a project with the provisional title *Studies on George Seferis, Poet, Critic, Diarist.* I am grateful to the University of Toronto and the Canada Council for the Humanities and Social Sciences for financial support towards the completion of the project. In the present paper, extensive use is made, in my translation, of Seferis' diary *Meres B* [Days B], which covers the period 24 August 1931-12 February 1934, published in Athens by Ikaros, 1975. I quote the poetry of Seferis in the translation by E. Keeley and Ph. Sherrard from: *George Seferis, Collected Poems.* Expanded Edition (Princeton

University Press, 1981) with the permission of the translators. All other translations from Greek sources in this paper are my own, unless indicated.

1. See below, p. 96.

2. Here the Greek word *dískos* carries its double meaning, "phonograph record" and "serving tray."

3. Cf. with what Seferis wrote to his sister Ioanna (Tsatsos 1982: 203): "But I so long for Attica. The pines and the sea. These two things are before my eyes every day, like mythological creatures, in their changing aspects always new. A man must be away from his country at a mature age if he is to understand the *Odyssey*."

4. Allusion to E. A. Poe's *A Narrative of A. Gordon Pym*, from the tenth chapter of which Seferis had borrowed the epigraph of his poem "The Mood of a Day" (*Turning Point*).

5. Seferis had talked about Ramon Gomez de la Serna in a bad sleep during a restless night he spent after an antityphus injection. L. Durrell became interested in the subject and mentioned the Spaniard in his autobiographical poem "Mythology, II," which Seferis translated into Greek.

6. Both Vayenas (198-200, and *passim*) and D. Maronitis (1984: 97-107) have commented extensively and perceptively on "Hampstead," especially in contrast to the poem by Angelos Sikelianos, "Thalero."

7. In Beaton's "Life at Close Range," review of *Meres B*, in *T.L.S.*[*Times Literary Supplement*], 3888 (17 September 1976): 1179.

8. Harvard University Press, 1970. Seferis' introduction to this book may have been a partial compensation to Harvard for Seferis' refusal to deliver a similar lecture series at Harvard for 1969, on which point, see below, p. 97.

9. The last simile may be likened with another involving El Greco. Under 20 December 1931, Seferis wrote: "The other day I found an old note of mine: 'National Gallery, 1924: A brush-stroke of Theotokopoulos [El Greco] like a Cretan fifteen-syllable line.'" The matter of this simile, which was not in fact made by Seferis but by a friend of his, is clarified in Seferis' *On the Greek Style* (1966: 94-95). On Seferis and El Greco, see also below, p. 27.

10. A similar turn of phrase was used, many years later, by the Greek writer Nikos Gabriel Pentzikis, in reference to Seferis' pessimism, against which Pentzikis proposed the alternative of Christian faith (Thaniel 1983: 129): "The acceptance of the 'surreal' enables man to dance off the storms of life. [According to Pentzikis], Seferis does not dare to dance; his ego is too strong for that. 'And yet,' Pentzikis says, 'the whole thing is no more complicated than an inoculation.'"

11. A listing of parallels in the essays of Eliot and Seferis is provided by Nakas (1978). See also Nakas' essay on Eliot in *I Lexi*, 43 (1985), 271-276.

12. Cf. the relevant passage in Part IV of the poem (in *Turning Point*):

> Two serpents, beautiful, apart, tentacles of separation
> crawl and search, in the night of the trees,
> for a secret love in hidden bowers;
> sleepless they search, they neither drink nor eat.
>
> Circling, twisting, their insatiable intent
> spins, multiplies, turns, spreads rings on the body
> which the laws of the starry dome silently govern,
> stirring its hot, irrepressible frenzy.

13. *Sic* in the original, after "I read."

14. Cf. with "Seferis and the 'Mythical Method,'" in Keeley (1983: 68-94).

15. See above, p. 89.

16. In fact, the column, whose drums are still strewn on the ground where they fell, was a casualty of a violent windstorm in 1852. Several Greek poets wrote poems on the fallen column.

17. The 1940 edition of *Book of Exercises* and subsequent editions of Seferis' poetry did not include the poems for Tuesday and Wednesday, which had been lost and found again in the 1960s. These were first published in Italy, and are now included in the expanded *Seferis* by Keeley-Sherrard.

18. The Greek *arkíto Víos* (enough of life) are the words which Cassandra utters last (in Aeschylus *Agamemnon*, 1324), before she enters the palace at Mycenae to die.

19. *On the Greek Style* (1966: 69): "We went out into the empty streets of the becalmed city. On the wet pavement we could see, painted in multicolor crayons, the figure of Christ, with a discolored crimson forehead and heart. . . ."

20. In *Le jour et la nuit, Cahiers 1917-52* (Paris: Gallimard, 1952).

21. In Seferis-Diamantis (1985: 16).

References Cited

Seferis, George. 1981 *Collected Poems*. Trans. E. Keeley and Ph. Sherrard. Expanded Edition. Princeton University Press.

————. 1966 *On the Greek Style. Selected Essays in Poetry and Hellenism*. Trans. R. Warner and Th. Frangópoulos. Boston: Little Brown and Co.

————. 1973 *Méres E (Days E) [1945-51]*. Athens: 'Ikaros.

————. 1975 *Méres B (Days B) [1931-34]*. Athens: 'Ikaros.

————. 1977 *Méres C (Days C) [1934-40]*. Athens: 'Ikaros.

————. 1977 *Méres D (Days D) [1941-44]*. Athens: 'Ikaros.

————. 1986 *Méres F (Days F) [1951-56]*. Athens: 'Ikaros.

————. 1975 *Seferis and Theotokás: Allilografía (Correspondence)*. Athens: Ermís.

————. 1985 *Seferis and Diamantís: Allilografía (Correspondence)*. Athens: Stigmí.

Beaton, R. 1976 *Life at Close Range* (Review of Seferis' Méres B). Times Literary Supplement 3888: 1179.

Keeley, E. M. 1983 *Modern Greek Poetry: Voice and Myth*. Princeton University Press.

Maronítis, D. 1984 *I Píissi tu Yiórgu Seféri (The poetry of George Seferis)*. Athens: Ermís.

Miller, H. 1941 *The Colossus of Maroussi*. New York: New Directions.

Nákas, Th. 1978 *Parállila Horía sta Dokímia tu Seféri ke tu Éliot (Parallel passages in the essays of Seferis and the essays of Eliot)*. Athens: Privately pr.

Stanford, W. B. 1954 *The Ulysses Theme: A Study in the Adaptability of a Traditional Hero*. Oxford University Press.

Thaniel G. 1983 *Homage to Byzantium: The Life and Work of Nikos Gabriel Pentzikis*. Minneapolis: North Central Publ. Co.

Tsátsos, I. 1982 *My Brother George Seferis*. Trans. J. Demos. Minneapolis: North Central Publ. Co.

Vayenás, N. 1979 *O Piitís ke o Horeftís (The poet and the dancer)*. Athens: Kédros.

Roderick Beaton (essay date October 1987)

SOURCE: Beaton, Roderick. "From Mythos to Logos: The Poetics of George Seferis." *Journal of Modern Greek Studies* 5, no. 2 (October 1987): 135-52.

[In the following essay, Beaton explores the blending of mythology and history that characterizes much of Seferis's poetry.]

"It was its two component parts that made me choose the title of this piece of work; MYTHOS[1] (myth), because I have used quite plainly a certain mythology; ISTORIA (history/story), because I have tried to express, with some coherence, a situation as independent of myself as the characters in a novel" (Seféris 1972: 314). With this note to the sequence of 24 poems published in 1935 under the title **Mithistórima** or *Novel*, Seferis drew attention to the references to ancient Greek mythology which abound in the poems and also to the strategy which some of the texts, at least, pursue of juxtaposing this mythology with the world of real experience (history or story). This strategy owes an acknowledged debt to that of T. S. Eliot in *The Waste Land*, but rather more to Eliot's now famous review of James Joyce's novel *Ulysses*, which had been published in the same year (1922). There Eliot credits Joyce with the achievement of a new "method," which he contrasts with the "narrative method" of the obsolescent genre of the novel. This method uses a myth (here the paradigmatic story of the *Odyssey*) as "a way of controlling, of ordering, of giving a shape and a significance to the immense panorama of futility and anarchy which is contemporary history" (Eliot 1970: 270).

The relevance of Eliot's conception of myth, distilled from Joyce's novel, to a reading of Seferis' sequence of poems goes beyond the disputed question of how far this "mythical method" is actually used in individual sections of **Mithistórima**.[2] The link between the mythical and the real that Seferis proposes in his note, if it is to be effected, as he put it, "with some coherence," demands a literary form able to encompass a range of objectively presented events and capable of imposing a coherent structure upon them. Lyric poetry, particularly in the almost telegraphic form in which both Eliot and Seferis had inherited it from the French Symbolists, is not well equipped for this task. For Seferis, who unlike Eliot had been trying for ten years to write a novel, the example of Joyce becomes only the final, clinching, reason for invoking that genre: only the larger literary structure of the novel can encompass the avowed program of Seferis' note on **Mithistórima**, of effectively linking myth and history "with some coherence."[3]

The title of **Mithistórima** alludes to a literary space in which *mythos* and *istoría* (myth and history/story) are capable of being reconciled within a coherent structure. This space however remains imaginary, or at best vestigial: **Mithistórima**, in defiance of its title, is not a novel, although its 24 sections might be read either as the fragments of a lost novel or as the inchoate material for a novel yet to be written. In any case the poems, through their title and the note on it, delineate at the level of discourse a literary space which they do not fill, or not fully.

At the level of "story,"[4] that is, within each of the 24 poems, this delineation of a space that can only inadequately be filled, if at all, is reduplicated. The multiple personae whose disembodied voices are heard in the poems are repeatedly and explicitly aware of a lack, of the lack of something which is never named in the poems but which can plausibly be identified with the term *mythos,* which appears only in the note attributable not to any of the poems' narrators but to the poet in his "own" persona as "implied author." To see how this lack is defined within the poems, I propose to look in detail at Poem 1 of the sequence before turning outside of the text for evidence of the significance that Seferis' contemporaries attached to the term "myth."

> The angel messenger
> three years we waited intently for him
> peering very closely
> at the pines the shore and the stars.
> Mingling with the plough's furrow or the keel of the
>   ship
> seeking to rediscover the primal seed
> once more to set in train the immemorial drama.
>
> We returned to our homes shattered
> with palsied limbs, our mouths ravaged
> by the taste of rust and brine.
> When we awoke we traveled northwards, strangers
> plunged into mists by the immaculate wings of swans
>   that savaged us.
> On winter nights a mighty wind from the East would
>   fray our senses
> in summer we would fade into the agony of a day
>   incapable of giving up the ghost.
>
> We brought back
> these carvings of a humble art.

The *ángelos* of the first line is the elusive object (grammatically in the accusative case) of a quest made more fully explicit in 1. 6: "seeking to rediscover." *Angelos* means two things in Greek tradition: angel and messenger, both of them bringers of tidings, that is, of words. The messenger in ancient tragedy was invariably the bearer of bad news; in Christian texts the angels are the messengers of a benign God and bring "good tidings of great joy." In ancient tragedy the *ángelos* announces the "catastrophe," or the resolution of a story which had a special status as a *mythos,* one of the tales about gods and heroes by means of which ancient Greeks tried to come to terms with the cosmos and their place in it. In the Christian story, on the other hand, at the Annunciation (*Evangelismós*), the *good* news which crucially separates Christianity from all that had gone before in the religious tradition of Judaism is brought by an angel. The *ángelos* then is the speaking representative of the two great groups of myths which have shaped Greek and European civilisation.

If "myth," in a sense yet to be defined, represents the object of the quest adumbrated in the first paragraph, the second indicates the route taken in pursuit of this quest: that is, northwards. As it happens, this was the route taken by the poet himself, but metaphorically it applies to any Greek in search of the remotest origins of his culture. Lines 6-8 already imply an analogy between this second-order quest for myth and the mythical adventures of such heroes as Odysseus and Jason. Northern Europe (especially France and England), as Seferis acknowledged in an essay, had preserved—and given a new lease of life to—ancient Greek learning in the Renaissance and its aftermath, a revival from which the Greeks themselves were for the most part excluded under Ottoman rule (Seféris 1974a: I. 215-217). Northern Europe represented the principal repository where the "primal seed" underlying the ancient Greek achievement could now be sought, but where the Greek speakers in the poem, like Seferis himself, find themselves paradoxically *kséni* (strangers/foreigners).[5]

But if the mythical and primeval substrata beneath classical culture are the object of the quest, they can only with difficulty be reconciled with received notions of "high art." The poem concludes gloomily, and baldly: "We brought back / these carvings of a humble art." Seferis' words here echo those of Kariotákis, who had committed suicide in 1928: "Humble art devoid of style, / How late have I learnt to learn from you;"[6] but I suspect that there is also a more important allusion, if not directly to a passage in D. H. Lawrence's *Women in Love,* then certainly to the contemporary intellectual debate upon which it touches. A group of men in a London flat are looking at a totemic figurine (the carving of a "humble art") from the South Pacific:

> Birkin, white and strangely ghostly, went over to the carved figure of the savage woman in labour. Her nude, protuberant body crouched in a strange, clutching posture, her hands gripping the ends of the band, above her breast.
>
> "It is art," said Birkin . . .
>
> "Why is it art?" Gerald asked, shocked, resentful.
>
> "It conveys a complete truth," said Birkin. "It contains the whole truth of that state, whatever you feel about it."
>
> "But you can't call it *high* art," said Gerald.
>
> "High! There are centuries and hundreds of centuries of development in a straight line, behind that carving; it is an awful pitch of culture, of a definite sort.
>
>   (Lawrence 1960: 87)

It is precisely this kind of culture and this kind of art, possessed of a primitive power, encapsulating a "complete truth," and at the same time the culmination of an agelong tradition, that **Mithistórima** as a whole attempts to recapture for the modern world.

The parallel reading of the last two lines of Seferis' poem alongside an extract from D. H. Lawrence's novel begins to suggest a context for the whole of **Mithis-**

tórima, and this context must now be examined. At the end of the 19th century James Frazer, in *The Golden Bough,* had shown how ancient literature and recorded beliefs could be read as the traces of much more ancient and primitive beliefs and practices, and anthropologists in the decades up until World War II often aimed to fill out this version of a lost childhood of man with their interpretations of contemporary primitive societies (Frazer 1961). Often the work of anthropologists in the 1920s reads uncannily like the poetry of an Eliot or a Seferis, none more so than the influential work on myth in primitive societies by Bronislaw Malinowski. "Myth as it exists in a savage community," wrote Malinowski in 1926:

> that is, in its living primitive form, is not merely a story told but a reality lived. It is not of the nature of fiction, such as we read today in a novel, but it is a living reality, believed to have once happened in primeval times, and continuing ever since to influence the world and human destinies . . . It is necessary to go back to primitive mythology in order to learn the secret of its life in the study of a myth which is still alive—before, mummified in priestly wisdom, it has been enshrined in the indestructible but lifeless repository of dead religions.
>
> (Malinowski 1974: 100-1)

Just such a backward progress toward a "living reality" beyond the "lifeless repository" of codified art and religion—represented for Seferis by the statues and ruins of ancient Greece—is depicted in the first poem of *Mithistórima* and indeed in that sequence as a whole.

And lest it be thought that Lawrence and Malinowski are improbably remote from Athens and Seferis in the early 30s, here is Seferis himself on the same subject, in his introduction to his translation, published a year after *Mithistórima,* of Eliot's *The Waste Land:*

> It seems to me . . . that with this technique [sc. of "continuous extinction of personality"], Eliot has tried to find in his times something that would play the role of mythology, even if only for a restricted public. When myth was an experience common to all, the poet had at his disposal a living vehicle, an emotional atmosphere ready prepared, in which he could move freely in order to reach out to those around him; in which he himself could be inscribed *[na diatipothí].* One word, irrespective of the skill of the artist, could awake in [his hearers'] souls a whole world of fear or hope. We have nothing in our contemporary languages to equal in weight or catholicity or emotional wealth the simple word *Semnai* at the time of Aischylos, or the two words *eterno* [sic] *dolore* at the time of Dante. I suppose that what Eliot has sought before everything else, out of the verses that he transposes or paraphrases, was this common vehicle, which once upon a time was given to the poet by the natural functioning of mythology.
>
> (1974a: I. 43-44)

And a few pages earlier Seferis had quoted with approval Eliot's comments of 1923 on the decline of the traditional way of life in the South Pacific (1974a: I. 27-28).

It was not only classical learning that the modern Greek had to learn from northern Europe at this time; it was also this whole idea that the "primal seed" of classical and by implication all later Hellenism lay buried in the textual and archeological record. The myth that is the object of the quest is itself, although a Greek word and to be sought among the relics of a Greek civilization, the discovery of northern Europe. Indeed it was in English and French that the project described in the opening paragraph of *Mithistórima* 1, of revitalizing an enervated tradition by seeking the creative force attributed to primitive myth, was first attempted in literature. The most famous literary text which proceeds in this way is of course Joyce's *Ulysses,* whose relation to *Mithistórima* has already been discussed.[7] Another is alluded to, I believe, in Poem I's second paragraph, which describes the journey to the north.

The 12th line of this poem—"plunged into mists by the immaculate wings of swans that savaged us"—is extremely puzzling: one may suspect an allusion to the myth of Leda, seduced by Zeus in the guise of a swan, so as to conceive Helen of Troy. But more interestingly, the *savagery* and physicality of the image used by Seferis can most satisfactorily be accounted for as an allusion to the recreation of that myth by W. B. Yeats in the poem "Leda and the Swan" (Yeats 1957: 441). Yeats was one of the first poets to adapt Frazer's anthropological insights for poetry. "Leda and the Swan" evokes the savagery of a bestial union between the human and the divine that metaphorically generates both myth and history:

> A sudden blow: the great wings beating still
> Above the staggering girl, her thighs caressed
> By the dark webs, her nape caught in his bill,
> He holds her helpless breast upon his breast.

The brutally physical terms in which Zeus' rape of Leda in the guise of a swan is envisaged here fits exactly with the concept of the "living reality" behind classical myth which the generation after *The Golden Bough* had learned to look for behind the ancient texts. The relevance of Yeats' poem to the quest for the "primal seed" behind "the immemorial drama" in *Mithistórima* becomes fully clear in its third stanza:

> A shudder in the loins engenders there
> The broken wall, the burning roof and tower
> And Agamemnon dead.

The seed implanted in this myth grew into Helen of Troy, but for whom the whole cycle of myths and legends about the Trojan War could never have come into being. In the allusion to Yeats' poem and the reference to northern Europe, Seferis pays tribute to the role of western culture in nurturing and interpreting the ancient tradition that offers the only road open to the modern Greek to rediscover his own "primal seed"—although the image alluded to may also imply something less than natural about the process.

The close reading of Poem 1 of *Mithistórima* alongside the discourse of Seferis and his older contemporaries about myth enables us to describe with a degree of fullness what it is, at the level of story, that the speakers in that poem experience as a lack. Throughout the rest of the sequence each poem, with the possible exception of the last two, represents a new beginning. Each separate poem, at the level of its story, delineates the contours of an absence, of something that is lacking, although the "space" so defined is far from identical each time. What is certain is that, always at the level of "story," the revitalizing power of myth is never regained: toward the end of the sequence the cessation from the quest is several times linked with the term *galíni* (serenity), which in a series of contexts acquires a sinister ambiguity:

> "Give us, outside of sleep, serenity"
>
> (Poem 15)

> ". . . I see the trees that breathe the black serenity of
>   the dead
> and then the smiles, without progression, of the
>   statues"
>
> (Poem 20)

> "We who had nothing shall teach them serenity"
>
> (Poem 24)

The serenity which is the final word of the entire sequence is far from representing a resolution of the quest. It too represents only an absence: the absence of striving, the cessation of effort, the suspension of consciousness, perhaps even of life.

The overt use of classical mythology in many of the poems, an element that has often enough been discussed, makes no great contribution to filling the gap opened up by the very first verb in Poem 1, *periméname* ("we were waiting for"). Rather, the abundance of mythological allusions[8] serves as a series of pointers to their common denominator of a (lost) myth in the Malinowskian sense, a myth which the poems' diversified personae fail to recover.

So far I have been considering *Mithistórima* only in relation to the discourses of its time. If these discourses are viewed from a somewhat later perspective, it

becomes possible to place the sequence of poems alongside a number of literary and anthropological writings of the 1920s and 1930s in which the classic dilemma of the Romantic or post-Romantic writer is formulated in a distinctive way. This dilemma, which has been variously articulated since the 1950s by M. H. Abrams (1953), Fredric Jameson (1972) and Paul de Man (1984), is posed for the writer by the nature of his medium: how can the bounds of language be transcended within a text which itself consists only of language? The invocation of myth in the writings of Yeats, Joyce, Eliot and Seferis, as an originating and controlling power, was an attempt to break out of what Jameson has termed (after Wordsworth) the "prison-house of language." The attempt belongs fully to what Paul de Man called the "rhetoric of Romanticism," that is to the "adventure of a failure" of language, as a constitutive system, ever to achieve "the absolute identity with itself that exists in the natural object" or to match, without losing that constitutive power, the "ontological status of the object" (De Man 1984: 6-7).

In the period up until World War II the appeal to myth appears as a strategy for resolving this dilemma, since primitive myth in the discourse of anthropologists such as Frazer and Jessie Weston[9] was seen as simultaneously a linguistic construct like literature and a real presence and constitutive force *in the world*—something which literature, if one follows the rhetoric of de Man, cannot ever be. For whatever reason—and this is not the place to embark on the wider question—after World War II myth ceases to occupy such a key position either in anthropology or in literature.

Seferis after *Mithistórima* never again used "a certain mythology" to point the way towards "myth" as an ideal status to which a text could or should aspire. In later poems such as **"Thrush"** and certain of the poems of *Logbook III,* a single myth (not "mythology" in general) is used as a specific point of reference and departure. In **"Thrush"** the abstract and purely textual quest for "the light" is anchored in the reader's more familiar (but still textual) experience by sustained allusion to the parallel quest of Odysseus for his homeland[10] but at the levels of both story and discourse what is sought is not the mythical status of the *Odyssey,* still less of whatever more primitive myths may lie behind it, but *to fos* (the light). Indeed from this time on, when a poem by Seferis adopts an ancient myth in this way, the myth comes increasingly to be equated with an ancient *literary text*: Euripides' *Helen* in **"Helen,"** Aeschylus' *Persians* and the Psalms in **"Salamis in Cyprus,"** in allusions which are no longer, properly speaking, to myths at all. By the time of *Logbook III,* mythical reference has become fully assimilated as one strand among many in the intertextual (that is, literary) web of references and allusions that constitute Seferis' text.

But the "rhetoric of Romanticism," the "adventure of a failure" of language to reach out beyond the limitations of its own condition, continues unabated in the poems that Seferis wrote after *Mithistórima.* An absence which the text delineates but can never quite fill is evident again in **"Thrush,"** where it is named as "the light," and in *Logbook III,* where the term *thávma* (miracle) used by the poet in a note to the first edition, would be appropriate.[11] But in order to follow through the postwar development of Seferis' poetics, I shall turn now to his final completed poetic statement, the *Three Secret Poems.*

Published in 1966, the *Three Secret Poems* have been much translated but almost wholly ignored in critical discussions of Seferis. Their terseness and the apparent absence of a principal, unifying theme seem to have retarded recognition of the *Three Secret Poems* as a final testament of some complexity.[12] The fragmentary sections that make up these poems offer a secular vision of a world in dissolution, set against a background of a Greek landscape and Greek literary allusions. Repeated metamorphoses, some but not all inspired by classical mythology, fill out the sinister picture of a world gone awry: dancers are turned into trees (I. 1), ancient sea-nymphs, the Graeae, appear as monstrosities without eyelids (I. 2); voices turn into pebbles and playthings for children (I. 5); a murderess becomes rooted, apparently literally, in the earth, colored pebbles taking the place of nipples as she becomes, perhaps, a statue (II. 3); sea and land fester like putrid bodies (II. 4; III. 4); a crime has no witnesses because "they have abolished their eyes" (II. 5); everything is being ground down by millstones in order to turn into stars (III. 1); a great rose is implanted deep in the side of someone addressed (an unexpected allusion, surely, to Jean Genet's novel, *The Miracle of the Rose*) (III. 2); Pasiphae, merging in the epithet *kimatóferti* with Europa abducted by a bull, conceives the Minotaur in the hide of a cow (III. 3); the pine resin, caught in the heat of noon, longs to turn into flame and in an ultimate conflagration everything together "must burn / this noontide when the sun is transfixed / to the heart of the centifoliate rose" (III. 14).

In this final transformation, Poem III ends with an evident allusion to Eliot's final statement as a poet, "Little Gidding":

> And all shall be well and all manner of thing shall be
>   well
> When the tongues of flame are in-folded
> Into the crowned knot of fire
> And the fire and the rose are one.
>
> (Eliot 1963: 223)

The *three* secret poems do certainly invite comparison with the older poet's *four* quartets. But the relationship is more complex. Seferis never underwent a religious conversion such as Eliot publicized in his writings from "Ash Wednesday" onwards. Indeed in one of Seferis' earliest diary entries to mention Eliot, in which he records his increasing admiration for the Anglo-American poet, he makes a point of saying, "The only thing that stands in my way, and it is substantial, is his Christianity, because he is a rampant Anglo-Catholic" (Seféris 1975b: II. 108). Seferis by the 1960s would doubtless have toned down this criticism, but there is no evidence for a public change of attitude to religion. Seferis does however follow a path parallel with Eliot's later development in two important respects. The philosophy of Heraclitus makes its appearance in Seferis' texts only *after* Eliot had published *Four Quartets* with two fragments from Heraclitus (in Greek) as an epigraph.[13] Although Biblical texts make a steady appearance, most evidently in the diaries, from the late 1920s until the 1960s and although references to the Christian "myth" in *Mithistórima* should not be underestimated, nonetheless it is only in *Logbook III* and *Three Secret Poems* that allusion to Christian religious literature plays a major part in Seferis' poetry.

Heraclitus first appears in Seferis' essays by name in 1947, in a note referring the reader to the epigraph of *Four Quartets* (1974a: I. 512) and then in two published letters of 1949, one again on the subject of Eliot (1974a: II. 9-24), the other the famous "scenario" which purports to elucidate the poem **"Thrush"** (1974a: II. 30-56). In the second the quoted fragment of Heraclitus—"The sun shall not overstep his measure; otherwise the Erinyes, handmaidens of justice, will hunt him down"—is a gloss on a passage in **"Thrush"** which had been written three years before (in October 1946); and both that part of **"Thrush"** and the later comment on it are clearly foreshadowed in a passage written in 1941 in a preface to an edition of Kalvos' *Odes* published the following year.[14]

Heraclitus reappears in *Logbook III,* in the two poems **"Memory A"** and **"Memory B."** In the first of these, an allusion to the Furies, possibly recalling the passages just cited, is significantly ranged alongside several allusions to the Apocalypse of St. John. In the *Three Secret Poems* he reappears again: the final line of the first poem, "the guiding of the thunderbolt" alludes to the fragment, "All things are guided / governed by the thunderbolt," and Poem III, Section 2, opens with an unacknowledged translation of one of the two fragments of Heraclitus that Eliot had used as an epigraph to the *Four Quartets*:

> They all see visions
> but no one admits to them:
> they go on thinking they are alone.

Seferis has made one important change here, to which I shall return. The original contains the word *logos* where Seferis has substituted *orámata* (visions).[15]

But if Heraclitus is an important, and relatively new, point of reference in the *Three Secret Poems,* the central reference and unifying principle of the whole work is derived from the Biblical text of the Apocalypse of St. John the Divine, or the Book of Revelation as it is called in the English Bible. In parallel with the writing of the *Three Secret Poems,* Seferis was engaged in translating the Apocalypse into modern Greek, and his version appeared in 1966, the same year as the poems. His account of the genesis of that translation also links St. John with Heraclitus, as the poem **"Memory A"** had done, and has significant points of contact with the *Three Secret Poems*:

> This work is the fruit of a moment: dawn on Friday 16th September 1955. The day before, a little before midnight, *I was in the isle that is called Patmos [Apoc.* I: 9]. As day was about to break I was up in the citadel. The sea, motionless as metal [cf. *Apoc.* IV: 6 and *Three Secret Poems* I. 3; III. 6, 10], bound the neighbouring islands together. Not a leaf breathed in the growing light. The stillness *[galíni]* was an unbroken shell . . . In this way I was drawn back to feelings I had been given before at other times by the Greek light: to that terrible blackness I had felt powerfully present behind the blue, when in October 1944 I returned to my country . . .
>
> The Eumenides were waiting once again behind the sun as Herakleitos had imagined them. A mechanism of self-destruction was there, in motion, crushing every spark of goodwill and dedication."

(Seféris 1966: 9)

It is not primarily by verbal allusion that the reference of the poems to the Apocalypse is established: the explicit allusions are all to Greek mythology, not Christian. The few close verbal echoes of the Apocalypse are woven unobtrusively into the text: a lyrical evocation of the Greek landscape in the 6th section of Poem III contains the line, "the sea all of glass at our feet," an echo of "the sea of glass like unto crystal" before the throne in Chapter 4 (v. 6) of the Apocalypse, while the briefly lyrical tenth section of the same poem repeats the imagery and some of the vocabulary of the harvest of dreams in Chapter 14. The fundamental relation of the poem to the Apocalypse is established first of all by its title, *Three Secret Poems,* which is semantically a precise inversion of "Apocalypse," meaning "revelation," and by the numerical structure of the text. *Three* poems are made up of *four* groups of *seven* sections (the first two poems contain seven sections each, the third fourteen), and the *three* poems and the *four* groups of seven add up to yet another seven. Indeed if the numerical relation to Eliot's *Four Quartets* previously mentioned is taken into account, the magic number of the Apocalypse is reduplicated once again. All this places the text as a whole in a special relation to the Biblical revelation of the end of the world. Yet another link is supplied by the title of the third "Secret

Poem," **"Summer Solstice,"** which in Greece is St. John's Day (24th June); and although the name of St. John never appears in the text, there are references in the first and last sections of the poem to the popular Greek practice of divination using molten lead on the eve of midsummer's day, which had furnished Seferis with the title of a poem written as long ago as 1932, **"Fotiés tu Ai-Yiánni"**—Fires of *St. John.*

This further reference to a popular custom, a reference that underlies the whole of the third poem, **"Summer Solstice,"** increases the range of the allusion well beyond the text of the Apocalypse. The folk custom traditionally associated with the name of St. John affords a link between the conflagration that ends the world (in the Apocalypse) and its nearest Heraclitean equivalent—the point in the sun's cycle where the sun by "overstepping its measure" would provoke the spontaneous combustion of the entire natural world. St. John, however, is nowhere mentioned in the text. As a consequence, the absent signifier ("St. John") is the more easily extended to cover several signifieds—to connect Midsummer's Day, in defiance of the categories of the real world, with St. John the Divine.

But behind the absent signifier "St. John," which unites disparate signifieds, is a further signifier, likewise absent in the text, of far greater potential power in defying the categories of the real and contingent world. The same signifier "St. John" is naturally attached also to the signified "St. John the Evangelist," which comes into play in relation to the reference to Heraclitus. Both Heraclitus and St. John the Evangelist had declared the first principle governing the contingent world to be the *logos*—the Word. The multiple juxtapositions that constitute the text of the *Three Secret Poems* are united by this ultimate but absent signifier which they collectively presuppose. The juxtaposition of the numerical symbolism of Revelation with more direct allusion to the fragments of Heraclitus, and the portrayal of a dissolving world simultaneously in terms of the Christian Last Judgment and of a catastrophic disruption in the Heraclitean order of nature, point inexorably to a synthesis of the pagan Hellenic and Christian concepts of *logos* as the first principle of the universe. The catalyst for this process is indeed reference to a modern Greek folk custom which, although dedicated to the festival of a Christian saint, is commonly thought of as a pagan "survival."

"In the beginning was the *logos*" was in fact quoted by Seferis as far back as 1941 in the same preface to Kalvos' *Odes* in which we detected the earliest implicit allusion to Heraclitus, and specifically to the fragment about the sun overstepping his measure (Seferis 1974a: I. 189, see note 14); so there is nothing sudden or strange about the reading proposed for the *Three Secret Poems.* What remains to be discussed is the significance that the absent *logos* has in these poems.

Seferis' increased interest in Biblical texts in his later years has nothing to do, as we saw, with religious conversion. Interestingly, he explains it himself in terms of *language*—and the choice of the two texts which (both of them in the 1960s) he translated from the Greek Bible bears this out. The Apocalypse and the Song of Songs (Seféris 1965) are traditionally regarded as the two most "poetic" or literary parts of the Bible. In his introduction to the translation of the Apocalypse Seferis justifies his interest, and tries to arouse that of his readers, in the Greek Bible as a monument to a crucial stage in the continuous development of the Greek language; and he further justifies translation into the modern language (a course not generally favored by the Greek Church) by reference to the *literary* influence exercised by Bible translations in Anglo-Saxon countries since the Renaissance. He concludes:

> I have never claimed, nor ever considered, that it is possible for the translation to replace the original, either when it comes to dogma or to worship. These matters belong exclusively to the Church and we lay people have no grounds for comment. However *concern for our language* [my emphasis] is a thing that interests every one of us in whatever corner of the earth he finds himself.
>
> (Seféris 1966: 18)

Seferis is careful, in a way that contrasts strikingly with Eliot's remarks on poetry and religion, to separate the secular concerns of the poet from religious practice and belief. The *Three Secret Poems* constitute an unambiguously secular and textual quest for the ultimate signifier, a "Word" which will be the ultimate origin and the ultimate validation both of language and of the world which it seeks to approach. As in *Mithistórima,* the strategy Seferis adopts for reaching this ultimate point—a strategy which must by definition end in at least partial failure—consists in delineating a void, an empty space into which language can reach for the object of its quest but never quite reach that object itself. The eighth section of Poem III is a meditation on the poet's task which considerably strengthens the reading of the poems outlined here.

> Your life is what you gave
> this void is what you gave
> the white paper.

Throughout Seferis' poetic career, it may be suggested, his strategy remained constant: the aim of his poetics was to delineate the shape of an absence in the modern world (at the level of "story"), in the text itself at the level of discourse, which cannot therefore ever appear within the text, but is implicitly invoked as its ultimate validation. In the early *Mithistórima* what is absent is "myth" in a specifically post-Frazerian sense. In Seferis' postwar poems a radical shift occurs from the primitive and irrational "first seed" that was sought in

the poems of *Mithistórima* to a validating and originating principle that can be sought rather through the rational tradition and through the rhetoric, although not the doctrines, of Christianity. The word for this principle, as it is found in Heraclitus and the Gospel of St. John, is *logos,* which links the linguistic unit, the basis of poetry, with human reason and the creation of the real world. The moment when this shift occurs can perhaps be identified in the final part of the poem **"Thrush,"** where the narrator, following a course parallel with that of Odysseus, listens to the voices of the dead in his search for a home that is to be "the light." The voice of "the old man" that comes to him here—which should according to Homer and to Eliot's mythology in *The Waste Land* be that of the shaman or prophet, Teiresias—is instead the voice of Socrates, the representative par excellence of rational philosophy. This moment in **"Thrush"** is marked by several lines translated from Socrates' words in the *Apology*; it draws attention to itself as the moment of transition from *mythos* in the Frazerian sense to *logos* in the Heraclitean and rational senses in which it was to dominate the rest of Seferis' poetry.

Seferis' final variation on the "rhetoric of Romanticism" which constitutes, I believe, the poetics of his later work, is summed up, less cryptically perhaps, in a lecture he gave at the University of Thessaloníki in 1964, when the *Three Secret Poems* must have been in the final stages of completion:

> It is the most difficult moment of all, this struggle to locate just the voice which coincides, and is identified, with the things he [the poet] wishes to create, or, if we prefer, which *creates these things in naming them* [my emphasis]. The ultimate point toward which the poet aims is to be able to say, 'Let there be light,' and for there to be light
>
> (Seféris 1974a: II. 164)[16]

Notes

Versions of this paper were read at Queens College, City University of New York; Princeton University; Brown University; and the University of Cambridge during the Fall of 1985, and at the University of Oxford in 1986. I am grateful to participants in discussion on all of these occasions, whose suggestions and comments have helped me in many ways, and particularly to Elisabeth Constantinides, Dorothy Gregory, Edmund Keeley, William Wyatt, Jr., Lucia Athanasaki, David Holton, Ruth Padel, Peter Mackridge, and Oliver Dickinson. Needless to say all errors and omissions remain my sole responsibility.

1. The Greek terms used in the title of this paper are treated throughout for purposes of transliteration as belonging to ancient Greek.

2. On the "mythical method" in Seferis see Keeley 1956, 1969, 1983; Vayenás 1979: 148-155; Beaton 1985: 33-4 and n. 8.

3. The posthumously published *Six Nights on the Acropolis* (Seféris 1974b) was largely written in 1928 and itself contains many references to the significance that Seferis at the time attached to the genre. Other abortive plans for novels between 1924 and 1931 are mentioned in the diaries (Seféris 1975a; cf. Vayenás 1987).

An intermediate role in the genesis of *Mithistórima* was in fact played by George Theotokás' novel *Argó,* published in two volumes in 1933 and 1936 respectively. I have shown elsewhere how something very similar to Eliot's "mythical method" is used in this novel, adapted to a contemporary Greek context (Beaton 1985). Close textual comparison of *Argó* with *Mithistórima* reveals an interesting and complex relation between the two texts. Apart from the adoption of an ancient myth as the organizing principle of the text, *Argó* Vol. 1 anticipates *Mithistórima* in the significance given to the word *galíni* (serenity) as the final word in the text and in a number of key passages. Near the end of Vol. 1 the writer's alter ego, Lámbros Hristídis, meditates in terms very similar to those used in Seferis' poems: "Alas! we'll never achieve the ideal work. Nor will we find the ideal woman. Nor will we make poetry real in our lives. Nor ideas either . . . That was all mere childishness, the dreams of youth. There isn't a Golden Fleece anywhere to be found. But there's still the voyage of the Argo" (Theotokás 1933: 309-10). This part of *Argó* was published in the summer of 1933, and the poems that comprise *Mithistórima* are dated in the published text "December '33-December '34." However, an even larger number of correspondences can be observed between Seferis' poems and the second volume of Theotokás' novel (which again ends with the word *galíni*). This time, of course (Theotokás 1936), it was Theotokás who had read Seferis.

4. The terms "discourse" and "story" are used in the sense defined by Gérard Genette (1980). The former refers to the linguistic and textual aspects of the text, the latter to the supposed reality or events referred to within it. It should be emphasised that both story and discourse, so understood, belong fully to the literary text as a signifying system and correspond analogically to the terms "signified" and "signifier" as applied to the linguistic sign. See also Chatman 1978.

5. The dependence of Seferis and other 20th-century Greek poets on European classical scholarship has been ably demonstrated by Dr. David Ricks in an unpublished doctoral thesis (Ricks 1986).

6. Kariotákis 1972: 113, where the word "carving" *(anáglifo)* is also used in the immediate context.

The allusion is pointed out by G. P. Savvídis in his notes to Seféris 1972.

7. For a reference to a French example which briefly excited Seferis, see Seféris 1975a: 14-5.

8. More or less explicit allusions are made to the house of Atreus (Poems 3, 16), to Jason and the Argonauts (Poems 4, 10); to the fate of Odysseus' companions (Poems 4, 15), to the visit to the underworld (Poems 9, 24), to the death of Adonis (Poem 9), to Narcissus (Poem 15, 11. 16-18), to Astyanax (Poem 17) and to the ordeal of Andromeda (Poem 20).

9. The work of both anthropologists, but particularly Weston (1920), is explicitly invoked by Eliot in the Notes to *The Waste Land* (Eliot 1963: 80).

10. Vayenás has shown that the Homeric superstructure of this poem was adopted late in the process of composition and was probably prompted by an essay of Matthew Arnold which emphasizes the nature of myth in ancient tragedy as a fixed reference point known to playwright and audience alike (Vayenás 1979: 264-265).

11. "The poems of this collection . . . were given to me [cf. the similar expression used in Seferis' note to his translation of the Apocalypse, quoted below, and 'Poems Given' (Dosména) as the title of a group of poems in *Book of Exercises*] in the fall of '53 when I traveled for the first time to Cyprus. It was the revelation *[apokálipsi]* of a world and the experience of a human drama which, whatever the expediencies of daily interchange, measures and judges our humanity. . . . And I consider that if I was lucky enough to find in Cyprus such a gift of grace, it is perhaps because this island gave me what it had to give me within a framework sufficiently restricted for every sensation not to evaporate, as happens in the capitals of the great world, but sufficiently broad to make room for miracle. A strange thing to say today; Cyprus is a land where miracle still functions. . . ." (Seféris 1972: 336).

12. See the excellently produced bilingual edition with translation and introduction by Walter Kaiser (Seferis 1969). As far as criticism is concerned the only exception is the enthusiastic but unsystematic monograph by Kóstas Papayeoryíou (1973).

13. A quotation of Fr 75 as cited by Marcus Aurelius appears in Seferis' posthumously published novel, *Eksi Níhtes stin Akrópoli* (Seféris 1974b: 46) and presumably dates from 1928 when most of that text was written. Interestingly this fragment is not picked up again in the postwar poems that allude ever more frequently to Heraclitus: it might be

suggested that at this stage of Seferis' career the citation has more to do with his interest in Marcus Aurelius (on which see Ricks 1986) than with his later use of Heraclitus.

14. The particular stanza which Seferis picks out for comment in 1941 (Seferis 1974a: I 208-9) he had earlier admired in an essay of 1936 (Seféris 1974: I 60-1), but the implicitly "Heraclitean" reading of Kálvos' stanza is entirely new in the later essay. By 1941 three of the *Four Quartets* had already appeared. It may further be noted in passing that the same 1941 essay contains the quotation from the *Pervigilium Veneris* which was later to be used in Part III of "Thrush" (Seféris 1974a, I 206). I am grateful to an anonymous peer-reviewer for the *Journal* for pointing to another Heraclitean allusion in a poem of the same period: 'Enas Yéros stin Akropotamiá' (1942), *11*. 13-15. I am less convinced, however, by the same reviewer's suggestion that lines 14-15 of 'Les Anges Sont Blancs' (1939) also allude to Heraclitus. These lines are an amplification of ideas already found in *Mithistórima* 15 and *The Waste Land* V respectively.

15. "The word *[logos]* being common to all, the majority live as though they have private wisdom" (Fr. 2, quoted in Eliot 1963: 189).

16. The quotation is taken from a translation by Peter Thompson of this essay (= Seferis 1983: 36).

References Cited

Abrams, M. H. 1953 *The Mirror and the Lamp: Romantic Theory and the Critical Tradition*. New York and Oxford: Oxford University Press.

Beaton, Roderick 1985 "Myth and Text: Readings in the Modern Greek Novel." *Byzantine and Modern Greek Studies* 9: 29-53.

Chatman, Seymour 1978 *Story and Discourse: Narrative Structure in Fiction and Film*. Ithaca and London: Cornell University Press.

De Man, Paul 1984 *The Rhetoric of Romanticism*. New York and Guildford: Columbia University Press.

Eliot, T. S. 1963 *Collected Poems 1909-1962*. London: Faber and Faber.

———. 1970 "*Ulysses*: Order and Myth." *In James Joyce, The Critical Heritage,* ed. R. Deming, Vol. 1, pp. 268-271. London: Routledge and Kegan Paul (¹1923).

Frazer, James G. 1961 *The New Golden Bough*. New York: Anchor.

Genette, Gérard 1980 *Narrative Discourse*. Oxford: Blackwell (¹1972).

Jameson, Fredric 1972 *The Prison-House of Language: A Critical Account of Structuralism and Russian Formalism*. Princeton and Guildford: Princeton University Press.

Kariotákis, Kóstas 1972 *Piímata ke Pezá, Epimélia G. P. Savvídis*. Athens: Ermís.

Keeley, Edmund 1956 "T. S. Eliot and the Poetry of George Seferis." *Comparative Literature* 8: 214-226.

———. 1969 "Seferis and the 'Mythical Method.'" *Comparative Literature Studies* 6: 109-125. Reprinted in *Modern Greek Poetry: Voice and Myth,* pp. 68-86. Princeton and Guildford: Princeton University Press, 1983.

———. 1983 Addendum [to Keeley 1969]. *In Modern Greek Poetry, Voice and Myth,* pp. 86-94.

Lawrence, D. H. 1960 *Women in Love*. Harmondsworth (Middlesex): Penguin Books (¹1921).

Malinowski, Bronislaw 1974 "Myth in Primitive Psychology." Reprinted in *Myth, Magic and Religion*. London: Souvenir Press.

Papayeoryíou, K. G. 1973 *Simiósis Páno sta "Tría Krifá Piímata" tou G. Seféri*. Athens: Ekdósis Bukumáni.

Ricks, David 1986 *Homer and Greek poetry, 1888-1940: Cavafy, Sikelianos, Seferis*. University of London: Unpublished PhD thesis.

Seféris, George 1965 *'Asma Asmáton: Metagrafí*. Athens: Ikaros.

———. 1966 *I Apokálipsi tu Ioánni: Metagrafí*. Athens: Ikaros.

———. 1969 *Tría Krifá Piímata. Three Secret Poems*. Tr. Walter Kaiser. Cambridge, MA: Harvard University Press.

———. 1972 *Piímata* (8th ed). Athens: Ikaros.

———. 1974a *Dokimés* (2 vols). Athens: Ikaros.

———. 1974b *'Eksi Níhtes stin Akrópoli, Epimélia G. Savvídis*. Athens: Ikaros.

———. 1975a *Méres A': 16 Fevruaríu 1925-17 Avgústu 1931*. Athens: Ikaros.

———. 1975b *Méres B': 24 Avgústu 1931-12 Fevruaríu 1934*. Athens: Ikaros.

———. 1983 *Language in Our Poetry*. Tr. Peter Thompson. *Labrys* 8: 35-45.

Theotokás, George 1933, 1936 *Argó* (2 vols). Athens: Estía.

Vayenás, Násos 1979 *O Piitís ke o Horeftís: Mia Exétasi tis Piitikís ke tis Píisis tu Seféri*. Athens: Kédros.

————. 1987 *Seferis' Six Nights on the Acropolis: The Diary as Novel.* In*The Greek Novel A.D. 1-1985,* ed. Roderick Beaton. London: Croom Helm.

Weston, Jessie 1920 *From Ritual to Romance.* Cambridge: Cambridge University Press.

Yeats, W. B. 1957 *The Variorum Edition of the Poems of W. B. Yeats,* ed. Peter Allt and Russell K. Alspach. New York: Macmillan.

George Dandoulakis (essay date 1989)

SOURCE: Dandoulakis, George. "George Seferis and Dictatorship." *Journal of European Studies* 19 (1989): 135-47.

[*In the following essay, Dandoulakis traces Seferis's reaction to the dictatorial regime that came to power in Greece in 1967.*]

Until recently, any attempt to define the extent of George Seferis's attitude to the Greek regime which seized power on 21 April 1967 seemed to be exhausted by a consideration of a few key documents. They are, first, his poem **"The Cats of Saint Nickolas"**, completed on 5 February 1969; second, his famous Statement of 28 March 1969; third his two-line poem **"Out of Stupidity"**; and fourth, his last poem, **"On Aspalathoi"**, which he wrote on 31 March 1971 after an excursion to Sounio. Now, however, with the publication of "Manuscript October 68" in June 1986, it is necessary to take into account a number of its entries, for they throw new light on Seferis's progress from a reluctance to sign manifestos against the regime to the moment of the Statement itself, in which he emerges as a major critic of the junta. They also provide the context for his last, great poem.

Given Seferis's awareness of his pre-eminent position as a Greek poet, it was inevitable that he should wish to be cautious about committing himself to public statement. For whatever he said was bound to be widely reported, discussed and variously interpreted. At the time of the junta, Greek poets still spoke with the accent of authority, as indeed they still do so. This authority, which in a sense is endlessly part of Greek culture, had been especially pointed at the time when the struggle for liberation against Turkey reached its height. (Hence the Greek veneration of Byron. He had spoken out for Greece and could even be presented as having died for the cause.) The emergence of Solomos as Greece's "national poet" coincided with the triumph of that struggle, and inevitably meant that he gave utterance to the nation's newly-forged aspirations. Solomos bequeathed his image and its burden to his successors. As with other Greek poets, therefore, Seferis found it

impossible to deny his national identity. Whatever he might say, he spoke "for Greece". At the time of the Metaxas dictatorship he had written a poem, **"In the Manner of G. S."** whose first line, "Wherever I travel Greece keeps wounding me", had become a virtual rallying cry for all those who yearned for the restoration of democratic government. That poem had been written in the late 1930s. Thirty years later there was another dictatorship. What was the poet to do?

The text of "Manuscript 68" shows Seferis worrying at this question. It includes a number of entries and notes made during the period 26 September-29 December 1968, when the poet was in America at the Institute of Advanced Studies, Princeton. According to the editor's preface, "Manuscript October 68" is made up of a number of perforated sheets of paper, separate from the two diary note-pads which cover the period 1967-1971. The latter still remain unpublished, and undoubtedly there will be need for further revision and reconsideration of the issues in question when they appear. Seferis transferred some of his entries in the first note-pad (it covers the period 22 February 1967-29 December 1968) to "Manuscript October 1968" which he intended to form a sequel to "Synomilla me ton Favricio" (Dialogue with Fabricius) published in January 1967. That "Dialogue" threw some light on aspects of Seferis's politics and revealed his disgust at the Greek political world, as it had existed from 1940-41. Apart from the diary entries, the text of "Manuscript October 68" also contains extracts from newspapers which Seferis either copied or cut out. Some passages from "Manuscript October 68" were for the first time presented in an English translation by Kay Cicellis at the Cambridge Poetry Festival in April 1983. The complete text was read at a lecture in Salonica on 26 February 1986, and initially published in the journal *Diavazo* on 23 April of the same year, and then in an annotated edition by Pavlos Zannas.

"Manuscript October 68" opens with a brief description of Seferis's house near the Princeton University Campus. There are mentions of the students, boys with beards and girls in mini skirts, and reference to the wedding of Onassis and Jackie Kennedy at Scorpio, which Seferis watched on a friend's TV. Seferis confesses that his feelings are those of an outcast, a man in exile with no connections. He realizes that what he had written many years previously, under an earlier junta, as an epigraph to *Logbook I*, is still relevant:

> Meanwhile it sometimes seems better to me to sleep than to be so completely without companions as we are, to be always waiting like this: and what's to be done or said in the meanwhile I don't know, and what is the use of poets in a mean-spirited time.[1]

This latter time is also mean-spirited, but Seferis is not ready yet to condemn it publicly. Instead, he openly declares that he is against the involvement of poets with, and commitment to, politics, so that although he is hurt by the political situation in Greece, he refuses to use his art as a weapon:

> I underlined the words that are still hurting me today. Don't tell me that it is a sign of my arrogance to think that poets self-flattered with political or party rhetoric are unworthy. My writings till this day show the whole of my thought on this matter.[2]

He then refers to his present reading and work on Plato's Myths (published under the title *Metagraphes* in 1980). Plato, indeed, seems to have acted as a kind of medicine for him in hard times. He mentions his decision not to publish anything as long as censorship lasts and points out that the advent of the dictatorship has greatly distressed him:

> A few days later the tanks and cannons of the military regime made everything fade, except for the habit of informing. This flourished to an unexpected degree whatsoever. You are greatly surprised when you begin to realise that we have the skills for such an achievement.[3]

His next entry, dated "Sunday, 20.X.1968", concerns Onassis's wedding. Seferis remarks that the signs of luxury in the ceremony are symptoms of the time and inserts an extract on the occasion from the *New York Times* as a prelude to his bitter remark, "These are the present 'Great Ideas of the Greeks'", a comment which leads to two short verses showing how much he felt a stranger at home. There is also an extract from the first junta referendum from the *New York Times,* followed by the mordant verses:

> How distant is Greece
> in the land of Christian Greeks!
>
> Patission Street was a country road in those years.
> I was an adolescent then.[4]

There follow two earlier entries in the diary, dated 28 and 29 April 1967 (Holy Week), which Seferis enters here in order to convey his feelings one week after the imposition of dictatorship. The two passages illuminate his convictions and express his disgust for the politicians as well as his disapproval of the communists' practices in 1944. The first passage is straightforward:

> It's a week today. They might be right: possibly like those others in '44 they are filled with fear because they hold arms and like the other ones they do not want to let arms go from their hands. They are probably right. But I beg God, I don't want to be like them or the other ones.
>
> To hell with these days! All the old wounds from this land have opened again, and the years are gone.

Here Seferis compares the protagonists of the coup to the communist leaders during the civil war. What he finds common to them is their thirst for power.

The second passage is allusive and less particularized. Nevertheless, Seferis's invective shows his anger and indignation against the main protagonists of the junta:

> Cheap politicians, mere rhetoricians just to make themselves heard, midwives of non-pregnant women. These concern yesterday's telephone call. Yesterday, a man inexperienced and uneducated in politics said "since they force me to face the dilemma: their dictatorship or . . .", but there is need for further development here.[5]

Seferis then records a number of apparently random memories of the junta's early days. He begins with a sentence written by a schoolgirl, who was instructed to add the letter "n" at the end of each word in order to write the purist form of Greek. This resulted in an ungrammatical sentence. Here Seferis shows his concern for the education of Greek students, which was in the hands of the junta. As a result of their nonsensical rhetoric, the colonels further distorted that pedantic form of Greek they had adopted:

> —Education!
> What can anyone do about it?
> Passive resistance, o altria cosa.

But what is of greater importance here is that Seferis picks out three extracts from the colonels' speeches and adds his own withering comments in order to expose the pretensions of the regime. The first extract is from General Spandidaklis's speech and refers to the sacrifice of the Greek fighters at Arkadi (Crete) during the Tourkokratia. Being surrounded by Turkish forces and as further resistance was hopeless, they chose to die by exploding their shelter rather than surrender to the enemy. Seferis's remarks show how it feels when the men who deprived the Greeks of democracy put themselves forward as propagators of freedom:

> The land we have loved is now doing whatever it can to kick us.
>
> I have a country, which, to save itself, as they say, (but from what?) tries hard to give birth to informers, traitors, Police Officers, Ptolemies etc.
>
> Difference between 67 and the years 38-39.[6]

In addition, he refers sadly to all those who collaborated with the regime and parallels the present dictatorship to that of Metaxas.

Then Seferis comments on an extract from Patakos's speech, (Kozani, 19 July 1967) which claims that the officers are motivated purely by good intentions, that they desire to be the saviours of the nation.

> Terrific demagogues would daily abolish democracy with their shamelessness and tread on every sacred symbol of the nation.[7]

And then he condemns the shallowly patriotic sentiments of General Spandidakis's speech at Samos on 7
August 1967, when the coup was called an historical
necessity.

> As we are free to make up such rhetoric, we became
> the anomaly of the western world.

> Suddenly in Greece we all became subjects. The
> military regime needs a victory: for the rest of us a
> defeat would suit.[8]

Seferis broods over his own attitude as a man of letters
to the regime, which at the time amounted to passive
non-acceptance, and he yet again declares his anti-
communist views:

> Of what significance is it when an author stops writing,
> if it is for the good of the country? But if I am against
> communism, this is because I think it is significant.[9]

Seferis obviously associates the authoritarianism of
military regimes with the governments of communist
countries:

> It is our destiny to be the land of thoughtless political
> actions. In 1943 when Italy started fighting on our side
> and the left guerillas (EM) could collect arms from the
> surrendering Italians, they thought they were given the
> opportunity to exterminate their opponents.[10]

Seferis is admittedly here offering a very personal and
tentative view, but it has to be said that he was wrong
to associate what had happened in the civil war with
what happened in April 1967. On the former occasion,
there had been an armed conflict between the left and
the right, while on the latter occasion a minority of
extreme right-wing Greek officers turned against all
democratic Greeks, irrespective of their politics.

Seferis defines his own attitude:

> "Consider reputation", an author said to me, before I
> left Athens, in order to persuade me to make a state-
> ment against the junta. He was apparently considering
> reputation himself; as for me, reputation does not define
> my actions, nor do people who know me expect, at
> least I hope not, manifestations like those of Helen
> Vlachos, or those of Melina (Mercouri) or even those
> of Andreas Papandreou, in order to understand my
> political convictions. (See for instance *Epoches,* Janu-
> ary 1967, "Dialogue with Favricious" (at the end, p6)
> and my letter to Franklin Ford, The Dean, Faculty of
> Arts and Sciences at Harvard University, on
> 27.XIII.1967, in which I refuse his offer to become
> Charles Elliot Norton Professor of Poetry).[11]

The reference here is to a letter in which the poet makes
it clear that his refusal to accept the post was due to the
political situation in Greece. He points out that since
1962 he has abstained from politics and belongs to no
party; and as the case is, since there is no freedom of
speech at home, he feels it cannot exist anywhere: thus,
if he cannot work productively at home, he cannot work
abroad either.

After this declaration, Seferis makes four short remarks
which reveal his disappointment and the frustration of
his hopes for Greece's future:

> We have come to a point that the National Holiday will
> mean not celebrations but repentance for what we
> thoughtlessly did in the years of our freedom.

> Our wounds again and again.

> Our hopes in the time of war.

> Our land, the land of Karagiozis.

Then, having read Karl Jasper's English version of *The
Question of German Guilt,* which touches on the distinction between political freedom and political dictatorship, Seferis notes down his own views in relation to
the situation in Greece:

> I thought that all those efforts and all those sacrifices
> had at least brought us to maturity. I was wrong. The
> class of the military has established dictatorship even
> today in 1967-1968: the class of the anti-military will
> unavoidably establish its own dictatorship. The country
> will go on like this.[12]

In addition, Seferis explains the reason why he has so
far avoided a public condemnation of the regime:

> But I want to go back to my country and I don't want
> to give anyone the means to prevent me from returning
> to my country.[13]

He goes on to defend himself against the accusations
published in *Ellinocandikon Vima,* a weekly of the
Greek diaspora. The paper blamed Seferis for remaining silent while other writers in Greece were prepared
to suffer imprisonment and exile: it also accused him of
having gone to Africa some time before the German
invasion in 1941. Seferis asserts that in 1941 he joined
the Free Government in moving to Crete, Egypt and
then South Africa, because he had had information that
the Germans had already proscribed him for being pro-
British, and concludes with an outline of the tragedy he
feels is in store for Greece:

> Unfortunately, it seems that the junta has not cured us
> of rhetoric. That's what has been worrying me since 21
> April. On that day, I felt great horror as we were enter-
> ing into a situation with no way out. Once more a civil
> war, much worse that those we have had, was opening
> before us.[14]

Of particular interest are two incidents that took place
before Seferis left for America on 26 September 1968.
He recalls M. Theodorakis's visit to him and comments
on the composer's suggestion to ask the junta for
permission to give a public concert in the Stadium, as
Theodorakis had set some of Seferis's poems to music:

> I wondered what he had in mind by making this sug-
> gestion: Answer A: mere superficiality. Answer B: I am
> the winner either with a positive answer from the

authorities or with a negative one. Because, if it is positive, there will be a first rate personal success for me as musician and a party-man: If it is negative, the attempt itself will bring me some benefit, and I will have involved S (Seferis).[15]

Unfortunately, we do not know M. Theodorakis's motives, and thus cannot say whether Seferis' interpretation of them is unfair to him or not.

The second incident concerns an ex-minister's wife who asked Seferis to plead with the junta for clemency for the poet Yannis Ritsos. Ritsos was due to be operated on, and the authorities had refused his wife permission to be near him at that time. Seferis points out that he finds Ritsos consistent to his ideology and that for a moment he felt like doing this favour. On second thoughts, however, he was forced to consider what the junta would ask of him in return. After this, the ex-minister's wife said she would contact him again, but two days later she telephoned and asked him to forget everything they had said. Perhaps she feared for her own safety, perhaps for his peace of mind. Either way, it is an incident which brings starkly before us the terrible dilemmas facing the Greeks during the junta.

At the end of "Manuscript October 68", Seferis poses an issue that is a matter of conscience for himself as well as for others: to abandon Greece or to stay on despite the dictatorship. He finds a parallel between the present situation and the time of an earlier ordeal, in 1941, when he was forced to emigrate to the Middle East. He feels that it is better for all the Greeks to stay, unless there are particular reasons to leave because by going abroad as immigrants they degrade themselves. He points out that the experience of the dictatorship will direct the Greeks' thoughts and actions, argues for honesty and right judgement, and condemns all pompous exclamations. His answer to the question "How can you live in Greece under the present circumstances?" is:

> I don't know your family's circumstances, but if I knew, would you allow me to ask you "How can you live with your family"? It is my country and I love it, and I don't recognize in anyone the right to prevent me from living in my country and hearing my language spoken, whether he is a General or a Colonel. As for the accusations, they are easily made by those who sit at ease abroad or whisper maliciously within the country.[16]

Seferis then makes two interesting remarks:

> The military (the ones here, of America) caused the coup in Greece—
>
> (A friend Senator, Wash)
>
> After Vietnam, for a long time this land will not intervene in any foreign country.
>
> (22 Dec)

Seferis does not give the name of the Senator and 'Wash' is most probably an abbreviation for 'Washington'. Yet these remarks verify some of the claims that the USA government or its agents were partly responsible for the coup, claims which Seferis must have thought justified, otherwise there could have been no reason for quoting them. Nevertheless, he strongly believed that the Greeks were not exempt from responsibility for the fate which had overtaken them. Referring to the coup, he says "I hope that these deeds will give us the opportunity to ponder our foolish actions".

Now, however, the problem is what to do. He quotes from a letter he received from a younger Greek writer in London (once again we are not told who the writer is):

> In the end, the only solution is abstention (from writing) or escape . . . I begin to feel disgusted with all these. But I don't know if Greece will ever be saved by disgust only. Perhaps what is left is to save ourselves as much as possible.[17]

Seferis may have shared the young writer's disgust, but he did not share his escapism and the need which he felt to save himself. He quotes the letter in order to focus his disapproval, for his intention has always been to remain in Greece and share its people's misfortunes. At the same time the situation in Greece filled him with pain and anger, and these emotions are evident in the two-line poem **"Out of Stupidity"** with which "Manuscript October 68" closes:

> Greece, Fire! of Christian, Fire! Greeks, Fire!
> Three dead words, Why did you kill them?[18]

Seferis is known to have altered the second line into "Dead Words! Why did you kill them?", which changes the implication. He might simply be criticizing the Colonels for adopting the three words as a means of putting forward their false ideology and appearing as true patriots and Christians, or he might be attacking all manifestations of theocratic patriotism, which means that these words had already lost their meaning through overuse in slogans.

On 28 March 1968 Seferis's famous statement appeared. A tape with his recorded voice had been sent to London and given to the BBC and other radio and newspaper correspondents. The broadcast of the Statement and the publication in the press created a sensation all over the world. In Greece, the regime was, not surprisingly, outraged, and immediately sent out a press release in which it attempted to defend itself in the name of the Greek nation against Seferis's "unfair accusations". Following orders, the press gave the governmental critique sensational headlines such as "Mr Seferis Attacks His Own Country" while avoiding publication of

the statement itself, with the result that the Greek reading public remained ignorant of what Seferis had actually said. Seferis was scathingly criticized as a man and
a poet. He was denounced as an enemy within who
shared the evil views of foreign enemies of Greece,
such as Nenni, the Italian Minister of Foreign Affairs,
who had officially invited Andreas Papandreou to Rome
some days before Seferis's Statement appeared. The
junta considered such a meeting to constitute an act of
interference in the political affairs of Greece.

The attack against Seferis was carried on for some days
by the pro-junta newspapers *Nea Politeia* and *Estia*
with equally scathing articles: "The Freedom of Spirit
and Mr Seferis" (*Nea Politeia,* 2 April 1969), "The
Razor-blade of his Silence" (*Estia,* 29 March 1969); but
mainly by a series of articles in *Eleftheros Cosmos*: "A
Reply to George Seferis" (1 April 1969), "The Ideas of
our Struggles" (2 April 1969), "Responsibilities Past
and Present" (3 April 1969), "Some Questions" (5 April
1969).

Nea Politeia and *Eleftheros Cosmos* did, however,
consent to publish Seferis's Statement, because their
readers could not be contaminated by the Seferian evil.

It is noteworthy that no newspaper dared publish any
article in Seferis's defence because of the Pre-censorship
Law, which was still in force. It was a year later that
the occasion of Seferis's seventieth birthday offered the
newspapers *To Vima, Ta Nea* and *Ethnos* the opportunity to publish dedicatory articles commending both the
man and his work.

But what of the Statement itself? Why did it so upset
the Colonels? The answer is that in his Statement Seferis condemns the junta and makes a plea for the end of
"hamartia", the anamoly of the western world, which
has brought Greece to the edge of the precipice. Seferis
once again mentions his decision to keep away from
politics, though he insists that he is in no sense indifferent to the fate of Greece. He also makes plain his decision not to publish anything as long as there is no
freedom of speech in his country. It is his sense of duty,
he therefore says, that makes him speak out in order
unambiguously to condemn the regime. "A regime has
been imposed on us which is entirely opposed to the
ideals for which our world fought during the last War".
As a result, all spiritual values in Greece "have been
submerged in the muddy and stagnant waters of a
swamp". Seferis points out that as in all dictatorships,
tragedy awaits at the end, so "the longer this abnormal
situation lasts, the worse it becomes".

Seferis was well aware that the junta which proclaimed
at one and the same time its exclusiveness and its
absolute cultural and moral value was a malign

contradiction, an insult to the very Greekness it
pretended to embody: it had to go. Therefore, his decision to speak out was, as the novelist Costas Tachtsis
very rightly pointed out, the product of mature consideration and inner struggle. Seferis's stay in America,
which gave him the opportunity to examine the whole
situation from a distance, must have helped him towards
taking it.

Eighteen Texts—a collection of poems, short stories and
articles by eighteen different contributors intending to
condemn the regime through implication and analogy—
came out in July 1970. Seferis's exquisite poem **"The
Cats of Saint Nickolas"** was given the position of honour. The poem is a testimony to freedom of the intellect as the highest virtue. This masterpiece of allegory
dramatizes the misfortunes of Greece through the ages,
and outlines a history filled with political passions, civil
wars, and manslaughter. It is a poem in which the forces
of good fight against the forces of evil, win, but suffer
casualties in the struggle: "Centuries of poison, generations of poison". Seferis uses an epigraph from Aeschylus's *Agamemnon* to bring to us the atmosphere of
drama:

> But deep inside me sings
> the fury's lyreless threnody:
> my heart, self taught, has lost
> the previous confidence of hope.

It is the mood of a man in despair, of a man whose
mind carries broken memories. Seferis adopts a narrator, the captain, who brings forth memories from
medieval Cyprus: the helmsman stands indifferent
beside him, while the traveller (the poet) listens. Though
it is Christmas Day, the memories that come forth, as
the boat sails past the Cape of Cats, are associated with
death. "And old Ramazan, how he would look death
square in the eyes / whole days long in the snow of the
East". This is the setting where the drama of Greece is
re-enacted, first through the mouth of the half-mad
monk, "a kind of dreamer", and then through the mouth
of the captain:

> It was the time of the great drought
> forty years without rain,
> the whole island devastated,
> people died and snakes were born.
> This cape had millions of snakes
> thick as a man's leg
> and full of poison.
> In those days the monastery of St Nicholas
> was held by the monks of St Basil,
> and they couldn't work their fields
> and they couldn't put their flocks to pasture;
> in the end they were saved by the cats they raised.
> Every day at dawn a bell would strike
> and the crew of cats would move out to battle.
> They'd fight the day long, until

the bell could sound the evening feed.
Supper done, the bell would sound again
and out they'd go to fight the night's war.
They say it was a wonderful thing to see them,
some lame, some twisted, others missing
a nose, an ear, their hides in shreds.
So to the sound of four bells a day
months went by, years, season after season.
Wildly obstinate, always wounded,
they annihilated the snakes; but in the end they disap-
      peared:
they just couldn't take in that much poison.
Like a sunken ship
they didn't leave a thing behind them on the surface:
no meow, no bell even.
Steady as you go!
      What could the poor devils do?
fighting like that day and night, drinking in
the poisonous blood of those reptiles?
Centuries of poison: generations of poison.
'Steady as you go', echoed the indifferent helmsman.[19]

Above all, the poem expresses Seferis's certainly, a prophetic one, that the forces of evil, the snakes, will finally be crushed. The wounds of Greece will, however, remain.

Seferis wrote his last poem **"On Aspalathoi"** on 31 March 1971, after an outing to Sounio, and it was first published in the newspaper *To Vima* on 23 September of the same year. The title of the poem refers to a wild thorny plant and its theme is the punishment of an ancient tyrant whose body is dragged among thorny aspalathoi. The lovely spring setting is dominated by the presence of these plants with their sinister connotations, and the ancient columns "strings of a harp / still resounding", a token of the classical world from which Seferis draws his parallel with the modern tyranny of Greece. The poem ends with the punishment of the ancient tyrant, one whose application to the present tyranny resonates within its lines. It is the catharsis in the drama Seferis had spoken of in his statement:

Sounio was beautiful again in Spring
      On Anunciation Day.
Few green leaves round the rusty stones,
      red clay and aspalathoi,
pointing their big thorns and yellow flowers.

At a distance, the ancient columns,
strings of a harp, still resounding.
Serenity.

What can it be that reminded me of Ardiaios?
One word in Plato, perhaps,
lost in the channels of my brain.
The name of the yellow bush
hasn't changed since that time.
In the evening I came across the passage:
"They tied him up", it says,
"they forced him down and flayed him;
they dragged him along and thorny aspalathoi

tore his flesh: they took him to Tartarus
and threw him there, a wretch".

That's how the Pamphylian Ardiaios,
that most vicious tyrant,
paid for his crimes in the nether world.[20]

The poem is not a warning. It does not naively point out to the colonels what is in store for them. Seferis was not naive; nor did the colonels take the poem as a threat. It is rather a poem whose language provides its own judgement on the barbarians, those tyrants who tried to wreck a nation and its culture. Seferis is telling the colonels what they are and what they deserve.

The poem thus triumphantly vindicates Seferis's decision to speak out on behalf of his vision of Greece, the beloved republic. As is so typical of his great poems, **"On Aspalathoi"** provides a reading of the Greek landscape in a manner which allows access to the nation's multi-layered history. Myth and legend are alluded to as a means of authenticating Seferis's certainty that, no matter what the difficulties, the ideal Greece, home and inspiration of democracy, will survive the worst that can be done to it or that it can do to itself.

Notes

1. George Seferis, *Poems 1924-1955,* translated by E. Keeley & P. Sherrard, (Jonathan Cape, 1969), 197.

2. All references are made to the Greek edition of *Manuscript October 68,* ed. Pavlos Zannos, Diaton, Athens, 1986, of which I give my own translation, 29.

3. *Ibid.,* 31.

4. *Ibid.,* 33.

5. *Ibid.,* 34.

6. *Ibid.,* 34-5.

7. *Ibid.,* 36.

8. *Ibid.,* 37.

9. *Ibid.,* 35.

10. *Ibid.,* 37.

11. *Ibid.,* 38.

12. *Ibid.,* 38-9.

13. *Ibid.,* 42.

14. *Ibid.,* 43.

15. *Ibid.,* 45.

16. *Ibid.,* 51.

17. *Ibid.,* 51-2.

18. *Ibid.*, 53.

19. *Eighteen Texts,* 1-3 (English edition).

20. Here I give my own translation.

Roderick Beaton (essay date 1991)

SOURCE: Beaton, Roderick. "The Modern World: Technology, History, and Politics." In *George Seferis,* pp. 50-65. Bristol, U.K.: Bristol Classical Press, 1991.

[*In the following excerpt, Beaton discusses Seferis's preoccupation with the ancient past and his dissatisfaction with his own era.*]

A simple way to explain the intensity of Seferis' interest in the ancient past, that we examined in the last chapter, would be to say that he did not think very highly of the present. Certainly, Seferis' public pronouncements on the state of the nation are almost invariably gloomy, and frequently seem rather pompous today. But there is no question of Seferis merely seeking refuge from the modern world among the myths and statues of the past. Not only as a diplomat, but as a poet as well, Seferis was deeply involved in the current affairs of his country and the political fate of his fellow-Greeks. It is true that the only good things he has to say of the contemporary world relate to the inner world of the individual (the landscapes, voices and visions of the poetry), while contemporary man and society are presented in a pretty depressing light. But Seferis blamed the limitations of human nature for the lack of vision of his contemporaries; and for all his pessimism he never retreated into the world of private fantasy represented by the traditional phrase, the 'ivory tower'.

The modern world in Seferis' poetry constantly rubs shoulders with the ancient—and indeed as we have seen, Seferis believed that the legacy of the ancients was merely a lifeless burden unless there were living people ready and willing to breathe new life into it. Apart from the inner life of the individual, the modern world makes its presence felt in Seferis' poetry in three main ways: in allusions (i) to technological progress, which Seferis invariably links with moral decline; (ii) to the major historical events in Greece that he lived through; and (iii) to internal political problems in Greece.

I. TECHNOLOGY AND MORAL DECLINE

Seferis' attitude to these widely recognised characteristics of twentieth-century life is neither especially unusual nor especially subtle. But they appear so often throughout the poetry, as to provide a necessary backdrop for other kinds of reference to the modern world. And they appear so often together as to make it clear that, for Seferis at least, the one automatically implies the other. This attitude is already present in the earliest to be written of the published *Poems,* '**Fog**', written in London in 1924:

> "Πες της το μ' ένα γιουκαλίλι . . ."
> γρινιάζει κάποιος φωνογράφος·
> έ
> πες μου τι να της πω, Χριστέ μου,
> τώρα συνήθισα μονάχος.
>
> (1-4)

> 'Say it with a ukulele . . .'
> grumbles some gramophone;
> Christ, tell me what to say to her
> now that I'm used to my loneliness?

The reference is to a popular song of the time; the ukulele is a kind of banjo. The words of the song refer to a real musical instrument, but the words themselves come in disembodied, mechanical form. The poet retorts, sarcastically—'Christ' looks like something between a blasphemy and a prayer—yes, but what am I to say; in a world of mechanical, disembodied voices, everyone is alone. Real communication, like the 'real' song of the ukulele, has become difficult or even impossible in the modern technological world.

The gramophones make a regular series of appearances in Seferis' poems of the 1930s and 1940s, and always with the same negative associations. The women described as huddled on to boats in pursuit of 'unreal pilgrimages' in section 8 of *Mythistorema* are 'grated by gramophone records' (8: 6); the same technology appears as representative of a degraded civilisation in the Δεκαέξι χάι-κάι ('**Sixteen Haiku**') 4; in the σημειώσεις για μια "Εβδομάδα" ('**Notes for a Week**'): Δευτέρα ('**Monday**') 8-10; Τρίτη ('**Tuesday**') 10-16; Τετάρτη ('**Wednesday**') 18-26; in Ένας λόγος για το καλοκαίρι ('**A word for summer**') 6, 9, all from Τετράδιο γυμνασμάτων (*Book of Exercises*); and in *Logbook I* in the poem Αφήγηση ('**Narration**') 5. It reappears in "Κίχλη" ('**Thrush**') in the form of the radio whose song ends section II. In the later poems a slightly wider range of scientific and technological expertise is again linked to an absence of moral awareness or human feeling. This is especially evident in the poems Μνήμη Α' ('**Memory I**') 9-12 and Έγκωμη ('**Engomi**') 12-13, from Ημερολόγιο καταστρώματος Γ' (*Logbook III*). It makes a final appearance in the Τρία κρυφά ποιήματα (*Three Secret Poems*), in Πάνω σε μια χειμωνιάτικη αχτίνα ('**Upon a Ray of Winter Sun**') 3: 1-5.

II. HISTORICAL EVENTS

It is not surprising that contemporary history should play some part in the poetry of Seferis, himself one of a million and half Greeks displaced from Asia Minor after the disaster of 1922, and for the rest of his life, as a diplomat, with a relatively privileged view of the great events of his time. The distinction between history and politics in Seferis' poetry is not fully clearcut; but under this heading I shall be considering the actual events of history and their impact on the poet and his country, while the following section will be concerned with political attitudes and conflicts which had not necessarily resulted in action. The historical events to be considered now are: the Asia Minor disaster (1922); Greece's involvement in the Second World War (1940-4); and the civil war which followed (1944-9).

THE ASIA MINOR DISASTER

The poem which can most obviously be connected with this historical experience is the sequence *Mythistorema*, written 1933-4 and published in 1935. This is not to say that *Mythistorema* is a poem about the disaster: in fact neither this nor any other modern event is ever mentioned quite explicitly in a poem of Seferis.[1] The few clear references to the modern world in that poem point only indirectly in the direction of the recent national disaster. The description of the women and children crowded on to boats in section 8: 3-8 recall the refugee ships of 1922-3, and references to rusted cannons in section 4: 5 and to cannon shots on the island of Ydra (13: 1) serve as reminders of the earlier conflict between Greeks and Turks, in which the Greeks had won their independence.

But apart from the prevailing disorientation of the modern world that this poem describes, the most telling allusion to the Asia Minor disaster is also the most indirect. Section 17 refers to the capture of Troy by the Greeks in ancient, legendary times. It is entirely implicit, but an important element in that section of the poem, that ancient Troy stood near the coast of Asia Minor, in the area from which the Greeks had only recently been uprooted, just as their legendary ancestors had destroyed the city of their enemies and taken their women and children as captives to Greece. Section 17 gains much of its point through suggesting this comparison between a legendary victory and a modern defeat (see pp. 104-5), and through the further implication that the human consequences of each were equally tragic. This is another example of Seferis' 'allusive method' in action, and helps further to explain the poet's fascination with the remote past. It is through parallels and contrasts between different periods of history, that Seferis most often refers, indirectly, to recent and contemporary experience.

WORLD WAR II

[World War II] appears directly in a poem of the collection Ημερολόγιο καταστρώματος Α' (*Logbook I*), written shortly after the outbreak of war in Europe, in November 1939. This is the poem **'Les Anges Sont Blancs'**, which contains a reference to the map of Poland changing shape like a stain of ink on blotting paper (the consequence of Hitler's attack on that country in September 1939, in defiance of an ultimatum from Britain and France, and his subsequent pact with Stalin). The more direct effects of the war in Greece are less visible in Seferis' poetry. There is no allusion to the heroic campaign against the Italians in Albania in the winter of 1940-1. On the other hand the war is to be assumed as the essential background of all the poems in Ημερολόγιο καταστρώματος Β' (*Logbook II*), written between May 1941 and October 1944. Indeed the date of composition given at the end of each of them, usually with the place also, is itself a reminder of this background. References to identifiable events in these wartime poems, however, are rare. The first poem, which was actually begun during the German attack on Crete in May 1941, describes the event, but in general terms:

Και τώρα βγήκε το νέο φεγγάρι αγκαλιασμένο
με το παλιό· με τ' όμορφο νησί ματώνοντας
λαβωμένο· το ήρεμο νησί, το δυνατό νησί, το
  αθώο.
Και τα κορμιά σαν τσακισμένα κλαδιά
και σαν ξεριζωμένες ρίζες . . .

                                                    10-15

And now the new moon has come out embracing
the old; and the beautiful island bleeding,
wounded; the calm island—the strong, the innocent
  island.
And the bodies like broken branches,
like roots uprooted. . . .

The physical and moral damage inflicted by the war is more clearly evoked in poems which look back on the events from a distance: in **'Thrush'** (1946), and in a memorable passage from σαλαμίνα της Κύπρος (**'Salamis in Cyprus'**, dated November 1953):

Φίλοι του άλλου πολέμου,
σ' αυτή την έρημη συννεφιασμένη ακρογιαλιά
σας συλλογίζομαι καθώς γυρίζει η μέρα—
Εκείνοι που έπεσαν πολεμώντας κι εκείνοι που
  έπεσαν χρόνια μετά τη μάχη·
εκείνοι που είδαν την αυγή μες απ' την πάχνη
  του θανάτου
ή, μες στην άγρια μοναξιά κάτω από τ' άστρα,
νιώσανε πάνω τους μαβιά μεγάλα
τα μάτια της ολόκληρης καταστροφής·
κι ακόμη εκείνοι που προσεύχονταν
όταν το φλογισμένο ατσάλι πριόνιζε τα καράβια:
"Κύριε, βόηθα να θυμόμαστε
πώς έγινε τούτο το φονικό·
την αρπαγή το δόλο την ιδιοτέλεια,
το στέγνωμα της αγάπης·
Κύριε, βόηθα να τα ξεριζώσουμε . . ."

                                                    35-49

Friends from the other war,
on this deserted and cloudy beach
I think of you as the day turns—
those who fell fighting and those who fell years after
   the battle,
those who saw dawn through the mist of death
or, in wild solitude under the stars,
felt upon them the huge dark eyes
of total disaster;
and those again who prayed
when flaming steel sawed the ships:
'Lord, help us to keep in mind
the causes of this slaughter:
greed, dishonesty, selfishness,
the desiccation of love;
Lord, help us to root these out . . .'

In fact Seferis' wartime poems have more to do with the politics of the Greek government in exile than with the more immediate horrors of the war, and this will be discussed in the next section.

THE CIVIL WAR

The 'first round' of the Greek civil war had already been fought between rival groups of resistance fighters in the mountains before Seferis returned to Athens with the Greek government in October 1944. But Seferis was in Greece throughout the 'second round', that is the brief uprising of 3 December 1944 and its suppression by British troops, and the long third round from 1946 to 1949, in which superior American firepower finally put an end to the political hopes of the communist left in Greece. Yet the traumatic events of these years find only one single echo in Seferis' published writings up until the time of his death.

This occurs in the last section of the poem **'Thrush'** (see pp. 115-17), in a reference so fleeting that it has usually been overlooked (III 62).[2] The allusion is to the sons of Oedipus, Eteocles and Polynices, who fought one another to the death, and it is of considerable importance for our understanding of that poem. **'Thrush'** was written at a time when war in its most 'unnatural' form was beginning once again—civil war in which Greek was pitted against Greek, and the political balance between Left and Right that Seferis had sought during his exile in the Middle East had exploded into a conflict of rival ideologies. It was at precisely that moment that he wrote **'Thrush'**, the first of a number of poems that looks forward, in visionary rather than in practical terms, to the reconciliation of conflict and the rebirth of love. The Oedipus myth provides Seferis with an example of unnatural love within the family (in the incest of Oedipus with his mother Jocasta), and also of unnatural, civil conflict (in the fatal war between the two brothers). And it is out of this worst of all possible worlds, in **'Thrush'**, that the poet's vision is able, despite or even because of this latest degradation of the Greek historical experience, to look beyond it to a vision of love:

Τραγούδησε μικρή Αντιγόνη, τραγούδησε,
  τραγούδησε . . .
δε σου μιλώ για περασμένα, μιλώ για την
  αγάπη· . . .

                       (3: 66-7)

Sing, little Antigone, sing, O sing . . .
I'm not speaking to you about things past, I'm speaking about love; . . .

Among the poems which Seferis wrote during the civil war period but did not publish are several which attempt to come to grips, in poetic terms, with the conflict of Greek against Greek. These poems were published only after the poet's death, in Τετράδιο γυμνασμάτων Β' (***Book of Exercises II***). That he chose not to publish them in his lifetime suggests rather that Seferis was dissatisfied with the artistic success of the attempt, than any political motive. (It is possible, though, that the absolute refusal of these poems to express a preference for either side in the conflict would have been thought subversive in the circles in which Seferis moved professionally, during the civil war itself.) In these poems the ancient myth of Oedipus makes its only other appearances in Seferis' poetry apart from the allusion in **'Thrush'** just mentioned: in the poems entitled Τυφλός (**'Blind Man'**, dated December 1945) and Οιδιπόδειο, '48 (**'Oedipal '48'**), written in Ankara in October of that year. Other poems which allude to the civil war draw implicitly on this allusion to the Oedipus myth: in all of them a fratricidal war is seen as a perversion of nature, and, like the fight to the death between the sons of Oedipus, as the consequence of love perverted from its natural course. (The sons of Oedipus were the issue of the incestuous marriage between Oedipus and his mother.)

The last of these poems to be written dates from the end of the civil war, and its title **'Canzona'**, is an allusion to the Italian title given by Beethoven to a movement in one of his quartets: 'Song of thanksgiving, by one who has come through an illness, in the Lydian mode.' Seferis as it happened was in the Turkish town of Bursa (Prousa) at the time (this was the period of his posting to Turkey); and Bursa lies in the ancient province of Lydia after which the musical mode is named. But the more important allusion of the title is to 'one who has come through an illness'. The poem, as its title leads us to expect, is in the form of a prayer of thanksgiving. But it is not the poet himself who has 'come through'; it is, by implication, divided Greece. The most direct reference to the civil war comes in the following lines:

Κι ανάμεσα στ' αδέρφια μας που κλώθουν
στις φλέβες τους το δίκλωνο αίμα,
στον άγριο φόβο της αγάπης
στην τρυφερότητα του μίσους

στην κατηφόρα του σκοταδιού,
βοήθησέ μας.³

And among our brothers who spin
in their veins the twin-branched blood,
in the wild fear of love
in the tenderness of hatred
in the descent into darkness,
grant us aid.

The 'twin-branched blood' alludes to the sons of
Oedipus, born of the same blood but fighting one
against the other. It is noticeable how once again in this
poem, as in **'Thrush'** and the Oedipus poems of ***Book
of Exercises II,*** the theme of fratricidal conflict is
juxtaposed to that of love, in this case love gone wrong,
love which turns into its opposite, hatred. These poems
attribute no blame for the state of affairs: through human weakness of a kind familiar from Seferis' poetry,
man's natural capacity for love has been diverted from
its normal course and the result, as in the ancient dramas
on the Oedipus story, is tragedy. In that story, Oedipus
willingly married Jocasta, but did not know that she
was his mother. Oedipus broke the law of nature unwittingly; but once that law had been broken the destructive consequences became inescapable—and that is
what makes the tragedy. Seferis' poems which deal
with the civil war offer a view of that conflict in
similarly tragic terms.

III. POLITICS

Under this heading I shall consider the dictatorship of
Metaxas imposed on 4 August 1936; the politics of the
Greek government in exile in Egypt during the Second
World War; the early stages of the Cyprus conflict in
1953 and 1954; and the dictatorship of the Colonels,
imposed in 1967 and still in force at the time of Seferis' death in 1971.

THE METAXAS DICTATORSHIP.

Seferis' principled disapproval of the regime of General
Ioannis Metaxas, who seized power in Greece on 4
August 1936 is clear from the personal account he wrote
in exile, after Metaxas' death in January 1941 and the
Nazi occupation of Greece in April of that year.⁴ This
account was not published until after Seferis' death,
and it would have been dangerous, as well as unprofes-
sional, for him to have made any public comment on
Metaxas' seizure of power at the time. As a senior civil
servant, Seferis nonetheless served the regime, first in a
foreign posting to Albania (1936-8) and then as Director of the Foreign Press up until the Nazi invasion.
Ironically enough, for a poet committed to the ideals of
freedom and free speech, Seferis was actually in charge
of censoring foreign press reports going out of Greece.
In poems written during this period we occasionally
find Seferis using and developing his 'allusive method'

in order to evade the censorship he was also obliged to
practise in his professional life. The last group of poems
which make up ***Book of Exercises*** (published in 1940)
have the general title σχέδια για ένα καλοκαίρι
(**'Sketches for a Summer'**), and most were written
during the first two years of the Metaxas regime.

The first of these, **'A Word for Summer'**, is dated
'Autumn, 1936' and describes the glum 'back to school'
feelings of city life being resumed after the summer
break. But there are hints that the end of that particular
summer (after the military *coup d' état* of 4 August—
although of course this is not mentioned in the poem) is
the end of something more profound; and the resump-
tion of a familiar routine begins to sound, by the end of
the poem, more and more sinister:

Μένει ακόμα η κίτρινη έρημο το καλοκαίρι
κύματα της άμμου φεύγοντας ως τον τελευταίο
  κύκλο
ένας ρυθμός τυμπάνου αλύπητος ατέλειωτος
μάτια φλογισμένα βουλιάζοντας μέσα στον ήλιο
χέρια με φερσίματα πουλιών χαράζοντας τον
  ουρανό
χαιρετώντας στίχους νεκρών σε στάση προσοχής
χαμένα σ' ένα σημείο που δεν τ' ορίζω και με
  κυβερνά·
τα χέρια σου γγίζοντας το ελεύθερο κύμα.

                                                    55-62

There still remains the yellow desert, summer,
waves of sand receding to the final circle
a *drum's beat, merciless, endless,*
flaming eyes sinking into the sun
hands in the manner of birds cutting the sky
saluting ranks of the dead who stand at attention
hands *lost* at a point *beyond my control and mastering*
  me:
your hands touching the *free wave.*

This is how the poem ends, and I have underlined the
words and phrases which seem to me to contain indirect
hints of the recent political change and its implications.
The summer recedes before the 'drum's beat, merciless,
endless', even the dead are called to take the salute in a
military manner,⁵ the poet sees everything as lost now
that he has no power of action but is merely ruled, and
the final words of the poem are surely a backward
glance at the relative political freedoms of the early
30s, in the words the 'free wave'.

Two other poems of the same period also probably
contain allusions to the loss of political freedom in
Greece at the hands of Metaxas, and like the previous
poem were published while Metaxas was still in power
(in 1940, in ***Logbook I***). Ο δικός μας ήλιος (**'Our
Sun'**) is a cryptic poem which shares the mood of
foreboding and even of warning that dominates this collection written under the shadow of impending world

war. The poet addresses another person: 'This sun was mine and yours,' he begins. But out of sight behind the sun seen by both:

ποιος υποφέρει πίσω από το χρυσαφί μεταξωτό
ποιος πεθαίνει;

(2)

Who's suffering behind the golden silk, who's dying?

The sun (or the sunlight, perhaps) is golden, but also silken; we accept it because we have to but we can't see what it hides. What it does turn out to hide are the atrocities of the police state (3-6). There may be a pun implied between the word μεταξωτό (silk) and the name of Metaxas. Later the poems speaks of the 'gold embroidery' (χρυσά κεντίδια) of this particular sun, and this image of military power helps to explain the curious choice of 'silk' (which is repeated at the end of the poem). Messengers arrive, apparently with a warning, but the other person, addressed as 'you' is 'blinded by the light' and tells them to rest before delivering their message. As a result, they die before they can say more than, 'We don't have time'. The other person ('you') at the end of the poem holds on to 'our sun' and 'kept all of it' (22), while the poet has taken a different path and learnt the terrible secrets that lie:

. . . πίσω από το χρυσάφι και το μετάξι·
δεν έχουμε καιρό. σωστά μιλήσαν οι
μαντατοφόροι.

23-4

. . . behind the gold and the silk:
we don't have time. The messengers were right.

If this poem contains a warning, the subject of that warning surely lies closer to home than the impending world war. Or rather, if it warns against the dictatorial methods and the police states of Hitler in Germany and Mussolini in Italy, that were later to become Greece's enemies in that war, it also warns even more strongly of the dangers of these same evils as practised in Greece by Metaxas.[6]

The other poem of this period which seems to allude to the Metaxas regime is Ο γυρισμός του ξενιτεμένου (**'The Return of the Exile'**), dated to spring 1938 on the poet's return to Athens from Albania. This poem can be read on a number of levels, and is certainly not *only* about the Metaxas dictatorship.[7] However its dialogue-form seems to be a development of the situation in **'Our Sun'** (which it immediately follows in *Logbook I*), in which the poet had addressed another character whose perception of things turned out to be very different from his. And in this poem the speeches of this other character, the interlocutor, have a sinister

refrain in their insistence on 'getting used to things' (15, 33, 44). The poet, returning to his native land, sees everyone about him reduced to their knees as though praying (30-31); even his final friend sinks out of sight while scythe-bearing chariot wheels cut down everything above ground. This is one way of describing a return to a country under military rule.

THE POLITICS OF THE GREEK GOVERNMENT IN EXILE (1941-4).

Now that both Seferis' personal and his 'political' diaries for the period have been published, we can see more clearly than many contemporary readers would have been able to do, how the poems of *Logbook II* are the tip of a very large iceberg indeed. This is not the place to attempt to disentangle the political complexities of the Greek government in exile in Egypt, nor of Seferis' own principled but contorted efforts to maintain a kind of personal balance in all this.[8] Symptomatic is the following exchange with a French observer, just after Seferis had lost his job as Director of the Press Office for alleged left-wing sympathies:

"Περίεργο", είπε, "ως τώρα κατηγορούσαν το γραφείο σας ως συντηρητικό, τώρα ως αριστερό, περίεργο—δεν καταλαβαίνω." "Ίσως να πρέπει να καταλάβετε ότι κάναμε καλά τη δουλειά μας", του είπα.[9]

'It's strange,' he said, 'up till now your office has been accused of being conservative, now it's supposed to be leftwing, it's strange—I don't understand.' 'Perhaps you ought to understand that we've been doing our job well,' I told him.

The same lonely stance, together with a sarcastic scorn for politicians of whatever party, can be seen in poems of *Logbook II* such as Υστερόγραφο (**'Postscript'**), **'Kerk str. Oost, Pretoria, Transvaal'** (13-17), Μέρες τ' Απρίλη '43 (**'Days of April '43'**), and Θεατρίνοι, M.A. (**'Actors, Middle East'**). But the poet's personal search for a political balance between the extremes of Left and Right, that can be traced in the poems and diaries of this period, undoubtedly helped to shape his fascination, in later poems and essays, with the harsh norms of justice that he found in the ancient writings of Herakleitos and Aeschylus.

CYPRUS, 1953-4.

The 'tragic' understanding of human conflict which Seferis seemed to be working towards in his poems written in exile during World War II and during the Greek civil war period is developed far more, and fully linked to the poet's concept of justice as a natural force (see pp. 42-3), in the poems he wrote as a result of two visits to Cyprus in the autumn of 1953 and 1954. This was the time when Greek-Cypriot and mainland Greek demands for the island to be unified with Greece were gathering momentum, and being rebuffed with increasing finality by the British government, which had ruled Cyprus since 1878.

The armed struggle by a section of the Greek-Cypriot population under the banner of EOKA did not begin until after Seferis' visits to the island that formed the basis for *Logbook III,* published in 1955. But the tensions were clear to see, as Seferis noted in his diaries; and the grim warning contained in the poem **'Salamis in Cyprus'**, of the 'drying up of love' and the hardening of attitudes that leads to a chain of violence, has proved prophetically true. Although Seferis could hardly have predicted the precise form that events would take, he well understood the causes, as they were visible then, that would lead in the late fifties to violence and repression, then, after the island's independence, in the sixties to intercommunal strife between Greek and Turkish Cypriots, and finally, in 1974, to the enforced partition of Cyprus after the Turkish invasion. The insights into the nature and causes of war that Seferis began to develop during the time of his political balancing act in the Middle East during the Second World War, and which took shape in his poems of the civil war period, reach their fullest development in this collection, and are most apparent in two poems, Ελένη (**'Helen'**), and **'Salamis in Cyprus'**.

'Helen' takes as its starting point the ancient play of the same name by Euripides (fifth century BC), which had set out to cast doubt on the heroic legends of the war of Troy that the Greeks of that time believed in as history. According to this play, Helen of Troy—the most beautiful woman in the world, over whom the Greeks and Trojans were supposed to have fought for ten years—never went there at all, but had been spirited off by a god to Egypt. The play tells of the incredulous meeting of her there, by a group of Greeks who have lost their home as the indirect cause of the Trojan war, and are now on their way to Cyprus to found a new city. This city will be called Salamis, which figures in the next poem to be discussed, and so provides a point of contact between Euripides' play and Cyprus where this poem was written. Euripides' Greeks, in his play, are still shattered by the effects of a long war recently over, and are understandably horrified to be discovering, too late for it to make any difference to their lives, that what they had fought for was only an illusion. The woman they had fought for ten years to recapture was only a shadow in the likeness of Helen, put there by the gods to make fools of them, while the real Helen has been doing no harm to anybody in Egypt. The ways of the ancient Greek gods are indeed mysterious—and not necessarily well meant either. This is the dilemma of Euripides' **'Helen'**.

Seferis' poem is a sustained allusion to this ancient text, but grounded in the actual landscape of contemporary Cyprus, as is clear from the refrain that occurs three times in the poem:

"Τ' αηδόνια δε σ' αφήνουνε να κοιμηθείς στις Πλάτρες."

'The nightingales won't let you sleep in Platres.'

Platres, in the Troodos mountains, was then the summer residence of the colonial governor, and so the line contains an allusion also to the political situation at the time when it was written. In this indirect but unmistakable manner, Seferis updates the dilemma of Euripides' play: for the Trojan war fought, so the story goes, for a beautiful woman, we are invited to substitute the Second World War, fought for freedom from oppression. Greece and Britain had been allies in that war, but Britain was now refusing the freedom that both peoples had fought for, to the Greeks of Cyprus. The poem takes a bleak view of history, implying that wars may be fought again and again for false goals or for goals that cannot be achieved, no matter how great the sacrifice. It all depends—will human beings ever be wise enough not to fall for the bait laid for them by the gods?[10]

'Salamis in Cyprus' has already been discussed. . . . With its appeal to the 'friends from the other war' and its paraphrase, in Greek, of a prayer by a British Royal Navy commander during the Second World War, this poem makes one of the most direct references to a political situation that can be found in Seferis' poetry. It also, . . . , refines the idea discussed earlier, that violence is the inevitable result of the 'drying up of love'. In its place, the poem warns, repression will only breed violence:

Δεν αργεί να καρπίσει τ' αστάχυ
δεν χρειάζεται μακρύ καιρό
για να φουσκώσει της πίκρας το προζύμι,
δεν χρειάζεται μακρύ καιρό
το κακό για να σηκώσει το κεφάλι,
κι ο άρρωστος νους που αδειάζει
δε χρειάζεται μακρύ καιρό
για να γεμίσει με την τρέλα,
νῆσός τις ἔστι . . .

26-34

Wheat doesn't take long to ripen,
it doesn't take much time
for the yeast of bitterness to rise,
it doesn't take much time
for evil to raise its head,
and the sick mind emptying
doesn't take much time
to fill with madness:
there is an island . . .

Another important element in this poem is the concept of 'the lesser evil'. Near the end of the poem two opposing voices propose different solutions. The first invokes the doctrine of political expediency (the 'art of the possible') and opts for acceptance of the situation. 'It is better to forget', this voice begins; and by now there have been many poems by Seferis in which the verb 'to forget' has been linked to sinister, even disastrous, consequences. The other voice is the one that insists on the 'terrible message from Salamis'.

The choice of the lesser of two evils—the politician's choice—is central to another poem of *Logbook III*, O δαίμων της πορνείας ('**The Demon of Fornication**'). This poem follows Cavafy's manner of using a historical source: in form it is a straightforward narrative (in itself something very unusual for Seferis). In content it retells a steamy episode from the history of Cyprus in the fourteenth century, from the fifteenth-century chronicle of Leontios Macheras. The essence of this story has strong parallels with other poems of Seferis that we have been discussing: a king's passionate love for his queen turns sour when it is alleged that she is unfaithful. As a result corruption spreads through the court and the whole island, until the king is brutally murdered. The moral dilemma faced by the courtiers in this poem, is whether to try to cover up for the queen's infidelity or risk the king's anger. They choose 'the lesser evil' (46), and inadvertently oil the wheels that lead to disaster. This poem (again following the manner of Cavafy) makes no direct reference to contemporary Cyprus at all; the action is entirely set in the rather exotic past of the medieval Kingdom of Cyprus and Jerusalem. The dangers of choosing the 'lesser evil', however, clearly allude to the same contemporary political dilemma as does the poem '**Salamis in Cyprus**'. And in portraying the root cause of corruption and violence as love perverted, it develops and deepens the attitude to contemporary conflicts that we have already seen in other poems of Seferis of this period.

The Regime of the Colonels (1967-74).

Seferis' last collection of poems published during his lifetime, ***Three Secret Poems,*** makes no detectable allusions at all to the political events of the decade during which the poems were written. However, as we have seen, the imposition of military rule in 1967 provoked from Seferis a rare explicit statement . . . , and the poems Οι γάτες τ' 'Αη Νικόλα ('**The Cats of St Nicholas**'), "Επί ασπαλάθων . . ." ('**On Aspalathoi . . .**' or '**On Gorse . . .**'), and 'Ίππιος Κολωνός ('**Hippios Colonus**'[11]). Only the first of these appeared in print before the poet's death in August 1971, in the protest volume Δεκαοχτώ κείμενα (*Eighteen Texts*). '**On Aspalathoi . . .**' was first published in the newspaper *To Vima* a month later (23 September), and '**Hippios Colonus**' in the following year, although it had been written earlier, in 1970. '**The Cats of St Nicholas**' belongs with the other Cyprus poems in *Logbook III,* to which it has been added in later editions of the Ποιήματα (*Poems*).

'**On Aspalathoi . . .**', which is dated 31 March 1971, is Seferis' last poem. Like '**The Demon of Fornication**'

it alludes to contemporary events indirectly, by using a method characteristic of Cavafy. The title consists of a fragment of ancient Greek, quoted out of context from Plato's *Republic*. The development of the poem then follows quite closely that of Cavafy's poem about the son of Julius Caesar and Cleopatra, Καισαρίων ('Caesarion').[12] The poet describes a visit to the ancient temple at Sounion near Athens, where as well as the ruins he notices the spiky plants called, in ancient Greek, *aspalathoi* (gorse). The word '*aspalathoi*' then reminds the poet of a little-known passage in an ancient text (a favourite way for Cavafy to introduce a theme), in which a notorious tyrant was punished eternally in the underworld by being dragged across these same spiky bushes. The continued existence in Greece of both the name and the thing it refers to, forges a link between Plato's time and ours, suggesting that the punishment for tyrants will still be as terrible in the modern world as it was in the ancient. It is interesting too, to notice that in this poem Seferis focusses on the *plant* which is a relatively insignificant detail amid other more terrible tortures in Plato's account. The link between the natural world and justice, and between the modern world and the ancient, is again present in this poem. By highlighting the '*aspalathoi*' Seferis is able to hint that the natural world itself punishes the tyrant, and so redresses the balance of nature in which tyranny (and of course the torture practised by the Colonels) are unnatural.[13]

In all of Seferis' poems which comment on contemporary history and/or politics the contemporary allusions never seem to be made for their own sake or in isolation from other characteristic themes of the poet's work. Indeed the reader with no knowledge of twentieth-century Greek history would learn little, if anything, from Seferis. And although, as I have tried to show in this chapter, a knowledge of events contemporary with the poems does in some cases add something to our understanding of a poem, Seferis' handling of contemporary themes always leads away from the topical and the local, to set it in a context of justice, nature, time, or all of these. And it is striking that up until the end of his career, if Seferis is going to allude to contemporary events, he will almost always do so by way of allusion to the distant past.

Notes

1. Some of the critical discussion of the relation between the poem and the historical events of 1922 is summarised and discussed by Capri-Karka (1985: 24-6), who concludes that:

   There is no doubt that the poem is permeated by a feeling of defeat, loss and agony and that this feeling is not unrelated to the national disaster . . . But the interpretation of the whole poem as an expression of a particular historical event is rather simplistic . . . [The] poem works also on a universal level because it can express the feelings of the defeated, the exiled, the victims of any war.

2. An exception is Vitti (1989: 229-30).

3. 'Canzona' 18-23. The other clear allusions to the civil war in *Book of Exercises II* are in Γυμνοπαιδία, Υ. Γ. 1945 (19-27), Μεροληψία, Το χιόνι εδώ δεν τελειώνει (5-13), and Με λαμπυρίσματα γυαλιού.

4. See Seferis 1972b.

5. The line could also be interpreted as meaning that the verses (στίχοι) of dead *poets* are called to stand to attention (before a military ruler).

6. At the time when this poem was written many people in Greece, including Seferis, feared that if it came to war, Metaxas would be more likely to join with Hitler and Mussolini, some of whose totalitarian methods he imitated in Greece, than with democratic countries like Britain and France. In the event, Metaxas took the opposite course, when on 28 October 1940 he sent the one-word telegram 'No' to Mussolini and so brought Greece into the war on the Allied side. This action, which briefly united almost all Greeks in fighting off the Italian invaders in the winter of 1940-1, belatedly turned Metaxas into a truly national leader in the eyes of many Greeks, again including Seferis. But there was no Ochi Day in 1938, and good reason to fear the consequences of the Metaxas dictatorship for Greece.

7. For detailed discussion of this poem see Maronitis 1984: 29-43 and Ricks 1989: 147-57.

8. This can now be seen with greater clarity, when the poems are set alongside passages from the diaries which relate to the same situations and events: see Krikos-Davis 1989.

9. Seferis 1979: 221 (Wed. 3 May 1944).

10. For detailed discussion of this poem and its treatment of its 'source' in Euripides, see Krikos-Davis 1979.

11. For an English translation of this poem see Seferis 1983c: 18.

12. For an analysis of this poem see Robinson 1988: 81-6.

13. On this poem see Krikos-Davis 1984.

References

Capri-Karka, C. 1985 *War in the poetry of George Seferis: a poem-by-poem analysis,* New York: Pella.

Krikos-Davis, K. 1979 'On Seferis' "Helen"', *Byzantine and Modern Greek Studies* 5: 57-76.

————. 1984 'Notes on Seferis' last poem', *Scandinavian Studies in Modern Greek* 7-8: 101-6.

Maronitis 1984 Μαρωνίτης, Δ.Ν. Η ποίηση του Γιώργου σεφέρη: μελέτες και μαθήματα, Αθήνα: Ερμής.

Ricks, David 1989 *The shade of Homer: a study in Modern Greek poetry,* Cambridge: Cambridge University Press.

Robinson, Christopher 1988 *C. P. Cavafy* (Studies in Modern Greek), Bristol: Bristol Classical Press.

Seferis, G. 1964 *Le Discours de Stockholm.* Institut Français d' Athènes.

————. 1965 σεφέρης, Γ. Αντιγραφές, Αθήνα: Ίκαρος.

————. 1966 *On the Greek style* [selected essays from Dokimes], translated by Rex Warner and Th. D. Frangopoulos, Boston and London.

————. 1972a σεφέρης, Γ. Ποιήματα (8η έκδοση), επιμ. Γ.Π. σαββίδη, Αθήνα: Ίκαρος.

————. 1972b σεφέρης, Γ. Χειρόγραφο σεπ. '41, Αθήνα: Ίκαρος.

————. 1972c σεφέρης, Γ. Άσμα ασμάτων, Αθήνα: Ίκαρος.

————. 1973; 1975a; 1975b; 1977a; 1977b; 1986a. σεφέρης, Γ. Μέρες (6 volumes), Αθήνα: Ίκαρος.

————. 1974a *A poet's journal: days of 1945-1951.* Translated by Athan Anagnostopoulos, Cambridge, Mass.: Harvard University Press.

————. 1974b σεφέρης, Γ. Έξι νύχτες στην Ακρόπολη, επιμ. Γ.Π. σαββίδη, Αθήνα: Ίκαρος.

————. 1975c σεφέρης, Γ. Η Αποκάλυψη του Ιωάννη, Αθήνα: Ίκαρος.

————. 1976 σεφέρης, Γ. Τετράδιο γυμνασμάτων, Β', επιμ. Γ.Π. σαββίδη, Αθήνα: Ίκαρος.

————. 1979, 1986b σεφέρης, Γ. Πολιτικό ημερολόγιο (2 volumes), Αθήνα: Ίκαρος.

————. 1980 σεφέρης, Γ. Μεταγραφές, επιμ. Γ. Γιατρομανωλάκη, Αθήνα: Λέσχη.

————. 1982 *Collected poems,* translated, edited, and introduced by Edmund Keeley and Philip Sherrard [revised and expanded edition], London: Anvil Press Poetry.

————. 1983a 'Poems in new translations by John Stathatos', *Labrys* 8: 2-16.

————. 1983b 'Language in our poetry,' translated by Peter Thompson, *Labrys* 8: 35-45.

————. 1983c 'Three last poems', translated by Peter Thompson, *Labrys* 8: 17-20.

―――. 1984 σεφέρης, Γ. Δοκιμές, (5η έκδοση), Αθήνα: Ίκαρος.

―――. 1990 George Seferis: *Complete poems, translated, edited and introduced by E. Keeley and P. Sherrard,* Princeton and Guildford: Princeton University Press.

Vitti, M. 1989 Φθορά και λόγος: εισαγωγή στην ποίηση του Γιώργου σεφέρη (νέα έκδοση, αναθεωρημένη), Αθήνα: Εστία.

Kostas Myrsiades (essay date 2000)

SOURCE: Myrsiades, Kostas. "Odysseus in the Poetry of George Seferis." *Journal of the Hellenic Diaspora* 26, no. 1 (2000): 65-70.

[*In the following essay, Myrsiades examines Seferis's position in the modern debate between the Hellenic and the Romeic perspectives on Greek identity.*]

The new vitality in modern Greek poetry, which has resulted in several nominations for the Nobel Prize in literature (all for poetry) since the early fifties and the awarding of two Nobel Prizes—in 1963 to George Seferis and again in 1979 to Odysseus Elytis—has had several beginnings.

The movement we call modern Greek poetry begins with the vernacular Akritic epic cycle, composed between the ninth and eleventh centuries and handed down from generation to generation until it was finally committed to writing in the nineteenth century.

But it was not until the poet Kostis Palamas (1859-1943) that a completely new kind of life was infused into Greek poetry. It was Palamas who rejected the romantics and the "purist" form of Greek (*katharevousa*), to lead his contemporaries and younger poets (George Seferis among them, along with Odysseus Elytis and Yannis Ritsos) into a fresh world of literature in which the full possibilities of the modern Greek language and its rhythms were explored.

Finally, the proper beginning of modern Greek poetry as we understand it today, can be said to have occurred in the early 1930s. It was during this period that George Seferis's first book of poetry, perceptively titled **Turning Point** (1931), was published to mark the beginning of the strongest wave of symbolism to enter Greece. This period was also the key moment for Greek surrealist poetry, with the founding of the periodical *Ta Nea Grammata* (1935). In March of that same year there appeared two more seminal texts of modern poetry—George Seferis's **Mythistorema** and Andreas Embirikos's *Ypsikaminos*—while in November of the same

year, *Ta Nea Grammata* published the first poems of Odysseus Elytis. A year earlier in 1934, Yannis Ritsos's first book of poetry, *Tractor,* had appeared.

In this new poetry of the thirties, which clearly and definitively turned from old Greek forms to the more avant garde techniques of western Europe, in particular to French Symbolism and Surrealism, modern Greek poets were to create a poetry so heavily imbued with the past of that nation, that the body of their work cannot be seriously discussed without giving that past significant consideration.

During this period modern Greek poetry was caught in the great debate over Greek identity—a debate on-going since before the Greek Revolution of 1821. It involved distinctions drawn between two attitudes toward Greek identity. The European or foreign view (referred to as the Hellenic view) was characterized by a long-term love affair with the distant classical past, as a source of the values that informed European culture, and a distinct distaste for modern Greece, since Byzantium, as an ethnically mixed grab-bag of largely oriental attitudes. The European view was shared by intellectual Greeks of the Diaspora, who were to provide the new leaders of what they regarded as a backward native population.

In opposition to the Hellenic view was the Romeic view. Adopted by the autochthonous or indigenous native Greeks who populated the Turkish lands, it accepted the mixed demography of Greek lands that resulted from the variety of invasions and migrations that afflicted Greece across its history. The Romeic view defined itself as a pluralistic, largely lower-class oral culture, whose origins could be effectively traced to the Byzantine and Ottoman empires.

It was this unresolved debate that we find reflected in the poetry of the 1930s. Preoccupation with the past as opposed to insistence on living in the present, became a dominant theme, which was shared by the poets of this period. Attempts to define Greek identity during this time are torn between the Europeanized approach (exemplified by George Seferis) and its reliance on the classical past for modern meaning; the Christian approach adopted by Takis Papatsonis, which carries us forward to an essentially Byzantine world view, but one still tempered by classical influences and European forms; a third, largely internal, subconcious view illustrated by Odysseus Elytis, which finds its direction by indirection, effectively resolving the issue by avoiding it; and finally Yannis Ritsos's view, which places the debate squarely in modern times, with the firm insistence that the value of the past lies only in the present.

Of the poets mentioned, it is George Seferis who most completely exemplifies the use of the Greek classical past and who sets the standard for its use in the Greek present. Using the Homeric hero Odysseus as a continuing figure throughout his poetry, Seferis finds for his modern Greek audience a persona at home in the global world, a man of action who, certain of his eventual return to Ithaca, does not know despair. Seferis takes this very literal Odysseus and transforms him into an exile, a fatherly sea captain, a pilgrim. His Odysseus, unlike Homer's, cannot return to the world of society and physical reality—to Ithaca—for he is incapable of communication with the dead, who alone hold the secret of his return. The secret of how he is to return home is withheld from Seferis's Odysseus, a pathetic sufferer who bends to his fate, unlike his ancestor, Homer's character, the man of action, who wrestles old Proteus as he transforms into various beasts until, at the end, exhausted, Proteus is compelled to reveal Odysseus's future.

Again in the underworld, Homer's Odysseus approaches the dead to learn from the prophet Tiresias the fate that awaits him in Ithaca. Seferis's modern Odysseus, by contrast, unable to return home, must persist in his never-ending quest, without issue, overwhelmed by the memories of lost friends and relatives, weak companions submerged or dying. The poet reminds us that in modern times, Homeric Odysseus has become a shadow of regret, a ghost that haunts us "with eyes reddened by the salt of the sea." This twentieth-century hero conveys the inadequacy of the present-day Greek in equaling the feats of his forefathers. He serves as a voice for all men tormented by alienation, and the futile search for a paradise, which is no more. A surrogate for the poet himself, Odysseus is cut off from his homeland by two world wars and a lifetime career in the foreign diplomatic corps.

If a counterpart to this Odysseus exists in Homer's world, Seferis suggests, then Elpenor—a common sailor in Odysseus's crew—must be he. It is Elpenor who succumbs to the fatal charms of the goddess Circe. Trapped by Homer in a foreign mythic landscape that he does not understand, Elpenor, at a loss in heroic times, is very much at home in Seferis's world. In the poet's words, "Sentimental, mediocre, wasted," Elpenor is the "poor devil" that modern man has become, while the classical Odysseus is only the shadow of what modern man "should be." Coordinate with Seferis's groping hero of resignation and defeat, the landscape of his poetic world is one of mutilated statues and altars. Hulks of ships coated with rust and brine, a harsh and ruined legacy. These echoes of the past torment the dislocated in Seferis's own *Odyssey*, his twenty-four part poem, *Mythistorema*:

> What are they after, our souls, traveling
> on rotten brine-soaked timbers
> from harbor to harbor?

> (*Mythistorema* 8:9-11)[1]

Seferis retreats to the past in his own life as well as in the life of his poetry. Going back into his childhood to create an individual mythology, he becomes himself a lonely island in time. In a letter written in 1941, he refers to the conditions of creation that feed into his poetry: "There are nights," he says, "when I wake with the feeling that I am a golden fish in a bottle of electric liquid. It is an atmosphere of sick childhood; stimulating with dryness, stimulating in a bad way." This childhood world, this past, this source of his own creativity, as well as the creativity of his people, becomes identified in the poet's mind with the world of the dead, a world he finds more real than that of the living. Past and present become confused, fragments of history floating like memories of waking life in our dreams. He says in *Mythistorema*:

> I woke with this marble head in my hands;
> It exhausts my elbows and I don't know where to put
>   it down.
> It was falling into the dream as I was coming out of
>   the dream
> So our life became one and it will be very
> difficult for it to separate again.

> (*Mythistorema* 3:1-4)

And only in death does the possibility exist that the past might become present again, the "appearance" of the former fusing with the "reality" of the latter. Perhaps the ruins will become full again, in "the hour of death," Seferis muses in his poem **"Memory II."**

Thus, in Seferis, where the echo of the past is constant, one can never be certain whether he is in the company of the living or the dead. The quest is for the past, for an end to the perennial dislocations in time. It is a persistent search for the lost world of the now-dead, which somehow is yet alive, for an insistent and yet anonymous racial memory that is at the same time now a part of past history. Memory leads to disorientation and to interiorization of the external event; it leads to fatalism and to a sense of the unreliability of real time. It is the interpenetration of the inherited past and time-present removed from the accidents of time, that represents, for Seferis, essential reality.

Seferis's view is a tragically paradoxical one; there can be no hope of an end, save in cessation of the search, no likelihood of a resolution, save in catastrophe. The sense of present loss and of imminent failure is constant. Again in *Mythistorema* he states,

> What are they after, our souls, traveling
> on the decks of decayed ships
> crowded in with sallow women and crying babies
> unable to forget themselves either with the flying fish
> or with the stars that masts point out at their tips
> grated by gramophone records
> committed to non-existent pilgrimages unwillingly,
> murmuring broken thoughts from foreign languages?

> (*Mythistorema* 8:1-9)

Seferis's hero is a passive figure, his *Odyssey* a resigned event that merely poses fatalistically the question of deliverance. He says in **Mythistorema,**

> Having known this fate of ours so well
> wandering around among broken stones, three or six
>   thousand years
> searching in collapsed buildings that might have been
>   our homes
> trying to remember dates and heroic deeds:
> will we be able?
>
> (***Mythistorema*** 22:11-15)

The poet's final answer to the quest comes in his poem, **"The Thrush."** Here, he paraphrases from Plato's *Apology,* Socrates's response at his trial,

> "And if you condemn me to drink poison, I thank you
> Your law will be my law; how can I go
> wandering from one foreign country to another, a roll-
>   ing stone.
> I prefer death.
> Who'll come out best only God knows."
>
> (**"The Thrush,"** 3:21-25)

Such a reduction in stature of Odysseus, the man of action, to acquiescence in his own death—the only end to his quest in modern times—leads Seferis to pathos. Through Socrates's response, Odysseus is reduced to an Elpenor.

Note

1. Translations of Seferis's poems are from *George Seferis: Collected Poems (1924-1955),* trans. Edmund Keeley and Philip Sherrard (Princeton: Princeton University Press, 1971).

Martha Klironomos (essay date October 2002)

SOURCE: Klironomos, Martha. "Ancient *Anamnesis,* National *Mneme* in the Poetry of Giorgos Seferis." *Journal of Modern Greek Studies* 20, no. 2 (October 2002): 216-39.

[*In the following essay, Klironomos explores the importance of memory in Seferis's poetry.*]

> Προχωρώ ανάμεσα στην ανάμνηση ℵαι στη
> συνείδηση
>
> *I advance between memory and consciousness*
>
> *Seferis,* Μέρες Γ' *(1977)*

ANCIENT ανάμνησις—μνήμη

In his discussion of Eliot's preoccupation with the past, Seferis remarks that the mark of a good poet is based on "the feeling for history," innate "within ourselves,"

which is contingent upon understanding the whole of human experience. We particularly engage such a historical consciousness in the reading of literary texts from which can we simulate—not a mere flash back in the archaeology of time—but the essence of lived history (Seferis 1974:142-143).[1] «Διαβάστε μια ραψωδία του Ομήρου», he writes, «ℵαι ℵοιτάχτε αν, στα σημεία του σας συγℵινούν, αυτό που αισθανόσαστε είναι απλά ℵαι μόνο μια αρχαιολογιℵή αναδρομή ή μήπως είναι ένα συναίσθημα θρεμμένο από όλην την ανθρώπινη πείρα που μεσολάβησε από την παλιά εℵείνη εποχή ως τη σημερινή στιγμή σας» (Seferis, 1996:169).[2]

At the base of this claim, Seferis affirms the ancient premise of memory as cognition:[3] «για να θυμηθούμε τον αρχαίο σοφό: "γνώση είναι ανάμνηση"» (1977:167).[4] Elsewhere, in Μεταγραφές (1980), Seferis translates a passage from the *Phaedrus* (274c-275a) that defines "memory" («μνήμη») as true "wisdom" («σοφία»). In these instances, Seferis calls up how recollection in antiquity is identified as the basis for truth, that is, learning or knowledge. In the *Meno,* Plato says that "research and learning" («μάθησιν») are wholly "recollection" («ανάμνησις») (*Meno* 81 b3-82). Aristotle also lists memory as a principal component of wisdom (see Small 1997:238).

Whether this recalled knowledge is already inherently innate or nurtured by experience, however, remained an essential question for Plato and Aristotle in each of their respective definitions of memory.[5] These ancient authors are viewed as antecedents for the distinction between "innatist" and "empiricist"[6] theories of learning and recollection: between theories that are indicative of the mind's inner cognitive capabilities as opposed to those that can be attributed to experience and the outer stimuli of sense perception (D. Scott 1995:4). It is a dichotomy that resurfaces throughout Western thought, ranging from epistemological and scientific concepts to ordinary everyday thinking.[7]

How traces of this dichotomy between innatism and experience address historical consciousness in Seferis's own poetics underlies the premise of the first part of this essay. Seferis certainly looks to ancient precedent to validate his understanding of "knowledge is memory"—«γνώση είναι ανάμνηση»—to delineate powerful foundational myths that can be held in the national psyche to ground its identity, a project that relies heavily on a reading of the classics. While he does not present a systematic reading on the subject of knowledge and recollection, Seferis's integration of ancient formulations of memory into his poetry taps into this dichotomy between innatist and empiricist forms of remembrance: a contrast that emerges between presenting the basis of recalled knowledge as *anamnesis,* that is, an inward gaze into the soul's self-knowledge, on the one hand; or, on the other hand, as *mneme,* that is, the preservation of lived experience, subsumed in emblematic images, practices, and beliefs, upon which society constructs its collective identity.

Placing memory at the forefront defines our interpretive task in two ways: it looks at the interplay between ancient and modern texts but does so in a manner that moves beyond a consideration of "intertextuality" in the limited sense in which it has been discussed in previous commentary;[8] it also offers a way in which we can explore elements associated with the memory process that are grounded in the rhetoric of the poetic language itself—those which vacillate from metaphors representing the mind's insight vs. those that stem from reconstructed experience.

A consideration of memory in the modernist text, then, need not merely restrict itself to explication of the devices used to recall ancient literary tradition.[9] Such a method posits the relationship between ancient and modern texts solely as a unidirectional one in which the former is viewed as originary and authoritative, and the latter as derivative and revisionist. Rather, the approach presented here views the relationship between such texts as an interactive one—both *dialogical,*[10] in the sense that it recalls several historical and social meanings of memory at *play* with each other; and, *agonistic,* in recognizing how competing mnemonic concepts embodied in a poetic text can both connote and frustrate meaning.

In this way the reader of the poetry can pursue a number of interpretive paths that are contingent upon similarities and differences between antiquity and modernity in terms of mnemonic concepts, modes of historical consciousness, and the function of the text in representing values privileged in collective consciousness. Yet, because these concepts of *anamnesis* and *mneme* are not fully integrated into the writing of the text, and are often rendered in fragmented form, the attainment of total understanding is often found to be as fleeting as the process of remembering itself.[11]

Platonic *anamnesis* refers to recollection as reminiscence, that is, it is a calling to mind of pre-existing knowledge, latent within our soul, which it had acquired in its prenatal state.[12] By contrast, Aristotelian *anamnesis* is "not the recovery or acquisition of memory," for it rejects the Platonic claim of a prenatal state, but it is the conscious recall of a *lived* past based upon sensory perception.[13] One "remembers now what one saw or otherwise experienced formerly" (Aristotle, *On Memory,* 2.1ff).[14]

While Aristotle develops his ideas in a non-mythical context, myths revolving around memory in Plato's thought become adapted into a general theory of knowl-edge.[15] In the Platonic conception of *anamnesis, Mnemosyne,* the supernatural power, establishes itself "within man to become the very faculty of knowing" (Vernant 1983:92).[16] A process that had once been relegated to mystic exercise, recollection now becomes identified with the quest for truth.[17]

The function of memory, as exhibited in this schema, however, does not reconstruct past time; nor is it concerned with a chronology of events, but, rather, as J. P. Vernant points out, in the search for truth, "it reveals the eternal and unchangeable being" (1983:92). *Mnemosyne* enables the escape from the life of the temporal, mortal world and facilitates contact with the divine realm of the soul, a world of "ideas." Memory does not exemplify a temporal consciousness as much as its transcendence; its objective is not to chronicle the history of the self but to attach the soul to the divine (Vernant, 1983:92).

Separated from inner man upon his death, the soul, for Plato, is a daemon, a divine principle, the function of which is to connect individual destiny to the cosmic order. The demiurge assigns a star to each immortal soul to which it returns once it has been purified through the process of remembering. In its negation of chronological time, *anamnesis* posits the acquisition of knowledge and transforms human existence by connecting it to the broader cosmic order (Vernant 1983:93-94).

What distinguishes the body of ideas revolving around memory in Platonic thought is how it radically changed the concept of the human soul and advanced it towards the idea of an "inner" being.[18] In the *Alcibiades,* an early source,[19] Plato discusses the nature of the soul and says that it is the soul that defines the individual self. As the soul is identified with the self, it is also identified with cognition: for "the soul is the seat of knowledge and thought" (*Alc.* I.133B).

In its definition of self-knowledge as the power to "look into ourselves," the *Alcibiades* upholds the notion that knowledge looms innately "inside" or within the soul.[20] It recalls other Platonic dialogues in which the idea of innateness is viewed within the broader theory of recollection.[21] In the *Meno* Socrates, in the midst of an inquiry into virtue, says that the soul pre-exists in the body and was consciously in possession of knowledge in its earlier state. But, upon entering the body, it "forgets" its knowledge, retaining it "latently" in the form of a memory. What makes discovery possible, he maintains, is our ability to recollect and revive these memories within us.[22] Socrates concludes that in recollecting, Meno, his interlocutor, will be recovering knowledge that is already within him (D. Scott 1995:15-16).

In defining innateness, then, the *Meno* emphasizes our power of recollection and learning as an accumulated knowledge but one that is already stored "inside" or "within" the soul.[23] Among reformulations of Platonic *anamnesis* that underlie modern theories of innatism, are also those that inform recent psychological research. As Westbury and Dennett point out, modern psychology still addresses an aspect of innatism initially raised by Platonic *anamnesis*—that "there can be no learning—and so no knowledge—from the base of a tabula rasa" (2000:18).[24]

The innatism of the soul serves as a foundation upon which Seferis bases his own understanding of recalled knowledge as insight and discovery in Μυθιστόρημα Δ', «'Αργοναῦτες». The poem begins with a quote from the passage in the *Alcibiades* that refers to the soul "knowing" itself:[25]

Ναὶ ψυχὴ
εἰ μέλλει γνώσεσθαι αὑτὴν
εἰς ψυχὴν
αὑτῇ βλεπτέον:[26]

(CP [Collected Poems of George Seferis, tr. by Edmund Keeley and Phillip Sherrard, Princeton: Princeton University Press, 1981], 8)[27]

In the *Alcibiades* (I.132c-133c), Socrates presents the analogy between the eye and the soul, vision and self-knowledge. He draws a parallel between the eye seeing itself in its own reflection and seeing itself reflected in another's eye; in a similar way, the soul knows itself when it focuses its gaze upon another's soul in which wisdom, or knowledge, is reflected.[28] But rather than refer to the "other" of the soul reflected in the mirror, as another self or God, Seferis identifies the other in demotic Greek as "τον ξένο Ναι τον εχθρό" ("the stranger and the enemy") (*CP,* 8, 9). In its "translation" into a modern context, the Platonic idea of self-knowledge in Seferis's poem is reformulated into terms with which the modern subject grapples to resolve its estrangement and discover its identity—by transcendence or through experience.

Platonic self-knowledge, as a metaphor for insight and the inward gaze, is recited by the traveling companions, the Argonauts:

Εἰ μέλλει γνώσεσθαι αὑτὴν, έλεγαν
εἰς ψυχὴν βλεπτέον, έλεγαν
Ναι τα Νουπιά χτυπούσαν το χρυσάφι του πελάγου

(*CP,* 8)[29]

The Delphic maxim of "know thyself" is not only integrated into the narrators' collective consciousness but also embodied in the act of journeying with the striking of the oars into the sea's luminosity. The journey becomes an enactment of the quest for identity: "Their souls become one with the oars and the oarlocks" (*CP,* 9, 11). Yet the journey takes the form of a passage

into their collective mind's memory bank as it encounters a sea of recollected images, a panoramic survey of the vast *topoi* of the past perceived throughout time:

Δυστυχισμέες γυναίΝες Νάποτε με ολολυγμούς
Νλαίγανε τα χαμένα τους παιδιά
Νι' άλλες αγριεμένες γύρευαν το ΜεγαλέξαντρΝο
Ναι δόξες βυθισμένες στα βάθη της Ασίας.
Αράξαμε σ' αΝρογιαλιές γεμάτες αρώματα
    νυχτερινά
με Νελαϊδίσματα πουλιών, νερά που αφήνανε στα
    χέρια
τη μνήμη μιας μεγάλης ευτυχίας.

(*CP,* 10)[30]

The emphasis here is not to recount the past with historical accuracy, for the narrators avoid designating specific moments in time. The text represents both a transcendence from history into mythic time for the acquisition of self-knowledge and a grounding of experience acquired from the essence of lived history.

The Argonauts go on to recount the past through sense perception and associative emotive states. But what they recall is not what is actually experienced but rather a reconstruction of what was experienced that accords with their knowledge and beliefs.[31] The foremost example is the way in which memories are transcribed: as the loss of former "glories" and "the memory of great happiness." Such mediations of past experience exude a national consciousness in demarcating and interpreting key episodes that exemplify the losses and achievements of its past experience. The task of those who remember their ancestors is to assess and imbue with meaning residual sensory data and other remnants left from the past, which, in Seferis's poetry, often ranges from broken marbles to fragmented texts, a point to which we shall return at the conclusion of this section when we consider the function of art.

In its re-discovery of images and *axiomata* from the past, the poem also alludes to death rituals, which are closely associated with archaic forms of social memory. Yet, these are also viable ways in which the modern subject engages itself in traditional forms of experiencing that promote the anchoring of social identity through the link with the past. An example is the externalizing of trauma and loss through tears and lament in the previously quoted passage.

The poem concludes with the passage:

Οι σύντροφοι τέλειωσαν με τη σειρά,
με χαμηλωμένα μάτια. Τα Νουπιά τους
δείχνουν το μέρος που Νοιμούνται στ' αΝρογιάλι.
Κανείς δεν τους θυμάται. ΔιΝαιοσύνη.

(*CP,* 10)[32]

The passage calls to mind archaic burial practices and how memory is conventionally marked by the gravesite, the *sema*, a physical reminder of the warrior's existence. In archaic sources the warrior strives his entire life to attain glory by virtue of leaving behind a good memory. Yet, in this instance, oars mark the site of the companions' demise, ensuring that their memory will not be properly honored. The fear that haunts the Argonauts in ancient sources is one that also vexes the narrators of Seferis's poem—that they might die «νώνυμοι Ϗαι ἀφαντοι» ("unknown and forgotten") (see Detienne 1999: 155, n.2).

Seferis, then, chooses not to recall what Vernant has coined the "beautiful death" of the archaic Greek warrior as it is typically represented in ancient epic (1991:50ff.). It is inscribed in archaic social memory in two related forms: the hero is both recalled through epic song and memorialized in the grave marker. Such an image is said to celebrate the *kleos* and reputation of the fallen aristocratic figure. Preserved in poetic utterance and remembered in every act of its recitation and performance, the recalled image is one of perfection to be revered by society; it becomes a marker of social cohesion. Despite his demise, the hero lives on through the continual invocation of his name and in the endurance of his reputation, both of which command a presence not only in the remembrance of those left behind but also in the consciousness of generations to come (Vernant 1991:68-69).

But just as the memory of death is a way in which to preserve images and *axiomata* from the past to promote the unifying ideals of the *polis,* it is also a way in which to remember civic crisis. Seferis recalls the calamity revolving around Agamemnon's murder. He quotes Orestes's cry at his father's gravesite, «μέμνησο λουτρῶν οἷς ἐνοσφίσθης» ("remember the bath, where you were robbed of life"), a line taken from Aeschylus's *Libation-Bearers* (491), which serves as an epigraph to Μυθιστόρημα Γ'.[33] Orestes remembers the specific place where his father was murdered; but in exacting justice, Orestes's vengeance perpetuates the cycle of violence and disorder that plagues the House of Atreus and its wider society. Seferis's citing of the line can be seen as pointing to the tragic consequences befallen on this society because of its *hubris,* a didactic example from which parallels can be drawn to the modern age.

Seferis uses the same line from the *Libation-Bearers* in a draft of a poem published in Μέρες Ε' wherein he associates it with a potent symbol through which national memory is commonly preserved. Written in the aftermath of WWII, here the speaker cries out the line in demotic Greek at the tomb of the "Unknown Soldier" in Syntagma Square:

στο σύνταγμα μπροστά στον Ἄγνωστο στρατιώτη:
Πόσα λεπτά σιωπῆς Ϗοστίζει μια ζωή;
«θυμήσου τα λουτρά που σε θανάτωσαν πατέρα»·

(1996:55-56)[34]

Despite its anonymity, the tomb of the "Unknown Soldier," becomes a consecrated emblem of national endurance and perseverance in the face of adversity. As an image of continuity, the tomb comes to signify the eternal nation.[35] Through its perpetual remembrance, it reveals the nation's desire to vanquish death.

In the poem **"Last Stop,"** for Seferis, *mneme,* as the collective remembrance of pain and suffering, articulated in the phrase «μνησιπήμων πόνος» ("the pain of remembrance of suffering")[36] (*Agam.* 180), is continuously experienced by humanity within a historical continuum. The poem, which makes overt references to the Revolution of 1821 as well as to WWII, refers to the commonality of war shared among cultures across epochs, the horror of which is always "alive" and "growing":

Κι' α σου μιλώ με παραμύθια Ϗαι παραβολές
είναι γιατί τ' αϏούς γλυϏότερα, Ϗι' η φρίϗη
δεν Ϗουβεντιάζεται γιατί είναι ζωντανή
γιατί είναι αμίλητη Ϗαι προχωράει·
στάζει τη μέρα στάζει στον ύπνο
μνησιπήμων πόνος

(*CP*, 314)[37]

cf. «στάζει δ' ἐν θ' ὕπνῳ πρὸ Ϗαρδίας μνησιπήμων πόνος· Ϗαὶ παρ' ἄϗοντας ἦλθε σωφρονεῖν» (*Agam.* 179-181) ("Instead of sleep there trickles before the heart the pain of remembrance of suffering: even to the unwilling discretion comes")

(Fraenkel, 1962:I.101)

In Aeschylus, the phrase «μνησιπήμων πόνος», in which the recollection of pain is compared to a wound, suggested by the word στάζει, implies that long afterwards it "will ache at times and even break out again, reminding the sufferer of the original hurt" (Fraenkel 1962: II.106).[38] The phrase is uttered by the chorus of Argive elders who refer to Zeus' ordinance that "wisdom" comes from "suffering."

Wisdom gained from the testimony of suffering is acquired not only from the reading of ancient but also popular texts. Such a stance permeates the prologue of Makrygiannes's *Memoirs,* which Seferis cites in the first stanza of the poem to frame the theme of reading and remembering. Consciously aware of how it differs from official written historical accounts of the Revolution of 1821, Makrygiannes remarks how the *Memoirs* articulate empirical "truth."[39] It is a basis upon which Seferis assesses the value of the *Memoirs* in his literary criticism. In the recounting of the history of the trials of the nation, the "spiritual wisdom" represented in Makrygiannes, as Seferis puts it, "is the common lot, the spiritual wealth of a race, handed on through the ages from millennium to millennium, from generation to generation . . . persecuted and always alive, ignored and always present—the common lot of Greek popular tradition" (Seferis 1966:35-36).[40]

How can we assess this valuation of the empirical in the project of the Greek national poet, and what is the function of art therein? In reading both ancient and popular texts, and in integrating variant modes of remembrance in his poetics, Seferis, too, promotes a model of historical experience that differentiates itself from the conventional narrative representation of history. His example illustrates how literature in Greek society approximates what Agnes Heller calls "primary lived history": a mode of historical consciousness that engages the collective "re-presentation" of experience, enabling one "to remember together with others" and to "re-live" experiences "under the spell of the same *a priori* form of historical experiencing (of art, religion and philosophy)" (1993:43). Within this framework, his work offers us, then, a renewed understanding of the residual function of literature in Greek society and of its continual relevance as a mechanism for the preservation of memory and a symbolic medium of societal reconciliation.[41]

The search for a mechanism through which the modern subject can relive history together with others is exemplified in Seferis's poem, **"The King of Asine,"** which is based upon an obscure textual reference in Homer's *Iliad*. It features the contemporary poet in search of the lost king, walking among ruins in an archaeological site, a metaphor for delving into the past. He attempts to interpret these broken fragments—which can be read simultaneously as the attempt to endow meaning to the archaeological ruins themselves as well as to the textual fragments upon which the poem is constructed. Seferis calls up how a whole understanding of the ancient past underlying the discourse of European Hellenism from the nineteenth to the twentieth centuries was actually founded upon the reading of fragments—be it unearthed marbles resulting from an archaeological excavation, rediscovered papyri of ancient texts, models of philological exegesis which were based on reascribing holistic interpretations to ancient, fragmented texts.[42]

Yet the poet moves beyond these fragments to culminate his search in contemplating the meaning of lived experience:

> ανάμεσα στις χαλασμένες τούτες γραμμές τις
> αχμές τις αιχμές τα χοίλα χαι τις χαμπύλες
> υπάρχουν άραγε . . .
> υπάρχουν, η χίνηση του προσώπου το σχήμα της
> στοργής
> εχείνων που λιγόστεψαν τόσο παράξενα μες στη
> ζωή μας
> αυτών που απόμειναν σχιές χυμάτων χαι
> στοχασμοί με την απεραντοσύνη του πελάγου
> ή μήπως όχι δεν απομένει τίποτε παρά μόνο το
> βάρος
> η νοσταλγία του βάρους μιας ύπαρξης
> ζωντανής . . .

> ειχόνα μορφής που μαρμάρωσε με την απόφαση
> μιας πίχρας παντοτινής
> Ο ποιητής ένα χενό.

(*CP*, 268)[43]

The fragments instill a "void" in the poet. Disconnected as they are, the "fragments," for Heller a distinctive metaphor of modern historical consciousness, do not represent the totality of a past which can be collectively recounted by those who can actually remember it. Whatever is left of the past is not retained in the memory of the living (see Heller 1993:40). History is far too remote and inaccessible. The text, then, presents us with how modern historical consciousness confronts the remoteness of the past and the ways in which it can be made accessible.

It is only through nostalgia that the past can become revived; a "nostalgia," as Seferis puts it, "for the weight of a living existence." Nostalgia revives the fragments and renders them meaningful to modern consciousness.[44] As Heller remarks, "Many a modern man and woman have their moments of nostalgia. . . . They enliven the past on the common ground of their lived history" (1993:40). In this way, nostalgia approximates the ideal mode of historical experiencing simulated in art, religion, and philosophy: the Hegelian notion of the "living Spirit" and of "living (*lebendige*) History" (Heller:1993:40-41).[45] It is through art, religion and philosophy that our ancestors can be resurrected for they "unite presentation with re-presentation, re-collection and re-membrance." Through these and other forms of ritual, the modern subject can be reconnected spiritually to its predecessors. In this sense, we can recognize how the shared myths and memories of a nation as expressed in literature can be seen as ideal forms of representation (see Heller 1993:40-41).

Seferis's poetry presents the "recollective spectacle," one that references not only "primary" but also "secondary" modes of lived history to use Heller's formulations:[46] between a past actually lived by individuals which is collectively remembered and a past that is not directly experienced, recalled, or shared by others and, as such, is subject to reconstruction and interpretation. For Heller, primary "lived history" is something that can actually be remembered and shared with others. In remembering, "one follows the traces left on the membrane of one's own memory and on the memory of others" (1993:43).

If primary lived history is the continuous sharing of experiences which are often kept alive by reminiscence (1993:43), this differs from "recollection," that is, secondary lived history, which "re-collects" past stories, once connected, but which will be reconfigured later into a coherent whole. Unlike remembrance, recollection re-collects its stories, not from the traces on the membrane of memory, but from those who not only recollect but also selectively interpret the lived history of others (1993:36). Keeping this distinction in mind, we can consider, then, how Seferis's poetics address historicism and national memory as modes of secondary lived history.

HISTORICISM—NATIONAL Μνήμη

How memory as variant modes of secondary lived history emerges in Seferis's poetics underlies the premise of the second part of this essay. Returning to the poem «Ἀργοναῦτες», with the experience of loss comes the quest for self-knowledge in the recovery of the variant histories and glories of the past. In this sense the poem speaks to the view of memory that has evolved within European modernity: a new-found self-consciousness in thinking about one's relationship to the past, which posits a new construct of time by virtue of its very historicism.

Such a historicism is rooted in classical idealism: the identity of the self, its self-knowledge, cannot be defined without taking its past experience into account. For Hegel, as Richard Terdiman succinctly puts it, recollection embodies the self's "triumphant self-absorption at the end of history" (1985:14). Recollection constitutes an "epiphany" that harmonizes "self and world, past and present, being and becoming" (Terdiman 1985:14; see also Hegel 1966:807).

But the schemata that dominate historicist discourse in European modernity follow along several paths. World-historical paradigms clash between the model of the holistic universality of all cultures vs. that of the totality of particular ones.[47] The latter model, inspired by Johann Gottfried Herder's thought, underlies the writing of local national histories, imbuing the idea of *nation* with the notion of a "restrictively defined culture or a mystically determined collectivity, a people or *Volk*" (North 1991:11).[48] In the case of Greece, we can trace the writing, dissemination, and institutionalization of knowledge of the past to Herder's example. Such divergent strands within historicist discourse should pose questions to our understanding of how memory is constructed in modernist literature across national cultures, and what we can learn from the particularities of a given case.

Seferis's poetry certainly dismantles the idea of total recall and illustrates how the self-consciousness over time in Greek Modernism has also resulted in a questioning of traditional conceptualizations of memory. It invites comparison on a general thematic and rhetorical level to writers in the Anglo-Irish and American traditions, such as Yeats, Pound, and Eliot, or in the French, such as Proust, who conceived the problem of the past in terms of a "mnemonic" or "memory crisis,"

to use Terdiman's formulations (1985; 1993), one that manifested itself in systematic perturbations of memory, which indicate how the past "evades our memory" and how "recollection has ceased to integrate with consciousness." Because of the past's "paradoxical inaccessibility," past and present become mutually reinvented. Thus Seferis's text, like others of this period, reveals "a failure of diachronicity" through "subjective epistemic rupture." The preoccupation with memory, and, by association, with history, then, can be considered as the attempt to confront the "crisis of diachronicity" (Terdiman 1985:15).

Seferis's poetry simulates the representation of such overt disruptions of time and the fragmenting of knowledge. In illustrating a comparable crisis of diachronicity, it reveals the fissures of epistemological rupture that emulate the memory process—«τα χάσματα της μνήμης» ("the chasms of memory") (*CP*, 276, 277) as Seferis refers to it in the poem «Υστερόγραφο» ("**Postscript**"), its "gaps" and "lacunae" (1974:174), those that signify its inevitable break with continuity. His example verifies how in Greek Modernism memory is also fraught with fleeting images, that ever deepen the chasms between remembering and forgetting, those, as he puts it in the poem, «Η Απόφαση της Λησμονιάς» ("**The Decision to Forget**"), «που ταξιδεύουν σαν άσπρα Νουρέλια μέσα στο νου σου/ Ναι σε ξυπνάνε σε πράγματα που έζησες Ναι που δε θυμάσαι» (*CP*, 262).[49]

But when the Seferian poetic text laments memory loss and expresses the continual desire towards its recovery, it has cultural nationalist implications.[50] Μυθιστόρημα, a word in Modern Greek that means novel, that is, narrative, and is made up of the terms μύθος ("myth") and ιστορία ("history" or "story"), explores the limits of collective memory in which the rhetorical play of the text centers on the ideas of remembering and forgetting experienced by both self and nation, whose perspectives within the poem are inextricably linked. In Μυθιστόρημα, Seferis highlights—not the continuity of the collective novel, narrative, history, or myth—but the disjunction of time and repeated perturbations of memory that mark the nation's collective consciousness, obsessively anxious over the subject of the past and over its proper recall:

> Γιατί πέρασαν τόσα Ναι τόσα μπροστά στα μάτια μας
> που Ναι τα μάτια μας δεν είδαν τίποτε, μα πάρα-πέρα
> Ναι πίσω η μνήμη σαν το άσπρο πανί μια νύχτα σε μια μάντρα
> που είδαμε οράματα παράξενα . . .
> να περνούν Ναι να χάνουνται . . .
> γιατί γνωρίσαμε τόσο πολύ τούτη τη μοίρα μας
> στριφογυρίζοντας μέσα σε σπασμένες πέτρες,
> τρεις ή έξι χιλιάδες χρόνια

ψάχνοντας σε οιΝοδομέ]s γΝρεμισμένες που θα
  είταν ίσως το διΝό μας σπίτι
προσπαθώντας να θυμηθούμε χρονολογίες Ναι
  ηρωιΝές πράξεις·
θα μπορέσουμε;

(*CP*, 54)[51]

The text illustrates the nation's desire to find a shared sense of the past, to define and to draw on a reservoir of commonly held historical memories, "dates" and "deeds"; yet, at the same time, it bewails the impending absence and loss that results in acknowledging the remoteness of the past and its continued inaccessibility. Using the modernist mode of writing, with its penchant for dislocating time, Seferis does not identify a concrete or distinct historical period, and often conflates vast and disparate moments of historical time within a single phrase—"three or six thousand years." Memory thus surfaces into a crisis of cultural amnesia in its questioning of the premise of historical fact as a stable and reliable interpretation of reality.

Assuredly, Seferis's poetry reflects how memory continued to remain a privileged *topos* in Neohellenic thinking as it had been in the nineteenth century. But his preoccupation with memory takes on an important ideological charge, especially writing a decade after the Asia Minor Catastrophe. It was a period in which the question of the appropriation of history—and the viability of the continuity thesis that had dominated Greek thinking since the nineteenth century—comes to a crossroads and becomes problematized.

A main goal of the Greek cultural nationalist project of the nineteenth century in the area of historiography was to refute Western skepticism of Greece's claims to its past by producing evidence to trace the thread of cultural continuity from the ancient to the modern age, as a number of critics have already commented.[52] Greece's "memory project," that is, how the society reconstructed its past, from the pedagogy of educational institutions and historians' accounts to the popular beliefs of ordinary people, became fixated not on the failure but, rather, on the creation and promotion of the diachronic model. Konstantinos Paparrigopoulos's *History of the Greek Nation* (1850-1874), the most important national history of Greece that the nineteenth century produced, based its premise on presenting the collective memory of the *ethnos* as an organic unity and continuity that had historically evolved since antiquity. The presupposition underlying such writing approximated the historical method outlined by Hegel in which the nation represents an incomplete present, which cannot develop an integrated consciousness without reference to the past.[53]

The example of historiography and the valorization of the continuity thesis illustrates how the case of Greece in "remembering" its nation's past is no different than the example of other nations in which the process of selection and reinvention comes into play in both its political and cultural nationalist programs: at the expense of "forgetting" other epochs, in Ernest Renan's sense,[54] the ancient past was often privileged in the diachronic model. Collective memories range from references to an idealized golden age (Periclean Athens, the Age of Alexander, the Byzantine Empire) to the painful recollections of the nation's later defeats (the Fall of Constantinople in 1453, the wars of 1897, 1922, and WWII).

But these "memories"—whether recollections of wars and their heroes, or of migrations and colonizations—constitute the nation's conscious ideological choices, ones that had become revised continuously since the nineteenth century to appeal to popular consciousness and to its mobilization within changing conditions caused by modernization.[55] Collective memory in the case of Greece, perhaps most cogently, illustrates what Edward Said has recently argued in reference to *fin-de-siècle* national historiography—that it is not merely "an inert and passive thing, but a field of activity in which past events are selected, reconstructed, maintained, modified, and endowed with political meaning." Memory and its multiple strategies, for historians, private citizens, and institutions is, Said observes, not only something invented but also something used and misused. It is not merely a matter of simple access and recall as if memory "sits inertly there for each person to possess and contain" (Said 2000:185).

Indeed, Greek historicist discourse not only promoted a cohesive sense of national identity and provided a model for unity and for a defense of tradition, but it also justified political nationalist, i.e., expansionist, campaigns. From the nineteenth to the twentieth century Greek political culture appropriated the realm of history, using the premise of the diachronic model, as it underlay the basis for irrendentism in the form of the *Megali Idea*.[56] The *Megali Idea* culminated in the war between Greece and Turkey from 1920-1922, which sought to restore to Greece the territorial boundaries of the former Byzantine Empire; however, the program was beset by overwhelming defeat in 1922.

When Seferis refers to the nation's anxiety over being unable to recall "dates and heroic deeds," he reflects the age's re-theorizing of history at a critical point in its evolution as a nation. The text reflects the psyche of post-1922 Greece, a period that met massive social and political change—one that had to re-think its relationship to its past and to search for new political, moral and aesthetic directives within the realm of collective memory to cope with such transformation. But collective memory in the decades after 1922 often takes form in a myriad of personal memoirs, oral histories, newspaper eye-witness accounts, and in fiction novels rather than in massive official historical accounts of events that refer to the catastrophe itself, for example.[57] What dominates the narration of these aforementioned genres is the violent confrontations that marked the conflict between the warring nations. By stark contrast, the determinism, causality, and rationalism that dominates official historical accounts of the national collective past[58] are obliterated in the poem as if to universalize all individual moments in history into one relative totality.

Collective memory in poems such as Μυθιστόρημα undercuts the rule of the diachronic model by the repeated dissolution of the memory process and the fragmenting of the mythical and historical narrativities of the poem. At the same time, however, the poetry reflects how in the wider context of Greek society, history as collective memory is consciously posited as a stabilizing factor for it responds to societal needs for "continuity," which are symbolically enacted through tradition, seeking an integrated vision between past and present.[59] Seferis explores the realms of tradition through citations of ancient texts. Yet what distinguishes him from his Anglo-American and European counterparts is the Greek poet's empirical claim to antiquity as a living legacy.

While Seferis explores these entities through high culture in the form of the literary text, Renée Hirschon discusses the reasons why memory is ascribed such significance in Greek popular consciousness.[60] Memory's powerful images recall a past "containing the lost but meaningful patterns of life" (1989:17). It plays an adaptive function, as in the example of the displaced, non-literate Greek refugees who fled Turkey in 1922, the subjects of her study, who turn to the past to deal with the chaos that comes with resettlement. Memory within this group becomes a bridge to reconcile the traumatic break caused by their expulsion (1989:17). It "becomes a critical link, the means of a cultural survival, a kind of capital without which their identity would be lost" (1989:15).

There are elements in Μυθιστόρημα that refer to the experience of an uprooted group and the significance memory plays in the retention of their identity, although we should be wary in identifying the poem strictly with the circumstances of the 1922 evacuation as the poem is fluid in its historical reference points. Despite their expulsion and the loss of the homeland, the consciousness of time, the primary of memory as a constant, prevails in the collective voice of the displaced who are "unable to forget themselves":

. . . ταξιδεύοντας
πάνω σε Καταστρώματα Κατελυμένων Καραβιών
στριμωγμένες με γυναίκες Κίτρινες Και μωρά που Κλαίνε
χωρίς να μπορούν να ξεχαστούν. . . .

(*CP,* 20)[61]

Placing memory at the forefront, an alternative to previous discussions of Seferis's use of the classics, provides us with an interpretive model that extends beyond a mere conventional study of sources. Rather, the approach presented here views the relationship between ancient and modern texts as a *dialogical* and *agonistic* one and offers a number of interpretive paths to explore that include similarities and differences between antiquity and modernity in terms of mnemonic concepts, modes of historical consciousness, and the function of the text in representing values privileged in collective consciousness.

Considering, in particular, how the Seferian text manifests empirical forms of remembrance as both primary and secondary lived experience, shared modes of private remembrance and public recollection, enables us to see how literature in the case of Greece continues to fulfill a function in the preservation of memory in offering a mode of historical experiencing akin to that of ritual and religion, beyond important ideological and aesthetic considerations that have been argued in recent scholarship. The potential for further analysis in a discussion of memory in the case of Seferis, beyond textual analysis of his criticism, journals and memoirs, is warranted in examining how memory in his historical context is defined in complex social networks and as well as in political and cultural institutions.

Notes

Acknowledgements. I am very grateful to Anne Carson and Alan Kim for their comments and thoughtful suggestions.

1. These comments, sketched in Seferis's Μέρες Ε' (1977), are prefatory remarks to a proposed monograph edition of his essay on Cavafy and Eliot in which he discusses their shared affinity for experience, learning, and history. See «Κ.Π. Καβάφης, θ.σ. Ελιοτ: παράλληλοι» in Δοκιμές Α' (Seferis 1984:324-363).

2. "Read a rhapsode from Homer," Seferis writes, "and see if whether, at the parts that move you, what you feel is merely an archaeological reference alone, or if perhaps it is a sentiment nurtured by all the human experience that has occurred from that ancient era down to your present moment" (1974:143).

3. Memory, represented typically through the medium of poetry, reveals to us, as commentators have noted, an entire epistemology with systems of classification and taxonomies that exemplify archaic modes of cognition. See Vernant (1983) and Small (1997). Poetry served both a mimetic and mnemonic function; memory was equated with poetic utterance, as the verb μιμνήσκω in ancient Greek means not only "to recall" but "to mention" (Detienne 1999:150, n. 2).

4. "to remember the ancient sage, 'knowledge is memory'" (Seferis 1974:142).

5. Much has been written on the general distinction between Platonic and Aristotelian definitions of memory, only a fraction of which we can point to here. See, for example, Klein (1965) and Yates (1999); Dominic Scott (1995) discusses how Platonic *anamnesis* generated a number of responses and interpretations by several successors, including Aristotle, Epicurus, and the Stoics (1995:3ff.).

6. I borrow these terms from Dominic Scott (1995).

7. In his discussion of the dichotomy between innatist and empiricist theories in later Western thought, Dominic Scott (1995:4ff.) surveys thinkers from Descartes to Chomsky. See also Westbury and Dennett (2000), who discuss the relevance of Platonic and Aristotelian mnemonic ideas in psychological research.

8. For a discussion of various meanings of the term "intertextuality" and how these compare and contrast with the more conventional meanings of "influence," see Clayton and Rothstein (1991).

9. Well-known modes of textual recall include quotes, allusions, paraphrase, and the use of myth and history.

10. See Terdiman's application of Bakhtinian dialogism as a "memory model" (1993:45).

11. See Dimiroulis (1999) for a discussion of the interpretive challenges posed by the Seferian text.

12. See Plato, *Phaedo* 72e, 92d, and *Phil.* 34c. For more detailed discussion of mythical ideas revolving around Platonic *anamnesis,* see Vernant (1983:92ff.). See also Dominic Scott's (1995) extensive discussion of Platonic recollection and learning.

13. Aristotle contends that there is a knowledge based upon sense perceptions, see *On Memory,* I.24ff. Plato, however, believes that there are, latent in an individual's memory, forms or molds of the ideas the realities of which the soul knew in its prenatal existence. The Platonic conception of true knowledge, as Yates puts it, "consists in fitting the imprints from sense impressions on to the mould or imprint of the higher reality of which the things here below are reflections" (1999:36). See Plato, *Phaedo* 75b-d. In the *Phaedrus* (249 e-250 d), Plato presents his view of the function of rhetoric, i.e., to persuade one to the knowledge of truth. There he discusses how knowledge of the truth and of the soul is attained by remembering and by the recollection of the ideas once seen by the soul of which all things on earth are but mere confused imitations. All kinds of knowledge or learning are thus an attempt to recollect these realities (Yates 1999:36-37).

14. Klein offers the following translation of this line: "When one is [actively] learning ($\mu\acute\alpha\theta\eta$) or passively experiencing ($\pi\acute\alpha\theta\eta$) [something] for the first time one is neither reacquiring a memory [of that something], for there was none before, nor is one acquiring one initially; but when the [firm] possession ($\acute\epsilon\xi\iota\varsigma$) [of what is being learned] or . . . the [full] experience is achieved, then there is memory . . ." (1965:110). Klein points out how Aristotle does not clearly distinguish between his use of the term $\mu\nu\acute\eta\mu\eta$ from $\alpha\nu\acute\alpha\mu\nu\eta\sigma\iota\varsigma,$ and this accounts for the fluidity in their translation, i.e., "recollection," "reminiscence," "remembrance," and "memory" (1965:111). Vernant, however, makes the distinction between Aristotelian *mneme,* which he views as the ability to preserve the past (i.e., in terms of mnemonic exercise) vs. Aristotelian *anamnesis,* which refers to the power of the mind in its "deliberate and effective recall" (1983:94-95). See Aristotle, *On Memory.*

15. See Vernant's discussion (1983:84, 92ff).

16. Such an identification is most readily understood in Platonic language whereby "to know" is "to remember" (Vernant 1983:92).

17. On this point, see, for example, Vernant's discussion of Pythagorean "memory exercises" (1983:86ff). Fischer draws a parallel between such ancient mnemonic practices and post-modern ethnic re-creations of identity (1986:197).

18. In the *Alcibiades* (I.130c) Plato treats the soul as our own spiritual being—not as "a spiritual being that is foreign to us" (Vernant 1983:92). See also the *Phaedo* (72e), which discusses the immortality of the soul. Cf. Seferis, Μεταγραφέ]ς, 1980:59-65.

19. Plato's authorship of the *Alcibiadis* has been contested. See Denyer (2001:14ff).

20. The *Phaedo* (73 a9) also talks of knowledge present within us («ἐμιστήμη ἐνοῦσα»). See Dominic Scott (1995:16, n. 2).

21. On the question of self-knowledge, the dialogue also presents the contrast between learning from others and discovering knowledge for oneself (*Alcibiades* I.106d ff.). There is disagreement in the commentary over whether the subtext of this point in the dialogue presupposes the doctrine of recollection expounded in the *Meno.* See Denyer (2001: 25, n. 20; 101-102). For more discussion on the *Meno,* see Gulley (1962), Klein (1965), Vlastos (1965), and Nehamas (1984).

22. See, for example, a key passage provided here in translation with minor changes:

    > Seeing then that the soul is immortal and has been born many times, and has beheld all things both in this world and in the nether realms, [it] has acquired knowledge of all and everything; so that it is no wonder that [it] should be able to recollect all that [it] knew before about virtue and other things. For as all nature is akin, and the soul has learned all things, there is no reason why we should not, by remembering but one single thing—an act which men call learning—discover everything else, if we have courage and faith not in the search; since, it would seem, research and learning are wholly recollection.

    (Plato, *Meno* 81 c-d)

23. The text reflects upon our ability to recollect forgotten things, particularly when we are conscious of their having been forgotten; and to do this consciously, with effort, is contingent upon our power to "look within ourselves." See Klein's commentary on the *Meno* 81 b3-d4 (1965: 96, n. 5). Yates points to the argument presented in the *Phaedo* (75 b-d) wherein "all sensible objects are referable to certain types of which they are likenesses." While we have not seen or learned these types in our present life, we saw them before birth and knowledge of them is "innate" in our memories (Yates, 1999:36). See also Dominic Scott's discussion of the *Phaedo* (72e ff.) (1995:15-16).

24. While the theory of innateness in Platonic *anamnesis* is found to be somewhat inadequate, Westbury and Dennett point out that a central question raised in the *Meno* still preoccupies contemporary researchers on memory: "to recall something, we must already know what it is we are trying to recall (and therefore have no reason to recall it) or else not know it (and so have no ability to recall it)" (2000:15).

25. See Tagopoulos's insights on Platonic *anamnesis* in reference to this passage (1997:168-169).

26. cf. the full passage of the Lamb translation of *Alcibiades* I.133B, which is provided here with minor changes:

SOCRATES:

"And if the soul, too, my dear Alcibiades, is to know [itself,] [it] must surely look [into] a soul, and especially at that region of it in which occurs the virtue of soul—wisdom, and at any other part of a soul which resembles this?"

ALCIBIADES:

"I agree Socrates."

SOCRATES:

"And can we find any part of the soul that we can call more divine that this, which is the seat of knowledge and thought?"

ALCIBIADES:

"We cannot."

SOCRATES:

"Then this part of [it] resembles God, and whoever looks at this, and comes to know all that is divine will gain thereby the best knowledge of himself."

ALCIBIADES:

"Apparently."

SOCRATES:

"And self-knowledge we admitted to be temperance (σωφροσύνη)."

27. All translations of Seferis's poetry are taken from the Keeley and Sherrard edition of the *Collected Poems* (1981), abbreviated from here on as *CP*.

    And if the soul,
    is to know itself,
    it must look
    into a soul:

    (*CP*, 9)

28. See Gary Alan Scott's discussion of this passage (2000:96) in relation to Socratic *paideusis*.

29. If it is to know itself, they said
    it must look into a soul, they said
    and the oars struck the sea's gold

    (*CP*, 9)

30. Sometimes unfortunate women wept
    lamenting their lost children
    and others raging sought Alexander the Great
    and glories buried in the heart of Asia.
    We moored on shores full of night-scents
    with birds singing, waters that left on the hands
    the memory of great happiness.

    (*CP*, 11)

31. cf. Westbury and Dennett who point out how what we recall "is not what we actually experienced, but rather a reconstruction of what we experienced that is consistent with our current goals and knowledge about the world" (2000:19). For a discussion of memory, sense perception, and Greek popular consciousness, see Seremetakis (1994).

32. The companions died one by one,
    with lowered eyes. Their oars
    mark the place where they sleep on the shore.
    No one remembers them. Justice.

    (*CP*, 11)

33. Line 491 from Aeschylus' *Libation-Bearers* is the Smyth translation with minor changes. At the site of Agamemnon's tomb, Orestes is reminding his father of the bath where he was slain by Clytem-

nestra upon his return from Troy. The site had been envisioned differently by Menelaos in *Odyssey* 4. 1. 584, where he orders the erection of a tomb for Agamemnon "so that his glory [*kleos*] might remain forever" (Vernant 1991:69, n. 34).

34.   at Syntagma, before the Unknown Soldier.
        How many moments of silence does a life cost?
        'Remember, Father, the baths where you were slain!'

                                          (Seferis 1974:43)

35. See Anderson's discussion of the cultural roots of nationalism in reference to the tomb of the unknown soldier (1991).

36. cf. Keeley and Sherrard's translation of this phrase as "memory-wounding pain" (*CP*, 315).

37.   And if I talk to you in fables and parables
        it's because it's more gentle for you that way; and horror
        really can't be talked about because it's alive,
        because it's mute and goes on growing:
        memory-wounding pain
        drips by day drips in sleep.

                                          (*CP*, 315)

38. Fraenkel offers a more literal translation: "'instead of sleep' (or 'in the place where if things ran their untroubled course one would find sleep') one finds 'the slow drip, drip of pain'" (1962: II.107). See Giatromanolakis's remarks in Μεταγραφές 1980:258-259, n. 3.

39. In the prologue to his *Memoirs,* Makrygiannes writes "I shall record the naked truth. . . . History will tell of the causes of evil, and the newspapers speak of them every day" (1966:5).

40. See Sultan (1999) and Tsoucalas (1999). Seferis views Makrygiannes as "a surefooted messenger of the long and unbroken tradition of the people, which, because it is so deeply rooted in him, can teach us not just through one man's voice but in the voice of many, and can tell us what we are and how we are in our deepest selves. It tells us that his anger, his pain, his tragedy are not private affairs of his own, but concern all of us; they are affairs of yours, of mine, of all of us; they are affairs in which all of us together, the living and the dead, have our individual and our joint share and responsibility" (Seferis 1966:63).

41. See Jusdanis (1991) for a discussion of national literature as a symbolic medium of societal reconciliation.

42. See Heller's discussion of "archaeological" recollection and the unearthing of fragments as a dominant metaphor of the past in modern consciousness (1993:38-40).

43.   does there really exist
        among these ruined lines, edges, points, hollows, and curves
        does there really exist . . .
        does there exist the movement of the face, shape of the tenderness
        of those who've shrunk so strangely in our lives,
        those who remained the shadow of waves and thoughts with the sea's boundlessness
        or perhaps no, nothing is left but the weight
        the nostalgia for the weight of a living existence . . .
        image of form that the sentence to everlasting bitterness
        has turned to stone:
        the poet a void.

                                          (*CP*, 269)

44. See Heller's discussion of the heap of fragments as a metaphor for historical consciousness in Benjamin's work (1993:43). What distinguishes Seferis's example from Benjamin's is the former's claim to history as a "living" medium.

45. Heller's source is Hegel's *Philosophy of Religion.*

46. Heller adds another perspective to current discussions on "social" and "cultural" memory. The existing literature is prolific, and only a few recent examples will be mentioned here, such as Bal, Crewe, and Spitzer (1999), Ben-Amos and Weissberg (1999). Those that specifically look at the Greek case include Benveniste and Paradellis (1999), and Papailias (2001). For an overview of discussions on historical consciousness in anthropological literature, see Sutton (1998:1-14).

47. In *A Theory of History* (1980), Heller provides a schematic outline of the major manifestations of modern historical consciousness through three seminal reference points: everyday historical consciousness; the *episteme* of historiography, i.e., the writing of history; and a *philosophy* of history. She surveys here the evolution of mythic to historical consciousness, spanning the ancient to the post-modern periods. See, in particular, the schemata outlined in nineteenth century historiography (1982:250-251).

48. See Meinecke, especially his discussion of Herder's understanding of the national spirit and his historical model (1972:356ff).

49. "that travel like white tatters through your mind / and waken you to things you lived yet don't remember" (*CP*, 263).

50. For background on Greek Modernism's cultural nationalism, see Tziovas (1989) and Leontis (1995).

51.   So very much having passed before our eyes
        that our eyes in the end saw nothing, but beyond

and behind was memory like the white sheet one night
in an enclosure
where we saw strange visions . . .
pass by and vanish . . .
having known this fate of ours so well
wandering among broken stones, three or six
thousand years
searching in collapsed buildings that might have been
our homes
trying to remember dates and heroic deeds:
will we be able?

(CP, 55)

52. See, for example, Herzfeld (1986), Danforth (1984), and Kitroeff (1990:143-144). Kitroeff argues that Paparriogopoulos relied on historicist presuppositions of the nineteenth century, something he held in common with other variant nationalist historians in Europe. Not only was Paparrigopoulos's theory the rule for well over a century in Greece, but so was his methodological approach, which Kitroeff describes as "a form of Rankean hermeneuticism" (1990:143-144).

53. In *Lectures on the Philosophy of World History,* Hegel remarks on the writing of national history:

> But it is the state which first supplies a content which not only lends itself to the prose of history but actually helps to produce it. . . . It thereby creates a record of its own development, and an interest in intelligible, determinate, and—in their results—enduring deeds and events, on which Mnemosyne, for the benefit of the perennial aim which underlies the present form and constitution of the state, is impelled to confer a lasting memory. . . . [T]he external existence of the state, despite the rational laws and principles it contains, is an incomplete present which cannot understand itself and develop an integrated consciousness without reference to the past.

(1975:36)

54. "Forgetting, I would even go as far as to say historical error," Renan argues, "is a crucial factor in the creation of a nation, which is why progress in historical studies often constitutes a danger for [the principle of] nationality" (1990:11).

55. See Smith (1999:262-266) and Jusdanis (1991).

56. For background on the *Megali Idea,* see Skopetea (1985).

57. See Doulis (1977:74). Even though Kitroeff's article was published in 1990, his general conclusions on the limited historiography produced on the Asia Minor Campaign, including some of the ideological problems posed by existing scholarship, are still relevant (1990:144, 155).

58. See Heller (1982, 1993) for a discussion of teleological historical models.

59. See Klironomos for remarks on Seferis's defense of tradition in his literary criticism (2000:111).

60. For a discussion of history and popular memory in recalling the events of WWII, see Sutton (1998). For a discussion of memory and homeland in Seferis, see Dracopoulos (2000).

61.   . . . traveling
on the decks of decayed ships
crowded in with sallow women and crying babies
unable to forget themselves . . .

(CP, 21)

References Cited

Aeschylus 1952 *The Oresteia.* Vol. II. The Loeb Classical Library. Translated by Herbert Weir Smyth. Cambridge: Harvard University Press.

Anderson, Benedict 1991 *Imagined Communities.* New York: Verso.

Aristotle 1995 *On Memory.* In *The Complete Works of Aristotle. The Revised Oxford Translation,* ed. Jonathan Barnes, Vol. 1, 714-720. Princeton Bolligen Series LXXI. Princeton: Princeton University Press.

Bal, Mieke, Jonathan Crewe, and Leo Spitzer, editors 1999 *Acts of Memory: Cultural Recall in the Present.* Hanover and London: University Press of New England.

Ben-Amos, Dan, and Liliane Weissberg, editors 1999 *Cultural Memory and the Reconstruction of Identity.* Detroit: Wayne State University Press.

Benveniste, Rika and Theodore Paradellis, editors 1999 Διαδρομές Και τόποι της μνήμης· Ιστορικές Και ανθρωπολογικές προσεγγύσεις. Athens: Alexandreia.

Clayton, Jay and Eric Rothstein 1991 *Influence and Intertextuality in Literary History.* Madison: The University of Wisconsin Press.

Danforth, Loring 1984 "The Ideological Context of the Search for Continuities in Greek Culture." *Journal of Modern Greek Studies* 2:53-85.

Denyer, Nicholas, editor 2001 Plato: *Alcibiades. Cambridge Greek and Latin Classics Series.* Cambridge: Cambridge University Press.

Detienne, Marcel 1999 *The Masters of Truth in Archaic Greece.* Translated Janet Lloyd. New York: Zone Books. [1967].

Dimiroulis, Dimitris 1999 Δημήτρης Δημηρούλης, «Ο φοβερός παλασμός»· Κριτικό αφήγημα για τα «Τρία Κρυφά ποιήματα»του Γ. σεφέρη. Athens: Plethron.

Doulis, Thomas 1977 *Disaster and Fiction: Modern Greek Fiction and the Impact of the Asia Minor Disaster of 1922.* Berkeley: University of California Press.

Dracopoulos, Antonis 2000 Αντώνης Δρακόπουλος, «Τι είδε ο σεφέρης στα μοναστήρια της Καππαδοκίας.» Special issue on Giorgos Seferis, ed. Vrasidas Karalis. Διαβάζω 410 (September):112-117.

Fischer, Michael M. J. 1986 "Ethnicity and the Arts of Memory." In *Writing Culture: The Poetics and Politics of Ethnography,* ed. James Clifford and George E. Marcus, 194-233. Berkeley, Los Angeles and London: University of California Press.

Fraenkel, E., ed. 1962 *Agamemnon.* 3 vols. London: Oxford.

Gulley, Norman 1962 *Plato's Theory of Knowledge.* London: Methuen.

Hegel, George Wilhelm Friedrich 1966 *The Phenomenology of Mind.* London: George Allen and Unwin.

Hegel, George Wilhelm Friedrich 1975 *Lectures on the Philosophy of World History.* Cambridge: Cambridge University Press.

Heller, Agnes 1982 *A Theory of History.* London, Boston, and Henley: Routledge and Kegan Paul.

Heller, Agnes 1993 *A Philosophy of History in Fragments.* Oxford and Cambridge: Blackwell Publishers.

Herzfeld, Michael 1986 *Ours Once More: Folklore, Ideology and the Making of Modern Greece.* New York: Pella.

Hirschon, Renée 1989 *Heirs of the Greek Catastrophe: The Social Life of Asia Minor Refugees in Piraeus.* Oxford: Clarendon Press.

Jusdanis, Gregory 1991 *Belated Modernity and Aesthetic Culture: Inventing National Literature.* Minneapolis: University of Minnesota Press.

Kitroeff, Alexander 1990 "Continuity and Change in Contemporary Greek Historiography." In *Modern Greece: Nationalism and Nationality,* ed. Martin Blinkhorn and Thanos Veremis, 143-172. Athens: Sage, ELIAAMEP.

Klein, Jacob 1965 *A Commentary on Plato's Meno.* Chapel Hill: The University of North Carolina Press.

Klironomos, Martha 2000 Μάρθα Κληρονόμου, «Η μνήμη στο έργο του Γιώργου Σεφέρη.» Special issue on Giorgos Seferis, ed. and trans. Vrasidas Karalis. Διαβάζω 410 (September):105-111.

Leontis, Artemis 1995 *Topographies of Hellenism: Mapping the Homeland.* Ithaca and London: Cornell University Press.

Makrygiannes, I. 1966 *The Memoirs of General Makrygiannes.* Ed. and trans. H. A. Lidderdale. London: Oxford University Press.

Meinecke, Friedrich 1984 *Historicism: The Rise of a New Historical Outlook.* New York: Herder and Herder.

Nehamas, Alexander 1985 "Meno's Paradox and Socrates as a Teacher." *Oxford Studies in Ancient Philosophy* 3:1-30.

North, Michael 1991 *The Political Aesthetic of Yeats, Eliot, and Pound.* Cambridge and New York: Cambridge University Press.

Papailias, Penelope C. 2001 *Genres of Recollection: History, Testimony and Archive in Contemporary Greece.* Ph.D. dissertation. University of Michigan.

Plato 1986 *Alcibiades.* In *Plato.* Vol. XII. Translated by W. R. M. Lamb. The Loeb Classical Library. Cambridge: Harvard University.

———. 1999 *Meno.* In *Plato.* Vol. II. Translated by W. R. M. Lamb. The Loeb Classical Library. Cambridge: Harvard University.

———. 1999 *Phaedo* and *Phaedrus.* In *Plato.* Vol. I. Translated by Harold North Fowler. The Loeb Classical Library. Cambridge: Harvard University Press.

Renan, Ernest 1990 "What Is A Nation?" In *Nation and Narration,* edited by Homi Bhabba, 8-22. London and New York: Routledge.

Said, Edward W. 2000 "Invention, Memory, and Place." *Critical Inquiry,* Winter 26(2):175-192.

Scott, Dominic 1995 *Recollection and Experience: Plato's Theory of Learning and Its Successors.* Cambridge: Cambridge University Press.

Scott, Gary Alan 2000 *Plato's Socrates As Educator.* Albany: State University of New York Press.

Seferis, George 1966 *On the Greek Style: Selected Essays in Poetry and Hellenism.* Translated by Rex Warner and Th. D. Frangopoulos. Boston: Little, Brown.

———. 1974 *A Poet's Journal. Days of 1945-1951.* Translated by Athan Anagnostopoulos. Cambridge: Harvard University Press.

———. 1980 Γιώργος σεφέρης. Μεταγραφές. Ed. G. Giatromanolakakis. Athens: Lesche.

———. *1981 Collected Poems of George Seferis.* Translated by Edmund Keeley and Phillip Sherrard. Princeton: Princeton University Press.

———. 1984 Δοϰιμές. τομ. Α'-Β'. Athens: Ikaros.

———. 1996 [1977] Μέρες. τομ. Α'-Ζ'. Athens: Ikaros.

Seremetakis, C. Nadia 1994 *The Senses Still: Perception and Memory as Material Culture in Modernity.* Chicago: University of Chicago Press.

Skopetea, Elli 1985 Ελλη σϰοπετέα, Το «πρότυπο βασίλειο» ϰαι η μεγάλη ιδέα. Όψεις του εθνιϰού προβλήματος στην Ελλάδα *(1830-1880).* Athens: Polytypo.

Small, Jocelyn Penny 1997 *Wax Tablets of the Mind: Cognitive Studies of Memory and Literacy in Classical Antiquity.* London and New York: Routledge.

Smith, Anthony D. 1999 *Myths and Memories of the Nation.* Oxford: Oxford University Press.

Sultan, Nancy 1999 *Exile and the Poetics of Loss in Greek Tradition.* Lanham, MD: Rowman and Littlefield.

Sutton, David E. 1998 *Memories Cast in Stone: The Relevance of the Past in Everyday Life.* Oxford: Berg.

Tagopoulos, Constance V. 1997 *Myth, Memory, and Love in Plato, Seferis and Joyce: The Quest for Language and Balance.* Ph.D. dissertation, City University of New York.

Terdiman, Richard 1985 "Deconstructing Memory: On Representing the Past and Theorizing Culture in France Since the Revolution." *Diacritics* Winter 15(4):13-36.

————. 1993 *Present Past: Modernity and the Memory Crisis.* Ithaca: Cornell University Press.

Tsoucalas, Konstantinos 1999 Κωνσταντίνος Τσουϗαλάς, Η εξουσία ως λαός ϗι ως έθνος. Athens: Themelio.

Tziovas, Dimitris 1989 Δημήτρης Τζιόβας. Οι μεταμορφώσεις του εθνισμού ϗαι το ιδεολόγημα της ελληνικϗότητας στο μεσοπόλεμο. Athens: Odysseas.

Vernant, Jean Pierre 1983 *Myth and Thought Among the Greeks.* London: Routledge. [1965].

Vernant, Jean Pierre 1991 *Mortals and Immortals: Collected Essays.* Edited by Froma I. Zeitlin. Princeton: Princeton University Press.

Vlastos, Gregory 1965 "Anamnesis in the Meno." *Dialogue* 4:143-167. Reprinted in *Studies in Greek Philosophy,* Vol. II, *Socrates, Plato, and Their Tradition,* 147-165. Princeton: Princeton University Press, 1995.

Westbury, Chris and Daniel C. Dennett 2000 "Mining the Past to Construct the Future: Memory and Belief as Forms of Knowledge." In *Memory, Brain, and Belief,* edited by Daniel L. Schacter and Elaine Scarry, 11-32. Cambridge: Harvard University Press.

Yates, Frances 1999 *The Art of Memory. Selected Works.* Vol. III, 1-49. New York and London: Routledge.

FURTHER READING

Biography

Beaton, Roderick. *George Seferis: Waiting for the Angel.* New Haven, Conn.: Yale University Press, 2003, 512 p.
    Comprehensive account of Seferis's life and career.

Criticism

Argyros, Alexander. "The Hollow King: A Heideggerian Approach to George Seferis's 'The King of Asini.'" *Boundary 2* 15, nos. 1, 2 (fall/winter 1986/1987): 305-21.
    Examination of Seferis's poem within the context of the idealized version of Greek history formulated by the nineteenth-century European humanists.

Charalambidou, Nadia. "Seferis's *Six Nights on the Acropolis*: A Modernist Tale?" In *Greek Modernism and Beyond,* edited by Dimitris Tziovas, pp. 163-76. Lanham, Md.: Rowman & Littlefield, 1997.
    Contends that Seferis's *Six Nights on the Acropolis,* which includes poetry as well as diary entries, is more modernist than many critics believe.

Kaiser, Walter. "Translator's Foreword." In *Three Secret Poems* by George Seferis, translated by Walter Kaiser, pp. vii-xix. Cambridge, Mass.: Harvard University Press, 1969.
    Discussion of the first poetry written by Seferis after his 1962 retirement from public life.

Keeley, Edmund, and Philip Sherrard. "Foreword." In *George Seferis: Collected Poems,* translated, edited, and introduced by Edmund Keeley and Philip Sherrard, pp xi-xix. Princeton, N.J.: Princeton University Press, 1995.
    Introduction to Seferis's poetry, placing his work within the context of the Greek literary tradition.

Savidis, George P. "The Tragic Vision of Seferis." *Grand Street* 5, no. 2 (winter 1986): 153-74.
    Analysis of the tragic elements of Seferis's verse and the poet's own aversion to being labeled as a pessimist.

Thaniel, George. "George Seferis's 'Thrush': A Modern Descent." *Canadian Review of Comparative Literature* (winter 1977): 89-102.
    Contends that the poem "The Thrush" is an example of Descent poetry, in which the hero travels to the underworld and returns a changed man.

John Wilmot, Earl of Rochester
1647-1680

English poet and playwright.

INTRODUCTION

Rochester was an accomplished poet whose critical reputation has been adversely influenced by the details of his personal life. His reputation for drunkenness and debauchery—as well as his many "unprintable" poems—has often interfered with serious evaluations of his verse on its own merits. Modern scholars, however, have demonstrated renewed interest in Rochester's career; several new editions of his poetry appeared in the late twentieth century and a film based on his life, *The Libertine*, was released in 2004.

BIOGRAPHICAL INFORMATION

Wilmot was born on April 1, 1647, in Oxfordshire, to Anne and Henry Wilmot. His mother was a parliamentarian and his father a Royalist who was named Earl of Rochester for his military service to the exiled Charles II. When his father died serving in Holland in 1658, young Wilmot succeeded him in the title, becoming the second Earl of Rochester. Initially he was educated at home and then at the Burford Grammar School. He entered Oxford at the age of twelve and began writing poetry; he earned his Master of Arts degree two years later. After a tour of the continent, Rochester assumed his place in the court of the restored monarchy at the age of seventeen. He was imprisoned briefly in the Tower of London for abducting Elizabeth Malet, a wealthy heiress who would later become his wife. In 1665 Rochester served in the military in Holland, returned briefly to England, and one year later again served in battle against the Dutch, distinguishing himself as a hero.

Rochester's career as a courtier was solidified by his marriage to Malet in 1667, but he was becoming even more famous as a drunkard—he reportedly had been drinking heavily since his student days at Oxford—and a libertine. Stories of lavish spending, numerous fights, and outrageous sexual exploits circulated throughout the court, and his unsavory reputation was further enhanced by the bawdy verse attributed to him, only some of which he actually wrote. In 1668 Rochester and his wife had their first child, a daughter, and

although the couple had three more children together, they never maintained the same residence after that. Since his wife's family retained control over her fortune, Rochester spent most of his life in debt.

Rochester was banished from court in 1671 for having lampooned the King and his mistress in verse. During his banishment he posed as Dr. Bendo, an Italian doctor, and established a successful medical practice. A year later, he regained the King's favor and returned to court, apparently without tempering his flamboyant behavior. Rochester continued writing and throughout the 1670s his poetry was appearing in more and more publications—often without his authorization or even his knowledge. He also began writing for the stage, occasionally producing original work, but more often adapting the work of other playwrights or penning scenes for plays by his contemporaries. By 1680 Rochester was on his deathbed, apparently suffering from syphilis; he died a month later, at the age of thirty-three, having renounced his atheism. Religious leaders used the story of Rochester's deathbed repentance and conversion to Christianity as an inspirational lesson for the next several generations of young English libertines.

MAJOR WORKS

Rochester's most famous and most highly acclaimed poem is *A Satyr against Mankind,* sometimes known as *A Satyr against Reason and Mankind* (1679), in which he suggests that animals are superior to humans. In the epistolary poem *Letter from Artemisia in the Towne to Chloe in the Country* (1679) Rochester adopts a female persona to satirize social attitudes about love and lust. One of his most notorious poems, "A Ramble in St. James's Park," is often considered a poetic response to Edmund Waller's *On St. James's Park: As Lately Improved by His Majesty,* which describes a romantic pastoral setting populated by the finest lords and ladies of the court. Rochester's version is far more coarse— and apparently far more accurate, since the park was the designated meeting place for prostitutes and their customers from all social classes during the Restoration era.

Other noteworthy poems include "The Disabled Debauchee" (c. 1675), also called "The Maim'd Debauchee," an ironic dramatic monologue predicting a bleak future for the narrator who is bound to suffer increasing impotence and enfeeblement; "Tunbridge Wells" (1675) describing the grotesque visitors to a popular rural watering place outside of London; and "Timon," a satiric look at London life under the restored monarchy of Charles II. Its subject is a dinner party the title character attends with the court wits and their ladies—where the food and wine are bad and the conversation worse. In "An Allusion to Horace" (1675) Rochester adapts one of Horace's satires to reflect his own time, taking on the admirers of John Dryden just as Horace had taken on the admirers of Lucilius. The poem was the apparent cause of Dryden's lifelong animosity towards Rochester. The majority of these works were published anonymously in collections and broadsides during Rochester's lifetime—often without his approval. In 1680, soon after the poet's death, a collection of his works was published, *Poems on Several Occasions By the Right Honourable The E. of R—.* More collections followed, many of them containing bowdlerized versions of Rochester's more explicit verses. It was not until the twentieth century that scholars began sorting out the poetry erroneously attributed to Rochester from that actually written by him and publishing more reliable editions of his work.

CRITICAL RECEPTION

Early criticism of Rochester's work concentrated on the more outrageous aspects of his life and on those poems considered obscene by many critics of the eighteenth and nineteenth centuries. During his lifetime, he was the target of numerous satires and lampoons according to David M. Vieth, who notes that Rochester had countless enemies and that "his questionable manner of life made him an inviting target." Still, his poetry garnered some praise by his contemporaries, although David Farley-Hills suggests that some of it consisted of politically motivated flattery and is, therefore, suspect. In the early eighteenth century, François-Marie Arouet Voltaire's estimate of Rochester as "a man of genius and a great poet" was influential in encouraging an appreciation of his wit. By mid-century, however, his reputation for debauchery was gaining far more attention than his poetry. For almost two hundred years thereafter, Rochester's work was, for the most part, completely ignored—unfairly so, in the opinion of Ronald Duncan, who complains that "the somewhat colourful escapades in his life have almost wholly blinded the public (the reading public) to the solid and sober achievements of his pen."

Modern critics have begun to separate Rochester's life from his writing career. Several collections of his work have been published in the twentieth century, along with a number of critical studies reevaluating his reputation as a poet. One of the first critics to recognize Rochester's importance was Vivian de Sola Pinto, who claimed that "his was the representative mind of the English aristocracy under Charles II," combining the pride associated with the Renaissance with the "impassioned and bitter self-criticism" of the coming age. Samuel J. Rogal calls him "the rare breed of literary animal who, although clearly typifying the age in which he lived, at the same time appeared to be struggling ferociously against its ideas and institutions." Raymond K. Whitley contends that Rochester "is one of the first satirists of the Restoration period with a philosophical focus, as opposed to a social one" and notes that the poet was "about as pessimistic as it is possible to be within the limits of satire."

Critics have also recently begun questioning Rochester's true feelings toward the bawdy life he seemed to be advocating in his poetry. Dustin H. Griffin, in his analysis of *A Satyr against Mankind,* suggests that the poem is both stylistically and thematically ambiguous: "Although we may extract from one part of the poem a sensationalist ethic, in other parts we find that such an ethic does not produce good or happy men." Whitley notes that Rochester was traditional enough "to find the sensationalist universe inadequate, and to attack, from a largely traditional perspective, the vices of his age, even the very libertine code he elsewhere espouses." Carole Fabricant points to an ambiguous attitude in Rochester's poetry, maintaining that most of the works deal with sexual frustration rather than sexual satisfaction. According to Fabricant, "throughout Rochester's poetry the sexual takes on increasingly sinister overtones until it finally emerges as mechanical grotesquerie." Reba Wilcoxon has studied "A Ramble in St. James's Park" and reports that many critics find the work "impressive and brilliant," despite its sexually explicit language. She considers the work an ironic burlesque of the pastoral poem in which "the poetry of praise and the celebration of place are completely deflated"; Rochester instead presents a scene of decay and disease, purporting to depict what those who frequented the park were really like.

The subject of Rochester's deathbed confession and conversion to Christianity has been a topic of scholarly and theological debate since the late seventeenth century, reports Robert G. Walker. Biographers wondered whether Rochester's last-minute repentance was sincere, and churchmen questioned the efficacy of his renunciation of debauchery at a time when his physical limitations made debauchery no longer possible anyway. Nonetheless, Walker notes that the story of Rochester's deathbed repentance was hailed by many Christian leaders for its polemic value.

PRINCIPAL WORKS

Poetry

Letter from Artemisia in the Towne to Chloe in the Country 1679

A Satyr against Mankind [*A Satyr against Reason and Mankind*] 1679

Upon Nothing, A Poem 1679

A Very Heroical Epistle from My Lord All-Pride to Dol-Common 1679

Poems on Several Occasions By the Right Honourable The E. of R— 1680

Poems on Several Occasions. Written by a Late Person of Honour 1685

The Poetical Works of That Witty Lord John Earl of Rochester, Left in Ranger's Lodge in Woodstock Park, where His Lordship Died, and never before Printed: with Some Account of the Life of That Ingenious Nobleman. Extracted from Bishop Burnet, and other Eminent Writers 1761

John Wilmot, Earl of Rochester: His Life and Writings [edited by Johannes Prinz] 1927

Rochester's Poems on Several Occasions [edited by James Thorpe] 1950

Poems by John Wilmot, Earl of Rochester [edited by Vivian de Sola Pinto] 1953

Sodom, or the Quintessence of Debauchery. Written for the Royall Company of Whoremasters, possibly by Rochester 1957

The Complete Poems of John Wilmot, Earl of Rochester [edited by David M. Vieth] 1968

Lyrics and Satires of John Wilmot, Earl of Rochester [edited by David Brooks] 1980

John Wilmot, Earl of Rochester: Selected Poems [edited by Paul Hammond] 1982

The Poems of John Wilmot, Earl of Rochester [edited by Keith Walker] 1984

Other Major Works

Valentinian: A Tragedy. As 'tis Alter'd by the late Earl of Rochester. And Acted at the Theatre-Royal [adapted from a play by John Fletcher] (play) 1685

Collected Works of John Wilmot, Earl of Rochester [edited by John Hayward] (play, poems, letters) 1926

The Letters of John Wilmot, Earl of Rochester [edited by Jeremy Treglown] (letters) 1980

John Wilmot, Earl of Rochester: The Complete Works [edited by Frank H. Ellis] (poems, plays, letters) 1994

CRITICISM

Ronald Duncan (essay date 1948)

SOURCE: Duncan, Ronald. Introduction to *Selected Lyrics and Satires of John Wilmot, 2nd Earl of Rochester,* edited by Ronald Duncan, pp. 9-29. Welwyn Garden City, Herts, England: Forge Press, 1948.

[*In the following introduction, Duncan contends that Rochester's critical reputation has suffered because his critics have placed undue emphasis on the details of his personal life rather than judging his poetry on its own merits.*]

One cannot define good poetry; it defies precise formulation. Those who attempt to make an exact science of literary criticism, or pretend that they have some formula up their sleeve to which good poetry will fit and bad poetry will not, generally end either by stretching their formula to cover their taste, or, what is even more dangerous, sacrificing the remnants of their taste for the sake of their precious formula.

If beauty could be defined it would not exist; it would be manufactured. And the facility with which it could then be reproduced would, I suggest, make us reject the replica almost as soon as we had approved of the model.

We seek conformity in nature; the unique in art. And by definition, that which is copied cannot be unique, or art—though it may well be nature.

I cannot prove that Rochester is a good poet. And this admission at least saves me the vain effort of attempting to do so. But he is a poet to my taste; and in poetry taste is the only foot rule.

The best one can do is to present what one likes and leave it at that. The most one can do is to try and describe one artistic experience in terms of another—by drawing comparisons with the works of other poets etc. and, useful as comparative criticism is in the moulding of one's own taste or the education of others, neither a description nor a comparison constitutes a definition.

My main concern has been to get Rochester into print again. There are too many books about poetry, yet half our poets are out of print. And I have pursued this aim for the last twelve years, ever since I stumbled across a copy of the Nonesuch Edition[1] which even then was, I understand, already out of print.

There never has been a popular cheap edition of Rochester; he has always been condemned to the comparative obscurity of a limited deluxe edition, and has been inaccessible to the Tripos student. And even when published under these circumstances he has more often than not been presented as a naughty oddity rather than as the serious poet he is. Anthologies, too, have tended to ignore him altogether, or, as the Oxford Book of English verse does, confine him to four brief lyrics.

For my part I cannot recall any University lecturer ever mentioning the poet's existence to me. Perhaps the label 'Restoration poet' was sufficient to cover him. Once docketed do not let us delay. . . .

Not only has Rochester suffered from neglect, but when mentioned he has been the victim of false and superficial emphasis. The somewhat colourful escapades in his life have almost wholly blinded the public (the reading public) to the solid and sober achievements of his pen.

His notoriety as 'the leading libertine in the gay Court of Charles II' and as the aristocrat whose tongue would tempt the angels to a second fall has obscured his literary reputation. So cheap and vicious have such comments been that it is perhaps not surprising that he has not been read—though it is strange his life has not been filmed. . . .

Whether all this moral obloquy is relevant or deserved is another matter. Criticism, or what passes as such, of this category, reveals the critic's private prejudices but does little to evaluate the poet.

As Johnson[2] says, 'Rochester had an early inclination towards intemperance which he totally subdued in his travels; but, when he became a courtier, he unhappily addicted himself to dissolute and vicious company, by which his principles were corrupted and his manners depraved. He lost all sense of religious restraint, and, finding it not convenient to admit the authority of laws which he was resolved not to obey, sheltered his wickedness behind infidelity.'

This judgment is probably quite true, not only of Rochester but of many others; yet were we to ignore the works of every poet to whom the same might superficially apply, our anthologies would look considerably reduced, not to say a trifle lean.

But whereas this charge of 'moral looseness' has caused Rochester to remain so long unpublished, a similar extraliterary notoriety has thrust considerably lesser figures, such as Wilde, into innumerable editions. It is indeed strange that a country which, at one of its most narrow-minded periods, witnessed Tennyson reading 'In Memoriam' to Queen Victoria and rewarded him with a peerage, should have banished Rochester from the Reading Room of the British Museum. Perhaps 'In Memoriam' has never been understood? Perhaps Rochester has never been read at all?

For I can find nothing offensive in him. His most bawdy poems do not shock me, his pornography delights me. This is an admission, not a confession. I do not think my taste is either elastic or eclectic, for I find much of Swinburne's sentiment obscene and Ruskin's lyricism disgusts me as a commercial traveller's smutty story.

Fortunately I need not stop to re-argue the difference between pornography and obscenity. Lawrence's pamphlet, is, if I remember, adequate.[3] Though perhaps one might add that pornography is the art which attracts you towards sex; obscenity the nauseous substitute for sex which repels you from the actual experience. The former moves you towards sex, the latter from it. Apart from answering the pertinent question raised by Mr. Thurber: '*Is sex really necessary?*' this distinction is I think sufficient.

A great deal of the most obscene lavatory-wall scribblings have been falsely attributed to Rochester. This pirating under his name began whilst the poet was still alive. Such a filthy and illiterate piece as the so-called five-act play *Sodom* was laid at his door or, one might say, on his step, causing the poet to attack the author:

> Tell me abandoned miscreant, prithee tell
> What damned Power invoked and sent from Hell
> ———did thee inspire———
> Thou covetest to be lewd but wantest the might
> And art all over devil but in wit,
> Week, feeble, strainer at mere ribaldry
> Whose muse is impotent to that degree
> It must like Age be whipped to Lechery.[4]

Many gossip-column critics have, in spite of the above, still attributed this play to him merely because the transcript in Hamburg bears the inscription 'By the E of R'.

POETRY CRITICISM, Vol. 66

However, I have laboured through this obscene doggerel and there cannot be the slightest doubt that
Rochester is not the author. It was impossible for him
to write three lines without spilling his wit or displaying his competence as a literary craftsman.

And so it is with the whole mass of dreary coarseness
which was passed round the coffee houses under his
name. Many of these laboured efforts at lewdness such
as **'A Ramble in St. James' Park'**[5] and **'Signor
Dildoe'**[6] still exist in manuscript copy books, but
Rochester's style is wholly missing from them, and
these and many others must be rejected both as spurious and indecent. They have achieved nothing, but damaged the reputation of the poet who certainly did not
write them.

On the other hand, copies of one or two poems still exist, such as the song: **"Oh, What damned Age do we
live in"**[7] which, from the run of the verse and its wit, I
would ascribe to Rochester. Unfortunately, however, I
cannot include this song in this edition; for, though its
title alone would suggest that it is particularly pertinent
to contemporary readers, I am informed that 'it might
undermine public morals'—so precariously are we
poised. The same applies to the **'Satyr on King Charles
II'** for which Rochester was banished for a time from
court.

Johnson, writing from an age which supported him on a
more secure perch, giving him standards to which he
could refer, and by which he could judge others, wrote
most ungenerously of the poet: 'Thus in a course of
drunken gaiety and gross sensuality with intervals of
study perhaps yet more criminal, with an avowed
contempt for all decency and order, a total disregard to
every moral, and a resolute denial of every religious
obligation, he lived worthless and useless, and blazed
out his health in lavish voluptuousness, till at the age of
one and thirty, he had exhausted the fund of life, and
reduced himself to a state of weakness and decay.'[8]

True as most of the above may be, Rochester is a serious poet.

One regrets that Johnson who was a major poet himself
and, with Dryden and Ben Jonson behind him, is
certainly one of the greatest literary critics, should have
concerned himself in one or two of his briefer Essays
so much with the Lives of the Poets, and so little with
their poetry. (I am of course not referring to his essays
on Milton, Dryden or Pope.)

When one realizes that a mind as profound as Johnson's
should have been turned from the proper consideration
of Rochester's poetry by the fog of the poet's reputation, one is forced to remark that it seems a pity that an
artist need have a life at all; since, no sooner has he lost

it, than frivolous or vicious minds scrabble over the
details of his biography rather than strain their concentration by studying his work. (A book reaches me this
morning from the United States on *The Works of
Beethoven.* One is not surprised to see that it reproduces
the composer's laundry list.)

What biographical facts I set down here are, I know,
largely irrelevant in evaluating the poet's work. Experiences do not describe an artist; an artist describes his
experiences. Rochester observed his own life as though
it were a play in which he took no part. The excesses in
it were also the excesses of his environment.

No man can do less than live in the age in which he is
born.

Rochester was born in 1647 or 1648, succeeding his
father to the earldom at the age of ten. After Oxford he
proceeded to make a tour, as was the custom of people
of his class, in France and Italy. On his return, at the
age of eighteen, he was presented to the Court at Whitehall where on account of 'his ready wit and pleasing
appearance' he was well received by 'the pleasure-
loving monarch', Charles II.

It is a platitude to refer to this period, and the Stuart
Court in particular, as one of 'squalor and vice'. But I
suspect this accepted description is not wholly deserved.
Political propaganda is not only a contemporary
phenomenon.

Yet for all the so-called moral squalor of the Court, we
know that it did constitute a centre of gravity for the
arts.[9] The palace was decorated with the paintings of
the Italian and Dutch schools; the music of Lawes, Purcell and Lully was played from the galleries by day,
and at night the Court supported the theatre where the
plays of Dryden, Etheredge etc. were well received. If
it was squalid it was certainly not dull. As for 'the
profligate empty-headed' monarch—whose French
background and love of wit led him to appoint the
philosopher St. Everemond to the Governorship of Duck
Island in St. James's Park—one suspects that he was no
more empty-headed than his most maligned father. (In
my opinion the ΕΙΚΟΝ ΒΑΣΙΛΙΚΗ not only displays
Charles I as a responsible monarch, it reveals a deeply
religious mind and a master of English prose.)

However, this is no place to revalue the Stuarts, nor
have I the equipment with which to do so; but I suggest
that our accepted notions concerning this period derive
as much from libel as they do from fact.

Soon after taking his place at this 'licentious' court,
Rochester was imprisoned in the Tower by the amoral
monarch for the 'High Misdemeanour' of abducting
Miss Mallet—whom he later married.

Released from the Tower, he volunteered for service in the Fleet and saw action at Bergen. On his return he was appointed a Gentleman of the Bedchamber. He married Miss Mallet in the same year. The correspondence between Lord Rochester, his wife, his mother and his friend, Henry Savile, should be published as they constitute a most readable history of the period, besides which they show the poet as not only a devoted husband, but a person who took his position as a peer more seriously than is generally supposed. His speeches delivered in the House of Lords are hardly those of a man 'whose principles were corrupt and his manner depraved'.

Certain it is that during his brief life at Court Rochester got up to many youthful escapades. He also wrote many libels.

> Mine host drinks to the Best in Christendom
> And decently my Lady quits the Room.
> Left to our selves, of several things we prate,
> Some regulate the *Stage,* and some the *State*;
> *Halfwit* cries up my Lord of *Orrery,*
> Ah, how well *Mustapha* and *Zanger* dye!
> His sense so little forced, that by one Line
> You may the other easily divine!
>   *And which is worse, if any worse can be,*
>   *He never said one word of it to me.*
> There's fine Poetry! you'd swear 'twere *Prose,*
> So little on the Sense the Rhymes impose. . . .

('Timon')

In such lampoons (a form which any healthy age might carry) Rochester succeeds in capturing the run of conversation within his verse. No small achievement within the couplet—'*So little on the Sense the Rhymes impose*'.

In 1673 the poet was again banished, this time for writing the famous satire on the King which he apparently inadvertently handed to the monarch himself, believing he had put some other firework in his pocket. During this period of exile there is a legend that Rochester and his friend, the Duke of Buckingham, leased an Inn on the Newmarket Road where they set up as publicans. Which exploit seems no more vicious than when he took up residence in the City of London under an assumed name, disguised as a well-to-do tradesman. When tired of this charade he took to the name of Dr. Alexander Bendo, lived in Tower Hill, claiming to be a master of quackery and astrology. Here he issued a pamphlet as an advertisement. It cannot be suggested that it was influenced by Swift.

> The Knowledge of these Secrets I gathered in my Travels abroad (where I have spent my Time ever since I was Fifteen Years Old, to this my Nine and Twentieth Year) in *France* and *Italy*: Those that have travelled in *Italy,* will tell you to what a Miracle Art does there assist Nature in the Preservation of Beauty; how Women of Forty bear the same Countenance with those of Fifteen; Ages are no way distinguished by Faces; Whereas here in *England,* look a Horse in the Mouth, and a Woman in the Face, you presently know both their Ages to a Year. I will therefore give you such Remedies, that without destroying your Complexion (as most of your Paints and Dawbings do) shall render them purely Fair, clearing and preserving them from all Spots, Freckles, Heats and Pimples, any Marks of the Small-Pox, or any other accidental ones, so the Face be not seamed or scarred.
>
> I will also preserve and cleanse your Teeth, white and round as Pearls, fastening them that are loose; your Gums shall be kept entire and red as Coral, your Lips of the same Colour and soft as you could wish your lawful Kisses.
>
> I will likewise administer that which shall cure the worst of Breaths, provided the Lungs are not totally perished and imposthumated; as also certain and infallible Remedies for those whose Breaths are yet untainted, so that nothing but either a very long Sickness, or Old Age itself, shall ever be able to spoil them.
>
> I will besides (if it be desired) take away from their Fatness who have over-much, and add Flesh to those that want it, without the least Detriment to their Constitutions.
>
> Now should *Galen* himself look out of his Grave, and tell me these were Bawbles below the Profession of a Physician, I would boldly answer him, that I take more Glory in preserving God's Image in its unblemished Beauty, upon one good Face, than I should do in patching up all the decayed Carcasses in the World.
>
> They that will do me the Favour to come to me, shall be sure from Three of the Clock in the Afternoon, till Eight at Night, at my Lodgings in *Tower-Street,* next door to the sign of the *Black Swan,* at a *Goldsmith's House,* to find—
>
> *Their Humble Servant*
> Alexander Bendo.

And the following passage is I think a good example of the run of Restoration prose:

> Consider, pray, the Valiant and the coward, the wealthy Merchant and the Bankrupt, the Politician and the Fool; they are the same in many things, and differ in but one alone. The Valiant Man holds up his Head, looks confidently round about him, wears a Sword, courts a Lord's Wife, and owns it: So does the Coward, one only point of Honour, and that's Courage (which, like false Metal, one only trial can discover) makes the distinction.

Rochester not only wrote satire, he lived it too. This dualism was a habit of his.

After the Dr. Bendo episode, he continued to live at Court and interested himself in the stage, writing an adaptation of Fletcher's *Valentinian* and contributing a scene to be inserted in Sir Robert Howard's play *The*

Conquest of China. Rochester was for a time an intimate friend and patron of Dryden and *Marriage à La Mode* is dedicated to him.

In 1677 Rochester's health began to worsen. He retired for a time to the country and now began to doubt his doubts and repent his ways. Like many professing atheists he was essentially of a religious frame of mind. In the same year it was reported that the poet had died, 'which rumour,' he wrote, 'increased my passion for living and I am now resolved to live out of spite'.

In 1679 he spoke against the Exclusion Bill in the House of Lords. But this was his last appearance in London. The final brief period of his life covers his intense spiritual introspection and the religious experience he underwent whilst hearing Isaiah read to him as he lay ill in bed. Burnet reports the experience as the poet described it:

> As he heard it (the chapter of Isaiah) read, he felt an inward Force upon him, which did so enlighten his Mind, and convince him, that he could resist it no longer. For the words had an Authority which did shoot like Rays or Beams in his Mind; so he was not only satisfied in his Understanding, but by a Power which did so effectually constrain him, that he did ever after firmly believe in his Saviour, as if he had seen him in the clouds.[10]

This return to faith subsequent to his conversations with Dr. Burnet on the nature of Immortality and the Resurrection was not another superficial youthful enthusiasm, but represented what he had sought all his life. Sometimes his search looks like derision, sometimes like angry negation, but it is always desperation, the desperate thirst for spiritual affirmation. Like Donne, the dissipation of his youth was no more than a manifestation of unattached vitality seeking its attachment. It is probable that this physical vitality and mental vigour are minimum attributes if faith is to be grasped firmly; it is certain that their sense of sin contributed towards their appreciation of redemption. It is the same road that St. Augustine trod.

Before his death Rochester recanted all his poems which had been based on Hobbes' materialism and reviled his former way of life:

> For the benefit of all those whom I may have drawn into sin by my example and encouragement, I leave to the World this my last declaration, which I deliver in the presence of the Great God, who knows the secrets of all hearts, and before whom I am now appearing to be judged.
>
> That, from the bottom of my soul, I detest and abhor the whole course of my former wicked life; that I think I can never sufficiently admire the goodness of God, who has given me a true sense of my pernicious opinions and vile practices, by which I have hitherto

lived without hope and without God in the world; have been an open enemy to Jesus Christ, doing the utmost despite to the Holy Spirit of Grace. And that the greatest testimony of my charity to such is, to warn them, in the name of God, and as they regard the welfare of their immortal souls, no more to deny his being or his providence, or despite his goodness; no more to make a mock of sin, or condemn the pure and excellent religion of my ever blessed Redeemer, through whose merits alone, I, one of the greatest sinners, do yet hope for mercy and forgiveness. Amen.

Declared and signed in the presence of

> Anne Rochester, Robert Parsons.
> J. Rochester. June 1680.

Rochester died a few days later at the age of thirty-two—at which age few poets have made such a solid contribution to literature.

To appraise his verse it is more important to study the intellectual background of the Restoration than to observe the dates and incidents of his brief career. Professor Pinto covers this background most thoroughly.

Without doubt the key to it lies in the publication of Hobbes' *Leviathan* in 1651—with Descartes behind it. It was this lucid materialism which set the intellectual temper to Rochester's youth and to his period as a whole. Hobbes' philosophy went to the heads of Restoration England: it was taken as an excuse for license and irresponsibility which, as Rochester found, led to the tyranny of sensual gratification and boredom.

There is a distinct parallel between Restoration cynicism and the intellectual temper of our own 1920's. Hobbes did for the seventeenth century what Marx did for the twentieth.

A chronological table shows certain other directions in the poet's background:

	1616	Shakespeare dies
	1631	Donne dies; Dryden born
	1637	Ben Jonson dies
Rochester born	1648	
	1651	Hobbes' 'Leviathan' published (Hobbes was Francis Bacon's secretary)
	1670	Pascal's Pensées published
	1674	Milton dies: Herrick also
	1678	Marvel dies
Rochester's death	1680	
	1688	Pope born.

The usual method of literary (and musical) criticism is, from my observation, very similar to that which takes place at my local market when I send bullocks in to be slaughtered. The animals are given a cursory once-over by a triumvirate: the auctioneer, a farmer, and a butcher; and according to their weight and age, are graded into one or other of three classes. Once marked on their rump with the brand A, B or C, they are despatched with no further enquiry into their quality.

This method is, I suppose, better than no method, for it does establish some sort of order in the bellowing and panic-stricken herd. But as the vet often says to me as we lean upon the rails, 'some of those fat cows graded as "A" are full of tuberculosis if they bothered to look; and, I daresay, some of those lean devils classed as "C" are as healthy as antelopes, with the best quality meat'.

A distinction serves a useful purpose when it is first made: but when it becomes a mere label it may obscure more than it clarifies.

It is a commonplace to talk about Elizabethan, Metaphysical, Restoration and Augustan poets. These schools have been well defined and are of course entities . . . but a glance at the table I have given may serve to show how difficult and dangerous it is to draw precise frontiers.

It is too easy to talk of Rochester as a Restoration poet and then stamp him on the rump—such may serve as a guide to culture but I doubt if it constitutes it or even an appreciation of it. Not all the labels in the world can direct a purblind taste.

In poetry it is not easy to distinguish between the root and the flower. Where does the Augustan Age begin? Who are its precursors? I do not see how you can avoid Rochester—or Marvel. The latter's *Horatian Ode* is certainly behind it, as is the following in which I also hear the hoofs of Volpone:

> As some brave *Admiral,* in former War
> Deprived of Force, but prest with Courage still,
> Two Rival Fleets appearing from afar,
> Crawls to the top of an adjacent Hill. . . .

and so to the end:

> Thus Bravo-like I'll sawcily impose
> And, safe from danger, valiantly advise;
> Sheltered in Impotence urge you to blows,
> And, being good for nothing else, be wise.

The visual quality of this imagery is in the same tradition as parts of the Dunciad. . . .

Who is the last metaphysical poet? Again I do not see how you can avoid Rochester. The poem **On nothing** is an obvious but I do not think a particularly good example. For metaphysical poetry is not merely a question of complicated imagery or range of reference but poetry in which the emotions and the intellect are engaged at one and the same time.

But to trace Cowley's or Donne's influence on Rochester or Rochester's influence on Pope is all very well so long as it does not distract from the actual reading of either. No poet can be considered properly in vacuo. Each poem presents all poetry. Its references are both forward and backward in time and these are part of its dimensions.

In short what I am trying to do here is to persuade people to read Rochester's poetry rather than go off satisfied with my opinion about him. A great deal of so-called literary (and musical) criticism now consists in nothing more than a parlour game 'Hunt the Origin' or 'Trace the Influence'. All of which helps to cover many paragraphs and eventually trains the mind to a proper appreciation of detective novels. Crabbe's portrait studies can be seen in embryo in **"Tunbridge Wells,"** and in *A letter fancied from Artemisa in The Town to Cloe in the Country*; as Ben Jonson can be seen as the foundation of Rochester's excellent poem **"Upon His Drinking Bowl."**

But the danger of pointing to an influence in a writer is that the reader then takes that as a derogatory criticism, for there is a passion to pigeon-hole poets, especially amongst those who like talking about but not reading poetry. . . .

> Were I, who to my cost already am,
> One of those strange, prodigious Creatures *Man,*
> A Spirit free to choose for my own share
> What case of Flesh and Blood I'd please to wear,
> I'd be a *Dog,* a *Monkey* or a *Bear,*
> Or any thing but that vain *Animal*
> Who is so proud of being Rational.
> The Senses are too gross, and he'll contrive
> A sixth, to contradict the other five.

> (*A Satyr Against Reason and Mankind*)

Johnson's only comment on the above satire is: 'Rochester can only claim when all Boileau is taken Away'. Certainly Rochester's poem derives from Boileau.

> De tous les Animaux qui s'élèvent dans l'air
> Qui marchant sur la terre ou nagent dans la mer,
> De Paris, au Perau, du Japon juscu'a Rome
> Le plus sot animal, à mon avis, c'est l'homme.

And Pope's 'Essay on Man' leans back on Rochester. As Mr. Hayward has commented: 'Rochester's version has merits worthy of more praise than Johnson's curt criticism expresses.' That puts it mildly. Rochester's parenthesis in his first line adds wit, an improvement on *à mon avis.*

Also Mr. Pound pointed out[11] that Rochester's:

> After Death nothing is, and nothing Death;
> The utmost Limits of a gasp of Breath.

Let the ambitious Zealot lay aside
His hopes of Heaven (whose Faith is but his
      Pride). . . .

                              (trans. from Seneca's *Troas*)

'improves on Boileau, but not on Seneca':

      Post mortem nihil est, ipsaque mors nihil.

One could, if one wanted to amuse oneself, fill a whole volume of quotations of echoes. But as Johnson certainly knew more goes to making an omelette than just taking a bowl full of eggs. We all know that both a diamond and coal are compounds of carbon but an explanation does not detract from a miracle of synthesis. So it is with poetry. And Rochester is a serious poet.

What do I mean by serious? I do not regard Tennyson as serious even at his most pontifical or lyrical. Whereas Rochester is serious at his most flippant. Seriousness is not a question of choice of subject; it is something to do with the relation of the poet to his experience; an immediacy which charges the verse with emotion and, at the same time, a detachment which engages an objective intelligence towards that experience.

There is no value in originally *per se*. Rochester may be more derivative than Tennyson but I suspect that that is part of his strength. It is not a disadvantage for a poet to be either consciously or unconsciously aware of other poets—indeed the solidity of his verse depends largely on this kind of integration. But it is another matter when his experiences and emotions are derivative too—which is not the same thing as merely being aware of other people's experiences. Tennyson's verse may be original in the sense that it is not an adaptation but it is his experiences which are second-hand. He stands on emotional tip-toe. Whereas Rochester wrote in the manner of Boileau, Tennyson only succeeded in writing in the manner of Tennyson.

However, one does not of necessity establish one reputation merely by destroying another.

Rochester's positive achievement is his contribution to the tradition of SONG. Not every poem printed in the anthologies under the loose title of 'Song' is capable of being sung. It is not that such poems have not been set to music; it is that the clumsy arrangement of their syllables defy articulation in song. Rochester probably absorbed his technical proficiency in writing songs by listening to Purcell and Lawes whilst in the 'squalid' court.

      All my past Life is mine no more,
          The flying Hours are gone;
      Like transitory Dreams given o'er,
      Whose Images are kept in store
          By Memory alone.

      Whatever is to come, is not;
          How can it then be mine?
      The present Moment's all my Lot,
      And that, as fast as it is got,
          Phillis is wholly thine.

      Then talk not of Inconstancy,
          False Hearts and broken vows;
      If I by Miracle can be
          This live-long Minute true to thee
          'Tis all that Heav'n allows.

Rochester wrote half-a-dozen songs as good as this. Apart from Ben Jonson's lyrics in his Masques, and Campion, there is very little within this particular form to equal his achievement. One cannot read these songs without being aware that they are meant to be sung. They are suitable for setting to music in that the first verse suggests a melody the development and realization of which the rest of the poem does not impede or obstruct. They are *cantabile* in the way that troubadour verse is. Their rhythm does not depend on some rule-of-thumb method of arranging syllables but is a question of weight felt in the ear. And that is the essence of metre without which scansion is a positive hindrance. What is the prime necessity for words which are to be sung? A sufficiency and spacing of vowels with an avoidance of weak female endings at the end of a phrase.

Apart from their value as words to be sung, they have an ironic content which, if I am not mistaken, looks to Pope:

      Love a woman! You're an *Ass*,
          'Tis a most insipid Passion
      To choose out for your Happiness
          The silliest Part of God's Creation.

      Let the Porter and the Groom,
          Things designed for duty Slaves,
      Drudge in fair *Aurelia's* womb,
          To get supplies for Age and Graves:

      Farewell, Woman, I intend
          Henceforth every night to sit
      With my lewd well-natured Friend,
          Drinking to engender Wit.

                                          (Rochester)

      I know a thing that's most uncommon
          (Envy be silent and attend).
      I know a reasonable woman
          Handsome and witty, yet a friend.

      Not warped by passion, awed by rumour
          Not grave through pride, nor gay through folly
      An equal mixture of good humour
          And sensible soft melancholy.

      'Has she no fault then (Envy says), Sir?'
          Yes, she has one, I must aver;

When all the world conspires to praise her
The woman's deaf, and does not hear.

(Pope)

I think the juxtaposition of these two poems shows Rochester's virtues and his limitations. He has not Pope's control, but there is no doubt that Rochester helped to mould the pastoral tradition of song to a more urbane and mature attitude. His shepherds are not simple, nor are his nymphs dull with virtue. He was, with Flaubert, aware that *Elle retrouvait dans l'adultère toutes les platitudes du marriage.*

Phillis, be gentler, I advise,
    Make up for time mis-spent;
When Beauty on its Death-bed lies
    'Tis high time to repent.

Such is the Malice of your Fate
    That makes you old so soon,
Your Pleasure ever comes too late,
    How early e'er begun.

Think what a wretched thing is she
    Whose Stars contrive in spight
That Morning of her Love should be
    Her fading Beauty's Night.

Then if, to make your ruin more,
    You'll peevishly be coy,
Die with the Scandal of a Whore
    And never know the Joy.

To quote Johnson: 'His songs have no particular character: they tell like other songs, in smooth and easy language, of scorn and kindness, dismission and desertion, absence and inconstancy, with the commonplace of artificial courtship. They are commonly smooth and easy but have little nature and little sentiment.'

The above song is hardly 'commonplace courtship', whatever it is—and allowing all Rochester's faults, lack of 'character' is not one of them.

How can one exclude Rochester? Certainly not on his inability to write verse. One is I suppose driven back to this question of his content—which is supposed to be so obscene. Let us compare this libertine with two of our most respectable lyricists. . . .

Airy, fairy Lilian
Flitting, fairy Lilian
When I ask her if she loves me,
Claps her tiny hands above me,
    Laughing all she can;
She'll not tell me if she loves me,
    Cruel little Lilian.

(Tennyson)

And vital feelings of delight
Shall rear her form to stately height,

Her virgin bosom swell;
Such thoughts to Lucy I will give
While she and I together live
    Here in this happy dell.

(Wordsworth: Lucy IV)

Naked she lay, clasped in my longing Arms,
I filled with Love, and she all over Charms,
Both equally inspired with eager fire,
Melting through kindness, flaming in desire;
With *Arms, Legs, Lips,* close clinging in embrace,
She clips me to her Breast, and sucks me to her Face.
The nimble *Tongue* (Love's lesser Lightning) plaid
Within my *Mouth,* and to my thoughts conveyed
Swift Orders, that I should prepare to throw
The All-dissolving *Thunderbolt* below.

(Rochester)

Although the above extracts may not be entirely representative of their respective authors, they do serve to show the impotent decline in amorous verse. And I take it that a love poem can with advantage contain reference to the reality of amorous experience. To my mind Rochester's reference to the 'nobler part', 'the all-dissolving thunderbolt', is decent, and Tennyson's 'Airy, fairy Lilian' to say the least, is a false description of the lady incompatible with the creak of her corsets. . . .

Poets cannot be measured. It does not get you very far to say Villon is greater than Rochester. Rochester is a poet in his own right. By reading other poets you do not cover his contribution; and by reading him you are not just reading somebody else at one remove. And if, as I hope, contemporary verse, having digested the reforms which the Imagists brought in, should now look more to rhythm and form, I do not see how it can ignore Rochester.

Notes

1. See Bibliography.
2. *Lives of the Poets: Rochester.*
3. *Pornography and Obscenity* by D. H. Lawrence.
4. "Upon the Author of a Play called *Sodom.*"
5. *and*
6. Manuscripts in British Museum.
7. Manuscripts in British Museum.
8. Johnson's essay on Rochester, in *Lives of the Poets.*
9. See *Rochester* by V. de Sola Pinto (Bodley Head.)
10. *Life of Rochester,* by Gilbert Burnet, D.D.
11. *A.B.C. of Reading,* Ezra Pound. (Routledge).

Bibliography

Rochester Manuscripts in British Museum.

The Works of John Wilmot, Earl of Rochester, edited by John Hayward. (Nonesuch Press 1926.)

A.B.C. of Reading, by Ezra Pound. (Routledge & Son 1934.)

Life of Rochester, by Gilbert Burnet, D.D. (William Pickering.)

Lives of the Poets, by Samuel Johnson.

Transactions of the Royal Society of Literature of the United Kingdom. Vol. XIII. Paper by Vivian de Sola Pinto. (Humphrey Milford 1934.)

Rochester: Portrait of a Restoration Poet, by Vivian de Sola Pinto. (John Lane: The Bodley Head 1935.)

A Sermon preached at the funeral of John Earl of Rochester by Robert Parsons, M.A.

The Sacred Wood, by T. S. Eliot. (Faber and Faber 1920.)

David M. Vieth (essay date 1963)

SOURCE: Vieth, David M. "Verse Satires on Rochester: The Myth and the Man." In *Attribution in Restoration Poetry: A Study of Rochester's Poems of 1680,* pp. 164-203. New Haven, Conn.: Yale University Press, 1963.

[*In the following excerpt, Vieth examines the many satirical verses and lampoons written about Rochester, some originally attributed to the poet himself.*]

I

An important ingredient in the biography of any prominent Restoration figure is the way he or she was portrayed in the lampoons of the day. These lampoons cannot, of course, be relied upon for literal accuracy; hostile by their very nature, they tend to exaggerate unfavorable personality traits and to oversimplify or even falsify facts. Nevertheless, if their distortions are corrected by reference to more trustworthy data, Restoration lampoons can supply an added dimension which the biographer would be foolish to ignore. At the very least, they preserve evanescent gossip or emphasize base motives that are not clearly revealed in other sources. Often they afford a vivid glimpse of a person as he was seen by large numbers of his contemporaries—resembling, in this respect, political cartoons of the twentieth century. At their best, they offer the biographer the sort of imaginative projection of his subject's identity which he may seek in vain in the dry records that ordinarily constitute much of his raw material.

Many influences combined to make the personal satire of the Restoration what it was: contemporary stage comedy, the technique of the prose "character," earlier English traditions of satire,[1] and, increasingly, the

examples of Horace, Juvenal, and Persius, whether studied directly or absorbed through the medium of adapters like Boileau. In addition, however, the peculiar worth of Restoration lampoons to the biographer and historian probably stems from two developments, superficially opposite in tendency, which were both strong during this formative period in English literature.

Evidently one of these developments amounted to a compelling desire for concreteness in poetical expression. Such a tendency seems to be urgently present during the initial stages of a major literary movement, when poets are trying to get back to essentials. To a degree, this tendency is a reaction against the unreal "poetic diction" of a previous literary mode; the preface to the *Lyrical Ballads* and *The Love Song of J. Alfred Prufrock* come quickly to mind, and the emerging Augustan sensibility was partly a revolt against the excesses of late Metaphysical poetry. A normal aspect of the desire to be concrete is a felt need for a poetical style modeled upon the spoken language of whatever segment of society best embodies the half-realized values of the new sensibility; thus Wordsworth wished to imitate the language of peasants. In the Restoration, the model was the conversation of the fashionable rakes who surrounded Charles II, or even of mere aspirants to membership in this circle. To illustrate the pungently realistic idiom which resulted, no better example could be found than Rochester's satires, especially **"Timon"** and **"Tunbridge Wells."**[2]

Furthermore, just as Wordsworth depicted particular rocks, trees, and flowers because he felt these objects of "nature" were most real, so the Restoration satirist, a hypersensitive member of a civilized community, apparently felt constrained to achieve concreteness by attacking actual *people.* Despite the dictum that satire should be general—that it should scourge the sin rather than the sinner—the Restoration satirist, and even a later Augustan like Alexander Pope, must have been impelled to write personal satire by pressures in the prevailing sensibility that made the critical doctrine very difficult to observe. The satirist's conscience may have been uneasy, but his urge to use actual persons is a circumstance for which the biographer and historian can be grateful.

Good poetry cannot, however, be only a "slice of life" composed of realistic colloquial idiom, specific names, and particularities of personal behavior; even a mediocre poet knows, or feels, that he must strive for a universality transcending these incidents of the surface. Accordingly, we also find a tendency in Restoration satire to elevate its particular personages to the status of myth. Moreover, as befitted a socially centered age, the myths were usually not the work of a single poet, but were communal products. After a semi-mythic characterization had been outlined by one satirist, other satirists frequently incorporated it into their own lampoons and filled out its details. Though this process may strike a twentieth-century reader as mere borrowing, it more nearly resembles creative participation in a ritual.

Restoration satirists did not often achieve full success in their myth-making, but their few triumphs are so effective that the myth is more memorable than the real person on whom it is based. One remembers the Earl of Mulgrave as the haughty ass who complacently thought himself the ideal soldier and lover; or one remembers Sir Carr Scroope as the feckless fop who, though half-blind and repulsively ugly, sent his amatory verses to countless women and was so absorbed in writing poetry that he fought in rhyme rather than with his sword. Even individual performances like Dryden's portraits of Shadwell and Buckingham owe something to the tradition of myth-making in Restoration lampoons. Evidently the tradition carried over into later practice, for the curious semi-mythic world of Restoration satire seems closely akin to the half-real, half-fictional existence which Aubrey Williams has found characteristic of the personages in Pope's *Dunciad*.[3] Thus two tendencies in Restoration lampoons, the tendency to concreteness and the countertendency to myth, probably account for much of their colorful portraiture and their resultant usefulness to the biographer.

Oddly, none of Rochester's numerous biographers has provided so much as a list of the lampoons written against him during his lifetime. Though, as we shall see, there may be good reasons for this neglect, even a casual reader could guess that Rochester sustained frequent personal attacks which offer knowledge of the way he was viewed by his less sympathetic contemporaries. He was sufficiently prominent, and his questionable manner of life made him an inviting target. Also, the satirists had part of their myth already available, for Rochester's social position was somewhat like that of a cinema star in twentieth-century America, nor was he reluctant to perpetuate the myth through his considerable talents as a *poseur*. A survey of the surviving lampoons on Rochester seems long overdue.

This survey is further necessitated by a strange irony: of the satires written against him, about half were ultimately attributed to Rochester himself. This happened largely because some of them found their way into the first edition of 1680, the Huntington edition (A-1680-HU). In the lost archetype of the Huntington edition and the Yale MS., the scribe included several such lampoons in his section of poems by or concerning Rochester; the Huntington edition, in turn, printed almost all of these lampoons as Rochester's own compositions. A study of the collection represented by the Yale MS. and the Huntington edition must therefore attempt to separate this group of satires from the poems which can be accepted as genuine Rochester.

II

The earliest lampoons on Rochester apparently originated, as so many things did in Restoration poetry, among the gentlemen-wits at Court. During 1670-75, and probably before, the Wits seem to have amused themselves by writing jocular, bawdy poems about each other. The first datable poem of this type on Rochester is a clever satirical song headed, in some eighteenth-century editions, "The Debauchee." Its entire text is here reproduced as an example, since the next few poems to be discussed are so obscene that full quotation is not desirable. Though "The Debauchee" is traditionally printed as seven rhymed couplets of anapestic tetrameter, the usual arrangement has been altered to emphasize the rhyming of the half-lines (except lines 5 and 7, which may be corrupt). "Rochester" is speaking:

> I Rise at Eleven,
>   I Dine about Two,
> I get drunk before Seven,
>   and the next thing I do;
> I send for my *Whore*,
>   when for fear of a *Clap*,
> I Spend in her hand,
>   and I Spew in her *Lap*:
> <Then> we quarrel, and scold,
>   till I fall <fast> asleep,
> When the *Bitch,* growing bold,
>   to my Pocket does creep;
> Then slyly she leaves me,
>   and to revenge th' affront,
> At once she bereaves me
>   of *Money,* and *Cunt.*
> If by chance then I wake,
>   hot-headed, and drunk,
> What a coyle do I make
>   for the loss of my *Punck?*
> I storm, and I roar,
>   and I fall in a rage,
> And missing my *Whore,*
>   I bugger my *Page*:
> Then crop-sick, all *Morning,*
> I rail at my *Men,*
> And in Bed I lye Yawning,
>   till Eleven again.[4]

This song is not unfriendly to Rochester. Nevertheless, it anticipates what we shall find to have been his standard satiric character as whoremaster, toper, idler, and bully.

Most students of Rochester have supposed that "The Debauchee" is his own composition—a natural assumption, since it is written in the first person, and Rochester was quite capable of satirizing himself. The poem was accepted as genuine by John Hayward, Quilter Johns, Johannes Prinz, and James Thorpe; Vivian de Sola Pinto doubted its authenticity, however, since he omitted it from his edition.[5] Actually, as Thorpe conceded, there is only "slight evidence" of Rochester's authorship (*Rochester's Poems,* p. 177). "The Debauchee" was first printed as Rochester's in the Huntington edition, from which it was reprinted with the same ascription in the other 1680 editions and the later editions of 1685 (A-1685), 1701 (A-1701), 1713 (A-1713), and 1731 (A-1731). From one of the 1680 editions, apparently, it was also printed as Rochester's in Edmund Curll's *The Works Of the Earls of Rochester, Roscommon, Dorset, & c.,* 1714 (C-1714-1), and succeeding editions of this collection. No text is extant in the Yale MS., for the poem was probably among those removed by the fourth gap. Two manuscript versions, in Bodl. MS. Rawl. Poet. 152 and Edinburgh MS. DC.1.3, carry no ascriptions. Thus the only evidence of Rochester's authorship is the ambiguous testimony of the Huntington edition.

Since the Huntington edition prints "The Debauchee" in the section of poems by or concerning Rochester, any internal evidence that it satirizes the Earl is sufficient to question its authenticity. This evidence exists, for the poem depicts a typical day in the life of just such a rake as Rochester was popularly believed to be. Moreover, as von Römer noted years ago,[6] an experience like the one described in "The Debauchee" actually happened to Rochester. Pepys records that on 2 December 1668, he

> heard the silly discourse of the King, with his people about him, telling a story of my Lord Rochester's having of his clothes stole, while he was with a wench; and his gold all gone, but his clothes found afterwards stuffed into a feather bed by the wench that stole them.

Even if "The Debauchee" does not refer to this particular incident, it might allude to a similar occurrence at some other date.

Fortunately, a newly discovered piece of external evidence seems to indicate both the true author of "The Debauchee" and its approximate date of composition. Early in 1673, the Earl of Huntingdon applied to his cousin Godfrey Thacker, in London, for the latest gossip concerning Rochester. In Thacker's reply, dated 20 March 1672/3, a postscript offers the following story:

> My Lord Buckhurst and Lord Rochester being in company, a suddaine Malancholly possest him Rochester inquiring the reason hee answered hee was troubled at Rochesters lude way of living, and in thes verses over the leafe exprest it[7]

On the reverse side of the leaf, Thacker quotes the first eight lines of "The Debauchee." Though the anecdotal quality of Thacker's account may not inspire confidence in the accuracy of all its details, the portion most likely to be true is his ascription of the poem to Buckhurst; conceivably the rest of the story might be a fabrication to explain this ascription. The point is scarcely important, however, for Thacker's statement is the only real evidence we possess on the authorship of "The Debauchee."

Similar to "The Debauchee" is an obscene satirical "Song" beginning "In the Fields of Lincolns Inn," which may also emanate from the Court Wits and which may have been written about the same date, though clear evidence is lacking. The "Song" even resembles "The Debauchee" in attempting a prosodic *tour de force,* since it consists of four eight-line stanzas of trochaic tetrameter rhymed *abbacdcd,* with the *a* and *d* rhymes masculine and the *b* and *c* rhymes feminine.

Though the early printed texts of the "Song" attribute it to Rochester, few students of his poetry have believed that he wrote it. His authorship was rejected by Hayward, Johns, Prinz, and Pinto. Thorpe, accepting the poem as genuine, nevertheless added that "it may very possibly have been falsely attracted into the Rochester canon; but no evidence appears to disprove his authorship" (*Rochester's Poems,* p. 176). The "Song" was first printed as Rochester's in the Huntington edition, where it is found in the section of poems by or concerning Rochester. It was reprinted with the same ascription in the other editions of 1680 but was omitted from later editions. In the Yale MS. it seems, like "The Debauchee," to have been among the poems removed by the fourth gap. Two manuscript versions furnish ascriptions: Harvard MS. Eng. 636F assigns the poem to Rochester, whereas Bodl. MS. Don. b. 8, unknown to Thorpe, ascribes it to Sir Charles Sedley.

Besides the ascription to Sedley, internal evidence casts doubt on Rochester's authorship of the "Song." Its style is not strikingly Rochesterian, and in places its author apparently had difficulty maintaining his intricate rhyme scheme, as in the opening lines:

> In the *Fields* of *Lincolns Inn,*
> 　Underneath a tatter'd *Blanket,*
> 　On a *Flock-Bed, God* be thanked,
> Feats of Active Love were seen.[8]

"*God* be thanked," with the last word pronounced as two syllables, is a feeble way to fill out a line and supply a rhyme. One wonders whether Rochester's talents would have been so severely strained.

More important, the "Song" may be a genial lampoon on Rochester, for it seems to reflect the popular image of the Earl as a sort of archetypal whoremonger. In vaguely mock-pastoral terms, the poem describes how two men, Corydon and Strephon, attempt simultaneous sexual intercourse with one woman. Strephon was a pseudonym commonly used for Rochester; also, in contrast to Corydon, a mere neophyte, Strephon possesses extraordinary qualifications:

> *Coridon's* aspiring *Tarse,*
> 　Which to *Cunt,* had ne're submitted;
> 　Wet with Am'rous Kiss she fitted,
> To her less frequented Ar———

> *Strephon*'s, was a handful longer,
>   Stiffly propt with eager *Lust*;
> None for *Champion,* was more stronger,
>   This into her *Cunt* he thrust.

These arguments help to clarify the external evidence on the authorship of the "Song." The ascription in the Huntington edition is ambiguous, since the scribe of the archetype may have included the "Song" in his section of poems by or concerning Rochester in the belief that it satirized the Earl. The ascription in Harvard MS. Eng. 636F is likewise suspect, for this manuscript tends to attribute too much to Rochester, as is shown by the next poem to be discussed. Moreover, in the independently descended texts of the "Song," the character of the variants suggests that most of them resulted from memorial transmission; possibly someone who tried to carry the poem in his head confused its subject with its author, and the false ascription then passed into the Harvard manuscript.

No external evidence remains except the ascription to Sedley in Bodl. MS. Don. b. 8, a volume whose attributions are unusually trustworthy. Though Pinto questions this ascription because "there is no other evidence" of Sedley's authorship (*Works of Sedley, 1,* xxvii), there is likewise no reliable testimony that anyone else wrote the "Song." Sedley may have composed it under circumstances similar to those which led Buckhurst to write "The Debauchee."

Probably written more than a year after "The Debauchee" is a long, extremely bawdy narrative satire in heroic couplets beginning "Say Heav'n-born Muse, for only thou canst tell." The earliest texts entitle this satire "The Argument," a heading which properly belongs only to its introductory four-line synopsis; with better reason but no visible authority, eighteenth-century editions call the poem "Bath Intrigues." This witty, if sometimes rough and incoherent lampoon relates how Rochester is tricked by three lascivious women at Bath, how he resolves to break up their friendship, and how he carries out his obscene revenge. As in "The Debauchee" and the "Song," the portrayal of Rochester, while not very attractive, is not perceptibly hostile. Indeed, far from being primarily a lampoon on Rochester, "The Argument" is more interesting for its antireligious attitudes. It also deserves special mention as a thoroughgoing attempt to use mock-epic devices for satirical purposes, a relatively rare phenomenon at this early date.[9]

Students of Rochester have unanimously concluded that he did not write "The Argument": the poem was rejected by Hayward, Johns, Prinz, Pinto, and Thorpe. Its textual history resembles those of "The Debauchee" and the "Song." First printed as Rochester's in the Huntington edition, where it appears in the section of poems by or concerning Rochester, it was reprinted with the same ascription in the other 1680 editions but drops out of later editions in this series. From one of the 1680 editions it was again printed as Rochester's in Curll's edition of 1714 and in later editions of this collection; from the edition of 1714, in turn, Giles Jacob derived his attribution. In the Yale MS., where only the title, the four-line "argument," and the first eight lines of text are extant, "The Argument" carries no ascription—though, significantly, all preceding genuine poems are ascribed to Rochester. An ascription to Rochester occurs, however, in Harvard MS. Eng. 636F.

As Thorpe has demonstrated (*Rochester's Poems,* p. 174), the ascriptions to Rochester in the Huntington edition and the Harvard manuscript cannot be correct, for "The Argument" satirizes Rochester and also reproduces the traditional satiric image of the Earl as the legendary lecher. Though the poem's principal male character is identified merely as *"R———"* in the printed texts (A-1680-HU, p. 35), the Harvard manuscript gives his full name as "Rochester," as does a marginal note in a contemporary hand in the Sterling copy of the 1680 editions (A-1680-S-S). The poem further calls him "Peer" and "Spiney *Lord,*" alluding to Rochester's slender physique. There is even a sarcastic reference to Rochester's "lasting *Verse.*" Interestingly, "The Argument" augments the mythic characterization of Rochester by describing him as malicious; we are told that "his Heart with rancour swell'd" as he cast his "evil *Eye*" upon the three women whose lewd pleasures he vowed to destroy.

No evidence is forthcoming on the true author of "The Argument," though its religious skepticism and its familiarity with the Court seemingly point to one of the Wits. Prinz felt that the poem "looks like a production of Alexander Radcliffe" (*Rochester,* p. 150), an opinion which Thorpe thought "reasonable" even if "only a guess" (*Rochester's Poems,* p. 174). Without more facts, however, speculation is futile.

Evidently "The Argument" was not in existence before spring of 1674. Several topical allusions occur in the poem. Unfortunately, little help is afforded by references to breaking the Triple League and to the Duke of Luxemburg, one of Louis XIV's generals, since either might have been mentioned after the early 1670s. A likely *terminus post quem* is, however, provided by the following passage:

> To th' Tree she leads him, from a *Bough* pulls down,
> A mighty Tool, a *Dildoe* of renown;
> A *Dildoe,* long, and large, as *Hectors Launce,*
> Inscrib'd, *Honi Soit Qui Mal y' Pence.*
> *Knight* of the *Garter,* made for's vast deserts,
> As *Modern Heroe,* was for's monstrous parts.

The last couplet probably satirizes the Earl of Mulgrave, who became Knight of the Garter on 23 April

1674.[10] The couplet reflects the satirists' usual charges against Mulgrave: "monstrous parts" apparently sneers at his boasted exploits as a lover, while *"Modern Heroe"* may allude both to his arrogance and to his ambitions as a military commander. Some support for this limiting date can be found in the poem's assertion that *"Men* of *God* to *Betty B<ewly>* go"; according to Thomas Duffet's *The Empress of Morocco. A Farce,* acted about December 1673, Betty Bewly had then begun "the Trade but newly."[11] "The Argument" may have been written soon after 23 April 1674, though this cannot, of course, be certainly established.

III

The spring of 1676, when Rochester celebrated his twenty-ninth birthday, marks a subtle yet definite change in the direction of his life, as appears even in the lampoons written against him. Generally this was a season of triumph. March 1676 was the month of Rochester's apotheosis as the half-angelic, half-diabolical Dorimant of Etherege's *Man of Mode.* By this date Rochester had produced most of his best poetry, which contemporaries were acclaiming as work of enduring merit. *A Satyr against Mankind* was certainly written by March, and during this winter Rochester challenged Dryden's supremacy by skillfully satirizing the laureate in **"An Allusion to Horace."**

On the other hand, Rochester's career now begins a gradual downward movement. The mood of pessimistic probing which lent tragic maturity to many of Rochester's poems of 1674 and 1675 was deepening into the misanthropy which partly explains his lessening literary activity during his remaining four years of life and which led finally to his dramatic deathbed repentance. In late summer of 1675, probably because he had offended the Duchess of Portsmouth in his "scepter" lampoon on King Charles, Rochester had suffered the prolonged banishment from Court during which he masqueraded as the mountebank Alexander Bendo; this banishment was a period of disillusionment, as his letters reveal.[12] In June 1676, Rochester indirectly caused the death of a companion in the notorious riot at Epsom which his enemies never forgot. Lampoons on Rochester multiplied, and no longer were they *jeux d'esprit* by close friends. While their portrayal of the Earl preserves a continuity with earlier satires, they become increasingly serious and hostile.

Among these lampoons should be listed two of the three surviving verse answers to *A Satyr against Mankind,* even though both poems, the productions of clergymen far removed from the Court scene, are somewhat tangential to the tradition. The better and more widely circulated of the two, beginning "Were I to chuse what sort of Corps I'd wear," is ascribed in independently derived texts to "P," "Dr. P———," and "Dr.

P———ck"; Edward Pococke, the well-known Oxford divine and orientalist, may be intended. Anthony Wood, however, assigns the poem to "one Mr. Griffith a minister." Probably Wood's authority should be preferred, though Pococke's claim cannot be ruled out entirely.[13] The second answer, a cruder effort beginning "Were I a Sp'rit, to chuse for my own share," was written by Thomas Lessey, a fellow of Wadham College, Oxford.[14]

Griffith and Lessey address themselves chiefly to the philosophic issues raised by *A Satyr against Mankind,* but both smuggle in a good deal of *argumentum ad hominem* by insinuating that Rochester's poem was merely an attempt to rationalize his carnal pleasures. Griffith sees Rochester primarily as a voluptuary. After a loaded statement (echoing one of Rochester's lines) that he would not wish to be "Baron Dog, Lord Monkey, or Earl Bear," Griffith decries Rochester's endeavor to "Defend Debaucheries" and make men "drunk and pockey." He pointedly alludes to philosophies ending "In Notions of Venereal Mysteries," to "the madder Taverns lewder stews" of London, and to Court physicians with nothing to do except "compounding Lusts." Nevertheless, Griffith backhandedly compliments Rochester's "Wit, Extravagance and Mode" and numbers him among those "acutest Wits" who "when they're defil'd / Turn most extravagant, prophane and wild."

Lessey plainly has Rochester in mind in the long, rambling, rather silly description of fashionable "Hobbists" which constitutes the second half of his poem. Fortunately, his attitude is epitomized by an earlier short passage which, in the context, must glance at Rochester. This passage, besides illustrating the continuity of the semi-mythic image found in earlier satires, shows the hostile turn which lampoons on Rochester were taking. Notable new features are the references to cowardice, blasphemy, and deceit, as well as the suggestion that Rochester was considered a devil:

> 'Tis guilt alone breeds cow'rdise and distrust,
> For all Men wou'd be Valiant if they durst;
> Those only can't, who swear, and whore, and cheat,
> And sell their *Honour* at the cheapest rate:
> Whom brawling Surfeits, Drunkenness and Claps;
> Hurry on head-long to the *Grave* perhaps:
> Such some call *Devils,* but we think the least,
> And therefore kindly head them with the be<a>st.
> Chuse they themselves whose *Case* they'll please to
>   wear,
> The Case of Dog, the Monkey, or the Bear.

Squarely in the tradition is a satirical song entitled "The Bully" which Thomas D'Urfey wrote for his comedy *The Fool Turn'd Critick,* acted 18 November 1676. Ironically, George Sherburn, believing this song to be Rochester's own composition, recently singled it out as a striking expression of Rochester's "metrically boisterous self";[15] Sherburn's slip perhaps demonstrates the Restoration satirist's ability to trick his readers, even in the twentieth century, into acceptance of a mythic substitute for his victim's real identity. "The Bully" repeats the traditional characterization of Rochester, depicting him as whoremaster, idler, brawler, and coward. It also criticizes the King's continued tolerance toward Rochester's escapades, and it concludes with a prediction (not borne out in the event) concerning the manner of the Earl's death. The poem is reproduced in full from the earliest known text:

> Room, room, room for a man of the Town,
>   that takes delight in roring;
> That daily rambles up and down,
>   and spends his nights in whoring:
> That for the noble name of Spark
>   does his companions rally:
> Commits an out-rage in the dark,
>   then sneaks into an Ally.
>
> To every female that he meets,
>   he swears he bears affection;
> Defies all Laws, arrests, or fears,
>   by help of kind protection.
> Then he, intending further wrongs,
>   by some resenting Cully,
> Is decently run through the Lungs,
>   and there's an end of Bully.[16]

The fifth through the eighth lines of this song appear to be one of several contemporary attacks on Rochester for his part in the brawl at Epsom on the night of 17 June 1676, five months before D'Urfey's song was performed. This episode was discussed in detail in the preceding chapter. . . . D'Urfey's quatrain parallels the Epsom incident: Rochester, for whatever reason, tried to "rally" his companions by drawing his sword, this "out-rage" was committed in the dark, and Rochester immediately absconded.

Students of Rochester were slow to discover that "The Bully" was written by D'Urfey. Hayward and Johns both printed it as Rochester's, while Prinz, though he suspected that the poem alluded to the Epsom affair and might therefore satirize Rochester, did not know its true author. Norman Ault cautiously assigned the poem to "Rochester or D'Urfey." Thorpe, putting the relevant bits of evidence together for the first time, concluded that "The Bully" was "probably" by D'Urfey, and Pinto subsequently omitted it from his edition of Rochester.

D'Urfey's authorship of "The Bully" is scarcely open to question. Though the poem does not appear in the only edition of D'Urfey's comedy, published in 1678, it had previously been printed in *The Last and Best Edition of New Songs,* 1677, as a song "In the Fool turn'd Critick." Any ambiguity in this implied ascription is resolved by D'Urfey's inclusion of the poem in his authoritative *A New Collection of Songs and Poems. By Thomas D'Urfey, Gent.,* 1683, under the heading "The Bully, a Song in the Fool turned Critick." There is no admissible evidence that "The Bully" was written by anyone other than D'Urfey. The poem is unfortunately not extant in the Yale MS., since it was probably part of the material removed by the fifth gap. Its position in the Huntington edition indicates, however, that it came to be printed under Rochester's name only because the scribe of the archetype included it in his section of poems by or concerning Rochester as a satire on the Earl. From the Huntington edition, it was reprinted as Rochester's in the other 1680 editions and in the later editions of 1685 (A-1685), 1701 (A-1701), 1713 (A-1713), and 1731 (A-1731). From one of the 1680 editions, apparently, it was also printed as Rochester's in Benjamin Bragge's *Miscellaneous Works* of Rochester and Roscommon, 1707 (C-1707-a), and later editions in this series (C series). A single manuscript text assigning the poem to Rochester, in Bodl. MS. Rawl. Poet. 173, was probably copied from one of the 1680 editions. Aside from a worthless attribution to "Ephelia" in her *Female Poems,* 1682, no other early texts of "The Bully" carry ascriptions.

The Epsom affair also figures prominently in the passage which Sir Carr Scroope directed against Rochester in his "In defence of Satyr," probably written during the summer of 1676. Since this passage was quoted in full in the preceding chapter, it need not be given again. Scroope reproduces the usual mythic image of Rochester with a few inconspicuous additions and with a mild tone that is characteristic of his writing: Rochester is described as an irresponsible buffoon who is also malicious, scurrilous, treacherous to his friends, debauched, dangerously quarrelsome, and cowardly. Nevertheless, Scroope complains that Rochester is esteemed by the fashionable rakes as the pleasantest, wittiest man in town. After Rochester's scorching retort in "On the suppos'd Authour of a late Poem in defence of Satyr," Scroope's brief "Answer," probably written before the end of 1676, deftly dismisses Rochester as too disreputable, too cowardly, too pox-ridden, and too impotent in his malice to deserve any reply.

While Scroope and D'Urfey were planning their attacks, a far more ambitious verse assault on Rochester was brought to completion in a quiet town in Surrey. Fortunately for literary scholars, the date of *A Satyr against Vertue* can be established with certainty: John Oldham's poetical notebook (Bodl. MS. Rawl. Poet. 123) meticulously records that he composed this poem in "July 1676 at Croydon," where he was teaching school.

Though *A Satyr against Vertue,* like other lampoons considered in this chapter, was printed as Rochester's own composition in 1680, Thorpe is probably wrong in speculating that it was included in the Huntington edition because of an evident connection with Rochester (*Rochester's Poems*, p. 188). If this were true, we should expect to find it in the section of poems by or concerning Rochester; instead, it appears in the section of poems by miscellaneous authors. Evidently the fact that Oldham designed his poem as a satire on Rochester was unknown to the scribe of the archetype, as it was also unknown to the Restoration audience at large. The information was suppressed in all early printed texts of the poem and is, indeed, known today only because of notations in two manuscripts, one of them Oldham's holograph. Opposite the title of the poem, Oldham wrote, "Suppos'd to be spoken by a Court-Hector at Breaking of ye Dial in Privy-Garden." Similarly, B. M. Add. MS. 14047 describes the poem as "Supposed to be spoken by ye Court-Hector who demolised ye sund-Diall." Both notations refer to an escapade which Rochester perpetrated on Friday, 25 June 1675. Bursting into the Privy Garden after a night's revelry, Rochester, Buckhurst, Fleetwood Shepherd, and several other Wits suddenly found themselves confronted by the King's sundial, an elaborate confection of glass spheres arranged in a phallic shape. Seized by a drunken inspiration, Rochester shouted, "What! Dost thou stand here to———time?" and in a moment he had demolished the offending instrument.[17]

Besides being both horrified and fascinated by Rochester's personal life—lurid as it must have seemed from the perspective of Croydon—Oldham secretly admired Rochester's poetry, which at this stage of his career he studied and tried to imitate.[18] The technique of *A Satyr against Vertue* finds its closest analogues among Rochester's satires. Oldham's lampoon specially resembles the ironic structure which Rochester had used to satirize Mulgrave in ***A Very Heroical Epistle in Answer to Ephelia,*** written less than a year earlier; possibly Oldham was imitating this particular poem, though there is no documentary evidence that he was familiar with it. Drawing heavily upon the concepts of *le libertinage*,[19] Oldham depicts Rochester as *persona* arguing for a life of pure sensuality and repudiating all traditional social conventions, moral codes, and religious principles. When this kind of ironic technique is successful, as it is in Rochester's spoof of Mulgrave, the *persona* appears ridiculous by his implicit violation of the shared values of the contemporary audience. Regrettably, *A Satyr against Vertue* misses full effectiveness, partly because it tends to be pedantic, partly because Oldham lacked the requisite light touch, and partly because of his besetting sin of never saying in one line what he could say in two. Oldham succeeds, however, at one point where all other satirists failed: he endows the mythic image of Rochester with some of the stature which the man possessed in real life. The ironic technique of Oldham's long lampoon is well illustrated by the first of its twelve sections:

> Now curses on ye all, ye virtuous *Fools,*
> Who think to fetter free born *Souls,*
> And tye 'em up to dull *Morality,* and *Rules.*
> The *Stagyrite,* be damn'd, and all the Crew,
> Of learned *Idiots,* who his steps pursue;
> And those more silly *Proselites,* whom his fond
> Precepts drew!
> Oh had his *Ethicks,* been with their <vile> *Author*
> drown'd
> Or a like fate, with those lost Writings found,
> Which that grand *Plagiary,* doom'd to *Fire,*
> And made by unjust *Flames* expire,
> They ne're had then seduc'd *Mortality,*
> Ne're lasted to debauch the *World,* with their lewd
> *Pedantry.*
> But damn'd and more (if *Hell* can do't) be that Thrice
> cursed name,
> Who e're the rudiments of Law design'd;
> Who e're did the First *Model* of *Religion,* frame,
> And by that double *Vassalage* enthrall'd *Mankind;*
> By nought before, but their own Pow'r, or will
> confin'd:
> Now quite abridg'd of all their Primitive liberty.
> And *Slaves,* to each capricious *Monarchs,* Tyranny.
> More happy *Brutes*! who the great Rule of sense
> observe,
> And ne're from their First Charter swerve.
> Happy whose lives are meerly to enjoy,
> And feel no stings of Sin, which may their Bliss
> annoy;
> Still unconcern'd, at *Epithets* of ill, or good,
> Distinctions unadult'rate *Nature,* never understood.[20]

In succeeding sections of the poem, "Rochester" envies the legendary exploits of such sinners as Nero, Guy Fawkes, and Satan.

Since the *persona* of *A Satyr against Vertue* represents Rochester, it is difficult to read Oldham's "Apology" for his lampoon without peculiar reference to the Earl. Speaking now in his own person, Oldham seemingly contrasts his poetical morality with Rochester's:

> Our *Poet,* has a diff'rent taste of Wit,
> Nor will to th' common Vogue, himself submit.
> Let some admire the *Fops,* whose Talents lye,
> In venting dull insipid *Blasphemy*; . . .
> Wits name, was never to profaness due,
> For then you see, he cou'd be witty too:
> He cou'd *Lampoon* the *State,* and *Libel Kings,*
> But that he's *Loyal,* and knows better things,
> Than *Fame,* whose guilty *Birth* from *Treason*
> springs. . . .
> He cou'd be *Baudy* toe, and nick the times,
> In what they dearly love, damn'd *Placket* Rhymes
> Such as our *Nobles* write———
> Whose nauseous *Poetry,* can reach no higher,
> Than what the *Cod-peice,* or its *God* inspire:
> So lewd they spend at Quill, you'd justly think,
> They wrote with something nastier than Ink.
>
> (A-1680-HU, pp. 127, 128)

The phrase *"Libel Kings"* may allude to Rochester's "scepter" lampoon on Charles II, which was probably written during the preceding summer.

A fact little known to students of Rochester is that more than a year after *A Satyr against Vertue,* Oldham again used the Earl as *persona* in a long ironical satire in pindarics. This satire was first published in Oldham's *Poems, and Translations,* 1683, as "A Dithyrambick. The Drunkards Speech in a Mask" (p. 206). As with *A Satyr against Vertue,* the early printed texts suppress any indication that the poem satirizes Rochester. According to Oldham's notebook, however, where it is headed "A Dithyrambique on Drinking" and includes some lines lacking in the printed version, this poem is "Suppos'd to be Spoken by Rochester at ye Guinny Club" (p. 206). The printed version states that "A Dithyrambick" was "Written in Aug. 1677"; the holograph text dates it more precisely "Aug. 5. 1677." As an ironic defence of drunkenness, "A Dithyrambick" has less range than *A Satyr against Vertue* and is therefore markedly inferior. Since its technique is otherwise identical with that of *A Satyr against Vertue,* illustrative quotations would be superfluous.[21]

IV

After the concentrated satirical bombardment of Rochester between spring of 1676 and autumn of 1677, an unexplained two-year armistice set in until late 1679. Dryden's preface to *All for Love* was published in March 1678, but this attack is not in verse, and it owes little to the image of Rochester in the verse satires. Hostilities were resumed with Mulgrave's passage on Rochester in "An Essay upon Satyr," a copy of which was in Rochester's hands on 21 November 1679 (Wilson, *Rochester-Savile Letters,* p. 73). Familiar though this long passage is, it should be given in full to illustrate its continuity with the tradition:

> Roches<te>r I despise for his meer want of wit,
> Though thought to have a Tail and Cloven Feet;
> For while he mischief means to all mankind,
> Himself alone the ill effects does find;
> And so like Witches justly suffers shame,
> Whose harmless malice is so much the same;
> False are his words, affected is his wit,
> So often he does aim, so seldom hit;
> To every face he cringes while he speaks,
> But when the Back is turn'd the head he breaks;
> Mean in each Action, lewd in every Limb,
> Manners·themselves are mischievous in him:
> A proof that chance alone makes every Creature,
> A very *Killig<re>w* without good Nature;
> For what a *Bessus* has he always liv'd,
> And his own *Kickings* notably contriv'd:
> (For there's the folly that's still mixt with fear)
> Cowards more blows than any Heroe bear;
> Of fighting sparks some may her pleasures say,
> But 'tis a bolder thing to run away:
> The World may well forgive him all his ill,
> For ev'ry fault does prove his penance still;
> Falsly he falls into some dangerous Noose,
> And then as meanly labours to get loose;
> A life so infamous is better quitting,

> Spent in base injury and low submitting:
> I'd like to have left out his Poetry;
> Forgot by all almost as well as me.
> Sometimes he has some humour, never wit,
> And if it rarely, very rarely hit:
> 'Tis under so much nasty rubbish laid,
> To find it out's the Cinder-womans trade;
> Who for the wretched remnants of a fire,
> Must toil all day in ashes and in mire;
> So lewdly dull his idle works appear,
> The wretched Texts deserve no Comments here;
> Where one poor thought sometimes left all alone,
> For a whole page of dulness to attone:
> 'Mongst forty bad, one tolerable line,
> Without expression, fancy, or design.[22]

Virtually every feature of this portrait, even the suggestion that Rochester was a devil, had appeared in earlier lampoons. Nevertheless, Mulgrave has arranged his inherited material so as to emphasize three alleged aspects of Rochester's character: (1) impotent malice, chiefly flattery as preparation for attempted treachery; (2) cowardice; (3) poor obscene poetry. Doubtless these three emphases were adopted partly to give coherence to the portrait, but it is interesting that each had a possible source in Mulgrave's personal experiences with Rochester. Since he cherished literary aspirations despite his limited talent, Mulgrave had reason to depreciate the poetry of an overpowering rival. Moreover, since Rochester was directly or indirectly responsible for attacks on Mulgrave in a multitude of lampoons, Mulgrave might well think it advantageous to accuse his adversary of malice, especially ineffectual malice. The charge of cowardice may allude to the brawl at Epsom, but it probably refers also to Rochester's behavior when Mulgrave challenged him to a duel in November 1669.

Similar in tone to Mulgrave's passage, though less artful, is a lengthy attack on Rochester in a Tory lampoon of unknown authorship written about two months later. This poem, which the manuscript text quoted below describes as "A Satyr ag^t. L^d. Roch. & Petitionings 1679/80," has hitherto escaped identification as a satire on Rochester. The date supplied in the manuscript is remarkably accurate, for internal evidence indicates that this lampoon was probably composed in January 1679/80. Both its title and its text mention Whig "Petitionings" for an early meeting of Parliament, a political maneuver which Shaftesbury initiated about December 1679 and brought to a climax the following month. Moreover, since the lampoon exhorts the King to "Call home thy banish'd brother," it could scarcely have been written after 28 January, when Charles announced in Council that he was recalling James from Scotland. The passage on Rochester constitutes the first half of the poem:

> Amongst the Race of England's modern Peers,
> There's one whose looks, betray his lewder Years.
> Whome early Nature for all Ill did frame,

And time increas'd not faster than his Fame.
Unheard of vices were his studied care,
The effects of which his rotten ruins wear.
His sight's a terror to the boldest Punk,
Who shunn's him more y^n. Pembroke, when hee's
    drunk.
But tho' to Pox, & Impotence confin'd,
His bodye's less corrupted then his Mind.
Both Politick, & Heroe hee'd be thought,
But Jamese's ruine has his Judgement bought,
And Epsom Hedg can wittness how he fought.
To a Soul so mean ev'n Shadwell is a stranger,
Nay little Sid: (it seems) less values danger.
(The most hen-heart-d wretches of the Age,
Who ne're durst give offence but on y^e stage,)
But on such trash my time is ill bestow'd,
Those Hackney Cowards in the comon Road.
The man whose Caracter I would relate,
From Infamy refin'd derives his Fate.
As France can tell where he the broyl begann,
Engaged his freind, & then away he ran.
This is that worship'd Idoll who w$^{th's}$ Pen,
Detracts the best of Monarchs, best of Men.
Whose Libells wholly tend to move sedition,
(Like those good men who now adays petition.)
Falshood & knavery do his Moralls guide,
(A stain to Honor, & a slave to Pride.)
Yett courts & flatters you in ev'ry place
And all the while's designing y^r disgrace
The most Fantastick of all fools 'ith' Nation,
Industrious onely to be out of fashion.[23]

Despite the information in the heading of this lampoon, the passage may not at first look much like a description of Rochester, which is perhaps the reason why its subject has remained unidentified. Every detail is explicable as a reference to Rochester, however, and it is doubtful that any other contemporary nobleman could fill the specifications so well. Generally the portrait incorporates the features we have observed in earlier lampoons. Its subject is described as malicious, sycophantic, treacherous, cowardly, impotent, sexually perverted, and disfigured by venereal disease. He has written poetry, including at least one satire on King Charles—probably Rochester's "scepter" lampoon. He is admittedly a "worship'd Idoll," as Rochester was among such friends as Shadwell and Sedley ("little Sid," the nickname used also in "An Essay upon Satyr"). Possibly derived from Mulgrave's passage is the picture of this nobleman as a decayed gallant whose formerly fashionable manners now make him a parody of the true gentleman. Positive identification is afforded by the accusation that "Epsom Hedg can wittness how he fought": Rochester was the only peer who participated in the brawl at Epsom.

Other features of the portrait are more difficult. So far as is known, no single incident in Rochester's career fully satisfies the allegation that

. . . France can tell where he the broyl begann,
Engaged his freind, & then away he ran.

Most details in this couplet could refer to the Epsom affair: Rochester recommended that "broyl" by drawing his sword, thereby fatally engaging his friend Downs, after which he ran away. But why "France"? Possibly the unknown satirist has tried to impose the circumstances of the Epsom brawl upon an earlier altercation in Paris which achieved international notoriety at the time, though Rochester's part in it was secondary. At the Paris opera in late June 1669, as Rochester was sitting on the stage with William Lord Cavendish (later Earl and Duke of Devonshire), one of a group of drunken French officers began to insult Cavendish, who thereupon struck the Frenchman in the face. Swords were quickly out of their sheaths, and Cavendish, badly outnumbered, found himself backed against the side scenes with several dangerous wounds. He was saved by a Swiss servant of Ralph Montagu (the English ambassador), who seized him and threw him into the pit. Rochester's actions during this melee are less fully recorded (he may have been slightly wounded while attempting to aid his companion), but the episode was widely remembered to Cavendish's credit.[24]

Equally problematic, but far more important, is the charge that Rochester was a moving spirit in the Whig campaign to exclude the Duke of York from the royal succession. This information, if true, would be highly significant. Throughout most of his life, Rochester seems to have avoided the quarrels of political parties. To be sure, there is no evidence that he ever broke off his close friendships with prominent Whigs like Dorset and Buckingham. Also, parliamentary records provide some support for the accusation in the lampoon: during 1679, Rochester voted consistently with the Whig leaders.[25] That Rochester helped to *lead* the fight for exclusion is, however, difficult to accept; such action on his part would inevitably be documented in numerous contemporary sources besides the lampoon. Possibly its Tory author, gambling that his readers would consider Rochester totally disreputable, hoped to convict the entire Whig party of guilt by association.

The two portraits just discussed are the work of an unimaginative prig and a party hack, but one may wonder whether their forbidding picture of Rochester as a superannuated debauchee was entirely the result of personal and political enmity. Rochester had little more than six months to live; by this time, his protracted devotion to Bacchus and Venus, attractive enough ten years before, may have left visibly repellent marks on the aging thirty-two-year-old libertine.

Apart from a possible allusion to Rochester as "*Lord Lampoon* and *Monsieur Song*" in Otway's *The Poet's Complaint of his Muse,* published about 22 January 1679/80,[26] no other satires on Rochester are known to have been written during his lifetime. His name turns up occasionally in lampoons composed after his death on 26 July 1680, but such references are better considered an aspect of his posthumous reputation and therefore find no place in this discussion.

V

A significant conclusion should emerge from the foregoing quotations of lampoons on Rochester: though the satirists created a consistent cartoon portrait of the Earl which developed discernibly over the years, it never approached the success of their characterizations of other Restoration figures like Mulgrave and Scroope. One aim of the satirists' rhetorical strategy was to persuade the reader to substitute their mythic image for the real person. Thus a measure of their failure with Rochester is that the man remains more fascinating than the myth.

Some understanding of the satirists' plight may be gleaned from Dryden's prose attack on the Earl in the preface to *All for Love,* which can scarcely be ignored in this chapter. Though Dryden's partisans have doubtless felt obliged to defend it, his passage on Rochester suffers by comparison either with **"An Allusion to Horace,"** which it answers, or with Dryden's own brilliant mythic portrayal of Shadwell in *Mac Flecknoe,* written about this same date. Whatever the root cause of Dryden's difficulty, one reason why Rochester's attack on the laureate is so convincing is that it mingles praise with its censure, whereas Dryden allows his opponent nothing. With ingratiating generosity (real or feigned), Rochester concedes Dryden's merits as a poet:

> But to be just, 'twill to his praise be found,
> His *Excellencies* more than faults abound
> Nor dare I from his sacred Temples tear,
> That *Lawrel,* which he best deserves to wear.

(A-1680-HU, p. 43)

By contrast, Dryden's description of Rochester, "this Rhyming Judge of the Twelve-penny Gallery, this Legitimate Son of *Sternhold*" who allegedly cannot write his own name,[27] is so patently unfair that the objective reader could not accept it in imagination or as fact, especially if **"An Allusion to Horace"** lies open before him as implicit testimony against Dryden's accusations.

Various reasons may explain why Dryden and the verse satirists had such trouble creating a serviceable mythic image of Rochester. Twentieth-century readers forget too readily the commanding advantages which Rochester possessed over most of his opponents. Besides *scandalum magnatum,* not a risk to be taken lightly by a commoner, Rochester's position as literary dictator and arbiter of fashion was formidable, nor did he hesitate to crush an opposing satirist with the satirist's own weapons, if he thought the man worth the trouble. Possibly the danger of legal reprisal led Dryden, after

meditating his attack a full two years, to portray Rochester's character in a form distorted almost beyond recognition. Similar fears may have cramped the creative urges of some of the verse satirists.

Along other lines, the satirists may have found an obstacle imposed by the origin of their mythic image of Rochester, which apparently began its existence among his cronies as a form of joshing. Once established, the clichés of this flippant characterization would be difficult to alter. Altered and developed they must be, however, if a hostile satirist expected his serious image of Rochester to carry conviction with an audience.

Even if these two causes were not operative, Restoration satirists would still have faced a severe challenge, for Rochester's real-life personality, especially as viewed by friendly observers, embodied unique qualities which only a very gifted writer could incorporate successfully into a satirical portrait. Most of the lampoons (D'Urfey's lyric, for example) tend to portray Rochester as little more than an ordinary rakehell who happened to be a peer—a mere bully like Philip Herbert, Earl of Pembroke, to whom Rochester is compared in the Tory tirade at the end of the preceding section of this chapter. Such a characterization impales the satirist on the horns of a dilemma: if Rochester is so insignificant, why bother to attack him? Only two poets apparently recognized the problem and took measures to solve it. Oldham, we have seen, tried to invest his mythic image of Rochester with some of the man's actual stature. Scroope took an opposite tack by denying, in a tone of sweet reasonableness, that Rochester possessed this stature. His epigrammatic "Answer" to Rochester's abuse of him beautifully illustrates his strategy:

> Raile on poore feeble *Scribler,* speak of me,
> In as bad Terms, as the *World* speaks of thee.
> Sit swelling in thy Hole, like a vext *Toad,*
> And full of *Pox,* and *Malice,* spit abroad.
> Thou can'st <blast> no *Mans Fame,* with thy ill word,
> Thy Pen, is full as harmless as thy Sword.[28]

Frustrating target that Rochester must have been for his fellow satirists, their final humiliation is that none of them equaled the skill of a brief poem in which he apparently satirized himself. In sixteen dramatically compressed lines, this poem presents a fictitious dialogue between Rochester and a postboy:

[ROCHESTER]

> Son of A whore God dam you can you tell
> A Peerless Peer the Readyest way to Hell
> Ive out swilld Baccus sworn of my own make
> Oaths wod fright furies & make Pluto quake
> Ive swived more whores more ways y[n] Sodoms
>   walls
> Ere knew or the College of Romes Cardinalls

Witness Heroick scars, look here nere go
sear cloaths & ulcers from ye top to toe
frighted at my own mischeifes I have fled
and bravely left my lifes defender dead
Broke houses to break chastity & died
that floor with murder which my lust denyed
Pox on it why do I speak of these poor things
I have blasphemed my god & libelld Kings
the readyest way to Hell come quick

BOY

                                    nere stirr
The readyest way my Lords by Rochester[29]

Though several early texts assign the poem to 1674, this date can scarcely be correct, for the ninth and tenth lines almost certainly allude to the Epsom affair of 17 June 1676. While his "lifes defender," Downs, tried to quell the "mischeifes" which Rochester had set in motion by drawing his sword upon the constable, the "frighted" Rochester not very bravely fled, leaving Downs "dead" or at least mortally injured. This identification is further supported by marginal notations in three manuscripts: in Victoria and Albert Museum MS. Dyce 43, "lifes defender" is glossed as "Downs," in Vienna MS. 14090 as "Cap. Downs," and in B. M. Harl. MS. 6914 as "[C]aptn [D]owns" (with the initial letters of both words removed by trimming of the leaf). Moreover, the succeeding couplet of the poem may be a lurid exaggeration of the portion of this episode in which Rochester and his companions, searching for a whore, broke into the constable's house and beat him. Since the verses to the postboy describe Downs as "dead," they were probably written after he finally succumbed on 27 June. Probably, too, they were not written much later, for they evidently figure in "In defence of Satyr" as the "*Buffoone* Conceit" with which (so Scroope alleges) Rochester attempted to shrug off his responsibility in the Epsom imbroglio. Very late June or early July 1676 seems the likeliest date for these verses, which, if Rochester wrote them, are surely one of the strangest acts of contrition on record.

The poem to the postboy has a curious textual history. Though it circulated in manuscript among Rochester's contemporaries, no portion of the poem reached print until 1926, nor has any twentieth-century editor of Rochester accorded it an unqualified status in the canon; indeed, its text has never before been published in full. Hayward and Prinz both printed only the first six lines, Hayward in the introduction to his edition and Prinz, using a different text, in his *Rochesteriana*. Subsequently, in an article, John Harold Wilson claimed the poem for Rochester but printed a version which lacks two lines. Pinto, adopting Wilson's version for his edition, nevertheless consigned it to his appendix of doubtful poems.[30]

These disagreements concerning the poem's authenticity may be due to titles in some early texts which could imply either that Rochester wrote the poem or that it was composed by some unnamed author as a lampoon on the Earl. Examples of these ambiguous titles are "Earle of Rochester's Conference with a Post Boy" and "Roch: to a Post boy." Other headings, however, seem to identify Rochester as author—for instance, "To the Post Boy by L^d: Rochester" and "Verses to y^e. Post-boy by Roch^r." Also, two texts drop the last word of the poem ("Rochester") below the line, apparently to make it serve as an ascription. There is no clear evidence that Rochester did not write the poem, nor is there any ascription to another author. Considerations of style further strengthen the case for Rochester's authorship: few poets writing in 1676 had such a flair for the dramatic or could reproduce Rochester's distinctive heroic-couplet manner so well. One can hardly quarrel with Wilson's judgment:

> Although it seems incredible that a poet could write so viciously of himself, I am persuaded that Rochester did so write. The poem is clearly his style of rough, vigorous verse, and his sense of irony was perfectly capable of such an attitude.

Pinto's inference that the poem is a kind of tape-recording of an actual episode—he printed it as an impromptu—scarcely merits serious attention. Experiences in real life do not occur in finished heroic couplets and perfect dramatic form, nor would postboys ordinarily be so clever.

An astonishing feature of these half-boastful, half-penitential verses is that Rochester is working in the tradition propagated by the lampoons written against him. Indeed, he composed his lines during a period when hostile lampoons were specially numerous. Rochester's poem focuses upon the Epsom affair, the incident most frequently cited to his disfavor by his enemies. He had "libelld Kings" in his "scepter" lampoon, mentioned by several satirists, and he possibly "blasphemed my god" in **"A Satyr against Mankind,"** which called forth such lengthy disquisitions from Griffith and Lessey. Almost every detail of the familiar mythic image is here, slightly exaggerated: Rochester depicts himself as blasphemer, drunkard, brawler, bully (even a murderer), coward, whoremaster, and sexual degenerate covered with sores from venereal disease. Rochester succeeds, however, in transcending the limitations inherent in the traditional image of himself. Following much the same line adopted by Oldham, but far more effectively, Rochester infuses his self-portrait with almost Satanic energy and grandeur. The result gives the electrifying impression of being simultaneously in contact with both myth and reality. It is as if Rochester turned to his brother satirists with a mocking smile, saying, "Look! This is how it should be done!"

Notes

1. For a stimulating discussion of these earlier traditions, see Alvin Kernan, *The Cankered Muse:*

Satire of the English Renaissance (New Haven, Yale Univ. Press, 1959).

2. Some of the points raised in this paragraph are developed in other directions by T. S. Eliot in his fine essay "The Music of Poetry," in *On Poetry and Poets* (London, Faber and Faber, 1957), pp. 26-38.

3. Aubrey L. Williams, *Pope's Dunciad: A Study of its Meaning* (Baton Rouge, Louisiana State Univ. Press, 1955), pp. 5, 60-86.

4. The text is that of A-1680-HU, p. 59, with two emended readings taken from Bodl. MS. Rawl. Poet. 152 and Edinburgh MS. DC.1.3. In l. 9 A-1680-HU reads "There" for "Then," and in l. 10 it omits "fast." See Part III for detailed lists of the early texts and ascriptions of most of the poems discussed in this chapter.

5. See Part III for documentation of the previous scholarship on most of the poems discussed in this chapter.

6. L. S. A. M. v. Römer, *Rochester's Sodom Herausgegeben nach dem Hamburger Manuscript* (Paris, H. Welter, 1904), p. xx.

7. Huntington MS. HA 12525. See Lucyle Hook, "Something More About Rochester," *Modern Language Notes, 75* (1960), 478-85.

8. The text is that of A-1680-HU, p. 55, except that indention is introduced to emphasize the rhyme scheme, and the eight four-line stanzas of the copy-text are combined into four stanzas of eight lines each.

9. Dryden is supposed to have said of *Mac Flecknoe* that it was "the first piece of ridicule written in Heroics" (Joseph Spence, *Anecdotes,* ed. Samuel Weller Singer, London, 1820, p. 60). Though not strictly accurate, Dryden's remark underscores the novelty of the mock-heroic satire in "The Argument."

10. William A. Shaw, *The Knights of England* (London, Sherratt and Hughes, 1906), *1,* 37.

11. *The Empress of Morocco. A Farce,* 1674, p. 34. In this chapter, all dates of dramatic performances and publication of plays are taken from Nicoll, *Restoration Drama.*

12. For the circumstances surrounding the "scepter" lampoon, see my article, "Rochester's 'Scepter' Lampoon on Charles II," *Philological Quarterly, 37* (1958), 424-32. See also *The Famous Pathologist or The Noble Mountebank by Thomas Alcock and John Wilmot, Earl of Rochester,* ed. Vivian de Sola Pinto, Nottingham University Miscellany No. 1 (Nottingham, Sisson and Parker, 1961).

13. The poem appears without ascription in the Yale MS., p. 22; Taylor MS. 3, p. 222; Harvard MS. Eng. 623F, p. 20; B. M. Harl. MS. 6207, fol. 66ʳ; Bodl. MS. Don. b. 8, p. 564; Edinburgh MS. DC.1.3, p. 27; and the undated folio leaflet *An Answer to the Satyr against Mankind,* which was published, according to Anthony Wood, in July 1679 (*Athenae Oxonienses, 3,* 1229).

The poem is ascribed to "a Countrey Parson" in Cambridge MS. Add. 6339, fol. 17ʳ, and to "P" in Harvard MS. Eng. 636F, p. 91. It is assigned to "Dr. P———" in *Poems on Affairs of State,* 1699 (Case 211-1-d), p. ²254, and reprinted with this ascription in 1702 (Case 211-1-e), p. ²254; 1703 (Case 211-1-f), p. ²254; 1710 (Case 211-1-g), p. ²254; 1716 (Case 211-1-h), p. ²254; and *A New Collection of Poems Relating to State Affairs,* 1705 (Case 237), p. 267. Evidently one of these volumes is the source of Giles Jacob's ascription to "Dr. P———" (*Poetical Register, 2,* 236). The poem is attributed to "Dr. P———ck" in *Poems on Affairs of State,* 1703 (Case 211-2-a), p. 432, reprinted with the same ascription in 1703 (Case 211-2-b), p. 432, and reissued in 1716 (Case 211-2-c), p. 432.

Wood, as noted in the text above, attributes the poem to "one Mr. Griffith a minister" (*3,* 1229). Horace Walpole also assigns it to Griffith but cites Wood as his source (*Catalogue of Royal and Noble Authors, 2,* 39). The poem is ascribed to "the Reverend Mr. Griffith" in Tonson's edition of 1714 (B-1714), p. 59, and reprinted with this ascription in 1732 (B-1732), p. 59. Tonson's ascription may derive from Wood; his text was printed from the folio leaflet of 1679 with a few readings corrected from some other source, possibly *Poems on Affairs of State,* 1699, or a later edition of this miscellany.

My quotations from the poem in the next paragraph are taken from *Poems on Affairs of State,* 1699.

14. Lessey's poem is ascribed to him in *Poetical Recreations,* 1688 (Case 186), p. ²67; B. M. Sloane MS. 1458, fol. 43ʳ; and B. M. Harl. MS. 6207, fol. 60ʳ. The printed version, from which my quotation in the next paragraph is taken, lacks two long passages preserved in the manuscripts.

The third answer to "A Satyr against Mankind," beginning "Were I a Spirit free (which Thought's as Vain,") contains no personal allusions to Rochester. It is printed without ascription in *Corinna; or, Humane Frailty. A Poem. With an Answer to the E. of R———'s Satyr against Man,* 1699, p. 17.

15. *A Literary History of England,* ed. Albert C. Baugh (New York and London, Appleton-Century-Crofts, 1948), p. 743.

16. *The Last and Best Edition of New Songs,* 1677 (Case 163), sig. A2ᵛ.

17. HMC, *Laing, 1,* 405. John Aubrey, *Brief Lives,* ed. Andrew Clark (Oxford, Clarendon Press, 1898), *2,* 34. *The Poems and Letters of Andrew Marvell,* ed. H. M. Margoliouth (Oxford, Clarendon Press, 1927), *1,* 190. Arthur Bryant, *King Charles II* (London, New York, and Toronto, Longmans, Green, 1932), p. 260. Wilson, *Court Wits,* pp. 37-38. The inventor of the sundial, Francis Hall (or Francis Line, or Franciscus Linus), published *An Explication of the Diall Sett up in the Kings Garden at London, an. 1669,* Liège, 1673; a drawing of the dial is included as a fold-out frontispiece.

18. In an undated satirical fragment in his notebook, Oldham apparently calls Rochester "our great witty bawdy Peer" (p. 225).

19. This aspect of Oldham's poem is discussed by Dale Underwood, *Etherege and the Seventeenth-Century Comedy of Manners* (New Haven, Yale Univ. Press, 1957), pp. 10 ff.

20. A-1680-HU, p. 115. "Vile" in l. 7, the reading of Oldham's holograph draft, has been substituted for "wild."

21. Passages on Rochester occur in two more lampoons written about this date. One passage is not itself satirical, while the other is of slight importance.

The authorship of "Advice to Apollo" ("I've heard the Muses were still soft and kind") is unknown, but its attitudes suggest an origin in Rochester's circle of Wits. Though many early texts assign it to 1678, internal evidence shows that "Advice to Apollo" was composed during Dryden's "retirement" from the stage between the production of *Aureng-Zebe* (17 Nov. 1675) and that of *All for Love* (12 Dec. 1677). As Wilson conjectured, the poem may have been a joint effort by the group of Rochester's cronies who assembled at Woodstock in autumn of 1677 (*Court Wits,* p. 195). "Advice to Apollo" is a satire against satires in which Rochester is praised for writing love poems:

> *Rochester*'s easie Muse does still improve,
> Each hour thy little wealthy World of Love,
> (That World in which each Muse is thought a Queen)
> That he must be forgiven in charity then;
> Though his sharp Satyrs have offended thee;
> In charity to Love who will decay,
> When his delightfull Muse (its only stay)
> Is by thy Power severely ta'ne away.

> Forbear (then) Civil Wars, and strike not down
> Love, who alone supports thy tottering Crown.

> (*Poems on Affairs of State,* 1697 [Case 211-1-a], p. ¹212)

The other passage, written sometime during the middle 1670s, is found in James Carkesse's *Lucida Intervalla,* 1679 (p. 51), a collection of verses purportedly composed by an inmate of Bedlam. Carkesse whimsically predicts that he will soon be welcoming various authors of lampoons:

> *Bucks* both and *Rochester,* unless they mend,
> Hither the *King* designs forthwith to send:
> *Shepherd* and *Dreyden* too, must on 'em wait;
> For he's resolved at once to rid the State,
> Of this *Poetick, Wanton, Mad-like* Tribe,
> Whose *Rampant Muse* does *Court* and *City* Gibe.

For information on Carkesse, see Hugh Macdonald, "The Attacks on Dryden," *Essays and Studies by Members of the English Association,* 21 (1936), 41-74.

22. *The Fourth (and Last) Collection of Poems, Satyrs, Songs, & c.,* 1689 (Case 189-4), p. 31.

23. B. M. Add. MS. 23722, fol. 73ʳ. The lampoon also appears in Folger MS. M. b. 12, fol. 2ʳ; B. M. Sloane MS. 655, fol. 8ʳ; Victoria and Albert Museum MS. Dyce 43, p. 8; Edinburgh MS. DC.1.3, p. 25; Vienna MS. 14090, fol. 10ᵛ; and *Poems on Affairs of State,* 1704 (Case 211-3-a), p. 144, reprinted 1716 (Case 211-3-b), p. 128. None of these texts carries an ascription. The Folger, Dyce, and Vienna manuscripts may all be in the same handwriting.

The Tory lampoon was followed by "An Answer to the former Satyr" ("Amongst the writeing race of Modern Witts"), whose unknown Whig author was so intent on echoing his opponent's phraseology that his passage on Rochester fails to offer anything new. Because of his wobbly irony, not even his real attitude toward Rochester is clear:

> The first whose Character he would relate,
> For want of Witt, & Fashion finds his Fate.
> Theres not so false, so in famous a Thing,
> So lew'd a Wretch ith' Court (God bless the King)
> To Pox, & Impotence as much confin'd,
> As little Politick, & no more refind.
> In's heart the Honor, & in's Bones the dryness,
> Just such a Heroe is his Royall Highness,
> Had this dull wretch but his deserved fall,
> Witt then and truth might flourish at Whitehall.

The quotation is from B. M. Add. MS. 23722, fol. 74ʳ. The poem is printed in *Poems on Affairs of State,* 1704 (Case 211-3-a), p. 147.

24. HMC, *Sixth Report,* p. 366; *Buccleuch and Queensberry, 1,* 429-30. Sir William Temple, *Letters,* ed. Jonathan Swift, 1700, *2,* 70-71. Grove,

The Lives of All the Earls and Dukes of Devonshire, 1764, pp. 31-32. Francis Bickley, *The Cavendish Family* (London, Constable, 1911), pp. 150-51.

25. *Journals of the House of Lords, 13,* 565, 587, 594.

26. *The Works of Thomas Otway,* ed. J. C. Ghosh (Oxford, Clarendon Press, 1932), 2, 412. *Narcissus Luttrell's Popish Plot Catalogues,* intro. by F. C. Francis (Oxford, Basil Blackwell, 1956), p. [2]18. Otway's poem was advertised in the *Term Catalogues* in February 1679/80.

27. *All for Love: or, The World well Lost,* 1678, sigs. b3^v-b4^v.

28. A-1680-HU, p. 50. Since "blast" in l. 5 is the reading of all early manuscripts including the Yale MS., the reading of A-1680-HU, "hurt," must be a corruption.

29. The text is that of B. M. Harl. MS. 6914, fol. 21^r, with the following alterations: the heading, "To the Post Boy by L^d: Rochester 1674," is omitted, as is the marginal gloss opposite ll. 9-10; l. 15 is divided to signify the change of speakers; and the marginal note "Boy" is placed at l. 15 instead of l. 16.

The poem is headed "Verses to the Post Boy" in Victoria and Albert Museum MS. Dyce 43, p. 241, and "To y^e. Post Boy" in Vienna MS. 14090, fol. 128^r, where the table of contents lists it as "Verses to y^e. Post-boy by Roch^r." Both of these manuscripts, which are probably in the same handwriting, drop the last word of the poem ("Rochester") below the line, evidently to make it serve as an ascription. The poem is headed "E: of Rochesters Conference With a Post Boy. 1674" in Bodl. MS. Firth C. 15, p. 15; "Earle of Rochester's Conference with a Post Boy. 1674" in the Ohio MS., p. 16 (the Wilson-Pinto text); and "Earle of Rochesters Conference with a Post Boy" in Taylor MS. 2, p. 8. These three manuscripts are almost certainly in the same handwriting. Taylor MS. 3, p. 254, gives the poem as "Roch: to a Post boy," and it appears as "To A Postboy: E: of R." in an uncatalogued manuscript at the University of Illinois.

Prinz published the first six lines of the poem as "Spoken to a Postboy, 1674" and described them as "Extempore to a Post-boy, reproduced from an old manuscript entry in vol. I of my copy of The Poetical Works of the Earls of Rochester, Roscomon, Dorset, etc. London, 1739" (*Rochesteriana: Being Some Anecdotes Concerning John Wilmot Earl of Rochester,* Leipzig, privately printed, 1926, pp. 9, 56). Hayward printed the same six lines and said of them: "These lines,

spoken extempore, to a Post-boy, are attributed to him [Rochester] in a MS. commonplace book, and dated 1674" (*Collected Works,* p. xlix). Hayward does not identify his commonplace book.

30. Wilson, "Rochester's 'Buffoon Conceit,'" *Modern Language Notes, 56* (1941), 372-73. Pinto, *Poems,* p. 147.

Works Cited

Because the titles of Rochester editions are inadequate for precise identification, some form of bibliographical notation is essential. The following scheme, which has proved practicable in informal use, will be cited when necessary in subsequent chapters. All early editions of Rochester belong either to one of three major series, which began publication in 1680, 1691, and 1707, or to a single minor series beginning in 1718. These four series will be designated A, B, C, and D respectively. Within each series, individual editions are ordinarily designated by the dates of their imprints. Except for the 1680 editions, which are more complicated, different editions appearing in the same series in the same year are designated a, b, c in order of their publication. If an edition is in more than one volume, a volume number may be indicated by an arabic numeral. Thus the first volume of the second of two editions published in the C series in 1721 becomes C-1721-b-1. Piracies are designated by the letter P. Unlike systems based upon a consecutive numbering, this scheme will usually allow newly discovered editions to be integrated smoothly into their proper series. Also, it is compatible with Thorpe's set of symbols for the 1680 editions. Thus the Huntington edition becomes A-1680-HU, while the two known copies of this edition become A-1680-HU-HU and A-1680-HU-PE.

Works Cited by Cue Titles

Athenae Oxonienses and *Fasti Oxonienses*: Anthony à Wood, *Athenae Oxonienses. . . . To Which Are Added The Fasti,* ed. Philip Bliss, London, F. C. and J. Rivington, 1813-20.

Case: Arthur E. Case, *A Bibliography of English Poetical Miscellanies 1521-1750,* Oxford, The Bibliographical Society, 1935.

Catalogue of Royal and Noble Authors: Horace Walpole, *A Catalogue of the Royal and Noble Authors of England,* Strawberry Hill, 1758.

Collected Works: *Collected Works of John Wilmot, Earl of Rochester,* ed. John Hayward, London, Nonesuch Press, 1926.

Court Wits: John Harold Wilson, *The Court Wits of the Restoration,* Princeton Univ. Press, 1948.

CSPD: *Calendar of State Papers, Domestic Series.*

CTB: *Calendar of Treasury Books.*

Day and Murrie: Cyrus Lawrence Day and Eleanore Boswell Murrie, *English Song-Books 1651-1702,* Oxford, The Bibliographical Society, 1940.

Dorset: Brice Harris, *Charles Sackville, Sixth Earl of Dorset,* Urbana, Univ. of Illinois Press, 1940.

Dryden Bibliography: Hugh Macdonald, *John Dryden: A Bibliography of Early Editions and of Drydeniana,* Oxford, Clarendon Press, 1939.

HMC: Reports of the Royal Commission on Historical Manuscripts.

Sixth Report: *Sixth Report.*

Seventh Report: *Seventh Report.*

Bath: *Manuscripts of the Marquis of Bath.*

Buccleuch and Queensberry: *Manuscripts of the Duke of Buccleuch and Queensberry.*

Dartmouth: *Manuscripts of the Earl of Dartmouth.*

Kenyon: *Manuscripts of Lord Kenyon.*

Laing: *Laing Manuscripts Preserved in the University of Edinburgh.*

Le Fleming: *Manuscripts of S. H. Le Fleming, Esq., of Rydal Hall.*

Montagu: *Manuscripts of Lord Montagu of Beaulieu.*

Ormonde: *Manuscripts of the Marquess of Ormonde.*

Rutland: *Manuscripts of His Grace the Duke of Rutland.*

Stopford-Sackville: *Manuscripts of Mrs. Stopford-Sackville, of Drayton House, Northamptonshire.*

Lives of the Poets: Theophilus Cibber, *The Lives of the Poets of Great Britain and Ireland,* London, R. Griffiths, 1753.

"Oldham Bibliography": Harold F. Brooks, "A Bibliography of John Oldham," *Oxford Bibliographical Society Proceedings and Papers,* 5 (1940), 1-38.

Pepys: *The Diary of Samuel Pepys,* ed. Henry B. Wheatley, London, George Bell and Sons, 1893-99.

Poems: *Poems by John Wilmot, Earl of Rochester,* ed. Vivian de Sola Pinto, London, Routledge and Kegan Paul, 1953.

Poetical Register: Giles Jacob, *The Poetical Register: or, the Lives and Characters of the English Dramatick Poets,* London, E. Curll, 1719-20.

Poetical Works: *The Poetical Works of John Wilmot, Earl of Rochester,* ed. Quilter Johns, Halifax, Eng., Haworth Press, 1933.

Restoration Drama: Allardyce Nicoll, *A History of English Drama 1660-1900*: vol. *1, Restoration Drama,* 4th ed., Cambridge Univ. Press, 1955.

Pinto, Rochester: Vivian de Sola Pinto, *Rochester: Portrait of a Restoration Poet,* London, John Lane the Bodley Head, 1935.

Prinz, Rochester: Johannes Prinz, *John Wilmot, Earl of Rochester: His Life and Writings,* Leipzig, Mayer and Müller, 1927.

Rochester-Savile Letters: *The Rochester-Savile Letters,* ed. John Harold Wilson, Columbus, Ohio State Univ. Press, 1941.

Rochester's Poems: *Rochester's Poems on Several Occasions,* ed. James Thorpe, Princeton Univ. Press, 1950.

Stationers' Register: *A Transcript of the Registers of the Worshipful Company of Stationers; from 1640-1708,* London, privately printed, 1913-14.

Term Catalogues: *The Term Catalogues, 1668-1709,* ed. Edward Arber, London, privately printed, 1903-06.

"Text of Rochester": David M. Vieth, "The Text of Rochester and the Editions of 1680," *Papers of the Bibliographical Society of America, 50* (1956), 243-63.

Works of Etheredge: *The Works of Sir George Etheredge,* ed. A. Wilson Verity, London, J. C. Nimmo, 1888.

Works of Sedley: *The Poetical and Dramatic Works of Sir Charles Sedley,* ed. V. de Sola Pinto, London, Constable, 1928.

David Farley-Hills (essay date 1972)

SOURCE: Farley-Hills, David. Introduction to *Rochester: The Critical Heritage,* edited by David Farley-Hills, pp. 1-26. London: Routledge & Kegan Paul, 1972.

[*In the following introduction, Farley-Hills provides an overview of the critical reception of Rochester's poetry from his own time through the mid-twentieth century.*]

The history of Rochester criticism illustrates almost all the ways imaginable in which the critic can be deflected from a reasonably objective view of the poetry. Accordingly, this collection of critical comments on Rochester from his contemporaries through to the beginning of the twentieth century contains comparatively little that can help the modern reader to come to a fair estimate of the poems as poems, but is a mine of information both about the ways criticism can be deflected by non-critical considerations—ethical or religious bias, the inadequate or ill-judged application of historical or biographical information—and at the same time it is a record of changing attitudes, moral and aesthetic, over more than two centuries. In selecting the material I have been concerned firstly to give an adequate and representative coverage of critical opinion over these years. To have confined myself to the contemporary response to Rochester's poetry would have been to record critical judgment at its most partial, for during his lifetime Rochester was even more controversial as a man than as a poet. While he was alive, it was almost impossible to judge his literary achievement without entering into the controversies that surrounded him as a patron of literature, notorious rake, reputed atheist and finally Christian penitent; and even after his death criticism remained as much concerned with his character as with his poetry.

A surprising amount of comment on his own contemporaries is still extant, more perhaps than for any other literary figure of the Restoration, though by modern standards the record is meagre and confusingly mixed with biographical tittle-tattle and non-literary polemic. I have tried to include as much of this early material as possible, both because of its intrinsic interest and because some of it is hard to come by. Just as interesting, though often just as confused, is the response of subsequent generations, and there are valiant attempts over the years, by Thomas Rymer, by Dr Johnson to some extent, by Emile Forgues, for instance, to free literary judgments from the religious and moral dogma. Modern criticism can be dated roughly from the time when the critic could escape from the clutch of moral bigotry and read the poetry without either being excited by the promise of pornography or being blinkered by the assumption of moral superiority. By 1903—the date of the last two pieces in this collection—to defend Rochester's poetry was no longer regarded as perverse; nor was there a virtue in simply condemning it. But it is not finally, I think, until Whibley's excellent essay on 'The Court Poets' in volume 8 of the *Cambridge History of English Literature* (1912) that one gets the feeling, at least in extended critical discussion, that here at last is a critic willing to take the poetry on its own merits and quite independently of the myth that had grown up round Rochester's life. It is appropriate therefore to end on the threshold of modern critical attitudes with two pieces that show vividly both the continuing prejudices that surrounded the poet, illustrated from Thomas Longueville's book (No. 78), and a fair example of the attempts being made to see Rochester's work for its true worth. Courthorpe in this last extract (No. 79) is still referring to 'floods of indescribable filth' in the accepted nineteenth-century manner, but he is also attempting to come to genuinely literary judgments. With Whibley therefore I feel we arrive at a new phase of Rochester criticism, the modern phase, with its increasing understanding of Rochester as a literary artist.

EDITIONS OF THE POETRY

The availability of Rochester's poetry and the critical comments follow a related pattern: until the middle of the eighteenth century there were many editions; then came a gradual falling off, until the nineteenth century, when there were very few reprints; and it is not until the twentieth century that his poetry has become readily available again. Similarly, during his lifetime and in the first part of the eighteenth century he was a much discussed figure both as man and poet; between 1750 and 1850 interest waned, and what comment there was tended to become increasingly hostile. Thomas Park's judgment in 1806 that 'This Lord's licentious productions too forcibly warrant the sentence of outlawry that decorum and taste have passed upon them' (No. 52) seems to sum up the prevailing opinion. After 1850 interest begins to pick up and once again the record becomes fuller and more rewarding.

There is no complete bibliography of Rochester's writings, and the complex relationship of the various texts has never been thoroughly explored, although in *Attribution in Restoration Poetry* David Vieth has established three major lines of descent for the seventeenth- and earlier eighteenth-century editions. The overall picture is clear, however. The publications in the seventeenth century are more or less honest attempts to collect together what was known or assumed to be by Rochester. No collection of the poetry was published during his lifetime, though some of his lyrics found their way into miscellanies and several of his poems were printed in single sheet issues, 'broadsides', before 1680. Almost immediately after his death a collection of poems was issued described as ***Poems on several Occasions by the Right Honourable the E. of R———.***[1] This purported to come from Antwerp, though it, and several subsequent editions, were in fact printed surreptitiously in London. The 1680 'editions', of which there were at least ten, provide the best editions before the twentieth century in spite of their surreptitious entry into the world, their obvious bid for the market in pornography, and though they are in fact anthologies and not solely Rochester's work. A new and in some ways more careful edition of the poetry, heavily bowdlerized, and therefore less comprehensive or authentic, was published by Jacob Tonson with an (unsigned) introduction by Thomas Rymer in 1691. These two texts, with reprints in 1695 and 1696, are the chief seventeenth-century printed sources. A large number of manuscript collections containing Rochester's poetry also survive from the period. Gentlemen writers were not expected to publish for profit and besides, censorship laws during Charles II's reign discouraged publication of the satire and pornography that featured largely in this court poetry. In addition to the poems, Rochester's play *Valentinian* was published separately in 1685 and a collection of letters in 1697 and 1699.

The beginning of the eighteenth century saw a flood of Rochester publications. These editions can be divided into those that are primarily concerned to make Rochester's poetry available as literature and those supplying the pornographic market. In the early eighteenth century, the literary texts derive from Tonson's edition, six reprints of which were published, with alterations, up to 1732. Next, in 1779, came Steevens's extensive selection with a preface by Dr Johnson (No. 47). A number of later selections are based on this edition. The pornographic texts were mostly published under the title *The Works of the Earls of Rochester and Roscommon,* of which there are at least twenty-eight separate editions following the first in 1707. Altogether between 1700 and 1750 there were at least twenty-seven editions of the poetry, excluding smaller selections; and between 1750 and 1800 there were about seventeen, if we include the extensive selection in Steevens's edition and the selections that derive from it. Between 1800 and 1850 there were only five editions—all selections— and between 1850 and 1900 only two extensive selections, though a few of his poems appeared in anthologies. Since 1900 the number of editions has risen again and there have been at least eleven editions either of the complete poems or of a substantial selection of them. There have also been editions of the complete works and of the Rochester-Savile correspondence.

BIOGRAPHICAL LITERATURE

Like the editions, the literature on Rochester himself can be divided into the clean and the unclean. On the one hand there is the series of religious homilies, which retell the story of Rochester's death-bed suffering and repentance, both to warn the reader of the dangers of the immoral life and to illustrate the Christian thesis that it is never too late to repent. On the other hand there are the accounts of Rochester's life that lay stress on his amatory or bacchic adventures (with incidents often invented by the writer) clearly designed for the same readers that bought the pornographic poetry. This titillating 'Rochesteriana', which continues throughout the eighteenth century and into the nineteenth, often threw up works of almost pure invention, such as William Dugdale's obscene *Singular Life, Amatory Adventures and Extraordinary Intrigues of John Wilmot* (1864). In the nineteenth century, too, there were a number of novels concerning Rochester's life. Perhaps the oddest of all these fictions is the series of stories said by a certain Mlle Kruizhanovskaya, a medium, to have been dictated to her, presumably in French, by the poet's spirit.[2] Apparently Rochester was a name to conjure with even in the reign of Queen Victoria.

Just as odd in their own way are the religious tracts that tell of Rochester's wicked life and spectacular conversion. These too went on into the nineteenth century with such publications as *The Repentance and Happy*

Death of the Celebrated Earl of Rochester (1814), several times reprinted, and *The Conversion of the Earl of Rochester* (1840), a Religious Tract Society publication (No. 61). The earliest attempt to present Rochester's life as a religious parable was Gilbert Burnet's *Some Passages of the Life and Death . . . of Rochester* (No. 10), which Johnson extolled as a masterpiece in its own right. This is the most informative and valuable early document on Rochester, but we should remember that its prime purpose, like the later tracts, was to disseminate Christian propaganda. It was immensely popular and went on reprinting until the second half of the nineteenth century. Its popularity seems to have been at a height between 1800 and 1820, at the very time when interest in the poetry was at its nadir. Obviously it was thought that the poetry and the piety did not mix. Almost as popular as Burnet's work, and often reprinted with it, was Robert Parsons's funeral sermon (No. 9).

Because attitudes towards Rochester's poetry were closely bound up with attitudes towards him as a man, the editor faces the problem of where to draw the line between biographical and critical material. Generally I have tried to avoid the salacious or hagiological gossip, but occasionally I have included biographical excerpts either because they contain interesting observations on Rochester's writings or because they throw light on Rochester's literary personality. Aubrey's brief life (No. 29) and the excerpt from Wood's *Athenae Oxonienses* (No. 27) also provide the basic facts of Rochester's life and can be used as points of reference whenever biographical information is wanted. Burnet's *Life* is given entire as a key document for the understanding of Rochester's state of mind. It is not really a conventional *Life* but a series of interviews in which Rochester talks about his own attitudes and is given the orthodox, if sometimes cooked-up, replies point by point by Burnet.

EARLY PRAISE

The critical material falls into four main periods. The early period, running roughly from the early 1670s, when his poetry is first commented on, to the end of the seventeenth century, is distinguished by its partisanship. Writers are either strongly for or equally strongly against Rochester as both man and writer. We can never know whether men like Sir Francis Fane or John Crowne really believed their flattery of Rochester's genius; they were interested parties; and when Dryden tells Rochester he is 'above any incense I can give you' (No. 3b), we can only recall that within four or five years he is referring to Rochester's poetic gifts as 'a trifling kind of fancy' (No. 3c). There is, however, rather more consistency about Dryden's attitude to Rochester than might be supposed from this contrast. Even in the flattering Dedication of *Marriage à la Mode,* Dryden slily puts the emphasis not on Rochester's achievement, but on his potential and this, it is suggested, will remain as potential because Rochester is 'above the narrow praises which poesy could give you' (No. 3a). For Dryden, Rochester is the amateur, the dilettante, who can afford to dabble in poetry but whose dabblings no self-respecting professional would take too seriously. Dryden with his sense of the high seriousness of poetry was also expert at demolishing a rival's reputation (poor Shadwell, of enviable talents, has still not recovered from the drubbing he got in *Mac Flecknoe*) and Rochester, a much more formidable opponent in every way, has also suffered in his literary reputation through Dryden's well calculated slurs. The exact cause of Dryden's quarrel with Rochester is unknown, but on the evidence of his Preface to *All for Love*, Dryden took great offence at Rochester's lines in the **"Allusion to Horace"** (1675). This poem is a clever adaptation of the tenth satire of book one of Horace's *Satires*. It begins:

> Well Sir, 'tis granted, I said D[*ryden's*] Rhimes,
> Were stoln, unequal, nay, dull many times:
> What foolish *Patron,* is there found of his,
> So blindly partial, to deny me this?
> But that his *Plays,* embroider'd up and down,
> With *Wit* and *Learning,* justly pleas'd the *Town,*
> In the same *Paper,* I as freely own,
> Yet having this allow'd, the heavy *Mass,*
> That stuffs up his loose volumes must not pass.[3]

Later in the poem Rochester returns to his attack to scoff at Dryden's attempts to emulate the humour of the Wits. The following lines (71-80), however, are complimentary by the standards of the age:

> D[*ryden*], in vain try'd this nice way of wit,
> For he to be a tearing *Blade* thought fit,
> But when he would be sharp, he still was blunt:
> To frisk his frollique fancy, he'd cry Cunt,
> Wou'd give the *Ladies,* a dry *Bawdy* bob,
> And thus he got the name of *Poet Squab.*
> But to be just, 'twill to his praise be found,
> His *Excellencies* more than faults abound;
> Nor dare I from his sacred temples tear
> That *Lawrel,* which he best deserves to wear.

In his Preface Dryden pretends that he thinks the author of the **"Allusion"** is one of Rochester's 'zanies' but he must have known its real author. In fact, Rochester's attack was not as severe as it has been made out to be by the satirical standards of the time, and Dryden is perhaps being a little over-touchy.

Sometimes the contemporary compliments to Rochester are sincere. In the opinion of Marvell (recorded in Aubrey's *Brief Life of Marvell*) 'the Earl of Rochester was the only man in England that had the true veine of satyre'. Marvell's compliment is that of the sophisticated practitioner of poetry, while Pepys's regretful 'As he is past writing any more so bad in one sense, so I despair

of any man surviving him to write so good in another' (Letter to W. Hewer, 4 November 1680) probably reflects the feelings of countless ordinary readers until well on into the eighteenth century, to judge by the frequency of the editions. The other great Restoration diarist, John Evelyn, merely records that Rochester was 'a very profane wit'. Allusions to Rochester are frequent in the popular satire of the time as we can see in the recent Yale collection of *Poems on Affairs of State* as well as excerpts given in this collection (Nos. 6, 20). An anonymous commentator has scrawled on a copy of Mulgrave's *An Essay upon Satire* now in the British Museum library (Harleian MS 7317) a reference to Rochester as 'One of the finest men England ever bred, a great and admir'd Wit . . .'[4] Another less complimentary remark from a satire of the late 1680s, 'The Reformation of Manners', tells us 'One man reads Milton, forty Rochester' (*Poems on Affairs of State,* 1703, ii. 371). There is a record, even at this early date, of Rochester's poetry crossing the Atlantic. In a commonplace book of a New Englander, John Saffin (1632-1740), ten rather garbled lines of the poem **Upon Nothing** are written down without comment, suggesting perhaps oral transmission.[5]

During his lifetime any compliment to Rochester, like Lee's dedication of his tragedy *Nero* (No. 2a), is clearly suspect, but Lee's praise in the *Princess of Cleves* (No. 2b) referring to his death, is a touching public tribute. The spate of funeral elegies in 1680 are perhaps the most eloquent witness to his popularity as a poet. These are from a wide ranging section of the literary world. It was not only courtiers who lamented 'Strephon's' passing: Oldham and Aphra Behn were professional poets—Oldham, a staunchly independent moralist, Aphra Behn a playwright with some aspirations towards inclusion among the wits. Anne Wharton, a relative of Rochester, was an aristocratic amateur poet of melancholic rather than witty tendencies. Flatman was an Oxford academic far removed from the London Court, while his friend Samuel Woodford was an Anglican priest. Of the prose commemorators Burnet and Parsons also were priests. The only tribute from the circle of wit proper was Wolseley's Preface to *Valentinian.*

All this suggests that Rochester was accepted as a major poet by a wide cross-section of the reading public of his day and not just by a small fashionable clique, as has sometimes been assumed. Some of the elegies—those of Flatman (No. 17), Samuel Woodford (No. 18), Samuel Holland (No. 19)—stress the Christian significance of his life; as such, they give little information on Rochester as a writer, except to witness for his great reputation as a literary figure. Much more interesting are the tour elegies that concentrate on his literary achievement and influence, and of these Oldham's *Bion* (No. 12) is the most interesting of all. Oldham, in the *Satire against Virtue,* 1676, had brilliantly attacked the poet's immorality by using Rochester's own technique of impersonation: the poem takes the form of a speech by Rochester himself attacking virtue. In the elegy Oldham has paid generous homage to the man who taught him how to write poetry:

If I am reckon'd not unblest in Song,
'Tis what I ow to thy all-teaching tongue,
Others thy Flocks, thy Lands, thy Riches have,
To me thou didst thy Pipe, and Skill vouchsafe.

Aphra Behn's elegy, in sprightly verse, concentrates on the loss of a great satirist:

Satyr has lost its art, its sting is gone,
The Fop and Cully now may be undone; [i.e. unportrayed]
That dear instructing Rage is now allay'd,
And no sharp Pen does tell 'em how they've stray'd
. . .

It is surprising how often contemporaries of 'the mad Earl' (as Hearne liked to call him) stress his role as teacher and reformer. Anne Wharton's lines have this emphasis, celebrating his learning, his natural ability and his 'instructing' purpose, but like Aphra Behn she seems to think of him first as a satirist. Of all these elegies hers had the longest currency, still appearing in nineteenth-century editions of Rochester's poems (for example *The Cabinet of Love*, 1821) and the complimentary lines it inspired from Waller, Jack Howe and Robert Wolseley (Nos. 14b-d) seem to suggest that it was regarded with special favour by her contemporaries. Anne Wharton was a relative of Rochester and presumably knew him personally. The fourth elegy, the anonymous 'Alas what dark benighting Clouds or shade' (No. 15), while it also mentions that Rochester's purpose was 'to correct the proud' and celebrates his great poetic talent, hovers between a literary and eschatalogical interest in Rochester. Its account of Rochester's personal virtues strains our credulity, but here and there there are some informative hints about the contemporary response to the poetry, such as the suggestion that some found the verse obscure and needing the author's exposition (possibly a reference to the paradoxical **Satire against Mankind**).

Burnet's so-called *Life* and Parsons's funeral sermon on Rochester must also be considered as elegies (in his Preface Burnet refers to his work as 'celebrating the praises of the dead') and like some of the verse elegies their purpose is to stress the Christian significance of Rochester's life and death. Rochester had only been dead a couple of months when we find John Tillotson, later Archbishop of Canterbury, entering into his commonplace book for 1 October 1680: 'My Lord of Rochester . . . the greatest instance any age hath af-

forded: not for his own sake, as St. Paul was not, who yet was no enemy to God and religion, but by mistake. I cannot think, but that it was intended for some greater good to others' (Birch's *Life of Tillotson*, 1752, p. 74). And Rochester was scarcely dead when Tillotson was writing to a friend on 2 August, 'I am sorry, that an example, which might have been of so much use and advantage to the world, is so soon taken from us' (Birch, p. 73). Similarly Rochester's friend George Saville, Earl of Halifax, referring to Rochester's death in a letter to Burnet, is more concerned with the repentance than with the poetry (Marshall, *A Supplement to the History of Woodstock Manor*, 1874, p. 28). It was inevitable in an age as dominated by Christian thinking as the Restoration that this emphasis should be placed on the religious significance of Rochester's life. Burnet's most valuable contribution is the insight he gives us into the kind of mind that produced the poetry, a mind which combines an earnest, almost desperate desire to believe in something, with a tough scepticism that refuses to allow him to accept anything that his intellect does not fully understand. Burnet brings out Rochester's honesty both in his understanding of his own motives and in his frankness in talking about them: 'he would often break forth into such hard expressions concerning himself, as would be indecent for another to repeat' (p. 73). A remarkable example of this self-criticism is preserved in the gruesome 'Conference with a Post Boy' (Pinto, lxxx). Burnet takes Rochester's poetic genius for granted, remarking that 'few men ever had a bolder flight of fancy more steadily governed by judgment than he had.' The mention of judgment (intellectual control) is worth remarking and conforms with the picture Burnet gives of Rochester as a studious and not unlearned man, as well as a debauchee. Parsons's much shorter sermon (No. 9), though it is much less informative about the man, is as informative about the poet. Again the poetry is highly praised, Parsons singling out the importance of paradox. But his rather questionable belief that Rochester would have become a great religious poet is prompted by his desire to emphasize the sincerity of Rochester's conversion to Christianity. It is Parsons who records Rochester's death-bed wish that his 'profane and lewd writings' should be burnt (*Sermon*, 1680, pp. 28-9). Like Anne Wharton, Burnet and later Antony Wood (echoing Parsons), Parsons emphasizes not only Rochester's natural talents, but his learning and application 'rare, if not peculiar to him, amongst those of his quality'. Others who knew him differed about this. Dryden, we have already seen, had no great opinion of the seriousness of his attitudes and Rochester's tutor, Gifford, maintained that 'my Lord understood very little or no Greek, and that he had but little Latin, and therefore 'tis a great mistake in making him (as Burnet and Wood have done) so great a Master of Classick Learning' (*Hearne's Remarks and Collections,* ed. C. E. Doble, 1889, iii. 263). Hearne backs this up with an opinion of a 'Mr. Collins of Magdalen' that Rochester 'understood little or nothing of Greek' (*ibid.* iii. 273).

ATTACK AND DEFENCE

Just as Rochester inspired eulogy from his contemporaries, so he also found himself under constant attack. It would have been surprising if a man whose opinions and behaviour were so unorthodox had escaped censure, given the authoritarian temper of the age. The attacks are usually of two kinds: attacks on his personality (accusations of cowardice, malice, atheism, licentiousness) or attacks, like Dryden's and Mulgrave's, on his alleged incompetence as a poet. His controversial personality gave rise to a large number of poems in which he is satirized, sometimes gently and sympathetically by friends like Sedley and the Earl of Dorset, sometimes with great asperity, as in the attacks of Scroope and Mulgrave. Rochester's ability to inspire enmity among the professional writers is illustrated not only by Dryden's attack, but also in Otway's bitter condemnation of him as 'Lord Lampoon' in *The Poet's Complaint to his Muse.* Employing a device Rochester had himself developed, Oldham, in the *Satire on Virtue,* uses Rochester as a persona for condemning himself. The convention was continued after his death in poems like *Rochester's Ghost* (1682) and the poem of Thomas Durfey included in this collection (No. 25). In these poems Rochester's ghost returns to earth to condemn his own past life and the conduct of other debauchees. Sometimes the device is used simply to condemn others, as in 'Rochester's Farewell' (1680). Vieth gives a full account of this anti-Rochester literature in his *Attribution in Restoration Poetry* (ch. 6).

Robert Wolseley's 'Preface', attached to the publication of Rochester's play *Valentinian* in 1685, is the first extended criticism of Rochester's work. It is not an attempt at an impartial assessment but a defence of the poetry against Mulgrave's attacks in the *Essay upon Poetry* (1682) (No. 7b) and to a lesser extent in the *Essay upon Satire* (1679) (No. 7a). In the *Essay upon Poetry* Mulgrave concentrates his attention on the bawdiness of Rochester's songs and implies that Rochester lacked wit (meaning poetic invention). Wolseley, though he refers to Rochester's fame as a satirist, is primarily concerned to defend the lyric poetry on the grounds that excellence in poetry is independent of content and that the ability to make a good poem out of uncongenial material is the hallmark of the great poet. The ingenuity or wit of the poet to make something out of nothing is a common theme in Renaissance criticism. It is well expressed in Philip Massinger's lines in praise of a burlesque poem:

> It shewed more art in Virgil to relate,
> And make it worth the hearing, his Gnat's fate;
> Then to conceive what those great Mindes must be
> That sought and found out fruit full Italie.[6]

Paradoxical poetry, praising 'things without honour', was an established genre in the sixteenth and seventeenth centuries—Rochester's **Upon Nothing** and Donne's *Nocturnal upon St. Lucie's Day* are two widely differing examples of this kind.[7] Wolseley's defence is thus couched in aesthetic terms; he defends Rochester's poetic inventiveness. While he concedes that objection may be made against the content of Rochester's poetry on moral grounds (pp. 195-6), he argues that his poetic genius is too well known and too widely admitted to be brought into question. Throughout the essay he is not so much attempting to demonstrate Rochester's greatness as a poet as trying to demolish Mulgrave's objections.

Rymer's 'Preface' to the 1691 edition of the poems attempts a more dispassionately critical approach to the poetry. Unfortunately the exact circumstances of Rymer's commission are unknown. The 1691 volume of Rochester's poems, **Poems etc. on Several Occasions,** published by Jacob Tonson, has until recently been treated as the best early edition of the poetry. Prinz and Pinto suggest that it may have been 'produced with the approval of the Earl's family and friends' (Pinto ed., xli), but there is no real evidence for this. There is no doubt that it was a genuine attempt to produce a standard collection of Rochester's poetry that would be acceptable to the reading public at large, and Rymer's 'Preface', with its stress on the literary value of the poems, would help to establish the serious nature of the publication. Tonson, who was presumably the editor, was a reputable publisher and the bowdlerization that characterizes it would certainly be regarded as a virtue in the 1690s. Thomas Rymer seems to have known one of Rochester's intimates, Sir Fleetwood Shepherd; it is not known whether he knew Rochester himself. He is most likely to have been asked to contribute the Preface as the most distinguished English critic of literature next to Dryden—who could hardly have been expected to praise his old enemy. Whether Rymer was chosen because he was sympathetic, or was sympathetic because he was chosen there is no way of telling. The Preface is objective in its approach, hinting at Rochester's lack of discipline as a poet, a charge related to the earlier charge of 'amateurism', but also—and correctly—stressing the extraordinary energy, 'a strength, a spirit, and manly vigour' of Rochester's style. This is the central quality of Rochester's satire (as it must be of any great poet) and significantly, it is primarily the satire that Rymer discusses. In a more general way at the end of the Preface he mentions the paradoxical element in Rochester's poetry, the enigmatic interplay of serious and comic, so perceptively that we wish the Preface had been longer.

REPUTATION IN THE EARLY EIGHTEENTH
CENTURY

In the last decade of the seventeenth century Rochester's reputation seemed to suffer a minor eclipse. This can be understood partly as the effect of the piety and seriousness of the court of William and Mary. The new poetic fashions persuaded even Swift, the greatest comic genius of the age, to try his hand at solemn Pindarics. For this short period the cultural climate was characterized by a prudery more Victorian than Restoration or Augustan. We should not be surprised that the young Addison (whom C. S. Lewis has characterized as a Victorian before his time) fails to mention John Wilmot in his galaxy of English Poets in *An Account of the Greatest English Poets* (1694), and that Samuel Cobb omits him from his *Poetae Britannici* of 1700. In spite of this temporary eclipse, there is evidence at the turn of the century that Rochester is still being widely read and some evidence about who is reading him. Joseph Addison later occasionally mentions Rochester and acknowledges (in a *Spectator* essay, 1712), that **Upon Nothing** is an 'admirable Poem' though 'upon that barren subject'. His friend Steele twice quotes the lines on Sedley from the **"Allusion to Horace"** in the same *Spectator* essays, for Steele Rochester's poetry seems to have had a particular fascination, and there are a number of references to Rochester in Steele's work.[8] That another popular writer, Daniel Defoe, held Rochester in great esteem can be seen from the excerpts from the *Review* quoted (No. 35). Moll Flanders twice refers to Rochester, quoting two lines from **Artemesia** on love (Everyman ed., p. 62) and lines from the song 'Phyllis, be gentler, I advise' (Everyman ed., p. 55). That Moll could be expected to know Rochester's poetry so well, and that readers of Defoe's novels should be able to pick up the allusion suggests a very wide reading audience for Rochester in the 1720s. Even as late as 1749 Fielding expects his reader to pick up a casual reference in *Tom Jones* (Everyman. i. 104). This, however, like Rochester's influence on the libertine heroes in Richardson's *Pamela* and *Clarissa,* is more a tribute to Rochester's notoriety as a man than to his fame as a poet. References to Rochester over the period are more common in popular than in polite literature, but it is strange that Swift makes no references to him, because his work shows Rochester's influence.

Rochester's reputation as a poet reached a peak in the 1720s. Voltaire's estimate of him as a man of genius and great poet (No. 41), a view that was no doubt picked up during his stay in England between 1726 and 1729, probably reflects the prevailing opinion of polite society at that time in England. His assertion in the epistle on Rochester and Waller that Rochester's name is 'universally known' is exaggerated, but Rochester was familiar to French-speaking audiences not only through the writings of St Evremond which Voltaire mentions, but in Hamilton's *Memoirs of Grammont* (No. 36). St Evremond held Rochester in high esteem, writing in a letter to Ninon de Lanclos in 1698 that he 'had more wit than any man in England' (*Letters of Saint Evremond,* ed. Hayward, (1930), p. 323). Grammont, a French nobleman who spent some time in exile at Charles II's Court, expresses his admiration for Rochester more equivocally. Edmund Waller, in a letter to St Evremond, recalls a dinner conversation in which Grammont told Rochester that 'if he could by any means divest himself of one half of his wit, the other half would make him the most agreeable man in the world' ('Stephen Collet' [Thomas Byerley] *Relics of Literature,* (1823), p. 52). Rochester is also briefly mentioned in Bayle's encyclopaedic *Dictionary* (No. 33), and there were translations into French of Burnet's *Life* published in 1716 and 1743. There were also translations of the *Life* into German in 1698, 1732, 1735 and 1775 and into Dutch. None of Rochester's poetry was available in French until 1753 and the **Satire against Mankind** was published in a German prose translation in 1757.

In England Rochester continued to be championed as a poet and wit throughout the first half of the eighteenth century. The veteran critic John Dennis uses Rochester's name to illustrate the brilliance of the Restoration literary scene in contrast to what he regarded as the literary decadence of his own generation (No. 32). In *The Advancement and Reformation of Modern Poetry* (1701), (No. 32b) Dennis attacks Rochester's immorality, but this work is addressed to Rochester's archenemy Mulgrave and is not consistent with Dennis's usual attitudes. Comment on Rochester's poetry from 1700 to 1750 is almost always complimentary and even Giles Jacob (No. 38), while he deplores the immorality of the Restoration, is nonetheless full of admiration for Rochester's poetry. Most indicative of the general esteem of the 1720s and '30s is the learned Spence's shocked reaction to Pope's suggestion that the Earl of Dorset was the better poet: 'What, better than Rochester?' (1734), (No. 40). Spence's high regard for Rochester's poetry is evident in the *Historical Remarks on the English Poets* (1732-3), (No. 40) where he is singled out for praise as exceptional even in an age that was 'very rich in satire'.

There were, in this period, as we might expect, strong reservations about Rochester's character as a man and about the immorality of some of his poetry. These doubts are illustrated by a delightful remark of the Duchess of Montagu in a letter to her daughter-in-law Lady Mary in 1724: the Duchess describes a marriage of which she disapproves as 'the nastiest thing I ever heard in my life . . . There is nothing in my Lord Rochester's verses that makes one more ashamed.' But generally reservations about the immorality of the man and his poetry are not allowed to qualify the praise for the quality of the verse.

Pope's attitudes to Rochester are equivocal. The remarks recorded by Spence are mostly unflattering, or, at best, faint praise. Like Dryden, Pope seems to have considered Rochester a dilettante in literature, calling him a 'holiday writer' (No. 40d) and dismissing the whole tradition of the courtly wit of 'either Charles's days' (*Imitations of Horace II,* i. 108) as 'The Mob of Gentlemen who wrote with ease'. Elsewhere Pope comments on Rochester's 'bad versification' (No. 40e), though from Pope's point of view this meant not adopting as strict a view of the heroic couplet as his own. His early verses *On Silence* are deliberately modelled on **Upon Nothing** and his allusions to Rochester in the *Imitations of Horace,* written between 1733 and 1738, show that the poetry recurred to him late in life. At some stage in his career, too, he took the trouble to annotate his copy of the 1696 edition of Rochester's poems (now in the New York Public Library). Even more interestingly Pope took considerable pains in his own revised version of Mulgrave's *Essay upon Satire,* which he published in his edition of Mulgrave's works (1723), to omit all censure of Rochester's poetry. For instance Mulgrave's line:

Rochester I despise for his mere want of wit.

becomes in Pope's version:

Last enters Rochester of sprightly wit.

A curious poem written about 1739 shows Pope's ambivalent attitude to Rochester. He calls the poem 'On lying in the Earl of Rochester's Bed at Atterbury' and tells us rather contradictorily:

That here he lov'd, or here expir'd,
Begets no numbers grave or gay.

Another of Pope's friends (later his enemy) Lady Mary Wortley Montagu shows a knowledge of Rochester's poetry: in a letter of 1759 alluding (it seems) to **Artemesia** and expecting the allusion to be understood, and in an earlier letter (1752), she gives it as her opinion that Richardson's *Pamela* will do more harm than the works of Rochester.

OPINIONS 1750-1800

By the 1750s, however, Lady Mary's views were definitely behind the times, for by now sympathy with Rochester's libertine attitudes and comic view of life was on the wane. Not only his immoral career, but the poetry itself, tended to be condemned outright on moral

grounds. Even among his contemporaries there were people who attacked the poetry as immoral. Mulgrave we have already seen, attacked Rochester for the obscenity of his songs. But more typical of this early period is the equivocal attitude that Pepys expresses of a writer so good in one sense, so bad in another. Anthony Wood records the same mixed reaction:

They [the poems of the 1680 volume] are full of obscenity and prophaneness, and are more fit (tho' excellent in their kind) to be read by Bedlamites, than pretenders to vertue and modesty.

The paradox of a man who would have been better if he had written worse came to be resolved by denying that he wrote well; to Walpole as we shall see he was a bad poet as well as a bad man. The shift towards this simple solution to the problem, which Wolseley had tried to tackle in the Preface to *Valentinian,* is already noticeable in the *Life of Sedley* of 1722 (No. 39):

They [the poems of Rochester and the other Court Wits] are not fit to be read by People whose Religion and Modesty have not quite forsaken them; and which, had those grosser Parts been left out, would justly have passed for the most polite Poetry that the World ever saw.

The confusion between aesthetic and moral standards may be accepted as inevitable, but writers were obviously determined to ignore the truth that Wolseley had pointed out that 'my Lord writ a great number [of poems] without the least obsceneness in 'em.' Besides, a selection of carefully gelded poems were readily available both in the Tonson editions and later in Steevens's selection.

The first out-and-out condemnation of both man and poems was Robert Shiels's account in *'Mr. Cibber's' Lives of the Poets* (1753) (No. 43). Shiels was not averse to profiting from Rochester's scandalous reputation, for he reproduced many of the anecdotes—some spurious—that had gathered round Rochester's life, but his dislike of the poems was unequivocal, though he acknowledged the exceptional natural talents of the man. He was concerned not to allow the vicious influence of the poetry to spread and refused to discuss it. By 1757 another Scot, the great David Hume, was informing his readers that 'the very name of Rochester is offensive to modern ears.' This did not, incidentally, prevent his contemporaries from buying copies of the poems in large numbers. Hume acknowledged Rochester's great talent as a poet, but refused to discuss the poetry except to condemn it—admittedly, here Hume was merely making a catalogue of Restoration poets as part of his general history of the period and therefore an extended discussion was anyway not his intention. He placed Rochester second, after Dryden, in his list of literary figures of the age. Walpole's attack on Rochester, 1758 (No. 45), took the process of denigration a stage further. Walpole was not willing to concede even natural talent and made his condemnation more severe by accepting the possibility that poetry could be both good *and* indecent: 'Indecency is far from conferring wit; but it does not destroy it neither.' Having said this he then goes on to argue that Rochester's poetry is without merit. The age which produced Rochester was barbarous, the favourable judgments of his contemporaries Wood and Marvell, absurd. Walpole, though he purports to judge the poetry as poetry, bases his criticism on a narrow moral judgment, a judgment that ignores Wolseley's caveat and the evidence of the bowdlerized editions. Walpole's determination to condemn is an excellent if sad example of the way in which a sensitive and intelligent man can adopt the unreasoned prejudices of an increasingly moralistic climate of opinion.

Not all comment in this period, however, is hostile. The *Biographia Britannica* (1766) article on Rochester, which records his waywardness as a man and quotes Walpole's opinions, also expresses admiration for the poetry: 'His style was clear and strong, and when he used figures they were very lively, yet far enough out of the common road.' This article, it should be noted, is reserved for a supplement of the *Biographia,* suggesting that Rochester is no longer regarded as an inevitable inclusion even in such an extensive compilation. In this growing climate of disapproval and neglect Johnson's *Life of Rochester* (No. 47) stands out as something of an exception. He is at any rate determined not to be misled by the cant of the period. Johnson's own highly moral view of life permits him no sympathy with the Restoration libertine's attitudes, but he is willing to try to separate his opinion of the poet's morals from his opinion of the morality of the poetry, though he is not entirely successful in this. As in the other *Lives of the Poets,* Johnson adopts a threefold division in this essay, first giving us the more important biographical facts and discussing Rochester's character (though these two parts are not kept separate) and then turning to a discussion of literary merits. The biographical material is largely taken from Burnet's *Life,* which Johnson mentions as a book 'the critick ought to read for its elegance, the philosopher for its arguments, and the saint for its piety'—I have followed Johnson in regarding it as 'an injury to the reader to offer him an abridgement'. The critical section is independent of earlier sources, though the judgments Johnson offers are open to question. It is possible that Johnson did not closely look at Rochester's work. At this time, although Rochester editions were still selling well, they were mostly of the popular, salacious kind which a critic like Johnson would disregard. At a more sophisticated level one would guess that Rochester was read as light entertainment and would therefore no longer warrant the treatment that Johnson gave to the poets like Mil-

ton, Dryden and Pope, though Steevens's selection shows that the polite reader expected Rochester to be represented in an extended collection of English poetry. Symptomatic of Johnson's lack of interest is his over-reliance on his memory. He misquotes Scroope's *Defence of Satire* and a line of the *Satire against Mankind* as 'a saying' of Rochester. Imperfect memory also probably explains Johnson's extraordinary judgment that Rochester's songs 'have no particular character', for had he re-examined them he could hardly have come to this conclusion. He mentions none of them specifically and possibly he was simply working on an impression he had formed of Restoration lyric in general. Most modern critics agree that Rochester's songs are, in Dr Leavis's words, 'peculiarly individual utterances' (*Revaluation,* p. 35), and this seems also to have been the view of Rochester's contemporaries. For example Parsons stresses Rochester's originality in the funeral sermon (No. 9):

> Whoever reads his composures, will find all things in them so peculiarly Great, New, and Excellent, that he will easily pronounce, that tho he has lent to many others, yet he has borrowed of none.

Johnson's comments on the satire are more specific. He shows his customary shrewdness in his caution about what can be accepted as Rochester's, mentioning only poems that are certainly authentic. He is complimentary about the **"Allusion to Horace,"** approving the ingenuity with which Rochester has manipulated Horace's verse to fit his own times. *Upon Nothing* he regards as 'the strongest effort of his [Rochester's] Muse'. Johnson was not the first to single out *Upon Nothing* for special praise. Giles Jacob thought it 'an excellent piece' (No. 38), but no one had hitherto suggested that it was the best of Rochester's poems. It is clever and has moments of power, yet it is essentially a play poem—as Forgues and Whibley later pointed out—and not to be seriously compared with the great satires. Unfortunately Johnson's judgment was followed by many later critics.

Of the other satires Johnson mentions some **'Verses to Lord Mulgrave'** without comment. A lampoon in reply to Carr Scroope's *Defence of Satire* (presumably the lines beginning 'To rack and torture thy unmeaning Brain') is described as a vigorous piece. On the great *Satire against Mankind* Johnson remarks that 'Rochester can only claim what remains when all Boileau's part is taken away'—an argument he had disregarded in dealing with the more closely imitative **"Allusion to Horace."**

At the root of Johnson's failure in this essay lies, one would guess, his great hurry to complete his commission. He had been given only a few weeks to prepare the first volume of *Lives.* The essay also suffers in spite of Johnson's relative detachment, from the prevalent weakness of Rochester criticism, of judging the poetry in terms of the man. For instance, Johnson takes it for granted that Rochester was too preoccupied with his debaucheries to take his writing seriously and goes on to argue from this that 'his pieces are commonly short'. Even if we did not have textual and biographical information to suggest that Rochester worked over his poetry it is apparent enough that his finest works—**Artemesia, "Timon," "Tunbridge Wells"** and the *Satire against Mankind* are his longest. Also underlying Johnson's judgment is the Renaissance dogma that a good writer must be a good man. Though Johnson is too wise to adopt a sentimental or simple-minded view of what a good man is, not surprisingly he finds it difficult to include John Wilmot in that category. This prejudice colours the whole of Johnson's *Life* and is nowhere more evident than in the last lines:

> In all his works there is a spriteliness and vigour, and every where may be found tokens of a mind which study might have carried to excellence. What more can be expected from a life spent in ostentatious contempt of regularity, and ended before the abilities of many other men began to be displayed?

Johnson's opinions, expressed with their customary force and air of conviction, echo through the comments of writers throughout the nineteenth century. (See for example Nos. 49, 50 and the quotation from Stephen Collet, p. 20.)

The Early Nineteenth Century

For all its faults Johnson's *Life of Rochester* is the last extended assessment of Rochester for many years to show any sympathy with his poetry. The new century witnessed both a steady decline not just in sympathetic comment but in any comment at all. Editions of the poetry became fewer. Silence is as significant as comment. Coleridge, for instance, for all his great interest in the seventeenth century, never mentions Rochester. This neglect is not easy to explain. Possibly Coleridge never entirely grew out of his youthful dislike of 'that school of French poetry, condensed and invigorated by English understanding': as he describes the Augustan poets in Chapter I of the *Biographia Literaria*. We might have expected Byron to be sympathetic, yet he only mentions Rochester once or twice in passing. What comment there is on the poetry is largely hostile, even when there is some interest in the man. There is still a glimmer of appreciation from Malone in his edition of Dryden's prose (1800). He gives a very unflattering picture of Rochester's literary relationships, but he does concede that he is a poet of distinction who 'wanted not [Dryden's] aid to be remembered'. Ree's *Cyclopedia* (1819) is more damning, it quotes Walpole's strictures with approval and adds, inaccurately, 'as for his poetical compositions they were for the most part lampoons or amatory effusions, the titles of which would stain the page of biography.' Thomas Byerley, under the pseudonym of Stephen Collet, sums up the attitude of his contemporaries in his *Relics of Literature* (1823). The opening phrase is taken from Johnson's *Life*: 'Although the blaze of this nobleman's reputation is not yet quite extinguished, it is principally as a great wit, a great libertine, and a great penitent, that he is at present known.' There are still however, interesting asides and signs that some intelligent readers are finding enjoyment in this Augustan poet. Isaac D'Israeli, for instance, calls Rochester 'a great satirist', a remark splendidly independent of the prejudices of his age. In his *Quarrels of Authors* (1814) (No. 53) he remarks that Rochester gives us an important insight into the nature of satire in suggesting to Burnet that it is prompted by revenge. In the same year a noble compliment to Rochester comes from Germany's greatest poet. It is not apparent whether Goethe knew the author of the passage he quotes from the *Satire against Mankind* in his *Autobiography* (1814) (No. 54). That he admired it profoundly and felt its full force is indicated by the context, where he uses the lines to illustrate the habitual melancholy of poets, remarking that 'whole volumes' could be written as a commentary on the text. A little later, in the lectures on the English poets of 1818, Hazlitt says just enough about Rochester to make us wish he had said much more. Hazlitt seems on the point of turning Rochester into a Romantic cult hero: 'his contempt for everything that others respect, almost amounts to sublimity.' Almost, but not quite, for there is in his poetry an Augustan decorum and restraint that was coming under bitter attack from some of Hazlitt's contemporaries—though Pope was the chief target. It is surprising, nevertheless, as Street remarks at the end of the nineteenth century (No. 74), that a romantic Rochester was not created, for his rebelliousness and outspokenness would have fitted him for the role. Possibly the neo-classicism in Restoration literature and art did not provide the right background for a Romantic hero, and Rochester, for all his rebelliousness, was very much a man and poet of his age. For whatever reason, then, Rochester was not accepted as a substitute for Lord Byron, with whom he was occasionally compared.

1850-1900

By the time Forgues came to write his two fascinating essays on Rochester for the French (and French-speaking European) public in 1857, there were signs that some of the old puritanical prejudices were dying. Exactly why this gradual shift towards more tolerant attitudes was taking place it is impossible to say. Why, for instance, did Henry Hallam (No. 60) read Rochester's satirical poetry (along with most of the other satire of the day) 'with nothing but disgust' in 1839, yet twenty-five years later not only admit Rochester's 'considerable and varied genius', but praise the lyrics, which he had not discussed in his earlier edition, as doing 'credit to the Caroline period'? It was not merely a personal change of opinion, and Hallam is still not *very* complimentary; it is a gradual changing of the general climate of opinion. This change is possibly reflected in an interesting comment by Gilchrist in his *Life of Blake* (1864) that society in Blake's day was much more puritanical than it was in his own. Additional evidence is provided by the change in the article on Rochester in the *Encyclopaedia Britannica* from the seventh edition (1842) to the ninth (1886). The article in the seventh edition is similar to those of earlier editions; it is largely biographical and confines itself, in commenting on the poetry, to quoting Walpole's strictures. The edition of 1860, the eighth, though still largely biographical, describes the poetry as possessing 'liveliness and vigour' and quotes Dr Johnson's qualified approval in place of Walpole. The ninth edition (No. 72) is still more complimentary. Condemnation of Rochester's poetry on narrow moral grounds is still quite common to the end of the nineteenth century, but more commentators are willing to be tolerant, to treat the verse on its merits and especially to admire the lyrics. These fifty years up to about 1900 are the only time in the history of Rochester criticism that we find the lyrics preferred to the satires.

The article by 'S.H.' in the *Gentleman's Magazine* of 1851 (No. 63) on Rochester and Nell Gwyn is a good example of the cautious tolerance that appears at mid-century. The usual comments are made about Rochester's indecency, but his poetry is also recognized as a valuable record of Restoration society and although this is a historical rather than a critical interest, it acknowledges the realism of the satires, an important quality that had been lost sight of. 'S.H.' is even willing, as few commentators have been, to take sides with Rochester against Dryden, by pointing out that the comments on Dryden in the **"Allusion to Horace"** are not unjust.

Forgues's articles in the *Revue des Deux Mondes* (August and September 1857) also stress the realism of Rochester's attitudes and the value of the verse as a record of Restoration society. Accordingly he is interested in the satire, and especially in two satires that had previously received little critical attention, **"Timon"** and **"Tunbridge Wells."** His view of Rochester as a poet is uncomplimentary: though the best of the Restoration poets, he is of an inferior order, a Petronius, not a Juvenal or Persius. The value of the poems, he says, exists 'only for literary history and for studious explorers of former times'. The historical interest partly explains why he is willing to devote two long articles to this largely unknown English poet at a time when nothing comparable was to be found in English. Knowledge of Rochester on the Continent had never entirely died out, as we know from Goethe's quotation from the *Satire against Mankind* (No. 54). In France,

Victor Hugo had included Rochester anachronistically as a character in his early drama *Cromwell* (1827), and he had appeared as a character in several slightly earlier plays (see Prinz *Rochester,* pp. 440-1), but the more serious French interest had evaporated. Forgues's concern with Rochester is something new. He is not without the kind of moral bias that had blinkered English judgments for so long, and he is just as ready as his English contemporaries to raise his hands in horror at the profligacy of Charles' reign, but he is also willing to look beyond this. From time to time he ventures critical judgments, and these are not entirely consistent with his overall view of Rochester's poetry as only of historical importance. In this literary criticism he shows independence of mind. The poem that Johnson extols, **Upon Nothing,** he considered 'of secondary importance', objecting to its epigrammatic method and that it is satirical where it ought to be philosophical. He dislikes the *Satire against Mankind* largely because of its pessimistic view of mankind. In this he shows his chief weakness as a critical commentator, his concern purely with what is being said and his lack of sensitivity about the poetic method. He shows an inability to respond to the force and energy of this poem, an energy that had so obviously impressed Goethe (No. 54) and, a little later, Tennyson (No. 68). It is not surprising then that he values more highly what he calls the 'humbler pieces', the comic satire, where he can enjoy the social comment without being called upon to respond to the ingenuity and power of the verse.

There is no evidence that Forgues was read by nineteenth-century English commentators, but in England too there is an increase in serious interest in Rochester's work at this date. Gilfillan (No. 66) and Taine (No. 67) might complain about Rochester's wickedness; Henry Morley might be contemptuous (No. 70); the well-read might ignore and misquote, but things were changing. On the one side there is some cruel evidence of just how little he was read: in Abbott and Campbell's *Life of Jowett,* the authors admit that they had to get learned help to identify three (garbled) lines of the *Satire against Mankind* (No. 68) and the letter from which the lines are recorded refers to them as 'some eighteenth-century verses'. An avid reader like Joseph Hunter can pass Rochester by without more than a glance. In his extensive manuscript collection of comments on the English poets Hunter reports of Rochester: 'I have cared so little about this person that I have not a single notice of him in the original book of notes for these articles.' On the other hand Jowett is seen enjoying the *Satire against Mankind* and Tennyson was fond of quoting from the poem (No. 68). Charles Cowden Clarke in the *Comic Writers of England* (1871) (No. 69) deals with Rochester at some length; interested as he is in the gossip surrounding Rochester, he does not ignore the poetry and is not uncomplimentary about it. It is interesting that he assumes, unjustifiably, that Marvell must have shared the nineteenth century's high estimate of Butler in preference to Rochester. By 1880 Edmund Gosse, though concerned with Rochester's nastiness, can present him as an exquisite lyrical poet and this view is echoed again by Oliver Elton in the last year of the century (No. 76). But nineteenth-century criticism of Rochester suffered from errors and misinformation. Elton, for example, accepts the story that Rochester had behaved spitefully towards Settle, Crowne and Otway, though it is not supported by the evidence. He is also handicapped by the uncertainty of the Rochester canon at this date. Like most of his predecessors he accepts poems that are probably not Rochester's (for instance *The Session of the Poets* and the lyric 'I cannot change as others do'). But then it is only since the publication of Vieth's edition of the poems in 1968, that the critic has been able to accept or reject poems with some degree of confidence.

MODERN CRITICISM

Rochester's reputation as a poet, never very high in the nineteenth century, has at last come into its own, though there is still no outstanding critical assessment. With the new edition of the poems by Vieth and the pioneering work of scholars like Prinz, Pinto, Thorpe and Wilson good texts are now available. The first modern edition was the *Collected Works* edited by John Hayward in 1926. This contains Rochester's play *Valentinian* as well as the poems and an extensive selection of letters, but suffers from the inclusion of much spurious material. Pinto's edition of the poetry in 1953, the first to establish the canon of Rochester's work, has now been superseded by Vieth's edition of the *Complete Poems* (1968). There have also been several extensive selections of the poetry and a facsimile edition of *Poems on Several Occasions, 1680,* with an excellent introduction, by James Thorpe. A scholarly edition of the correspondence between Rochester and his friend Henry Savile edited by J. H. Wilson was published in 1941. The publication of these editions was greatly facilitated by the important bibliographical work of J. Prinz, *John Wilmot, Earl of Rochester: His Life and Writings* (1926). There has also been a distinct advance in sifting the authentic from the spurious in the details of Rochester's life. The most notable contributions to this are the book of Prinz already mentioned, Pinto's biography *Enthusiast in Wit,* a revised version of a biography first published in 1935 under the title *Rochester, Portrait of a Restoration Poet,* and J. H. Wilson's *The Court Wits of the Restoration* (1948).

Modern criticism, however, begins before these editions became available in Whibley's essay on the Court Poets in the *Cambridge History of English Literature* (vol. 8, 1912). The essay covers the work of the poets of Charles II's Court and gives us a resumé of Rochester's life. Whibley makes the inevitable mistakes of attribu-

tion and of accepting apocryphal biographical material, but when he writes about the poetry (pp. 213-15) he has a sure touch. He dismisses Johnson's praise of *Upon Nothing* by calling the poem, perhaps rather immoderately, 'a piece of ingenuity, unworthy his talent' and makes the point that Wolseley had made 227 years earlier and that hardly anyone had heeded, that a great many of Rochester's poems are unsalacious and can safely be judged 'upon their very high merits'. He sees that Rochester's claim to be a major poet must rest on the satire and argues that his skill as a satirist is a combination of 'nature' and 'art'. Nor is he to be put off by Pope's accusations of Rochester's 'incorrectness'—'He wrote the heroic couplet with a life and freedom that few have excelled'—though he acknowledges, as any honest critic must, that Rochester was no perfectionist. Rochester's use of the heroic couplet is much freer than either Pope's or Dryden's, and while this loses sometimes in precision it often gains in the wider range of rhythmic effects it allows. Whibley seems to have been the first modern critic to notice this. It is worth mentioning in passing that Rochester's flexible use of the couplet is to be explained in terms of the Renaissance theory of decorum which required a rough metre for satire. For Whibley the *Satire against Mankind* is Rochester's finest achievement, and he praises it for its energy and power. The lyrics he considers far less important, and his comments on them are fewer and less interesting. His praise of the 'imitation' of Quarles, for instance, **'Why do'st thou shade thy lovely face?'** seems exaggerated. There is, in any case, considerable uncertainty that this poem is by Rochester; Vieth does not include it in his new edition, describing it as 'merely an adaptation of Quarles's *Emblemes*'. Whibley is the first critic of Rochester's poetry since the earlier eighteenth century to appreciate something of Rochester's true stature as a poet and to understand where his strength lies. He rejects as irrelevant to the poetry both the diabolical rake and the careless gentleman of the Rochester legends and sees him as a poet of both natural gifts and great technical skill. Much is inevitably left out in such a short space and Whibley's essay contains no more than a sketch of a thorough appreciation of the poetry.

With the appearance of the new editions there have been important contributions towards a re-assessment of the poetry. These have tended to be more concerned with sources and influences than with critical evaluation. There have been explorations of Rochester's thought, especially in the *Satire against Mankind,* of his use of conventional verse forms and of his place in literary history. Inevitably too, there has been continuing discussion of the problems concerned with the authenticity of the poems and the biography. Critical evaluation, until very recently, has tended to interpret the poetry from what we know of the man. Rochester's personality has obvious fascinations for a generation like ours that has grown up to regard his libertinism as morally acceptable. Critics, of which Pinto is perhaps the most distinguished, find Rochester highly sympathetic as a man and prefer those poems where he seems to be speaking in his own person. Thus Pinto gives high praise to the lyrics like **'Absent from thee I languish still'** and **'All my past life is mine no more'** where strong emotion is expressed. This is the 'romantic' Rochester, and certainly these occasional outbursts of emotion are one facet of his work. They are, however, one extreme of a range that extends in the other direction to the complete disengagement of poems like **"The Maim'd Debauchee,"** the **"Song of a Young Lady to her Ancient Lover"** and the mock song **'I cannot swive as others do'**.

In more recent criticism some attempt has been made to redress the bias towards a personal interpretation of the poems by stressing Rochester's skill in disengaging himself from his work, the quality that Keats called 'negative capability'. In a recent British Academy lecture, for instance, Anne Righter demonstrates Rochester's use of irony. David Vieth is also largely concerned with this detachment in his *Attribution in Restoration Poetry* (1963). This is primarily a bibliographical work, but contains a number of important critical observations. He shows that in both *A Very Heroicall Epistle in Answer to Ephelia* and in **"An Epistolary Essay from M.G. to O.B."** the comic hero is a caricature of the Earl of Mulgrave and not, as was often assumed earlier, Rochester speaking in his own person. What were earlier taken to be autobiographical poems are shown to be mock heroic, in which the absurd boasting of the hero is the object of satire. The tendency of Vieth's critical comments, even clearer in the introduction to his edition of the poems, is to demonstrate the ironic detachment of Rochester's satirical techniques, and in showing this he has done more than any other critic to free the poetry from the shadow of the poet. Vieth, however, tends to ignore the more passionate, personal utterances that from an essential part of both lyric and satire and the critic is still awaited who can see the interplay of the two sides of Rochester's art, the emotion and the detachment, as part of the complex unity of his work.

Notes

1. The earliest known version of this, the 'Huntington' edition, was published in photographic facsimile by James Thorpe, *Princeton Studies in English,* No. 30, 1950.

2. *Episode de la Vie de Tibère, œuvre medianimique dictée par l'esprit de J.-W. Rochester* (1886), *Le Pharaon Mernephtah* (1888), *Herculanum* (1889) etc.

3. Pinto, lv. ll. 1-9. The 'patron' of line 3 is Rochester's enemy the Earl of Mulgrave.

4. Recorded in John Hayward's edition of *Letters of Saint Evremond* (1930), p. 323.

5. N. S. Grabo, *Notes and Queries* 207 (1962), pp. 392-3.

6. *Wit Restor'd* (1658), p. 142.

7. For an excellent account of this tradition see Rosalie Colie's *Paradoxia Epidemica* (1966).

8. See *The Occasional Verse of Richard Steele,* ed. Blanchard (1952), p. xv.

Bibliography

HORNE, C. J., Appendix to *Pelican Guide to English Literature 4: From Dryden to Johnson* (1957), contains short list of works on Rochester.

PINTO, V. DE S., *The English Renaissance 1510-1688,* London (1938), pp. 351-2, contains short bibliography of Rochester's work and Rochester criticism.

———, *The Restoration Court Poets,* London (1965) (Writers and their Works No. 186), pp. 41-4, gives a short list of works on Rochester.

PRINZ, J., *John Wilmot, Earl of Rochester,* Leipzig (1927), pp. 309-443, contain a fairly thorough, but by no means complete, list of editions of Rochester's writings as well as lists of works on Rochester and his poetry.

SUTHERLAND, J., *English Literature of the Late Seventeenth Century,* Oxford (1969), pp. 561-3.

VIETH, D. M., *Attribution in Restoration Poetry,* Yale Studies in English No. 153 (1963), gives lists of manuscript and printed sources of poems by and attributed to Rochester as well as a check list (Appendix B) of manuscripts, early editions and anthologies where Rochester's poetry is to be found.

———, *Complete Poems of John Wilmot,* London (1968). The introduction includes a list of editions, biographies and critical works on Rochester written between 1925-67, bringing Prinz's bibliography up to date.

WILSON, J. H., *The Court Wits of the Restoration,* London (1948), pp. 218-22, contain a short list of works on Rochester.

Carole Fabricant (essay date July 1974)

SOURCE: Fabricant, Carole. "Rochester's World of Imperfect Enjoyment." *Journal of English and Germanic Philology* 73, no. 3 (July 1974): 338-50.

[*In the following essay, Fabricant maintains that the sexual imagery in Rochester's poetry is more often grotesque than erotic.*]

The durability of the Earl of Rochester's reputation as libertine and sensualist is hardly surprising under the circumstances. Even apart from the extravagant exploits attributed to him by numerous chroniclers both during and after his brief life,[1] we have the testimony of his poems, which abound in the drama of copulation much in the way that major Augustan works abound in the great drama of Chaos' triumph over Western civilization. The poems focus to such an extent upon genitalia of various sizes and capacities that these, by their sheer quantity, emerge as the central objects of Rochester's world. There seems to be little if anything which occurs outside their general aegis. Thus all political affairs are ascribed directly to the length and comportment of King Charles's sexual organ (**"The Scepter Lampoon"**). Consistently the poems reflect a conversion of spiritual and philosophical phenomena into concrete objects or actions: a kind of counter "transubstantiation" which exposes the wine as nothing but water after all. Hence Incarnation is despiritualized into fornication and religious rituals are acted out in sexual terms. Rochester, for example, talks of serving up his "dram of sperm" as a "grace cup" (**"A Ramble in St. James's Park"**)—his semen, in other words, will take the place of the liquor traditionally served after grace at a meal's end. His outlook is affirmed most explicitly in *A Satyr Against Reason and Mankind,* where the speaker, in his rebuttal to the clergyman who functions as *adversarius,* proclaims the realm of everyday physical activity as the only valid context for human endeavor—"Our sphere of action is life's happiness, / And he who thinks beyond, thinks like an ass" (ll. 96-97).[2] In addition, he redefines the notion of right reason so that it becomes specifically the ally of the senses, renewing appetites rather than destroying them and intensifying instead of denying worldly pleasures.

Yet the fact of the matter is that Rochester's writings deal less with orgasm than with its obstruction; less with sexuality than with the *failure* of sexuality. Although the author stoutly maintains that "Our sphere of action is life's happiness," this sphere—namely the phenomenal world—is portrayed in extremely bleak terms. Its postulated plenitude concerning sensual matters contrasts sharply with the sparseness, if not indeed the absence, of descriptions asserting nature's fruitfulness and beauty. Even in those instances where Rochester exalts the body's functioning, the language of his verse tends to undermine the physical ideal presented. Thus, in **"The Fall,"** the poet imagines a paradisal realm marked by absolute and unlimited sexuality but depicts the eternal lovemaking in abstract and completely unerotic terms:

> Naked beneath cool shades they lay;
> Enjoyment waited on desire;
> Each member did their wills obey,
> Nor could a wish set pleasure higher.

The extreme terseness of the passage subverts the sense of erotic dalliance and the luxurious prolongation without end of what purports to be the perfect sex act. Moreover, the vision of "enjoyment wait[ing] on desire" occurs, after all, in a poem entitled **"The Fall."** The focus is thus made clear from the outset; indeed, the passage describing unlimited sexual pleasure is immediately followed by a lament for the present:

> But we, poor slaves to hope and fear,
> Are never of our joys secure;
> They lessen still as they draw near,
> And none but dull delights endure.

The idyllic conditions described at the beginning belong irrevocably to a remote, perhaps mythical past. Rochester's temporal distancing of the paradisal state in this poem suggests the mental and spatial distancing it undergoes in *Valentinian,* his adaptation of Fletcher's drama. While remaining faithful to Fletcher's depiction of Lucina as a chaste wife stoutly defending her threatened virtue, Rochester nevertheless discards the prudishness of the original character and allows his own Lucina to expound the dream of a sensually appetizing Eden compatible (though not identical) with the libertine's.[3] Yet the reader is impressed less with the seductiveness than with the unreality of the dream. Lucina's Eden exists solely in her mind, conceived as a place removed in every way from her present circumstances. Throughout Rochester's writings, delineations of a perfect sexuality are carefully, even emphatically, distanced from everyday Restoration reality.

I

Perhaps the most remarkable aspect of these writings is the extent to which intercourse is contemplated, discussed, and aspired to while rarely executed in fact. The absence of sex in the early love lyrics is due, generally speaking, to the proverbial chaste maiden whose excessive fear or pride prevents the imploring lover from consummating his desire. The Corinna of **"A Pastoral Dialogue between Alexis and Strephon"** and the Phyllis of **"Woman's Honor"** exemplify such women. These poems paint a world of sterility *before* sex, created by the willful, misguided denial of it—a subject, of course, completely in keeping with Rochester's presumed outlook. But subsequent poems, peopled with the worldliest and least modest of women, likewise emerge as studies in sterility: this time, a sterility arising *after* the body has made its commitment to the world of the senses but suddenly proved itself hopelessly inadequate for the task. In a poem like **"Woman's Honor,"** sexual love per se can be invoked as the panacea for absurd pride and false honor—implicitly, as the panacea for all obstacles to a substantive human relationship. Subsequently, poem after poem—**"The Imperfect Enjoyment," "Timon," "Tunbridge Wells"** —dramatizes the ludicrous simplicity of such a belief.

Each consistently distinguishes between true passion (merely assumed, never actually realized) and the sterile gestures into which it has evolved.

In *A Letter from Artemisia to Chloe,* Artemisia extols sexual love but notes that it has "grown, like play, to be an arrant trade." This degeneration is mirrored in the behavior of women who, now "deaf to nature's rule, or love's advice, / Forsake the pleasure to pursue the vice. / To an exact perfection they have wrought / The action, love; the passion is forgot" (ll. 60-63). As opposed to the speaker of *A Satyr Against Reason and Mankind,* Artemisia uses the word "action" pejoratively, as a pitiful substitute for the "passion" it can do no more than imitate. In most of Rochester's writings action, though initially vital and rejuvenating, turns inextricably into the dull repetition of meaningless motions; sexual activity, into mechanical gestures or masturbation. The Fine Lady of *A Letter from Artemisia* turns first to her automaton-like escort, the "necessary thing" whose sole function seems to be to "bow and be gone," and then to her monkey, that "curious miniature of man" whose actions markedly resemble those of the humble knight. In terms of the poetic fiction it hardly matters which of the pair the Lady decides to make love to, since the absurdity of the act is assured in either case. The Lady and the monkey's embracing more or less parallels the two women in **"Tunbridge Wells"** who hold hands "lovingly" while most appropriately discussing their own barrenness and the arrested sexual development of their offspring.

In Rochester's poetry, while the solution at first seems to lie in rejecting the empty abstractions of the mind for the body's living substance, the body ultimately proves wholly incapable of perpetuating the vitality of genuine passion. The prudish maiden who rejects all physical love emerges as a counterpart, not contrast, to the supposedly sophisticated courtier turned fop for whom physical love is a commodity, an item of goods like clothing or furniture; one who "would have a passion, for 'twas fine! / That, a new suit, and what he next must say / Runs in his idle head the livelong day" ("Could I but make my wishes insolent," ll. 14-16). The latter is but one of numerous figures slinking through Rochester's verse who reflect the malady of what we might term "sex in the head"—in this case quite literally. Other examples of this disease, dramatized through similar wording, occur in **"A Ramble in St. James's Park,"** where the speaker's mistress is chided for being "a whore in understanding," and in the verses **"On Mrs. Willis,"** who is portrayed as "Bawdy in thoughts." Even pregnancies are able to take place only in the head (and the male head at that):

> Poor foolish fribble, who by subtlety
> Of midwife, truest friend to lechery,
> Persuaded art to be at pains and charge

> To give thy wife occasion to enlarge
> Thy silly head. . . .

(**"Tunbridge Wells,"** ll. 139-43)

Although liberated from the repressive control of mental abstractions and embraced as a physical reality, sex inevitably winds up back in the realm of mind, whether as the daily thoughts of the dull fop, the drunken thoughts of the derelict, or the pitiful yearnings of the aged belles. The speaker and his companions in **"A Ramble"** spend their time converting sexuality into an object of leering thoughts. While imbibing in the Bear, they engage in "grave discourse" on the various sexual pairings for the night. The speaker then goes to St. James's Park to survey the goings-on in an unmistakably voyeuristic manner. Considering the nature of the "all-sin-sheltering grove," remarkably little action takes place. We view attempted though unexecuted seductions, absurd social affectations, and the act of spying through someone else's eyes, but nothing more. The situation is similar in **"Tunbridge Wells,"** another site noted for its sexual assignations, since it regularly lures women who wish "new life bestowed on half-dead wombs." Here too sex is acted out solely in the thoughts, words, and stilted gestures of a variety of wives and fops, who in effect dramatize their own hopeless lack of sexuality amidst strenuous attempts to rejuvenate it.

The vicarious quality of sexual indulgence becomes clearest in **"The Disabled Debauchee,"** where the speaker, looking ahead to his increasing impotence, makes plans to continue his lascivious activities through the surrogate of some youth whose blood he will "fire" by "telling what [he] did / When [he] was strong and able to bear arms." Again we are struck by the rather conspicuous lack of emphasis upon the immediate and realized pleasures of sex. Although the Debauchee is presumably at the moment still in possession of his health and vigor, he chooses not to sing the praises of a *carpe diem* philosophy but instead to dwell upon his future incapacities: specifically, the inevitable prospect of the body's disintegration. Such figures dramatize, with extreme literalness, the Hobbesian notion of the imagination as "decaying sense."[4] It is an imagination which preys upon the debilitated body, and which for the most part lacks any creative or redemptive powers.

The situation is similar with respect to the host's wife depicted in **"Timon."** Rochester deviates from his source—Boileau's Third Satire—when he presents her at the dinner table.[5] The focus of Boileau's poem alternates solely between a lengthy description of the "banquet" fare and a portrayal of the dull, pretentious fops who in turn eat, drink, converse, and battle with one another. The scene is devoid of all female figures, and in no way treats the sexual implications of the absurd gathering. Rochester changes the poem's focus considerably when he introduces the host's wife, one more in the long line of *memento mori*'s who permeate his writings. She readily brings to mind the Corinna described in *A Letter from Artemisia,* for whom "Gay were the hours, and winged with joys . . . / When first the town her early beauties knew," but who declines to the point where she is "scorned by all, forsaken, and oppressed, / . . . Diseased, [and] decayed . . ." (ll. 193-94, 201-203). Although the host's wife does not find herself in quite such dire straits, her plight does not differ significantly. Like the other, she had once been fair and generous in her lovemaking, "But age, beauty's incurable disease, / Had left her more desire than power to please. / As cocks will strike although their spurs be gone, / She with her old blear eyes to smite begun" (ll. 49-52). Her situation epitomizes the movement from genuine passion to sterile form, since "Though nothing else, she in despight of time / Preserved the affectation of her prime," and demonstrates how social behavior can become a mode of sexual sublimation. Either activity—social or sexual—proves hopelessly vacuous and unfulfilling. Timon's inability to satisfy his appetite at the dinner table because of the poor fare implicitly parallels the "starvation" of the host in his marriage bed. Food, like sex, has degenerated into mere semblance, a vague facsimile of the real thing.[6]

Thus in instance after instance Rochester's poetry is characterized, not by the exaltation of sexuality as commonly assumed, but by an unequivocal demonstration of the latter's transience and futility. This demonstration takes many forms. Often a poem dramatizes the separateness of each bodily part and the body's consequent inability to function successfully as a whole. By a variety of images and techniques, the ideal of totality is invoked merely to be subverted in the next moment. A typical example occurs in **"The Imperfect Enjoyment,"** where intertwining arms, legs, lips, and breasts turn abruptly into an exclusive focus upon the mistress's hand and the lover's sexual organ, each seeming peculiarly autonomous and disembodied. The "distance" between them, symbolic if not literal, is clear: "Ev'n her fair hand, which might bid heat return / To frozen age, and make cold hermits burn, / Applied to my dead cinder, warms no more / Than fire to ashes could past flames restore" (ll. 31-34). This description recalls a passage in **"A Song of a Young Lady to Her Ancient Lover,"** which presents an ostensibly more optimistic picture of the same basic situation: "Thy nobler part . . . / From [his] ice shall be released, / And soothed by my reviving hand, / In former warmth and vigor stand" (ll. 15-20). Similarly, in **"A Satyr on Charles II,"** the poet sympathizes with "The pains it costs to poor, laborious Nelly, / Whilst she employs hands, fingers, mouth, and thighs, / Ere she can raise the member she enjoys." In all such cases, farcically mechanical exertions replace natural lovemaking.

To be sure, the **"Song of a Young Lady"** cited above reflects a hopeful note in its suggestion of a kind of *felix culpa* through which the fallen penis will subsequently rise to its former heights. Yet, despite the seeming optimism, the Young Lady's **"Song"** proves characteristic of its author in that it utterly fails to substantiate the promise of rebirth through its language. The Song deliberately reverses the poetic convention whereby an old man addresses a young girl, transforming her into a symbol of physical and spiritual revival.[7] The emphasis in such poems remains focused upon the promise inherent in youth while at the same time age is portrayed as the natural culmination of youth's potentiality, in much the same way that the flower embodies the fulfillment of the bud. Waller's and Etherege's respective verses "To a Very Young Lady" well exemplify this genre.[8] Rochester's poem, by contrast, does not support its promise of renewal with descriptions embodying in themselves the fact of nature's fertility, beauty's power, and youth's exaltation. The possibility of a sexual revival is stated rather than triumphantly demonstrated through images of natural and human regeneration. We know that the speaker is young primarily because of the title; the poem itself fails to present an attractive vision of youth associated with energy and rebirth. The speaker's "brooding kisses" are likened to the "kind showers in autumn" which "a second spring recall." However, the image of the Ancient Lover's "dry, withered lips" resembling "barren furrows" and the prospect of his soon becoming "Aching, shaking, crazy, [and] cold" counteract the life-giving kisses and set the tone for the poem as a whole. In the final analysis **"A Song of a Young Lady"** has little to do with either sexual rebirth or longevity. Its theme concerns an ailing organism which retains some hope of approximating its former state. But the promise held out rests primarily with the possibility that a disintegrating machine can be patched together again for another few performances.

II

I do not randomly choose the image of a disintegrating machine. For throughout Rochester's poetry the sexual takes on increasingly sinister overtones until it finally emerges as mechanical grotesquerie.[9] In a frightening extension of Descartes' view that animals are simply machines, Rochester at times posits the vision of man himself as the ultimate machine. In this connection it is interesting that he specifically draws a parallel between human and animal behavior on several occasions. We have already seen the interchangeability of the Fine Lady's "necessary thing" and the "curious miniature of man" in *A Letter from Artemisia.* An even more striking example occurs in **"The Imperfect Enjoyment,"** where the speaker likens his mistresses' sterile, meaningless performances of sexual intercourse to hogs who "on gates do rub themselves and grunt" (l. 65).

The animals in this passage symbolize not uncontrolled bestiality but something far worse: automaton-like motions inimical to any genuine passion and incapable of yielding sensual delight. These motions equally characterize the human figures depicted by Rochester. Thus the speaker of **"A Ramble"** reviles his mistress bitterly for having rendered sex a mere mechanical process by "turn[ing] damned abandoned jade, / When neither head nor tail persuade" (ll. 99-100). Just as, in **"The Imperfect Enjoyment,"** he is a "common fucking post" for whores' relief, so she is here "A passive pot for fools to spend in." Mrs. Willis in a similar manner betrays the sanctity of "generous" passion through her dreary executions of joyless lust: "She rails and scolds when she lies down, / And curses when she spends" (**"On Mrs. Willis"**).

Although in a poem like **"A Satyr on Charles II"** the somewhat laborious efforts required to execute the sexual act are treated in a mildly ironic and humorous manner, elsewhere they are offered as the irrefutable proof that the human body is a mechanism slowly but surely falling apart. The application of the female hand to the male member becomes much like the manual repair of a defective vehicle or instrument part. The men in Rochester's verse are at one point accurately characterized as "Poor broken properties" ("Fragment: What vain, unnecessary things are men"). Sexuality for them is little more than automaton-like movement. The same is true of the Emperor's bawd, Chylax, to whom Valentinian contemptuously declares, "A meer perpetual Motion makes you happy." Rochester's implicit "answer" to Donne's "Licence my roaving hands, and let them go, / Behind, before, above, between, below. / O my America! my new-found-land"[10] is his scornful assertion:

> Let the porter and the groom,
>   Things designed for dirty slaves,
> Drudge in fair Aurelia's womb
>   To get supplies for age and graves.
>
> ("**Song: Love a woman? You're an ass!**")

Sexual intercourse involves not eager exploration but tedious drudgery; it is here as laborious an activity from the male viewpoint as it is elsewhere shown to be from the female's.

While contemporary poems of other Court Wits—for example, the epistles of Etherege and Buckhurst[11]—likewise often depict sexual activity in highly unattractive terms, stressing an aftermath of exhaustion and possible disease, none goes as far as Rochester's in showing how a world of dynamic potency can turn abruptly into a universe of irreparable decay. The poet in "Mr. Etherege's Answer" draws a repulsive picture of the act of love, making the sexual organs into grotesque objects. However, his disgust is quickly erased by a full day's sleep. He awakens the next morning "fresh and gay / As citizen on holiday." Renewed appetite replaces sexual weariness, so that the stench-ridden "pool of harlot" now seems "fresh and wholesome gear." Sexuality becomes part of an eternal cycle of recurrence, with revulsion and surfeit giving way to the birth of new desires along with the prospect of new conquests. Thus while Etherege's poem mildly undercuts the libertine ideal of unlimited sensuality, it reflects little of the devastating irony to which Rochester subjects the same ideal. Etherege's perpetual round of sexual exhaustion followed by erotic arousal, which leaves the vision of physical plenitude basically intact, becomes at times in Rochester a sexual cul-de-sac, heralding the annihilation of even the slightest possibility of continued physical pleasure. The horror which the poet experiences upon viewing the events in St. James's Park and the violent denunciations he heaps on the scene have the effect of rendering carefree lovemaking obsolete and future sexual escapades almost inconceivable.

III

Rochester's attitude toward the body reveals itself most strikingly and dramatically in **"The Imperfect Enjoyment."** Works dealing with the theme of impotence constituted an important genre during the seventeenth century, so we can examine closely how Rochester accommodated poetic convention to his own unique perspective.[12] **"The Imperfect Enjoyment"** is distinctive for the bitterness of its tone, which differs from the calmly ironic or resigned tone of the other versions. Only Rochester ends his poem with an emphatic curse, which suggests much more than the momentary surprise or disappointment voiced by Etherege, Aphra Behn, Wycherley, and others. Whereas Behn extends description of the sex foreplay over eighty lines, enhancing thereby the titillating effects upon the reader and making the impotence seem something of an afterthought, Rochester arrives at the critical moment—premature ejaculation—at line 15, and thus reserves the remaining fifty-seven lines to dwell upon the terrifying fact of impotence in all its ramifications. What results is a profound revulsion of sexuality itself which almost assumes the magnitude of an all-encompassing contempt for the world. The speaker ends by lashing out vitriolically against his penis and verbally transforming it into a repulsive object—"Through all the town a common fucking post"—which he violently dismisses as "Worst part of me, and henceforth hated most" (l. 62).

In Etherege's "The Imperfect Enjoyment" there is no isolation whatever of the penis, hence no hint of its evolution into a dehumanized thing separate from the living organism. Far from betraying revulsion against the sexual act itself or hatred directed toward the male organ, Etherege very quietly and dispassionately blames his mistress, who displayed "too much modesty," and then calmly philosophizes about the general situation:

> From my defeat your glory does arise,
> My weakness proves the vigor of your eyes;
> They did consume the victim, ere it came
> Unto the altar, with a purer flame.

(ll. 45-48)

Wycherley's "The Double Disappointment" and the anonymous poem beginning "Fruition was the Question in Debate" likewise end on a note of serene philosophic reflection. Thus the latter soberly observes: "For Love turns impotent, when strain'd too high, / This very Cordial makes him sooner die, / Evaporates in Flame the Fire so great; / Love's Chemistry thrives best with equal Heat." Another of Wycherley's poems on this theme, "The Unperforming Lover's Apology," is almost ludicrous in its leisurely and meticulously symmetrical explanation of what went wrong ("Your too much Beauty, my too much Desire, / Your too much Warmth in Love, my too much Fire," etc.) and in its gleeful playing with paradox. One would almost think the speaker deliberately failed to "perform" just so that he could deliver his elaborate apology.

"The Disappointment" by Aphra Behn, modeled closely on Ovid's *Amores,* III.7, ends somewhat more dramatically than the foregoing works, with the lover "curs-[ing] his Birth, his Fate, [and] his Stars" for having been damned to "the Hell, of Impotence," but even here there is no real stridency or truculence, no overwhelming sense of horror at the body's inadequacy. We do not hear the lover cry out in his own voice, as is the case in Rochester's poem; instead, the narrator detachedly observes that he does so. All of the works cited here differ radically from Rochester's verse in both specific detail and pervasive tone.

Other related points of contrast prove equally illuminating. Many of the non-Rochesterian "Imperfect Enjoyment" poems suggest, at least implicitly, the temporary nature of the failure and the promise of greater success in the future. (None in any case denies the latter's possibility.) The speaker in one specifically looks forward to his subsequent bedroom endeavors and prays: "When next in such Assaults I chance to be, / Give me more Vigour, less Activity" ("Fruition was the Question in Debate"). The title of another anonymous poem, "The Lost Opportunity Recovered," speaks for itself. While it describes Lysander's initial impotence in rather graphic detail, its final 120 lines are reserved for an ecstatic depiction of his restored vigor, when, "With a proud Courage and with stiffness blest," he more than compensates for his previous lapse with a sexual stamina worthy of Chanticleer. Rochester's version, however, conveys a sense of finality which seems to preclude not only future successes but even further at-

tempts. The violent repudiation of his member in many ways calls to mind the bitter outcry against Corinna in **"A Ramble."** Both endings suggest an unequivocal termination of all physical pleasure. Rochester's portrayal of impotence implies that it is not so much the temporary result of particular circumstances as the inevitable condition of all human existence: a comprehensive metaphor of man's failure to realize his desires in the mortal world. This interpretation is underscored by the fact that no clearly delineated reasons are offered for the lover's sexual inadequacy; it simply asserts itself, with neither forewarning nor excuse.

Other treatments of this theme make it clear that the impotence results specifically from the unnecessary dalliance of the coy maiden or the lover's overly vivid imagination, or else a combination of these factors—both of which, incidentally, are singled out by Montaigne as prime causes of male impotence in his essay, "Of the Force of Imagination."[13] Etherege relates how "After a pretty amorous discourse, / She does resist my love with pleasing force, / Moved not with anger but with modesty: / Against her will she is my enemy" (ll. 1-4). Aphra Behn puts stress on Cloris' ambivalence, emblematized by "Her bright Eyes sweet, and yet severe, / Where Love, and shame, confus'dly strive." She both desires and fears sexual intercourse, and consequently repulses even as she lures on the unfortunate lover. Added to this are the latter's wildly extravagant expectations of possessing his goddess and entering "That awful Throne! that Paradice!" which make the coming disappointment seem almost inevitable: "Ready to taste a Thousand joys / The too transported hapless Swayne, / Found the vast pleasure, turn'd to pain." The anonymous author of "Fruition . . ." likewise ascribes the failure at least partially to his mistress's affected modesty—the "feigned Vertue [that is] but a Bawd to Vice"—which fans his desires to a disproportionate extent.

In Rochester's poem, however, there is seemingly no obstacle preventing the physical consummation. Corinna, far from playing the coy maiden, shows great enthusiasm for the venture—"Both [are] equally inspired with eager fire"—while the lover applies himself immediately to the task at hand, without first constructing an elaborate mental anticipation by its nature incapable of fulfillment. The poet makes a point of stressing the rapidity of the sexual advances and the way that they seem to translate themselves directly into action:

> Her nimble tongue, Love's lesser lightning, played
> Within my mouth, and to my thoughts conveyed
> Swift orders that I should prepare to throw
> The all-dissolving thunderbolt below.

(ll. 7-10)

And yet, when the critical moment arrives, the body fails as it does so often in Rochester's poetry. To be sure, an explanation for this failure is offered *ex post facto* by the lover:

> Eager desires confound my first intent,
> Succeeding shame does more success prevent,
> And rage at last confirms me impotent.

(ll. 28-30)

But the pronouncement comes as rather an afterthought, unsupported by prior description and inadequate as an elucidation of the specific circumstances described. The dramatic effect of the verse, therefore, is to make impotence seem fundamentally inexplicable and uncontrollable, an inevitable fact of life liable to appear at any moment without warning and without particular reason. Elsewhere, in **"The Disabled Debauchee,"** we view impotence as the unavoidable state produced by a gradual, extended lapse of time, hence located in the indeterminate future; here we see it dramatized as immanent in each and every instant, capable of apocalyptically asserting itself at any time, whether in youth or old age. Impotence sheds its fixed temporal associations and becomes an eternal present.

It should seem clear by now that, despite Rochester's libertinism (or perhaps in some curious way because of it), his writings are at their most convincing and eloquent when registering disgust with the physical world, especially as it relates to sexuality. Starting from a theoretical premise which maintains the unqualified exaltation of worldly phenomena and the total embrace of sensual pleasures, Rochester reveals an underlying repulsion against all worldly and sensual things as these repeatedly betray initial expectations. The basic tenor of his work bears affinities not so much with Donne's early songs and sonnets, their seemingly natural kin, as with his *Devotions,* where we find a similar emphasis on bodily failure (in this case the author's own sickness) as a primary characteristic—and comprehensive metaphor—of human existence. The wretched consequences ensuing upon the Fall, represented by Donne as a condition whereby "one half [of mankind] lacks meat, and the other stomach," have equal relevance to Restoration life as Rochester depicts it.[14] We should no longer be surprised at the extent to which the experience of joy and the awareness of earthly beauty are absent from Rochester's writings. Not only do such writers as Lovelace and Herrick paint earthly delights in a manner foreign to Rochester, but even religious poets like Vaughan and Traherne convey a sensuous bliss nonexistent in his work. The "sprightliness" and "vigor" that Samuel Johnson discerns in Rochester's poetry,[15] while unquestionably present on one level, seem ultimately rather incongruous when applied to a body of writings so obsessed with its vision of impotence and decay.

Notes

1. See, for example, Gilbert Burnet, *Some Passages on the Life and Death of the Right Honourable John Earl of Rochester* (London, 1680) and *History of His Own Time* (London, 1724), I, where he asserts that Rochester "gave himself up to all sorts of extravagance, and to the wildest follies that a wanton could devise" (pp. 264-65). For further elaboration of this view, see Robert Parsons, *A Sermon Preached at the Funeral of the Right Honorable John Earl of Rochester* (Oxford, 1680); *The Rochester-Savile Letters,* ed. John H. Wilson (Columbus, 1941); "Some Memoirs of the Earl of Rochester," *The Works of Rochester,* ed. Quilter Johns (Halifax, Eng., 1933); Samuel Johnson, *Lives of the English Poets,* ed. L. Archer-Hind, Everyman ed. (London and New York, 1964), I, 127-31; *Memoirs of the Comte de Gramont* by Anthony Hamilton, ed. Cyril Hughes Hartmann (New York, 1930), pp. 234-48, 256-58, *et passim.* Twentieth-century writers who stress the libertine aspects of Rochester's life include Johannes Prinz, *John Wilmot, Earl of Rochester: His Life and Writings* (Leipzig, 1927); John Harold Wilson, *The Court Wits of the Restoration* (Princeton, 1948); Vivian de Sola Pinto, *Enthusiast in Wit: A Portrait of John Wilmot, Earl of Rochester, 1647-1680* (London, 1962); Don Cameron Allen, *Doubt's Boundless Sea: Skepticism and Faith in the Renaissance* (Baltimore, 1964).

2. All quotations from Rochester's poetry are taken from *The Complete Poems of John Wilmot, Earl of Rochester,* ed. David M. Vieth (New Haven and London, 1968).

3. In the *Collected Works of John Wilmot, Earl of Rochester,* ed. John Hayward (London, 1926), pp. 188-89.

4. *Hobbes' Leviathan, Reprinted from the Edition of 1651* (Oxford, 1909), p. 13.

5. Cf. Boileau-Despréaux, *Oeuvres complètes,* Gallimard ed. (Bruges, 1966), pp. 20-25. Although there have been several attempts to assess the relationship between Rochester's *Satyr Against Reason and Mankind* and Boileau's Eighth Satire, no one has examined with any thoroughness the similarities and contrasts between *Timon* and the Third Satire. I can here only point to one small difference which, however, suggests a much broader disparity in outlook.

6. The analogy between food and sex in this respect is bolstered by the carrots' resemblance to the Countess's dildo: "A dish of carrots, each of them as long / As tool that to fair countess did belong, / Which her small pillow could not so well hide /

But visitors his flaming head espied" (ll. 79-82). The meaning of "tool" becomes clear in light of a passage from "Signior Dildo" concerning the Countess of Northumberland: "She stifled him almost beneath her pillow, / So closely sh' embraced Signior Dildo" (ll. 31-32).

7. For a brief description of poems utilizing this convention, see Warren Chernaik, *The Poetry of Limitation: A Study of Edmund Waller* (New Haven and London, 1968), pp. 99-102.

8. See *The Poems of Edmund Waller,* ed. G. Thorn Drury (London, 1893), p. 57, and *The Poems of Sir George Etherege,* ed. James Thorpe (Princeton, 1963), p. 1.

9. This aspect of Rochester's poetry has been noted by Ronald Berman, "Rochester and the Defeat of the Senses," *Kenyon Review,* 26 (1964), 357.

10. *John Donne: The Elegies and the Songs and Sonnets,* ed. Helen Gardner (Oxford, 1965), p. 15.

11. These may be found in *The Poems of Etherege,* ed. Thorpe, pp. 35-45.

12. The "Imperfect Enjoyment" poems written during the Restoration include Etherege's "The Imperfect Enjoyment," in *Poems,* ed. Thorpe, pp. 77-78; Aphra Behn's "The Disappointment," in *Rochester's Poems on Several Occasions,* ed. James Thorpe (Princeton, 1950), pp. 92-97; Wycherley's "The Double Disappointment," in *The Complete Works of William Wycherley,* ed. Montague Summers (London, 1924), III, 37, and "The Unperforming Lover's Apology" (IV, 249-50); "The Lost Opportunity Recovered," in *Wit and Drollery* (London, 1682), pp. 1-16; "Fruition was the Question in Debate," in *Collected Works of Rochester,* ed. Hayward, p. 117. For information on other non-English versions, see Richard Quaintance, "French Sources of the Restoration 'Imperfect Enjoyment' Poem," *PQ* [*Philological Quarterly*], 42 (1963), 190-99.

13. Montaigne, for example, declares of the female sex: "Now they wrong us, to receive and admit us with their wanton, squeamish, querellous countenances, which setting us a fire, extinguish us." He cites a favorite saying of Pythagoras' niece: "That a woman which lies with a man ought together with her petie-coate, leave off all bashfulnesse." In addition, and to a much greater extent, he stresses the harms wreaked by an excessively vivid imagination overrun by assorted false beliefs and superstitions. Relating one incident from his own experience and another about King Amasis of Egypt with his young Greek bride Laodice, Montaigne convincingly argues that sexual impotence almost always involves mind over matter—the intervention of the mental faculties in a specifically physical activity. He offers repeated illustrations to prove that "The minde of the assailant molested with sundry different alarums, is easily dismaid." See *Montaigne's Essays,* trans. John Florio, Everyman ed. (London and New York, 1910), I, 97.

14. See *Devotions upon Emergent Occasions,* ed. John Sparrow (Cambridge, 1923).

15. Johnson, *Lives,* ed. Archer-Hind, I, 131.

Ronald W. Johnson (essay date summer 1975)

SOURCE: Johnson, Ronald W. "Rhetoric and Drama in Rochester's *Satyr against Reason and Mankind.*" *Studies in English Literature 1500-1900* 15, no. 3 (summer 1975): 365-73.

[*In the following essay, Johnson praises Rochester's creation of an ambivalent persona in his* Satyr against Reason and Mankind, *as well as his use of complementary rhetorical and dramatic structures.*]

A satirist chooses an object—a target—and proceeds to criticize. But in order to make the criticism palatable and entertaining, the satirist needs to adopt a role which can simultaneously effect mockery toward a target and amiability in an audience. If the target is fairly small, that is if few in the audience are likely to be sympathetic to the target of satire or if the satirist addresses a rather select audience, the satirist can be relatively straightforward. If, however, the satirist aims at a more comprehensive target, one which is likely to touch nerves in most or all of his audience, the satirist must work more subtly.[1] Rochester is straightforward enough in these lines on John Sheffield, Earl of Mulgrave:

> And, with his arm and head, his brain's so weak
> That his starved fancy is compelled to rake
> Among the excrements of others' wit
> To make a stinking meal of what they shit;
> So swine, for nasty meat, to dunghill run,
> And toss their gruntling snouts up when they've done.[2]

But to attack reason and mankind is a much more difficult task if the satirist intends to reach many men. We have a stake in reason and mankind; Rochester's intended audience had no special stake in Mulgrave. The satirist who directs his attack primarily at an individual can hardly count on entertaining or enlightening that individual; but he can hope to amuse a broader audience while projecting his target from a new perspective. Dryden's *Mac Flecknoe* presents Shadwell from an entertaining and even enlightening perspective, but there is no evidence that Shadwell was entertained or enlightened by it. So what can be said for Rochester's *Satyr,* aimed at us?

The problem that Rochester faced is important because its solution is the key to the structure of the poem. R. S. Crane offers considerable good sense when he suggests concerning the critic that "his first business, whatever else he may do, is to consider literary works, without prejudice, in the light of the specific ends or principles of construction, whatever they may be, which have in fact, on the best hypothesis he can form, governed their composition. . . ."[3] Such a task, of course, tends to attract more moral than practical critical support. The task of determining ends and principles of construction is as Crane points out a large one. But in the case of Rochester's *Satyr* a beginning is made easier by the fact that the fundamental problem of structuring the poem is clear: Rochester had to devise a structure which would allow him simultaneously to mock and entertain mankind. The following paragraphs argue that Rochester succeeds in that paradoxical task by constructing his poem on rhetorical and dramatic principles. He unites the rhetorical and the dramatic in a persona who elicits our support but figures forth Rochester's satiric aims.

Critical accounts of Rochester's *Satyr against Reason and Mankind* have largely dealt with the problem of originality and its corollary, the problem of sources. Instead, then, of focusing directly on Rochester, criticism has tended to explore Johnson's dictum: "Of the *Satire against Man* Rochester can only claim what remains when all Boileau's part is taken away."[4] The poem has also been found indebted to such authors as Hobbes, Montaigne, and La Rochefoucauld, not to mention Boileau. Insofar as the *Satyr* is merely a translation or even an imitation of Boileau's Eighth Satire—or of any work—any attempt to understand the satiric structure of the poem must surely consult the sources. Johnson's "London," for example, obviously owes much by way of formal arrangement to Juvenal's Third Satire. A good many parallels in thought and expression have been discovered between Rochester and other authors.[5] Yet Crane's "specific ends and principles of construction" which govern the making of an individual poem are clearly not to be found for Rochester in Boileau, or Hobbes, or Montaigne. As John F. Moore concludes in his article on Rochester's originality, "Rochester must be credited with the same degree of eclectic originality accorded to other writers who absorb ideas from extensive reading and develop them into an essentially original synthesis."[6] Rochester was surely familiar with Boileau's poetry, and he was surely familiar with the ideas propagated by Hobbes or Montaigne. But so were most educated men of the age. What is important for our purposes is the fact that Rochester shaped ideas for his own artistic end. As suggested above, for example, the thrust of the *Satyr against Reason and Mankind* is not aimed at just this or that man but at all mankind. Boileau limits his target to

certain men; Rochester does not. The special end Rochester attempted prompts one to explore his specific principles of construction.

The *Satyr against Reason and Mankind* appears first of all to be a debate. But, insofar as it is a debate, it is loaded in favor of Rochester's persona. The cleric, the opposition, is barely allowed to state his case before he is interrupted; nor is he allowed a rebuttal as is the persona. In fact, Rochester has created a declamation carefully organized on the principles of classical rhetoric. The cleric is only allowed to act out one aspect of the neat rhetorical organization. There is the exordium (ll. 1-7), the narration of the "facts" in the case (ll. 8-45), the argument displaying objections (where the cleric acts out his role) and answers to objections (ll. 46-167), the remarks supplementary to the main argument (ll. 168-173), and the epilogue (ll. 174 to the end).

The exordium (ll. 1-7) succinctly introduces the persona's thesis: that he would prefer to be a beast rather than a man. It is worth noting, though, that the persona is acutely aware that such a separation from his fellow man is beyond hope. His thesis is conditional and admittedly impossible: "Were I (who to my cost already am / One of those strange, prodigious creatures, man) / A spirit free to choose. . . ." His acute sense of his own humanity is important although easily overlooked because of the devastating attacks against mankind which follow. But the persona's role in the poem takes on ironic complexity and subtlety if his own humanity is remembered. He is no Houyhnhnm surveying the Yahoos; more like Gulliver, he is uncomfortably aware of the Yahoo within himself. That predicament helps explain the next section of the poem and the next section of the rhetorical structure, the narration. The persona begins the prosecution in the classic manner; he lays out his facts. As he pictures the case, man is so enamored of his own invention, reason, that he follows reason wherever it takes him. The scene is curiously laughable and pathetic. Reason is metaphorically presented as an *ignis fatuus* (fool's fire, a flickering light associated with swamp gas); it leads man on a lifelong misadventure through the bogs and thorns of error, over mountains of whimseys, and into the boundless sea of doubt where mankind attempts to stay afloat by clinging to bladders (urinary receptacles) which are books of philosophy. The narration of the facts and man's Quixotic life are brought to a conclusion that contains more pathos than humor:

> Then old age and experience, hand in hand,
> Lead him to death, and make him understand,
> After a search so painful and so long,
> That all his life he has been in the wrong.
> Huddled in dirt the reasoning engine lies,
> Who was so proud, so witty, and so wise.

The idea, the image, and the tone conjure irony: the formerly pompous "reasoning engine," "proud," "witty," "wise," is now "huddled in dirt" after a "search so painful and so long." Again, the lines produce not laughter but pity. The persona is not merely critical; his presentation is also sympathetic.

Important also in this narration is the dramatic movement. Man, the main character, of course, in the persona's presentation, imitates the movement of the classic tragic hero. Man's journey begins with rising from bogs and brakes (up to "mountains of whimseys") and ends with falling ("into doubt's boundless sea") and finally death. The action does not involve an Aristotelian hero—after all, it is only a "vain animal" which undergoes the action—but, if man's fate is not on that account tragic, it is pathetic. The movement at this point does not directly involve the persona; he merely recites his case, sums up with some observations on man's pride, wisdom, and wit, then introduces the interrupting cleric. But just as man becomes a pathetic character in the dramatic action of the persona's narration, the persona becomes a pathetic character in his rhetorical role within Rochester's poem. That development emerges in the third section of the poem, the argument (ll. 46-167).

The argument's organization is rhetorically simple enough. The cleric, objecting to the persona who would "rail at reason and mankind" (l. 59), articulates a traditional vision of reason as the attribute which raises mankind above the beast and beyond. The persona's answer to the objections divides into two parts: the cleric's mistaken notion of reason is attacked and put right in a series of contrasts which emphasizes the superiority of empiricism over speculative system building (ll. 72-111);[7] the cleric's mistaken notion of mankind's superiority to the beasts is attacked in a series of contrasts which, after a transitional section suggesting that the beasts have a better sense of reason than mankind (ll. 112-122), emphasizes man's moral inferiority to the beasts (ll. 123-167). But if the organization of this argumentative section is simple, the argument is enlivened by dramatization. Rochester could have had the persona merely state possible objections at this point in his speech; instead, Rochester chose to create a foil. The cleric never has a chance. He is pompous and witless on wit:

> Perhaps my muse were fitter for this part,
> For I profess I can be very smart
> On wit, which I abhor with all my heart.
>
> (ll. 52-54)

The persona, on the contrary, has already achieved exactly the opposite effect, writing on the same subject, in lines such as these:

> For wits are treated just like common whores:
> First they're enjoyed, and then kicked out of doors.

> The pleasure past, a threatening doubt remains
> That frights th' enjoyer with succeeding pains.
>
> (ll. 37-40)

The cleric seems already disarmed as a debater when he turns his attention toward the debate (his ink, likened to the tide in l. 57, is presumably swayed by the moon). In any case, the imagery with which the cleric pictures man's fate makes use of the rising and falling motif which the persona has, as we have seen, already initiated. This time, however, instead of climbing, stumbling, and falling after an *ignis fatuus,* man flies, dives, and soars on wings of reason. Man is not pathetic in this pattern, but triumphant. Such a vision is obviously too much for the persona: he breaks into the cleric's speech in order to crush the cleric's notion that reason allows us to soar beyond earth. Quite the opposite is true of reason:

> This made a whimsical philosopher
> Before the spacious world, his tub prefer,
> And we have modern cloistered coxcombs who
> Retire to think, 'cause they have nought to do.
>
> (ll. 90-93)

The cleric's vision of man soaring is supplanted by the persona's more earthly vision involving "frantic crowds," "thinking fools," "bedlams," a "heavy sot," an "old witch," a "crippled carcass," a "tub," and "cloistered coxcombs" (ll. 82-92).

But even if the persona's rhetorical prowess allows him to make a mere foil of the cleric, there is cause to suspect that Rochester toys a bit with his persona. After the persona's attack on the cleric's notion of reason, the persona has managed, he announces (l. 112), to make reason right. The persona's right reason is not the traditional right reason of scholastic philosophy (grounded in a one, true, and good universe, perceiving essences, oriented toward metaphysics as much as ethics); on the contrary, the persona's right reason is epistemologically empirical ("That reason which distinguishes by sense") and ethically pragmatic ("Those creatures are the wisest who attain / By surest means, the ends at which they aim"). The persona's triumph in righting reason is short lived, however, when he turns toward man. What the persona perceives and articulates is that, first of all, an empirical approach to man reveals that man is corrupt; secondly, if one is going to achieve what he wants, be pragmatic, in a corrupt society, then he will himself be corrupt. Thus the persona's rise to the role of the assured rhetorician who has righted reason is swiftly followed by the revelation of the ironic predicament at the end of the argument. His remarks supplementary to the main argument reflect on himself as much as on other men:

> Thus, sir, you see what human nature craves:
> Most men are cowards, all men should be knaves.

The difference lies, as far as I can see,
Not in the thing itself, but the degree,
And all the subject matter of debate
Is only: Who's a knave of the first rate?

(ll. 168-173)

While we identify with the winning debater as he pillories the pompous cleric, Rochester is able to mask his satire against us in the rise and fall of the persona himself. After all, we follow a kind of *ignis fatuus* when we side with the persona. The persona's role is reflexively ironic throughout: he wants to be a beast but knows he is a man; he satirizes wits but is himself witty; he rights reason only to perceive that reason demands one be a knave; he initiates and dominates the debate but suggests the subject being debated is not the issue. Rochester creates a persona who is a confident, aloof, and cynical rhetorician; but that is only a mask for the persona's identity as a pathetic human in Rochester's bleak vision of mankind. The winning rhetorician, whose case has been persuasive, must himself be a knave; he may even be a first-rate knave. The persona's convincing empiricism suggests that "most men are cowards"; his pragmatism concludes that "all men should be knaves" (l. 169). The only question remaining: who is best at it? In any case, the persona is clearly an *ignis fatuus* who has led us to our own sea of doubt; we cannot rely on a persona who gives us every reason to believe that he is merely exercising his powers of knavery. Laughter, for the reader, again is lost to the pathetic irony of the persona's denouement. The great debater has, in the last act of the debate, been deflated to the point of becoming merely a fellow knave. We who admired the debater's skill (his pride, his wit, his wisdom?) are left without anything positive or affirmative: there is only the knavery suggested by the persona or the foolishness suggested by the cleric. And, of course, it is not the cleric who finally stands for the reason and mankind satirized in Rochester's poem; it is the persona and, hence, ourselves. The cleric and what he stands for are merely facilely burlesqued; we, through the persona, are subtly caught in satiric irony. We know what is wrong without knowing what is right (very much like the persona's pathetic man who, after a painful and long search, discovers that all his life has been in the wrong).

Rochester's ability to mask his identity in real life was and is, of course, legendary; he played several roles in his brief lifetime. But his ability to create the ambivalent persona is perhaps less well known. For example, there is the oddly proud and pathetic persona of the **"Disabled Debauchee"**; or there is the ambivalent persona of **"To the Postboy,"** which poem Vieth briefly introduces as "strange half-boastful, half-penitential verses";[8] surely the **Satyr against Reason and Mankind** contains its own reflexively ironic persona—attractive in his debating triumph, disappointing in his too human denoue-

ment. In fact, irony of a particularly broad scope often relies on an ambivalent persona; one is reminded of the complexities surrounding Swift's Gulliver of the Fourth Book, or even Browning's persona in "My Last Duchess," or Twain's Theodor Fischer in *The Mysterious Stranger* and the Boss in *A Connecticut Yankee in King Arthur's Court*. All of these personae tend to end as *alazons* who have—perhaps against their will—become their own *eirons*; the persona in Rochester's **Satyr** is no exception.

Finally, there is Rochester's ambivalent, if on that account consistent, epilogue (ll. 174 to the end). The epilogue begins with an apparent qualification or delimiting of the original target, reason and mankind:

All this with indignation have I hurled
At the pretending part of the proud world,
Who, swollen with selfish vanity, devise
False freedoms, holy cheats, and formal lies
Over their fellow slaves to tyrannize.

(ll. 174-178)

The persona seems to be suggesting that his attack on reason and mankind was actually only aimed at "part" of mankind. As has been seen, that is ostensibly if not actually true. He appeared only to attack the pompous principles associated with the cleric and his kind. But more was at stake, and even here the persona is talking about those men who attempt to tyrannize "their fellow slaves." We are all slaves, presumably, in the sense that "Men must be knaves, 'tis in their own defence" (l. 160). Furthermore, the persona has just concluded that none of us can afford to "be less a villain than the rest" (l. 167). Since all men are villains, distinguishing one type of villain from the whole world would appear to be only a matter of degree. The target, rather than being narrowed as at first appears, is only actually being brought into focus in a slightly different manner. In this case the persona again offers a conditional proposition; it seems to contain the possibility of a recantation of all that has gone before. If a just courtier can be found or if a faithful churchman can be found, the persona will admit he has been wrong. He is in little danger: "If such there be, yet grant me this at least: / Man differs more from man, than man from beast." Clearly, he again sees his conditional proposition as quite impossible. In effect, he is suggesting that such a man could not be a man at all. Granting that any man differs more from mankind than mankind differs from the beast is, in the context of the poem, akin to granting the famous proposition that all generalizations are false including this one. Affirmation ends in absurdity.

The ending, like the poem, even like Rochester himself, is enigmatic. The rhetorical and dramatic structures within the poem constitute Rochester's fundamental principles of construction. Perception of the major irony of the poem depends upon grasping the relationship between the two structures. The poem appears to be one thing, an indictment of those who regard mankind as superior to beasts on the basis of reason; but the poem is quite another thing, an indictment of all mankind as inevitably dishonest on the basis of common sense. Rochester is able to criticize us while entertaining us because the rhetorical and the dramatic structures complement one another and thereby produce satire of the widest scope.

Notes

1. Cf. David Worcester, *The Art of Satire* (New York, 1960), pp. 13ff.

2. From "My Lord All-Pride." All quotations from Rochester are taken from *The Complete Poems of John Wilmot, Earl of Rochester,* ed. David M. Vieth (New Haven, 1968).

3. R. S. Crane, "Critical and Historical Principles of Literary History," *The Idea of the Humanities* (Chicago, 1967), II, 60.

4. *Lives of the English Poets,* ed. George Birkbeck Hill (Oxford, 1905), I, 226.

5. See, for example: S. F. Crocker, "Rochester's Satire against Mankind: A Study of Certain Aspects of the Background," *West Virginia University Studies* III, *Philological Papers,* II (May, 1937), 57-73; John F. Moore, "The Originality of Rochester's *Satyr against Mankind,*" *PMLA,* 58 (1943), 393-401; Thomas H. Fujimura, "Rochester's 'Satyr against Mankind'; An Analysis," *Studies in Philology,* 55 (1958), 576-590; Paul C. Davies, "Rochester and Boileau: A Reconsideration," *Comparative Literature,* 21 (1969), 348-355.

6. "The Originality of Rochester's *Satyr against Mankind,*" *PMLA,* 58 (1943), 401. Recently, attention has begun to turn toward the workings of that originality in the poem itself: Charles A. Knight, "The Paradox of Reason: Argument in Rochester's 'Satyr against Mankind,'" *Modern Language Review,* 65 (1970), 254-260; David M. Vieth, "Toward an Anti-Aristotelian Poetic: Rochester's *Satyr Against Mankind* and *Artemisia to Chloe,* with Notes on Swift's *Tale of a Tub* and *Gulliver's Travels,*" *Language and Style,* 5 (1972), 123-145; Dustin H. Griffin, *Satires Against Man: The Poems of Rochester* (Berkeley, 1973), pp. 197-245.

7. See Thomas H. Fujimura's article, cited above, for a more detailed commentary on the persona's right reason vs. speculative reason.

8. Cf. Anne Righter, "John Wilmot, Earl of Rochester," *Proceedings of the British Academy,* 53 (1967), 47-69. Righter discusses "To the Postboy" and, in general, argues convincingly for the notion that Rochester's characteristic mode is one of disguise.

Reba Wilcoxon (essay date summer 1976)

SOURCE: Wilcoxon, Reba. "The Rhetoric of Sex in Rochester's Burlesque." *Papers on Language & Literature* 12, no. 3 (summer 1976): 273-84.

[*In the following essay, Wilcoxon discusses Rochester's satirizing of romantic conventions and sexual behavior in his poetry.*]

Among the few poems that have survived in Rochester's own handwriting is a free translation of the first five lines of Lucretius's *De Rerum Natura,* an invocation to Venus as the "delight of mankind" by whom "all things live."[1] The fragment is an ironic contrast to the anti-sublime treatment of love for which Rochester is notorious. For him, the "delight of mankind" could be painful, nasty, or ridiculous; and, though all things live by Love, Sex is usually her right name. The images and obscenities of sex are particularly destructive to the romantic ideal in some of Rochester's burlesques of popular seventeenth-century forms.

Such burlesque was popular in the Restoration, and practiced by other Court Wits; but Rochester was unequalled in using sexual satire to a double purpose. Working within the rhetorical and conceptual schemes of the pastoral, the song, and the panegyric, he ridiculed the genres themselves for their reductive and euphemistic visions of sexual relations, and, at the same time, poked fun at the tendency to see sexual candor equally as false as sexual romanticism—if taken at face value. As W. K. Wimsatt has said of the Augustan mode, Rochester challenges the reader with "by no means an easy burlesque nihilism."[2]

In poems satirizing sexual behavior Rochester takes rhetorical advantage of the decorum of the genres, while violating, in the cause of advancing his own "truth," the decorum of content. At this level Rochester's images and obscenities function as a symbol of the naturalism and empiricism for which he stands, in opposition to the traditional rationalism that stands behind the pastoral, the love lyric, and the panegyric. In the cognitive process Rochester thus sets in motion, one sees only the degradation of sex—and women. Yet the rule of order, for form and content, doubles back on this interpretation to modify the judgment of degradation: the burlesque implies something positive. A true dialectic is not involved, for there is no synthesis. Rather, one feels confronted with a swinging door between two philosophical perspectives, opening one way and then the other. Not all burlesque works this way; more commonly, the tradition of form and content is a backdrop that effects incongruity either for social satire or simple fun. Thus, the *Aeneid* suffers no diminution in the *Dunciad*; Milton loses no stature in "The Splendid Shilling"; Ovid's story of Baucis and Philemon is not itself attacked in Swift's poem.

By contrast, in Rochester's rhetoric of sex, values on both sides of the door remain constant: on the one hand, sex degrades the romantic ideal, but, on the other, the pressure of the ideal forces a reassessment of the vehicle, sex itself. Once the barrier of obscenity falls away, one detects degrees of attack and the distinctions made that point to sexual standards rather than, as Ronald Berman has held, "the defeat of the senses."[3] Yet the obscenity continues to erode the traditional romantic values. The best examples of this reciprocating process appear among the poems that have long been categorized as "unprintable" or "unquotable"—for example, **"Fair Chloris in a pigsty lay," "The Mock Song," "By all love's soft, yet mighty powers,"** and the more substantial **"A Ramble in St. James's Park."**

Although **"Fair Chloris in a pigsty lay"** is entitled **"Song to Chloris"** in the 1680 edition of ***Poems on Several Occasions,*** the poem is more exactly a mock-pastoral narrative rather than a song, if the song is considered as a short lyric on love. The pastoral, the idyllic vision of country life generally recognized as an urban literary invention, had all but run its course by the time of the Restoration. To the Court Wits, love in the countryside was a patent joke, and Rochester plumbs the joke to its Freudian limits in **"Fair Chloris."** It is the *reductio ad absurdum* of the pastoral, in terms of setting and sex. A pigsty is, after all, as indigenous to a rural setting as lambs and willow trees. "Romance" in Arcadia should, if one is honest about it, accommodate sexual fantasies and masturbation, as much as "romance" in the real world.

Swift's *Go, go, you're bit* is recalled in **"Fair Chloris"**: first, in the reader's inclination to interpret the rape by the crafty swain as real rather than as a dream; and, secondly, in the reversal occurring in the last stanza, which is the ultimate degeneration of the pastoral and of the romantic trappings which precede it. Pigsty though it is, the pastoral epithets are deceptively persuasive, and the description of Fair Chloris rushing to the aid of her "bosom pig" is reminiscent of a Homeric goddess bent upon divine intervention. But since "not one god took care to save" her from the swain's ploy to lure her to the cave and there violate her "honor" (a virtue that Rochester often makes light of when it refers to chastity), the battle is lost—in epic terms: "Now piercèd is her virgin zone; / She feels the foe within it" (31-32). This end of the chase is an ironic

contrast to metamorphosis in classic myth, in which case, a Daphne or an Arethusa is saved by the gods at the last minute, and being a tree or a fountain is preferable to "dishonor."

Rochester's semantic trap closes on a final *reductio* of pastoral, a grotesque happy ending in the stanza that is often suppressed:

> Frighted she wakes, and waking frigs.
> Nature thus kindly eased
> In dreams raised by her murmuring pigs
> And her own thumb between her legs,
> She's innocent and pleased.
>
> [36-40]

The word "innocent" is the kind of jolt—typical of the parodic technique—which Anne Righter has commented on: "Nothing is more characteristic of Rochester than the way a single word, particularly in the final stanza of a poem, will suddenly move into focus and reveal its possession of a variety of warring meanings."[4] Chloris is innocent in the conventional sense, for the rape is after all only a dream. She is innocent in a more unconventional sense, for her action is a natural response to sexual arousal. At the same time, the irony of her innocence is that she is guilty of the dream, which expresses her own unconscious desires.

Thus Rochester alternates between two planes of values. Rhetorically, his readers are forced to consider the incongruity between the ideal pastoral nymph and the real demand of female sexuality, which makes common notions of chastity a joke. Sex pokes fun at the pastoral, and, conversely, the burlesque of the pastoral pokes fun at sex. Out of this complementary function emerges an implication that sexual acts—and sexual language—are essentially natural (though not necessarily attractive), and that repression and false ideas of "honor" are, like "fair Chloris," rather foolish.

Unlike the pastoral, the song or lyric had little historical stature as a literary genre in the seventeenth century. Nevertheless, it was widely practiced, very popular, and judged by fairly consistent formal criteria: to be clear, smooth, controlled, and brief.[5] Since the seventeenth century, critics of various moral persuasions show a remarkable consensus in praising Rochester not only for his mastery of the form but also for the intensely personal and passionate quality that separated him from his colleagues. To speak of Rochester's "burlesque" of the song is to speak in terms of content, not structure. In the **"Mock Song"** and **"By all love's soft, yet mighty powers,"** Rochester holds firmly to the form of the song while subverting the sweet, the ideal, and even the urbanely cynical content. In terms of technique, these poems are, in Dr. Johnson's terms, "smooth and easy," but contrary to his judgment that Rochester's songs "have little nature," they often have too much for comfort.[6]

The **"Mock Song"** has been established as a travesty of a love song probably written by Sir Carr Scroope and addressed to the Maid of Honor whom he courted, Cary Frazier.[7] Rochester's metrical pattern is identical with Scroope's, and the verbal parallels are similar, although the **"Mock Song"** is a dialogue and Scroope's song is not. Scroope writes in the tradition of such "sweet singers" as Edmund Waller;[8] whereas Rochester transforms the speaker into a sentimental fool who does not understand the kind of female he courts. Scroope's avowal that he "will still love on, will still love on, and die," is parodied by Rochester's creation of a mistress who is compelled to "love on, and die"—the usual pun for orgasm—with "forty lovers more." Phyllis's reply to her plaintive lover completes the poem:

> "Can I," said she, "with nature strive?
>   Alas I am, alas I am a whore!
>
> Were all my body larded o'er
>   With darts of love, so thick
> That you might find in every pore
>   A well-stuck standing prick,
> Whilst yet my eyes alone were free,
>   My heart would never doubt,
> In amorous rage and ecstasy,
>   To wish those eyes, to wish those eyes fucked out."
>
> [7-16]

The mark of Rochester is typical in "Can I with nature strive?" It is in keeping with Fair Chloris of the pigsty, and with the "divine" Corinna of **"A Ramble in St. James's Park."** The imagery of eating is also consistent with **"A Ramble"**; that is, the verb "larded" evokes associations with cooking and meat, or flesh. In the poem the interplay of "larded" with "well-stuck standing prick" transforms Phyllis into "meat," seventeenth-century slang for the female pudendum. The picture of Phyllis is comic; yet the serious effect is to equate the sex act with eating, with no more than a bodily function, and to make Phyllis a bizarre sexual glutton, whose capacity extends even to her eyes.

To the extent that the **"Mock Song"** portrays Cary Frazier, it is a lampoon. But it rises above the topical level of a feud with Sir Carr Scroope or any particular animus toward Cary Frazier, for without these references the poem stands on its own as a gem of burlesque. If the convex side of the satire shows the folly of sentimental love songs and lovers, the concave shows the grossness of ungovernable sexual appetite. The unnatural image of Phyllis prevents taking seriously the excuse, "Can I with nature strive?" Rochester is not satirizing natural sexual desire, but excessive and indiscriminate sexual indulgence.

The satire on women takes a different turn in the song, **"By all love's soft, yet mighty powers."** No other burlesque by Rochester comes closer to exemplifying

what Norman Brown has said of Swift's "unprintable" poems: "For their real theme—quite obvious on a dispassionate reading—is the conflict between our animal body, appropriately epitomized in the anal function, and our pretentious sublimations, more specifically the pretensions of sublimated or romantic-Platonic love."[9] The difference between the two poets is that Rochester's orientation is genital rather than anal, as **"By all love's soft, yet mighty powers"** demonstrates. His mockery of the sublimations in the love song is simultaneously mockery of the potential foulness of the female body, combined in a rather remarkable technical way.

Contrapuntal to the smoothness of sounds and rhythm (apparent when the poem is read aloud without attention to meaning) are well-paced cognitive jolts effected by the obscene imagery:

> By all love's soft, yet mighty powers,
>   It is a thing unfit
> That men should fuck in time of flowers,
>   Or when the smock's beshit.
>
> [1-4]

The opening line sounds the chord of ideal love, which sets up one expectation; the harmony of the verse sets up another. The harmony continues in the euphonic alliteration of "fuck in time of flowers" and "when the smock's beshit," while the language of copulation, menstruation, and excretion violates the conventional mode of the ideal. The dissonance of the concrete negation is especially disturbing because the poetry seems to move smoothly forward all the while. The technique is maintained in each stanza. The tired adjectives of the love song undergo an oxymoronic revival as the poet adjures his "fair nasty nymph" to be "clean and kind" (5) with the aid of paper and sponges. The old metaphor that love is a battle is recast when he says that his passion will not decay if his "smoking prick escape the fray / Without a bloody nose." (11-12). The theme of cleanliness is concluded with:

> If thou wouldst have me true, be wise
>   And take to cleanly sinning;
> None but fresh lovers' pricks can rise
>   At Phyllis in foul linen.
>
> [13-16]

Vieth comments that "the key phrase advising Phyllis to 'take to cleanly sinning' brings together the planes of morality and hygiene."[10] "Sinning" was, and still is, a common term for fornication, but it is clear from Burnet's report of his conversations with Rochester that fornication per se was not a moral issue for the poet.[11] In other words, the intent seems to be pragmatic: Rochester is not attacking women or sex, but dirty women; and, in view of the standards of hygiene of the time, no doubt the cleanliness of female partners was a common concern. Other Court Wits, at least, have left records of such concern. Etherege, for example, in a verse letter to Buckhurst complains that after a night of whoring "neither shirt nor water could / Remove the stench of lecherous mud." And Henry Savile, writing to Rochester from Paris in 1679, announces he is sending a gift of *"poudre de cypre* to keep the ladyes heades sweet, and a bottle of myrtle water to keep theire tailes streight." The same interest in cleanliness recurs in Swift's *Strephon and Chloe* and also in Pope's *Sober Advice.* Pope writes: "Give me a willing Nymph! 'tis all I care, / Extremely clean, and tolerably fair."[12] Vulgar and slight though it is, **"By all love's soft, yet mighty powers"** exhibits complete control of form and tone. Rochester's insistence on the foul details, while interweaving them with the language of civilized male-female relationships (love's powers, joys, truth, wisdom), not only strips away the false illusions of romance but also implies that satisfactory sexual gratification requires more than the physical act itself. Thus, the same exchange of rhetorical functions occurs here as in the **"Mock Song."** Conventions of the love lyric are attacked through the insistence on physical reality while, at the same time, these same conventions contribute to the emergence of a sexual standard that justifies the ugliness and even makes it funny.

A similar reciprocating process is set in motion in **"A Ramble in St. James's Park."** A poem of 166 lines, **"A Ramble"** is a hybrid, owing much to Butler's *Hudibras* and to formal verse satire, yet qualifying in several ways as a mock-panegyric. No less than pastoral and the sweet song, panegyric serves the incomplete—and ideal—interpretation of reality. The panegyrist attempts "to turn historical fact into symbol, to do justice to his occasion and yet transcend it, turning the local and particular into the general and universal."[13] In **"A Ramble in St. James's Park,"** Rochester's rebellion transforms the local historical fact of Restoration life into a universal sexual symbol. In so doing, Rochester exemplifies Earl Miner's observation that when "we examine the employment of the usual *topoi* of praise (origin, ancestry, great acts, testimony from others, testimony from the speaker, etc.), we soon come to see that satire and panegyric invert each other along very similar rhetorical lines."[14]

Underlying Rochester's obscene vision of St. James's Park is Edmund Waller's *On St. James's Park: As Lately Improved by his Majesty,* and more than one critic has detected parallels between the two.[15] The radical difference between St. James's Park as depicted by Waller in 1661 and by Rochester in 1673 centers on the human use of the setting. Waller describes a noble park visited by romantic gallants and ladies, graced with the presence of a wise ruler, Charles II, and conducive to man's highest activity: "Free from the impediments of light

and noise, / Man, thus retired, his nobler thoughts employs."[16] By the time of Rochester's poem, the reputation of the park as a place of assignation and solicitation had become a common joke, a joke already exploited in Restoration comedy. Out of this indecent use of the park, Rochester paints over Waller's canvas a coarse sexual scene. In both Waller's and Rochester's versions man and nature are in harmony, but the character of that harmony changes from an ordered nobility to a disordered promiscuity.

Waller initiates his praise of the park and of Charles II with allusions to Paradise, Heaven, and Eden, in a kind of elevation of association. Rochester picks up the religious overtones with: "But though St. James has th' honor on 't, / 'Tis consecrate to prick and cunt" (9-10). The mock-religious note of "consecrate" sounds repeatedly in the poem: in "hallowed walks," in the comparison of Corinna to a goddess "dropped from heaven," in references to the "grace cup," to "grace divine," to the devil, the Jesuits, and Jesus (33, 38, 122, 147). The mockery works both ways: against religious clichés common to the panegyric, and against the sexual corruption of the park.

Similarly, Rochester caricatures Waller's prophecy that the young trees will become a "living gallery of aged trees" commensurate with the historical destiny of Charles II. Waller uses the trees to underwrite the heritage and wisdom of Charles:

> Bold sons of earth, that thrust their arms so high,
> As if once more they would invade the sky.
> In such green palaces the first kings reigned,
> Slept in their shades, and angels entertained;
> With such old counsellors they did advise.
> And, by frequenting sacred groves, grew wise.
>
> [70-75]

Rochester ridicules these *topoi* of praise of ancestry and great acts:

> There, by a most incestuous birth,
> Strange woods spring from the teeming earth;
> For they relate how heretofore,
> When ancient Pict began to whore,
> Deluded of his assignation
> (Jilting, it seems, was then in fashion),
> Poor pensive lover, in this place
> Would frig upon his mother's face;
> Whence rows of mandrakes tall did rise
> Whose lewd tops fucked the very skies.
> Each imitative branch does twine
> In some loved fold of Aretine.
>
> [11-22]

Rochester burlesques man's unity with nature in the Pict's sperm spilled on Mother Earth giving rise to the mandrakes with their human-shaped roots, which, by tradition, arouse sexual desire in man. They are, as in

Waller, "sons of earth," but their invasion of the skies effects the infinite interpenetration of sex in time and space. Rochester also subverts with irony Waller's prediction, "Methinks I see the love that shall be made, / The lovers walking in that amorous shade" (21-22), by describing, in an "all-sin-sheltering grove" (25), a chaotic conjunction of human bodies engaged in "buggeries, rapes, and incests" (24).

Having made sex the emblem of all nature, Rochester introduces another mock substitution for the panegyric. In the "spacious alleys" of Waller's St. James's Park moves the figure of the Prince, Charles II, exemplar of divine right and recipient of divine favor. In Rochester's park the "hallowed walks" yield up the proud Corinna, seemingly of divine origin. Just as there has been a sexual inversion of the noble park, so is there an inversion of the proud goddess to a proud bitch—she is at one with the true nature of the park, and is subsequently revealed, in Ronald Berman's terms, as the "vessel of Nature." This is to be construed in the vilest sense as she exits with the three fops.[17]

Whereas in the first half of the poem the obscenity is a seriocomic device for burlesquing panegyric to reveal brutal reality, in the last half it makes repulsive the ends of mindless pleasure, of mechanical coupling. What emerges is a measure for "love" that can be found elsewhere in Rochester and that is not far removed from the stage of Restoration comedy. When Dorimant says to Loveit in *The Man of Mode*, "To be seen publickly so transported with the Vain Follies of that Notorious Fop, to me is an infamy below the sin of prostitution with another man,"[18] he recreates the Rochester who writes in **"A Ramble"**:

> Had she picked out, to rub her arse on,
> Some stiff-pricked clown or well-hung parson,
> Each job of whose spermatic sluice
> Had filled her cunt with wholesome juice,
> I the proceeding should have praised
> In hope sh' had quenched a fire I raised.
> Such natural freedoms are but just:
> There's something generous in mere lust.
> But to turn damned abandoned jade
> When neither head nor tail persuade;
> To be a whore in understanding,
> A passive pot for fools to spend in!
>
> [91-102]

Lust itself is not denounced; the speaker asks instead a discrimination in its exercise, as implied by the "whore in understanding" and the "passive pot." Further, although there is some sarcasm in the reference to the "wholesome juice" of clown and parson, the verb "picked" suggests an act of will above the passivity where "neither head nor tail persuade." And, however low on the scale of sexual partnership, the clown is "stiff-pricked" and the parson "well-hung"; whereas the

fops are dishonest, affected, and, by Restoration standards, effeminate. The lover here is not necessarily deviant: literature and experience testify to the common feeling of men that if they must have a rival, it not be someone sexually inferior to themselves.

The libertine then expounds on his tolerance toward inconstancy in a passage replete with obscene images that suggest the grosser side of his relationship with Corinna. He has not complained when

> Full gorgèd at another time
> With a vast meal of nasty slime
> Which your devouring cunt had drawn
> From porters' backs and footmen's brawn,
> I was content to serve you up
> My ballock-full for your grace cup.
>
> [117-22]

The "grace cup" is a semantic tie with the fallen goddess image and with the earlier mock-religious description of the park, "consecrate to prick and cunt." As in the **"Mock Song,"** the allusions to a sexual feast create the impression that eating and copulating are but primitive physical functions to be satisfied. This is not to deny that they are pleasurable, "Nor ever thought it in abuse / While you had pleasure for excuse" (123-24), but to suggest that something more is required.

Wherein, then, lies the cause of the lover's charge of "treachery" (107)? It is a betrayal of "tender hours," which are more significant than sexual intercourse, and of something that can be labelled "love":

> When, leaning on your faithless breast,
> Wrapped in security and rest,
> Soft kindness all my powers did move,
> And reason lay dissolved in love!
>
> [129-32]

The tenderness is a meaningful contrast with the nastiness of the immediately preceding sexual description. Thus the obscenity in lines 111-22 affirms the inescapable demands of physical nature, a naturalism opposed to Waller's vision, while it simultaneously makes way for another plane of human relationship, described without obscenity and not inconsonant, after all, with the vision of Waller.

The speaker in **"A Ramble"** closes with a vow of revenge and a curse delivered upon Corinna. Although it is a device of classical satire, the curse burlesques the customary conclusion in panegyrics: a good wish for the future of the celebrated person, such as Waller expressed for Charles II after his description of St. James's Park. The wretched future of her who "dares prophane the cunt I swive" negates the romantic ideal of love, but at the same time implies there ought to be a better world in which such profanation does not exist.

Critics have judged **"A Ramble"** to be impressive and brilliant.[19] Contributing to that brilliance is the burlesque dimension; as the sexual images are blown to outlandish size, and ironically expressed in religious terms, the poetry of praise and the celebration of place are completely deflated. Here, Rochester says, is what St. James's Park, heroes, and heroines are really like. Concurrently, Waller's panegyric reciprocates with a **"A Ramble"** by its contrasting tranquillity and order so that the Restoration world of violent sex, fops, and fallen Corinnas—all betray the love that provides "security and rest."

These examples of Rochester's burlesque of pastoral, song, and panegyric, illustrate, on the one hand, how the mockery of received forms served his drive toward empiricism, or toward realism; and, on the other, how this drive takes a satiric direction that appears to denigrate women and sexual acts. I have maintained that the denigration is itself partly an illusion. Just as Rochester exposes the false face of romantic conventions, so in the double mirror does the rhetorical tradition of form and order cast a reflection upon his sexual imagery and obscenity. In other words, there is a form and order for sexuality as well, which can be reached through candor, but not candor alone. The candor testifies that sex is a given of nature, with its own demands. That fact of nature belies false notions of chastity in a Fair Chloris of the pigsty and creates whores who cannot with nature strive. It must contend with the realities of menstruation and excretion, and drives all levels of society to the all-sin-sheltering grove.

But that is not all. To stop there is to be as much deceived by Rochester as by romantic conventions. The naturalism he would not deny has its own vice, namely, indiscriminate sex—bodies without aesthetic regard, couplings without choice, and intimacy without emotional investment. This is the same Rochester who wrote, outside his "veine of satire":

> When, wearied with a world of woe,
>   To thy safe bosom I retire
> Where love and peace and truth does flow,
>   May I contented there expire.[20]

Expire, of course, is the common pun of the time. Sexuality is still in place, and the standards are those I have found to be immanent in the burlesques: love, peace, and truth. Whether one labels such sexual standards "morality" or not is immaterial to an understanding of Rochester's technique. For him, the rhetoric of sex in these burlesques served both the art of poetry and the art of love.

Notes

1. All verse quotations are from *The Complete Poems of John Wilmot, Earl of Rochester,* ed. David M. Vieth (New Haven, 1968); for the lines from Lucretius, see pp. 34-35.

2. "The Augustan Mode in English Poetry," *Hateful Contraries: Studies in Literature and Criticism* (Lexington, Ky., 1966), p. 150.

3. "Rochester and the Defeat of the Senses," *Kenyon Review* 26 (1964): 354-68.

4. "John Wilmot, Earl of Rochester," *Proceedings of the British Academy* 53 (1967): 62.

5. Catharine Walsh Peltz, "The Neo-Classic Lyric 1660-1725," *ELH* 11 (1944): 93-96.

6. *Lives of the English Poets,* ed. George Birkbeck Hill, 3 vols. (Oxford, 1905), 1: 224.

7. Vieth, *Complete Poems,* p. 136.

8. Henry Savile classed the "old bard Waller" as one of the "sweet singers" in a letter of 1677; see *The Rochester-Savile Letters 1671-1680,* ed. John Harold Wilson (Columbus, Ohio, 1941), p. 48 (hereafter cited as *Letters*).

9. "The Excremental Vision," *Discussions of Jonathan Swift,* ed. John Traugott (Boston, 1962), p. 96; cited here from *Life Against Death: The Psychoanalytical Meaning of History* (Middletown, Conn., 1959).

10. Vieth, *Complete Poems,* p. xxxv.

11. Gilbert Burnet, *Some Passages of the Life and Death of the Right Honourable John Earl of Rochester* (1680; facsimile rpt. Hildesheim, W. Germ., 1968), pp. 38-39.

12. *The Poems of Sir George Etherege,* ed. James Thorpe (Princeton, 1963), p. 38; *Letters,* p. 67; *The Twickenham Edition of the Poems of Alexander Pope,* ed. John Butt, 2d ed., vol. 4, *Imitations of Horace, "Sermon II"* (London, 1953), p. 89, ll. 161-62.

13. Warren L. Chernaik, *The Poetry of Limitation: A Study of Edmund Waller* (New Haven, 1968), p. 125.

14. "In Satire's Falling City," *The Satirist's Art,* ed. H. James Jensen and Malvin R. Zirker, Jr. (Bloomington, Ind., 1972), p. 13.

15. A discussion of some of the parallels and a good analysis of the poem in general appear in Dustin Griffin's *Satires Against Man: The Poems of Rochester* (Berkeley, 1973), pp. 25-35.

16. *The Poems of Edmund Waller,* ed. G. Thorn-Drury, 2 vols. (London, 1893), 2:42, ll. 75-76. Future references are to this edition and are cited by line in the text.

17. Berman, p. 362.

18. George Etherege, *The Man of Mode, or, Sir Fopling Flutter, The Dramatic Works of Sir George Etherege,* ed. H. F. B. Brett-Smith, 2 vols.

(Oxford, 1927), 2:270, act 2, sc. 1. The character of Dorimant has, since the play was first performed in 1676, been regarded as a representation of Rochester.

19. Berman, p. 362, writes of the "brilliance of this unprintable poem"; Vieth, *Complete Poems,* p. xxvi, and Anne Righter, "John Wilmot, Earl of Rochester," p. 55, use the adjective "impressive."

20. Vieth, *Complete Poems,* p. 89.

Raymond K. Whitley (essay date summer 1978)

SOURCE: Whitley, Raymond K. "Rochester: A Cosmological Pessimist." *English Studies in Canada* 4, no. 2 (summer 1978): 179-92.

[*In the following essay, Whitley contends that Rochester was one of the first of the philosophical satirists.*]

The Earl of Rochester is one of the first satirists of the Restoration period with a philosophical focus, as opposed to a social one. The satire of, say, Dryden or the Restoration dramatists focuses largely on human morality in a social context. Moreover, except where libertine "naturalism" obtains limited expression in early Restoration comedy, these satirists confidently embrace more or less conventional normative values. They have already accepted, before writing, that traditional apprehension of the human position in a moral cosmos which, from the social values they champion, we may infer at a distance in their works. However, Rochester's approach to satire is a good deal more sceptical and questioning; for that reason, philosophical and cosmological issues are nearer the surface in his work. This is not to claim that other poets and dramatists contemporary with Rochester are in some way limited or inferior because of their more confident emphasis. Rather, it is to point out a distinction in tone and feeling between those men and Rochester.

John Wilmot, too, treats major moral, political, and aesthetic issues of his period, but in such a way as to emphasize their relationship to the human position in the cosmos at large. In addition to exhibiting that renewed interest in pagan philosophers which had become a standard feature of intellectual life by his time, he is amongst the first English poets to respond wholeheartedly to the implications of the empirical revolution in science and philosophy as it began to affect the outlook of seventeenth-century man. As a highly educated, intelligent young courtier, he joined his fellow wits in a rigorous sceptical examination of traditional moral and theological authorities, and he came to accept the empirical epistemology of Thomas Hobbes as a rational analysis of human nature and,

almost certainly, as a justification of personal hedonism. Moreover, he toyed with the moral and cosmological pessimism which many of Hobbes's readers found consequent on the *Leviathan*'s largely political arguments. At the same time, however, traditional habits of thought were still strong enough in Rochester—perhaps as a result of what was no doubt a conventional religious education—for him to find the sensationalist universe inadequate, and to attack, from a largely traditional perspective, the vices of his age, even the very libertine code he elsewhere espouses. As Vivian de Sola Pinto has it, Rochester's poetry "makes us feel what it was like to live in a world suddenly transformed by the scientists into a vast machine governed by mathematical laws, where God has become a remote first cause and man an insignificant 'reas'ning Engine.'"[1] This disjunction of values by no means disrupts his satires, though it is present in them; in fact, some derive their grim power from it. In the light of these remarks, I should like to discuss the effect and meaning of five of His Lordship's works, starting with a group of three social satires and finishing with two black and universal philosophic ones.

Rochester's social satires, like others of the period, ridicule popular vice and affectation in society on traditional moral grounds. The coquette whose speeches constitute much of the **Letter From Artemisia in the Town, To Chloe in the Country,**[2] for example, is ridiculed for the boundless pride exhibited in her affected conduct. In her "fifty antic postures" (94) of introduction to Artemisia, she apes all the fashionable trivia of courtly gesture. So enamoured is she of her own utterance that her voice is "more loud / Than a great-bellied woman's in a crowd" (78-79), and she stops nattering only "Through want of breath" (136). Her protestation of ignorance and innocence as a result of her stay in the country (95-100) is the obvious pretense of a woman possessing the highest opinion of her own sagacity and sophistication. But most material of all, she is Artemisia's example of the kind of women who have perverted "Love, the most gen'rous passion of the mind" (40) into "an arrant trade" (51) by means of "many little cheats and tricks" (53) intended to increase physical pleasure at the expense of spiritual solace: "To an exact perfection they have brought / The action love: the passion is forgot" (62-63).

The country lady espouses a totally egotistical theory of love that bears out Artemisia's contention point for point. For the coquette, love is a mere game, in which the object is to dupe lovers and husbands with "gross, dull, common flatteries" (129), while using them for material support and ego aggrandizement. In this scheme, men of wit, "Slow of belief and fickle in desire, / Who ere they'll be persuaded, must enquire" (105-6), are dangers to be avoided, even though they are normally valued as the best choice in lovers, while a fool who "Vain of his proper merit . . . with ease / believes we love him best who best can please" (127-28) becomes the proper object of the coquette's dark design. The wits' intelligence presents the threat that they will detect the women's baseness and use them as Corinna's wit does in the coquette's exemplum (198-200), but fools such as those the bumpkin Corinna subsequently picks up (210-14) are a fertile source of revenge and money. What makes this vicious confession ironic, of course, is that its speaker is unaware that she addresses in Artemisia not a fellow conspirator but a hostile audience who will present her statements as she makes them for contemptuous comparison to accepted morals.

A Very Heroical Epistle in Answer to Ephelia (p 113) and **"An Epistolary Essay from M.G. to O.B. upon Their Mutual Poems"** (p 144) present another persona like that of *Artemesia to Chloe.* Scholarship has shown the two speakers of these works to have the same topical referent in the Earl of Mulgrave.[3] Certainly, both speakers utter the same selfish, complacent nonsense applied in two different realms of activity. The technique is the same as that of *Artemesia to Chloe*; Rochester just has his butt speak in a situation (here two private letters) where he is most likely to be frank, and lets the sheer egoism and perversion of his opinions rebound ironically upon him as the reader applies conventional moral values to them.

In the *Heroical Epistle,* for example, Bajazet (the name which the first lampoon of the pair gives Mulgrave) confidently declares his exemption from all moral responsibility in love because of his "greatness" and principled hedonism. He has not been inconstant or unkind to his mistress because it is against his theory of the sovereignty of appetites. As he explains:

> Well manner'd, honest, generous, and stout
> (Names by dull fools to plague mankind found out)
> Should I regard, I must myself constrain,
> And 'tis my maxim to avoid all pain.

> (10-13)

In the course of this revelation, he exhibits a singular and ridiculous arrogance. He reduces every aspect of his life to self (7-9); compares himself to heavenly bodies, the sun (18) and the comet (21), in his importance; reduces love—like the speaker of *Artemesia to Chloe*—to a matter of acquisition and economics (25-31); and finishes with an egotistical day-dream about the utter tyrant in love he would like to be. His sultan, "like a god" in the Lucretian sense, adored but unadoring, can enjoy his passive seraglio just as he pleases, for should they complain, he can simply have them killed (35-52). That Bajazet is powerless to make this dream come true, as the *Heroical Epistle*'s closing lines (53-56) admit, that he is in fact in opposite straits, beset

by Ephelia's (Mall Kirke's) relatives, adds just that final touch of irony which perfects his unwitting self-confession.

Much the same process occurs in **"M.G. to O.B."** In protesting to O.B. that the criticism he has received for his part in their mutual efforts disturbs him not at all, M.G. proposes a critical theory that is as insolent and perverted in terms of conventional, contemporary ideas as Bajazet's theory of love. Just as Bajazet blithely reduces all his life to self, so M.G. reduces all his art to the same measure: "To my dear self a pleasure I beget, / No matter though the censuring critic fret" (19-20). "Instead of submitting his verses to the collective good taste and judgement of educated readers, as a poet was expected to do, M.G. disavows any ambition 'to be admir'd' . . . He rejects the notion that poetry is better written by those few geniuses who are 'inspir'd' with 'wit'—here appropriately equated with God-given 'Grace.'"[4] Verse becomes, to him, merely more or less foetid verbal excrement, whose production is the right and necessity of every man. "Must none," he asks, "but civet cats have leave to shit?" (43). This low estimate of art successfully reduces the significance of the superiority he is forced to acknowledge in O.B.'s verse (40-42), but it rebounds ironically on the quality of M.G.'s own poetry. So does his claim that it is in some way unique; when M.G. boasts "that's my end, for man can wish no more / Than so to write, as none e'er writ before" (48-49), he fails to see the "pejorative implication that M.G.'s verses are unique only in their silliness."[5] Once again, then, the "straight" speeches of Rochester's persona ironically expose his own arrogance to ridicule.

Yet there is something more than this typical pattern of contemporary social satire at work in **"M.G. to O.B.,"** as well as in the other two pieces I have mentioned. All three exhibit an awareness on the part of their author of the philosophical questions antecedent to the immoralities they satirize; the butts of these poems, like their counterparts in other authors, transgress not just personal morality but the cosmological prerogatives of God in the Christian humanist tradition. So arrogant is M.G., for example, that he openly accuses Providence of being niggardly in its poetic gifts to him: "Unequally the partial hand of heaven / Has all but this one only blessing given" (54-55). Thus, he challenges normative values at a much higher level than that of mundane literary criticism.

Similarly, the coquette of *Artemisia to Chloe* is not just a proud and selfish slut. Artemisia is careful to explain that her friend is "an ass through choice, not want of wit" (151), that is, she is vicious of her own depraved free will, like Eve; God does not make fools—they make themselves. The introduction of God and will into Artemisia's discussion of the coquette's perverted reason suggests that her individual failings contribute to that cosmological disjunction consequent on the Fall. Furthermore, her primary fault, the perversion of Love, is the perversion of the sole Heavenly consolation for a world fraught with evil. Love, to Artemisia, is "that cordial drop heaven in our cup has thrown, / To make the nauseous draught of life go down" (44-45). The coquette, in debasing its use, sins not just against society, but also against Divine order.

This care on Rochester's part to place vice in a cosmological perspective is most clearly evident, however, in the **Heroical Epistle.** Bajazet's egoism manifests itself not in mere social irresponsibility, but also in a universal disruption of that traditional Renaissance scheme of cosmology, the Chain of Being, which was in Rochester's time still a basic assumption of popular thought. I have noted already that Bajazet's arrogance leads him to compare himself with celestial bodies high above his station in that chain, but the terms of the passage in which he reduces his life to self indicate that he pretends to usurp the whole system of the ordered universe. The human order, from his inferiors (the servants) to his equals (his friends), and superiors (his mistress and king), he claims, exists only for him (8); thus he rejects the complex system of rights, dependency, and responsibility by means of which humanity is related to the Divinely-ordered universe. Unsatisfied with that presumption, he goes on to include the order of that universe at large, "heaven and earth" (9), in his rejection. He yearns for literally universal self-indulgence. As Robert Vieth suggests,[6] the sultan passage is a climax of limitless egoism, a vision of Bajazet as both king and indifferent god, the impious focal point of a perverted state and cosmos. The overtly cosmological terms in which Bajazet's pride and selfishness are figured forth transcend his relationship with Ephelia, and even his situation at court, to relate directly his personal vices with the forces of evil and uncreation in the universe as a whole.

This sort of philosophical interest is exhibited neither so frequently nor so overtly by the social satires of Dryden. Of course, the vices Dryden ridicules can be analyzed in terms of the traditional cosmological model which informs both his normative values and Rochester's, but to carry out such analysis, the reader must more consistently supply the system himself; it seldom appears obviously in the works. Perhaps that omission is a measure of Dryden's confidence in the continued efficacy of traditional constructs as a basis for moral judgement amongst his public. Certainly, it scarcely indicates doubt; as Louis Bredvold suggests, Dryden's plays and religious verse exhibit a sceptical turn of mind, but Dryden's scepticism led him more and more strongly to a conservatism in ethics, religion, and politics[7] which his satires reflect. I believe that whereas Dryden had worked out his normative system before

writing, Rochester is still construing it as he writes. His compulsion to link private vice emphatically to cosmological evil in his social satires reflects his profound desire for a moral universe, and the depth of his philosophical interest in morality and human nature—a range of concern which, as I shall try to show, finds full expression in **Upon Nothing** and **A Satyr against Reason and Mankind.**

Curiously enough, in addition to connecting the butts of his social satires with cosmological evil, Rochester also accords them a surprising satiric insight of their own. The coquette of **Artemisia to Chloe,** for instance, is devastating at the expense of the fools that are her victims. Fools in love, she points out, are made as much by their pride as by feminine designs:

> ". . . the kind, easy fool, apt to admire
> Himself, trusts us; his follies all conspire
> To flatter his, and favour our desire.
> Vain of his proper merit, he with ease
> Believes we love him best, who best can please."

> (124-28)

Certainly, she depicts the buffoon that is her friend Corinna's victim as being full of his own importance despite the reality of his callow ignorance:

> "When my young master's worship comes to town:
> From pedagogue and mother just set free
> The heir and hopes of a great family;
> Which with strong ale and beef, the country rules;
> And ever since the Conquest have been fools."

> (210-24)

Similarly, M.G., the persona of **"M.G. to O.B.,"** makes a very convincing thrust at the value which, he claims, inverts all virtue into vice out of ignorance and dishonesty:

> It calls the courtier knave, the plain man rude,
> Haughty the grave, and the delightful lewd,
> Impertinent the brisk, morose the sad,
> Mean the familiar, the reserved one mad.
> Poor helpless woman is not favoured more:
> She's a sly hypocrite, or public whore.

> (91-96)

The opinions of these personae, as a result of their occasional wisdom, are ridiculously self-contradictory. One might argue that these sallies on the part of Rochester's satirized characters are undermined by their own vices, yet both accord so well with the ethical locus of the satires in which they occur that they must remain proof against the suggestion of invalidity. This telescoping of ridicule is more than a clever technique by means of which Rochester broadens his satire; it is more than that justice which Dryden vouchsafes Achitophel, because the redeeming insight of Rochester's characters contributes actively to his satiric argument, whereas Dryden's mention of Achitophel's virtue is only a mollifying aside, albeit with a satiric intent. Rather, Rochester's butts make the contribution they do because his attitude towards their mode of thought is ambiguous. Both the Mulgrave persona and the coquette are discerning wits; it is not idly that Artemisia remarks of the latter figure, "to her was known / Everyone's fault, or merit, but her own" (164-65). Rochester recognizes the value of the libertine's cynical intelligence—its ability to detect vice and folly in others, if not in itself.

In fact, his concession to the satiric butts of his social satires is only an oblique indication of the libertine principles he himself preaches elsewhere. The sensational life of the moment which Bajazet calls natural, for example, is the system on which Rochester bases his famous lyric, **"Love and Life"** (p 90). In it, having proven that the past and future are not real, and that all value reposes in the "present moment," he says:

> Then talk not of inconstancy,
> False hearts, and broken vows;
> If I, by miracle, can be
> This live-long minute true to thee
> 'Tis all that heaven allows.

> (11-15)

But for the humble tone in which they are expressed, the principles exhibited in these lines might have been Bajazet's. Indeed, so close to Rochester's own opinions are those of the Mulgrave persona that in the absence of external evidence both the ***Heroical Epistle*** and **"M.G. to O.B."** were read, until recently, as Rochester's unfeigned expressions of swaggering hedonism.[8] Certainly the facts of Rochester's life suggest anything but a satirical moralist; the question of his sincerity is bound to loom large in his readers' minds.

However, the discrepancy between the principles of his life and those informing his satires is largely a biographical difficulty. In those works already mentioned, Rochester's softening towards his victims results only in an addition to the satiric depth of his argument, so that its impact is enhanced rather than damaged. Similarly, in his two overtly philosophical satires, ***Upon Nothing*** and ***A Satyr against Reason and Mankind,*** the tension between traditional normative values and Rochester's response to the implications of the new philosophy, both of which are simultaneously present, results in a moving, comprehensive savagery.

Admittedly, ***Upon Nothing*** (p 118) is superficially a satire on human vices. It depends for its effect on a pun on "nothing," which word signifies in the poem both the state of everything before being, Milton's "Chaos and old Night," and vacuity of value and meaning. So

worthless are those things human which have being, argues Rochester, that they bring back the rule of chaos with their vicious, uncreative energy. Thus, kings take advice from "persons highly thought at best for nothing fit" (39),

> Whilst weighty Something modestly abstains
> From Princes' coffers, and from statesmen's brains,
> And Nothing there like stately Nothing reigns.

> (40-42)

In nations, kings, because they entertain the advice of statesmen who lack morality and intelligence, have nothing materially—in their treasuries—and attain nothing of moral or spiritual value by their administrations, so that their reigns, like that of primal chaos, "stately Nothing," are vacuous and chaotic. Rochester repeats this pattern at various levels of human endeavour, but in each case the verdict is the same; human endeavours are worthless pretense because they amount to nothing and tend toward chaos.

This cosmological joke on vicious men, however, is backed by a profound pessimism. The jest depends upon a system of being in which even God is a creation of chaos, of Nothing:

> Ere Time and Place were, Time and Place were not,
> When Primitive Nothing Something straight begot;
> Then all proceeded from the great united What.

> (4-6)

"The great united What," as well as signifying the philosophical abstract—being—is also the vague "Something" that creates the material universe, "men, beasts, birds, fire, water, air, and land" (12). Rochester obviously intends "Something" to mean, in the vaguest terms, Deity, and this Deity is *not* eternal. He has a beginning in Nothingness, and there is no indication that he can avoid ending the same way:

> Something, the general attribute of all,
> Severed from thee, its sole original,
> Into thy boundless self must undistinguished fall.

> (7-9)

Moreover, this "Something," this God surrogate, is only a first cause of creation; he, or it, has no power in shaping and maintaining the universe. Once Something has uttered the first fiat, those philosophical attributes of the universe which in the Christian humanist tradition would be the tools of God in the act of creation become in Rochester's satire foes of primal chaos, acting against it independent of Divine will, in a struggle which is itself finally reduced to nothing:

> Matter, the wicked'st offspring of thy race,
> By Form assisted, flew from thy embrace,
> And rebel Light obscured thy reverend dusky face.

With Form and Matter, Time and Place did join;
Body, thy foe, with these did leagues combine
To spoil thy peaceful realm, and ruin all thy line.

(13-18)

Nor does "Something" exercise a continuing Providential guidance in the creation; human worthlessness exists because "Something," God by implication, permits it (37). God, in effect, is himself reduced to nothing, while Nothing, who had "a being ere the world was made / And well fixed, art alone of ending not afraid" (2-3), takes over the Divine functions of eternity, omnipresence, and first creation.

Once that fundamental reversal has been made in the poem's opening stanzas, it is easy for Rochester to ridicule bitterly the worthlessness of all mundane endeavours. If there is Nothing in God and the cosmos, how should there be any value on earth? Thus, the priests pry into the bosom, not of God, but of Nothing, to find where the Truth—Nothing—"in private lies" (22-24), while Nothing informs the theories of the philosophers (28-30), and the "vast designs of state" which "have rack'd the politician's breast" are "least unsafe and best" when reduced to Nothing (31-36). Having dealt with man's attempts to explain his existence meaningfully, Rochester then turns his rage toward various levels of human society. Just as the king and his cabinet are worthless (see 41), so the judiciary, "Lawn sleeves and furs and gowns" (45) merely devise shapes and forms for Nothing in attempting to "look wise." All manner of national virtues—"Hibernian learning, Scotch civility" (47), and so forth—are next reduced to nothing, followed by virtues of private morality: gratitude, generosity, and good faith (49-51). Ultimately, Rochester reduces the entire hierarchic cosmos, through its nothingness, to a common metaphorical level with the baseness of the "whores' vows" that conclude the pattern. The emotional effect of this grim winding down of all human value is remarkably similar to the frightening conclusion of *Dunciad* IV, and the passage has the same import as Pope's last words: the return of Chaos, of Nothingness, in an apocalypse of vice.

Clearly, ***Upon Nothing*** is neither an immoral poem nor bad satire, even though it mixes a traditional revulsion of vice with a cosmological model that excludes moral absolutes. The vehement disgust with which Rochester figures forth his system of human and cosmological vacuity indicates that his position as satirist remains eminently moral; that there *should* be virtue in the world is as clear as the fact that Rochester sees none. However, unlike Dryden or Congreve, who intend correction by the ridicule of vice, Rochester sees no end to human worthlessness, because the universe itself, as he apprehends it, has become an amoral mechanism which no longer offers a basis for moral action. The upshot of this tension between his convictions and his desires is

an impressively ferocious satire that includes all things human, and even God.

This vehemence and the dislocation of value from which it is derived occur again in ***A Satyr against Reason and Mankind*** (p 94), only this time the satire is more sharply focused on humanity, and the philosophical bases of Rochester's position are more consistently worked out. In it, he uses some of the epistemological and political analyses of Thomas Hobbes to attack not just the vicious, but man in general, both for presuming to be more than the creature of sensation he is, and for failing in the virtuous existence which is the end of such a presumption.

The poem opens with an attack on man's pride of reason, which Rochester ridicules by exposing the inefficiency of rationality. Having described reason as an *ignis fatuus,* he pursues the image as man, the benighted traveller, is led by reason through "error's fenny bogs and thorny brakes" (15), up "Mountains of whimsies" (17), "Into doubt's boundless sea" (21), and is left to die with the knowledge of his presumption in the couplet which has become the cliché epitome of Rochester's verse: "Huddled in dirt, the reasoning engine lies, / Who was so proud, so witty and so wise" (29-30). Meanwhile, wit, the external manifestation of intellectual power, is merely a "vain, frivolous pretense" (35) contributing to man's misery, for though it pleases others for a time, it calls down hatred on its possessor's head when his audience begins to fear that they will be the object of his next raillery (37-45). Thus, Rochester identifies reason with confusion and misery so that men, to rely on it, must be fools.

At this point, Rochester introduces a straw-man, a "formal band and beard" (46) who mouths the standard Christian-humanist view of man as the image of God, adorned with reason "To dignify his nature above beast" (65) and to inspire piety in him by a just apprehension of the Divinely ordered universe. Of course, Rochester exposes these statements as platitudes which ". . . we know / From the pathetic pen of Ingelo / From Patrick's *Pilgrim,* Sibbes' soliloquies" (72-74), all of which were popular seventeenth-century books of devotion. However, the interruption does put Rochester's contentions in perspective and gives him the excuse he needs to clarify his criticism of reason and humanity.

It is man's speculative reason, Rochester explains, on which is based the conventional world-view of his interlocutor, that he finds so repellently arrogant:

And 'tis this very reason I despise,
This supernatural gift, that makes a mite
Think he's the image of the infinite
Comparing his short life, void of all rest,
To the eternal and the ever blest.

(75-79)

That sort of reason, he claims, leads to madness, "Filling with fanatic crowds of thinking fools / Those reverend bedlams, colleges and schools" (82-83). Rochester's scorn, even so, extends only to discursive reason; as Thomas Fujimura points out, the good Earl is himself too rationalistic to deny reason completely.[9]

What he offers in the place of "the morally suasive reason of the Christian humanist"[10] is a pragmatic faculty based on Hobbesian epistemology. Like Hobbes, Rochester sees man as a creature limited to sense impressions for his ideas, and to appetites for motivation. Just as Hobbes claims that "there is no conception in a man's mind which has not at first, totally or by parts, been begotten upon the organs of sense,"[11] so Rochester establishes that sense is the "light of nature" (13) from which speculative reason leads man astray. Just as Hobbes posits "for a general inclination of all mankind a perpetual and restless desire for power after power that ceases only in death,"[12] Rochester sees his own motivation as a desire to satisfy appetites. In these circumstances, reason, to both writers, is properly limited by those psychological bounds. To Hobbes, reasoning is simply an addition or subtraction of sense impressions,[13] to be employed as a method of satisfying desires. "From desire," he says, "arises the thought of some means we have seen produce the like of that which we aim at: and from the thought of that, the thought of means to that means; and so continually till we come to some beginning within our own power."[14] Similarly, Rochester's right reason "distinguishes by sense, / And gives us rules of good and ill from thence" (100-1) and is limited to "action's government" (94), where action is taken primarily to maximize pleasure. In his scheme, the moral reason of the traditional thinker, in addition to its presumption, becomes an unnatural check on the appetites which man should satisfy:

> My reason is my friend, yours is a cheat;
> Hunger calls out, my reason bids me eat;
> Perversely, yours your appetite does mock:
> This asks for food, that answers, 'What's o'clock?'

> (106-9)

In the first part of the *Satyr against Mankind,* humanity stands indicted of pride in speculative reason and foolishness in following it, because of that limited realm of knowledge and action to which Rochester claims human nature restricts mankind. In the second part, he uses some of the consequences of Hobbesian thought to pillory man for being less than the moral ideal which traditional speculative reasoning suggests.

Rochester realizes, for example, that if the satisfaction of appetites is the end of human life, and reason is a means to that end, efficiency becomes the most important test of wisdom, and efficiency is a criterion on which animals and men may be compared: "Those creatures are the wisest who attain, / By surest means, the ends at which they aim" (117-18). Thus, since beasts attain their ends as efficiently as man, they are, Rochester claims, as wise as man, if not wiser. With the help of the Hobbesian conception of man, he reduces the Christian humanist's sacred tenet, that man is superior to beast, to absurdity.

Similarly, he claims that men are morally less than the animals as well. Animals kill for food out of honest, natural instinct: "With teeth and claws by Nature armed, they hunt / Nature's allowance, to supply their want" (133-34). Man, on the other hand, while professing morality, kills his fellow men, not out of natural necessity, but prodigality of appetite:

> But man with smiles, embraces, friendships, praise,
> Inhumanly his fellow's life betrays;
> With voluntary pains works his distress,
> Not through necessity, but wantonness.

> (133-37)

Rochester's ironic distinction is "between the natural, instinctive, straightforward state of war in the animal world, and the perverse, hypocritical treachery of man."[15] In order to make it, he has moved the violent, sociological chaos that in Hobbes's view characterized man in a state of nature[16] from the theoretical past to the actual present, where it should not exist, since the advent of society in the *Leviathan* meant the end of the debilitating insecurity of the state of war. "In Rochester's satire . . . the commonwealth of men has not achieved the peace and security that Hobbes depicts."[17] In addition to being less efficient than the beast, then, man is morally baser than his wholly instinctive fellow creatures.

Having shown this, Rochester moves on to indicate that all positive human values depend not on altruism, but self-interest. He derives from Hobbes the notion that fear and the lust for power are the bases of all human virtue. According to that philosopher, fear and desire motivate men to avoid their natural state of war: "The passions that incline men to peace are fear of death, desire of such things as are necessary to commodious living, and a hope by their industry to obtain them."[18] Furthermore, it is the society of men which establishes virtue and vice; "in the condition of men that have no other law but their own appetites," he says, "there can be no general rule of good and evil actions. But in a commonwealth this measure is false: not the appetite of private men but the law, which is the will and appetite of the state is the measure."[19] Rochester has simply short-circuited this line of reasoning to arrive at his contention that men are primarily evil.

According to a strictly Hobbesian outlook, this analysis of the origins of morality is not pejorative. The self-interest which drives Hobbesian man into society and virtue has no moral implication, just as the virtues to which he is driven are naturally relative to the society he forms. But a moral satire on the baseness of mankind is impossible to a moral relativist, and Rochester is no moral relativist, for all his Hobbesian philosophizing. In fact, he applies to the moral relativism of Hobbesian man the moral absolutes of the traditional perspective, with devastating effects much to the detriment of humanity's complacent self-esteem.

The fear on which all human values depend becomes "base" (143), and all man's values, "His boasted honour, and his dear-bought fame; / That lust of power, to which he's such a slave" (144-45), all become functions of a low cowardice: "For all men would be cowards if they durst" (158). Meanwhile, man's positive appetites, "for the which alone he dares be brave" (146), make him wear a mask of virtue in the social context which amounts to hypocrisy (150-51). In such a society, held together by weak cowardice and featuring the voracious self-interest of the Hobbesian state of nature continuing surreptitiously under an uncomfortable veneer of morality, any real virtue is impossible; "honesty's against all common sense: / Men must be knaves, 'tis in their own defence" (159-60), for they will suffer at the hands of their fellow men if they are not. This notion completes Rochester's exposure of the baseness of humanity; when he excludes all virtue from man, he completes the utter deflation of human self-esteem begun with the attack on speculative reason.

What makes the satire so savage and universal is the same dualism of values and philosophical profundity that characterizes **Upon Nothing.** On the one hand, Rochester uses the new philosophy to attack the traditional presumptions of man. On the other, he uses moral absolutes derived from those presumptions to crucify the nature of humanity according to the new philosophy. The result is a moving judgement against the conception, "whenever and by whomever held, that man is by nature intelligent and noble."[20]

Of course, the existence of **A Satyr against Mankind** suggests that man is not hopelessly corrupt and that there is yet some value in the universe, however slight. Were Rochester a complete pessimist, he would not bother to write; there would be no point. In this light, it is useful to consider the postscript added to the poem in the 1680 edition of **Poems on Several Occasions,** and found in a number of the later seventeenth- and eighteenth-century editions of Rochester's work. Beginning after the otherwise final pessimism of "And all the subject matter of debate, / Is only: Who's a knave of the first rate" (172-73), Rochester continues for fifty-one lines, enumerating the moral conditions under which he will retract his vilifications and "Adore those shrines of virtue, homage pay, / And with the Rabble World, their Laws obey" (218-19). If, he says, his

detractors can find him one just courtier, "Who does his needful flattery direct, / Not to oppress and ruin, but protect" (181-82), one upright statesman, "Who does his arts and policies apply, / To raise his country, not his family" (187-88), or one humble, disingenuous priest,

> Not one blown up with vain prelatic pride,
> Who, for reproof of sins, does man deride;
> Whose envious heart makes preaching a pretense,
> With his obstreperous, saucy eloquence,
> To chide at kings, and rail at men of sense . . .
>
> 　　　　　　　　　　　　　　　　　　(193-97)

"if," in short, "upon earth there dwell such God-like men" (216), Rochester will recant.

However, in view of his previous contentions about human nature, his conditions remain little short of impossible. The implied corollary to all the specific vices which the honest man must shun is their overwhelming frequency in general. In large measure, this conclusion becomes a continuation of his previous attack at the specific levels of courtier, statesman, and priest. It is more important that most courtiers flatter "to oppress and ruin," that the average statesman "Receives close bribes through friends' corrupted hands" (190), and that priests' "talents lie / In avarice, pride, sloth, and gluttony" (198-99), than it is that one of them may in fact be virtuous. Significantly, such a man would be, to Rochester, "God-like," not human, and would have to believe "Mysterious truths, which no man can conceive" (215). The possibility scarcely exists at all.

Rochester, then, remains, even in this slightly less vituperative denouement, about as pessimistic as it is possible to be within the limits of satire. In the face of what he felt was overwhelming rational evidence of a mechanistic, amoral universe, his satires represent the desperate efforts of a moralist who doubts the validity of his own ideas to assert absolute values. In this desperation, he sees at once the presumption, under the new philosophy, of man's traditionally superior moral being in an ordered cosmos, and the galling failure of what is now inherently frail man to live up to his moral ideals. This double frustration, that of the new philosopher and old moralist combined, results in that savagery of tone that distinguishes Rochester's best work.

Notes

1. "Introduction" to *Poems by John Wilmot, Earl of Rochester* (London 1953), p xxxix.

2. *The Complete Poems of John Wilmot, Earl of Rochester,* ed David M. Vieth (New Haven 1968), p 104. All subsequent references are to this edition, with line numbers given in parentheses after each quotation.

3. See George de Forrest Lord, ed *Poems on Affairs of State,* (London and New Haven 1963), I, 345, 348; also David M. Vieth, *Attribution in Restoration Poetry* (New Haven 1963), pp 107, 129. *The Heroical Epistle* is the second of a pair of lampoons, the first, *The Complaint of Ephelia,* having been written by "Gentle George" Etherege, ridiculing Mulgrave's enormity in love with reference to his disastrous affair with Mall Kirke. *The Epistolary Essay* is Rochester's extension of the *Heroical Epistle*'s method of ridicule to Mulgrave's poetic endeavours, particularly the *Essay on Satire* on which he and Dryden (the "Old Boys" of the *Epistolary Essay*) collaborated to produce some lines critical of Rochester.

4. Vieth, *Attribution,* p 122.

5. Ibid, p 125.

6. Ibid, p 116.

7. *The Intellectual Milieu of John Dryden* (Ann Arbor 1962), p 15.

8. Vieth, *Attribution,* p 120.

9. "Rochester's *Satyr Against Mankind*: An Analysis," SP [*Studies in Philology*], 55 (1958), 578.

10. Ibid, 579.

11. *Leviathan,* Parts I and II (New York 1958), p 25.

12. *Leviathan,* p 86.

13. Ibid, p 45.

14. Ibid, p 33.

15. John F. Moore, "Rochester's *Satyr Against Mankind,*" PMLA, 58 (1943), 395.

16. *Leviathan,* pp 106-7.

17. Fujimura, 586.

18. *Leviathan,* p 109.

19. Ibid, p 15.

20. Moore, 399.

Thomas K. Pasch (essay date spring 1979)

SOURCE: Pasch, Thomas K. "Concentricity, Christian Myth, and the Self-Incriminating Narrator in Rochester's 'A Ramble in St. James's Park.'" *Essays in Literature* 6, no. 1 (spring 1979): 21-8.

[*In the following essay, Pasch claims that in "A Ramble in St. James's Park," Rochester frustrates the reader's expectations as he introduces standard poetic conventions only to overturn them.*]

Rochester's **"A Ramble in St. James's Park"** is an assault on the reader's sensibilities. It is a series of confrontations between the reader's expectations and Rochester's intentions. Conventional poetic modes are projected and then destroyed. The total effect is a disordering journey through one hundred sixty-six lines of poetry in the company of a narrator who turns the world upside down in a chaotic look at libertine life in Restoration England. Imagery, verse form, and the device of the narrator, which in poetry are normally used to create meaning, are used by Rochester to destroy any traditional concept of meaning. The order and meaning which the structure, biblical metaphors, and persona should provide are turned back upon themselves to force the reader to re-evaluate his relationship with the poem at every level.

Structurally, the **"Ramble"** consists of five verse units.[1] These five units are arranged concentrically; that is, the first section balances the fifth, the second balances the fourth, and the third is the center. The poem's structural configuration, ABCBA, like an Aristotelian cosmos of concentric spheres, seems—however delusively—to provide a basis in the poem for a sense of order and relationship between the poem's sections and also between the reader and the poem. The concentric organization gives the poem a specious sense of wholeness and unity which the symbol of the circle provides. As David Vieth states, "In this kind of structure, passages on either side of the physical center of a literary work are balanced against each other so as to bring them into specially close relationship, with the center itself receiving significantly heavy emphasis."[2]

Articulated in the central section is the ideal of lust as "natural freedom," which appears both to inform and be informed by the surrounding sections. In the first section (the first 42 lines), the speaker establishes a tone of sexual promise, reveals the park's sexual history, describes the modern sexual activities of the park and its inhabitants, and places Corinna within the park. These elements are balanced with the last section of the poem (lines 133-66), where the narrator establishes a tone of sexual despair, curses Corinna with sexual frustration, alludes to the debased sexual activities of various groups within the Town, and banishes Corinna from the park. The second and fourth sections (lines 43-86 and 105-32) are also matched. The three milquetoast beaus of the second section are paired with Corinna's three types of sexual partners of the fourth section (porters, footmen, and "half the town") whose sexual potency makes them the male equivalents of the female described in **"The Imperfect Enjoyment."** In each pair of sections, the sexual promise of the poem's first half turns into the sexual despair of the poem's latter half.[3] The narrator's reaction in the final two sections, in situations explicitly parallel to the first two sections, appears to be a direct consequence of Corinna's violation of the libertine's creed which is interposed between the poem's two halves.

The physical center of the poem (lines 87-104) is also the philosophical center where the speaker's positive values are expressed. Corinna's sexual excesses with "half the town" are commendable in terms of the reversed values of the libertine's creed; that is, promiscuity, lust, and vice are evidence of life and vitality and consequently are good. Energy, lust, passion, and voracious sexual appetite are all natural extensions of such a system and should be indulged: "Such natural freedoms are but just: / There's something generous in mere lust."[4] Passionless whoring, "When neither head nor tail persuade" (l. 100), is condemned. The beaus are imitations of life unlike the lusty clown or parson who ooze life and vitality. Apparently, as Dustin Griffin concludes, "Honest, generous lust, then, becomes the ideal" against which the decadent world of those who feel nothing is measured.[5] The presence of the libertine's value system throughout the poem is confirmed by the concentric structure; however, the structure also denies the system's validity as it is practiced by the speaker. Although Griffin sees the "possibility" of self-deception in the narrator's defense of Corinna's lust, he continues to place blame on Corinna, resulting in only a subtle qualification of the speaker (p. 32). Rochester, however, is actually presenting a very real and pervasive undercutting of the speaker through the self-incriminating evidence revealed in the poem's concentricity, as we shall see.

Closely linked with the concentric structure is the biblical imagery in **"A Ramble in St. James's Park,"** which further clarifies the undercutting of the speaker. The metaphors of Creation, Fall, Redemption, and Last Judgment are used by the narrator to describe his relationship with Corinna. These four metaphors encircle the central section where the creative power, the narrator-poet, resides like a Deity presiding over his creation, the cosmos of his poem. Section one, which describes the creation of the garden and places Adam and Eve within it, is in apposition to section five, the Last Judgment, where the apocalypse results in Corinna's judgment, damnation, and oblivion. The temptation and fall of section two are balanced by section four's Christ-like suffering for mankind's excesses, last supper-like communion, and redemption through remission of sins. Despite this symmetry, however, there is a disjunction between the order and meaning implied in the speaker's metaphors and the order and meaning revealed by the structure.

The narrator begins the poem walking, like Adam, through St. James's Park, the ornamental garden improved by Charles and opened to the Town about 1661.[6] Critics have noted the difference between Waller's pastoral description in his *On St. James's Park*

and Rochester's sexual concerns.[7] Yet, as Reba Wilcoxon has noticed, the two versions remain similar: "In both Waller's and Rochester's versions man and nature are in harmony, but the character of that harmony changes from an ordered nobility to a disordered promiscuity" (p. 280). The park remains pastoral, but the concept of what makes pastoral has changed. In Rochester's poem, the creation myth of St. James's Park places the emphasis, not on the creating divine word, but on a real physical act of frustrated mortal and pagan Pict.[8] *Fiat lux* has become *fiat coitus*. The result is a perverse world of unnatural acts in nature and in humanity—where, for example, trees are replaced by overgrown mandrakes. The "imitative" branches, "Whose lewd tops fucked the very skies" (l. 20), mirror the actions of the park's society: "And nightly now beneath their shade / Are buggeries, rapes, and incests made" (ll. 23-24). It is a garden of frustration, and of lust not love. The narrator is a reflection of the sexual preoccupation of this Eden; he is a sexual predator, in the garden "to see / Drunkenness relieved by lechery" (ll. 5-6). Like the biblical Adam, the narrator names the creatures of his "Eden" (ll. 25-35) and is a product of the earth of the garden. But where Adam was created from the "dust of the ground," the speaker is a product of the "teeming earth" of the park.[9]

To the Adam-narrator comes Eve. Corinna passes and, as is the nature of the sterile environment of the park, ignores and thereby frustrates the aroused speaker's sexual intentions. Corinna, the Eve of this perverted paradise, is a strumpet who, instead of being created by God as a helpmate for man, "dropped from heaven . . . In scorn of some despairing god" (ll. 38-40). She descends to the garden in order that the sexual frustration begun in heaven may continue in the garden of frustration.

"With wriggling tails" (l. 44) the three "knights" make their snake-like approach, and the temptation occurs. This temptation, however, is not the promise of the knowledge of good and evil. It is only an indirect proposition by three minor figures who are evil because of their inability to fit naturally into this unnatural society. Each of them, in Griffin's words, seeks "to force nature, to satisfy not instinctual desires, but invented and inappropriate ones" (p. 32). The diner eats only what he considers fashionable food;[10] the Gray's Inn wit steals handkerchiefs and phrases interchangeably; and the boy copies the foolish fashions of his foolish mentors. Their "abortive imitation" and "universal affectation" reduce the proposition to a parody of polite conversation:

> One, in a strain 'twixt tune and nonsense,
> Cries, "Madam, I have loved you long since.
> Permit me your fair hand to kiss."
>
> (ll. 75-77)

The temptation has occurred; Corinna's exit with the beaus marks her "fall to so much infamy" (l. 90).

In section four of the poem, Corinna's past relations with the narrator are described in terms which recall the salvation offered by Christ. A pattern is established and repeated in her debauches: Corinna goes whoring, returns, has sex with the narrator, and only then is satisfied. The speaker projects himself as the necessary part in the completion of the process; without his "surfeit water," she cannot be content. This cycle is the speaker's metaphorical extension of Christ's redemptive function. The narrator has been singled out "of all mankind, / To so severe a fate designed" (ll. 105-06) and must suffer for Corinna's sins: "Did ever I refuse to bear / The meanest part your lust could spare?" (ll. 111-12). His love for her removes her sins, and, in a corollary to the fall in section two, Corinna can now be saved. The pattern of her debauchery assumes the Christic metaphor: Corinna's whoring is a sin against the speaker's love (ll. 109-10); her return is her repentance; through communion with the narrator, who provides the "grace cup," she is granted remission of her sins with half of London; and she is redeemed as "reason lay dissolved in love" (ll. 132). Corinna, however, has not yet returned from her most recent escapade with the three beaus. The redemptive cycle is incomplete. The consequence is a replacement of the Christ-like image of love and forgiveness of section four by the narrator's self-image as the God of judgment and retribution of section five.

Corinna has once again sinned against the speaker. The First Commandment, "Thou shalt love the Lord thy God and Him only shalt thou serve," read in sexual terms, has been broken. Her failure to return for redemption signals her damnation. The implication is that the wrath of God is the product of sexual frustration. This is reinforced by the concentric structure which places the narrator-god of section five in juxtaposition with the "despairing god" of section one. Corinna is damned in a combination of images from the Old and New Testament, like Eve being driven from the garden, and like an apocalyptic Last Judgment.

Corinna is judged for her sin, cursed, and damned. She is to be cast into oblivion like the whore of Babylon: ". . . God hath remembered her iniquities. Reward her even as she rewarded you, and double unto her double according to her works: in the cup which she hath filled, fill to her double. How much she hath glorified, and lived deliciously, so much torment and sorrow give her" (Revelation 18:5-7). The narrator paraphrases this curse and, in accordance with the concerns of his world, translates it into sexual "torment and sorrow" in an image of aeolian intercourse (ll. 133-42). If Corinna's hell is banishment from his presence, her oblivion is removal from the society of St. James's Park:

> Loathed and despised, kicked out o' th' Town
> Into some dirty hole alone,
> To chew the cud of misery
> And know she owes it all to me.

(ll. 161-64)

This is like Eve being driven from Eden. Corinna will be cast out of the garden, out of the London society of St. James's Park, and into the country. The city is the pastoral dream. Her hell, a common theme in Restoration comedies, is the social and sexual disadvantages associated with country life.

The most important device in the poem is the narrator. His view is ostensibly the reader's view. He controls the structure, metaphors, and tone as the reader's only link to the events and judgments in the poem. To remind the reader of this, at the exact midpoint of the central section the speaker and his values are emphasized: "I the proceeding should have praised / In hope sh' had quenched a fire I raised" (ll. 95-96). The couplet, like the poem itself (ll. 5 and 166), begins and ends with "I." Section three, in addition to being the philosophical center, is the ego center of the poem. The speaker's ego colors the poem's events and, consequently, its value system.

The narrator's view does not, however, correspond with reality. The facts in the poem deny the narrator's charge that Corinna engages in sex with fools unfeelingly.[11] It is Corinna who transforms the beau's nonsense into a sexual encounter. Her entire body responds: "When at her mouth her cunt cries, 'Yes!'" (l. 78). The facts in the poem also contradict the self-image of the narrator. He portrays himself as the necessary finale to Corinna's debauches. Suspicions should be aroused, however, when he claims to satisfy Corinna after one-half million Londoners have tried. A dram, after all, is only one eighth of an ounce. Further, although he claims to dominate the relationship with his sexuality, he is powerless. It is Corinna who is confessed to and believed in. It is Corinna who chooses whether or not to come to him. And, ultimately, it is Corinna who provides "security and rest" and evokes love in him through her grace (ll. 108 and 127). She, too, it seems, is Christ. The narrator's view is contradicted by the facts he presents. His ego demands that he create a fiction to allow himself to remain at the center of his universe, just as he creates a poem with himself at the structural center.

When seen in the context of the speaker's "egotistic fantasies,"[12] the poem's inconsistent activity and values make sense. It is the betrayal of the narrator's ego, not just his sexual needs, which makes this encounter different. It is acceptable for Corinna to have sex with half of London because that makes the narrator, in his own mind, the sexual equal of one-half million men; he has deluded himself with the belief that he alone can satisfy her. However, for Corinna to scorn the narrator for three affected fops destroys his fiction and his ego. The beaus, for the speaker, are living, breathing, identifiable people, unlike the glorious ambiguity of "half the town," "porters," and "footmen." The speaker must compete with three real social inferiors, and he loses.

The ego center shows the real value system at work in the poem. The emphasis is not upon espousing a libertine creed or looking for value in metaphors, verse form, or structure. Each poetic device is denied the reader. The confused and confusing comparisons and parallels generated by the concentric structure are a result of the speaker's attempt to rationalize the events of the poem and formulate them into a pattern of values which will spare his ego by altering the perception of reality for himself and the reader. The distinction the narrator makes between himself and the others at the Bear, in the opening lines, is indicative of this Rochesterian trick. The inhabitants of the Bear are depicted as only speaking of sex while the narrator is out doing something about it. Yet the narrator, too, only *speaks* of "who fucks who, and who does worse" in his talk of Corinna. And further incriminating evidence of the narrator's self-deception is revealed in the poem's concentricity. Everywhere in the last two sections of the poem the narrator is implicitly equated with all the images of frustration and violation of the rake's code which occurred in the first two sections. Pict, frustrated god, debased inhabitants of Park and Town, the three beaus, and Corinna are all equated with the narrator's own actions. The distinctions made between the narrator and the other characters in the poem exist only in his own mind.[13]

The narrator makes a one-dimensional response to Corinna, for she is his ego-satisfying whore. The narrowness of his response results in a lack of correspondence between what Corinna is and what he has made her in his fictional world where he reigns as narrator-poet-god.[14] Separated from reality, he deludes himself. The narrator, then, is no different from the three beaus who live in an unreal, self-contained, self-created imitation of the social scene. Both the beaus and the narrator create their own worlds out of touch with reality because they have reduced life to one dimension. The beaus are consumed with being in the mode; the narrator is obsessed with being the consummate libertine. The narrator, like the beaus, is a fool. But the narrator is also the reader's guide through the poem. The danger is that the reader will respond to this foolish narrator only on one level.[15] The reader is challenged to recognize and to respond to the poem's affective push and pull at every level.

While the absurdity of the metaphors pushes the reader out of the poem, the concentric structure promises to draw him back by making sense of the imagery. But the surface value of the structure and the glaring inconsistency of the speaker's position push the reader away once again to ponder his relationship with such a poem. Vieth describes a similar process in another of Rochester's poems: "Assuming the reader responds favorably to the *Satyr,* as most readers initially do, he will next try to apprehend the poem as exhibiting some kind of Aristotelian unity, if only because it is printed as a single work. Deprived of sufficient consistency in those logical and conceptual terms which the *Satyr* urges so prominently, he is driven as he reads to supply whatever kind of unity his imagination affords, thereby involving himself as co-participant along with the poet in the experiential process of creating the poem"—what Vieth also describes as Rochester's "simultaneous manipulation of several conflicting levels or planes of experience."[16] This Rochesterian device forces the reader to participate in the poetic process and to constantly re-evaluate his relationship with each element of the **"Ramble."**

Notes

1. Other structures are evident in the *Ramble*. These include the parody of Waller's *On St. James's Park,* the pattern of an actual "ramble" through the park, and mock heroic. While the first two are commonly pointed out, the mock heroic has not been discussed in print. The action begins *in medias res,* and the poem parodies the heroic in its concern for idealized lust, libertine sexual honor, and knighthood (the beaus are referred to as "knights o' th' elbow and the slur"). None of these three structures gives more than a localized effect in the poem.

2. David M. Vieth, "Concept as Metaphor: Dryden's Attempted Stylistic Revolution," *Language and Style,* 3 (1970), 201. Although he does not refer to the *Ramble,* Vieth does notice concentric structure in Rochester's *Artemisia to Chloe*: see his "Toward an Anti-Aristotelian Poetic: Rochester's *Satyr Against Mankind* and *Artemisia to Chloe,* with Notes on Swift's *Tale of a Tub* and *Gulliver's Travels,*" *Language and Style,* 5 (1972), 123-45. R. G. Peterson also emphasizes the importance of the interdependent relationship between the parts of a concentric work: "The criterion to be observed in counting books (or anything else) is this: the element to be counted should be in fruitful relationship (harmony, contrast, conflict, etc.) with obvious narrative, thematic, or symbolic concerns in the work"; see his "Critical Calculations: Measure and Symmetry in Literature," *PMLA,* 91 (1976), 370.

3. Within the five sections there are rather precise parallels: the pastoral scene of the Park (ll. 1-10) with the pastoral country (ll. 161-66), the frustra-

tion of the Pict (ll. 11-20) with Corinna as a "dog-drawn bitch" (ll. 153-60), the catalog of deviant inhabitants of the Park (ll. 21-32) with the deviant behaviors associated with certain stereotyped classes (ll. 143-53), the frustration of a god by Corinna (ll. 33-40) with the aeolian image of frustration (ll. 133-42), and the sexual encounter of the three beaus and their proposition (ll. 41-86) with the speaker's history of Corinna's past sexual encounters and his own relationship with her (ll. 105-32).

4. *The Complete Poems of John Wilmot, Earl of Rochester,* ed. David M. Vieth (New Haven, Conn.: Yale Univ. Press, 1968), p. 43, ll. 97-98. All subsequent references will be to this edition.

5. Dustin H. Griffin, *Satires Against Man: The Poems of Rochester,* (Berkeley: Univ. of California Press, 1973), p. 32.

6. Griffin, p. 28.

7. Griffin, pp. 28-29, and Reba Wilcoxon, "The Rhetoric of Sex in Rochester's Burlesque," *Papers on Language and Literature,* 12 (1976), 280-84.

8. At least seven different creative acts are alluded to in this section of the poem (ll. 1-42): the creation myth of Genesis, the procreative acts of the Pict, the mythology of the park's origins, the actual re-creation of St. James's Park by Charles (God's viceregent), the narrator who creates the Pict myth, and the creative act of the poet (Rochester and the narrator).

9. Biblical allusions are used extensively in the poem: the elevation of St. James's Park to Ede-nesque proportions through words like "honor" (l. 9), "consecrate" (l. 10), "all-sin-sheltering grove" (l. 25), and "hallowed walks" (l. 33); the concept of *felix culpa* (ll. 91-96); free will (ll. 109-10); the Twenty-Third Psalm (ll. 129-30); and the parable of passing a camel through the eye of a needle (ll. 143-53). Also, the central section ends with a paradox like the paradox central to Christian belief—the fortunate fall.

10. The beau demonstrates his ignorance of the mode by failing to understand that "Banstead mutton" is not a culinary delight but a reference to King Charles's whores; see Vieth's note, *Complete Poems,* p. 42.

11. Noting that the speaker is "partly self-deceived" and "outraged when the principle [of mutual inconstancy] is put into practice," Griffin nevertheless misses the proper emphasis by returning to the view that the main point in the poem remains "that unfeeling sex with fools is far worse than lust" (p. 35). He shares the narrator's view of Corinna: "Lust at least indicates passion, but Corinna indulges in sex unfeelingly" (p. 31).

12. John E. Sitter arrives at a similar recognition of the narrator's ego (although he limits it to the final lines of the poem): "The poem concludes with some thirty-four lines of invective ('May stinking vapors choke your womb . . .'), in which the speaker evidently forgets the reader altogether and finally appears to forget even Corinna, as he ends his outburst wrapped securely in egotistic fantasies." See "Rochester's Reader and the Problem of Satiric Audience," *Papers on Language and Literature,* 12 (1976), 292.

13. Also intruding between the reader and the poem is the narrator's fondness for paradoxes: ll. 41-42 and 104. The paradoxes promise great insights into the narrator's view of the world. They too, however, are just another trick. If women are "vile" when "fair," how does this apply to Corinna, and what is the exact nature of her vileness? How is it possible to put a blot on infamy? Does one blot it by doing good? If so, this is not the charge against Corinna; and if she is evil, how is it possible to be worse than the worst? The paradoxes demonstrate how confused the narrator is and how careful the reader must be.

14. In addition, the failure of the exact physical center (l. 83) to correspond with the central section (ll. 87-104) further undercuts the narrator's self-concept of god-like omnipotence which the concentric structure helps create. Ideally, as Peterson states, the image of the circle seems to allow "escape from the chaos of raw experience, to make [a] poem 'nature methodiz'd,' the work of 'art, not chance'" (p. 372). However, the narrator's "little world made cunningly" is lopsided. The resulting balanced imbalance of the off-center center is emblematic of the pseudo-rational narrator's unbalanced condition. Vieth notes a similar situation in *Artemisia to Chloe* and concludes that the off-center "center" is "possibly symptomatic of a put-on" (p. 142).

15. Sitter is concerned with the language, but he also notes the implication of a passive response to the poem: "The reader becomes a partner (a 'whore in understanding') as well as observer to the [speaker's self-delusion] unless he responds to the poem's implied challenge to assume a more active role as reader than a 'passive pot for fools to spend in'" (p. 292).

16. "Towards an Anti-Aristotelian Poetic," pp. 128-29, and *Complete Poems,* Introduction, p. xxxv.

James E. Gill (essay date winter 1981)

SOURCE: Gill, James E. "Mind against Itself: Theme and Structure in Rochester's *Satyr against Reason and*

Mankind." Texas Studies in Literature and Language 23, no. 4 (winter 1981): 555-76.

[*In the following essay, Gill refutes the prevalent critical view that* Satyr against Reason and Mankind, *Rochester's most famous poem, lacks unity and coherence.*]

Rochester's ***Satyr Against Reason and Mankind*** is surely the witty earl's best-known poem and one of his most powerful ones; our appreciation of it has been greatly enhanced by modern scholars, especially by Vivian de Sola Pinto, David M. Vieth, and Dustin H. Griffin, who have helped establish the facts of the author's life, the text of his poems, and a basic knowledge of their literary and intellectual background.[1] Still, a survey of these and other studies reveals that there is considerable disagreement about the poem, about the origin and nature of its ideas, and especially about its structure and unity. Particularly at issue in these readings are questions about the place of Hobbesian and "naturalistic" ideas in the poem, about the nature and the relationships to each other of the various concepts of *reason* broached in the ***Satyr,*** and about the poem's strategy and coherence.[2]

Although these problems are not identical, their interrelationship can be seen in the fact that most critics see the poem as inconsistent and contradictory. One influential critic has argued that the poem lacks "Aristotelian" unity because it consists of a "libertine" half and a Hobbesian half, each of which is logically incompatible with the other. In arguing that the poem must be understood as a special case of "anti-Aristotelian" structure, Vieth contends that Rochester initially presents man as capable of achieving a "norm of pleasure" identified with true wisdom but later sees man as "victimized by his depraved nature" and unable to "rise to the moral level of animals."[3] According to Vieth, the poem thus drives the reader "to supply whatever kind of unity his imagination affords, thereby involving himself as coparticipant along with the poet in the experiential process of creating the poem."[4]

Perhaps not so extreme in its views, another recent interpretation of the *Satyr* sees the work as an eclectic "combination of formal satire and formal defense of heterodox opinion."[5] Although Dustin H. Griffin claims that the poem is well integrated through Rochester's use of paradox, like Vieth he also perceives unresolved internal inconsistencies or contradictions in the poem. For example, as the opening lines of the poem show, "the speaker is on the one hand a commentator on the human condition, and at the same time imprisoned in it. . . . A possibility of change or freedom is offered only to be taken away immediately. The whole poem operates in this fashion . . . , an illogical pattern always working against the clear logic of the poem's four-part structure."[6] Here Griffin identifies one of the crucial problems in the poem—a problem of point of view; but he fails to analyze the implications of the fact that he so ably establishes—that the satirist (as distinct from the poet) in some way represents as well as discusses the human mind's propensity to involve itself in self-defeating hypothesis. As a consequence, Griffin finds the speaker's later remarks about reason to be inconsistent and confusing—again doubtless part of "an illogical pattern."[7] And as a final consequence, Griffin sees a not much greater unity in the poem than does Vieth: he contends that "no one factor suffices to account for the ebb and flow of statement and qualification which is such a marked feature of the ***Satyr.*** . . ."[8] Of course, what is wanted is a formal principle which governs such ebb and flow.

Some critics who have squarely confronted the problem of the poem's speaker have also produced interesting insights which are difficult nevertheless to harmonize with all the poem's facts. Charles A. Knight, for example, holds that the poem's speaker sees himself as inextricably caught by his view of the human situation as it is presented in lines 1-122 and that he presents alternative choices which he knows are equally impossible. Thus according to Knight, the speaker is comically aware that he is trapped in a dilemma, the speaker's awareness of which the poem is said comically to develop.[9] In contrast, Ronald A. Johnson argues that the persona develops from the outset an argument through which he "rights" reason but that his triumph in doing so is short-lived. "The persona's rise to the role of rhetorician who has righted reason is swiftly followed by the revelation of the ironic predicament at the end of the argument":[10] because we identify with the persona as he triumphs over the "formal band and beard," we are necessarily trapped with him as he is forced to admit that all men are merely knaves. Thus Rochester leaves us "without anything which is positive or affirmative," and the satirist is satirized.[11]

These readings illustrate some of the principal difficulties of interpreting the poem. One critic sees the poem's speaker as the formulator of inconsistencies which the reader is invited to contemplate with the poet (and which may victimize both reader and writer, I might add). Another reader, who is aware that the speaker seems at the poem's beginning to confess the impossibility of his task, virtually ignores this fact in his explanation of the poem's later apparent inconsistencies. Yet another reader sees the poem's persona as the formulator of a case who eventually succumbs to his own argument, and yet a fourth reader sees the satirist as being from the outset a victim of his own views. We are invited by the poet, according to these views, either to contemplate with him apparently irreconcilable views, or to contemplate in him or in his satirist an ebb and flow of opinion or the comedy or satiric irony of self-contradiction or self-entrapment.

Against these several current interpretations I believe that the *Satyr* is a thoroughly well unified poem and a deeply moving one as well. I believe that its so-called Hobbesian and libertine sections are parts of an intelligible whole and that the poem gathers its various disparities or incongruities or its "ebb and flow" within a unifying "reflexive" framework. Among these incongruities several appear so prominent that various critics have hinged their readings of the poem on them. They include the following perceptions: (1) that the satirist in his opening lines seems to deny the possibility of his undertaking and thereby creates a problem of point of view in the poem; (2) that he builds a case against human reason via his human reason; (3) that he achieves, after considerable argument, the spontaneous wisdom of the beasts; (4) that he then apparently denies the relevance of that wisdom to human conduct; (5) that the satirist seems to employ the term "reason" in several different senses; (6) that he is thus the comic victim of his own diatribe or the satiric victim of his own satire; and (7) that he at last conditionally recants his original contentions and provisionally holds that man may differ from man more than man differs from beasts. A good number of disparities for one poem!

If we are to see the poem as something greater than a mere succession of contradictions which are effective chiefly in the reader's response to them as such, then we must be prepared to see the poem as *dramatizing* in a complex way the problems of self-reflection or reflexivity in which criticism and diatribe are themselves treated critically as well as performed. Especially important in this respect is an awareness of what Rosalie L. Colie has called "epistemological paradox, in which the mind, by its own operation, attempts to say something about its own operation."[12] Such paradoxes redirect "thoughtful attention to faulty or limited structures of thought," and "operating at the limits of discourse, [they] play back and forth across terminal and categorical boundaries. . . ."[13] As Professor Colie and others show in analyzing the "all-Cretans-are-liars" paradox, such paradoxes are often not merely self-canceling but may be truly "speculative" and are sometimes "so balanced that one meaning can never outweigh the other, though weighed to eternity."[14] In other words, such paradoxes are not inevitably merely "disjunctive" but may be "constructive." Paradox which is not merely disjunctive may, in other words, lead to a *controlled acceptance of incongruities* and may therefore link as well as separate its elements in a bond not easily dissolved.[15]

In this respect the reader of the *Satyr* needs also to be reminded of the single most important historically identifiable paradoxical argument contributing to the poem—the theriophilic paradox. Griffin and others have, of course, already established the relevance of this tradition to the *Satyr* and delineated some of its major features.[16] What these scholars have not considered adequately is the importance of certain strategies of the argument that beasts are more reasonable and better than men.

In order to understand those strategies, however, it is necessary to comprehend the underlying structure of the theriophily as it was developed in some of its principal sources. Historical and formal analysis of these works reveals that the argument is based on the primitivistic dissociation of human nature and human reason from nature and the reason implicit in it—from the Logos, which is immanent in the orderly behavior of animals.[17] Thus, while theriophiles argue that beasts are more natural, and therefore that they are better than man, they can also contend that beasts are more reasonable than men, even, paradoxically, if beasts do not reason as well as men or if they do not reason at all. Human reason in such cases is often seen as indirect, complex, abstract, and remote from the simple natural life.[18]

The aim of such arguments is at least twofold. First, they are designed to humiliate human pride: they attack human viciousness, folly, and deviousness by contrasting human behavior with the much less complicated behavior of animals. Second, they are designed to humiliate pride in reason not only by observing its excesses and failures but also by representing the action of human reason in considering itself; thus the reader of the theriophilic argument is often the witness of a formidable fit of reason against itself and of prodigious mental efforts to render plausible an obviously outrageous contention—that animals are superior to men. Theriophily is therefore almost always "reflexive" (i.e., self-criticizing as well as self-proving).[19] If man is not obviously inferior to animals, one may ask what man proves when he argues that man is inferior to brute beasts. He is, of course, twice proving the vanities of human reason—vanities which humble beasts do not thoroughly mimic. But the very fact of self-reflection is of such ambiguous value that it may entail some saving grace or virtue since self-awareness—knowledge of human vanities—need not itself be wholly useless. Indeed, self-knowledge seems to constitute the chief value of the theriophilic exercise to most of its perpetrators. In any case, it is not easy to see it as being often merely "disjunctive."

Several reasons exist for emphasizing these features of the tradition to a reading of the *Satyr*. First, the reader is sensitized to the general reflexive and self-criticizing features of the paradox and is better prepared to observe them at work in the poem. Second, an awareness of the form and order of successive paradoxical maneuvers of theriophily can help account for some of the *Satyr*'s puzzling passages and twists. For example, Vieth's division of the poem into two irreconcilable halves at line 122 corresponds almost exactly to that part of the traditional argument which concedes that even if animals do not reason any better than men or if they do not reason at all, they are better off for it. This point in the poem is also the one that makes Griffin question whether Rochester has not shifted the grounds of his argument and employed a concept of reason different from the one he has previously been using.[20] Here, one will recall, the satirist has through a long argument managed to "right" reason but still finds animals "at least as wise and better far" than men. The traditional shift is, of course, one from *logos prophorikos* or "uttered reason" to *logos endiathetos* or "the reason inherent in nature." One is discursive reason, whereas the other is the reason of things implicit in them. One is abstract, indirect, and fallible; the other is inherent and direct.[21] The shift at this point in the **Satyr** from a discussion of human and bestial wisdom to contemplation of human and bestial natures falls entirely within the boundaries of the theriophilic paradox; and whatever values we may wish to give it, it is nevertheless an entirely traditional development within the theriophilic paradox, not an extraordinary shift peculiar to Rochester's poem. Rochester's achievement lies rather in his exploitation of the possibilities within the traditional paradoxical argument of the dialectical play and poise of ideas about reason and nature within the human mind.

A second feature of theriophilic arguments, their reflexivity, also helps account for the fact that the satirist, after he has made his case against reason and mankind, finally brings himself to look critically at his own contentions, to establish provisionally counter-contentions also of a "what if" nature, and to recant his paradox conditionally. Indeed, the poem's epilogue reminds us of the poem's puzzling, "what if" beginnings and makes us, as well as the poem's speaker, realize that the entire poem has been conducted as a series of hypotheses which from the outset emphasize its reflexivity. At several points, in fact—in his initial strange paradox, in his fit of reason against reason, in the imagery of ascending and falling, in the description of wit as victimizing both the wit and the enjoyer of wit, in the appearance of the adversary and his fits of wit against wit and of reason for reason, in the satirist's all but useless "righting" of reason, in his forthright strictures on human duplicity and his honest discounting of honesty, and finally in his apparent willingness to give up much of his case under certain conditions—one can see the possibility that Rochester not only has his satirist enumerate traditional paradoxes but also dramatizes them through the speaker's paradoxical train of thought. He does so by showing how in him the mind turns against itself. In other words, the speaker performs as well as remains aware of his own paradoxi-

cal thought. Such internalizing of the "external" criticisms of mankind reveals Rochester's original use of traditional materials and suggests that the poem has a consistency and internal coherence not often attributed to it.

The poem's structure has been variously described as falling into two or more parts. Vieth's text, as opposed to his argument, recognizes the two main parts of the poem as including the principal arguments (ll. 1-173) and the epilogue (ll. 174-221). This division, admittedly the fruit of only rudimentary analysis, nevertheless reveals an important feature of the poem—that everything up to the epilogue (to ll. 173) is part of a case built against mankind: as the satirist states, "All this with indignation have I hurled / At the pretending part of the proud world . . ." (ll. 174-75).[22] In other words, the first major section of the poem consists of the building of a case against man's use of his speculative reason, his pride, and his wit; moreover, it includes the defense of speculative reason by the adversarius and its refutation, and the case against man's practical social behavior (ll. 1-122, 123-73, respectively). One of the chief difficulties of this section is that the orderly progression of the satirist's case against reason and mankind is dramatically interrupted by the adversarius, who may be merely imagined and whose defense of reason prompts the satirist to define a "right" or practical reason (ll. 1-45, 46-71, 72-111). It is the sharp contrast of man's habitual "indirectness" with the simplicity and directness of bestial "right reason" (ll. 112-22) that leads to what Vieth has called the "Hobbesian" analysis of man's social behavior as being based on fear and "wantonness" (ll. 123-73). The "Hobbesian" section, it should be added, can be seen as a continuation of an argument begun as early as the "Hobbesian" analysis of wit in lines 35-45. In this section hope of pleasing and fear of being victimized not only parallel the theological "grounds of hope and fear" mentioned later by the adversarius but anticipate the fear and wantonness of the later Hobbesian section of the poem. Moreover, as Wilcoxon has suggested, the skepticism of the first section of the poem may be as much grounded in Hobbes's nominalism as in libertine Pyrrhonism. Such observations, however, are only the initial indications of the coherence denied to the poem by Vieth and glimpsed only partially by other critics.

The "fabricated" or "hypothetical" nature of the case built by the satirist against man's self-defeating qualities is first indicated by the poem's opening passage. These lines are puzzling in the extreme, but properly read, they convey a complex message. First, they announce that the satirist is constructing a case against mankind by adopting hypothetical or theoretical points of view of man from both above ("a spirit free") and below (the beasts). In brief, the speaker implies, "If I were capable of looking at mankind from certain positions, I would probably condemn him in the following ways. . . ."

Second, the opening lines deny what they assert—the possibility of achieving the condition of a "spirit free." Even the form of the utterance involves the speaker in impossible implications. The implicit order of the passage is the conventional one in which beings range from corporeal to incorporeal and one in which man is seen as the middle link between these realms of being; but the passage also implies that the mixing of these two orders of being in man has resulted in a monstrosity possessing neither the hypothetical freedom of incorporeality nor the certainty and "unanimity" of the beasts. Spirit and beast are, paradoxically, capable of simplicity and clarity which elude man's reason—a "Reason, which fifty times for one does err."[23] But the lines seem to imply a further paradox—that ascent up the chain of being from man to free spirit would entail the choosing of a lower bodily form since if the "cost" of being a man is great, then the cost of being a free spirit may paradoxically even be greater:

> Were I (who to my cost already am
> One of those strange, prodigious creatures, man)
> A spirit free to choose, for my own share,
> What case of flesh and blood I pleased to wear,
> I'd be a dog, a monkey, or a bear.
>
> (ll. 1-5)

This passage not only anticipates the poem's later paradoxical rising and falling—of rising only to fall—but also represents or enacts as well as states the perplexities of human thought and the human condition. The coveted states of spiritual freedom and bestial certainty are, as the conditional tense and the strange initial parenthesis suggest, self-conscious projections, hypotheses, or theoretical constructs of the skeptical human mind which thus defines the poles or extremes between which all human possibilities exist. Yet, as we have seen, the use of such dialectical extremes involves the satirist in unavoidable paradox and self-contradiction at the very beginning of his enterprise. The poet thus represents the satirist and all men as trapped between imaginable extremes: first, the satirist recognizes his plight through explicit statements which threaten coherence itself; second, it is obvious that man would, and would not, have a body; third, man's plight is thereafter seen in the description of humanity's tragic pursuit of knowledge through reason (ll. 8-30)—a plight represented most graphically in the imagery of rising and falling, of rising only to fall; and finally, man's paradoxical situation is further represented by the opposition of a "formal band and beard" to the satirist. On the one hand, the adversarius argues on behalf of a reason which pierces "the flaming limits of the uni-

verse," whereas the satirist condemns the speculative reason and favors only a limited "right reason" appropriate to the beasts. The form of these contentions parallels and in a sense enacts through its dialectical oppositions the complex paradox of the opening lines: what man desires is inimical to what man desires. The pattern thus established defines the self-canceling, self-defeating qualities of human thought and action. It is a pattern which is reflexive and which dramatizes its content. Thus as the satirist builds a case about mankind's confusion, he also in a sense enacts it.

The second and third verse paragraphs of the poem explore then the self-defeating qualities of the principal faculties of the human mind—reason and wit. Reason is seen as the will-o'-the-wisp which misleads men in the interior wilderness of the mind where it creates obstacles which it then strives vainly to surmount. Images of rising and falling combine with images of swimming and sinking and of dazzling and darkening to reveal reason as a bog as well as an uncertain light and as that which impedes man as well as that which impels him toward experiences successively more remote from the life of the senses and progressively nearer to the tragic understanding that "all his life has had been in the wrong" and to death. Man thus to his cost prefers "Reason, which fifty times for one does err," to "certain instinct," presumably that of the beasts. But reason is also the bog, the area of experience in which men drown. Reason is both subjective power and objective realm of experience. If Rochester is following the theriophilic paradox, however, such "bestial" instinct is the equivalent of the "reason of nature," what the ancient Stoics and skeptics called *logos endiathetos*. According to theriophiles, this reason is implicit in the behavior of beasts and accounts for their "oneness" with nature and with themselves whether or not they reason discursively. If such instincts are implanted in animals, the senses are the means to natural ends, according to many theriophiles.[24]

The vain search for knowledge described in these lines is a solitary and "interior" undertaking, as the images of the lonely figure climbing self-erected mountains and falling in previously prepared bogs reveal. The "reasoning engine," "so proud, so witty, and so wise," is thus isolated and alienated from the "world he should enjoy." Yet in keeping with Rochester's practice in the poem of multiplying ironies, the satirist also finds man's social experience as alienating as man's speculative efforts: "wit," the eminently social exercise of intelligence in its associativeness, also ironically alienates man from his own kind and cuts him off from happiness. Wits and those who enjoy wit make up the social world and are likened to whores and their clients, who are each the victims and the exploiters of the other.

> For wits are treated just like common whores:
> First they're enjoyed, and then kicked out of doors.

The pleasure past, a threatening doubt remains
That frights the enjoyer with succeeding pains.
Women and men of wit are dangerous tools,
And ever fatal to admiring fools:
Pleasure allures, and when the fops escape,
'Tis not that they're beloved, but fortunate,
And therefore what they fear at heart, they hate.

(ll. 37-45)

In both the case of speculative reason and the case of social wit—of the inner life and the social life—the mind's faculties are turned against themselves and thus against human happiness. And it is this state of affairs— the self-destructiveness of human thought as it is induced by solitary and social pride—that renders men the fearful, hateful, vainglorious creatures who are later discussed in what Vieth has called the poem's "Hobbesian half." The speaker in fact hints here that the internal forces which destroy inner certainty and happiness are mirrored in human society.[25] This analogy between inner lack of coherence and an underlying lack of social cohesion cannot, I think, be overstressed as a source of the poem's own cohesiveness. Moreover, the mere fact of such an analogy at this point belies the facile division of the poem into two separate contradictory halves since it obviously anticipates the description of man's behavior in lines 123-73.

The apparent interruption by "the formal band and beard" at this point is thus rather ironic because the clergyman concedes at once that wit is intolerable and even reveals his abilities in a notorious fit of wit against wit—itself an implicit example of the paradox or irony of human self-negation through self-assertion (ll. 48-57) just as the satirist's fits of reason against reason establish and reinforce the pattern. It is thus all the more ironic that the adversarius then defends human reason and those social instincts which wit both serves and subverts. With a similar ironic effect, the imagery of the clergyman's harangue implicitly conveys a satiric judgment on itself. For just as the satirist had earlier described man's futile search for certainty in terms of "wandering," "climbing," and "huddling" in dirt, so the preacher now speaks of taking "flight," of "diving," and (in an ironic pun) of the "true *grounds* of hope and fear," (i.e., of "rewards and punishments" in the hereafter). The initial images of rising and falling—of rising only to fall—ironically frame the clergyman's inflated claims on reason's behalf so that his denial of limit is everywhere circumscribed by the language of limitation.

In his rejoinder the satirist picks up this theme again. He depicts the clergyman as "this busy, puzzling stirrer up of doubt" framing mysteries so that others can unriddle them: on reason's wings every "heavy sot" believes he "can pierce / The limits of the boundless universe." (The limits of language—"limits of the

boundless"—are approached and in a sense overcome in this passage.) The clergyman's rationalism is ultimately likened by the satirist to body-withering, rank superstition: reason elevates rational man in the same way that magical unguents are said to enable the withered carcass of a witch to fly. It is no wonder that the satirist's rebuttal concludes with another image of man fallen away from the active world. The image of Diogenes' tub as a place of cynical retreat may perhaps be conflated here with the image of the sweating tub (a cure for the pox). Commitment to speculative reason destroys bodies as well as nonplusses minds; thus "modern cloistered coxcombs who / Retire to think 'cause they have nought to do" spend their time in "nonsense and Impossibilities" in the same way that active men are eventually debilitated by the pox. Devotion or speculation eventually renders one inactive and impotent. If one reflects at this point on the satirist's own strategies for stirring up doubt and thinks of the satirist's plight at the poem's conclusion, it becomes easier to see how Rochester intertwines and reinforces in various ways the theme and the enactment of the mind's self-defeat as well as its defeat of the body.

The theme of thought's betrayal of thought and its subversion of the capacity to act in the search for natural pleasures satisfying natural ends doubtless belongs in part to the revival of Epicurus in the seventeenth century, but it also belongs to the theriophilic argument in which human duality is contrasted with bestial *unanimity*. And it is so with Rochester's satirist, who sees both theoretical reason (based on vain hope and fear) and social wit—and later the active life (based on self-defeating wantonness and fear)—as lacking the unanimity or integrity which, according to theriophiles, the beasts so abundantly manifest. That unanimity is represented by the satirist as consisting of direct natural responses, uncluttered by custom and speculation, to natural appetites. Reason, heretofore paradoxically stretching toward the "limits of the boundless universe, now is "righted" and "bounds desires with a reforming will / To keep 'em more in vogue, not to kill." Now the speculative reason's destructive lack of discipline is contrasted with the satirist's much more reasonable acknowledgment of limits.

As we have already suggested, however, the satirist's "reason righted" need not have any value other than as a dialectical counterpart of the speculative reason or social custom which it mocks here: "Hunger calls out, my reason bids me eat; / Perversely, yours your appetite does mock: / This asks for food, that answers, 'What's o'clock?'" (ll. 107-09). The satirist's hypothetical "right reason," unlike his adversary's speculative reason, may thus be at least *theoretically* suited to the active life, for it is like the humble law of the natural life as lived by animals: "Those creatures are the wisest who attain / By surest means, the ends at which they aim" (ll. 117-

18). But the fatal gap between thought and action in man is nevertheless revealed by the fact that men must argue to achieve what beasts, without reflection, achieve directly. If man may plausibly argue that men may profitably follow the beasts' example, he may then achieve their wisdom, but he may not at the same time be able to act as they act: "'Tis evident beasts are, in their degree / As wise at least, and better far than he" (ll. 115-16).

Yet, as we have seen before and now observe, the means for attaining this conclusion have hardly been the "surest." There is a fatal gap between thought and action in man which is revealed by the gap that men must argue extensively to discover what beasts, without argument, know immediately. And even if man may plausibly *argue* that men may profitably follow the beasts' example, he may *then* approach their wisdom and *still be unable to act* as they act. Indeed, the very necessity of an intervening discursive process like the one we are witnessing in the satirist precludes our genuinely following the model of the animals: "'Tis evident beasts are, in their degree / As wise at least, and better far then he" (ll. 115-16). The satirist's case is an example of its contention, and it is self-proving. That is, even though man may achieve a vision of an ideal of spontaneous "rational" response—of unanimity or integrity—he may not realize his ideal through his actions simply because of his dual, doubting, "reasoning" nature. The satirist's ideal of right reason may not cohere, as Vieth argues, with his subsequent description of the hypocrisy of human action; but the satirist's *example*—his initial doubts, his fit of reason against reason, his development of a counterreason, and his awareness of the ironies of these procedures—do cohere with, support, and even paradoxically may cast some doubt on his "Hobbesian" description of human action in lines 123-73.

The self-evident gap between thought and action, between means and ends, is not eliminated by the "righting of reason" because the necessity of righting reason is the surest sign of the gap. If, therefore, man may achieve with labor the wisdom of animals, that very achievement precludes the practice of such wisdom, for in contrast to bestial directness, concreteness, and unanimity, his typical ways of thinking are characterized by struggle, indirectness, abstraction, and duality.

Thus, from one point of view, the satirist *must* both set up a norm for reasonable behavior and then imply that men cannot attain it. He is able to do so without loss of "reason" because of the inveterate fallibility of human reason in the first place. We see, in other words, the reflexivity of man in the paradox that he simultaneously asserts, denies, and exemplifies or enacts the capacities and incapacities of human reason.

In a quite limited sense, then, the satirist does do what Vieth and Griffin have claimed for him at this point: he has set up a standard which he then reveals cannot be achieved; he does assert the possibility of reason and then seems to deny it; and he has suffered the meanings of terms of shift or at least has rendered them ambiguous. But as we have shown, these maneuvers are controlled by the poem's reflexive framework, by its developing contexts, and by the fact that the satirist dramatically enacts as well as discusses the self-contradictoriness of human reason. Rather than perceiving any special discord at this crucial point in the poem, the reader can with fewer assumptions and greater consistency perceive in the satirist's case a continuous enactment and awareness of the multiple ironies of human thought and experience in a poem built completely on paradox.

In recapitulation, then, we see that the satirist builds a case against reason in lines 1-122 based on his perception of his own and other men's propensities to create obstacles so that they can surmount them, to do what must be later undone, and to undo what has already been achieved. The mind, struggling for a point of view, becomes preoccupied with problems of its own making; and its efforts to get outside itself—to make contact with the world and with other beings—are frustrated in a thoroughly debilitating self-consciousness. The higher man tries to soar, the lower he falls. At the poem's outset, his search for a point of entry into man's condition involves a leap upward which also involves a descent to the condition of the beasts. By the end of his argument with the adversarius, he has arrived discursively at this very same point—the wisdom of the beasts, that which animals know directly and which man only indirectly discovers through argument. In every point and angle of this process, one perceives mankind's lack of unanimity—its failure to be at one with itself. The point is both argued and enacted.

The succeeding section of the poem—the so-called Hobbesian portion—parallels the theme of the deviousness of human thought with a discussion of the deviousness of active human behavior. It does so now by contrasting the ruling desires of animals and their efficient securing of natural ends through natural means with the ruling fears and caprices of men and their typical indirectness. The desires of animals are furthermore identified with necessity, whereas those of men are seen as supererogatory. Like man's speculative reason, human fears and caprice deviously exceed all limits. Animals hunt

> Nature's allowance, to supply their want.
> But man, with smiles, embraces, friendship, praise,
> Inhumanly his fellow's life betrays;
> With voluntary pains works his distress,
> Not through necessity, but wantonness.

(ll. 134-37)

The emphasis on the "voluntary pains" which men take to vex their fellow creatures carries a step further the theme of the perversities of human ways developed and represented in the earlier sections of the poem. There the speculative reason only tortures itself; and the wit, who strains to give others pleasure "at his own expense," only accidentally victimizes them. Here, however, man is teased with a "righted" reason which it seems is, after all the fuss about it, quite beyond him; and his violence is seen as subtle and completely gratuitous, a voluntary product of his deviousness and chronic fearfulness. Whereas bestial wisdom consists of the direct perception and securing of desiderata, human behavior consists of the devious securing of the unnecessary through fear and sheer "wantonness." Smiles conceal treachery; a military posture, fame, and honor are built on fear; power is slavery; the social virtues arise from hypocrisy: all apparent virtue arises from vice. And not even honesty seems possible, since it is quickly identified by men as the greatest folly or possibly as the greatest knavery of all. Besides, the law of self-defense in this fear-ridden, hypocritical society means that "All the subject of debate / Is only: Who's a knave of the first rate?" (ll. 172-73). Truth against truth, honesty against honesty, reason against reason—all are parts of a vicious circularity from which neither mankind nor the satirist seems able to escape.

Instead of the "vertical" antitheses of the satirist's attacks on the speculative reason (mite / infinite, void of all rest / ever blest), the attack on man's social behavior exploits the irony of appearances often associated with theriophilic arguments: appearances to the contrary notwithstanding, men are more rapacious than beasts. Both devices appear in the poem's opening paradox, and these devices are analogous in their effects. In the first part it is implied that the higher one rises, the lower one will fall; in the second part it is implied that apparent virtues arise from and conceal fear and wantonness operating on thoroughly vicious human propensities. Thus cowardice yields a spurious courage, and traits or qualities ordinarily assumed to be good— honesty and "weak truth"—are desperately impractical.

The satirist's attack on men's active social behavior thus parallels in certain ways his attack on their speculative or contemplative lives, even though there is no exact, logical paralleling of epistemological or psychological categories in the two sections (e.g., the speculative with the practical understanding). Man's hopes and fears in his speculative life seem to correspond, however, to his wantonness and fearfulness in society, and his intellectual uncertainties and self-contradictoriness cohere with his political determinations "by committee." His intellectual indirectness and frustrations cohere with his social hypocrisies and frustrations, and a vicious circularity characterizes all of his determinations. These considerations and the

important earlier lines on wit's victimization of others and of self link sections of a poem well designed to explore the self-destructiveness of all human thought and activity.

In retrospect we can see how Rochester has built into the satirist's argument the secondary paradoxical contention of the theriophilic argument: after insisting that animals reason better than men, the theriophile often shifts to the contention that even if beasts do not "reason" at all, or if their "reason" is not so subtle as man's, still they are better off for it. Rochester's satirist in fact shows that if man, with all his powers of "reason," has to contend mightily to achieve what beasts know and do without effort, then surely human reason is a curse, since it has so little to do with the reason implicit in the nature of things. Yet if man can with great labor utilize the speculative reason to achieve the wisdom of the beasts, as the satirist does, it nevertheless remains true that such reason is often abused and in any event may make very little practical difference in the government of human affairs because it is so often its own enemy. The human nature which is explored in the so-called Hobbesian section of the poem (ll. 123-73) is then in its indirectness, doubleness, and circularity like the human reason explored in the so-called libertine section (ll. 1-122). Both human reason and human nature are so devious that even the consciousness of such crookedness may make no practical difference in one's conduct and may indeed convince one of its unavoidability. In such a world, survival makes crookedness necessary, and the greatest honesty man can achieve is the stark awareness of his thoroughgoing dishonesty.

Thus, if, as Vieth and Griffin have argued of lines 123-73, the satirist is "not simply extending the comparison between men and beasts, [but] is changing the terms" of it,[26] he does so within a traditional framework and follows faithfully yet creatively the "logic" of the traditional argument as it is based on ancient distinctions between the reason of nature and the reason of men. One can plausibly argue, however, that the "change of terms" is implied in the poem's opening paradox, in the early description of "reason" as irrelevant or inimical to life's real business, in the lines on wit, and in the dialectic generated by the quarrel between the satirist and the adversarius—the last perhaps amounting to a quarrel between a man and himself—between the conflicting claims of two kinds of reason, and finally by the strange doubleness and self-defeating indirections of human thought and action.

The third and last major section of the poem, the Epilogue, continues this paradoxical strategy with a vengeance and reemphasizes the poem's reflexivity. First, it at once reminds the reader of the highly stipulative, conditional, hypothetical, and self-critical nature of the foregoing arguments condemning human reason and human nature—"All this with indignation have I hurled / At the pretending part of the proud world." The satirist has built a case to counter the usual pretenses of mankind to intellectual and moral preeminence in the universe. Second, the Epilogue is itself developed out of a counterstipulation, as it were, which, while reasserting the already pungent satire of mankind, allows at the same time for exceptions to the satiric hypothesis. All the while that these possible exceptions are being discussed, it is clear that the *possibilities* of an honest nobleman and a meek, humble clergyman are purely mental phenomena, antitheses arising principally from the dialectical play of mind characteristic of the entire poem. Just as the satirist can imagine the arguments of the *adversarius* and just as theoretical "righted" reason can be poised against speculative reason, so can imagined virtuous men be poised against the knaves of lines 159-73.

The Epilogue thus (1) reverses the tendency of the previous satire of man; (2) continues that satire by defining the ideal in terms of what it is *not,* that is, in terms of current vicious practices and types; and (3) unifies these by broaching the paradoxical possibility that the ingrained human deviousness hitherto explored in the poem might at once be admitted and employed—mirabile dictu!—for unselfish ends: it may be just possible for a nobleman to acknowledge his avarice and at the same time to withstand bribery or for a "man of honest sense" to prove by his *actions* that "he does believe / Mysterious truths which no man can conceive" (ll. 214-15). It is significant that such men are themselves seen as paradoxical or as embodying, like all men, the basic contradictoriness revealed at the poem's outset; for "sense" and mystery are as much at odds as "avarice" is with honesty and patriotism. Sheer contrariety and deviousness render possible what is improbable.

Again stressing the highly tentative, even hypothetical nature of his utterance ("If such there be . . ."), the satirist now agrees to recant his original paradox *if* he can anywhere find these ideals. As we have seen, however, there are no guarantees that they exist anywhere but in the satirist's mind: he may imagine them or create them just as he has earlier created a case against human reason and society and just as he has earlier imaginatively "righted" reason. In view of these earlier arguments, the realization of even a perverse ideal involves one in a paradox as great as all those other paradoxes which the poem develops and enacts.

"Man differs more from man, than man from beast." Can there be any doubt that such a paradox applies to the internal divisions within man as well as to the hypothetical differences among men? Thus the satirist in turning on his previous argument not only suggests

how men may differ from each other while he continues to assert that there is a common human nature. He also represents and dramatizes the ways in which the human mind, in all its indirections and dubieties, argues with and defeats itself. That defeat is so thorough that it even paradoxically may give us a gleam of hope, so that it is not wrong to say that human hopes and fears pervade the poem in ways both destructive and now perhaps even creative.

These final paradoxes and the paradox with which the poem opens are posed as hypothetical constructs; and as such they can be seen as questions—questions not resolved or dissipated simply in comedy or by means of the satirist being satirized, rather they are confirmed as questions by the tortured consciousness of the satirist. Because the poem presents them, enacts them and confirms them as questions, it achieves a poise and richness which a poem lacking unity cannot achieve. In other words, it supports "the intent at totality of the interpretive process [which] may be seen as the literary version of the Gestaltist law of Prägnanz: that the richest organization compatible with the data is to be preferred."[27] The fact that the satirist can construct a devastating case against reason and man makes one point. The fact that he can provisionally doubt that case makes another. Similar sets of points can be seen in the poem's successive questions. For example, is "righted" reason beyond man? Is the meek altruistic man merely a delusion created by the human imagination or by "reason's" tantalizing, tortuous action on man's hopes and fears in his search for certainty and happiness and glory? If indeed the poem does through its ironies pose such questions among other questions, then I believe that it does successfully combine "libertine" and skeptical thought with certain aspects of Hobbesian psychology in a well-unified structure. It is not that Rochester merely at one point speaks of man as corrigible and at another as incorrigible. It is that from first to last the poem everywhere questions man's knowledge and corrigibility through both hypotheses and hypothesizing. Seen in this way, the poem is the well-constructed expression and dramatization of the fundamental perplexities of a mind aware that mind itself is the source of all perplexity and all imagined virtue and all real vice.[28]

The poem may then be well described as "open-ended," since it poses a final fundamental question. But because the poem questions both directly through statement of paradox or hypothesis on the one hand and indirectly through representation of the self-conscious perplexities of the paradoxist on the other hand, it "performs" its message or embodies it in a highly imaginative way through both strategy and structure. The poem is highly ironic, but these ironies are not limited to a comic awareness of the persona's insufficiency or to the contrived irony of the satirist satirized. Nor need that irony be necessarily seen in terms of an anti-Aristotelian poetic or any poetic substantially different from those whereby many other splendid ironic works have been described. More important, our awareness of the poem's pervasive ironies preserves in it a measure of self-knowledge, humility, and tragic pathos as well as wit—in short, a measure of humanity.

Notes

1. I refer, of course, to Vivian de Sola Pinto's *Enthusiast in Wit* (Lincoln: Univ. of Nebraska Press, 1962); to David M. Vieth's *Attribution in Restoration Poetry: A Study of Rochester's Poem of 1680* (New Haven: Yale Univ. Press, 1963) and to his splendid edition of *The Complete Poems of John Wilmot, Earl of Rochester* (New Haven: Yale Univ. Press, 1968); and to Dustin H. Griffin's stimulating and well-informed *Satires Against Man: The Poems of Rochester* (Berkeley: Univ. of California Press, 1973).

2. See especially Thomas H. Fujimura, "Rochester's 'Satyr Against Mankind,' An Analysis," *Studies in Philology*, 55 (1958), 576-90; and David M. Vieth, "Toward an Anti-Aristotelian Poetic: Rochester's *Satyr Against Mankind* and *Artemisia to Chloe*, with Notes on Swift's *Tale of a Tub* and *Gulliver's Travels*," *Language and Style*, 5 (1972), 123-45. Vieth also acknowledges some indebtedness to Peter Thorpe, "The Nonstructure of Augustan Verse," *Papers on Language and Literature*, 5 (1969), 235-51, which also briefly discusses Rochester's *Satyr*. Some points of Vieth's argument were anticipated as early as Irène Simon, "'Pride of Reason' in the Restoration," *Revenue des langues vivantes*, 25 (1959), 375-97, esp. 376 n.3.

   One of the most recent contributions to the ongoing discussion is the fine study by Reba Wilcoxon, "Rochester's Philosophical Premises: A Case for Consistency," *Eighteenth-Century Studies*, 8 (1974-75), 183-201. Other important studies are Charles A. Knight, "The Paradox of Reason: Argument in Rochester's 'Satyr against Mankind,'" *Modern Language Review*, 65 (1979), 254-60; and Ronald W. Johnson, "Rhetoric and Drama in Rochester's 'Satyr against Reason and Mankind,'" *Studies in English Literature, 1500-1900*, 15 (1975), 365-73. For Vieth's critique of other studies of the poem, see "Toward an Anti-Aristotelian Poetic," pp. 125 ff. and 143-44 pp 13-16

3. Vieth, "Toward an Anti-Aristotelian Poetic," pp. 125-27. Other scholars who have investigated the poem's ideas apparently do not agree entirely with Vieth's description of lines 1-122 as predominantly "libertine" or "Epicurean" and of lines 123-73 as predominantly "Hobbesian." For example, Wil-

coxon's interesting and thoughtful study agrees in part with the earlier view of Fujimura that the *Satyr* is "most Hobbesian" in its "reliance on the senses and in its rejection of the hypostatized entities that are the corruptions of language" (Wilcoxon, p. 194). In other words, she finds with Fujimura the presence of Hobbesian influence in what Vieth calls the "libertine half" of the poem. She disagrees with Fujimura, however, and agrees with Vieth in finding also Hobbesian influence in what Vieth has called the poem's Hobbesian section: "the Hobbesian Shadow hovers over Rochester's lines [on fear-driven man, l. 128]. . . . They suggest that man has not left Hobbes's state of nature—and by extension what passes for civilization is a hollow sham. As we have seen, Rochester does not say this is a necessary state of affairs" (p. 197). But one should also note that Wilcoxon sees, rightly I think, in both sections of the poem an Epicurean as well as Hobbesian emphasis on fear (pp. 197-98).

   Such considerations, it seems to me, further weaken Vieth's contention—which, after all, he asserts primarily through his criticism of others rather than through any direct proof of his own— that the poem falls into two irreconcilable halves.

4. Vieth, "Toward an Anti-Aristotelian Poetic," pp. 128-29. Vieth describes the poem as providing a special case of "Rochesterian irony," "Rochester's discovery of the way to link discontinuous modes of experience" (p. 129). Yet Vieth's point is that the poem does *not* link such modes but rather merely presents them to us. It is my contention that the *Satyr* does link rather than merely juxtapose.

5. Griffin, p. 206. Griffin (pp. 205-06) finds the poem to consist of four parts: "(1) the statement of the thesis (ll. 1-45); (2) the imagined objections by the adversarius (ll. 48-71); (3) the reply to the objections, concerning first reason (ll. 72-111) and then mankind, both with respect to his 'wisdom' (ll. 112-22) and 'human nature' (ll. 123-73); and (4) an epilogue, containing a summary (ll. 174-78) and peroration, in which the speaker conditionally recants (ll. 179-219) and conditionally reformulates his paradox (ll. 220-21)."

6. Griffin, p. 209.

7. Griffin, p. 209.

8. Griffin, pp. 244-45.

9. Knight, pp. 254-60, esp. p. 255. Knight's analysis of the poem's opening lines is very skillful, and I am indebted to it. His commentary tends to become less enlightening as he moves toward the poem's critique of man in society and the Epilogue.

10. Johnson, p. 370.

11. Johnson, p. 371.

12. Rosalie L. Colie, *Paradoxia Epidemica: The Renaissance Tradition of Paradox* (Princeton: Princeton Univ. Press, 1966), pp. 6-8.

13. Colie, p. 7.

14. Colie, p. 6.

15. Colie, pp. 20 and passim. This definition also applies to irony which is not merely simple irony. On the relationship of paradox to irony, see Colie, pp. 10 and 517: "The formal structure of paradox is of course dialectic: therefore it inevitably is a figure of thought." The same can be said of irony. On the fusing power of paradox and irony, see p. 520.

16. Griffin, pp. 158 ff. The most important study of theriophily is George Boas, *The Happy Beast in French Thought of the Seventeenth Century* (Baltimore: Johns Hopkins Univ. Press, 1933); for discussion and examples of the double paradox of theriophily, see esp. pp. 1-2, 58-59, and 124-25. For other important studies, see the bibliographical notes in James E. Gill, "Theriophily in Antiquity: A Supplementary Account," *Journal of the History of Ideas,* 30 (1969), 401-12; and "Beast over Man: Theriophilic Paradox in Gulliver's 'Voyage to the Country of the Houyhnhnms,'" *Studies in Philology,* 67 (1970), 532-49. Especially informative are Henri Busson—three works—*La Pensée religieuse françaiseaise de Charron à Pascal* (Paris: J. Vrin, 1933), *Le Rationalisme dans la littérature française de la renaissance (1533-1601),* rev. ed. (Paris: J. Vrin, 1957); and *La Religion des classiques (1660-1685)* (Paris: J. Vrin, 1948).

17. For a generalized statement of this common strategy, see Boas, pp. 1-2; and for the evolution of theriophilic topics of criticism and their typical structure in the principal source of theriophily in antiquity, Plutarch's *Gryllus,* see Gill, "Theriophily in Antiquity," esp. p. 412.

18. For an early discussion of the "unanimity" of animals—as opposed to human multiplicity and confusion—see Diogenes Laertius, "Life of Zeno" in *The Lives and Opinions of Eminent Philosophers,* trans. C. D. Yonge (London, 1853), p. 290. Pascal—who interestingly enough both refutes and then utilizes the theriophilic paradox (and thereby creates his own distinctive version of it)—emphasizes man's lack of integrity or "unanimity." See Blaise Pascal, *Pensées,* trans. J. M. Cohen (Baltimore: Penguin Books, 1961), p. 114, Nos. 327-30. Also see St. Evremond's exclamation: "Nature! éleve-nous à la clarté des anges, / Ou nous abaisse au sens des simples animaux." In *Oeuvres mélées de St. Evremond,* ed. Charles Giraud, 2 vols. (Paris, 1865), II, 536. For a curious English version of the argument, see Walter Charleton's Introduction to his translation of J. B. Van Helmont's *A Ternary of Paradoxes* (London, 1650), sigs. f2-f4v, where Charleton seems to combine Baconian and Gassendist thought when he praises the "Clarity of Abstracted and Intuitive Intellection" (i.e., clear perception and firm induction) and condemns "Reason . . . as a caduce, spurious Faculty, accidentally Advenient upon the Degradation of our Nature. . . ." (sig. f2). Similarly he argues elsewhere that "the Science of the Praemises, is always more certain than the Science of Conclusion . . . and that Science is radically seated in Intellect, without the concurrence of *Reason,* because we find it older than the Demonstration." Truth, therefore, is fact, and the product of reason is only opinion: one is *"ens reale, verum,"* whereas the other is only *"ens mentale, problematicum"* (sig. f4). He then goes on to suggest that animals may make even better use of the faculty of discourse than men do and to insist that this realization is bound to humiliate human pretensions.

19. The term "reflexive" I use to describe thought or reflection which is about itself—"enquiry into the character of . . . psychic experience and what that enquiry reveals about structure and nature of . . . being." I adapt for my purposes the language of James E. Swearingen in *Reflexivity in* Tristram Shandy: *An Essay in Phenomenological Criticism* (New Haven: Yale Univ. Press, 1977), p. 49. Swearingen's concept is much more intricately articulated than my own, however, and I do not claim that my views are based on his interesting attack on the problems of reading *Tristram Shandy.*

Rochester's originality is perhaps best seen in the fact that the theriophilic argument in Rochester's poem is more reflexive than Boileau's in his *Satire VIII* the poem which Rochester imitates. For example, Boileau's poem—which contains the simplest extended version of theriophily on record—has no real paradoxical critique of human reason as Rochester's does. It is, furthermore, interesting to observe that though many readers have argued for Rochester's originality vis-à-vis Boileau (see, e.g., Pinto, p. 151), few critics have understood the crucial differences in their respective praises of animals. The most important difference is that, because of his reflexive development of the theriophilic paradox, Rochester's satirist is, as it were, arguing with himself as well as with others; in Boileau there is very little of this kind of drama.

20. Griffin, pp. 158 ff.

21. Gill, "Theriophily in Antiquity," pp. 406-07.

22. This point is made well by Johnson.

23. It is interesting to note that some theriophiles argue that animals reason more like angels or even like God than like men. In such comparisons we see an emphasis on the *directness* of bestial perception, thought, and action as opposed to the *indirectness* of human thought and action. See, for example, the enlightening discussion of this matter by Bernard le Bouvier de Fontenelle in the group of essays and fragments ranging from "Du Bonheur" through "Sur l'Instinct" in *Fontenelle: Oeuvres,* ed. G. B. Depping, II (Paris, 1818; rpt. Genève: Sklatine Reprints, 1966), pp. 379-424.

24. This reading at least resolves Griffin's problem (pp. 227-28) in reading ll. 8 ff., where he is puzzled about whether instinct is linked to the senses and opposed to reason and the "sixth sense" or whether instinct and speculative reason are to be imagined as polar opposites, with the senses somewhere in a middle ground. The solution of this problem depends on the discrimination among "reasons," as we see, and not on the determination of a single "reason." See also Gill, "Theriophily in Antiquity," esp. pp. 406-07; and J. S. Spink, *French Free-Thought from Gassendi to Voltaire* (New York: Greenwood Press, 1969), pp. 80-84 and 91-102, on instinct and "sense" in animals.

An analogous situation occurs in *Gulliver's Travels,* IV, where Houyhnhnm reason and the reason of Nature are contrasted with human reason. See Gill, "Beast over Man," pp. 544-48; and *The Prose Works of Jonathan Swift,* ed. Herbert Davis et al., Vol. XI (Oxford: Basil Blackwell, 1941), p. 251: "Neither is *Reason* among them a Point problematical as with us, where men can argue with Plausibility on both Sides of a Question."

25. The satirist's perception of wit seems to me to be fairly close to Hobbes' analysis of laughter, which he describes as the result of sudden

> *Joy* [which], arising from imagination of a man's own power and ability; is that exultation of the mind which called *Glorying*; which if grounded upon the experience of his own former actions, is the same with Confidence; but if grounded on the flattery of others; or onely [*sic*] supposed by himself, for delight in the consequences of it, is called Vaine-Glory. . . . Sudden Glory, is the passion which maketh those Grimaces called Laughter; and is caused either by some sudden act of their own, that pleaseth them; or by the apprehension of some deformed thing in another, by comparison whereof they suddenly applaud themselves. And it is incident most to them that are conscious of the fewest abilities in themselves who are forced to keep themselves in their own favour, by observing the imperfections of other men.

Quoted from *Leviathan* in *The English Works of Thomas Hobbes of Malmesbury,* ed. Sir William Molesworth, Vol. III (London, 1839), pp. 45-46). That Hobbes' contemporaries were aware of the cynical nature of his theory of laughter and could critically reflect on its social uses and misuses can be seen in Samuel Butler's early critique of it in his "A Modern Politician" (*Samuel Butler (1612-1680): Characters,* ed. Charles W. Daves [Cleveland: Press of Case Western Reserve Univ., 1970], pp. 43-44).

26. The terms are Griffin's (pp. 236-37), but the idea also pervades Vieth's essay and was suggested first by Simon, p. 376 n. 3.

27. Jonathan Culler, *Structuralist Poetics: Structuralism, Linguistics, and the Study of Literature* (Ithaca: Cornell Univ. Press, 1975), p. 174.

28. Cf. Wilcoxon's statement (p. 198): "The absence of *ataraxia* in Rochester is, I would argue, the source of his art." To state the matter another way, one might say that through the poem Rochester protests in an uncommon way what many commonly complain of. First, he protests the tyranny of abstraction as it carries us away from the concrete texture of our lives. Second, he complains of the equally misleading appearances which society presents and compels us to present to each other. The unfruitfulness of man's efforts at private speculation and of his resorts to social intercourse may leave him very little fresh and vital space in which to live. And in fact much of the vitality which Rochester's satirist manifests is generated by his inability not to react against the tyrannies which he so rigorously describes.

John D. Patterson (essay date spring 1981)

SOURCE: Patterson, John D. "Rochester's Second Bottle: Attitudes to Drink and Drinking in the Works of John Wilmot, Earl of Rochester." *Restoration* 5, no. 1 (spring 1981): 6-15.

[*In the following essay, Patterson explores the theme of drinking and its relationship to sex, friendship, and wisdom—which, he maintains, constitute major motifs in Rochester's work.*]

On June 22, 1674, Rochester wrote a letter for his friend Henry Savile beginning, "Whether Love, Wine, or Wisdome (wch. rule you by turnes) have the present ascendent, I cannott pretend to determine att this distance," and going on to express his belief that Savile will not have forgotten his "Absent freinds."[1] This opening juxtaposition of love, wine, and wisdom is not only a rhetorical device sweeping the reader into the panegyric on drinking that the letter becomes. The relationship of these three concepts to each other and to friendship constitutes a theme that is continually explored and developed by Rochester throughout his letters and poetry.

While discussion of the conflicting claims of love and wine is something of a commonplace in Restoration literature, particularly in the comedies, Rochester seems to have had more than a casual interest in the subject. Indeed in **"Upon His Drinking a Bowl"** he declares, "Cupid and Bacchus my saints are,"[2] and it seems curious to me that while a great deal of attention has been given to this worship of Cupid, little or no serious attention has been given to his equally devout worship of Bacchus. Rochester's witty and urbane letter of June 22, 1674, is a good starting point for an examination of the different attitudes towards drink and drinking expressed throughout his works. And it is worth bearing in mind that while there is some truth in Vieth's "To a greater or lesser degree the 'I' of each poem is always Rochester,"[3] one can never be sure that the voice of any poem is Rochester's true voice. With the letters one can be more certain. At least if Rochester did not believe what he wrote in his letters, he wanted Savile to believe that he did, and that is as close as we shall ever get to hearing the real Rochester.

The opening of the letter implies that love, wine, and wisdom are three "humours" that dominate Savile in turns. Although it might be assumed that when one of the humours is dominant the other two are entirely repressed, the cyclical nature of the process means that Savile only temporarily renounces women, wine, or sober judgment (as wisdom might be defined in this context) in favor of any one of the rest. Rochester continues with a reference to a time when, after he had revealed to the women concerned Savile's infidelity to "the Black & faire Countesses," Savile forgave him "upon the first Bottle & upon the second on my conscience wou'd have renounc'd them and the whole sex." This could mean either that when drinking the second bottle of wine Savile announced his intention to give up women and Rochester persuaded him of the folly of such a procedure, or that Savile was on the point of making the announcement and would have done so had occasion arisen. Either way, the combination of wine and Rochester's company mellowed Savile's anger and almost, but not quite, led to a renunciation of women in favor of wine.

A panegyric on the merits of alcohol follows, eulogizing wine's power to break down both psychological and social barriers: "Oh that second bottle Harry is the sincerest, wisest, & most impartiall downright freind wee have, tells us truth of our selves. . . ." It is the second bottle, the one that brings stimulation without stupefaction, that Rochester praises.[4] Sincere, truly wise, and impartial, it removes those barriers and buttresses that, although developed for our own protection, are necessarily deceptive. Wine is personified as a friend (indeed it performs the duty of a best friend as it "tells us truth of our selves"), but it is inextricably associated with human friends when the presence of plain-dealing drinking companions is implied: "[Wine] forces us to speake truths of others, banishes flattery from our Hearts, setts us above the meane Policy of Court prudence, wch. makes us lye to one another all day, for feare of being betray'd by each other att night. . . ." The dissimulation of everyday conduct, which for Rochester and Savile meant courtly etiquette, is explicitly contrasted with the speech and behavior of a company of friends drinking. One is the state of war of each against each posited by Hobbes, the other a society where false barriers have been broken down, a brave new world of honesty, forthrightness and sincere friendship. In this world even "the errantest villain breathing is honest as long as that bottle lives," although typically, once he has suggested the ideal, Rochester points out that this very rarely comes about in real life because "few of that tribe [the dishonest] dare venture upon him [the bottle], att least among the Courtiers and statesmen."

Real life brings Rochester to consider "the three businesses of this Age, Woemen, Polliticks & drinking," at which only in the latter have Rochester and Savile not proved themselves "Errant fumblers." A "fumbler" at this time could mean "an unperforming Husband, one that is insufficient" (*OED* definition b), and it is not unlikely that Rochester intended the play on words, principally because he makes the obvious sexual pun on "dye" later in the sentence, but also because, as we shall see, for Rochester there was a particular relationship between the generative powers of sex and alcohol. The main part of the letter concludes with a light-hearted proposal that he and Savile should "live & dye sheere drunkards, or entire lovers" rather than attempt to be both lovers and drinkers. This proposal is not to be taken too seriously as it appears to be rather a lead up to the chiastic joke about "wch. is the most tiresome creature, the loving drunkard or the drunken lover" than a genuine plea. Rochester, who admitted to Burnet that he introduced lies into his poems to enhance their aesthetic appeal, was never too concerned with accuracy when there was a jest in the offing.[5]

In fact there is only one work in the Rochester canon in which a definite preference between wine and women is seriously asserted. In the song beginning **"Love a woman? You're an ass!"** Rochester's persona declares his intention to renounce women entirely in favor of male company and drink. This is probably an early poem, since Rochester employs the traditional form of the Cavalier drinking song, which also means that the persona's views are not necessarily Rochester's. Certainly the sentiment expressed is atypical of Rochester and indeed is contradicted by almost every other statement he makes on the relationship between wine and women:

> Love a woman? You're an ass!
> 'Tis a most insipid passion
> To choose out for your happiness
> The silliest part of God's creation.
>
> Let the porter and the groom,
> Things designed for dirty slaves,
> Drudge in fair Aurelia's womb
> To get supplies for age and graves.
>
> Farewell, woman! I intend
> Henceforth every night to sit
> With my Lewd, well-natured friend,
> Drinking to engender wit.
>
> Then give me health, wealth, mirth, and wine,
> And, if busy love entrenches,
> There's a sweet, soft page of mine
> Does the trick worth forty wenches.

There may well be, as David Farley-Hills points out, "a metaphysic of rejection far stronger than the conventional rejection of women for wine" in the last line of the second stanza;[6] but the reason for this, I think, is not so much "the anti-feminist malevolence" of stanzas two and four as the positive attractions presented in stanzas three and four. Critics have often seen Rochester using drink as a refuge, as sanctuary from something (usually women) that he is fleeing. Farley-Hills comments, "Drinking is more likely to be an anodyne than a pleasure in such a world, a desperate remedy in an attempt to retain some hold on some meaning." However, Rochester's speaker uses drink for positive rather than negative reasons. He wants to use it "to engender wit" and he wants to use it in the company of a friend. It is wit and friendship that give meaning to Rochester's world, and drink is a means to that end, not an end in itself. It is a positive pleasure rather than a desperate remedy.

According to the speaker, to love a woman is a dull pleasure characterized by drudgery and futility. Perhaps he thinks this because, like Rochester in the letter discussed above, he is an unperforming "fumbler" with women. Like Rochester in the letter, though, the speaker is no fumbler when it comes to drinking, which he associates with fertility. The basic procreative function of the species he assigns to those who cannot think, to the lower orders and women. He and his friend will indulge in the higher pleasures of mental procreation, a function stimulated by alcohol. Recognizing that man cannot live without some sexual release, he announces his intention to indulge in homosexual acts, which are presented in physical rather than emotional terms: the page, who is a possession of the speaker's rather than a lover, is "sweet" to the sight and "soft" to the touch, and their encounter is a "trick," in the sense of a bout of physical sex, rather than an emotional experience. The speaker, then, requires only wine and male company of one sort or another.

More frequently, though, Rochester's works give the impression that wine and women provide equal and complementary pleasures. A good illustration is **"To a Lady in a Letter,"** a poem that has generally been incorrectly categorized with **"Love a woman?"** as expressing a preference for wine over women.[7] The poem is an attempt to give intellectual justification to a life of pleasure in which the writer can drink with his friends and his mistress can take lovers: "Let us, since wit has taught us how, / Raise pleasure to the top" is the central theme of the poem:

> Such perfect bliss, fair Chloris, we
> In our enjoyments prove,
> 'Tis pity restless jealously
> Should mingle with our love.
>
> Let us, since wit has taught us how,
> Raise pleasure to the top:
> You rival bottle must allow,
> I'll suffer rival fop.
>
> Think not in this that I design
> A treason 'gainst love's charms,
> When, following the god of wine,
> I leave my Chloris' arms. . . .[8]

The letter-writer is not seeking to abandon Chloris in favor of the bottle. Their sex life is still satisfactory as far as he is concerned: their enjoyments result in "perfect bliss" and he will "ne'er repine" at her love-making. He is writing in the present, not the past, tense, about the situation as it now stands and as it will continue if she accepts his interpretation of it. He wants to use his intellect ("wit") to overcome the natural feelings of mutual jealousy aroused by Chloris' lovers and his drinking, and there follows a witty comparison between their respective tipples, wine and semen, which again reveals a correspondence between the generative powers of sex and alcohol. The writer declares that Chloris' sexual organs can take off semen as quickly as he can drink wine:

> Since you have that, for all your haste
> (At which I'll ne'er repine),
> Will take his liquor off as fast
> As I can take off mine.

In the last stanza he uses chiasmus to make a witty comparison between his drinking and her love-making:

> Whilst I, my pleasure to pursue,
> Whole nights am taking in
> The lusty juice of grapes, take you
> The juice of lusty men.

The description of the bottle and the fop as rivals to the mistress and the writer respectively implies a continuation of the relationship between them. Bottle and fop are rivals to, not replacements of, the originals. The writer explicitly states that he does not intend any "treason 'gainst love's charms" by his proposal, and maintains a tone of urbane reasonableness throughout. In stanza seven, for instance, Chloris "freely may confess" the truth of his argument, and they will "ne'er disagree" because they are equals in their desire to maximize pleasure. Chloris will satisfy her sexual lust with her empty-headed fops while the writer, as we shall see, will satisfy his intellectual desires with the help of drink and, presumably, the company of his friends. He is not, then, announcing his intention to escape from women by drinking. Although he will leave Chloris' arms to follow Bacchus, the implications, as in "Absent from thee, I languish still," are that the straying lover will return. To indulge in the two pleasures of love and wine is to "raise pleasure to the top," which is the object of his philosophy of life.

It is interesting to note that throughout the three basic texts of the poem the lines referring to the mutual desire of the writer and his mistress to maximize pleasure retain the same meaning and virtually the same wording:

> Let us, since wit has taught us how,
>   Raise pleasure to the top:
>   . . . . .
>
> For did you love your pleasure less,
>   You were no match for me.

(Versions A and B, the earliest, read "instructs" for "has taught" and "not fitt for" instead of "no match for.") This indicates the importance of the pleasure principle to Rochester's analysis of the writer's situation. But the final version of the poem does not give any indication why the writer should consider drinking a pleasure, let alone one of the two "top" pleasures. The last stanza of version B, however, reads:

> For wine (whose power alone can raise
>   Our thoughts soe farr above)
> Affords Idea's fitt to praise.
>   What wee thinke fitt to Love.[9]

As the writer loves wine and his mistress equally, though in different ways and for different reasons, the last line could apply to either. But the reason he considers drinking to be a pleasure is made clear: wine has the power to heighten the mental faculties. Wine stimulates one's thoughts to produce "Ideas" or conceptions that are "fit" for or on appropriate level to the subject under consideration. Wine is able to do this, as Rochester explained in the letter examined above, because it enables one to perceive truth.

The word "Ideas" might be used in the seventeenth-century sense of figures of speech (see *OED* definition 7, c) in which case drinking is seen as an essential part of poetic creation, helping the poet to find the exact words he needs to express his feelings. In **"The Disabled Debauchee"** there is a similar ambiguity. The Debauchee talks of "When fleets of glasses sail about the board, / From whose broadsides volleys of wit shall rain." While obviously comparing sallies of wit to the discharge of a ship's gun, he might also be punning on "broadside" in the sense of libel-sheet or satire, the poetic product of the wit engendered by drinking. In this light Robert Wolseley's defence of Rochester's wit in his preface to *Valentinian* appears particularly appropriate. Wolseley defines wit as "a *true and lively expression of Nature.* By *Nature* I do not only mean all sorts of material Objects, and species of Substance whatsoever, but also general Notions and abstracted Truths" (in *Critical Heritage,* p. 52). Wine not only enables one to penetrate through superficiality to truth, as Rochester explained in his letter, but also gives one the ability to express these truths in "a true and lively" form by stimulating the intellect and the powers of poetic creativity, as the speakers suggest in **"Love a woman?"** and the Portland stanza of **"To a Lady in a Letter."**

The speaker of **"Upon his Drinking a Bowl,"** however, has a different attitude towards wine. The poem is an adaptation of Anacreon's Odes XVII and XVIII or lines thirteen to forty of Ronsard's adaptation of these odes beginning "Du grand Turc je n'ay souci." In his edition of Ronsard's *Oeuvres complètes* Paul Laumonier explains that the Greek text used by Ronsard ran the two odes together and that Ronsard himself followed this format.[10] This accounts for the rather misleading information supplied by C. A. Zimansky and repeated by Vieth in a headnote that Rochester's poem is "a translation of Ronsard's poem beginning, 'Vulcan! En faveur de moy . . . .'." Ronsard's poem was first published in 1553 but was substantially altered by Ronsard for its many subsequent appearances from 1555 onwards (see *Oeuvres complètes,* V, 79-80, for original text and variants). Rochester's poem has more in common with the altered version than the first; particularly noticeable is the adaptation of Ronsard's "viellard Nestor" into a reference to the cup that "Nestor used of old." But as always with Rochester's adaptations, a number of original elements are introduced: the imagery of the sea, the contemporary details of the Dutch wars and Butler's astrologer Sir Sidrophel, and most significantly, the attitudes towards drink and sex expressed in stanzas five and six. In stanza five the speaker describes the scene he would like to see upon his bowl:

> But carve thereon a spreading vine,
>   Then add two lovely boys;

>   Their limbs in amorous folds entwine,
>   The type of future joys.

The homosexual implications are obvious, and as in the last stanza of **"Love a woman?"** it is the physical rather than the emotional experience of homosexuality that is emphasized. The descriptions are unashamedly sensual: the boys are seductively "lovely"; "limbs" implies the activity of all members of the body; "amorous folds" has sexual connotations; "entwine" is more sensual than, say, "embrace." Neither Ronsard nor later translators of Anacreon describe such a physical homosexual encounter,[11] but for Rochester's speaker this is the example of "future joys."

As Anne Righter has pointed out, though, it is characteristic of Rochester's poetry that a revelation in the last stanza exposes a variety of meanings in the poem,[12] and here it is revealed that the "lovely boys" are in fact Bacchus (cf. Dryden's "Alexander's Feast," l.48, where the musician sings "Of Bacchus ever fair, and ever young") and Cupid the winged boy:

>   Cupid and Bacchus my saints are:
>   May drink and love still reign.
>   With wine I wash away my cares,
>   And then to cunt again.

This is truly wine as anodyne. Perhaps Rochester was influenced by his sources. Anacreon frequently washes away his cares with wine, as does Ronsard in his anacreontic "Odette, ou plus Tost folie" (*Oeuvres complètes*, VI, 243-44). More importantly, perhaps the "cares" the speaker is washing away are worries about the loveless, mechanical attitude to sex that "And then to cunt again" implies. If so, "The type of future joys" becomes more significant. It might simply refer to the joys of cunt that he goes to when drunk, but the disembodied attitude suggested by the synecdochical "cunt," particularly when this is compared with the sensuousness of stanza five, implies that this holds little joy for him. More likely, "The type of future joys" is some ideal state of love, either the homosexual love (associated with wine, male friendship, and sensuality) of stanza five and **"Love a woman?"** or a heterosexual love, presumably like that posited in **"The Fall"**:

>   How blest was the created state
>   Of man and woman, ere they fell,
>   Compared to our unhappy fate:
>   We need not fear another hell.
>
>   Naked beneath cool shades they lay;
>   Enjoyment waited on desire;
>   Each member did there wills obey,
>   Nor could a wish set pleasure higher.

Whatever its nature, it is typical that a speaker of Rochester's should think that this ideal state does not exist at the moment; such "joys" are in the future. The present condition is that described in **"The Fall"**:

>   But we, poor slaves to hope and fear,
>   Are never of our joys secure;
>   They lessen still as they draw near,
>   And none but dull delights endure.

The most one can do is to vary the sensations of the present. The speaker goes "to cunt again," which implies that he is returning from where he has just been. "[D]rink and love" might rule his life in turns, but drink is an anodyne and love is earthly, mechanical, and inevitable. The sensual round of cunt/drink/cunt might not "Raise pleasure to the top," but it can alleviate the boredom and fears inherent in a society fallen into dullness.

A more positive attitude, paradoxically, is expressed in **"The Disabled Debauchee,"** in which Rochester founds a demoniac religion on the debilitation of drink and pox. The "wise" Debauchee is a god-like figure who, "absent" yet present, exults in his own glory. Like some pagan god, "From his fierce eyes flashes of fire he throws, / As from black clouds when lightning breaks away." He is the god of a demoniac religion of drinking, a religion of "vice" that scorns "dull morals." He looks forward to engineering the fall of an innocent youth into sexual and alcoholic temptation:

>   Should any youth (worth being drunk) prove nice,
>   And from his fair inviter meanly shrink,
>   'Twill please the ghost of my departed vice
>   If, at my counsel, he repent and drink.

The two temptations are neatly combined when the Debauchee refers to a time when he "was strong and able to bear arms." This phrase not only echoes the images of battle in earlier stanzas but also connotes the weapons of love and drink, naked limbs and full glasses (cf. Wycherley's *The Country Wife,* 1675, where Lady Fidget encourages her companions to raise their glasses by urging them to "take up these arms" [V, iv, 33]). The religious atmosphere evoked by suggestions of temptation, counselling, repentance, and communion is maintained when the Debauchee announces his intention to "inspire" the youth to a distinctly satanic calling involving violence, desecration, and indiscriminate sexuality. The Debauchee glorifies his religion by presenting such acts of inversion and evil as "important mischief" and "handsome ills":

>   I'll tell of whores attacked, their lords at home;
>   Bawds' quarters beaten up, and fortress won;
>   Windows demolished, watches overcome;
>   And handsome ills by my contrivance done.
>
>   Nor shall our love-fits, Chloris, be forgot,
>   When each the well-looked linkboy strove t'enjoy,
>   And the best kiss was the deciding lot
>   Whether the boy fucked you, or I the boy.
>
>   With tales like these I will such thoughts inspire
>   As to important mischief shall incline:

I'll make him long some ancient church to fire,
  And fear no lewdness he's called to by wine.

The character is similar to the one that Rochester adopts for his demoniac tirade **"To the Postboy,"** written about a year later in 1676. Here the "peerless peer" who has "outswilled Bacchus" demands to be told the quickest way to Hell. The crimes he boasts of might be the ten commandments of the Disabled Debauchee's religion: drinking, swearing, fornication, buggery, cowardice, violence, rape, murder, blasphemy and libel.

However, the Debauchee is not yet disabled, for the poem is a proleptic fantasy. Perhaps Rochester shared the fantasy: **"To the Postboy"** might suggest that he did. More likely it suggests that Rochester was adopting his own caricature,[13] an image itself no doubt fostered by poems such as **"The Disabled Debauchee."** The public image of Rochester the demoniac drinker is well developed in Oldham's "A Dithyrambic. The Drunkards Speech in a Mask," first published in *Poems and Translations* (London, 1683, pp. 206-15). According to Oldham's notebook "A Dithyrambic" is "Suppos'd to be Spoken by Rochester at ye Guinny Club" (see *ARP*, [*Attribution in Restoration Poetry* (New Haven: Yale Univ. Press, 1963)] p. 188). As the poem was written in August, 1677, the Drunkard might even be based upon Rochester's Disabled Debauchee. Oldham's Drunkard begins by addressing the religious, sarcastically calling them "wise" and suggesting that they might be able to beguile "some unexperienc'd Fop" or "raw ent'ring Sinner" but not him who is, by implication, an experienced rake and sinner. Like Rochester in **"The Mock Song,"** the Drunkard parodies Sir Carr Scroope's song beginning "I cannot change as others do." Scroope's lover declares that he "Will still love on, will still love on, and die" while Oldham's Drunkard announces, "It is resolv'd, I will drink on, and die." He declares "Drunkenness and Wine" to be "Divine" and sees drink as an invigorating "Soul" which he will "invoke" as "almighty Wine . . . the World's great Soul, that heav'nly Fire" (st. 3). Drink is "the best of Vice" and he compares with his drunken self prophets "Drunk with the Spirits of infus'd Divinity" who "with holy Frenzy reel . . . rave, stagger, and are mad, like me" (st. 6). Finally he contemplates staggering down to Hell "in triumph" (st. 7).

In Rochester's poetry, though, the drunkard is not always a witty or powerful and overwhelming figure. In **"Timon"** Rochester shows the effects of alcohol on the unintelligent mind. Timon is waylaid by "a dull dining sot" who takes him home to dinner with a company of bullies and promises that when drunk the company will "write and fight" (ll. 5, 30). The implication is plainly that of alcohol leading to poetic inspiration. In the event the company fight but do not write, and the fact that they fight physically as well as verbally is symptomatic

of their low level of intelligence. Whatever else it might engender, alcohol here could not produce wit because, apart from Timon, there are no intelligent minds to work upon. The effect of alcohol upon the dull imagination is to break down the social restraints and barriers without encouraging the perceptions that intelligent minds are capable of at such times.

The drunkenness described in **"Timon,"** where the drinkers reveal their foolishness through their arguments and resort to physical violence (ll. 111-75), is similar to that referred to by Hobbes when he considers the effects of alcohol on the mind in *Leviathan*, I, 8:

> For the variety of behavior in men that have drunk too much, is the same with that of mad-men: some of them Raging, others Loving, others Laughing, all extravagantly, but according to their Severall domineering Passions: For the effect of the wine, does but remove Dissimulation; and take from them the sight of the deformity of their Passions. For (I believe) the most sober men, when they walk alone without care and employment of the mind, would be unwilling the vanity and Extravagance of their thoughts at this time should be so publiquely seen.[14]

This in turn is similar to the proverbial "In Vino Veritas." Rochester had certainly read *Leviathan* and presumably knew the proverb as it had come into popular usage during Elizabeth's reign.[15] Most likely his ideas were grounded in practice. What is important is the variety of attitudes that Rochester reveals towards the old adage. Like Hobbes he realizes that drink releases passions that are normally represented for social reasons. But although he demonstrates the anti-social passions released by drink in **"Timon"** and the demoniac potential latent in this in **"The Disabled Debauchee,"** he is more often concerned to express the beneficial results of this breakdown in terms of plain-dealing between friends and the heightened perception of the intelligent mind.

Certain biographical evidence would appear to suggest that Rochester's wit was indeed sharpened by alcohol: "And the natural heat of his fancy, being inflamed by Wine, made him so extravagantly pleasant, that many, to be more diverted by that humor, studied to engage him deeper and deeper in intemperance," reports Burnet in *Some Passages*. There then follows the notorious passage in which Rochester claims that "for five years together he was continually Drunk: not all the while under the visible effect of it, but his blood was so inflamed, that he was not in all that time cool enough to be perfectly master of himself" (*Critical Heritage*, p. 50). It must be remembered, though, that Rochester was prone to exaggeration; in a letter of August, 1975, for instance, he writes, "I was newly brought in dead of a Fall from my Horse" (*Letters*, p. 35). The validity of the statement is also called into question when Burnet continues, "By this, [i.e. by being drunk for five years] he said, he had broke the firm constitution of his Health, that seemed so strong, that nothing was too hard for it." This is a strange comment to make in view of the fact that other biographical evidence would suggest that Rochester's constitution had never been "firm" or "strong": he was a delicate child and Pinto thinks it likely that he contracted venereal disease at the age of fourteen, which would have further weakened a constitution that was not naturally robust.[16] That Rochester claimed otherwise might imply that his view of the circumstances was confused if not incorrect. If there is any truth in the statement, it does not seem unreasonable to suggest that any drunkenness would not have to be severe or continuous for five years to break his health.

Even at the end of his life in these conversations with Burnet, Rochester saw pleasure in terms of "the free use of Wine and Women" which he refers to as "the gratification of our natural Appetites" (*Critical Heritage*, p. 57). Each is a complement to the other, because for Rochester the love and sexual stimulation of women and the intellectual stimulation of wine together with friendship were the natural requirements of man. In July, 1678, he wrote a letter to Savile that ends:

> . . . and now I fear, I must fall, that it may be fulfilled which was long since written for Instruction in a good old Ballad,

> But he who lives not Wise and Sober
> Falls with the Leaf still in October.

> About which time, in all probability, there may be a period added to the ridiculous being of
> Your humble Servant, Rochester.

In fact he was to live for another two years. The old ballad associates drunkenness with folly, showing the antithesis of wine and wisdom. This is the traditional view, the view of Hobbes, the view of Burnet, the view of the wise and the sober. By traditional standards Rochester's attitudes and actions were not wise. They were hardly even comprehensible:

> it is a miraculous thing (as the wise have it) when a Man, half in the Grave, cannot leave off playing the Fool, and the Buffoon; but so it falls out of my comfort.
> (This and above, *Letters*, p. 65)

But for Rochester, who extolled the merits of the second bottle in 1674, explored the relationship between sex and alcohol in **"Love a woman?"** and **"To a Lady in a Letter,"** and still regarded "the free use of Wine and Women" as "the gratification of our natural Appetites" in 1680, there was some reason in madness.

Notes

1. *The Rochester-Savile Letters, 1671-1678,* ed. John H. Wilson (Columbus: Ohio State Univ. Press, 1941), p. 33. Hereafter referred to as *Letters*.

2. *The Complete Poems of John Wilmot, Earl of Rochester,* ed. David M. Vieth (New Haven: Yale Univ. Press, 1968), p. 53. Hereafter all quotations of Rochester's poetry are from this edition unless otherwise stated.

3. Ibid., p. xli.

4. Incidentally, Rochester's use of "bottle" to mean the quantity of liquor held by a bottle comes thirteen years before the earliest example quoted in the *OED* (definition b). See O. F. Babler and Editor, "The Second and Later Bottles," *N&Q* [*Notes and Queries*], 197 (1952), 389-90.

5. Gilbert Burnet, *Some Passages in the Life and Death of Rochester,* in *Rochester: the Critical Heritage,* ed. David Farley-Hills (London: Routledge and Kegan Paul, 1972), p. 54.

6. For this and the following two quotations see David Farley-Hills, *Rochester's Poetry* (Totowa, N.J.: Rowman and Littlefield, 1978), pp. 69-70.

7. Ibid., pp. 71-72. See also Dustin H. Griffin, *Satires Against Man* (Berkeley: Univ. of California Press, 1973), p. 128.

8. Professor Vieth has informed me that for the *textus receptus* of the final version he has now returned to that printed at the very end of his article, "A Textual Paradox: Rochester's 'To a Lady in a Letter,'" *PBSA* [*Papers of the Bibliographical Society of America*], 54 (1960), 147-62. I quote from this text, which differs from the final version in *Complete Poems* only in that 1. 15 reads, "Will take his [instead of "its"] liquor off as fast." The masculine possessive adjective, which might appear strange or archaic in a reference to a woman's genitals, was perhaps suggested by Rochester's belief that drinking was an essentially masculine occupation.

9. "A Textual Paradox," p. 152. All three texts are printed in this article.

10. *Pierre de Ronsard, Oeuvres complètes,* ed. Paul Laumonier, V (Paris: Hachette, 1928), 79n; hereafter cited as *Oeuvres complètes*.

11. Cf. Thomas Stanley, "The Cup, XVII" and "Another, XVIII" in *Anacreon. Bion. Moschus. Kisses by Secundus, etc.* (London, 1651), pp. 11-12; John Oldham, "The Cup" in *Poems and Translations* (London, 1683), pp. 116-19.

12. Anne Righter, "John Wilmot, Earl of Rochester," *Proc. Brit. Acad.,* 53 (1967), 62.

13. See D. M. Vieth, *Attribution in Restoration Poetry* (New Haven: Yale Univ. Press, 1963), pp. 202-03. Hereafter *ARP*.

14. Thomas Hobbes, *Leviathan,* ed. C. B. Macpherson (Harmondsworth, Eng.: Penguin, 1968), pp. 141-42.

15. See M. P. Tilley, *A Dictionary of the Proverbs in England in the Sixteenth and Seventeenth Centuries* (Ann Arbor: Univ. of Michigan Press, 1950), W 465. See also Wycherley's *The Country Wife* (1675) where "two bottles" lead to "the truth of our hearts" and the ladies drink "By this brimmer, for truth is nowhere else to be found" (V, iv, ll. 19-20, 22).

16. See Vivian de Sola Pinto, *Enthusiast in Wit* (Lincoln: Univ. of Nebraska Press, 1962), pp. 4, 5, 8-9; Johannes Prinz, *John Wilmot, Earl of Rochester* (Leipzig: Mayer & Müller, 1927), p. 41; D. M. Vieth, Introd., *Complete Poems,* p. xx.

Robert G. Walker (essay date January 1982)

SOURCE: Walker, Robert G. "Rochester and the Issue of Deathbed Repentance in Restoration and Eighteenth-Century England." *South Atlantic Review* 47, no. 1 (January 1982): 21-37.

[*In the following essay, Walker discusses Rochester's deathbed repentance and its relevance to seventeenth- and eighteenth-century theological debates regarding the efficacy of such last-minute conversions.*]

No one in Samuel Johnson's time and no one today would likely find much similarity between Johnson's life and the life of debauchery led by John Wilmot, Earl of Rochester. At first, then, it is a bit surprising to find the two linked in an anonymous pamphlet published in London in 1791 and entitled *Reflections on the Last Scene of the Late Doctor Johnson's Life: As Exhibited by His Biographer Sir John Hawkins; Shewing the Real Goodness of His State; and That His Friends Had No Just Ground To Be Shocked at Expressions Arising from a Truly Broken and Contrite Heart.* The pamphlet argues that in Johnson's final days he received an education in "the school of repentance" (p. 8) in a way that parallels Rochester's end: "When the witty Earl of Rochester in the days of Charles the second was brought into the school of repentance, we find him sunk into the lowest state of humility. His grief was so great for having offended God, that he wished he had been a poor crawling Leper in a ditch" (p. 10). The link is forged, obviously enough, by the two men's contrite Christian deaths, but that the anonymous writer chose to leap backward 111 years to the "days of Charles the second" for the only non-biblical allusion in his work suggests that Rochester's final days exerted an important and long-lasting influence that has not been fully recognized on a significant aspect of eighteenth-century theological thought.

From the late Restoration period to the end of the eighteenth century in England several theological issues were in heated debate. Christian and anti-Christian argued about God's particular providence, about the immortality of the human soul, and about the nature and validity of traditional religious proofs—to name three of the most important issues—with a passion and a perseverance that may be difficult to understand from our contemporary secular point of view. Discussions and disputes about deathbed repentance formed part of the contentious atmosphere of the age, but this debate was primarily intramural: Christians differed greatly among themselves as to whether a deathbed repentance was efficacious. Moreover, arguments about deathbed repentance were fuelled and shaped by contemporary events to a much greater extent than other theological arguments. Perhaps the most important of these shaping events was the death of Rochester.

I

The following anecdote is told of the illustrious seventeenth-century divine Isaac Barrow: "He was attending at court as the king's chaplain, when he met the famous Earl of Rochester, who thus accosted him: 'Doctor, I am yours to the shoetie.' Barrow: 'My lord, I am yours to the ground.' Rochester: 'Doctor, I am yours to the centre.' Barrow: 'My lord, I am yours to the antipodes.' Rochester (scorning to be foiled by a musty old piece of divinity, as he termed him): 'Doctor, I am yours to the lowest pit of hell.' Barrow (turning on his heel): 'There, my lord, I leave you.'"[1] Barrow, who died in 1677, would have been surprised indeed at the subsequent comments of his friend, Anglican colleague, and posthumous editor John Tillotson, who wrote in 1680 on the occasion of Rochester's death, "I am sorry, that an example, which might have been of so much use and advantage to the world, is so soon taken from us." Rochester, Tillotson believed, was "the greatest instance any age hath afforded" of repentance.[2] The rest of Tillotson's remark is a bit elliptical, but worth deciphering, I think: "The greatest instance any age hath afforded: not for his own sake, as St. Paul was not, who yet was no enemy to God and religion, but by mistake. I cannot think, but that it was intended for some greater good to others." Clearly Tillotson views Rochester's late conversion to Christianity as a moral exemplum of great importance, greater even than a major biblical paradigm for conversion, since Rochester, unlike Paul, was not an enemy to religion merely "by mistake." So Rochester's previous notorious and deliberate profligacy heightened the impact of his repentance. Tillotson also seems to suggest that the story is important not so much as an unusual and interesting piece of private biography ("not for his own sake") but as a public polemic "intended for some greater good to others." And as polemic, it turns out, is exactly the way Tillotson and others used the story of Rochester's final days.

The most famous account of those days is Gilbert Burnet's *Some Passages of the Life and Death of the Right Honourable John Earl of Rochester* (London, 1680), an enormously popular book which, according to Samuel Johnson, "the critick ought to read for its elegance, the philosopher for its arguments, and the saint for its piety."[3] Regardless of whether Tillotson "revised and improved" Burnet's book (as Thomas Birch believed),[4] he certainly approved it as much as Johnson would later, but perhaps not with Johnson's critically trained eye. For the seemingly insignificant Johnsonian triplet I have just quoted in fact describes the structure as well as the content of Burnet's work, and even the order in which the various parts appear. The first of the three major sections of the work—approximately one-sixth of the whole—is a brief life of Rochester, as elegantly written as any secular biography; the middle section and by far the longest—roughly half the book—consists of the philosophical arguments on behalf of the Christian religion made by Burnet to Rochester; the final section treats in detail Rochester's last days in a way inspirational of responses like Samuel Holland's couplet,

> The Mighty *Rochester* a *Convert* Dies,
> He fell a Poet, but a Saint shall Rise.[5]

In this hagiographical section of Burnet's work we find Rochester conspicuously curious about the theological implications of deathbed repentance. In a letter to Burnet on 25 June 1680 he asks Burnet to pray that God "would mercifully accept of my Death-Bed Repentance" (p. 81). Later Burnet writes that "he was very anxious to know my Opinion of a Death-Bed Repentance. I told him, That before I gave any Resolution in that, it would be convenient that I should be acquainted more particularly with the Circumstances and Progress of his Repentance" (p. 82). Both Rochester's questioning and Burnet's reluctance to answer hastily suggest the problematic nature of the issue of deathbed repentance in England at the end of the seventeenth century.

Burnet next describes how he became convinced of the sincerity of Rochester's repentance. Rochester affirmed that he was persuaded of the truth of Christianity; gave an account of the inward working of God's grace on him; took the Sacrament with great satisfaction and with the increased pleasure of having his wife receive it with him—she had been "for some years misled into the Communion of the Church of *Rome*"; and expressed content with God's will either to have him live or die (pp. 82-83). All these things—and Burnet mentions others in the same vein—are rather what we would expect from a tardy convert and indeed are rather more private

than public. But notice what seems finally to assure Burnet, or at least what he uses as a climax to his list of Rochester's penitential behavior and as an introduction to his discussion of the theological implications of late conversion: "All these things at several times, I had from him, besides some Messages, which very well became a dying Penitent to some of his former Friends, and a Charge to publish any thing concerning him, that might be a mean to reclaim others. *Praying God, that as his life had done much hurt, so his death might do some good*" (pp. 83-84). Rochester went public with his repentance through Burnet's book and through the similarly popular sermon preached at his funeral by Robert Parsons, his family chaplain. Parsons lists as one of several signs of the sincerity of the repentance "his commands to me, to preach abroad, and to let all men know . . . how severely God had disciplined him for his sins by his afflicting hand." Parsons then prints Rochester's dying remonstrance in which he declares his abhorrence of the whole course of his former life "For the benefit of all those whom I may have drawn into sin by my example and encouragement."[6] As we shall soon see, the promulgation of his deathbed repentance that Rochester desired and that Burnet and Parsons effected was probably inspired by the parameters of seventeenth-century Anglican doctrine concerning the efficacy of late conversions; furthermore, a recent precedent for Rochester's behavior existed in the case of James Ley, third Earl of Marlborough.

Marlborough, a royalist naval captain killed in a seabattle with the Dutch on 3 June 1665, shortly before his death "wrote several letters to his friends, whom he was conscious of having injured by his ill example and impiety, urging them to return to virtue and religion."[7] One of these letters, written to Sir Hugh Pollard, found its way into print in several different vehicles, including the broadside *Two Noble Converts; or the Earl of Marlborough and the Earl of Rochester. Their Dying Requests and Remonstrance, to the Atheists and Debauchees of this Age* (London, 1680), and Josiah Woodward's *Fair Warnings to a Careless World, or the Serious Practice of Religion Recommended by the Admonitions of Dying Men, and the Sentiments of All People in Their Most Serious Hours* (1707). The publication history of Woodward's book can tell us something about the persistence of the ideas I am tracing. The copy I shall quote is designated the third edition, London, 1723. The work apparently continued to be popular and to be reissued: the Beinecke Library (Yale) has a "fourth" edition dated 1729 and the *BLC* [*British Library Catalogue*] lists a "fourth" edition in 1736. The frontispiece of the 1723 edition is entitled "John Earl of Rochester a Penitent" and shows a deathbed scene with a man (Burnet?) kneeling and reading to the supine nobleman. Although the frontispiece suggests that Rochester had now become the bigger drawing card, Marlborough's story occupies a conspicuous place in Woodward's work, taking up the first chapter, pp. 1-10. In the letter to Pollard quoted by Woodward, Marlborough states that he is writing "from a *sober resolution* of what concerns my self, and earnest desire to do you more good after my death, than mine example (God of his mercy pardon the badness of it) in my lifetime may do you harm" (p. 3). He concludes the letter by expressing belief in Christian immortality and writes in a postscript, "I beseech you commend my love to all mine acquaintance; particularly, I pray you that my cousin *Glascock* may have a sight of this letter, and as many friends besides as you will, or any else that desire it" (p. 4).

The rough parallel between the late conversions of the two noblemen was exploited, then, by a writer like Woodward,[8] and one suspects that Marlborough's story lived as long as it did primarily because of its association with Rochester's. It is now certainly dead: the *DNB,* [*Dictionary of National Biography*] for instance, makes mention neither of Marlborough's conversion nor of his letter-writing. Rochester's story was to have a much stronger and longer-lasting hold on the popular imagination, in part because his pre-conversion behavior was much more notoriously sinful than Marlborough's (though Tillotson's biographer Thomas Birch calls Marlborough a "contemner of religion"),[9] and in part because Rochester's situation more clearly centered on the theological issue of the efficacy of deathbed repentance. Going into battle, Marlborough might have viewed his death as possible, even probable, but not inevitable. Rochester's illness, on the other hand, made his death as certain as any event can be and thus prompted his questioning of Burnet about the relevant Christian doctrine.

Burnet's answer to Rochester is important enough to be quoted at some length:

> I told him, That, though the Promises of the Gospel did all depend upon a real change of Heart and Life, as the indispensible condition upon which they were made; and that it was scarce possible to know certainly whether our Hearts are changed, unless it appeared in our lives; and the Repentance of most dying men being like the howlings of condemned Prisoners for Pardon, which flowed from no sense of their Crimes, but from the horrour of approaching Death; there was little reason to encourage any to hope much from such Sorrowings: Yet certainly, if the Mind of a Sinner, even on a Death-Bed, be truly renewed and turned to God, so great is His Mercy, that He will receive him, even in that extremity.
>
> (p. 84)

In his conclusion Burnet shows no doubt that Rochester's is one of those rare efficacious late conversions: "Now he is at rest, and I am very confident enjoys the Fruits of his late, but sincere Repentance. . . . Here is a publick Instance of One who lived of [the libertines'] Side, but could not die of it" (p. 87).

The crux of the matter, obviously, was how to determine whether the dying person's Christian sentiments were a function of a true conversion (a turning of the heart away from sin) or merely the product of the horrible fear of death to be expected from a sinner and thus signals of despair rather than true repentance. The determination in the days before Rochester's famous conversion was usually made along a rather hard line for the would-be convert, as sermons by the noted seventeenth-century Anglican minister Jeremy Taylor indicate. Illustrative is a two-part sermon entitled "The Invalidity of a Late, or Death-bed Repentance," published as sermons five and six of *XXVIII Sermons Preached at Golden Grove* (London, 1651). Taylor couches his discussion in terms of the distinction between sorrow for sins and the duty of repentance. Repentance begins with a deep sorrow, but "sorrow for sins, is not Repentance; not that duty which gives glory to God. . . . Repentance is a great volume of duty; and Godly sorrow is but the frontispiece or title page" (pp. 56-57). Repentance is not accomplished until it bears fruit in the world, Taylor argues, that is, until we "have acquired the habits of all those Christian graces which are necessary in the transaction of our affairs, in all relations to God, and our neighbour, and our own person" (p. 63). Since a dying man has no time for the "holy living" which Taylor believes is an "absolute necessity" for repentance (p. 72), his salvation seems "little lesse then absolutely impossible" (p. 65). The only recourse for a dying sinner is to "pray, and groan, and call to God, and resolve to live well when he is dying; but this is but just as the Nobles of Xerxes, when in a storm they were to lighten the ship to preserve their Kings life, they . . . leaped into the sea: so (I fear) doe these men, pray and mourn, and worship and so leap overboard into an ocean of eternal and intolerable calamity" (p. 79).

Taylor reinforces his semantic argument with appropriate biblical analogues. The cases of Ahab and Judas illustrate that mere sorrow is not repentance (p. 57). The parable of the foolish virgins points up the folly of waiting too late to follow God (p. 76), and according to Taylor this, rather than the story of the penitent thief, is the applicable biblical exemplum: "But why may not we be saved as well as the thief upon the crosse? even because our case is nothing alike. When Christ dies once more for us, we may look for such another instance; not till then. But this thiefe did but then come to Christ. . . . The thief had made no contract with God in Jesus Christ, and therefore failed of none. . . . But we that have made a covenant with God in baptisme, and failed of it all our dayes, and then returne at night, when we cannot work; have nothing to plead for our selves" (p. 78).

Even before the death of Rochester the Anglican position on deathbed repentance had softened somewhat from Taylor's stance. Those two famous seventeenth-century divines who were mentioned at the outset of this essay, John Tillotson and Isaac Barrow, wrestled with the knotty issue in remarkably similar sermons on the identical biblical text, Psalm cxix.60—"I made haste, and delayed not to keep thy commandments."[10] As this text suggests, both clergymen wish to encourage early rather than late repentance, and to this end both compare the procrastinating sinner to Horace's foolish rustic (*Epistle* i.2) who, in Barrow's words, "stayed by the river-side waiting till it had done running, so that he might pass dry-foot over the channel" (p. 310; p. 117 in Tillotson). For the most part what Tillotson and Barrow write coincides with Jeremy Taylor's view; however, here is Barrow calling attention to an opening in the walls of heaven that Taylor had done his best to hide: "God is ever ready, upon our true conversion, to receive us into favour; . . . even . . . a lewd strumpet, as Magdalene, a notable thief, as he upon the cross, a timorous renouncer, as St Peter, a furious persecutor, as St Paul, a stupid idolater, as all the heathen world, when the Gospel came to them, . . . if he be disposed to repent, is capable of mercy; . . . those instances peremptorily do evince, that repentance is never superannuated; that if we can turn at all, we shall not turn too late" (pp. 318-19). By lumping together the penitent thief with St. Paul, Barrow seriously undermines the argument advanced by Taylor that repentance is not accomplished until it bears fruit in the world. Nor does Barrow see the need to maintain that the thief is not a good analogy to the present-day dying sinner.

Tillotson, especially in his other sermons, is a bit closer to Taylor than to Barrow. In a sermon preached 2 September 1688, he remarks, "I will not pronounce any thing concerning the impossibility of a death-bed repentance: but I am sure that it is very difficult, and I believe very rare. We have but one example, that I know of, in the whole Bible, of the repentance of a dying sinner; I mean that of the penitent thief upon the cross: and the circumstances of his case are so peculiar and extraordinary, that I cannot see that it affords any ground of hope and encouragement to men in ordinary cases."[11] The parable of the wise and foolish virgins Tillotson regards as the more pertinent biblical analogy. But Tillotson is willing, as we have seen, to make Rochester the exception that proves the rule, and he is willing to do so, I believe, because the publicity attached to Rochester's death made it an excellent polemical weapon for the Christian apologist, a weapon so powerful that Tillotson and others were persuaded to risk its obvious potential backfire. Moreover, the publicity which made the weapon so strong could also be viewed as a way of satisfying Taylor's (and others') insistence on fruits of repentance as a sign of its sincerity and efficacy. So increasing toleration of deathbed repentance favored both the dying sinner and the polemical divine, at least for a time.

II

The issue of deathbed repentance continued to be discussed frequently in tracts and sermons at the end of the seventeenth and beginning of the eighteenth century, but these discussions were largely derivative and redundant. Christian writers divided into two camps. Hardliners like William Payne, Samuel Clarke, and Benjamin Hoadley stressed a definition of repentance which necessarily included "performing and practising the Vertues contrary to those Sins" that the penitent had forsaken; and invariably they dismissed as irrelevant to the question the story of the thief on the cross and the parable of the laborers in the vineyard.[12] Interestingly though, none of these writers disputed specifically the repentance of Rochester. Softliners like Robert South and Richard Fiddes, on the other hand, emphasized the problematic nature of the question. Each man wrote a sermon which listed first the arguments against and then the arguments in favor of the possibility of a deathbed repentance. Despite this illusion of balanced treatment South and Fiddes were both more inclined to accept than to reject that possibility, as a comparison of their views with those of Payne, Clarke, and Hoadley makes clear. For example, Payne believed that the episode of the penitent thief had erroneously "from a matter of History and Circumstance been improved to Teach and Advance a new Doctrine, no where else to be found in the Bible" (p. 317); South, conversely, found the singularity and even the obscurity of this biblical episode reasons to accept it as a validating precedent: "And who knows, but that God intended this signal instance to remain as a perpetual remedy against despair, to sinners repenting in any part of their lives? . . . [It] might be the design of the Spirit here, not to make any such declaration of pardon openly and expressly to death-bed penitents, lest by accident it might open a door of licence to sin; but rather to preach it more tacitly to our reasons, in the example of the thief upon the cross."[13] To prevent their being accused of opening that licentious door, both South and Fiddes concluded that, although deathbed repentance was possible, it was highly improbable: as Fiddes put it, "And therefore *admitting* that a Death-bed Repentance, if sincere, may be available to Salvation; yet there are so many Blanks against this one Prize, that no Man, one would think, who might other ways be secure of it, should run the Hazard, the almost desperate Hazard, of drawing it" (p. 172).

Thus the controversy stood, unresolved but not en-flamed, until the appearance of White Kennet's *Sermon Preach'd at the Funeral of the Right Noble William Duke of Devonshire . . . Fryday Septemb. 5th MDC-CVII*, a work now known to students of English literature primarily as a footnote to the following lines from Alexander Pope's *Essay on Criticism*:

Then Unbelieving Priests reform'd the Nation,
And taught more *Pleasant* Methods of Salvation;
Where Heav'ns Free Subjects might their *Rights*
  dispute,
Lest God himself shou'd seem too *Absolute.*
Pulpits their *Sacred Satire* learn'd to spare,
And Vice *admir'd* to find a *Flatt'rer there!*[14]

In their annotation of these lines Pope's Twickenham editors write that "portions of [Kennet's] argument are so ineptly presented as to invite attack," and this is putting it mildly. William Cavendish, first Duke of Devonshire, was notorious for his sexual promiscuity. It is not farfetched at all, I think, to speculate that Kennet, seeing Devonshire as a third noble convert in the Marlborough-Rochester tradition, consciously plays Burnet to Devonshire's Rochester when he writes, "And possibly for wicked Livers there is a Door of Hope, by a late Repentance work'd out with godly Sorrow in a time of need, in extremity, upon a Bed of Sickness, and the nearest Views of Death: A Repentance, that if eminent and exemplary, may be accepted by a gracious God who knoweth the Heart, from whence it proceedeth."[15] But Kennet fails miserably in his adopted role for two reasons. First, he asserts but is unable to explain that Devonshire's late repentance is exemplary but not a widely-applicable precedent. Instead of escaping the dilemma as South and Fiddes do by stressing the long odds against tardy conversion, Kennet turns the Christian God into an elitist: "Not that a late Repentance is by any means to be depended on. . . . O my Brethren, it is not a Precedent to follow, it is rather a Miracle, stand still and adore the Goodness of God in it! This rarely happens but in Men of distinguish'd Sence and Judgment. Ordinary Abilities may be altogether sunk by a long Virtuous [vicious?] Course of Life. . . . while the nobler and brighter parts have an Advantage of understanding the worth of their Soul before they resign it" (p. 12). Kennet realizes he is not on firm ground here, but the more he struggles, the deeper he sinks: "Not that God is a Respecter of Persons, but the Difference is in Men; and the more intelligent Nature is the more suseptive of divine Grace" (p. 12). Kennet's second failure is a function of his first: while concentrating on the refined and elevated nature of Devonshire, he discreetly draws a veil over the Duke's riotous past and deals with his sins vaguely and quickly. The flatterer had indeed replaced the satirist in the pulpit.

Eighteenth-century polemicists rarely eschewed breaking the butterfly. Kennet's ludicrous position was attacked by Henry Sacheverell (according to Pope's Twickenham editors) as well as by Pope, and it is hard to tell how many sermons and tracts on the subject of deathbed repentance written early in the eighteenth century were inspired directly or indirectly by the Kennet controversy. John Dunton's certainly was. His spirited *Hazard of a Death-Bed-Repentance, Fairly*

Argued, from the Late Remorse of W———Late D———of D——— is expressly a response to Kennet's sermon. Dunton first hits sardonically at Kennet's elitism: "Reader, I shall only add, I cou'd have swell'd this *Essay on a Death-Bed-Repentance* (in Answer to *Dr. K———*) to a *Larger Bulk,* but I was loth to tire thy Patience, and was also willing to consult *the Convenience of the Poorer Buyers,* who tho' they have Souls of as great Value as the Souls of the *Rich,* yet can't purchase such *Large Volumes* as they can."[16] Since Kennet had neglected to mention Devonshire's sins, Dunton chronicles them at length and concludes that Devonshire's "Adulterous Life, to the Time of his last Sickness, gives us Reason to think he never intended to repent, 'till he cou'd Whore no longer" (p. 11). That his sins were not publicly exposed at his death becomes a major reason to doubt the sincerity of Devonshire's repentance: "tho' wicked Men will not be willing to have their Infirmities laid out at their *Funeral,* yet the greatest Sinner, if he dies a sincere Penitent, will be willing, with the *Earl of Rochester,* not only to sign a *Dying Remonstrance* against the whole Course of his former wicked Life, but will have it Publish'd at his *Funeral* what a great Sinner he had been. Had we had such a *Dying Remonstrance from the late D———of D———* as we had from the Lord *Rochester,* I shou'd have thought him Sincere in his *late Repentance,* (as the late D———calls it)" (pp. 13-14). A farrago of the relevant literature, Dunton's tract includes quotations from Parson's sermon on Rochester's death and from the penitential letters of James Ley, Earl of Marlborough (pp. 32-34), as Dunton tries to distinguish between legitimate and illegitimate late conversion. Dunton knew how to milk a popular topic. Later in the same year he published *The Hazard of a Death-Bed-Repentance, Further Argued . . . Being a Second Answer to Dr. K———'s Sermon Preach'd at the D———'s Funeral* (London, 1708), in which he boasted that his first answer had come to a third edition in six weeks (p. i). In the sequel Dunton takes the familiar hardline on the biblical precedent, arguing that the thief's repentance, "generally taken as an Instance of great Favour to a *late conversion,*" is not so at all, but a miracle (p. 4). Dunton, moreover, relies on the notion of St. Augustine that the thief's conversion was not really late, for he took the first possible opportunity to convert (p. 11). Finally, Dunton laments that, while in scripture almost all repentances are followed by reformed lives, deathbed repentance "is now become . . . the only Repentance in Use, and hath devour'd the other" (p. 13).

Even when we allow for hyperbole, Dunton's last remark clearly indicates the increasing tolerance of deathbed repentance in England during the eighteenth century. By mid-century, when the Kennet controversy had completely died down, this increasing tolerance is evident in the writings of, among others, John Wesley and Samuel Johnson. Wesley's stance on the issue was obviously dictated by the Methodist tendency to stress faith over works more than it was felt Roman Catholicism and right-wing Anglicanism did in that ancient seesawing controversy. In a sermon first published in 1765 and probably delivered in March 1764, Wesley held that "God does undoubtedly command us both to repent, and to bring forth fruits meet for repentance; . . . [but] those fruits are only necessary *conditionally*; if there be time and opportunity for them. Otherwise a man may be justified without them, as was the *thief* upon the cross (if we may call him so; for a late writer has discovered that he was no thief, but a very honest and respectable person!); but he cannot be justified without faith; this is impossible."[17] The "late writer" Wesley refers to parenthetically has not, to my knowledge, been identified. He may be John Jortin (1698-1770), Archdeacon of London, who sought latent qualities in the thief that would solve the difficulty of using his story as an indication of God's infinite mercy without encouraging hardened sinners to procrastinate their repentance: Jortin assumed "that there was something particular in him that qualified him for such a favour."[18] Wesley, with his Augustinian emphasis on justification and sanctification by faith alone, would certainly have found Jortin's speculations irrelevant, and even if Jortin is not the particular writer to whom Wesley alluded, that writer was undoubtedly trying to exonerate the thief for the same reason as Jortin.

Wesley's stance, then, is not surprising in the light of his overall religious principles. But that Samuel Johnson should stand with Wesley is perhaps less expected. For one thing, Johnson's position on other debated and changing religious topics is usually conservative: he resisted the dulcification of the doctrine of damnation and eternal punishments and his views on the proofs of Christianity were distinctly of the seventeenth rather than the late eighteenth century.[19] Moreover, as Richard E. Brantley has recently noted, "Scholars seem to wince at the very idea that [Johnson] could have inclined to the Methodist heart of Anglican faith, and it is not that they misunderstand Johnson's belief—they apparently misunderstand Wesley's kind of Evangelical belief."[20] Brantley makes a cogent case that Johnson and Wesley share the established religious tradition in many areas, including the Evangelical emphasis on conversion. My point here is that in a somewhat narrower area— deathbed repentance—Johnson's and Wesley's views again coincide, although those views are at variance with what was the usual Anglican view in the late seventeenth century. In this case, in other words, Johnson and Wesley share the newer, more tolerant position.

Johnson's statements on the efficacy of deathbed repentance contain little of the hesitancy or hedging that marked the statements even of softliners South and Fiddes at the beginning of the century. When Boswell assumed that the malevolent aggressor in a duel had little hope of salvation should he be killed, Johnson replied, "Sir, we are not to judge determinately of the state in which a man leaves this life. He may in a moment have repented effectually, and it is possible may have been accepted by God. There is in 'Camden's Remains,' an epitaph upon a very wicked man, who was killed by a fall from his horse, in which he is supposed to say,

> 'Between the stirrup and the ground,
> I mercy ask'd, I mercy found.'"[21]

Johnson's opinion is the same in his sermons as in his conversation. To the question of "whether a repentance begun in sickness, and prevented by death from exerting its influence upon the conduct, will avail in the sight of God," Johnson replies simply, "if God who sees the heart, sees it rectified in such a manner as would consequently produce a good life, he will accept that repentance."[22] Clearly a firm belief in the omniscience of God and the finite knowledge of man is one of the bases for Johnson's opinion. Another seems to be his willingness to allow any motive, even fear of damnation, to pull the sinner back to the breast of his God. In the same sermon Johnson writes, "An amendation of life is the chief and essential part of repentance. He that has performed that great work, needs not disturb his conscience with subtle scruples, or nice distinctions. He need not recollect, whether he was awakened from the lethargy of sin, by the love of God, or the fear of punishment" (p. 24).

Perhaps Johnson's most extensive and deliberate statement about deathbed repentance occurs in *The Convict's Address to His Unhappy Brethren,* a sermon written for and delivered by Reverend William Dodd in 1777 as Dodd awaited execution for forgery. Assuming the role of a convicted prisoner, Johnson notes, "Our repentance is like that of other sinners on the deathbed,"[23] and then goes on in a typically Johnsonian manner to reconcile theological doctrine with practical morality:

> Of the efficacy of a death-bed repentance many have disputed; but we have no leisure for controversy. Fix in your minds this decision, 'Repentance is a change of the heart, of an evil to a good disposition.' When that change is made, repentance is complete. God will consider that life as amended, which would have been amended if he had spared it. Repentance in the sight of man, even of the penitent, is not known but by its *fruits*: but our Creator sees the fruit, in the blossom, or the seed. He knows those resolutions which are fixed, those conversions which would be permanent; and will receive them who are qualified by holy desires for works of righteousness, without exacting from them those outward duties which the shortness of their lives hindered them from performing.
>
> (p. 308)

Johnson's concluding remark in this sermon only reinforces his tolerant position with the biblical paradigms he cites: "And, finally, we must commend and entrust our souls to him, who died for the sins of men; with earnest wishes and humble hopes, that he will admit us with the labourers who entered the vineyard at the *last hour,* and associate us with the *thief* whom he pardoned on the cross!" (p. 311).

The tendency to accept more readily a deathbed repentance is unmistakably and increasingly present in the century following Rochester's death, but the acceptance is never unanimous. Conspicuous hardline points of view continue to crop up, even into the nineteenth century.[24] Perhaps more important, by the end of the eighteenth and beginning of the nineteenth century the nature of the issue had changed. In 1776 David Hume, an avowed sceptic, died as pacific a death as any lifelong or recently repentant Christian. In 1809 Thomas Paine, a vociferous deist, disappointed the fanatical Christians who continually intruded into his death-chamber by ending his life without either recanting his heresies or suffering mental torment for them.[25] In the light of these new and threatening public paradigms, the argument *among Christians* about deathbed repentance must have paled in importance. I shall quote at some length from the nineteenth-century Scottish evangelical writer Thomas Chalmers, for his words are illustrative not only of an antipathy toward deathbed repentance but also of a weariness of the whole topic:

> There is often, in the pencilled descriptions of the moralist, a kind of poetical and high-wrought imagery thrown around the chamber of death; and that, whether it be the terrors of guilt, or the triumphs of conscious virtue, which are conceived to mark this closing scene of our history in the world. It is well to know what the plain and experimental truth is, upon the subject. In the case of a worldly and alienated life, the remorse is not nearly so pungent, the apprehensions not nearly so vivid and terrifying, the impression of future and eternal realities not nearly so overpowering, as we are apt to fancy upon such an occasion. The truth is, that as it was throughout the whole of his living, so it is generally in dying. He is still engrossed with present and sensible things; and there is positively nothing in the mere approach of dissolution that can raise up the ascendancy of faith, or render him less the slave of sight, and of the body, than he was before. There is the present pain, there is the present thirst, there is the present breathlessness; and if, amid the tumults of his earthly fabric giving way, and the last irregular movements of its deranged mechanism fast drawing to their cessation, he send for the minister to soothe him by his prayers, even he forms but one of the present varieties. There is no actual going forth of the patient's mind towards the things which are above.[26]

How much the spectres of Hume and Paine haunt the vision of someone like Chalmers is rather difficult to determine, but certainly present here is a desire to regard the death scene as indicative of "present" rather than future concerns. Such a secularization of death has the advantage, for the Christian side, of diverting much of the polemical force of public and peaceful deaths by anti-Christians like Hume and Paine. Concomitant with this secularization of death, however, was a devaluation of conspicuous last-minute repentance like that of the Earl of Rochester. After a century of intestine argument about this issue and in the face of an increasing external threat, this was apparently a price that Christian apologists like Chalmers were willing to pay.[27]

Notes

1. *DNB,* s.v. "Barrow."

2. "Life of the Author," *Works of Dr. John Tillotson* (London, 1820), I, l. The first quotation is from a letter from Tillotson to a Mr. Nelson dated 2 August 1680, the second from Tillotson's commonplace book entry of 1 October 1680. Rochester died 26 July 1680.

3. "Life of Rochester," *Works of Samuel Johnson* (Troy, New York: Pafraets, 1903), VIII, 137.

4. "Life of the Author," Tillotson's *Works,* I, lii.

5. "An Elegie Humbly Offered to the Memory of That Matchless Wit, and Unparallel'd Example of Sincere Penitency, the Right Honorable John Earl of Rochester" (1680), rpt. in *Rochester: The Critical Heritage,* ed. David Farley-Hills (New York: Barnes & Noble, 1972), p. 128. Holland's is one of eight elegies for Rochester published in 1680; all are conveniently reprinted in this volume. Farley-Hills' work is also my source for Burnet's biography of Rochester, hereafter cited parenthetically in the text.

6. *A Sermon Preached at the Funeral of the Right Honourable John Earl of Rochester* (London, 1787), pp. 130, 131. "First published in 1680, it had achieved its fourteenth edition by around 1730 and went on being published throughout the eighteenth and into the nineteenth century; the last edition (with Burnet's *Life*) is dated 1820" (*Rochester: The Critical Heritage,* p. 45).

7. "Life of the Author," Tillotson's *Works,* I, li.

8. Such exploitation probably precedes Woodward. In his preface Woodward notes a debt to "a little Tract" by David Lloyd, the incompleteness and mistakes of which cause Woodward to regard it merely as a "rough Draught" (p. A5ᵛ). Lloyd's *Dying and Dead Mens Living Words, or Fair Warnings to a Careless World* was first published in 1665, with a second edition in 1682. I have not seen Lloyd's work, but it seems likely from the dates that Marlborough's death was at least in part the occasion of its initial publication, and Rochester's death the reason for its reissuance.

9. "Life of the Author," Tillotson's *Works,* I, li.

10. "Sermon XIV: The Folly and Danger of Irresolution and Delaying," Tillotson's *Works,* II, 104-22; "Sermon XLIII: The Danger and Mischief of Delaying Repentance," *Theological Works of Isaac Barrow,* ed. Alexander Napier (Cambridge, 1859), III, 301-43. Tillotson's sermon was first published in 1675, two years before Barrow's death. A comparative reading of the sermons indicates that one writer has borrowed rather heavily from the other, but the direction of this borrowing I have been unable to determine.

11. "Sermon XXXI: The Parable of the Ten Virgins," Tillotson's *Works,* II, 557.

12. William Payne, *A Practical Discourse of Repentance . . . Demonstrating the Invalidity of a Death-Bed Repentance* (London, 1693), p. 26. See also Samuel Clarke, *Three Practical Essays, on Baptism, Confirmation, and Repentance,* 4th ed. (London, 1721), esp. pp. 195-96; and Benjamin Hoadley, *Several Discourses concerning the Terms of Acceptance with God.* (London, 1711), esp. sermons XV-XVIII. Hoadley's four sermons refuting the validity of deathbed repentance serve as an ideational climax to his series of eighteen discourses, and Payne's chapter, "Of a Death-Bed Repentance," makes up 126 of his work's 559 pages.

13. Robert South, *Sermons Preached upon Several Occasions* (London: Reeves & Turner, n.d.), II, 315 (from Sermon XXXVI, part two). See also Richard Fiddes, Sermon VII in *Practical Discourses on Several Subjects,* 2nd ed. (London, 1713).

14. Ll. 546-51; quoted from *Pastoral Poetry and An Essay on Criticism,* ed. E. Audra and Aubrey Williams (Twickenham ed., 1961), pp. 300-04.

15. (London, 1707), p. 12.

16. (London, 1708), p. 5; italics reversed.

17. "Sermon L: The Scripture Way of Salvation," *Wesley's Standard Sermons,* ed. Edward H. Sugden (London, 1921), II, 451-52.

18. "Sermon VII: The Penitent Thief," *Sermons on Different Subjects* (London, 1809), II, 88.

19. See Paul C. Davies, "The Debate on Eternal Punishment in Late Seventeenth-and Eighteenth-Century English Literature." *ECS* [*Eighteenth Century Studies*], 4 (1971), 269-70, 275; and Robert G. Walker, "Johnson in the 'Age of Evidences,'" *HLQ* [*Huntington Library Quarterly*], 44 (1980), 27-41.

20. "Johnson's Wesleyan Connection," *ECS,* 10 (1976-77), 150. For a thorough survey of eighteenth-century views of conversion, see Donald J. Greene, "Dr. Johnson's 'Late Conversion': A Reconsideration," *Johnsonian Studies,* ed. Magdi Wahba (Cairo, 1962), pp. 61-92. Regardless of the nature of the conversion Johnson experienced in the last months of his life, it resists classification as a deathbed repentance in the same sense as Rochester's; my essay treats Johnson's thoughts only on this related, but distinct issue.

21. *Boswell's Life of Johnson* (Hill-Powell ed., 1934), IV, 212.

22. Sermon 2, *Samuel Johnson: Sermons,* ed. Jean Hagstrum and James Gray (New Haven: Yale Univ. Press, 1978), pp. 24-25; hereafter cited in the text.

23. Sermon 28, *Samuel Johnson: Sermons,* p. 307.

24. See, for instance, Sydney Smith, "On Repentance," *Two Volumes of Sermons* (London, 1809), I, 14-16.

25. For a more detailed study of the polemical nature of Hume's and Paine's deaths, see Robert G. Walker, "Public Death in the Eighteenth Century," *Research Studies,* 48 (1980), 11-24.

26. "Introductory Essay to *Serious Reflections on Time and Eternity . . .* and *On the Consideration of Our Latter End . . . ,*" *Works of Thomas Chalmers* (Glasgow, [1836]), XIII, 272; in the same volume see also Chalmers' "Introductory Essay to *Call to the Unconverted,*" esp. pp. 126-27.

27. The research and writing of this essay were generously assisted by a Research Fellowship from the American Council of Learned Societies and by two summer stipends from the Research Grants Committee of the University of Alabama in Huntsville.

Larry Carver (essay date fall 1982)

SOURCE: Carver, Larry. "Rascal before the Lord: Rochester's Religious Rhetoric." *Essays in Literature* 9, no. 2 (fall 1982): 155-69.

[*In the following essay, Carver insists that a careful examination of Rochester's poetry yields evidence that the poet did not reject Christianity as most critics believe.*]

> The things of this world
> can only be truly perceived
> by looking at them backwards.[1]
>
> Gracian, *The Critic*

Recently Reba Wilcoxon, after scrutinizing five of Rochester's poems, concluded that the poet's work shows a "rejection of Christian orthodoxy."[2] Rochester certainly had a speculative mind, and by focusing on the "philosophical premises which seem to shape" (1.183) his thought, Wilcoxon has provided a useful context for understanding Rochester's skepticism. But the narrowed focus has intensified light in one area only to leave others in greater darkness, particularly Rochester's stance toward Christianity. Rochester often does satirize Christianity; at times, however, he uses Christian values as satiric norm. On still other occasions the satire directed at Christianity slips into irony through which he simultaneously affirms and negates orthodox tenets while linguistically exploring their very nature. "Rejection" does not adequately describe the complexity with which Rochester deals with Christianity, nor does it accurately delineate his religious stance which is less a matter of philosophy than of rhetoric; and if we are to understand it properly we need to account for the enormous energy and ingenuity with which Rochester's speakers negate Christian teachings. Once we do, we will find, I think, that Wilcoxon has it just backwards. We will find that Rochester's poetry everywhere reflects his Christian and God-fearing upbringing and provides evidence, if anything, of an excessive preoccupation with and acceptance of Christian orthodoxy which Rochester, for all his efforts, could never banish with pagan reasons.[3]

I

One such example of pagan reason, is the translation from Lucretius's *De Rerum Natura,* I. 44-49.

> The gods, by right of nature, must possess
> An everlasting age of perfect peace;
> Far off removed from us and our affairs;
> Neither approached by dangers, or by cares;
> Rich in themselves, to whom we cannot add;
> Not pleased by good deeds, nor provoked by bad.[4]

Wilcoxon takes this fragment to be evidence of Rochester's rejection of Christianity. It would be more accurate to say that these lines along with evidence from other poems suggest that Rochester believed, or wanted to believe, that God and man are radically other. Unlike Milton, Rochester needed a God removed from earthly experience, a God remote and mysterious, or as I think he would have put it, it is better in principle that God and man be radically other and for three reasons.

For one, given his depraved nature, man is not worthy. Man debases whatever is good. Love, for example, seems the one proof that a benevolent God exists. As Artemisia tells Chloe,

> Love . . .
> That cordial drop heaven in our cup has thrown
> To make the nauseous draught of life go down;
> On which the only blessing, God might raise
> In lands of atheists, subsidies of praise.

(11.40, 44-47)

Yet man has turned "This only joy for which poor we were made" into "an arrant trade" (11.50-51). The spiritual becomes debased. Man inhabits and is part of a world of seamy physicality that affords no transcendence. Like the speaker in **"A Ramble in St. James's Park,"** the only "grace cup" man can know is a "devouring cunt" (11.122,119). Even Artemisia's reference to cup suggests the female anatomy that leads us to this world rather than the cup of communion the drinking from which allows participation in the holy other. Apparently because of his very nature, the only communion man can know is a parodic one, exemplified by the concluding prayer of the speaker in **"On the Women About Town"**:

> O ye merciful powers who of mortals take care,
> Make the women more modest, more sound, or less fair!
> Is it just that with death cruel love should conspire,
> And our tarses be burnt by our hearts taking fire?
> There's an end of communion if humble believers
> Must be damned in the cup like unworthy receivers.

(11.13-18)

Here too the Eucharistic cup, a promise of spiritual communion, has become a cup of flesh. Although the speaker embraces a discourse in which earthly love can stand for a type of divine, the incongruity between experience and his language suggests the enormous distance between divine and secular. Even if the speaker were aware of the total incommensurability of language and experience, which his possible allusion to I Corinthians 11:27-29 intimates, his awareness does not promise transcendence, simply greater depravity. If communion between God and man exists in Rochester's poetry, it is debased and much diseased.

If man is unworthy of God in Rochester's poetry, so too a worthy God could have nothing to do with the human. "The gods, by right of nature, must possess / An everlasting age of perfect peace" because if they entered into the world, they would become subject to its laws, the primary one being Rochester's version of a material and ethical entropy, the world in a constant flux that defeats attempts to shape and to give it purpose. As the speaker in the fragment **"Sab: Lost"** explains:

> She yields, she yields! Pale envy said amen:
> The first of women to the last of men.
> Just so those frailer beings, angels, fell;
> There's no midway, it seems, 'twixt heaven and hell.
> Was it your end, in making her, to show
> Things must be raised so high to fall so low?
> Since her nor angels their own worth secures,
> Look to it, gods! the next turn must be yours.

God must remain remote; if he did not, he would become part of this ceaseless undoing process.

The third reason behind this need for a remote God can be seen in Rochester's adoption of a Lucretian stance toward the divine. Lucretius believed all human ills arise from man's fear of the arbitrary power of the gods, of death, and of the afterlife. His arguments that man's soul, a mere complex of atoms, does not exist after death and that the gods live pleasant lives divorced from human concerns were meant to banish these fears. It seems reasonable to speculate that a man leading Rochester's life would seek solace in a belief that the gods would pursue him neither in this life nor in the hereafter, that he would want to believe the gods are neither "pleased by good deeds, nor provoked by bad." If so, the seeking becomes evidence of pagan reason attempting to deal, probably on a conscious level, with Christian guilt.

This interpretation would be in keeping with what I take to be Rochester's awareness of the paradoxes in Lucretius. Though a materialist, Lucretius felt he had sure knowledge of much the senses cannot know, atoms, for example. Claiming to show what man can and cannot know, Lucretius, morever, praises Epicurus for having a mind and spirit that "went far beyond the flaming walls of our world, traversing all of unmeasured space. Returning in triumph, he reported to us what can come into being and what cannot, and by what law there is for each thing a power that is limited, and a boundary that is firmly fixed."[5] The irony of this empiricist swelling into speculation was not lost on Rochester as he has the *adversarius* in *A Satyr against Reason and Mankind* paraphrase the passage.

> Reason, by whose aspiring influence
> We take a flight beyond material sense,
> Dive into mysteries, then soaring pierce
> The flaming limits of the universe,
> Search heaven and hell, find out what's acted there,
> And give the world true grounds of hope and fear.
>
> (11.66-71)

This religious man does not know he is quoting a materialist and an enemy of religion, nor does the speaker in the poem, an irony that undercuts both of their positions. Moreover, in order to combat such speculations and prove his materialistic stance, he must resort, as did Lucretius, to speculation.

As Rochester sifted through the past—Ovid, Catullus, Livy, and Seneca—seeking models from which to construct an intelligible world in the present, the Lucretian incongruities and their Rochesterian parallels must have amused and disturbed him. Lucretius claimed that all knowledge comes from the senses, that nothing does not exist, that one need not fear death or the power of the gods, and that his work would assuage fear, yet he indulged in speculative thought, dwelt excessively on nothing, death, and the gods, and gave every indication of being racked with anxiety.[6] Similarly, Rochester's adoption of a Lucretian stance toward the relationship of God to man reveals a deep ambivalence, a conscious rejection of yet attraction to Christianity.

Rochester's parodies of religious vocabulary provide further evidence of his ambivalence toward Christianity. Artemisia informs Chloe that "Bedlam has many mansions . . ." (1. 17). The dissipated lady in **"Timon"** with "more desire than power to please" (1. 50) wonders "how heaven could bless / A man [Louis XIV] that loved two women at one time" (11. 58-59). Given the speaker, reference, and tone, heaven and its blessings have been reduced to verbal tics.

These examples, though they parody the religious, serve to revivify it. In such cases Rochester should be looked upon as a poet violating convention in order to re-establish it. Like any good poet, he participates in that radical attempt that gives language meaning. It is not just that many of these poems require knowledge of the traditional meanings of religious words or references in order to appreciate the mockery, but that the religious comes to be used in a positive sense.[7]

The world Artemisia describes is a Bedlam, a mad parody of the divine order symbolized by the Father's house of many mansions. This parodic world at once mocks that divine order and is judged by it. Seen from a perspective "As true as heaven," Artemisia's fallen world would be "more infamous than hell" (1. 112). Though she is in part aware that her words condemn her, the lady in **"Timon"** is not; she unwittingly judges herself by her own references. In his use of religious vocabulary the speaker in *A Very Heroical Epistle* also condemns himself. He compares himself to the sun; he is a "blazing star" (1. 21), and he grants grace and charity. He wants nothing less than to be God. But as he reduces Christian values to an amoral materialism, we are given a norm by which to judge his fantastic egocentricity.[8]

Rochester, however, does not consistently employ religious values as satiric norm. More often, religion itself becomes a satiric object because its content is human and physical rather than divine and spiritual. Throughout his poetry, Rochester "discloses the ways in which material interests are masked by 'eulogistic coverings.'"[9] Love is but a compensation for lust or bodily functions. As Huff puts it when asked "if love's flame he never felt / He answered bluntly, 'Do you think I'm gelt?'" (**"Timon,"** 11. 61-62). Corinna, in "What cruel pains Corinna takes," learns that honor is but "affected rules" (1. 11) masking physical desires. The **"Disabled Debauchee"** concludes that wisdom springs from impotence. Like love, honor, and wisdom, religious vocabulary, for Rochester, fits into this category of "eulogistic coverings."

The *Satyr* affords the clearest example of Rochester attacking the motivation inherent in religious vocabulary and of pointing out pernicious effects of this vocabulary. The first half of the poem argues that instead of being created in God's image, a creature of spirit endowed with right reason, man is, like the dog Jowler, a material being driven by physical appetite. The language of religion not only fails to account for human motivation, it leads man away from his real nature and in turn perverts it. Religious vocabulary is a fiction which disguises man's true nature from himself. Such fictions are dangerous in that man, thinking he is pursuing truth, learns "After a search so painful and so long / That all his life he has been in the wrong" (11. 27-28). In the hands of the unscrupulous, such fictions can be used to exploit others. The unscrupulous are "the pretending part of the proud world" at whom, at least in this interpretation, the *Satyr* is directed, those "Who, swollen with selfish vanity, devise / False freedoms, holy cheats, and formal lies / Over their fellow slaves to tyrannize" (11. 175-78).

Such satire certainly seems to indicate a rejection of Christianity, but only in part and in no simple way. Another interpretation, equally valid, could show the norm by which religious vocabulary is criticized itself being undermined. Rochester's satire simply does not have the stability of philosophical definition; to read the poetry is to experience, more often than not, stable irony, to use Wayne Booth's distinction, becoming unstable. As this movement takes place, we find religious vocabulary being used not so much as norm or butt of satire as a vehicle for exploring the nature of Christianity linguistically. A good illustration of this movement and of what happens to religion under its impact is **"Written in a Lady's Prayer Book."**

I

Fling this useless book away,
And presume no more to pray.
Heaven is just, and can bestow
Mercy on none but those that mercy show.
With a proud heart maliciously inclined
Not to increase, but to subdue mankind,
In vain you vex the gods with your petition;
Without repentance and sincere contrition,
You're in a reprobate condition.

II

Phyllis, to calm the angry powers
And save my soul as well as yours,
Relieve poor mortals from despair,
And justify the gods that made you fair;
And in those bright and charming eyes
Let pity first appear, then love,
That we by easy steps may rise
Through all the joys on earth to those above.

Phyllis believes one thing, the male speaker quite another, and he attempts to convince her about his attitude toward something of great importance, her salvation. Both speaker and Phyllis appear to inhabit the same order of discourse, the words employed, "Heaven,"

"Mercy," "repentance," and "contrition," ostensibly having the same meaning for him as for her. As the speaker's argument progresses, the religious words, however, change meaning. The Christian heaven evoked at the beginning becomes sexual intercourse at the end. The speaker's operational definition of "mercy" is equally topsy-turvy. His argument is one of plentitude where multiplication of the things of God's world is good, and he has the rhetoric if not the content of virtue. According to him, Phyllis has erred because her "proud heart" is "maliciously inclined / Not to increase, but subdue mankind." What in a traditional frame of values—exercising control and being chaste—would be good, the speaker makes blameworthy. Perhaps Phyllis's pride does make her culpable, but given the choice of sexual indulgence or chastity, she clearly should choose the latter, though according to the speaker she is wrong to do so. Should the lady, on his terms, prove merciful, he would no doubt find hers a "heavenly reward," but then mercy would have quite a different meaning.

The witty redefinition of what it means to be merciful sets other definitions askew. As the speaker would have it, the woman is "reprobate," morally unprincipled, if she does not agree with his proposition. To repent and to be sincerely contrite, would be, of all things, to give into him. In a casuistical way the speaker is right. By giving into him, Phyllis will have something about which to be contrite. She will have something to repent. Paradoxically, her religious vocabulary will have meaning only when it has been violated.[10] There is yet another way in which the speaker's argument is wittily plausible. We, and probably Phyllis, take "contrite" in its figurative sense, but the speaker has the literal sense in mind: "contrition" meaning the action of rubbing things together, or against each other: grinding, pounding, or bruising. The sexual connotations are clear, and just as clearly, the congruence between language and what is being described has become problematic.

The traditional meanings and the speaker's redefinitions are kept in constant play, the latter undermining the former yet still being judged by them, depending upon them for meaning yet attacking them at the same time. This interaction makes the humor possible, the humor arising from incongruity, but it also calls into question the function of language, points out how problematic signification really is. The lady's tacit argument and belief depend on the word, yet if she listens closely, she finds the linguistic basis for her belief being dissolved.

In breaking apart words the speaker furthers his rhetorical aim: the here and now, actions, the physical are important, are useful, not the afterlife, prayer, or the spirit. Just as mercy moves in definition from heavenly to fleshly reward in one line, so the other religious words become translated into the physical. The poem is a blasphemous commentary on the word become flesh, on the incarnation. Linguistically, the speaker has made the words contrite; he has broken their spirit, despiritualized them. This linguistic process mirrors his advice to Phyllis not to use the book and not to pray. These activities are spiritual ways to salvation, and this seduction poem also satirizes the doctrine of salvation by faith. As we learn in the second stanza, the speaker wants the two of them to ascend to heaven through the flesh not the word. Good deeds, at least as the speaker defines them, not faith, lead to salvation. Words, book, and prayer have all lost in the speaker's logic their efficacy, and the traditional dialectic of Christian-Platonism embodied in the movement from body to soul, from the senses to reason to understanding, from woman to beauty to the idea of God has been turned upside down.

It could be argued that this poem, like examples cited earlier, derives its meaning by a travesty of conventional meanings. And while it is true that the poem cannot mean without a knowledge of religious vocabulary and doctrines, our experience of reading the poem tells us, I think, that re-establishing the meaning of religious concepts is not central. While the speaker is being satirized—his blasphemous wit condemning him unawares—what we intuit to be Phyllis's (and our own) naive faith in the efficacy of words is also being held up to ridicule. The poem itself involves us in the process of how we establish meaning: and in its attack on language, it leaves us no secure ground upon which to make our assessment. It displays a radical distrust of language, particularly of religious language. By theme and philosophy, the poem points away from language toward action. The successful *carpe diem* poem, of course, leads to silence and action. It uses language to get beyond language. In the poem, too, the attitude toward language would suggest that words can mean only when attached to actions and the physical world. In its spiritual, or metaphorical, form language leads away from the useful. The poem, beginning with the onomatopoetic "Fling," embodies a positivistic theory of language. Yet, in using words to defeat words the speaker exemplifies just how effective language can be. Moreover, he will transcend the reality of Phyllis's objections, if at all, through the word.

From the evidence we have garnered so far one would certainly argue, as Wilcoxon has, that Rochester rejected Christian orthodoxy. He uses orthodox religious tenets sparingly as positive norms in his satire while often attacking them or rendering them equivocable through irony. As I have been suggesting, however, this evidence can be made to support the opposite case, that rejection signalizes affirmation. Rochester's ambivalence toward Christianity, his using it both as the norm and butt of satire as well as his resorting to irony accords with what we know of the satirist: what he attacks is always

more than a little part of himself. Such an explanation not only has a generic rightness to it, but it is in keeping with those early lives of Rochester which transform his rakish self into a Christian exemplum of sinner in service of the Lord. Our post-Freudian sensibilities, moreover, find no problem in accepting that the blasphemous should form the obverse of the truly religious. But such a reading, it might be countered, is simply an exercise in ironic recuperation, making a writer say what you want him to say by claiming that he is being ironic and nothing is easier. Furthermore, to draw upon generic, biographical, and psychoanalytical systems of meaning is to make a highly problematic interpretation even more so. Besides, the question is not whether Rochester had a religious sensibility but whether that sensibility took orthodox paths.

These objections are not without force, but whether we read Rochester's use of Christianity straightforwardly or with an ironic eye, we are still missing something of great importance, and that is the remarkable energy with which Rochester treats religious subjects, the intensity with which he attempts to deny the validity of Christianity. The best description of this characteristic so central to the man and his work remains that of Robert Parsons who astutely noted that Rochester

> seem'd to affect something singular and paradoxical in his Impieties, as well as his Writings, above the reach and thought of other men; taking as much pains to draw others in, and to pervert the right ways of virtue, as the Apostles and Primitive Saints, *to save their own souls, and them that heard them.* For this was the heightening and amazing circumstances of his sins, that he was so diligent and industrious to recommend and propagate them: . . . framing Arguments for Sin, making Proselytes to it, and writing Panegyricks upon Vice; singing Praises to the great enemy of God, and casting down Coronets and Crowns before his Throne.[11]

All that a saint might wish to affirm, Rochester attempts to negate and with saintly zeal. He opposes religion with such energy and ingenuity. He is so splendidly, completely wicked; his speakers are so debased, so far gone in their sin. He is "singular" in his negation. If we are going to describe accurately the place of Christianity in Rochester's poetry, whether our interpretative model employs irony or not, we must account for this excessive negativity.

II

When Artemisia writes that she is "Pleased with the contradiction and the sin" (1. 30), she could well have been describing Rochester's poetry as the state of her mind. So much of the poetry involves a "saying against," and it contradicts with pleasure. The negative permeates Rochester's poetry, its techniques as well as its subject matter, its personae as well as their settings, until finally it becomes the subject itself. Save for a few exceptions, when we read an affirmation in Rochester's poetry, we know either to take it negatively or simply to remain uncertain about how to take it at all. The **"Impromptu on the English Court"** exemplifies our reading for the negative.

> Here's Monmouth the witty,
> And Lauderdale the pretty,
> And Frazier, that learned physician;
> But above all the rest,
> Here's the Duke for a jest,
> And the King for a grand politician.

Without knowing the historical context, we might read these as straightforward statements; it would be wrong to do so. For Monmouth was notoriously lacking in wit, Lauderdale not pretty, the Duke incapable of jest, and we have no reason to suspect Rochester thought otherwise. But we also know from the experience of reading other poems by Rochester that the most satisfying interpretations do not emerge unless we expect, for example, punning. Monmouth, following this line of reading, is not witty, that is, is not a "mouth man," nor is Lauderdale pretty as a pretty valley. To read Rochester's poetry intelligently, however, we need more than anything else a feel for the ironic. A handsome duke should be witty; he is not. The king's physician should be learned, capable of caring for the body physical, just as a king should be politically astute so as to be able to care for the body politic, but neither Frazier nor Charles fit the bill. As Kenneth Burke reminds us: "Irony is the most obvious specific example of the implied feeling for the negative."[12] It is Rochester's principal mode.

Negative in technique, the poetry is also negative in subject matter. This point comes through at its simplest if we think how much of the poetry deals with taboo topics. Impotence, sodomy, masturbation, promiscuity go against normal biology or conventional morality, and the apparently biologically normal lovers never get together: Rochester's speakers are forever leaving their mistresses (**"Love and Live"** and some nine other poems). They find enjoyment in not being together (**"Absent From Thee"**) and in not consummating their love (**"The Platonic Lady"**). For them it is better not to have than to have (**"The Mistress"**). And finally they would rather know pain than pleasure, pain having become their pleasure (**"The Mistress,"** ll. 25-32). So many of the speakers are debased that they are incapable of acting—the Disabled Debauchee and the speaker in **"The Imperfect Enjoyment"**—or act against themselves. Though he has clues enough to know better, the speaker in **"A Ramble"** chases after Corinna. Artemisia plunges into verse, and Timon goes off to dinner. They rail at and punish themselves; indeed, one of the central images of Rochester's poetry involves willing sacrifice, slavery, and victimization, all presages of the great negative: death.

As with the characters, so with the world they inhabit; both are infused with the negative. Though the speaker in the **Satyr** attempts to establish nature as a positive, it is a positive no one can follow and may not be a positive at all. The speaker claims that one in tune with the senses, with nature, will be guided so that his will can make choices that lead to the pleasurable. Yet save for the example of eating whenever one likes, he gives no other evidence of man in harmony with his senses (ll. 99-111).[13] He condemns men, moreover, for acting in accord with nature, for following their physical appetites, in the second half of the poem, but then he has shifted his definition (or the poet, debunking the speaker's argument, has shifted it) of nature from the following of instinct to the following of cultural norms, nature having become our "second" or "social" nature. It would seem that nature is more a hypothetical, than a real, good. For the emphasis on the senses, on following nature, leads in the other poems as well as in the **Satyr** not to the blissful and pleasurable but to the seamy and painful.

The negative, Bergson points out, is a function of expectation. You expect the day to be hot, but it isn't. Things are as they are unless an act of mind posits, expects, that they should be other.[14] Behind Rochester's poetry lies a sensibility that expected ever so much. One letter to his wife, only a fragment of which survives, succinctly captures Rochester's sense of the gulf between expectation and reality:

> —soe great a disproportion t'wixt our desires and what is ordained to content them; but you will say this is pride and madness, for theire are those soe intirely satisfyed with theire shares in this world that theire wishes nor theire thoughts have not a farther prospect of felicity and glory. I'le tell you, were that mans soule plac't in a body fitt for it, hee were a dogg, that could count any thing a benefit obtain'd wth flattery, feare and service.[15]

From this distance between desire and reality springs the attitude in the poetry toward nature, lovers, politicians, and yes, Christianity—none of which are what Rochester expects them to be.[16]

Rochester responds to the gap between what should be and what is with comedy, satire, and irony, all of which arise, it seems to me, from what Burke has called the "aesthetic negative, whereby any moralistic thou-shalt-not provides material for our entertainment, as we pay to follow imaginary accounts of 'deviants' who, in all sorts of ingenious ways are represented as violating those very Don'ts".[17] Readers are entertained as both Rochester and his characters violate cultural and religious standards. Such violations can be instrumental, ludic, or destructive, though these categories overlap. To violate the social or divine order instrumentally is to protest against it with an intention of preserving and strengthening it. But violation can also be ludic, an entering into a realm of possibility with rules shattered, a saturnalia, or it can be destructive, criminal. Though it seems right to read Rochester, as Wilcoxon has, as more ludic and destructive than instrumental, in matters of religion he is *serio ludere,* playing most seriously. Underlying his poetry is just not the aesthetic but also the religious negative whose principle energy is to convert the negative into a positive.

Dustin Griffin has written that "Rochester's life and poems offer us not images of the rake's mastery, but images of a failure to attain mastery." He goes on to observe that Rochester "explores the possibilities of the rake only to discover pain and perplexity, insecurity, and enslavement. . . ."[18] But Rochester does more than discover pain and perplexity; he pursues them, desires and needs them. If he had not found them in abundance in the Restoration Court, he would have had to invent them. For Rochester, failure is mastery, pain a sign of pleasure, absence of presence, impotence of potence, nothing of something. Whether by way of philosophical disposition, experience, or both, Rochester found that the positive state does not exist in human affairs, not at least in a pure enough form for him. As he told Burnet, religion is either the "most important thing" or it is not; if it is, human beings have done and always will do it disservice. Better "there should be no other Religious Worship, but a general Celebration of that Being, in some short Hymn. . . ." (*Some Passages,* 11. 61,77). Better that God not exist in human terms, except in the negative. Any human formulation of the ideal is a debasement and limitation. The negative is the realm of the unlimited, where ideals can exist beyond the foreclosure that human experience places upon them. Rochester wants, expects, the ideal, but because he is human, he has to pursue it through the negative.

Indeed, to assure that the ideal will exist, he creates the interference of his own negative.[19] He attempts to remain in the world of pure possibility, always to court but never to know the ideal, a man in perpetual motion, never to stop. For as Rochester well knew, a perfect persuasion leads to death, just as anyone motionless falls out of his Descartian universe. Thus a God who would love him must be fanciful, just as a woman who would give in to him must be resisted, and any enjoyment must be imperfect. Rochester's negative courtship of God implicitly informs all the poetry, whether the subject is God, kings, or mistresses. His entire work is a paradoxical encomium, a praise of impiety that is really pious; but in at least two poems his courting of the Lord *via negativa* is explicit.

The first, **"Rochester Extempore,"** is ostensibly doggerel:

> And after singing Psalm the Twelfth,
> He laid his book upon the shelf

> And looked much simply like himself;
> With eyes turned up, as white as ghosts,
> He cried, "Ah, Lard! ah, Lard of Hosts!
> I am a rascal, that thou know'st!"

In truth, this is rather complex, though the rhetoric outshines the poetry. There are a number of observations in Psalm 12 applicable to a rascal such as Rochester. The Psalm tells of those that "speak vanity every one with his neighbor: with flattering lips and with a double heart do they speak," a blow at the courtier and ironist. The promise is that "The Lord shall cut off all flattering lips, and the tongue that speaketh proud things . . ." The poem would seem, if hardly an Ignatian meditation, at least a recognition and condemnation, the speaker seeing himself in the mirror of the text all too clearly. Yet the childish rhythm suggests a playfulness out of keeping with serious self-judgment. In his impudence, the speaker has all the makings of a true rascal. We could leave it at that; our awareness is greater than the speaker's and his own words judge him. Yet, the theatricality—looking simply, white as a ghost, the mocking "Lard"—also suggests that the speaker is aware of what he is doing. The poem is reported, and the observer is to the persona as we are to him and as presumably his other audience, the Lord, is too. Yes, the speaker is saying, I am bad, but I know it, and because I do, I am not really that bad. Mine is play, an act; you—the audience being the Lord—"know'st" what I am really. In one sense, I suppose I am a rascal, but my awareness should make you see that in this charge there is no "serious implication of bad qualities" (OED, definition 3). It is the rhetorical stance of a naughty boy before a chastizing father, joking and clowning being a form of covert communication between father and son that allows them at once to acknowledge the interference between them created by the son and yet to overcome it. Indeed, the joking itself is part of the interference which makes communication necessary; the son hopes the wit makes it also intimate. To others it may appear that I am just a rascal, a member of "the rabble of an army or of the populace; common soldiers or camp-followers, persons of the lowest class" (OED, definition 1). But you know, father, that I am of that army over which you as "Lord of Hosts" preside, "Hosts" referring to the "armies of Israel" and by analogy to "angels that attend God" (OED, definition 3). Self-debasement becomes self-enhancement; the negative becomes a positive. Rochester is clowning before the Lord and apparently in the process making his debased circumstances worse but actually through his own negative interference showing why he should march in his father's army. Joking, ostensibly a form of impiety, becomes religious. The attempt of religion is "religare," to bind back, to unite once again man and God; and as Freud reminds us, jokes can be, and are in Rochester's hands, a means of re-establishing the original power of words. Rochester's poem aptly fits into the category of jokes described by Freud as "'ready repartees.' For repartee consists in the defence going to meet the aggression, in 'turning the tables on someone' or 'paying someone back in his own coin'—that is, in establishing an unexpected unity between attack and counter-attack."[20] Through his wit, Rochester turns guilt into redemption. Through wit, he is both separating himself from god—the very separation being proof of God's existence—and binding himself to Him.

The magnificently wicked speaker in **"To the Postboy"** adopts a similar rhetorical stance. The poem plays upon the paradox that the logic of Christianity leads to the perfect crime being redeemed by the perfect act of love. Therefore, in a virtuoso display of rhetoric, Rochester offers himself as the "greatest of sinners" (Parsons' phrase)—drunkard, liar, Sodomite, murderer. The ploy is that God, as Charles II often did, will see the wit, will perceive that here corruption is conscientiousness, and will forgive him who is in reality his perfect servant. A Pauline paradox is being pushed to the limits: "Therefore I take pleasure in infirmities, in reproaches, in necessities, in persecutions, in distresses for Christ's sake: for when I am weak, then I am strong" (II Corinthians 12:10). This speaker, seemingly the very sign of Hell, is on the same road as the "Postboy," who as Bunyan tells us, "in his haste an emblem is / Of those; that are set out for lasting bliss."[21] The paradox is further exemplified in the poem's last two lines. Rochester asks:

The readiest way to Hell—come quick!

BOY

Ne'er stir:
The readiest way, my Lord, 's by Rochester.

Vieth's punctuation makes sense, but the poem's paradoxicality calls for another. "The readiest way? My Lord's, by Rochester." The Lord's and Rochester's ways would be one and the same, the road to Hell also the road to Heaven.

It is impossible to paraphrase the paradoxes at work here, the combination of Christian humility with aristocratic pride, the simultaneous provoking of criticism and the guilt it involves with an attempt through self-awareness to foreclose that criticism, the attempt to be both victim and judge. It is quite dazzling and meant to be, the rhetorical paradox having as its purpose "to show off the skill of an orator and to arouse the admiration of an audience, both at the outlandishness of the subject and the technical brilliance of the rhetorician."[22] Rochester audaciously challenges his conventional audience of Christian believers, saying in effect, that if your religion is true, this is what it requires of you: to become

great sinners. But what is paradox to the multitudes will be, Rochester hopes, orthodox to his other audience, the Lord.[23]

Both these poems exemplify Rochester's negative theology. Both mock the God of Christianity but do so with an ingenious perversity that show that the speakers understand God's way ever so well. If He does exist, He will see such perversity for what it is, a perfection of his system, and thus He will forgive. Prodigal son psychology was perhaps never so finely employed again until the days of Kierkegaard. Just as the materialistic determinism and the filthy words which inform and identify Rochester's poetry are a perverse imitation of God's holy order, so too the rhetorical stance of these two poems is a travesty of Christianity which also affirms its possibilities.

The question remains whether this religious stance is orthodox. I think it is, that Rochester's skepticism towards language betrays a Puritanical concern for definition and exactitude, the same concern that fueled the Royal society, and so does his negative theology. "For the Puritans," Sacvan Bercovitch writes, man "must 'be soaked and boiled in afflictions,' as Job was . . . 'Would you wash your face clean?' asks John Bunyan—well, 'first take a glass and see where it is durty': 'labour' to discern your every crime, 'experimentally' persuade yourself that you are 'the biggest sinner in the world,' 'plunge' yourself into the foul waters of your heart till you know there is 'none worse than thyself.' 'You must be empty, if ever Christ fill you,' went the pulpit refrain: 'You must be nothing, if you would have Christ.'"[24] One smiles. Surely Rochester experimented and labored all too willingly to prove himself the "biggest sinner"? Yet without this understanding of the negative way, the pathos if not much of the ironic genius of say **"To the Postboy"** escapes us. Rochester followed the Puritan injunction to become "nothing." Like so many theologians, he knew that perhaps the only way for a human being to know God is to know Him by what he is not, to know Him, that is, as Moses did, from the backside.

Notes

1. Barbara Babcock uses this suggestive quotation as epigram for her brilliant introduction to *The Reversible World: Symbolic Inversion in Art and Society* (Ithaca, N. Y.: Cornell Univ. Press, 1978).

2. "Rochester's Philosophical Premises: A Case for Consistency," *Eighteenth-Century Studies,* 8 (1974/75), 200. Wilcoxon's argument is similar to Dustin Griffin's (*Satires Against Man, The Poems of Rochester* [Berkeley, Calif: Univ. of California Press, 1973]). Rochester is a skeptic, partaking fully in the libertine heterodoxy described by Bredvold and Underwood (p. 16). He is a moral-

ist, believes in a Supreme Being and the immortality of the soul, but is doubtful of "the other tenets of orthodox Christianity" (p. 9). Both Wilcoxon and Griffin have made valuable contributions to a lively, often acerbic debate that began the day Rochester died and that has continued on into modern criticism. Assessing Prinz's biography, Montague Summers with characteristic bluntness wrote that "for all his boundless and indeed exaggerated enthusiasm Herr Prinz has certainly not gone to the lengths of proclaiming that Rochester had a 'religious' mind, that he was a man who 'pondered long and deeply on the ultimate problems of philosophy and religion.' This absurdity was put forward in all apparent seriousness by a writer in an article 'Unpublished Poem Attributed to Rochester' in *The Times Literary Supplement,* 22nd November, 1934" (*The Playhouse of Samuel Pepys* [London: Kegan Paul, 1935,], p. 302). The author of this letter was Vivian de Sola Pinto; undaunted by Summers' blast, he went on to make his case in book length form, one of the central arguments of *Enthusiast in Wit* (Lincoln: Univ. of Nebraska Press, 1962; a revision of *Rochester, Portrait of a Restoration Poet,* 1935) being that Rochester's "celebrated conversion to religion was no sudden *volte-face*; it was the culminating point of a dialectical process which had been going on in his mind for years" (p. 186). George Williamson came down on Pinto's side, writing in *The Proper Wit of Poetry* (Chicago: Univ. of Chicago Press, 1961) that "For all his agnostic wit, Rochester's best love poems are haunted by ideas of religion" (p. 126). Howard Weinbrot quoted this observation in a recent article and labeled it shrewd, "The Swelling Volume: The Apocalytic Satire of Rochester's Letter from Artemisia . . . ," *Studies in the Literary Imagination,* 5 (October 1972), 23. Equally shrewd to my mind is Raman Selden's comment that "Much of Rochester's finest poetry takes the form of inverted religion," *English Verse Satire 1590-1765* (London: George Allen & Unwin, 1978), p. 94. The debate goes on.

3. See James William Johnson's fascinating chapter, "A Christian Upbringing, 1647-1656," in his forthcoming biography, *"Mad" Rochester: The Life and Times of John Wilmot 1647-1680.*

4. *The Complete Poems of John Wilmot, Earl of Rochester,* ed. David Vieth (New Haven: Yale Univ. Press, 1968), p. 35. I use this edition throughout citing line numbers parenthetically.

5. Lucretius, *On Nature,* trans. Russel M. Geer (New York: Bobbs-Merrill, 1965), I. 73-77.

6. In composing "Upon Nothing," Rochester obviously had in mind Lucretius I. 150-60, an observation I owe to James William Johnson. For a sug-

gestive analysis of Lucretius's motives, see Kenneth Burke, *A Grammar of Motives* (1945; rpt. Berkeley, Calif.: Univ. of California Press, 1969), pp. 162-65.

7. Such an instrumental reading of Rochester's use of Christianity is finally where I wind up in this paper, but in the cases just cited the instrumental is, I think, obvious. In other poems, it is far less so; therefore, they have to be approached in a roundabout way, nearly backwards.

8. I am following David Vieth's fine reading of the poem in *Attribution in Restoration Poetry* (New Haven: Yale Univ. Press, 1963), pp. 107-19.

9. Kenneth Burke, *The Philosophy of Literary Form* (1941; rpt. Berkeley, Calif.: Univ. of California Press, 1973), p. 168.

10. Cf. Umberto Eco's ingenious "is there a way of generating aesthetic messages in a Edenic Language," in which he asserts that Adam first understands the structure of his language and of the world about him when he violates the initial Edenic language system. Like Eco's Adam, Phyllis may arrive "at a comprehension of the system at the very moment in which he is calling the system into question and therefore destroying it" (*Russian Formalism,* ed. Stephen Bann and John Bowlt [Edinburgh: Scottish Academic Press, 1973], p. 173). Rochester had an intuitive sense that any order demands a disorder, that inherent in Christianity is crime. At times, he seems to see language as a symptom of that crime, at other times, a means of overcoming it.

11. Robert Parsons, *A Sermon Preached At the Funeral of . . . John Earl of Rochester* (Oxford, at the Theatre, Printed for Richard Davis and Thomas Bowman, 1680), p. 9.

12. Kenneth Burke, *Language as Symbolic Action* (Berkeley, Calif.: Univ. of California Press, 1966), p. 461.

13. The eating example, it seems to me, is the speaker's attempt to say no to God's original "Thou shalt not," the Edenic interdiction against apples. He is attempting to negate God's word and the power of abstract language in general. If one eliminates all but positivistic language, there can be no moral disobedience.

14. Henri Bergson, *Creative Evolution* (New York: Henry Holt, 1911), pp. 272-98. Bergson's thoughts on "nothing" influenced Kenneth Burke and for his brilliant treatment of the negative see *Language as Symbolic Action,* particularly pp. 9-13 and 453-79; and *The Rhetoric of Religion* (1961; rpt. Berkeley, Calif.: Univ. of California Press, 1970), *passim.*

15. *The Collected Works of John Wilmot Earl of Roch-ester,* ed. John Hayward (London: Nonesuch Press, 1926), p. 288.

16. As Burnet tells us: "He upon that told me plainly, There was nothing that gave him, and many oth-ers, a more secret encouragement in their ill ways, than that those who pretended to believe, lived so that they could not be thought to be in earnest, when they said it" (*Some Passages of The Life and Death of John Earl of Rochester* in *Rochester, The Critical Heritage,* ed. David Farley-Hills [New York: Barnes and Noble, 1972], p. 77).

17. *Language as Symbolic Action,* p. 13.

18. Dustin Griffin, p. 20.

19. If his world is already suffused with the negative, why should Rochester create his own negatives? One might speculate that there is more than a little aristocratic hauteur in such a stance; nothing hu-man will do. There is also self-protection; one need not commit oneself for nothing is worthy. One escapes responsibility. But here also seems to be, in religion at least, a desire to use the negative to correct the errors of others and thus preserve the integrity and perhaps mystery of religion. In effect, Rochester is saying I do not know what true religion would be but it is not what is being practiced. Cf. Kant's observation that "From the point of view of our knowledge in general . . . the peculiar function of negative proposition is simply to prevent error" (cited by Bergson, *Cre-ative Evolution,* p. 287).

20. Sigmund Freud, *Jokes and Their Relationship to the Unconscious,* trans. James Strachey (New York: Norton, 1963), p. 68.

21. John Bunyan, "On the Post-boy," in *A Book For Boys and Girls: or Country Rhimes For Children* (London, 1686; facsimile rpt. London: Elliot Stock, 1889), p. 35. I owe this illuminating refer-ence to James William Johnson.

22. Rosalie Colie, *Paradoxia Epidemica, The Renais-sance Tradition of Paradox* (Princeton, N.J.: Prin-ceton Univ. Press, 1966), p. 3. Cf. what Rochester told Parsons: "One day at an Atheistical Meeting, at a person of Qualitie's, I undertook to manage the Cause, and was the principal Disputant against God and Piety, and for my performances received the applause of the whole company . . ." (*Sermon,* p. 23).

23. Rochester would have smiled to see Parsons wrestle with this same paradox in his funeral sermon. Preaching on the text of the prodigal son, Parsons is too ingenious in defending Rochester's life and his death-bed repentance. Thus he has to spend much of the sermon explaining why it is better not to be a Rochester when he has given every evidence that it is.

24. Sacvan Bercovitch, *The Puritan Origins of the American Self* (New Haven: Yale Univ. Press, 1975), pp. 14-15.

A. D. Cousins (essay date summer 1984)

SOURCE: Cousins, A. D. "The Context, Design, and Argument of Rochester's *A Satyr against Reason and Mankind." Studies in English Literature 1500-1900* 24, no. 3 (summer 1984): 429-39.

[*In the following essay, Cousins analyzes the structure and meaning of Rochester's* A Satyr against Reason and Mankind, *maintaining that in it he offers a possible solution to the problem of disorder—both public and private—raised throughout his work.*]

Recent interpretations of Rochester's **A Satyr against Reason and Mankind** have tended to emphasize the philosophical and literary associations of the poem. Neither its place in the context of Rochester's other poems, nor how design and argument interrelate in it, has been so distinctly elucidated.[1] The following discus-sion suggests that **A Satyr** indicates Rochester's tenta-tive solution to the private and social disorder recur-rently analyzed in his other poems, and that to understand the solution it implies one must recognize how it redefines "right reason" (and relates that to the personality) within an ironically deliberative design. The discussion hopes to show that seeing the context, design, and argument of **A Satyr** in this way helps at once to illuminate the poem and to clarify our sense of Rochester's achievement as a poet.

If **A Satyr** develops from the European libertine tradi-tion, perhaps also being indebted to the English tradi-tion running from Donne through the cavalier poets, it emerges as well from Rochester's own pattern of libertine thought. Repeatedly in his other poems he characterizes human nature in terms of the impulse to pleasure and shows that unreason is inseparable from it. So too is the problem of power. Rochester demonstrates that the impulse to pleasure not only dominates people but drives them to dominate each other—or to submit to control by others. This is crystallized in his love poems' recurring images of tyranny and enslavement, which are not outworn conventions but expressions of one of Rochester's elemental beliefs. As he says in the opening quatrain of the poem on the whore Sue Willis:

> Against the charms our ballocks have
> How weak all human skill is,
> Since they can make a man a slave
> To such a bitch as Willis![2]

He similarly considers the intrinsic disorderliness of human nature in **"A Pastoral Dialogue between Alexis and Strephon"** (esp. lines 51-70), **"A Dialogue between Strephon and Daphne"** (esp. lines 13-16 and 57-72), **"The Advice," "As Chloris full of harmless thought," "What cruel pains Corinna takes,"** the two translations from Lucretius, **"To Love"** (esp. lines 9-12 and 27-60), **"The Imperfect Enjoyment"** (esp. lines 50-61), **"A Ramble in St. James's Park," "Upon His Drinking a Bowl"** (esp. lines 21-24), **"The Fall," "What vain, unnecessary things are men!"** (esp. lines 31-40), **A Very Heroical Epistle in Answer to Ephelia, "The Disabled Debauchee,"** and **"I swive as well as others do."** In those poems Rochester may criticize or advocate reason's submission to passion, and praise or attack the power-play of love; nonetheless, his varying attitudes to how people behave center on a consistent, and essentially serious, analysis of why they do so.

That analysis of human nature's disorderliness is writ large in Rochester's thinking on the discord he sees as pervading Restoration society. It can be seen in his farcical surveys of Carolean courtly love, where its political implications seem clear as through it Rochester explains the sexual anarchy he perceives at the heart of England's government.[3] Here one could cite **"On the Women about Town," "Quoth the Duchess of Cleveland to counselor Knight," "The Second Prologue at Court to 'The Empress of Morocco,' Spoken by the Lady Elizabeth Howard"** (esp. lines 23-45), **"Signior Dildo,"** and **"When to the King I bid good morrow."** But most important here is **"A Satyr on Charles II,"** where the political criticism implicit in the courtly love poems becomes explicit in Rochester's account of the king's rule and personality. Rochester says of the king: "Nor are his high desires above his strength: / His scepter and his prick are of a length" (lines 10-11). He continues: "Poor prince! thy prick, like thy buffoons at Court, / Will govern thee because it makes thee sport" (lines 14-15). Charles is characterized as "A merry monarch, scandalous and poor" (line 21, see lines 18-20). Dominated by his "high desires" for pleasure, the king rules—and becomes an irrational victim—to gain it. The impulse to pleasure, unreason, and the misdirection of power disorder Charles, and in him that disorder becomes institutionalized for society.

The relationship of **A Satyr** to Rochester's critique of private and social disorder can be suggested by a glance at the other verse satires in which he explores how society is pervaded by a discord of the kind Charles embodies. Two are representative, **"Tunbridge Wells"** and **A Letter from Artemisia in the Town to Chloe in the Country**; the most significant thing seems to be that in them Rochester traces society's discords and confusions yet offers no remedies for the ills he observes.

"Tunbridge Wells" is a series of character sketches given by the speaker whose presence unifies the poem.

(He is a contemptuous observer of visitors to the resort which lends the poem its name.) Vivid, clever, and funny as the character sketches are, they do not tell us much. Rather it is their variety, and how they are given importance in the poem, that are most revealing. By setting his poem at a fashionable resort, Rochester can let us examine a cross-section of society (see lines 4-5). Standing out from the crowd are influential representatives of State (lines 11-24) and Church (lines 41-69), as well as embodiments of triviality (lines 86-113), sterility (lines 114-48), and naive imposture (lines 149-65). All act irrationally, seek to dominate others, and show in some way that their lives are sensual. To illustrate the stupidity, lechery, and grossness of the various characters would be easy, but it is more useful to indicate how the relatively simple sketches of these characters are made important in the poem. The cross-section of society at the resort is ruled by the only figure Rochester draws with a sophisticated rhetoric.[4] This "buckram puppet" with his pretense to wisdom (lines 33-35) is "Master o' th' Ceremonies, yet can dispense / With the formality of talking sense" (lines 39-40). Seeing this, we realize at once what the character sketches mean. They image the flaws Rochester discerns at the heart of his world, but they also imply that men prefer to be governed by a parody of order; men choose to be ruled by irrational ceremony from without, and by disorder from within. This thoroughly develops the argument of the satire on Charles II.

A Letter from Artemisia does so with more sophistication.[5] Artemisia remarks early in her letter that "Bedlam has many mansions" (line 17); in effect she goes on to show Chloe and us that the town is one of them. Her letter focuses on love, both because it impels the lives around her (lines 32-33) and because she thinks it "That cordial drop heaven in our cup has thrown / To make the nauseous draught of life go down" (lines 44-45). Believing in love's value, she is angered to see it "debauched by ill-bred customs" (line 39) so that women especially "To an exact perfection . . . have wrought / The action, love; the passion is forgot" (lines 62-63). In the town, love means only the impulse to pleasure (lines 50-69); driven by it, people now calculatingly abuse reason to control and ruin each other's lives. Corinna's story, which concludes the poem (lines 189-251), persuasively dramatizes this: she is seduced and abandoned by a "man of wit" (line 198), becomes a whore, then turns adventuress, finally outwitting a wealthy lover and murdering him to secure his money. The satire pictures a Hobbesian world—but one that is anarchic and predatory in the name of love.

Those satires imply that Rochester sees disorder as intrinsic to society, and as insistently manifested in his society's conventions of manners and speech. His libertine critique of this in terms of the impulse to pleasure, unreason, and domination, seems to acknowledge no principle of order in existence; to be sure, an angry reasonableness guides observation and judgment in Rochester's satiric personae, but their reasonableness serves merely to isolate them in a world seen as anarchic. Moreover, insofar as those satires elaborate the argument of **"A Satyr on Charles II,"** they affirm what the picturing of Charles as a comic emblem of misrule suggests indirectly but forcefully: that Rochester's preoccupation with the discords and confusions of his world reflects his comprehensive sense that the Restoration has in fact been the reverse of what his contemporaries hoped and claimed. His view of the Restoration appears to be that disorder has been variously stylized and institutionalized with the king's return—there has been anything but the establishing of order in society with the return of Charles to the throne. These things would seem to indicate where *A Satyr against Reason and Mankind* lies in the context of Rochester's other poems.

A Satyr shows Rochester again analyzing human nature in those libertine terms which pervade his other poems. Here, however, he does so with two significant differences. First, he considers the intellect and the personality both directly and at length. Second, in doing so he tries to find a starting point for order in existence; tentatively and with strong reservations—and with whatever degree of conscious intent—he seeks a solution to the discord for which elsewhere he has no answer. While that suggests how *A Satyr* relates immediately to Rochester's other poems, perhaps a more oblique relationship could also be suggested. Rochester's other poems imply that his view of the Restoration is as pessimistic as Butler's.[6] *A Satyr* might well be, in effect, Rochester's attempt to locate, within the world of Charles's failed rule, a basis for a genuine restoration of order to the individual and society. All this seems to be confirmed by the poem's design and argument.

In *A Satyr,* Rochester redirects our thinking on "right reason" and relates his version of "right reason" to the apparent disorder of the personality. He does so to suggest that if what is really "right reason" were followed and made to guide the impulse to pleasure, then we could probably make a start at overcoming disorder in ourselves and our relations with others. Proposing even a starting point for order is quite an achievement for Rochester, given his view of experience, and the more so because in *A Satyr* he continues to assert, as he does in his other poems, that meanness and selfishness are elemental to human nature, and therefore the prospect of orderly living must be remote. But to appreciate exactly what Rochester argues and attempts in *A Satyr,* one needs first to recognize his poem's design. Rochester designs it as two linked "deliberative orations," to the second of which (and so to the poem as a whole) he adds a long and paradoxical epilogue. He organizes his

poem, then, on the traditional principles for shaping an argument which expresses right reason persuasively. The very form of his poem implies that it should embody "right reason," and that is significant because within the traditional design for an argument expressing "right reason" Rochester subversively redefines what "right reason" (and man's relationship to it) is. The poem's ironic design is tactically precise.

A description of the poem's design will show how Rochester adapts the familiar five or six part structure of the deliberative oration: *exordium* (lines 1-7); *propositio* (lines 8-11); *narratio/confirmatio*—first part (lines 12-30); [*transitio,* lines 31-36]; *narratio/confirmatio*—second part (lines 37-45); [*transitio,* lines 46-47]; *confutatio* (lines 48-93); *conclusio* (lines 94-111)//[*transitio,* lines 112-13]; *propositio* (lines 114-16); *confirmatio*—first part (lines 117-22); [*transitio,* lines 123-27]; *confirmatio*—second part (lines 128-38); *confutatio* (lines 139-67); *conclusio* (lines 168-73)//[*transitio,* (lines 174-78)]; *promissio* (lines 179-221)]: *notatio* (lines 179-90); *notatio* (lines 191-215); *contrarium* (lines 216-21).[7] This form should not be thought of as rigid or as simply mechanical, but rather as a judged pattern of argument through whose coherence Rochester tries to establish a basis for coherence in his world. How the poem's design and argument interrelate to that end becomes clear if one traces the poem's development.

In the introduction to the satire's argument (lines 1-7), the poem's speaker defines himself and at the same time provokes us to look afresh at our place in the chain of being. We have to look closely at what he says because it really forms the basis of all that follows. The speaker begins by wondering what "case of flesh" (line 4) he would inhabit if he were a "spirit free to choose" (line 3) and not that "strange" creature, man (line 2). He decides that he would rather inhabit a beast (line 5) than live as what he now is—the final rhymes of the introduction chiming out in mockery the conventional definition of man: "animal/rational" (lines 6-7). The implications of this are intriguing. A spirit (being incorporeal) is traditionally considered to be a thing of "pure" intellect, that is, to be a thing not really dependent on sense perception for knowledge. Rochester indicates in this passage that the "spirit" inhabiting the human body is not a "pure" intellect ("vain" suggesting man to be an "animal" which, though "rational," is "useless" or "futile" as well as "conceited," and thus pointing to the imperfection of the so-called reason by which man is "proud" to conduct his life—see lines 8-9) and so implies his rejection of the conventional idea that man can be defined as a "pure" intellect informing a "case of flesh."[8] The neoplatonic/ Augustinian view of man (dwelt on in lines 58-71) is being obliquely satirized from the poem's beginning.

We have discovered that we are not medially between beast and angel; we are eccentric, and nearer beasts than anything.

From there, Rochester goes on to state the initial premise for his redefinition of "right reason" (lines 8-11): instead of relying on direct contact with experience through the senses for guidance, man foolishly guides himself by the misleading abstractions of the so-called "reason" we now employ (lines 8, 10-11). That premise is confirmed through two narratives (lines 12-30, 37-45). The first of these is tactically brilliant, for Rochester defies the logical procedures devised by the reason we now have and tries to persuade us by a vivid appeal to the senses. He depicts our reason not as a God-given inner light but as "an *ignis fatuus* in the mind" (line 12). Misled rather than illuminated by his inner light, man "climbs with pain / Mountains of whimseys, heaped in his own brain" (lines 16-17). Lost on his journey within, man reasons his way on till he falls into the hopeless skepticism of "doubt's boundless sea" (line 19), from which he emerges only at death (lines 25-26) with the certain knowledge of his lifelong mistakenness (line 28). Through the senses we are forced to recognize the nature of what we call reason. No wonder, then, that Rochester mocks the contemporary idea of man as a "reasoning engine" (line 29), as a neat, rational automaton. In the second narrative (lines 37-45) he goes on to suggest that our wit—the "vain, frivolous" (line 35), and dangerous play of the "reasoning engine['s]" intellect—threatens to ruin us in society (lines 36-37) as surely as the exercise of "reason" in the mind's inner world destroys us. So far, Rochester has obliquely attacked the neoplatonic/Augustinian view of man, and directly attacked the contemporary view of man as a "reasoning engine." He has demonstrated how what we call reason works inside us and within society. But he has not yet considered our prevailing idea of what reason is: he confutes the orthodox idea of human reason in lines 48-93.

In lines 48-71 a cleric appears as the speaker's "adversary." "I profess I can be very smart / On wit," he says (lines 53-54). His conceit and his paradoxical Enthusiasm ("I profess") for wit aimed at wit deftly characterize him. He enters the poem, however, mainly to celebrate "reason" as our distinguishing feature, which gives us a divine nescience. He claims blandly that God "in shining reason dressed" the soul "To dignify [man's] nature above beast" (lines 64-65). By the "aspiring influence" of reason, he goes on, "We take a flight beyond material sense" (lines 66-67). At last we know what Rochester means exactly by the "reason" he satirizes. He is in fact attacking the neoplatonic idea of reason as being ultimately the means by which we come to perceive the intelligible; that is, he attacks the idea of the mind as having a higher rational faculty than one which just organizes sense-perception. According

especially to the Augustinian development of the neo-platonic tradition, this "higher reason" leads to knowledge of the transcendent, and so to wisdom (*sapientia*).[9] The "adversary" who overstates that view may be a fool, but he represents a powerful orthodoxy, and so when the speaker begins his reply with "Hold, mighty man" (line 72), he is not just joking.

Having summarized what has long been claimed for human reason by orthodox Christianity (and recently restated by the Cambridge Platonists), Rochester then has his speaker bluntly repudiate it. He snaps: "'tis this very reason I despise" (line 75). His opposition to it eschews subtleties to make three points. First, because he imagines reason a "supernatural gift" (line 76), man foolishly compares his brief and self-disordered life with the calm existence of God (lines 76-80). Second, trusting in this concept of reason, man sets his mind towards the irrational, which he mistakes for wisdom (lines 81-89). Third, he therefore values the contemplative life as a supreme good, whereas to all appearances it is fantastic (lines 90-93). The last point mocks the idea of the isolated mind's questing for *sapientia*; in the conclusion to the first of the satire's deliberative orations, Rochester proceeds to argue that "right reason" aims at *prudentia*: the sane conduct of our lives in themselves and in relation to others. "But thoughts are given for action's government" (line 94), we are told, and "Our sphere of action is life's happiness" (line 96). Only a reason which deals with those two things—"action's government" for "life's happiness"—is said to be "right reason" (line 99), which "distinguishes by sense / And gives us rules of good and ill from thence" (lines 100-101). So within the traditional design for an argument expressing "right reason," Rochester has subversively redefined "right reason" in terms like Hobbes's. He has done so to indicate a starting point for a way of life which may be both libertine and ordered, because "right reason" and the impulse to pleasure (lines 102-105) have become harmonious, benignly excluding extremes from the conduct of life (lines 102-109).

The following argument on man's personality is both simpler and less hopeful than that on his intellect. Rochester says: "Thus I think reason righted, but for man, / I'll ne'er recant; defend him if you can" (lines 112-13). The argument on the personality takes up the issue of *prudentia*—the sane conduct of life—as the true wisdom at which we should aim, but its premise is the topos, "beasts are, in their degree, / As wise at least, and better far than [man]" (lines 115-16, see line 114). Two passages confirm the premise (lines 117-22, 128-38), as was the case earlier. The first of these proposes a syllogism in the vein of Sextus Empiricus, to prove that if a hunting dog acts more successfully than a politician, then it must fairly be thought the wiser (more prudent) of the two.[10] The second passage stresses that only man destroys his kind for the delight of it (line

131-32); Rochester intensifies Hobbes's view of man as by nature predatory and anarchic. The two passages confirming the premise, then, severally suggest that man has no distinctive capacity to achieve *prudentia* and, more important, that his personality in fact shows him as having a distinctive capacity to negate it. That depreciation of the human personality is developed in the ensuing set-piece. The famous set-piece on human motivation (lines 139-67) tries to confute a belief that the essentially mean personality of man can allow him to be truly altruistic, truly virtuous. Fear, in all its selfishness (line 148), underlies what seems virtuous in man: "The good he acts, the ill he does endure, / 'Tis all from fear, to make himself secure" (lines 155-56).[11] Through a series of striking epigrams, Rochester denies man an innate nobility; in so doing he denies man's intrinsic aspiration to high ideals and thus makes *prudentia* seem yet further from achievement by man than has been earlier implied. Moreover, having asserted the lack of altruistic virtue in human nature, Rochester at once proposes a major implication of such an attitude to man: "honesty's against all common sense: / Men must be knaves, 'tis in their own defence" (lines 159-60). Disorder, then, would seem to be built into human life; in the poem's second part, disorder and human meanness stand out as the only two constant things in society. In the conclusion to the satire's second deliberative oration (lines 168-73) Rochester neatly sums this up: "you see what human nature craves: / Most men are cowards, all men should be knaves" (lines 168-69). For Rochester, *prudentia* is a very qualified ideal.

Rochester's argument on the intellect seems to define a starting point for order in life by harmonizing "right reason" (newly understood) and the impulse to pleasure. The following argument on the personality suggests that man's nature breeds disorder. The two arguments seem to come down to this: reason can be righted and can order human behavior, but man cannot be essentially changed. In other words, there is a possibility of order in life, but that order will come from true reason co-operating with human meanness, and not from reason altering or dominating it. Any order achieved in life, then, will be precarious. In fact, the poem seems to imply that what order man does achieve will be personal, while his behavior towards others will tend to be much as it always has. So it would appear too easy to say that a reading of Hobbes explains Rochester's poem away; on the contrary, Rochester seems to be making his distinct interpretation of Hobbes's thinking on reason and man.[12]

Rochester's cautious balancing of ideas in the satire is emphasized by his epilogue to it.[13] Earlier in the poem, he has implied a universal meanness; now, he says that altruistic virtue may possibly exist (lines 179-215). The possibility, according to Rochester, is faint, but he grants that there may really be a good man in State (lines 179-

90) or Church (lines 191-215). However, Rochester pictures such a man by sequences of negatives. He seems to feel that a "good man" can be drawn only through contrasts with more familiar types. The point is simply that while a "good man" may exist, Rochester has yet to see one. So, given the counterpoise of its ideas, the satire understandably ends with juxtaposed contraries (lines 216-19, 220-21): if a "good man" (or, even, more than one) exists, Rochester will "recant" his earlier paradox of beasts' superiority to men, taking that "good man" as a moral guide—but whether or not such a person can be found, Rochester still asserts paradoxically that "Man differs more from man, than man from beast" (line 221). He stresses that we must have no illusions about what we are or where we are in the scheme of things.

Rochester's *A Satyr against Reason and Mankind* cannot be seen as a statement of mere nihilism; the poem's shrewdly designed argument is too poised and various for that familiar interpretation to be accurate. The poem may be wary in seeking a basis for order in existence, and it may indicate that the order we could hope for must necessarily be limited and precarious; nonetheless, it shows Rochester's pessimistic view of his world to be neither facile nor unbalanced. In the artistic circles of Charles's court, where libertine attitudes are much in vogue, Rochester alone uses libertine ideas both playfully and to offer a comprehensive analysis of experience, arguing what "right reason" and *prudentia* are within its contained anarchy.

Notes

1. This is not to impugn the well-known studies of the poem by Moore, Fujimura, and Main. Nor is it to impugn those studies of the Rochester canon which examine it among the other poems. See esp. V. De S. Pinto, "John Wilmot, Earl of Rochester," in *The Pelican Guide to English Literature,* ed. Boris Ford, 6 vols. (1957; rpt. Harmondsworth: Penguin, 1966), 4:142-55; Rachel Trickett, *The Honest Muse: A Study in Augustan Verse* (Oxford: Clarendon Press, 1967), esp. pp. 20-21, 82-84, 88-89; Harold Love, "Rochester and the Traditions of Satire," in *Restoration Literature: Critical Approaches,* ed. idem (London: Methuen, 1972), pp. 145-77; Dustin H. Griffin, *Satires Against Man: The Poems of Rochester* (Berkeley and London: Univ. of California Press, 1973); Earl Miner, *The Restoration Mode from Milton to Dryden* (Princeton: Princeton Univ. Press, 1974), pp. 373-76, 380-86, 388-90, 412-22; David Farley-Hills, *The Benevolence of Laughter: Comic Poetry of the Commonwealth and Restoration* (London: Macmillan, 1974), pp. 132-84; Raman Selden, *English Verse Satire 1590-1765* (London: Allen and Unwin, 1978), pp. 92-100.

2. Reference here and throughout is to David M. Vieth, ed., *The Complete Poems of John Wilmot, Earl of Rochester* (New Haven and London: Yale Univ. Press, 1968). For contrasting ideas in other poems by Rochester, see "The Submission," "Absent from thee," "The Mistress," and especially "'Twas a dispute," which are exceptional. For similar thinking by his contemporaries, see especially Mulgrave and Dryden, *An Essay upon Satire,* lines 168-79, 230-69.

3. I borrow the term "Carolean" from Robert D. Hume, as it is useful for distinguishing "Caroline" works from the later "Carolean." (I owe this reference to Professor Harold Brooks.)

4. See lines 32-40; for example, the vivid trope of line 33, the sly *sermocinatio* of line 35, *comprehensio* in line 36, and esp. the neat play of "Ceremonies" against "formality," lines 39-40.

5. David M. Vieth, whose chronology in his edition is the best we have, places *A Letter* after *A Satyr* while suggesting that both could have been written in 1675. For the purposes of my argument it doesn't matter which has precedence—though if *A Letter* does follow *A Satyr* it would seem that when Rochester had proposed where order might start in life, he nonetheless kept a clear eye on his society as it was, not as he thought it should be.

6. See Butler's *Satyr upon the Licentious Age of Charles the Second,* and discussion of it in my essay, "The Idea of a 'Restoration' and the Verse Satires of Butler and Marvell," *Southern Review* 14 (July 1981):131-42, pp. 134-36.

7. *Divisio* is the sixth part added to the more usual five. Rochester has *propositio* rather than *divisio*; he omits both *exordium* and *narratio* in the second section of the satire (some rhetoricians agree that *narratio* can be dispersed throughout the whole or omitted). For other accounts of the satire's design, see esp. Peter Thorpe, "The Non-Structure of Augustan Verse," *Papers on Language and Literature* 5 (Summer 1969):235-51, and Dustin H. Griffin, *Satires Against Man,* pp. 205-206. Eric Rothstein's *Restoration and Eighteenth-Century Poetry 1660-1780* (London: Routledge and Kegan Paul, 1981) appeared after the completion of this essay. Professor Rothstein also views the poem as having a deliberative design, but as forming a single and simply "Aristotelian oration" (p. 31, see p. 32). His view of the poem's argument and context also differs from that proposed in this essay.

8. This implies a rejection of St. Augustine's idea that the mind has a "higher intellect" able to perceive things eternal and so to achieve *sapientia*. For a different view of the intellectual contexts immediately relevant to the poem, see R. Wilcoxon, "Rochester's Philosophical Premises: A Case for Consistency," *ECS* [*Eighteenth-Century Studies*] 8 (Winter 1974-1975):183-201.

9. The argument for this is developed especially in *De Trinitate* (see *De Magistro*).

10. A fine irony, as Aristotle describes *prudentia* as the special virtue of the politician.

11. Graham Wallas has a useful account of fear in Hobbes's psychology in *The Great Society,* ch. 6. (This reference I owe also to Professor Brooks.)

12. This is not to ignore the influence of Montaigne, Boileau, et al. Boileau's eighth satire, especially, provides Rochester with a model for his attack on conventional views of reason. For all that, Rochester's poem has a scope and ambitiousness beyond the range of Boileau's.

13. On the probable origin of the epilogue, see Kristoffer F. Paulson, "The Reverend Edward Stillingfleet and the 'Epilogue' to Rochester's *A Satyr against Reason and Mankind,*" *PQ* [*Philological Quarterly*] 50 (October 1971):657-63.

Samuel J. Rogal (essay date September 1988)

SOURCE: Rogal, Samuel J. "The Earl of Rochester: 'Why Am I No Poet of the Times?'" *CLA Journal* 32, no. 1 (September 1988): 91-102.

[*In the following essay, Rogal examines Rochester's attitude towards his society and the Restoration monarchy.*]

If one were in a hurry to form a critical attitude toward John Wilmot, Second Earl of Rochester, he would simply observe that the most notorious resident of Charles II's Parnassian stable came into the world on the first day of April, and let it go at that. Should such a hasty approach prove unrealistic, one can always fall back upon Samuel Johnson's method; that great man admittedly gave over Rochester's poems to his amanuensis, George Steevens, "to castrate for the edition of the poets," an act that caused Dr. John Taylor to observe that "if Rochester had been castrated himself, his exceptionable poems would not have been written."[1] In the event that the Johnsonian system becomes too heavy a burden upon the critical conscience, one may, in the end, seek safety in the profundity of Edmund Gosse, who concluded that "the muse of Rochester resembles nothing so much as a beautiful child which had wontonly rolled itself in the mud, and which has grown so dirty that the ordinary wayfarer would rather pass it hurriedly by, than do justice to its native charms."[2]

Unfortunately, characterizations as those just cited, although not entirely inaccurate, have stood far too long as the principal means for describing the poet's life and then relating it to his literary career. Even more unfortunate, they become clichés, serving only to stamp the man a rake or a profligate, failing to consider the more important issues of how and why he became so.

At the risk of reducing matters of biography and literary history to a single paragraph, it seems sufficient to identify John Wilmot as the rare breed of literary animal who, although clearly typifying the age in which he lived, at the same time appeared to be struggling ferociously against its ideas and institutions. He was not so much a product of the Restoration as of the monarch who reaped the benefits from that event: an easygoing, pleasure-loving, and overly amorous Charles II, who tended more in the direction of his personal friends' affairs than he did toward matters concerning the nation; an extravagant man more interested in dumping public money into the purses of his male and female companions than in spending it for the good of all his subjects. Thus, in February 1661, Charles granted to the thirteen-year-old Rochester a pension of £500 per annum, retroactive to the preceding spring, as a token of appreciation for military and personal services rendered by the boy's father. Eight months later, after having received—simultaneously, as it were—a kiss on the left cheek from the Lord Chancellor of England and an M.A. from Oxford—the young earl and his tutor, Sir Andrew Balfour, embarked upon a four-year tour of France and Italy, a journey paid for by the Crown.

On Christmas day 1664, Rochester, now seventeen, but with his life more than half spent, presented himself to court. The next dozen years have become legend and certainly deserving of the highest rank in the chronicles of libertine living: the attempted abduction of Elizabeth Malet, participation in the Second Dutch War, marriage and maintenance of mistresses, immature pranks, duels, riotous drinking bouts, and involvement in at least two killings. Although the King never publicly expressed approval of those activities, he did little that was effective in discouraging them; his reactions ranged from pardons to short assignments outside London, to extended periods of exile from court. The ever grateful Rochester rarely wasted an opportunity to thank his sovereign: "All monarchs I hate, and the thrones they sit on. / From the hector of France to the cully of Great Britain" (ll. 32-33).[3]

Lest the young Earl be censured for bad rhythm, lack of respect, absence of taste, or all three, the point must be driven home immediately that the lines cited above indeed represent the essence of his attitude toward Charles and the nation—or at least that part of the nation with which the King chose to concern himself. For, despite his bold expeditions into the deepest recesses of London's dens of debauchery, Rochester's brief tenure on earth comes forth, especially in his poetry, as a serious struggle to find expression within the suffocating confines of "this saucy world," wherein "my prostituted sense be drawn / To every rule their misty customs spawn" (ll. 83, 85-86).[4] What compounded the struggle, of course, was a pattern of existence in which his intellect waged constant war with his appetites. Thus, when he lashed out at Charles, as the leader of a world comprised of fops, rakes, and whores, he could not escapes criticizing his own weaknesses and the erosion of his own intellect. Naturally, the struggle within him raised serious questions about the state and direction of his art: whether to obscure the shortcomings of imperfect world and riotous existence, thereby achieving qualified success as a flatterer, or to depict reality in sharp and harsh terms, thus condemning both himself and his verse.

Surely the route to fame and comfort would have proven no problem for the quick-witted Rochester. In fact, almost at the very moment the last spark from the pyre of Puritanism had extinguished itself, John Dryden flung open the gates and stepped onto the fertile fields of Augustan orthodoxy, a new world "Which in soft Centuries shall smoothly run." The restored Stuart prince could rest easy, for

> At home the hatful names of Parties cease
> And factious Souls are weary'd into Peace.
> The discontented now are only they
> Whose Crimes before did your Just Cause betray:
> Of those your Edicts some reclaim from sins,
> But most your Life and Blest Example wins.
> Oh Happy Prince, whom Heav'n hath taught the way
> By paying Vows, to have more Vows to pay!
> Oh Happy Age! Oh times like those alone,
> By Fate reserv'd for Great *Augustus* Throne!
> When the joint growth of Arms and Arts foreshew
> The World a Monarch, and that Monarch *You.*
>
> (ll. 293, 312-23)[5]

Hard on Dryden's heels, almost as though he feared that neoclassicism would deny him membership, came Edmund Waller. The post-parliamentarian, who had served both the first Charles and the first and last Lord Protector, cast his imitative eye upon St. James's Park and quickly determined his future course of action:

> Here a well-polish't Mall gives us the joy
> To see our Prince his matchless force imploy;
> His manly posture and his graceful meen
> Vigor and Youth in all his motion seen,
> His shape so lovely, and his limbs so strong,
> Confirm our hopes we shall obey him long.
>
> (ll. 57-62)[6]

One must not be too hasty to fling *Astraea Redux* or *On St. James's Park* into the same wastebin with later, mere windblown pieces of flattery as, for instance, Colley Cibber's birthday odes to George II. Neither Dryden nor Waller is particularly enamored of Charles; instead, each found himself drawn by an enthusiastic vision of a fresh beginning for British society, a world in which poet and merchant, courtier and minister, might promenade to the same tune while engaged in serious business and indulging in profitable recreation. If such a world should and could exist, it were far better to have it led by a Stuart than by a Cromwell.

From a certain but very limited point of view, the Restoration did indeed produce, especially for the nation's capital, a way of life governed by reason, dignity, and grace. The nightingales sang in Vauxhall Gardens; Charles fed his ducks and taught his spaniels to swim in St. James's Park; coaches paraded in the Ring in Hyde Park; *The London Gazette* came forth on Mondays and Thursdays; the great wits of the day gathered in the large coffee-houses in Covent Garden to gossip or to recite *Hudibras* and *Annus Mirabilis*; Dryden, Etherege, Wycherley, and Sedley hoisted London society upon the stage; Purcell made music at the Chapel Royal; Newton watched apples fall at Woolsthorpe; and South, Stillingfleet, Barrow, and Ken blessed God, King, and Nation from their pulpits. As long as people could keep their eyes and chins inclined toward Heaven, they would never lose sight of the best of all possible worlds.

Nevertheless, there existed another view of life, a world of pretension, poverty, and general ugliness that presented a sharp contrast to the order and beauty heralded by Dryden and Waller. The London of Charles II was a foul-smelling sewer of humanity: the breaths of its citizens reeked from too much bad wine, and its gutters overflowed with the contents of thousands of chamber pots. Its streets suffered from lack of decent paying and even worse lighting; the gentlemen of the road and the ladies of the night plied their trades in almost complete freedom, since an adequate police force had yet to be organized and the watchmen were practically useless. In the East End, a new diversion emerged, as London weavers rioted and smashed the looms of French Protestant silk weavers, the latter having supposedly been rescued from the bigotry of Louis XIV. If one grew tired of that activity, he could saunter down to the port of London and observe the most recent branch of British trade with the other side of the world that had developed seriously since the end of the Commonwealth—the slave traffic! Certainly, it is not altogether incorrect to assume that the plague of 1665 and the great fire in the following year were, in terms of the social and physical conditions of the town, blessings in disguise.

Little wonder, then, that Rochester, even in his most intemperate moments, could not possibly imagine or pay tribute to such a world as Waller and Dryden had

conjured forth. Toward the end of *Annus Mirabilis,* the latter peers through the thick smoke of the great fire and proclaims,

> Methinks already, from this chymic flame,
>   I see a city of more precious mold,
> Rich as the town which gave the Indies name,
>   With silver pav'd, and all divine with gold.
>
> (ll. 1169-72)[7]

John Wilmot dared not commit himself to that pot of gold at the end of Augustus's rainbow, since he had little idea of and even less concern for the London prior to the devastation of 1666. His focus, although often blurred, nonetheless hones in upon the ever present; because he cared only to see reality, he did not require a vision of the ideal. Society, as Rochester perceived it, belonged to the fops, the rakes, and the whores; the honest poet must identify its qualities and satirize its pretention—even if that meant condemnation of himself and his art. Thus, he smears Waller's mirage of St. James's Park with bold streaks from his realistic brush to produce an "all-sin-sheltering grove," populated by

> Whores of the bulk and the alcove,
> Great ladies, chambermaids, and drudges,
> The ragpicker, and heiress trudges.
> Carmen, divines, great lords, and tailors,
> Prentices, poets, pimps, and jailers,
> Footmen, fine fops do here arrive,
> And here promiscuously they swive.
>
> (ll. 25-32)[8]

Even the compiler of this catalogue of Restoration London society belongs in the list, as at the outset of the poem he readily identifies himself as one who will "still take care to see / Drunkenness relieved by lechery . . ." (ll. 5-6).

One need not read too deeply into Rochester's poetry before realizing that the key aspect of his struggle as would-be artist in a third-rate society was not so much what to criticize, but the manner by which to express the criticism. The poet may have been guilty of a thousand sins, but there is no doubting his honesty; he comes forth as a striking example of disillusioned man: bitter, disgusted, and irritable at himself for playing a leading role in the grand but meaningless game of Restoration life. To couch his bitterness and disgust in irrelevant platitudes would have been, at best, absurd, especially for the courtier who looked upon his contemporaries as fundamentally envious and dull. Rather, Rochester saw himself "Born to myself, myself I like alone / And must conclude my judgment good, or none." Therefore,

> If I designed to please, the way were then
> To amend my manners rather than my pen.
> The first's unnatural, therefore unfit,

And for the second, I despair of it,
Since grace is not so hard to get as wit.

(ll. 73-74, 25-29)[9]

The method, then, consisted mainly of peeling back the layers of silk and powder from the bodies of polite citizens, of chipping away the images and metaphors from classical poetry, revealing the obscene but authentic qualities of life by giving the hypocrite, the whore, and the devil their day in court.

If the center of Rochester's struggle with himself and his society can be easily located, the plan of his satiric forays is no less discernible. While his contemporaries strive for heaven (or for what they believe is heaven), he wallows in the slime of pure, realistic satire, a world in which nothing appears to be safe or sacred. At one moment he unfolds the image of **"Fair Chloris in a pigsty lay,"** lulled to sleep by the grunts of her unwashed charges; the dream consists of a violation upon the maid by a lustful swain, which, of course, causes her to awake. Chloris's return to consciousness constitutes an almost perfect solution to the grand moral dilemma that goes by the name of virginity:

> Frighted she wakes, and waking frigs.
>   Nature thus kindly eased
> In dreams raised by her murmuring pigs
> And her own thumb between her legs,
>   She's innocent and pleased.

(ll. 1, 36-40)[10]

On another occasion, Rochester pays a visit to Tunbridge Wells, seemingly the popular watering trough for persons of fashion, but actually a "rendezvous of fools, buffoons, and praters, / Cuckolds, whores, citizens, their wives and daughters." For all but ten of the 175 lines, the poet parades before the reader all manner of foppery; in the end, he can only sound the obvious note of exasperation: "what thing is man, that thus / In all his shapes, he is ridiculous?" The one consolation is found in his horse that will carry him away from the place: "For he, doing only things fit for his nature, / Did seem to me by much the wiser creature" (ll. 4-5, 166-67, 174-75).[11] From Tunbridge Wells the road leads directly to Whitehall Palace, surely for Rochester the most demoralizing sign of his ill-witted society. Why, he asks, in one of his frequent outbursts of pure frustration,

>   does something still permit
> That sacred monarchs should in council sit
> With persons highly thought at best for nothing fit,
> While weighty Something modestly abstains
> From princes' coffers, and from statesmen's brains,
> And Nothing there like stately Nothing reigns?

(ll. 37-42)[12]

Like Milton's Satan, the intellect of the Restoration court has been hurled headlong, down through chaoes;

its temple of Pandemonium exists not necessarily near the imaginative fiery lake, but in all too real locales: a dirty farmyard, Tunbridge Wells, and Whitehall Palace.

Rochester achieves the best results in attempting to express his personal displeasure with Restoration society in two of his more controlled pieces, *A Letter from Artemisia in the Town to Chloe in the Country* and *A Satyr Against Reason and Mankind.* Although the first effort focuses once again upon the sordid state of love in a third-rate society, where folly is attained "[b]y studious search, and labour of the brain," it contains, as well, some acid commentary upon the state of poets and poetry. Against a background of self-appointed wits who vie for praise and fame—and who ultimately fail in their attempts to produce legitimate art—the writer of the epistle early reaches the conclusion that "poetry's a snare." Under such conditions, the poet can only hope to become a court jester, "[c]ursed if you fail, and scorned though you succeed!" The device of a female persona allows Rochester to comment upon the shortcomings of his own intellectual art, for he realizes only too well that "Readers must reap the dullness writers sow." In his own instance, then, the epithet of "whore is scarce a more reproachful name / Than poetess—"(ll. 157, 16, 23, 260, 26-27).[13]

In the *Satyr Against Reason and Mankind,* where the poet appears at once classical, profound, and deeply disturbed, the emphasis is upon the superiority of unerring animal instinct over fallible human reason. Simply, Rochester distrusts reason; therefore, man—especially the poet's contemporaries—exists as a stupid creature. As a practitioner of murder and general cruelty even beyond the degree of animals, the late seventeenth-century version of the species unconsciously transforms his cherished reason into pure folly. Of course, the essence of the poem could hardly be termed original, since Rochester develops themes common to his age: the unreliability of speculative reasoning as an aid to solving problems beyond the scope of man, the preponderance of human error, and the eventual triumph of false pride. Learning may "bear him up awhile, and make him try / To swim with bladders of philosophy," but for man, eventually, "The vapour dances in his dazzling sight / Till, spent, it leaves him to eternal night" (ll. 20-21, 23-24).[14] Throughout, the poet surveys, with his distrusting eye, a wide range of mankind, from the clergy to the fools at court, concluding, first, that all men are knaves and, second, that "Man differs more from man, than man from beast" (l. 221). If nothing else, those ideas cast a clear beacon into the next century; they allow us to understand better the dilemma of Lemuel Gulliver among the Houyhnhnms and to trace the outline of Pope's "isthmus of a middle state."

However, there are two aspects of the *Satyr* that point to the very heart of Rochester's struggle with himself and with his own class. Fairly early in the piece, the poet offers a thinly veiled summary of his own misdirected existence:

> Then old age and experience, hand in hand,
> Lead him to death, and make him understand,
> After a search so painful and so long,
> That all his life he has been in the wrong.
> Huddled in dirt the reasoning engine lies,
> Who was so proud, so witty, and so wise.
>
> (ll. 25-30)

Aside from the opening reference to old age—one state in life that Rochester never came close to reaching—the lines exist as a harsh measure of self-criticism. Wit and pride gave him pleasure, but eventually that pleasure destroyed his happiness and only "made him venture to be made a wretch" (l. 32). The lament over his own failings, over the waste that has characterized his life, leads Rochester to seek out an ethical hero, one who might yet save the church, the court, the nation, and even himself from being completely overrun by pride. He asks for

> a meek, humble man of honest sense,
> Who, preaching peace, does practice continence,
> Whose pious life's a proof he does believe
> Mysterious truths, which no man can conceive.
>
> (ll. 212-15)

Whether such an ethical messiah could have calmed the fires of Rochester's dissatisfaction with himself and his world is another matter; at least the lines cited directly above provide some indication of the poet moving in the general direction of the spiritual conversion that would come only a few weeks prior to his death. Thus, almost four years after the ***Satyr*** he can demand of the world, "Let the ambitious zealot lay aside / His hopes of heaven, whose faith is but his pride . . ." (ll 3-4).[15]

Midway through his *Epistolary Essay* satirizing John Sheffield, Rochester inquires, "But why am I no poet of the times?" (l. 50). From the simplest point of view and, perhaps, the only one worth examining, the answer is to be found in the poet himself. "I have blasphemed by God, and libeled Kings," proclaims the Earl to the postboy, and then requests the most direct route to Hell. The boy quickly replies, "Ne'er stir: / The readiest way, my Lord, 's by Rochester" (ll. 14-17).[16] Actually, the quickest way to perdition was probably a merciful end for Rochester's struggles with himself and his times; what else could have been expected from one who seemed determined not to yield to form and custom? Certainly, he would never have become a flatterer,

> Half witty, and half mad, and scarce half brave;
> Half honest, which is very much a knave—
> Made up of all those halves, thou canst not pass
> For anything entirely but an ass.
>
> (ll. 31-34)[17]

Nor would he have permitted himself the luxury of old age, a state shut up within "the dull shore of lazy temperance" (l. 16).[18] For Rochester, the only legitimate existence, and thus the only valid form of expression, focused upon man's right to live in accordance with his natural impulses. He allowed himself little in the way of direction or even purpose; instead, he chose to be pushed along by "the pleasing billows of debauch" (l. 15). Nevertheless, as he sailed through one reckless experience after another, Rochester proved that English verse could accommodate the vitality that was so much a part of his nature. The unfortunate aspect of his life and art, as well as of his reputation as person and poet, was that this vitality remained muffled throughout much of his lifetime, since the first collection of his poems did not appear until after his death. But at least John Wilmot was able to supply future generations with a hard earned lesson. Perhaps the Age of Reason really became reasonable when, in 1733, the principal poet of the Augustan Age cautioned,

> Nature's road must never be preferred;
> Reason is here no guide, but still a guard:
> 'Tis here to rectify, not overthrow,
> And treat this passion more as friend than foe.
>
> (ll. 161-64)[19]

Notes

1. R. W. Chapman, ed., *Boswell's Life of Johnson* (London: Oxford Univ. Press, 1953), p. 869.

2. Edmund W. Gosse, "Rochester," in *The English Poets,* ed. Thomas Humphry Ward (London: Macmillan, 1898), II, 425.

3. "A Satyr on Charles II," in *The Complete Poems of John Wilmot, Earl of Rochester,* ed. David M. Vieth (New Haven: Yale Univ. Press, 1968), p. 61, lines 32-33; all references to Rochester's poems in my text are to this edition.

4. "An Epistolary Essay from M. G. to O. B. upon Their Mutual Poems," p. 147, lines 83, 85-86.

5. John Dryden, "Astraea Redux: A Poem on the Happy Restoration and Return of His Sacred Majesty Charles the Second," in *A Collection of English Poems, 1660-1800,* ed. Ronald S. Crane (New York: Harper and Row, 1932), p. 58.

6. Edmund Waller, "On St. James's Park, as Lately Improved by His Majesty," in Crane, p. 37.

7. John Dryden, "Annus Mirabilis: The Year of Wonders, 1666," in *John Dryden: Selected Works,* ed. William Frost, 2nd. ed. (San Francisco: Rinehart, 1971), p. 377.

8. "A Ramble in St. James's Park," p. 41, lines 25-32.

9. "An Epistolary Essay," pp. 147, 145.

10. "Song," pp. 27-28.

11. "Tunbridge Wells," pp. 73, 80.

12. "Upon Nothing," p. 119.

13. "A Letter from Artemisia in the Town to Chloe in the Country," pp. 104-12.

14. "A Satyr Against Reason and Mankind," p. 95.

15. "A Translation from Seneca's 'Troades,' Act II, Chorus," p. 150.

16. "To the Postboy," p. 131.

17. "On the Supposed Author of a Late Poem in Defence of Satyr," p. 133.

18. "The Disabled Debauchee," p. 116.

19. Alexander Pope, "An Essay on Man," in *Selected Poetry and Prose,* ed. W. K. Wimsatt, 2nd ed. (New York: Holt, 1972), p. 207.

Marianne Thormählen (essay date October 1988)

SOURCE: Thormählen, Marianne. "Rochester and *The Fall*: The Roots of Discontent." *English Studies* 69, no. 5 (October 1988): 396-409.

[*In the following essay, Thormählen explores the late-twentieth-century resurgence of interest in Rochester's poetry.*]

When Vivian de Sola Pinto suggested that John Wilmot, the second Earl of Rochester, should be called 'the great poet of unbelief' (as compared to Milton, 'the great poet of belief'), F. R. Leavis testily retorted, 'Rochester is not a great poet of any kind'.[1] In the succeeding decades, the question of Rochester's greatness was less interesting to critics than his artistic-cum-philosophical affiliations. The attribute 'major poet' is sometimes seen in discussions of the extent to which he may be said to represent such concepts as 'Augustan', 'Epicurean', 'Neo-Classicist', etc.; but it is usually incidental to the argumentation.

Still, the reasons for the current surge of interest in Rochester are worth considering. What is it about the writings of this gifted amateur, with their representations of late-seventeenth-century mores, that attracts so many late-twentieth-century scholars and students? The availability of two useful modern editions[2] of his poems has obviously made his work more accessible than it used to be, but then accessibility is not, on its own, a purveyor of interest. The patent obscenity of some poems which used to be difficult for non-scholars to obtain is no novelty to modern readers and thus insufficient as an explanation of Rochester's power of attrac-

tion. If the skill and elegance of his craftsmanship were the prime feature of that attraction, some of his contemporaries—Sedley and Dorset, for instance, the latter with the matchless ballad 'To all you ladies now at land' to his credit—should share the attention given to Rochester to a far greater extent than they do. And, of course, other seventeenth-century poets aimed highly enjoyable satiric volleys at hypocrisy, stupidity, and vanity without rousing anything like the comprehensive interest now given to Rochester.

All these aspects, and others too—the recent tercentenary of the poet's death is obviously a factor—are surely relevant to the contemporary appreciation of Rochester. But a study of Rochester scholarship in the last few decades reveals that his peculiar restlessness, his lack of equilibrium and harmony, constitutes the critical impulse in many studies devoted to his work. Some Rochester critics are themselves fully aware of the prevalence of an element of disquiet in the poet and describe this trait in clarifying remarks on his turbulent mind.[3] Others are less explicit on this point, but their discussions indicate their preoccupation with Rochester's unwillingness—or inability—to found his entire poetic utterance on a secure, affirmative, and readily paraphrasable argumentative basis. It is hardly unreasonable to assume that this poet, in whose work the pursuit of sensual pleasure often meets with disappointment and frustration, must appeal strongly to readers and critics whose formative years, three centuries later, were accompanied by an I-can't-get-no-satisfaction obbligato.[4]

Paradoxically enough, though, the element of disharmony that is so potent in Rochester's poetry is one that his critics tend to be reluctant to acknowledge as omnipresent and unmitigated. Much has been said about Rochester's values, but the general contention seems to be that even if they are sometimes hard to ascertain, and occasionally non-existent, Rochester was determined to achieve tenable ones. It is also usually felt that the direction which that determination took is discernible in his poetry. The wish to subject his work to some sort of classification on the basis of the values evinced in it is evident in a number of Rochester studies.[5]

However, a careful reading of the entire Rochester canon (for the purposes of this article, the poems which both David Vieth and Keith Walker attribute to him) fails to produce a reliable set of ethical conceptions. Aberrations in human behaviour are freely castigated, but a corresponding code of desirable conduct is lacking. Rochester offers no consistent system of values to hold on to; what is also absent in his oeuvre is, it seems to me, a manifest *desire* for such a system. Did Rochester, in Harold Love's words, 'struggle heroically to establish values of some kind'?[6] Knowledge of his

death-bed conversion and preceding conversations with Burnet makes such a struggle on the part of the man himself seem likely. It is curious, however, that his poetry contains so little in the way of evidence.

In my view, Rochester's pervasive restlessness and discontent do not appear to be rooted in an awareness of a lack of belief (in a wide sense) and an inability to attain unshakeable convictions. The speaker of the famous *Satyr,* for instance, is nothing if not sure of himself. His scathing condemnation of the aspirations, dealings, and motives of mankind does not betray the slightest doubt of the justness of his opinions. Even *if* his bleak picture of the human race were to be contradicted by the existence of some good and virtuous man, or men—and the speaker clearly does not think much of the possibility—such a paragon would not invalidate the argumentation in general, but serve to emphasise the viciousness of the rest of mankind. The cynicisms of *Upon Nothing* remain perfectly controlled and argued to the end; nothing in the poem suggests a desire for an affirmative antithesis to Nothing.[7]

If doubt and fruitless yearning for stable convictions do not account for the absence of peace, fulfilment, and achievement in Rochester's poetry, what are the causes of his discontent? Put briefly and simply, I think they are to be found in his realisation that sensual pleasure, which is repeatedly held up as the *summum bonum*[8] in his poems, is in itself so feeble, impermanent, and flawed. The poems that purport to advocate pleasure have little to say about the actual delights of drinking and lovemaking, the favoured pastimes. If a reluctant would-be mistress prefers honour and virtue to love, she is merely threatened (like so many other obdurate literary ladies) with the ravages of time, future infamy, or the impending demise of her adoring slave. No voluptuously detailed descriptions of the joys of the flesh (such as those with which Jonson's and Carew's Celias were to be enticed) are offered as bait. And the man who envisages his disreputable old age in **"The Disabled Debauchee"** can hardly expect to inspire young men to adopt the life of a rake by boasting about ill-natured pranks vaguely reminiscent of the anything-but-glorious Epsom brawl.[9] Rochester's Celia (in **"Upon his leaving his Mistriss"**), encouraged to become 'the Mistriss of *Mankind*', is depicted as a passive goddess of plenty; the pleasures she is capable of bestowing and receiving are never described. And when, in **"Against Constancy,"** the speaker argues that youth and sexual prowess inspire a wish to 'be often try'd', actual enjoyment seems to be less important than a high performance rating. The conclusion of this lyric is less than rapturous,

> Ile change a Mistress till i'me dead,
> and fate change me for worms.

Having urged the unrestrained pursuit of unrestricted pleasure, the speaker does not linger in descriptions of it, and of fulfilment in pleasure; instead, the 'change' metaphor is given a physical dimension that could not very well be grimmer.

Characteristically, too, the speaker in **"The Submission"** 'dissolves in a Rapture of Charms' not in the celebrated lady's actual embrace, but 'At the thought of those Joyes I should meet in her Arms'. Anticipation, not enjoyment, accounts for his ecstasy.

When the purveyor of **"The Advice"** speaks about harmony and the power of passion in lines 15-28, the attractive representation of the conventional image of the kissing brooks is incidental to his argumentation, which is geared to persuading a lady to yield to love. And when Artemiza pens those beautiful lines on 'Love, the most gen'rous passion of the mynde' that have caused so much debate as to whether this is what Rochester himself felt, she is not so much extolling this 'onely Joy' as deploring its debasement.

Why, then, do Rochester's poems urge addressees and readers to pursue sensual pleasure when they have so little to say about the rewards of that pursuit? Those who resist it due to various ethical considerations, or sheer anxiety about concomitant hazards, are berated and ridiculed, less because they deprive themselves of the best things in life than because they are stupid enough to let instinct be repressed by the tyranny of mere concepts (Virtue, Honour). Failure to pursue sensual gratification is thus primarily the result of a cognitive weakness, not a physical or an emotional one.

This does not explain why Rochester's poems sometimes deprecate those pleasures that are so passionately advocated. The paradox comes to a head, and to a certain extent resolves itself, in one of his finest lyrics, **"The Fall"**:

> How blest was the Created State
>   Of Man and Woman, e're they fell,
> Compar'd to our unhappy ffate!
>   We need not fear another Hell:
>
> Naked beneath cool Shades they lay,
>   Enjoyment waited on desire;
> Each member did their wills obey:
>   Nor could a wish set pleasure higher.
>
> But we, poor Slaves to hope and fear,
>   Are never of our Joys secure:
> They lessen still, as they draw near;
>   And none but dull delights endure.
>
> Then, Cloris, while I duty pay,
>   The nobler Tribute of a heart;
> Be not you so severe, to say
>   You Love me for a frailer part.

Rochester critics discussing this poem have drawn attention to the mechanical aspects of lovemaking in Paradise,[10] to the reciprocity that characterises those proceedings,[11] and to the comic dimension inherent in Rochester's representation of current, and traditional, ideas.[12] But **"The Fall"** offers more than a discourse on post-lapsarian love as compared to the perfection of Eden. These four stanzas relate the one to the other, showing how present pain and insufficiency are in fact bound up with the transgression of Adam and Eve.

The first three lines of the poem are traditional enough, but the fourth is startling: our 'unhappy ffate' is so miserable as to constitute a living hell, the only hell we shall ever know.[13] The idea that a languishing suitor's torment could be characterised as a hell on earth had been a commonplace for centuries, and many authors had borrowed the infernal motif in order to emphasise the sorrows of earthly existence. But Rochester's poem argues that a man and a woman who are lovers, and clearly committed to each other, are so far from reaping the enjoyment that should attend their relationship that the discrepancy between the ideal and the actual literally hurts like hell.

The next two stanzas embody the comparison between enjoyment in Paradise and the delights available to post-lapsarian lovers. The pivot on which the comparison turns is that the bliss that was Adam and Eve's was undisturbed by 'hope and fear'. Unworried by speculation and anticipation, as well as by notions of impermanence and unreliability (in the loved one and in the freshly-created body), the pre-lapsarian lovers possessed the ability to gratify their desires as soon as they arose, without impediments and delay, and without taking thought. Their bodies were completely subservient to their 'wills', and their minds in perfect harmony with both—the question of 'parts' in stanza four does not arise at all in this indivisible enjoyment. The line 'Nor could a wish set pleasure higher' could be related to Adam and Eve and taken to mean that they could conceive of no greater joy; but the applicability of the sentence seems to be more general than that: it is impossible for anyone to aim higher than that harmony of instant, unfailing compliance.

Consequently, the insistence of some critics on the 'mechanical copulation' of Adam and Eve in Rochester's poem is somewhat misleading. The second stanza is not merely concerned with smooth physical performance but with harmony—the harmony that was shattered by the Fall.

In calling pre-lapsarian existence 'blest', Rochester conforms to traditional usage; 'bliss' as a designation of life in Paradise is predominant in literary representations of Eden both before and after his time. Thomas Traherne's *Blisse* argues that 'All Blisse / Consists in

this, / To do as Adam did / And not to know those Superficial Toys / Which in the Garden once were hid'.[14] Sir Charles Sedley's *The Happy Pair* praises pre-lapsarian Man before the coming of 'PRIDE, that Architect of Hell' and 'plunging Avarice', affirming, 'Then then the new Inhabitant was blest, / Ease watch'd his Heart, and Peace secur'd his Breast'.[15] Both these poems deplore the subsequent advent of materialistic greed. The development in **"The Fall,"** on the other hand, is more strikingly reminiscent of the implications inherent in two quotations from *Paradise Lost*: Satan's resentment at Adam and Eve's enjoying 'thir full / Of bliss on bliss, while I to Hell am thrust, / Where neither joy nor love, but fierce desire' (IV. 508-9); and the injunction, some 270 lines later, 'Sleep on, / Blest pair; and O yet happiest if ye seek / No happier state, and know to know no more'.

As Ronald Berman pointed out, Rochester's Paradise is not Milton's;[16] but the ruinous effect of knowledge and desire is made abundantly clear in the third stanza of **"The Fall."** The tasting of the fruit from the Tree of Knowledge ended the blissful state where satisfaction attended on inclination and the inclinations of man and woman were in harmony with one another. The nature of sensual pleasure itself has changed. Enjoyment has become a thing to be coveted, while the glories it would hold in anticipation are tarnished and faded in fulfilment. In other words, 'our Joys' must be actively pursued, prove to be less than we hoped, and will not stay. Post-lapsarian existence thus has a temporal dimension unknown to the lovers in Eden. Permanent joy is now as impossible as permanent life; 'none but dull delights endure', whereas the slavery to hope and fear is a lasting condition. Rochester does not expressly state that this development was the result of purchasing knowledge, but that sad bargain is implied throughout the poem, and its title emphasises the event. The poet will have known Cowley's poem *The Tree of Knowledge*, whose third strophe is relevant not only to **"The Fall,"** but to Rochester's *Satyr* as well:

> The onely *Science* Man by this did get,
>> Was but to *know* he nothing *Knew*:
>> He straight his *Nakedness* did view,
> His ign'orant poor estate, and was asham'd of it.
>> Yet searches *Probabilities*,
>> And *Rhetorick*, and *Fallacies*,
>> And seeks by useless pride
> With slight and withering *Leaves* that *Nakedness* to hide.[17]

The account of man's loss of his happiness in lines 31-4 of the *Satyr* recalls the Fall while stressing the pernicious workings of pride:[18]

> *Pride* drew him in, as *Cheats*, their *Bubbles* catch,
> And makes him venture, to be made a *Wretch*.
> His wisdom did his happiness destroy,
> Aiming to know that *World* he shou'd enjoy.

Other authors had warned their audiences not to search for potentially harmful knowledge. Suckling, for instance, advised his 'fond youth' to 'stay here . . . and ask no more; be wise: / Knowing too much long since lost paradise'.[19] Montaigne's *Apologie de Raymond Sebond,* whose relevance to the *Satyr* has been suggested by several critics, bitterly denounced man's intellectual aspirations, stating that 'La presomption est nostre maladie naturelle et originelle' and that 'La peste de l'homme, c'est l'opinion de science'. The *Apologie* praises ignorance as being 'tant recommandée par nostre religion' and describes the Fall as the failure of man to comply with God's simple 'loy de pure obeïssance', brought on by the devil's promises of 'science et . . . cognoissance'.[20]

On the whole, however, sixteenth- and seventeenth-century accounts of the Fall and its consequences do not feature the debasement of sensual pleasure as the most important result of man's transgression. **"The Fall"** does. Not the loss of pre-lapsarian man's closeness to God, nor the forfeiture of immortality is what is rued by Rochester's speaker; the wreck of innocence and virtue does not provoke his lamentations, nor does the transformation of pure connubial raptures to 'foul concupiscence' or the harsh terms imposed by God on human existence. The quality of pleasure is his sole concern, and the fact that it has suffered is the cause of his distress.

The third stanza of **"The Fall,"** then, laments the diminution of pleasure due to the advent of 'hope and fear' and the discrepancy between anticipation and fulfilment. Post-lapsarian lovers are cursed with thoughts, insights, and emotions that were unknown in Paradise, where the perfect harmony of the Creation precluded their existence.

In affirming that the lovers in Paradise had sexual intercourse before the Fall, Rochester conforms to a tradition which includes St. Augustine, representatives of mediaeval scholasticism such as Peter Comestor's *Historia Scholastica,* and, of course, Milton.[21] In fact, Book XIV of *De Civitate Dei*—especially §§ xxiii and xxiv—contains expressions which strongly resemble certain turns of phrase in **"The Fall."** Speaking about the permissibility of procreation if nobody had sinned, St. Augustine said,

> Et ideo illae nuptiae dignae felicitate paradisi, si peccatum non fuisset, et diligendam prolem gignerent et pudendam libidinem non haberent. Sed quo modo id fieri posset, nunc non est quo demonstretur exemplo. Nec ideo tamen incredibile debet videri etiam illud unum sine ista libidine voluntati potuisse servire, cui tot membra nunc serviunt.

The English translation of the last sentence (in the Loeb edition of 1966, by Philip Levine) underlines the resemblance, 'Nevertheless, that is no reason why it should seem incredible that the will, which is now obeyed by so many members, might also have been obeyed in the absence of this lust by that one part as well'.[22]

St. Augustine's emphasis, however, is on procreation brought about as a result of sexual intercourse taking place at a proper time, and to a proper extent, to ensure conception. This utilitarian view of erotic activity is so far removed from Rochester's picture of the pleasures of Paradise as to provoke a suspicion that the resemblance noted above might even embody a subtle mockery of the Augustinian point of view. As for *Paradise Lost,* Milton's encomium on 'wedded Love' (IV. 743 ff.) certainly employs some sensuous imagery—'Here Love his golden shafts employs', etc.—but the pertinence of procreation is clearly stated in lines such as 'Our Maker bids increase, who bids abstain / But our destroyer, foe to God and man?'

Rochester's portrayal of the sensual bliss enjoyed by Adam and Eve contains no hints of men being made by and by. There is no purpose to their pleasures except the immediate, effortless satisfaction of their appetites. In this respect, Rochester's pre-lapsarian lovers resemble the happy animals of seventeenth-century literature in France and England more than contemporary accounts of Adam and Eve. A well-known example is supplied by Rochester's contemporary, Mme. Deshoulières, in her eulogy on sheep, *Les Moutons*:[23]

> Hélas! petits Moutons, que vous êtes heureux!
> Vous paissez dans vos champs sans souci, sans allarmes
>   Aussi-tôt aimés qu'amoureux,
> On ne vous force point à rêpandre des larmes;
> Vous ne formez jamais d'inutiles désirs.
> Dans vos tranquilles coeurs l'amour suit la nature;
> Sans ressentir ses maux, vous avez ses plaisirs.

Mme. Deshoulières' sheep need not envy man 'cette fière raison dont on fait tant de bruit', and she reassures them that they are far happier than human beings, who have to recognise that 'Il n'est dans ce vaste Univers / Rien d'assûré, rien de solide'. Clearly, the insistence in the *Satyr* on beasts being 'As wise at least, and better far than [man]' need not be exclusively indebted to the 'theriophily' (Boas's term) of Montaigne and Boileau.[24]

The representations of ideal human love found in those classical authors with whom Rochester was familiar do not usually depict sexual enjoyment as being devoid of effort, the lovers being 'aussi-tôt aimés qu'amoureux'. Ovid, for instance, argues that 'quod licet, ingratum est', issuing the following recommendation, 'speremus pariter, pariter metuamus amantes, / et faciat voto rara repulsa locum' (*Amores* II.xix). Lucretius' description of primitive man in Book V of *De Rerum Natura* speaks of Venus uniting rambling lovers in the woods, which certainly suggests uninhibited enjoyment. Still, although such unions would sometimes have been due to mutual passion, Lucretius says that the woman might have been forced or bribed ('vel violenta viri vis atque impensa libido / vel pretium, glandes atque arbita vel pira lecta'; V.964-5. Of course, the glum description of the fallacies of sexual love in Book IV offers a rather depressing picture of the realm of Venus). Pleasure as defined by Epicurus is far too passive and too closely associated with the avoidance of pain of fit in with Rochester's concentration on the joys of the flesh.[25] Profligacy was not advocated by Epicurus, and he insisted that 'Every desire must be confronted with this question: what will happen to me, if the object of my desire is accomplished and what if it is not?'[26]—deliberations of a kind that Rochester's Adam and Eve were mercifully spared.

It should perhaps be added that the effortless gratification of sexual desire was not a prime feature in classical descriptions of the Golden Age. The loss of primitive man's blissful state is more often contemplated in connexion with the advent of strife and avarice (as in Traherne's and Sedley's poems), and of toil, than in conjunction with the decrease of sensual pleasure and sexual capacity.[27]

When domestic poets of the sixteenth and seventeenth centuries lament the passing of a golden age of uninhibited love, there are two main reasons for their regret: one is that the despised laws of civilisation have restricted the choice of partners; the other that present-day lovers have to submit to the irksome preliminaries of wooing. When, for instance, the speaker of Donne's XVIIth *Elegy* ('Variety') exclaims, 'How happy were our Syres in ancient times', he is thinking of the freedom from 'honour' and 'opinion' enjoyed by promiscuous primitive man—a freedom the loss of which Dryden would later regret in the opening lines of *Absalom and Achitophel*. (The line 'Women were then no sooner asked then won' may seem to recall line 6 in **"The Fall,"** but Donne's elegy has much more in common with other poems of Rochester's—for instance **"Womans Honor"** and the *Very Heroicall Epistle in Answer to Ephelia*—than with **"The Fall."**) Richard Lovelace's *Love made in the first Age: To Chloris* vents the would-be lover's weariness of a particularly tedious pursuit, that of persuading a prospective mistress by means of lavishing praise on her (Rochester satirised this universal occupation in **"A Ramble in Saint James's Parke,"** lines 75-9, and **"Tunbridge Wells,"** lines 104-9): 'Thrice happy was that golden Age, / When Complement was constru'd Rage'.[28]

One poem which also applauds spontaneous lovemaking, and which does so against the background of pre-lapsarian bliss, is Edmund Waller's *The Fall*. Farley-Hills rightly brings this poem into conjunction with Rochester's; there can be little doubt that Rochester

knew it. Waller's lyric outlines a 'happy chance' where a youth accidentally falls on top of a girl. The result is commended in the conclusion, addressed to the 'nymph', 'If aught by him amiss were done, / 'Twas that he let you rise so soon'. The situation resembles the one in Rochester's **"Song"** beginning 'As Chloris full of harmless thought' more than the latter's **"The Fall."** In Waller's poem, the new lovers are compared to Adam and Eve:

> 'Twas such a chance as this made all
> The world into this order fall;
> Thus the first lovers, on the clay,
> Of which they were composed, lay.
> So in their prime, with equal grace,
> Met the first patterns of our race.[29]

There is no suggestion here that post-lapsarian love is inferior to the joys of Paradise; on the contrary, Waller's young lovers are seen as recreating the pleasures of Eden.

A comparison between Waller's and Rochester's poems with the same title demonstrates the latter's independence in handling traditional motifs. The preceding review of literary texts dealing with the bliss enjoyed by lovers of past ages has testified to that independence, too. Rochester has made use of imagery and vocabulary found in a large number of seventeenth-century literary discourses on love, adapting them to his own poetical concerns. **"The Fall"** is a particularly instructive instance of his originality. An awareness of this originality serves to sharpen the reader's attention to Rochester's distinctive mode of argumentation.

As Farley-Hills points out, Rochester's poem makes it clear that it is impossible to return to Paradise. In the final stanza of **"The Fall,"** the contrast between love in Eden on the one hand and post-lapsarian joys on the other is followed by a sombre conclusion, a conclusion whose scope is narrower than that of the preceding discussions. It focuses on the speaker's own relationship with his lady. The application is concrete, but the relationship itself is not without ambiguities. Why, for instance, is the tribute of the speaker's heart said to be 'nobler' than his *pars pessima*, that 'worst part of me' (**"The Imperfect Enjoyment"**) whose failure to perform according to its owner's will is implicit in the whole poem? Is the 'nobility' merely ironical, as Farley-Hills suggests (*Rochester's Poetry*, p. 51), and the whole situation patently ridiculous? Does the stanza allow for theorising on a subject of interest to more than one recent Rochester critic, namely the question of the ascendancy of either sex over the other ('sexual politics' or, to borrow the term used by a mediaeval expert, 'maistrye')?

On the face of it, the argumentation seems straightforward enough. The male speaker asserts his devotion to his mistress, begging her to refrain from expecting physical performance in excess of what he is able to supply. To the extent that the final stanza relies on the previous one ('Then . . .'), he is suggesting that this physical weakness is no fault of his; it is an aspect of post-lapsarian existence. He reminds her of the superiority of the tribute he bestows on her, hoping that she will, in consequence, bear with the short-comings of his 'frailer part'. But this bald review of the lover's plea does not do full justice to the underlying subtlety of these ostensibly simple lines.

To begin with, the word 'duty' sets the key for the individual man-woman relationship which provides the core of the poem's conclusion. Reinforced by 'pay' and 'Tribute', it imparts a feudal dimension to that relationship, according to the OED definition 'payment made in recognition of feudal superiority'.[30] (This element is weakened in David Vieth's edition, where the copy-text has 'duly' instead of 'duty'—'Then, Chloris, while I duly pay / The nobler tribute of my heart'. This reading appears less rugged to present-day readers, and other modern editors have also adopted it; but the pertinent vassalage aspect suffers badly in consequence.)

It should be noted that **"The Fall"** is not the only Rochester poem to suggest that a woman plays the part of a feudal lord, served by a male vassal. The **"Song"** beginning 'What Cruel pains *Corinna* takes' ends in an ironic twist:

> The Scorn she bears so helpless proves,
>   When I plead Passion to her,
> That much she fears, (but more she loves,)
>   Her Vassal should undo her.

In his imitation of Ovid's *Amores* II.ix, Rochester renders the conclusion 'ambobus populis sic venerandus eris' as 'The Vassall World, is then thy owne', introducing a feudal element in the adoration of the ruler Cupid by both sexes.

Finally, Rochester's second **"Prologue to The Empress of Morocco"** includes a humorous reference to vassalage in the elaborate, and double-edged, compliments to Charles II. The woman speaker reminds the monarch that he may, if he neglects the just claims of the ladies, find that they 'are things / Born to kil Vassals, and to conquer Kings'.

These representations of vassalage (with the exception of the Ovid translation) also attest to female superiority; but it is qualified by suggestions of the vassal's triumph (**"Song"**) and of the supremacy of the King and Love (the **"Prologue"**). As Reba Wilcoxon pointed out,[31] Rochester's sardonic lines **"To his more than Meritorious Wife"** (where, incidentally, the word 'Duty' also has feudal connotations) make fun of the notion of the woman as a feudal lord. Is the sway of the mistress in **"The Fall"** similarly undercut by implied limitations?

While the third stanza seemed to include mankind as a whole in its dejected account of quotidian pleasures, the female addressee is undoubtedly better off than her lover in the fourth. What, then, are the reasons for her advantage?

In a careful and interesting discussion of 'Libertinism and Sexual Politics' in Rochester's poetry (see n. 10), Sarah Wintle argues that

> Rochester in this poem seems to see women's greater sexual strength as a result of the Fall. Either way, what one might call the political implications are grim. Sexual equality, even in Paradise, points to a bleak notion of contract: I use you, you use me. Otherwise, in a fallen world, the man can pretend to the nobler virtues of culture, but natural female dominance threatens.

There can be little doubt of the essential truth of the first statement. Female superiority is a result of the Fall, but whether it can be referred to as 'greater sexual strength' is perhaps debatable. As Wintle pointed out in a previous passage, the 'human instrument is untrustworthy' outside Paradise. In view of plain and fundamental biological facts, the fallibility of the body is a greater source of anxiety to men. This, however, hardly gives women greater sexual *strength*; and I am not certain that 'natural female dominance' is altogether adequate as a designation for the advantages inherent in the option of passivity. But the main question raised by Wintle's discussion is whether the issue of sexual equality involves a 'bleak notion of contract: I use you, you use me'. Surely the second stanza of **"The Fall"** presents the joys of Paradise as indivisible and mutual (cf. above on pre-lapsarian harmony). If there is any bargaining in the poem, it consists in the lover's wish that his 'duty', the 'Tribute of a heart', will be accepted by his mistress as an adequate compensation for physical inadequacy.

The absence of any clues as to the state of *her* heart does not augur well for him. She clearly matters to him as a person (as Corinna does to the speaker in **"The Imperfect Enjoyment"**); that is why it worries him that he might not be able to satisfy her, and he is afraid that *she* only wants him for whatever sexual services he can render her. It is somewhat surprising that this reversal of the classic only-want-one-thing pattern has not been given more attention by critics interested in Rochester's views on relations between the sexes.

The lover's anxiety lends a deeper dimension to the feudal aspect of the relationship. A vassal offers service to his feudal lord in return for security and the use of property. If Cloris finds the services of her lover unsatisfactory, and his duty insufficient, he must fear that she will withdraw the privileges she has granted.

This reading of **"The Fall"** sees the poem as a fundamentally serious admission of personal, and painful, inadequacy, complemented by an excuse for it and a plea for mercy. By contrast, Farley-Hills stresses the irony of the concluding stanza, arguing that the lover's '"frailer part", inhibited by hopes and fears, has failed to rise to the occasion. The situation is ribald and ludicrous. Man is made to look a fool standing there with his fool's bauble. But the poet (and we, too, the readers) can laugh' (*Rochester's Poetry,* p. 51).[32] How sincere is **"The Fall"**?

A definite reply presupposes that certainty in respect of Rochester's personal feelings and convictions which, as I have maintained elsewhere (see n. 5), we do not and cannot possess. It is characteristic of Rochester's 'spirit of wit' that an ironic dimension can be felt in everything he wrote. This is one reason for the shakiness of claims (to quote an instance with some relevance to this discussion) that Rochester really favoured equality between the sexes and that whenever a poem seems to suggest something else, the poet is merely joking.[33]

Farley-Hills states that the word 'nobler' is indebted to 'the conventional, platonic assumption that spiritual love is superior to sexual love', which is surely true. Unfortunately, however, his reading of 'duty'—'the lover's miserable offer of his duty as the best he can do'—misses the point of the feudal tribute; 'duty' is taken to mean 'obligation' and given highly unfavourable connotations as a result.

The word 'nobler' need not be quite as ironic as Farley-Hills feels it to be. In the first place, the heart is one of those parts of the body 'without which life cannot be maintained' and hence by definition 'noble' (OED s.v. 'noble', II.7.c; the OED lists three seventeenth-century instances). Secondly, in the context of this poem—the **"SONG of a young LADY To her Ancient Lover"** is a different case—'nobler' refers to a part of the lover which he is able to control and free to bestow on his mistress. His heart is thus invested with the capacity and liberality that are lacking in his 'frailer part' and hence by comparison 'nobler'. (The OED states that the word 'noble' is frequently found 'in the comparative and superlative, denoting superiority to other things of the same name'. It might be added that Dr. Johnson includes the definition 'free, generous, liberal' under 'noble'.)

Whatever view one takes of deliberations of this kind, the chivalrous attitude of the lover in **"The Fall"** cannot be proved to be a more genuine representation of Rochester's own feelings than, for instance, the expostulations in the **"Song"** beginning **'Love a Woman! y'are an Ass'**. (After all, it is hardly unnatural for a man whose life was largely dominated by women—not only mistresses but also his wife, mother, and daughters, all with claims on him—should sometimes erupt in imprecations against the whole sex and gratefully flee to all-male company, dispensing with the

pain and uncertainties that attend upon intercourse with women.) It can, however, be argued that the views and emotions articulated in **"The Fall"** are more profoundly relevant to the body of the poet's work. When it seems to me that **"The Fall"** is particularly interesting in the context of Rochester's poetry as a whole, it is because it sheds light on a central preoccupation in his poetry: the superiority of sensual pleasure over all other sources of gratification in life *and* the nagging realisation that sensual pleasure is sadly apt to fall short of human desire.

No other poem of Rochester's outlines this clash of convictions as starkly as **"The Fall."** In addition, this poem offers an ideal (pre-lapsarian harmony in love) and an explanation for the loss of that ideal (the Fall, the result of the fatal pursuit of knowledge). Despite the constant inconsistencies in Rochester's poetry, the contentions voiced in the first three stanzas of **"The Fall"** are not invalidated by any other poem; and his letters contain a fair number of similar statements. While this defence of the basic sincerity of **"The Fall"** is a highly limited as well as an essentially negative one, it is still unusually solid where Rochester is concerned.

To return to the point of departure, a search for Rochester's 'values' involves an assumption that the poet—explicitly or implicitly—proposes certain philosophical or ethical standards. Such an assumption hardly seems relevant to the pressing concerns contained in lyrics such as **"The Fall."** Rochester appears to me to express a condition rather than to suggest remedies for one. As Barbara Everett showed, mockery and denial are facets of that condition; but so is, I think, a realisation that although even the best parts of it are vastly inferior to that paradise that was lost when human beings were no longer content with the perfect harmony of bodies and wills, those best parts are still—in the words of a twentieth-century poet sometimes reminiscent of Rochester—'not to be despised'.

Notes

1. In 'The Line of Wit', published in Leavis's *Revaluation.*

2. David M. Vieth (ed.), *The Complete Poems of John Wilmot, Earl of Rochester* (New Haven and London, 1968); Keith Walker (ed.), *The Poems of John Wilmot Earl of Rochester* (Oxford, 1984). Quotations in this article are from the latter edition.

3. See, for example, Dustin Griffin's informative introductory chapter in his *Satires Against Man: The Poems of Rochester* (Berkeley/Los Angeles/ London, 1973), esp. pp. 10-20, and Reba Wilcoxon, 'Rochester's Philosophical Premises: A

Case for Consistency', *Eighteenth-Century Studies* 8 (Winter 1974/75), 198 ('The absence of *ataraxia* [previously defined as "imperturbability"] in Rochester is, I would argue, the source of his art, and, paradoxically, the reason that some commentators see him as a poet in search of belief or of identity'). See also K. E. Robinson, 'Rochester's Dilemma', *The Durham University Journal* LXXI.2 (N.S. XL.2), June 1979, 223-31, and David M. Vieth, '"Pleased with the Contradiction and the Sin": The Perverse Artistry of Rochester's Lyrics', *Tennessee Studies in Literature* 25 (1980), 35-56.

4. Previous generations of critics were alive to this dimension in Rochester's work, too; see for instance Fredelle Bruser, 'Disproportion: A Study in the Work of John Wilmot, Earl of Rochester', *University of Toronto Quarterly* XV.4 (July 1946), 384-96 and Ronald Berman, 'Rochester and the Defeat of the Senses', *The Kenyon Review* XXVI.2 (Spring 1964), 354-68.

5. The persistent contradictions and inconsistencies in Rochester's poetry are commented on in an article by the present author, 'Rochester and Jealousy: Consistent Inconsistencies', *The Durham University Journal* LXXX.2 (N.S. XLIX.2), June 1988, 213-223. This article contains detailed discussions of *A Ramble in Saint James's Parke* and *The Mistress.*

6. See the Introduction to *The Penguin Book of Restoration Verse* (Harmondsworth, 1968), p. 27. (Love's words regarding Rochester's 'cult of vandalism', some fifteen lines earlier, made an important point; cf. n. 7 on Barbara Everett's essay.)

7. While I agree with Paul C. Davies that Rochester's verses possess 'moral assurance', I cannot see that his 'weighty Somthing' constitutes a 'positive standard'. See 'Rochester: Augustan and Explorer', *The Durham University Journal* LXI.2 (N.S. XXX.2), March 1969, 60. In a highly stimulating discussion of 'The Sense of Nothing' in Rochester's poetry, Barbara Everett established that even Rochester's best critics tend to 'over-stress the "positive" aspects of his work'; in Jeremy Treglown (ed.), *Spirit of Wit: Reconsiderations of Rochester* (Oxford, 1982), p. 27. David Vieth has recently expressed the hope that 'more critics will recognise that the temptation to find a consistent philosophy in Rochester is a simplistic delusion'; see *Rochester Studies 1925-1982: an Annotated Bibliography* (New York/London, 1984), p. xvii.

8. See Reba Wilcoxon, 'Rochester's Philosophical Premises', 200.

9. This incident is described in many Rochester studies; see for example Vivian de Sola Pinto, *Enthusiast in Wit: A Portrait of John Wilmot Earl of Rochester 1647-1680* (London, 1962; a revised edition of Pinto's *Rochester: Portrait of a Restoration Poet*), pp. 162-3.

10. See Berman, 'Rochester', 357, and Sarah Wintle, 'Libertinism and Sexual Politics' in Treglown (ed.), *Spirit of Wit,* pp. 154-5.

11. Wintle, loc. cit.

12. See David Farley-Hills, *Rochester's Poetry* (London, 1978), pp. 47-51. (Cf. also below.)

13. The contention that death ends all human life is also expressed in *Upon Nothing* and in Rochester's translation of a fragment from Seneca's *Troades,* beginning, 'After Death, nothing is, and nothing Death'.

14. In the *Penguin Book of Restoration Verse,* p. 79.

15. In *The Poetical and Dramatic Works of Sir Charles Sedley,* Vol. I, ed. by Vivian de Sola Pinto (London, 1928), 65.

16. 'Rochester', 357. Griffin says that Rochester may well have read *Paradise Lost* (*Satires Against Man,* p. 215n), and it is likely that he did.

17. *The English Writings of Abraham Cowley,* ed. A. R. Waller (Cambridge, 1905), *Cambridge English Classics,* p. 45.

18. The importance of pride as a cause of the Fall is related to Restoration literature in Dale Underwood's *Etherege and the Seventeenth-Century Comedy of Manners* (New Haven and London, 1957); see especially pp. 31-6.

19. 'Against Fruition' in *The Poems, Plays and Other Remains of Sir John Suckling,* Vol. I, ed. by W. Carew Hazlitt (London, 1892, the second rev. ed.), 18. An informative scholarly discussion of the against-fruition convention, and Suckling's importance to it, is found in a study by Richard E. Quaintance Jr., 'Passion and Reason in Restoration Love Poetry' (diss., Yale 1962), pp. 70-158.

20. Pp. 28 and 83-4 in Paul Porteau's 1937 edition of *L'Apologie.*

21. See J. M. Evans, *Paradise Lost and the Genesis Tradition* (Oxford, 1968), pp. 46, 94, and 169, and Joseph E. Duncan, *Milton's Earthly Paradise: A Historical Study of Eden* (Minneapolis, 1972), p. 180.

22. Quaintance draws attention to the relevance of *De Civitate Dei* in 'Passion and Reason', p. 218n, quoting a pertinent passage from § xxiv.

23. Quoted in George Boas, *The Happy Beast in French Thought of the Seventeenth Century* (New York, 1966; a reprint of the 1933 edition), pp. 147-8. This poem would seem to have been an early work, and Rochester may have come across it during one of his visits to the French Court.

24. It is interesting that Rochester's *Tunbridge Wells,* believed by Vieth to have been written in 1674, should refer to animals as 'Thrice happy beasts'. In that same year, Flatman's Pindaric ode *The Disappointed* was printed in a collection of poems by this poet, whom Rochester accused of being a 'Slow Drudge, in swift Pindarique straines'. The last strophe of *The Disappointed* begins, 'Thrice happy then are beasts, said I . . . They only sleep, and eat, and drink, / They never meditate, nor think'. In Saintsbury (ed.), *Minor Poets of the Caroline Period,* Vol. III (Oxford, 1921), 360.

25. Cf. Thomas Franklin Mayo, *Epicurus in England (1650-1725),* (Dallas, 1934), pp. 174-5.

26. *Epicurus: The Extant Remains,* ed. Cyril Bailey (Oxford, 1926), pp. 116-17.

27. See Arthur O. Lovejoy and George Boas, *Primitivism and Related Ideas in Antiquity* (Baltimore, 1935), Vol. I of *A Documentary History of Primitivism and Related Ideas, passim.*

28. *The Poems of Richard Lovelace,* ed. by C. H. Wilkinson (Oxford, 1930; I have used the reprinted edition of 1953), p. 146.

29. In *The Poetical Works of Edmund Waller,* ed. Thomas Park (London, 1806), Vol. I, 60. See Farley-Hills, *Rochester's Poetry,* pp. 49-51.

30. A well-known example of 'duty' being used to denote a vassal's tribute is found in the opening sonnet of Daniel's *Delia,* where the third line reads, 'Returning thee the tribute of my dutie' (about the poet's labours). On the feudal significance of 'dutie' in this context, see Lars-Håkan Svensson, *Silent Art: Rhetorical and Thematic Patterns in Samuel Daniel's* Delia (Lund, 1980), pp. 35-6.

31. In 'Rochester's Sexual Politics', *Studies in Eighteenth-Century Culture* 8, ed. Roseann Runte (Madison, 1979), 139-40.

32. The nature of the actual situation is a debatable matter. Farley-Hills, following Quaintance, feels that the title of the poem embodies a reference to 'the detumescence of the uncompliant penis'. Griffin, in his short but lucid account of *The Fall* (*Satires Against Man,* pp. 108-9), implicitly questions this view and asserts that 'the poem expresses a general disillusion, felt by both man and woman, with all sensual pleasures'. As far as I can see, *The Fall* does not outline any particular erotic predicament.

33. This is a somewhat drastic summary of Reba Wilcoxon's main argument in 'Rochester's Sexual Politics'.

Germaine Greer (essay date 2000)

SOURCE: Greer, Germaine. "The Female Impersonator." In *John Wilmot, Earl of Rochester,* pp. 45-53. Devon, U.K.: Northcote House, 2000.

[*In the following excerpt, Greer discusses instances in Rochester's poetry in which he adopts a female persona.*]

Nowadays few male poets would dare to adopt a female voice, but in the seventeenth century poets as apparently macho as Ben Jonson, who had killed a man, did not shrink from speaking as women of women's affairs. Marvell could be a nymph upon occasion. Rochester had no hesitation in writing in a female voice; indeed, adopting a female persona seems to have permitted a kind of paradoxicality in his thinking that was not accessible to masculine authority. The classical precedent was to be found in the *Heroides,* Ovid's impersonation of the most famous heroines of antiquity, although every dramatist of every age has written for heroic female characters.

In 1673 Rochester impersonated a real woman in order to chastise a fellow-courtier. Negotiations for the marriage of Henrietta Maria Price, one of Queen Catherine's Maids of Honour, had been jeopardized by the boasting of Lord Chesterfield, erstwhile Chamberlain to the Queen, that the lady was in love with him. Miss Price could not afford to antagonize so powerful a personage but she had somehow to stop his mouth. Rochester came to the rescue by penning a note for her to include with the rich present of a pair of Italian gloves:

> My Lord—
> These are the gloves that I did mention
> Last night and 'twas with the intention
> That you should give me thanks and wear them,
> For I most willingly can spare them.

Having impersonated the embarrassed young woman, it was easy to switch to impersonating the presumptuous grandee himself.

> When you this packet first do see,
> 'Damn me,' cry you, 'she has writ to me;
> I'd better be at Bretby still
> Than troubled with love against my will.
> Besides, this is not all my sorrow:
> She's writ today, she'll come tomorrow.'

Chesterfield took the present and the point that it was prompted by

> neither love nor passion
> But only for your recreation.
>
> (Walker, 61-2, ll. 1-4, 5-10, 15-16)

Miss Price's marriage with his kinsman Alexander Stanhope went ahead. Chesterfield copied the poem into his letter-book and, we may hope, behaved with more circumspection thereafter.

Rochester was unusually aware that for his female contemporaries sex was a blood-sport. Daphne, in the eclogue **'A Dialogue between Strephon and Daphne'**, probably the first of his female impersonations, in love with Strephon who is tired of her, woos him in vain. He crushes her with the observation that 'Change has greater charms than you'. Daphne learns from this to follow the Rochesterian principle:

> Womankind more joy discovers
> Making fools than keeping lovers.
>
> (Walker, 14, ll. 71-2)

The speaker of the song 'Injurious charmer of my vanquished heart' from *Valentinian* is a nymph who regrets the easiness with which she entered into intimacy. She asks her lover to 'invent some gentle way to let [her] go'

> For what with joy thou didst obtain,
> And I with more did give,
> In time will make thee false and vain,
> And me unfit to live.
>
> (Walker, 28, ll. 5-8)

By no means all of Rochester's female selves are victims; some are aggressors. In the song **'To her Ancient Lover'** a very young Lady proposes to take very un-ladylike liberties:

> On thy withered lips and dry,
> Which like barren furrows lie,
> Brooding kisses I will pour,
> Shall thy youthful heat restore
>   . . . . .
>
> Thy nobler part, which but to name
> In our sex would be counted shame,
> By age's frozen grasp possessed,
> From his ice shall be released:
> And soothed by my reviving hand
> In former warmth and vigour stand . . .
>
> (Walker, 33, ll. 7-10, 13-20)

Rochester's **'Platonic Lady'** is another who actively seeks her own pleasure. The poem is a variation on the pseudo-Petronian theme *Foeda est in coitu et brevis voluptas* with its implied rejection of vulgar notions of sexual prowess.

> I love a youth will give me leave
> His body in my arms to wreathe,
> To press him gently and to kiss . . .
>   . . . . .

> I'd give him liberty to toy
> And play with me and count it joy.
> Our freedom should be full complete
> And nothing wanting but the feat.
>
> (Walker, 24, ll. 13-15, 19-22)

Stranger, and undeniably authentic, are the fifty-five lines of dramatic monologue in Rochester's holograph, that begin

> What vaine unnecessary things are men
> How well we do with out 'em, tell me then
> Whence comes that meane submissivness wee finde
> This ill bred age has wrought on womankinde . . .
>
> (Walker, 90, ll. 1-4)

In the late 1670s occurred a set of circumstances that produced the literary figure of 'Ephelia', a jilted Maid of Honour, who may or may not have had an actual historic counterpart. The court wits went into battle for her against their sworn enemy Mulgrave; first Etherege penned an epistle from Ephelia to her unconstant gallant or 'Bajazet', then Rochester weighed in with Bajazet's answer or *A Very Heroical Epistle from My Lord All-Pride to Dol-Common*:

> Madam,
> If you're deceived, it is not by my cheat,
> For all disguises are below the great.
> What man or woman upon earth can say
> I ever used 'em well above a day?
> How is it then that I inconstant am?
> He changes not who always is the same.
> In my dear self I centre everything,
> My servants, friends, my mistress and my King,
> Nay, heaven and earth to that one point I bring.
>
> (Walker, 112, ll. 1-9)

There is little doubt that while Rochester disappointed his mother, his wife, his mistress and his daughters, he was obsessed and fascinated by women. It is not surprising that the sensitive son of a woman like Anne Rochester should be aware of his spiritual self as female. This was one of the many things about Rochester that Burnet could not understand. Most of Rochester's utterance as reported in *Some Passages in the Life and Death of the Right Honourable John Earl of Rochester* is uncomprehending paraphrase, but occasionally Rochester's frame of reference shows through: 'But for the next state', Burnet wrote, 'he thought it more likely that the soul began anew, and that her sense of what she had done in this body, lying in the figures that are made in the Brain, as soon as she dislodged, all these perished'. Nowhere else does Burnet write of the soul as female. The dying Rochester is supposed to have asked:

> What a pox have the Women to do with the Muses? I grant you the Poets call the nine Muses by the names of Women, but why so? not because the Sex has anything to do with Poetry, but because in the Sex they're much fitter for prostitution.[1]

These words are usually understood to reflect on women; they actually reflect on poetry. Rochester had explained the parallel before, in the epilogue he wrote for Charles Davenant's play, *Circe*:

Poets and women have an equal right
To hate the dull who, dead to all delight,
Feel pain alone and have no joy but spite . . .

. . . . .

Since therefore to the women it appears
That all these enemies of wit are theirs,
Our poet the dull herd no longer fears.

(Walker, 58, ll. 10-12, 17-19)

As Artemis sprang fully armed from the head of Zeus, Rochester brought forth Artemisa, virgin poet and wit. The verse epistle Rochester wrote in her persona, ***Artemisa to Cloe,*** was first printed as a broadside in 1679. It seems that 1679 was the year of the female poet: both *Ephelia to Bajazet* and Rochester's **'Very Heroicall Epistle in Answer'** as well as the first issue of *Female Poems on Several Occasions by Ephelia* appeared that year. Rochester's Artemisa is better known than any of these; *Female Poems on Several Occasions* did not sell; it was reissued in 1682 plumped out with an added section of poems associated with Rochester, whereas the broadside of ***Artemisa to Cloe*** sold out and was reprinted in the same year. A better indication of the intense interest Rochester's poem aroused is that it is to be found in no fewer than twenty-three contemporary manuscripts (Walker, 190-1). By 1700 it had appeared in six further printings. Quotations from it can be found embedded in all kinds of writing.

What Artemisa writes to Cloe is a Horatian epistle in a low and familiar style. She disparages herself, as Horace does, by invoking an implicit standard of right feeling and common sense which she herself cannot claim to have attained. Having curtsied to the convention that she should write only in response to a command, she rattles on into a comparison of versifying with such masculine pastimes as riding astride and fighting, only to pitch poetry rather higher, invoking the subliminal image of Pegasus in her reference to the 'lofty flights of dangerous poetry'. The image gallops on into a pathless stormy world which becomes an ocean where poet privateers dare destruction for the bays.

When I reflect on this, I straight grow wise
And my own self thus gravely I advise,
'Dear Artemisa, poetry's a snare.
Bedlam has many mansions—have a care.
Your Muse diverts you, makes the reader sad;
You fancy you're inspired, he thinks you mad . . .'

(Walker, 83, ll. 14-19)

Rochester, like Artemisa, was a poet against his better judgement. His itch to show off plus his verbal incontinence pushed him time and again into cata-

strophic indiscretions which brought swift and condign punishment in their train. When it came to defending himself he had no remedy but Jonson's:

Thou callst me poet, as a term of shame:
But I have my revenge made, in thy name.[2]

So he might have considered himself revenged against Mulgrave in lampooning him as 'Lord All-Pride'.

Artemisa knows that

Whore is scarce a more reproachful name
Than Poetesse:

(Walker, 83, ll. 26-7)

but 'arrant woman' as she is, she cannot cure her itch to write. Though Artemisa expresses the problem in terms of gender, gender was not the crucial factor. The imputation of immodesty, of seeking praise by a promiscuous display of wit, could have been levelled at Rochester himself. If Rochester had been able to rein in his wit he might have become a rich and powerful man, and he could have been a great poet if his rank had not impeded his full development as effectively as Artemisa's sex would impede hers. He could not sit and toil over his lines as Dryden or Cowley might do. He might like nothing better than showing in a brilliant couplet or two what was wrong with both of them, but he was not permitted to care what became of his efforts. He accepted contributions and collaboration from less gifted men, and never troubled himself to record an authorized version of even his most deeply felt poetry.

The break in the regularity of the couplets between lines 27 and 28 of ***Artemisa to Cloe,*** and the slightly awkward bridging passage that follows before the poem as it were restarts at line 32, could be a sign that the poem was begun as part of an interchange to which Cloe too would contribute, rather in the manner of the interchanges between Ephelia and Bajazet. In a *Miscellany* of 1720 appears a fragment called 'Cloe to Artemisa':

While vulgar souls their vulgar love pursue,
And in the common way themselves undo;
Impairing health and fame and risking life,
To be a mistress, or, what's worse, a wife:
We whom a nicer taste has raised above
The dangerous follies of such slavish love,
Despite the sex, and in ourselves we find
Pleasures for their gross senses too refined . . .[3]

In the poem which appears next in the miscellany, 'The Return', the lines in praise of love from ***Artemisa to Cloe*** are quoted and credited to 'Bion', the poetic sobriquet that the poetaster Robert Wolseley used for Rochester.[4] In Bodleian MS Don b. 8, the most authoritative source for the ***Artemisa to Cloe,*** a note opposite line 251 says: 'This poeme is supposed to bee made by the Earle of Rochester, or Mr Wolseley.' The insertion of the note at one of the several passages in the poem where the energy seems to flag might provide a clue to some of the structural weaknesses that cause the taut thread of Artemisa's thought to slacken and even to sag into lampoon (e.g. ll. 66-72). 'The lyric poet with the sevenfold skull' may have been involved in the original project and interpolated contributions of his own, supplying duller connective tissue for brilliant fragments by Rochester.[5]

Artemisa begins her letter *in propria persona,* then, as a mirror within a mirror, introduces the fine lady to whom was known 'Every one's fault and merit but her own', who in turn introduces Corinna.

> That wretched thing Corinna who had run
> Through all the several ways of being undone,
> Cozened at first by love, and living then
> By turning the too dear bought trick on men.
>
> . . . . .
>
> Courted, admired, loved, with presents fed,
> Youth in her looks and pleasure in her bed,
> Till Fate or her ill angel thought it fit
> To make her dote upon a man of wit,
> Who found 'twas dull to love above a day,
> Made his ill-natured jest and went away.
> Now scorned by all, forsaken and oppressed,
> She's a memento mori to the rest;
> Diseased, decayed, to take up half a crown
> Must mortgage her long scarf and mantua gown.
> Poor creature who, unheard of, as a fly
> In some dark hole must all the winter lie,
> That for one month she tawdry may appear.
>
> (Walker, 88, ll. 189-92, 195-208)

The scorn here is the fine lady's, but the pity comes from Rochester. This vignette is truer to the actual circumstances of a woman of wit like Aphra Behn, whom Rochester certainly knew and may have collaborated with, than any suffragette version of her as a woman of independent means or late twentieth-century triumphalist vision of her as a feisty feminist bisexual.

In 1676 Rochester created a heroine of the feistiest and most feminist, namely Amocoa, Empress of China, in the scene that he wrote for Sir Robert Howard's 'Conquest of China by the Tartars', probably simply to oblige the man who in 1644 had rescued the poet's father when he was wounded and taken prisoner at Cropredy Bridge. Howard, who was appointed auditor of the Exchequer in 1677, did not find the time to finish his play. Rochester's contribution, which survives in two manuscripts, can be authenticated from Howard's letter to the poet, dated 7 April 1676.[6]

Amocoa, who appears on stage at the head of an army, rejects any suggestion that she is unfit for command:

> Woman is born
> With equal thirst of honour and of fame,

> But treacherous man misguides her in her aim,
> Makes her believe that all her glories lie
> In dull obedience, truth and modesty,
> That to be beautiful is to be brave,
> And calls her conqueror when she's most his slave,
> Forbidding her those noble paths to tread
> Which through bold daring deeds to glory lead,
> With the poor hypocritical pretence
> That woman's merit is her innocence,
> Who treacherously advised retaining thus
> The sole ambition to be virtuous
> Thinks 'tis enough if she's not infamous.
>
> (Ellis, 184, ll. 9-22)

Amocoa announces the dawn of a new era in which

> Woman henceforth by [her] example taught
> To vaster heights of virtue shall be wrought.
> Trained up in war and arts she shall despise
> The mean pretended conquests of her eyes,
> Nor be contented with the low applause
> Left to her sex by man's tyrannic laws.
>
> (Ellis, 185, ll. 25-30)

When she selects Hyachian for her general, passing over Lycungus, he rails against her:

> Who in the dumb greensickness of her mind
> Still hungers for the trash of all mankind.
> Not an insipid fop on earth does move
> For whom some woman does not die in love.
>
> (Ellis, 187, ll. 122-5)

So are we brought back via Artemisa's commonplace to the chagrin of the rejected wit in St James's Park.

Notes

1. Gilbert Burnet, in Farley-Hills, [*Rochester: The Critical Heritage,* ed. D. Farley-Hills (London and New York, 1972; repr. 1995)], 64.

2. 'To my Lord Ignorant', in Ben Jonson, *The Complete Poems,* ed. George Parfitt (London, 1988), 37.

3. 'Cloe to Artimesa', in *Eighteenth Century Women Poets: An Oxford Anthology,* ed. Roger Lonsdale (Oxford, 1989), 83.

4. *A New Miscellany* (1720), 124-5.

5. See the account of Wolseley in *The Surviving Works of Anne Wharton,* ed. G. Greer and S. Hastings (Stump Cross, 1997), 87-90.

6. *Letters,* [*The Letters of John Wilmot Earl of Rochester,* ed. Jeremy Treglown (Oxford, 1980)], 115-16.

Select Bibliography

EDITIONS

Ellis, Frank H. (ed.), *John Wilmot, Earl of Rochester. The Complete Works* (Harmondsworth and New York, 1994).

Walker, Keith (ed.), *The Poems of John Wilmot, Earl of Rochester* (Oxford and New York, 1984).

Jonathan Brody Kramnick (essay date summer 2002)

SOURCE: Kramnick, Jonathan Brody. "Rochester and the History of Sexuality." *ELH* 69, no. 2 (summer 2002): 277-301.

[*In the following essay, Kramnick positions Rochester's erotic poetry within the history of sexuality by tracing its reception and use by eighteenth-century writers.*]

How do we understand older models of desire? The question haunts the literary history of sexuality because it raises the problem of change, the depiction of erotic relations over time. Once we pause to look, we see that the past's ways of wanting are not our own. The language of human motivation and the practices of embodied intimacy have a different cast. Scholarship has rightly been wary of bending these antique thoughts and behaviors to fit contemporary notions of sexual identity. As elsewhere, the rule has been always to historicize. One recently prominent approach in Restoration and eighteenth-century studies has been to concentrate on the way in which modern sexuality gradually takes shape. The past is unlike the present but still holds the key to our origins. History is therapeutic: it yields our most cherished notions of ourselves. This essay suggests a different way of encountering the erotics of the past. I situate Rochester's erotic poetry within its philosophical and literary contexts and then observe how that poetry was read in later decades. Rochester provides an important example not simply because he is so explicit in depicting acts and desires, but also because sexuality is for him such a distinctive and vexing feature of the self and world. Sex troubles human willing, perception, and desire. It thus raises problems of wide significance for Restoration culture. One of them is the nature of agency in an increasingly secular world. Like many of his contemporaries, Rochester makes desire our presiding faculty, the cause behind our actions. But desire for him is a peculiar thing. Rarely do inner wants match worldly practice. Sex leads to shame, erotic love to disappointment. The trick of many of his poems is to expose how our habits of mind and bodily appetites are experienced as private even though they begin in public, in the space where people and poems circulate. Rochester's sense of the public is specific to the court and manuscript culture of the 1670s. A great deal changes when writers attempt to imagine the civil society and print culture of later years. Rochester's language does not vanish under a politer age, as has often been assumed. Rather, his language gets turned out to different ends. The semantics of desire change with the literary and political systems to which they are tied. One name for this change is the history of sexuality.

Let me begin with a typical moment in the literary culture of the Restoration. Retired to the country during the summer of 1678, Rochester writes wearily to his friend Savile at court about how he would counsel Nell Gwynn, the royal mistress, to maintain her advantage with the king: "it will disgrace my politics to differ from yours, who have wrought now some time under the best and keenest statesmen our cabinet boasts of. But to confess the truth, my advice to the lady you wot of has ever been this . . . Cherish his love wherever it inclines and be assured you can't commit greater folly than pretending to be jealous; but on the contrary, with hand, body, head, heart, and all the faculties you have, contribute to his pleasure all you can and comply with his desires throughout."[1] By "politics" Rochester apparently means both the vocation of "statesmen" and the erotic arts of insinuation. Each is a means of personal advancement in a culture still dominated by the court. Desire follows the footsteps of ambition. Rochester's peculiar insight is to make ambition work by apathy. Complying with the desires of another turns out to be the way of getting what you want. Politics of this order saturate the self: personal matters of embodiment and consciousness take shape from desires that are not one's own. Charles and Nell Gwynn alike have their wants spelled out elsewhere, and that is because neither one's actions proceed from their passions. As we shall see, Rochester returns habitually to this disclosure, within desire, of external sources of motivation. Like his contemporaries, he aligns selfhood with desire and desire with drive. Unlike many of them, he locates agency on the outside of things.

Rochester's political advice to Nell Gwynn might lead one to think that he considered the king to be the source of all desire, the prime manipulator of ambition. His writings on Charles's sexuality, however, are entirely within the model of erotic passivity sketched above. Consider the notorious portrait limned by **"In the Isle of Brittain,"** a poem Rochester apparently passed to Charles by mistake late in 1673:

> Him no Ambition mov'd to get Renowne
> Like a French Foole still wandring up and downe,
> Starving his People, hazarding his Crowne.
> Peace was his Aime, his gentleness was such
> And Love, he lov'd, For he lov'd fucking much,
> Nor was his high desire above his Strength:
> His Scepter and his Prick were of a length,
> And she may sway the one who plays with t'other
> Which makes him litle wiser then his Brother.[2]

Charles's desire is obstreperous and timid, a paradox worked by the poem to considerable effect. We are led to consider that his political docility follows his erotic assertiveness, that he has fallen supine to the French because he prefers sexual conquest, and thus that "Ambition," of which he has none, is separate from "desire," of which he has plenty. But then the poem goes on to say the opposite. Charles's sexual desire is "of a length" with his foreign policy. Both come from elsewhere: the seductive arts of mistresses, the wiling strategies of France. For all his apparent turgidity, his "prowdest peremptory Prick" (17), his "limber tarse" (28), Charles shows himself to be pliant, easily swayed. His wants are simple to manipulate and difficult to fulfill. On one level, the worry is over royal succession and Charles's inability to produce an heir, a situation that lent sexual politics a rare and unmatched specificity throughout the 1670s and 1680s.[3] On another, the lines introduce a philosophical problem that will concern Rochester over the course of his career: how to correlate the inner workings of the self—its desires or passions—with intentional behavior, a dilemma posed with some intensity by the intellectual culture of the period, as we shall see. It is interesting, for this reason, that one version of the poem, found in four separate manuscript copies, substitutes "designs" for "desire" in line 14.[4] Considering the overall scheme, the effect of the substitution is less to desexualize or censor the poem—the "fucking" of line 13 is retained—than to clarify the question of willing and to tighten even further the bind of statecraft to erotics. That is, "designs," with its implications of forethought and strategy, underscores how the "desire" spelled out by the rest of the poem is about mental and political volition.

The poem ends with a preview of the letter Rochester will later send to Savile, where the self is parsed and given over to another as a sign of its striving assiduity.

> This to evince wou'd be too long to tell yee
> The painfull Tricks of the laborious Nelly,
> Imploying Hands, Armes, Fingers, Mouth and Thighs
> To raise the Limb which shee each Night enjoyes.
>
>   (30-34)

The ambitious Nell Gwynn manages to excite the yielding king, but only by surrendering her body to the arduous drudgery of enjoyment. This image of sex as assertive dispossession will reappear in several guises in Rochester's poetry. Consider the discussion of the origin of love that runs through ***Artemiza to Chloe***. As elsewhere, the question at hand concerns the provenance of sexual desire, but in this case the treatment is considerably more abstract. A verse epistle from a woman "in the countrey" to a woman "in the city," the poem shuttles between private life—the emotions one confesses to another in a letter, the gossipy goings on about town, the desires besetting one's heart—and urban living. The task that Artemiza sets for herself is to estimate the relation between the two. She begins with a long, mawkish tribute to a love now lost on "this lewd Towne" (33):

> But how, my dearest Chloe, shall I sett
> My pen to write, what I would faine forgett,

> Or name that lost thing (Love) without a teare,
> Synce soe debauch'd by ill-bred Customes heare?
> *Love,* the most gen'rous Passion of the mynde,
> The softest refuge Innocence can fynde,
> The safe directour of unguided youth,
> Fraught with kind wishes, and secur'd by Trueth,
>
>   (36-43)

These lines have often been read as Rochester's most sentimental and least characteristic utterance.[5] Yet their place in the Restoration's semantics of desire is more complicated than one might assume. Few words are more overlaid with allusive meaning in the period than "passion" (a painful transport of feeling, the suffering of Christ, the emotions of the mind). Artemiza's use in these lines appears to narrow the meaning to the passions of contemporary philosophical discourse: fear, hope, envy, shame, and so forth. She draws upon a tradition of thought that dates back to the ancients and places the poem within one of the great philosophical controversies of the seventeenth century.[6] What are the origins of our emotions? What role do they play in knowledge? How do they shape our behavior? Love is more "gen'rous" than other passions because it directs our "unguided" actions to other people without apparent origins in self-regard or the desire for power.[7]

Because love appeared to imply a transcendence of self-interest, and because love appeared to involve at least two people, it was of habitual interests to writers attempting to understand the shape and origins of societies. For example, Artemiza would seem to cite and disagree with the view presented by Thomas Hobbes that love follows upon the possession of what one desires. Hobbes's logic is inexorable: "small beginnings of Motion, within the body of man, before they appear in walking, speaking, striking, and other visible actions, are commonly called Endeavor . . . This Endeavour, when it is toward something which causes it, is called Appetite or Desire . . . That which men Desire they are also said to Love . . . So that Desire, and Love, are the same thing; save that by Desire we always signifie the Absence of the Object; by Love, most commonly the Presence of the same."[8] In this passage from *Leviathan*, Hobbes makes the important move of placing love within the restless pursuit after power. Love springs from a desire that is satisfied by what it possesses. In an earlier work, Hobbes states the point even more baldly: "This is that love which is the great theme of the poets: but notwithstanding their praises, it must be defined by the word need; for it is a conception of the need a man hath of that one person desired."[9] On this view, love is an insufficient basis for civil society because different people's desires inevitably come into conflict. Society is imposed by the state, which mandates we cede our rights to things and thus fall out of love.

When Artemiza describes love as "gen'rous" and "kind," she makes what would appear to be a point counter to Hobbes: love transcends interest. She is closer perhaps to Rochester's exact contemporary, Walter Charleton, the Royal physician, whose 1674 treatise *A Natural History of the Passions* claims love "is the most agreeable and complacent of all Passions." Alone among the passions, love cannot be explained by the regard we have for ourselves or by our need to secure personal safety. In love, we will sacrifice our welfare, our safety, even our lives. This is because when we are in love "we consider ourselves as *already* joyned to the thing loved, by a certain conception of ourselves to be as it were a part thereof." Love is agreeable because it causes us to surrender interest in solitary cares for an interest in the cares of other people. Or to be more precise, we are able to feel more than for ourselves because we have become part of someone else, our initial interest in whom derives from our own needs: "I should define Love," he closes, "to be a Commotion of the Soul, produced by a motion of the Spirits, which inciteth her to joyn herself, by her will, to objects that appear convenient and gratefull to her."[10] According to Charelton, love transfigures the self and hence lays the basis for lasting bonds. According to Hobbes, appetitive desire ultimately discomposes these bonds to the extent that they require the state to hold them in place. In either case, the burden is to imagine how inwardness—"small beginnings of Motion, within the body of man"—initiates the attachments of civil society.

What then happens when love fails to name inner wants but is the result of outer fashion? This appears to be the substance of Artemiza's long complaint to Chloe. Love has become "debauch'd" and "lost" not because we are too egotistical, as the lines have often been read, but rather because we are not egotistical enough. What is lost is, in fact, a passion that begins within the precincts of the self. Artemiza works over this point enough to warrant a long citation:

> This onely Joy, for which poore Wee were made,
> Is growne like Play, to be an Arrant Trade;
> The Rookes creepe in, and it has gott of late
> As many little Cheates, and Trickes, as that.
> But what yet more a Womans heart would vexe,
> 'Tis cheifely carry'd on by our owne Sexe,
> Our silly Sexe, who borne, like Monarchs, free,
> Turne Gipsyes for a meaner liberty,
> And hate restraint, though but from Infamy.
> They call whatever is not Common, nice,
> And deafe to Natures rule, or *Loves* advice,
> Forsake the Pleasure, to pursue the Vice.
> To an exact perfection they have wrought
> The Action *Love,* the Passion is forgott.
> 'Tis below Witt, they tell you, to admire,
> And e'ne without approving they desire.
> Their private wish obeys the publicke Voyce,
> 'Twixt good, and bad Whimsey decides, not Choyce.
> Fashions grow up for tast, att Formes they strike;
> They know, what they would have, not what they like.

(50-69)

We are reminded that the correspondence is from one woman to another, this time in order to place the dilemma of love in a series of reflections on misdirected feeling. Women are the subject of private emotions made public, in poem's like *Artemiza to Chloe*; they are also the bearers of private emotions misshapen by the public. The lines slide the one into the other. The blush of "poor Wee" lovers, beheld by whomever may read this poem, is put at risk of being made into a "Trade." Turning love out in public in this fashion is a hallmark of the times, according to Artemiza, who embellishes the image by making the commerce sexual; many women "Turn Gipsyes" and sell their favors, she writes, and then lists the ways in which publicity warps the circuit of desire.[11] Our thoughts and feelings proceed from the external circumstances of urban living, including the very correspondence and circulation that underwrite the poem. Agency is turned over on itself, as the will becomes a hollowed out aftereffect of the "publicke Voyce." The result is a curious blend of inwardness and anomie, where "Whimsey decides, not Choyce."

As is often the case in Rochester's poetry, sexuality turns into a drawn out mistake. When Artemiza complains that the townsfolk have forsaken "Pleasure" for "Vice" she seems to accuse an odd variety of sex that is wholly public, that has neither beginning nor end in the privacy of the self. One could make a good case that this is the most common motif of all of Rochester's erotic verse, where the image of modernity as the scurrying about of bodies rift from their wants occurs regularly in shameful scenes of mechanized copulation. In Carole Fabricant's influential formulation, "Rochester's poetry is characterized not by an exaltation of sexuality as commonly assumed, but by an unequivocal demonstration of the latter's transience and futility." For Fabricant, sex is Rochester's "comprehensive metaphor of man's failure to realize his desires in the mortal world."[12] I'd like to suggest that the precise opposite is the case; the failure of sex lies in the world's strange realization, indeed its fabrication, of desire. We may see this in a couplet worth pausing over, Artemiza's oft-quoted complaint, "To an exact perfection they have wrought / The Action Love, the passion is forgot." The couplet articulates two types of love in the form of a broken pair: action and passion, doing and feeling. Each term takes its meaning from the absence of the other: passion is forsaken by the action that proceeds in its stead; action is cut loose from its anchor in the subject. Sex in town is depraved because no one wants to be having it. The citizens are "lewd," oddly, because they have too little desire; "e'ne without approving they desire"; "They know, what they would have, not what they like." The action of love manufactures its cause in the privation of the self.

As we have seen, the category of action is no less implicated in the thick of seventeenth-century discourse than passion. The term describes the churning procession of the will from thought to formulated behavior in the world. "The action love" is a distinctive take on this problem. If love names the tissue of feeling that binds or sunders one person and another, then sex is love in action, a procession from the self outward. Rochester bends action to show how it is initiated and put in peril by the "publicke" in all of that term's allusive richness: citizens in town, readers of poetry, followers of fashion, denizens of Whitehall. Considered this way, we can see the special charge that sexual disgrace carries for him. Erotic relations are the means by which Rochester attempts to understand our habits of mind and action now that their anchors in tradition have been cut loose.[13] Or so the poem would seem to suggest, as it holds out the unity of passion and action as the never to be found meeting of desire and worldliness. (The term for this meeting is pleasure, which is as absent in *Artemiza to Chloe* as elsewhere in Rochester's poetry.) Rochester's meaning may be clarified if we turn to his more abstract consideration in the *Satyr on Reason and Mankind.*

Keyed to the philosophical idiom of its time, this poem makes the problem of agency central to its break from traditional modes of understanding human psychology.[14] The poem makes this clear, in fact, by distilling and simplifying philosophical conflict into a neat rupture with the twin institutions of Religion and Scholasticism, whose dreary procedures of detachment—"Reason, by whose aspiring Influence / We take a flight beyond Material sense" (66-67)—provide Rochester with an antithetical model of the self. His modern response lies with Hobbes in the attempt to ground personality and desire in "sense."[15] Thought is useful to the degree to which it leads to action in the world. When the speaker of the poem attempts to articulate this position, however, he encounters a familiar problem. Once we dismiss traditional modes of explaining how thought becomes an action, the precise relation between the two is difficult to pin down. For Hobbes, the answer lay in what he proposed as the material nature of consciousness. A "[m]otion, within the body of man," thought is itself already an action.[16] With his simpler and more secondary level of argument, Rochester's speaker cannot afford such fine distinctions. He prefers to let the problem wind its way across his couplets:

> . . . Thoughts are given for Actions government,
> Where Action ceases, Thought's impertinent.
> Our sphere of Action is Life's happiness,
> And he who thinks beyond, thinks like an Asse.
>
> (94-97)

Four lines crosshatch thought and action in a variety of relations; thinking first governs, then requires, then opposes acting.[17] The effort is to join the two in a sustained

mixture. Eventually, this results in a tentative reconciliation with a "right reason" (99)

> That bounds Desires with a reforming Will,
> To keep them more in vigour, not to kill.
>
> (102-3)

Set against the extended dismissal of Scholastic rationality, this recourse to "right reason" has long struck readers as curious. The effect is to reenact the tension between private and public as a conflict within the self, a conflict between mental faculties where reason corresponds to the public, desire the private. Seen this way, the lines repeat in miniature the troubled relation of passion to action in town, except here desire is encouraged not shrunken by something outside itself. The passion forgotten by the action at town is brought into being by a rational faculty that lies on passion's exterior. The speaker explains matters to his "Scholiast" interlocutor as follows:

> Your Reason hinders, mine helps enjoy,
> Renewing appetites yours would destroy.
> My Reason is my friend, Yours is a cheat,
> Hunger calls out, my Reason bids me eat;
>
> (104-7)

Scholastic reason "hinders" and "destroy[s]" presumably because it stands apart from—is unaware of—the wants of the body. In contrast, the speaker's right reason "bounds" then "bids" desire and does so in verbs ("reforms," "renews," "helps") that suggest a transitive agency. Through this simple feat of consonance, we are invited to glimpse how an act of repression turns into an act of excitation. The result is a delayed urgency. Desire is twice represented (in Hobbesian language) as appetite, an unalterable precondition to willing.[18] Yet, its course is oddly circuitous, as if one must be reminded to be hungry. The speaker presents his self-love as if it comes from somewhere other than himself, and on a certain sense of things this is so. Public desire has so burrowed into the psyche that the generative power of right reason comes to seem like it is the presence of an alien form.

At this point, one might reasonably object that I have so abstracted sexuality from the body that it has become indistinguishable from the more pristine regions of the mind. Yet, if my reading has demonstrated anything, it is, I hope, that the turning of sex into a problem of thought (and thought into sex) is a central preoccupation of Rochester's poetry. The fateful split of passion and action animates well-known scandal poems like **"A Ramble in St. James's Park,"** where the abjected Corinna stands guilty of being a *"Whore* in understanding" (101). By this, the poem seems to mean that Corinna, like the citizens of *Artemiza to Chloe,* is having sex without wanting to. She circulates in public and freely disposes her body to others while apparently not ever choosing to do so. How should we understand this insistent separation of sexual activity from volition? We might begin by observing that sex in the poem takes place in the anonymous setting of a park and is defined by contact with strangers. The "All-sin-sheltering Grove" is a place of profligate social mingling, where

> Great *Ladies, Chamber-Maids,* and *Drudges,*
> The *Rag-picker,* and *Heiriesse* trudges:
> *Carr-men, Divines, great Lords,* and *Taylors,*
> *Prentices, Poets, Pimps,* and *Gaolers;*
> *Foot-Men,* fine *Fops,* do here arrive,
> And here promiscuously they swive.
>
> (27-32)

This is Rochester at his most Juvenalian.[19] Rome has been replaced by London, but the image of urban chaos remains in certain respects the same; the satirist recoils in fascination from a cityscape of promiscuous intercourse. Sex is sociality gone awry, as a cross-section of the social order blends at its most sensitive points of contact. When Corinna forswears the speaker and joins the rabble, she illustrates how public forms of erotic concourse shape the desire alleged to precede them.

What kind of choice has Corinna made? Recent criticism has tried to rescue her decision for an incipient feminism. "Corinna retains initiative," according to one reader; hers is a "considered female libertinism," according to another.[20] But the poem seems to resist making her decision anything like a purposive act. Here is the moment of volition:

> One in a strain 'twixt Tune and *Nonsense,*
> Cries, *Madam, I have lov'd you long since,*
> *Permit me your fair hand to kiss.*
> When at her *Mouth* her *Cunt* says yes.
>
> (75-78)

Startling and disquieting as the final line of this verse paragraph may be, it is difficult to reclaim its resonance for embodied, female agency. Rather, the line's peculiar intensity lies in its frustrated splitting of Corinna's body from itself. Her cunt belies her mouth and speaks out of turn. The synecdoche is less about an impetuous and crafty desire than the difficulty of locating desire's origin, or, that is, the beguiling sense that the latter dwells in the fluid relations of city living itself. Corinna's leap into the vortex of public sex thus becomes, in the outraged language of the speaker, a leap into relations that, like the social circulation first noticed at the park's entrance, refuse to stand still.

> And with these Three confounded *Asses,*
> From *Park,* to *Hackney-Couch,* she passes,
> So a proud *Bitch* does lead about,
> Of humble *Currs,* the Amorous rout;
> Who most obsequiously do hunt,
> The sav'ry scent of Salt-swolne *Cunt.*
>
> (81-86)

Urbanity turns sex into a roundabout chase, an image the poem insists upon so strenuously as to make it difficult to see how bodies ever stop moving long enough to come into contact. While this satire of disruptive urban life is readily taken from Juvenal, Rochester turns it to his own ends when he shows how urbanity scuttles choice making. The back and forth between park and hackney couch quickens action and freezes passion. The speaker does not condemn Corinna so much for the recklessness of her sex therefore as the inanition of her will:

> Had she pickt out to rub her Arse on,
> Some stiff-Prick'd *Clown,* or well hung *Parson,*
> Each job of whose Spermatick Sluce,
> Had fill'd her *Cunt* with wholsome Juice,
> I the proceeding shou'd have prais'd,
> In hope she had quencht a Fire I rais'd:
> Such nat'rall freedoms are but just,
> There's something gen'rous in meer Lust.
> But to turn damn'd abandon'd *Jade,*
> When neither *Head* nor *Tail* perswade;
> To be a *Whore,* in understanding,
> A Passive *Pot* for *Fools* to spend in.
> The *Devil* plaid booty, sure with thee,
> To bring a blot on infamy.[21]
>
> (91-104)

Once again, what does it mean to have desire without volition, to act without choosing, to be a whore in understanding? The first sentence presents an alternative case of passionate action. Had Corinna chose—"pickt out"—her assignation, the speaker would be content. She would have, as he puts it later, "pleasure for excuse" (124). As with love, lust is apparently "gen'rous," a "nat'rall freedom" of appetitive self-regard. This hypothetical libertinism is circumscribed, however, by its conditional syntax. The point is not to celebrate women libertines. The point is to offset and augment Corrina's eerily frozen will. Her many actions are entirely "passive" because she does not initiate or participate in their cause. Recruited by a world outside herself, she remains immune to reason and passion, head and tail alike.

We are led to suspect that sex in the modern moment can result in nothing other than the will's infirmity. This is still the case, I would argue, when the precise opposite occurs in Rochester's ***Imperfect Enjoyment,*** a poem in which the passionless action of public sex is replaced by the actionless passion of private impotence.[22] Whatever else one might choose to say about this frequently discussed poem, one might observe that Rochester describes the moment of spectacular failure, strangely, as a victory of the emotions:

> Eager desires Confound, the first intent,
> Succeeding shame does more success prevent
> And Rage at last confirms me impotent.
>
> (28-30)

The triplet makes impotence of philosophical interest by showing how it troubles our expected sense of causation.[23] Within the philosophical milieu from which this poem takes its catalog of the passions, action is either a direct or mediated result of an emotional antecedent. According to Hobbes, it would be logically impossible for desire to confound "intent" because the two are the same thing. When we desire something we call upon the will to bring it to us: *Respice finem,"* he recites as a maxim, "in all your actions, look often upon what you would have, as the thing that directs all your thoughts in the way to attain it."[24] On Charleton's view the procession of passion and action is nature's tricky plan to secure positive behavior in the world: "her design in instating our Passions, was in the general this; that they might dispose and incite the Soul to affect and desire those things, which Nature by secret dictates teaches to be good and profitable to her, and to persist in that desire." Man is "constituted propens to Passions," Charleton reasons; yet "he is not therefore the less perfect, but rather the more capable of pleasure from the right use of the good things of this life."[25] Rochester turns this line of thinking over and, famously, makes it "imperfect." He traces a curious breakdown or stutter at the threshold of volition: passion does not issue in an action, but folds back on itself. The result is a remarkable forfeiture of the very pleasure that marks our secular being in the world.

I've attempted to demonstrate thus far how sexuality is a privileged means by which Rochester's poetry stages problems around agency, publicity, and privacy specific to the philosophical and literary culture of the late seventeenth century. I would like now to discuss how Rochester's categories are transformed under the different conditions of his successors. Before doing so, however, it may be useful to distinguish this essay's sense of Rochester's place in the history of sexuality from recent treatments of the same. Recent scholarship has tended to understand Rochester in terms of what comes after him; I shall do the opposite. According to Randolph Trumbach, the influential historian of eighteenth-century sexuality, Rochester is the last great example of a world that has not yet divided itself into homo and heterosexual modes of being. Rochester was comfortable describing sexual relations with men because, on Trumbach's view, these relations did not yet carry the negative stigma of effeminacy but were, rather, signs of libertine extravagance. By the early eighteenth century, however, "Rochester's bisexual sodomy . . . could no longer be used as the supreme symbol of license; it had come instead to be seen as incompatible with a libertine's driving interest in women."[26] Critics following Trumbach's lead have attempted to fill in the image of Rochester's premodernity by comparing his rebarbative and ambidextrous

erotics to the system of polite sexual difference that would, on this account, follow in his wake.[27] Much of this discussion has centered on the poem **"Love to a Woman"**:

> Love a Woman! Th'rt an Ass:
> Tis a most insipid passion
> To Chuse out for thy Happiness
> The dullest part of Gods Creation.
>
> Let the Porter and the Groom,
> Things design'd for dirty slaves,
> Drudg in fair *Aurelias* womb
> To gett supplies for Age and Graves.
>
> Farewell *Woman*—I entend
> Henceforth every Night to sitt
> With my lewd well natur'd Friend
> Drinking to engender witt.
>
> Then give me health, wealth, Mirth, and wine,
> And if buizy Love intrenches
> There's a sweet soft Page of mine
> Can doe the Trick worth Forty wenches.

(1-16)

According to Harold Weber, this poem isn't really about sex at all, or at most uses sex as a vehicle to express the gloaming days of an aristocratic order: "Boys and lower class substitutes, firmly fixed in an economic system that is far less fluid and dynamic than the sexual economy, can stand in for women precisely because they do not question the distinction between active and passive, superiority and subordination." To the variable world of sexual desire and difference that will issue in only after him, Rochester prefers the rigid taxonomy of traditional society. In Duane Coltharp's similar terms, "sexual difference yields to class difference."[28] Even if we accept for a moment Trumbach's historical argument—that the modern system of gender and sexuality emerged near the turn of the eighteenth century and put to rest the coarse uncertainty of writers like Rochester—it would seem strange to derive the meaning of the poem from a world to which it logically had no access. It would seem strange, too, to read out of the poem its own vocabulary of the sexual. The first thing that one might notice along these lines is the unusual way in which the opening stanza makes desire a matter of volition. Lovers of women "Chuse" an "insipid passion," while lovers of drink allow "witt" to come to them. The turn in the final stanza from drinking to sex is thus made to seem predictable. Love "intrenches" from outside the self and takes shape from the male sociability the speaker prefers to the dreary work of desire. The upshot is dramatic: Rochester eroticizes the courtly reception framework of the poem itself. But what happens to the vocabulary of desire once this framework forever changes?

The difficult relation of passion and action was Rochester's bequeathment to the eighteenth century. In 1709 alone, the **Artemiza** couplet "To an exact perfection they have wrought / The Action *Love,* the Passion is forgot" was cited twice by Steele in the *Tatler* and in the opening pages of Manley's *New Atalantas;* soon it cropped up in the oddest places. Between Rochester and the *Tatler* lies a remarkable change in the nature of the public. Rochester circulated his poems in manuscript; Addison and Steele marketed their papers in print. Rochester wrote for an audience lodged at court; Addison and Steele wrote for the urban coffee houses.[29] Rochester's poems bristle with the topicality of an audience that knows, or claims to know, its individual members; Addison and Steele's audience could include anyone who knew how to read. In each respect, the citation of Rochester importantly transforms the meaning. The public whose actions of love put passion in peril is the very audience of the *Tatler* itself, an audience who consumes print daily, and who enjoys discussing small chestnuts of the national literature, like several lines from **Artemiza to Chloe.** This draws sex on a different parabola. When Steele discusses the importance of these lines from "long ago," he coaches his readers in common habits of desire and common habits of speech, a conversation that stretches to include the very limits of civil society. In *Tatler* 5, the lines sit atop the paper as an epigraph. Why is this paper introduced with a citation from Rochester? Steele turns to his reader and responds: "ask Mrs. Meddle, who is a Confident, or Spy, upon all the Passions in Town, and she'll tell you, that the Whole is a game of cross purposes: the Lover is generally pursuing one, who is in pursuit of another, and running from one that desires to meet him."[30] The clue to Steele's reading lies in the direct address: ask Mrs. Meddle, dear reader, and she'll tell you. Simply to accept this address is to recognize oneself in the world of the *Tatler,* where love rebounds across the passions in town. Steele is writing to me and also to readers who are like me. Our love has the same strange destiny as the *Tatler*: it crisscrosses the public.

When Steele returns to Rochester's couplet three months later, he gives a much fuller sense of what the action and passion of love signified for his culture. As befits a journal designed for widespread circulation in print, Steele begins *Tatler* 49 with an attempt to pin down terms for general consumption. We must get beyond our particular understanding of things and agree upon certain shared meanings. Apparently, no single term "has suffer'd so much in this Kind as Love; under which rever'd Name, a brutal Desire call'd Lust is frequently concealed and admitted." The effort to distinguish the two obliges Steele once more to discuss the meaning of Rochester's elusive couplet: "Philander the other day was bewailing this Misfortune with much Indignation and upbraided me for having some time since quoted these excellent lines of the satyrist:

To an exact Perfection they have brought
The action love, the passion is forgot.

How could you (said he) leave such an hint so coldly?" (1:348). In response, Steele interprets "The action love" to mean lust, "passion" to mean love, and both to augur a specific type of feeling. Love weaves and lust tears apart the fabric of civil society. Like Rochester and his contemporaries, Steele ponders the emotional bonds of a secular community. Yet, his sharp division between love and lust reworks self and desire alike. Love is no longer a possession or assimilation of the beloved; these are now the fervent qualities of lust. Rather, the improbable attachment of one person to another is secured through "benevolence," the becalmed darts of respect. To be in love, on this view, is to feel a lasting "concern and fondness" for someone. To be consumed by lust is, oddly, to feel a lasting aversion: "lawless desire . . . has something so unnatural in it, that it hates its own make, and shuns the object it lov'd, as soon as it has made it like it self" (1:348-49). Where love secures selfhood by discovering feelings for others, lust destroys the very same. In each case, the relation to the object surpasses what we might initially expect. Lust eagerly consumes, love respectfully shies from the beloved: "Love . . . is a Child that complains and bewails its inability to help itself, and weeps for Assistance, without an immediate Reflection or Knowledge of the Food it wants: Lust, a watchful Thief which seizes its Prey, and lays Snares for its own Relief; and its principal Object being Innocence, it never robs, but it murders at the same Time" (1:349). The passion of love, once so unable to find an equivalent action in the world, now is the basis of sociability, a surrender of personal appetite that marks true concern for others. Meanwhile, the action of love, once so defining of life in town, now marks the fatality of a self that only labors for possession.

To this new account of agency and desire, Steele matches a new account of society. "We may settle our Notion of these different Desires," he continues, "and accordingly rank their followers," first among whom is the angelic woman we all know, "Aspasia." "In this accomplished Lady, Love is the constant Effect, because it is never the Design" (1:349). Here Steele resolves the problem of desire and worldliness, the unlikely joining of one person's wants with other people's happiness, simply by leaching desire out of the passion of love. To be in love is to lack "Design," which is why Aspasia makes good citizens out of her lovers: "to behold her is an immediate Check to immoderate Behaviour, and to love her, is a liberal Education . . . A Regard for Aspasia naturally produces Decency of Manners, and a good Conduct of Life, in her admirers." Love is the very spring of social cohesion, feeling the root of civility. As Steele explains, "Love is the happy composition of all the Accomplishments that make a Fine Gentleman." This is because the passion is really not that passionate, nor the action that vigorous. Love makes citizens once we've cooled its idiom: "The Motive of a Man's Life is seen in all his Actions; and such as have the beauteous Boy for their Inspirer, have a Simplicity of Behaviour, and a certain Evenness of Desire, which burns like the Lamp of Life in their Bosoms" (1:349). Passionate action is gentility unbound, a meeting of inwardness and volition to last the length of one's days. Lust fails on both scores; its devotees "often desire what they scorn, and as often consciously and knowingly embrace where they are mutually indifferent" (1:349-50). Fervent desire is doubly antithetical, paired with hatred and apathy at turns. Through these various distinctions and their exemplary figures (Aspasia, Florio, Amanda, Limberham, among others), Steele bends the Rochester citation to suit his public. We accede to the model of this journal because in it we find the love that shapes our society.

Steele's rival Delarivier Manley published her scandal novel, the *New Atalantas,* a month after the *Tatler*'s first citation of Rochester. Her exposé of the intimate lives of prominent Whig politicians begins with the goddess Astrea's return to Atalantas and reunion with her neglected mother Virtue. Virtue's first words to her daughter on the sad state of affairs at home include the following:

> Innocence is banished by the first dawn of early knowledge. Sensual corruptions and hasty enjoyments affright me from their habitation. They embellish not the heart to make it worthy of the God; their whole care is outward and transferred to the person. By a diabolical way of argument they prove the body is only necessary to the pleasures of enjoyment; that love resides not in the heart, but in the face, and as certain of their poets have it,
>
> To an exact Perfection they have brought
> The Action Love, the Passion is forgot.[31]

Rochester's couplet has become an occasion of party politics. On Steele's Whig reading, the passion of love allows us to imagine a society built on the pleasant deferral of appetite. Manley's Tory response concentrates on an action of love set loose on a fallen world. She thus returns to the couplet a portion of the corrosive sexuality bled out of Steele's reading. Rochester illustrates how the modern, Whig regime has split desire from interiority and made it subject to "outward" cares. Manley makes some use of this reading. In many respects, her novel is nothing other than a series of instances in which desire takes shape from politics. The various examples of debauched court life follow the careers of crafty citizens who manipulate sexuality for personal advancement. Soon after the Rochester citation, for example, we are told how Fortunas and Germanicus plot their ascents at court by surrendering to the desires of others, Fortunas to the Dutchess, Germanicus to the Prince. Neither has "desire" to speak of,

but each burns with insatiable "ambition."[32] In the hollowed out precincts of Manley's subject Rochester echoes loudly. Yet, Manley retrieves this account of political sexuality across the gulf that separates the two writers. Rochester wrote his poetry for an audience at court. The framework of reading included the state, even when the poems were read elsewhere. As we saw in the scepter poem, the verse understands no firm distinction between polity and audience. In contrast, Manley writes to the civil society that judges the state. She exploits the media of print and novel to circulate a kind of sexualized political propaganda.[33] Rochester's world of passionless action no longer projects an image of the state onto the town, but in the opposite vein, provides a way for an urban, reading public to glimpse and criticize its politicians.

Steele and Manley twist the Rochester couplet to fit their different political allegiances. The twin citations reveal how ideological argument led to rival accounts of the reading public and rival models of desire. Four years later, Jane Barker further twists the couplet to explore the fate of inwardness in the new form of the popular novel. Barker's *Love Intrigues* begins by establishing itself as a pleasing retreat from the sort of party conflict that embroiled Steele and Manley. The "little novel," as she calls it in the dedication, recounts the ill-fated courtship of Galasia and Bosvil, two lovers who never quite manage to understand each other's intentions.[34] Framing the narrative is a discussion between Galasia and her friend Lucasia, who meet in the St. Germains Garden while war rages abroad and political conflict percolates at home. Exhausted from discussing "the Several Adventures of the former and late War, and what they had to hope or fear from the Success, or Overthrow of either or both Parties," Lucasia "desired Lucasia to recount to her the Adventures of her early Years, of which she had already heard some Part, and therefore believed the whole to be a diverting Novel" (83). Barker does not simply shift away from Manleyan political allegory; she stages this shift as the essential importance of the novel. The frame provides a set of instructions on how to read the novel as leisurely diversion.

Galasia and Bosvil navigate the shoals of a modern courtship whose rituals constrain the articulation of feeling. Galasia's modesty, for example, belies a churning unease: "tho' in Bosvil's Presence I made a shift to keep up this Outside of a seeming Insensibility of Love; but interiorily I was tormented with a thousand Anxieties, which made me seek Solitude where I might without Witness or Controul, disburden my overcharged Heart of Sighs and Tears" (87). And Bosvil's expressiveness belies an inner disregard: "he made the outward Grimaces of Lover, with an indifferent Interior; whilst I bore up an outside Indifferency, with a Heart full of Passion" (90). The novel resolves this split by providing the "Interior" life of its characters, or at least promises to do so at such moments of sheer exposition. Galasia in fact follows the insight with a small lesson in reading: "Thus a Mask is put on, sometimes to conceal an ill Face, and sometimes to preserve a good one: And the most part of Mankind are in reality different from what they seem, and affect to be thought what they are not" (90). Novels show people as they really are, apparently, by mapping the warped circuit of action and passion, behavior and interiority. Since she is in a position to instruct us how to read the novel, it is no surprise that Galasia thinks she has finally learned how to read Bosvil's character. When Bosvil discovers he has a rival for Galasia's affection, one Mr. Brafort, he asserts the priority of his affection. Brafort easily complies and slinks away, causing Galasia to reflect:

> To an exact Perfection he had brought
> The Action Love, the Passion be forgot.

> (91)

The Rochester couplet helps to explain Brafort's bluff indifference, compared to which Bosvil's recent attention appears genuine: "This transaction . . . gave me a strong Belief of Bosvil's Sincerity and made me interpret every little dubious Word, which he sometimes mixed with his fond Actions, to be Demonstrations of a real Passion" (91). Soon thereafter, Bosvil again forsakes Galasia. The momentary correspondence of passion and action turns out to be yet another ruse, and Galasia receives an education in the modern semantics of desire: "My Grammar Rules now became harsh Impertinences, for I thought I had learned *Amo,* and *Amor,* by a shorter and surer Method; and the only syntax I studied, was how to make suitable Answers to my father, and to him, when the longed-for Question should be proposed" (91). For Galasia, traditional marriage is the period of all romantic sentences. The new language of desire provides nothing but bafflement, as Bosvil's actions run athwart the grammar of matrimony and Bosvil's passions sink into unknowable inwardness. The rules she had expected to govern his behavior and structure her feelings have failed her, and she is unable, as yet, to understand what has come to replace them. In this failure, of course, lies the success of the novel, which unfolds the process of her love in the secular time of narrative.

Barker cites Rochester on one of those occasions—typical for the early novel—when the peculiar intentions of the genre rise to a point of didactic articulation. She wants to tell us what she is doing so we are sure to read her correctly. Yet, the riddle of passion and action is ultimately solved at the level of the story, where it is strung across the history of lovers. We follow lovers as they confront irresolvable differences between their subjective experiences of the world. For Barker, love refers only to itself. She is interested neither in the

political allegory of Manley, nor the social modeling of Addison. With this reduction of scale, Barker's adaptation of Rochester assumes its widest significance. Self-referential in time, the bonds of intimacy are more the stuff of stories than the springs of society. Secular love has become an enclosed system—a "grammar" as Galasia puts it—and in so doing it has deepened the problems encountered by Rochester. How are we to understand the wayward drift of our own passions, let alone the intentions of another person? Barker makes no attempt to answer the question, but she does aim to exploit its difficulty. It should come as no surprise, then, that the separating out of intimate relations from the relations of society and politics comes with the development of a form adequate to their exploration.

We would be hard pressed to map these citations on a single arc: Barker, Steele, and Manley are contemporaries; each makes use of formal and institutional developments particular to the age: a market for print, a system of politics, a grammar of love, a theory of society. Rochester's categories are made to serve a new culture. The move from Rochester to his reception in the eighteenth century covers forty important years in the history of sexuality. Recent criticism has emphasized how Rochester's depiction of sexual relations was unlike those brought about by the modern system that took shape after him. With sufficient dexterity, this argument could perhaps be made for any writer at any time. I have emphasized, therefore, the details of Rochesterian usage and their survival into the next age. I have dwelled on passion and action because they provide a semantic context for Rochester's model of sexuality, and its eighteenth-century aftermath. The terms bring us into the language world in which private and public motivation were secularized and made uncertain at an important moment of change. These were terms understood to have a wide implication for the fate of the self and the contours of desire. Doubtless there were others. The history of sexuality consists in nothing less than reconstructing this language and measuring its change over time. I hope to have provided in this essay a preliminary sense of what that project might look like.

Notes

1. "Rochester in the Country to Savile in London," June 1678, in *The Letters of John Wilmot, Earl of Rochester,* ed. Jeremy Treglown (Chicago: Univ. of Chicago Press, 1980), 189.

2. John Wilmot, Earl of Rochester, *In the Isle of Brittain,* in *The Works of John Wilmot, Earl of Rochester,* ed. Harold Love (Oxford: Clarendon, 1999), 5-13. All citations of Rochester's poetry are from this edition and are hereafter cited parenthetically by line number.

3. For Rochester's place in this context see Ronald Paulson, "Rochester: The Body Politic and the

Body Private," in *The Author in his Works: A Problem in Criticism,* ed. Lewis Martz and Aubrey Williams (New Haven: Yale Univ. Press, 1978), 103-21. For the context of Charles's sexuality, see Rachel Weil, "Sometimes a Scepter is Only a Scepter: Pornography and Politics in Restoration England," in *The Invention of Pornography: Obscenity and the Origins of Modernity, 1500-1800,* ed. Lynn Hunt (New York: Zone, 1996), 125-53.

4. See Rochester, "Group-E. text," in *Works of Rochester,* 89.

5. For a recent treatment, see Marienne Thormählen, *Rochester: The Poems in Context* (Cambridge: Cambridge Univ. Press, 1993), and her subsequent discussion "Dissolver of Reason: Rochester and the Nature of Love," in *That Second Bottle: Essays on John Wilmot Earl of Rochester,* ed. Nicholas Fisher (Manchester: Univ. of Manchester Press, 2000), 21-34.

6. See Susan James's definitive and brilliant study, *Passion and Action: The Emotions in Seventeenth-Century Philosophy* (Oxford: Oxford Univ. Press, 1997). "Our affective life," on James's account, was subject to a "strong synthesizing urge" over the course of the century. The passions were drawn into "pairs of negative and positive emotions . . . variously characterized in terms of inclination and aversion" (6, 7).

7. Pity and compassion offer similarly other-directed aims but are easier, ultimately, to reconcile with protection of our fragile sense of ourselves.

8. Thomas Hobbes, *Leviathan, or the Matter, Forme, & Power of a Common-Wealth Ecclesiasticall and Civill,* ed. Richard Tuck (Cambridge: Cambridge Univ. Press, 1996), 38.

9. Hobbes, *Human Nature: Or the Fundamental Elements of Policy,* in *The English Works of Thomas Hobbes,* vol. 4, ed. William Molesworth (London: John Bohn, 1839), 48.

10. Walter Charleton, *A Natural History of the Passions* (1674), 100 ("is the most"), 101 ("we consider"; "I should").

11. In a tantalizingly titled essay, "On Not Being a Very Punctual Subject: Rochester and the Invention of Modernity" (in *Reading Rochester,* ed. Edward Burns [New York: St. Martins, 1995]), Nick Davis makes the following point about the nature of desire in *Artemiza:* "The poem is structured as a series of disappearances (flights or headlong pursuits) into ego's compelling counterpart to ego, on the principle that social desire (we might say 'socialized' desire, which for the Freud-

ian tradition desire always already is) consists of accession to the desire of the other; this calls into play a relationship of aggressivity towards an other whose attitude to 'self' one has somehow to take on without having the remotest chance of displacing it—'it' is where 'you' find yourself having to be" (130). As I've attempted to demonstrate, the "aggressive" accession to the other was central to the seventeenth century's sense of its own modernity. If there is a connection to Freud to be found here, it lies only in psychoanalysis's philosophical prehistory, not as Davis suggests, its transhistorical veracity.

12. Fabricant, 343, 348.

13. Artemiza's quasi-religious thoughts on love that lead into the lament, in this respect, are placed at an ironic distance from the rest of the poem.

14. Thormählen's discussion of the intellectual context (*Poems in Context,* 162-89) is the most recent and lengthy account of his debts, although I think she mistakes the nature of Hobbes's materialism, as I discuss below.

15. *Leviathan* (1651) opens with the following clarification:

> The cause of Sense, is the Externall Body, or Object, which presseth the organ proper to each Sense, either immediately, as in the Tast and Touch; or mediately, as in Seeing, Hearing, and Smelling: which pressure, by the mediation of Nerves, and other strings, and membranes of the body, continued inwards to the Brain, and Heart, causeth there a resistance, or counter-pressure, or endeavour of the heart, to deliver itself: which endeavour because *Outward,* seemeth to be some matter without. And this *seeming,* or *fancy,* is that which men call *Sense;* and consisteth, as to the Eye, in a *Light,* or *Colour figured*; To the Eare, in a *Sound*; To the Nostrill, in an *Odour*; To the Tongue and Palat, in a *Savour*; And to the rest of the body, in *Heat, Cold, Hardnesse, Softnesse,* and such qualities, as we discern by *Feeling.*
>
> (13-14)

Within these churning sentences lies a two-part movement set to define the rigor of modern philosophy. Sense binds thought to "external bodies or objects," but these are known only through the mind's reflection on itself, the "seeming or fancy" tied to an outside whose presence must always only be supposed. We are a tissue of impressions left by objects; our minds are involved in understanding these objects. Both the world and the self become subject to intensive deliberation. On this account, Hobbes intends to correct "the Philosophy-schooles, through all the Universities of Christendome," whose misguided authority is "grounded upon certain Texts of Aristotle" (14). Where the schools argue that matter alone causes sensation, Hobbes postulates that the mind represents sensation to itself. Thoughts and passions are motions within the self and the beginnings of actions in the world. In contrast, matter can neither do nor think anything. The accusation that Scholasticism entailed a "thinking" nature, one endowed with agency, was common to the modern polemic, not just to Hobbes but to his antagonist Robert Boyle as well. See, for example, Boyle's *A Free Enquiry into the Vulgarly Receiv'd Notion of Nature* (1687).

16. On thinking as motion in Hobbes's philosophy, see James, *Passion and Action,* 126-31.

17. Glossing these lines, Dustin Griffin has written that "[m]orality, for Rochester, was the product of rational thought, not revelation" (*Satire Against Mankind: The Poems of Rochester* [Berkeley: Univ. of California Press, 1973], 8). This strikes me as half correct. While it is surely right to say that the poem prefers the secular to the religious, it is nevertheless misleading to suggest that the solution dwells in the very category the poem insists upon questioning.

18. Hobbes writes frequently of the "beginnings of motion, within the mind of man" as "Desire or Appetite" (*Leviathan,* 38).

19. The model would be Juvenal's third satire.

20. Stephen Clark, "'Something Gen'rous in Mere Lust': Rochester and Misogyny," in *Reading Rochester,* 27; and Sarah Wintle, "Libertinism and Sexual Politics," in *Spirit of Wit: Reconsiderations of Rochester,* ed. Jeremy Treglown (Hamden: Archon, 1982), 165.

21. Thormählen argues that "[w]hat motivates her is one of the three defects which are always seen as inexcusable in Rochester's oeuvre: vanity, or pride" (*Poems in Context,* 98). I think, rather, she has no motivation at all.

22. I owe this observation to Kathleen Lubey.

23. Griffin makes the opposite point: "The mind, the nonsensual faculties, have nothing to do with the lover's failure; indeed, the culprit is the unruly member which is imagined to have a will of its own. It is the offending organ, not the meddling mind, that is cursed" (95).

24. Hobbes, *Leviathan,* 21.

25. Charleton, 169-70.

26. Randolph Trumbach, *Sex and the Gender Revolution 1: Heterosexuality and the Third Gender in Enlightenment London* (Chicago: Univ. of Chicago Press, 1998), 75. Trumbach's model looms large

over the recent discussion of sexuality in eighteenth-century Britain. His account runs something like this: before the modern age, sodomy was unrelated to effeminacy but understood to be an act between men of different ages or with unequal degrees of power; as relations between men and women gradually became more equal, male-male desire grew equated with effeminacy in the person of the "molly." The emergence of the molly as a social type thus depends upon the larger reshuffling of gender roles Trumbach assigns as the hallmark of the modern age. In the past, masculinity and femininity existed in a relation of hierarchical similitude. Over the course of the eighteenth century, masculinity and femininity split into a reciprocal difference that has the molly as a stigmatized "third gender" at its constitutive threshold.

Influential as this model has been, it seems to me tendentious in several respects. According to Trumbach, eighteenth-century men had to "prove" they weren't mollies by sleeping with prostitutes or through non-consensual sex. Nascent homosexual identity is thus deduced from the alleged (and never quite demonstrated) prominence of the molly, which is in turn deduced from the alleged, compensatory behavior of men: arrests for rape and prostitution increase, ergo homosexuality! Setting aside for a moment this curious logic, we should not be surprised to find that arrests for these crimes increased over the century since arrests for all crimes increased. Trumbach does not account for changes in record keeping or inquire whether arrests for these crimes increased disproportionately. The gap between evidence and argument in this respect is massive, and one suspects that the numbers are ushered in after the fact.

27. In addition to the articles below, see Trumbach's early discussion of the poem in his "The Birth of the Queen: Sodomy and the Emergence of Gender Equality in Modern Culture, 1660-1750," in *Hidden From History: Reclaiming the Gay and Lesbian Past,* ed. Martin Duberman and Martha Vicinus (New York: New American Library, 1989), 129-40. Cameron McFarlane criticizes Trumbach's reading in *The Sodomite in Fiction and Satire, 1660-1750* (New York: Columbia, 1997) for overemphasizing the significance of the poem, but wrongly bases this point on the fact that, like all of Rochester's poetry, the poem wasn't "published" (by which he means printed) during Rochester's life. As for the larger point, McFarlane is certainly correct to point to Trumbach's schematized narrative, but the alternative he proposes—sodomy as "transgression" both now and then—hardly seems more rigorous or historical.

28. Harold Weber, "'Drudging in Fair Aurelia's Womb': Constructing Homosexual Economies in Rochester's Poetry," *The Eighteenth Century: Theory and Interpretation* 33 (1992): 114; Duane Colthorp, "Rivall Fopps, Rambling Rakes, Wild Women: Homosocial Desire and Courtly Crisis in Rochester's Poetry," *The Eighteenth Century: Theory and Interpretation* 38 (1997): 27. Weber builds his argument on Trumbach's model: "Though his poetry does register some of the specific historical ambiguities and contradictions of male sexuality in a patrilineal society that led to the establishment of a 'new' sexual identity, it belongs instead to . . . an older mode of sexual discourse concerned with 'hierarchy' rather than 'difference'" (102). Colthorp's reading is less reliant on Trumbach's narrative than Weber's and more interested in situating Rochester's "homosocial desire" in the politics of the Restoration. For further thoughts along these lines, see Sarah Ellenzweig's incisive essay "*Hitherto Propertied*: Rochester's Aristocratic Alienation and the Paradox of Class Formation in Restoration England" (*ELH*, forthcoming 2002).

29. Compare Steele's sense of audience below to that provided by Rochester at the end of the "Allusion to Horace":

    I loath the Rabble, 'tis enough for me
    If Sydley, Shadwell, Shepheard, Wicherley,
    Godolphin, Butler, Buckhurst, Buckinghame
    And some few more, whome I omitt to name
    Approve my sence, I count their Censure Fame.

    (120-24)

30. Richard Steele, *The Tatler*, ed. Donald Bond, 3 vols. (Oxford: Oxford Univ. Press, 1987), 1:27. Hereafter cited parenthetically by volume and page number.

31. Delarivier Manley, *New Atalantas* (1709), ed. Ros Ballaster (London: Penguin, 1991), 5.

32. Here is part of Manley's long exposition of how Fortunas's "ambition would not rest": "The lovely youth knew punctually how to improve those first and precious moments of good fortune whilst yet the gloss of novelty remained, whist desire was unsated, and love in the high sprint-tide of full delight; having an early forecast, a chain of thought, unusual at his years, a length of view before him, not born a slave to love, so as to reckon the possession of the charmingist woman of the court as a zenith of his fortune, but rather the auspicious, ruddy streaks of an early morning, an earnest to the meridian of the brightest day" (15).

33. My argument here is indebted to Paula McDowell's *The Women of Grub Street: Press, Politics, and Gender in the London Literary Marketplace 1678-1730* (Oxford: Oxford Univ. Press, 1998).

34. Jane Barker, *Love Intrigues: Or, the History of the Amours of Bosvil and Galesia, As Related to Lucasia in St. Germains Garden. A Novel* (1713), in *Popular Fiction by Women, 1688-1750*, ed. Paula Backsheider and John Richetti (Oxford: Oxford Univ. Press, 1998), 84. Hereafter cited parenthetically by page number.

Sarah Ellenzweig (essay date fall 2002)

SOURCE: Ellenzweig, Sarah. "*Hitherto Propertied*: Rochester's Aristocratic Alienation and the Paradox of Class Formation in Restoration England." *ELH* 69, no. 3 (fall 2002): 703-25.

[*In the following essay, Ellenzweig discusses Rochester's status as an impoverished member of the aristocracy and the relationship of his social position to the poems "A Ramble in St. James's Park" and "Love to a Woman."*]

ANTONIO:

> You must disrobe anon, and don your Native habiliaments and in the Equipage give that fair Viscountess to understand the true quality of her Husband.

GUILLOM:

> Hum—I'm afraid, 'tis a harder task to leap from a Lord to a Rogue, than tis from a Rogue to a Lord.

ANTONIO:

> Not at all, we have Examples of both dayly.

> —Aphra Behn, *The False Count* (1681)[1]

On the evening of 26 May 1665, John Wilmot, Second Earl of Rochester, abducted the much sought after heiress Elizabeth Malet in a coach-and-six, thereby inaugurating what would be an infamous reputation for aristocratic bravado. After dining in Whitehall with a Maid of Honor of Charles II's, Malet was returning home with her grandfather, the ex-Cavalier Lord Hawley, when their coach was stopped at Charing Cross by a party of armed men. Malet was captured and spirited into the night.[2] Pepys described the scandal in his diary a few days later:

> she was seized on by both horse and foot-men and forcibly taken from [her grandfather] and put into a coach with six horses and two women provided to receive her; and carried away. Upon immediate pursuit, my Lord of Rochester (for whom the King had spoke to the Lady often, but with no success) was taken at Uxbridge; but the lady is not yet heard of, and the King mighty angry and the Lord sent to the Tower.[3]

Pepys, himself "carried away" by the romance and excess of the exploit, leaves to a terse parenthetical comment what most deserves attention: "the King had spoke [of Rochester] to the Lady often, but with no success." Why the lack of success?

The Lady's affections, it appeared, were with Rochester, and in keeping with the scandal and intrigue which the incident precipitated, the couple eloped without the permission of Malet's guardians two years later.[4] In an overdetermined culmination to the drama, Pepys spotted the newlyweds at the theater, six days after the marriage, and his comment goes far to answer the above question: "Here I saw my Lord Rochester and his Lady, Mrs. Mallet, who hath after all this ado married him; and, as I hear some say in the pit, it is a great act of charity, *for he hath no estate.*"[5] The Parliamentarians had seized the royalist Wilmots' land at Adderbury during the Interregnum, and as Gilbert Burnet astutely remarked, Rochester's father, the celebrated Cavalier general, Henry Wilmot, "left his son little other inheritance but the honour and title derived to him." At Henry Wilmot's death in 1657, the ten-year-old John Wilmot became the second Earl of Rochester, Baron Wilmot of Adderbury, and Viscount Wilmot of Athlone in Ireland, but the series of titles, though markers of glorified status, were of negligible economic value. In debt and propertyless, with no income except a small perpetually-in-arrears pension from the king, Rochester was far from an attractive suitor in the eyes of Malet's guardians. Even the king's favor could not make up for his lack of "cash and acres."[6]

For Rochester's biographers, the Malet abduction represents a chivalric effort to rescue a Lady from the mercenary manipulations of her guardians. For Daniel Defoe writing in 1727, however, the abductor "within the Times of our Memory" was hardly a gallant Cavalier:

> The Arts and Tricks made use of to Trapan, and as it were, Kidnap young Women . . . were very scandalous . . . the young Lady . . . was watch'd, laid in wait for, and, as it were, besieged by a continual Gang of Rogues, Cheats, Gamesters, and such like starving Crew.[7]

Defoe's commentary is suggestive of the way in which the reckless excesses of the post-Restoration aristocrat point more to his abasement and degradation than to his honor and elevation. Indeed, just as Malet was no helpless damsel but rather a confident heiress who declared she would *"choose for herselfe,"* Rochester was not the free and independent nobleman of earlier eras.[8] Once the balance of the constitution was in favor of the new men of property, and the Crown dependent on their support, an unpropertied "favorite" like Rochester had little influence and less institutional power, and the king had no political need for his loyalty. When he arrived at

court in 1664 at the age of seventeen, Rochester was short of money and at the mercy of the court's favor, in the uncertain position of having to rely on the king's munificence and sense of personal obligation to the Wilmot family. Charles awarded him an annual salary as Gentleman of the Bedchamber, along with Buckingham, Sackville, and Mulgrave, but Rochester was the only one of this noble group without a large income from landed property.[9]

At the historical moment when the emergent standard of class first began to challenge and infiltrate a social order traditionally stratified in terms of rank, the Malet abduction attests to the crisis of aristocratic dominance. When it became all too apparent that despite his titles, Rochester was simply not a good match financially, the collision between his elevated rank and degraded class position exploded in a flagrantly theatrical act that invoked an idealized and irredeemable world of heroic romance.[10] By inhabiting the posture of the intrepid knight, Rochester attempts to showcase his internal honor—courage and valor—precisely because its external signifiers—power and wealth—had been unprecedentedly attenuated. Rochester's ambiguous position in a culture newly readable in socioeconomic terms will be my concern in the following essay.

I begin my discussion with the Malet abduction because it affords a particularly illustrative example of the conflict between Rochester's elevated status and decreased material power. This conflict, though perhaps not articulated in these terms, is familiar to readers of Rochester's poetry and represented most instructively in the two Rochester poems I will consider at length—**"A Ramble in St. James's Park"** and **"Love to a Woman."**[11] Rochester's cavalier stance, as readers have long recognized, asserts certain age-old privileges of the aristocracy at the same time as it registers the demise of those privileges. It will be my argument that such bluff and bluster have a way of proleptically laying bare an emergent logic of class, a logic that will eventually displace earlier rationales of social rank and status.

* * *

Dryden's dedication to Rochester in *Marriage-A-la-Mode* (1673) provides a powerful instance of this dynamic at work. The exemplary aristocratic amateur, as described by Dryden, displays neither spite nor ill will toward professional poets, his role being that of beneficent patron rather than jealous competitor. On the contrary, "There are a *midling* sort of Courtiers, who . . . supply [their want of wit] by an excess of malice to those who have it." While Rochester, it appears, stands as the model of "Generosity," "Delicacy," and "Decency of Behaviour," Dryden adds ambiguously "that I should have fear'd you, for my Critick, if I had not with some policy given you the trouble of being my Protector." He continues, "Wit seems to have lodg'd it self more Nobly in this Age, than in any of the former: and people of my mean condition, are onely Writers, because some of the Nobility, and your Lordship in the first place, are above the narrow praises which Poesie could give you."[12] Dryden deftly turns Rochester's infamous tendency to "lay down the law" to other writers to his own advantage here: snobbish aristocratic disdain for entrepreneurial activity threatens to become a marker of a "midling" status position in which the amateur implicitly would no longer enjoy the privilege of remaining "above the narrow praises which Poesie could give you."[13] Dryden insinuates, then, that his noble patron ought to be prudent in his faultfinding, since any hint of "malice" toward a common client presupposes a horizontal playing field that the properly vertical patron/ client relationship would preclude. In other words, imperious disapprobation now assumes the equalizing processes of class. Dryden's closing comment reveals the precariousness of Rochester's position: "Your Lordship has but another step to make, and from the Patron of Wit, you may become its Tyrant: and Oppress our little Reputations with more ease then you now protect them."[14] This is an elegant compliment with a lethal edge: in indulging in aristocratic "tyranny," Dryden warns, Rochester will be obliged to submit to a realm in which the customary privileges of status no longer hold.

If the censure of social inferiors, as Dryden suggests, exposes an uncomfortable proximity to those from whom the aristocratic amateur is supposed to remain distanced, how do we read Rochester's libertine satire **"A Ramble in St. James's Park,"** a poem whose organizing preoccupation is this very problem of increased proximity? The poem begins famously with a stunning description of sexual and social mixing:

> Unto this All-sin-sheltring Grove,
> Whores of the Bulk, and the Alcove,
> Great Ladies, Chamber-Maids, and Drudges,
> The Rag-picker, and Heiresse trudges:
> Carr-men, Divines, great Lords, and Taylors,
> Prentices, Poets, Pimps and Gaolers;
> Foot-Men, fine Fops, do here arrive,
> And here promiscuosly they swive.
>
> (25-32)

As long as the above amalgam involves players whose social position is either comparable or obviously different, the aristocratic speaker of **"A Ramble"** appears to condone the Park's liberal ethos. Trouble arises, however, when he witnesses three fops make off with his mistress, Corinna. The fops represent a threat because their status is distinctly nebulous. They are "neither lower class nor fully aristocratic," but aspirants to elevated status.[15] The speaker describes them as gamblers and speculators—"Knights, o'th' Elbow, and

the slurr" (43)—characterizing them from the start as ambitious and opportunistic self-promoters, part of the new ruling elite at court that benefited from the opening up of governmental careers to "talents" and not just to nobility.[16] It is just this increase in patronage between the Crown and the rising gentry that has placed the rakish speaker on the losing end of opportunity.

Moreover, whereas libertine promiscuity and extravagance formerly demonstrated the ex-Cavalier's denunciation of the "more private, 'domestic' activities of the rising gentry," those same excesses have now been appropriated by and made to fit the logic of a new social dispensation.[17] In the words of Davenant's Tom Double, once the inheritors of Civil War Puritanism "began to smell at a court, which was towards the middle of the late King's reign, they . . . laid aside all their former sobriety and gravity of manners, and are become as expensive and vicious as we are." The libertine ex-Cavalier thus finds himself surrounded by "a hierarchy of pretenders to [his] qualities."[18] As James Turner argues, "Whereas in France the sexual sublime served to rationalize and defend the libertinism of the aristocracy, in England it could be assumed even by the minor gentry and apprentice wits who crowded into the pit, for whom it conveyed a kind of surrogate class-privilege."[19] Henry Bulkeley articulates the rake's frustration in a letter to Rochester in which he laments that "the fop is the only fine Gentlman of the Times":

> It is thay are the hopeful spriggs of the Nation whose knowledge lyes in their light Periwiggs and trimed shoes, who herd with one another not because they love [each other], but understand no body else, whose Honour, Honesty and Freindship is like the consent of Hounds, who knowe not why thay runn together, but that thay hunt the same sent . . . My Lord all I can say is that since wee who reverence bottle and bold Truth are contemned, these Creatures have Interest enough to invade our Ease and our reputation.[20]

Much like Bulkeley, the speaker responds to the fops' invasion of his territory by attempting to expose them as undeserving imposters. The first fop, "Near Kin to th' Mother of the Maids" (46), is described as a grotesque version of an aristocratic courtier like Rochester himself, and the speaker struggles to disentangle himself from such confusing nearness to this "Whitehall blade" (45):

> He ventures to do like the best.
> But wanting common Sence, th'ingredient,
> In choosing well, not least expedient,
> Converts Abortive imitation,
> To Universal affectation;
> So he not only eats, and talks,
> But feels, and smells, sits down and walks;
> Nay looks, and lives, and loves by Rote.
>
> (54-61)

Striving to reinstate correct status boundaries, the speaker here insists on his difference from a crass and illegitimate poseur, but his affirmation of difference betrays an anxiety that in fact, he is indistinguishable from and interchangeable with his imitators.

The speaker feels less need to separate himself out from more obvious social inferiors, with whom he grants Corinna full libertine license to fornicate. Status difference thus appears to be the organizing principle of the speaker's code of social/sexual mixing—sex with the non-upwardly mobile is permissible, even approved, while sex with the socially ambitious fops is contemptible and denounced—but the character of Corinna's desire is equally, if not more important here. Whereas Corinna's sex with social inferiors is always fueled by lust, she appears to offer up her body to the fops without bodily desire:

> Had she pickt out to rub her Arse on,
> Some stiff-Prick'd Clown, or well-hung Parson,
> Each job of whose Spermatick Sluce,
> Had filled her Cunt with wholsome Juice,
> I the proceeding shou'd have prais'd,
> In hope she had quencht a Fire I rais'd:
> Such nat'rall freedoms are but just,
> There's something gen'rous in meer Lust.
> But to turn damn'd abandon'd Jade,
> When neither Head nor Tail perswade;
> To be a Whore, in understanding,
> A Passive Pot for Fools to spend in.
> The Devil plaid booty, sure with thee,
> To bring a blot on infamy.
>
> (91-104)

When the speaker describes Corinna as "a Whore, in understanding," he attacks her, it would seem, for falling prey to social rather than sexual urges. But her offense is more complicated. Lacking the carnal physical potency of the hardy underclasses, the fops don't compel at the raw and immediate level of the body, but neither, it would seem, did the speaker, who learned at best to "hope" that Corinna's escapades with other men "had quencht a Fire I rais'd." But what is the "Fire" raised by the speaker? Is it not pride in being the desired object, linked through several steps of remove to Corinna's sexual desire? It is precisely this power to produce pride and thereby raise fire in one's chosen object that should, in the eyes of the speaker, be his exclusive privilege. Previously the sole executive of this role, the speaker faces the prospect of the fops replacing him. "Joyful, and pleas'd" (80) at the fops' attention, Corinna is gratified to have been chosen by them. The fops now share an equal power to "raise a Fire" in Corinna, a fire, moreover, that they, like the speaker, might not directly "quench." We can infer that the fops, like other social inferiors, could allowably serve to satisfy Corinna's lust—in imagining the hypothetical encounter between Corinna and the "stiff prickt Clown or well hung Parson," the speaker explains that he would have "prais'd" just such a proceeding—but they cannot ignite more exalted sources of pleasure.

Despite his swashbuckling sexual bravado, the speaker suggests that what he values in his relationship with Corinna, perhaps more than the embodied physicality of sex, is precisely this more exquisite and intricate register of love and passion.

> You that cou'd make my Heart away,
> For Noise and Colours, and betray,
> The Secrets of my tender hours,
> To such Knight Errant Paramours;
> When leaning on your Faithless Breast,
> Wrapt in security, and rest,
> Soft kindness all my pow'rs did move,
> And Reason lay dissolv'd in Love.
>
> (125-32)

The above posture of the abject metaphysical "believer" betrayed by his heartless Lady, while in part ironic, also points nostalgically to the loss of a sovereignty whose absolute and singular status is threatened by the fops' encroachments. Turner observes that the physical pleasures of libertinism "are often disparaged as 'slimy drudgeries' or 'wearisome obligations,'" and it is indeed notable that once the speaker sparks a fire in Corinna, as the poem recounts it, he is then often involved only in a secondary way with the physical satisfaction of this fire:

> When your lew'd Cunt, came spewing home,
> Drencht with the Seed of half the Town,
> My Dram of Sperme, was supt up after,
> For the digestive Surfeit Water.
> Full gorged at another time,
> With a vast Meal of Nasty Slime;
> Which your devouring Cunt had drawn
> From Porters Backs and Foot-mens Brawn;
> I was content to serve you up,
> My ballock full, for your Grace Cup;
> Nor ever thought it an abuse,
> While you had pleasure for excuse.
>
> (113-24)[21]

The parsons, porters, and footmen serve as the degraded objects on whom the fire raised by the speaker is satiated, but the danger of the fops lies in their equivalence to him—their status as subjects with a comparable power. That Corinna is *not* motivated by lust in her choice of the fops, but rather flattered by their hackneyed compliments and rote mimicry of the aristocratic rake, constitutes a direct threat to the speaker. For once the fops move Corinna, not in body but in "understanding," he has no sovereign role to play.

The speaker is incensed that "a thing admir'd by me, / Shou'd taste so much of Infamy" (89-90), and after a virulent 31 line rant against Corinna, the poem ends with the following decree:

> And may no Woman better thrive,
> That dares prophane the Cunt I Swive.
>
> (165-66)

These lines mark the culmination of the speaker's aristocratic and masculine presumption, bearing testament to Rochester's long-standing reputation as a misogynist poet. I want to suggest, however, that the speaker's outrage at being situated by Corinna as just one among many consumers in St. James's Park, and his emphasis, however insolent, on the qualitative difference between individual lovers, perhaps serves a more subversive purpose. For the fops' efforts to ape the aristocracy reflect the familiar contradictions of upward mobility commented upon by social historians and Marxist critics: the rise of the middle classes depends upon the increased possibilities for mobility which follow the demystification of status hierarchies, but the defining feature of the new class is not so much its celebration of a specific class identity, but rather its desire, as often as not, to acquire status privilege, to become absorbed within the upper gentry and aristocracy.[22] One sees evidence of this dialectic in Bulkeley's complaint to Rochester that though the fops "herd" together, they "knowe not why thay runn together, but that thay hunt the same sent." The acquisition of status insidiously denies not only the reality of economic relationships and actual inequalities, but the existence of the category of class altogether. To put it another way, the upstarts' pretensions to social distinction, to status, are tenable only by obscuring the very economic relations on which the class system depends. As Georg Lukacs has noted, "status conciousness," precisely because it denies the centrality of the economic, not only "masks class consciousness; in fact it prevents it from emerging at all." In this light, Rochester's aristocratic speaker is not so different from the radical worker who insists upon the qualitative specificity of his labor in the face of the market's obscurations. The speaker and the upstart fops with whom he competes can be said to be engaged in a social conflict "reflected in an ideological struggle . . . for the veiling or the exposure of the class character of society."[23]

* * *

Finding himself deprived of sexual and social supremacy, the speaker of **"A Ramble"** reveals the purported equality of individuals within a class system of social organization to be an abstraction. The demystification of aristocratic difference allows the fops to identify with the formerly inaccessible rake, and yet the speaker does not share in their rising fortunes. His consequent embrace of difference thus serves to disrupt an identification which suppresses concrete inequalities. It is notable, however, that the speaker's insistence on difference and inexchangeability is extended more to the fops than to the unambitious parsons and footmen. For though the speaker seems assured that between the parson and himself the strict hierarchies of status are maintained, it is with just these commoners that he also shares an unexpected class identification. The Rochester

poem that appears most unequivocally to express the confidence of stable aristocratic hierarchy demonstrates this paradox.[24]

> Love a Woman! Th'rt an Ass:
>   Tis a most insipid passion
> To Chuse out for thy Happiness
>   The dullest part of Gods Creation.
>
> Let the Porter and the Groom,
>   Things design'd for dirty slaves,
> Drudg in fair Aurelias womb
>   To gett supplies for Age and Graves.
>
> Farewell Woman—I entend
>   Henceforth every Night to sitt
> With my lewd well natur'd Friend
>   Drinking to engender witt.
>
> Then give me health, wealth, Mirth, and wine,
>   And if buizy Love intrenches
> There's a sweet soft Page of mine
>   Can doe the Trick worth Forty wenches.

It would seem difficult to argue that **"Love to a Woman"** troubles a traditional social hierarchy. Brashly contemptuous of both women and laborers, the imperious speaker appears to exist in a stable world of privilege and homosocial decadence. As Randolph Trumbach argues, in the sexual culture of the Restoration, "the most daringly masculine men had sexual relations with both women and adolescent males," and many of these men were aristocrats. Indeed, sodomizing a passive and socially inferior male partner was an accustomed prerogative of the aristocratic rake; sex with the "sweet soft Page" (15) thus becomes a forceful assertion of both masculine and social hierarchy. Each man knows his proper place in relations between a nobleman and a servant, and homosocial principles are here extended so far that women are excluded entirely.[25] And yet by refusing sex with women, the haughty speaker obstructs the primary mechanism of the aristocratic ideology he seems to support—the transmission of honor through the patriline. The noble injunction to make heirs is relegated to ignoble workers, and the sacred "work" of reproduction transmogrified into the slavish toil of manual labor.

Indeed, what is most striking in **"Love to a Woman"** is the way in which the sacred and time-old duty of making heirs is represented in distinctly modern terms as a type of alienated labor. Not only is the producer of heirs a "dirty slave," he is also reified as a disembodied mechanism that has sex instrumentally rather than sensuously. The passing on of the patriline is refigured as a type of organized expropriation of sexuality for the equally abstract and immaterial use of "Age and Graves," and the product of man's fashioning reflects not life but death.[26] While the speaker's proclamation expresses familiar aristocratic disdain for the slavish porter and groom, it also points to a curious identification with them. It is only because the speaker understands himself to be an objectified conduit in the service of aristocratic reproduction that he passes off the dirty work of alienated labor to those for whom the drudgery would be deemed appropriate.

It is not surprising, then, that the speaker abandons the production of heirs, choosing instead to "engender witt." Even the illicit sexuality that would replace the sanctioned appears as almost an afterthought in the poem's last three lines. For what will replace generative sexuality with women is not so much nonprocreative sex with male servants, but rather a spiritual entity that is fostered and intensified by "drink." The social aspect of work that has become mystified in Rochester's desolate envisioning of procreative sexuality reemerges in the lively homosociality evoked in the third and final stanzas. And by the final couplet of the poem, the speaker and his common page foreclose the possibility of production and the alienation of its output altogether. When we remember that the aristocracy's chief means of consolidating and perpetuating its power was through marriage and procreation, the speaker's abdication from sustaining legitimate succession—from reproducing aristocratic difference—represents, however ambivalently, an unmistakable censure of the traditional social and sexual hierarchy which his status group would have him maintain. In other words, the seeming extension of status and sex persecution becomes the means through which the reproduction of aristocratic and patriarchal hierarchy breaks down.

Recent critical treatments of the aristocratic rake have begun to illuminate the peculiar modernity of the alienated aristocracy in the early modern period, and the way in which it is deeply cynical not only about the new social formation from which it feels excluded, but also about the very traditional values it would seem to uphold. As Peter Porter observes, "Certainly their privileges meant much to them, but they had few illusions about them."[27] This skeptical disillusionment was particularly profound in landless noblemen like Rochester, who in 1660 failed to see the restoration of their property along with the monarchy, and complained that "the Old Cavaliers, who had stood most firm to the Royal Cause . . . had been utterly ruin'd in Endeavouring its support."[28] The royalist ideal at the Restoration has been described as a longing to "escape into . . . a stable, hierarchical society dominated by loyal Anglican landowners prepared to live on their country estates, supported by the labor of a contented, obedient populace."[29] To the extent that Rochester condemned what he saw to be the corrupt machinations of court politics—the transformation of political courtiership into a quest for financial gain—he may in part be seen to identify with the loyal Anglican landowner and the landed interest. As he writes to his friend Henry Savile in the spring

of 1676, "They who would be great in our little government seem as ridiculous to me as school-boys who with much endeavour and some danger climb a crab-tree, venturing their necks for fruit which solid pigs would disdain if they were not starving." And, in a 1678 letter, Savile expresses ironic concern over Rochester's "fall-[ing] to the ordinary ignorance of a meer Country gentleman."[30]

Rochester can thus appear to be a precursor of the irate Tory squire who, in his resistance to capitalism's incursion in the countryside, anachronistically insists on upholding paternalist benevolence in all dealings. But, as Savile well knew, Rochester was not a country gentleman. The group of gentry and noblemen who opposed the corruption of court bureaucracy and the rural entrepreneurs' connections to the financial interest were landowners living on income from rents.[31] Moreover, the royalist gentry and aristocrats who did recover after the Civil Wars were those who successfully redeemed their lands in 1660 and adapted to the newly innovative methods of estate management and land improvement and investment. The end of feudalism was for the most part best for the middle men: the abolition of feudal tenures in 1646 confirmed in possession the well-to-do yeomen and tenant farmers who had acquired property during the Civil Wars and Interregnum, as well as the tradesmen, merchants, and soldiers who had bought estates with their savings.[32] But it was not only the laboring poor who failed to win protection. One satirist wrote these disenchanted lines on Charles's restoration, suggesting the volatile association between the ex-Cavalier and the common poor that Christopher Hill has called "radical royalism":

> His father's foes he doth reward,
> Preferring those cut off his head;
> Old Cavaliers, the crown's best guard,
> He leaves to starve for want of bread.
> Never was any prince endued
> With so much grace and gratitude.[33]

Excluded from both the monied court interest and the conservative country interest, Rochester's social positioning is not readily apparent. Having lost privileges, property, and fortune, the dispossessed ex-Cavalier suffers from an acute sense of displacement and homelessness. It is this sense of displacement, documented in Rochester's **"Love to a Woman,"** that marks the Restoration aristocrat as the figure of the period perhaps most attuned to what Marx, nearly two centuries later, will characterize as the alienation of the working class.

* * *

In **"Love to a Woman,"** the aristocratic speaker's claim to status difference from the porter and the groom in fact bespeaks a class identification with them. In **"A**

Ramble," the appeal to difference serves to disturb identification, precisely because the reduced speaker does *not* share a class identification with the fops who aspire to his still-elevated rank. My readings in both instances have sought to establish that poems which have been seen to represent the apotheosis of the male aristocrat's affirmation of status privilege in fact point in a rather opposite direction. Current scholarship has shown similar interest in interrogating Rochester's place in the canon as the paradigmatic aristocratic amateur of the Restoration, and some has situated his poetry in the context of class. A recent essay by Duane Coltharp, for example, argues that in reaction to the growing political and economic power of the gentry and merchant classes, embattled early-modern aristocrats like Rochester attempted to "define a class identity" by defensively asserting aristocratic hauteur against "the social climbers who threatened their position." Such class conflict, as Coltharp understands it, "converge[s] upon the body of a contested woman, who becomes the focal point of masculine struggles for power and prestige."[34]

The objective of the male, aristocratic personae of Rochester's poetry is, more often than not, to achieve dominance over the degraded bodies of women, but how exactly is this pursuit connected to the early workings of class? For one, as Coltharp and others have suggested, much of Rochester's verse fails to reflect this kind of mastery.[35] Indeed, the interest of Rochester's poetry, as Harold Weber argues, lies in its tendency both to assert and reverse expected hierarchies, transforming male and aristocratic preeminence into its opposite.[36] In **"Love to a Woman,"** it is not remarkable to find women situated as "breeding machines," responsible for the smooth perpetuation of power and property of which they will have no share, legal or otherwise.[37] We have long recognized the way in which the patrilineal system of inheritance commodified the female virgin for her value as breeder of the legal heir. And yet it is the poem's male speaker who refuses to be a disembodied mechanism procreating "supplies" of no use-value to him personally: his understanding of *himself* as an objectified conduit for the transmission of property is what motivates his transferal of the dirty work of alienated labor to those whose demeaned status would render the drudgery suitable.[38] This group includes porters and grooms, and also women. That Rochester figures the male aristocrat and his alienation from power and property not simply through an analogy to a menial laborer, but also by calling attention to his alienated ownership of his body and its reproductive function, signifies, I want to suggest, a vexed parity between the position of the alienated speaker and the position of the woman he so disgustedly rejects.[39] Rochester's speaker recognizes that his predicament is not so unlike that of a woman or a commoner, his alienated ownership of his body and its reproductive function serving to position him as their counterpart. Class

identity, then, would seem to coalesce in more ambiguous relation to women than we might expect.

Because the bodies of women and lower-class men and boys are largely undifferentiated and interchangeable in Rochester's verse—the specificity of sex subjection not yet clearly separated out from social subjection—the male aristocrat's class disenfranchisement is also figured in gendered terms.[40] To be in a position of social inferiority in a Rochester poem is also, more often than not, to be in a position of "feminized" sexual abjection. Alternatively, what Weber has termed the "sexual underclass" in Rochester is almost always represented by an "economic underclass."[41] This analogy is perhaps most famously suggested in Rochester's **"Imperfect Enjoyment,"** in which the Cavalier speaker, looking back on his past sexual potency, brags that his "Dart of Love" (37) "t'would Carelessly invade / Woman, nor Man, nor ought its fury stayd—/ Where ere it pierc'd a Cunt it found or made—" (41-43). His present impotence, however, forces him to reevaluate his self-perception as a heroic sexual conqueror of women and boys: by the poem's end, the speaker concedes that he is not the elevated "all dissolving Thunderbolt" (10) who "Breaks every stew" (59), but rather "a Common Fucking Post, / On whom each Whore Relieves her tingling Cunt" (63-64). Most notable in these lines is not only the speaker's class reversal from heroic conqueror to common sexual tool, but also the gender reversal between the whore and the speaker: the whore moves from a state of degradation to one of autonomous activity, while the speaker degenerates into a passive and exploited implement.

This crossing of expected gender boundaries is entirely consistent with the pre-modern understanding of sex and status as overlapping structures.[42] Indeed, the fluidity in Rochester's poetry between sex and social status also characterizes the logic of the patriarchalist analogy between the family and the state, in which a wife's subjection to her husband is understood as homologous to a servant's subjection to his master and to the subject's subjection under the monarch.[43] For Rochester, then, men and women are situated along a vertical axis of hierarchy, according to which women's difference from men is understood as social, cultural, and juridical rather than organic and sexual. As Thomas Laqueur has argued, "During much of the seventeenth century, to be a man or a woman was to hold a social rank, to assume a cultural role, and not to be organically one or the other of two sexes. Sex was still a sociological, not an ontological category." It was not until the eighteenth century, Laqueur maintains, "that there was something concrete and specific inside, outside, and throughout the body that defined male as opposed to female." Although tied to a rigidly hierarchical social and political order, the "one sex" model of sexual stratification paradoxically allowed for a flexibility in gender roles that did not survive the eighteenth century's grounding of sex in the bedrock of biology. As Laqueur explains, "In this world, the body with its one elastic sex was far freer to express theatrical gender and the anxieties thereby produced than it would be when it came to be regarded as the foundation of gender."[44]

Situating both the sexual and social politics of Rochester's poetry within the context of a one-sex model is critical to our effort to understand what "class identity" might entail in Rochester's verse. Coltharp argues that such class identity is constituted through the shoring up of aristocratic and masculine hauteur, and yet might not these moments of bravado be more indicative of an effort to protect a *status identity* at a point when class awareness would foster a vexed alliance with the commoners and women over whom the Rochesterian personae is seen to command power?[45] Indeed, it is largely because Rochester's patriarchalism *cannot* differentiate between class and sex subjection that his disenfranchised speakers identify with the social predicament of women at the same time as they attempt to assert mastery over them.[46]

The implications of this argument for our understanding of Rochester's sexual politics are at least twofold. In his attempts to persuade Rochester of the moral opprobrium of "the free use of wine and women," Bishop Burnet reminds him "that men have a property in their wives and daughters, so that to defile the one, or corrupt the other, is an unjust and injurious thing." But Rochester's notion of ownership and freedom has little to do with the "possessive individualism" which characterizes Burnet's model. To Burnet's great mortification, Rochester had an entirely different conception of what property, in self and in others, might mean, and it is telling that his response to Burnet's catechizing was, in Burnet's words, that it "sounded . . . like enthusiasm or canting: he had no notion of it, and so could not understand it."[47] When the speaker of **"A Ramble"** reminds Corinna that he "gave [her] privilege above / The nice allowances of love" (109-10), he refers to her equal power as an active sexual agent both with commoners and with him. Like many women in Rochester's poetry, Corinna is, in Coltharp's words, "saturated with subjective qualities, endowed with desire, vision, and will." Rochester's speakers degrade their feminine objects, but they simultaneously acknowledge their autonomy.[48]

It is tempting, thus, to see Rochester's rejection of the commodification of (sexual) labor as anticipating an argument that Marxist feminism will make centuries later—that sexual objectification can also be a form of alienation. And yet as **"A Ramble"** makes obvious, to position another or to be positioned oneself as an object of desire is not perforce alienating. Sexual alienation, like the alienation of labor for Marx, results when one's

sexuality (or one's labor) exists as an object for another without also existing as such for oneself.[49] This is the predicament of the speaker of **"Love to a Woman"**: the producer of heirs becomes a thing whose sexuality is appropriated for someone else—namely, for the social hierarchy from which he is already excluded. Interestingly, in a paradoxical reversal, the alienation of sexual objectification, the critique of which feminism tends to assume, is disclosed through Rochester's radical royalist imagining of patrilineage as the drudgery of alienated labor. For Rochester, to be positioned as a woman—commodified for the purposes of sexual reproduction—or to be positioned as a common wage-laborer—alienated from the products of his work—seems to amount to the same thing.

The parallel between social and sexual subjection in Rochester's poetry meets its test case, however, in a poem like **"The Disabled Debauchee,"** in which a woman who appears to share the libertine speaker's social status is permitted entrance into the poem's homosocial economy as a kind of stand-in for a male equal.

> Nor shall our Love-fits Cloris be forgot,
> When each the well-look'd Linkboy strove t' enjoy;
> And the best Kiss was the deciding Lot,
> Whether the Boy Fuck'd you, or I the Boy.

> (37-40)

The fluidity between male and female is particularly emphasized in the above lines, for as Paul Hammond notes, the speaker's second person address to "Cloris" follows two earlier second person addresses to implicitly male companions.[50] Cloris is thus aligned, not with the subjugated body of the "Linkboy," but rather with the supremacy of the aristocratic speaker, the speaker and Cloris each competing on equal terms for the power to exercise sexual dominance over the underclass. As Cloris's and Corinna's example indicates, some women can approximate social equality with aristocratic men, but the poem's effort to posit an equivalence between who "Fuck[s]" whom suffers a paradigm trauma in line 40 when the speaker is faced with the prospect of Cloris "Fuck[ing]" the linkboy. The poem is then forced to concede that Cloris is not a seamless stand-in for one of the aristocratic speaker's rakish cronies precisely because within its terms of intelligibility she cannot "Fuck . . . the Boy." Given the implied status equivalence between Cloris and the speaker, if, in the end, Cloris can only be "Fuck'd" *by* the boy, the poem would seem to betray an awareness that in Weber's words, "women, in fact, remain the permanent underclass."[51] However, to the extent that we see the variables of sex and class begin to become partially distinguished in this instance, to use the word "class" to describe the position of women is perhaps misleading. Since sex subjection in Rochester's poetry is coherent largely within the hierarchical terms of social status, **"The Disabled Debauchee"** suggests that Rochester's identification with the position of women is tempered by his inability to see women as other than versions of men with whom an aristocratic speaker is either equal or not. If women's inferiority, regardless of their status position, is understood in terms of an analogy to the position of commoners, the case of aristocratic women poses a nagging problem, for they undeniably share certain privileges with men of their status group. Thus the lack of distinction between social and sexual subjection in Rochester's poetry represents both the conditions of possibility for his sympathy for women, and its limits.

* * *

Through poetic forms and parodic self-presentations which call for literary-critical interpretation, Rochester acts out the complexity of a stance which historical description and analysis have proven less able to represent and decipher. Part of this difficulty arises from a critical resistance to using class analysis before class is a developed and stabilized category, i.e., before the nineteenth century. One exception to this tendency is E. P. Thompson's invaluable consideration of class struggle in the eighteenth century, a study that has provided a framework through which early modern critics can make sense of otherwise often unintelligible social phenomena. Thompson's definition of class situates itself in opposition to what he calls "a new generation of Marxist theorists" whom he implies eschew "the fatigue of historical practice" in favor of static theories: "it is only too often the case that the theory takes precedence over the historical evidence which it is intended to theorize. It is easy to suppose that class takes place, not as historical process, but inside our heads." Such an opening up of the category of class is precisely what allows "important kinds of social protest" to become visible in periods before the nineteenth century, forms of protest, like Rochester's, which might look quite different from what we see in later periods.[52]

Although Thompson sees his usage of class as a heuristic historical category to be consonant with Marx's own usage, the fact that Marx had so little to say on the subject of the aristocracy brings to view Marx's own capacity to neglect history in favor of philosophy. In *The German Ideology,* he explains that "the bourgeoisie itself . . . finally absorbs all propertied classes it finds in existence (while it develops the majority of the earlier propertyless and a part of the hitherto propertied classes into a new class, the proletariat)." By "hitherto propertied," Marx refers mainly to the formerly independent agriculturists who were expropriated from the land after the 1646 abolition of feudal tenures and the consequent development of modern private property. One wonders, however, whether Marx also had in mind the other group for whom the end of

feudalism and the emergence of absolute private property amounted to disenfranchisement and alienation: aristocratic ex-Cavaliers, like Rochester, who found themselves newly landless after the 1660 Act of Indemnity and Oblivion failed to restore their sequestered property.[53]

Rochester's appeals to status difference may appear to affirm the biological essentialism of "birth equals worth" and signify nothing more than reactionary aristocratic petulance at the loss of social preeminence. However, it has been a particularly intractable historical contradiction that the anti-essentialism that bespoke the liberatory promise of class represents, at the same time, the insidious obscurations of class's reign: it is precisely because class anathematized essential difference that the bourgeoisie were eventually able to universalize their rule and conceal the traces of their dominance by denying the existence of the very category that allowed for their rise.[54] Caught historically in the vortex of status and class, in a volatile social group for whom the essentialisms of aristocratic difference (though demystified) are still available as a social strategy, and for whom the inaugural exploitations of class are especially raw and outrageous, Rochester has a paradoxical purchase on a historically specific form of class-consciousness.[55]

Notes

1. Aphra Behn, *The False Count* (1681), in *The Works of Aphra Behn,* ed. Janet Todd (Columbus: Ohio State Univ. Press, 1996), 5.1.194-99.

2. Graham Greene, *Lord Rochester's Monkey* (New York: Viking Press, 1974), 41-43; Vivian deSola Pinto, *Enthusiast in Wit* (Lincoln: Univ. of Nebraska Press, 1962), 35-37.

3. Samuel Pepys, *The Diary of Samuel Pepys,* ed. Robert Latham, 11 vols. (Berkeley: Univ. of California Press, 1970-83), 6:110.

4. Harold Wilson, "Rochester's Marriage," *RES* [*Review of English Studies*] 19 (1943): 401-2.

5. Pepys, 8:4, my emphasis. James Turner ends his discussion of sexual heroism with the observation that a history of the period must address "the ambiguous class-position of the sexual hero" ("The Libertine Sublime," *SECC* [*Studies in Eighteenth-Century Culture*] 19 [1989]: 112).

6. Gilbert Burnet, *Some Passages of the Life of John Earl of Rochester,* in *Lives of Sir Matthew Hale and John Earl of Rochester* (London: William Pickering, 1829), 191. Wilson, "Rochester's Marriage," 401.

7. Daniel Defoe, *Conjugal Lewdness* (Gainesville: Scholars' Facsimiles & Reprints, 1967), 366.

8. F. R. Harris, *The Life of Edward Mountagu, R. G. First Earl of Sandwich,* vol. 2 (London: John Murray, 1912), 176, my emphasis.

9. On the growth of patronage between the Crown and the rising gentry, see Linda Levy Peck, *Court Patronage and Corruption in Early Stuart England* (Boston: Unwin Hyman, 1990), 49, 91; Basil Greenslade, "Affairs of State," in *Spirit of Wit,* ed. Jeremy Treglown (Hamden, Conn.: Archon Books, 1982), 95, 102; and Wilson, *The Court Wits of the Restoration* (Princeton: Princeton Univ. Press, 1948), 52, 10.

10. On the transition from status to class, see Max Weber, *From Max Weber,* trans. and ed. H. H. Gerth and C. Wright Mills (New York: Oxford Univ. Press, 1974), 181-87; Michael McKeon, *Origins of the English Novel* (Baltimore: The Johns Hopkins Univ. Press, 1987), 133, 162-64. On the rake as a displaced heroic figure, symptomatic of the breakdown of a traditional social order, see Richard Braverman, "Libertines and Parasites," *Restoration* 2.2 (1987): 73-86.

11. On the always contested question of the relationship between poet and speaker, I concur with Dustin Griffin's assertion that "the libertine speakers of [Rochester's] poems are too much like the historical Rochester to be personae, and too self-consciously, too knowingly, scandalous to be, simply, the man himself" (*Satires Against Man: The Poems of Rochester* [Berkeley: Univ. of California Press, 1973], 24-25).

12. John Dryden, *Marriage A-la-Mode* (1673), in *The Works of John Dryden,* ed. Edward Niles Hooker and H. T. Swedenberg, Jr., 20 vols. (Berkeley: Univ. of California Press, 1956), 11:222, 221, 223.

13. Christopher Hill, "Two Radical Royalists," in *The Collected Essays,* vol. 1 (Amherst: Univ. of Massachusetts Press, 1985), 301. It is just this reputation for censuring other writers that the speaker of Rochester's social satire "Timon" endeavors to disprove, though the mild and dispassionate persona is so flagrantly ironic that only the most naive of readers would have missed Rochester's patent self-mockery.

> I vow'd, I was noe more a Witt than he,
> Unpractic'd, and unblest in Poetry:
> A song to Phillis, I perhaps might make,
> But never Rhym'd but for my Pintles sake;
> I envy'd noe Man's Fortune, nor his Fame,
> Nor ever thought of a Revenge soe tame.

"Timon," in *The Works of John Wilmot, Earl of Rochester,* ed. Harold Love (New York: Oxford Univ. Press, 1999), 19-24. All references to Rochester's poetry are from this edition. Poems are hereafter cited parenthetically by line number.

Circulated in manuscript during Rochester's lifetime, his poetry is notoriously difficult and often impossible to date.

14. Dryden, 11:223-24.

15. Robert Holton, "Sexuality and Social Hierarchy in Sidney and Rochester," *Mosaic* 24 (1991): 61.

16. On the seventeenth-century shift in patronage, see David Ogg, *England in the Reign of Charles II,* vol. 1 (Oxford: Clarendon Press, 1934), 110-11; McKeon, *Origins,* 186.

17. Braverman, 78. On the redefinition of libertinism, see also Angeline Goreau, "'Last Night's Rambles': Restoration Literature and the War Between the Sexes," in *The Sexual Dimension in Literature,* ed. Alan Bold (Totowa, N.J.: Barnes & Noble, 1982), 50.

18. Charles Davenant, *The True Picture of a Modern Whig,* in his *Political and Commercial Works* (1771), ed. Charles Whitworth, vol. 4 (Farnborough: Gregg Press, 1967), 185. John Trangott, "The Rake's Progress From Court to Comedy," *SEL* [*Studies in English Literature 1500-1900*] 6 (1966): 389.

19. Turner, "The Libertine Sublime," 102.

20. To Rochester in London from Henry Bulkeley, May-June, 1676, in *The Letters of John Wilmot, Earl of Rochester,* ed. Treglown (Oxford: Blackwell, 1980), 124-27.

21. Turner, "The Properties of Libertinism," *Eighteenth-Century Life* 9.3 (1995): 82.

22. See McKeon, *Origins,* 174.

23. Georg Lukacs, *History and Class Consciousness: Studies in Marxist Dialectics,* trans. Rodney Livingstone (Cambridge: MIT Press, 1968), 58, 59. My reading of "A Ramble" is informed by E. P. Thompson's argument that class struggle predates the existence of the categories we know today as classes, that indeed, class categories only emerge through the process of class struggle ("Eighteenth-Century English Society: Class Struggle Without Class?" *Social History* 3 [1978]: 149).

24. Harold Weber argues that "Love to a Woman" "comes closest to achieving . . . masculine self-sufficiency . . . constructing a male homosexual universe which simply excludes women" ("Drudging in Fair Aurelia's Womb: Constructing Homosexual Economies in Rochester's Poetry," *The Eighteenth Century* 33 [1992]: 110).

25. Randolph Trumbach, "Sex, Gender, and Sexual Identity in Modern Culture: Male Sodomy and Female Prostitution in Enlightenment London," *Journal of the History of Sexuality* 2 (1991): 188.

On sodomy and the aristocratic libertine, see also Trumbach, "Sodomy Transformed: Aristocratic Libertinage, Public Reputation and the Gender Revolution of the 18th Century," *Journal of Homosexuality* 19 (1990): 105-24; and *Sex and the Gender Revolution,* vol. 1 (Chicago: Univ. of Chicago Press, 1998), 73-76. On same-sex love as an assertion of social hierarchy in "Love to a Woman," see McKeon, "Historicizing Patriarchy: the Emergence of Gender Difference in England, 1660-1760," *ECS [Eighteenth-Century Studies]* 28 (1995): 309.

26. Ros Ballaster has also noted the contradictory way in which the aristocracy succeeds in reproducing itself only by "stoop[ing] . . . to the menial task of marital reproduction" ("John Wilmot, Earl of Rochester," in *The Cambridge Companion to English Literature, 1650-1740,* ed. Steven N. Zwicker [Cambridge: Cambridge Univ. Press, 1998], 212.) On the demographic crisis of 1650-1750 which contributed to the decline of the aristocracy, see Lawrence Stone and Jeanne C. Fawther Stone, *An Open Elite?: England, 1540-1880* (Oxford: Clarendon, 1984), 100-9, 276-77. On man's estrangement from bodily sensuousness under conditions of alienated labor, see Karl Marx, *Economic and Philosophic Manuscripts of 1844,* trans. Martin Milligan (New York: International Publishers, 1964), 114, 138.

27. Peter Porter, "The Professional Amateur," in *Spirit of Wit,* 59. On aristocratic cynicism, see Holton, 58-59; and McKeon, *Origins,* 169, 171. The term "alienated aristocrat" is Hill's ("Two Radical Royalists," 301).

28. Davenant, *The True Picture of an Ancient Tory, in a Dialogue Between Vassal a Tory, and Freeman a Whig* (London, 1702), 29. On the disaffected ex-Cavalier, see also Keith Feiling, *A History of the Tory Party 1640-1714* (Oxford: Clarendon Press, 1924), 98-101.

29. R. Malcolm Smuts, *Court Culture and the Origins of A Royalist Tradition in Early Stuart England* (Philadelphia: Univ. of Pennsylvania Press, 1987), 291.

30. Rochester in the country to Savile in London, Spring 1676, in *Letters,* 119; To Rochester in the country from Savile in London, 2 July 1678, in *Letters,* 201. On the landed interest in the eighteenth century, see Thompson, "Eighteenth-Century English Society," 139-40; and his *Idem, Customs in Common* (New York: The New Press, 1993), 79.

31. See McKeon, *Origins,* 166.

32. Hill, *The World Turned Upside Down: Radical Ideas During the English Revolution* (New York: Penguin, 1972), 107; Ogg, 163.

33. John Freke, "The History of Insipids" (1674), in *Anthology of Poems on Affairs of State,* ed. G. de-Forest Lord (New Haven: Yale Univ. Press, 1975), 37-42. (The poem was attributed to Rochester until Frank Ellis discovered two sources in 1965 citing Freke as author.) A melancholy letter from Savile to Rochester provides further support of the association between aristocratic ex-Cavaliers and the poor at the Restoration. Savile writes, "Since the death of poor Sir Simon Fanshaw that sorte of excellent breed is almost extinguished, or att least soe farr decayed that except an old Cavalier Corporall that I beleeve you have seen begging in St. James's parke, there is noe more any such person" (To Rochester at Adderbury from Savile, 25 June 1678," in *Letters,* 194).

34. Duane Coltharp, "Rivall Fopps, Rambling Rakes, Wild Women: Homosocial Desire and Courtly Crisis in Rochester's Poetry," *The Eighteenth Century* 38 (1997): 30, 29, 24.

35. See Coltharp, 27; Harold Weber, 104; Warren Chernaik, *Sexual Freedom in Restoration Literature* (New York: Cambridge Univ. Press, 1995), 59; Stephen Clark, "'Something Genrous in Meer Lust?' Rochester and Misogyny," in *Reading Rochester,* ed. Edward Burns (New York: St. Martin's Press, 1995), 39; Griffin, 11-12, 20.

36. Harold Weber, 108.

37. Margaret Ezell, *The Patriarch's Wife* (Chapel Hill: Univ. of North California Press, 1987), 2.

38. Many women poets of the period repeatedly invoked the class-inflected language of "drudgery" to describe female subordination. See Lady Mary Chudleigh's "To the Ladies" (1703) and "Ladies Defence" (1701), *The Poems and Prose of Mary, Lady Chudleigh,* ed. Ezell (New York: Oxford Univ. Press, 1993.) See also "The Emulation" (1683), in *Kissing the Rod: An Anthology of Seventeenth-Century Women's Verse,* ed. Germaine Greer et. al. (New York: Farrar Straus Giroux, 1988).

39. "Signior Dildo," a poem variously attributed to Rochester, also implies that reproductive capacity can be the locus of exclusion and denigration for men as well as for women. The poem's speaker unfolds a kind of comical reverse scenario from "Love to a Woman" in which a sequence of aristocratic ladies choose sex with a dildo over the "Flesh and Blood" (80) of aristocratic men. The poem would seem to intimate that the gender reversal makes no difference: just as women are rejected in "Love to a Woman" due to the inseparability in heterosexual sex between pleasure and procreation, in "Signior Dildo," the cast out "Rabble of Pricks" (81) are laughably undesirable because of their bodily ties to reproduction, ties which the women in the poem have happily thrown off:

The good Lady Sands burst into a Laughter,
To see how the Bollox came wabling after;
And had not their weight retarded the Foe
Indeed, 't had gone hard with Signior Dildo.

(89-92)

40. On the lack of differentiation between women and boys in Rochester's verse, see Harold Weber, 102; Reba Wilcoxon, "Rochester's Sexual Politics," *SECC* 8 (1979): 138.

41. Harold Weber, 114.

42. See Anthony Fletcher, *Gender, Sex and Subordination in England, 1500-1800* (New Haven: Yale Univ. Press, 1995).

43. As John Locke later complains of the confusion of social and sexual subjection in Filmer's *Patriarcha* (1680), "Let the words Rule and Subject be but found in the Text or Margent, and it immediately signifies the Duty of a Subject to his Prince, the Relation is changed, and though God says Husband, Sir Robert will have it King" (*Two Treatises of Government,* ed. Peter Laslett [Cambridge: Cambridge Univ. Press, 1988], 1.5.49).

44. Thomas Laqueur, *Making Sex: Body and Gender From the Greeks to Freud* (Cambridge: Harvard Univ. Press, 1990), 142, 133, 125. On sex as a sociological category, see also Fletcher, 30-43, 60-98. Harold Weber also observes that Rochester's poetry "belongs . . . to what Thomas Laqueur has identified as an older mode of sexual discourse concerned with 'hierarchy' rather than 'difference'" (102). For more on the shift in sexual discourse from hierarchy to difference, see McKeon, "Historicizing Patriarchy," 301-4.

45. In suggesting an interconnection between Rochester's identification with commoners and with women, it will not be my intent to collapse the distinction between categories of sex and class. My point is rather to remind us that such a distinction meant something different in Restoration England than it does in our modern context. Though Rochester's poetry reflects the breakdown of belief in the essential difference of aristocratic blood, it predates the corollary investment in the essential difference between male and female. On the opposite trajectories of these two forms of essentialism, see McKeon, "Historicizing Patriarchy."

46. Feminist critics have long been divided on Rochester's attitude towards women. See Sarah Wintle, "Libertinism and Sexual Politics," in *Spirit of Wit,* 133-65; Wilcoxon; Goreau; Chernaik, 52-79; and Clark.

47. Burnet, 211, 249, 215.

48. Coltharp, 32, 33.

49. As Marx explains, it is only under the conditions of estranged labor that objectification is experienced as alienation. Otherwise, objectification may be the foundation of human freedom whereby the subject becomes embodied in products and relationships (See *Economic and Philosophic Manuscripts,* 114; and *Gundrisse: Foundations of the Critique of Political Economy,* trans. Martin Nicolaus [Harmondsworth: Penguin, 1973], 832).

50. Paul Hammond, "Rochester's Homoeroticism," in *That Second Bottle: Essays on John Wilmot, Earl of Rochester,* ed. Nicholas Fisher (New York: Manchester Univ. Press, 2000), 54.

51. Harold Weber, 114.

52. Thompson, "Eighteenth-Century Society," 147, 150.

53. Marx and Frederick Engels, *The German Ideology,* part 1 (New York: International Publishers, 1970), 82. On the developments leading to the emergence of modern private property, see Marx, *Capital,* vol. 1, trans. Ben Fowkes (New York: Vintage Books, 1977), 883-85.

54. On the bourgeoisie's effort to efface the reality of class conflict in society, see Lukacs, 61.

55. E. J. Hobsbawm has argued that "the nobility and gentry may develop something like a class consciousness much sooner than the rest." However, to the extent that class consciousness by definition implies awareness of one's economic position in society, Hobsbawm's assumption that "the criterion of self-definition will be primarily non-economic" confuses class consciousness with what would more accurately be described as status consciousness. This confusion stems from Hobsbawm's prior assumption that the nobility's status privilege is coequal with class privilege, that "legal or quasi-legal privilege implies economic advantage" ("Class Consciousness in History," in *Aspects of History and Class Consciousness,* ed. Istvan Meszaros [London: Routledge, 1971], 8, 10).

FURTHER READING

Criticism

Bruce, Susan. "'Rolling about from Whore to Whore': Rochester's Satirico-Sexual Self and the Art of Conspicuous Consumption." *Forum for Modern Language Studies* 30, no. 4 (October 1994): 305-15.

Analysis of the relationship between the satiric narrator of Rochester's poems and the world the poet is satirizing.

Crumb, Michael. "Dialog, Decadence, and Expressionism: Petronius and Rochester." In *Compendious Conversations: The Method of Dialogue in the Early Enlightenment,* edited by Kevin L. Cope, pp. 139-5 Frankfurt am Main, Germany: Peter Lang, 1992.

Compares the treatment of decadence and resistance to authority in Petronius's *Satyricon* and in Rochester's poetry.

Farley-Hills, David. "Heaven in Hell's Despair—The Anatomy of Love in Rochester's Lyric Poetry." In *Rochester's Poetry*, pp. 36-88. Totowa, N.J.: Rowman and Littlefield, 1978.
  Explores Rochester's love poetry within the context of the courtly tradition.

Gill, James E. "The Fragmented Self in Three of Rochester's Poems." *Modern Language Quarterly* 49, no. 1 (March 1988): 19-37.
  Discussion of fragmented and threatened subjectivity as it relates to "Love and Life," *A Letter from Artemisia in the Town to Chloe in the Country,* and *A Satyr Against Reason and Mankind.*

Gill, Pat. "'Filth of All Hues and Odors': Public Parks, City Showers, and Promiscuous Acquaintance in Rochester and Swift." *Genre* 27, no. 4 (winter 1994): 333-50.
  Explores similarities in Jonathan Swift's and Rochester's treatments of the social mixing of classes.

Griffin, Dustin H. "A Reading of the *Satyr against Mankind.*" In *Satires against Man: The Poems of Rochester,* pp. 197-245. Berkeley: University of California Press, 1973.
  Discusses the thematic and stylistic ambiguities of *Satyr against Mankind,* Rochester's most famous poem.

Hammond, Paul. "Censorship in the Manuscript Transmission of Restoration Poetry." In *Literature and Censorship,* edited by Nigel Smith, pp. 39-62. Cambridge, U.K.: D. S. Brewer, 1993.
  Discusses the contemporary censorship of Restoration oppositional poems, among them Rochester's satire on Charles II.

Johnson, J. W. "Lord Rochester and the Tradition of Cyrenaic Hedonism, 1670-1790." *Studies on Voltaire and the Eighteenth Century* 153 (1976): 1151-167.
  Examines Rochester's work within the tradition of universalist, or classical, hedonism.

Pinto, Vivian de Sola. "The Right Veine." In *Portrait of a Restoration Poet,* pp. 127-58. London: John Lane The Bodley Head, 1935.
  Presents Rochester as a witty satirist who completely captured the spirit of his age.

Rogal, Samuel J. "The Control of Honest Expression: Offensive Language in Rochester's Poetry." *Forum* 30, no. 1 (winter 1989): 33-8.
  Examination of seventeenth- and eighteenth-century negative reactions to Rochester's use of offensive language.

Sitter, John E. "Rochester's Reader and the Problem of Satiric Audience." *Papers on Language & Literature* 12, no. 3 (summer 1976): 285-98.
  Discussion of the relationship between author and reader in the reception of Rochester's poetry.

Wilders, John. "Rochester and the Metaphysicals." In *Spirit of Wit: Reconsiderations of Rochester,* edited by Jeremy Treglown, pp. 42-57. Oxford, U.K.: Basil Blackwell, 1982.
  Refutes critics who consider Rochester's poetry narrow and simplistic.

Additional coverage of Rochester's life and career is contained in the following sources published by Thomson Gale: *British Writers,* **Vol. 2;** *Dictionary of Literary Biography,* **Vol. 131;** *Literature Criticism from 1400 to 1800,* **Vol. 75;** *Literature Resource Center*; **and** *Poets: American and British.*

How to Use This Index

The main references

```
Calvino, Italo
     1923-1985 ....... CLC 5, 8, 11, 22, 33, 39,
                            73; SSC 3, 48
```

list all author entries in the following Gale Literary Criticism series:

AAL = *Asian American Literature*
BG = *The Beat Generation: A Gale Critical Companion*
BLC = *Black Literature Criticism*
BLCS = *Black Literature Criticism Supplement*
CLC = *Contemporary Literary Criticism*
CLR = *Children's Literature Review*
CMLC = *Classical and Medieval Literature Criticism*
DC = *Drama Criticism*
HLC = *Hispanic Literature Criticism*
HLCS = *Hispanic Literature Criticism Supplement*
HR = *Harlem Renaissance: A Gale Critical Companion*
LC = *Literature Criticism from 1400 to 1800*
NCLC = *Nineteenth-Century Literature Criticism*
NNAL = *Native North American Literature*
PC = *Poetry Criticism*
SSC = *Short Story Criticism*
TCLC = *Twentieth-Century Literary Criticism*
WLC = *World Literature Criticism, 1500 to the Present*
WLCS = *World Literature Criticism Supplement*

The cross-references

```
See also CA 85-88, 116; CANR 23, 61;
DAM NOV; DLB 196; EW 13; MTCW 1, 2;
RGSF 2; RGWL 2; SFW 4; SSFS 12
```

list all author entries in the following Gale biographical and literary sources:

AAYA = *Authors & Artists for Young Adults*
AFAW = *African American Writers*
AFW = *African Writers*
AITN = *Authors in the News*
AMW = *American Writers*
AMWR = *American Writers Retrospective Supplement*
AMWS = *American Writers Supplement*
ANW = *American Nature Writers*
AW = *Ancient Writers*
BEST = *Bestsellers*
BPFB = *Beacham's Encyclopedia of Popular Fiction: Biography and Resources*
BRW = *British Writers*
BRWS = *British Writers Supplement*
BW = *Black Writers*
BYA = *Beacham's Guide to Literature for Young Adults*
CA = *Contemporary Authors*
CAAS = *Contemporary Authors Autobiography Series*
CABS = *Contemporary Authors Bibliographical Series*
CAD = *Contemporary American Dramatists*
CANR = *Contemporary Authors New Revision Series*
CAP = *Contemporary Authors Permanent Series*
CBD = *Contemporary British Dramatists*
CCA = *Contemporary Canadian Authors*
CD = *Contemporary Dramatists*
CDALB = *Concise Dictionary of American Literary Biography*
CDALBS = *Concise Dictionary of American Literary Biography Supplement*
CDBLB = *Concise Dictionary of British Literary Biography*

CMW = St. James Guide to Crime & Mystery Writers
CN = Contemporary Novelists
CP = Contemporary Poets
CPW = Contemporary Popular Writers
CSW = Contemporary Southern Writers
CWD = Contemporary Women Dramatists
CWP = Contemporary Women Poets
CWRI = St. James Guide to Children's Writers
CWW = Contemporary World Writers
DA = DISCovering Authors
DA3 = DISCovering Authors 3.0
DAB = DISCovering Authors: British Edition
DAC = DISCovering Authors: Canadian Edition
DAM = DISCovering Authors: Modules
   DRAM: Dramatists Module; *MST:* Most-studied Authors Module;
   MULT: Multicultural Authors Module; *NOV:* Novelists Module;
   POET: Poets Module; *POP:* Popular Fiction and Genre Authors Module
DFS = Drama for Students
DLB = Dictionary of Literary Biography
DLBD = Dictionary of Literary Biography Documentary Series
DLBY = Dictionary of Literary Biography Yearbook
DNFS = Literature of Developing Nations for Students
EFS = Epics for Students
EXPN = Exploring Novels
EXPP = Exploring Poetry
EXPS = Exploring Short Stories
EW = European Writers
FANT = St. James Guide to Fantasy Writers
FW = Feminist Writers
GFL = Guide to French Literature, Beginnings to 1789, 1798 to the Present
GLL = Gay and Lesbian Literature
HGG = St. James Guide to Horror, Ghost & Gothic Writers
HW = Hispanic Writers
IDFW = International Dictionary of Films and Filmmakers: Writers and Production Artists
IDTP = International Dictionary of Theatre: Playwrights
LAIT = Literature and Its Times
LAW = Latin American Writers
JRDA = Junior DISCovering Authors
MAICYA = Major Authors and Illustrators for Children and Young Adults
MAICYAS = Major Authors and Illustrators for Children and Young Adults Supplement
MAWW = Modern American Women Writers
MJW = Modern Japanese Writers
MTCW = Major 20th-Century Writers
NCFS = Nonfiction Classics for Students
NFS = Novels for Students
PAB = Poets: American and British
PFS = Poetry for Students
RGAL = Reference Guide to American Literature
RGEL = Reference Guide to English Literature
RGSF = Reference Guide to Short Fiction
RGWL = Reference Guide to World Literature
RHW = Twentieth-Century Romance and Historical Writers
SAAS = Something about the Author Autobiography Series
SATA = Something about the Author
SFW = St. James Guide to Science Fiction Writers
SSFS = Short Stories for Students
TCWW = Twentieth-Century Western Writers
WLIT = World Literature and Its Times
WP = World Poets
YABC = Yesterday's Authors of Books for Children
YAW = St. James Guide to Young Adult Writers

Literary Criticism Series
Cumulative Author Index

Armah, Ayi Kwei 1939- . **BLC 1; CLC 5, 33, 136**
See also AFW; BRWS 10; BW 1; CA 61-64; CANR 21, 64; CDWLB 3; CN 7; DAM MULT, POET; DLB 117; EWL 3; MTCW 1; WLIT 2

Armatrading, Joan 1950- .... **CLC 17**
See also CA 114; 186

Armitage, Frank
See Carpenter, John (Howard)

Armstrong, Jeannette (C.) 1948- .... **NNAL**
See also CA 149; CCA 1; CN 7; DAC; SATA 102

Arnette, Robert
See Silverberg, Robert

Arnim, Achim von (Ludwig Joachim von Arnim) 1781-1831 ..... **NCLC 5; SSC 29**
See also DLB 90

Arnim, Bettina von 1785-1859 ...... **NCLC 38, 123**
See also DLB 90; RGWL 2, 3

Arnold, Matthew 1822-1888 ..... **NCLC 6, 29, 89, 126; PC 5; WLC**
See also BRW 5; CDBLB 1832-1890; DA; DAB; DAC; DAM MST, POET; DLB 32, 57; EXPP; PAB; PFS 2; TEA; WP

Arnold, Thomas 1795-1842 .... **NCLC 18**
See also DLB 55

Arnow, Harriette (Louisa) Simpson 1908-1986 .... **CLC 2, 7, 18**
See also BPFB 1; CA 9-12R; 118; CANR 14; DLB 6; FW; MTCW 1, 2; RHW; SATA 42; SATA-Obit 47

Arouet, Francois-Marie
See Voltaire

Arp, Hans
See Arp, Jean

Arp, Jean 1887-1966 .... **CLC 5; TCLC 115**
See also CA 81-84; 25-28R; CANR 42, 77; EW 10

Arrabal
See Arrabal, Fernando

Arrabal, Fernando 1932- ... **CLC 2, 9, 18, 58**
See Arrabal (Teran), Fernando
See also CA 9-12R; CANR 15; EWL 3; LMFS 2

Arrabal (Teran), Fernando 1932-
See Arrabal, Fernando
See also CWW 2

Arreola, Juan Jose 1918-2001 .... **CLC 147; HLC 1; SSC 38**
See also CA 113; 131; 200; CANR 81; CWW 2; DAM MULT; DLB 113; DNFS 2; EWL 3; HW 1, 2; LAW; RGSF 2

Arrian c. 89(?)-c. 155(?) .... **CMLC 43**
See also DLB 176

Arrick, Fran .... **CLC 30**
See Gaberman, Judie Angell
See also BYA 6

Arley, Richmond
See Delany, Samuel R(ay), Jr.

Artaud, Antonin (Marie Joseph) 1896-1948 .... **DC 14; TCLC 3, 36**
See also CA 104; 149; DA3; DAM DRAM; DLB 258; EW 11; EWL 3; GFL 1789 to the Present; MTCW 1; RGWL 2, 3

Arthur, Ruth M(abel) 1905-1979 ..... **CLC 12**
See also CA 9-12R; 85-88; CANR 4; CWRI 5; SATA 7, 26

Artsybashev, Mikhail (Petrovich) 1878-1927 .... **TCLC 31**
See also CA 170; DLB 295

Arundel, Honor (Morfydd) 1919-1973 .... **CLC 17**
See also CA 21-22; 41-44R; CAP 2; CLR 35; CWRI 5; SATA 4; SATA-Obit 24

Arzner, Dorothy 1900-1979 .... **CLC 98**

Asch, Sholem 1880-1957 .... **TCLC 3**
See also CA 105; EWL 3; GLL 2

Ascham, Roger 1516(?)-1568 .... **LC 101**
See also DLB 236

Ash, Shalom
See Asch, Sholem

Ashbery, John (Lawrence) 1927- .. **CLC 2, 3, 4, 6, 9, 13, 15, 25, 41, 77, 125; PC 26**
See Berry, Jonas
See also AMWS 3; CA 5-8R; CANR 9, 37, 66, 102, 132; CP 7; DA3; DAM POET; DLB 5, 165; DLBY 1981; EWL 3; INT CANR-9; MTCW 1, 2; PAB; PFS 11; RGAL 4; WP

Ashdown, Clifford
See Freeman, R(ichard) Austin

Ashe, Gordon
See Creasey, John

Ashton-Warner, Sylvia (Constance) 1908-1984 .... **CLC 19**
See also CA 69-72; 112; CANR 29; MTCW 1, 2

Asimov, Isaac 1920-1992 ..... **CLC 1, 3, 9, 19, 26, 76, 92**
See also AAYA 13; BEST 90:2; BPFB 1; BYA 4, 6, 7, 9; CA 1-4R; 137; CANR 2, 19, 36, 60, 125; CLR 12, 79; CMW 4; CPW; DA3; DAM POP; DLB 8; DLBY 1992; INT CANR-19; JRDA; LAIT 5; LMFS 2; MAICYA 1, 2; MTCW 1, 2; RGAL 4; SATA 1, 26, 74; SCFW 2; SFW 4; SSFS 17; TUS; YAW

Askew, Anne 1521(?)-1546 .... **LC 81**
See also DLB 136

Assis, Joaquim Maria Machado de
See Machado de Assis, Joaquim Maria

Astell, Mary 1666-1731 .... **LC 68**
See also DLB 252; FW

Astley, Thea (Beatrice May) 1925-2004 .... **CLC 41**
See also CA 65-68; 229; CANR 11, 43, 78; CN 7; DLB 289; EWL 3

Astley, William 1855-1911
See Warung, Price

Aston, James
See White, T(erence) H(anbury)

Asturias, Miguel Angel 1899-1974 .... **CLC 3, 8, 13; HLC 1**
See also CA 25-28; 49-52; CANR 32; CAP 2; CDWLB 3; DA3; DAM MULT, NOV; DLB 113, 290; EWL 3; HW 1; LAW; LMFS 2; MTCW 1, 2; RGWL 2, 3; WLIT 1

Atares, Carlos Saura
See Saura (Atares), Carlos

Athanasius c. 295-c. 373 .... **CMLC 48**

Atheling, William
See Pound, Ezra (Weston Loomis)

Atheling, William, Jr.
See Blish, James (Benjamin)

Atherton, Gertrude (Franklin Horn) 1857-1948 .... **TCLC 2**
See also CA 104; 155; DLB 9, 78, 186; HGG; RGAL 4; SUFW 1; TCWW 2

Atherton, Lucius
See Masters, Edgar Lee

Atkins, Jack
See Harris, Mark

Atkinson, Kate 1951- .... **CLC 99**
See also CA 166; CANR 101; DLB 267

Attaway, William (Alexander) 1911-1986 .... **BLC 1; CLC 92**
See also BW 2, 3; CA 143; CANR 82; DAM MULT; DLB 76

Atticus
See Fleming, Ian (Lancaster); Wilson, (Thomas) Woodrow

Atwood, Margaret (Eleanor) 1939- ... **CLC 2, 3, 4, 8, 13, 15, 25, 44, 84, 135; PC 8; SSC 2, 46; WLC**
See also AAYA 12, 47; AMWS 13; BEST 89:2; BPFB 1; CA 49-52; CANR 3, 24, 33, 59, 95, 133; CN 7; CP 7; CPW; CWP; DA; DA3; DAB; DAC; DAM MST, NOV, POET; DLB 53, 251; EWL 3; EXPN; FW; INT CANR-24; LAIT 5; MTCW 1, 2; NFS 4, 12, 13, 14, 19; PFS 7; RGSF 2; SATA 50; SSFS 3, 13; TWA; WWE 1; YAW

Aubigny, Pierre d'
See Mencken, H(enry) L(ouis)

Aubin, Penelope 1685-1731(?) .... **LC 9**
See also DLB 39

Auchincloss, Louis (Stanton) 1917- .. **CLC 4, 6, 9, 18, 45; SSC 22**
See also AMWS 4; CA 1-4R; CANR 6, 29, 55, 87, 130; CN 7; DAM NOV; DLB 2, 244; DLBY 1980; EWL 3; INT CANR-29; MTCW 1; RGAL 4

Auden, W(ystan) H(ugh) 1907-1973 . **CLC 1, 2, 3, 4, 6, 9, 11, 14, 43, 123; PC 1; WLC**
See also AAYA 18; AMWS 2; BRW 7; BRWR 1; CA 9-12R; 45-48; CANR 5, 61, 105; CDBLB 1914-1945; DA; DA3; DAB; DAC; DAM DRAM, MST, POET; DLB 10, 20; EWL 3; EXPP; MTCW 1, 2; PAB; PFS 1, 3, 4, 10; TUS; WP

Audiberti, Jacques 1899-1965 .... **CLC 38**
See also CA 25-28R; DAM DRAM; EWL 3

Audubon, John James 1785-1851 . **NCLC 47**
See also ANW; DLB 248

Auel, Jean M(arie) 1936- .... **CLC 31, 107**
See also AAYA 7, 51; BEST 90:4; BPFB 1; CA 103; CANR 21, 64, 115; CPW; DA3; DAM POP; INT CANR-21; NFS 11; RHW; SATA 91

Auerbach, Erich 1892-1957 .... **TCLC 43**
See also CA 118; 155; EWL 3

Augier, Emile 1820-1889 .... **NCLC 31**
See also DLB 192; GFL 1789 to the Present

August, John
See De Voto, Bernard (Augustine)

Augustine, St. 354-430 .... **CMLC 6; WLCS**
See also DA; DA3; DAB; DAC; DAM MST; DLB 115; EW 1; RGWL 2, 3

Aunt Belinda
See Braddon, Mary Elizabeth

Aunt Weedy
See Alcott, Louisa May

Aurelius
See Bourne, Randolph S(illiman)

Aurelius, Marcus 121-180 .... **CMLC 45**
See Marcus Aurelius
See also RGWL 2, 3

Aurobindo, Sri
See Ghose, Aurabinda

Aurobindo Ghose
See Ghose, Aurabinda

Austen, Jane 1775-1817 ...... **NCLC 1, 13, 19, 33, 51, 81, 95, 119, 150; WLC**
See also AAYA 19; BRW 4; BRWC 1; BRWR 2; BYA 3; CDBLB 1789-1832; DA; DA3; DAB; DAC; DAM MST, NOV; DLB 116; EXPN; LAIT 2; LATS 1:1; LMFS 1; NFS 1, 14, 18, 20; TEA; WLIT 3; WYAS 1

Auster, Paul 1947- .... **CLC 47, 131**
See also AMWS 12; CA 69-72; CANR 23, 52, 75, 129; CMW 4; CN 7; DA3; DLB 227; MTCW 1; SUFW 2

Austin, Frank
See Faust, Frederick (Schiller)
See also TCWW 2

Austin, Mary (Hunter) 1868-1934 . **TCLC 25**
See Stairs, Gordon
See also ANW; CA 109; 178; DLB 9, 78,
206, 221, 275; FW; TCWW 2

Averroes 1126-1198 .... **CMLC 7**
See also DLB 115

Avicenna 980-1037 .... **CMLC 16**
See also DLB 115

Avison, Margaret (Kirkland) 1918- .. **CLC 2,
4, 97**
See also CA 17-20R; CANR 134; CP 7;
DAC; DAM POET; DLB 53; MTCW 1

Axton, David
See Koontz, Dean R(ay)

Ayckbourn, Alan 1939- ...... **CLC 5, 8, 18, 33,
74; DC 13**
See also BRWS 5; CA 21-24R; CANR 31,
59, 118; CBD; CD 5; DAB; DAM DRAM;
DFS 7; DLB 13, 245; EWL 3; MTCW 1,
2

Aydy, Catherine
See Tennant, Emma (Christina)

Ayme, Marcel (Andre) 1902-1967 ... **CLC 11;
SSC 41**
See also CA 89-92; CANR 67; CLR 25;
DLB 72; EW 12; EWL 3; GFL 1789 to
the Present; RGSF 2; RGWL 2, 3; SATA
91

Ayrton, Michael 1921-1975 .... **CLC 7**
See also CA 5-8R; 61-64; CANR 9, 21

Aytmatov, Chingiz
See Aitmatov, Chingiz (Torekulovich)
See also EWL 3

Azorin .... **CLC 11**
See Martinez Ruiz, Jose
See also EW 9; EWL 3

Azuela, Mariano 1873-1952 .. **HLC 1; TCLC
3, 145**
See also CA 104; 131; CANR 81; DAM
MULT; EWL 3; HW 1, 2; LAW; MTCW
1, 2

Ba, Mariama 1929-1981 .... **BLCS**
See also AFW; BW 2; CA 141; CANR 87;
DNFS 2; WLIT 2

Baastad, Babbis Friis
See Friis-Baastad, Babbis Ellinor

Bab
See Gilbert, W(illiam) S(chwenck)

Babbis, Eleanor
See Friis-Baastad, Babbis Ellinor

Babel, Isaac
See Babel, Isaak (Emmanuilovich)
See also EW 11; SSFS 10

Babel, Isaak (Emmanuilovich)
1894-1941(?) .. **SSC 16, 78; TCLC 2, 13**
See Babel, Isaac
See also CA 104; 155; CANR 113; DLB
272; EWL 3; MTCW 1; RGSF 2; RGWL
2, 3; TWA

Babits, Mihaly 1883-1941 .... **TCLC 14**
See also CA 114; CDWLB 4; DLB 215;
EWL 3

Babur 1483-1530 .... **LC 18**

Babylas 1898-1962
See Ghelderode, Michel de

Baca, Jimmy Santiago 1952- . **HLC 1; PC 41**
See also CA 131; CANR 81, 90; CP 7;
DAM MULT; DLB 122; HW 1, 2; LLW 1

Baca, Jose Santiago
See Baca, Jimmy Santiago

Bacchelli, Riccardo 1891-1985 .... **CLC 19**
See also CA 29-32R; 117; DLB 264; EWL
3

Bach, Richard (David) 1936- .... **CLC 14**
See also AITN 1; BEST 89:2; BPFB 1; BYA
5; CA 9-12R; CANR 18, 93; CPW; DAM
NOV, POP; FANT; MTCW 1; SATA 13

Bache, Benjamin Franklin
1769-1798 .... **LC 74**
See also DLB 43

Bachelard, Gaston 1884-1962 ...... **TCLC 128**
See also CA 97-100; 89-92; DLB 296; GFL
1789 to the Present

Bachman, Richard
See King, Stephen (Edwin)

Bachmann, Ingeborg 1926-1973 .... **CLC 69**
See also CA 93-96; 45-48; CANR 69; DLB
85; EWL 3; RGWL 2, 3

Bacon, Francis 1561-1626 .... **LC 18, 32**
See also BRW 1; CDBLB Before 1660;
DLB 151, 236, 252; RGEL 2; TEA

Bacon, Roger 1214(?)-1294 .... **CMLC 14**
See also DLB 115

Bacovia, George 1881-1957 .... **TCLC 24**
See Vasiliu, Gheorghe
See also CDWLB 4; DLB 220; EWL 3

Badanes, Jerome 1937-1995 .... **CLC 59**

Bagehot, Walter 1826-1877 .... **NCLC 10**
See also DLB 55

Bagnold, Enid 1889-1981 .... **CLC 25**
See also BYA 2; CA 5-8R; 103; CANR 5,
40; CBD; CWD; CWRI 5; DAM DRAM;
DLB 13, 160, 191, 245; FW; MAICYA 1,
2; RGEL 2; SATA 1, 25

Bagritsky, Eduard .... **TCLC 60**
See Dzyubin, Eduard Georgievich

Bagrjana, Elisaveta
See Belcheva, Elisaveta Lyubomirova

Bagryana, Elisaveta .... **CLC 10**
See Belcheva, Elisaveta Lyubomirova
See also CA 178; CDWLB 4; DLB 147;
EWL 3

Bailey, Paul 1937- .... **CLC 45**
See also CA 21-24R; CANR 16, 62, 124;
CN 7; DLB 14, 271; GLL 2

Baillie, Joanna 1762-1851 ...... **NCLC 71, 151**
See also DLB 93; RGEL 2

Bainbridge, Beryl (Margaret) 1934- . **CLC 4,
5, 8, 10, 14, 18, 22, 62, 130**
See also BRWS 6; CA 21-24R; CANR 24,
55, 75, 88, 128; CN 7; DAM NOV; DLB
14, 231; EWL 3; MTCW 1, 2

Baker, Carlos (Heard)
1909-1987 .... **TCLC 119**
See also CA 5-8R; 122; CANR 3, 63; DLB
103

Baker, Elliott 1922- .... **CLC 8**
See also CA 45-48; CANR 2, 63; CN 7

Baker, Jean H. .... **TCLC 3, 10**
See Russell, George William

Baker, Nicholson 1957- .... **CLC 61, 165**
See also AMWS 13; CA 135; CANR 63,
120; CN 7; CPW; DA3; DAM POP; DLB
227

Baker, Ray Stannard 1870-1946 .... **TCLC 47**
See also CA 118

Baker, Russell (Wayne) 1925- .... **CLC 31**
See also BEST 89:4; CA 57-60; CANR 11,
41, 59; MTCW 1, 2

Bakhtin, M.
See Bakhtin, Mikhail Mikhailovich

Bakhtin, M. M.
See Bakhtin, Mikhail Mikhailovich

Bakhtin, Mikhail
See Bakhtin, Mikhail Mikhailovich

Bakhtin, Mikhail Mikhailovich
1895-1975 .... **CLC 83; TCLC 160**
See also CA 128; 113; DLB 242; EWL 3

Bakshi, Ralph 1938(?)- .... **CLC 26**
See also CA 112; 138; IDFW 3

Bakunin, Mikhail (Alexandrovich)
1814-1876 .... **NCLC 25, 58**
See also DLB 277

Baldwin, James (Arthur) 1924-1987 . **BLC 1;
CLC 1, 2, 3, 4, 5, 8, 13, 15, 17, 42, 50,
67, 90, 127; DC 1; SSC 10, 33; WLC**
See also AAYA 4, 34; AFAW 1, 2; AMWR
2; AMWS 1; BPFB 1; BW 1; CA 1-4R;
124; CABS 1; CAD; CANR 3, 24;
CDALB 1941-1968; CPW; DA; DA3;
DAB; DAC; DAM MST, MULT, NOV,
POP; DFS 11, 15; DLB 2, 7, 33, 249, 278;
DLBY 1987; EWL 3; EXPS; LAIT 5;
MTCW 1, 2; NCFS 4; NFS 4; RGAL 4;
RGSF 2; SATA 9; SATA-Obit 54; SSFS
2, 18; TUS

Baldwin, William c. 1515-c. 1563 ...... **LC 113**
See also DLB 132

Bale, John 1495-1563 .... **LC 62**
See also DLB 132; RGEL 2; TEA

Ball, Hugo 1886-1927 .... **TCLC 104**

Ballard, J(ames) G(raham) 1930- . **CLC 3, 6,
14, 36, 137; SSC 1, 53**
See also AAYA 3, 52; BRWS 5; CA 5-8R;
CANR 15, 39, 65, 107, 133; CN 7; DA3;
DAM NOV, POP; DLB 14, 207, 261;
EWL 3; HGG; MTCW 1, 2; NFS 8;
RGEL 2; RGSF 2; SATA 93; SFW 4

Balmont, Konstantin (Dmitriyevich)
1867-1943 .... **TCLC 11**
See also CA 109; 155; DLB 295; EWL 3

Baltausis, Vincas 1847-1910
See Mikszath, Kalman

Balzac, Honore de 1799-1850 ... **NCLC 5, 35,
53, 153; SSC 5, 59; WLC**
See also DA; DA3; DAB; DAC; DAM
MST, NOV; DLB 119; EW 5; GFL 1789
to the Present; LMFS 1; RGSF 2; RGWL
2, 3; SSFS 10; SUFW; TWA

Bambara, Toni Cade 1939-1995 .... **BLC 1;
CLC 19, 88; SSC 35; TCLC 116;
WLCS**
See also AAYA 5, 49; AFAW 2; AMWS 11;
BW 2, 3; BYA 12, 14; CA 29-32R; 150;
CANR 24, 49, 81; CDALBS; DA; DA3;
DAC; DAM MST, MULT; DLB 38, 218;
EXPS; MTCW 1, 2; RGAL 4; RGSF 2;
SATA 112; SSFS 4, 7, 12

Bamdad, A.
See Shamlu, Ahmad

Bamdad, Alef
See Shamlu, Ahmad

Banat, D. R.
See Bradbury, Ray (Douglas)

Bancroft, Laura
See Baum, L(yman) Frank

Banim, John 1798-1842 .... **NCLC 13**
See also DLB 116, 158, 159; RGEL 2

Banim, Michael 1796-1874 .... **NCLC 13**
See also DLB 158, 159

Banjo, The
See Paterson, A(ndrew) B(arton)

Banks, Iain
See Banks, Iain M(enzies)

Banks, Iain M(enzies) 1954- .... **CLC 34**
See also CA 123; 128; CANR 61, 106; DLB
194, 261; EWL 3; HGG; INT CA-128;
SFW 4

Banks, Lynne Reid .... **CLC 23**
See Reid Banks, Lynne
See also AAYA 6; BYA 7; CLR 86

Banks, Russell (Earl) 1940- .... **CLC 37, 72,
187; SSC 42**
See also AAYA 45; AMWS 5; CA 65-68;
CAAS 15; CANR 19, 52, 73, 118; CN 7;
DLB 130, 278; EWL 3; NFS 13

Banville, John 1945- .... **CLC 46, 118**
See also CA 117; 128; CANR 104; CN 7;
DLB 14, 271; INT CA-128

Banville, Theodore (Faullain) de
1832-1891 .... **NCLC 9**
See also DLB 217; GFL 1789 to the Present

Benary-Isbert, Margot 1889-1979 .... **CLC 12**
  See also CA 5-8R; 89-92; CANR 4, 72;
  CLR 12; MAICYA 1, 2; SATA 2; SATA-
  Obit 21

Benavente (y Martinez), Jacinto
  1866-1954 .... **DC 26; HLCS 1; TCLC 3**
  See also CA 106; 131; CANR 81; DAM
  DRAM, MULT; EWL 3; GLL 2; HW 1,
  2; MTCW 1, 2

Benchley, Peter (Bradford) 1940- .. **CLC 4, 8**
  See also AAYA 14; AITN 2; BPFB 1; CA
  17-20R; CANR 12, 35, 66, 115; CPW;
  DAM NOV, POP; HGG; MTCW 1, 2;
  SATA 3, 89

Benchley, Robert (Charles)
  1889-1945 .... **TCLC 1, 55**
  See also CA 105; 153; DLB 11; RGAL 4

Benda, Julien 1867-1956 .... **TCLC 60**
  See also CA 120; 154; GFL 1789 to the
  Present

Benedict, Ruth (Fulton)
  1887-1948 .... **TCLC 60**
  See also CA 158; DLB 246

Benedikt, Michael 1935- .... **CLC 4, 14**
  See also CA 13-16R; CANR 7; CP 7; DLB
  5

Benet, Juan 1927-1993 .... **CLC 28**
  See also CA 143; EWL 3

Benet, Stephen Vincent 1898-1943 ..... **PC 64;**
  SSC 10; TCLC 7
  See also AMWS 11; CA 104; 152; DA3;
  DAM POET; DLB 4, 48, 102, 249, 284;
  DLBY 1997; EWL 3; HGG; MTCW 1;
  RGAL 4; RGSF; SUFW; WP; YABC 1

Benet, William Rose 1886-1950 ..... **TCLC 28**
  See also CA 118; 152; DAM POET; DLB
  45; RGAL 4

Benford, Gregory (Albert) 1941- ..... **CLC 52**
  See also BPFB 1; CA 69-72, 175; CAAE
  175; CAAS 27; CANR 12, 24, 49, 95,
  134; CSW; DLBY 1982; SCFW 2; SFW
  4

Bengtsson, Frans (Gunnar)
  1894-1954 .... **TCLC 48**
  See also CA 170; EWL 3

Benjamin, David
  See Slavitt, David R(ytman)

Benjamin, Lois
  See Gould, Lois

Benjamin, Walter 1892-1940 .... **TCLC 39**
  See also CA 164; DLB 242; EW 11; EWL
  3

Ben Jelloun, Tahar 1944-
  See Jelloun, Tahar ben
  See also CA 135; CWW 2; EWL 3; RGWL
  3; WLIT 2

Benn, Gottfried 1886-1956 .. **PC 35; TCLC 3**
  See also CA 106; 153; DLB 56; EWL 3;
  RGWL 2, 3

Bennett, Alan 1934- .... **CLC 45, 77**
  See also BRWS 8; CA 103; CANR 35, 55,
  106; CBD; CD 5; DAB; DAM MST;
  MTCW 1, 2

Bennett, (Enoch) Arnold
  1867-1931 .... **TCLC 5, 20**
  See also BRW 6; CA 106; 155; CDBLB
  1890-1914; DLB 10, 34, 98, 135; EWL 3;
  MTCW 2

Bennett, Elizabeth
  See Mitchell, Margaret (Munnerlyn)

Bennett, George Harold 1930-
  See Bennett, Hal
  See also BW 1; CA 97-100; CANR 87

Bennett, Gwendolyn B. 1902-1981 .... **HR 2**
  See also BW 1; CA 125; DLB 51; WP

Bennett, Hal .... **CLC 5**
  See Bennett, George Harold
  See also DLB 33

Bennett, Jay 1912- .... **CLC 35**
  See also AAYA 10; CA 69-72; CANR 11,
  42, 79; JRDA; SAAS 4; SATA 41, 87;
  SATA-Brief 27; WYA; YAW

Bennett, Louise (Simone) 1919- .... **BLC 1;**
  CLC 28
  See also BW 2, 3; CA 151; CDWLB 3; CP
  7; DAM MULT; DLB 117; EWL 3

Benson, A. C. 1862-1925 .... **TCLC 123**
  See also DLB 98

Benson, E(dward) F(rederic)
  1867-1940 .... **TCLC 27**
  See also CA 114; 157; DLB 135, 153;
  HGG; SUFW 1

Benson, Jackson J. 1930- .... **CLC 34**
  See also CA 25-28R; DLB 111

Benson, Sally 1900-1972 .... **CLC 17**
  See also CA 19-20; 37-40R; CAP 1; SATA
  1, 35; SATA-Obit 27

Benson, Stella 1892-1933 .... **TCLC 17**
  See also CA 117; 154, 155; DLB 36, 162;
  FANT; TEA

Bentham, Jeremy 1748-1832 .... **NCLC 38**
  See also DLB 107, 158, 252

Bentley, E(dmund) C(lerihew)
  1875-1956 .... **TCLC 12**
  See also CA 108; DLB 70; MSW

Bentley, Eric (Russell) 1916- .... **CLC 24**
  See also CA 5-8R; CAD; CANR 6, 67;
  CBD; CD 5; INT CANR-6

ben Uzair, Salem
  See Horne, Richard Henry Hengist

Beranger, Pierre Jean de
  1780-1857 .... **NCLC 34**

Berdyaev, Nicolas
  See Berdyaev, Nikolai (Aleksandrovich)

Berdyaev, Nikolai (Aleksandrovich)
  1874-1948 .... **TCLC 67**
  See also CA 120; 157

Berdyayev, Nikolai (Aleksandrovich)
  See Berdyaev, Nikolai (Aleksandrovich)

Berendt, John (Lawrence) 1939- ...... **CLC 86**
  See also CA 146; CANR 75, 93; DA3;
  MTCW 1

Beresford, J(ohn) D(avys)
  1873-1947 .... **TCLC 81**
  See also CA 112; 155; DLB 162, 178, 197;
  SFW 4; SUFW 1

Bergelson, David (Rafailovich)
  1884-1952 .... **TCLC 81**
  See Bergelson, Dovid
  See also CA 220

Bergelson, Dovid
  See Bergelson, David (Rafailovich)
  See also EWL 3

Berger, Colonel
  See Malraux, (Georges-)Andre

Berger, John (Peter) 1926- .... **CLC 2, 19**
  See also BRWS 4; CA 81-84; CANR 51,
  78, 117; CN 7; DLB 14, 207

Berger, Melvin H. 1927- .... **CLC 12**
  See also CA 5-8R; CANR 4; CLR 32;
  SAAS 2; SATA 5, 88; SATA-Essay 124

Berger, Thomas (Louis) 1924- .. **CLC 3, 5, 8,**
  11, 18, 38
  See also BPFB 1; CA 1-4R; CANR 5, 28,
  51, 128; CN 7; DAM NOV; DLB 2;
  DLBY 1980; EWL 3; FANT; INT CANR-
  28; MTCW 1, 2; RHW; TCWW 2

Bergman, (Ernst) Ingmar 1918- ...... **CLC 16,**
  72, 219
  See also CA 81-84; CANR 33, 70; CWW
  2; DLB 257; MTCW 2

Bergson, Henri(-Louis) 1859-1941 . **TCLC 32**
  See also CA 164; EW 8; EWL 3; GFL 1789
  to the Present

Bergstein, Eleanor 1938- .... **CLC 4**
  See also CA 53-56; CANR 5

Berkeley, George 1685-1753 .... **LC 65**
  See also DLB 31, 101, 252

Berkoff, Steven 1937- .... **CLC 56**
  See also CA 104; CANR 72; CBD; CD 5

Berlin, Isaiah 1909-1997 .... **TCLC 105**
  See also CA 85-88; 162

Bermant, Chaim (Icyk) 1929-1998 ... **CLC 40**
  See also CA 57-60; CANR 6, 31, 57, 105;
  CN 7

Bern, Victoria
  See Fisher, M(ary) F(rances) K(ennedy)

Bernanos, (Paul Louis) Georges
  1888-1948 .... **TCLC 3**
  See also CA 104; 130; CANR 94; DLB 72;
  EWL 3; GFL 1789 to the Present; RGWL
  2, 3

Bernard, April 1956- .... **CLC 59**
  See also CA 131

Bernard of Clairvaux 1090-1153 .. **CMLC 71**
  See also DLB 208

Berne, Victoria
  See Fisher, M(ary) F(rances) K(ennedy)

Bernhard, Thomas 1931-1989 ..... **CLC 3, 32,**
  61; DC 14; TCLC 165
  See also CA 85-88; 127; CANR 32, 57; CD-
  WLB 2; DLB 85, 124; EWL 3; MTCW 1;
  RGWL 2, 3

Bernhardt, Sarah (Henriette Rosine)
  1844-1923 .... **TCLC 75**
  See also CA 157

Bernstein, Charles 1950- .... **CLC 142,**
  See also CA 129; CAAS 24; CANR 90; CP
  7; DLB 169

Bernstein, Ingrid
  See Kirsch, Sarah

Beroul fl. c. 1150- .... **CMLC 75**

Berriault, Gina 1926-1999 .... **CLC 54, 109;**
  SSC 30
  See also CA 116; 129; 185; CANR 66; DLB
  130; SSFS 7,11

Berrigan, Daniel 1921- .... **CLC 4**
  See also CA 33-36R, 187; CAAE 187;
  CAAS 1; CANR 11, 43, 78; CP 7; DLB 5

Berrigan, Edmund Joseph Michael, Jr.
  1934-1983
  See Berrigan, Ted
  See also CA 61-64; 110; CANR 14, 102

Berrigan, Ted .... **CLC 37**
  See Berrigan, Edmund Joseph Michael, Jr.
  See also DLB 5, 169; WP

Berry, Charles Edward Anderson 1931-
  See Berry, Chuck
  See also CA 115

Berry, Chuck .... **CLC 17**
  See Berry, Charles Edward Anderson

Berry, Jonas
  See Ashbery, John (Lawrence)
  See also GLL 1

Berry, Wendell (Erdman) 1934- ... **CLC 4, 6,**
  8, 27, 46; PC 28
  See also AITN 1; AMWS 10; ANW; CA
  73-76; CANR 50, 73, 101, 132; CP 7;
  CSW; DAM POET; DLB 5, 6, 234, 275;
  MTCW 1

Berryman, John 1914-1972 ... **CLC 1, 2, 3, 4,**
  6, 8, 10, 13, 25, 62; PC 64
  See also AMW; CA 13-16; 33-36R; CABS
  2; CANR 35; CAP 1; CDALB 1941-1968;
  DAM POET; DLB 48; EWL 3; MTCW 1,
  2; PAB; RGAL 4; WP

Bertolucci, Bernardo 1940- ...... **CLC 16, 157**
  See also CA 106; CANR 125

Berton, Pierre (Francis Demarigny)
  1920-2004 .... **CLC 104**
  See also CA 1-4R; CANR 2, 56; CPW;
  DLB 68; SATA 99

Bertrand, Aloysius 1807-1841 .... **NCLC 31**
  See Bertrand, Louis oAloysiusc

Breton, Andre 1896-1966 .. CLC 2, 9, 15, 54;
PC 15
See also CA 19-20; 25-28R; CANR 40, 60;
CAP 2; DLB 65, 258; EW 11; EWL 3;
GFL 1789 to the Present; LMFS 2;
MTCW 1, 2; RGWL 2, 3; TWA; WP

Breytenbach, Breyten 1939(?)- .. CLC 23, 37,
126
See also CA 113; 129; CANR 61, 122;
CWW 2; DAM POET; DLB 225; EWL 3

Bridgers, Sue Ellen 1942- .... CLC 26
See also AAYA 8, 49; BYA 7, 8; CA 65-68;
CANR 11, 36; CLR 18; DLB 52; JRDA;
MAICYA 1, 2; SAAS 1; SATA 22, 90;
SATA-Essay 109; WYA; YAW

Bridges, Robert (Seymour)
1844-1930 .... PC 28; TCLC 1
See also BRW 6; CA 104; 152; CDBLB
1890-1914; DAM POET; DLB 19, 98

Bridie, James .... TCLC 3
See Mavor, Osborne Henry
See also DLB 10; EWL 3

Brin, David 1950- .... CLC 34
See also AAYA 21; CA 102; CANR 24, 70,
125, 127; INT CANR-24; SATA 65;
SCFW 2; SFW 4

Brink, Andre (Philippus) 1935- . CLC 18, 36,
106
See also AFW; BRWS 6; CA 104; CANR
39, 62, 109, 133; CN 7; DLB 225; EWL
3; INT CA-103; LATS 1:2; MTCW 1, 2;
WLIT 2

Brinsmead, H. F(ay)
See Brinsmead, H(esba) F(ay)

Brinsmead, H. F.
See Brinsmead, H(esba) F(ay)

Brinsmead, H(esba) F(ay) 1922- ...... CLC 21
See also CA 21-24R; CANR 10; CLR 47;
CWRI 5; MAICYA 1, 2; SAAS 5; SATA
18, 78

Brittain, Vera (Mary) 1893(?)-1970 . CLC 23
See also BRWS 10; CA 13-16; 25-28R;
CANR 58; CAP 1; DLB 191; FW; MTCW
1, 2

Broch, Hermann 1886-1951 .... TCLC 20
See also CA 117; 211; CDWLB 2; DLB 85,
124; EW 10; EWL 3; RGWL 2, 3

Brock, Rose
See Hansen, Joseph
See also GLL 1

Brod, Max 1884-1968 .... TCLC 115
See also CA 5-8R; 25-28R; CANR 7; DLB
81; EWL 3

Brodkey, Harold (Roy) 1930-1996 .. CLC 56;
TCLC 123
See also CA 111; 151; CANR 71; CN 7;
DLB 130

Brodsky, Iosif Alexandrovich 1940-1996
See Brodsky, Joseph
See also AITN 1; CA 41-44R; 151; CANR
37, 106; DA3; DAM POET; MTCW 1, 2;
RGWL 2, 3

Brodsky, Joseph . CLC 4, 6, 13, 36, 100; PC
9
See Brodsky, Iosif Alexandrovich
See also AMWS 8; CWW 2; DLB 285;
EWL 3; MTCW 1

Brodsky, Michael (Mark) 1948- ...... CLC 19
See also CA 102; CANR 18, 41, 58; DLB
244

Brodzki, Bella ed. .... CLC 65

Brome, Richard 1590(?)-1652 .... LC 61
See also BRWS 10; DLB 58

Bromell, Henry 1947- .... CLC 5
See also CA 53-56; CANR 9, 115, 116

Bromfield, Louis (Brucker)
1896-1956 .... TCLC 11
See also CA 107; 155; DLB 4, 9, 86; RGAL
4; RHW

Broner, E(sther) M(asserman)
1930- .... CLC 19
See also CA 17-20R; CANR 8, 25, 72; CN
7; DLB 28

Bronk, William (M.) 1918-1999 .... CLC 10
See also CA 89-92; 177; CANR 23; CP 7;
DLB 165

Bronstein, Lev Davidovich
See Trotsky, Leon

Bronte, Anne 1820-1849 ..... NCLC 4, 71, 102
See also BRW 5; BRWR 1; DA3; DLB 21,
199; TEA

Bronte, (Patrick) Branwell
1817-1848 .... NCLC 109

Bronte, Charlotte 1816-1855 ...... NCLC 3, 8,
33, 58, 105, 155; WLC
See also AAYA 17; BRW 5; BRWC 2;
BRWR 1; BYA 2; CDBLB 1832-1890;
DA; DA3; DAB; DAC; DAM MST, NOV;
DLB 21, 159, 199; EXPN; LAIT 2; NFS
4; TEA; WLIT 4

Bronte, Emily (Jane) 1818-1848 ... NCLC 16,
35; PC 8; WLC
See also AAYA 17; BPFB 1; BRW 5;
BRWC 1; BRWR 1; BYA 3; CDBLB
1832-1890; DA; DA3; DAB; DAC; DAM
MST, NOV, POET; DLB 21, 32, 199;
EXPN; LAIT 1; TEA; WLIT 3

Brontes
See Bronte, Anne; Bronte, Charlotte; Bronte,
Emily (Jane)

Brooke, Frances 1724-1789 .... LC 6, 48
See also DLB 39, 99

Brooke, Henry 1703(?)-1783 .... LC 1
See also DLB 39

Brooke, Rupert (Chawner)
1887-1915 ..... PC 24; TCLC 2, 7; WLC
See also BRWS 3; CA 104; 132; CANR 61;
CDBLB 1914-1945; DA; DAB; DAC;
DAM MST, POET; DLB 19, 216; EXPP;
GLL 2; MTCW 1, 2; PFS 7; TEA

Brooke-Haven, P.
See Wodehouse, P(elham) G(renville)

Brooke-Rose, Christine 1926(?)- ..... CLC 40,
184
See also BRWS 4; CA 13-16R; CANR 58;
118; CN 7; DLB 14, 231; EWL 3; SFW 4

Brookner, Anita 1928- .. CLC 32, 34, 51, 136
See also BRWS 4; CA 114; 120; CANR 37,
56, 87, 130; CN 7; CPW; DA3; DAB;
DAM POP; DLB 194; DLBY 1987; EWL
3; MTCW 1, 2; TEA

Brooks, Cleanth 1906-1994 . CLC 24, 86, 110
See also AMWS 14; CA 17-20R; 145;
CANR 33, 35; CSW; DLB 63; DLBY
1994; EWL 3; INT CANR-35; MTCW 1,
2

Brooks, George
See Baum, L(yman) Frank

Brooks, Gwendolyn (Elizabeth)
1917-2000 ... BLC 1; CLC 1, 2, 4, 5, 15,
49, 125; PC 7; WLC
See also AAYA 20; AFAW 1, 2; AITN 1;
AMWS 3; BW 2, 3; CA 1-4R; 190; CANR
1, 27, 52, 75, 132; CDALB 1941-1968;
CLR 27; CP 7; CWP; DA; DA3; DAC;
DAM MST, MULT, POET; DLB 5, 76,
165; EWL 3; EXPP; MAWW; MTCW 1,
2; PFS 1, 2, 4, 6; RGAL 4; SATA 6;
SATA-Obit 123; TUS; WP

Brooks, Mel .... CLC 12
See Kaminsky, Melvin
See also AAYA 13, 48; DLB 26

Brooks, Peter (Preston) 1938- .... CLC 34
See also CA 45-48; CANR 1, 107

Brooks, Van Wyck 1886-1963 .... CLC 29
See also AMW; CA 1-4R; CANR 6; DLB
45, 63, 103; TUS

Brophy, Brigid (Antonia)
1929-1995 .... CLC 6, 11, 29, 105
See also CA 5-8R; 149; CAAS 4; CANR
25, 53; CBD; CN 7; CWD; DA3; DLB
14, 271; EWL 3; MTCW 1, 2

Brosman, Catharine Savage 1934- ..... CLC 9
See also CA 61-64; CANR 21, 46

Brossard, Nicole 1943- .... CLC 115, 169
See also CA 122; CAAS 16; CCA 1; CWP;
CWW 2; DLB 53; EWL 3; FW; GLL 2;
RGWL 3

Brother Antoninus
See Everson, William (Oliver)

The Brothers Quay
See Quay, Stephen; Quay, Timothy

Broughton, T(homas) Alan 1936- ..... CLC 19
See also CA 45-48; CANR 2, 23, 48, 111

Broumas, Olga 1949- .... CLC 10, 73
See also CA 85-88; CANR 20, 69, 110; CP
7; CWP; GLL 2

Broun, Heywood 1888-1939 .... TCLC 104
See also DLB 29, 171

Brown, Alan 1950- .... CLC 99
See also CA 156

Brown, Charles Brockden
1771-1810 .... NCLC 22, 74, 122
See also AMWS 1; CDALB 1640-1865;
DLB 37, 59, 73; FW; HGG; LMFS 1;
RGAL 4; TUS

Brown, Christy 1932-1981 .... CLC 63
See also BYA 13; CA 105; 104; CANR 72;
DLB 14

Brown, Claude 1937-2002 ... BLC 1; CLC 30
See also AAYA 7; BW 1, 3; CA 73-76; 205;
CANR 81; DAM MULT

Brown, Dan .... CLC 209
See also AAYA 55; CA 217; MTFW

Brown, Dee (Alexander)
1908-2002 .... CLC 18, 47
See also AAYA 30; CA 13-16R; 212; CAAS
6; CANR 11, 45, 60; CPW; CSW; DA3;
DAM POP; DLBY 1980; LAIT 2; MTCW
1, 2; NCFS 5; SATA 5, 110; SATA-Obit
141; TCWW 2

Brown, George
See Wertmueller, Lina

Brown, George Douglas
1869-1902 .... TCLC 28
See Douglas, George
See also CA 162

Brown, George Mackay 1921-1996 ... CLC 5,
48, 100
See also BRWS 6; CA 21-24R; 151; CAAS
6; CANR 12, 37, 67; CN 7; CP 7; DLB
14, 27, 139, 271; MTCW 1; RGSF 2;
SATA 35

Brown, (William) Larry 1951-2004 . CLC 73
See also CA 130; 134; CANR 117; CSW;
DLB 234; INT CA-134

Brown, Moses
See Barrett, William (Christopher)

Brown, Rita Mae 1944- .... CLC 18, 43, 79
See also BPFB 1; CA 45-48; CANR 2, 11,
35, 62, 95; CN 7; CPW; CSW; DA3;
DAM NOV, POP; FW; INT CANR-11;
MTCW 1, 2; NFS 9; RGAL 4; TUS

Brown, Roderick (Langmere) Haig-
See Haig-Brown, Roderick (Langmere)

Brown, Rosellen 1939- .... CLC 32, 170
See also CA 77-80; CAAS 10; CANR 14,
44, 98; CN 7

Brown, Sterling Allen 1901-1989 ...... BLC 1;
CLC 1, 23, 59; HR 2; PC 55
See also AFAW 1, 2; BW 1, 3; CA 85-88;
127; CANR 26; DA3; DAM MULT,
POET; DLB 48, 51, 63; MTCW 1, 2;
RGAL 4; WP

Brown, Will
See Ainsworth, William Harrison

Burroughs, William S(eward)
1914-1997 .. **CLC 1, 2, 5, 15, 22, 42, 75, 109; TCLC 121; WLC**
See Lee, William; Lee, Willy
See also AAYA 60; AITN 2; AMWS 3; BG 2; BPFB 1; CA 9-12R; 160; CANR 20, 52, 104; CN 7; CPW; DA; DA3; DAB; DAC; DAM MST, NOV, POP; DLB 2, 8, 16, 152, 237; DLBY 1981, 1997; EWL 3; HGG; LMFS 2; MTCW 1, 2; RGAL 4; SFW 4

Burton, Sir Richard F(rancis)
1821-1890 .... **NCLC 42**
See also DLB 55, 166, 184

Burton, Robert 1577-1640 .... **LC 74**
See also DLB 151; RGEL 2

Buruma, Ian 1951- .... **CLC 163**
See also CA 128; CANR 65

Busch, Frederick 1941- ... **CLC 7, 10, 18, 47, 166**
See also CA 33-36R; CAAS 1; CANR 45, 73, 92; CN 7; DLB 6, 218

Bush, Barney (Furman) 1946- .... **NNAL**
See also CA 145

Bush, Ronald 1946- .... **CLC 34**
See also CA 136

Bustos, F(rancisco)
See Borges, Jorge Luis

Bustos Domecq, H(onorio)
See Bioy Casares, Adolfo; Borges, Jorge Luis

Butler, Octavia E(stelle) 1947- .. **BLCS; CLC 38, 121**
See also AAYA 18, 48; AFAW 2; AMWS 13; BPFB 1; BW 2, 3; CA 73-76; CANR 12, 24, 38, 73; CLR 65; CPW; DA3; DAM MULT, POP; DLB 33; LATS 1:2; MTCW 1, 2; NFS 8; SATA 84; SCFW 2; SFW 4; SSFS 6; YAW

Butler, Robert Olen, (Jr.) 1945- ...... **CLC 81, 162**
See also AMWS 12; BPFB 1; CA 112; CANR 66; CSW; DAM POP; DLB 173; INT CA-112; SSFS 11

Butler, Samuel 1612-1680 .... **LC 16, 43**
See also DLB 101, 126; RGEL 2

Butler, Samuel 1835-1902 .... **TCLC 1, 33; WLC**
See also BRWS 2; CA 143; CDBLB 1890-1914; DA; DA3; DAB; DAC; DAM MST, NOV; DLB 18, 57, 174; RGEL 2; SFW 4; TEA

Butler, Walter C.
See Faust, Frederick (Schiller)

Butor, Michel (Marie Francois)
1926- .... **CLC 1, 3, 8, 11, 15, 161**
See also CA 9-12R; CANR 33, 66; CWW 2; DLB 83; EW 13; EWL 3; GFL 1789 to the Present; MTCW 1, 2

Butts, Mary 1890(?)-1937 .... **TCLC 77**
See also CA 148; DLB 240

Buxton, Ralph
See Silverstein, Alvin; Silverstein, Virginia B(arbara Opshelor)

Buzo, Alex
See Buzo, Alexander (John)
See also DLB 289

Buzo, Alexander (John) 1944- .... **CLC 61**
See also CA 97-100; CANR 17, 39, 69; CD 5

Buzzati, Dino 1906-1972 .... **CLC 36**
See also CA 160; 33-36R; DLB 177; RGWL 2, 3; SFW 4

Byars, Betsy (Cromer) 1928- .... **CLC 35**
See also AAYA 19; BYA 3; CA 33-36R, 183; CAAE 183; CANR 18, 36, 57, 102; CLR 1, 16, 72; DLB 52; INT CANR-18; JRDA; MAICYA 1, 2; MAICYAS 1; MTCW 1; SAAS 1; SATA 4, 46, 80; SATA-Essay 108; WYA; YAW

Byatt, A(ntonia) S(usan Drabble)
1936- .... **CLC 19, 65, 136**
See also BPFB 1; BRWC 2; BRWS 4; CA 13-16R; CANR 13, 33, 50, 75, 96, 133; DA3; DAM NOV, POP; DLB 14, 194; EWL 3; MTCW 1, 2; RGSF 2; RHW; TEA

Byrd, Willam II 1674-1744 .... **LC 112**
See also DLB 24, 140; RGAL 4

Byrne, David 1952- .... **CLC 26**
See also CA 127

Byrne, John Keyes 1926-
See Leonard, Hugh
See also CA 102; CANR 78; INT CA-102

Byron, George Gordon (Noel)
1788-1824 ..... **DC 24; NCLC 2, 12, 109, 149; PC 16; WLC**
See also BRW 4; BRWC 2; CDBLB 1789-1832; DA; DA3; DAB; DAC; DAM MST, POET; DLB 96, 110; EXPP; LMFS 1; PAB; PFS 1, 14; RGEL 2; TEA; WLIT 3; WP

Byron, Robert 1905-1941 .... **TCLC 67**
See also CA 160; DLB 195

C. 3. 3.
See Wilde, Oscar (Fingal O'Flahertie Wills)

Caballero, Fernan 1796-1877 .... **NCLC 10**

Cabell, Branch
See Cabell, James Branch

Cabell, James Branch 1879-1958 .... **TCLC 6**
See also CA 105; 152; DLB 9, 78; FANT; MTCW 1; RGAL 4; SUFW 1

Cabeza de Vaca, Alvar Nunez
1490-1557(?) .... **LC 61**

Cable, George Washington
1844-1925 .... **SSC 4; TCLC 4**
See also CA 104; 155; DLB 12, 74; DLBD 13; RGAL 4; TUS

Cabral de Melo Neto, Joao
1920-1999 .... **CLC 76**
See Melo Neto, Joao Cabral de
See also CA 151; DAM MULT; DLB 307; LAW; LAWS 1

Cabrera Infante, G(uillermo) 1929- . **CLC 5, 25, 45, 120; HLC 1; SSC 39**
See also CA 85-88; CANR 29, 65, 110; CD-WLB 3; CWW 2; DA3; DAM MULT; DLB 113; EWL 3; HW 1, 2; LAW; LAWS 1; MTCW 1, 2; RGSF 2; WLIT 1

Cade, Toni
See Bambara, Toni Cade

Cadmus and Harmonia
See Buchan, John

Caedmon fl. 658-680 .... **CMLC 7**
See also DLB 146

Caeiro, Alberto
See Pessoa, Fernando (Antonio Nogueira)

Caesar, Julius .... **CMLC 47**
See Julius Caesar
See also AW 1; RGWL 2, 3

Cage, John (Milton, Jr.)
1912-1992 .... **CLC 41; PC 58**
See also CA 13-16R; 169; CANR 9, 78; DLB 193; INT CANR-9

Cahan, Abraham 1860-1951 .... **TCLC 71**
See also CA 108; 154; DLB 9, 25, 28; RGAL 4

Cain, G.
See Cabrera Infante, G(uillermo)

Cain, Guillermo
See Cabrera Infante, G(uillermo)

Cain, James M(allahan) 1892-1977 .. **CLC 3, 11, 28**
See also AITN 1; BPFB 1; CA 17-20R; 73-76; CANR 8, 34, 61; CMW 4; DLB 226; EWL 3; MSW; MTCW 1; RGAL 4

Caine, Hall 1853-1931 .... **TCLC 97**
See also RHW

Caine, Mark
See Raphael, Frederic (Michael)

Calasso, Roberto 1941- .... **CLC 81**
See also CA 143; CANR 89

Calderon de la Barca, Pedro
1600-1681 .... **DC 3; HLCS 1; LC 23**
See also EW 2; RGWL 2, 3; TWA

Caldwell, Erskine (Preston)
1903-1987 .... **CLC 1, 8, 14, 50, 60; SSC 19; TCLC 117**
See also AITN 1; AMW; BPFB 1; CA 1-4R; 121; CAAS 1; CANR 2, 33; DA3; DAM NOV; DLB 9, 86; EWL 3; MTCW 1, 2; RGAL 4; RGSF 2; TUS

Caldwell, (Janet Miriam) Taylor (Holland)
1900-1985 .... **CLC 2, 28, 39**
See also BPFB 1; CA 5-8R; 116; CANR 5; DA3; DAM NOV, POP; DLBD 17; RHW

Calhoun, John Caldwell
1782-1850 .... **NCLC 15**
See also DLB 3, 248

Calisher, Hortense 1911- ..... **CLC 2, 4, 8, 38, 134; SSC 15**
See also CA 1-4R; CANR 1, 22, 117; CN 7; DA3; DAM NOV; DLB 2, 218; INT CANR-22; MTCW 1, 2; RGAL 4; RGSF 2

Callaghan, Morley Edward
1903-1990 ..... **CLC 3, 14, 41, 65; TCLC 145**
See also CA 9-12R; 132; CANR 33, 73; DAC; DAM MST; DLB 68; EWL 3; MTCW 1, 2; RGEL 2; RGSF 2; SSFS 19

Callimachus c. 305B.C.-c.
240B.C. .... **CMLC 18**
See also AW 1; DLB 176; RGWL 2, 3

Calvin, Jean
See Calvin, John
See also GFL Beginnings to 1789

Calvin, John 1509-1564 .... **LC 37**
See Calvin, Jean

Calvino, Italo 1923-1985 .... **CLC 5, 8, 11, 22, 33, 39, 73; SSC 3, 48**
See also AAYA 58; CA 85-88; 116; CANR 23, 61, 132; DAM NOV; DLB 196; EW 13; EWL 3; MTCW 1, 2; RGSF 2; RGWL 2, 3; SFW 4; SSFS 12

Camara Laye
See Laye, Camara
See also EWL 3

Camden, William 1551-1623 .... **LC 77**
See also DLB 172

Cameron, Carey 1952- .... **CLC 59**
See also CA 135

Cameron, Peter 1959- .... **CLC 44**
See also AMWS 12; CA 125; CANR 50, 117; DLB 234; GLL 2

Camoens, Luis Vaz de 1524(?)-1580
See Camoes, Luis de
See also EW 2

Camoes, Luis de 1524(?)-1580 . **HLCS 1; LC 62; PC 31**
See Camoens, Luis Vaz de
See also DLB 287; RGWL 2, 3

Campana, Dino 1885-1932 .... **TCLC 20**
See also CA 117; DLB 114; EWL 3

Campanella, Tommaso 1568-1639 .... **LC 32**
See also RGWL 2, 3

Campbell, John W(ood, Jr.)
1910-1971 .... **CLC 32**
See also CA 21-22; 29-32R; CANR 34; CAP 2; DLB 8; MTCW 1; SCFW; SFW 4

Campbell, Joseph 1904-1987 .... **CLC 69; TCLC 140**
See also AAYA 3; BEST 89:2; CA 1-4R; 124; CANR 3, 28, 61, 107; DA3; MTCW 1, 2

Campbell, Maria 1940- .... **CLC 85; NNAL**
See also CA 102; CANR 54; CCA 1; DAC

Casas, Bartolome de las 1474-1566
  See Las Casas, Bartolome de
  See also WLIT 1
Casely-Hayford, J(oseph) E(phraim)
  1866-1903 .... **BLC 1; TCLC 24**
  See also BW 2; CA 123; 152; DAM MULT
Casey, John (Dudley) 1939- .... **CLC 59**
  See also BEST 90:2; CA 69-72; CANR 23,
  100
Casey, Michael 1947- .... **CLC 2**
  See also CA 65-68; CANR 109; DLB 5
Casey, Patrick
  See Thurman, Wallace (Henry)
Casey, Warren (Peter) 1935-1988 .... **CLC 12**
  See also CA 101; 127; INT CA-101
Casona, Alejandro .... **CLC 49**
  See Alvarez, Alejandro Rodriguez
  See also EWL 3
Cassavetes, John 1929-1989 .... **CLC 20**
  See also CA 85-88; 127; CANR 82
Cassian, Nina 1924- .... **PC 17**
  See also CWP; CWW 2
Cassill, R(onald) V(erlin)
  1919-2002 .... **CLC 4, 23**
  See also CA 9-12R; 208; CAAS 1; CANR
  7, 45; CN 7; DLB 6, 218; DLBY 2002
Cassiodorus, Flavius Magnus c. 490(?)-c.
  583(?) .... **CMLC 43**
Cassirer, Ernst 1874-1945 .... **TCLC 61**
  See also CA 157
Cassity, (Allen) Turner 1929- .... **CLC 6, 42**
  See also CA 17-20R; 223; CAAE 223;
  CAAS 8; CANR 11; CSW; DLB 105
Castaneda, Carlos (Cesar Aranha)
  1931(?)-1998 .... **CLC 12, 119**
  See also CA 25-28R; CANR 32, 66, 105;
  DNFS 1; HW 1; MTCW 1
Castedo, Elena 1937- .... **CLC 65**
  See also CA 132
Castedo-Ellerman, Elena
  See Castedo, Elena
Castellanos, Rosario 1925-1974 .... **CLC 66;**
    HLC 1; SSC 39, 68
  See also CA 131; 53-56; CANR 58; CD-
  WLB 3; DAM MULT; DLB 113, 290;
  EWL 3; FW; HW 1; LAW; MTCW 1;
  RGSF 2; RGWL 2, 3
Castelvetro, Lodovico 1505-1571 .... **LC 12**
Castiglione, Baldassare 1478-1529 ...... **LC 12**
  See Castiglione, Baldesar
  See also LMFS 1; RGWL 2, 3
Castiglione, Baldesar
  See Castiglione, Baldassare
  See also EW 2
Castillo, Ana (Hernandez Del)
  1953- .... **CLC 151**
  See also AAYA 42; CA 131; CANR 51, 86,
  128; CWP; DLB 122, 227; DNFS 2; FW;
  HW 1; LLW 1; PFS 21
Castle, Robert
  See Hamilton, Edmond
Castro (Ruz), Fidel 1926(?)- .... **HLC 1**
  See also CA 110; 129; CANR 81; DAM
  MULT; HW 2
Castro, Guillen de 1569-1631 .... **LC 19**
Castro, Rosalia de 1837-1885 ... **NCLC 3, 78;**
    PC 41
  See also DAM MULT
Cather, Willa (Sibert) 1873-1947 . **SSC 2, 50;**
    TCLC 1, 11, 31, 99, 132, 152; WLC
  See also AAYA 24; AMW; AMWC 1;
  AMWR 1; BPFB 1; CA 104; 128; CDALB
  1865-1917; CLR 98; DA; DA3; DAB;
  DAC; DAM MST, NOV; DLB 9, 54, 78,
  256; DLBD 1; EWL 3; EXPN; EXPS;
  LAIT 3; LATS 1:1; MAWW; MTCW 1,
  2; NFS 2, 19; RGAL 4; RGSF 2; RHW;
  SATA 30; SSFS 2, 7, 16; TCWW 2; TUS

Catherine II
  See Catherine the Great
  See also DLB 150
Catherine the Great 1729-1796 .... **LC 69**
  See Catherine II
Cato, Marcus Porcius
  234B.C.-149B.C. .... **CMLC 21**
  See Cato the Elder
Cato, Marcus Porcius, the Elder
  See Cato, Marcus Porcius
Cato the Elder
  See Cato, Marcus Porcius
  See also DLB 211
Catton, (Charles) Bruce 1899-1978 . **CLC 35**
  See also AITN 1; CA 5-8R; 81-84; CANR
  7, 74; DLB 17; SATA 2; SATA-Obit 24
Catullus c. 84B.C.-54B.C. .... **CMLC 18**
  See also AW 2; CDWLB 1; DLB 211;
  RGWL 2, 3
Cauldwell, Frank
  See King, Francis (Henry)
Caunitz, William J. 1933-1996 .... **CLC 34**
  See also BEST 89:3; CA 125; 130; 152;
  CANR 73; INT CA-130
Causley, Charles (Stanley)
  1917-2003 .... **CLC 7**
  See also CA 9-12R; 223; CANR 5, 35, 94;
  CLR 30; CWRI 5; DLB 27; MTCW 1;
  SATA 3, 66; SATA-Obit 149
Caute, (John) David 1936- .... **CLC 29**
  See also CA 1-4R; CAAS 4; CANR 1, 33,
  64, 120; CBD; CD 5; CN 7; DAM NOV;
  DLB 14, 231
Cavafy, C(onstantine) P(eter) .... **PC 36;**
    TCLC 2, 7
  See Kavafis, Konstantinos Petrou
  See also CA 148; DA3; DAM POET; EW
  8; EWL 3; MTCW 1; PFS 19; RGWL 2,
  3; WP
Cavalcanti, Guido c. 1250-c.
  1300 .... **CMLC 54**
  See also RGWL 2, 3
Cavallo, Evelyn
  See Spark, Muriel (Sarah)
Cavanna, Betty .... **CLC 12**
  See Harrison, Elizabeth (Allen) Cavanna
  See also JRDA; MAICYA 1; SAAS 4;
  SATA 1, 30
Cavendish, Margaret Lucas
  1623-1673 .... **LC 30**
  See also DLB 131, 252, 281; RGEL 2
Caxton, William 1421(?)-1491(?) .... **LC 17**
  See also DLB 170
Cayer, D. M.
  See Duffy, Maureen
Cayrol, Jean 1911- .... **CLC 11**
  See also CA 89-92; DLB 83; EWL 3
Cela (y Trulock), Camilo Jose
  See Cela, Camilo Jose
  See also CWW 2
Cela, Camilo Jose 1916-2002 .... **CLC 4, 13,**
    59, 122; HLC 1; SSC 71
  See Cela (y Trulock), Camilo Jose
  See also BEST 90:2; CA 21-24R; 206;
  CAAS 10; CANR 21, 32, 76; DAM
  MULT; DLBY 1989; EW 13; EWL 3; HW
  1; MTCW 1, 2; RGSF 2; RGWL 2, 3
Celan, Paul .... **CLC 10, 19, 53, 82; PC 10**
  See Antschel, Paul
  See also CDWLB 2; DLB 69; EWL 3;
  RGWL 2, 3
Celine, Louis-Ferdinand .. **CLC 1, 3, 4, 7, 9,**
    15, 47, 124
  See Destouches, Louis-Ferdinand
  See also DLB 72; EW 11; EWL 3; GFL
  1789 to the Present; RGWL 2, 3

Cellini, Benvenuto 1500-1571 .... **LC 7**
Cendrars, Blaise .... **CLC 18, 106**
  See Sauser-Hall, Frederic
  See also DLB 258; EWL 3; GFL 1789 to
  the Present; RGWL 2, 3; WP
Centlivre, Susanna 1669(?)-1723 .... **DC 25;**
    LC 65
  See also DLB 84; RGEL 2
Cernuda (y Bidon), Luis
  1902-1963 .... **CLC 54; PC 62**
  See also CA 131; 89-92; DAM POET; DLB
  134; EWL 3; GLL 1; HW 1; RGWL 2, 3
Cervantes, Lorna Dee 1954- ..... **HLCS 1; PC
  35**
  See also CA 131; CANR 80; CWP; DLB
  82; EXPP; HW 1; LLW 1
Cervantes (Saavedra), Miguel de
  1547-1616 .... **HLCS; LC 6, 23, 93; SSC
  12; WLC**
  See also AAYA 56; BYA 1, 14; DA; DAB;
  DAC; DAM MST, NOV; EW 2; LAIT 1;
  LATS 1:1; LMFS 1; NFS 8; RGSF 2;
  RGWL 2, 3; TWA
Cesaire, Aime (Fernand) 1913- .... **BLC 1;
  CLC 19, 32, 112; DC 22; PC 25**
  See also BW 2, 3; CA 65-68; CANR 24,
  43, 81; CWW 2; DA3; DAM MULT,
  POET; EWL 3; GFL 1789 to the Present;
  MTCW 1, 2; WP
Chabon, Michael 1963- ... **CLC 55, 149; SSC
  59**
  See also AAYA 45; AMWS 11; CA 139;
  CANR 57, 96, 127; DLB 278; SATA 145
Chabrol, Claude 1930- .... **CLC 16**
  See also CA 110
Chairil Anwar
  See Anwar, Chairil
  See also EWL 3
Challans, Mary 1905-1983
  See Renault, Mary
  See also CA 81-84; 111; CANR 74; DA3;
  MTCW 2; SATA 23; SATA-Obit 36; TEA
Challis, George
  See Faust, Frederick (Schiller)
  See also TCWW 2
Chambers, Aidan 1934- .... **CLC 35**
  See also AAYA 27; CA 25-28R; CANR 12,
  31, 58, 116; JRDA; MAICYA 1, 2; SAAS
  12; SATA 1, 69, 108; WYA; YAW
Chambers, James 1948-
  See Cliff, Jimmy
  See also CA 124
Chambers, Jessie
  See Lawrence, D(avid) H(erbert Richards)
  See also GLL 1
Chambers, Robert W(illiam)
  1865-1933 .... **TCLC 41**
  See also CA 165; DLB 202; HGG; SATA
  107; SUFW 1
Chambers, (David) Whittaker
  1901-1961 .... **TCLC 129**
  See also CA 89-92; DLB 303
Chamisso, Adelbert von
  1781-1838 .... **NCLC 82**
  See also DLB 90; RGWL 2, 3; SUFW 1
Chance, James T.
  See Carpenter, John (Howard)
Chance, John T.
  See Carpenter, John (Howard)
Chandler, Raymond (Thornton)
  1888-1959 .... **SSC 23; TCLC 1, 7**
  See also AAYA 25; AMWC 2; AMWS 4;
  BPFB 1; CA 104; 129; CANR 60, 107;
  CDALB 1929-1941; CMW 4; DA3; DLB
  226, 253; DLBD 6; EWL 3; MSW;
  MTCW 1, 2; NFS 17; RGAL 4; TUS
Chang, Diana 1934- .... **AAL**
  See also CA 228; CWP; EXPP

Chomsky, (Avram) Noam 1928- ..... **CLC 132**
See also CA 17-20R; CANR 28, 62, 110, 132; DA3; DLB 246; MTCW 1, 2

Chona, Maria 1845(?)-1936 .... **NNAL**
See also CA 144

Chopin, Kate .... **SSC 8, 68; TCLC 127; WLCS**
See Chopin, Katherine
See also AAYA 33; AMWR 2; AMWS 1; BYA 11, 15; CDALB 1865-1917; DA; DAB; DLB 12, 78; EXPN; EXPS; FW; LAIT 3; MAWW; NFS 3; RGAL 4; RGSF 2; SSFS 17; TUS

Chopin, Katherine 1851-1904
See Chopin, Kate
See also CA 104; 122; DA3; DAC; DAM MST, NOV

Chretien de Troyes c. 12th cent. - . **CMLC 10**
See also DLB 208; EW 1; RGWL 2, 3; TWA

Christie
See Ichikawa, Kon

Christie, Agatha (Mary Clarissa) 1890-1976 .. **CLC 1, 6, 8, 12, 39, 48, 110**
See also AAYA 9; AITN 1, 2; BPFB 1; BRWS 2; CA 17-20R; 61-64; CANR 10, 37, 108; CBD; CDBLB 1914-1945; CMW 4; CPW; CWD; DA3; DAB; DAC; DAM NOV; DFS 2; DLB 13, 77, 245; MSW; MTCW 1, 2; NFS 8; RGEL 2; RHW; SATA 36; TEA; YAW

Christie, Philippa .... **CLC 21**
See Pearce, Philippa
See also BYA 5; CANR 109; CLR 9; DLB 161; MAICYA 1; SATA 1, 67, 129

Christine de Pizan 1365(?)-1431(?) .... **LC 9**
See also DLB 208; RGWL 2, 3

Chuang Tzu c. 369B.C.-c. 286B.C. .... **CMLC 57**

Chubb, Elmer
See Masters, Edgar Lee

Chulkov, Mikhail Dmitrievich 1743-1792 .... **LC 2**
See also DLB 150

Churchill, Caryl 1938- .... **CLC 31, 55, 157; DC 5**
See Churchill, Chick
See also BRWS 4; CA 102; CANR 22, 46, 108; CBD; CWD; DFS 12, 16; DLB 13; EWL 3; FW; MTCW 1; RGEL 2

Churchill, Charles 1731-1764 .... **LC 3**
See also DLB 109; RGEL 2

Churchill, Chick
See Churchill, Caryl
See also CD 5

Churchill, Sir Winston (Leonard Spencer) 1874-1965 .... **TCLC 113**
See also BRW 6; CA 97-100; CDBLB 1890-1914; DA3; DLB 100; DLBD 16; LAIT 4; MTCW 1, 2

Chute, Carolyn 1947- .... **CLC 39**
See also CA 123; CANR 135

Ciardi, John (Anthony) 1916-1986 . **CLC 10, 40, 44, 129**
See also CA 5-8R; 118; CAAS 2; CANR 5, 33; CLR 19; CWRI 5; DAM POET; DLB 5; DLBY 1986; INT CANR-5; MAICYA 1, 2; MTCW 1, 2; RGAL 4; SAAS 26; SATA 1, 65; SATA-Obit 46

Cibber, Colley 1671-1757 .... **LC 66**
See also DLB 84; RGEL 2

Cicero, Marcus Tullius 106B.C.-43B.C. .... **CMLC 3**
See also AW 1; CDWLB 1; DLB 211; RGWL 2, 3

Cimino, Michael 1943- .... **CLC 16**
See also CA 105

Cioran, E(mil) M. 1911-1995 .... **CLC 64**
See also CA 25-28R; 149; CANR 91; DLB 220; EWL 3

Cisneros, Sandra 1954- .... **CLC 69, 118, 193; HLC 1; PC 52; SSC 32, 72**
See also AAYA 9, 53; AMWS 7; CA 131; CANR 64, 118; CWP; DA3; DAM MULT; DLB 122, 152; EWL 3; EXPN; FW; HW 1, 2; LAIT 5; LATS 1:2; LLW 1; MAICYA 2; MTCW 2; NFS 2; PFS 19; RGAL 4; RGSF 2; SSFS 3, 13; WLIT 1; YAW

Cixous, Helene 1937- .... **CLC 92**
See also CA 126; CANR 55, 123; CWW 2; DLB 83, 242; EWL 3; FW; GLL 2; MTCW 1, 2; TWA

Clair, Rene .... **CLC 20**
See Chomette, Rene Lucien

Clampitt, Amy 1920-1994 .... **CLC 32; PC 19**
See also AMWS 9; CA 110; 146; CANR 29, 79; DLB 105

Clancy, Thomas L., Jr. 1947-
See Clancy, Tom
See also CA 125; 131; CANR 62, 105; DA3; INT CA-131; MTCW 1, 2

Clancy, Tom .... **CLC 45, 112**
See Clancy, Thomas L., Jr.
See also AAYA 9, 51; BEST 89:1, 90:1; BPFB 1; BYA 10, 11; CANR 132; CMW 4; CPW; DAM NOV, POP; DLB 227

Clare, John 1793-1864 .. **NCLC 9, 86; PC 23**
See also DAB; DAM POET; DLB 55, 96; RGEL 2

Clarin
See Alas (y Urena), Leopoldo (Enrique Garcia)

Clark, Al C.
See Goines, Donald

Clark, (Robert) Brian 1932- .... **CLC 29**
See also CA 41-44R; CANR 67; CBD; CD 5

Clark, Curt
See Westlake, Donald E(dwin)

Clark, Eleanor 1913-1996 .... **CLC 5, 19**
See also CA 9-12R; 151; CANR 41; CN 7; DLB 6

Clark, J. P.
See Clark Bekederemo, J(ohnson) P(epper)
See also CDWLB 3; DLB 117

Clark, John Pepper
See Clark Bekederemo, J(ohnson) P(epper)
See also AFW; CD 5; CP 7; RGEL 2

Clark, Kenneth (Mackenzie) 1903-1983 .... **TCLC 147**
See also CA 93-96; 109; CANR 36; MTCW 1, 2

Clark, M. R.
See Clark, Mavis Thorpe

Clark, Mavis Thorpe 1909-1999 ...... **CLC 12**
See also CA 57-60; CANR 8, 37, 107; CLR 30; CWRI 5; MAICYA 1, 2; SAAS 5; SATA 8, 74

Clark, Walter Van Tilburg 1909-1971 .... **CLC 28**
See also CA 9-12R; 33-36R; CANR 63, 113; DLB 9, 206; LAIT 2; RGAL 4; SATA 8

Clark Bekederemo, J(ohnson) P(epper) 1935- .... **BLC 1; CLC 38; DC 5**
See Clark, J. P.; Clark, John Pepper
See also BW 1; CA 65-68; CANR 16, 72; DAM DRAM, MULT; DFS 13; EWL 3; MTCW 1

Clarke, Arthur C(harles) 1917- .... **CLC 1, 4, 13, 18, 35, 136; SSC 3**
See also AAYA 4, 33; BPFB 1; BYA 13; CA 1-4R; CANR 2, 28, 55, 74, 130; CN 7; CPW; DA3; DAM POP; DLB 261; JRDA; LAIT 5; MAICYA 1, 2; MTCW 1, 2; SATA 13, 70, 115; SCFW; SFW 4; SSFS 4, 18; YAW

Clarke, Austin 1896-1974 .... **CLC 6, 9**
See also CA 29-32; 49-52; CAP 2; DAM POET; DLB 10, 20; EWL 3; RGEL 2

Clarke, Austin C(hesterfield) 1934- .. **BLC 1; CLC 8, 53; SSC 45**
See also BW 1; CA 25-28R; CAAS 16; CANR 14, 32, 68; CN 7; DAC; DAM MULT; DLB 53, 125; DNFS 2; RGSF 2

Clarke, Gillian 1937- .... **CLC 61**
See also CA 106; CP 7; CWP; DLB 40

Clarke, Marcus (Andrew Hislop) 1846-1881 .... **NCLC 19**
See also DLB 230; RGEL 2; RGSF 2

Clarke, Shirley 1925-1997 .... **CLC 16**
See also CA 189

Clash, The
See Headon, (Nicky) Topper; Jones, Mick; Simonon, Paul; Strummer, Joe

Claudel, Paul (Louis Charles Marie) 1868-1955 .... **TCLC 2, 10**
See also CA 104; 165; DLB 192, 258; EW 8; EWL 3; GFL 1789 to the Present; RGWL 2, 3; TWA

Claudian 370(?)-404(?) .... **CMLC 46**
See also RGWL 2, 3

Claudius, Matthias 1740-1815 .... **NCLC 75**
See also DLB 97

Clavell, James (duMaresq) 1925-1994 .... **CLC 6, 25, 87**
See also BPFB 1; CA 25-28R; 146; CANR 26, 48; CPW; DA3; DAM NOV, POP; MTCW 1, 2; NFS 10; RHW

Clayman, Gregory .... **CLC 65**

Cleaver, (Leroy) Eldridge 1935-1998 .... **BLC 1; CLC 30, 119**
See also BW 1, 3; CA 21-24R; 167; CANR 16, 75; DA3; DAM MULT; MTCW 2; YAW

Cleese, John (Marwood) 1939- .... **CLC 21**
See Monty Python
See also CA 112; 116; CANR 35; MTCW 1

Cleishbotham, Jebediah
See Scott, Sir Walter

Cleland, John 1710-1789 .... **LC 2, 48**
See also DLB 39; RGEL 2

Clemens, Samuel Langhorne 1835-1910
See Twain, Mark
See also CA 104; 135; CDALB 1865-1917; DA; DA3; DAB; DAC; DAM MST, NOV; DLB 12, 23, 64, 74, 186, 189; JRDA; LMFS 1; MAICYA 1; NCFS 4; NFS 20; SATA 100; SSFS 16; YABC 2

Clement of Alexandria 150(?)-215(?) .... **CMLC 41**

Cleophil
See Congreve, William

Clerihew, E.
See Bentley, E(dmund) C(lerihew)

Clerk, N. W.
See Lewis, C(live) S(taples)

Cleveland, John 1613-1658 .... **LC 106**
See also DLB 126; RGEL 2

Cliff, Jimmy .... **CLC 21**
See Chambers, James
See also CA 193

Cliff, Michelle 1946- .... **BLCS; CLC 120**
See also BW 2; CA 116; CANR 39, 72; CD-WLB 3; DLB 157; FW; GLL 2

Clifford, Lady Anne 1590-1676 .... **LC 76**
See also DLB 151

Clifton, (Thelma) Lucille 1936- .... **BLC 1; CLC 19, 66, 162; PC 17**
See also AFAW 2; BW 2, 3; CA 49-52; CANR 2, 24, 42, 76, 97; CLR 5; CP 7; CSW; CWP; CWRI 5; DA3; DAM MULT, POET; DLB 5, 41; EXPP; MAICYA 1, 2; MTCW 1, 2; PFS 1, 14; SATA 20, 69, 128; WP

Conrad, Robert Arnold
See Hart, Moss

Conroy, (Donald) Pat(rick) 1945- ... **CLC 30, 74**
See also AAYA 8, 52; AITN 1; BPFB 1; CA 85-88; CANR 24, 53, 129; CPW; CSW; DA3; DAM NOV, POP; DLB 6; LAIT 5; MTCW 1, 2

Constant (de Rebecque), (Henri) Benjamin
1767-1830 .... **NCLC 6**
See also DLB 119; EW 4; GFL 1789 to the Present

Conway, Jill K(er) 1934- .... **CLC 152**
See also CA 130; CANR 94

Conybeare, Charles Augustus
See Eliot, T(homas) S(tearns)

Cook, Michael 1933-1994 .... **CLC 58**
See also CA 93-96; CANR 68; DLB 53

Cook, Robin 1940- .... **CLC 14**
See also AAYA 32; BEST 90:2; BPFB 1; CA 108; 111; CANR 41, 90, 109; CPW; DA3; DAM POP; HGG; INT CA-111

Cook, Roy
See Silverberg, Robert

Cooke, Elizabeth 1948- .... **CLC 55**
See also CA 129

Cooke, John Esten 1830-1886 .... **NCLC 5**
See also DLB 3, 248; RGAL 4

Cooke, John Estes
See Baum, L(yman) Frank

Cooke, M. E.
See Creasey, John

Cooke, Margaret
See Creasey, John

Cooke, Rose Terry 1827-1892 ...... **NCLC 110**
See also DLB 12, 74

Cook-Lynn, Elizabeth 1930- .... **CLC 93; NNAL**
See also CA 133; DAM MULT; DLB 175

Cooney, Ray .... **CLC 62**
See also CBD

Cooper, Anthony Ashley 1671-1713 .. **LC 107**
See also DLB 101

Cooper, Dennis 1953- .... **CLC 203**
See also CA 133; CANR 72, 86; GLL 1; St. James Guide to Horror, Ghost, and Gothic Writers.

Cooper, Douglas 1960- .... **CLC 86**

Cooper, Henry St. John
See Creasey, John

Cooper, J(oan) California (?)- .... **CLC 56**
See also AAYA 12; BW 1; CA 125; CANR 55; DAM MULT; DLB 212

Cooper, James Fenimore
1789-1851 .... **NCLC 1, 27, 54**
See also AAYA 22; AMW; BPFB 1; CDALB 1640-1865; DA3; DLB 3, 183, 250, 254; LAIT 1; NFS 9; RGAL 4; SATA 19; TUS; WCH

Cooper, Susan Fenimore
1813-1894 .... **NCLC 129**
See also ANW; DLB 239, 254

Coover, Robert (Lowell) 1932- ...... **CLC 3, 7, 15, 32, 46, 87, 161; SSC 15**
See also AMWS 5; BPFB 1; CA 45-48; CANR 3, 37, 58, 115; CN 7; DAM NOV; DLB 2, 227; DLBY 1981; EWL 3; MTCW 1, 2; RGAL 4; RGSF 2

Copeland, Stewart (Armstrong)
1952- .... **CLC 26**

Copernicus, Nicolaus 1473-1543 .... **LC 45**

Coppard, A(lfred) E(dgar)
1878-1957 .... **SSC 21; TCLC 5**
See also BRWS 8; CA 114; 167; DLB 162; EWL 3; HGG; RGEL 2; RGSF 2; SUFW 1; YABC 1

Coppee, Francois 1842-1908 .... **TCLC 25**
See also CA 170; DLB 217

Coppola, Francis Ford 1939- ... **CLC 16, 126**
See also AAYA 39; CA 77-80; CANR 40, 78; DLB 44

Copway, George 1818-1869 .... **NNAL**
See also DAM MULT; DLB 175, 183

Corbiere, Tristan 1845-1875 .... **NCLC 43**
See also DLB 217; GFL 1789 to the Present

Corcoran, Barbara (Asenath)
1911- .... **CLC 17**
See also AAYA 14; CA 21-24R, 191; CAAE 191; CAAS 2; CANR 11, 28, 48; CLR 50; DLB 52; JRDA; MAICYA 2; MAIC-YAS 1; RHW; SAAS 20; SATA 3, 77; SATA-Essay 125

Cordelier, Maurice
See Giraudoux, Jean(-Hippolyte)

Corelli, Marie .... **TCLC 51**
See Mackay, Mary
See also DLB 34, 156; RGEL 2; SUFW 1

Corinna c. 225B.C.-c. 305B.C. ...... **CMLC 72**

Corman, Cid .... **CLC 9**
See Corman, Sidney
See also CAAS 2; DLB 5, 193

Corman, Sidney 1924-2004
See Corman, Cid
See also CA 85-88; 225; CANR 44; CP 7; DAM POET

Cormier, Robert (Edmund)
1925-2000 .... **CLC 12, 30**
See also AAYA 3, 19; BYA 1, 2, 6, 8, 9; CA 1-4R; CANR 5, 23, 76, 93; CDALB 1968-1988; CLR 12, 55; DA; DAB; DAC; DAM MST, NOV; DLB 52; EXPN; INT CANR-23; JRDA; LAIT 5; MAICYA 1, 2; MTCW 1, 2; NFS 2, 18; SATA 10, 45, 83; SATA-Obit 122; WYA; YAW

Corn, Alfred (DeWitt III) 1943- .... **CLC 33**
See also CA 179; CAAE 179; CAAS 25; CANR 44; CP 7; CSW; DLB 120, 282; DLBY 1980

Corneille, Pierre 1606-1684 ... **DC 21; LC 28**
See also DAB; DAM MST; DLB 268; EW 3; GFL Beginnings to 1789; RGWL 2, 3; TWA

Cornwell, David (John Moore)
1931- .... **CLC 9, 15**
See le Carre, John
See also CA 5-8R; CANR 13, 33, 59, 107, 132; DA3; DAM POP; MTCW 1, 2

Cornwell, Patricia (Daniels) 1956- . **CLC 155**
See also AAYA 16, 56; BPFB 1; CA 134; CANR 53, 131; CMW 4; CPW; CSW; DAM POP; DLB 306; MSW; MTCW 1

Corso, (Nunzio) Gregory 1930-2001 . **CLC 1, 11; PC 33**
See also AMWS 12; BG 2; CA 5-8R; 193; CANR 41, 76, 132; CP 7; DA3; DLB 5, 16, 237; LMFS 2; MTCW 1, 2; WP

Cortazar, Julio 1914-1984 ... **CLC 2, 3, 5, 10, 13, 15, 33, 34, 92; HLC 1; SSC 7, 76**
See also BPFB 1; CA 21-24R; CANR 12, 32, 81; CDWLB 3; DA3; DAM MULT, NOV; DLB 113; EWL 3; EXPS; HW 1, 2; LAW; MTCW 1, 2; RGSF 2; RGWL 2, 3; SSFS 3, 20; TWA; WLIT 1

Cortes, Hernan 1485-1547 .... **LC 31**

Corvinus, Jakob
See Raabe, Wilhelm (Karl)

Corwin, Cecil
See Kornbluth, C(yril) M.

Cosic, Dobrica 1921- .... **CLC 14**
See also CA 122; 138; CDWLB 4; CWW 2; DLB 181; EWL 3

Costain, Thomas B(ertram)
1885-1965 .... **CLC 30**
See also BYA 3; CA 5-8R; 25-28R; DLB 9; RHW

Costantini, Humberto 1924(?)-1987 . **CLC 49**
See also CA 131; 122; EWL 3; HW 1

Costello, Elvis 1954- .... **CLC 21**
See also CA 204

Costenoble, Philostene
See Ghelderode, Michel de

Cotes, Cecil V.
See Duncan, Sara Jeannette

Cotter, Joseph Seamon Sr.
1861-1949 .... **BLC 1; TCLC 28**
See also BW 1; CA 124; DAM MULT; DLB 50

Couch, Arthur Thomas Quiller
See Quiller-Couch, Sir Arthur (Thomas)

Coulton, James
See Hansen, Joseph

Couperus, Louis (Marie Anne)
1863-1923 .... **TCLC 15**
See also CA 115; EWL 3; RGWL 2, 3

Coupland, Douglas 1961- .... **CLC 85, 133**
See also AAYA 34; CA 142; CANR 57, 90, 130; CCA 1; CPW; DAC; DAM POP

Court, Wesli
See Turco, Lewis (Putnam)

Courtenay, Bryce 1933- .... **CLC 59**
See also CA 138; CPW

Courtney, Robert
See Ellison, Harlan (Jay)

Cousteau, Jacques-Yves 1910-1997 .. **CLC 30**
See also CA 65-68; 159; CANR 15, 67; MTCW 1; SATA 38, 98

Coventry, Francis 1725-1754 .... **LC 46**

Coverdale, Miles c. 1487-1569 .... **LC 77**
See also DLB 167

Cowan, Peter (Walkinshaw)
1914-2002 .... **SSC 28**
See also CA 21-24R; CANR 9, 25, 50, 83; CN 7; DLB 260; RGSF 2

Coward, Noel (Peirce) 1899-1973 . **CLC 1, 9, 29, 51**
See also AITN 1; BRWS 2; CA 17-18; 41-44R; CANR 35, 132; CAP 2; CDBLB 1914-1945; DA3; DAM DRAM; DFS 3, 6; DLB 10, 245; EWL 3; IDFW 3, 4; MTCW 1, 2; RGEL 2; TEA

Cowley, Abraham 1618-1667 .... **LC 43**
See also BRW 2; DLB 131, 151; PAB; RGEL 2

Cowley, Malcolm 1898-1989 .... **CLC 39**
See also AMWS 2; CA 5-8R; 128; CANR 3, 55; DLB 4, 48; DLBY 1981, 1989; EWL 3; MTCW 1, 2

Cowper, William 1731-1800 ..... **NCLC 8, 94; PC 40**
See also BRW 3; DA3; DAM POET; DLB 104, 109; RGEL 2

Cox, William Trevor 1928-
See Trevor, William
See also CA 9-12R; CANR 4, 37, 55, 76, 102; DAM NOV; INT CANR-37; MTCW 1, 2; TEA

Coyne, P. J.
See Masters, Hilary

Cozzens, James Gould 1903-1978 . **CLC 1, 4, 11, 92**
See also AMW; BPFB 1; CA 9-12R; 81-84; CANR 19; CDALB 1941-1968; DLB 9, 294; DLBD 2; DLBY 1984, 1997; EWL 3; MTCW 1, 2; RGAL 4

Crabbe, George 1754-1832 .... **NCLC 26, 121**
See also BRW 3; DLB 93; RGEL 2

Crace, Jim 1946- .... **CLC 157; SSC 61**
See also CA 128; 135; CANR 55, 70, 123; CN 7; DLB 231; INT CA-135

Craddock, Charles Egbert
See Murfree, Mary Noailles

Craig, A. A.
See Anderson, Poul (William)

Craik, Mrs.
See Craik, Dinah Maria (Mulock)
See also RGEL 2

Doblin, Alfred .... **TCLC 13**
   See Doeblin, Alfred
   See also CDWLB 2; EWL 3; RGWL 2, 3
Dobroliubov, Nikolai Aleksandrovich
   See Dobrolyubov, Nikolai Alexandrovich
   See also DLB 277
Dobrolyubov, Nikolai Alexandrovich
   1836-1861 .... **NCLC 5**
   See Dobroliubov, Nikolai Aleksandrovich
Dobson, Austin 1840-1921 .... **TCLC 79**
   See also DLB 35, 144
Dobyns, Stephen 1941- .... **CLC 37**
   See also AMWS 13; CA 45-48; CANR 2, 18, 99; CMW 4; CP 7
Doctorow, E(dgar) L(aurence)
   1931- .... **CLC 6, 11, 15, 18, 37, 44, 65, 113**
   See also AAYA 22; AITN 2; AMWS 4; BEST 89:3; BPFB 1; CA 45-48; CANR 2, 33, 51, 76, 97, 133; CDALB 1968-1988; CN 7; CPW; DA3; DAM NOV, POP; DLB 2, 28, 173; DLBY 1980; EWL 3; LAIT 3; MTCW 1, 2; NFS 6; RGAL 4; RHW; TUS
Dodgson, Charles L(utwidge) 1832-1898
   See Carroll, Lewis
   See also CLR 2; DA; DA3; DAB; DAC; DAM MST, NOV, POET; MAICYA 1, 2; SATA 100; YABC 2
Dodsley, Robert 1703-1764 .... **LC 97**
   See also DLB 95; RGEL 2
Dodson, Owen (Vincent) 1914-1983 .. **BLC 1; CLC 79**
   See also BW 1; CA 65-68; 110; CANR 24; DAM MULT; DLB 76
Doeblin, Alfred 1878-1957 .... **TCLC 13**
   See Doblin, Alfred
   See also CA 110; 141; DLB 66
Doerr, Harriet 1910-2002 .... **CLC 34**
   See also CA 117; 122; 213; CANR 47; INT CA-122; LATS 1:2
Domecq, H(onorio Bustos)
   See Bioy Casares, Adolfo
Domecq, H(onorio) Bustos
   See Bioy Casares, Adolfo; Borges, Jorge Luis
Domini, Rey
   See Lorde, Audre (Geraldine)
   See also GLL 1
Dominique
   See Proust, (Valentin-Louis-George-Eugene) Marcel
Don, A
   See Stephen, Sir Leslie
Donaldson, Stephen R(eeder)
   1947- .... **CLC 46, 138**
   See also AAYA 36; BPFB 1; CA 89-92; CANR 13, 55, 99; CPW; DAM POP; FANT; INT CANR-13; SATA 121; SFW 4; SUFW 1, 2
Donleavy, J(ames) P(atrick) 1926- .... **CLC 1, 4, 6, 10, 45**
   See also AITN 2; BPFB 1; CA 9-12R; CANR 24, 49, 62, 80, 124; CBD; CD 5; CN 7; DLB 6, 173; INT CANR-24; MTCW 1, 2; RGAL 4
Donnadieu, Marguerite
   See Duras, Marguerite
Donne, John 1572-1631 ... **LC 10, 24, 91; PC 1, 43; WLC**
   See also BRW 1; BRWC 1; BRWR 2; CD-BLB Before 1660; DA; DAB; DAC; DAM MST, POET; DLB 121, 151; EXPP; PAB; PFS 2, 11; RGEL 3; TEA; WLIT 3; WP
Donnell, David 1939(?)- .... **CLC 34**
   See also CA 197
Donoghue, Denis 1928- .... **CLC 209**
   See also CA 17-20R; CANR 16, 102

Donoghue, P. S.
   See Hunt, E(verette) Howard, (Jr.)
Donoso (Yanez), Jose 1924-1996 ... **CLC 4, 8, 11, 32, 99; HLC 1; SSC 34; TCLC 133**
   See also CA 81-84; 155; CANR 32, 73; CD-WLB 3; CWW 2; DAM MULT; DLB 113; EWL 3; HW 1, 2; LAW; LAWS 1; MTCW 1, 2; RGSF 2; WLIT 1
Donovan, John 1928-1992 .... **CLC 35**
   See also AAYA 20; CA 97-100; 137; CLR 3; MAICYA 1, 2; SATA 72; SATA-Brief 29; YAW
Don Roberto
   See Cunninghame Graham, Robert (Gallnigad) Bontine
Doolittle, Hilda 1886-1961 . **CLC 3, 8, 14, 31, 34, 73; PC 5; WLC**
   See H. D.
   See also AMWS 1; CA 97-100; CANR 35, 131; DA; DAC; DAM MST, POET; DLB 4, 45; EWL 3; FW; GLL 1; LMFS 2; MAWW; MTCW 1, 2; PFS 6; RGAL 4
Doppo, Kunikida .... **TCLC 99**
   See Kunikida Doppo
Dorfman, Ariel 1942- .... **CLC 48, 77, 189; HLC 1**
   See also CA 124; 130; CANR 67, 70, 135; CWW 2; DAM MULT; DFS 4; EWL 3; HW 1, 2; INT CA-130; WLIT 1
Dorn, Edward (Merton)
   1929-1999 .... **CLC 10, 18**
   See also CA 93-96; 187; CANR 42, 79; CP 7; DLB 5; INT CA-93-96; WP
Dor-Ner, Zvi .... **CLC 70**
Dorris, Michael (Anthony)
   1945-1997 .... **CLC 109; NNAL**
   See also AAYA 20; BEST 90:1; BYA 12; CA 102; 157; CANR 19, 46, 75; CLR 58; DA3; DAM MULT, NOV; DLB 175; LAIT 5; MTCW 2; NFS 3; RGAL 4; SATA 75; SATA-Obit 94; TCWW 2; YAW
Dorris, Michael A.
   See Dorris, Michael (Anthony)
Dorsan, Luc
   See Simenon, Georges (Jacques Christian)
Dorsange, Jean
   See Simenon, Georges (Jacques Christian)
Dorset
   See Sackville, Thomas
Dos Passos, John (Roderigo)
   1896-1970 ... **CLC 1, 4, 8, 11, 15, 25, 34, 82; WLC**
   See also AMW; BPFB 1; CA 1-4R; 29-32R; CANR 3; CDALB 1929-1941; DA; DA3; DAB; DAC; DAM MST, NOV; DLB 4, 9, 274; DLBD 1, 15; DLBY 1996; EWL 3; MTCW 1, 2; NFS 14; RGAL 4; TUS
Dossage, Jean
   See Simenon, Georges (Jacques Christian)
Dostoevsky, Fedor Mikhailovich
   1821-1881 .. **NCLC 2, 7, 21, 33, 43, 119; SSC 2, 33, 44; WLC**
   See Dostoevsky, Fyodor
   See also AAYA 40; DA; DA3; DAB; DAC; DAM MST, NOV; EW 7; EXPN; NFS 3, 8; RGSF 2; RGWL 2, 3; SSFS 8; TWA
Dostoevsky, Fyodor
   See Dostoevsky, Fedor Mikhailovich
   See also DLB 238; LATS 1:1; LMFS 1, 2
Doty, M. R.
   See Doty, Mark (Alan)
Doty, Mark
   See Doty, Mark (Alan)
Doty, Mark (Alan) 1953(?)- .... **CLC 176; PC 53**
   See also AMWS 11; CA 161, 183; CAAE 183; CANR 110
Doty, Mark A.
   See Doty, Mark (Alan)

Doughty, Charles M(ontagu)
   1843-1926 .... **TCLC 27**
   See also CA 115; 178; DLB 19, 57, 174
Douglas, Ellen .... **CLC 73**
   See Haxton, Josephine Ayres; Williamson, Ellen Douglas
   See also CN 7; CSW; DLB 292
Douglas, Gavin 1475(?)-1522 .... **LC 20**
   See also DLB 132; RGEL 2
Douglas, George
   See Brown, George Douglas
   See also RGEL 2
Douglas, Keith (Castellain)
   1920-1944 .... **TCLC 40**
   See also BRW 7; CA 160; DLB 27; EWL 3; PAB; RGEL 2
Douglas, Leonard
   See Bradbury, Ray (Douglas)
Douglas, Michael
   See Crichton, (John) Michael
Douglas, (George) Norman
   1868-1952 .... **TCLC 68**
   See also BRW 6; CA 119; 157; DLB 34, 195; RGEL 2
Douglas, William
   See Brown, George Douglas
Douglass, Frederick 1817(?)-1895 ..... **BLC 1; NCLC 7, 55, 141; WLC**
   See also AAYA 48; AFAW 1, 2; AMWC 1; AMWS 3; CDALB 1640-1865; DA; DA3; DAC; DAM MST, MULT; DLB 1, 43, 50, 79, 243; FW; LAIT 2; NCFS 2; RGAL 4; SATA 29
Dourado, (Waldomiro Freitas) Autran
   1926- .... **CLC 23, 60**
   See also CA 25-28R; 179; CANR 34, 81; DLB 145, 307; HW 2
Dourado, Waldomiro Freitas Autran
   See Dourado, (Waldomiro Freitas) Autran
Dove, Rita (Frances) 1952- . **BLCS; CLC 50, 81; PC 6**
   See also AAYA 46; AMWS 4; BW 2; CA 109; CAAS 19; CANR 27, 42, 68, 76, 97, 132; CDALBS; CP 7; CSW; CWP; DA3; DAM MULT, POET; DLB 120; EWL 3; EXPP; MTCW 1; PFS 1, 15; RGAL 4
Doveglion
   See Villa, Jose Garcia
Dowell, Coleman 1925-1985 .... **CLC 60**
   See also CA 25-28R; 117; CANR 10; DLB 130; GLL 2
Dowson, Ernest (Christopher)
   1867-1900 .... **TCLC 4**
   See also CA 105; 150; DLB 19, 135; RGEL 2
Doyle, A. Conan
   See Doyle, Sir Arthur Conan
Doyle, Sir Arthur Conan
   1859-1930 . **SSC 12, 83; TCLC 7; WLC**
   See Conan Doyle, Arthur
   See also AAYA 14; BRWS 2; CA 104; 122; CANR 131; CDBLB 1890-1914; CMW 4; DA; DA3; DAB; DAC; DAM MST, NOV; DLB 18, 70, 156, 178; EXPS; HGG; LAIT 2; MSW; MTCW 1, 2; RGEL 2; RGSF 2; RHW; SATA 24; SCFW 2; SFW 4; SSFS 2; TEA; WCH; WLIT 4; WYA; YAW
Doyle, Conan
   See Doyle, Sir Arthur Conan
Doyle, John
   See Graves, Robert (von Ranke)
Doyle, Roddy 1958(?)- .... **CLC 81, 178**
   See also AAYA 14; BRWS 5; CA 143; CANR 73, 128; CN 7; DA3; DLB 194
Doyle, Sir A. Conan
   See Doyle, Sir Arthur Conan

Ekwensi, Cyprian (Odiatu Duaka)
1921- .... **BLC 1; CLC 4**
See also AFW; BW 2, 3; CA 29-32R;
CANR 18, 42, 74, 125; CDWLB 3; CN
7; CWRI 5; DAM MULT; DLB 117; EWL
3; MTCW 1, 2; RGEL 2; SATA 66; WLIT
2

Elaine .... **TCLC 18**
See Leverson, Ada Esther

El Crummo
See Crumb, R(obert)

Elder, Lonne III 1931-1996 ..... **BLC 1; DC 8**
See also BW 1, 3; CA 81-84; 152; CAD;
CANR 25; DAM MULT; DLB 7, 38, 44

Eleanor of Aquitaine 1122-1204 ... **CMLC 39**

Elia
See Lamb, Charles

Eliade, Mircea 1907-1986 .... **CLC 19**
See also CA 65-68; 119; CANR 30, 62; CD-
WLB 4; DLB 220; EWL 3; MTCW 1;
RGWL 3; SFW 4

Eliot, A. D.
See Jewett, (Theodora) Sarah Orne

Eliot, Alice
See Jewett, (Theodora) Sarah Orne

Eliot, Dan
See Silverberg, Robert

Eliot, George 1819-1880 ...... **NCLC 4, 13, 23,
41, 49, 89, 118; PC 20; SSC 72; WLC**
See Evans, Mary Ann
See also BRW 5; BRWC 1, 2; BRWR 2;
CDBLB 1832-1890; CN 7; CPW; DA;
DA3; DAB; DAC; DAM MST, NOV;
DLB 21, 35, 55; LATS 1:1; LMFS 1; NFS
17; RGEL 2; RGSF 2; SSFS 8; TEA;
WLIT 3

Eliot, John 1604-1690 .... **LC 5**
See also DLB 24

Eliot, T(homas) S(tearns)
1888-1965 ...... **CLC 1, 2, 3, 6, 9, 10, 13,
15, 24, 34, 41, 55, 57, 113; PC 5, 31;
WLC**
See also AAYA 28; AMW; AMWC 1;
AMWR 1; BRW 7; BRWR 2; CA 5-8R;
25-28R; CANR 41; CDALB 1929-1941;
DA; DA3; DAB; DAC; DAM DRAM,
MST, POET; DFS 4, 13; DLB 7, 10, 45,
63, 245; DLBY 1988; EWL 3; EXPP;
LAIT 3; LATS 1:1; LMFS 2; MTCW 1,
2; NCFS 5; PAB; PFS 1, 7, 20; RGAL 4;
RGEL 2; TUS; WLIT 4; WP

Elizabeth 1866-1941 .... **TCLC 41**

Elkin, Stanley L(awrence)
1930-1995 .. **CLC 4, 6, 9, 14, 27, 51, 91;
SSC 12**
See also AMWS 6; BPFB 1; CA 9-12R;
148; CANR 8, 46; CN 7; CPW; DAM
NOV, POP; DLB 2, 28, 218, 278; DLBY
1980; EWL 3; INT CANR-8; MTCW 1,
2; RGAL 4

Elledge, Scott .... **CLC 34**

Elliott, Don
See Silverberg, Robert

Elliott, George P(aul) 1918-1980 .... **CLC 2**
See also CA 1-4R; 97-100; CANR 2; DLB
244

Elliott, Janice 1931-1995 .... **CLC 47**
See also CA 13-16R; CANR 8, 29, 84; CN
7; DLB 14; SATA 119

Elliott, Sumner Locke 1917-1991 ..... **CLC 38**
See also CA 5-8R; 134; CANR 2, 21; DLB
289

Elliott, William
See Bradbury, Ray (Douglas)

Ellis, A. E. .... **CLC 7**

Ellis, Alice Thomas .... **CLC 40**
See Haycraft, Anna (Margaret)
See also DLB 194; MTCW 1

Ellis, Bret Easton 1964- ...... **CLC 39, 71, 117**
See also AAYA 2, 43; CA 118; 123; CANR
51, 74, 126; CN 7; CPW; DA3; DAM
POP; DLB 292; HGG; INT CA-123;
MTCW 1; NFS 11

Ellis, (Henry) Havelock
1859-1939 .... **TCLC 14**
See also CA 109; 169; DLB 190

Ellis, Landon
See Ellison, Harlan (Jay)

Ellis, Trey 1962- .... **CLC 55**
See also CA 146; CANR 92

Ellison, Harlan (Jay) 1934- ... **CLC 1, 13, 42,
139; SSC 14**
See also AAYA 29; BPFB 1; BYA 14; CA
5-8R; CANR 5, 46, 115; CPW; DAM
POP; DLB 8; HGG; INT CANR-5;
MTCW 1, 2; SCFW 2; SFW 4; SSFS 13,
14, 15; SUFW 1, 2

Ellison, Ralph (Waldo) 1914-1994 .... **BLC 1;
CLC 1, 3, 11, 54, 86, 114; SSC 26, 79;
WLC**
See also AAYA 19; AFAW 1, 2; AMWC 2;
AMWR 2; AMWS 2; BPFB 1; BW 1, 3;
BYA 2; CA 9-12R; 145; CANR 24, 53;
CDALB 1941-1968; CSW; DA; DA3;
DAB; DAC; DAM MST, MULT, NOV;
DLB 2, 76, 227; DLBY 1994; EWL 3;
EXPN; EXPS; LAIT 4; MTCW 1, 2;
NCFS 3; NFS 2; RGAL 4; RGSF 2; SSFS
1, 11; YAW

Ellmann, Lucy (Elizabeth) 1956- ..... **CLC 61**
See also CA 128

Ellmann, Richard (David)
1918-1987 .... **CLC 50**
See also BEST 89:2; CA 1-4R; 122; CANR
2, 28, 61; DLB 103; DLBY 1987; MTCW
1, 2

Elman, Richard (Martin)
1934-1997 .... **CLC 19**
See also CA 17-20R; 163; CAAS 3; CANR
47

Elron
See Hubbard, L(afayette) Ron(ald)

El Saadawi, Nawal 1931- .... **CLC 196**
See al'Sadaawi, Nawal; Sa'adawi, al-
Nawal; Saadawi, Nawal El; Sa'dawi,
Nawal al-
See also CA 118; CAAS 11; CANR 44, 92

Eluard, Paul .... **PC 38; TCLC 7, 41**
See Grindel, Eugene
See also EWL 3; GFL 1789 to the Present;
RGWL 2, 3

Elyot, Thomas 1490(?)-1546 .... **LC 11**
See also DLB 136; RGEL 2

Elytis, Odysseus 1911-1996 .... **CLC 15, 49,
100; PC 21**
See Alepoudelis, Odysseus
See also CA 102; 151; CANR 94; CWW 2;
DAM POET; EW 13; EWL 3; MTCW 1,
2; RGWL 2, 3

Emecheta, (Florence Onye) Buchi
1944- .... **BLC 2; CLC 14, 48, 128**
See also AFW; BW 2, 3; CA 81-84; CANR
27, 81, 126; CDWLB 3; CN 7; CWRI 5;
DA3; DAM MULT; DLB 117; EWL 3;
FW; MTCW 1, 2; NFS 12, 14; SATA 66;
WLIT 2

Emerson, Mary Moody
1774-1863 .... **NCLC 66**

Emerson, Ralph Waldo 1803-1882 . **NCLC 1,
38, 98; PC 18; WLC**
See also AAYA 60; AMW; ANW; CDALB
1640-1865; DA; DA3; DAB; DAC; DAM
MST, POET; DLB 1, 59, 73, 183, 223,
270; EXPP; LAIT 2; LMFS 1; NCFS 3;
PFS 4, 17; RGAL 4; TUS; WP

Eminescu, Mihail 1850-1889 .. **NCLC 33, 131**

Empedocles 5th cent. B.C.- .... **CMLC 50**
See also DLB 176

Empson, William 1906-1984 ... **CLC 3, 8, 19,
33, 34**
See also BRWS 2; CA 17-20R; 112; CANR
31, 61; DLB 20; EWL 3; MTCW 1, 2;
RGEL 2

Enchi, Fumiko (Ueda) 1905-1986 ..... **CLC 31**
See Enchi Fumiko
See also CA 129; 121; FW; MJW

Enchi Fumiko
See Enchi, Fumiko (Ueda)
See also DLB 182; EWL 3

Ende, Michael (Andreas Helmuth)
1929-1995 .... **CLC 31**
See also BYA 5; CA 118; 124; 149; CANR
36, 110; CLR 14; DLB 75; MAICYA 1,
2; MAICYAS 1; SATA 61, 130; SATA-
Brief 42; SATA-Obit 86

Endo, Shusaku 1923-1996 ..... **CLC 7, 14, 19,
54, 99; SSC 48; TCLC 152**
See Endo Shusaku
See also CA 29-32R; 153; CANR 21, 54,
131; DA3; DAM NOV; MTCW 1, 2;
RGSF 2; RGWL 2, 3

Endo Shusaku
See Endo, Shusaku
See also CWW 2; DLB 182; EWL 3

Engel, Marian 1933-1985 .... **CLC 36; TCLC
137**
See also CA 25-28R; CANR 12; DLB 53;
FW; INT CANR-12

Engelhardt, Frederick
See Hubbard, L(afayette) Ron(ald)

Engels, Friedrich 1820-1895 .. **NCLC 85, 114**
See also DLB 129; LATS 1:1

Enright, D(ennis) J(oseph)
1920-2002 .... **CLC 4, 8, 31**
See also CA 1-4R; 211; CANR 1, 42, 83;
CP 7; DLB 27; EWL 3; SATA 25; SATA-
Obit 140

Enzensberger, Hans Magnus
1929- .... **CLC 43; PC 28**
See also CA 116; 119; CANR 103; CWW
2; EWL 3

Ephron, Nora 1941- .... **CLC 17, 31**
See also AAYA 35; AITN 2; CA 65-68;
CANR 12, 39, 83

Epicurus 341B.C.-270B.C. .... **CMLC 21**
See also DLB 176

Epsilon
See Betjeman, John

Epstein, Daniel Mark 1948- .... **CLC 7**
See also CA 49-52; CANR 2, 53, 90

Epstein, Jacob 1956- .... **CLC 19**
See also CA 114

Epstein, Jean 1897-1953 .... **TCLC 92**

Epstein, Joseph 1937- .... **CLC 39, 204**
See also AMWS 14; CA 112; 119; CANR
50, 65, 117

Epstein, Leslie 1938- .... **CLC 27**
See also AMWS 12; CA 73-76, 215; CAAE
215; CAAS 12; CANR 23, 69; DLB 299

Equiano, Olaudah 1745(?)-1797 . **BLC 2; LC
16**
See also AFAW 1, 2; CDWLB 3; DAM
MULT; DLB 37, 50; WLIT 2

Erasmus, Desiderius 1469(?)-1536 ..... **LC 16,
93**
See also DLB 136; EW 2; LMFS 1; RGWL
2, 3; TWA

Erdman, Paul E(mil) 1932- .... **CLC 25**
See also AITN 1; CA 61-64; CANR 13, 43,
84

Erdrich, Louise 1954- .... **CLC 39, 54, 120,
176; NNAL; PC 52**
See also AAYA 10, 47; AMWS 4; BEST
89:1; BPFB 1; CA 114; CANR 41, 62,
118; CDALBS; CN 7; CP 7; CPW; CWP;
DA3; DAM MULT, NOV, POP; DLB 152,

Fitzgerald, F(rancis) Scott (Key)
1896-1940 ... **SSC 6, 31, 75; TCLC 1, 6, 14, 28, 55, 157; WLC**
See also AAYA 24; AITN 1; AMW; AMWC 2; AMWR 1; BPFB 1; CA 110; 123; CDALB 1917-1929; DA; DA3; DAB; DAC; DAM MST, NOV; DLB 4, 9, 86, 219, 273; DLBD 1, 15, 16; DLBY 1981, 1996; EWL 3; EXPN; EXPS; LAIT 3; MTCW 1, 2; NFS 2, 19, 20; RGAL 4; RGSF 2; SSFS 4, 15; TUS

Fitzgerald, Penelope 1916-2000 . **CLC 19, 51, 61, 143**
See also BRWS 5; CA 85-88; 190; CAAS 10; CANR 56, 86, 131; CN 7; DLB 14, 194; EWL 3; MTCW 2

Fitzgerald, Robert (Stuart)
1910-1985 .... **CLC 39**
See also CA 1-4R; 114; CANR 1; DLBY 1980

FitzGerald, Robert D(avid)
1902-1987 .... **CLC 19**
See also CA 17-20R; DLB 260; RGEL 2

Fitzgerald, Zelda (Sayre)
1900-1948 .... **TCLC 52**
See also AMWS 9; CA 117; 126; DLBY 1984

Flanagan, Thomas (James Bonner)
1923-2002 .... **CLC 25, 52**
See also CA 108; 206; CANR 55; CN 7; DLBY 1980; INT CA-108; MTCW 1; RHW

Flaubert, Gustave 1821-1880 .... **NCLC 2, 10, 19, 62, 66, 135; SSC 11, 60; WLC**
See also DA; DA3; DAB; DAC; DAM MST, NOV; DLB 119, 301; EW 7; EXPS; GFL 1789 to the Present; LAIT 2; LMFS 1; NFS 14; RGSF 2; RGWL 2, 3; SSFS 6; TWA

Flavius Josephus
See Josephus, Flavius

Flecker, Herman Elroy
See Flecker, (Herman) James Elroy

Flecker, (Herman) James Elroy
1884-1915 .... **TCLC 43**
See also CA 109; 150; DLB 10, 19; RGEL 2

Fleming, Ian (Lancaster) 1908-1964 . **CLC 3, 30**
See also AAYA 26; BPFB 1; CA 5-8R; CANR 59; CDBLB 1945-1960; CMW 4; CPW; DA3; DAM POP; DLB 87, 201; MSW; MTCW 1, 2; RGEL 2; SATA 9; TEA; YAW

Fleming, Thomas (James) 1927- ...... **CLC 37**
See also CA 5-8R; CANR 10, 102; INT CANR-10; SATA 8

Fletcher, John 1579-1625 .... **DC 6; LC 33**
See also BRW 2; CDBLB Before 1660; DLB 58; RGEL 2; TEA

Fletcher, John Gould 1886-1950 .... **TCLC 35**
See also CA 107; 167; DLB 4, 45; LMFS 2; RGAL 4

Fleur, Paul
See Pohl, Frederik

Flieg, Helmut
See Heym, Stefan

Flooglebuckle, Al
See Spiegelman, Art

Flora, Fletcher 1914-1969
See Queen, Ellery
See also CA 1-4R; CANR 3, 85

Flying Officer X
See Bates, H(erbert) E(rnest)

Fo, Dario 1926- .... **CLC 32, 109; DC 10**
See also CA 116; 128; CANR 68, 114, 134; CWW 2; DA3; DAM DRAM; DLBY 1997; EWL 3; MTCW 1, 2

Fogarty, Jonathan Titulescu Esq.
See Farrell, James T(homas)

Follett, Ken(neth Martin) 1949- .... **CLC 18**
See also AAYA 6, 50; BEST 89:4; BPFB 1; CA 81-84; CANR 13, 33, 54, 102; CMW 4; CPW; DA3; DAM NOV, POP; DLB 87; DLBY 1981; INT CANR-33; MTCW 1

Fondane, Benjamin 1898-1944 ..... **TCLC 159**

Fontane, Theodor 1819-1898 .... **NCLC 26**
See also CDWLB 2; DLB 129; EW 6; RGWL 2, 3; TWA

Fontenot, Chester .... **CLC 65**

Fonvizin, Denis Ivanovich
1744(?)-1792 .... **LC 81**
See also DLB 150; RGWL 2, 3

Foote, Horton 1916- .... **CLC 51, 91**
See also CA 73-76; CAD; CANR 34, 51, 110; CD 5; CSW; DA3; DAM DRAM; DFS 20; DLB 26, 266; EWL 3; INT CANR-34

Foote, Mary Hallock 1847-1938 .. **TCLC 108**
See also DLB 186, 188, 202, 221

Foote, Samuel 1721-1777 .... **LC 106**
See also DLB 89; RGEL 2

Foote, Shelby 1916- .... **CLC 75**
See also AAYA 40; CA 5-8R; CANR 3, 45, 74, 131; CN 7; CPW; CSW; DA3; DAM NOV, POP; DLB 2, 17; MTCW 2; RHW

Forbes, Cosmo
See Lewton, Val

Forbes, Esther 1891-1967 .... **CLC 12**
See also AAYA 17; BYA 2; CA 13-14; 25-28R; CAP 1; CLR 27; DLB 22; JRDA; MAICYA 1, 2; RHW; SATA 2, 100; YAW

Forche, Carolyn (Louise) 1950- .... **CLC 25, 83, 86; PC 10**
See also CA 109; 117; CANR 50, 74; CP 7; CWP; DA3; DAM POET; DLB 5, 193; INT CA-117; MTCW 1; PFS 18; RGAL 4

Ford, Elbur
See Hibbert, Eleanor Alice Burford

Ford, Ford Madox 1873-1939 ... **TCLC 1, 15, 39, 57**
See Chaucer, Daniel
See also BRW 6; CA 104; 132; CANR 74; CDBLB 1914-1945; DA3; DAM NOV; DLB 34, 98, 162; EWL 3; MTCW 1, 2; RGEL 2; TEA

Ford, Henry 1863-1947 .... **TCLC 73**
See also CA 115; 148

Ford, Jack
See Ford, John

Ford, John 1586-1639 .... **DC 8; LC 68**
See also BRW 2; CDBLB Before 1660; DA3; DAM DRAM; DFS 7; DLB 58; IDTP; RGEL 2

Ford, John 1895-1973 .... **CLC 16**
See also CA 187; 45-48

Ford, Richard 1944- .... **CLC 46, 99, 205**
See also AMWS 5; CA 69-72; CANR 11, 47, 86, 128; CN 7; CSW; DLB 227; EWL 3; MTCW 1; RGAL 4; RGSF 2

Ford, Webster
See Masters, Edgar Lee

Foreman, Richard 1937- .... **CLC 50**
See also CA 65-68; CAD; CANR 32, 63; CD 5

Forester, C(ecil) S(cott) 1899-1966 . **CLC 35; TCLC 152**
See also CA 73-76; 25-28R; CANR 83; DLB 191; RGEL 2; RHW; SATA 13

Forez
See Mauriac, Francois (Charles)

Forman, James
See Forman, James D(ouglas)

Forman, James D(ouglas) 1932- .... **CLC 21**
See also AAYA 17; CA 9-12R; CANR 4, 19, 42; JRDA; MAICYA 1, 2; SATA 8, 70; YAW

Forman, Milos 1932- .... **CLC 164**
See also CA 109

Fornes, Maria Irene 1930- .... **CLC 39, 61, 187; DC 10; HLCS 1**
See also CA 25-28R; CAD; CANR 28, 81; CD 5; CWD; DLB 7; HW 1, 2; INT CANR-28; LLW 1; MTCW 1; RGAL 4

Forrest, Leon (Richard)
1937-1997 .... **BLCS; CLC 4**
See also AFAW 2; BW 2; CA 89-92; 162; CAAS 7; CANR 25, 52, 87; CN 7; DLB 33

Forster, E(dward) M(organ)
1879-1970 ...... **CLC 1, 2, 3, 4, 9, 10, 13, 15, 22, 45, 77; SSC 27; TCLC 125; WLC**
See also AAYA 2, 37; BRW 6; BRWR 2; BYA 12; CA 13-14; 25-28R; CANR 45; CAP 1; CDBLB 1914-1945; DA; DA3; DAB; DAC; DAM MST, NOV; DLB 34, 98, 162, 178, 195; DLBD 10; EWL 3; EXPN; LAIT 3; LMFS 1; MTCW 1, 2; NCFS 1; NFS 3, 10, 11; RGEL 2; RGSF 2; SATA 57; SUFW 1; TEA; WLIT 4

Forster, John 1812-1876 .... **NCLC 11**
See also DLB 144, 184

Forster, Margaret 1938- .... **CLC 149**
See also CA 133; CANR 62, 115; CN 7; DLB 155, 271

Forsyth, Frederick 1938- .... **CLC 2, 5, 36**
See also BEST 89:4; CA 85-88; CANR 38, 62, 115; CMW 4; CN 7; CPW; DAM NOV, POP; DLB 87; MTCW 1, 2

Forten, Charlotte L. 1837-1914 .... **BLC 2; TCLC 16**
See Grimke, Charlotte L(ottie) Forten
See also DLB 50, 239

Fortinbras
See Grieg, (Johan) Nordahl (Brun)

Foscolo, Ugo 1778-1827 .... **NCLC 8, 97**
See also EW 5

Fosse, Bob .... **CLC 20**
See Fosse, Robert Louis

Fosse, Robert Louis 1927-1987
See Fosse, Bob
See also CA 110; 123

Foster, Hannah Webster
1758-1840 .... **NCLC 99**
See also DLB 37, 200; RGAL 4

Foster, Stephen Collins
1826-1864 .... **NCLC 26**
See also RGAL 4

Foucault, Michel 1926-1984 . **CLC 31, 34, 69**
See also CA 105; 113; CANR 34; DLB 242; EW 13; EWL 3; GFL 1789 to the Present; GLL 1; LMFS 2; MTCW 1, 2; TWA

Fouque, Friedrich (Heinrich Karl) de la Motte 1777-1843 .... **NCLC 2**
See also DLB 90; RGWL 2, 3; SUFW 1

Fourier, Charles 1772-1837 .... **NCLC 51**

Fournier, Henri-Alban 1886-1914
See Alain-Fournier
See also CA 104; 179

Fournier, Pierre 1916- .... **CLC 11**
See Gascar, Pierre
See also CA 89-92; CANR 16, 40

Fowles, John (Robert) 1926- . **CLC 1, 2, 3, 4, 6, 9, 10, 15, 33, 87; SSC 33**
See also BPFB 1; BRWS 1; CA 5-8R; CANR 25, 71, 103; CDBLB 1960 to Present; CN 7; DA3; DAB; DAC; DAM MST; DLB 14, 139, 207; EWL 3; HGG; MTCW 1, 2; RGEL 2; RHW; SATA 22; TEA; WLIT 4

Fox, Paula 1923- .... **CLC 2, 8, 121**
See also AAYA 3, 37; BYA 3, 8; CA 73-76; CANR 20, 36, 62, 105; CLR 1, 44, 96; DLB 52; JRDA; MAICYA 1, 2; MTCW 1; NFS 12; SATA 17, 60, 120; WYA; YAW

Fox, William Price (Jr.) 1926- .... **CLC 22**
See also CA 17-20R; CAAS 19; CANR 11; CSW; DLB 2; DLBY 1981

Foxe, John 1517(?)-1587 ...... **LC 14**
See also DLB 132

Frame, Janet .. **CLC 2, 3, 6, 22, 66, 96; SSC 29**
See Clutha, Janet Paterson Frame
See also CN 7; CWP; EWL 3; RGEL 2; RGSF 2; TWA

France, Anatole .... **TCLC 9**
See Thibault, Jacques Anatole Francois
See also DLB 123; EWL 3; GFL 1789 to the Present; MTCW 1; RGWL 2, 3; SUFW 1

Francis, Claude .... **CLC 50**
See also CA 192

Francis, Richard Stanley 1920- ... **CLC 2, 22, 42, 102**
See also AAYA 5, 21; BEST 89:3; BPFB 1; CA 5-8R; CANR 9, 42, 68, 100; CDBLB 1960 to Present; CMW 4; CN 7; DA3; DAM POP; DLB 87; INT CANR-9; MSW; MTCW 1, 2

Francis, Robert (Churchill) 1901-1987 .... **CLC 15; PC 34**
See also AMWS 9; CA 1-4R; 123; CANR 1; EXPP; PFS 12

Francis, Lord Jeffrey
See Jeffrey, Francis
See also DLB 107

Frank, Anne(lies Marie) 1929-1945 .... **TCLC 17; WLC**
See also AAYA 12; BYA 1; CA 113; 133; CANR 68; CLR 101; DA; DA3; DAB; DAC; DAM MST; LAIT 4; MAICYA 2; MAICYAS 1; MTCW 1, 2; NCFS 2; SATA 87; SATA-Brief 42; WYA; YAW

Frank, Bruno 1887-1945 .... **TCLC 81**
See also CA 189; DLB 118; EWL 3

Frank, Elizabeth 1945- .... **CLC 39**
See also CA 121; 126; CANR 78; INT CA-126

Frankl, Viktor E(mil) 1905-1997 ...... **CLC 93**
See also CA 65-68; 161

Franklin, Benjamin
See Hasek, Jaroslav (Matej Frantisek)

Franklin, Benjamin 1706-1790 .... **LC 25; WLCS**
See also AMW; CDALB 1640-1865; DA; DA3; DAB; DAC; DAM MST; DLB 24, 43, 73, 183; LAIT 1; RGAL 4; TUS

Franklin, (Stella Maria Sarah) Miles (Lampe) 1879-1954 .... **TCLC 7**
See also CA 104; 164; DLB 230; FW; MTCW 2; RGEL 2; TWA

Franzen, Jonathan 1959- .... **CLC 202**
See also CA 129; CANR 105

Fraser, Antonia (Pakenham) 1932- . **CLC 32, 107**
See also AAYA 57; CA 85-88; CANR 44, 65, 119; CMW; DLB 276; MTCW 1, 2; SATA-Brief 32

Fraser, George MacDonald 1925- ...... **CLC 7**
See also AAYA 48; CA 45-48, 180; CAAE 180; CANR 2, 48, 74; MTCW 1; RHW

Fraser, Sylvia 1935- .... **CLC 64**
See also CA 45-48; CANR 1, 16, 60; CCA 1

Frayn, Michael 1933- . **CLC 3, 7, 31, 47, 176**
See also BRWC 2; BRWS 7; CA 5-8R; CANR 30, 69, 114, 133; CBD; CD 5; CN 7; DAM DRAM, NOV; DLB 13, 14, 194, 245; FANT; MTCW 1, 2; SFW 4

Fraze, Candida (Merrill) 1945- .... **CLC 50**
See also CA 126

Frazer, Andrew
See Marlowe, Stephen

Frazer, J(ames) G(eorge) 1854-1941 .... **TCLC 32**
See also BRWS 3; CA 118; NCFS 5

Frazer, Robert Caine
See Creasey, John

Frazer, Sir James George
See Frazer, J(ames) G(eorge)

Frazier, Charles 1950- .... **CLC 109**
See also AAYA 34; CA 161; CANR 126; CSW; DLB 292

Frazier, Ian 1951- .... **CLC 46**
See also CA 130; CANR 54, 93

Frederic, Harold 1856-1898 .... **NCLC 10**
See also AMW; DLB 12, 23; DLBD 13; RGAL 4

Frederick, John
See Faust, Frederick (Schiller)
See also TCWW 2

Frederick the Great 1712-1786 .... **LC 14**

Fredro, Aleksander 1793-1876 .... **NCLC 8**

Freeling, Nicolas 1927-2003 .... **CLC 38**
See also CA 49-52; 218; CAAS 12; CANR 1, 17, 50, 84; CMW 4; CN 7; DLB 87

Freeman, Douglas Southall 1886-1953 .... **TCLC 11**
See also CA 109; 195; DLB 17; DLBD 17

Freeman, Judith 1946- .... **CLC 55**
See also CA 148; CANR 120; DLB 256

Freeman, Mary E(leanor) Wilkins 1852-1930 .... **SSC 1, 47; TCLC 9**
See also CA 106; 177; DLB 12, 78, 221; EXPS; FW; HGG; MAWW; RGAL 4; RGSF 2; SSFS 4, 8; SUFW 1; TUS

Freeman, R(ichard) Austin 1862-1943 .... **TCLC 21**
See also CA 113; CANR 84; CMW 4; DLB 70

French, Albert 1943- .... **CLC 86**
See also BW 3; CA 167

French, Antonia
See Kureishi, Hanif

French, Marilyn 1929- .. **CLC 10, 18, 60, 177**
See also BPFB 1; CA 69-72; CANR 3, 31, 134; CN 7; CPW; DAM DRAM, NOV, POP; FW; INT CANR-31; MTCW 1, 2

French, Paul
See Asimov, Isaac

Freneau, Philip Morin 1752-1832 .. **NCLC 1, 111**
See also AMWS 2; DLB 37, 43; RGAL 4

Freud, Sigmund 1856-1939 .... **TCLC 52**
See also CA 115; 133; CANR 69; DLB 296; EW 8; EWL 3; LATS 1:1; MTCW 1, 2; NCFS 3; TWA

Freytag, Gustav 1816-1895 .... **NCLC 109**
See also DLB 129

Friedan, Betty (Naomi) 1921- .... **CLC 74**
See also CA 65-68; CANR 18, 45, 74; DLB 246; FW; MTCW 1, 2; NCFS 5

Friedlander, Saul 1932- .... **CLC 90**
See also CA 117; 130; CANR 72

Friedman, B(ernard) H(arper) 1926- .... **CLC 7**
See also CA 1-4R; CANR 3, 48

Friedman, Bruce Jay 1930- ...... **CLC 3, 5, 56**
See also CA 9-12R; CAD; CANR 25, 52, 101; CD 5; CN 7; DLB 2, 28, 244; INT CANR-25; SSFS 18

Friel, Brian 1929- .... **CLC 5, 42, 59, 115; DC 8; SSC 76**
See also BRWS 5; CA 21-24R; CANR 33, 69, 131; CBD; CD 5; DFS 11; DLB 13; EWL 3; MTCW 1; RGEL 2; TEA

Friis-Baastad, Babbis Ellinor 1921-1970 .... **CLC 12**
See also CA 17-20R; 134; SATA 7

Frisch, Max (Rudolf) 1911-1991 ... **CLC 3, 9, 14, 18, 32, 44; TCLC 121**
See also CA 85-88; 134; CANR 32, 74; CD-WLB 2; DAM DRAM, NOV; DLB 69, 124; EW 13; EWL 3; MTCW 1, 2; RGWL 2, 3

Fromentin, Eugene (Samuel Auguste) 1820-1876 .... **NCLC 10, 125**
See also DLB 123; GFL 1789 to the Present

Frost, Frederick
See Faust, Frederick (Schiller)
See also TCWW 2

Frost, Robert (Lee) 1874-1963 .. **CLC 1, 3, 4, 9, 10, 13, 15, 26, 34, 44; PC 1, 39; WLC**
See also AAYA 21; AMW; AMWR 1; CA 89-92; CANR 33; CDALB 1917-1929; CLR 67; DA; DA3; DAB; DAC; DAM MST, POET; DLB 54, 284; DLBD 7; EWL 3; EXPP; MTCW 1, 2; PAB; PFS 1, 2, 3, 4, 5, 6, 7, 10, 13; RGAL 4; SATA 14; TUS; WP; WYA

Froude, James Anthony 1818-1894 .... **NCLC 43**
See also DLB 18, 57, 144

Froy, Herald
See Waterhouse, Keith (Spencer)

Fry, Christopher 1907- .... **CLC 2, 10, 14**
See also BRWS 3; CA 17-20R; CAAS 23; CANR 9, 30, 74, 132; CBD; CD 5; CP 7; DAM DRAM; DLB 13; EWL 3; MTCW 1, 2; RGEL 2; SATA 66; TEA

Frye, (Herman) Northrop 1912-1991 .... **CLC 24, 70; TCLC 165**
See also CA 5-8R; 133; CANR 8, 37; DLB 67, 68, 246; EWL 3; MTCW 1, 2; RGAL 4; TWA

Fuchs, Daniel 1909-1993 .... **CLC 8, 22**
See also CA 81-84; 142; CAAS 5; CANR 40; DLB 9, 26, 28; DLBY 1993

Fuchs, Daniel 1934- .... **CLC 34**
See also CA 37-40R; CANR 14, 48

Fuentes, Carlos 1928- .. **CLC 3, 8, 10, 13, 22, 41, 60, 113; HLC 1; SSC 24; WLC**
See also AAYA 4, 45; AITN 2; BPFB 1; CA 69-72; CANR 10, 32, 68, 104; CD-WLB 3; CWW 2; DA; DA3; DAB; DAC; DAM MST, MULT, NOV; DLB 113; DNFS 2; EWL 3; HW 1, 2; LAIT 3; LATS 1:2; LAW; LAWS 1; LMFS 2; MTCW 1, 2; NFS 8; RGSF 2; RGWL 2, 3; TWA; WLIT 1

Fuentes, Gregorio Lopez y
See Lopez y Fuentes, Gregorio

Fuertes, Gloria 1918-1998 .... **PC 27**
See also CA 178; 180; DLB 108; HW 2; SATA 115

Fugard, (Harold) Athol 1932- . **CLC 5, 9, 14, 25, 40, 80; DC 3**
See also AAYA 17; AFW; CA 85-88; CANR 32, 54, 118; CD 5; DAM DRAM; DFS 3, 6, 10; DLB 225; DNFS 1, 2; EWL 3; LATS 1:2; MTCW 1; RGEL 2; WLIT 2

Fugard, Sheila 1932- .... **CLC 48**
See also CA 125

Fukuyama, Francis 1952- .... **CLC 131**
See also CA 140; CANR 72, 125

Fuller, Charles (H.), (Jr.) 1939- .... **BLC 2; CLC 25; DC 1**
See also BW 2; CA 108; 112; CAD; CANR 87; CD 5; DAM DRAM, MULT; DFS 8; DLB 38, 266; EWL 3; INT CA-112; MTCW 1

Fuller, Henry Blake 1857-1929 .... **TCLC 103**
See also CA 108; 177; DLB 12; RGAL 4

Fuller, John (Leopold) 1937- .... **CLC 62**
See also CA 21-24R; CANR 9, 44; CP 7; DLB 40

Fuller, Margaret
See Ossoli, Sarah Margaret (Fuller)
See also AMWS 2; DLB 183, 223, 239

Fuller, Roy (Broadbent) 1912-1991 ... **CLC 4, 28**
See also BRWS 7; CA 5-8R; 135; CAAS 10; CANR 53, 83; CWRI 5; DLB 15, 20; EWL 3; RGEL 2; SATA 87

Fuller, Sarah Margaret
See Ossoli, Sarah Margaret (Fuller)

Fuller, Sarah Margaret
See Ossoli, Sarah Margaret (Fuller)
See also DLB 1, 59, 73

Fuller, Thomas 1608-1661 .... **LC 111**
See also DLB 151

Fulton, Alice 1952- .... **CLC 52**
See also CA 116; CANR 57, 88; CP 7; CWP; DLB 193

Furphy, Joseph 1843-1912 .... **TCLC 25**
See Collins, Tom
See also CA 163; DLB 230; EWL 3; RGEL 2

Fuson, Robert H(enderson) 1927- .... **CLC 70**
See also CA 89-92; CANR 103

Fussell, Paul 1924- .... **CLC 74**
See also BEST 90:1; CA 17-20R; CANR 8, 21, 35, 69, 135; INT CANR-21; MTCW 1, 2

Futabatei, Shimei 1864-1909 .... **TCLC 44**
See Futabatei Shimei
See also CA 162; MJW

Futabatei Shimei
See Futabatei, Shimei
See also DLB 180; EWL 3

Futrelle, Jacques 1875-1912 .... **TCLC 19**
See also CA 113; 155; CMW 4

Gaboriau, Emile 1835-1873 .... **NCLC 14**
See also CMW 4; MSW

Gadda, Carlo Emilio 1893-1973 ...... **CLC 11; TCLC 144**
See also CA 89-92; DLB 177; EWL 3

Gaddis, William 1922-1998 ... **CLC 1, 3, 6, 8, 10, 19, 43, 86**
See also AMWS 4; BPFB 1; CA 17-20R; 172; CANR 21, 48; CN 7; DLB 2, 278; EWL 3; MTCW 1, 2; RGAL 4

Gaelique, Moruen le
See Jacob, (Cyprien-)Max

Gage, Walter
See Inge, William (Motter)

Gaiman, Neil (Richard) 1960- .... **CLC 195**
See also AAYA 19, 42; CA 133; CANR 81, 129; DLB 261; HGG; SATA 85, 146; SFW 4; SUFW 2

Gaines, Ernest J(ames) 1933- .. **BLC 2; CLC 3, 11, 18, 86, 181; SSC 68**
See also AAYA 18; AFAW 1, 2; AITN 1; BPFB 2; BW 2, 3; BYA 6; CA 9-12R; CANR 6, 24, 42, 75, 126; CDALB 1968-1988; CLR 62; CN 7; CSW; DA3; DAM MULT; DLB 2, 33, 152; DLBY 1980; EWL 3; EXPN; LAIT 5; LATS 1:2; MTCW 1, 2; NFS 5, 7, 16; RGAL 4; RGSF 2; RHW; SATA 86; SSFS 5; YAW

Gaitskill, Mary (Lawrence) 1954- .... **CLC 69**
See also CA 128; CANR 61; DLB 244

Gaius Suetonius Tranquillus
See Suetonius

Galdos, Benito Perez
See Perez Galdos, Benito
See also EW 7

Gale, Zona 1874-1938 .... **TCLC 7**
See also CA 105; 153; CANR 84; DAM DRAM; DFS 17; DLB 9, 78, 228; RGAL 4

Galeano, Eduardo (Hughes) 1940- . **CLC 72; HLCS 1**
See also CA 29-32R; CANR 13, 32, 100; HW 1

Galiano, Juan Valera y Alcala
See Valera y Alcala-Galiano, Juan

Galilei, Galileo 1564-1642 .... **LC 45**

Gallagher, Tess 1943- .... **CLC 18, 63; PC 9**
See also CA 106; CP 7; CWP; DAM POET; DLB 120, 212, 244; PFS 16

Gallant, Mavis 1922- ..... **CLC 7, 18, 38, 172; SSC 5, 78**
See also CA 69-72; CANR 29, 69, 117; CCA 1; CN 7; DAC; DAM MST; DLB 53; EWL 3; MTCW 1, 2; RGEL 2; RGSF 2

Gallant, Roy A(rthur) 1924- .... **CLC 17**
See also CA 5-8R; CANR 4, 29, 54, 117; CLR 30; MAICYA 1, 2; SATA 4, 68, 110

Gallico, Paul (William) 1897-1976 ..... **CLC 2**
See also AITN 1; CA 5-8R; 69-72; CANR 23; DLB 9, 171; FANT; MAICYA 1, 2; SATA 13

Gallo, Max Louis 1932- .... **CLC 95**
See also CA 85-88

Gallois, Lucien
See Desnos, Robert

Gallup, Ralph
See Whitemore, Hugh (John)

Galsworthy, John 1867-1933 .... **SSC 22; TCLC 1, 45; WLC**
See also BRW 6; CA 104; 141; CANR 75; CDBLB 1890-1914; DA; DA3; DAB; DAC; DAM DRAM, MST, NOV; DLB 10, 34, 98, 162; DLBD 16; EWL 3; MTCW 1; RGEL 2; SSFS 3; TEA

Galt, John 1779-1839 .... **NCLC 1, 110**
See also DLB 99, 116, 159; RGEL 2; RGSF 2

Galvin, James 1951- .... **CLC 38**
See also CA 108; CANR 26

Gamboa, Federico 1864-1939 .... **TCLC 36**
See also CA 167; HW 2; LAW

Gandhi, M. K.
See Gandhi, Mohandas Karamchand

Gandhi, Mahatma
See Gandhi, Mohandas Karamchand

Gandhi, Mohandas Karamchand
1869-1948 .... **TCLC 59**
See also CA 121; 132; DA3; DAM MULT; MTCW 1, 2

Gann, Ernest Kellogg 1910-1991 ..... **CLC 23**
See also AITN 1; BPFB 2; CA 1-4R; 136; CANR 1, 83; RHW

Gao Xingjian 1940- .... **CLC 167**
See Xingjian, Gao

Garber, Eric 1943(?)-
See Holleran, Andrew
See also CANR 89

Garcia, Cristina 1958- .... **CLC 76**
See also AMWS 11; CA 141; CANR 73, 130; DLB 292; DNFS 1; EWL 3; HW 2; LLW 1

Garcia Lorca, Federico 1898-1936 ...... **DC 2; HLC 2; PC 3; TCLC 1, 7, 49; WLC**
See Lorca, Federico Garcia
See also AAYA 46; CA 104; 131; CANR 81; DA; DA3; DAB; DAC; DAM DRAM, MST, MULT, POET; DFS 4, 10; DLB 108; EWL 3; HW 1, 2; LATS 1:2; MTCW 1, 2; TWA

Garcia Marquez, Gabriel (Jose)
1928- .... **CLC 2, 3, 8, 10, 15, 27, 47, 55, 68, 170; HLC 1; SSC 8, 83; WLC**
See also AAYA 3, 33; BEST 89:1, 90:4; BPFB 2; BYA 12, 16; CA 33-36R; CANR 10, 28, 50, 75, 82, 128; CDWLB 3; CPW; CWW 2; DA; DA3; DAB; DAC; DAM MST, MULT, NOV, POP; DLB 113; DNFS 1, 2; EWL 3; EXPN; EXPS; HW

1, 2; LAIT 2; LATS 1:2; LAW; LAWS 1; LMFS 2; MTCW 1, 2; NCFS 3; NFS 1, 5, 10; RGSF 2; RGWL 2, 3; SSFS 1, 6, 16; TWA; WLIT 1

Garcilaso de la Vega, El Inca
1503-1536 .... **HLCS 1**
See also LAW

Gard, Janice
See Latham, Jean Lee

Gard, Roger Martin du
See Martin du Gard, Roger

Gardam, Jane (Mary) 1928- .... **CLC 43**
See also CA 49-52; CANR 2, 18, 33, 54, 106; CLR 12; DLB 14, 161, 231; MAICYA 1, 2; MTCW 1; SAAS 9; SATA 39, 76, 130; SATA-Brief 28; YAW

Gardner, Herb(ert George)
1934-2003 .... **CLC 44**
See also CA 149; 220; CAD; CANR 119; CD 5; DFS 18, 20

Gardner, John (Champlin), Jr.
1933-1982 ...... **CLC 2, 3, 5, 7, 8, 10, 18, 28, 34; SSC 7**
See also AAYA 45; AITN 1; AMWS 6; BPFB 2; CA 65-68; 107; CANR 33, 73; CDALBS; CPW; DA3; DAM NOV, POP; DLB 2; DLBY 1982; EWL 3; FANT; LATS 1:2; MTCW 1; NFS 3; RGAL 4; RGSF 2; SATA 40; SATA-Obit 31; SSFS 8

Gardner, John (Edmund) 1926- .... **CLC 30**
See also CA 103; CANR 15, 69, 127; CMW 4; CPW; DAM POP; MTCW 1

Gardner, Miriam
See Bradley, Marion Zimmer
See also GLL 1

Gardner, Noel
See Kuttner, Henry

Gardons, S. S.
See Snodgrass, W(illiam) D(e Witt)

Garfield, Leon 1921-1996 .... **CLC 12**
See also AAYA 8; BYA 1, 3; CA 17-20R; 152; CANR 38, 41, 78; CLR 21; DLB 161; JRDA; MAICYA 1, 2; MAICYAS 1; SATA 1, 32, 76; SATA-Obit 90; TEA; WYA; YAW

Garland, (Hannibal) Hamlin
1860-1940 .... **SSC 18; TCLC 3**
See also CA 104; DLB 12, 71, 78, 186; RGAL 4; RGSF 2; TCWW 2

Garneau, (Hector de) Saint-Denys
1912-1943 .... **TCLC 13**
See also CA 111; DLB 88

Garner, Alan 1934- .... **CLC 17**
See also AAYA 18; BYA 3, 5; CA 73-76, 178; CAAE 178; CANR 15, 64, 134; CLR 20; CPW; DAB; DAM POP; DLB 161, 261; FANT; MAICYA 1, 2; MTCW 1, 2; SATA 18, 69; SATA-Essay 108; SUFW 1, 2; YAW

Garner, Hugh 1913-1979 .... **CLC 13**
See Warwick, Jarvis
See also CA 69-72; CANR 31; CCA 1; DLB 68

Garnett, David 1892-1981 .... **CLC 3**
See also CA 5-8R; 103; CANR 17, 79; DLB 34; FANT; MTCW 2; RGEL 2; SFW 4; SUFW 1

Garos, Stephanie
See Katz, Steve

Garrett, George (Palmer) 1929- .. **CLC 3, 11, 51; SSC 30**
See also AMWS 7; BPFB 2; CA 1-4R; 202; CAAE 202; CAAS 5; CANR 1, 42, 67, 109; CN 7; CP 7; CSW; DLB 2, 5, 130, 152; DLBY 1983

Garrick, David 1717-1779 .... **LC 15**
See also DAM DRAM; DLB 84, 213; RGEL 2

Garrigue, Jean 1914-1972 .... **CLC 2, 8**
  See also CA 5-8R; 37-40R; CANR 20
Garrison, Frederick
  See Sinclair, Upton (Beall)
Garrison, William Lloyd
  1805-1879 .... **NCLC 149**
  See also CDALB 1640-1865; DLB 1, 43,
  235
Garro, Elena 1920(?)-1998 .. **HLCS 1; TCLC
  153**
  See also CA 131; 169; CWW 2; DLB 145;
  EWL 3; HW 1; LAWS 1; WLIT 1
Garth, Will
  See Hamilton, Edmond; Kuttner, Henry
Garvey, Marcus (Moziah, Jr.)
  1887-1940 .... **BLC 2; HR 2; TCLC 41**
  See also BW 1; CA 120; 124; CANR 79;
  DAM MULT
Gary, Romain .... **CLC 25**
  See Kacew, Romain
  See also DLB 83, 299
Gascar, Pierre .... **CLC 11**
  See Fournier, Pierre
  See also EWL 3
Gascoigne, George 1539-1577 .... **LC 108**
  See also DLB 136; RGEL 2
Gascoyne, David (Emery)
  1916-2001 .... **CLC 45**
  See also CA 65-68; 200; CANR 10, 28, 54;
  CP 7; DLB 20; MTCW 1; RGEL 2
Gaskell, Elizabeth Cleghorn
  1810-1865 .... **NCLC 5, 70, 97, 137; SSC
  25**
  See also BRW 5; CDBLB 1832-1890; DAB;
  DAM MST; DLB 21, 144, 159; RGEL 2;
  RGSF 2; TEA
Gass, William H(oward) 1924- . **CLC 1, 2, 8,
  11, 15, 39, 132; SSC 12**
  See also AMWS 6; CA 17-20R; CANR 30,
  71, 100; CN 7; DLB 2, 227; EWL 3;
  MTCW 1, 2; RGAL 4
Gassendi, Pierre 1592-1655 .... **LC 54**
  See also GFL Beginnings to 1789
Gasset, Jose Ortega y
  See Ortega y Gasset, Jose
Gates, Henry Louis, Jr. 1950- ... **BLCS; CLC
  65**
  See also BW 2, 3; CA 109; CANR 25, 53,
  75, 125; CSW; DA3; DAM MULT; DLB
  67; EWL 3; MTCW 1; RGAL 4
Gautier, Theophile 1811-1872 .. **NCLC 1, 59;
  PC 18; SSC 20**
  See also DAM POET; DLB 119; EW 6;
  GFL 1789 to the Present; RGWL 2, 3;
  SUFW; TWA
Gawsworth, John
  See Bates, H(erbert) E(rnest)
Gay, John 1685-1732 .... **LC 49**
  See also BRW 3; DAM DRAM; DLB 84,
  95; RGEL 2; WLIT 3
Gay, Oliver
  See Gogarty, Oliver St. John
Gay, Peter (Jack) 1923- .... **CLC 158**
  See also CA 13-16R; CANR 18, 41, 77;
  INT CANR-18
Gaye, Marvin (Pentz, Jr.)
  1939-1984 .... **CLC 26**
  See also CA 195; 112
Gebler, Carlo (Ernest) 1954- .... **CLC 39**
  See also CA 119; 133; CANR 96; DLB 271
Gee, Maggie (Mary) 1948- .... **CLC 57**
  See also CA 130; CANR 125; CN 7; DLB
  207
Gee, Maurice (Gough) 1931- .... **CLC 29**
  See also AAYA 42; CA 97-100; CANR 67,
  123; CLR 56; CN 7; CWRI 5; EWL 3;
  MAICYA 2; RGSF 2; SATA 46, 101
Geiogamah, Hanay 1945- .... **NNAL**
  See also CA 153; DAM MULT; DLB 175

Gelbart, Larry (Simon) 1928- .... **CLC 21, 61**
  See Gelbart, Larry
  See also CA 73-76; CANR 45, 94
Gelbart, Larry 1928-
  See Gelbart, Larry (Simon)
  See also CAD; CD 5
Gelber, Jack 1932-2003 ...... **CLC 1, 6, 14, 79**
  See also CA 1-4R; 216; CAD; CANR 2;
  DLB 7, 228
Gellhorn, Martha (Ellis)
  1908-1998 .... **CLC 14, 60**
  See also CA 77-80; 164; CANR 44; CN 7;
  DLBY 1982, 1998
Genet, Jean 1910-1986 . **DC 25; CLC 1, 2, 5,
  10, 14, 44, 46; TCLC 128**
  See also CA 13-16R; CANR 18; DA3;
  DAM DRAM; DFS 10; DLB 72; DLBY
  1986; EW 13; EWL 3; GFL 1789 to the
  Present; GLL 1; LMFS 2; MTCW 1, 2;
  RGWL 2, 3; TWA
Gent, Peter 1942- .... **CLC 29**
  See also AITN 1; CA 89-92; DLBY 1982
Gentile, Giovanni 1875-1944 .... **TCLC 96**
  See also CA 119
Gentlewoman in New England, A
  See Bradstreet, Anne
Gentlewoman in Those Parts, A
  See Bradstreet, Anne
Geoffrey of Monmouth c.
  1100-1155 .... **CMLC 44**
  See also DLB 146; TEA
George, Jean
  See George, Jean Craighead
George, Jean Craighead 1919- .... **CLC 35**
  See also AAYA 8; BYA 2, 4; CA 5-8R;
  CANR 25; CLR 1; 80; DLB 52; JRDA;
  MAICYA 1, 2; SATA 2, 68, 124; WYA;
  YAW
George, Stefan (Anton) 1868-1933 . **TCLC 2,
  14**
  See also CA 104; 193; EW 8; EWL 3
Georges, Georges Martin
  See Simenon, Georges (Jacques Christian)
Gerald of Wales c. 1146-c. 1223 ... **CMLC 60**
Gerhardi, William Alexander
  See Gerhardie, William Alexander
Gerhardie, William Alexander
  1895-1977 .... **CLC 5**
  See also CA 25-28R; 73-76; CANR 18;
  DLB 36; RGEL 2
Gerson, Jean 1363-1429 .... **LC 77**
  See also DLB 208
Gersonides 1288-1344 .... **CMLC 49**
  See also DLB 115
Gerstler, Amy 1956- .... **CLC 70**
  See also CA 146; CANR 99
Gertler, T. .... **CLC 34**
  See also CA 116; 121
Gertsen, Aleksandr Ivanovich
  See Herzen, Aleksandr Ivanovich
Ghalib .... **NCLC 39, 78**
  See Ghalib, Asadullah Khan
Ghalib, Asadullah Khan 1797-1869
  See Ghalib
  See also DAM POET; RGWL 2, 3
Ghelderode, Michel de 1898-1962 ..... **CLC 6,
  11; DC 15**
  See also CA 85-88; CANR 40, 77; DAM
  DRAM; EW 11; EWL 3; TWA
Ghiselin, Brewster 1903-2001 .... **CLC 23**
  See also CA 13-16R; CAAS 10; CANR 13;
  CP 7
Ghose, Aurabinda 1872-1950 .... **TCLC 63**
  See Ghose, Aurobindo
  See also CA 163
Ghose, Aurobindo
  See Ghose, Aurobinda
  See also EWL 3

Ghose, Zulfikar 1935- .... **CLC 42, 200**
  See also CA 65-68; CANR 67; CN 7; CP 7;
  EWL 3
Ghosh, Amitav 1956- .... **CLC 44, 153**
  See also CA 147; CANR 80; CN 7; WWE
  1
Giacosa, Giuseppe 1847-1906 .... **TCLC 7**
  See also CA 104
Gibb, Lee
  See Waterhouse, Keith (Spencer)
Gibbon, Edward 1737-1794 .... **LC 97**
  See also BRW 3; DLB 104; RGEL 2
Gibbon, Lewis Grassic .... **TCLC 4**
  See Mitchell, James Leslie
  See also RGEL 2
Gibbons, Kaye 1960- .... **CLC 50, 88, 145**
  See also AAYA 34; AMWS 10; CA 151;
  CANR 75, 127; CSW; DA3; DAM POP;
  DLB 292; MTCW 1; NFS 3; RGAL 4;
  SATA 117
Gibran, Kahlil 1883-1931 . **PC 9; TCLC 1, 9**
  See also CA 104; 150; DA3; DAM POET,
  POP; EWL 3; MTCW 2
Gibran, Khalil
  See Gibran, Kahlil
Gibson, William 1914- .... **CLC 23**
  See also CA 9-12R; CAD 2; CANR 9, 42,
  75, 125; CD 5; DA; DAB; DAC; DAM
  DRAM, MST; DFS 2; DLB 7; LAIT 2;
  MTCW 2; SATA 66; YAW
Gibson, William (Ford) 1948- ... **CLC 39, 63,
  186, 192; SSC 52**
  See also AAYA 12, 59; BPFB 2; CA 126;
  133; CANR 52, 90, 106; CN 7; CPW;
  DA3; DAM POP; DLB 251; MTCW 2;
  SCFW 2; SFW 4
Gide, Andre (Paul Guillaume)
  1869-1951 ..... **SSC 13; TCLC 5, 12, 36;
  WLC**
  See also CA 104; 124; DA; DA3; DAB;
  DAC; DAM MST, NOV; DLB 65; EW 8;
  EWL 3; GFL 1789 to the Present; MTCW
  1, 2; RGSF 2; RGWL 2, 3; TWA
Gifford, Barry (Colby) 1946- .... **CLC 34**
  See also CA 65-68; CANR 9, 30, 40, 90
Gilbert, Frank
  See De Voto, Bernard (Augustine)
Gilbert, W(illiam) S(chwenck)
  1836-1911 .... **TCLC 3**
  See also CA 104; 173; DAM DRAM, POET;
  RGEL 2; SATA 36
Gilbreth, Frank B(unker), Jr.
  1911-2001 .... **CLC 17**
  See also CA 9-12R; SATA 2
Gilchrist, Ellen (Louise) 1935- .. **CLC 34, 48,
  143; SSC 14, 63**
  See also BPFB 2; CA 113; 116; CANR 41,
  61, 104; CN 7; CPW; CSW; DAM POP;
  DLB 130; EWL 3; EXPS; MTCW 1, 2;
  RGAL 4; RGSF 2; SSFS 9
Giles, Molly 1942- .... **CLC 39**
  See also CA 126; CANR 98
Gill, Eric 1882-1940 .... **TCLC 85**
  See Gill, (Arthur) Eric (Rowton Peter
  Joseph)
Gill, (Arthur) Eric (Rowton Peter Joseph)
  1882-1940
  See Gill, Eric
  See also CA 120; DLB 98
Gill, Patrick
  See Creasey, John
Gillette, Douglas .... **CLC 70**
Gilliam, Terry (Vance) 1940- .... **CLC 21, 141**
  See Monty Python
  See also AAYA 19, 59; CA 108; 113; CANR
  35; INT CA-113
Gillian, Jerry
  See Gilliam, Terry (Vance)

Gilliatt, Penelope (Ann Douglass)
1932-1993 .... **CLC 2, 10, 13, 53**
See also AITN 2; CA 13-16R; 141; CANR
49; DLB 14

Gilligan, Carol 1936- .... **CLC 208**
See also CA 142; CANR 121; FW

Gilman, Charlotte (Anna) Perkins (Stetson)
1860-1935 ...... **SSC 13, 62; TCLC 9, 37, 117**
See also AMWS 11; BYA 11; CA 106; 150;
DLB 221; EXPS; FW; HGG; LAIT 2;
MAWW; MTCW 1; RGAL 4; RGSF 2;
SFW 4; SSFS 1, 18

Gilmour, David 1946- .... **CLC 35**

Gilpin, William 1724-1804 .... **NCLC 30**

Gilray, J. D.
See Mencken, H(enry) L(ouis)

Gilroy, Frank D(aniel) 1925- .... **CLC 2**
See also CA 81-84; CAD; CANR 32, 64,
86; CD 5; DFS 17; DLB 7

Gilstrap, John 1957(?)- .... **CLC 99**
See also CA 160; CANR 101

Ginsberg, Allen 1926-1997 .... **CLC 1, 2, 3, 4, 6, 13, 36, 69, 109; PC 4, 47; TCLC 120; WLC**
See also AAYA 33; AITN 1; AMWC 1;
AMWS 2; BG 2; CA 1-4R; 157; CANR
2, 41, 63, 95; CDALB 1941-1968; CP 7;
DA; DA3; DAB; DAC; DAM MST,
POET; DLB 5, 16, 169, 237; EWL 3; GLL
1; LMFS 2; MTCW 1, 2; PAB; PFS 5;
RGAL 4; TUS; WP

Ginzburg, Eugenia .... **CLC 59**
See Ginzburg, Evgeniia

Ginzburg, Evgeniia 1904-1977
See Ginzburg, Eugenia
See also DLB 302

Ginzburg, Natalia 1916-1991 .... **CLC 5, 11, 54, 70; SSC 65; TCLC 156**
See also CA 85-88; 135; CANR 33; DFS
14; DLB 177; EW 13; EWL 3; MTCW 1,
2; RGWL 2, 3

Giono, Jean 1895-1970 .... **CLC 4, 11; TCLC 124**
See also CA 45-48; 29-32R; CANR 2, 35;
DLB 72; EWL 3; GFL 1789 to the
Present; MTCW 1; RGWL 2, 3

Giovanni, Nikki 1943- ...... **BLC 2; CLC 2, 4, 19, 64, 117; PC 19; WLCS**
See also AAYA 22; AITN 1; BW 2, 3; CA
29-32R; CAAS 6; CANR 18, 41, 60, 91,
130; CDALBS; CLR 6, 73; CP 7; CSW;
CWP; CWRI 5; DA; DA3; DAB; DAC;
DAM MST, MULT, POET; DLB 5, 41;
EWL 3; EXPP; INT CANR-18; MAICYA
1, 2; MTCW 1, 2; PFS 17; RGAL 4;
SATA 24, 107; TUS; YAW

Giovene, Andrea 1904-1998 .... **CLC 7**
See also CA 85-88

Gippius, Zinaida (Nikolaevna) 1869-1945
See Hippius, Zinaida (Nikolaevna)
See also CA 106; 212

Giraudoux, Jean(-Hippolyte)
1882-1944 .... **TCLC 2, 7**
See also CA 104; 196; DAM DRAM; DLB
65; EW 9; EWL 3; GFL 1789 to the
Present; RGWL 2, 3; TWA

Gironella, Jose Maria (Pous)
1917-2003 .... **CLC 11**
See also CA 101; 212; EWL 3; RGWL 2, 3

Gissing, George (Robert)
1857-1903 .... **SSC 37; TCLC 3, 24, 47**
See also BRW 5; CA 105; 167; DLB 18,
135, 184; RGEL 2; TEA

Gitlin, Todd 1943- .... **CLC 201**
See also CA 29-32R; CANR 25, 50, 88

Giurlani, Aldo
See Palazzeschi, Aldo

Gladkov, Fedor Vasil'evich
See Gladkov, Fyodor (Vasilyevich)
See also DLB 272

Gladkov, Fyodor (Vasilyevich)
1883-1958 .... **TCLC 27**
See Gladkov, Fedor Vasil'evich
See also CA 170; EWL 3

Glancy, Diane 1941- .... **CLC 210; NNAL**
See also CA 136, 225; CAAE 225; CAAS
24; CANR 87; DLB 175

Glanville, Brian (Lester) 1931- .... **CLC 6**
See also CA 5-8R; CAAS 9; CANR 3, 70;
CN 7; DLB 15, 139; SATA 42

Glasgow, Ellen (Anderson Gholson)
1873-1945 .... **SSC 34; TCLC 2, 7**
See also AMW; CA 104; 164; DLB 9, 12;
MAWW; MTCW 2; RGAL 4; RHW;
SSFS 9; TUS

Glaspell, Susan 1882(?)-1948 ..... **DC 10; SSC 41; TCLC 55**
See also AMWS 3; CA 110; 154; DFS 8,
18; DLB 7, 9, 78, 228; MAWW; RGAL
4; SSFS 3; TCWW 2; TUS; YABC 2

Glassco, John 1909-1981 .... **CLC 9**
See also CA 13-16R; 102; CANR 15; DLB
68

Glasscock, Amnesia
See Steinbeck, John (Ernst)

Glasser, Ronald J. 1940(?)- .... **CLC 37**
See also CA 209

Glassman, Joyce
See Johnson, Joyce

Gleick, James (W.) 1954- .... **CLC 147**
See also CA 131; 137; CANR 97; INT CA-137

Glendinning, Victoria 1937- .... **CLC 50**
See also CA 120; 127; CANR 59, 89; DLB
155

Glissant, Edouard (Mathieu)
1928- .... **CLC 10, 68**
See also CA 153; CANR 111; CWW 2;
DAM MULT; EWL 3; RGWL 3

Gloag, Julian 1930- .... **CLC 40**
See also AITN 1; CA 65-68; CANR 10, 70;
CN 7

Glowacki, Aleksander
See Prus, Boleslaw

Gluck, Louise (Elisabeth) 1943- .. **CLC 7, 22, 44, 81, 160; PC 16**
See also AMWS 5; CA 33-36R; CANR 40,
69, 108, 133; CP 7; CWP; DA3; DAM
POET; DLB 5; MTCW 2; PFS 5, 15;
RGAL 4

Glyn, Elinor 1864-1943 .... **TCLC 72**
See also DLB 153; RHW

Gobineau, Joseph-Arthur
1816-1882 .... **NCLC 17**
See also DLB 123; GFL 1789 to the Present

Godard, Jean-Luc 1930- .... **CLC 20**
See also CA 93-96

Godden, (Margaret) Rumer
1907-1998 .... **CLC 53**
See also AAYA 6; BPFB 2; BYA 2, 5; CA
5-8R; 172; CANR 4, 27, 36, 55, 80; CLR
20; CN 7; CWRI 5; DLB 161; MAICYA
1, 2; RHW; SAAS 12; SATA 3, 36; SATA-Obit 109; TEA

Godoy Alcayaga, Lucila 1899-1957 .. **HLC 2; PC 32; TCLC 2**
See Mistral, Gabriela
See also BW 2; CA 104; 131; CANR 81;
DAM MULT; DNFS 1; HW 1, 2; MTCW 1,
2

Godwin, Gail (Kathleen) 1937- ..... **CLC 5, 8, 22, 31, 69, 125**
See also BPFB 2; CA 29-32R; CANR 15,
43, 69, 132; CN 7; CPW; CSW; DA3;
DAM POP; DLB 6, 234; INT CANR-15;
MTCW 1, 2

Godwin, William 1756-1836 .. **NCLC 14, 130**
See also CDBLB 1789-1832; CMW 4; DLB
39, 104, 142, 158, 163, 262; HGG; RGEL
2

Goebbels, Josef
See Goebbels, (Paul) Joseph

Goebbels, (Paul) Joseph
1897-1945 .... **TCLC 68**
See also CA 115; 148

Goebbels, Joseph Paul
See Goebbels, (Paul) Joseph

Goethe, Johann Wolfgang von
1749-1832 . **DC 20; NCLC 4, 22, 34, 90, 154; PC 5; SSC 38; WLC**
See also CDWLB 2; DA; DA3; DAB;
DAC; DAM DRAM, MST, POET; DLB
94; EW 5; LATS 1; LMFS 1:1; RGWL 2,
3; TWA

Gogarty, Oliver St. John
1878-1957 .... **TCLC 15**
See also CA 109; 150; DLB 15, 19; RGEL
2

Gogol, Nikolai (Vasilyevich)
1809-1852 .... **DC 1; NCLC 5, 15, 31; SSC 4, 29, 52; WLC**
See also DA; DAB; DAC; DAM DRAM,
MST; DFS 12; DLB 198; EW 6; EXPS;
RGSF 2; RGWL 2, 3; SSFS 7; TWA

Goines, Donald 1937(?)-1974 ... **BLC 2; CLC 80**
See also AITN 1; BW 1, 3; CA 124; 114;
CANR 82; CMW 4; DA3; DAM MULT,
POP; DLB 33

Gold, Herbert 1924- ... **CLC 4, 7, 14, 42, 152**
See also CA 9-12R; CANR 17, 45, 125; CN
7; DLB 2; DLBY 1981

Goldbarth, Albert 1948- .... **CLC 5, 38**
See also AMWS 12; CA 53-56; CANR 6,
40; CP 7; DLB 120

Goldberg, Anatol 1910-1982 .... **CLC 34**
See also CA 131; 117

Goldemberg, Isaac 1945- .... **CLC 52**
See also CA 69-72; CAAS 12; CANR 11,
32; EWL 3; HW 1; WLIT 1

Golding, Arthur 1536-1606 .... **LC 101**
See also DLB 136

Golding, William (Gerald)
1911-1993 ..... **CLC 1, 2, 3, 8, 10, 17, 27, 58, 81; WLC**
See also AAYA 5, 44; BPFB 2; BRWR 1;
BRWS 1; BYA 2; CA 5-8R; 141; CANR
13, 33, 54; CDBLB 1945-1960; CLR 94;
DA; DA3; DAB; DAC; DAM MST, NOV;
DLB 15, 100, 255; EWL 3; EXPN; HGG;
LAIT 4; MTCW 1, 2; NFS 2; RGEL 2;
RHW; SFW 4; TEA; WLIT 4; YAW

Goldman, Emma 1869-1940 .... **TCLC 13**
See also CA 110; 150; DLB 221; FW;
RGAL 4; TUS

Goldman, Francisco 1954- .... **CLC 76**
See also CA 162

Goldman, William (W.) 1931- ...... **CLC 1, 48**
See also BPFB 2; CA 9-12R; CANR 29,
69, 106; CN 7; DLB 44; FANT; IDFW 3,
4

Goldmann, Lucien 1913-1970 .... **CLC 24**
See also CA 25-28; CAP 2

Goldoni, Carlo 1707-1793 .... **LC 4**
See also DAM DRAM; EW 4; RGWL 2, 3

Goldsberry, Steven 1949- .... **CLC 34**
See also CA 131

Goldsmith, Oliver 1730-1774 .... **DC 8; LC 2, 48; WLC**
See also BRW 3; CDBLB 1660-1789; DA;
DAB; DAC; DAM DRAM, MST, NOV,
POET; DFS 1; DLB 39, 89, 104, 109, 142;
IDTP; RGEL 2; SATA 26; TEA; WLIT 3

Goldsmith, Peter
See Priestley, J(ohn) B(oynton)

Grove, Frederick Philip .... **TCLC 4**
See Greve, Felix Paul (Berthold Friedrich)
See also DLB 92; RGEL 2

Grubb
See Crumb, R(obert)

Grumbach, Doris (Isaac) 1918- . **CLC 13, 22, 64**
See also CA 5-8R; CAAS 2; CANR 9, 42, 70, 127; CN 7; INT CANR-9; MTCW 2

Grundtvig, Nicolai Frederik Severin
1783-1872 .... **NCLC 1**
See also DLB 300

Grunge
See Crumb, R(obert)

Grunwald, Lisa 1959- .... **CLC 44**
See also CA 120

Gryphius, Andreas 1616-1664 .... **LC 89**
See also CDWLB 2; DLB 164; RGWL 2, 3

Guare, John 1938- .... **CLC 8, 14, 29, 67; DC 20**
See also CA 73-76; CAD; CANR 21, 69, 118; CD 5; DAM DRAM; DFS 8, 13; DLB 7, 249; EWL 3; MTCW 1, 2; RGAL 4

Guarini, Battista 1537-1612 .... **LC 102**

Gubar, Susan (David) 1944- .... **CLC 145**
See also CA 108; CANR 45, 70; FW; MTCW 1; RGAL 4

Gudjonsson, Halldor Kiljan 1902-1998
See Halldor Laxness
See also CA 103; 164

Guenter, Erich
See Eich, Gunter

Guest, Barbara 1920- .... **CLC 34; PC 55**
See also BG 2; CA 25-28R; CANR 11, 44, 84; CP 7; CWP; DLB 5, 193

Guest, Edgar A(lbert) 1881-1959 ... **TCLC 95**
See also CA 112; 168

Guest, Judith (Ann) 1936- .... **CLC 8, 30**
See also AAYA 7; CA 77-80; CANR 15, 75; DA3; DAM NOV, POP; EXPN; INT CANR-15; LAIT 5; MTCW 1, 2; NFS 1

Guevara, Che .... **CLC 87; HLC 1**
See Guevara (Serna), Ernesto

Guevara (Serna), Ernesto
1928-1967 .... **CLC 87; HLC 1**
See Guevara, Che
See also CA 127; 111; CANR 56; DAM MULT; HW 1

Guicciardini, Francesco 1483-1540 ..... **LC 49**

Guild, Nicholas M. 1944- .... **CLC 33**
See also CA 93-96

Guillemin, Jacques
See Sartre, Jean-Paul

Guillen, Jorge 1893-1984 . **CLC 11; HLCS 1; PC 35**
See also CA 89-92; 112; DAM MULT, POET; DLB 108; EWL 3; HW 1; RGWL 2, 3

Guillen, Nicolas (Cristobal)
1902-1989 .... **BLC 2; CLC 48, 79; HLC 1; PC 23**
See also BW 2; CA 116; 125; 129; CANR 84; DAM MST, MULT, POET; DLB 283; EWL 3; HW 1; LAW; RGWL 2, 3; WP

Guillen y Alvarez, Jorge
See Guillen, Jorge

Guillevic, (Eugene) 1907-1997 .... **CLC 33**
See also CA 93-96; CWW 2

Guillois
See Desnos, Robert

Guillois, Valentin
See Desnos, Robert

Guimaraes Rosa, Joao 1908-1967 .... **HLCS 2**
See Rosa, Joao Guimaraes
See also CA 175; LAW; RGSF 2; RGWL 2, 3

Guiney, Louise Imogen
1861-1920 .... **TCLC 41**
See also CA 160; DLB 54; RGAL 4

Guinizelli, Guido c. 1230-1276 ...... **CMLC 49**

Guiraldes, Ricardo (Guillermo)
1886-1927 .... **TCLC 39**
See also CA 131; EWL 3; HW 1; LAW; MTCW 1

Gumilev, Nikolai (Stepanovich)
1886-1921 .... **TCLC 60**
See Gumilyov, Nikolay Stepanovich
See also CA 165; DLB 295

Gumilyov, Nikolay Stepanovich
See Gumilev, Nikolai (Stepanovich)
See also EWL 3

Gump, P. Q.
See Card, Orson Scott

Gunesekera, Romesh 1954- .... **CLC 91**
See also BRWS 10; CA 159; CN 7; DLB 267

Gunn, Bill .... **CLC 5**
See Gunn, William Harrison
See also DLB 38

Gunn, Thom(son William)
1929-2004 . **CLC 3, 6, 18, 32, 81; PC 26**
See also BRWS 4; CA 17-20R; 227; CANR 9, 33, 116; CDBLB 1960 to Present; CP 7; DAM POET; DLB 27; INT CANR-33; MTCW 1; PFS 9; RGEL 2

Gunn, William Harrison 1934(?)-1989
See Gunn, Bill
See also AITN 1; BW 1, 3; CA 13-16R; 128; CANR 12, 25, 76

Gunn Allen, Paula
See Allen, Paula Gunn

Gunnars, Kristjana 1948- .... **CLC 69**
See also CA 113; CCA 1; CP 7; CWP; DLB 60

Gunter, Erich
See Eich, Gunter

Gurdjieff, G(eorgei) I(vanovich)
1877(?)-1949 .... **TCLC 71**
See also CA 157

Gurganus, Allan 1947- .... **CLC 70**
See also BEST 90:1; CA 135; CANR 114; CN 7; CPW; CSW; DAM POP; GLL 1

Gurney, A. R.
See Gurney, A(lbert) R(amsdell), Jr.
See also DLB 266

Gurney, A(lbert) R(amsdell), Jr.
1930- .... **CLC 32, 50, 54**
See Gurney, A. R.
See also AMWS 5; CA 77-80; CAD; CANR 32, 64, 121; CD 5; DAM DRAM; EWL 3

Gurney, Ivor (Bertie) 1890-1937 ... **TCLC 33**
See also BRW 6; CA 167; DLBY 2002; PAB; RGEL 2

Gurney, Peter
See Gurney, A(lbert) R(amsdell), Jr.

Guro, Elena (Genrikhovna)
1877-1913 .... **TCLC 56**
See also DLB 295

Gustafson, James M(oody) 1925- ... **CLC 100**
See also CA 25-28R; CANR 37

Gustafson, Ralph (Barker)
1909-1995 .... **CLC 36**
See also CA 21-24R; CANR 8, 45, 84; CP 7; DLB 88; RGEL 2

Gut, Gom
See Simenon, Georges (Jacques Christian)

Guterson, David 1956- .... **CLC 91**
See also CA 132; CANR 73, 126; DLB 292; MTCW 2; NFS 13

Guthrie, A(lfred) B(ertram), Jr.
1901-1991 .... **CLC 23**
See also CA 57-60; 134; CANR 24; DLB 6, 212; SATA 62; SATA-Obit 67

Guthrie, Isobel
See Grieve, C(hristopher) M(urray)

Guthrie, Woodrow Wilson 1912-1967
See Guthrie, Woody
See also CA 113; 93-96

Guthrie, Woody .... **CLC 35**
See Guthrie, Woodrow Wilson
See also DLB 303; LAIT 3

Gutierrez Najera, Manuel
1859-1895 .... **HLCS 2; NCLC 133**
See also DLB 290; LAW

Guy, Rosa (Cuthbert) 1925- .... **CLC 26**
See also AAYA 4, 37; BW 2; CA 17-20R; CANR 14, 34, 83; CLR 13; DLB 33; DNFS 1; JRDA; MAICYA 1, 2; SATA 14, 62, 122; YAW

Gwendolyn
See Bennett, (Enoch) Arnold

H. D. .... **CLC 3, 8, 14, 31, 34, 73; PC 5**
See Doolittle, Hilda

H. de V.
See Buchan, John

Haavikko, Paavo Juhani 1931- .. **CLC 18, 34**
See also CA 106; CWW 2; EWL 3

Habbema, Koos
See Heijermans, Herman

Habermas, Juergen 1929- .... **CLC 104**
See also CA 109; CANR 85; DLB 242

Habermas, Jurgen
See Habermas, Juergen

Hacker, Marilyn 1942- ...... **CLC 5, 9, 23, 72, 91; PC 47**
See also CA 77-80; CANR 68, 129; CP 7; CWP; DAM POET; DLB 120, 282; FW; GLL 2; PFS 19

Hadewijch of Antwerp fl. 1250- ... **CMLC 61**
See also RGWL 3

Hadrian 76-138 .... **CMLC 52**

Haeckel, Ernst Heinrich (Philipp August)
1834-1919 .... **TCLC 83**
See also CA 157

Hafiz c. 1326-1389(?) .... **CMLC 34**
See also RGWL 2, 3

Hagedorn, Jessica T(arahata)
1949- .... **CLC 185**
See also CA 139; CANR 69; CWP; RGAL 4

Haggard, H(enry) Rider
1856-1925 .... **TCLC 11**
See also BRWS 3; BYA 4, 5; CA 108; 148; CANR 112; DLB 70, 156, 174, 178; FANT; LMFS 1; MTCW 2; RGEL 2; RHW; SATA 16; SCFW; SFW 4; SUFW 1; WLIT 4

Hagiosy, L.
See Larbaud, Valery (Nicolas)

Hagiwara, Sakutaro 1886-1942 .... **PC 18; TCLC 60**
See Hagiwara Sakutaro
See also CA 154; RGWL 3

Hagiwara Sakutaro
See Hagiwara, Sakutaro
See also EWL 3

Haig, Fenil
See Ford, Ford Madox

Haig-Brown, Roderick (Langmere)
1908-1976 .... **CLC 21**
See also CA 5-8R; 69-72; CANR 4, 38, 83; CLR 31; CWRI 5; DLB 88; MAICYA 1, 2; SATA 12

Haight, Rip
See Carpenter, John (Howard)

Hailey, Arthur 1920- .... **CLC 5**
See also AITN 2; BEST 90:3; BPFB 2; CA 1-4R; CANR 2, 36, 75; CCA 1; CN 7; CPW; DAM NOV, POP; DLB 88; DLBY 1982; MTCW 1, 2

Hailey, Elizabeth Forsythe 1938- ..... **CLC 40**
See also CA 93-96; 188; CAAE 188; CAAS 1; CANR 15, 48; INT CANR-15

Harris, George Washington
1814-1869 .... NCLC **23**
See also DLB 3, 11, 248; RGAL 4
Harris, Joel Chandler 1848-1908 ..... SSC **19**;
TCLC **2**
See also CA 104; 137; CANR 80; CLR 49;
DLB 11, 23, 42, 78, 91; LAIT 2; MAI-
CYA 1, 2; RGSF 2; SATA 100; WCH;
YABC 1
Harris, John (Wyndham Parkes Lucas)
Beynon 1903-1969
See Wyndham, John
See also CA 102; 89-92; CANR 84; SATA
118; SFW 4
Harris, MacDonald .... CLC **9**
See Heiney, Donald (William)
Harris, Mark 1922- .... CLC **19**
See also CA 5-8R; CAAS 3; CANR 2, 55,
83; CN 7; DLB 2; DLBY 1980
Harris, Norman .... CLC **65**
Harris, (Theodore) Wilson 1921- .... CLC **25,
159**
See also BRWS 5; BW 2, 3; CA 65-68;
CAAS 16; CANR 11, 27, 69, 114; CD-
WLB 3; CN 7; CP 7; DLB 117; EWL 3;
MTCW 1; RGEL 2
Harrison, Barbara Grizzuti
1934-2002 .... CLC **144**
See also CA 77-80; 205; CANR 15, 48; INT
CANR-15
Harrison, Elizabeth (Allen) Cavanna
1909-2001
See Cavanna, Betty
See also CA 9-12R; 200; CANR 6, 27, 85,
104, 121; MAICYA 2; SATA 142; YAW
Harrison, Harry (Max) 1925- .... CLC **42**
See also CA 1-4R; CANR 5, 21, 84; DLB
8; SATA 4; SCFW 2; SFW 4
Harrison, James (Thomas) 1937- ...... CLC **6,
14, 33, 66, 143; SSC 19**
See Harrison, Jim
See also CA 13-16R; CANR 8, 51, 79; CN
7; CP 7; DLBY 1982; INT CANR-8
Harrison, Jim
See Harrison, James (Thomas)
See also AMWS 8; RGAL 4; TCWW 2;
TUS
Harrison, Kathryn 1961- .... CLC **70, 151**
See also CA 144; CANR 68, 122
Harrison, Tony 1937- .... CLC **43, 129**
See also BRWS 5; CA 65-68; CANR 44,
98; CBD; CD 5; CP 7; DLB 40, 245;
MTCW 1; RGEL 2
Harriss, Will(ard Irvin) 1922- .... CLC **34**
See also CA 111
Hart, Ellis
See Ellison, Harlan (Jay)
Hart, Josephine 1942(?)- .... CLC **70**
See also CA 138; CANR 70; CPW; DAM
POP
Hart, Moss 1904-1961 .... CLC **66**
See also CA 109; 89-92; CANR 84; DAM
DRAM; DFS 1; DLB 7, 266; RGAL 4
Harte, (Francis) Bret(t)
1836(?)-1902 ... SSC **8, 59; TCLC 1, 25;
WLC**
See also AMWS 2; CA 104; 140; CANR
80; CDALB 1865-1917; DA; DA3; DAC;
DAM MST; DLB 12, 64, 74, 79, 186;
EXPS; LAIT 2; RGAL 4; RGSF 2; SATA
26; SSFS 3; TUS
Hartley, L(eslie) P(oles) 1895-1972 ... CLC **2,
22**
See also BRWS 7; CA 45-48; 37-40R;
CANR 33; DLB 15, 139; EWL 3; HGG;
MTCW 1, 2; RGEL 2; RGSF 2; SUFW 1
Hartman, Geoffrey H. 1929- .... CLC **27**
See also CA 117; 125; CANR 79; DLB 67

Hartmann, Sadakichi 1869-1944 ... TCLC **73**
See also CA 157; DLB 54
Hartmann von Aue c. 1170-c.
1210 .... CMLC **15**
See also CDWLB 2; DLB 138; RGWL 2, 3
Hartog, Jan de
See de Hartog, Jan
Haruf, Kent 1943- .... CLC **34**
See also AAYA 44; CA 149; CANR 91, 131
Harvey, Caroline
See Trollope, Joanna
Harvey, Gabriel 1550(?)-1631 .... LC **88**
See also DLB 167, 213, 281
Harwood, Ronald 1934- .... CLC **32**
See also CA 1-4R; CANR 4, 55; CBD; CD
5; DAM DRAM, MST; DLB 13
Hasegawa Tatsunosuke
See Futabatei, Shimei
Hasek, Jaroslav (Matej Frantisek)
1883-1923 .... SSC **69; TCLC 4**
See also CA 104; 129; CDWLB 4; DLB
215; EW 9; EWL 3; MTCW 1, 2; RGSF
2; RGWL 2, 3
Hass, Robert 1941- ... CLC **18, 39, 99; PC 16**
See also AMWS 6; CA 111; CANR 30, 50,
71; CP 7; DLB 105, 206; EWL 3; RGAL
4; SATA 94
Hastings, Hudson
See Kuttner, Henry
Hastings, Selina .... CLC **44**
Hathorne, John 1641-1717 .... LC **38**
Hatteras, Amelia
See Mencken, H(enry) L(ouis)
Hatteras, Owen .... TCLC **18**
See Mencken, H(enry) L(ouis); Nathan,
George Jean
Hauptmann, Gerhart (Johann Robert)
1862-1946 .... SSC **37; TCLC 4**
See also CA 104; 153; CDWLB 2; DAM
DRAM; DLB 66, 118; EW 8; EWL 3;
RGSF 2; RGWL 2, 3; TWA
Havel, Vaclav 1936- ..... CLC **25, 58, 65, 123;
DC 6**
See also CA 104; CANR 36, 63, 124; CD-
WLB 4; CWW 2; DA3; DAM DRAM;
DFS 10; DLB 232; EWL 3; LMFS 2;
MTCW 1, 2; RGWL 3
Haviaras, Stratis .... CLC **33**
See Chaviaras, Strates
Hawes, Stephen 1475(?)-1529(?) .... LC **17**
See also DLB 132; RGEL 2
Hawkes, John (Clendennin Burne, Jr.)
1925-1998 .. CLC **1, 2, 3, 4, 7, 9, 14, 15,
27, 49**
See also BPFB 2; CA 1-4R; 167; CANR 2,
47, 64; CN 7; DLB 2, 7, 227; DLBY
1980, 1998; EWL 3; MTCW 1, 2; RGAL
4
Hawking, S. W.
See Hawking, Stephen W(illiam)
Hawking, Stephen W(illiam) 1942- . CLC **63,
105**
See also AAYA 13; BEST 89:1; CA 126;
129; CANR 48, 115; CPW; DA3; MTCW
2
Hawkins, Anthony Hope
See Hope, Anthony
Hawthorne, Julian 1846-1934 .... TCLC **25**
See also CA 165; HGG
Hawthorne, Nathaniel 1804-1864 ... NCLC **2,
10, 17, 23, 39, 79, 95; SSC 3, 29, 39;
WLC**
See also AAYA 18; AMW; AMWC 1;
AMWR 1; BPFB 2; BYA 3; CDALB
1640-1865; DA; DA3; DAB; DAC; DAM
MST, NOV; DLB 1, 74, 183, 223, 269;
EXPN; EXPS; HGG; LAIT 1; NFS 1, 20;
RGAL 4; RGSF 2; SSFS 1, 7, 11, 15;
SUFW 1; TUS; WCH; YABC 2

Hawthorne, Sophia Peabody
1809-1871 .... NCLC **150**
See also DLB 183, 239
Haxton, Josephine Ayres 1921-
See Douglas, Ellen
See also CA 115; CANR 41, 83
Hayaseca y Eizaguirre, Jorge
See Echegaray (y Eizaguirre), Jose (Maria
Waldo)
Hayashi, Fumiko 1904-1951 .... TCLC **27**
See Hayashi Fumiko
See also CA 161
Hayashi Fumiko
See Hayashi, Fumiko
See also DLB 180; EWL 3
Haycraft, Anna (Margaret) 1932-
See Ellis, Alice Thomas
See also CA 122; CANR 85, 90; MTCW 2
Hayden, Robert E(arl) 1913-1980 ..... BLC **2;
CLC 5, 9, 14, 37; PC 6**
See also AFAW 1, 2; AMWS 2; BW 1, 3;
CA 69-72; 97-100; CABS 2; CANR 24,
75, 82; CDALB 1941-1968; DA; DAC;
DAM MST, MULT, POET; DLB 5, 76;
EWL 3; EXPP; MTCW 1, 2; PFS 1;
RGAL 4; SATA 19; SATA-Obit 26; WP
Haydon, Benjamin Robert
1786-1846 .... NCLC **146**
See also DLB 110
Hayek, F(riedrich) A(ugust von)
1899-1992 .... TCLC **109**
See also CA 93-96; 137; CANR 20; MTCW
1, 2
Hayford, J(oseph) E(phraim) Casely
See Casely-Hayford, J(oseph) E(phraim)
Hayman, Ronald 1932- .... CLC **44**
See also CA 25-28R; CANR 18, 50, 88; CD
5; DLB 155
Hayne, Paul Hamilton 1830-1886 . NCLC **94**
See also DLB 3, 64, 79, 248; RGAL 4
Hays, Mary 1760-1843 .... NCLC **114**
See also DLB 142, 158; RGEL 2
Haywood, Eliza (Fowler)
1693(?)-1756 .... LC **1, 44**
See also DLB 39; RGEL 2
Hazlitt, William 1778-1830 ...... NCLC **29, 82**
See also BRW 4; DLB 110, 158; RGEL 2;
TEA
Hazzard, Shirley 1931- .... CLC **18**
See also CA 9-12R; CANR 4, 70, 127; CN
7; DLB 289; DLBY 1982; MTCW 1
Head, Bessie 1937-1986 ...... BLC **2; CLC 25,
67; SSC 52**
See also AFW; BW 2, 3; CA 29-32R; 119;
CANR 25, 82; CDWLB 3; DA3; DAM
MULT; DLB 117, 225; EWL 3; EXPS;
FW; MTCW 1, 2; RGSF 2; SSFS 5, 13;
WLIT 2; WWE 1
Headon, (Nicky) Topper 1956(?)- ..... CLC **30**
Heaney, Seamus (Justin) 1939- ..... CLC **5, 7,
14, 25, 37, 74, 91, 171; PC 18; WLCS**
See also BRWR 1; BRWS 2; CA 85-88;
CANR 25, 48, 75, 91, 128; CDBLB 1960
to Present; CP 7; DA3; DAB; DAM
POET; DLB 40; DLBY 1995; EWL 3;
EXPP; MTCW 1, 2; PAB; PFS 2, 5, 8,
17; RGEL 2; TEA; WLIT 4
Hearn, (Patricio) Lafcadio (Tessima Carlos)
1850-1904 .... TCLC **9**
See also CA 105; 166; DLB 12, 78, 189;
HGG; RGAL 4
Hearne, Samuel 1745-1792 .... LC **95**
See also DLB 99
Hearne, Vicki 1946-2001 .... CLC **56**
See also CA 139; 201
Hearon, Shelby 1931- .... CLC **63**
See also AITN 2; AMWS 8; CA 25-28R;
CANR 18, 48, 103; CSW

Korolenko, Vladimir
   See Korolenko, Vladimir Galaktionovich
Korolenko, Vladimir G.
   See Korolenko, Vladimir Galaktionovich
Korolenko, Vladimir Galaktionovich
   1853-1921 .... **TCLC 22**
   See also CA 121; DLB 277
Korzybski, Alfred (Habdank Skarbek)
   1879-1950 .... **TCLC 61**
   See also CA 123; 160
Kosinski, Jerzy (Nikodem)
   1933-1991 .... **CLC 1, 2, 3, 6, 10, 15, 53, 70**
   See also AMWS 7; BPFB 2; CA 17-20R; 134; CANR 9, 46; DA3; DAM NOV; DLB 2, 299; DLBY 1982; EWL 3; HGG; MTCW 1, 2; NFS 12; RGAL 4; TUS
Kostelanetz, Richard (Cory) 1940- .. **CLC 28**
   See also CA 13-16R; CAAS 8; CANR 38, 77; CN 7; CP 7
Kostrowitzki, Wilhelm Apollinaris de
   1880-1918
   See Apollinaire, Guillaume
   See also CA 104
Kotlowitz, Robert 1924- .... **CLC 4**
   See also CA 33-36R; CANR 36
Kotzebue, August (Friedrich Ferdinand) von
   1761-1819 .... **NCLC 25**
   See also DLB 94
Kotzwinkle, William 1938- ..... **CLC 5, 14, 35**
   See also BPFB 2; CA 45-48; CANR 3, 44, 84, 129; CLR 6; DLB 173; FANT; MAICYA 1, 2; SATA 24, 70, 146; SFW 4; SUFW 2; YAW
Kowna, Stancy
   See Szymborska, Wislawa
Kozol, Jonathan 1936- .... **CLC 17**
   See also AAYA 46; CA 61-64; CANR 16, 45, 96
Kozoll, Michael 1940(?)- .... **CLC 35**
Kramer, Kathryn 19(?)- .... **CLC 34**
Kramer, Larry 1935- .... **CLC 42; DC 8**
   See also CA 124; 126; CANR 60, 132; DAM POP; DLB 249; GLL 1
Krasicki, Ignacy 1735-1801 .... **NCLC 8**
Krasinski, Zygmunt 1812-1859 .... **NCLC 4**
   See also RGWL 2, 3
Kraus, Karl 1874-1936 .... **TCLC 5**
   See also CA 104; 216; DLB 118; EWL 3
Kreve (Mickevicius), Vincas
   1882-1954 .... **TCLC 27**
   See also CA 170; DLB 220; EWL 3
Kristeva, Julia 1941- .... **CLC 77, 140**
   See also CA 154; CANR 99; DLB 242; EWL 3; FW; LMFS 2
Kristofferson, Kris 1936- .... **CLC 26**
   See also CA 104
Krizanc, John 1956- .... **CLC 57**
   See also CA 187
Krleza, Miroslav 1893-1981 .... **CLC 8, 114**
   See also CA 97-100; 105; CANR 50; CD-WLB 4; DLB 147; EW 11; RGWL 2, 3
Kroetsch, Robert 1927- .. **CLC 5, 23, 57, 132**
   See also CA 17-20R; CANR 8, 38; CCA 1; CN 7; CP 7; DAC; DAM POET; DLB 53; MTCW 1
Kroetz, Franz
   See Kroetz, Franz Xaver
Kroetz, Franz Xaver 1946- .... **CLC 41**
   See also CA 130; CWW 2; EWL 3
Kroker, Arthur (W.) 1945- .... **CLC 77**
   See also CA 161
Kropotkin, Peter (Aleksieevich)
   1842-1921 .... **TCLC 36**
   See Kropotkin, Petr Alekseevich
   See also CA 119; 219
Kropotkin, Petr Alekseevich
   See Kropotkin, Peter (Aleksieevich)
   See also DLB 277

Krotkov, Yuri 1917-1981 .... **CLC 19**
   See also CA 102
Krumb
   See Crumb, R(obert)
Krumgold, Joseph (Quincy)
   1908-1980 .... **CLC 12**
   See also BYA 1, 2; CA 9-12R; 101; CANR 7; MAICYA 1, 2; SATA 1, 48; SATA-Obit 23; YAW
Krumwitz
   See Crumb, R(obert)
Krutch, Joseph Wood 1893-1970 ..... **CLC 24**
   See also ANW; CA 1-4R; 25-28R; CANR 4; DLB 63, 206, 275
Krutzch, Gus
   See Eliot, T(homas) S(tearns)
Krylov, Ivan Andreevich
   1768(?)-1844 .... **NCLC 1**
   See also DLB 150
Kubin, Alfred (Leopold Isidor)
   1877-1959 .... **TCLC 23**
   See also CA 112; 149; CANR 104; DLB 81
Kubrick, Stanley 1928-1999 .... **CLC 16; TCLC 112**
   See also AAYA 30; CA 81-84; 177; CANR 33; DLB 26
Kumin, Maxine (Winokur) 1925- ..... **CLC 5, 13, 28, 164; PC 15**
   See also AITN 2; AMWS 4; ANW; CA 1-4R; CAAS 8; CANR 1, 21, 69, 115; CP 7; CWP; DA3; DAM POET; DLB 5; EWL 3; EXPP; MTCW 1, 2; PAB; PFS 18; SATA 12
Kundera, Milan 1929- . **CLC 4, 9, 19, 32, 68, 115, 135; SSC 24**
   See also AAYA 2; BPFB 2; CA 85-88; CANR 19, 52, 74; CDWLB 4; CWW 2; DA3; DAM NOV; DLB 232; EW 13; EWL 3; MTCW 1, 2; NFS 18; RGSF 2; RGWL 3; SSFS 10
Kunene, Mazisi (Raymond) 1930- ... **CLC 85**
   See also BW 1, 3; CA 125; CANR 81; CP 7; DLB 117
Kung, Hans .... **CLC 130**
   See Kung, Hans
Kung, Hans 1928-
   See Kung, Hans
   See also CA 53-56; CANR 66, 134; MTCW 1, 2
Kunikida Doppo 1869(?)-1908
   See Doppo, Kunikida
   See also DLB 180; EWL 3
Kunitz, Stanley (Jasspon) 1905- .. **CLC 6, 11, 14, 148; PC 19**
   See also AMWS 3; CA 41-44R; CANR 26, 57, 98; CP 7; DA3; DLB 48; INT CANR-26; MTCW 1, 2; PFS 11; RGAL 4
Kunze, Reiner 1933- .... **CLC 10**
   See also CA 93-96; CWW 2; DLB 75; EWL 3
Kuprin, Aleksander Ivanovich
   1870-1938 .... **TCLC 5**
   See Kuprin, Aleksandr Ivanovich; Kuprin, Alexandr Ivanovich
   See also CA 104; 182
Kuprin, Aleksandr Ivanovich
   See Kuprin, Aleksander Ivanovich
   See also DLB 295
Kuprin, Alexandr Ivanovich
   See Kuprin, Aleksander Ivanovich
   See also EWL 3
Kureishi, Hanif 1954(?)- ... **CLC 64, 135; DC 26**
   See also CA 139; CANR 113; CBD; CD 5; CN 7; DLB 194, 245; GLL 2; IDFW 4; WLIT 4; WWE 1
Kurosawa, Akira 1910-1998 ..... **CLC 16, 119**
   See also AAYA 11; CA 101; 170; CANR 46; DAM MULT

Kushner, Tony 1956(?)- ..... **CLC 81, 203; DC 10**
   See also AMWS 9; CA 144; CAD; CANR 74, 130; CD 5; DA3; DAM DRAM; DFS 5; DLB 228; EWL 3; GLL 1; LAIT 5; MTCW 2; RGAL 4
Kuttner, Henry 1915-1958 .... **TCLC 10**
   See also CA 107; 157; DLB 8; FANT; SCFW 2; SFW 4
Kutty, Madhavi
   See Das, Kamala
Kuzma, Greg 1944- .... **CLC 7**
   See also CA 33-36R; CANR 70
Kuzmin, Mikhail (Alekseevich)
   1872(?)-1936 .... **TCLC 40**
   See also CA 170; DLB 295; EWL 3
Kyd, Thomas 1558-1594 .... **DC 3; LC 22**
   See also BRW 1; DAM DRAM; DLB 62; IDTP; LMFS 1; RGEL 2; TEA; WLIT 3
Kyprianos, Iossif
   See Samarakis, Antonis
L. S.
   See Stephen, Sir Leslie
La3amon
   See Layamon
   See also DLB 146
Labrunie, Gerard
   See Nerval, Gerard de
La Bruyere, Jean de 1645-1696 .... **LC 17**
   See also DLB 268; EW 3; GFL Beginnings to 1789
Lacan, Jacques (Marie Emile)
   1901-1981 .... **CLC 75**
   See also CA 121; 104; DLB 296; EWL 3; TWA
Laclos, Pierre Ambroise Francois
   1741-1803 .... **NCLC 4, 87**
   See also EW 4; GFL Beginnings to 1789; RGWL 2, 3
Lacolere, Francois
   See Aragon, Louis
La Colere, Francois
   See Aragon, Louis
La Deshabilleuse
   See Simenon, Georges (Jacques Christian)
Lady Gregory
   See Gregory, Lady Isabella Augusta (Persse)
Lady of Quality, A
   See Bagnold, Enid
La Fayette, Marie-(Madelaine Pioche de la Vergne) 1634-1693 .... **LC 2**
   See Lafayette, Marie-Madeleine
   See also GFL Beginnings to 1789; RGWL 2, 3
Lafayette, Marie-Madeleine
   See La Fayette, Marie-(Madelaine Pioche de la Vergne)
   See also DLB 268
Lafayette, Rene
   See Hubbard, L(afayette) Ron(ald)
La Flesche, Francis 1857(?)-1932 ...... **NNAL**
   See also CA 144; CANR 83; DLB 175
La Fontaine, Jean de 1621-1695 .... **LC 50**
   See also DLB 268; EW 3; GFL Beginnings to 1789; MAICYA 1, 2; RGWL 2, 3; SATA 18
Laforgue, Jules 1860-1887 . **NCLC 5, 53; PC 14; SSC 20**
   See also DLB 217; EW 7; GFL 1789 to the Present; RGWL 2, 3
Lagerkvist, Paer (Fabian)
   1891-1974 ..... **CLC 7, 10, 13, 54; TCLC 144**
   See Lagerkvist, Par
   See also CA 85-88; 49-52; DA3; DAM DRAM, NOV; MTCW 1, 2; TWA

Longfellow, Henry Wadsworth
1807-1882 .... **NCLC 2, 45, 101, 103; PC 30; WLCS**
See also AMW; AMWR 2; CDALB 1640-1865; CLR 99; DA; DA3; DAB; DAC; DAM MST, POET; DLB 1, 59, 235; EXPP; PAB; PFS 2, 7, 17; RGAL 4; SATA 19; TUS; WP

Longinus c. 1st cent. - .... **CMLC 27**
See also AW 2; DLB 176

Longley, Michael 1939- .... **CLC 29**
See also BRWS 8; CA 102; CP 7; DLB 40

Longus fl. c. 2nd cent. - .... **CMLC 7**

Longway, A. Hugh
See Lang, Andrew

Lonnbohm, Armas Eino Leopold 1878-1926
See Leino, Eino
See also CA 123

Lonnrot, Elias 1802-1884 .... **NCLC 53**
See also EFS 1

Lonsdale, Roger ed. .... **CLC 65**

Lopate, Phillip 1943- .... **CLC 29**
See also CA 97-100; CANR 88; DLBY 1980; INT CA-97-100

Lopez, Barry (Holstun) 1945- .... **CLC 70**
See also AAYA 9; ANW; CA 65-68; CANR 7, 23, 47, 68, 92; DLB 256, 275; INT CANR-7, -23; MTCW 1; RGAL 4; SATA 67

Lopez Portillo (y Pacheco), Jose
1920-2004 .... **CLC 46**
See also CA 129; 224; HW 1

Lopez y Fuentes, Gregorio
1897(?)-1966 .... **CLC 32**
See also CA 131; EWL 3; HW 1

Lorca, Federico Garcia
See Garcia Lorca, Federico
See also DFS 4; EW 11; PFS 20; RGWL 2, 3; WP

Lord, Audre
See Lorde, Audre (Geraldine)
See also EWL 3

Lord, Bette Bao 1938- .... **AAL; CLC 23**
See also BEST 90:3; BPFB 2; CA 107; CANR 41, 79; INT CA-107; SATA 58

Lord Auch
See Bataille, Georges

Lord Brooke
See Greville, Fulke

Lord Byron
See Byron, George Gordon (Noel)

Lorde, Audre (Geraldine)
1934-1992 .. **BLC 2; CLC 18, 71; PC 12**
See Domini, Rey; Lord, Audre
See also AFAW 1, 2; BW 1, 3; CA 25-28R; 142; CANR 16, 26, 46, 82; DA3; DAM MULT, POET; DLB 41; FW; MTCW 1, 2; PFS 16; RGAL 4

Lord Houghton
See Milnes, Richard Monckton

Lord Jeffrey
See Jeffrey, Francis

Loreaux, Nichol .... **CLC 65**

Lorenzini, Carlo 1826-1890
See Collodi, Carlo
See also MAICYA 1, 2; SATA 29, 100

Lorenzo, Heberto Padilla
See Padilla (Lorenzo), Heberto

Loris
See Hofmannsthal, Hugo von

Loti, Pierre .... **TCLC 11**
See Viaud, (Louis Marie) Julien
See also DLB 123; GFL 1789 to the Present

Lou, Henri
See Andreas-Salome, Lou

Louie, David Wong 1954- .... **CLC 70**
See also CA 139; CANR 120

Louis, Adrian C. .... **NNAL**
See also CA 223

Louis, Father M.
See Merton, Thomas (James)

Louise, Heidi
See Erdrich, Louise

Lovecraft, H(oward) P(hillips)
1890-1937 .... **SSC 3, 52; TCLC 4, 22**
See also AAYA 14; BPFB 2; CA 104; 133; CANR 106; DA3; DAM POP; HGG; MTCW 1, 2; RGAL 4; SCFW; SFW 4; SUFW

Lovelace, Earl 1935- .... **CLC 51**
See also BW 2; CA 77-80; CANR 41, 72, 114; CD 5; CDWLB 3; CN 7; DLB 125; EWL 3; MTCW 1

Lovelace, Richard 1618-1657 .... **LC 24**
See also BRW 2; DLB 131; EXPP; PAB; RGEL 2

Lowe, Pardee 1904- .... **AAL**

Lowell, Amy 1874-1925 ... **PC 13; TCLC 1, 8**
See also AAYA 57; AMW; CA 104; 151; DAM POET; DLB 54, 140; EWL 3; EXPP; LMFS 2; MAWW; MTCW 2; RGAL 4; TUS

Lowell, James Russell 1819-1891 ... **NCLC 2, 90**
See also AMWS 1; CDALB 1640-1865; DLB 1, 11, 64, 79, 189, 235; RGAL 4

Lowell, Robert (Traill Spence, Jr.)
1917-1977 .... **CLC 1, 2, 3, 4, 5, 8, 9, 11, 15, 37, 124; PC 3; WLC**
See also AMW; AMWC 2; AMWR 2; CA 9-12R; 73-76; CABS 2; CANR 26, 60; CDALBS; DA; DA3; DAB; DAC; DAM MST, NOV; DLB 5, 169; EWL 3; MTCW 1, 2; PAB; PFS 6, 7; RGAL 4; WP

Lowenthal, Michael (Francis)
1969- .... **CLC 119**
See also CA 150; CANR 115

Lowndes, Marie Adelaide (Belloc)
1868-1947 .... **TCLC 12**
See also CA 107; CMW 4; DLB 70; RHW

Lowry, (Clarence) Malcolm
1909-1957 .... **SSC 31; TCLC 6, 40**
See also BPFB 2; BRWS 3; CA 105; 131; CANR 62, 105; CDBLB 1945-1960; DLB 15; EWL 3; MTCW 1, 2; RGEL 2

Lowry, Mina Gertrude 1882-1966
See Loy, Mina
See also CA 113

Loxsmith, John
See Brunner, John (Kilian Houston)

Loy, Mina .... **CLC 28; PC 16**
See Lowry, Mina Gertrude
See also DAM POET; DLB 4, 54; PFS 20

Loyson-Bridet
See Schwob, Marcel (Mayer Andre)

Lucan 39-65 .... **CMLC 33**
See also AW 2; DLB 211; EFS 2; RGWL 2, 3

Lucas, Craig 1951- .... **CLC 64**
See also CA 137; CAD; CANR 71, 109; CD 5; GLL 2

Lucas, E(dward) V(errall)
1868-1938 .... **TCLC 73**
See also CA 176; DLB 98, 149, 153; SATA 20

Lucas, George 1944- .... **CLC 16**
See also AAYA 1, 23; CA 77-80; CANR 30; SATA 56

Lucas, Hans
See Godard, Jean-Luc

Lucas, Victoria
See Plath, Sylvia

Lucian c. 125-c. 180 .... **CMLC 32**
See also AW 2; DLB 176; RGWL 2, 3

Lucretius c. 94B.C.-c. 49B.C. .... **CMLC 48**
See also AW 2; CDWLB 1; DLB 211; EFS 2; RGWL 2, 3

Ludlam, Charles 1943-1987 .... **CLC 46, 50**
See also CA 85-88; 122; CAD; CANR 72, 86; DLB 266

Ludlum, Robert 1927-2001 .... **CLC 22, 43**
See also AAYA 10, 59; BEST 89:1, 90:3; BPFB 2; CA 33-36R; 195; CANR 25, 41, 68, 105, 131; CMW 4; CPW; DA3; DAM NOV, POP; DLBY 1982; MSW; MTCW 1, 2

Ludwig, Ken .... **CLC 60**
See also CA 195; CAD

Ludwig, Otto 1813-1865 .... **NCLC 4**
See also DLB 129

Lugones, Leopoldo 1874-1938 .... **HLCS 2; TCLC 15**
See also CA 116; 131; CANR 104; DLB 283; EWL 3; HW 1; LAW

Lu Hsun .... **SSC 20; TCLC 3**
See Shu-Jen, Chou
See also EWL 3

Lukacs, George .... **CLC 24**
See Lukacs, Gyorgy (Szegeny von)

Lukacs, Gyorgy (Szegeny von) 1885-1971
See Lukacs, George
See also CA 101; 29-32R; CANR 62; CD-WLB 4; DLB 215, 242; EW 10; EWL 3; MTCW 2

Luke, Peter (Ambrose Cyprian)
1919-1995 .... **CLC 38**
See also CA 81-84; 147; CANR 72; CBD; CD 5; DLB 13

Lunar, Dennis
See Mungo, Raymond

Lurie, Alison 1926- ..... **CLC 4, 5, 18, 39, 175**
See also BPFB 2; CA 1-4R; CANR 2, 17, 50, 88; CN 7; DLB 2; MTCW 1; SATA 46, 112

Lustig, Arnost 1926- .... **CLC 56**
See also AAYA 3; CA 69-72; CANR 47, 102; CWW 2; DLB 232, 299; EWL 3; SATA 56

Luther, Martin 1483-1546 .... **LC 9, 37**
See also CDWLB 2; DLB 179; EW 2; RGWL 2, 3

Luxemburg, Rosa 1870(?)-1919 ..... **TCLC 63**
See also CA 118

Luzi, Mario 1914- .... **CLC 13**
See also CA 61-64; CANR 9, 70; CWW 2; DLB 128; EWL 3

L'vov, Arkady .... **CLC 59**

Lydgate, John c. 1370-1450(?) .... **LC 81**
See also BRW 1; DLB 146; RGEL 2

Lyly, John 1554(?)-1606 .... **DC 7; LC 41**
See also BRW 1; DAM DRAM; DLB 62, 167; RGEL 2

L'Ymagier
See Gourmont, Remy(-Marie-Charles) de

Lynch, B. Suarez
See Borges, Jorge Luis

Lynch, David (Keith) 1946- ...... **CLC 66, 162**
See also AAYA 55; CA 124; 129; CANR 111

Lynch, James
See Andreyev, Leonid (Nikolaevich)

Lyndsay, Sir David 1485-1555 .... **LC 20**
See also RGEL 2

Lynn, Kenneth S(chuyler)
1923-2001 .... **CLC 50**
See also CA 1-4R; 196; CANR 3, 27, 65

Lynx
See West, Rebecca

Lyons, Marcus
See Blish, James (Benjamin)

Lyotard, Jean-Francois
1924-1998 .... **TCLC 103**
See also DLB 242; EWL 3

Lyre, Pinchbeck
See Sassoon, Siegfried (Lorraine)

Lytle, Andrew (Nelson) 1902-1995 ... **CLC 22**
See also CA 9-12R; 150; CANR 70; CN 7;
CSW; DLB 6; DLBY 1995; RGAL 4;
RHW

Lyttelton, George 1709-1773 .... **LC 10**
See also RGEL 2

Lytton of Knebworth, Baron
See Bulwer-Lytton, Edward (George Earle
Lytton)

Maas, Peter 1929-2001 .... **CLC 29**
See also CA 93-96; 201; INT CA-93-96;
MTCW 2

Macaulay, Catherine 1731-1791 .... **LC 64**
See also DLB 104

Macaulay, (Emilie) Rose
1881(?)-1958 .... **TCLC 7, 44**
See also CA 104; DLB 36; EWL 3; RGEL
2; RHW

Macaulay, Thomas Babington
1800-1859 .... **NCLC 42**
See also BRW 4; CDBLB 1832-1890; DLB
32, 55; RGEL 2

MacBeth, George (Mann)
1932-1992 .... **CLC 2, 5, 9**
See also CA 25-28R; 136; CANR 61, 66;
DLB 40; MTCW 1; PFS 8; SATA 4;
SATA-Obit 70

MacCaig, Norman (Alexander)
1910-1996 .... **CLC 36**
See also BRWS 6; CA 9-12R; CANR 3, 34;
CP 7; DAB; DAM POET; DLB 27; EWL
3; RGEL 2

MacCarthy, Sir (Charles Otto) Desmond
1877-1952 .... **TCLC 36**
See also CA 167

MacDiarmid, Hugh .... **CLC 2, 4, 11, 19, 63;
PC 9**
See Grieve, C(hristopher) M(urray)
See also CDBLB 1945-1960; DLB 20;
EWL 3; RGEL 2

MacDonald, Anson
See Heinlein, Robert A(nson)

Macdonald, Cynthia 1928- .... **CLC 13, 19**
See also CA 49-52; CANR 4, 44; DLB 105

MacDonald, George 1824-1905 .... **TCLC 9,
113**
See also AAYA 57; BYA 5; CA 106; 137;
CANR 80; CLR 67; DLB 18, 163, 178;
FANT; MAICYA 1, 2; RGEL 2; SATA 33,
100; SFW 4; SUFW; WCH

Macdonald, John
See Millar, Kenneth

MacDonald, John D(ann)
1916-1986 .... **CLC 3, 27, 44**
See also BPFB 2; CA 1-4R; 121; CANR 1,
19, 60; CMW 4; CPW; DAM NOV, POP;
DLB 8, 306; DLBY 1986; MSW; MTCW
1, 2; SFW 4

Macdonald, John Ross
See Millar, Kenneth

Macdonald, Ross ..... **CLC 1, 2, 3, 14, 34, 41**
See Millar, Kenneth
See also AMWS 4; BPFB 2; DLBD 6;
MSW; RGAL 4

MacDougal, John
See Blish, James (Benjamin)

MacDougal, John
See Blish, James (Benjamin)

MacDowell, John
See Parks, Tim(othy Harold)

MacEwen, Gwendolyn (Margaret)
1941-1987 .... **CLC 13, 55**
See also CA 9-12R; 124; CANR 7, 22; DLB
53, 251; SATA 50; SATA-Obit 55

Macha, Karel Hynek 1810-1846 .... **NCLC 46**

Machado (y Ruiz), Antonio
1875-1939 .... **TCLC 3**
See also CA 104; 174; DLB 108; EW 9;
EWL 3; HW 2; RGWL 2, 3

Machado de Assis, Joaquim Maria
1839-1908 .... **BLC 2; HLCS 2; SSC 24;
TCLC 10**
See also CA 107; 153; CANR 91; DLB 307;
LAW; RGSF 2; RGWL 2, 3; TWA; WLIT
1

Machaut, Guillaume de c.
1300-1377 .... **CMLC 64**
See also DLB 208

Machen, Arthur .... **SSC 20; TCLC 4**
See Jones, Arthur Llewellyn
See also CA 179; DLB 156, 178; RGEL 2;
SUFW 1

Machiavelli, Niccolo 1469-1527 ... **DC 16; LC
8, 36; WLCS**
See also AAYA 58; DA; DAB; DAC; DAM
MST; EW 2; LAIT 1; LMFS 1; NFS 9;
RGWL 2, 3; TWA

MacInnes, Colin 1914-1976 .... **CLC 4, 23**
See also CA 69-72; 65-68; CANR 21; DLB
14; MTCW 1, 2; RGEL 2; RHW

MacInnes, Helen (Clark)
1907-1985 .... **CLC 27, 39**
See also BPFB 2; CA 1-4R; 117; CANR 1,
28, 58; CMW 4; CPW; DAM POP; DLB
87; MSW; MTCW 1, 2; SATA 22; SATA-
Obit 44

Mackay, Mary 1855-1924
See Corelli, Marie
See also CA 118; 177; FANT; RHW

Mackay, Shena 1944- .... **CLC 195**
See also CA 104; CANR 88; DLB 231

Mackenzie, Compton (Edward Montague)
1883-1972 .... **CLC 18; TCLC 116**
See also CA 21-22; 37-40R; CAP 2; DLB
34, 100; RGEL 2

Mackenzie, Henry 1745-1831 .... **NCLC 41**
See also DLB 39; RGEL 2

Mackey, Nathaniel (Ernest) 1947- .... **PC 49**
See also CA 153; CANR 114; CP 7; DLB
169

MacKinnon, Catharine A. 1946- .... **CLC 181**
See also CA 128; 132; CANR 73; FW;
MTCW 2

Mackintosh, Elizabeth 1896(?)-1952
See Tey, Josephine
See also CA 110; CMW 4

MacLaren, James
See Grieve, C(hristopher) M(urray)

Mac Laverty, Bernard 1942- .... **CLC 31**
See also CA 116; 118; CANR 43, 88; CN
7; DLB 267; INT CA-118; RGSF 2

MacLean, Alistair (Stuart)
1922(?)-1987 .... **CLC 3, 13, 50, 63**
See also CA 57-60; 121; CANR 28, 61;
CMW 4; CPW; DAM POP; DLB 276;
MTCW 1; SATA 23; SATA-Obit 50;
TCWW 2

Maclean, Norman (Fitzroy)
1902-1990 .... **CLC 78; SSC 13**
See also AMWS 14; CA 102; 132; CANR
49; CPW; DAM POP; DLB 206; TCWW
2

MacLeish, Archibald 1892-1982 ... **CLC 3, 8,
14, 68; PC 47**
See also AMW; CA 9-12R; 106; CAD;
CANR 33, 63; CDALBS; DAM POET;
DFS 15; DLB 4, 7, 45; DLBY 1982; EWL
3; EXPP; MTCW 1, 2; PAB; PFS 5;
RGAL 4; TUS

MacLennan, (John) Hugh
1907-1990 .... **CLC 2, 14, 92**
See also CA 5-8R; 142; CANR 33; DAC;
DAM MST; DLB 68; EWL 3; MTCW 1,
2; RGEL 2; TWA

MacLeod, Alistair 1936- .... **CLC 56, 165**
See also CA 123; CCA 1; DAC; DAM
MST; DLB 60; MTCW 2; RGSF 2

Macleod, Fiona
See Sharp, William
See also RGEL 2; SUFW

MacNeice, (Frederick) Louis
1907-1963 .... **CLC 1, 4, 10, 53; PC 61**
See also BRW 7; CA 85-88; CANR 61;
DAB; DAM POET; DLB 10, 20; EWL 3;
MTCW 1, 2; RGEL 2

MacNeill, Dand
See Fraser, George MacDonald

Macpherson, James 1736-1796 .... **LC 29**
See Ossian
See also BRWS 8; DLB 109; RGEL 2

Macpherson, (Jean) Jay 1931- .... **CLC 14**
See also CA 5-8R; CANR 90; CP 7; CWP;
DLB 53

Macrobius fl. 430- .... **CMLC 48**

MacShane, Frank 1927-1999 .... **CLC 39**
See also CA 9-12R; 186; CANR 3, 33; DLB
111

Macumber, Mari
See Sandoz, Mari(e Susette)

Madach, Imre 1823-1864 .... **NCLC 19**

Madden, (Jerry) David 1933- .... **CLC 5, 15**
See also CA 1-4R; CAAS 3; CANR 4, 45;
CN 7; CSW; DLB 6; MTCW 1

Maddern, Al(an)
See Ellison, Harlan (Jay)

Madhubuti, Haki R. 1942- ... **BLC 2; CLC 6,
73; PC 5**
See Lee, Don L.
See also BW 2, 3; CA 73-76; CANR 24,
51, 73; CP 7; CSW; DAM MULT, POET;
DLB 5, 41; DLBD 8; EWL 3; MTCW 2;
RGAL 4

Madison, James 1751-1836 .... **NCLC 126**
See also DLB 37

Maepenn, Hugh
See Kuttner, Henry

Maepenn, K. H.
See Kuttner, Henry

Maeterlinck, Maurice 1862-1949 ..... **TCLC 3**
See also CA 104; 136; CANR 80; DAM
DRAM; DLB 192; EW 8; EWL 3; GFL
1789 to the Present; LMFS 2; RGWL 2,
3; SATA 66; TWA

Maginn, William 1794-1842 .... **NCLC 8**
See also DLB 110, 159

Mahapatra, Jayanta 1928- .... **CLC 33**
See also CA 73-76; CAAS 9; CANR 15,
33, 66, 87; CP 7; DAM MULT

Mahfouz, Naguib (Abdel Aziz Al-Sabilgi)
1911(?)- .... **CLC 153; SSC 66**
See Mahfuz, Najib (Abdel Aziz al-Sabilgi)
See also AAYA 49; BEST 89:2; CA 128;
CANR 55, 101; DA3; DAM NOV;
MTCW 1, 2; RGWL 2, 3; SSFS 9

Mahfuz, Najib (Abdel Aziz al-Sabilgi)
.... **CLC 52, 55**
See Mahfouz, Naguib (Abdel Aziz Al-
Sabilgi)
See also AFW; CWW 2; DLBY 1988; EWL
3; RGSF 2; WLIT 2

Mahon, Derek 1941- .... **CLC 27; PC 60**
See also BRWS 6; CA 113; 128; CANR 88;
CP 7; DLB 40; EWL 3

Maiakovskii, Vladimir
See Mayakovski, Vladimir (Vladimirovich)
See also IDTP; RGWL 2, 3

Mailer, Norman (Kingsley) 1923- . **CLC 1, 2,
3, 4, 5, 8, 11, 14, 28, 39, 74, 111**
See also AAYA 31; AITN 2; AMW; AMWC
2; AMWR 2; BPFB 2; CA 9-12R; CABS
1; CANR 28, 74, 77, 130; CDALB 1968-
1988; CN 7; CPW; DA; DA3; DAB;
DAC; DAM MST, NOV, POP; DLB 2,
16, 28, 185, 278; DLBD 3; DLBY 1980,
1983; EWL 3; MTCW 1, 2; NFS 10;
RGAL 4; TUS

Merimee, Prosper 1803-1870 ... **NCLC 6, 65; SSC 7, 77**
See also DLB 119, 192; EW 6; EXPS; GFL 1789 to the Present; RGSF 2; RGWL 2, 3; SSFS 8; SUFW

Merkin, Daphne 1954- .... **CLC 44**
See also CA 123

Merleau-Ponty, Maurice
1908-1961 .... **TCLC 156**
See also CA 114; 89-92; DLB 296; GFL 1789 to the Present

Merlin, Arthur
See Blish, James (Benjamin)

Mernissi, Fatima 1940- .... **CLC 171**
See also CA 152; FW

Merrill, James (Ingram) 1926-1995 .. **CLC 2, 3, 6, 8, 13, 18, 34, 91; PC 28**
See also AMWS 3; CA 13-16R; 147; CANR 10, 49, 63, 108; DA3; DAM POET; DLB 5, 165; DLBY 1985; EWL 3; INT CANR-10; MTCW 1, 2; PAB; RGAL 4

Merriman, Alex
See Silverberg, Robert

Merriman, Brian 1747-1805 .... **NCLC 70**

Merritt, E. B.
See Waddington, Miriam

Merton, Thomas (James)
1915-1968 . **CLC 1, 3, 11, 34, 83; PC 10**
See also AMWS 8; CA 5-8R; 25-28R; CANR 22, 53, 111, 131; DA3; DLB 48; DLBY 1981; MTCW 1, 2

Merwin, W(illiam) S(tanley) 1927- ... **CLC 1, 2, 3, 5, 8, 13, 18, 45, 88; PC 45**
See also AMWS 3; CA 13-16R; CANR 15, 51, 112; CP 7; DA3; DAM POET; DLB 5, 169; EWL 3; INT CANR-15; MTCW 1, 2; PAB; PFS 5, 15; RGAL 4

Metastasio, Pietro 1698-1782 .... **LC 115**
See also RGWL 2, 3

Metcalf, John 1938- .... **CLC 37; SSC 43**
See also CA 113; CN 7; DLB 60; RGSF 2; TWA

Metcalf, Suzanne
See Baum, L(yman) Frank

Mew, Charlotte (Mary) 1870-1928 .. **TCLC 8**
See also CA 105; 189; DLB 19, 135; RGEL 2

Mewshaw, Michael 1943- .... **CLC 9**
See also CA 53-56; CANR 7, 47; DLBY 1980

Meyer, Conrad Ferdinand
1825-1898 .... **NCLC 81; SSC 30**
See also DLB 129; EW; RGWL 2, 3

Meyer, Gustav 1868-1932
See Meyrink, Gustav
See also CA 117; 190

Meyer, June
See Jordan, June (Meyer)

Meyer, Lynn
See Slavitt, David R(ytman)

Meyers, Jeffrey 1939- .... **CLC 39**
See also CA 73-76, 186; CAAE 186; CANR 54, 102; DLB 111

Meynell, Alice (Christina Gertrude Thompson) 1847-1922 .... **TCLC 6**
See also CA 104; 177; DLB 19, 98; RGEL 2

Meyrink, Gustav .... **TCLC 21**
See Meyer, Gustav
See also DLB 81; EWL 3

Michaels, Leonard 1933-2003 ..... **CLC 6, 25; SSC 16**
See also CA 61-64; 216; CANR 21, 62, 119; CN 7; DLB 130; MTCW 1

Michaux, Henri 1899-1984 .... **CLC 8, 19**
See also CA 85-88; 114; DLB 258; EWL 3; GFL 1789 to the Present; RGWL 2, 3

Micheaux, Oscar (Devereaux)
1884-1951 .... **TCLC 76**
See also BW 3; CA 174; DLB 50; TCWW 2

Michelangelo 1475-1564 .... **LC 12**
See also AAYA 43

Michelet, Jules 1798-1874 .... **NCLC 31**
See also EW 5; GFL 1789 to the Present

Michels, Robert 1876-1936 .... **TCLC 88**
See also CA 212

Michener, James A(lbert)
1907(?)-1997 .. **CLC 1, 5, 11, 29, 60, 109**
See also AAYA 27; AITN 1; BEST 90:1; BPFB 2; CA 5-8R; 161; CANR 21, 45, 68; CN 7; CPW; DA3; DAM NOV, POP; DLB 6; MTCW 1, 2; RHW

Mickiewicz, Adam 1798-1855 . **NCLC 3, 101; PC 38**
See also EW 5; RGWL 2, 3

Middleton, (John) Christopher
1926- .... **CLC 13**
See also CA 13-16R; CANR 29, 54, 117; CP 7; DLB 40

Middleton, Richard (Barham)
1882-1911 .... **TCLC 56**
See also CA 187; DLB 156; HGG

Middleton, Stanley 1919- .... **CLC 7, 38**
See also CA 25-28R; CAAS 23; CANR 21, 46, 81; CN 7; DLB 14

Middleton, Thomas 1580-1627 ...... **DC 5; LC 33**
See also BRW 2; DAM DRAM, MST; DFS 18; DLB 58; RGEL 2

Migueis, Jose Rodrigues 1901-1980 . **CLC 10**
See also DLB 287

Mikszath, Kalman 1847-1910 .... **TCLC 31**
See also CA 170

Miles, Jack .... **CLC 100**
See also CA 200

Miles, John Russiano
See Miles, Jack

Miles, Josephine (Louise)
1911-1985 .... **CLC 1, 2, 14, 34, 39**
See also CA 1-4R; 116; CANR 2, 55; DAM POET; DLB 48

Militant
See Sandburg, Carl (August)

Mill, Harriet (Hardy) Taylor
1807-1858 .... **NCLC 102**
See also FW

Mill, John Stuart 1806-1873 .... **NCLC 11, 58**
See also CDBLB 1832-1890; DLB 55, 190, 262; FW 1; RGEL 2; TEA

Millar, Kenneth 1915-1983 .... **CLC 14**
See Macdonald, Ross
See also CA 9-12R; 110; CANR 16, 63, 107; CMW 4; CPW; DA3; DAM POP; DLB 2, 226; DLBD 6; DLBY 1983; MTCW 1, 2

Millay, E. Vincent
See Millay, Edna St. Vincent

Millay, Edna St. Vincent 1892-1950 ..... **PC 6, 61; TCLC 4, 49; WLCS**
See Boyd, Nancy
See also AMW; CA 104; 130; CDALB 1917-1929; DA; DA3; DAB; DAC; DAM MST, POET; DLB 45, 249; EWL 3; EXPP; MAWW; MTCW 1, 2; PAB; PFS 3, 17; RGAL 4; TUS; WP

Miller, Arthur 1915- ...... **CLC 1, 2, 6, 10, 15, 26, 47, 78, 179; DC 1; WLC**
See also AAYA 15; AITN 1; AMW; AMWC 1; CA 1-4R; CABS 3; CAD; CANR 2, 30, 54, 76, 132; CD 5; CDALB 1941-1968; DA; DA3; DAB; DAC; DAM DRAM, MST; DFS 1, 3, 8; DLB 7, 266; EWL 3; LAIT 1, 4; LATS 1:2; MTCW 1, 2; RGAL 4; TUS; WYAS 1

Miller, Henry (Valentine)
1891-1980 .... **CLC 1, 2, 4, 9, 14, 43, 84; WLC**
See also AMW; BPFB 2; CA 9-12R; 97-100; CANR 33, 64; CDALB 1929-1941; DA; DA3; DAB; DAC; DAM MST, NOV; DLB 4, 9; DLBY 1980; EWL 3; MTCW 1, 2; RGAL 4; TUS

Miller, Hugh 1802-1856 .... **NCLC 143**
See also DLB 190

Miller, Jason 1939(?)-2001 .... **CLC 2**
See also AITN 1; CA 73-76; 197; CAD; CANR 130; DFS 12; DLB 7

Miller, Sue 1943- .... **CLC 44**
See also AMWS 12; BEST 90:3; CA 139; CANR 59, 91, 128; DA3; DAM POP; DLB 143

Miller, Walter M(ichael, Jr.)
1923-1996 .... **CLC 4, 30**
See also BPFB 2; CA 85-88; CANR 108; DLB 8; SCFW; SFW 4

Millett, Kate 1934- .... **CLC 67**
See also AITN 1; CA 73-76; CANR 32, 53, 76, 110; DA3; DLB 246; FW; GLL 1; MTCW 1, 2

Millhauser, Steven (Lewis) 1943- .... **CLC 21, 54, 109; SSC 57**
See also CA 110; 111; CANR 63, 114, 133; CN 7; DA3; DLB 2; FANT; INT CA-111; MTCW 2

Millin, Sarah Gertrude 1889-1968 ... **CLC 49**
See also CA 102; 93-96; DLB 225; EWL 3

Milne, A(lan) A(lexander)
1882-1956 .... **TCLC 6, 88**
See also BRWS 5; CA 104; 133; CLR 1, 26; CMW 4; CWRI 5; DA3; DAB; DAC; DAM MST; DLB 10, 77, 100, 160; FANT; MAICYA 1, 2; MTCW 1, 2; RGEL 2; SATA 100; WCH; YABC 1

Milner, Ron(ald) 1938-2004 ..... **BLC 3; CLC 56**
See also AITN 1; BW 1; CA 73-76; CAD; CANR 24, 81; CD 5; DAM MULT; DLB 38; MTCW 1

Milnes, Richard Monckton
1809-1885 .... **NCLC 61**
See also DLB 32, 184

Milosz, Czeslaw 1911- ...... **CLC 5, 11, 22, 31, 56, 82; PC 8; WLCS**
See also CA 81-84; CANR 23, 51, 91, 126; CDWLB 4; CWW 2; DA3; DAM MST, POET; DLB 215; EW 13; EWL 3; MTCW 1, 2; PFS 16; RGWL 2, 3

Milton, John 1608-1674 ..... **LC 9, 43, 92; PC 19, 29; WLC**
See also BRW 2; BRWR 2; CDBLB 1660-1789; DA; DA3; DAB; DAC; DAM MST, POET; DLB 131, 151, 281; EFS 1; EXPP; LAIT 1; PAB; PFS 3, 17; RGEL 2; TEA; WLIT 3; WP

Min, Anchee 1957- .... **CLC 86**
See also CA 146; CANR 94

Minehaha, Cornelius
See Wedekind, (Benjamin) Frank(lin)

Miner, Valerie 1947- .... **CLC 40**
See also CA 97-100; CANR 59; FW; GLL 2

Minimo, Duca
See D'Annunzio, Gabriele

Minot, Susan 1956- .... **CLC 44, 159**
See also AMWS 6; CA 134; CANR 118; CN 7

Minus, Ed 1938- .... **CLC 39**
See also CA 185

Mirabai 1498(?)-1550(?) .... **PC 48**

Miranda, Javier
See Bioy Casares, Adolfo
See also CWW 2

Moore, Marianne (Craig)
1887-1972 .... **CLC 1, 2, 4, 8, 10, 13, 19, 47; PC 4, 49; WLCS**
See also AMW; CA 1-4R; 33-36R; CANR 3, 61; CDALB 1929-1941; DA; DA3; DAB; DAC; DAM MST, POET; DLB 45; DLBD 7; EWL 3; EXPP; MAWW; MTCW 1, 2; PAB; PFS 14, 17; RGAL 4; SATA 20; TUS; WP

Moore, Marie Lorena 1957- .... **CLC 165**
See Moore, Lorrie
See also CA 116; CANR 39, 83; CN 7; DLB 234

Moore, Thomas 1779-1852 .... **NCLC 6, 110**
See also DLB 96, 144; RGEL 2

Moorhouse, Frank 1938- .... **SSC 40**
See also CA 118; CANR 92; CN 7; DLB 289; RGSF 2

Mora, Pat(ricia) 1942- .... **HLC 2**
See also AMWS 13; CA 129; CANR 57, 81, 112; CLR 58; DAM MULT; DLB 209; HW 1, 2; LLW 1; MAICYA 2; SATA 92, 134

Moraga, Cherríe 1952- ...... **CLC 126; DC 22**
See also CA 131; CANR 66; DAM MULT; DLB 82, 249; FW; GLL 1; HW 1, 2; LLW 1

Morand, Paul 1888-1976 .... **CLC 41; SSC 22**
See also CA 184; 69-72; DLB 65; EWL 3

Morante, Elsa 1918-1985 .... **CLC 8, 47**
See also CA 85-88; 117; CANR 35; DLB 177; MTCW 1, 2; RGWL 2, 3

Moravia, Alberto .... **CLC 2, 7, 11, 27, 46; SSC 26**
See Pincherle, Alberto
See also DLB 177; EW 12; EWL 3; MTCW 2; RGSF 2; RGWL 2, 3

More, Hannah 1745-1833 ...... **NCLC 27, 141**
See also DLB 107, 109, 116, 158; RGEL 2

More, Henry 1614-1687 .... **LC 9**
See also DLB 126, 252

More, Sir Thomas 1478(?)-1535 .... **LC 10, 32**
See also BRWC 1; BRWS 7; DLB 136, 281; LMFS 1; RGEL 2; TEA

Moreas, Jean .... **TCLC 18**
See Papadiamantopoulos, Johannes
See also GFL 1789 to the Present

Moreton, Andrew Esq.
See Defoe, Daniel

Morgan, Berry 1919-2002 .... **CLC 6**
See also CA 49-52; 208; DLB 6

Morgan, Claire
See Highsmith, (Mary) Patricia
See also GLL 1

Morgan, Edwin (George) 1920- .... **CLC 31**
See also BRWS 9; CA 5-8R; CANR 3, 43, 90; CP 7; DLB 27

Morgan, (George) Frederick
1922-2004 .... **CLC 23**
See also CA 17-20R; 224; CANR 21; CP 7

Morgan, Harriet
See Mencken, H(enry) L(ouis)

Morgan, Jane
See Cooper, James Fenimore

Morgan, Janet 1945- .... **CLC 39**
See also CA 65-68

Morgan, Lady 1776(?)-1859 .... **NCLC 29**
See also DLB 116, 158; RGEL 2

Morgan, Robin (Evonne) 1941- .... **CLC 2**
See also CA 69-72; CANR 29, 68; FW; GLL 2; MTCW 1; SATA 80

Morgan, Scott
See Kuttner, Henry

Morgan, Seth 1949(?)-1990 .... **CLC 65**
See also CA 185; 132

Morgenstern, Christian (Otto Josef Wolfgang) 1871-1914 .... **TCLC 8**
See also CA 105; 191; EWL 3

Morgenstern, S.
See Goldman, William (W.)

Mori, Rintaro
See Mori Ogai
See also CA 110

Mori, Toshio 1910-1980 .... **SSC 83**
See also AAL; CA 116; DLB 312; RGSF 2

Moricz, Zsigmond 1879-1942 .... **TCLC 33**
See also CA 165; DLB 215; EWL 3

Morike, Eduard (Friedrich)
1804-1875 .... **NCLC 10**
See also DLB 133; RGWL 2, 3

Mori Ogai 1862-1922 .... **TCLC 14**
See Ogai
See also CA 164; DLB 180; EWL 3; RGWL 3; TWA

Moritz, Karl Philipp 1756-1793 .... **LC 2**
See also DLB 94

Morland, Peter Henry
See Faust, Frederick (Schiller)

Morley, Christopher (Darlington)
1890-1957 .... **TCLC 87**
See also CA 112; 213; DLB 9; RGAL 4

Morren, Theophil
See Hofmannsthal, Hugo von

Morris, Bill 1952- .... **CLC 76**
See also CA 225

Morris, Julian
See West, Morris L(anglo)

Morris, Steveland Judkins 1950(?)-
See Wonder, Stevie
See also CA 111

Morris, William 1834-1896 . **NCLC 4; PC 55**
See also BRW 5; CDBLB 1832-1890; DLB 18, 35, 57, 156, 178, 184; FANT; RGEL 2; SFW 4; SUFW

Morris, Wright 1910-1998 .. **CLC 1, 3, 7, 18, 37; TCLC 107**
See also AMW; CA 9-12R; 167; CANR 21, 81; CN 7; DLB 2, 206, 218; DLBY 1981; EWL 3; MTCW 1, 2; RGAL 4; TCWW 2

Morrison, Arthur 1863-1945 .... **SSC 40; TCLC 72**
See also CA 120; 157; CMW 4; DLB 70, 135, 197; RGEL 2

Morrison, Chloe Anthony Wofford
See Morrison, Toni

Morrison, James Douglas 1943-1971
See Morrison, Jim
See also CA 73-76; CANR 40

Morrison, Jim .... **CLC 17**
See Morrison, James Douglas

Morrison, Toni 1931- ..... **BLC 3; CLC 4, 10, 22, 55, 81, 87, 173, 194**
See also AAYA 1, 22; AFAW 1, 2; AMWC 1; AMWS 3; BPFB 2; BW 2, 3; CA 29-32R; CANR 27, 42, 67, 113, 124; CDALB 1968-1988; CLR 99; CN 7; CPW; DA; DA3; DAB; DAC; DAM MST, MULT, NOV, POP; DLB 6, 33, 143; DLBY 1981; EWL 3; EXPN; FW; LAIT 2, 4; LATS 1:2; LMFS 2; MAWW; MTCW 1, 2; NFS 1, 6, 8, 14; RGAL 4; RHW; SATA 57, 144; SSFS 5; TUS; YAW

Morrison, Van 1945- .... **CLC 21**
See also CA 116; 168

Morrissy, Mary 1957- .... **CLC 99**
See also CA 205; DLB 267

Mortimer, John (Clifford) 1923- ..... **CLC 28, 43**
See also CA 13-16R; CANR 21, 69, 109; CD 5; CDBLB 1960 to Present; CMW 4; CN 7; CPW; DA3; DAM DRAM, POP; DLB 13, 245, 271; INT CANR-21; MSW; MTCW 1, 2; RGEL 2

Mortimer, Penelope (Ruth)
1918-1999 .... **CLC 5**
See also CA 57-60; 187; CANR 45, 88; CN 7

Mortimer, Sir John
See Mortimer, John (Clifford)

Morton, Anthony
See Creasey, John

Morton, Thomas 1579(?)-1647(?) .... **LC 72**
See also DLB 24; RGEL 2

Mosca, Gaetano 1858-1941 .... **TCLC 75**

Moses, Daniel David 1952- .... **NNAL**
See also CA 186

Mosher, Howard Frank 1943- .... **CLC 62**
See also CA 139; CANR 65, 115

Mosley, Nicholas 1923- .... **CLC 43, 70**
See also CA 69-72; CANR 41, 60, 108; CN 7; DLB 14, 207

Mosley, Walter 1952- .... **BLCS; CLC 97, 184**
See also AAYA 57; AMWS 13; BPFB 2; BW 2; CA 142; CANR 57, 92; CMW 4; CPW; DA3; DAM MULT, POP; DLB 306; MSW; MTCW 2

Moss, Howard 1922-1987 . **CLC 7, 14, 45, 50**
See also CA 1-4R; 123; CANR 1, 44; DAM POET; DLB 5

Mossgiel, Rab
See Burns, Robert

Motion, Andrew (Peter) 1952- .... **CLC 47**
See also BRWS 7; CA 146; CANR 90; CP 7; DLB 40

Motley, Willard (Francis)
1909-1965 .... **CLC 18**
See also BW 1; CA 117; 106; CANR 88; DLB 76, 143

Motoori, Norinaga 1730-1801 .... **NCLC 45**

Mott, Michael (Charles Alston)
1930- .... **CLC 15, 34**
See also CA 5-8R; CAAS 7; CANR 7, 29

Mountain Wolf Woman 1884-1960 . **CLC 92; NNAL**
See also CA 144; CANR 90

Moure, Erin 1955- .... **CLC 88**
See also CA 113; CP 7; CWP; DLB 60

Mourning Dove 1885(?)-1936 .... **NNAL**
See also CA 144; CANR 90; DAM MULT; DLB 175, 221

Mowat, Farley (McGill) 1921- .... **CLC 26**
See also AAYA 1, 50; BYA 2; CA 1-4R; CANR 4, 24, 42, 68, 108; CLR 20; CPW; DAC; DAM MST; DLB 68; INT CANR-24; JRDA; MAICYA 1, 2; MTCW 1, 2; SATA 3, 55; YAW

Mowatt, Anna Cora 1819-1870 ..... **NCLC 74**
See also RGAL 4

Moyers, Bill 1934- .... **CLC 74**
See also AITN 2; CA 61-64; CANR 31, 52

Mphahlele, Es'kia
See Mphahlele, Ezekiel
See also AFW; CDWLB 3; DLB 125, 225; RGSF 2; SSFS 11

Mphahlele, Ezekiel 1919- ... **BLC 3; CLC 25, 133**
See Mphahlele, Es'kia
See also BW 2, 3; CA 81-84; CANR 26, 76; CN 7; DA3; DAM MULT; EWL 3; MTCW 2; SATA 119

Mqhayi, S(amuel) E(dward) K(rune Loliwe)
1875-1945 .... **BLC 3; TCLC 25**
See also CA 153; CANR 87; DAM MULT

Mrozek, Slawomir 1930- .... **CLC 3, 13**
See also CA 13-16R; CAAS 10; CANR 29; CDWLB 4; CWW 2; DLB 232; EWL 3; MTCW 1

Mrs. Belloc-Lowndes
See Lowndes, Marie Adelaide (Belloc)

Mrs. Fairstar
See Horne, Richard Henry Hengist

M'Taggart, John M'Taggart Ellis
See McTaggart, John McTaggart Ellis

MST, MULT, NOV, POP; DLB 173; EWL
    3; FW; MTCW 1, 2; NFS 4, 7; RGAL 4;
    TUS
Neff, Debra .... **CLC 59**
Neihardt, John Gneisenau
    1881-1973 .... **CLC 32**
    See also CA 13-14; CANR 65; CAP 1; DLB
    9, 54, 256; LAIT 2
Nekrasov, Nikolai Alekseevich
    1821-1878 .... **NCLC 11**
    See also DLB 277
Nelligan, Emile 1879-1941 .... **TCLC 14**
    See also CA 114; 204; DLB 92; EWL 3
Nelson, Willie 1933- .... **CLC 17**
    See also CA 107; CANR 114
Nemerov, Howard (Stanley)
    1920-1991 .... **CLC 2, 6, 9, 36; PC 24;**
        TCLC 124
    See also AMW; CA 1-4R; 134; CABS 2;
    CANR 1, 27, 53; DAM POET; DLB 5, 6;
    DLBY 1983; EWL 3; INT CANR-27;
    MTCW 1, 2; PFS 10, 14; RGAL 4
Neruda, Pablo 1904-1973 .. **CLC 1, 2, 5, 7, 9,**
        28, 62; HLC 2; PC 4, 64; WLC
    See also CA 19-20; 45-48; CANR 131; CAP
    2; DA; DA3; DAB; DAC; DAM MST,
    MULT, POET; DLB 283; DNFS 2; EWL
    3; HW 1; LAW; MTCW 1, 2; PFS 11;
    RGWL 2, 3; TWA; WLIT 1; WP
Nerval, Gerard de 1808-1855 ... **NCLC 1, 67;**
        PC 13; SSC 18
    See also DLB 217; EW 6; GFL 1789 to the
    Present; RGSF 2; RGWL 2, 3
Nervo, (Jose) Amado (Ruiz de)
    1870-1919 .... **HLCS 2; TCLC 11**
    See also CA 109; 131; DLB 290; EWL 3;
    HW 1; LAW
Nesbit, Malcolm
    See Chester, Alfred
Nessi, Pio Baroja y
    See Baroja (y Nessi), Pio
Nestroy, Johann 1801-1862 .... **NCLC 42**
    See also DLB 133; RGWL 2, 3
Netterville, Luke
    See O'Grady, Standish (James)
Neufeld, John (Arthur) 1938- .... **CLC 17**
    See also AAYA 11; CA 25-28R; CANR 11,
    37, 56; CLR 52; MAICYA 1, 2; SAAS 3;
    SATA 6, 81, 131; SATA-Essay 131; YAW
Neumann, Alfred 1895-1952 .... **TCLC 100**
    See also CA 183; DLB 56
Neumann, Ferenc
    See Molnar, Ferenc
Neville, Emily Cheney 1919- .... **CLC 12**
    See also BYA 2; CA 5-8R; CANR 3, 37,
    85; JRDA; MAICYA 1, 2; SAAS 2; SATA
    1; YAW
Newbound, Bernard Slade 1930-
    See Slade, Bernard
    See also CA 81-84; CANR 49; CD 5; DAM
    DRAM
Newby, P(ercy) H(oward)
    1918-1997 .... **CLC 2, 13**
    See also CA 5-8R; 161; CANR 32, 67; CN
    7; DAM NOV; DLB 15; MTCW 1; RGEL
    2
Newcastle
    See Cavendish, Margaret Lucas
Newlove, Donald 1928- .... **CLC 6**
    See also CA 29-32R; CANR 25
Newlove, John (Herbert) 1938- .... **CLC 14**
    See also CA 21-24R; CANR 9, 25; CP 7
Newman, Charles 1938- .... **CLC 2, 8**
    See also CA 21-24R; CANR 84; CN 7
Newman, Edwin (Harold) 1919- ...... **CLC 14**
    See also AITN 1; CA 69-72; CANR 5

Newman, John Henry 1801-1890 . **NCLC 38,
    99**
    See also BRWS 7; DLB 18, 32, 55; RGEL
    2
Newton, (Sir) Isaac 1642-1727 ...... **LC 35, 53**
    See also DLB 252
Newton, Suzanne 1936- .... **CLC 35**
    See also BYA 7; CA 41-44R; CANR 14;
    JRDA; SATA 5, 77
New York Dept. of Ed. .... **CLC 70**
Nexo, Martin Andersen
    1869-1954 .... **TCLC 43**
    See also CA 202; DLB 214; EWL 3
Nezval, Vitezslav 1900-1958 .... **TCLC 44**
    See also CA 123; CDWLB 4; DLB 215;
    EWL 3
Ng, Fae Myenne 1957(?)- .... **CLC 81**
    See also BYA 11; CA 146
Ngema, Mbongeni 1955- .... **CLC 57**
    See also BW 2; CA 143; CANR 84; CD 5
Ngugi, James T(hiong'o) . **CLC 3, 7, 13, 182**
    See Ngugi wa Thiong'o
Ngugi wa Thiong'o
    See Ngugi wa Thiong'o
    See also DLB 125; EWL 3
Ngugi wa Thiong'o 1938- ... **BLC 3; CLC 36,
    182**
    See Ngugi, James T(hiong'o); Ngugi wa
    Thiong'o
    See also AFW; BRWS 8; BW 2; CA 81-84;
    CANR 27, 58; CDWLB 3; DAM MULT,
    NOV; DNFS 2; MTCW 1, 2; RGEL 2;
    WWE 1
Niatum, Duane 1938- .... **NNAL**
    See also CA 41-44R; CANR 21, 45, 83;
    DLB 175
Nichol, B(arrie) P(hillip) 1944-1988 . **CLC 18**
    See also CA 53-56; DLB 53; SATA 66
Nicholas of Cusa 1401-1464 .... **LC 80**
    See also DLB 115
Nichols, John (Treadwell) 1940- .... **CLC 38**
    See also AMWS 13; CA 9-12R, 190; CAAE
    190; CAAS 2; CANR 6, 70, 121; DLBY
    1982; LATS 1:2; TCWW 2
Nichols, Leigh
    See Koontz, Dean R(ay)
Nichols, Peter (Richard) 1927- .... **CLC 5, 36,
    65**
    See also CA 104; CANR 33, 86; CBD; CD
    5; DLB 13, 245; MTCW 1
Nicholson, Linda ed. .... **CLC 65**
Ni Chuilleanain, Eilean 1942- .... **PC 34**
    See also CA 126; CANR 53, 83; CP 7;
    CWP; DLB 40
Nicolas, F. R. E.
    See Freeling, Nicolas
Niedecker, Lorine 1903-1970 ..... **CLC 10, 42;
    PC 42**
    See also CA 25-28; CAP 2; DAM POET;
    DLB 48
Nietzsche, Friedrich (Wilhelm)
    1844-1900 .... **TCLC 10, 18, 55**
    See also CA 107; 121; CDWLB 2; DLB
    129; EW 7; RGWL 2, 3; TWA
Nievo, Ippolito 1831-1861 .... **NCLC 22**
Nightingale, Anne Redmon 1943-
    See Redmon, Anne
    See also CA 103
Nightingale, Florence 1820-1910 ... **TCLC 85**
    See also CA 188; DLB 166
Nijo Yoshimoto 1320-1388 .... **CMLC 49**
    See also DLB 203
Nik. T. O.
    See Annensky, Innokenty (Fyodorovich)

Nin, Anais 1903-1977 ..... **CLC 1, 4, 8, 11, 14,
    60, 127; SSC 10**
    See also AITN 2; AMWS 10; BPFB 2; CA
    13-16R; 69-72; CANR 22, 53; DAM
    NOV, POP; DLB 2, 4, 152; EWL 3; GLL
    2; MAWW; MTCW 1, 2; RGAL 4; RGSF
    2
Nisbet, Robert A(lexander)
    1913-1996 .... **TCLC 117**
    See also CA 25-28R; 153; CANR 17; INT
    CANR-17
Nishida, Kitaro 1870-1945 .... **TCLC 83**
Nishiwaki, Junzaburo
    See Nishiwaki, Junzaburo
    See also CA 194
Nishiwaki, Junzaburo 1894-1982 .... **PC 15**
    See Nishiwaki, Junzaburo; Nishiwaki
    Junzaburo
    See also CA 194; 107; MJW; RGWL 3
Nishiwaki Junzaburo
    See Nishiwaki, Junzaburo
    See also EWL 3
Nissenson, Hugh 1933- .... **CLC 4, 9**
    See also CA 17-20R; CANR 27, 108; CN
    7; DLB 28
Nister, Der
    See Der Nister
    See also EWL 3
Niven, Larry .... **CLC 8**
    See Niven, Laurence Van Cott
    See also AAYA 27; BPFB 2; BYA 10; DLB
    8; SCFW 2
Niven, Laurence Van Cott 1938-
    See Niven, Larry
    See also CA 21-24R, 207; CAAE 207;
    CAAS 12; CANR 14, 44, 66, 113; CPW;
    DAM POP; MTCW 1, 2; SATA 95; SFW
    4
Nixon, Agnes Eckhardt 1927- .... **CLC 21**
    See also CA 110
Nizan, Paul 1905-1940 .... **TCLC 40**
    See also CA 161; DLB 72; EWL 3; GFL
    1789 to the Present
Nkosi, Lewis 1936- .... **BLC 3; CLC 45**
    See also BW 1, 3; CA 65-68; CANR 27,
    81; CBD; CD 5; DAM MULT; DLB 157,
    225; WWE 1
Nodier, (Jean) Charles (Emmanuel)
    1780-1844 .... **NCLC 19**
    See also DLB 119; GFL 1789 to the Present
Noguchi, Yone 1875-1947 .... **TCLC 80**
Nolan, Christopher 1965- .... **CLC 58**
    See also CA 111; CANR 88
Noon, Jeff 1957- .... **CLC 91**
    See also CA 148; CANR 83; DLB 267;
    SFW 4
Norden, Charles
    See Durrell, Lawrence (George)
Nordhoff, Charles Bernard
    1887-1947 .... **TCLC 23**
    See also CA 108; 211; DLB 9; LAIT 1;
    RHW 1; SATA 23
Norfolk, Lawrence 1963- .... **CLC 76**
    See also CA 144; CANR 85; CN 7; DLB
    267
Norman, Marsha 1947- . **CLC 28, 186; DC 8**
    See also CA 105; CABS 3; CAD; CANR
    41, 131; CD 5; CSW; CWD; DAM
    DRAM; DFS 2; DLB 266; DLBY 1984;
    FW
Normyx
    See Douglas, (George) Norman
Norris, (Benjamin) Frank(lin, Jr.)
    1870-1902 .... **SSC 28; TCLC 24, 155**
    See also AMW; AMWC 2; BPFB
    2; CA 110; 160; CDALB 1865-1917; DLB
    12, 71, 186; LMFS 2; NFS 12; RGAL 4;
    TCWW 2; TUS

Peshkov, Alexei Maximovich 1868-1936
See Gorky, Maxim
See also CA 105; 141; CANR 83; DA;
DAC; DAM DRAM, MST, NOV; MTCW
2

Pessoa, Fernando (Antonio Nogueira)
1888-1935 ..... **HLC 2; PC 20; TCLC 27**
See also CA 125; 183; DAM MULT; DLB
287; EW 10; EWL 3; RGWL 2, 3; WP

Peterkin, Julia Mood 1880-1961 ...... **CLC 31**
See also CA 102; DLB 9

Peters, Joan K(aren) 1945- .... **CLC 39**
See also CA 158; CANR 109

Peters, Robert L(ouis) 1924- .... **CLC 7**
See also CA 13-16R; CAAS 8; CP 7; DLB
105

Petofi, Sandor 1823-1849 .... **NCLC 21**
See also RGWL 2, 3

Petrakis, Harry Mark 1923- .... **CLC 3**
See also CA 9-12R; CANR 4, 30, 85; CN 7

Petrarch 1304-1374 .... **CMLC 20; PC 8**
See also DA3; DAM POET; EW 2; LMFS
1; RGWL 2. 3

Petronius c. 20-66 .... **CMLC 34**
See also AW 2; CDWLB 1; DLB 211;
RGWL 2, 3

Petrov, Evgeny .... **TCLC 21**
See Kataev, Evgeny Petrovich

Petry, Ann (Lane) 1908-1997 .. **CLC 1, 7, 18;**
TCLC 112
See also AFAW 1, 2; BPFB 3; BW 1, 3;
BYA 2; CA 5-8R; 157; CAAS 6; CANR
4, 46; CLR 12; CN 7; DLB 76; EWL 3;
JRDA; LAIT 1; MAICYA 1, 2; MAIC-
YAS 1; MTCW 1; RGAL 4; SATA 5;
SATA-Obit 94; TUS

Petursson, Halligrimur 1614-1674 .... **LC 8**

Peychinovich
See Vazov, Ivan (Minchov)

Phaedrus c. 15B.C.-c. 50 .... **CMLC 25**
See also DLB 211

Phelps (Ward), Elizabeth Stuart
See Phelps, Elizabeth Stuart
See also FW

Phelps, Elizabeth Stuart
1844-1911 .... **TCLC 113**
See Phelps (Ward), Elizabeth Stuart
See also DLB 74

Philips, Katherine 1632-1664 . **LC 30; PC 40**
See also DLB 131; RGEL 2

Philipson, Morris H. 1926- .... **CLC 53**
See also CA 1-4R; CANR 4

Phillips, Caryl 1958- .... **BLCS; CLC 96**
See also BRWS 5; BW 2; CA 141; CANR
63, 104; CBD; CD 5; CN 7; DA3; DAM
MULT; DLB 157; EWL 3; MTCW 2;
WLIT 4; WWE 1

Phillips, David Graham
1867-1911 .... **TCLC 44**
See also CA 108; 176; DLB 9, 12, 303;
RGAL 4

Phillips, Jack
See Sandburg, Carl (August)

Phillips, Jayne Anne 1952- .... **CLC 15, 33,**
139; SSC 16
See also AAYA 57; BPFB 3; CA 101;
CANR 24, 50, 96; CN 7; CSW; DLBY
1980; INT CANR-24; MTCW 1, 2; RGAL
4; RGSF 2; SSFS 4

Phillips, Richard
See Dick, Philip K(indred)

Phillips, Robert (Schaeffer) 1938- .... **CLC 28**
See also CA 17-20R; CAAS 13; CANR 8;
DLB 105

Phillips, Ward
See Lovecraft, H(oward) P(hillips)

Philostratus, Flavius c. 179-c.
244 .... **CMLC 62**

Piccolo, Lucio 1901-1969 .... **CLC 13**
See also CA 97-100; DLB 114; EWL 3

Pickthall, Marjorie L(owry) C(hristie)
1883-1922 .... **TCLC 21**
See also CA 107; DLB 92

Pico della Mirandola, Giovanni
1463-1494 .... **LC 15**
See also LMFS 1

Piercy, Marge 1936- .... **CLC 3, 6, 14, 18, 27,**
62, 128; PC 29
See also BPFB 3; CA 21-24R, 187; CAAE
187; CAAS 1; CANR 13, 43, 66, 111; CN
7; CP 7; CWP; DLB 120, 227; EXPP;
FW; MTCW 1, 2; PFS 9; SFW 4

Piers, Robert
See Anthony, Piers

Pieyre de Mandiargues, Andre 1909-1991
See Mandiargues, Andre Pieyre de
See also CA 103; 136; CANR 22, 82; EWL
3; GFL 1789 to the Present

Pilnyak, Boris 1894-1938 . **SSC 48; TCLC 23**
See Vogau, Boris Andreyevich
See also EWL 3

Pinchback, Eugene
See Toomer, Jean

Pincherle, Alberto 1907-1990 ...... **CLC 11, 18**
See Moravia, Alberto
See also CA 25-28R; 132; CANR 33, 63;
DAM NOV; MTCW 1

Pinckney, Darryl 1953- .... **CLC 76**
See also BW 2, 3; CA 143; CANR 79

Pindar 518(?)B.C.-438(?)B.C. .... **CMLC 12;**
PC 19
See also AW 1; CDWLB 1; DLB 176;
RGWL 2

Pineda, Cecile 1942- .... **CLC 39**
See also CA 118; DLB 209

Pinero, Arthur Wing 1855-1934 .... **TCLC 32**
See also CA 110; 153; DAM DRAM; DLB
10; RGEL 2

Pinero, Miguel (Antonio Gomez)
1946-1988 .... **CLC 4, 55**
See also CA 61-64; 125; CAD; CANR 29,
90; DLB 266; HW 1; LLW 1

Pinget, Robert 1919-1997 .... **CLC 7, 13, 37**
See also CA 85-88; 160; CWW 2; DLB 83;
EWL 3; GFL 1789 to the Present

Pink Floyd
See Barrett, (Roger) Syd; Gilmour, David;
Mason, Nick; Waters, Roger; Wright, Rick

Pinkney, Edward 1802-1828 .... **NCLC 31**
See also DLB 248

Pinkwater, Daniel
See Pinkwater, Daniel Manus

Pinkwater, Daniel Manus 1941- .... **CLC 35**
See also AAYA 1, 46; BYA 9; CA 29-32R;
CANR 12, 38, 89; CLR 4; CSW; FANT;
JRDA; MAICYA 1, 2; SAAS 3; SATA 8,
46, 76, 114; SFW 4; YAW

Pinkwater, Manus
See Pinkwater, Daniel Manus

Pinsky, Robert 1940- .... **CLC 9, 19, 38, 94,**
121; PC 27
See also AMWS 6; CA 29-32R; CAAS 4;
CANR 58, 97; CP 7; DA3; DAM POET;
DLBY 1982, 1998; MTCW 2; PFS 18;
RGAL 4

Pinta, Harold
See Pinter, Harold

Pinter, Harold 1930- .. **CLC 1, 3, 6, 9, 11, 15,**
27, 58, 73, 199; DC 15; WLC
See also BRWR 1; BRWS 1; CA 5-8R;
CANR 33, 65, 112; CBD; CD 5; CDBLB
1960 to Present; DA; DA3; DAB; DAC;
DAM DRAM, MST; DFS 3, 5, 7, 14;
DLB 13; EWL 3; IDFW 3, 4; LMFS 2;
MTCW 1, 2; RGEL 2; TEA

Piozzi, Hester Lynch (Thrale)
1741-1821 .... **NCLC 57**
See also DLB 104, 142

Pirandello, Luigi 1867-1936 .. **DC 5; SSC 22;**
TCLC 4, 29; WLC
See also CA 104; 153; CANR 103; DA;
DA3; DAB; DAC; DAM DRAM, MST;
DFS 4, 9; DLB 264; EW 8; EWL 3;
MTCW 2; RGSF 2; RGWL 2, 3

Pirsig, Robert M(aynard) 1928- ... **CLC 4, 6,**
73
See also CA 53-56; CANR 42, 74; CPW 1;
DA3; DAM POP; MTCW 1, 2; SATA 39

Pisarev, Dmitrii Ivanovich
See Pisarev, Dmitry Ivanovich
See also DLB 277

Pisarev, Dmitry Ivanovich
1840-1868 .... **NCLC 25**
See Pisarev, Dmitrii Ivanovich

Pix, Mary (Griffith) 1666-1709 .... **LC 8**
See also DLB 80

Pixerecourt, (Rene Charles) Guilbert de
1773-1844 .... **NCLC 39**
See also DLB 192; GFL 1789 to the Present

Plaatje, Sol(omon) T(shekisho)
1878-1932 .... **BLCS; TCLC 73**
See also BW 2, 3; CA 141; CANR 79; DLB
125, 225

Plaidy, Jean
See Hibbert, Eleanor Alice Burford

Planche, James Robinson
1796-1880 .... **NCLC 42**
See also RGEL 2

Plant, Robert 1948- .... **CLC 12**

Plante, David (Robert) 1940- . **CLC 7, 23, 38**
See also CA 37-40R; CANR 12, 36, 58, 82;
CN 7; DAM NOV; DLBY 1983; INT
CANR-12; MTCW 1

Plath, Sylvia 1932-1963 ..... **CLC 1, 2, 3, 5, 9,**
11, 14, 17, 50, 51, 62, 111; PC 1, 37;
WLC
See also AAYA 13; AMWR 2; AMWS 1;
BPFB 3; CA 19-20; CANR 34, 101; CAP
2; CDALB 1941-1968; DA; DA3; DAB;
DAC; DAM MST, POET; DLB 5, 6, 152;
EWL 3; EXPN; EXPP; FW; LAIT 4;
MAWW; MTCW 1, 2; NFS 1; PAB; PFS
1, 15; RGAL 4; SATA 96; TUS; WP;
YAW

Plato c. 428B.C.-347B.C. .... **CMLC 8, 75;**
WLCS
See also AW 1; CDWLB 1; DA; DA3;
DAB; DAC; DAM MST; DLB 176; LAIT
1; LATS 1:1; RGWL 2, 3

Platonov, Andrei
See Klimentov, Andrei Platonovich

Platonov, Andrei Platonovich
See Klimentov, Andrei Platonovich
See also DLB 272

Platonov, Andrey Platonovich
See Klimentov, Andrei Platonovich
See also EWL 3

Platt, Kin 1911- .... **CLC 26**
See also AAYA 11; CA 17-20R; CANR 11;
JRDA; SAAS 17; SATA 21, 86; WYA

Plautus c. 254B.C.-c. 184B.C. ...... **CMLC 24;**
DC 6
See also AW 1; CDWLB 1; DLB 211;
RGWL 2, 3

Plick et Plock
See Simenon, Georges (Jacques Christian)

Plieksans, Janis
See Rainis, Janis

Plimpton, George (Ames)
1927-2003 .... **CLC 36**
See also AITN 1; CA 21-24R; 224; CANR
32, 70, 103, 133; DLB 185, 241; MTCW
1, 2; SATA 10; SATA-Obit 150

Pliny the Elder c. 23-79 .... **CMLC 23**
See also DLB 211

Pliny the Younger c. 61-c. 112 ...... **CMLC 62**
See also AW 2; DLB 211

Plomer, William Charles Franklin
1903-1973 .... **CLC 4, 8**
See also AFW; CA 21-22; CANR 34; CAP 2; DLB 20, 162, 191, 225; EWL 3; MTCW 1; RGEL 2; RGSF 2; SATA 24

Plotinus 204-270 .... **CMLC 46**
See also CDWLB 1; DLB 176

Plowman, Piers
See Kavanagh, Patrick (Joseph)

Plum, J.
See Wodehouse, P(elham) G(renville)

Plumly, Stanley (Ross) 1939- .... **CLC 33**
See also CA 108; 110; CANR 97; CP 7; DLB 5, 193; INT CA-110

Plumpe, Friedrich Wilhelm
1888-1931 .... **TCLC 53**
See also CA 112

Plutarch c. 46-c. 120 .... **CMLC 60**
See also AW 2; CDWLB 1; DLB 176; RGWL 2, 3; TWA

Po Chu-i 772-846 .... **CMLC 24**

Podhoretz, Norman 1930- .... **CLC 189**
See also AMWS 8; CA 9-12R; CANR 7, 78, 135

Poe, Edgar Allan 1809-1849 ..... **NCLC 1, 16, 55, 78, 94, 97, 117; PC 1, 54; SSC 1, 22, 34, 35, 54; WLC**
See also AAYA 14; AMW; AMWC 1; AMWR 2; BPFB 3; BYA 5, 11; CDALB 1640-1865; CMW 4; DA; DA3; DAB; DAC; DAM MST, POET; DLB 3, 59, 73, 74, 248, 254; EXPP; EXPS; HGG; LAIT 2; LATS 1:1; LMFS 1; MSW; PAB; PFS 1, 3, 9; RGAL 4; RGSF 2; SATA 23; SCFW 2; SFW 4; SSFS 2, 4, 7, 8, 16; SUFW; TUS; WP; WYA

Poet of Titchfield Street, The
See Pound, Ezra (Weston Loomis)

Pohl, Frederik 1919- .... **CLC 18; SSC 25**
See also AAYA 24; CA 61-64, 188; CAAE 188; CAAS 1; CANR 11, 37, 81; CN 7; DLB 8; INT CANR-11; MTCW 1, 2; SATA 24; SCFW 2; SFW 4

Poirier, Louis 1910-
See Gracq, Julien
See also CA 122; 126

Poitier, Sidney 1927- .... **CLC 26**
See also AAYA 60; BW 1; CA 117; CANR 94

Pokagon, Simon 1830-1899 .... **NNAL**
See also DAM MULT

Polanski, Roman 1933- .... **CLC 16, 178**
See also CA 77-80

Poliakoff, Stephen 1952- .... **CLC 38**
See also CA 106; CANR 116; CBD; CD 5; DLB 13

Police, The
See Copeland, Stewart (Armstrong); Summers, Andrew James

Polidori, John William 1795-1821 . **NCLC 51**
See also DLB 116; HGG

Pollitt, Katha 1949- .... **CLC 28, 122**
See also CA 120; 122; CANR 66, 108; MTCW 1, 2

Pollock, (Mary) Sharon 1936- .... **CLC 50**
See also CA 141; CANR 132; CD 5; CWD; DAC; DAM DRAM, MST; DFS 3; DLB 60; FW

Pollock, Sharon 1936- .... **DC 20**

Polo, Marco 1254-1324 .... **CMLC 15**

Polonsky, Abraham (Lincoln)
1910-1999 .... **CLC 92**
See also CA 104; 187; DLB 26; INT CA-104

Polybius c. 200B.C.-c. 118B.C. ...... **CMLC 17**
See also AW 1; DLB 176; RGWL 2, 3

Pomerance, Bernard 1940- .... **CLC 13**
See also CA 101; CAD; CANR 49, 134; CD 5; DAM DRAM; DFS 9; LAIT 2

Ponge, Francis 1899-1988 .... **CLC 6, 18**
See also CA 85-88; 126; CANR 40, 86; DAM POET; DLBY 2002; EWL 3; GFL 1789 to the Present; RGWL 2, 3

Poniatowska, Elena 1933- . **CLC 140; HLC 2**
See also CA 101; CANR 32, 66, 107; CD-WLB 3; CWW 2; DAM MULT; DLB 113; EWL 3; HW 1, 2; LAWS 1; WLIT 1

Pontoppidan, Henrik 1857-1943 .... **TCLC 29**
See also CA 170; DLB 300

Ponty, Maurice Merleau
See Merleau-Ponty, Maurice

Poole, Josephine .... **CLC 17**
See Helyar, Jane Penelope Josephine
See also SAAS 2; SATA 5

Popa, Vasko 1922-1991 . **CLC 19; TCLC 167**
See also CA 112; 148; CDWLB 4; DLB 181; EWL 3; RGWL 2, 3

Pope, Alexander 1688-1744 ...... **LC 3, 58, 60, 64; PC 26; WLC**
See also BRW 3; BRWC 1; BRWR 1; CD-BLB 1660-1789; DA; DA3; DAB; DAC; DAM MST, POET; DLB 95, 101, 213; EXPP; PAB; PFS 12; RGEL 2; WLIT 3; WP

Popov, Evgenii Anatol'evich
See Popov, Yevgeny
See also DLB 285

Popov, Yevgeny .... **CLC 59**
See Popov, Evgenii Anatol'evich

Poquelin, Jean-Baptiste
See Moliere

Porete, Marguerite c. 1250-1310 .. **CMLC 73**
See also DLB 208

Porphyry c. 233-c. 305 .... **CMLC 71**

Porter, Connie (Rose) 1959(?)- .... **CLC 70**
See also BW 2, 3; CA 142; CANR 90, 109; SATA 81, 129

Porter, Gene(va Grace) Stratton .. **TCLC 21**
See Stratton-Porter, Gene(va Grace)
See also BPFB 3; CA 112; CWRI 5; RHW

Porter, Katherine Anne 1890-1980 ... **CLC 1, 3, 7, 10, 13, 15, 27, 101; SSC 4, 31, 43**
See also AAYA 42; AITN 2; AMW; BPFB 3; CA 1-4R; 101; CANR 1, 65; CDALBS; DA; DA3; DAB; DAC; DAM MST, NOV; DLB 4, 9, 102; DLBD 12; DLBY 1980; EWL 3; EXPS; LAIT 3; MAWW; MTCW 1, 2; NFS 14; RGAL 4; RGSF 2; SATA 39; SATA-Obit 23; SSFS 1, 8, 11, 16; TUS

Porter, Peter (Neville Frederick)
1929- .... **CLC 5, 13, 33**
See also CA 85-88; CP 7; DLB 40, 289; WWE 1

Porter, William Sydney 1862-1910
See Henry, O.
See also CA 104; 131; CDALB 1865-1917; DA; DA3; DAB; DAC; DAM MST; DLB 12, 78, 79; MTCW 1, 2; TUS; YABC 2

Portillo (y Pacheco), Jose Lopez
See Lopez Portillo (y Pacheco), Jose

Portillo Trambley, Estela
1927-1998 .... **HLC 2; TCLC 163**
See Trambley, Estela Portillo
See also CANR 32; DAM MULT; DLB 209; HW 1

Posey, Alexander (Lawrence)
1873-1908 .... **NNAL**
See also CA 144; CANR 80; DAM MULT; DLB 175

Posse, Abel .... **CLC 70**

Post, Melville Davisson
1869-1930 .... **TCLC 39**
See also CA 110; 202; CMW 4

Potok, Chaim 1929-2002 ... **CLC 2, 7, 14, 26, 112**
See also AAYA 15, 50; AITN 1, 2; BPFB 3; BYA 1; CA 17-20R; 208; CANR 19, 35, 64, 98; CLR 92; CN 7; DA3; DAM NOV; DLB 28, 152; EXPN; INT CANR-19; LAIT 4; MTCW 1, 2; NFS 4; SATA 33, 106; SATA-Obit 134; TUS; YAW

Potok, Herbert Harold -2002
See Potok, Chaim

Potok, Herman Harold
See Potok, Chaim

Potter, Dennis (Christopher George)
1935-1994 .... **CLC 58, 86, 123**
See also BRWS 10; CA 107; 145; CANR 33, 61; CBD; DLB 233; MTCW 1

Pound, Ezra (Weston Loomis)
1885-1972 .. **CLC 1, 2, 3, 4, 5, 7, 10, 13, 18, 34, 48, 50, 112; PC 4; WLC**
See also AAYA 47; AMW; AMWR 1; CA 5-8R; 37-40R; CANR 40; CDALB 1917-1929; DA; DA3; DAB; DAC; DAM MST, POET; DLB 4, 45, 63; DLBD 15; EFS 2; EWL 3; EXPP; LMFS 2; MTCW 1, 2; PAB; PFS 2, 8, 16; RGAL 4; TUS; WP

Povod, Reinaldo 1959-1994 .... **CLC 44**
See also CA 136; 146; CANR 83

Powell, Adam Clayton, Jr.
1908-1972 .... **BLC 3; CLC 89**
See also BW 1, 3; CA 102; 33-36R; CANR 86; DAM MULT

Powell, Anthony (Dymoke)
1905-2000 ..... **CLC 1, 3, 7, 9, 10, 31**
See also BRW 7; CA 1-4R; 189; CANR 1, 32, 62, 107; CDBLB 1945-1960; CN 7; DLB 15; EWL 3; MTCW 1, 2; RGEL 2; TEA

Powell, Dawn 1896(?)-1965 .... **CLC 66**
See also CA 5-8R; CANR 121; DLBY 1997

Powell, Padgett 1952- .... **CLC 34**
See also CA 126; CANR 63, 101; CSW; DLB 234; DLBY 01

Powell, (Oval) Talmage 1920-2000
See Queen, Ellery
See also CA 5-8R; CANR 2, 80

Power, Susan 1961- .... **CLC 91**
See also BYA 14; CA 160; CANR 135; NFS 11

Powers, J(ames) F(arl) 1917-1999 ..... **CLC 1, 4, 8, 57; SSC 4**
See also CA 1-4R; 181; CANR 2, 61; CN 7; DLB 130; MTCW 1; RGAL 4; RGSF 2

Powers, John J(ames) 1945-
See Powers, John R.
See also CA 69-72

Powers, John R. .... **CLC 66**
See Powers, John J(ames)

Powers, Richard (S.) 1957- .... **CLC 93**
See also AMWS 9; BPFB 3; CA 148; CANR 80; CN 7

Pownall, David 1938- .... **CLC 10**
See also CA 89-92; 180; CAAS 18; CANR 49, 101; CBD; CD 5; CN 7; DLB 14

Powys, John Cowper 1872-1963 ... **CLC 7, 9, 15, 46, 125**
See also CA 85-88; CANR 106; DLB 15, 255; EWL 3; FANT; MTCW 1, 2; RGEL 2; SUFW

Powys, T(heodore) F(rancis)
1875-1953 .... **TCLC 9**
See also BRWS 8; CA 106; 189; DLB 36, 162; EWL 3; FANT; RGEL 2; SUFW

Prado (Calvo), Pedro 1886-1952 ... **TCLC 75**
See also CA 131; DLB 283; HW 1; LAW

Prager, Emily 1952- .... **CLC 56**
See also CA 204

Pratchett, Terry 1948- .... **CLC 197**
See also AAYA 19, 54; BPFB 3; CA 143;
CANR 87, 126; CLR 64; CN 7; CPW;
CWRI 5; FANT; SATA 82, 139; SFW 4;
SUFW 2

Pratolini, Vasco 1913-1991 .... **TCLC 124**
See also CA 211; DLB 177; EWL 3; RGWL
2, 3

Pratt, E(dwin) J(ohn) 1883(?)-1964 . **CLC 19**
See also CA 141; 93-96; CANR 77; DAC;
DAM POET; DLB 92; EWL 3; RGEL 2;
TWA

Premchand .... **TCLC 21**
See Srivastava, Dhanpat Rai
See also EWL 3

Preseren, France 1800-1849 .... **NCLC 127**
See also CDWLB 4; DLB 147

Preussler, Otfried 1923- .... **CLC 17**
See also CA 77-80; SATA 24

Prevert, Jacques (Henri Marie)
1900-1977 .... **CLC 15**
See also CA 77-80; 69-72; CANR 29, 61;
DLB 258; EWL 3; GFL 1789 to the
Present; IDFW 3, 4; MTCW 1; RGWL 2,
3; SATA-Obit 30

Prevost, (Antoine Francois)
1697-1763 .... **LC 1**
See also EW 4; GFL Beginnings to 1789;
RGWL 2, 3

Price, (Edward) Reynolds 1933- ... **CLC 3, 6,
13, 43, 50, 63; SSC 22**
See also AMWS 6; CA 1-4R; CANR 1, 37,
57, 87, 128; CN 7; CSW; DAM NOV;
DLB 2, 218, 278; EWL 3; INT CANR-
37; NFS 18

Price, Richard 1949- .... **CLC 6, 12**
See also CA 49-52; CANR 3; DLBY 1981

Prichard, Katharine Susannah
1883-1969 .... **CLC 46**
See also CA 11-12; CANR 33; CAP 1; DLB
260; MTCW 1; RGEL 2; RGSF 2; SATA
66

Priestley, J(ohn) B(oynton)
1894-1984 .... **CLC 2, 5, 9, 34**
See also BRW 7; CA 9-12R; 113; CANR
33; CDBLB 1914-1945; DA3; DAM
DRAM, NOV; DLB 10, 34, 77, 100, 139;
DLBY 1984; EWL 3; MTCW 1, 2; RGEL
2; SFW 4

Prince 1958- .... **CLC 35**
See also CA 213

Prince, F(rank) T(empleton)
1912-2003 .... **CLC 22**
See also CA 101; 219; CANR 43, 79; CP 7;
DLB 20

Prince Kropotkin
See Kropotkin, Peter (Aleksieevich)

Prior, Matthew 1664-1721 .... **LC 4**
See also DLB 95; RGEL 2

Prishvin, Mikhail 1873-1954 .... **TCLC 75**
See Prishvin, Mikhail Mikhailovich

Prishvin, Mikhail Mikhailovich
See Prishvin, Mikhail
See also DLB 272; EWL 3

Pritchard, William H(arrison)
1932- .... **CLC 34**
See also CA 65-68; CANR 23, 95; DLB
111

Pritchett, V(ictor) S(awdon)
1900-1997 ... **CLC 5, 13, 15, 41; SSC 14**
See also BPFB 3; BRWS 3; CA 61-64; 157;
CANR 31, 63; CN 7; DA3; DAM NOV;
DLB 15, 139; EWL 3; MTCW 1, 2;
RGEL 2; RGSF 2; TEA

Private 19022
See Manning, Frederic

Probst, Mark 1925- .... **CLC 59**
See also CA 130

Prokosch, Frederic 1908-1989 ...... **CLC 4, 48**
See also CA 73-76; 128; CANR 82; DLB
48; MTCW 2

Propertius, Sextus c. 50B.C.-c.
16B.C. .... **CMLC 32**
See also AW 2; CDWLB 1; DLB 211;
RGWL 2, 3

Prophet, The
See Dreiser, Theodore (Herman Albert)

Prose, Francine 1947- .... **CLC 45**
See also CA 109; 112; CANR 46, 95, 132;
DLB 234; SATA 101, 149

Proudhon
See Cunha, Euclides (Rodrigues Pimenta)
da

Proulx, Annie
See Proulx, E(dna) Annie

Proulx, E(dna) Annie 1935- ...... **CLC 81, 158**
See also AMWS 7; BPFB 3; CA 145;
CANR 65, 110; CN 7; CPW 1; DA3;
DAM POP; MTCW 2; SSFS 18

Proust, (Valentin-Louis-George-Eugene)
Marcel 1871-1922 ..... **SSC 75; TCLC 7,
13, 33, 161; WLC**
See also AAYA 58; BPFB 3; CA 104; 120;
CANR 110; DA; DA3; DAB; DAC; DAM
MST, NOV; DLB 65; EW 8; EWL 3; GFL
1789 to the Present; MTCW 1, 2; RGWL
2, 3; TWA

Prowler, Harley
See Masters, Edgar Lee

Prus, Boleslaw 1845-1912 .... **TCLC 48**
See also RGWL 2, 3

Pryor, Richard (Franklin Lenox Thomas)
1940- .... **CLC 26**
See also CA 122; 152

Przybyszewski, Stanislaw
1868-1927 .... **TCLC 36**
See also CA 160; DLB 66; EWL 3

Pteleon
See Grieve, C(hristopher) M(urray)
See also DAM POET

Puckett, Lute
See Masters, Edgar Lee

Puig, Manuel 1932-1990 .... **CLC 3, 5, 10, 28,
65, 133; HLC 2**
See also BPFB 3; CA 45-48; CANR 2, 32,
63; CDWLB 3; DA3; DAM MULT; DLB
113; DNFS 1; EWL 3; GLL 1; HW 1, 2;
LAW; MTCW 1, 2; RGWL 2, 3; TWA;
WLIT 1

Pulitzer, Joseph 1847-1911 .... **TCLC 76**
See also CA 114; DLB 23

Purchas, Samuel 1577(?)-1626 .... **LC 70**
See also DLB 151

Purdy, A(lfred) W(ellington)
1918-2000 .... **CLC 3, 6, 14, 50**
See also CA 81-84; 189; CAAS 17; CANR
42, 66; CP 7; DAC; DAM MST, POET;
DLB 88; PFS 5; RGEL 2

Purdy, James (Amos) 1923- .... **CLC 2, 4, 10,
28, 52**
See also AMWS 7; CA 33-36R; CAAS 1;
CANR 19, 51; CN 7; DLB 2, 218;
EWL 3; INT CANR-19; MTCW 1; RGAL
4

Pure, Simon
See Swinnerton, Frank Arthur

Pushkin, Aleksandr Sergeevich
See Pushkin, Alexander (Sergeyevich)
See also DLB 205

Pushkin, Alexander (Sergeyevich)
1799-1837 .... **NCLC 3, 27, 83; PC 10;
SSC 27, 55; WLC**
See Pushkin, Aleksandr Sergeevich
See also DA; DA3; DAB; DAC; DAM
DRAM, MST, POET; EW 5; EXPS; RGSF
2; RGWL 2, 3; SATA 61; SSFS 9; TWA

P'u Sung-ling 1640-1715 .... **LC 49; SSC 31**

Putnam, Arthur Lee
See Alger, Horatio, Jr.

Puttenham, George 1529-1590 .... **LC 116**
See also DLB 281

Puzo, Mario 1920-1999 .... **CLC 1, 2, 6, 36,
107**
See also BPFB 3; CA 65-68; 185; CANR 4,
42, 65, 99, 131; CN 7; CPW; DA3; DAM
NOV, POP; DLB 6; MTCW 1, 2; NFS 16;
RGAL 4

Pygge, Edward
See Barnes, Julian (Patrick)

Pyle, Ernest Taylor 1900-1945
See Pyle, Ernie
See also CA 115; 160

Pyle, Ernie .... **TCLC 75**
See Pyle, Ernest Taylor
See also DLB 29; MTCW 2

Pyle, Howard 1853-1911 .... **TCLC 81**
See also AAYA 57; BYA 2, 4; CA 109; 137;
CLR 22; DLB 42, 188; DLBD 13; LAIT
1; MAICYA 1, 2; SATA 16, 100; WCH;
YAW

Pym, Barbara (Mary Crampton)
1913-1980 .... **CLC 13, 19, 37, 111**
See also BPFB 3; BRWS 2; CA 13-14; 97-
100; CANR 13, 34; CAP 1; DLB 14, 207;
DLBY 1987; EWL 3; MTCW 1, 2; RGEL
2; TEA

Pynchon, Thomas (Ruggles, Jr.)
1937- ...... **CLC 2, 3, 6, 9, 11, 18, 33, 62,
72, 123, 192; SSC 14; WLC**
See also AMWS 2; BEST 90:2; BPFB 3;
CA 17-20R; CANR 22, 46, 73; CN 7;
CPW 1; DA; DA3; DAB; DAC; DAM
MST, NOV, POP; DLB 2, 173; EWL 3;
MTCW 1, 2; RGAL 4; SFW 4; TUS

Pythagoras c. 582B.C.-c. 507B.C. . **CMLC 22**
See also DLB 176

Q
See Quiller-Couch, Sir Arthur (Thomas)

Qian, Chongzhu
See Ch'ien, Chung-shu

Qian, Sima 145B.C.-c. 89B.C. .... **CMLC 72**

Qian Zhongshu
See Ch'ien, Chung-shu
See also CWW 2

Qroll
See Dagerman, Stig (Halvard)

Quarles, Francis 1592-1644 .... **LC 117**
See also DLB 126; RGEL 2

Quarrington, Paul (Lewis) 1953- ..... **CLC 65**
See also CA 129; CANR 62, 95

Quasimodo, Salvatore 1901-1968 .... **CLC 10;
PC 47**
See also CA 13-16; 25-28R; CAP 1; DLB
114; EW 12; EWL 3; MTCW 1; RGWL
2, 3

Quatermass, Martin
See Carpenter, John (Howard)

Quay, Stephen 1947- .... **CLC 95**
See also CA 189

Quay, Timothy 1947- .... **CLC 95**
See also CA 189

Queen, Ellery .... **CLC 3, 11**
See Dannay, Frederic; Davidson, Avram
(James); Deming, Richard; Fairman, Paul
W.; Flora, Fletcher; Hoch, Edward
D(entinger); Kane, Henry; Lee, Manfred
B(ennington); Marlowe, Stephen; Powell,
(Oval) Talmage; Sheldon, Walter J(ames);
Sturgeon, Theodore (Hamilton); Tracy,
Don(ald Fiske); Vance, John Holbrook
See also BPFB 3; CMW 4; MSW; RGAL 4

Queen, Ellery, Jr.
See Dannay, Frederic; Lee, Manfred
B(ennington)

Queneau, Raymond 1903-1976 ..... **CLC 2, 5, 10, 42**
See also CA 77-80; 69-72; CANR 32; DLB 72, 258; EW 12; EWL 3; GFL 1789 to the Present; MTCW 1, 2; RGWL 2, 3

Quevedo, Francisco de 1580-1645 .... **LC 23**

Quiller-Couch, Sir Arthur (Thomas) 1863-1944 .... **TCLC 53**
See also CA 118; 166; DLB 135, 153, 190; HGG; RGEL 2; SUFW 1

Quin, Ann (Marie) 1936-1973 .... **CLC 6**
See also CA 9-12R; 45-48; DLB 14, 231

Quincey, Thomas de
See De Quincey, Thomas

Quindlen, Anna 1953- .... **CLC 191**
See also AAYA 35; CA 138; CANR 73, 126; DA3; DLB 292; MTCW 2

Quinn, Martin
See Smith, Martin Cruz

Quinn, Peter 1947- .... **CLC 91**
See also CA 197

Quinn, Simon
See Smith, Martin Cruz

Quintana, Leroy V. 1944- ...... **HLC 2; PC 36**
See also CA 131; CANR 65; DAM MULT; DLB 82; HW 1, 2

Quintilian c. 35-40–c. 96. .... **CMLC 77**
See also AW 2; DLB 211; RGWL 2, 3

Quiroga, Horacio (Sylvestre) 1878-1937 .... **HLC 2; TCLC 20**
See also CA 117; 131; DAM MULT; EWL 3; HW 1; LAW; MTCW 1; RGSF 2; WLIT 1

Quoirez, Françoise 1935- .... **CLC 9**
See Sagan, Françoise
See also CA 49-52; CANR 6, 39, 73; MTCW 1, 2; TWA

Raabe, Wilhelm (Karl) 1831-1910 . **TCLC 45**
See also CA 167; DLB 129

Rabe, David (William) 1940- .. **CLC 4, 8, 33, 200; DC 16**
See also CA 85-88; CABS 3; CAD; CANR 59, 129; CD 5; DAM DRAM; DFS 3, 8, 13; DLB 7, 228; EWL 3

Rabelais, Francois 1494-1553 .... **LC 5, 60; WLC**
See also DA; DAB; DAC; DAM MST; EW 2; GFL Beginnings to 1789; LMFS 1; RGWL 2, 3; TWA

Rabinovitch, Sholem 1859-1916
See Aleichem, Sholom
See also CA 104

Rabinyan, Dorit 1972- .... **CLC 119**
See also CA 170

Rachilde
See Vallette, Marguerite Eymery; Vallette, Marguerite Eymery
See also EWL 3

Racine, Jean 1639-1699 .... **LC 28, 113**
See also DA3; DAB; DAM MST; DLB 268; EW 3; GFL Beginnings to 1789; LMFS 1; RGWL 2, 3; TWA

Radcliffe, Ann (Ward) 1764-1823 ... **NCLC 6, 55, 106**
See also DLB 39, 178; HGG; LMFS 1; RGEL 2; SUFW; WLIT 3

Radclyffe-Hall, Marguerite
See Hall, (Marguerite) Radclyffe

Radiguet, Raymond 1903-1923 ...... **TCLC 29**
See also CA 162; DLB 65; EWL 3; GFL 1789 to the Present; RGWL 2, 3

Radnoti, Miklos 1909-1944 .... **TCLC 16**
See also CA 118; 212; CDWLB 4; DLB 215; EWL 3; RGWL 2, 3

Rado, James 1939- .... **CLC 17**
See also CA 105

Radvanyi, Netty 1900-1983
See Seghers, Anna
See also CA 85-88; 110; CANR 82

Rae, Ben
See Griffiths, Trevor

Raeburn, John (Hay) 1941- .... **CLC 34**
See also CA 57-60

Ragni, Gerome 1942-1991 .... **CLC 17**
See also CA 105; 134

Rahv, Philip .... **CLC 24**
See Greenberg, Ivan
See also DLB 137

Raimund, Ferdinand Jakob 1790-1836 .... **NCLC 69**
See also DLB 90

Raine, Craig (Anthony) 1944- .. **CLC 32, 103**
See also CA 108; CANR 29, 51, 103; CP 7; DLB 40; PFS 7

Raine, Kathleen (Jessie) 1908-2003 .. **CLC 7, 45**
See also CA 85-88; 218; CANR 46, 109; CP 7; DLB 20; EWL 3; MTCW 1; RGEL 2

Rainis, Janis 1865-1929 .... **TCLC 29**
See also CA 170; CDWLB 4; DLB 220; EWL 3

Rakosi, Carl .... **CLC 47**
See Rawley, Callman
See also CA 228; CAAS 5; CP 7; DLB 193

Ralegh, Sir Walter
See Raleigh, Sir Walter
See also BRW 1; RGEL 2; WP

Raleigh, Richard
See Lovecraft, H(oward) P(hillips)

Raleigh, Sir Walter 1554(?)-1618 .... **LC 31, 39; PC 31**
See Ralegh, Sir Walter
See also CDBLB Before 1660; DLB 172; EXPP; PFS 14; TEA

Rallentando, H. P.
See Sayers, Dorothy L(eigh)

Ramal, Walter
See de la Mare, Walter (John)

Ramana Maharshi 1879-1950 .... **TCLC 84**

Ramoacn y Cajal, Santiago 1852-1934 .... **TCLC 93**

Ramon, Juan
See Jimenez (Mantecon), Juan Ramon

Ramos, Graciliano 1892-1953 .... **TCLC 32**
See also CA 167; DLB 307; EWL 3; HW 2; LAW; WLIT 1

Rampersad, Arnold 1941- .... **CLC 44**
See also BW 2, 3; CA 127; 133; CANR 81; DLB 111; INT CA-133

Rampling, Anne
See Rice, Anne
See also GLL 2

Ramsay, Allan 1686(?)-1758 .... **LC 29**
See also DLB 95; RGEL 2

Ramsay, Jay
See Campbell, (John) Ramsey

Ramuz, Charles-Ferdinand 1878-1947 .... **TCLC 33**
See also CA 165; EWL 3

Rand, Ayn 1905-1982 ...... **CLC 3, 30, 44, 79; WLC**
See also AAYA 10; AMWS 4; BPFB 3; BYA 12; CA 13-16R; 105; CANR 27, 73; CDALBS; CPW; DA; DA3; DAC; DAM MST, NOV, POP; DLB 227, 279; MTCW 1, 2; NFS 10, 16; RGAL 4; SFW 4; TUS; YAW

Randall, Dudley (Felker) 1914-2000 . **BLC 3; CLC 1, 135**
See also BW 1, 3; CA 25-28R; 189; CANR 23, 82; DAM MULT; DLB 41; PFS 5

Randall, Robert
See Silverberg, Robert

Ranger, Ken
See Creasey, John

Rank, Otto 1884-1939 .... **TCLC 115**

Ransom, John Crowe 1888-1974 .. **CLC 2, 4, 5, 11, 24; PC 61**
See also AMW; CA 5-8R; 49-52; CANR 6, 34; CDALBS; DA3; DAM POET; DLB 45, 63; EWL 3; EXPP; MTCW 1, 2; RGAL 4; TUS

Rao, Raja 1909- .... **CLC 25, 56**
See also CA 73-76; CANR 51; CN 7; DAM NOV; EWL 3; MTCW 1, 2; RGEL 2; RGSF 2

Raphael, Frederic (Michael) 1931- ... **CLC 2, 14**
See also CA 1-4R; CANR 1, 86; CN 7; DLB 14

Ratcliffe, James P.
See Mencken, H(enry) L(ouis)

Rathbone, Julian 1935- .... **CLC 41**
See also CA 101; CANR 34, 73

Rattigan, Terence (Mervyn) 1911-1977 .... **CLC 7; DC 18**
See also BRWS 7; CA 85-88; 73-76; CBD; CDBLB 1945-1960; DAM DRAM; DFS 8; DLB 13; IDFW 3, 4; MTCW 1, 2; RGEL 2

Ratushinskaya, Irina 1954- .... **CLC 54**
See also CA 129; CANR 68; CWW 2

Raven, Simon (Arthur Noel) 1927-2001 .... **CLC 14**
See also CA 81-84; 197; CANR 86; CN 7; DLB 271

Ravenna, Michael
See Welty, Eudora (Alice)

Rawley, Callman 1903-2004
See Rakosi, Carl
See also CA 21-24R; CANR 12, 32, 91

Rawlings, Marjorie Kinnan 1896-1953 .... **TCLC 4**
See also AAYA 20; AMWS 10; ANW; BPFB 3; BYA 3; CA 104; 137; CANR 74; CLR 63; DLB 9, 22, 102; DLBD 17; JRDA; MAICYA 1, 2; MTCW 2; RGAL 4; SATA 100; WCH; YABC 1; YAW

Ray, Satyajit 1921-1992 .... **CLC 16, 76**
See also CA 114; 137; DAM MULT

Read, Herbert Edward 1893-1968 ..... **CLC 4**
See also BRW 6; CA 85-88; 25-28R; DLB 20, 149; EWL 3; PAB; RGEL 2

Read, Piers Paul 1941- .... **CLC 4, 10, 25**
See also CA 21-24R; CANR 38, 86; CN 7; DLB 14; SATA 21

Reade, Charles 1814-1884 .... **NCLC 2, 74**
See also DLB 21; RGEL 2

Reade, Hamish
See Gray, Simon (James Holliday)

Reading, Peter 1946- .... **CLC 47**
See also BRWS 8; CA 103; CANR 46, 96; CP 7; DLB 40

Reaney, James 1926- .... **CLC 13**
See also CA 41-44R; CAAS 15; CANR 42; CD 5; CP 7; DAC; DAM MST; DLB 68; RGEL 2; SATA 43

Rebreanu, Liviu 1885-1944 .... **TCLC 28**
See also CA 165; DLB 220; EWL 3

Rechy, John (Francisco) 1934- ...... **CLC 1, 7, 14, 18, 107; HLC 2**
See also CA 5-8R, 195; CAAE 195; CAAS 4; CANR 6, 32, 64; CN 7; DAM MULT; DLB 122, 278; DLBY 1982; HW 1, 2; INT CANR-6; LLW 1; RGAL 4

Redcam, Tom 1870-1933 .... **TCLC 25**

Reddin, Keith .... **CLC 67**
See also CAD

Redgrove, Peter (William) 1932-2003 .... **CLC 6, 41**
See also BRWS 6; CA 1-4R; 217; CANR 3, 39, 77; CP 7; DLB 40

Ridge, John Rollin 1827-1867 ...... **NCLC 82;**
NNAL
See also CA 144; DAM MULT; DLB 175
Ridgeway, Jason
See Marlowe, Stephen
Ridgway, Keith 1965- .... **CLC 119**
See also CA 172
Riding, Laura .... **CLC 3, 7**
See Jackson, Laura (Riding)
See also RGAL 4
Riefenstahl, Berta Helene Amalia 1902-2003
See Riefenstahl, Leni
See also CA 108; 220
Riefenstahl, Leni .... **CLC 16, 190**
See Riefenstahl, Berta Helene Amalia
Riffe, Ernest
See Bergman, (Ernst) Ingmar
Riggs, (Rolla) Lynn
1899-1954 .... **NNAL; TCLC 56**
See also CA 144; DAM MULT; DLB 175
Riis, Jacob A(ugust) 1849-1914 ..... **TCLC 80**
See also CA 113; 168; DLB 23
Riley, James Whitcomb 1849-1916 .... **PC 48;**
TCLC 51
See also CA 118; 137; DAM POET; MAI-
CYA 1, 2; RGAL 4; SATA 17
Riley, Tex
See Creasey, John
Rilke, Rainer Maria 1875-1926 .... **PC 2;**
TCLC 1, 6, 19
See also CA 104; 132; CANR 62, 99; CD-
WLB 2; DA3; DAM POET; DLB 81; EW
9; EWL 3; MTCW 1, 2; PFS 19; RGWL
2, 3; TWA; WP
Rimbaud, (Jean Nicolas) Arthur
1854-1891 ... **NCLC 4, 35, 82; PC 3, 57;**
WLC
See also DA; DA3; DAB; DAC; DAM
MST, POET; DLB 217; EW 7; GFL 1789
to the Present; LMFS 2; RGWL 2, 3;
TWA; WP
Rinehart, Mary Roberts
1876-1958 .... **TCLC 52**
See also BPFB 3; CA 108; 166; RGAL 4;
RHW
Ringmaster, The
See Mencken, H(enry) L(ouis)
Ringwood, Gwen(dolyn Margaret) Pharis
1910-1984 .... **CLC 48**
See also CA 148; 112; DLB 88
Rio, Michel 1945(?)- .... **CLC 43**
See also CA 201
Rios, Alberto (Alvaro) 1952- .... **PC 57**
See also AMWS 4; CA 113; CANR 34, 79;
CP 7; DLB 122; HW 2; PFS 11
Ritsos, Giannes
See Ritsos, Yannis
Ritsos, Yannis 1909-1990 .... **CLC 6, 13, 31**
See also CA 77-80; 133; CANR 39, 61; EW
12; EWL 3; MTCW 1; RGWL 2, 3
Ritter, Erika 1948(?)- .... **CLC 52**
See also CD 5; CWD
Rivera, Jose Eustasio 1889-1928 ... **TCLC 35**
See also CA 162; EWL 3; HW 1, 2; LAW
Rivera, Tomas 1935-1984 .... **HLCS 2**
See also CA 49-52; CANR 32; DLB 82;
HW 1; LLW 1; RGAL 4; SSFS 15;
TCWW 2; WLIT 1
Rivers, Conrad Kent 1933-1968 .... **CLC 1**
See also BW 1; CA 85-88; DLB 41
Rivers, Elfrida
See Bradley, Marion Zimmer
See also GLL 1
Riverside, John
See Heinlein, Robert A(nson)

Rizal, Jose 1861-1896 .... **NCLC 27**
Roa Bastos, Augusto (Antonio)
1917- .... **CLC 45; HLC 2**
See also CA 131; CWW 2; DAM MULT;
DLB 113; EWL 3; HW 1; LAW; RGSF 2;
WLIT 1
Robbe-Grillet, Alain 1922- .... **CLC 1, 2, 4, 6,**
8, 10, 14, 43, 128
See also BPFB 3; CA 9-12R; CANR 33,
65, 115; CWW 2; DLB 83; EW 13; EWL
3; GFL 1789 to the Present; IDFW 3, 4;
MTCW 1, 2; RGWL 2, 3; SSFS 15
Robbins, Harold 1916-1997 .... **CLC 5**
See also BPFB 3; CA 73-76; 162; CANR
26, 54, 112; DA3; DAM NOV; MTCW 1,
2
Robbins, Thomas Eugene 1936-
See Robbins, Tom
See also CA 81-84; CANR 29, 59, 95; CN
7; CPW; CSW; DA3; DAM NOV, POP;
MTCW 1, 2
Robbins, Tom .... **CLC 9, 32, 64**
See Robbins, Thomas Eugene
See also AAYA 32; AMWS 10; BEST 90:3;
BPFB 3; DLBY 1980; MTCW 2
Robbins, Trina 1938- .... **CLC 21**
See also CA 128
Roberts, Charles G(eorge) D(ouglas)
1860-1943 .... **TCLC 8**
See also CA 105; 188; CLR 33; CWRI 5;
DLB 92; RGEL 2; RGSF 2; SATA 88;
SATA-Brief 29
Roberts, Elizabeth Madox
1886-1941 .... **TCLC 68**
See also CA 111; 166; CLR 100; CWRI 5;
DLB 9, 54, 102; RGAL 4; RHW; SATA
33; SATA-Brief 27; WCH
Roberts, Kate 1891-1985 .... **CLC 15**
See also CA 107; 116
Roberts, Keith (John Kingston)
1935-2000 .... **CLC 14**
See also BRWS 10; CA 25-28R; CANR 46;
DLB 261; SFW 4
Roberts, Kenneth (Lewis)
1885-1957 .... **TCLC 23**
See also CA 109; 199; DLB 9; RGAL 4;
RHW
Roberts, Michele (Brigitte) 1949- .... **CLC 48,**
178
See also CA 115; CANR 58, 120; CN 7;
DLB 231; FW
Robertson, Ellis
See Ellison, Harlan (Jay); Silverberg, Robert
Robertson, Thomas William
1829-1871 .... **NCLC 35**
See Robertson, Tom
See also DAM DRAM
Robertson, Tom
See Robertson, Thomas William
See also RGEL 2
Robeson, Kenneth
See Dent, Lester
Robinson, Edwin Arlington
1869-1935 .... **PC 1, 35; TCLC 5, 101**
See also AMW; CA 104; 133; CDALB
1865-1917; DA; DAC; DAM MST,
POET; DLB 54; EWL 3; EXPP; MTCW
1, 2; PAB; PFS 4; RGAL 4; WP
Robinson, Henry Crabb
1775-1867 .... **NCLC 15**
See also DLB 107
Robinson, Jill 1936- .... **CLC 10**
See also CA 102; CANR 120; INT CA-102
Robinson, Kim Stanley 1952- .... **CLC 34**
See also AAYA 26; CA 126; CANR 113;
CN 7; SATA 109; SCFW 2; SFW 4
Robinson, Lloyd
See Silverberg, Robert

Robinson, Marilynne 1944- ...... **CLC 25, 180**
See also CA 116; CANR 80; CN 7; DLB
206
Robinson, Mary 1758-1800 .... **NCLC 142**
See also DLB 158; FW
Robinson, Smokey .... **CLC 21**
See Robinson, William, Jr.
Robinson, William, Jr. 1940-
See Robinson, Smokey
See also CA 116
Robison, Mary 1949- .... **CLC 42, 98**
See also CA 113; 116; CANR 87; CN 7;
DLB 130; INT CA-116; RGSF 2
Rochester
See Wilmot, John
See also RGEL 2
Rod, Edouard 1857-1910 .... **TCLC 52**
Roddenberry, Eugene Wesley 1921-1991
See Roddenberry, Gene
See also CA 110; 135; CANR 37; SATA 45;
SATA-Obit 69
Roddenberry, Gene .... **CLC 17**
See Roddenberry, Eugene Wesley
See also AAYA 5; SATA-Obit 69
Rodgers, Mary 1931- .... **CLC 12**
See also BYA 5; CA 49-52; CANR 8, 55,
90; CLR 20; CWRI 5; INT CANR-8;
JRDA; MAICYA 1, 2; SATA 8, 130
Rodgers, W(illiam) R(obert)
1909-1969 .... **CLC 7**
See also CA 85-88; DLB 20; RGEL 2
Rodman, Eric
See Silverberg, Robert
Rodman, Howard 1920(?)-1985 .... **CLC 65**
See also CA 118
Rodman, Maia
See Wojciechowska, Maia (Teresa)
Rodo, Jose Enrique 1871(?)-1917 .... **HLCS 2**
See also CA 178; EWL 3; HW 2; LAW
Rodolph, Utto
See Ouologuem, Yambo
Rodriguez, Claudio 1934-1999 .... **CLC 10**
See also CA 188; DLB 134
Rodriguez, Richard 1944- .... **CLC 155; HLC**
2
See also AMWS 14; CA 110; CANR 66,
116; DAM MULT; DLB 82, 256; HW 1,
2; LAIT 5; LLW 1; NCFS 3; WLIT 1
Roelvaag, O(le) E(dvart) 1876-1931
See Rolvaag, O(le) E(dvart)
See also CA 117; 171
Roethke, Theodore (Huebner)
1908-1963 .... **CLC 1, 3, 8, 11, 19, 46,**
101; PC 15
See also AMW; CA 81-84; CABS 2;
CDALB 1941-1968; DA3; DAM POET;
DLB 5, 206; EWL 3; EXPP; MTCW 1, 2;
PAB; PFS 3; RGAL 4; WP
Rogers, Carl R(ansom)
1902-1987 .... **TCLC 125**
See also CA 1-4R; 121; CANR 1, 18;
MTCW 1
Rogers, Samuel 1763-1855 .... **NCLC 69**
See also DLB 93; RGEL 2
Rogers, Thomas Hunton 1927- .... **CLC 57**
See also CA 89-92; INT CA-89-92
Rogers, Will(iam Penn Adair)
1879-1935 .... **NNAL; TCLC 8, 71**
See also CA 105; 144; DA3; DAM MULT;
DLB 11; MTCW 2
Rogin, Gilbert 1929- .... **CLC 18**
See also CA 65-68; CANR 15
Rohan, Koda
See Koda Shigeyuki
Rohlfs, Anna Katharine Green
See Green, Anna Katharine
Rohmer, Eric .... **CLC 16**
See Scherer, Jean-Marie Maurice

Sheldon, Alice Hastings Bradley
1915(?)-1987
See Tiptree, James, Jr.
See also CA 108; 122; CANR 34; INT CA-108; MTCW 1

Sheldon, John
See Bloch, Robert (Albert)

Sheldon, Walter J(ames) 1917-1996
See Queen, Ellery
See also AITN 1; CA 25-28R; CANR 10

Shelley, Mary Wollstonecraft (Godwin)
1797-1851 ...... **NCLC 14, 59, 103; WLC**
See also AAYA 20; BPFB 3; BRW 3; BRWC 2; BRWS 3; BYA 5; CDBLB 1789-1832; DA; DA3; DAB; DAC; DAM MST, NOV; DLB 110, 116, 159, 178; EXPN; HGG; LAIT 1; LMFS 1, 2; NFS 1; RGEL 2; SATA 29; SCFW; SFW 4; TEA; WLIT 3

Shelley, Percy Bysshe 1792-1822 .. **NCLC 18, 93, 143; PC 14; WLC**
See also BRW 4; BRWR 1; CDBLB 1789-1832; DA; DA3; DAB; DAC; DAM MST, POET; DLB 96, 110, 158; EXPP; LMFS 1; PAB; PFS 2; RGEL 2; TEA; WLIT 3; WP

Shepard, Jim 1956- .... **CLC 36**
See also CA 137; CANR 59, 104; SATA 90

Shepard, Lucius 1947- .... **CLC 34**
See also CA 128; 141; CANR 81, 124; HGG; SCFW 2; SFW 4; SUFW 2

Shepard, Sam 1943- .... **CLC 4, 6, 17, 34, 41, 44, 169; DC 5**
See also AAYA 1, 58; AMWS 3; CA 69-72; CABS 3; CAD; CANR 22, 120; CD 5; DA3; DAM DRAM; DFS 3, 6, 7, 14; DLB 7, 212; EWL 3; IDFW 3, 4; MTCW 1, 2; RGAL 4

Shepherd, Michael
See Ludlum, Robert

Sherburne, Zoa (Lillian Morin)
1912-1995 .... **CLC 30**
See also AAYA 13; CA 1-4R; 176; CANR 3, 37; MAICYA 1, 2; SAAS 18; SATA 3; YAW

Sheridan, Frances 1724-1766 .... **LC 7**
See also DLB 39, 84

Sheridan, Richard Brinsley
1751-1816 .... **DC 1; NCLC 5, 91; WLC**
See also BRW 3; CDBLB 1660-1789; DA; DAB; DAC; DAM DRAM, MST; DFS 15; DLB 89; WLIT 3

Sherman, Jonathan Marc .... **CLC 55**

Sherman, Martin 1941(?)- .... **CLC 19**
See also CA 116; 123; CAD; CANR 86; CD 5; DFS 20; DLB 228; GLL 1; IDTP

Sherwin, Judith Johnson
See Johnson, Judith (Emlyn)
See also CANR 85; CP 7; CWP

Sherwood, Frances 1940- .... **CLC 81**
See also CA 146, 220; CAAE 220

Sherwood, Robert E(mmet)
1896-1955 .... **TCLC 3**
See also CA 104; 153; CANR 86; DAM DRAM; DFS 11, 15, 17; DLB 7, 26, 249; IDFW 3, 4; RGAL 4

Shestov, Lev 1866-1938 .... **TCLC 56**

Shevchenko, Taras 1814-1861 .... **NCLC 54**

Shiel, M(atthew) P(hipps)
1865-1947 .... **TCLC 8**
See Holmes, Gordon
See also CA 106; 160; DLB 153; HGG; MTCW 2; SFW 4; SUFW

Shields, Carol (Ann) 1935-2003 ...... **CLC 91, 113, 193**
See also AMWS 7; CA 81-84; 218; CANR 51, 74, 98, 133; CCA 1; CN 7; CPW; DA3; DAC; MTCW 2

Shields, David (Jonathan) 1956- ...... **CLC 97**
See also CA 124; CANR 48, 99, 112

Shiga, Naoya 1883-1971 ..... **CLC 33; SSC 23**
See Shiga Naoya
See also CA 101; 33-36R; MJW; RGWL 3

Shiga Naoya
See Shiga, Naoya
See also DLB 180; EWL 3; RGWL 3

Shilts, Randy 1951-1994 .... **CLC 85**
See also AAYA 19; CA 115; 127; 144; CANR 45; DA3; GLL 1; INT CA-127; MTCW 1

Shimazaki, Haruki 1872-1943
See Shimazaki Toson
See also CA 105; 134; CANR 84; RGWL 3

Shimazaki Toson .... **TCLC 5**
See Shimazaki, Haruki
See also DLB 180; EWL 3

Shirley, James 1596-1666 .... **DC 25; LC 96**
See also DLB 58; RGEL 2

Sholokhov, Mikhail (Aleksandrovich)
1905-1984 .... **CLC 7, 15**
See also CA 101; 112; DLB 272; EWL 3; MTCW 1, 2; RGWL 2, 3; SATA-Obit 36

Shone, Patric
See Hanley, James

Showalter, Elaine 1941- .... **CLC 169**
See also CA 57-60; CANR 58, 106; DLB 67; FW; GLL 2

Shreve, Susan
See Shreve, Susan Richards

Shreve, Susan Richards 1939- .... **CLC 23**
See also CA 49-52; CAAS 5; CANR 5, 38, 69, 100; MAICYA 1, 2; SATA 46, 95, 152; SATA-Brief 41

Shue, Larry 1946-1985 .... **CLC 52**
See also CA 145; 117; DAM DRAM; DFS 7

Shu-Jen, Chou 1881-1936
See Lu Hsun
See also CA 104

Shulman, Alix Kates 1932- .... **CLC 2, 10**
See also CA 29-32R; CANR 43; FW; SATA 7

Shuster, Joe 1914-1992 .... **CLC 21**
See also AAYA 50

Shute, Nevil .... **CLC 30**
See Norway, Nevil Shute
See also BPFB 3; DLB 255; NFS 9; RHW; SFW 4

Shuttle, Penelope (Diane) 1947- .... **CLC 7**
See also CA 93-96; CANR 39, 84, 92, 108; CP 7; CWP; DLB 14, 40

Shvarts, Elena 1948- .... **PC 50**
See also CA 147

Sidhwa, Bapsy (N.) 1938- .... **CLC 168**
See also CA 108; CANR 25, 57; CN 7; FW

Sidney, Mary 1561-1621 .... **LC 19, 39**
See Sidney Herbert, Mary

Sidney, Sir Philip 1554-1586 . **LC 19, 39; PC 32**
See also BRW 1; BRWR 2; CDBLB Before 1660; DA; DA3; DAB; DAC; DAM MST, POET; DLB 167; EXPP; PAB; RGEL 2; TEA; WP

Sidney Herbert, Mary
See Sidney, Mary
See also DLB 167

Siegel, Jerome 1914-1996 .... **CLC 21**
See Siegel, Jerry
See also CA 116; 169; 151

Siegel, Jerry
See Siegel, Jerome
See also AAYA 50

Sienkiewicz, Henryk (Adam Alexander Pius)
1846-1916 .... **TCLC 3**
See also CA 104; 134; CANR 84; EWL 3; RGSF 2; RGWL 2, 3

Sierra, Gregorio Martinez
See Martinez Sierra, Gregorio

Sierra, Maria (de la O'LeJarraga) Martinez
See Martinez Sierra, Maria (de la O'LeJarraga)

Sigal, Clancy 1926- .... **CLC 7**
See also CA 1-4R; CANR 85; CN 7

Siger of Brabant 1240(?)-1284(?) . **CMLC 69**
See also DLB 115

Sigourney, Lydia H.
See Sigourney, Lydia Howard (Huntley)
See also DLB 73, 183

Sigourney, Lydia Howard (Huntley)
1791-1865 .... **NCLC 21, 87**
See Sigourney, Lydia H.; Sigourney, Lydia Huntley
See also DLB 1

Sigourney, Lydia Huntley
See Sigourney, Lydia Howard (Huntley)
See also DLB 42, 239, 243

Siguenza y Gongora, Carlos de
1645-1700 .... **HLCS 2; LC 8**
See also LAW

Sigurjonsson, Johann
See Sigurjonsson, Johann

Sigurjonsson, Johann 1880-1919 ... **TCLC 27**
See also CA 170; DLB 293; EWL 3

Sikelianos, Angelos 1884-1951 .... **PC 29; TCLC 39**
See also EWL 3; RGWL 2, 3

Silkin, Jon 1930-1997 .... **CLC 2, 6, 43**
See also CA 5-8R; CAAS 5; CANR 89; CP 7; DLB 27

Silko, Leslie (Marmon) 1948- .... **CLC 23, 74, 114; NNAL; SSC 37, 66; WLCS**
See also AAYA 14; AMWS 4; ANW; BYA 12; CA 115; 122; CANR 45, 65, 118; CN 7; CP 7; CPW; CWP; DA; DA3; DAC; DAM MST, MULT, POP; DLB 143, 175, 256, 275; EWL 3; EXPP; EXPS; LAIT 4; MTCW 2; NFS 4; PFS 9, 16; RGAL 4; RGSF 2; SSFS 4, 8, 10, 11

Sillanpaa, Frans Eemil 1888-1964 ... **CLC 19**
See also CA 129; 93-96; EWL 3; MTCW 1

Sillitoe, Alan 1928- .. **CLC 1, 3, 6, 10, 19, 57, 148**
See also AITN 1; BRWS 5; CA 9-12R, 191; CAAE 191; CAAS 2; CANR 8, 26, 55; CDBLB 1960 to Present; CN 7; DLB 14, 139; EWL 3; MTCW 1, 2; RGEL 2; RGSF 2; SATA 61

Silone, Ignazio 1900-1978 .... **CLC 4**
See also CA 25-28; 81-84; CANR 34; CAP 2; DLB 264; EW 12; EWL 3; MTCW 1; RGSF 2; RGWL 2, 3

Silone, Ignazione
See Silone, Ignazio

Silver, Joan Micklin 1935- .... **CLC 20**
See also CA 114; 121; INT CA-121

Silver, Nicholas
See Faust, Frederick (Schiller)
See also TCWW 2

Silverberg, Robert 1935- .... **CLC 7, 140**
See also AAYA 24; BPFB 3; BYA 7, 9; CA 1-4R, 186; CAAE 186; CAAS 3; CANR 1, 20, 36, 85; CLR 59; CN 7; CPW; DAM POP; DLB 8; INT CANR-20; MAICYA 1, 2; MTCW 1, 2; SATA 13, 91; SATA-Essay 104; SCFW 2; SFW 4; SUFW 2

Silverstein, Alvin 1933- .... **CLC 17**
See also CA 49-52; CANR 2; CLR 25; JRDA; MAICYA 1, 2; SATA 8, 69, 124

Silverstein, Shel(don Allan)
1932-1999 .... **PC 49**
See also AAYA 40; BW 3; CA 107; 179; CANR 47, 74, 81; CLR 5, 96; CWRI 5; JRDA; MAICYA 1, 2; MTCW 2; SATA 33, 92; SATA-Brief 27; SATA-Obit 116

Stephens, James 1882(?)-1950 .... **SSC 50; TCLC 4**
See also CA 104; 192; DLB 19, 153, 162; EWL 3; FANT; RGEL 2; SUFW

Stephens, Reed
See Donaldson, Stephen R(eeder)

Steptoe, Lydia
See Barnes, Djuna
See also GLL 1

Sterchi, Beat 1949- .... **CLC 65**
See also CA 203

Sterling, Brett
See Bradbury, Ray (Douglas); Hamilton, Edmond

Sterling, Bruce 1954- .... **CLC 72**
See also CA 119; CANR 44, 135; SCFW 2; SFW 4

Sterling, George 1869-1926 .... **TCLC 20**
See also CA 117; 165; DLB 54

Stern, Gerald 1925- .... **CLC 40, 100**
See also AMWS 9; CA 81-84; CANR 28, 94; CP 7; DLB 105; RGAL 4

Stern, Richard (Gustave) 1928- ... **CLC 4, 39**
See also CA 1-4R; CANR 1, 25, 52, 120; CN 7; DLB 218; DLBY 1987; INT CANR-25

Sternberg, Josef von 1894-1969 .... **CLC 20**
See also CA 81-84

Sterne, Laurence 1713-1768 .... **LC 2, 48; WLC**
See also BRW 3; BRWC 1; CDBLB 1660-1789; DA; DAB; DAC; DAM MST, NOV; DLB 39; RGEL 2; TEA

Sternheim, (William Adolf) Carl
1878-1942 .... **TCLC 8**
See also CA 105; 193; DLB 56, 118; EWL 3; RGWL 2, 3

Stevens, Mark 1951- .... **CLC 34**
See also CA 122

Stevens, Wallace 1879-1955 . **PC 6; TCLC 3, 12, 45; WLC**
See also AMW; AMWR 1; CA 104; 124; CDALB 1929-1941; DA; DA3; DAB; DAC; DAM MST, POET; DLB 54; EWL 3; EXPP; MTCW 1, 2; PAB; PFS 13, 16; RGAL 4; TUS; WP

Stevenson, Anne (Katharine) 1933- .. **CLC 7, 33**
See also BRWS 6; CA 17-20R; CAAS 9; CANR 9, 33, 123; CP 7; CWP; DLB 40; MTCW 1; RHW

Stevenson, Robert Louis (Balfour)
1850-1894 ...... **NCLC 5, 14, 63; SSC 11, 51; WLC**
See also AAYA 24; BPFB 3; BRW 5; BRWC 1; BRWR 1; BYA 1, 2, 4, 13; CD-BLB 1890-1914; CLR 10, 11; DA; DA3; DAB; DAC; DAM MST, NOV; DLB 18, 57, 141, 156, 174; DLBD 13; HGG; JRDA; LAIT 1, 3; MAICYA 1, 2; NFS 11, 20; RGEL 2; RGSF 2; SATA 100; SUFW; TEA; WCH; WLIT 4; WYA; YABC 2; YAW

Stewart, J(ohn) I(nnes) M(ackintosh)
1906-1994 .... **CLC 7, 14, 32**
See Innes, Michael
See also CA 85-88; 147; CAAS 3; CANR 47; CMW 4; MTCW 1, 2

Stewart, Mary (Florence Elinor)
1916- .... **CLC 7, 35, 117**
See also AAYA 29; BPFB 3; CA 1-4R; CANR 1, 59, 130; CMW 4; CPW; DAB; FANT; RHW; SATA 12; YAW

Stewart, Mary Rainbow
See Stewart, Mary (Florence Elinor)

Stifle, June
See Campbell, Maria

Stifter, Adalbert 1805-1868 .. **NCLC 41; SSC 28**
See also CDWLB 2; DLB 133; RGSF 2; RGWL 2, 3

Still, James 1906-2001 .... **CLC 49**
See also CA 65-68; 195; CAAS 17; CANR 10, 26; CSW; DLB 9; DLBY 01; SATA 29; SATA-Obit 127

Sting 1951-
See Sumner, Gordon Matthew
See also CA 167

Stirling, Arthur
See Sinclair, Upton (Beall)

Stitt, Milan 1941- .... **CLC 29**
See also CA 69-72

Stockton, Francis Richard 1834-1902
See Stockton, Frank R.
See also CA 108; 137; MAICYA 1, 2; SATA 44; SFW 4

Stockton, Frank R. .... **TCLC 47**
See Stockton, Francis Richard
See also BYA 4, 13; DLB 42, 74; DLBD 13; EXPS; SATA-Brief 32; SSFS 3; SUFW; WCH

Stoddard, Charles
See Kuttner, Henry

Stoker, Abraham 1847-1912
See Stoker, Bram
See also CA 105; 150; DA; DA3; DAC; DAM MST, NOV; HGG; SATA 29

Stoker, Bram . **SSC 62; TCLC 8, 144; WLC**
See Stoker, Abraham
See also AAYA 23; BPFB 3; BRWS 3; BYA 5; CDBLB 1890-1914; DAB; DLB 304; LATS 1:1; NFS 18; RGEL 2; SUFW; TEA; WLIT 4

Stolz, Mary (Slattery) 1920- .... **CLC 12**
See also AAYA 8; AITN 1; CA 5-8R; CANR 13, 41, 112; JRDA; MAICYA 1, 2; SAAS 3; SATA 10, 71, 133; YAW

Stone, Irving 1903-1989 .... **CLC 7**
See also AITN 1; BPFB 3; CA 1-4R; 129; CAAS 3; CANR 1, 23; CPW; DA3; DAM POP; INT CANR-23; MTCW 1, 2; RHW; SATA 3; SATA-Obit 64

Stone, Oliver (William) 1946- .... **CLC 73**
See also AAYA 15; CA 110; CANR 55, 125

Stone, Robert (Anthony) 1937- ... **CLC 5, 23, 42, 175**
See also AMWS 5; BPFB 3; CA 85-88; CANR 23, 66, 95; CN 7; DLB 152; EWL 3; INT CANR-23; MTCW 1

Stone, Ruth 1915- .... **PC 53**
See also CA 45-48; CANR 2, 91; CP 7; CSW; DLB 105; PFS 19

Stone, Zachary
See Follett, Ken(neth Martin)

Stoppard, Tom 1937- ... **CLC 1, 3, 4, 5, 8, 15, 29, 34, 63, 91; DC 6; WLC**
See also BRWC 1; BRWR 2; BRWS 1; CA 81-84; CANR 39, 67, 125; CBD; CD 5; CDBLB 1960 to Present; DA; DA3; DAB; DAC; DAM DRAM, MST; DFS 2, 5, 8, 11, 13, 16; DLB 13, 233; DLBY 1985; EWL 3; LATS 1:2; MTCW 1, 2; RGEL 2; TEA; WLIT 4

Storey, David (Malcolm) 1933- . **CLC 2, 4, 5, 8**
See also BRWS 1; CA 81-84; CANR 36; CBD; CD 5; CN 7; DAM DRAM; DLB 13, 14, 207, 245; EWL 3; MTCW 1; RGEL 2

Storm, Hyemeyohsts 1935- ... **CLC 3; NNAL**
See also CA 81-84; CANR 45; DAM MULT

Storm, (Hans) Theodor (Woldsen)
1817-1888 .... **NCLC 1; SSC 27**
See also CDWLB 2; DLB 129; EW; RGSF 2; RGWL 2, 3

Storni, Alfonsina 1892-1938 . **HLC 2; PC 33; TCLC 5**
See also CA 104; 131; DAM MULT; DLB 283; HW 1; LAW

Stoughton, William 1631-1701 .... **LC 38**
See also DLB 24

Stout, Rex (Todhunter) 1886-1975 ..... **CLC 3**
See also AITN 2; BPFB 3; CA 61-64; CANR 71; CMW 4; DLB 306; MSW; RGAL 4

Stow, (Julian) Randolph 1935- ... **CLC 23, 48**
See also CA 13-16R; CANR 33; CN 7; DLB 260; MTCW 1; RGEL 2

Stowe, Harriet (Elizabeth) Beecher
1811-1896 .... **NCLC 3, 50, 133; WLC**
See also AAYA 53; AMWS 1; CDALB 1865-1917; DA; DA3; DAB; DAC; DAM MST, NOV; DLB 1, 12, 42, 74, 189, 239, 243; EXPN; JRDA; LAIT 2; MAICYA 1, 2; NFS 6; RGAL 4; TUS; YABC 1

Strabo c. 64B.C.-c. 25 .... **CMLC 37**
See also DLB 176

Strachey, (Giles) Lytton
1880-1932 .... **TCLC 12**
See also BRWS 2; CA 110; 178; DLB 149; DLBD 10; EWL 3; MTCW 2; NCFS 4

Stramm, August 1874-1915 .... **PC 50**
See also CA 195; EWL 3

Strand, Mark 1934- .. **CLC 6, 18, 41, 71; PC 63**
See also AMWS 4; CA 21-24R; CANR 40, 65, 100; CP 7; DAM POET; DLB 5; EWL 3; PAB; PFS 9, 18; RGAL 4; SATA 41

Stratton-Porter, Gene(va Grace) 1863-1924
See Porter, Gene(va Grace) Stratton
See also ANW; CA 137; CLR 87; DLB 221; DLBD 14; MAICYA 1, 2; SATA 15

Straub, Peter (Francis) 1943- ... **CLC 28, 107**
See also BEST 89:1; BPFB 3; CA 85-88; CANR 28, 65, 109; CPW; DAM POP; DLBY 1984; HGG; MTCW 1, 2; SUFW 2

Strauss, Botho 1944- .... **CLC 22**
See also CA 157; CWW 2; DLB 124

Strauss, Leo 1899-1973 .... **TCLC 141**
See also CA 101; 45-48; CANR 122

Streatfeild, (Mary) Noel
1897(?)-1986 .... **CLC 21**
See also CA 81-84; 120; CANR 31; CLR 17, 83; CWRI 5; DLB 160; MAICYA 1, 2; SATA 20; SATA-Obit 48

Stribling, T(homas) S(igismund)
1881-1965 .... **CLC 23**
See also CA 189; 107; CMW 4; DLB 9; RGAL 4

Strindberg, (Johan) August
1849-1912 ... **DC 18; TCLC 1, 8, 21, 47; WLC**
See also CA 104; 135; DA; DA3; DAB; DAC; DAM DRAM, MST; DFS 4, 9; DLB 259; EW 7; EWL 3; IDTP; LMFS 2; MTCW 2; RGWL 2, 3; TWA

Stringer, Arthur 1874-1950 .... **TCLC 37**
See also CA 161; DLB 92

Stringer, David
See Roberts, Keith (John Kingston)

Stroheim, Erich von 1885-1957 ..... **TCLC 71**

Strugatskii, Arkadii (Natanovich)
1925-1991 .... **CLC 27**
See Strugatsky, Arkadii Natanovich
See also CA 106; 135; SFW 4

Strugatskii, Boris (Natanovich)
1933- .... **CLC 27**
See Strugatsky, Boris (Natanovich)
See also CA 106; SFW 4

Strugatsky, Arkadii Natanovich
See Strugatskii, Arkadii (Natanovich)
See also DLB 302

Author Index

Tolstoy, Count Leo
See Tolstoy, Leo (Nikolaevich)
Tomalin, Claire 1933- .... **CLC 166**
See also CA 89-92; CANR 52, 88; DLB
155
Tomasi di Lampedusa, Giuseppe 1896-1957
See Lampedusa, Giuseppe (Tomasi) di
See also CA 111; DLB 177; EWL 3
Tomlin, Lily .... **CLC 17**
See Tomlin, Mary Jean
Tomlin, Mary Jean 1939(?)-
See Tomlin, Lily
See also CA 117
Tomline, F. Latour
See Gilbert, W(illiam) S(chwenck)
Tomlinson, (Alfred) Charles 1927- .... **CLC 2,
4, 6, 13, 45; PC 17**
See also CA 5-8R; CANR 33; CP 7; DAM
POET; DLB 40
Tomlinson, H(enry) M(ajor)
1873-1958 .... **TCLC 71**
See also CA 118; 161; DLB 36, 100, 195
Tonna, Charlotte Elizabeth
1790-1846 .... **NCLC 135**
See also DLB 163
Tonson, Jacob fl. 1655(?)-1736 .... **LC 86**
See also DLB 170
Toole, John Kennedy 1937-1969 ..... **CLC 19,
64**
See also BPFB 3; CA 104; DLBY 1981;
MTCW 2
Toomer, Eugene
See Toomer, Jean
Toomer, Eugene Pinchback
See Toomer, Jean
Toomer, Jean 1894-1967 .. **BLC 3; CLC 1, 4,
13, 22; HR 3; PC 7; SSC 1, 45; WLCS**
See also AFAW 1, 2; AMWS 3; BW 1;
CA 85-88; CDALB 1917-1929; DA3;
DAM MULT; DLB 45, 51; EWL 3; EXPP;
EXPS; LMFS 2; MTCW 1, 2; NFS 11;
RGAL 4; RGSF 2; SSFS 5
Toomer, Nathan Jean
See Toomer, Jean
Toomer, Nathan Pinchback
See Toomer, Jean
Torley, Luke
See Blish, James (Benjamin)
Tornimparte, Alessandra
See Ginzburg, Natalia
Torre, Raoul della
See Mencken, H(enry) L(ouis)
Torrence, Ridgely 1874-1950 .... **TCLC 97**
See also DLB 54, 249
Torrey, E(dwin) Fuller 1937- .... **CLC 34**
See also CA 119; CANR 71
Torsvan, Ben Traven
See Traven, B.
Torsvan, Benno Traven
See Traven, B.
Torsvan, Berick Traven
See Traven, B.
Torsvan, Berwick Traven
See Traven, B.
Torsvan, Bruno Traven
See Traven, B.
Torsvan, Traven
See Traven, B.
Tourneur, Cyril 1575(?)-1626 .... **LC 66**
See also BRW 2; DAM DRAM; DLB 58;
RGEL 2
Tournier, Michel (Edouard) 1924- .... **CLC 6,
23, 36, 95**
See also CA 49-52; CANR 3, 36, 74; CWW
2; DLB 83; EWL 3; GFL 1789 to the
Present; MTCW 1, 2; SATA 23
Tournimparte, Alessandra
See Ginzburg, Natalia

Towers, Ivar
See Kornbluth, C(yril) M.
Towne, Robert (Burton) 1936(?)- ..... **CLC 87**
See also CA 108; DLB 44; IDFW 3, 4
Townsend, Sue .... **CLC 61**
See Townsend, Susan Lilian
See also AAYA 28; CA 119; 127; CANR
65, 107; CBD; CD 5; CPW; CWD; DAB;
DAC; DAM MST; DLB 271; INT CA-
127; SATA 55, 93; SATA-Brief 48; YAW
Townsend, Susan Lilian 1946-
See Townsend, Sue
Townshend, Pete
See Townshend, Peter (Dennis Blandford)
Townshend, Peter (Dennis Blandford)
1945- .... **CLC 17, 42**
See also CA 107
Tozzi, Federigo 1883-1920 .... **TCLC 31**
See also CA 160; CANR 110; DLB 264;
EWL 3
Tracy, Don(ald Fiske) 1905-1970(?)
See Queen, Ellery
See also CA 1-4R; 176; CANR 2
Trafford, F. G.
See Riddell, Charlotte
Traherne, Thomas 1637(?)-1674 .... **LC 99**
See also BRW 2; DLB 131; PAB; RGEL 2
Traill, Catharine Parr 1802-1899 .. **NCLC 31**
See also DLB 99
Trakl, Georg 1887-1914 .... **PC 20; TCLC 5**
See also CA 104; 165; EW 10; EWL 3;
LMFS 2; MTCW 2; RGWL 2, 3
Tranquilli, Secondino
See Silone, Ignazio
Transtroemer, Tomas Gosta
See Transtromer, Tomas (Goesta)
Transtromer, Tomas (Gosta)
See Transtromer, Tomas (Goesta)
See also CWW 2
Transtromer, Tomas (Goesta)
1931- .... **CLC 52, 65**
See Transtromer, Tomas (Gosta)
See also CA 117; 129; CAAS 17; CANR
115; DAM POET; DLB 257; EWL 3; PFS
21
Transtromer, Tomas Gosta
See Transtromer, Tomas (Goesta)
Traven, B. 1882(?)-1969 .... **CLC 8, 11**
See also CA 19-20; 25-28R; CAP 2; DLB
9, 56; EWL 3; MTCW 1; RGAL 4
Trediakovsky, Vasilii Kirillovich
1703-1769 .... **LC 68**
See also DLB 150
Treitel, Jonathan 1959- .... **CLC 70**
See also CA 210; DLB 267
Trelawny, Edward John
1792-1881 .... **NCLC 85**
See also DLB 110, 116, 144
Tremain, Rose 1943- .... **CLC 42**
See also CA 97-100; CANR 44, 95; CN 7;
DLB 14, 271; RGSF 2; RHW
Tremblay, Michel 1942- .... **CLC 29, 102**
See also CA 116; 128; CCA 1; CWW 2;
DAC; DAM MST; DLB 60; EWL 3; GLL
1; MTCW 1, 2
Trevanian .... **CLC 29**
See Whitaker, Rod(ney)
Trevor, Glen
See Hilton, James
Trevor, William .. **CLC 7, 9, 14, 25, 71, 116;
SSC 21, 58**
See Cox, William Trevor
See also BRWS 4; CBD; CD 5; CN 7; DLB
14, 139; EWL 3; LATS 1:2; MTCW 2;
RGEL 2; RGSF 2; SSFS 10
Trifonov, Iurii (Valentinovich)
See Trifonov, Yuri (Valentinovich)
See also DLB 302; RGWL 2, 3

Trifonov, Yuri (Valentinovich)
1925-1981 .... **CLC 45**
See Trifonov, Iurii (Valentinovich); Tri-
fonov, Yury Valentinovich
See also CA 126; 103; MTCW 1
Trifonov, Yury Valentinovich
See Trifonov, Yuri (Valentinovich)
See also EWL 3
Trilling, Diana (Rubin) 1905-1996 . **CLC 129**
See also CA 5-8R; 154; CANR 10, 46; INT
CANR-10; MTCW 1, 2
Trilling, Lionel 1905-1975 ..... **CLC 9, 11, 24;
SSC 75**
See also AMWS 3; CA 9-12R; 61-64;
CANR 10, 105; DLB 28, 63; EWL 3; INT
CANR-10; MTCW 1, 2; RGAL 4; TUS
Trimball, W. H.
See Mencken, H(enry) L(ouis)
Tristan
See Gomez de la Serna, Ramon
Tristram
See Housman, A(lfred) E(dward)
Trogdon, William (Lewis) 1939-
See Heat-Moon, William Least
See also CA 115; 119; CANR 47, 89; CPW;
INT CA-119
Trollope, Anthony 1815-1882 .... **NCLC 6, 33,
101; SSC 28; WLC**
See also BRW 5; CDBLB 1832-1890; DA;
DA3; DAB; DAC; DAM MST, NOV;
DLB 21, 57, 159; RGEL 2; RGSF 2;
SATA 22
Trollope, Frances 1779-1863 .... **NCLC 30**
See also DLB 21, 166
Trollope, Joanna 1943- .... **CLC 186**
See also CA 101; CANR 58, 95; CPW;
DLB 207; RHW
Trotsky, Leon 1879-1940 .... **TCLC 22**
See also CA 118; 167
Trotter (Cockburn), Catharine
1679-1749 .... **LC 8**
See also DLB 84, 252
Trotter, Wilfred 1872-1939 .... **TCLC 97**
Trout, Kilgore
See Farmer, Philip Jose
Trow, George W. S. 1943- .... **CLC 52**
See also CA 126; CANR 91
Troyat, Henri 1911- .... **CLC 23**
See also CA 45-48; CANR 2, 33, 67, 117;
GFL 1789 to the Present; MTCW 1
Trudeau, G(arretson) B(eekman) 1948-
See Trudeau, Garry B.
See also AAYA 60; CA 81-84; CANR 31;
SATA 35
Trudeau, Garry B. .... **CLC 12**
See Trudeau, G(arretson) B(eekman)
See also AAYA 10; AITN 2
Truffaut, Francois 1932-1984 ... **CLC 20, 101**
See also CA 81-84; 113; CANR 34
Trumbo, Dalton 1905-1976 .... **CLC 19**
See also CA 21-24R; 69-72; CANR 10;
DLB 26; IDFW 3, 4; YAW
Trumbull, John 1750-1831 .... **NCLC 30**
See also DLB 31; RGAL 4
Trundlett, Helen B.
See Eliot, T(homas) S(tearns)
Truth, Sojourner 1797(?)-1883 ...... **NCLC 94**
See also DLB 239; FW; LAIT 2
Tryon, Thomas 1926-1991 .... **CLC 3, 11**
See also AITN 1; BPFB 3; CA 29-32R; 135;
CANR 32, 77; CPW; DA3; DAM POP;
HGG; MTCW 1
Tryon, Tom
See Tryon, Thomas
Ts'ao Hsueh-ch'in 1715(?)-1763 .... **LC 1**
Tsushima, Shuji 1909-1948
See Dazai Osamu
See also CA 107

Vanbrugh, Sir John 1664-1726 .... **LC 21**
See also BRW 2; DAM DRAM; DLB 80;
IDTP; RGEL 2
Van Campen, Karl
See Campbell, John W(ood, Jr.)
Vance, Gerald
See Silverberg, Robert
Vance, Jack .... **CLC 35**
See Vance, John Holbrook
See also DLB 8; FANT; SCFW 2; SFW 4;
SUFW 1, 2
Vance, John Holbrook 1916-
See Queen, Ellery; Vance, Jack
See also CA 29-32R; CANR 17, 65; CMW
4; MTCW 1
**Van Den Bogarde, Derek Jules Gaspard
Ulric Niven** 1921-1999 .... **CLC 14**
See Bogarde, Dirk
See also CA 77-80; 179
Vandenburgh, Jane .... **CLC 59**
See also CA 168
Vanderhaeghe, Guy 1951- .... **CLC 41**
See also BPFB 3; CA 113; CANR 72
van der Post, Laurens (Jan)
1906-1996 .... **CLC 5**
See also AFW; CA 5-8R; 155; CANR 35;
CN 7; DLB 204; RGEL 2
van de Wetering, Janwillem 1931- ... **CLC 47**
See also CA 49-52; CANR 4, 62, 90; CMW
4
Van Dine, S. S. .... **TCLC 23**
See Wright, Willard Huntington
See also DLB 306; MSW
Van Doren, Carl (Clinton)
1885-1950 .... **TCLC 18**
See also CA 111; 168
Van Doren, Mark 1894-1972 .... **CLC 6, 10**
See also CA 1-4R; 37-40R; CANR 3; DLB
45, 284; MTCW 1, 2; RGAL 4
Van Druten, John (William)
1901-1957 .... **TCLC 2**
See also CA 104; 161; DLB 10; RGAL 4
Van Duyn, Mona (Jane) 1921- ...... **CLC 3, 7,
63, 116**
See also CA 9-12R; CANR 7, 38, 60, 116;
CP 7; CWP; DAM POET; DLB 5; PFS
20
Van Dyne, Edith
See Baum, L(yman) Frank
van Itallie, Jean-Claude 1936- .... **CLC 3**
See also CA 45-48; CAAS 2; CAD; CANR
1, 48; CD 5; DLB 7
Van Loot, Cornelius Obenchain
See Roberts, Kenneth (Lewis)
van Ostaijen, Paul 1896-1928 .... **TCLC 33**
See also CA 163
Van Peebles, Melvin 1932- .... **CLC 2, 20**
See also BW 2, 3; CA 85-88; CANR 27,
67, 82; DAM MULT
van Schendel, Arthur(-Francois-Emile)
1874-1946 .... **TCLC 56**
See also EWL 3
Vansittart, Peter 1920- .... **CLC 42**
See also CA 1-4R; CANR 3, 49, 90; CN 7;
RHW
Van Vechten, Carl 1880-1964 ... **CLC 33; HR
3**
See also AMWS 2; CA 183; 89-92; DLB 4,
9, 51; RGAL 4
van Vogt, A(lfred) E(lton) 1912-2000 . **CLC 1**
See also BPFB 3; BYA 13, 14; CA 21-24R;
190; CANR 28; DLB 8, 251; SATA 14;
SATA-Obit 124; SCFW; SFW 4
Vara, Madeleine
See Jackson, Laura (Riding)
Varda, Agnes 1928- .... **CLC 16**
See also CA 116; 122

Vargas Llosa, (Jorge) Mario (Pedro)
1939- ... **CLC 3, 6, 9, 10, 15, 31, 42, 85,
181; HLC 2**
See Llosa, (Jorge) Mario (Pedro) Vargas
See also BPFB 3; CA 73-76; CANR 18, 32,
42, 67, 116; CDWLB 3; CWW 2; DA;
DA3; DAB; DAC; DAM MST, MULT,
NOV; DLB 145; DNFS 2; EWL 3; HW 1,
2; LAIT 5; LATS 1:2; LAW; LAWS 1;
MTCW 1, 2; RGWL 2; SSFS 14; TWA;
WLIT 1
Varnhagen von Ense, Rahel
1771-1833 .... **NCLC 130**
See also DLB 90
Vasari, Giorgio 1511-1574 .... **LC 114**
Vasiliu, George
See Bacovia, George
Vasiliu, Gheorghe
See Bacovia, George
See also CA 123; 189
Vassa, Gustavus
See Equiano, Olaudah
Vassilikos, Vassilis 1933- .... **CLC 4, 8**
See also CA 81-84; CANR 75; EWL 3
Vaughan, Henry 1621-1695 .... **LC 27**
See also BRW 2; DLB 131; PAB; RGEL 2
Vaughn, Stephanie .... **CLC 62**
Vazov, Ivan (Minchov) 1850-1921 . **TCLC 25**
See also CA 121; 167; CDWLB 4; DLB
147
Veblen, Thorstein B(unde)
1857-1929 .... **TCLC 31**
See also AMWS 1; CA 115; 165; DLB 246
Vega, Lope de 1562-1635 .... **HLCS 2; LC 23**
See also EW 2; RGWL 2, 3
Vendler, Helen (Hennessy) 1933- ... **CLC 138**
See also CA 41-44R; CANR 25, 72; MTCW
1, 2
Venison, Alfred
See Pound, Ezra (Weston Loomis)
Ventsel, Elena Sergeevna 1907-2002
See Grekova, I.
See also CA 154
Verdi, Marie de
See Mencken, H(enry) L(ouis)
Verdu, Matilde
See Cela, Camilo Jose
Verga, Giovanni (Carmelo)
1840-1922 .... **SSC 21; TCLC 3**
See also CA 104; 123; CANR 101; EW 7;
EWL 3; RGSF 2; RGWL 2, 3
Vergil 70B.C.-19B.C. ... **CMLC 9, 40; PC 12;
WLCS**
See Virgil
See also AW 2; DA; DA3; DAB; DAC;
DAM MST, POET; EFS 1; LMFS 1
Vergil, Polydore c. 1470-1555 .... **LC 108**
See also DLB 132
Verhaeren, Emile (Adolphe Gustave)
1855-1916 .... **TCLC 12**
See also CA 109; EWL 3; GFL 1789 to the
Present
Verlaine, Paul (Marie) 1844-1896 .. **NCLC 2,
51; PC 2, 32**
See also DAM POET; DLB 217; EW 7;
GFL 1789 to the Present; LMFS 2; RGWL
2, 3; TWA
Verne, Jules (Gabriel) 1828-1905 ... **TCLC 6,
52**
See also AAYA 16; BYA 4; CA 110; 131;
CLR 88; DA3; DLB 123; GFL 1789 to
the Present; JRDA; LAIT 2; LMFS 2;
MAICYA 1, 2; RGWL 2, 3; SATA 21;
SCFW; SFW 4; TWA; WCH
Verus, Marcus Annius
See Aurelius, Marcus
Very, Jones 1813-1880 .... **NCLC 9**
See also DLB 1, 243; RGAL 4

Vesaas, Tarjei 1897-1970 .... **CLC 48**
See also CA 190; 29-32R; DLB 297; EW
11; EWL 3; RGWL 3
Vialis, Gaston
See Simenon, Georges (Jacques Christian)
Vian, Boris 1920-1959(?) .... **TCLC 9**
See also CA 106; 164; CANR 111; DLB
72; EWL 3; GFL 1789 to the Present;
MTCW 2; RGWL 2, 3
Viaud, (Louis Marie) Julien 1850-1923
See Loti, Pierre
See also CA 107
Vicar, Henry
See Felsen, Henry Gregor
Vicente, Gil 1465-c. 1536 .... **LC 99**
See also DLB 287; RGWL 2, 3
Vicker, Angus
See Felsen, Henry Gregor
Vidal, (Eugene Luther) Gore 1925- .. **CLC 2,
4, 6, 8, 10, 22, 33, 72, 142**
See Box, Edgar
See also AITN 1; AMWS 4; BEST 90:2;
BPFB 3; CA 5-8R; CAD; CANR 13, 45,
65, 100, 132; CD 5; CDALBS; CN 7;
CPW; DA3; DAM NOV, POP; DFS 2;
DLB 6, 152; EWL 3; INT CANR-13;
MTCW 1, 2; RGAL 4; RHW; TUS
Viereck, Peter (Robert Edwin)
1916- .... **CLC 4; PC 27**
See also CA 1-4R; CANR 1, 47; CP 7; DLB
5; PFS 9, 14
Vigny, Alfred (Victor) de
1797-1863 .... **NCLC 7, 102; PC 26**
See also DAM POET; DLB 119, 192, 217;
EW 5; GFL 1789 to the Present; RGWL
2, 3
Vilakazi, Benedict Wallet
1906-1947 .... **TCLC 37**
See also CA 168
Villa, Jose Garcia 1914-1997 .... **AAL; PC 22**
See also CA 25-28R; CANR 12, 118; EWL
3; EXPP
Villa, Jose Garcia 1914-1997
See Villa, Jose Garcia
Villa, Jose Garcia 1914-1997 .... **AAL; PC 22**
See also CA 25-28R; CANR 12, 118; EWL
3; EXPP
Villard, Oswald Garrison
1872-1949 .... **TCLC 160**
See also CA 113, 162; DLB 25, 91
Villaurrutia, Xavier 1903-1950 ...... **TCLC 80**
See also CA 192; EWL 3; HW 1; LAW
Villaverde, Cirilo 1812-1894 .... **NCLC 121**
See also LAW
Villehardouin, Geoffroi de
1150(?)-1218(?) .... **CMLC 38**
Villiers, George 1628-1687 .... **LC 107**
See also DLB 80; RGEL 2
**Villiers de l'Isle Adam, Jean Marie Mathias
Philippe Auguste** 1838-1889 ... **NCLC 3;
SSC 14**
See also DLB 123, 192; GFL 1789 to the
Present; RGSF 2
Villon, Francois 1431-1463(?) . **LC 62; PC 13**
See also DLB 208; EW 2; RGWL 2, 3;
TWA
Vine, Barbara .... **CLC 50**
See Rendell, Ruth (Barbara)
See also BEST 90:4
Vinge, Joan (Carol) D(ennison)
1948- .... **CLC 30; SSC 24**
See also AAYA 32; BPFB 3; CA 93-96;
CANR 72; SATA 36, 113; SFW 4; YAW
Viola, Herman J(oseph) 1938- .... **CLC 70**
See also CA 61-64; CANR 8, 23, 48, 91;
SATA 126
Violis, G.
See Simenon, Georges (Jacques Christian)

Viramontes, Helena Maria 1954- .... **HLCS 2**
See also CA 159; DLB 122; HW 2; LLW 1

Virgil
See Vergil
See also CDWLB 1; DLB 211; LAIT 1; RGWL 2, 3; WP

Visconti, Luchino 1906-1976 .... **CLC 16**
See also CA 81-84; 65-68; CANR 39

Vitry, Jacques de
See Jacques de Vitry

Vittorini, Elio 1908-1966 .... **CLC 6, 9, 14**
See also CA 133; 25-28R; DLB 264; EW 12; EWL 3; RGWL 2, 3

Vivekananda, Swami 1863-1902 .... **TCLC 88**

Vizenor, Gerald Robert 1934- .... **CLC 103; NNAL**
See also CA 13-16R, 205; CAAE 205; CAAS 22; CANR 5, 21, 44, 67; DAM MULT; DLB 175, 227; MTCW 2; TCWW 2

Vizinczey, Stephen 1933- .... **CLC 40**
See also CA 128; CCA 1; INT CA-128

Vliet, R(ussell) G(ordon)
1929-1984 .... **CLC 22**
See also CA 37-40R; 112; CANR 18

Vogau, Boris Andreyevich 1894-1938
See Pilnyak, Boris
See also CA 123; 218

Vogel, Paula A(nne) 1951- ... **CLC 76; DC 19**
See also CA 108; CAD; CANR 119; CD 5; CWD; DFS 14; RGAL 4

Voigt, Cynthia 1942- .... **CLC 30**
See also AAYA 3, 30; BYA 1, 3, 6, 7, 8; CA 106; CANR 18, 37, 40, 94; CLR 13, 48; INT CANR-18; JRDA; LAIT 5; MAICYA 1, 2; MAICYAS 1; SATA 48, 79, 116; SATA-Brief 33; WYA; YAW

Voigt, Ellen Bryant 1943- .... **CLC 54**
See also CA 69-72; CANR 11, 29, 55, 115; CP 7; CSW; CWP; DLB 120

Voinovich, Vladimir (Nikolaevich)
1932- .... **CLC 10, 49, 147**
See also CA 81-84; CAAS 12; CANR 33, 67; CWW 2; DLB 302; MTCW 1

Vollmann, William T. 1959- .... **CLC 89**
See also CA 134; CANR 67, 116; CPW; DA3; DAM NOV, POP; MTCW 2

Voloshinov, V. N.
See Bakhtin, Mikhail Mikhailovich

Voltaire 1694-1778 . **LC 14, 79, 110; SSC 12; WLC**
See also BYA 13; DA; DA3; DAB; DAC; DAM DRAM, MST; EW 4; GFL Beginnings to 1789; LATS 1:1; LMFS 1; NFS 7; RGWL 2, 3; TWA

von Aschendrof, Baron Ignatz
See Ford, Ford Madox

von Chamisso, Adelbert
See Chamisso, Adelbert von

von Daeniken, Erich 1935- .... **CLC 30**
See also AITN 1; CA 37-40R; CANR 17, 44

von Daniken, Erich
See von Daeniken, Erich

von Hartmann, Eduard
1842-1906 .... **TCLC 96**

von Hayek, Friedrich August
See Hayek, F(riedrich) A(ugust von)

von Heidenstam, (Carl Gustaf) Verner
See Heidenstam, (Carl Gustaf) Verner von

von Heyse, Paul (Johann Ludwig)
See Heyse, Paul (Johann Ludwig von)

von Hofmannsthal, Hugo
See Hofmannsthal, Hugo von

von Horvath, Odon
See von Horvath, Odon

von Horvath, Odon
See von Horvath, Odon

von Horvath, Odon 1901-1938 .... **TCLC 45**
See von Horvath, Oedoen
See also CA 118; 194; DLB 85, 124; RGWL 2, 3

von Horvath, Oedoen
See von Horvath, Odon
See also CA 184

von Kleist, Heinrich
See Kleist, Heinrich von

von Liliencron, (Friedrich Adolf Axel) Detlev
See Liliencron, (Friedrich Adolf Axel) Detlev von

Vonnegut, Kurt, Jr. 1922- . **CLC 1, 2, 3, 4, 5, 8, 12, 22, 40, 60, 111; SSC 8; WLC**
See also AAYA 6, 44; AITN 1; AMWS 2; BEST 90:4; BPFB 3; BYA 3, 14; CA 1-4R; CANR 1, 25, 49, 75, 92; CDALB 1968-1988; CN 7; CPW 1; DA; DA3; DAB; DAC; DAM MST, NOV, POP; DLB 2, 8, 152; DLBD 3; DLBY 1980; EWL 3; EXPN; EXPS; LAIT 4; LMFS 2; MTCW 1, 2; NFS 3; RGAL 4; SCFW; SFW 4; SSFS 5; TUS; YAW

Von Rachen, Kurt
See Hubbard, L(afayette) Ron(ald)

von Rezzori (d'Arezzo), Gregor
See Rezzori (d'Arezzo), Gregor von

von Sternberg, Josef
See Sternberg, Josef von

Vorster, Gordon 1924- .... **CLC 34**
See also CA 133

Vosce, Trudie
See Ozick, Cynthia

Voznesensky, Andrei (Andreievich)
1933- .... **CLC 1, 15, 57**
See Voznesensky, Andrey
See also CA 89-92; CANR 37; CWW 2; DAM POET; MTCW 1

Voznesensky, Andrey
See Voznesensky, Andrei (Andreievich)
See also EWL 3

Wace, Robert c. 1100-c. 1175 .... **CMLC 55**
See also DLB 146

Waddington, Miriam 1917-2004 .... **CLC 28**
See also CA 21-24R; 225; CANR 12, 30; CCA 1; CP 7; DLB 68

Wagman, Fredrica 1937- .... **CLC 7**
See also CA 97-100; INT CA-97-100

Wagner, Linda W.
See Wagner-Martin, Linda (C.)

Wagner, Linda Welshimer
See Wagner-Martin, Linda (C.)

Wagner, Richard 1813-1883 ..... **NCLC 9, 119**
See also DLB 129; EW 6

Wagner-Martin, Linda (C.) 1936- .... **CLC 50**
See also CA 159; CANR 135

Wagoner, David (Russell) 1926- .... **CLC 3, 5, 15; PC 33**
See also AMWS 9; CA 1-4R; CAAS 3; CANR 2, 71; CN 7; CP 7; DLB 5, 256; SATA 14; TCWW 2

Wah, Fred(erick James) 1939- .... **CLC 44**
See also CA 107; 141; CP 7; DLB 60

Wahloo, Per 1926-1975 .... **CLC 7**
See also BPFB 3; CA 61-64; CANR 73; CMW 4; MSW

Wahloo, Peter
See Wahloo, Per

Wain, John (Barrington) 1925-1994 . **CLC 2, 11, 15, 46**
See also CA 5-8R; 145; CAAS 4; CANR 23, 54; CDBLB 1960 to Present; DLB 15, 27, 139, 155; EWL 3; MTCW 1, 2

Wajda, Andrzej 1926- .... **CLC 16**
See also CA 102

Wakefield, Dan 1932- .... **CLC 7**
See also CA 21-24R, 211; CAAE 211; CAAS 7; CN 7

Wakefield, Herbert Russell
1888-1965 .... **TCLC 120**
See also CA 5-8R; CANR 77; HGG; SUFW

Wakoski, Diane 1937- ...... **CLC 2, 4, 7, 9, 11, 40; PC 15**
See also CA 13-16R, 216; CAAE 216; CAAS 1; CANR 9, 60, 106; CP 7; CWP; DAM POET; DLB 5; INT CANR-9; MTCW 2

Wakoski-Sherbell, Diane
See Wakoski, Diane

Walcott, Derek (Alton) 1930- .. **BLC 3; CLC 2, 4, 9, 14, 25, 42, 67, 76, 160; DC 7; PC 46**
See also BW 2; CA 89-92; CANR 26, 47, 75, 80, 130; CBD; CD 5; CDWLB 3; CP 7; DA3; DAB; DAC; DAM MST, MULT, POET; DLB 117; DLBY 1981; DNFS 1; EFS 1; EWL 3; LMFS 2; MTCW 1, 2; PFS 6; RGEL 2; TWA; WWE 1

Waldman, Anne (Lesley) 1945- .... **CLC 7**
See also BG 3; CA 37-40R; CAAS 17; CANR 34, 69, 116; CP 7; CWP; DLB 16

Waldo, E. Hunter
See Sturgeon, Theodore (Hamilton)

Waldo, Edward Hamilton
See Sturgeon, Theodore (Hamilton)

Walker, Alice (Malsenior) 1944- .... **BLC 3; CLC 5, 6, 9, 19, 27, 46, 58, 103, 167; PC 30; SSC 5; WLCS**
See also AAYA 3, 33; AFAW 1, 2; AMWS 3; BEST 89:4; BPFB 3; BW 2, 3; CA 37-40R; CANR 9, 27, 49, 66, 82, 131; CDALB 1968-1988; CN 7; CPW; CSW; DA; DA3; DAB; DAC; DAM MST, MULT, NOV, POET, POP; DLB 6, 33, 143; EWL 3; EXPN; EXPS; FW; INT CANR-27; LAIT 3; MAWW; MTCW 1, 2; NFS 5; RGAL 4; RGSF 2; SATA 31; SSFS 2, 11; TUS; YAW

Walker, David Harry 1911-1992 ...... **CLC 14**
See also CA 1-4R; 137; CANR 1; CWRI 5; SATA 8; SATA-Obit 71

Walker, Edward Joseph 1934-2004
See Walker, Ted
See also CA 21-24R; 226; CANR 12, 28, 53; CP 7

Walker, George F. 1947- .... **CLC 44, 61**
See also CA 103; CANR 21, 43, 59; CD 5; DAB; DAC; DAM MST; DLB 60

Walker, Joseph A. 1935- .... **CLC 19**
See also BW 1, 3; CA 89-92; CAD; CANR 26; CD 5; DAM DRAM, MST; DFS 12; DLB 38

Walker, Margaret (Abigail)
1915-1998 .... **BLC; CLC 1, 6; PC 20; TCLC 129**
See also AFAW 1, 2; BW 2, 3; CA 73-76; 172; CANR 26, 54, 76; CN 7; CP 7; CSW; DAM MULT; DLB 76, 152; EXPP; FW; MTCW 1, 2; RGAL 4; RHW

Walker, Ted .... **CLC 13**
See Walker, Edward Joseph
See also DLB 40

Wallace, David Foster 1962- ... **CLC 50, 114; SSC 68**
See also AAYA 50; AMWS 10; CA 132; CANR 59, 133; DA3; MTCW 2

Wallace, Dexter
See Masters, Edgar Lee

Wallace, (Richard Horatio) Edgar
1875-1932 .... **TCLC 57**
See also CA 115; 218; CMW 4; DLB 70; MSW; RGEL 2

Wallace, Irving 1916-1990 .... **CLC 7, 13**
See also AITN 1; BPFB 3; CA 1-4R; 132; CAAS 1; CANR 1, 27; CPW; DAM NOV, POP; INT CANR-27; MTCW 1, 2

Weil, Simone (Adolphine)
1909-1943 .... **TCLC 23**
See also CA 117; 159; EW 12; EWL 3; FW; GFL 1789 to the Present; MTCW 2

Weininger, Otto 1880-1903 .... **TCLC 84**

Weinstein, Nathan
See West, Nathanael

Weinstein, Nathan von Wallenstein
See West, Nathanael

Weir, Peter (Lindsay) 1944- .... **CLC 20**
See also CA 113; 123

Weiss, Peter (Ulrich) 1916-1982 .. **CLC 3, 15, 51; TCLC 152**
See also CA 45-48; 106; CANR 3; DAM DRAM; DFS 3; DLB 69, 124; EWL 3; RGWL 2, 3

Weiss, Theodore (Russell)
1916-2003 .... **CLC 3, 8, 14**
See also CA 9-12R, 189; 216; CAAE 189; CAAS 2; CANR 46, 94; CP 7; DLB 5

Welch, (Maurice) Denton
1915-1948 .... **TCLC 22**
See also BRWS 8, 9; CA 121; 148; RGEL 2

Welch, James (Phillip) 1940-2003 ..... **CLC 6, 14, 52; NNAL; PC 62**
See also CA 85-88; 219; CANR 42, 66, 107; CN 7; CP 7; CPW; DAM MULT, POP; DLB 175, 256; LATS 1:1; RGAL 4; TCWW 2

Weldon, Fay 1931- . **CLC 6, 9, 11, 19, 36, 59, 122**
See also BRWS 4; CA 21-24R; CANR 16, 46, 63, 97; CDBLB 1960 to Present; CN 7; CPW; DAM POP; DLB 14, 194; EWL 3; FW; HGG; INT CANR-16; MTCW 1, 2; RGEL 2; RGSF 2

Wellek, Rene 1903-1995 .... **CLC 28**
See also CA 5-8R; 150; CAAS 7; CANR 8; DLB 63; EWL 3; INT CANR-8

Weller, Michael 1942- .... **CLC 10, 53**
See also CA 85-88; CAD; CD 5

Weller, Paul 1958- .... **CLC 26**

Wellershoff, Dieter 1925- .... **CLC 46**
See also CA 89-92; CANR 16, 37

Welles, (George) Orson 1915-1985 .. **CLC 20, 80**
See also AAYA 40; CA 93-96; 117

Wellman, John McDowell 1945-
See Wellman, Mac
See also CA 166; CD 5

Wellman, Mac .... **CLC 65**
See Wellman, John McDowell; Wellman, John McDowell
See also CAD; RGAL 4

Wellman, Manly Wade 1903-1986 ... **CLC 49**
See also CA 1-4R; 118; CANR 6, 16, 44; FANT; SATA 6; SATA-Obit 47; SFW 4; SUFW

Wells, Carolyn 1869(?)-1942 .... **TCLC 35**
See also CA 113; 185; CMW 4; DLB 11

Wells, H(erbert) G(eorge) 1866-1946 . **SSC 6, 70; TCLC 6, 12, 19, 133; WLC**
See also AAYA 18; BPFB 3; BRW 6; CA 110; 121; CDBLB 1914-1945; CLR 64; DA; DA3; DAB; DAC; DAM MST, NOV; DLB 34, 70, 156, 178; EWL 3; EXPS; HGG; LAIT 3; LMFS 2; MTCW 1, 2; NFS 17, 20; RGEL 2; RGSF 2; SATA 20; SCFW; SFW 4; SSFS 3; SUFW; TEA; WCH; WLIT 4; YAW

Wells, Rosemary 1943- .... **CLC 12**
See also AAYA 13; BYA 7, 8; CA 85-88; CANR 48, 120; CLR 16, 69; CWRI 5; MAICYA 1, 2; SAAS 1; SATA 18, 69, 114; YAW

Wells-Barnett, Ida B(ell)
1862-1931 .... **TCLC 125**
See also CA 182; DLB 23, 221

Welsh, Irvine 1958- .... **CLC 144**
See also CA 173; DLB 271

Welty, Eudora (Alice) 1909-2001 .. **CLC 1, 2, 5, 14, 22, 33, 105; SSC 1, 27, 51; WLC**
See also AAYA 48; AMW; AMWR 1; BPFB 3; CA 9-12R; 199; CABS 1; CANR 32, 65, 128; CDALB 1941-1968; CN 7; CSW; DA; DA3; DAB; DAC; DAM MST, NOV; DLB 2, 102, 143; DLBD 12; DLBY 1987, 2001; EWL 3; EXPS; HGG; LAIT 3; MAWW; MTCW 1, 2; NFS 13, 15; RGAL 4; RGSF 2; RHW; SSFS 2, 10; TUS

Wen I-to 1899-1946 .... **TCLC 28**
See also EWL 3

Wentworth, Robert
See Hamilton, Edmond

Werfel, Franz (Viktor) 1890-1945 ... **TCLC 8**
See also CA 104; 161; DLB 81, 124; EWL 3; RGWL 2, 3

Wergeland, Henrik Arnold
1808-1845 .... **NCLC 5**

Wersba, Barbara 1932- .... **CLC 30**
See also AAYA 2, 30; BYA 6, 12, 13; CA 29-32R, 182; CAAE 182; CANR 16, 38; CLR 3, 78; DLB 52; JRDA; MAICYA 1, 2; SAAS 2; SATA 1, 58; SATA-Essay 103; WYA; YAW

Wertmueller, Lina 1928- .... **CLC 16**
See also CA 97-100; CANR 39, 78

Wescott, Glenway 1901-1987 .. **CLC 13; SSC 35**
See also CA 13-16R; 121; CANR 23, 70; DLB 4, 9, 102; RGAL 4

Wesker, Arnold 1932- .... **CLC 3, 5, 42**
See also CA 1-4R; CAAS 7; CANR 1, 33; CBD; CD 5; CDBLB 1960 to Present; DAB; DAM DRAM; DLB 13; EWL 3; MTCW 1; RGEL 2; TEA

Wesley, John 1703-1791 .... **LC 88**
See also DLB 104

Wesley, Richard (Errol) 1945- .... **CLC 7**
See also BW 1; CA 57-60; CAD; CANR 27; CD 5; DLB 38

Wessel, Johan Herman 1742-1785 .... **LC 7**
See also DLB 300

West, Anthony (Panther)
1914-1987 .... **CLC 50**
See also CA 45-48; 124; CANR 3, 19; DLB 15

West, C. P.
See Wodehouse, P(elham) G(renville)

West, Cornel (Ronald) 1953- .... **BLCS; CLC 134**
See also CA 144; CANR 91; DLB 246

West, Delno C(loyde), Jr. 1936- .... **CLC 70**
See also CA 57-60

West, Dorothy 1907-1998 .. **HR 3; TCLC 108**
See also BW 2; CA 143; 169; DLB 76

West, (Mary) Jessamyn 1902-1984 ... **CLC 7, 17**
See also CA 9-12R; 112; CANR 27; DLB 6; DLBY 1984; MTCW 1, 2; RGAL 4; RHW; SATA-Obit 37; TCWW 2; TUS; YAW

West, Morris
See West, Morris L(anglo)
See also DLB 289

West, Morris L(anglo) 1916-1999 ..... **CLC 6, 33**
See West, Morris
See also BPFB 3; CA 5-8R; 187; CANR 24, 49, 64; CN 7; CPW; MTCW 1, 2

West, Nathanael 1903-1940 .. **SSC 16; TCLC 1, 14, 44**
See also AMW; AMWR 2; BPFB 3; CA 104; 125; CDALB 1929-1941; DA3; DLB 4, 9, 28; EWL 3; MTCW 1, 2; NFS 16; RGAL 4; TUS

West, Owen
See Koontz, Dean R(ay)

West, Paul 1930- .... **CLC 7, 14, 96**
See also CA 13-16R; CAAS 7; CANR 22, 53, 76, 89; CN 7; DLB 14; INT CANR-22; MTCW 2

West, Rebecca 1892-1983 ... **CLC 7, 9, 31, 50**
See also BPFB 3; BRWS 3; CA 5-8R; 109; CANR 19; DLB 36; DLBY 1983; EWL 3; FW; MTCW 1, 2; NCFS 4; RGEL 2; TEA

Westall, Robert (Atkinson)
1929-1993 .... **CLC 17**
See also AAYA 12; BYA 2, 6, 7, 8, 9, 15; CA 69-72; 141; CANR 18, 68; CLR 13; FANT; JRDA; MAICYA 1, 2; MAICYAS 1; SAAS 2; SATA 23, 69; SATA-Obit 75; WYA; YAW

Westermarck, Edward 1862-1939 . **TCLC 87**

Westlake, Donald E(dwin) 1933- . **CLC 7, 33**
See also BPFB 3; CA 17-20R; CAAS 13; CANR 16, 44, 65, 94; CMW 4; CPW; DAM POP; INT CANR-16; MSW; MTCW 2

Westmacott, Mary
See Christie, Agatha (Mary Clarissa)

Weston, Allen
See Norton, Andre

Wetcheek, J. L.
See Feuchtwanger, Lion

Wetering, Janwillem van de
See van de Wetering, Janwillem

Wetherald, Agnes Ethelwyn
1857-1940 .... **TCLC 81**
See also CA 202; DLB 99

Wetherell, Elizabeth
See Warner, Susan (Bogert)

Whale, James 1889-1957 .... **TCLC 63**

Whalen, Philip (Glenn) 1923-2002 .... **CLC 6, 29**
See also BG 3; CA 9-12R; 209; CANR 5, 39; CP 7; DLB 16; WP

Wharton, Edith (Newbold Jones)
1862-1937 ... **SSC 6; TCLC 3, 9, 27, 53, 129, 149; WLC**
See also AAYA 25; AMW; AMWC 2; AMWR 1; BPFB 3; CA 104; 132; CDALB 1865-1917; DA; DA3; DAB; DAC; DAM MST, NOV; DLB 4, 9, 12, 78, 189; DLBD 13; EWL 3; EXPS; HGG; LAIT 2, 3; LATS 1:1; MAWW; MTCW 1, 2; NFS 5, 11, 15, 20; RGAL 4; RGSF 2; RHW; SSFS 6, 7; SUFW; TUS

Wharton, James
See Mencken, H(enry) L(ouis)

Wharton, William (a pseudonym) . **CLC 18, 37**
See also CA 93-96; DLBY 1980; INT CA-93-96

Wheatley (Peters), Phillis
1753(?)-1784 ... **BLC 3; LC 3, 50; PC 3; WLC**
See also AFAW 1, 2; CDALB 1640-1865; DA; DA3; DAC; DAM MST, MULT, POET; DLB 31, 50; EXPP; PFS 13; RGAL 4

Wheelock, John Hall 1886-1978 .... **CLC 14**
See also CA 13-16R; 77-80; CANR 14; DLB 45

Whim-Wham
See Curnow, (Thomas) Allen (Monro)

White, Babington
See Braddon, Mary Elizabeth

White, E(lwyn) B(rooks)
1899-1985 .... **CLC 10, 34, 39**
See also AITN 2; AMWS 1; CA 13-16R; 116; CANR 16, 37; CDALBS; CLR 1, 21; CPW; DA3; DAM POP; DLB 11, 22; EWL 3; FANT; MAICYA 1, 2; MTCW 1, 2; NCFS 5; RGAL 4; SATA 2, 29, 100; SATA-Obit 44; TUS

Wolfram von Eschenbach c. 1170-c. 1220 .... **CMLC 5**
See Eschenbach, Wolfram von
See also CDWLB 2; DLB 138; EW 1; RGWL 2

Wolitzer, Hilma 1930- .... **CLC 17**
See also CA 65-68; CANR 18, 40; INT CANR-18; SATA 31; YAW

Wollstonecraft, Mary 1759-1797 .... **LC 5, 50, 90**
See also BRWS 3; CDBLB 1789-1832; DLB 39, 104, 158, 252; FW; LAIT 1; RGEL 2; TEA; WLIT 3

Wonder, Stevie .... **CLC 12**
See Morris, Steveland Judkins

Wong, Jade Snow 1922- .... **CLC 17**
See also CA 109; CANR 91; SATA 112

Woodberry, George Edward 1855-1930 .... **TCLC 73**
See also CA 165; DLB 71, 103

Woodcott, Keith
See Brunner, John (Kilian Houston)

Woodruff, Robert W.
See Mencken, H(enry) L(ouis)

Woolf, (Adeline) Virginia 1882-1941 .. **SSC 7, 79; TCLC 1, 5, 20, 43, 56, 101, 123, 128; WLC**
See also AAYA 44; BPFB 3; BRW 7; BRWC 2; BRWR 1; CA 104; 130; CANR 64, 132; CDBLB 1914-1945; DA; DA3; DAB; DAC; DAM MST, NOV; DLB 36, 100, 162; DLBD 10; EWL 3; EXPS; FW; LAIT 3; LATS 1:1; LMFS 2; MTCW 1, 2; NCFS 8, 12; RGEL 2; RGSF 2; SSFS 4, 12; TEA; WLIT 4

Woollcott, Alexander (Humphreys) 1887-1943 .... **TCLC 5**
See also CA 105; 161; DLB 29

Woolrich, Cornell .... **CLC 77**
See Hopley-Woolrich, Cornell George
See also MSW

Woolson, Constance Fenimore 1840-1894 .... **NCLC 82**
See also DLB 12, 74, 189, 221; RGAL 4

Wordsworth, Dorothy 1771-1855 . **NCLC 25, 138**
See also DLB 107

Wordsworth, William 1770-1850 .. **NCLC 12, 38, 111; PC 4; WLC**
See also BRW 4; BRWC 1; CDBLB 1789-1832; DA; DA3; DAB; DAC; DAM MST, POET; DLB 93, 107; EXPP; LATS 1:1; LMFS 1; PAB; PFS 2; RGEL 2; TEA; WLIT 3; WP

Wotton, Sir Henry 1568-1639 .... **LC 68**
See also DLB 121; RGEL 2

Wouk, Herman 1915- .... **CLC 1, 9, 38**
See also BPFB 2, 3; CA 5-8R; CANR 6, 33, 67; CDALBS; CN 7; CPW; DA3; DAM NOV, POP; DLBY 1982; INT CANR-6; LAIT 4; MTCW 1, 2; NFS 7; TUS

Wright, Charles (Penzel, Jr.) 1935- .. **CLC 6, 13, 28, 119, 146**
See also AMWS 5; CA 29-32R; CAAS 7; CANR 23, 36, 62, 88, 135; CP 7; DLB 165; DLBY 1982; EWL 3; MTCW 1, 2; PFS 10

Wright, Charles Stevenson 1932- ..... **BLC 3; CLC 49**
See also BW 1; CA 9-12R; CANR 26; CN 7; DAM MULT, POET; DLB 33

Wright, Frances 1795-1852 .... **NCLC 74**
See also DLB 73

Wright, Frank Lloyd 1867-1959 .... **TCLC 95**
See also AAYA 33; CA 174

Wright, Jack R.
See Harris, Mark

Wright, James (Arlington) 1927-1980 .... **CLC 3, 5, 10, 28; PC 36**
See also AITN 2; AMWS 3; CA 49-52; 97-100; CANR 4, 34, 64; CDALBS; DAM POET; DLB 5, 169; EWL 3; EXPP; MTCW 1, 2; PFS 7, 8; RGAL 4; TUS; WP

Wright, Judith (Arundell) 1915-2000 .... **CLC 11, 53; PC 14**
See also CA 13-16R; 188; CANR 31, 76, 93; CP 7; CWP; DLB 260; EWL 3; MTCW 1, 2; PFS 8; RGEL 2; SATA 14; SATA-Obit 121

Wright, L(aurali) R. 1939- .... **CLC 44**
See also CA 138; CMW 4

Wright, Richard (Nathaniel) 1908-1960 ... **BLC 3; CLC 1, 3, 4, 9, 14, 21, 48, 74; SSC 2; TCLC 136; WLC**
See also AAYA 5, 42; AFAW 1, 2; AMW; BPFB 3; BW 1; BYA 2; CA 108; CANR 64; CDALB 1929-1941; DA; DA3; DAB; DAC; DAM MST, MULT, NOV; DLB 76, 102; DLBD 2; EWL 3; EXPN; LAIT 3, 4; MTCW 1, 2; NCFS 1; NFS 1, 7; RGAL 4; RGSF 2; SSFS 3, 9, 15, 20; TUS; YAW

Wright, Richard B(ruce) 1937- .... **CLC 6**
See also CA 85-88; CANR 120; DLB 53

Wright, Rick 1945- .... **CLC 35**

Wright, Rowland
See Wells, Carolyn

Wright, Stephen 1946- .... **CLC 33**

Wright, Willard Huntington 1888-1939
See Van Dine, S. S.
See also CA 115; 189; CMW 4; DLBD 16

Wright, William 1930- .... **CLC 44**
See also CA 53-56; CANR 7, 23

Wroth, Lady Mary 1587-1653(?) .... **LC 30; PC 38**
See also DLB 121

Wu Ch'eng-en 1500(?)-1582(?) .... **LC 7**

Wu Ching-tzu 1701-1754 .... **LC 2**

Wulfstan c. 10th cent. -1023 .... **CMLC 59**

Wurlitzer, Rudolph 1938(?)- .... **CLC 2, 4, 15**
See also CA 85-88; CN 7; DLB 173

Wyatt, Sir Thomas c. 1503-1542 . **LC 70; PC 27**
See also BRW 1; DLB 132; EXPP; RGEL 2; TEA

Wycherley, William 1640-1716 .... **LC 8, 21, 102**
See also BRW 2; CDBLB 1660-1789; DAM DRAM; DLB 80; RGEL 2

Wyclif, John c. 1330-1384 .... **CMLC 70**
See also DLB 146

Wylie, Elinor (Morton Hoyt) 1885-1928 .... **PC 23; TCLC 8**
See also AMWS 1; CA 105; 162; DLB 9, 45; EXPP; RGAL 4

Wylie, Philip (Gordon) 1902-1971 ... **CLC 43**
See also CA 21-22; 33-36R; CAP 2; DLB 9; SFW 4

Wyndham, John .... **CLC 19**
See Harris, John (Wyndham Parkes Lucas) Beynon
See also DLB 255; SCFW 2

Wyss, Johann David Von 1743-1818 .... **NCLC 10**
See also CLR 92; JRDA; MAICYA 1, 2; SATA 29; SATA-Brief 27

Xenophon c. 430B.C.-c. 354B.C. ... **CMLC 17**
See also AW 1; DLB 176; RGWL 2, 3

Xingjian, Gao 1940-
See Gao Xingjian
See also CA 193; RGWL 3

Yakamochi 718-785 .... **CMLC 45; PC 48**

Yakumo Koizumi
See Hearn, (Patricio) Lafcadio (Tessima Carlos)

Yamada, Mitsuye (May) 1923- .... **PC 44**
See also CA 77-80

Yamamoto, Hisaye 1921- .... **AAL; SSC 34**
See also CA 214; DAM MULT; LAIT 4; SSFS 14

Yamauchi, Wakako 1924- .... **AAL**
See also CA 214

Yanez, Jose Donoso
See Donoso (Yanez), Jose

Yanovsky, Basile S.
See Yanovsky, V(assily) S(emenovich)

Yanovsky, V(assily) S(emenovich) 1906-1989 .... **CLC 2, 18**
See also CA 97-100; 129

Yates, Richard 1926-1992 .... **CLC 7, 8, 23**
See also AMWS 11; CA 5-8R; 139; CANR 10, 43; DLB 2, 234; DLBY 1981, 1992; INT CANR-10

Yau, John 1950- .... **PC 61**
See also CA 154; CANR 89; CP 7; DLB 234

Yeats, W. B.
See Yeats, William Butler

Yeats, William Butler 1865-1939 . **PC 20, 51; TCLC 1, 11, 18, 31, 93, 116; WLC**
See also AAYA 48; BRW 6; BRWR 1; CA 104; 127; CANR 45; CDBLB 1890-1914; DA; DA3; DAB; DAC; DAM DRAM, MST, POET; DLB 10, 19, 98, 156; EWL 3; EXPP; MTCW 1, 2; NCFS 3; PAB; PFS 1, 2, 5, 7, 13, 15; RGEL 2; TEA; WLIT 4; WP

Yehoshua, A(braham) B. 1936- .. **CLC 13, 31**
See also CA 33-36R; CANR 43, 90; CWW 2; EWL 3; RGSF 2; RGWL 3

Yellow Bird
See Ridge, John Rollin

Yep, Laurence Michael 1948- .... **CLC 35**
See also AAYA 5, 31; BYA 7; CA 49-52; CANR 1, 46, 92; CLR 3, 17, 54; DLB 52; FANT; JRDA; MAICYA 1, 2; MAICYAS 1; SATA 7, 69, 123; WYA; YAW

Yerby, Frank G(arvin) 1916-1991 ..... **BLC 3; CLC 1, 7, 22**
See also BPFB 3; BW 1, 3; CA 9-12R; 136; CANR 16, 52; DAM MULT; DLB 76; INT CANR-16; MTCW 1; RGAL 4; RHW

Yesenin, Sergei Alexandrovich
See Esenin, Sergei (Alexandrovich)

Yesenin, Sergey
See Esenin, Sergei (Alexandrovich)
See also EWL 3

Yevtushenko, Yevgeny (Alexandrovich) 1933- ...... **CLC 1, 3, 13, 26, 51, 126; PC 40**
See Evtushenko, Evgenii Aleksandrovich
See also CA 81-84; CANR 33, 54; DAM POET; EWL 3; MTCW 1

Yezierska, Anzia 1885(?)-1970 .... **CLC 46**
See also CA 126; 89-92; DLB 28, 221; FW; MTCW 1; RGAL 4; SSFS 15

Yglesias, Helen 1915- .... **CLC 7, 22**
See also CA 37-40R; CAAS 20; CANR 15, 65, 95; CN 7; INT CANR-15; MTCW 1

Yokomitsu, Riichi 1898-1947 .... **TCLC 47**
See also CA 170; EWL 3

Yonge, Charlotte (Mary) 1823-1901 .... **TCLC 48**
See also CA 109; 163; DLB 18, 163; RGEL 2; SATA 17; WCH

York, Jeremy
See Creasey, John

York, Simon
See Heinlein, Robert A(nson)

Yorke, Henry Vincent 1905-1974 ..... **CLC 13**
See Green, Henry
See also CA 85-88; 49-52

Yosano Akiko 1878-1942 .... **PC 11; TCLC 59**
See also CA 161; EWL 3; RGWL 3

PC Cumulative Nationality Index

AMERICAN

Aiken, Conrad (Potter) **26**
Alexie, Sherman **53**
Ammons, A(rchie) R(andolph) **16**
Angelou, Maya **32**
Ashbery, John (Lawrence) **26**
Auden, W(ystan) H(ugh) **1**
Baca, Jimmy Santiago **41**
Baraka, Amiri **4**
Benét, Stephen Vincent **64**
Berry, Wendell (Erdman) **28**
Berryman, John **64**
Bishop, Elizabeth **3, 34**
Bly, Robert (Elwood) **39**
Bogan, Louise **12**
Bradstreet, Anne **10**
Braithwaite, William **52**
Brodsky, Joseph **9**
Brooks, Gwendolyn (Elizabeth) **7**
Brown, Sterling Allen **55**
Bryant, William Cullen **20**
Bukowski, Charles **18**
Cage, John **58**
Carruth, Hayden **10**
Carver, Raymond **54**
Cervantes, Lorna Dee **35**
Chin, Marilyn (Mei Ling) **40**
Cisneros, Sandra **52**
Clampitt, Amy **19**
Clifton, (Thelma) Lucille **17**
Corso, (Nunzio) Gregory **33**
Crane, (Harold) Hart **3**
Cullen, Countée **20**
Cummings, E(dward) E(stlin) **5**
Dickey, James (Lafayette) **40**
Dickinson, Emily (Elizabeth) **1**
Doolittle, Hilda **5**
Doty, Mark **53**
Dove, Rita (Frances) **6**
Dunbar, Paul Laurence **5**
Duncan, Robert (Edward) **2**
Dylan, Bob **37**
Eliot, T(homas) S(tearns) **5, 31**
Emerson, Ralph Waldo **18**
Erdrich, Louise **52**
Ferlinghetti, Lawrence (Monsanto) **1**
Forché, Carolyn (Louise) **10**
Francis, Robert (Churchill) **34**
Frost, Robert (Lee) **1, 39**
Gallagher, Tess **9**
Ginsberg, Allen **4, 47**
Giovanni, Nikki **19**
Glück, Louise (Elisabeth) **16**
Graham, Jorie **59**
Guest, Barbara **55**
Hacker, Marilyn **47**

Hammon, Jupiter **16**
Harjo, Joy **27**
Harper, Frances Ellen Watkins **21**
Hass, Robert **16**
Hayden, Robert E(arl) **6**
H. D. **5**
Hogan, Linda **35**
Hongo, Garrett Kaoru **23**
Howe, Susan **54**
Hughes, (James) Langston **1, 53**
Ignatow, David **34**
Jackson, Laura (Riding) **44**
Jacobsen, Josephine **62**
Jarrell, Randall **41**
Jeffers, (John) Robinson **17**
Johnson, James Weldon **24**
Jordan, June **38**
Justice, Donald **64**
Kenyon, Jane **57**
Kinnell, Galway **26**
Kizer, Carolyn **66**
Knight, Etheridge **14**
Komunyakaa, Yusef **51**
Kumin, Maxine (Winokur) **15**
Kunitz, Stanley (Jasspon) **19**
Lanier, Sidney **50**
Levertov, Denise **11**
Levine, Philip **22**
Lindsay, (Nicholas) Vachel **23**
Longfellow, Henry Wadsworth **30**
Lorde, Audre (Geraldine) **12**
Lowell, Amy **13**
Lowell, Robert (Traill Spence Jr.) **3**
Loy, Mina **16**
MacLeish, Archibald **47**
Mackey, Nathaniel **49**
Madhubuti, Haki R. **5**
Masters, Edgar Lee **1, 36**
McHugh, Heather **61**
Meredith, William (Morris) **28**
Merrill, James (Ingram) **28**
Merton, Thomas **10**
Merwin, W. S. **45**
Millay, Edna St. Vincent **6, 61**
Momaday, N(avarre) Scott **25**
Moore, Marianne (Craig) **4, 49**
Mueller, Lisel **33**
Nash, (Frediric) Ogden **21**
Nemerov, Howard (Stanley) **24**
Niedecker, Lorine **42**
O'Hara, Frank **45**
Olds, Sharon **22**
Olson, Charles (John) **19**
Oppen, George **35**
Ortiz, Simon J(oseph) **17**
Parker, Dorothy (Rothschild) **28**

Piercy, Marge **29**
Pinsky, Robert **27**
Plath, Sylvia **1, 37**
Poe, Edgar Allan **1, 54**
Pound, Ezra (Weston Loomis) **4**
Quintana, Leroy V. **36**
Ransom, John Crowe **61**
Reese, Lizette Woodworth **29**
Rexroth, Kenneth **20**
Rich, Adrienne (Cecile) **5**
Riley, James Whitcomb **48**
Ríos, Alberto **57**
Robinson, Edwin Arlington **1, 35**
Roethke, Theodore (Huebner) **15**
Rose, Wendy **13**
Rukeyser, Muriel **12**
Sanchez, Sonia **9**
Sandburg, Carl (August) **2, 41**
Sarton, (Eleanor) May **39**
Schwartz, Delmore (David) **8**
Schnackenberg, Gjertrud **45**
Schwerner, Armand **42**
Sexton, Anne (Harvey) **2**
Shapiro, Karl (Jay) **25**
Silverstein, Shel **49**
Snyder, Gary (Sherman) **21**
Song, Cathy **21**
Soto, Gary **28**
Stein, Gertrude **18**
Stevens, Wallace **6**
Stone, Ruth **53**
Strand, Mark **63**
Stryk, Lucien **27**
Swenson, May **14**
Tapahonso, Luci **65**
Tate, Allen **50**
Taylor, Edward **63**
Teasdale, Sara **31**
Thoreau, Henry David **30**
Toomer, Jean **7**
Urista, Alberto H. **34**
Viereck, Peter (Robert Edwin) **27**
Wagoner, David (Russell) **33**
Wakoski, Diane **15**
Walker, Alice (Malsenior) **30**
Walker, Margaret (Abigail) **20**
Warren, Robert Penn **37**
Welch, James **62**
Wheatley (Peters), Phillis **3**
Whitman, Walt(er) **3**
Wilbur, Richard **51**
Williams, William Carlos **7**
Wright, James (Arlington) **36**
Wylie, Elinor (Morton Hoyt) **23**
Yamada, Mitsuye **44**
Yau, John **61**

Nationality Index

PC-66 Title Index

ISBN 0-7876-8700-6

90000